THE
WISDEN
BOOK OF TEST CRICKET
2000-2009

THE
WISDEN
BOOK OF TEST CRICKET
2000–2009

Sixth edition Volume 3

Edited by
STEVEN LYNCH

THE
WISDEN
BOOK OF TEST CRICKET
2000-2009
Sixth edition, Volume 3

Edited by
STEVEN LYNCH

Dedicated to the memory of Bill Frindall, MBE (1939–2009)

First published in the UK in 2010 by
John Wisden & Co
An imprint of A & C Black Publishers Ltd
36 Soho Square, London W1D 3QY
www.wisden.com
www.acblack.com

ISBN 978 14081 2335 5

Cover by James Watson

This book is produced using paper that is made from wood grown in managed, sustainable
forests. It is natural, renewable and recyclable. The logging and manufacturing processes
conform to the environmental regulations of the country of origin.

Typeset in Minion by Palimpsest Book Production Limited,
Grangemouth, Stirlingshire

Printed and bound in the UK by MPG Books

Contents

Preface and Acknowledgements

This book follows on from the previous editions of *The Wisden Book of Test Cricket*, the most recent of which were published in 2000. Since then, over 400 Test matches have been played, taking the total number close to 2,000. This volume brings the series up to date, with scorecards of all the Tests played since the 2000 English season, up to the end of the 2009 one.

There are some changes from the previous volumes. The most obvious one is the name on the front: Bill Frindall, the BBC scorer who produced the first version of this book in 1979, passed away early in 2009. It seemed only fitting that this edition should be dedicated to his memory. And I hope, after almost 25 years of working for *Wisden*, that I have managed to produce a book of which he would approve.

There are other changes to the format. The scorecards are taken directly from *Wisden Cricketers' Almanack*, so are laid out differently to previous volumes. The match reports are longer than before: in many cases they are edited versions of *Wisden*'s own accounts, and include the Almanack's traditional mix of informative comment, facts and figures – and, occasionally, fun. Given for the first time are the winners of Man of the Match awards, while the fall-of-wicket information now includes the identity of the outgoing batsman.

This edition does not include a Test Records section, although individual Career Records are included, and there is an Index to show in which matches each player appeared. Readers will be able to find further, constantly updated records on the Cricinfo or Cricket Archive websites or in the Records section of the latest Almanack.

Each match has a reference number to show its overall position, and its place in that particular series. The first match in this volume, for example, is "Test No. 1510/9 (Z44/NZ280)", denoting that it was the 1510th Test played overall, and the ninth between Zimbabwe and New Zealand; furthermore it was Zimbabwe's 44th Test match and New Zealand's 280th. The overall numbers are arranged chronologically by series – so all the Tests of a particular series appear together and in numerical sequence, even if a Test started in another country before the end of the series in question.

Many people gave invaluable assistance in compiling this latest volume. Christopher Lane at Wisden had the original idea for an update, while my colleagues Scyld Berry, Hugh Chevallier and Harriet Monkhouse were always helpful, and didn't seem to mind that I was diverted from the task of producing next year's Almanack by constantly having my nose stuck in previous editions. Charlotte Atyeo and Kate Turvey at A&C Black Publishing saw the project through, while the typesetters Palimpsest dealt capably with the demanding layout. Philip Bailey produced the Test Career Records with his customary accuracy and speed, while Gordon Burling helped with the proofreading. My wife Karina, despite working on an important project of her own (our second son was born during the book's production), was also a great help. Finally, a great many people contributed to the accuracy of the original facts and figures in *Wisden*, and they are acknowledged in appropriate annual editions of the Almanack.

STEVEN LYNCH
November 2009

ZIMBABWE v NEW ZEALAND 2000–01 (1st Test)

At Queens Sports Club, Bulawayo, on 12, 13, 14, 15, 16 September.
Toss: Zimbabwe.   Result: NEW ZEALAND won by seven wickets.
Debuts: Zimbabwe – D. T. Mutendera. New Zealand – M. H. Richardson.
Man of the Match: P. J. Wiseman.

A draw looked likely shortly after lunch on the fourth day, when New Zealand were all out 12 behind on first innings, with Paul Strang recording what remain Zimbabwe's best bowling figures in a Test innings. But Zimbabwe collapsed to Cairns, who moved past Danny Morrison (161 wickets) into second place on New Zealand's wicket-taking lists. Just as important were Wiseman's offbreaks, which claimed five wickets in Zimbabwe's long first innings and another three in their second. New Zealand won shortly before tea on the final day, the main talking point of their innings coming when umpire Hair no-balled slow left-armer Grant Flower three times for throwing in his second over, which was completed by Rennie. Earlier, Campbell – who faced 307 balls in all – had reached 50 for the first time in 17 Tests (since Zimbabwe's last series against New Zealand), then Strang, in his first Test since May 1998 after a wrist injury, bowled superbly, eventually becoming only the second Zimbabwean to take ten wickets in a Test, after Adam Huckle (another legspinner) in 1997-98. Horne batted for more than five hours for his fourth Test century, the second against Zimbabwe. Before the match Guy Whittall withdrew from the Zimbabwean side, protesting that the inclusion of the black debutant David Mutendera instead of the white Craig Wishart was politically motivated – whereupon Wishart took Whittall's place. Zimbabwe were already without two other leading players: Murray Goodwin had returned to Western Australia, while Neil Johnson had joined South Africa's Western Province.

Zimbabwe

G. W. Flower c Parore b Vettori	24	– c Parore b O'Connor		3
G. J. Rennie c McMillan b Wiseman	36	– b Cairns		2
S. V. Carlisle c Horne b Wiseman	38	– b Wiseman		15
A. D. R. Campbell lbw b Astle	88	– lbw b Cairns		45
†A. Flower c Astle b Cairns	29	– lbw b Astle		22
C. B. Wishart c Richardson b Wiseman	17	– c Richardson b Wiseman		1
*H. H. Streak c Parore b Wiseman	51	– c McMillan b Wiseman		15
P. A. Strang c Richardson b Wiseman	0	– (9) not out		8
M. L. Nkala not out	30	– (8) c Sinclair b Cairns		0
B. C. Strang c Parore b O'Connor	10	– b Cairns		5
D. T. Mutendera b Cairns	10	– c Parore b Cairns		0
B 5, l-b 4, n-b 8	17	L-b 1, w 1, n-b 1		3

1/40 (1) 2/91 (2) 3/120 (3) 4/157 (5)   350   1/6 (2) 2/23 (3) 3/23 (1)   119
5/206 (6) 6/282 (4) 7/291 (8)   4/75 (5) 5/86 (6) 6/100 (4)
8/300 (7) 9/323 (10) 10/350 (11)   7/100 (8) 8/110 (7) 9/119 (10) 10/119 (11)

Cairns 28.2–9–77–2; O'Connor 30–7–63–1; McMillan 9–3–23–0; Vettori 52–23–79–1; Astle 11–6–9–1; Wiseman 45–16–90–5. *Second Innings*—Cairns 14.5–5–31–5; O'Connor 9–5–8–1; Wiseman 25–8–54–3; Richardson 1–0–1–0; Astle 18–10–24–1.

New Zealand

M. H. Richardson c Carlisle b Streak	6	– lbw b Rennie		13
M. J. Horne lbw b P. A. Strang	110			
M. S. Sinclair lbw b P. A. Strang	12	– (2) not out		43
P. J. Wiseman lbw b P. A. Strang	14			
*S. P. Fleming c Rennie b P. A. Strang	11	– (3) lbw b P. A. Strang		12
N. J. Astle c A. Flower b P. A. Strang	0	– (4) c Nkala b P. A. Strang		27
C. D. McMillan c A. Flower b P. A. Strang	58	– (5) not out		31
C. L. Cairns b Streak	33			
†A. C. Parore not out	32			
D. L. Vettori c and b P. A. Strang	49			
S. B. O'Connor c Campbell b P. A. Strang	4			
L-b 1, n-b 8	9	L-b 2, w 1, n-b 3		6

1/15 (1) 2/52 (3) 3/109 (4) 4/139 (5)   338   1/27 (1) 2/43 (3)   (3 wkts) 132
5/139 (6) 6/180 (2) 7/252 (7)   3/93 (4)
8/252 (8) 9/330 (10) 10/338 (11)

Streak 26–9–67–2; Nkala 21–7–43–0; P. A. Strang 51.5–12–109–8; B. C. Strang 25–7–63–0; Mutendera 14–4–29–0; G. W. Flower 16–4–26–0. *Second Innings*—Streak 5–0–21–0; Nkala 2–1–2–0; P. A. Strang 20.4–3–49–2; G. W. Flower 1.3–0–5–0; Rennie 13.3–0–40–1; Campbell 1–0–3–0; B. C. Strang 2–0–10–0.

Umpires: D. B. Hair *(Australia)* (33) and R. B. Tiffin *(Zimbabwe)* (17).
Third umpire: M. A. Esat *(Zimbabwe)*.   Referee: C. W. Smith *(West Indies)* (29).

Close of play: First day, Zimbabwe 185-4 (Campbell 37*, Wishart 10*); Second day, New Zealand 62-2 (Horne 40*, Wiseman 1*); Third day, New Zealand 252-7 (Cairns 33*); Fourth day, Zimbabwe 100-5 (Campbell 45*, Streak 9*).

1

ZIMBABWE v NEW ZEALAND 2000–01 (2nd Test)

At Harare Sports Club on 19, 20, 21, 22, 23 September.
Toss: New Zealand.   Result: NEW ZEALAND won by eight wickets.
Debuts: none.
Man of the Match: C. L. Cairns.

New Zealand took the short series despite a heroic effort from Whittall: back in the side after missing the first Test, he batted for 506 minutes in an attempt to stave off defeat after Zimbabwe were forced to follow on. Whittall, who hit 27 fours and two sixes, put on 131 with Andy Flower – who became the first Zimbabwean to reach 3,000 Test runs when 59 – and 151 with Streak, who himself survived for almost five hours. Last man Mbangwa (whose final Test batting average was 2.00) hung around for 39 minutes, but when he was eventually run out, there was just enough time for New Zealand to reach their target of 72, which they did with 16 balls to spare. It left Zimbabwe ruing the tame end to their first innings, when the last six wickets fell for 20 in 13 overs on the third afternoon. They followed on 299 behind and, at 48 for 4 next day, were looking down the barrel of an even heavier defeat before Whittall's heroics almost saved them. Earlier, Richardson – in only his second match – had become the sixth New Zealander to be dismissed for 99 in a Test, before Cairns hit 13 fours and three sixes in 124, his fourth Test century. He was also in at the climax, swiping Mbangwa one-handed over long leg for six shortly before the end. It was Fleming's 12th Test victory as captain, beating Geoff Howarth's previous New Zealand record of 11.

New Zealand

M. H. Richardson lbw b Nkala	99		
C. M. Spearman c A. Flower b Olonga	2	– (1) c Rennie b Streak	2
M. S. Sinclair c Carlisle b Olonga	44	– not out	35
*S. P. Fleming c Campbell b Mbangwa	9		
N. J. Astle run out	86		
C. D. McMillan lbw b Mbangwa	15		
C. L. Cairns st A. Flower b Strang	124	– (4) not out	19
†A. C. Parore c A. Flower b Olonga	4	– (2) c Carlisle b Streak	13
D. J. Nash c G. W. Flower b Strang	62		
P. J. Wiseman not out	1		
S. B. O'Connor c Whittall b G. W. Flower	2		
L-b 3, w 2, n-b 12	17	L-b 2, w 1, n-b 2	5

1/5 (2) 2/69 (3) 3/91 (4) 4/226 (1)   465   1/4 (1) 2/42 (2)   (2 wkts) 74
5/256 (5) 6/302 (6) 7/318 (8)
8/462 (9) 9/462 (7) 10/465 (11)

Olonga 27–5–115–3; Streak 29–6–74–0; Nkala 15–0–60–1; Mbangwa 28–10–58–2; Strang 38–11–80–2; G. W. Flower 20.3–6–59–1; Rennie 3–0–16–0. *Second Innings*—Streak 8–2–33–2; Nkala 3–0–17–0; Mbangwa 4.2–0–22–0.

Zimbabwe

G. W. Flower c Parore b Astle	49	– run out	10
G. J. Rennie c Spearman b Cairns	4	– c Spearman b O'Connor	1
S. V. Carlisle c Sinclair b Cairns	31	– c Fleming b Astle	20
A. D. R. Campbell c Fleming b O'Connor	0	– run out	10
†A. Flower lbw b McMillan	48	– c Sinclair b O'Connor	65
G. J. Whittall c Parore b Astle	9	– not out	188
*H. H. Streak c Wiseman b O'Connor	8	– lbw b Cairns	54
M. L. Nkala c Parore b McMillan	0	– lbw b O'Connor	0
P. A. Strang c Parore b O'Connor	5	– b Cairns	8
H. K. Olonga c Parore b Nash	4	– lbw b O'Connor	0
M. Mbangwa not out	0	– run out	5
B 3, l-b 3, w 1, n-b 1	8	B 4, l-b 4, n-b 1	9

1/5 (2) 2/76 (3) 3/77 (4) 4/118 (1)   166   1/1 (2) 2/27 (1) 3/39 (4)   370
5/146 (6) 6/151 (5) 7/151 (8)   4/48 (3) 5/179 (5) 6/330 (7)
8/157 (7) 9/164 (10) 10/166 (9)   7/335 (8) 8/348 (9) 9/349 (10) 10/370 (11)

Cairns 17.1–7–33–2; O'Connor 28–9–43–3; Nash 17–11–25–1; McMillan 12.5–2–29–2; Astle 14–9–22–2; Wiseman 3–0–8–0. *Second Innings*—O'Connor 45–17–73–4; Nash 17.3–8–28–0; McMillan 20–4–53–0; Astle 36–16–73–1; Cairns 33–7–80–2; Wiseman 27–11–55–0.

Umpires: I. D. Robinson *(Zimbabwe)* (23) and D. R. Shepherd *(England)* (53).
Third umpire: K. C. Barbour *(Zimbabwe)*.   Referee: C. W. Smith *(West Indies)* (30).

Close of play: First day, New Zealand 226-4 (Astle 64*); Second day, Zimbabwe 31-1 (G. W. Flower 11*, Carlisle 15*); Third day, Zimbabwe 6-1 (G. W. Flower 0*, Carlisle 5*); Fourth day, Zimbabwe 228-5 (Whittall 105*, Streak 10*).

BANGLADESH v INDIA 2000–01 (Only Test)

At Bangabandhu National Stadium, Dhaka, on 10, 11, 12, 13 November.
Toss: Bangladesh.   Result: INDIA won by nine wickets.
Debuts: Bangladesh – all. India – S. S. Das, S. S. Karim, Zaheer Khan.
Man of the Match: S. B. Joshi.

Bangladesh, who were elevated to Full (Test-playing) Membership of the ICC earlier in 2000, started their inaugural Test in style by running up 400, a total exceeded only once by a country in their first match (Zimbabwe's 456, also against India, in 1992-93). Aminul Islam, who batted for 535 minutes, became only the third player to score a century in his country's maiden Test, after Australia's Charles Bannerman (in the very first Test of all against England in 1876-77) and Dave Houghton of Zimbabwe. India struggled initially, especially against Bangladesh's captain, offspinner Naimur Rahman, whose eventual 6 for 132 had only been bettered once in a country's first Test (again in the first match of all, when Australia's Tom Kendall took 7 for 55). But, boosted by Joshi's highest Test score, India took a slender lead, and then Bangladesh gave an indication of the struggles which lay ahead of them over the coming decade by collapsing for 92, the second-lowest total by a country on debut after South Africa's 84 against England in 1888-89. India, led by Ganguly for the first time, completed a comfortable victory – their first in 22 away Tests since 1993-94 – under floodlights on the fourth evening. Dhaka's Bangabandhu Stadium became the first ground to stage home Tests for two different countries: Pakistan played seven Tests there before Bangladesh gained independence in 1971. It was also the "neutral" venue for the final of the Asian Test Championship between Pakistan and Sri Lanka in 1998-99.

Bangladesh

Shahriar Hossain c Ganguly b Joshi	12	– lbw b Joshi		7
Mehrab Hossain, sen. c Karim b Zaheer Khan	4	– c Kartik b Zaheer Khan		2
Habibul Bashar c Ganguly b Zaheer Khan	71	– c Zaheer Khan b Agarkar		30
Aminul Islam c Srinath b Agarkar	145	– lbw b Agarkar		6
Akram Khan c Dravid b Joshi	35	– (6) c Das b Joshi		2
Al Sahariar lbw b Agarkar	12	– (5) c and b Joshi		6
*Naimur Rahman c Das b Joshi	15	– (8) c Ganguly b Srinath		3
Khaled Mashud c Das b Joshi	32	– (7) not out		21
Mohammad Rafique c Das b Tendulkar	22	– c Ganguly b Srinath		4
Hasibul Hossain not out	28	– lbw b Srinath		0
Bikash Ranjan Das c Ganguly b Joshi	2	– c Das b Kartik		0
B 13, l-b 6, n-b 3	22	B 7, l-b 1, n-b 2		10

1/10 (2) 2/44 (1) 3/110 (3) 4/175 (5)   400   1/11 (2) 2/32 (4) 3/43 (5)   91
5/196 (6) 6/231 (7) 7/324 (8)   4/53 (3) 5/53 (6) 6/69 (8)
8/354 (9) 9/385 (4) 10/400 (11)   7/76 (1) 8/81 (9) 9/81 (10) 10/91 (11)

In the second innings Shahriar Hossain, when 3, retired hurt at 5 and resumed at 69.

Srinath 22–9–47–0; Zaheer Khan 21–6–49–2; Agarkar 31–13–68–2; Joshi 45.3–8–142–5; Kartik 24–9–41–0; Tendulkar 10–2–34–1. *Second Innings*—Srinath 11–3–19–3; Zaheer Khan 5–0–20–1; Agarkar 11–4–16–2; Joshi 18–5–27–3; Kartik 1.3–0–1–1.

India

S. S. Das b Naimur Rahman	29	– not out		22
S. Ramesh b Bikash Ranjan Das	58	– b Hasibul Hossain		1
M. Kartik c sub (Rajin Saleh) b Naimur Rahman	43			
R. Dravid c Al Sahariar b Mohammad Rafique	28	– (3) not out		41
S. R. Tendulkar c sub (Rajin Saleh) b Naimur Rahman	18			
*S. C. Ganguly c Al Sahariar b Naimur Rahman	84			
†S. S. Karim st Shahriar Hossain b Naimur Rahman	15			
S. B. Joshi c Al Sahariar b Mohammad Rafique	92			
A. B. Agarkar c Bikash Ranjan Das b Naimur Rahman	34			
J. Srinath c and b Mohammad Rafique	2			
Zaheer Khan not out	7			
B 13, l-b 4, w 2	19			

1/66 (1) 2/104 (2) 3/155 (4) 4/175 (3)   429   1/11 (2)   (1 wkt) 64
5/190 (5) 6/236 (7) 7/357 (6)
8/413 (8) 9/421 (10) 10/429 (9)

Hasibul Hossain 19–2–60–0; Bikash Ranjan Das 19–3–64–1; Naimur Rahman 44.3–9–132–6; Mohammad Rafique 51–12–117–3; Habibul Bashar 8–0–39–0. *Second Innings*—Hasibul Hossain 6–0–31–1; Bikash Ranjan Das 3–0–8–0; Naimur Rahman 4–0–22–0; Mohammad Rafique 2–0–3–0.

Umpires: S. A. Bucknor *(West Indies)* (52) and D. R. Shepherd *(England)* (54).
Third umpire: Mahbubur Rahman *(Bangladesh)*.   Referee: R. Subba Row *(England)* (35).

Close of play: First day, Bangladesh 239-6 (Aminul Islam 70*, Khaled Mashud 3*); Second day, India 81-1 (Ramesh 40*, Kartik 7*); Third day, India 366-7 (Joshi 71*, Agarkar 5*).

PAKISTAN v ENGLAND 2000–01 (1st Test)

At Gaddafi Stadium, Lahore, on 15, 16, 17, 18, 19 November.
Toss: England.   Result: MATCH DRAWN.
Debuts: Pakistan – Qaiser Abbas.
Man of the Match: Saqlain Mushtaq.

The first meeting between these two sides in Tests in Pakistan since the fractious 1987-88 series was dominated by patient, at times attritional, batting on a slow pitch on which the run-rate never exceeded 2.5 an over. Atherton (who passed 7,000 Test runs during his innings) and Trescothick started by adding 134 in 215 minutes, then Thorpe – dropped at slip by the debutant Qaiser Abbas when 2 – dug in for a six-hour century, and batted for 430 minutes in all, hitting just two fours (only Paul Gibb, with 120 for England v South Africa in the "Timeless Test" at Durban in 1938-39, has made a higher score with only two boundaries). Thorpe put on 166 with White, who just missed his maiden hundred on the third morning, before Hussain declared. Pakistan were similarly circumspect, although they dipped to 273 for 8 before Yousuf Youhana, who batted for 374 minutes in all, made an elegant century. He had only 37 when Saqlain Mushtaq came in at No. 10, but they put on 127, with Saqlain surviving more than four hours for his unbeaten 32. There were less than three hours remaining when England went in again. Hussain, who had dropped down the order in the first innings because of a back niggle, batted in his usual position at No. 3 – but he faced only three balls before he was hit on the wrist by a third successive bouncer from Wasim Akram and retired hurt.

England

M. A. Atherton c Yousuf Youhana b Saqlain Mushtaq . .	73	– lbw b Mushtaq Ahmed.	20
M. E. Trescothick c Salim Elahi b Saqlain Mushtaq . . .	71	– lbw b Wasim Akram	1
G. P. Thorpe c and b Saqlain Mushtaq.	118	– (4) c Abdul Razzaq b Saqlain Mushtaq	5
†A. J. Stewart lbw b Saqlain Mushtaq	3	– (5) not out.	27
*N. Hussain c Wasim Akram b Saqlain Mushtaq	7	– (3) retired hurt	0
G. A. Hick lbw b Saqlain Mushtaq.	16	– b Shahid Afridi.	14
C. White c Yousuf Youhana b Saqlain Mushtaq.	93		
I. D. K. Salisbury lbw b Saqlain Mushtaq	31		
A. F. Giles not out	37		
A. R. Caddick not out	5		
B 3, l-b 13, n-b 10.	26	L-b 7, n-b 3.	10

1/134 (2) 2/169 (1) 3/173 (4)   (8 wkts dec.) 480   1/4 (2) 2/29 (4)   (4 wkts dec.) 77
4/183 (5) 5/225 (6) 6/391 (3)   3/39 (1) 4/77 (6)
7/398 (7) 8/468 (8)

D. Gough did not bat.

In the second innings Hussain retired hurt at 13.

Wasim Akram 22–8–40–0; Abdul Razzaq 22–6–55–0; Saqlain Mushtaq 74–20–164–8; Mushtaq Ahmed 44–6–132–0; Shahid Afridi 18–6–38–0; Qaiser Abbas 16–3–35–0. *Second Innings*—Wasim Akram 6–5–1–1; Abdul Razzaq 7–0–21–0; Saqlain Mushtaq 10–2–14–1; Mushtaq Ahmed 8–0–32–1; Shahid Afridi 1.1–0–2–1.

Pakistan

Saeed Anwar lbw b Hick.	40	Saqlain Mushtaq not out	32
Shahid Afridi c Gough b Giles	52	Mushtaq Ahmed lbw b White	0
Salim Elahi b White	44		
Inzamam-ul-Haq b Giles	63	B 2, l-b 6, n-b 8.	16
Yousuf Youhana c Stewart b Giles	124		
Qaiser Abbas c Hick b White	2	1/63 (1) 2/101 (2) 3/199 (3)	401
*†Moin Khan lbw b Caddick	17	4/203 (4) 5/210 (6) 6/236 (7)	
Abdul Razzaq lbw b White	10	7/272 (8) 8/273 (9) 9/400 (5) 10/401 (11)	
Wasim Akram c White b Giles	1		

Gough 17–6–45–0; Caddick 24–4–68–1; Giles 59–20–113–4; Salisbury 31–5–71–0; Hick 8–0–42–1; White 24.3–5–54–4.

Umpires: D. B. Hair *(Australia)* (34) and Riazuddin *(Pakistan)* (8).
Third umpire: Salim Badar *(Pakistan)*.   Referee: R. S. Madugalle *(Sri Lanka)* (30).

Close of play: First day, England 195-4 (Thorpe 22*, Hick 6*); Second day, England 393-6 (White 89*, Salisbury 0*); Third day, Pakistan 119-2 (Salim Elahi 15*, Inzamam-ul-Haq 11*); Fourth day, Pakistan 333-8 (Yousuf Youhana 77*, Saqlain Mushtaq 14*).

PAKISTAN v ENGLAND 2000–01 (2nd Test)

At Iqbal Stadium, Faisalabad, on 29, 30 November, 1, 2, 3 December.
Toss: Pakistan.   Result: MATCH DRAWN.
Debuts: Pakistan – Danish Kaneria.
Man of the Match: Abdul Razzaq.

England ended up needing a watchful, technically superb vigil from Atherton to ensure defeat was avoided after slipping to 110 for 5 with a possible 13 overs remaining. The likelihood of a draw was increased by the loss of so much playing time: the daily ration of 83 overs was never completed because of rapidly fading light, and only 382 were bowled in a match unaffected by rain. England's return to the venue of the 1987-88 row between Mike Gatting and Shakoor Rana was not without further controversy. Hussain was given out lbw by Steve Bucknor when the TV replay clearly showed a thick edge; in the second innings, Mian Aslam gave him out caught behind off his pad, leaving Hussain stoical in public but distraught in private. These errors – obvious to the TV audience – increased the growing clamour for the third umpire to be consulted over borderline decisions. Thorpe again defended well: his 79 took 323 minutes, while Salisbury applied himself for 3½ hours as nightwatchman. England gained a lead of 26, helped by 32 no-balls. Then Abdul Razzaq, relishing his promotion to No. 3 (Saeed Anwar had an upset stomach), registered an accomplished maiden first Test century on his 21st birthday. England were set 244 in 62 overs, but a draw was their only realistic objective. Atherton battened down the hatches for 204 minutes. On a pitch where the spinners did most of the work, Wasim Akram had a quiet time in his 100th Test match.

Pakistan

Saeed Anwar c Thorpe b Giles	53		
Shahid Afridi c Thorpe b Gough	10	– c Giles b Gough	10
Salim Elahi c Atherton b Giles	41	– (1) c Stewart b Giles	72
Inzamam-ul-Haq b Giles	0	– c Hick b Salisbury	71
Yousuf Youhana c Thorpe b Gough	77		
Abdul Razzaq b White	9	– (3) not out	100
*†Moin Khan c Hussain b Giles	65		
Wasim Akram st Stewart b Giles	1	– (5) not out	4
Saqlain Mushtaq c Trescothick b Gough	34		
Arshad Khan c Thorpe b White	2		
Danish Kaneria not out	8		
B 1, l-b 12, n-b 3	16	B 6, l-b 5, n-b 1	12

1/33 (2) 2/96 (1) 3/96 (4) 4/130 (3)   316   1/13 (2) 2/111 (1)   (3 wkts dec.) 269
5/151 (6) 6/271 (5) 7/271 (7)   3/259 (4)
8/276 (8) 9/283 (10) 10/316 (9)

Gough 23.1–2–79–3; Caddick 15–3–49–0; White 25–6–71–2; Giles 35–13–75–5; Salisbury 10–0–29–0. *Second Innings*—Gough 10.2–1–32–1; Caddick 18–1–49–0; Giles 26–3–90–1; White 19–3–55–0; Salisbury 7–0–32–1.

England

M. A. Atherton c Yousuf Youhana b Saqlain Mushtaq	32	– not out	65
M. E. Trescothick st Moin Khan b Danish Kaneria	30	– b Saqlain Mushtaq	10
*N. Hussain lbw b Saqlain Mushtaq	23	– c Moin Khan b Arshad Khan	5
I. D. K. Salisbury c Yousuf Youhana b Arshad Khan	33		
G. P. Thorpe lbw b Wasim Akram	79	– (4) b Arshad Khan	0
†A. J. Stewart c Abdul Razzaq b Danish Kaneria	13	– (5) c Yousuf Youhana b Shahid Afridi	22
G. A. Hick c Yousuf Youhana b Abdul Razzaq	17	– (6) b Shahid Afridi	0
C. White b Saqlain Mushtaq	41	– (7) not out	9
A. F. Giles c Shahid Afridi b Abdul Razzaq	0		
A. R. Caddick c Moin Khan b Abdul Razzaq	5		
D. Gough not out	19		
B 4, l-b 14, n-b 32	50	L-b 4, n-b 10	14

1/49 (2) 2/105 (1) 3/106 (3) 4/203 (4)   342   1/44 (2) 2/57 (3)   (5 wkts) 125
5/235 (6) 6/274 (5) 7/274 (7)   3/57 (4) 4/108 (5) 5/110 (6)
8/275 (9) 9/295 (10) 10/342 (8)

Wasim Akram 26–6–69–1; Abdul Razzaq 20–0–74–3; Danish Kaneria 34–9–89–2; Saqlain Mushtaq 30.4–8–62–3; Arshad Khan 25–12–29–1; Shahid Afridi 1–0–1–0. *Second Innings*—Wasim Akram 5–1–13–0; Abdul Razzaq 1–1–0–0; Saqlain Mushtaq 19–4–26–1; Danish Kaneria 7–0–30–0; Arshad Khan 13–4–31–2; Shahid Afridi 12–3–21–2.

Umpires: S. A. Bucknor *(West Indies)* (53) and Mian Aslam *(Pakistan)* (6).
Third umpire: Shakeel Khan *(Pakistan)*.   Referee: R. S. Madugalle *(Sri Lanka)* (31).

Close of play: First day, Pakistan 243-5 (Yousuf Youhana 61*, Moin Khan 57*); Second day, England 110-3 (Salisbury 1*, Thorpe 2*); Third day, England 282-8 (White 6*, Caddick 2*); Fourth day, Pakistan 186-2 (Abdul Razzaq 60*, Inzamam-ul-Haq 33*).

PAKISTAN v ENGLAND 2000–01 (3rd Test)

At National Stadium, Karachi, on 7, 8, 9, 10, 11 December.
Toss: Pakistan.   Result: ENGLAND won by six wickets.
Debuts: none.
Man of the Match: M. A. Atherton.   Man of the Series: Yousuf Youhana.

England stole the series in the near-darkness, winning a Test in Pakistan for the first time in 39 years and inflicting Pakistan's first defeat in 35 Tests at the National Stadium. Moin Khan adopted desperate delaying tactics after Pakistan were bundled out for 158 on the final afternoon, leaving England to chase 176 in 44 overs. His bowlers took 40 minutes to send down the first seven, and almost 3½ hours to bowl a total of 41.3 nailbiting overs. Moin, who was warned for his go-slow strategy by the referee during tea, made three unsuccessful appeals for bad light as the batsmen resolutely stood their ground. Hick, after five successive failures, made a resolute 40 before being bowled when Waqar Younis was recalled for the 37th over. Waqar had come into the side only 15 minutes before the toss after Wasim Akram mysteriously withdrew, reportedly with a back spasm. With victory in sight (but little else), Thorpe edged the winning runs. Some of the Pakistani players thought he had been bowled, until the ball was spotted by a squinting fielder. England also owed much to Giles, whose seven wickets included the match-turning scalp of Inzamam-ul-Haq eight minutes before stumps on the fourth evening. Earlier in the match an England victory had looked a distant prospect as Inzamam and Yousuf Youhana shared a fourth-wicket stand of 259. Atherton responded with a marathon century, defying the heat and the bowlers for nine hours 38 minutes. It was Pakistan's fourth successive home series defeat.

Pakistan

Saeed Anwar lbw b Gough	8	– c Thorpe b Caddick	21
Imran Nazir c Giles b Trescothick	20	– c Stewart b Gough	4
Salim Elahi b Caddick	28	– c Thorpe b Giles	37
Inzamam-ul-Haq c Trescothick b White	142	– b Giles	27
Yousuf Youhana c and b Giles	117	– (6) c Stewart b White	24
Abdul Razzaq c Hussain b Giles	21	– (7) c Atherton b Giles	1
*†Moin Khan b Hick b Giles	13	– (8) c Hussain b White	14
Shahid Afridi b Giles	10	– (9) not out	15
Saqlain Mushtaq b Gough	16	– (5) lbw b Gough	4
Waqar Younis b Gough	17	– run out	0
Danish Kaneria not out	0	– lbw b Gough	0
B 3, l-b 3, n-b 7	13	B 3, l-b 5, n-b 3	11

1/8 (1) 2/44 (2) 3/64 (3) 4/323 (5)   405   1/24 (2) 2/26 (1) 3/71 (4)   158
5/325 (4) 6/340 (7) 7/359 (8)   4/78 (5) 5/128 (6) 6/128 (3)
8/374 (6) 9/402 (9) 10/405 (10)   7/139 (7) 8/143 (8) 9/149 (10) 10/158 (11)

Gough 27.4–5–82–3; Caddick 23–1–76–1; Trescothick 14–1–34–1; White 22–3–64–1; Salisbury 18–3–49–0; Giles 35–7–94–4. *Second Innings*—Gough 13–4–30–3; Caddick 15–2–40–1; Giles 27–12–38–3; Salisbury 3–0–12–0; White 12–4–30–2.

England

M. A. Atherton c Moin Khan b Abdul Razzaq	125	– c Saeed Anwar b Saqlain Mushtaq	26
M. E. Trescothick c Imran Nazir b Waqar Younis	13	– c Inzamam-ul-Haq b Saqlain Mushtaq	24
*N. Hussain c Inzamam-ul-Haq b Shahid Afridi	51	– (6) not out	6
G. P. Thorpe lbw b Waqar Younis	18	– not out	64
†A. J. Stewart c Yousuf Youhana b Saqlain Mushtaq	29	– (3) c Moin Khan b Saqlain Mushtaq	5
G. A. Hick c Shahid Afridi b Waqar Younis	12	– (5) b Waqar Younis	40
C. White st Moin Khan b Danish Kaneria	35		
A. F. Giles b Waqar Younis	19		
I. D. K. Salisbury not out	20		
A. R. Caddick c Moin Khan b Danish Kaneria	3		
D. Gough c Yousuf Youhana b Saqlain Mushtaq	18		
B 12, l-b 9, n-b 24	45	B 8, l-b 2, w 1	11

1/29 (2) 2/163 (3) 3/195 (4) 4/256 (5)   388   1/38 (1) 2/51 (2)   (4 wkts) 176
5/278 (6) 6/309 (1) 7/339 (8)   3/65 (3) 4/156 (5)
8/345 (7) 9/349 (10) 10/388 (11)

Waqar Younis 36–5–88–4; Abdul Razzaq 28–7–64–1; Shahid Afridi 16–3–34–1; Saqlain Mushtaq 52.1–17–101–2; Danish Kaneria 47–17–80–2. *Second Innings*—Waqar Younis 6–0–27–1; Abdul Razzaq 4–0–17–0; Saqlain Mushtaq 17.3–1–64–3; Danish Kaneria 3–0–18–0; Shahid Afridi 11–1–40–0.

Umpires: S. A. Bucknor *(West Indies)* (54) and Mohammad Nazir *(Pakistan)* (4).
Third umpire: Feroze Butt *(Pakistan)*.   Referee: R. S. Madugalle *(Sri Lanka)* (32).

Close of play: First day, Pakistan 292-3 (Inzamam-ul-Haq 123*, Yousuf Youhana 104*); Second day, England 79-1 (Atherton 43*, Hussain 13*); Third day, England 277-4 (Atherton 117*, Hick 12*); Fourth day, Pakistan 71-3 (Salim Elahi 14*, Saqlain Mushtaq 0*).

SOUTH AFRICA v NEW ZEALAND 2000–01 (1st Test)

At Springbok Park, Bloemfontein, on 17, 18, 19, 20, 21 November.
Toss: South Africa.   Result: SOUTH AFRICA won by five wickets.
Debuts: New Zealand – C. S. Martin, B. G. K. Walker.
Men of the Match: J. H. Kallis and M. Ntini.

Since winning in Zimbabwe New Zealand had gone down 5–0 in a one-day series to South Africa, and had also lost their first-choice new-ball pairing to injury. They duly lost here, too, first taken apart by Kallis, who collected his seventh Test century, then filleted by Donald, who became the first South African to take 300 Test wickets when he trapped O'Connor in front in the first innings, a feat acclaimed by his home crowd and a three-gun salute from an armoured car near the boundary. Kallis's 160, his highest Test score at the time, came from 289 balls and contained 26 fours: particularly on the opening day, he was given too much width. He came to the crease in the first over of the match, when Dippenaar fell to O'Connor's second ball. With Fleming leading the way before becoming the seventh from his country to be dismissed for 99 in a Test, New Zealand fared better in the follow-on, helped by the pitch playing slower and lower. Richardson (the previous entrant in New Zealand's 99 club, two months previously) again demonstrated his adhesive qualities, making 77 in 63 overs, while McMillan stuck it out for 67 overs. But Ntini demolished the tail with three wickets in three overs to leave his side needing only 101 to win. They lost five wickets in doing so, Boucher completing the victory after tea on the final day by sweeping three successive fours off the debutant legspinner Brooke Walker.

South Africa

H. H. Dippenaar c Astle b O'Connor	0	– c Parore b Tuffey	27
G. Kirsten c Astle b Martin	31	– lbw b O'Connor	1
J. H. Kallis c Parore b O'Connor	160	– lbw b Martin	13
D. J. Cullinan b Walker	29	– lbw b Tuffey	22
N. D. McKenzie c Parore b Martin	55	– not out	13
†M. V. Boucher lbw b Walker	76	– (7) not out	22
L. Klusener b O'Connor	9	– (6) c McMillan b Tuffey	4
N. Boje c Tuffey b Astle	43		
*S. M. Pollock c Sinclair b Martin	25		
A. A. Donald not out	21		
B 5, l-b 7, n-b 10	22	N-b 1	1

1/0 (1) 2/97 (2) 3/164 (4)   (9 wkts dec.) 471   1/3 (2) 2/16 (3) 3/55 (1)   (5 wkts) 103
4/279 (3) 5/304 (5) 6/330 (7)   4/69 (4) 5/75 (6)
7/409 (8) 8/429 (6) 9/471 (9)

M. Ntini did not bat.

O'Connor 30–4–87–3; Tuffey 26–6–96–0; Martin 22.1–4–89–3; Walker 27–4–92–2; Astle 24–5–57–1; McMillan 13–2–38–0. *Second Innings*—O'Connor 7–0–28–1; Martin 5–3–18–1; Tuffey 8–1–38–3; Walker 6.3–2–19–0.

New Zealand

M. H. Richardson b Donald	23	– lbw b Donald	77
C. M. Spearman c Klusener b Pollock	23	– c McKenzie b Ntini	15
M. S. Sinclair c Cullinan b Pollock	1	– c Klusener b Donald	20
*S. P. Fleming b Boje	57	– c Kirsten b Donald	99
N. J. Astle c Kallis b Ntini	37	– b Ntini	8
C. D. McMillan c Boucher b Donald	16	– c Kirsten b Kallis	78
†A. C. Parore lbw b Pollock	11	– (8) c Kallis b Ntini	12
B. G. K. Walker not out	27	– (7) c Boucher b Ntini	10
D. R. Tuffey b Pollock	0	– b Ntini	6
S. B. O'Connor lbw b Donald	15	– b Ntini	0
C. S. Martin c Boucher b Kallis	7	– not out	0
B 1, l-b 7, w 2, n-b 2	12	B 2, l-b 10, w 1, n-b 4	17

1/28 (1) 2/29 (3) 3/72 (2) 4/151 (4)   229   1/33 (2) 2/93 (3) 3/145 (1)   342
5/153 (5) 6/176 (6) 7/183 (7)   4/175 (5) 5/247 (4) 6/285 (7)
8/185 (9) 9/213 (10) 10/229 (11)   7/325 (6) 8/340 (9) 9/341 (8) 10/342 (10)

Donald 21–4–69–3; Pollock 22–10–37–4; Ntini 14–4–48–1; Kallis 13–5–30–1; Boje 16–4–35–1; Klusener 3–2–2–0. *Second Innings*—Donald 28–14–43–3; Pollock 25–11–47–0; Ntini 31.4–12–66–6; Kallis 23–4–88–1; Boje 40–14–61–0; Klusener 10–3–25–0.

Umpires: A. V. Jayaprakash *(India)* (6) and D. L. Orchard *(South Africa)* (20).
Third umpire: R. E. Koertzen *(South Africa)*.   Referee: Naushad Ali *(Pakistan)* (1).

Close of play: First day, South Africa 270-3 (Kallis 153*, McKenzie 42*); Second day, New Zealand 54-2 (Spearman 14*, Fleming 10*); Third day, New Zealand 82-1 (Richardson 50*, Sinclair 11*); Fourth day, New Zealand 260-5 (McMillan 25*, Walker 5*).

7

SOUTH AFRICA v NEW ZEALAND 2000–01 (2nd Test)

At St George's Park, Port Elizabeth, on 30 November, 1, 2, 3, 4 December.
Toss: South Africa.   Result: SOUTH AFRICA won by seven wickets.
Debuts: none.
Man of the Match: N. D. McKenzie.

With Sinclair making 150 and McKenzie responding with his maiden Test century, honours were roughly even until the fourth afternoon, when five New Zealand wickets tumbled for 69 between lunch and tea, with Pollock removing the stubborn Richardson and McMillan with successive deliveries. Klusener then polished off the innings with three wickets in ten balls, and South Africa were left needing only 86 to take the match and the series. "Poor batsmanship and poor option-taking," said Fleming of that disastrous session. New Zealand, in fact, had looked slight favourites midway through the match, when they reduced South Africa to 209 for 7. Martin took four wickets and Astle removed Kallis during an economical spell – but McKenzie, who hit 20 fours in a stylish display, and Boje then put on 136. Last out, Boje wasn't finished with the New Zealanders. He trapped Sinclair lbw shortly before lunch on the fourth day, and had Fleming caught at slip two overs later just after New Zealand had crept in front. The came the deciding session, which ensured Pollock's first series win as captain. The only shadow on the horizon was Donald's stomach-muscle strain, which kept him out of the final Test. Sinclair's 150, which lasted 397 minutes and included a six and 23 fours, was his first century since making 214 on debut against West Indies at Wellington in 1999-2000, and the highest for New Zealand against South Africa, beating John Reid's 142 at Johannesburg in 1961-62.

New Zealand

M. H. Richardson	b Ntini	26	– c Boucher b Pollock	60
C. M. Spearman	c Kirsten b Donald	16	– lbw b Donald	0
M. S. Sinclair	c Kirsten b Donald	150	– lbw b Boje	17
*S. P. Fleming	c and b Pollock	14	– c Cullinan b Boje	8
N. J. Astle	lbw b Pollock	2	– c Boucher b Ntini	18
C. D. McMillan	c Ntini b Pollock	39	– lbw b Pollock	0
†A. C. Parore	c Boucher b Donald	2	– c Kirsten b Ntini	5
B. G. K. Walker	c Cullinan b Pollock	3	– lbw b Klusener	19
S. B. O'Connor	b Kallis	20	– b Klusener	8
K. P. Walmsley	c Cullinan b Donald	5	– lbw b Klusener	5
C. S. Martin	not out	5	– not out	0
	B 4, l-b 5, w 2, n-b 5	16	B 6, l-b 3, n-b 4	13

1/43 (2) 2/55 (1) 3/95 (4) 4/101 (5)   298   1/4 (2) 2/54 (3) 3/64 (4)   148
5/172 (6) 6/194 (7) 7/203 (8)   4/111 (1) 5/111 (6) 6/115 (5)
8/276 (9) 9/291 (3) 10/298 (10)   7/122 (7) 8/147 (9) 9/147 (10) 10/148 (8)

Donald 26.3–2–69–4; Pollock 32–15–64–4; Kallis 21–8–44–1; Ntini 22–7–59–1; Klusener 6–2–8–0; Boje 19–5–45–0. *Second Innings*—Donald 7–1–16–1; Pollock 15–4–44–2; Ntini 16–6–24–2; Boje 15–2–30–2; Kallis 7–2–17–0; Klusener 9.3–5–8–3.

South Africa

H. H. Dippenaar	lbw b Martin	35	– lbw b O'Connor	0
G. Kirsten	c Parore b Walmsley	49	– not out	47
J. H. Kallis	c Parore b Astle	12	– c O'Connor b Martin	23
D. J. Cullinan	b Walker	33	– b Walmsley	11
*S. M. Pollock	c Spearman b Martin	33		
N. D. McKenzie	c Spearman b McMillan	120	– (5) not out	7
†M. V. Boucher	b O'Connor	0		
L. Klusener	c Parore b Martin	6		
N. Boje	c Parore b O'Connor	51		
A. A. Donald	lbw b Martin	9		
M. Ntini	not out	0		
	B 7, l-b 4, w 2	13	L-b 1	1

1/81 (1) 2/96 (3) 3/114 (2) 4/151 (4)   361   1/4 (1) 2/53 (3) 3/71 (4)   (3 wkts) 89
5/181 (5) 6/184 (7) 7/209 (8)
8/345 (6) 9/361 (10) 10/361 (9)

O'Connor 26.4–8–68–2; Martin 29–8–104–4; Walmsley 13–2–40–1; Walker 23–5–61–1; Astle 36–18–46–1; McMillan 17–6–31–1. *Second Innings*—O'Connor 8–4–9–1; Martin 12–3–32–1; Astle 2–0–8–0; Walker 7.1–1–32–0; Walmsley 5–2–7–1.

Umpires: R. E. Koertzen *(South Africa)* (20) and I. D. Robinson *(Zimbabwe)* (24).
Third umpire: D. L. Orchard *(South Africa)*.   Referee: Naushad Ali *(Pakistan)* (2).

Close of play: First day, New Zealand 206-7 (Sinclair 88*, O'Connor 3*); Second day, South Africa 123-3 (Cullinan 13*, Pollock 5*); Third day, South Africa 361-8 (Boje 51*, Donald 9*); Fourth day, South Africa 29-1 (Kirsten 22*, Kallis 6*).

SOUTH AFRICA v NEW ZEALAND 2000–01 (3rd Test)

At The Wanderers, Johannesburg, on 8 *(no play)*, 9, 10 *(no play)*, 11 *(no play)*, 12 December.
Toss: South Africa.   Result: MATCH DRAWN.
Debuts: South Africa – M. Ngam. New Zealand – H. J. H. Marshall.
Men of the Match: C. Scott and his groundstaff.   Man of the Series: M. Ntini.

South Africa's hopes of a clean sweep were washed away by rain, which prevented any play on the first, third and fourth days. When play did start New Zealand struggled against an attack lacking Donald, who had strained a stomach muscle in the previous Test. His replacement, Mfuneko "Chewing" Ngam, should have had a wicket in his first over. Cullinan, at slip, dropped makeshift opener Parore, and did it again in Ngam's third over. Dippenaar, at short leg, also gave each opener a life, and New Zealand could count their good fortune when they lunched at 83 for 1. They were unable to capitalise on it. Five wickets fell for 38 in the second session, starting with the dismissals of Richardson – Ngam's first victim, at last – and Sinclair immediately after the resumption. Ntini dismissed Fleming and Astle in successive overs, and only the debutant Hamish Marshall survived the collapse, if not without alarms. He was an hour and 38 balls over opening his Test account, and was struck on the helmet more than once, but without his three-hour struggle New Zealand would not have reached 200. When South Africa batted, Dippenaar hit 21 fours in his maiden Test century, then, as if the pointlessness of the proceedings needed accentuating, Kallis hung around after their century partnership to finish with 79 from 211 balls, while Cullinan faced 112 for his unbeaten 31. The match award deservedly went to the Wanderers' hard-working groundsman Chris Scott and his staff.

New Zealand

M. H. Richardson c Boucher b Ngam	46		S. B. O'Connor c Kallis b Pollock		9
†A. C. Parore c McKenzie b Ntini	10		C. S. Martin b Kallis		0
M. S. Sinclair c Klusener b Pollock	24				
*S. P. Fleming b Ntini	14		B 2, l-b 9, w 1, n-b 4		16
N. J. Astle c Kallis b Ntini	12				—
C. D. McMillan c Klusener b Kallis	4		1/37 (2) 2/83 (1) 3/83 (3)		200
H. J. H. Marshall not out	40		4/112 (4) 5/113 (5) 6/117 (6)		
B. G. K. Walker lbw b Klusener	17		7/148 (8) 8/174 (9)		
D. R. Tuffey c Boucher b Ngam	8		9/199 (10) 10/200 (11)		

Pollock 26–9–41–2; Ngam 19–8–34–2; Kallis 15.5–4–26–2; Ntini 18–9–29–3; Klusener 12–2–43–1; Boje 3–0–16–0.

South Africa

H. H. Dippenaar b O'Connor	100		D. J. Cullinan not out		31
G. Kirsten c Richardson b Martin	10		L-b 17, w 2		19
N. Boje c Sinclair b Martin	22				—
J. H. Kallis not out	79		1/18 (2) 2/87 (3) 3/187 (1)	(3 wkts dec.)	261

N. D. McKenzie, †M. V. Boucher, L. Klusener, *S. M. Pollock, M. Ntini and M. Ngam did not bat.

O'Connor 15–5–52–1; Martin 15–4–43–2; Tuffey 19–4–60–0; Astle 26–15–31–0; McMillan 17–5–41–0; Marshall 1–0–4–0; Sinclair 4–0–13–0.

Umpires: D. L. Orchard *(South Africa)* (21) and G. Sharp *(England)* (13).
Third umpire: R. E. Koertzen *(South Africa)*.   Referee: Naushad Ali *(Pakistan)* (3).

Close of play: First day, No play; Second day, South Africa 18-1 (Dippenaar 5*, Boje 0*); Third day, No play; Fourth day, No play.

INDIA v ZIMBABWE 2000–01 (1st Test)

At Feroz Shah Kotla, Delhi, on 18, 19, 20, 21, 22 November.
Toss: Zimbabwe.   Result: INDIA won by seven wickets.
Debuts: India – V. Dahiya.
Man of the Match: J. Srinath.

After two substantial first innings, the match was turned by the fiery bowling of Srinath, who demolished Zimbabwe's second innings. He dismissed both openers without scoring, then removed Campbell, who in the first innings had become the third Zimbabwean to score 2,000 Test runs, following the Flower brothers. Although Andy Flower then defended for 200 minutes, and Paul Strang survived for nearly two hours, India were eventually set 190 to win in 47 overs: they hurried home with almost ten to spare. Dravid was still there at the end: in all he scored 270 runs in the match without being out, passing 3,000 in Tests in the process. That included the first of his eventual five double-centuries in the first innings, during which he batted for 541 minutes (350 balls) and included 27 fours. He put on 213 with Tendulkar, who cruised to his 23rd Test century. Ganguly made a bold declaration immediately Dravid reached 200, just before tea on the fourth day: India were only 36 ahead, and the pitch was showing few signs of wear and tear. But Srinath blew away both openers for ducks, and Zimbabwe fizzled out for 225. In their first innings Andy Flower's 183 not out had occupied 466 minutes, and included 24 fours and two sixes ... and an unlikely tenth-wicket stand of 97 – still a national record – with Olonga, who kept his end up for 158 minutes.

Zimbabwe

G. W. Flower b Srinath	0	– c Dahiya b Srinath		0
G. J. Rennie c Dahiya b Srinath	13	– c Ganguly b Srinath		0
S. V. Carlisle c Joshi b Tendulkar	58	– c Ganguly b Joshi		32
A. D. R. Campbell c Laxman b Srinath	70	– c Dravid b Srinath		8
†A. Flower not out	183	– lbw b Agarkar		70
G. J. Whittall c Dravid b Joshi	0	– c Ramesh b Kartik		29
*H. H. Streak c Dravid b Srinath	25	– (8) lbw b Kartik		26
P. A. Strang c Ganguly b Joshi	19	– (9) not out		14
B. A. Murphy run out	13	– (7) c Dahiya b Srinath		6
B. C. Strang lbw b Agarkar	6	– c Tendulkar b Joshi		15
H. K. Olonga not out	11	– lbw b Srinath		10
B 8, l-b 10, w 4, n-b 2	24	B 4, l-b 9, w 1, n-b 1		15

1/0 (1) 2/15 (2) 3/134 (3)　　　　(9 wkts dec.) 422　　1/0 (1) 2/15 (2) 3/25 (4)　　　　　　225
4/154 (4) 5/155 (6) 6/232 (7)　　　　　　　　　　　　　　　4/47 (3) 5/109 (6) 6/144 (7)
7/266 (8) 8/312 (9) 9/325 (10)　　　　　　　　　　　　　　7/171 (5) 8/181 (8) 9/213 (10) 10/225 (11)

Srinath 35–9–81–4; Agarkar 35–13–89–1; Ganguly 8–1–26–0; Joshi 46–11–116–2; Tendulkar 19–5–51–1; Kartik 24–7–40–0; Laxman 1–0–1–0. *Second Innings*—Srinath 24.1–6–60–5; Agarkar 16–4–48–1; Joshi 25–7–68–2; Tendulkar 4–1–10–0; Kartik 11–2–26–2.

India

S. S. Das lbw b Olonga	58	– run out		4
S. Ramesh lbw b Streak	13	– c P. A. Strang b Streak		0
R. Dravid not out	200	– not out		70
S. R. Tendulkar c P. A. Strang b Murphy	122	– c Murphy b P. A. Strang		39
*S. C. Ganguly c A. Flower b Olonga	27	– not out		65
V. V. S. Laxman not out	18			
B 2, l-b 10, w 2, n-b 6	20	B 9, l-b 1, w 1, n-b 1		12

1/27 (2) 2/134 (1)　　　　　　　(4 wkts dec.) 458　　1/3 (2) 2/15 (1) 3/80 (4)　　　(3 wkts) 190
3/347 (4) 4/430 (5)

A. B. Agarkar, S. B. Joshi, †V. Dahiya, M. Kartik and J. Srinath did not bat.

Streak 30–9–78–1; B. C. Strang 28–9–95–0; Murphy 36–5–90–1; Olonga 20–3–79–2; P. A. Strang 15–1–52–0; G. W. Flower 13.4–3–52–0. *Second Innings*—Streak 5–2–18–1; B. C. Strang 3–0–20–0; Olonga 6–0–26–0; Murphy 11–0–56–0; P. A. Strang 4.2–0–26–1; G. W. Flower 1.4–0–10–0; Rennie 3.3–0–19–0; Campbell 3–1–5–0.

Umpires: J. H. Hampshire *(England)* (14) and S. Venkataraghavan *(India)* (40).
Third umpire: V. Chopra *(India)*.   Referee: B. N. Jarman *(Australia)* (22).

Close of play: First day, Zimbabwe 232-5 (A. Flower 55*, Streak 25*); Second day, India 9-0 (Das 4*, Ramesh 3*); Third day, India 275-2 (Dravid 118*, Tendulkar 70*); Fourth day, Zimbabwe 119-5 (A. Flower 41*, Murphy 0*).

INDIA v ZIMBABWE 2000–01 (2nd Test)

At Vidarbha C. A. Ground, Nagpur, on 25, 26, 27, 28, 29 November.
Toss: India.   Result: MATCH DRAWN.
Debuts: India – Sarandeep Singh.
Man of the Match: A. Flower.   Man of the Series: A. Flower.

Another magnificent display from Andy Flower denied India victory, although they still took the short series. Tendulkar's second Test double-century underpinned India's massive first innings, which lasted till ten overs after tea on the second day on a placid track. Tendulkar's innings lasted 392 minutes and 281 balls, and included 27 fours. He shared his second double-century stand in successive Tests with Dravid, who took his series aggregate to 432 before he was finally dismissed. Earlier, Das had made his maiden Test hundred. Zimbabwe were forced to follow on despite a dogged century from Grant Flower, who batted down the order after a king pair in the previous Test, but it was the other Flower brother who dominated the follow-on, taking Zimbabwe to safety with the highest Test score ever by a wicketkeeper, beating Taslim Arif's 210 not out for Pakistan v Australia at Faisalabad in 1979-80. After the debutant offspinner Sarandeep Singh had taken three quick wickets (including Carlisle and Rennie in the same over), Andy Flower batted for 544 minutes, facing 444 balls, and hit 30 fours and two sixes: he put on 209 with Campbell, who finally made his maiden century in his (and Zimbabwe's) 47th Test, and 113 with Viljoen (a last-minute fly-in for the injured Paul Strang) for the sixth wicket to ensure safety. Ganguly, who could have become the first Indian captain to win his first three Tests in charge, complained that the pitch was fit enough at the conclusion for another five-day match.

India

S. S. Das c Campbell b Murphy	110	†V. Dahiya not out 2
S. Ramesh run out	48	
R. Dravid c A. Flower b Streak	162	L-b 11, w 4, n-b 2 17
S. R. Tendulkar not out	201	
*S. C. Ganguly c Streak b G. W. Flower	30	1/72 (2) 2/227 (1) (6 wkts dec.) 609
A. B. Agarkar c Streak b Murphy	12	3/476 (3) 4/535 (5)
S. B. Joshi c Murphy b G. W. Flower	27	5/564 (6) 6/601 (7)

J. Srinath, Zaheer Khan and Sarandeep Singh did not bat.

Streak 31–7–87–1; Olonga 24–4–98–0; Nkala 22–2–86–0; Murphy 40.5–2–175–2; Viljoen 14–2–51–0; G. W. Flower 24–0–101–2.

Zimbabwe

G. J. Whittall c Dravid b Sarandeep Singh	84	– c Tendulkar b Sarandeep Singh	11
G. J. Rennie run out	19	– c Ganguly b Sarandeep Singh	37
S. V. Carlisle c and b Agarkar	51	– c Tendulkar b Sarandeep Singh	8
A. D. R. Campbell c Ramesh b Sarandeep Singh	4	– c Joshi b Zaheer Khan	102
†A. Flower c Dahiya b Agarkar	55	– not out	232
G. W. Flower not out	106	– c Ganguly b Joshi	16
D. P. Viljoen c Dahiya b Zaheer Khan	19	– c Ganguly b Sarandeep Singh	38
*H. H. Streak lbw b Srinath	16	– not out	29
M. L. Nkala c Dahiya b Srinath	6		
B. A. Murphy c Das b Joshi	0		
H. K. Olonga b Srinath	0		
B 6, l-b 12, w 1, n-b 3	22	B 12, l-b 14, n-b 4	30

1/43 (2) 2/144 (3) 3/165 (4) 4/166 (1)	382	1/24 (1) 2/60 (3)	(6 wkts) 503
5/262 (5) 6/324 (7) 7/359 (8)		3/61 (2) 4/270 (4)	
8/371 (9) 9/372 (10) 10/382 (11)		5/292 (6) 6/405 (7)	

Srinath 28.1–7–81–3; Zaheer Khan 21–3–78–1; Joshi 25–7–69–1; Agarkar 23–7–59–2; Sarandeep Singh 22–7–70–2; Tendulkar 1–0–7–0. *Second Innings*—Zaheer Khan 17–5–48–1; Agarkar 14–3–29–0; Sarandeep Singh 49–10–136–4; Joshi 41–5–153–1; Tendulkar 11–3–19–0; Srinath 15–5–53–0; Ramesh 3–0–14–0; Dravid 7–0–15–0; Ganguly 1–0–3–0; Das 3–0–7–0.

Umpires: R. S. Dunne *(New Zealand)* (36) and A. V. Jayaprakash *(India)* (7).
Third umpire: K. S. Giridharan *(India)*.   Referee: B. N. Jarman *(Australia)* (23).

Close of play: First day, India 306-2 (Dravid 93*, Tendulkar 49*); Second day, Zimbabwe 59-1 (Whittall 34*, Carlisle 4*); Third day, Zimbabwe 359-6 (G. W. Flower 91*, Streak 16*); Fourth day, Zimbabwe 238-3 (Campbell 83*, A. Flower 88*).

AUSTRALIA v WEST INDIES 2000–01 (1st Test)

At Woolloongabba, Brisbane, on 23, 24, 25 November.
Toss: Australia.   Result: AUSTRALIA won by an innings and 126 runs.
Debuts: West Indies – M. I. Black.
Man of the Match: G. D. McGrath.

Glenn McGrath took advantage of a slow, seaming wicket – Test cricket's first "drop-in" pitch (one prepared outside the ground and put in position by crane) – to take ten for 27 from 33 overs in a match which was over in around half the scheduled playing time. Only the Australian slow left-armer Bert Ironmonger, with 11 for 24 against South Africa on a rain-affected Melbourne strip in 1931-32, has taken ten wickets in a Test at a lower cost. McGrath's first-innings burst of six for eight in 68 balls helped shoot out West Indies for 82, their third sub-100 total in Tests since June: there were some wry smiles afterwards when the tourists' management insisted their problems were temperamental not technical, and called in psychologist Rudi Webster. Australia were in front by the end of the first day, and although they scored at less than three an over the eventual total – boosted by a maiden half-century from Lee – was more than enough for an innings win. Lara fell cheaply to McGrath in both innings, while Sarwan, chosen despite making two ducks in the preceding tour game against Victoria, bagged another pair. Only Chanderpaul, whose second innings spanned 229 minutes, held up Australia for long as they completed their 11th consecutive Test victory, equalling West Indies' own record from the mid-1980s. With Warne nursing a broken finger, Australia recalled legspinner Stuart MacGill after 19 months: he started the procession by taking the first wicket of the match, and bowled with impressive control throughout.

West Indies

S. L. Campbell	c M. E. Waugh b MacGill	10	– c Gilchrist b McGrath	0
D. Ganga	c Ponting b Bichel	20	– st Gilchrist b MacGill	8
B. C. Lara	c Gilchrist b McGrath	0	– c Gilchrist b McGrath	4
S. Chanderpaul	c Gilchrist b McGrath	18	– not out	62
*J. C. Adams	not out	16	– c Gilchrist b Lee	16
R. R. Sarwan	run out	0	– b Lee	0
†R. D. Jacobs	c M. E. Waugh b McGrath	2	– c M. E. Waugh b Bichel	4
N. A. M. McLean	lbw b McGrath	0	– lbw b Lee	13
M. Dillon	c Gilchrist b McGrath	0	– b McGrath	0
M. I. Black	c MacGill b McGrath	0	– c Gilchrist b McGrath	2
C. A. Walsh	c Langer b Lee	9	– c McGrath b MacGill	0
	L-b 6, n-b 1	7	B 8, l-b 3, n-b 4	15

1/21 (1) 2/25 (3) 3/53 (4) 4/59 (2)   82   1/0 (1) 2/10 (3) 3/29 (2) 4/62 (5)   124
5/60 (6) 6/63 (7) 7/63 (8)   5/66 (6) 6/81 (7) 7/98 (8)
8/67 (9) 9/67 (10) 10/82 (11)   8/117 (9) 9/119 (10) 10/124 (11)

McGrath 20–12–17–6; Lee 11.1–5–24–1; MacGill 5–1–10–1; Bichel 13–3–25–1. *Second Innings*—McGrath 13–9–10–4; Lee 18–9–40–3; MacGill 16–5–42–2; Bichel 11–4–21–1.

Australia

M. J. Slater	c Campbell b Black	54	S. C. G. MacGill	run out	19
M. L. Hayden	run out	44	G. D. McGrath	b Walsh	0
A. J. Bichel	c Jacobs b Black	8		L-b 5, n-b 4	9
J. L. Langer	c Jacobs b Black	3			
M. E. Waugh	c and b Dillon	24	1/101 (2) 2/111 (1) 3/112 (3)		332
*S. R. Waugh	c Campbell b Dillon	41	4/117 (4) 5/179 (5) 6/186 (6)		
R. T. Ponting	c Jacobs b Black	20	7/220 (7) 8/281 (8)		
†A. C. Gilchrist	c Jacobs b Dillon	48	9/331 (10) 10/332 (11)		
B. Lee	not out	62			

Walsh 31.4–7–78–1; Black 28–5–83–4; Dillon 25–8–79–3; McLean 25–5–79–0; Adams 5–2–8–0.

Umpires: D. B. Cowie *(New Zealand)* (19) and D. J. Harper *(Australia)* (10).
Third umpire: P. D. Parker *(Australia)*.   Referee: A. C. Smith *(England)* (5).

Close of play: First day, Australia 107-1 (Slater 54*, Bichel 4*); Second day, West Indies 25-2 (Ganga 8*, Chanderpaul 7*).

AUSTRALIA v WEST INDIES 2000–01 (2nd Test)

At W. A. C. A. Ground, Perth, on 1, 2, 3 December.
Toss: Australia.   Result: AUSTRALIA won by an innings and 27 runs.
Debuts: none.
Man of the Match: M. E. Waugh.

Within an hour of the start McGrath had taken a hat-trick, Lara had made a duck and West Indies had lost five wickets, and Australia's record 12th consecutive victory – beating the 11 of West Indies between March and December 1984 – was all but assured. McGrath's top-quality hat-trick, which included his 300th Test wicket, came when Campbell and Lara snicked away-cutters into the slips, then a mesmerised Adams popped a catch to short leg. Hinds and Jacobs, who was stranded just short of a maiden century, organised some sort of recovery, but a masterly century from Mark Waugh, combining classic batsmanship with limited-overs imagination, set up a lead of 200. Again it proved more than enough. Lara began the third day full of good intentions. He survived McGrath's barrage, but after almost an hour tried a horribly inappropriate pull at MacGill and was bowled. Hinds, Adams and Jacobs – left-handers all – put up more than six hours of stout-hearted resistance between them, raising a cheer of genuine appreciation from the crowd and causing Australia to experiment with part-time bowlers – but when Jacobs was foolishly run out, Lee fired out the last three in the same over to summarily finish the match. West Indies, who had won all their five previous Tests at the WACA, now lost within three days for the fourth time in their last six Test matches. Australia's sole setback was the torn buttock muscle that kept Steve Waugh, their captain, out of the next match.

West Indies

S. L. Campbell c Ponting b McGrath	3	– c Gillespie b Lee	4
D. Ganga lbw b Lee	0	– c Hayden b Gillespie	20
W. W. Hinds c M. E. Waugh b MacGill	50	– (4) b MacGill	41
B. C. Lara c MacGill b McGrath	0	– (5) b MacGill	17
*J. C. Adams c Langer b McGrath	0	– (6) not out	40
R. R. Sarwan c Slater b Lee	2	– (7) c Gilchrist b Lee	1
†R. D. Jacobs not out	96	– (8) run out	24
N. A. M. McLean b MacGill	7	– (9) b Lee	11
M. Dillon c Hayden b Gillespie	27	– (3) c Gilchrist b McGrath	3
M. I. Black c Hayden b Gillespie	0	– b Lee	0
C. A. Walsh c Gilchrist b Gillespie	1	– lbw b Lee	0
L-b 3, n-b 7	10	B 1, l-b 8, n-b 3	12

1/1 (2) 2/19 (1) 3/19 (4) 4/19 (5)   196   1/7 (1) 2/16 (3) 3/42 (2)   173
5/22 (6) 6/97 (3) 7/117 (8)   4/78 (5) 5/95 (4) 6/96 (7)
8/172 (9) 9/178 (10) 10/196 (11)   7/150 (8) 8/173 (9) 9/173 (10) 10/173 (11)

McGrath 19–2–48–3; Lee 15–5–52–2; Gillespie 12–2–46–3; MacGill 15–2–47–2. *Second Innings*—McGrath 18–7–26–1; Lee 15–2–61–5; MacGill 17–6–37–2; Gillespie 12–4–26–1; Hayden 2–0–9–0; M. E. Waugh 2–1–5–0.

Australia

M. L. Hayden b Black	69	B. Lee not out	41
M. J. Slater c Campbell b Dillon	19	S. C. G. MacGill not out	18
J. L. Langer c Sarwan b McLean	5	B 2, l-b 10, w 2, n-b 7	21
J. N. Gillespie c Lara b McLean	23		
M. E. Waugh c Adams b Dillon	119	1/52 (2) 2/62 (3) (8 wkts dec.) 396	
*S. R. Waugh c Campbell b Walsh	26	3/111 (1) 4/123 (4)	
R. T. Ponting b Black	5	5/188 (6) 6/208 (7)	
†A. C. Gilchrist c McLean b Walsh	50	7/303 (8) 8/348 (5)	

G. D. McGrath did not bat.

Walsh 31–10–74–2; Black 18–2–87–2; Dillon 29–4–130–2; McLean 22–3–78–2; Adams 8–3–15–0.

Umpires: J. H. Hampshire *(England)* (15) and P. D. Parker *(Australia)* (6).
Third umpire: R. J. Woolridge *(Australia)*.   Referee: A. C. Smith *(England)* (6).

Close of play: First day, Australia 72-2 (Hayden 46*, Gillespie 1*); Second day, West Indies 16-2 (Ganga 9*).

AUSTRALIA v WEST INDIES 2000–01 (3rd Test)

At Adelaide Oval on 15, 16, 17, 18, 19 December.
Toss: West Indies.   Result: AUSTRALIA won by five wickets.
Debuts: West Indies – M. N. Samuels.
Man of the Match: C. R. Miller.

Australia took the series and retained the Frank Worrell Trophy, although at least this time the match made it into the fifth day (just). Lara, who had just hammered 231 against Australia A, continued his return to form with a majestic 182, containing 29 fours and a six. Adams kept him company for almost three hours, contributing 49 to a partnership of 183. Gillespie took the first five wickets, then the debutant offspinner Colin "Funky" Miller took the last five, including Lara to a fine slip catch. Australia's openers put on a breezy 156, but the efforts of Ponting and Martyn (in his first home Test for nearly seven years) to build a lead were stymied when the last five wickets managed only 34. Lara threatened again, but when he turned Miller's arm-ball to short leg with the total 87 West Indies lost their last eight wickets for 54 to present Australia with a small target, although it looked rather bigger when they slipped to 48 for 4. Gilchrist was in at the end to complete victory: he was captain for the first time, in only his 12th Test, in the absence of the injured Steve Waugh. After the match, a retrospective ruling awarded the first penalty runs in a Test under the new 2000 Code of Laws. On the opening morning, a ball from Gillespie passed both Ganga and Gilchrist and struck a fieldsman's helmet; originally signalled as five byes, the runs were officially amended to penalties under Law 41.3.

West Indies

S. L. Campbell lbw b Gillespie	18	– c Gilchrist b McGrath	8
D. Ganga b Gillespie	23	– lbw b Miller	32
W. W. Hinds c Ponting b Gillespie	27	– c Martyn b MacGill	9
B. C. Lara c Waugh b Miller	182	– c Langer b Miller	39
*J. C. Adams c Gilchrist b Gillespie	49	– c Martyn b Miller	15
M. Dillon c Waugh b Gillespie	9	– (9) lbw b McGrath	19
M. N. Samuels lbw b Miller	35	– (6) c Hayden b MacGill	3
†R. D. Jacobs c Langer b Miller	21	– (7) c Ponting b Miller	2
N. A. M. McLean lbw b Miller	0	– (8) c Hayden b Miller	0
M. I. Black not out	1	– not out	3
C. A. Walsh lbw b Miller	0	– c Gilchrist b McGrath	0
B 3, l-b 12, n-b 6, p 5	26	B 6, l-b 3, w 1, n-b 1	11

1/45 (2) 2/52 (1) 3/86 (3) 4/269 (5)   391   1/26 (1) 2/36 (3) 3/87 (4) 4/96 (2)   141
5/280 (6) 6/354 (4) 7/376 (7)   5/109 (6) 6/109 (5) 7/109 (8)
8/382 (9) 9/391 (8) 10/391 (11)   8/116 (7) 9/137 (9) 10/141 (11)

McGrath 36–14–83–0; Gillespie 32–9–89–5; Miller 35.5–13–81–5; MacGill 24–5–118–0; Ponting 1–1–0–0. *Second Innings*—McGrath 9.5–1–27–3; Gillespie 13–5–18–0; MacGill 12–2–55–2; Miller 17–6–32–5.

Australia

M. J. Slater c sub (R. R. Sarwan) b Samuels	83	– (2) c Jacobs b Dillon	1
M. L. Hayden run out	58	– (1) c Jacobs b Walsh	14
J. L. Langer c Lara b Samuels	6	– c Jacobs b Dillon	48
M. E. Waugh lbw b Dillon	63	– c Jacobs b Dillon	5
J. N. Gillespie lbw b Walsh	4		
R. T. Ponting c Jacobs b Walsh	92	– (5) lbw b Walsh	11
D. R. Martyn not out	46	– (6) not out	34
*†A. C. Gilchrist c Jacobs b McLean	9	– (7) not out	10
S. C. G. MacGill c Jacobs b Dillon	6		
C. R. Miller c Campbell b McLean	1		
G. D. McGrath b Dillon	1		
B 5, l-b 13, w 5, n-b 11	34	B 3, l-b 1, n-b 3	7

1/156 (2) 2/160 (1) 3/169 (3) 4/187 (5)   403   1/8 (2) 2/22 (1) 3/27 (4)   (5 wkts) 130
5/310 (4) 6/369 (6) 7/386 (8)   4/48 (5) 5/111 (3)
8/397 (9) 9/398 (10) 10/403 (11)

Walsh 32–7–73–2; Black 18–1–75–0; Dillon 24.4–2–84–3; McLean 21–1–69–2; Adams 13–2–35–0; Samuels 19–6–49–2. *Second Innings*—Walsh 14–4–39–2; Dillon 12–3–42–3; Samuels 6–1–17–0; McLean 5–1–9–0; Adams 3–0–7–0; Black 3–0–12–0.

Umpires: S. J. Davis *(Australia)* (4) and S. Venkataraghavan *(India)* (41).
Third umpire: D. J. Harper *(Australia)*.   Referee: A. C. Smith *(England)* (7).

Close of play: First day, West Indies 274-4 (Lara 136*, Dillon 3*); Second day, Australia 180-3 (Waugh 10*, Gillespie 2*); Third day, Australia 403-9 (Martyn 46*, McGrath 1*); Fourth day, Australia 98-4 (Langer 43*, Martyn 18*).

AUSTRALIA v WEST INDIES 2000–01 (4th Test)

At Melbourne Cricket Ground on 26, 27, 28, 29 December.
Toss: West Indies.   Result: AUSTRALIA won by 352 runs.
Debuts: West Indies – C. E. L. Stuart.
Man of the Match: S. R. Waugh.

Australia won their 14th successive Test without much opposition from the once-mighty West Indies. Only a wild slog from Walsh, which saved the follow-on and compelled Australia to take a gratuitous second innings, stretched this match into a fourth day. Steve Waugh, back after injury, steadied his side after a slapdash start with his 23rd Test century. West Indies did not manage a run off the bat until the eighth over: McGrath began with eight overs for two runs, and Gillespie was scarcely more philanthropic. The wickets clattered – including Lara, flashing needlessly at Bichel – and, after little more than an hour and a half, it was 28 for 5. Eventually the bowlers tired, the ball was made squelchy by rain, and the siege was relaxed. Samuels and Jacobs (who had earlier equalled the Test wicketkeeping record with seven catches) put on 75, McLean lashed Bichel for six, and Walsh flailed twice, the first time to break his duck and the second to save the follow-on. This milestone so excited him that he ran himself out seeking a third run off the same ball. After claiming only four wickets in his previous four Tests, Bichel had now taken five in an afternoon. Australia calmly extended their lead to 461, then demolished West Indies again: Gillespie took all the wickets as they slumped to 23 for 6, Adams going first ball to complete a pair. For the first time in 58 Tests, McGrath did not take a wicket in either innings.

Australia

M. J. Slater c Jacobs b McLean	30	– (2) c Lara b Dillon	4
M. L. Hayden c Jacobs b Walsh	13	– (1) c Hinds b McLean	30
J. L. Langer c Jacobs b Stuart	31	– c Ganga b Adams	80
M. E. Waugh c Adams b Dillon	25	– not out	78
*S. R. Waugh not out	121	– c Jacobs b Stuart	20
R. T. Ponting c Hinds b McLean	23	– (7) not out	26
†A. C. Gilchrist c Campbell b Stuart	37		
A. J. Bichel c Jacobs b Dillon	3		
J. N. Gillespie c Jacobs b Walsh	19		
C. R. Miller c Jacobs b Dillon	29	– (6) st Jacobs b Adams	11
G. D. McGrath c Jacobs b Dillon	11		
L-b 4, w 1, n-b 17	22	B 5, l-b 4, w 1, n-b 3	13

1/41 (2) 2/47 (1) 3/101 (3) 4/105 (4)   364   1/8 (2) 2/49 (1)   (5 wkts dec.) 262
5/149 (6) 6/210 (7) 7/225 (8)   3/165 (3) 4/212 (5)
8/306 (9) 9/347 (10) 10/364 (11)   5/228 (6)

Walsh 33–6–62–2; Dillon 21–2–76–4; McLean 27–5–95–2; Stuart 15–4–52–2; Samuels 14–0–56–0; Adams 4–0–19–0. *Second Innings*—Walsh 18–3–46–0; Dillon 17–1–68–1; McLean 9–1–30–1; Stuart 15–2–66–1; Adams 18–8–43–2.

West Indies

S. L. Campbell c Hayden b Miller	5	– c Ponting b Gillespie	6
D. Ganga c Gilchrist b Gillespie	4	– lbw b Gillespie	0
W. W. Hinds c Slater b Gillespie	0	– c Bichel b Gillespie	4
B. C. Lara c M. E. Waugh b Bichel	16	– b Gillespie	0
*J. C. Adams c Gilchrist b Bichel	0	– (6) c M. E. Waugh b Gillespie	0
M. N. Samuels not out	60	– (7) c Gillespie b Miller	46
†R. D. Jacobs c M. E. Waugh b Bichel	42	– (8) c Gilchrist b Miller	23
N. A. M. McLean b Bichel	17	– (9) run out	1
M. Dillon b Gillespie	0	– (10) b Miller	15
C. E. L. Stuart b Bichel	1	– (5) lbw b Gillespie	4
C. A. Walsh run out	4	– not out	0
L-b 5, n-b 11	16	L-b 1, n-b 9	10

1/5 (2) 2/6 (3) 3/28 (4) 4/28 (1)   165   1/1 (2) 2/6 (3) 3/7 (4) 4/17 (1)   109
5/28 (5) 6/103 (7) 7/144 (8)   5/17 (6) 6/23 (5) 7/77 (8)
8/150 (9) 9/157 (10) 10/165 (11)   8/78 (9) 9/108 (10) 10/109 (7)

McGrath 13–7–15–0; Gillespie 18–6–48–3; Bichel 13.3–2–60–5; Miller 13–5–37–1. *Second Innings*—McGrath 12–6–10–0; Gillespie 17–5–40–6; Miller 14.3–2–40–3; Bichel 6–0–18–0.

Umpires: S. J. A. Taufel *(Australia)* (1) and S. Venkataraghavan *(India)* (42).
Third umpire: R. G. Patterson *(Australia)*.   Referee: A. C. Smith *(England)* (8).

Close of play: First day, Australia 295-7 (S. R. Waugh 98*, Gillespie 14*); Second day, West Indies 165; Third day, West Indies 10-3 (Campbell 0*, Stuart 3*).

AUSTRALIA v WEST INDIES 2000–01 (5th Test)

At Sydney Cricket Ground on 2, 3, 4, 5, 6 January.
Toss: West Indies.   Result: AUSTRALIA won by six wickets.
Debuts: none.
Man of the Match: M. J. Slater.   Man of the Series: G. D. McGrath.

Australia extended their record run of victories to 15 by completing only the eighth 5–0 whitewash in Test history: it was Australia's third such clean sweep, but only the second time West Indies had suffered one (also in South Africa in 1998-99). Here the West Indian openers made a confident start, putting on 147 before MacGill, who ended with seven wickets, dismissed both to trigger a collapse to a disappointing 272. Sarwan collected his third duck in five innings. Australia began hesitantly before a stand of 132 between Slater, who fell in the nineties for the ninth time in Tests, equalling Steve Waugh's record, while the captain himself went on to another century. Gilchrist, dropped first ball by Adams, thumped 87 out of 119 while he was in, as Australia stretched their lead to 180. When four wickets went down in 11 balls on the fourth morning a quick finish loomed, but the target was swelled to 173 by Sarwan's first innings of note in the series, allied to fighting fifties from Jacobs and Mahendra Nagamootoo, who numbers Rohan Kanhai and Alvin Kallicharran among his uncles. Australia won midway through the fifth day, with Slater again going close to three figures as the West Indians' lack of a wrist-spinner (Nagamootoo bowled as much with his fingers as his wrist) was again telling. The home side wore special caps during the match to mark the centenary of Australian federation, while the individualistic Miller dyed his hair blue.

West Indies

S. L. Campbell c and b MacGill	79	– c Gilchrist b Gillespie		54
W. W. Hinds b MacGill	70	– b McGrath		46
*J. C. Adams lbw b McGrath	10	– lbw b McGrath		5
B. C. Lara c M. E. Waugh b MacGill	35	– c Gilchrist b Miller		28
M. N. Samuels c Langer b MacGill	28	– lbw b Gillespie		0
R. R. Sarwan lbw b MacGill	0	– c Gilchrist b McGrath		51
†R. D. Jacobs st Gilchrist b MacGill	12	– lbw b M. E. Waugh		62
M. V. Nagamootoo c Slater b Miller	12	– c Hayden b Miller		68
N. A. M. McLean lbw b MacGill	0	– c M. E. Waugh b Miller		15
C. E. L. Stuart not out	12	– lbw b Miller		4
C. A. Walsh c Hayden b Miller	4	– not out		1
B 4, l-b 4, n-b 2	10	B 5, l-b 10, n-b 3		18

1/147 (1) 2/152 (2) 3/174 (3) 4/210 (4)   272   1/98 (2) 2/112 (3) 3/112 (1)   352
5/210 (6) 6/235 (5) 7/240 (7)   4/112 (5) 5/154 (4) 6/239 (6)
8/240 (9) 9/252 (8) 10/272 (11)   7/317 (7) 8/347 (8) 9/351 (9) 10/352 (10)

McGrath 19–7–43–1; Gillespie 16–4–44–0; MacGill 37–11–104–7; Miller 30.1–8–73–2. *Second Innings*—McGrath 24–4–80–3; Miller 32.5–3–102–4; MacGill 30–7–88–0; Gillespie 21–5–57–2; M. E. Waugh 9–3–10–1.

Australia

M. J. Slater c Samuels b Nagamootoo	96	– (2) not out	86
M. L. Hayden c Lara b Walsh	3	– (1) lbw b Stuart	5
J. L. Langer c Jacobs b McLean	20	– lbw b Walsh	10
M. E. Waugh run out	22	– c Adams b McLean	3
*S. R. Waugh b Nagamootoo	103	– lbw b Samuels	38
R. T. Ponting lbw b Stuart	51	– not out	14
†A. C. Gilchrist c Lara b Stuart	87		
J. N. Gillespie c Hinds b Nagamootoo	2		
C. R. Miller not out	37		
S. C. G. MacGill run out	1		
G. D. McGrath run out	13		
B 1, l-b 5, n-b 11	17	B 3, l-b 7, w 1, n-b 7	18

1/17 (2) 2/55 (3) 3/109 (4) 4/157 (1)   452   1/5 (1) 2/38 (3)   (4 wkts) 174
5/289 (6) 6/360 (5) 7/374 (8)   3/46 (4) 4/148 (5)
8/408 (7) 9/410 (10) 10/452 (11)

Walsh 25–4–74–1; Stuart 23–4–81–2; Nagamootoo 35–3–119–3; McLean 20–2–81–1; Adams 16.4–2–54–0; Samuels 16–5–37–0. *Second Innings*—Walsh 15–5–35–1; Stuart 7–0–40–1; McLean 8–1–35–1; Nagamootoo 9–1–28–0; Samuels 5.5–0–26–1.

Umpires: D. B. Hair *(Australia)* (35) and R. E. Koertzen *(South Africa)* (21).
Third umpire: S. J. A. Taufel *(Australia)*.   Referee: A. C. Smith *(England)* (9).

Close of play: First day, West Indies 256-9 (Stuart 0*, Walsh 0*); Second day, Australia 284-4 (S. R. Waugh 82*, Ponting 51*); Third day, West Indies 98-1 (Campbell 45*); Fourth day, Australia 44-2 (Slater 18*, M. E. Waugh 3*).

NEW ZEALAND v ZIMBABWE 2000–01 (Only Test)

At Basin Reserve, Wellington, on 26, 27, 28, 29, 30 December.
Toss: New Zealand.   Result: MATCH DRAWN.
Debuts: Zimbabwe – D. A. Marillier.
Man of the Match: C. D. McMillan.

A slow pitch and the loss of much of the third day to the weather effectively condemned this match to a draw. New Zealand took more than two days to amass their sizeable total, but only 190 of those came in 90 overs on the first day. Astle, previously so out of form that many had predicted this would be his last Test, gritted it out for 549 minutes (408 balls) for 141: his stand of 222 with McMillan remains a fifth-wicket record for New Zealand, beating the 183 of Mark Burgess and Robert Anderson against Pakistan at Lahore in 1976-77. Martin grabbed two early wickets in an opening spell of 8–6–15–2, but Zimbabwe grafted to safety, with Rennie going close to a maiden Test hundred and Flower hitting his sixth consecutive half-century, which took him past 1,000 runs in the calendar year in only nine Tests. With the pitch slow and tedious, and the home spinners toothless, Zimbabwe avoided the follow-on shortly before the fourth-day close. New Zealand's second innings showed more urgency, but they still could not manage four an over: Fleming's second declaration left Zimbabwe a notional target of 301 in 43 overs. Wiseman finally claimed his first wicket in the 16th over after tea on the final day, and the game ended by mutual consent shortly afterwards. Trevor Madondo, in his third and final Test, made a cultured maiden half-century: six months later he was to die of malaria.

New Zealand

M. H. Richardson run out	75			
M. J. Horne c Flower b Streak	1	– (1) c Flower b Streak		0
M. S. Sinclair lbw b Strang	9	– (2) c Flower b Murphy		18
*S. P. Fleming run out	22	– (3) run out		55
N. J. Astle c Carlisle b Strang	141	– (4) not out		51
C. D. McMillan b Murphy	142	– (5) c Madondo b Strang		10
†A. C. Parore not out	50	– (6) not out		3
B. G. K. Walker c Olonga b Strang	27			
P. J. Wiseman not out	0			
B 1, l-b 8, w 5, n-b 6	20	B 5, l-b 5, n-b 6		16

1/5 (2) 2/22 (3) 3/67 (4)   (7 wkts dec.) 487   1/4 (1) 2/44 (2)   (4 wkts dec.) 153
4/145 (1) 5/367 (6)   3/103 (3) 4/126 (5)
6/426 (5) 7/487 (8)

S. B. O'Connor and C. S. Martin did not bat.

Streak 37–10–74–1; Strang 46–16–116–3; Olonga 30–2–105–0; Murphy 46–9–128–1; Whittall 22–6–55–0. *Second Innings*—Streak 5–1–18–1; Strang 11–2–25–1; Murphy 18–0–86–1; Olonga 2–0–12–0; Whittall 4–3–2–0.

Zimbabwe

G. J. Whittall b Martin	9	– c Parore b O'Connor		6
G. J. Rennie c Parore b McMillan	93	– c Parore b Wiseman		37
S. V. Carlisle c Horne b Martin	0	– not out		16
A. D. R. Campbell lbw b Martin	24	– not out		0
†A. Flower c Parore b Martin	79			
T. N. Madondo not out	74			
D. A. Marillier c Parore b Martin	28			
*H. H. Streak not out	19			
B 3, l-b 9, n-b 2	14	L-b 1		1

1/21 (1) 2/23 (3) 3/66 (4)   (6 wkts dec.) 340   1/26 (1) 2/57 (2)   (2 wkts) 60
4/196 (5) 5/237 (2) 6/295 (7)

B. A. Murphy, B. C. Strang and H. K. Olonga did not bat.

Martin 32.5–11–71–5; O'Connor 16–7–29–0; Wiseman 54–13–131–0; Walker 22–1–68–0; McMillan 9–4–22–1; Astle 5–2–7–0. *Second Innings*—Martin 5–2–6–0; O'Connor 8–4–8–1; Wiseman 6–2–15–1; Walker 11–1–30–0.

Umpires: B. C. Cooray *(Sri Lanka)* (20) and R. S. Dunne *(New Zealand)* (37).
Third umpire: A. L. Hill *(New Zealand)*.   Referee: G. R. Viswanath *(India)* (2).

Close of play: First day, New Zealand 190-4 (Astle 56*, McMillan 20*); Second day, New Zealand 475-6 (Parore 44*, Walker 21*); Third day, Zimbabwe 48-2 (Rennie 20*, Campbell 15*); Fourth day, Zimbabwe 288-5 (Madondo 44*, Marillier 26*).

SOUTH AFRICA v SRI LANKA 2000–01 (1st Test)

At Kingsmead, Durban, on 26, 27, 28, 29 *(no play)*, 30 December.
Toss: South Africa.   Result: MATCH DRAWN.
Debuts: none.
Man of the Match: G. Kirsten.

The loss of the fourth day helped Sri Lanka save the game, and meant the match would be remembered more for the achievements of Muralitharan, whose 11 wickets included his 300th in Tests. South Africa started well, Kirsten extending his 11th Test century to a marathon 180 in 574 minutes. The extent he had to graft could be measured by the fact that eight of his 20 fours came in his first half-century. Sri Lanka, by contrast, struggled on South Africa's bounciest pitch: both openers made ducks, and although Sangakkara and Jayawardene added a defiant 168, their stand provided a remarkable 78% of the eventual total, as the last eight wickets clattered in 20 overs. Pollock claimed the final three wickets in five balls, becoming the second South African (after Allan Donald) to reach 200 in Tests. South Africa's decision not to enforce the follow-on was compromised when it rained. On the fifth morning Murali became the 17th player to reach 300 Test wickets when Pollock drove too early at a cunningly looped delivery. Only Dennis Lillee did it in fewer matches, taking 56 to Murali's 58. Sri Lanka's target was 345 in around 70 overs, sufficiently unappealing to suggest that Pollock remembered his mauling by Jayasuriya at Galle five months earlier. But Jayasuriya and Atapattu managed only 41 (their highest opening stand of the series), and Sri Lanka dipped to 80 for 4 in the 34th over before Arnold and Dilshan used up 30 overs to ensure the draw.

South Africa

H. H. Dippenaar c Kaluwitharana b Fernando	11	– lbw b Muralitharan	22
G. Kirsten c Kaluwitharana b Fernando	180	– c Arnold b Muralitharan	34
J. H. Kallis c Muralitharan b Fernando	21	– b Muralitharan	15
D. J. Cullinan c Atapattu b Muralitharan	59	– (9) not out	2
N. D. McKenzie c Dilshan b Muralitharan	9	– (7) lbw b Muralitharan	13
†M. V. Boucher c Arnold b Muralitharan	17	– c Vaas b Muralitharan	10
L. Klusener c Sangakkara b Muralitharan	50	– (8) not out	11
N. Boje b Muralitharan	32	– (5) c Sangakkara b Fernando	8
*S. M. Pollock c Kaluwitharana b Fernando	2	– (4) c Dilshan b Muralitharan	11
M. Ntini b Fernando	8		
M. Ngam not out	0		
B 5, l-b 10, w 1, n-b 15	31	B 4, l-b 3, n-b 7	14

1/31 (1) 2/86 (3) 3/194 (4) 4/238 (5)   420   1/46 (1) 2/75 (3)   (7 wkts dec.) 140
5/269 (6) 6/358 (7) 7/401 (2)   3/91 (2) 4/92 (4)
8/410 (9) 9/420 (10) 10/420 (8)   5/108 (6) 6/114 (5) 7/132 (7)

Vaas 26–1–84–0; Zoysa 20–3–62–0; Fernando 34–4–98–5; Muralitharan 58.3–16–122–5; Arnold 14–3–39–0.
Second Innings—Vaas 9–1–25–0; Zoysa 5–0–21–0; Fernando 10–0–48–1; Muralitharan 10–1–39–6.

Sri Lanka

M. S. Atapattu run out	0	– c Boucher b Boje	20
*S. T. Jayasuriya c McKenzie b Ngam	0	– c Cullinan b Ngam	26
K. C. Sangakkara c Kirsten b Boje	74	– st Boucher b Boje	17
D. P. M. D. Jayawardene c Boucher b Klusener	98	– c Boucher b Ntini	7
R. P. Arnold b Boje	3	– c Dippenaar b Pollock	30
T. M. Dilshan b Ngam	6	– not out	28
†R. S. Kaluwitharana c Boucher b Ntini	16	– c Boje b Pollock	1
W. P. U. J. C. Vaas c Boucher b Pollock	2	– not out	3
D. N. T. Zoysa c Ngam b Pollock	3		
C. R. D. Fernando not out	5		
M. Muralitharan c Boucher b Pollock	0		
N-b 9	9	B 4, l-b 7, n-b 6	17

1/0 (1) 2/2 (2) 3/170 (3) 4/184 (4)   216   1/41 (2) 2/69 (3)   (6 wkts) 149
5/184 (5) 6/201 (7) 7/208 (6)   3/80 (1) 4/80 (4)
8/208 (8) 9/215 (9) 10/216 (11)   5/132 (5) 6/140 (7)

Pollock 20.4–7–40–3; Ngam 12–0–59–2; Ntini 16–5–36–1; Kallis 9–3–17–0; Boje 19–4–44–2; Klusener 11–5–20–1. *Second Innings*—Pollock 16–5–35–2; Ngam 13–3–34–1; Ntini 10–4–18–1; Kallis 6–1–14–0; Boje 24–12–30–2; Klusener 5–1–7–0.

Umpires: D. L. Orchard *(South Africa)* (22) and Riazuddin *(Pakistan)* (9).
Third umpire: I. L. Howell *(South Africa)*.   Referee: R. Subba Row *(England)* (36).

Close of play: First day, South Africa 230-3 (Kirsten 112*, McKenzie 5*); Second day, Sri Lanka 62-2 (Sangakkara 25*, Jayawardene 31*); Third day, South Africa 47-1 (Kirsten 20*, Kallis 1*); Fourth day, No play.

SOUTH AFRICA v SRI LANKA 2000–01 (2nd Test)

At Newlands, Cape Town, on 2, 3, 4 January.
Toss: Sri Lanka.   Result: SOUTH AFRICA won by an innings and 229 runs.
Debuts: none.
Man of the Match: S. M. Pollock.

Sri Lanka might have got off the hook in the first Test, but there was no escape in the second as they crashed to their heaviest-ever defeat. They were soon in trouble: after choosing to bat on a pitch offering bounce and seam movement, they dissolved for a pitiful 95. Pollock despatched four shell-shocked top-order batsmen for 13, and the first eight were caught between slip and gully or at short leg. The rapid Ngam claimed three victims. He had to wait until the sixth wicket before the first one, but it was the top-scorer, Sangakkara, who dealt with the pace onslaught in a manner his team-mates could only dream about. South Africa's reply began in surreal style. Gibbs received a standing ovation from his home crowd as he walked out for his first international innings after a six-month suspension for involvement in Hansie Cronje's match-fixing schemes. The applause had hardly died down when he edged his second delivery to Sangakkara. Some felt this was poetic justice after the unseemly haste of Gibbs's recall at the expense of Boeta Dippenaar, who had scored a maiden Test century three weeks before against New Zealand. This was the end of Sri Lanka's success: Cullinan did as he pleased in his 12th Test century (a national record), while Boucher and Klusener fell just short of three figures. Sri Lankan hopes of a decent reply were derailed by Ngam and the left-arm spin of Boje as South Africa completed their most emphatic Test victory.

Sri Lanka

M. S. Atapattu c Kallis b Pollock	5	– lbw b Pollock	13
*S. T. Jayasuriya c Boucher b Pollock	8	– c Pollock b Ngam	0
†K. C. Sangakkara c Cullinan b Ngam	32	– c Boucher b Ngam	11
D. P. M. D. Jayawardene c Kallis b Pollock	0	– lbw b Boje	45
R. P. Arnold c Kirsten b Pollock	0	– c Gibbs b Boje	26
T. M. Dilshan c Pollock b Kallis	5	– c Boucher b Boje	17
D. A. Gunawardene c Kallis b Ngam	24	– b Ntini	13
W. P. U. J. C. Vaas c Pollock b Ngam	7	– c and b Boje	38
D. N. T. Zoysa c and b Pollock	10	– c Klusener b Ntini	0
C. R. D. Fernando not out	0	– c Boucher b Ngam	5
M. Muralitharan c Ntini b Pollock	0	– not out	1
W 1, n-b 3	4	L-b 6, w 1, n-b 4	11

1/12 (1) 2/13 (2) 3/13 (4) 4/13 (5)   95   1/4 (2) 2/18 (3) 3/53 (1) 4/99 (4)   180
5/33 (6) 6/66 (3) 7/84 (7)   5/112 (5) 6/119 (6) 7/131 (7)
8/95 (8) 9/95 (9) 10/95 (11)   8/135 (9) 9/172 (8) 10/180 (10)

Pollock 13.4–6–30–6; Ngam 13–3–26–3; Kallis 6–2–19–1; Ntini 6–2–20–0. *Second Innings*—Pollock 9–3–29–1; Ngam 8.2–1–36–3; Kallis 7–1–29–0; Ntini 11–2–52–2; Boje 10–3–28–4.

South Africa

G. Kirsten c Dilshan b Muralitharan	52	N. Boje not out	31
H. H. Gibbs c Sangakkara b Vaas	0	L-b 5, w 1, n-b 18	24
J. H. Kallis c Jayawardene b Fernando	49		
D. J. Cullinan run out	112	1/1 (2) 2/97 (1) (7 wkts dec.)	504
N. D. McKenzie c and b Arnold	47	3/130 (3) 4/231 (5)	
†M. V. Boucher c Jayawardene b Arnold	92	5/317 (4) 6/411 (6)	
L. Klusener c Jayasuriya b Arnold	97	7/504 (7)	

*S. M. Pollock, M. Ntini and M. Ngam did not bat.

Vaas 32–6–109–1; Zoysa 26–6–80–0; Fernando 25–2–105–1; Muralitharan 43–11–99–1; Jayasuriya 7–1–28–0; Arnold 24.2–4–76–3; Jayawardene 1–0–2–0.

Umpires: I. L. Howell *(South Africa)* (1) and E. A. Nicholls *(West Indies)* (13).
Third umpire: W. A. Diedricks *(South Africa)*.   Referee: R. Subba Row *(England)* (37).

Close of play: First day, South Africa 130-2 (Kallis 49*, Cullinan 17*); Second day, South Africa 426-6 (Klusener 44*, Boje 7*).

SOUTH AFRICA v SRI LANKA 2000–01 (3rd Test)

At Centurion Park, Pretoria, on 20, 21, 22 January.
Toss: Sri Lanka.   Result: SOUTH AFRICA won by an innings and seven runs.
Debuts: South Africa – J. M. Kemp.
Man of the Match: S. M. Pollock.   Man of the Series: S. M. Pollock.

Another three-day victory gave South Africa the series, although Sri Lanka had their moments. They seemed set to contain South Africa in the first innings before McKenzie and Pollock put on 150 for the eighth wicket. Pollock's maiden century – which came from only 95 balls, equalling Jonty Rhodes's national record – was only the ninth in Test history from No. 9 in the order (there have been five more since, including another by Pollock two months later, and also three from No. 10). He hit 16 fours, and three sixes that cleared the boundary with a dozen rows to spare. Then Atapattu was run out for the second time in the series, Jayasuriya fell to a blatantly obvious trap, carving a short, wide delivery straight to third man, and Sri Lanka (now including Aravinda de Silva, who had flown in as a reinforcement after being omitted from the original tour party) collapsed again, the only bright spot being Kaluwitharana's 30-ball 32. Sangakkara was promoted to open in the follow-on (partly because Jayasuriya had just learned of his wife's miscarriage) and responded magnificently by batting throughout before being the last out – trapped by a skidder just short of a maiden century – just when it looked as if South Africa might have to bat again. Sri Lanka were without both their leading bowlers: Muttiah Muralitharan tweaked a hamstring and pulled out on the morning of the match, while Chaminda Vaas had strained a groin muscle in a one-day international a few days beforehand.

South Africa

H. H. Dippenaar c Kaluwitharana b Perera	20	
H. H. Gibbs c Kaluwitharana b Zoysa	1	
J. H. Kallis c Arnold b Fernando	7	
D. J. Cullinan c Kaluwitharana b Wickremasinghe	48	
N. D. McKenzie c Wickremasinghe b Zoysa	103	
†M. V. Boucher c Kaluwitharana b Zoysa	38	
N. Boje c Jayasuriya b Arnold	6	
J. M. Kemp run out	2	
*S. M. Pollock c Sangakkara b Zoysa	111	
A. A. Donald not out	10	
M. Ntini c Kaluwitharana b Wickremasinghe	10	
B 4, l-b 2, w 1, n-b 15	22	
	378	

1/17 (2) 2/31 (1) 3/54 (3)
4/115 (4) 5/168 (6) 6/185 (7)
7/204 (8) 8/354 (5) 9/359 (9) 10/378 (11)

Zoysa 22–8–76–4; Perera 19–3–73–1; Fernando 16–1–107–1; Wickremasinghe 12.3–3–51–2; Arnold 14–2–50–1; Jayasuriya 6–3–10–0; de Silva 2–1–5–0.

Sri Lanka

M. S. Atapattu run out	3	– c Cullinan b Pollock	0
*S. T. Jayasuriya c McKenzie b Donald	16	– (6) b Donald	16
K. C. Sangakkara b Donald	3	– (2) lbw b Ntini	98
P. A. de Silva c Gibbs b Kallis	5	– (5) c Pollock b Kallis	22
D. P. M. D. Jayawardene c Boucher b Ntini	17	– (3) c Dippenaar b Kallis	23
R. P. Arnold b Ntini	13	– (4) c Pollock b Boje	71
†R. S. Kaluwitharana c Boucher b Ntini	32	– c Boucher b Kemp	10
D. N. T. Zoysa c Kallis b Ntini	1	– c and b Kemp	2
G. P. Wickremasinghe c Gibbs b Kemp	21	– c Boucher b Ntini	1
C. R. D. Fernando lbw b Kemp	0	– c Kallis b Kemp	1
P. D. R. L. Perera not out	1	– not out	0
L-b 3, w 3, n-b 1	7	L-b 2, w 2, n-b 4	8
	119		**252**

1/6 (1) 2/24 (2) 3/25 (3) 4/40 (4)   119
5/54 (5) 6/71 (6) 7/76 (8)
8/97 (7) 9/98 (10) 10/119 (9)

1/9 (1) 2/43 (3) 3/156 (4)   252
4/187 (5) 5/212 (6) 6/234 (7)
7/242 (8) 8/243 (9) 9/248 (10) 10/252 (2)

Donald 9–2–28–2; Pollock 7–3–15–0; Kallis 5–1–15–1; Ntini 11–5–39–4; Kemp 4.5–1–19–2. *Second Innings*— Pollock 17–5–43–1; Kallis 14–1–39–2; Donald 7–0–39–1; Kemp 13–2–33–3; Ntini 19.3–5–51–2; Boje 11–2–45–1.

Umpires: R. E. Koertzen *(South Africa)* (22) and P. Willey *(England)* (21).
Third umpire: D. L. Orchard *(South Africa)*.   Referee: R. Subba Row *(England)* (38).

Close of play: First day, South Africa 375-9 (Donald 10*, Ntini 8*); Second day, Sri Lanka 184-3 (Sangakkara 64*, de Silva 21*).

SRI LANKA v ENGLAND 2000–01 (1st Test)

At Galle International Stadium on 22, 23, 24, 25, 26 February.
Toss: Sri Lanka.   Result: SRI LANKA won by an innings and 28 runs.
Debuts: none.
Man of the Match: M. S. Atapattu.

England began the second leg of their winter tour the same way as the first, losing the opening Test. Sri Lanka's big total owed much to a stand of 230 between Atapattu, with his fourth double-century, and de Silva, who hit his 19th Test hundred. In stifling heat Atapattu remained at the crease for 684 minutes, and hit 18 fours from 536 balls. England were forced to follow on despite a dogged maiden century from Trescothick, who survived for 394 minutes: "He made the rest of us look like fools," lamented Atherton. Five wickets tumbled for 36 after Trescothick was fifth out, and he was back at the crease three-quarters of an hour later. Muralitharan toiled through more than 50 overs on a dustbowl, but the main destroyer was Jayasuriya, who took four wickets in an innings for only the third time in a Test – and promptly repeated the feat when England batted again. The openers put on 101 before a weary Trescothick departed after another 197 minutes of defiance, but that was just about the end of the resistance: all ten wickets fell for 88 as Sri Lanka marched to victory soon after lunch on the final day. After a bad-tempered match marred by inexperienced umpiring, five players were fined by the referee. The BBC radio team was banned from the ground on the second day after a quarrel over media rights, and forced to broadcast from the ramparts of the 17th-century Dutch fort overlooking the stadium.

Sri Lanka

M. S. Atapattu not out	201	R. P. Arnold not out		1
*S. T. Jayasuriya c White b Gough	14	B 9, l-b 2, n-b 10		21
†K. C. Sangakkara c White b Croft	58			—
P. A. de Silva run out	106	1/18 (2) 2/110 (3)	(5 wkts dec.)	470
D. P. M. D. Jayawardene run out	61	3/340 (4) 4/451 (5)		
W. P. U. J. C. Vaas c White b Giles	8	5/468 (6)		

T. M. Dilshan, H. D. P. K. Dharmasena, C. R. D. Fernando and M. Muralitharan did not bat.

Gough 26–3–95–1; Caddick 30–13–46–0; White 30–6–80–0; Giles 48–8–134–1; Croft 32–6–96–1; Hick 4–0–8–0.

England

M. A. Atherton lbw b Vaas	33	– c Sangakkara b Vaas	44
M. E. Trescothick c Sangakkara b Vaas	122	– c Sangakkara b Jayasuriya	57
*N. Hussain lbw b Muralitharan	3	– lbw b Muralitharan	1
G. P. Thorpe c Dilshan b Muralitharan	7	– lbw b Dharmasena	12
†A. J. Stewart lbw b Jayasuriya	19	– not out	34
R. D. B. Croft c Jayawardene b Jayasuriya	9	– (10) lbw b Jayasuriya	2
G. A. Hick c Sangakkara b Vaas	5	– (6) c Jayawardene b Jayasuriya	6
C. White c Sangakkara b Jayasuriya	25	– (7) lbw b Muralitharan	3
A. F. Giles c Dilshan b Muralitharan	4	– lbw b Muralitharan	1
A. R. Caddick c Jayawardene b Jayasuriya	0	– (8) b Jayasuriya	1
D. Gough not out	0	– b Muralitharan	0
B 2, l-b 3, n-b 21	26	B 11, l-b 6, n-b 11	28

1/83 (1) 2/93 (3) 3/117 (4) 4/197 (5)	253	1/101 (2) 2/105 (3) 3/121 (1)	189
5/206 (2) 6/217 (7) 7/239 (6)		4/145 (4) 5/167 (6) 6/176 (7)	
8/253 (8) 9/253 (10) 10/253 (9)		7/182 (8) 8/183 (9) 9/188 (10) 10/189 (11)	

Vaas 24–7–53–3; Muralitharan 54.3–14–79–3; Dharmasena 22–6–51–0; Fernando 2–0–10–0; Jayasuriya 27–7–50–4; de Silva 3–2–5–0. *Second Innings*—Vaas 15–6–29–1; Fernando 4–0–10–0; Jayasuriya 32–13–44–4; Dharmasena 16–6–21–1; Muralitharan 42.3–14–66–4; Arnold 1–0–2–0.

Umpires: A. V. Jayaprakash *(India)* (8) and P. T. Manuel *(Sri Lanka)* (8).
Third umpire: E. A. R. de Silva *(Sri Lanka)*.   Referee: Hanumant Singh *(India)* (5).

Close of play: First day, Sri Lanka 221-2 (Atapattu 85*, de Silva 56*); Second day, England 27-0 (Atherton 12*, Trescothick 11*); Third day, England 202-4 (Trescothick 119*, Croft 0*); Fourth day, England 118-2 (Atherton 44*, Thorpe 2*).

SRI LANKA v ENGLAND 2000–01 (2nd Test)

At Asgiriya Stadium, Kandy, on 7, 8, 9, 10, 11 March.
Toss: Sri Lanka.   Result: ENGLAND won by three wickets.
Debuts: none.
Man of the Match: D. Gough.

England just came out on top after a seesaw match which, like the previous one, was marred by poor umpiring: by some counts there were 15 errors, and afterwards the referee reprimanded Atherton and Sangakkara, and fined Jayasuriya 60% of his match fee for dissent. On the first morning, Sri Lanka sped to 69 for 2 in 16 overs, then White's third delivery induced two errors: first Sangakkara took his eye off the ball and deflected it, via his elbow, to gully, whereupon Rudi Koertzen gave him out. Ostentatious rubbing of his forearm earned Sangakkara the match's first reproof. Sri Lanka were rescued by a fine century from Jayawardene, who added 141 with Arnold, who was dropped by Trescothick at slip before he had scored. The fast bowlers claimed all the wickets, the last five of them for 20, then a long stand between Hussain and Thorpe put England very much in charge. Muralitharan, though, was convinced that Hussain was twice caught bat-pad – but the home umpire Cooray reprieved him both times, leading to the local newspaper headline "BC bats for England". Facing a deficit of 90, Sri Lanka were soon 88 for 6, but a superb counter-attack from Sangakkara – who just missed a maiden century for the second time in three Tests – and determined resistance from Dharmasena and Vaas meant England faced a tricky target of 161. Vaas the bowler then took four wickets, and it was left to the eighth-wicket pair to collect the last 19 runs required.

Sri Lanka

M. S. Atapattu b Gough	16	– c Stewart b Gough		2
*S. T. Jayasuriya c Giles b Caddick	9	– c Thorpe b Caddick		0
†K. C. Sangakkara c Trescothick b White	17	– st Stewart b Croft		95
P. A. de Silva c and b White	29	– c White b Gough		1
D. P. M. D. Jayawardene c Thorpe b Caddick	101	– b White		18
R. P. Arnold c White b Gough	65	– lbw b Croft		22
T. M. Dilshan c Atherton b Gough	36	– c Hick b Croft		0
H. D. P. K. Dharmasena c Thorpe b Gough	1	– c Hick b Gough		54
W. P. U. J. C. Vaas c Thorpe b Caddick	2	– c Croft b White		36
D. N. T. Zoysa c Stewart b Caddick	0	– c Hick b Gough		0
M. Muralitharan not out	10	– not out		6
B 1, l-b 3, n-b 7	11	B 2, l-b 3, n-b 11		16

1/21 (1) 2/29 (2) 3/69 (3) 4/80 (4)   297   1/2 (1) 2/2 (2) 3/3 (4)   250
5/221 (5) 6/277 (6) 7/279 (8)   4/42 (5) 5/81 (6) 6/88 (7)
8/282 (9) 9/286 (7) 10/297 (10)   7/181 (3) 8/234 (8) 9/242 (10) 10/250 (9)

Gough 14–1–73–4; Caddick 20–3–55–4; Giles 15–2–47–0; White 17–3–70–2; Croft 20–2–48–0.
Second Innings—Gough 22–6–50–4; Caddick 18–5–55–1; White 12.1–3–42–2; Croft 22–11–40–3; Giles 15–3–58–0.

England

M. A. Atherton lbw b Vaas	7	– c Sangakkara b Vaas		11
M. E. Trescothick c Sangakkara b Dharmasena	23	– lbw b Vaas		13
*N. Hussain b Muralitharan	109	– c Sangakkara b Vaas		15
G. P. Thorpe c Dilshan b Jayasuriya	59	– c Sangakkara b Muralitharan		46
†A. J. Stewart c Dilshan b Jayasuriya	54	– lbw b Vaas		7
G. A. Hick lbw b Muralitharan	0	– (7) b Jayasuriya		16
C. White st Sangakkara b Jayasuriya	39	– (8) not out		21
A. F. Giles b Muralitharan	5	– (9) not out		4
R. D. B. Croft not out	33	– (6) lbw b Dharmasena		17
A. R. Caddick b Muralitharan	7			
D. Gough lbw b Vaas	10			
B 16, l-b 20, w 1, n-b 4	41	B 1, l-b 8, n-b 2		11

1/16 (1) 2/37 (2) 3/204 (4) 4/232 (3)   387   1/24 (1) 2/25 (2) 3/86 (4)   (7 wkts) 161
5/236 (6) 6/323 (7) 7/330 (5)   4/89 (3) 5/97 (5)
8/336 (8) 9/346 (10) 10/387 (11)   6/122 (7) 7/142 (6)

Vaas 23–7–39–2; Zoysa 10–2–35–0; Muralitharan 63–21–127–4; Dharmasena 27–4–74–1; Jayasuriya 34–11–76–3.
Second Innings—Vaas 18–4–39–4; Zoysa 2–0–16–0; Dharmasena 8–0–25–1; Muralitharan 27–7–50–1; Jayasuriya 16.1–6–22–1.

Umpires: B. C. Cooray *(Sri Lanka)* (21) and R. E. Koertzen *(South Africa)* (23).
Third umpire: P. T. Manuel *(Sri Lanka)*.   Referee: Hanumant Singh *(India)* (6).

Close of play: First day, England 1-0 (Atherton 0*, Trescothick 1*); Second day, England 249-5 (Stewart 16*, White 6*); Third day, Sri Lanka 98-6 (Sangakkara 47*, Dharmasena 1*); Fourth day, England 91-4 (Stewart 2*, Croft 1*).

SRI LANKA v ENGLAND 2000–01 (3rd Test)

At Sinhalese Sports Club Ground, Colombo, on 15, 16, 17 March.
Toss: Sri Lanka.   Result: ENGLAND won by four wickets.
Debuts: Sri Lanka – D. Hettiarachchi.
Man of the Match: G. P. Thorpe.   Man of the Series: D. Gough.

England came from behind to take the series 2–1 after a thrilling match, on which 22 wickets fell on the third (and last) day for 229 runs. Crucially, that included Sri Lanka's whole second innings for just 81, their second-lowest in Tests, which left England only 74 to win ... but they lost six wickets in getting there, on a pitch offering increasing spin and generous bounce. On the first day Jayawardene had countered a fine spell from Croft to lift his side to a modest total. England were similarly indebted to Thorpe, who batted for 5½ hours in intense heat: he later said he had never played in such draining conditions. Trescothick provided slow left-armer Dinuka Hettiarachchi with a peculiar first Test wicket: he cracked a ball to leg, and everyone looked towards the boundary, only to discover it had lodged in the loose-fitting shirt of Arnold at short leg. The frenetic third day began with Vaas taking three for one in 16 balls, but England eked out a slender lead then, with Atapattu completing his third Test pair, claimed the upper hand through fine bowling. England had their own problems against the spin-ning ball as they chased their small target, but Thorpe held firm again. There were 11 ducks in the match, the seventh such instance in Tests: the last was bagged by Hussain, who limped in at No. 7 with a runner after pulling a thigh muscle. To widespread relief, the umpiring was of a high standard.

Sri Lanka

M. S. Atapattu b Caddick	0	– c Croft b Gough	0
*S. T. Jayasuriya c White b Croft	45	– lbw b Gough	23
†K. C. Sangakkara c Vaughan b Gough	45	– c Stewart b Caddick	0
P. A. de Silva c Vaughan b Giles	38	– c Thorpe b Caddick	23
D. P. M. D. Jayawardene c Stewart b Croft	71	– lbw b Giles	11
R. P. Arnold lbw b Giles	0	– c Hussain b Croft	0
T. M. Dilshan lbw b Croft	5	– b Giles	10
W. P. U. J. C. Vaas not out	19	– c Atherton b Giles	6
C. R. D. Fernando c Trescothick b Croft	2	– c Giles b Gough	5
D. Hettiarachchi b Gough	0	– not out	0
M. Muralitharan b Caddick	1	– lbw b Giles	1
B 4, l-b 4, w 1, n-b 6	15	N-b 2	2

1/2 (1) 2/88 (3) 3/108 (2) 4/205 (4)   241   1/21 (1) 2/24 (3) 3/24 (2)   81
5/209 (6) 6/216 (7) 7/219 (5)   4/57 (4) 5/59 (6) 6/59 (5)
8/225 (9) 9/240 (10) 10/241 (11)   7/69 (8) 8/76 (7) 9/80 (9) 10/81 (11)

Gough 14–5–33–2; Caddick 11.1–1–40–2; White 10–1–45–0; Giles 34–13–59–2; Croft 32–9–56–4. *Second Innings*—Gough 6–1–23–3; Caddick 8–2–29–2; Giles 9.1–4–11–4; Croft 5–0–18–1.

England

M. A. Atherton lbw b Vaas	21	– c and b Fernando	13
M. E. Trescothick c Arnold b Hettiarachchi	23	– c Sangakkara b Jayasuriya	10
*N. Hussain c Jayasuriya b Hettiarachchi	8	– (7) c Arnold b Jayasuriya	0
G. P. Thorpe not out	113	– not out	32
†A. J. Stewart b Muralitharan	3	– c Dilshan b Jayasuriya	0
M. P. Vaughan c Sangakkara b Vaas	26	– (3) b Muralitharan	8
C. White c Sangakkara b Vaas	0	– (6) c Jayawardene b Jayasuriya	8
A. F. Giles c Jayawardene b Vaas	0	– not out	1
R. D. B. Croft run out	16		
A. R. Caddick c Jayasuriya b Vaas	0		
D. Gough c Jayawardene b Vaas	14		
B 10, l-b 9, n-b 6	25	L-b 1, n-b 1	2

1/45 (1) 2/55 (2) 3/66 (3) 4/91 (5)   249   1/23 (1) 2/24 (2)   (6 wkts) 74
5/177 (6) 6/177 (7) 7/181 (8)   3/42 (3) 4/43 (5)
8/209 (9) 9/223 (10) 10/249 (11)   5/63 (6) 6/71 (7)

Vaas 27.5–6–73–6; Fernando 5–0–26–0; de Silva 3–1–2–0; Muralitharan 41–9–73–1; Hettiarachchi 24–6–36–2; Jayasuriya 9–1–20–0. *Second Innings*—Vaas 3–0–11–0; Hettiarachchi 3–1–5–0; Muralitharan 8–1–26–1; Fernando 2–0–7–1; Jayasuriya 8.3–0–24–4.

Umpires: E. A. R. de Silva *(Sri Lanka)* (2) and D. L. Orchard *(South Africa)* (23).
Third umpire: B. C. Cooray *(Sri Lanka)*.   Referee: Hanumant Singh *(India)* (7).

Close of play: First day, Sri Lanka 221-7 (Vaas 2*, Fernando 0*); Second day, England 175-4 (Thorpe 71*, Vaughan 26*).

INDIA v AUSTRALIA 2000–01 (1st Test)

At Wankhede Stadium, Mumbai, on 27, 28 February, 1 March.
Toss: Australia.   Result: AUSTRALIA won by ten wickets.
Debuts: India – R. L. Sanghvi.
Man of the Match: A. C. Gilchrist.

Australia extended their record sequence to 16 successive victories, winning in three days, although it was not as straightforward as the result suggests: they lost five first-innings wickets before reaching three figures. By then, though, India had been bowled out for 176, with McGrath characteristically accurate and Warne taking four wickets. They justified Steve Waugh's decision to put India in – a major gamble given doubts about the durability of the pitch, even though it traditionally helps the seamers early on. Australia slipped to 99 for 5 in reply on the second morning before Gilchrist changed the game with a rapid century, from 84 balls, hurtling from 50 in 100 in just 29: he gave Hayden a 30-over start yet beat him to three figures as they piled on 197 in 32 overs. Crucially, he had an escape at 44 – the substitute Hemang Badani, running back at midwicket, could not cling on to a top edge – then immediately survived an overhead chance to slip. In all Gilchrist hit 15 fours and four sixes as the lead swelled. India reached 154 for 2 (only 19 behind), but then Tendulkar fell for a cultured 65 to a superb catch from Ponting, who dived for a rebound after a pull struck short leg Langer on the shoulder, and the remaining wickets clattered for 65, including Agarkar's seventh successive Test duck against Australia. The openers needed only seven overs on the third evening to reach a modest target, Slater passing 5,000 Test runs in the process.

India

S. S. Das c Hayden b Gillespie	14	– c S. R. Waugh b Gillespie	7
S. Ramesh c Gilchrist b McGrath	2	– c Ponting b McGrath	44
R. Dravid c Gilchrist b Fleming	9	– b Warne	39
S. R. Tendulkar c Gilchrist b McGrath	76	– (5) c Ponting b M. E. Waugh	65
*S. C. Ganguly c Hayden b Warne	8	– (6) run out	1
V. V. S. Laxman c Ponting b McGrath	20	– (7) c Gilchrist b M. E. Waugh	12
†N. R. Mongia not out	26	– (4) c Gilchrist b Gillespie	28
A. B. Agarkar c and b Warne	0	– b M. E. Waugh	0
J. Srinath c M. E. Waugh b Warne	12	– (11) b McGrath	0
Harbhajan Singh c S. R. Waugh b Warne	0	– (9) not out	17
R. L. Sanghvi c Gilchrist b Gillespie	2	– (10) b Gillespie	0
B 4, l-b 1, w 1, n-b 1	7	B 5, n-b 1	6

1/7 (2) 2/25 (3) 3/31 (1) 4/55 (5)   176   1/33 (1) 2/57 (2) 3/154 (5)   219
5/130 (6) 6/139 (4) 7/140 (8)   4/156 (6) 5/174 (7) 6/174 (3)
8/165 (9) 9/166 (10) 10/176 (11)   7/193 (8) 8/210 (4) 9/216 (10) 10/219 (11)

In the second innings Mongia, when 0, retired hurt at 58 and resumed at 174-5.

McGrath 19–13–19–3; Fleming 15–3–55–1; Gillespie 15.3–4–50–2; Warne 22–7–47–4. *Second Innings*—McGrath 17.1–9–25–2; Fleming 15–1–44–0; Warne 28–11–60–1; Gillespie 19–8–45–3; M. E. Waugh 15–5–40–3.

Australia

M. J. Slater b Agarkar	10	– (2) not out	19
M. L. Hayden c Mongia b Srinath	119	– (1) not out	28
J. L. Langer c Dravid b Harbhajan Singh	19		
M. E. Waugh c Ganguly b Harbhajan Singh	0		
*S. R. Waugh c Dravid b Sanghvi	15		
R. T. Ponting c Das b Harbhajan Singh	0		
†A. C. Gilchrist st Mongia b Harbhajan Singh	122		
S. K. Warne c Tendulkar b Sanghvi	39		
J. N. Gillespie c Mongia b Srinath	0		
D. W. Fleming c Srinath b Agarkar	6		
G. D. McGrath not out	0		
B 13, l-b 3, n-b 3	19		

1/21 (1) 2/71 (3) 3/71 (4) 4/98 (5)   349   (no wkt) 47
5/99 (6) 6/296 (2) 7/326 (7)
8/327 (9) 9/349 (10) 10/349 (8)

Srinath 16–3–60–2; Agarkar 12–1–50–2; Harbhajan Singh 28–3–121–4; Sanghvi 10.2–2–67–2; Tendulkar 7–1–35–0. *Second Innings*—Srinath 2–0–17–0; Agarkar 1–0–8–0; Harbhajan Singh 2–0–11–0; Sanghvi 2–1–11–0.

Umpires: D. R. Shepherd *(England)* (55) and S. Venkataraghavan *(India)* (43).
Third umpire: N. N. Menon *(India)*.   Referee: C. W. Smith *(West Indies)* (31).

Close of play: First day, Australia 49-1 (Hayden 25*, Langer 10*); Second day, India 58-2 (Dravid 6*, Tendulkar 0*).

INDIA v AUSTRALIA 2000–01 (2nd Test)

At Eden Gardens, Kolkata, on 11, 12, 13, 14, 15 March.
Toss: Australia.　　Result: INDIA won by 171 runs.
Debuts: none.
Man of the Match: V. V. S. Laxman.

When India, following on, limped to 115 for 3, nothing seemed more certain than Australia's 17th successive Test victory: but Laxman and Dravid batted for the rest of the third day and throughout the fourth. They were eventually parted after 104 overs and 376 runs, an Indian fifth-wicket record. Australia were left needing 384 and, with Harbhajan Singh taking six wickets, subsided for 212. It was only the third time a Test had been won after following on: Australia were the previous victims too, losing to England at Sydney in 1894-95 and Headingley in 1981. It had been business as usual at the start: Hayden fell just short of his third Test century, but Steve Waugh made sure of his 25th, shoring things up after Harbhajan had taken India's first Test hat-trick, trapping Ponting and Gilchrist lbw before Warne glanced a full-toss to short leg. India struggled against McGrath, the only bright spot being Laxman's swash-buckling 59 – which earned him promotion to No. 3 in the follow-on. This time Laxman gave a flawless display that stretched over 631 minutes, during which he faced 452 balls, picked up 44 fours with a wide range of exciting shots, and comfortably surpassed India's previous-highest score, Sunil Gavaskar's 236 not out against West Indies at Madras in 1983-84. Australia had 75 overs to survive, but never looked like doing so as Harbhajan got to work again. Tendulkar chipped in with three wickets, including the crucial ones of Hayden and Gilchrist, who completed a king pair.

Australia

M. J. Slater c Mongia b Zaheer Khan	42	– (2) c Ganguly b Harbhajan Singh	43
M. L. Hayden c sub (H. K. Badani) b Harbhajan Singh	97	– (1) lbw b Tendulkar	67
J. L. Langer c Mongia b Zaheer Khan	58	– c Ramesh b Harbhajan Singh	28
M. E. Waugh c Mongia b Harbhajan Singh	22	– lbw b Raju	0
*S. R. Waugh lbw b Harbhajan Singh	110	– c sub (H. K. Badani) b Harbhajan Singh	24
R. T. Ponting lbw b Harbhajan Singh	6	c Das b Harbhajan Singh	0
†A. C. Gilchrist lbw b Harbhajan Singh	0	– lbw b Tendulkar	0
S. K. Warne c Ramesh b Harbhajan Singh	0	– (9) lbw b Tendulkar	0
M. S. Kasprowicz lbw b Ganguly	7	– (10) not out	13
J. N. Gillespie c Ramesh b Harbhajan Singh	46	– (8) c Das b Harbhajan Singh	6
G. D. McGrath not out	21	– lbw b Harbhajan Singh	12
B 19, l-b 10, n-b 7	36	B 6, n-b 8, p 5	19

1/103 (1) 2/193 (2) 3/214 (3) 4/236 (4)　　445　　1/74 (2) 2/106 (3) 3/116 (4)　　212
5/252 (6) 6/252 (7) 7/252 (8)　　　　　　　　　4/166 (5) 5/166 (6) 6/167 (7)
8/269 (9) 9/402 (10) 10/445 (5)　　　　　　　　7/173 (1) 8/174 (9) 9/191 (8) 10/212 (11)

Zaheer Khan 28.4–6–89–2; Prasad 30–5–95–0; Ganguly 13.2–3–44–1; Raju 20–2–58–0; Harbhajan Singh 37.5–7–123–7; Tendulkar 2–0–7–0. *Second Innings*—Zaheer Khan 8–4–30–0; Prasad 3–1–7–0; Harbhajan Singh 30.3–8–73–6; Raju 15–3–58–1; Tendulkar 11–3–31–3; Ganguly 1–0–2–0.

India

S. S. Das c Gilchrist b McGrath	20	– hit wkt b Gillespie	39
S. Ramesh c Ponting b Gillespie	0	– c M. E. Waugh b Warne	30
R. Dravid b Warne	25	– (6) run out	180
S. R. Tendulkar lbw b McGrath	10	– c Gilchrist b Gillespie	10
*S. C. Ganguly c S. R. Waugh b Kasprowicz	23	– c Gilchrist b McGrath	48
V. V. S. Laxman c Hayden b Warne	59	– (3) c Ponting b McGrath	281
†N. R. Mongia c Gilchrist b Kasprowicz	2	– b McGrath	4
Harbhajan Singh c Ponting b Gillespie	4	– (9) not out	8
Zaheer Khan b McGrath	3	– (8) not out	23
S. L. V. Raju lbw b McGrath	4		
B. K. V. Prasad not out	7		
L-b 2, n-b 12	14	B 6, l-b 12, w 2, n-b 14	34

1/0 (2) 2/34 (1) 3/48 (4) 4/88 (3)　　171　　1/52 (2) 2/97 (1)　　(7 wkts dec.) 657
5/88 (5) 6/92 (7) 7/97 (8)　　　　　　　　　　3/115 (4) 4/232 (5)
8/113 (9) 9/129 (10) 10/171 (6)　　　　　　　5/608 (3) 6/624 (7) 7/629 (6)

McGrath 14–8–18–4; Gillespie 11–0–47–2; Kasprowicz 13–2–39–2; Warne 20.1–3–65–2. *Second Innings*—McGrath 39–12–103–3; Gillespie 31–6–115–2; Warne 34–3–152–1; M. E. Waugh 18–1–58–0; Kasprowicz 35–6–139–0; Ponting 12–1–41–0; Hayden 6–0–24–0; Slater 2–1–4–0; Langer 1–0–3–0.

Umpires: S. K. Bansal *(India)* (6) and P. Willey *(England)* (22).
Third umpire: S. N. Bandekar *(India)*.　　Referee: C. W. Smith *(West Indies)* (32).

Close of play: First day, Australia 291-8 (S. R. Waugh 29*, Gillespie 6*); Second day, India 128-8 (Laxman 26*, Raju 3*); Third day, India 254-4 (Laxman 109*, Dravid 7*); Fourth day, India 589-4 (Laxman 275*, Dravid 155*).

INDIA v AUSTRALIA 2000–01 (3rd Test)

At M. A. Chidambaram Stadium, Chennai, on 18, 19, 20, 21, 22 March.
Toss: Australia.   Result: INDIA won by two wickets.
Debuts: India – S. V. Bahutule, S. S. Dighe.
Man of the Match: Harbhajan Singh and M. L. Hayden.   Man of the Series: Harbhajan Singh.

The deciding Test of an enthralling series, marked by dramatic shifts of fortune, produced a grandstand finish. Chasing 155, India seemed to be heading for a comfortable win, only to encounter a brave challenge from Australia's bowlers. The match started with another onslaught from Hayden, who was last out for 203, with 15 fours and an Australian-record six sixes. He shared hundred partnerships with both Waugh twins (Mark reached 7,000 runs during his 70), but the last seven wickets added only 51 – all but four of them from Hayden – as Harbhajan Singh flummoxed the later batsmen. The collapse was triggered when Steve Waugh became only the sixth batsman to be given out handled the ball in a Test, after he missed a sweep at Harbhajan and brushed away the ball when it looked as if it might spin back into the stumps. India claimed a handy lead, with Tendulkar making his 25th Test century, and although several of the Australians got set in their second innings, no-one exceeded Mark Waugh's 57 as Harbhajan worked his way through the order, ending up with 8 for 84 (and 15 in the match, second only to Narendra Hirwani's 16 on debut in 1987-88 for India). India reached 100 for the loss of only two wickets, but nerves jangled when six more went down in adding 50. Fittingly, Harbhajan was there to push the winning runs. Harbhajan finished with 32 wickets in the series: next for India were Tendulkar and Zaheer Khan, with three.

Australia

M. J. Slater c Laxman b Zaheer Khan	4	– (2) c Laxman b Harbhajan Singh	48
M. L. Hayden c Ganguly b Harbhajan Singh	203	– (1) c Zaheer Khan b Kulkarni	35
J. L. Langer c Dravid b Harbhajan Singh	35	– (4) c Laxman b Bahutule	21
M. E. Waugh c sub (H. K. Badani) b Bahutule	70	– (5) c Dravid b Harbhajan Singh	57
*S. R. Waugh handled the ball	47	– (6) c Das b Harbhajan Singh	47
R. T. Ponting st Dighe b Harbhajan Singh	0	– (7) c Dravid b Harbhajan Singh	11
†A. C. Gilchrist lbw b Harbhajan Singh	1	– (3) lbw b Harbhajan Singh	1
S. K. Warne c Das b Harbhajan Singh	0	– lbw b Harbhajan Singh	11
J. N. Gillespie c Ganguly b Harbhajan Singh	0	– c Dravid b Harbhajan Singh	2
C. R. Miller c Bahutule b Harbhajan Singh	0	– lbw b Harbhajan Singh	2
G. D. McGrath not out	3	– not out	11
B 8, l-b 10, n-b 10	28	B 8, l-b 6, n-b 4	18

1/4 (1) 2/67 (3) 3/217 (4) 4/340 (5)   391   1/82 (1) 2/84 (3) 3/93 (2)   264
5/340 (6) 6/344 (7) 7/374 (8)   4/141 (4) 5/193 (5) 6/211 (7)
8/376 (9) 9/385 (10) 10/391 (2)   7/241 (8) 8/246 (6) 9/251 (9) 10/264 (10)

Zaheer Khan 15–5–57–1; Ganguly 2–1–11–0; Harbhajan Singh 38.2–6–133–7; Kulkarni 23–5–67–0; Bahutule 21–3–70–1; Tendulkar 16–1–35–0. *Second Innings*—Zaheer Khan 4–0–13–0; Ganguly 1–0–8–0; Harbhajan Singh 41.5–20–84–8; Kulkarni 30–11–70–1; Tendulkar 12–0–43–0; Bahutule 9–0–32–1.

India

S. S. Das lbw b McGrath	84	– c and b McGrath	9
S. Ramesh c Ponting b Warne	61	– run out	25
V. V. S. Laxman c M. E. Waugh b McGrath	65	– c M. E. Waugh b Miller	66
S. R. Tendulkar c Gilchrist b Gillespie	126	– c M. E. Waugh b Gillespie	17
*S. C. Ganguly c Gilchrist b McGrath	22	– c M. E. Waugh b Gillespie	4
R. Dravid c Gilchrist b Gillespie	81	– c S. R. Waugh b Miller	4
†S. S. Dighe lbw b Warne	4	– not out	22
S. V. Bahutule not out	21	– c Warne b Miller	0
Zaheer Khan c and b Miller	4	– c M. E. Waugh b McGrath	0
Harbhajan Singh c M. E. Waugh b Miller	2	– not out	3
N. M. Kulkarni lbw b Miller	4		
B 19, l-b 2, w 1, n-b 5	27	L-b 3, n-b 2	5

1/123 (2) 2/211 (1) 3/237 (3) 4/284 (5)   501   1/18 (1) 2/76 (2)   (8 wkts) 155
5/453 (6) 6/468 (4) 7/470 (7)   3/101 (4) 4/117 (5)
8/475 (9) 9/477 (10) 10/501 (11)   5/122 (6) 6/135 (3) 7/135 (8) 8/151 (9)

McGrath 36–15–75–3; Gillespie 35–11–88–2; Miller 46–6–160–3; Warne 42–7–140–2; Ponting 2–1–2–0; M. E. Waugh 3–0–8–0; Hayden 1–0–7–0. *Second Innings*—McGrath 11.1–3–21–2; Gillespie 15–2–49–2; Miller 9–1–41–3; Warne 6–0–41–0.

Umpires: A. V. Jayaprakash *(India)* (9) and R. E. Koertzen *(South Africa)* (24).
Third umpire: C. R. Vijayaraghavan *(India)*.   Referee: C. W. Smith *(West Indies)* (33).

Close of play: First day, Australia 326-3 (Hayden 147*, S. R. Waugh 43*); Second day, India 211-1 (Das 84*, Laxman 59*); Third day, India 480-9 (Bahutule 4*, Kulkarni 0*); Fourth day, Australia 241-7 (S. R. Waugh 43*).

NEW ZEALAND v PAKISTAN 2000–01 (1st Test)

At Eden Park, Auckland, on 8, 9, 10, 11, 12 March.
Toss: New Zealand.   Result: PAKISTAN won by 299 runs.
Debuts: New Zealand – J. E. C. Franklin. Pakistan – Faisal Iqbal, Imran Farhat, Misbah-ul-Haq, Mohammad Sami.
Man of the Match: Mohammad Sami.

Mohammad Sami's Test career had a dream start: after a wicket with his fifth ball in the first innings, he demolished the second with five wickets for six runs in a seven-over spell of speed and reverse swing as New Zealand capitulated on the final morning. They had begun the day needing 326 more to win but, with nine wickets in hand, were confident they could secure the draw. However, Richardson lasted only four more balls, and although another ten overs passed without incident, Sami then entered the attack. Within 13 overs the game was over, with lunch still half an hour away. The final eight wickets fell for only ten runs, and the last five batsmen all failed to score. At the other end to Sami, Saqlain Mushtaq took four for three in 12.4 overs, on the first drop-in pitch for a Test in New Zealand – it was criticised for having no life, at least until the final dramatic collapse. Pakistan's batting star was Younis Khan, who just missed a hundred in the first innings but made sure of one in the second, taking his total for his last three Test innings to 356 for twice out. Younis shared century stands in both innings with another newcomer, Faisal Iqbal, the nephew of the team's coach, Javed Miandad. This was Pakistan's ninth victory over New Zealand in their last 11 Tests, and a devastating show of bowling firepower and bench strength, given that Wasim Akram and Shoaib Akhtar were both unavailable.

Pakistan

Imran Farhat c Parore b Martin	23	– c and b Wiseman		63
Salim Elahi c Parore b Tuffey	24	– c Wiseman b Tuffey		7
Misbah-ul-Haq c Sinclair b McMillan	28	– c Parore b Tuffey		10
Yousuf Youhana c Parore b Martin	51	– c Astle b Franklin		42
Younis Khan c McMillan b Tuffey	91	– (6) not out		149
Faisal Iqbal c Fleming b Tuffey	42	– (7) not out		52
*†Moin Khan c Parore b Tuffey	47			
Saqlain Mushtaq c Fleming b Martin	2	– (5) c Parore b Tuffey		2
Waqar Younis lbw b Martin	4			
Mushtaq Ahmed c Parore b Franklin	19			
Mohammad Sami not out	0			
B 2, l-b 7, n-b 6	15	B 4, l-b 6, n-b 1		11

1/46 (2) 2/52 (1) 3/130 (4) 4/138 (3)   346   1/21 (2) 2/59 (3)   (5 wkts dec.) 336
5/270 (5) 6/271 (6) 7/286 (8)   3/97 (1) 4/110 (5)
8/294 (9) 9/346 (7) 10/346 (10)   5/189 (4)

Tuffey 34–13–96–4; Martin 22–1–106–4; Franklin 21–6–55–1; Wiseman 7–0–35–0; McMillan 14–5–34–1; Astle 8–3–11–0. *Second Innings*—Tuffey 17–3–43–3; Martin 12–2–65–0; Franklin 18–2–59–1; Wiseman 36–6–107–1; McMillan 7–0–27–0; Astle 13–6–25–0.

New Zealand

M. H. Richardson b Mohammad Sami	1	– c Imran Farhat b Saqlain Mushtaq		59
M. D. Bell c Moin Khan b Waqar Younis	0	– run out		28
M. S. Sinclair c Imran Farhat b Mohammad Sami	34	– (4) c Yousuf Youhana b Mohammad Sami		10
*S. P. Fleming b Saqlain Mushtaq	86	– (5) lbw b Saqlain Mushtaq		5
N. J. Astle b Mushtaq Ahmed	0	– (6) b Saqlain Mushtaq		1
C. D. McMillan c Younis Khan b Waqar Younis	54	– (7) c Saqlain Mushtaq b Mohammad Sami		0
†A. C. Parore not out	32	– (8) not out		0
J. E. C. Franklin lbw b Saqlain Mushtaq	0	– (9) b Mohammad Sami		0
P. J. Wiseman lbw b Saqlain Mushtaq	9	– (3) b Mohammad Sami		8
D. R. Tuffey b Saqlain Mushtaq	2	– b Mohammad Sami		0
C. S. Martin b Mohammad Sami	0	– b Saqlain Mushtaq		0
B 8, l-b 20, n-b 6	34	B 12, l-b 7, n-b 1		20

1/1 (2) 2/1 (1) 3/82 (3) 4/83 (5)   252   1/91 (2) 2/105 (1) 3/121 (3)   131
5/194 (6) 6/217 (4) 7/217 (8)   4/126 (4) 5/127 (6) 6/130 (5)
8/237 (9) 9/251 (10) 10/252 (11)   7/130 (7) 8/130 (9) 9/130 (10) 10/131 (11)

Waqar Younis 22–8–44–2; Mohammad Sami 31.4–11–70–3; Saqlain Mushtaq 20–3–48–4; Mushtaq Ahmed 23–8–62–1. *Second Innings*—Waqar Younis 11–2–31–0; Mohammad Sami 15–4–36–5; Saqlain Mushtaq 25.4–12–24–4; Mushtaq Ahmed 8–2–21–0.

Umpires: D. B. Cowie *(New Zealand)* (20) and R. B. Tiffin *(Zimbabwe)* (18).
Third umpire: B. F. Bowden *(New Zealand)*.   Referee: R. S. Madugalle *(Sri Lanka)* (33).

Close of play: First day, Pakistan 270-4 (Younis Khan 91*, Faisal Iqbal 42*); Second day, New Zealand 65-2 (Sinclair 28*, Fleming 32*); Third day, Pakistan 98-3 (Yousuf Youhana 17*, Saqlain Mushtaq 0*); Fourth day, New Zealand 105-1 (Richardson 59*, Wiseman 2*).

NEW ZEALAND v PAKISTAN 2000–01 (2nd Test)

At Lancaster Park, Christchurch, on 15, 16, 17, 18, 19 March.
Toss: Pakistan.   Result: MATCH DRAWN.
Debuts: New Zealand – C. J. Drum.
Man of the Match: M. S. Sinclair.

A placid portable pitch produced a somnolent draw, with a match total of 1,243 runs for just 19 wickets. At least it gave the New Zealand batsmen a chance to rediscover some form: rather surprisingly, they had all survived intact despite the shocking collapse in the previous Test. Put in, Richardson and Bell completed the century stand they narrowly missed at Auckland, then Sinclair took centre stage, and rekindled expectations often disappointed since his 214 on debut against West Indies 15 months earlier. He reached his second double-hundred with a second six just before losing his final partner seven overs after tea on the second day: Glenn Turner was the only previous New Zealander to reach 200 twice in Tests. Sinclair's 520-minute innings, the first double-century for New Zealand against Pakistan, was matched by Yousuf Youhana, whose 203 (his first double-century) took eight minutes longer, although Youhana faced 429 balls to Sinclair's 348. Both hit 27 fours, while Youhana managed three sixes to Sinclair's two. Saqlain Mushtaq emphasised the pitch's placidity by sharing a stand of 248 with Youhana, and surviving more than seven hours for his own maiden Test century: his final batting average of 14.48 is the lowest by anyone who reached three figures in a Test. New Zealand quietly batted out the remaining 73 overs, latterly against occasional bowlers – one of whom, Younis Khan, claimed a first Test wicket with his legspin. This was the first draw between these countries since a run-fest at Auckland in 1988-89.

New Zealand

M. H. Richardson b Saqlain Mushtaq	46	– not out		73
M. D. Bell c Faisal Iqbal b Saqlain Mushtaq	75	– lbw b Younis Khan		40
M. S. Sinclair not out	204	– not out		50
*S. P. Fleming run out	32			
N. J. Astle c Moin Khan b Waqar Younis	6			
G. E. Bradburn c Imran Farhat b Fazl-e-Akbar	0			
C. D. McMillan c Younis Khan b Fazl-e-Akbar	20			
†A. C. Parore lbw b Saqlain Mushtaq	46			
D. R. Tuffey lbw b Fazl-e-Akbar	13			
C. J. Drum c Moin Khan b Waqar Younis	4			
C. S. Martin b Waqar Younis	0			
B 2, l-b 17, w 1, n-b 10	30	B 15, l-b 4, n-b 14		33

1/102 (1) 2/163 (2) 3/248 (4) 4/276 (5)   476   1/69 (2)   (1 wkt dec.) 196
5/282 (6) 6/327 (7) 7/428 (8)
8/449 (9) 9/468 (10) 10/476 (11)

Waqar Younis 34–6–114–3; Mohammad Sami 36–4–107–0; Fazl-e-Akbar 32–6–87–3; Saqlain Mushtaq 48–11–134–3; Younis Khan 6–1–15–0. *Second Innings*—Waqar Younis 8–1–18–0; Mohammad Sami 11–3–32–0; Fazl-e-Akbar 7–0–26–0; Saqlain Mushtaq 24–5–44–0; Younis Khan 21–6–47–1; Yousuf Youhana 1–0–3–0; Faisal Iqbal 1–0–7–0.

Pakistan

Imran Farhat c Drum b Martin	4	Waqar Younis c Parore b Tuffey	12
Ijaz Ahmed, sen. hit wkt b Drum	11	Fazl-e-Akbar not out	0
Faisal Iqbal c Fleming b McMillan	63	B 5, l-b 8, n-b 6	19
Inzamam-ul-Haq c Fleming b Martin	130		
Yousuf Youhana c and b Richardson	203	1/5 (1) 2/25 (2)	(8 wkts dec.) 571
Younis Khan c Parore b Tuffey	0	3/157 (3) 4/259 (4)	
*†Moin Khan c Martin b Bradburn	28	5/260 (6) 6/304 (7)	
Saqlain Mushtaq not out	101	7/552 (5) 8/569 (9)	

Mohammad Sami did not bat.

Tuffey 49–13–152–2; Martin 41–9–153–2; Drum 8–1–21–1; Bradburn 42–10–124–1; McMillan 31–13–47–1; Astle 30–12–45–0; Richardson 9–0–16–1.

Umpires: D. J. Harper *(Australia)* (11) and D. M. Quested *(New Zealand)* (5).
Third umpire: A. L. Hill *(New Zealand)*.   Referee: R. S. Madugalle *(Sri Lanka)* (34).

Close of play: First day, New Zealand 284-5 (Sinclair 100*, McMillan 1*); Second day, Pakistan 65-2 (Faisal Iqbal 22*, Inzamam-ul-Haq 26*); Third day, Pakistan 341-6 (Yousuf Youhana 73*, Saqlain Mushtaq 20*); Fourth day, Pakistan 561-7 (Saqlain Mushtaq 98*, Waqar Younis 5*).

NEW ZEALAND v PAKISTAN 2000–01 (3rd Test)

At Seddon Park, Hamilton, on 27, 28 *(no play)*, 29, 30 March.
Toss: New Zealand.   Result: NEW ZEALAND won by an innings and 185 runs.
Debuts: Pakistan – Humayun Farhat.
Man of the Match: D. R. Tuffey.

On a well-grassed pitch New Zealand levelled the series with their biggest Test victory, while the unpredictable Pakistanis went down to their heaviest defeat. It was a disastrous start for Inzamam-ul-Haq, deputising as captain for the injured Moin Khan. On the fourth day, McMillan inspired his team-mates by thumping 26 off a single over, a Test record at the time, after which a young pace attack cleaned Pakistan out. With the second day and half the third washed out, the entire match lasted less than 190 overs, barely two days' actual play. Pakistan started badly, only just avoiding their lowest total against New Zealand (102 at Faisalabad in 1990-91), then had to watch the home openers waltz past their total in 30 overs: both went on to maiden centuries. McMillan's burst against Younis Khan's only over of legspin – 444464 – was followed by a record seventh consecutive boundary when he hit his next ball, from Saqlain Mushtaq, for his third six. Having taken 80 deliveries for his fifty, he shot to 98 off another 16 before he was caught at deep third man. Fleming, who had helped him add 147, promptly declared with a lead of 303, which turned out to be more than enough when Pakistan collapsed again, all their wickets falling to catches. To add to their misery, they were later fined 75% of their match fees for a slow over-rate. Humayun Farhat, keeping wicket in what turned out to be his only Test, played alongside his brother Imran.

Pakistan

Imran Farhat c Astle b Martin	24	– c McMillan b Tuffey	1
Ijaz Ahmed, sen c Parore b Martin	5	– c Parore b Franklin	17
Faisal Iqbal c Bell b Martin	0	– c Bradburn b Tuffey	5
*Inzamam-ul-Haq lbw b Martin	5	– c Tuffey b Franklin	20
Yousuf Youhana c Parore b Tuffey	0	– c Parore b Martin	16
Younis Khan c Richardson b Tuffey	36	– c Astle b Tuffey	4
†Humayun Farhat c Parore b Tuffey	28	– c Bradburn b Martin	26
Saqlain Mushtaq run out	0	– c Martin b Franklin	14
Waqar Younis c Fleming b Franklin	0	– c Parore b McMillan	4
Fazl-e-Akbar c Parore b Tuffey	0	– not out	0
Mohammad Akram not out	1	– c and b Franklin	4
L-b 3, n-b 2	5	L-b 2, n-b 5	7

1/28 (2) 2/28 (3) 3/29 (1) 4/34 (4)   104   1/10 (1) 2/20 (3) 3/43 (2)   118
5/38 (5) 6/89 (7) 7/89 (8)   4/54 (4) 5/69 (5) 6/71 (6) 7/97 (7)
8/91 (9) 9/103 (10) 10/104 (6)   8/114 (9) 9/114 (8) 10/118 (11)

Tuffey 10.5–2–39–4; Martin 10–3–52–4; Franklin 6–2–10–1. *Second Innings*—Tuffey 19–5–38–3; Martin 15–2–48–2; Franklin 9.5–3–26–4; McMillan 5–3–2–1; Astle 1–0–2–0.

New Zealand

M. H. Richardson c Imran Farhat b Fazl-e-Akbar 106
M. D. Bell lbw b Waqar Younis 105
M. S. Sinclair c Waqar Younis b Fazl-e-Akbar........ 27
C. D. McMillan c Waqar Younis b Fazl-e-Akbar 98
*S. P. Fleming not out.......................... 51
L-b 10, n-b 10 20

1/181 (2) 2/239 (3)   (4 wkts dec.) 407
3/260 (1) 4/407 (4)

N. J. Astle, †A. C. Parore, G. E. Bradburn, J. E. C. Franklin, D. R. Tuffey and C. S. Martin did not bat.

Waqar Younis 31–2–98–1; Fazl-e-Akbar 27.2–6–85–3; Mohammad Akram 22–1–106–0; Saqlain Mushtaq 31–6–82–0; Younis Khan 1–0–26–0.

Umpires: R. S. Dunne *(New Zealand)* (38) and D. J. Harper *(Australia)* (12).
Third umpire: E. A. Watkin *(New Zealand)*.   Referee: R. S. Madugalle *(Sri Lanka)* (35).

Close of play: First day, New Zealand 160-0 (Richardson 64*, Bell 89*); Second day, No play; Third day, New Zealand 260-2 (Richardson 106*, McMillan 7*).

WEST INDIES v SOUTH AFRICA 2000–01 (1st Test)

At Bourda, Georgetown, Guyana, on 9, 10, 11, 12, 13 March.
Toss: West Indies.   Result: MATCH DRAWN.
Debuts: none.
Man of the Match: G. Kirsten.

Neither team could make enough headway on a slow, true pitch to claim an advantage. South Africa gained a first-innings lead of 28, thanks to Kirsten's 446-minute 150 (his 12th Test hundred, to equal Cullinan's national record), but there was encouragement for the home crowd when the Guyanese pair of Hooper and Sarwan set up a declaration. Hooper's two-year international "retirement" ended when he was appointed as captain in place of Jimmy Adams. He survived a close lbw shout from Kallis first ball and, after a cautious start, put on 62 with Sarwan in the last 11 overs of the fourth day. Both fell looking for quick runs next morning, with Sarwan unwisely testing Gibbs at square leg to be run out nine short of a classy maiden hundred. Hooper eventually gave South Africa a target of 306 and his bowlers 76 overs to press for victory. Neither was a realistic possibility. South Africa batted through without anxiety, while West Indies ended a run of seven Test defeats. The tourists might have had more anxious moments had Hooper not missed a regulation catch at second slip, off Gibbs, from Dillon's fifth ball. Gibbs took advantage to make his highest score since he was suspended for his part in the match-fixing affair. Earlier, Gayle had struck the ball with fierce power, especially through the off side, and had 14 fours in his 81 when he slashed to give Boucher his 150th dismissal in his 38th Test, beating Rod Marsh's record of 39.

West Indies

W. W. Hinds c Boje b Pollock	13	– c Boucher b Donald	14
C. H. Gayle c Boucher b Kallis	81	– c Boucher b Boje	44
M. N. Samuels b Boje	40	– b Kallis	51
B. C. Lara c Donald b Klusener	47	– c Pollock b Ntini	45
R. R. Sarwan b Donald	7	– run out	91
*C. L. Hooper c Klusener b Boje	69	– c Cullinan b Boje	35
†R. D. Jacobs lbw b Donald	0	– not out	18
N. A. M. McLean b Klusener	6	– lbw b Boje	0
D. Ramnarine run out	5		
M. Dillon c Cullinan b Ntini	9		
C. A. Walsh not out	2		
B 2, l-b 12, w 2, n-b 9	25	B 10, l-b 10, w 2, n-b 8, p 5	35

	304

1/43 (1) 2/131 (3) 3/165 (2) 4/206 (4)   304
5/221 (5) 6/221 (7) 7/228 (8)
8/238 (9) 9/300 (10) 10/304 (6)

1/51 (1) 2/78 (2)   (7 wkts dec.) 333
3/147 (4) 4/210 (3)
5/299 (6) 6/333 (5) 7/333 (8)

Donald 23–9–43–2; Pollock 18–2–54–1; Ntini 12–2–48–1; Kallis 17–2–33–1; Klusener 35–14–56–2; Boje 19.1–6–56–2. *Second Innings*—Donald 20–8–51–1; Pollock 17–4–51–0; Kallis 15–2–36–1; Boje 37–13–93–3; Ntini 20–5–50–1; Klusener 8–1–27–0.

South Africa

G. Kirsten c Jacobs b Walsh	150	– c Hinds b Ramnarine	24
H. H. Gibbs b Dillon	8	– not out	83
J. H. Kallis lbw b McLean	50	– lbw b McLean	30
D. J. Cullinan c Jacobs b Ramnarine	7	– not out	4
N. D. McKenzie b Ramnarine	4		
†M. V. Boucher lbw b Walsh	52		
L. Klusener lbw b McLean	5		
N. Boje c Hinds b Dillon	15		
*S. M. Pollock not out	17		
A. A. Donald c Lara b Ramnarine	2		
M. Ntini c Jacobs b Dillon	11		
B 4, l-b 5, n-b 2	11	B 1	1

1/25 (2) 2/171 (3) 3/186 (4) 4/198 (5)   332
5/274 (1) 6/285 (7) 7/287 (6)
8/310 (8) 9/315 (10) 10/332 (11)

1/66 (1) 2/134 (3)   (2 wkts) 142

Walsh 28–7–56–2; Dillon 27–5–64–3; McLean 22–0–75–2; Ramnarine 41–9–105–3; Hooper 8–0–21–0; Samuels 1–0–2–0. *Second Innings*—Walsh 10–3–19–0; Dillon 5–1–21–0; Ramnarine 27.3–14–46–1; McLean 10–3–25–1; Hooper 14–8–23–0; Sarwan 1–0–4–0; Samuels 2–0–3–0.

Umpires: J. H. Hampshire *(England)* (16) and E. A. Nicholls *(West Indies)* (14).
Third umpire: C. Alfred *(West Indies)*.   Referee: M. H. Denness *(England)* (6).

Close of play: First day, West Indies 232-7 (Hooper 12*, Ramnarine 4*); Second day, South Africa 130-1 (Kirsten 80*, Kallis 39*); Third day, West Indies 50-0 (Hinds 13*, Gayle 26*); Fourth day, West Indies 286-4 (Sarwan 71*, Hooper 31*).

WEST INDIES v SOUTH AFRICA 2000–01 (2nd Test)

At Queen's Park Oval, Port-of-Spain, Trinidad, on 17, 18, 19, 20, 21 March.
Toss: South Africa.   Result: SOUTH AFRICA won by 69 runs.
Debuts: none.
Man of the Match: D. J. Cullinan.

West Indies started the final day needing another 200 to win, but they lost four wickets for 19 at the start and five for 19 either side of tea to fall well short. In between, Hooper and Sarwan put on 92, but the captain was eventually left stranded and forlorn. For the locals, around 12,000 of whom turned up on the last day, it was a disappointing finale to the 50th Test at Queen's Park Oval, the eighth ground – the first outside England and Australia – to reach its half-century. The statistical highlight came midway through the third day, when Walsh became the first man to take 500 Test wickets, thanks to a dubious lbw decision against Kallis two balls after Kirsten had become No. 499. In the first innings Kallis had fallen to Hinds's third delivery in Tests, but Cullinan's 13th century pushed South Africa to 286, although their last five wickets tumbled for 30. Donald then made four important incisions, but Jacobs ushered West Indies into the lead, and when South Africa's second innings was only one run bigger than their first (Walsh finished with six wickets) a home victory looked on the cards ... but Lara bagged his first Test duck on his home ground, and Kallis made up for his two unusual dismissals with four wickets. Hooper and Sarwan kept the contest alive until Sarwan hooked a Kallis bouncer straight to square leg. Jacobs was run out by Gibbs's direct hit soon afterwards, and South Africa hurried to victory.

South Africa

H. H. Gibbs b Walsh	34	– c sub (S. Chanderpaul) b Walsh	87
G. Kirsten c Hooper b McLean	23	– c Jacobs b Walsh	22
J. H. Kallis c and b Hinds	53	– lbw b Walsh	0
D. J. Cullinan c Dillon b Ramnarine	103	– c Lara b Ramnarine	73
N. D. McKenzie c Gayle b Walsh	9	– c Jacobs b Dillon	25
†M. V. Boucher c Hooper b Hinds	16	– (7) b Dillon	38
L. Klusener c Jacobs b Ramnarine	15	– (6) c Gayle b Dillon	5
N. Boje c Jacobs b Ramnarine	3	– c Jacobs b Walsh	9
*S. M. Pollock not out	15	– b Walsh	8
A. A. Donald c Jacobs b McLean	0	– lbw b Walsh	1
M. Ntini c and b McLean	7	– not out	5
N-b 8	8	B 1, l-b 4, n-b 9	14

1/62 (2) 2/62 (1) 3/161 (3) 4/189 (5)   286   1/38 (2) 2/38 (3) 3/187 (4)   287
5/221 (6) 6/256 (7) 7/264 (8)   4/198 (1) 5/204 (6) 6/253 (5)
8/265 (4) 9/266 (10) 10/286 (11)   7/264 (7) 8/276 (8) 9/278 (10) 10/287 (9)

Walsh 21–5–47–2; Dillon 17–2–74–0; McLean 16.5–2–60–3; Ramnarine 18–6–57–3; Hooper 9–1–25–0; Hinds 5–0–23–2. *Second Innings*—Walsh 36.4–13–61–6; McLean 18–1–76–0; Dillon 28–8–58–3; Ramnarine 35–8–64–1; Hooper 13–4–23–0.

West Indies

W. W. Hinds c Boucher b Donald	56	– lbw b Kallis	2
C. H. Gayle lbw b Pollock	10	– c Boucher b Pollock	23
M. N. Samuels c Klusener b Donald	35	– (4) c Kallis b Donald	9
B. C. Lara c Kallis b Ntini	12	– (5) lbw b Ntini	0
R. R. Sarwan c Cullinan b Donald	34	– (6) c Boje b Kallis	39
*C. L. Hooper lbw b Donald	53	– (7) not out	54
†R. D. Jacobs not out	93	– (8) run out	4
N. A. M. McLean c Ntini b Pollock	3	– (9) c Boucher b Kallis	2
D. Ramnarine b Pollock	2	– (3) c Kallis b Donald	11
M. Dillon b Ntini	21	– lbw b Kallis	0
C. A. Walsh run out	0	– b Pollock	0
B 9, l-b 4, w 3, n-b 7	23	B 7, l-b 4, n-b 7	18

1/24 (2) 2/94 (3) 3/118 (1) 4/123 (4)   342   1/20 (1) 2/35 (3) 3/50 (4)   162
5/198 (5) 6/235 (6) 7/242 (8)   4/50 (2) 5/51 (5) 6/143 (6)
8/250 (9) 9/321 (10) 10/342 (11)   7/150 (8) 8/159 (9) 9/159 (10) 10/162 (11)

Donald 30–6–91–4; Pollock 28–11–55–3; Ntini 16–4–56–2; Kallis 21–10–44–0; Boje 19–2–65–0; Klusener 11–5–18–0. *Second Innings*—Donald 15–4–32–2; Pollock 23.1–8–35–2; Kallis 16–6–40–4; Ntini 16–4–22–1; Klusener 10–5–22–0.

Umpires: B. R. Doctrove *(West Indies)* (2) and D. B. Hair *(Australia)* (36).
Third umpire: C. E. Cumberbatch *(West Indies)*.   Referee: M. H. Denness *(England)* (7).

Close of play: First day, West Indies 2-0 (Hinds 0*, Gayle 0*); Second day, West Indies 250-7 (Jacobs 26*, Ramnarine 2*); Third day, South Africa 130-2 (Gibbs 57*, Cullinan 41*); Fourth day, West Indies 32-1 (Gayle 18*, Ramnarine 11*).

WEST INDIES v SOUTH AFRICA 2000–01 (3rd Test)

At Kensington Oval, Bridgetown, Barbados, on 29, 30, 31 March, 1, 2 April.
Toss: West Indies.   Result: MATCH DRAWN.
Debuts: none.
Man of the Match: D. J. Cullinan.

As the prospect of defeat unexpectedly crept up in the final session, West Indies resorted to blatant time-wasting. With seven wickets down and only Cuffy and Walsh to come, they stretched out the last five overs for 25 minutes. Ramnarine called for on-field treatment for a supposed hamstring strain, Dillon changed his boots, and there were other delays that brought a warning from umpire Bucknor. Mike Denness, the referee, took no action after speaking to the two players and team officials, but Pollock later revealed that some senior West Indians had apologised to him. Earlier in the day West Indies had sniffed victory when South Africa were reduced to 97 for 6, before Cullinan and Pollock dashed their hopes. These two had also reached centuries in the first innings, Pollock's being his second in two months from No. 9 in the order: he and Donald put on 132 for the ninth wicket. Jacobs had pushed his side close to first-innings parity, finally reaching a century – West Indies' first against South Africa – after several near-misses. He got there with a top-edged hook off Ntini, his fourth six to go with 11 fours, and remained unbeaten when Kallis wrapped up the innings with his sixth wicket. West Indies were eventually set 265: Gayle lashed 11 fours from 39 balls, but no-one else reached double figures. As Boje and Klusener found turn on the worn pitch, West Indies' slapdash approach almost cost them the match – but survival was guaranteed by games-manship at the expense of sportsmanship.

South Africa

G. Kirsten c Gayle b Walsh		0	– (2) c Samuels b Cuffy	0
H. H. Gibbs c Hooper b Dillon		34	– (1) c Sarwan b Hooper	19
J. H. Kallis c Jacobs b Dillon		11	– (5) c Sarwan b Hooper	20
D. J. Cullinan c and b Dillon		134	– c Lara b Ramnarine	82
N. D. McKenzie c Dillon b Hinds		72	– (3) c Jacobs b Ramnarine	12
†M. V. Boucher c Jacobs b Cuffy		3	– (7) c Jacobs b Ramnarine	0
N. Boje c Ramnarine b Dillon		34	– (9) not out	9
L. Klusener b Walsh		1	– (6) c Cuffy b Ramnarine	4
*S. M. Pollock not out		106	– (8) c Hooper b Walsh	40
A. A. Donald c Hooper b Walsh		37	– lbw b Ramnarine	0
M. Ntini c and b Ramnarine		0		
B 6, l-b 4, w 2, n-b 10		22	L-b 3, n-b 8	11

1/0 (1) 2/53 (2) 3/58 (3) 4/207 (5)   454   1/2 (2) 2/31 (1)   (9 wkts dec.) 197
5/230 (6) 6/306 (4) 7/307 (7)   3/36 (3) 4/80 (5)
8/315 (8) 9/447 (10) 10/454 (11)   5/95 (6) 6/97 (7) 7/167 (8) 8/197 (4) 9/197 (10)

Walsh 45–15–87–3; Dillon 34–1–147–4; Cuffy 30–7–71–1; Ramnarine 33.1–6–86–1; Hooper 18–5–31–0; Hinds 10–5–13–1; Samuels 2–0–6–0; Gayle 1–0–3–0. *Second Innings*—Walsh 14–3–28–1; Cuffy 10–4–28–1; Hooper 34–12–49–2; Dillon 4–2–7–0; Ramnarine 31.5–10–78–5; Samuels 2–1–4–0.

West Indies

W. W. Hinds c Boucher b Kallis		2	– (2) c Cullinan b Boje	8
C. H. Gayle c Cullinan b Ntini		40	– (1) c Boucher b Kallis	48
M. N. Samuels c McKenzie b Kallis		6	– c Cullinan b Boje	3
B. C. Lara c Boje b Kallis		83	– b Klusener	8
R. R. Sarwan c Gibbs b Ntini		16	– b Kallis	0
*C. L. Hooper c Boucher b Kallis		74	– c Boucher b Boje	5
†R. D. Jacobs not out		113	– c McKenzie b Boje	1
M. Dillon b Boje		14	– not out	2
D. Ramnarine lbw b Boje		6	– not out	0
C. E. Cuffy lbw b Kallis		4		
C. A. Walsh b Kallis		4		
B 4, l-b 9, n-b 12		25	B 8, l-b 1, n-b 4	13

1/37 (1) 2/49 (2) 3/57 (3) 4/102 (5)   387   1/34 (2) 2/59 (3) 3/64 (1)   (7 wkts) 88
5/218 (4) 6/252 (6) 7/316 (8)   4/64 (5) 5/72 (6)
8/353 (9) 9/381 (10) 10/387 (11)   6/82 (7) 7/82 (4)

Donald 14–7–30–0; Pollock 35–11–84–0; Kallis 36–17–67–6; Ntini 28–7–93–2; Boje 28–7–67–2; Klusener 10–3–33–0. *Second Innings*—Pollock 5–0–25–0; Kallis 8–1–34–2; Boje 16.4–10–17–4; Klusener 9–7–3–1.

Umpires: S. A. Bucknor *(West Indies)* (55) and D. B. Hair *(Australia)* (37).
Third umpire: H. A. Moore *(West Indies)*.   Referee: M. H. Denness *(England)* (8).

Close of play: First day, South Africa 244-5 (Cullinan 108*, Boje 3*); Second day, West Indies 7-0 (Hinds 0*, Gayle 5*); Third day, West Indies 252-5 (Hooper 74*, Jacobs 14*); Fourth day, South Africa 52-3 (Cullinan 12*, Kallis 5*).

WEST INDIES v SOUTH AFRICA 2000–01 (4th Test)

At Antigua Recreation Ground, St John's, Antigua, on 6, 7, 8, 9, 10 April.
Toss: West Indies.   Result: SOUTH AFRICA won by 82 runs.
Debuts: West Indies – N. C. McGarrell.
Man of the Match: S. M. Pollock.

South Africa claimed the series, and the new Sir Vivian Richards Trophy, just before tea on the last day. On a pitch expected to take spin, West Indies fielded only two fast bowlers for the first time since the Packer schism in 1977-78. Hooper's decision to bowl first, rather than offering his spinners the chance of a fourth-innings pitch, thus seemed to defy logic, but looked justified when South Africa were 152 for 7 at tea on the first day, six of the wickets falling to spin. The debutant slow left-armer Neil McGarrell claimed four, including three for seven in 23 balls. Only Gibbs, whose 85 included two sixes and 12 fours, batted with conviction before Pollock and Boje added 75; then West Indies collapsed, the last four wickets going for ten runs in 13.1 overs on the third morning. Their troubles worsened when Dillon went off after bowling just three balls, having sprained his right thumb in a collision with Lara. After South Africa dipped to 156 for 7 Kallis and Pollock extended the lead, and the eventual declaration set West Indies 323 in a minimum of 131 overs. While Lara was in – he clouted Boje for four leg-side sixes – home hopes still flickered. But at 91 he mistimed a drive off the new ball and was caught at extra cover: 11 balls later, South Africa became only the second team in 28 years, after Australia in 1994-95, to win a Test series in the Caribbean.

South Africa

G. Kirsten c Dillon b McGarrell		8	– (2) c Sarwan b Walsh	9
H. H. Gibbs c Jacobs b Hooper		85	– (1) c Gayle b Ramnarine	45
J. H. Kallis b Dillon		5	– (6) not out	30
D. J. Cullinan c Lara b Ramnarine		4	– (5) c Gayle b McGarrell	28
N. D. McKenzie c Jacobs b McGarrell		35	– (3) b Walsh	44
L. Klusener lbw b McGarrell		0	– (7) c Hinds b Walsh	1
†M. V. Boucher c Gayle b McGarrell		1	– (8) c Jacobs b Walsh	3
*S. M. Pollock not out		48	– (9) not out	41
N. Boje lbw b Walsh		36	– (4) c sub (S. C. Joseph) b Hooper	0
J. M. Kemp b Dillon		16		
M. Ntini b Dillon		0		
B 2, l-b 5, n-b 2		9	B 6, l-b 3, w 4, n-b 1	14

1/29 (1) 2/35 (3) 3/53 (4) 4/120 (5)   247   1/17 (2) 2/95 (1)   (7 wkts dec.) 215
5/126 (6) 6/136 (7) 7/148 (2)   3/96 (4) 4/123 (3)
8/223 (9) 9/247 (10) 10/247 (11)   5/135 (5) 6/146 (7) 7/156 (8)

Walsh 31–14–45–1; Dillon 18.2–4–47–3; McGarrell 43–19–72–4; Ramnarine 20–6–45–1; Hooper 10–2–31–1. *Second Innings*—Walsh 38–13–56–4; Dillon 0.3–0–3–0; Hinds 3.3–0–14–0; McGarrell 15–3–41–1; Hooper 24–7–37–1; Ramnarine 42–24–55–1.

West Indies

C. H. Gayle c Pollock b Kallis		11	– c McKenzie b Boje	12
W. W. Hinds c Boucher b Pollock		9	– c Kirsten b Boje	29
S. Chanderpaul c Cullinan b Kemp		40	– lbw b Boje	16
B. C. Lara c McKenzie b Kemp		19	– (5) c McKenzie b Kallis	91
R. R. Sarwan c Boje b Kallis		25	– (6) c Boucher b Pollock	26
*C. L. Hooper c Kirsten b Klusener		17	– (4) c McKenzie b Klusener	21
M. Dillon b Klusener		0	– (9) c Cullinan b Boje	1
†R. D. Jacobs not out		3	– (7) c Kirsten b Pollock	0
N. C. McGarrell lbw b Klusener		0	– (8) c Kemp b Pollock	6
D. Ramnarine run out		2	– c Kirsten b Kallis	9
C. A. Walsh lbw b Pollock		4	– not out	4
B 3, l-b 3, n-b 4		10	B 18, l-b 3, n-b 4	25

1/13 (1) 2/21 (2) 3/50 (4) 4/88 (5)   140   1/36 (1) 2/56 (2) 3/86 (4)   240
5/126 (3) 6/127 (7) 7/132 (6)   4/89 (3) 5/138 (6) 6/138 (7)
8/134 (9) 9/136 (10) 10/140 (11)   7/155 (8) 8/176 (9) 9/229 (5) 10/240 (10)

Pollock 22.1–11–25–2; Kallis 17–8–24–2; Ntini 6–2–27–0; Kemp 8–2–17–2; Boje 12–4–26–0; Klusener 11–4–15–3. *Second Innings*—Pollock 19–5–41–3; Kallis 15.4–6–23–2; Boje 45–9–118–4; Kemp 6–3–7–0; Klusener 14–6–30–1.

Umpires: E. A. Nicholls *(West Indies)* (15) and S. Venkataraghavan *(India)* (44).
Third umpire: P. C. Whyte *(West Indies)*.   Referee: M. H. Denness *(England)* (9).

Close of play: First day, South Africa 210-7 (Pollock 36*, Boje 28*); Second day, West Indies 130-6 (Hooper 16*, Jacobs 1*); Third day, South Africa 122-3 (McKenzie 44*, Cullinan 17*); Fourth day, West Indies 101-4 (Lara 5*, Sarwan 4*).

WEST INDIES v SOUTH AFRICA 2000–01 (5th Test)

At Sabina Park, Kingston, Jamaica, on 19, 20, 21, 22, 23 April.
Toss: West Indies.   Result: WEST INDIES won by 130 runs.
Debuts: West Indies – L. V. Garrick.
Man of the Match: R. D. Jacobs.

A welcome and deserved win was West Indies' first in 14 Tests since Birmingham the previous June. For South Africa, it was their first loss in 13 Tests since Galle in July. Victory was a fitting gift for Walsh in his last Test, and his six wickets carried his series total to 25, more than anyone else on either side, and lifted his Test record to 519. In spite of a pitch Pollock rated the best of the series, the scoring was again slow and low. Leon Garrick, rushed into the side for what turned out to be his only Test on the basis of an unbeaten 174 for Jamaica against the tourists, took the first ball – and cut it straight to gully, to become only the second debutant, after Jimmy Cook for South Africa against India at Durban in 1992-93, to fall to the opening delivery of a Test. A modest total of 225 still proved enough for a lead of 84 as South Africa subsided to their lowest total against West Indies, then another four-hour effort from the reliable Jacobs extended the home advantage to 385. South Africa briefly threatened, but three wickets from leg-spinner Ramnarine either side of lunch on the final day eased the tension. The new ball hastened the end, Dillon and Walsh taking two wickets apiece with it. Walsh's final victim was his opposite number, Donald. During South Africa's brief first innings Pollock completed the double of 2,000 runs and 200 wickets in Tests.

West Indies

L. V. Garrick c Pollock b Donald	0	– c Boucher b Donald	27
C. H. Gayle c Kemp b Donald	25	– b Pollock	32
S. Chanderpaul c Boucher b Kallis	7	– c Cullinan b Kemp	7
B. C. Lara c Kallis b Pollock	81	– b Adams	14
M. N. Samuels c Boucher b Donald	3	– b Pollock	59
*C. L. Hooper c Kirsten b Pollock	25	– c Pollock b Kallis	5
†R. D. Jacobs c Boucher b Pollock	0	– c McKenzie b Klusener	85
M. Dillon c Boucher b Donald	24	– c Gibbs b Pollock	13
D. Ramnarine not out	35	– c Cullinan b Pollock	9
C. E. Cuffy c Boucher b Pollock	3	– not out	13
C. A. Walsh c Adams b Pollock	4	– c Kirsten b Adams	3
B 4, l-b 12, w 2	18	B 14, l-b 13, w 4, n-b 3	34
	225		**301**

1/0 (1) 2/21 (3) 3/50 (2) 4/54 (5)   225
5/107 (6) 6/113 (7) 7/167 (4)
8/188 (8) 9/203 (10) 10/225 (11)

1/47 (1) 2/55 (3) 3/77 (4)   301
4/103 (2) 5/126 (6) 6/184 (5)
7/229 (8) 8/255 (9) 9/287 (7) 10/301 (11)

Donald 25–5–54–4; Pollock 26.5–17–28–5; Kallis 16–5–38–1; Kemp 16–3–45–0; Adams 11–1–43–0; Klusener 2–1–1–0. *Second Innings*—Donald 20–8–54–1; Pollock 34–8–66–4; Kallis 28–10–56–1; Adams 21.5–7–54–2; Kemp 18–9–30–1; Klusener 8–3–14–1.

South Africa

H. H. Gibbs c Jacobs b Cuffy	18	– (2) b Hooper	51
G. Kirsten c Gayle b Walsh	0	– (1) c Jacobs b Dillon	14
J. H. Kallis c and b Dillon	17	– (5) b Ramnarine	51
D. J. Cullinan c Lara b Cuffy	6	– lbw b Walsh	18
N. D. McKenzie lbw b Ramnarine	45	– (3) c Garrick b Ramnarine	55
L. Klusener b Walsh	13	– not out	31
†M. V. Boucher c Garrick b Walsh	13	– c Jacobs b Ramnarine	0
*S. M. Pollock c Jacobs b Dillon	24	– c Jacobs b Dillon	3
J. M. Kemp c Walsh b Dillon	0	– lbw b Walsh	0
A. A. Donald not out	1	– b Walsh	10
P. R. Adams c Hooper b Dillon	3	– c Samuels b Dillon	4
W 1	1	B 4, l-b 13, n-b 1	18
	141		**255**

1/9 (2) 2/24 (1) 3/35 (4) 4/51 (3)   141
5/77 (6) 6/97 (7) 7/137 (8)
8/137 (5) 9/137 (9) 10/141 (11)

1/37 (1) 2/102 (2) 3/124 (4)   255
4/190 (3) 5/209 (5) 6/209 (7)
7/235 (8) 8/236 (9) 9/250 (10) 10/255 (11)

Walsh 18–8–31–3; Cuffy 17–6–58–2; Dillon 15.1–5–32–4; Ramnarine 11–4–20–1. *Second Innings*—Walsh 22–6–62–3; Cuffy 10–3–13–0; Dillon 19–3–59–3; Ramnarine 31–6–61–3; Hooper 28–8–43–1.

Umpires: S. A. Bucknor *(West Indies)* (56) and S. Venkataraghavan *(India)* (45).
Third umpire: T. Wilson *(West Indies)*.   Referee: M. H. Denness *(England)* (10).

Close of play: First day, West Indies 214-9 (Ramnarine 28*, Walsh 0*); Second day, West Indies 34-0 (Garrick 21*, Gayle 10*); Third day, West Indies 255-7 (Jacobs 67*, Ramnarine 9*); Fourth day, South Africa 140-3 (McKenzie 40*, Kallis 5*).

ZIMBABWE v BANGLADESH 2000–01 (1st Test)

At Queens Sports Club, Bulawayo, on 19, 20, 21, 22 April.
Toss: Zimbabwe.   Result: ZIMBABWE won by an innings and 32 runs.
Debuts: Zimbabwe – A. M. Blignaut, D. D. Ebrahim, B. T. Watambwa. Bangladesh – Javed Omar,
Manjural Islam, Mohammad Sharif, Mushfiqur Rahman.
Man of the Match: Javed Omar.

Bangladesh's first overseas Test, like their home debut, ended in defeat. Blignaut, one of seven debutants, started
with some fine new-ball bowling, becoming the first Zimbabwean to take a five-for on debut (John Traicos did
so in their inaugural Test in 1992-93, but he had already played for South Africa). Put in, Bangladesh were 194
for 4 after tea on the first day, with Aminul Islam threatening to become the first to score centuries in his country's
first two Tests. But he fell to the new ball for 84, and the innings disintegrated. After that, Zimbabwe never really
released their grip, although left-arm seamer Manjural Islam (who finished with six wickets) was on a hat-trick
after dismissing Ebrahim with the last ball of his second over and Carlisle with the first ball of his third. Andy
Flower equalled Everton Weekes's 1940s record with his seventh consecutive Test fifty. Bangladesh's second
innings was virtually a procession from one end while Javed Omar carried his bat. He was only the third batsman,
and the first for more than 100 years, to do so on Test debut, following Jack Barrett for Australia at Lord's in
1890 and Pelham Warner for England at Johannesburg in 1898-99. Unusually for someone whose team lost by
an innings, Omar won the match award: he dedicated it to his brother Asif, a mentor until his early death in 1995.
Bangladesh's wicketkeeper Khaled Mashud broke his ankle during pre-match practice on the third day: Mehrab
Hossain took over behind the stumps.

Bangladesh

Javed Omar c Ebrahim b Murphy	62	– not out	85
Mehrab Hossain, sen. c Whittall b Blignaut	16	– b Streak	0
Habibul Bashar c Murphy b Blignaut	0	– c Murphy b Watambwa	24
Aminul Islam c A. Flower b Blignaut	84	– c Ebrahim b Streak	11
Akram Khan run out	21	– c Ebrahim b Blignaut	8
*Naimur Rahman c Blignaut b Watambwa	22	– c and b Nkala	6
†Khaled Mashud c A. Flower b Streak	30	– absent hurt	
Mushfiqur Rahman c Streak b Blignaut	4	– (7) c Nkala b Watambwa	2
Hasibul Hossain lbw b Streak	1	– (8) c G. W. Flower b Streak	6
Mohammad Sharif c Campbell b Blignaut	0	– (9) c Whittall b Blignaut	8
Manjural Islam not out	1	– (10) c and b Blignaut	6
L-b 1, w 6, n-b 9	16	L-b 2, w 6, n-b 4	12

1/26 (2) 2/30 (3) 3/114 (1) 4/149 (5)   257   1/6 (2) 2/61 (3) 3/105 (4)   168
5/194 (6) 6/226 (4) 7/253 (7)   4/116 (5) 5/129 (6) 6/138 (7)
8/256 (9) 9/256 (8) 10/257 (10)   7/149 (8) 8/160 (9) 9/168 (10)

Streak 21–7–47–2; Blignaut 23.3–5–73–5; Watambwa 17–4–38–1; Nkala 13–2–45–0; Murphy 17–2–53–1. *Second
Innings*—Streak 19–5–42–3; Blignaut 13.3–4–37–3; Nkala 9–0–34–1; Watambwa 13–3–44–2; Murphy 4–1–9–0.

Zimbabwe

G. J. Whittall c Mohammad Sharif b Hasibul Hossain	119	B. A. Murphy c Habibul Bashar	
D. D. Ebrahim c Khaled Mashud b Manjural Islam ...	2	b Naimur Rahman	30
S. V. Carlisle b Manjural Islam	3	B. T. Watambwa not out	4
A. D. R. Campbell c Khaled Mashud b Mohammad Sharif	19		
†A. Flower c Naimur Rahman b Manjural Islam	73	B 2, l-b 10, w 1, n-b 12	25
G. W. Flower c Mohammad Sharif b Hasibul Hossain .	68		
*H. H. Streak c sub (Mohammad Rafique)		1/18 (2) 2/27 (3) 3/66 (4)	457
b Manjural Islam	67	4/215 (5) 5/233 (1) 6/353 (7)	
A. M. Blignaut c and b Manjural Islam	0	7/353 (8) 8/389 (6)	
M. L. Nkala c Mehrab Hossain b Manjural Islam	47	7/353 (8) 8/389 (6)	

Hasibul Hossain 30–7–125–2; Manjural Islam 35–12–81–6; Mohammad Sharif 29–3–112–1; Mushfiqur Rahman
20–5–53–0; Naimur Rahman 24.4–7–74–1.

Umpires: K. C. Barbour *(Zimbabwe)* (2) and R. E. Koertzen *(South Africa)* (25).
Third umpire: C. K. Coventry *(Zimbabwe)*.   Referee: B. Warnapura *(Sri Lanka)* (1).

Close of play: First day, Bangladesh 256-9 (Mohammad Sharif 0*); Second day, Zimbabwe 287-5 (G. W. Flower
30*, Streak 25*); Third day, Bangladesh 91-2 (Javed Omar 47*, Aminul Islam 10*).

ZIMBABWE v BANGLADESH 2000–01 (2nd Test)

At Harare Sports Club on 26, 27, 28, 29, 30 April.
Toss: Zimbabwe.   Result: ZIMBABWE won by eight wickets.
Debuts: Bangladesh – Enamul Haque, sen.
Man of the Match: G. J. Whittall.   Man of the Series: H. H. Streak.

Another convincing victory, only their fifth in Tests, gave Zimbabwe their first proper series win (they beat India in a one-off Test at Harare in 1998-99), but Bangladesh gave an improved showing, taking the match into the final day and avoiding the innings defeat. This was Zimbabwe's 50th Test match: Campbell and Andy Flower had played in all of them, a unique achievement for any country, and Campbell set another record by becoming the first Zimbabwean fielder to take 50 catches. Mehrab Hossain anchored Bangladesh's innings for more than five hours, and on the second day the burly Akram Khan held the home attack off until after lunch – but then the last three wickets crashed in 11 balls. Slow left-armer Price was much the best of the bowlers, flighting the ball well. Zimbabwe batted solidly, although Andy Flower failed to break the Test record for successive fifties when he was run out for 23. As in the first Test, Zimbabwe lost five wickets before taking the lead, whereupon a determined stand between Grant Flower and Streak virtually decided the match; this time they added 133. Streak had a maiden Test century in his sights when he slashed at a wide ball from Mohammad Sharif, walked to a catch to the keeper, and immediately declared. Bangladesh avoided the innings defeat for the loss of only four wickets, and looked reasonably placed at 264 for 6 – but then lost their last four wickets for two, presenting Zimbabwe with exactly 100 to win.

Bangladesh

Javed Omar c Blignaut b Streak	1	– c G. W. Flower b Price	43
†Mehrab Hossain, sen. c Carlisle b Price	71	– c Blignaut b Watambwa	0
Al Sahariar c G. W. Flower b Streak	11	– c Streak b Watambwa	68
Aminul Islam c Campbell b Price	12	– lbw b Price	2
Habibul Bashar st A. Flower b Price	64	– c A. Flower b Streak	76
Akram Khan c Campbell b Streak	44	– c Campbell b Price	31
*Naimur Rahman lbw b Price	16	– run out	36
Mushfiqur Rahman c A. Flower b Streak	2	– (9) not out	2
Enamul Haque, sen. not out	20	– (8) c A. Flower b Watambwa	3
Mohammad Sharif c Carlisle b Watambwa	0	– c Carlisle b Streak	0
Manjural Islam c Campbell b Watambwa	0	– c A. Flower b Watambwa	0
L-b 8, w 3, n-b 2	13	L-b 2, w 1, n-b 2	5

1/1 (1) 2/23 (3) 3/48 (4) 4/162 (5)   254   1/2 (2) 2/97 (1) 3/99 (4)   266
5/171 (2) 6/196 (7) 7/207 (8)   4/127 (3) 5/203 (6) 6/246 (5)
8/253 (6) 9/254 (10) 10/254 (11)   7/264 (7) 8/264 (8) 9/265 (10) 10/266 (11)

Blignaut 27–6–67–0; Streak 30–12–38–4; Watambwa 14.5–3–48–2; Nkala 19–11–22–0; Price 30–9–71–4. *Second Innings*—Streak 21–7–47–2; Watambwa 22–5–64–4; Blignaut 15–6–27–0; Price 30–9–94–3; G. W. Flower 6–0–13–0; Nkala 6–0–19–0.

Zimbabwe

G. J. Whittall run out	59	– b Enamul Haque	60
D. D. Ebrahim c Akram Khan b Naimur Rahman	39	– run out	10
S. V. Carlisle c Habibul Bashar b Mohammad Sharif	21	– not out	29
A. D. R. Campbell c Mushfiqur Rahman b Naimur Rahman	73	– not out	0
†A. Flower run out	23		
G. W. Flower c Mohammad Sharif b Enamul Haque	84		
*H. H. Streak c Mehrab Hossain b Mohammad Sharif	87		
A. M. Blignaut run out	15		
M. L. Nkala c Mushfiqur Rahman b Enamul Haque	7		
R. W. Price not out	0		
B 7, l-b 6	13	L-b 1	1

1/90 (1) 2/104 (2) 3/164 (3)   (9 wkts dec.) 421   1/35 (2) 2/92 (1)   (2 wkts) 100
4/210 (5) 5/244 (4) 6/377 (6)
7/397 (8) 8/419 (9) 9/421 (7)

B. T. Watambwa did not bat.

Manjural Islam 34–9–113–0; Mohammad Sharif 28.4–6–108–2; Enamul Haque 46–15–94–2; Mushfiqur Rahman 11–1–33–0; Naimur Rahman 28–12–60–2. *Second Innings*—Manjural Islam 8–2–21–0; Mohammad Sharif 6–0–36–0; Enamul Haque 3–0–8–1; Mushfiqur Rahman 6–1–26–0; Naimur Rahman 0.3–0–8–0.

Umpires: D. B. Cowie *(New Zealand)* (21) and R. B. Tiffin *(Zimbabwe)* (19).
Third umpire: G. R. Evans *(Zimbabwe)*.   Referee: B. Warnapura *(Sri Lanka)* (2).

Close of play: First day, Bangladesh 198-6 (Akram Khan 15*, Mushfiqur Rahman 0*); Second day, Zimbabwe 144-2 (Carlisle 21*, Campbell 22*); Third day, Zimbabwe 377-6 (Streak 65*); Fourth day, Bangladesh 219-5 (Habibul Bashar 66*, Naimur Rahman 7*).

ENGLAND v PAKISTAN 2001 (1st Test)

At Lord's, London, on 17 *(no play)*, 18, 19, 20 May.
Toss: Pakistan.   Result: ENGLAND won by an innings and nine runs.
Debuts: England – R. J. Sidebottom, I. J. Ward.
Man of the Match: A. R. Caddick.

England comfortably won their 100th Test at Lord's – it was their 37th victory there – with Gough and Caddick taking 16 for 207 between them: Gough's eight wickets in his 50th Test included his 200th, when he had Rashid Latif caught behind in the first innings. This was the 12th time in the pair's 24 Tests together that England had won, testament to their combined potency and a record that compared favourably with Trueman and Statham (13 from 35). They were ably supported by assured close catching, notably from Thorpe, who also top-scored with 80, including a dozen fours. In the second innings he dived full length to his right at third slip for a superlative one-handed catch off Caddick's fifth ball to dismiss the luckless Salim Elahi for a pair. Law 13 proved unlucky for Pakistan when, after the first day was washed out, the follow-on target was reduced from 200 runs to 150; they struggled to close the gap to 188, then fell just short of making England bat again, losing 16 wickets in all on the fourth (and last) day. Shoaib Akhtar, playing his first Test in more than a year after injuries and investigations into his action, looked short of match fitness, although he did fracture Hussain's thumb an over before he was out for a five-hour 64. Ryan Sidebottom followed his father, Arnie (1985), as an England player: for six years he seemed destined also to follow him as a one-cap wonder, before returning in style in 2007.

England

M. A. Atherton b Azhar Mahmood	42	D. G. Cork c Younis Khan b Wasim Akram	25
M. E. Trescothick c Azhar Mahmood b Abdul Razzaq	36	A. R. Caddick b Azhar Mahmood	5
M. P. Vaughan c Rashid Latif b Azhar Mahmood	32	D. Gough not out	5
*N. Hussain c Rashid Latif b Azhar Mahmood	64	B 1, l-b 5, w 1, n-b 8	15
G. P. Thorpe c Abdul Razzaq b Waqar Younis	80		
R. J. Sidebottom c Inzamam-ul-Haq b Wasim Akram	4	1/60 (2) 2/105 (3) 3/114 (1)	391
†A. J. Stewart lbw b Shoaib Akhtar	44	4/246 (5) 5/254 (6) 6/307 (4)	
I. J. Ward c Abdul Razzaq b Waqar Younis	39	7/317 (7) 8/365 (9) 9/385 (10) 10/391 (8)	

Wasim Akram 34–9–99–2; Waqar Younis 25–5–77–2; Shoaib Akhtar 19–4–64–1; Abdul Razzaq 21–2–68–1; Younis Khan 5–0–27–0; Azhar Mahmood 26–12–50–4.

Pakistan

Saeed Anwar c Atherton b Gough	12	– c Thorpe b Caddick	8
Salim Elahi c Atherton b Caddick	0	– c Thorpe b Caddick	0
Abdul Razzaq c Stewart b Caddick	22	– c Atherton b Caddick	53
Inzamam-ul-Haq c Stewart b Caddick	13	– c Stewart b Cork	20
Yousuf Youhana lbw b Gough	26	– c Vaughan b Gough	6
Younis Khan b Cork	58	– lbw b Cork	1
Azhar Mahmood c Trescothick b Caddick	14	– c Stewart b Caddick	24
†Rashid Latif c Stewart b Gough	18	– c Stewart b Gough	20
Wasim Akram not out	19	– c Thorpe b Gough	12
*Waqar Younis c Thorpe b Gough	0	– c Stewart b Cork	21
Shoaib Akhtar b Gough	0	– not out	2
B 1, l-b 7, n-b 13	21	L-b 6, n-b 6	12

1/4 (2) 2/21 (1) 3/37 (4) 4/60 (3)	203	1/2 (2) 2/30 (1) 3/67 (4)	179
5/116 (5) 6/153 (7) 7/167 (6)		4/84 (5) 5/87 (6) 6/121 (3)	
8/203 (8) 9/203 (10) 10/203 (11)		7/122 (7) 8/147 (9) 9/167 (8) 10/179 (10)	

Gough 16–5–61–5; Caddick 17–3–52–4; Sidebottom 11–0–38–0; Cork 11–3–42–1; Trescothick 2–1–2–0. *Second Innings*—Gough 16–4–40–3; Caddick 18–3–54–4; Sidebottom 9–2–26–0; Cork 15.3–3–41–3; Vaughan 1–0–12–0.

Umpires: D. B. Hair *(Australia)* (38) and P. Willey *(England)* (23).
Third umpire: B. Dudleston *(England)*.   Referee: B. F. Hastings *(New Zealand)* (7).

Close of play: First day, No play; Second day, England 254-4 (Hussain 53*, Sidebottom 4*); Third day, Pakistan 115-4 (Yousuf Youhana 26*, Younis Khan 32*).

ENGLAND v PAKISTAN 2001 (2nd Test)

At Old Trafford, Manchester, on 31 May, 1, 2, 3, 4 June.
Toss: Pakistan.   Result: PAKISTAN won by 108 runs.
Debuts: none.
Man of the Match: Inzamam-ul-Haq.   Men of the Series: G. P. Thorpe and Inzamam-ul-Haq.

This was Test cricket at its twisting, turning best. At tea on the last day, England were 196 for 2, needing another 174 for an unlikely victory but on course for the draw that would have brought them a fifth consecutive series win for the first time in 30 years. But eight wickets fell in a frantic, fractious final session – four of them for one run in 13 balls – sparking scenes of jubilation from Pakistan's horn-blowing, flag-waving fans. Four batsmen were dismissed by no-balls which the umpires failed to spot amid the flurry of appeals – two of them, Ward and Caddick, to successive deliveries from Saqlain Mushtaq – and the end came with less than six overs remaining. This was bad luck for England, but couldn't detract from the truth that the better side had won, extending England's dismal record at Old Trafford to a solitary victory since 1981. The batting star was Inzamam-ul-Haq, who toyed with the bowlers like a cuddly lion pawing a mouse. He inspired Pakistan on the opening day and averted another mini-crisis in the second innings. Inzamam's 14th Test century helped Pakistan to 370 for eight by the first-day close: not since 1992, when Pakistan made 388 for three, also at Old Trafford, had any side scored so heavily on the opening day of a Test in England. Vaughan later reached his first Test hundred with a six – a two swelled by four overthrows. Stewart resumed the England captaincy in the absence of the injured Hussain.

Pakistan

Saeed Anwar c Atherton b Caddick	29	– c Thorpe b Gough		12
Abdul Razzaq b Caddick	1	– c Cork b Hoggard		22
Faisal Iqbal c Vaughan b Gough	16	– c Stewart b Caddick		14
Inzamam-ul-Haq c Ward b Hoggard	114	– c Trescothick b Hoggard		85
Yousuf Youhana c Knight b Caddick	4	– c Atherton b Caddick		49
Younis Khan lbw b Hoggard	65	– lbw b Cork		17
Azhar Mahmood c Knight b Hoggard	37	– b Caddick		14
†Rashid Latif run out	71	– c Atherton b Hoggard		25
Wasim Akram c Stewart b Gough	16	– b Gough		36
Saqlain Mushtaq not out	21	– c Stewart b Gough		5
*Waqar Younis lbw b Gough	5	– not out		14
L-b 9, n-b 15	24	L-b 11, n-b 19		30

1/6 (2) 2/39 (3) 3/86 (1) 4/92 (5)   403   1/24 (1) 2/41 (2) 3/63 (3)   323
5/233 (6) 6/255 (4) 7/308 (7)   4/204 (4) 5/208 (5) 6/232 (6)
8/357 (9) 9/380 (8) 10/403 (11)   7/241 (7) 8/300 (8) 9/306 (9) 10/323 (10)

Gough 23.4–2–94–3; Caddick 28–2–111–3; Hoggard 19–4–79–3; Cork 21–2–75–0; Trescothick 3–0–14–0; Vaughan 2–0–21–0. *Second Innings*—Gough 22.5–2–85–3; Caddick 22–4–92–3; Hoggard 29–4–93–3; Cork 25–9–42–1.

England

M. A. Atherton c Rashid Latif b Waqar Younis	5	– b Waqar Younis		51
M. E. Trescothick b Wasim Akram	10	– c Rashid Latif b Wasim Akram		117
M. P. Vaughan c Rashid Latif b Waqar Younis	120	– c Rashid Latif b Abdul Razzaq		14
G. P. Thorpe run out	138	– b Waqar Younis		10
*†A. J. Stewart not out	39	– lbw b Saqlain Mushtaq		19
I. J. Ward run out	12	– c Rashid Latif b Saqlain Mushtaq		10
N. V. Knight c Rashid Latif b Abdul Razzaq	15	– lbw b Wasim Akram		0
D. G. Cork c Saeed Anwar b Abdul Razzaq	2	– lbw b Saqlain Mushtaq		4
A. R. Caddick c Rashid Latif b Saqlain Mushtaq	1	– b Saqlain Mushtaq		0
D. Gough b Abdul Razzaq	0	– c sub (Imran Nazir) b Waqar Younis		23
M. J. Hoggard b Saqlain Mushtaq	0	– not out		0
L-b 5, w 2, n-b 8	15	B 6, l-b 4, w 1, n-b 2		13

1/15 (2) 2/15 (1) 3/282 (4) 4/283 (3)   357   1/146 (1) 2/174 (3) 3/201 (4)   261
5/309 (6) 6/348 (7) 7/353 (8)   4/213 (2) 5/229 (5) 6/230 (7)
8/354 (9) 9/356 (10) 10/357 (11)   7/230 (6) 8/230 (9) 9/261 (8) 10/261 (10)

Wasim Akram 30–7–89–1; Waqar Younis 24–3–87–2; Azhar Mahmood 8–0–35–0; Saqlain Mushtaq 30.2–7–80–2; Abdul Razzaq 19–2–61–3. *Second Innings*—Wasim Akram 23–4–59–2; Waqar Younis 22.1–3–85–3; Saqlain Mushtaq 47–20–74–4; Abdul Razzaq 13–5–33–1.

Umpires: E. A. Nicholls *(West Indies)* (16) and D. R. Shepherd *(England)* (56).
Third umpire: R. Julian *(England)*.   Referee: B. F. Hastings *(New Zealand)* (8).

Close of play: First day, Pakistan 370-8 (Rashid Latif 64*, Saqlain Mushtaq 2*); Second day, England 204-2 (Vaughan 84*, Thorpe 98*); Third day, Pakistan 87-3 (Inzamam-ul-Haq 25*, Yousuf Youhana 3*); Fourth day, England 85-0 (Atherton 30*, Trescothick 47*).

ZIMBABWE v INDIA 2001 (1st Test)

At Queens Sports Club, Bulawayo, on 7, 8, 9, 10 June.
Toss: Zimbabwe.   Result: INDIA won by eight wickets.
Debuts: none.
Man of the Match: S. S. Das.

Zimbabwe sealed their own fate with an inept batting performance on the opening day; from then on, they were engaged in a vain battle for survival in their country's first winter Test. They had struggled against some early life and movement, but this was no excuse for the poor shots that cost several wickets as Zimbabwe limped to their lowest total against India. Andy Flower, as so often, made the top score, but even his 45-ball 51 included an uncharacteristic array of daring strokes never suggesting permanence. Zimbabwe's bowlers struck back, but from 98 for 5 Tendulkar and Dravid took India into the lead, putting on 80 before Tendulkar was brilliantly caught by Carlisle at second slip. The last three wickets stretched the advantage to 145 as Harbhajan Singh hit out merrily for a maiden Test half-century. Both Flowers then made fighting fifties – Andy's was his ninth in ten Test innings – but no-one produced the big score required to turn the tables. Nehra, India's best bowler, was ordered out of the attack by umpire Harper after two warnings from umpire Tiffin for running on the pitch. His fellow left-arm seamer, Zaheer Khan, was also warned twice, arousing suspicions that this was a deliberate policy to rough up the pitch for Harbhajan's offspin. A tricky-looking target posed no problems in the end, although top-scorer Das might have been given out caught behind second ball, and was also dropped twice before India completed their first Test win outside Asia for 15 years.

Zimbabwe

G. J. Whittall b Nehra	6	– c Ramesh b Srinath	20
D. D. Ebrahim run out	12	– c Dravid b Srinath	0
S. V. Carlisle c Laxman b Zaheer Khan	29	– c Laxman b Nehra	52
A. D. R. Campbell c Dighe b Harbhajan Singh	21	– c Das b Harbhajan Singh	16
†A. Flower c Das b Nehra	51	– (6) c Ramesh b Nehra	83
G. W. Flower c Dighe b Srinath	5	– (7) run out	71
*H. H. Streak run out	16	– (8) lbw b Zaheer Khan	14
A. M. Blignaut lbw b Nehra	0	– (9) not out	32
B. A. Murphy c Dravid b Zaheer Khan	7	– (5) c Das b Zaheer Khan	10
H. K. Olonga c Dighe b Harbhajan Singh	16	– b Srinath	0
B. T. Watambwa not out	0	– run out	0
L-b 4, n-b 6	10	B 1, l-b 17, w 2, n-b 10	30

1/9 (1) 2/46 (2) 3/65 (3) 4/89 (4)   173   1/14 (2) 2/34 (1) 3/63 (4)   328
5/97 (6) 6/137 (5) 7/139 (8)   4/86 (5) 5/134 (3) 6/235 (6) ·
8/154 (7) 9/165 (9) 10/173 (10)   7/273 (8) 8/308 (7) 9/312 (10) 10/328 (11)

Srinath 15–5–47–1; Nehra 12–1–23–3; Zaheer Khan 11–1–54–2; Harbhajan Singh 20.5–6–45–2. *Second Innings*—Srinath 32.2–11–71–3; Nehra 26.4–4–77–2; Harbhajan Singh 37.5–8–92–1; Zaheer Khan 22–6–44–2; Tendulkar 6–0–23–0; Ganguly 1–0–3–0.

India

S. S. Das c Ebrahim b Murphy	30	– not out	82
S. Ramesh b Watambwa	2	– c Carlisle b Blignaut	17
V. V. S. Laxman c Whittall b Olonga	28	– c and b G. W. Flower	38
S. R. Tendulkar c Carlisle b Blignaut	74	– not out	36
J. Srinath c Whittall b Watambwa	1		
*S. C. Ganguly c A. Flower b Streak	5		
R. Dravid c A. Flower b Blignaut	44		
†S. S. Dighe c A. Flower b Streak	47		
Harbhajan Singh c Whittall b Watambwa	66		
Zaheer Khan b Streak	0		
A. Nehra not out	9		
L-b 4, w 1, n-b 7	12	B 4, w 1, n-b 6	11

1/2 (2) 2/54 (3) 3/81 (1) 4/83 (5)   318   1/71 (2) 2/132 (3)   (2 wkts) 184
5/98 (6) 6/178 (4) 7/208 (7)
8/280 (8) 9/280 (10) 10/318 (9)

Streak 24–7–63–3; Watambwa 25.5–6–94–3; Blignaut 16–2–68–2; Olonga 8–1–35–1; Murphy 16–3–54–1. *Second Innings*—Watambwa 15–4–54–0; Blignaut 12–3–25–1; Murphy 18.4–1–78–0; G. W. Flower 8–0–23–1.

Umpires: D. J. Harper *(Australia)* (13) and R. B. Tiffin *(Zimbabwe)* (20).
Third umpire: J. F. Fenwick *(Zimbabwe)*.   Referee: D. T. Lindsay *(South Africa)* (1).

Close of play: First day, India 83-3 (Tendulkar 16*, Srinath 1*); Second day, Zimbabwe 79-3 (Carlisle 27*, Murphy 10*); Third day, Zimbabwe 303-7 (G. W. Flower 67*, Blignaut 11*).

ZIMBABWE v INDIA 2001 (2nd Test)

At Harare Sports Club on 15, 16, 17, 18 June.
Toss: India.   Result: ZIMBABWE won by four wickets.
Debuts: Zimbabwe – T. J. Friend. India – H. K. Badani.
Man of the Match: A. M. Blignaut.   Man of the Series: S. S. Das.

India lost their chance of a rare overseas series win when, like Zimbabwe in the previous Test, they batted poorly in the first innings, and paid the penalty after a thrilling match of constant fluctuations. Das and Dravid stood out against an attack weakened when Watambwa limped off with a hamstring injury, but India's middle order imploded after lunch, before Dravid and Harbhajan Singh added 56 for the eighth wicket. Nehra's three quick strikes before the close gave India the upper hand, but Zimbabwe recovered well despite spirited bowling and fielding. India then appeared to be fighting their way out of trouble: the turning point came when Blignaut took the new ball one over before the close and had Dravid caught behind. Next morning four wickets tumbled for ten runs in six overs. The debutant Badani held out for 82 minutes, but Zimbabwe were left 157 to win. It was no simple task, but Carlisle played one of his country's most valuable innings, batting virtually without flaw for more than three hours to hold the innings together. Andy Flower, despite a serious thumb injury sustained while keeping wicket, hit two fours to complete Zimbabwe's sixth Test victory in 52 matches and square the series. The game had commenced with a minute's silence in memory of Zimbabwe's recent Test batsman Trevor Madondo, who had died of cerebral malaria only four days beforehand. The Zimbabwean team played in black armbands and, at the post-match ceremony, Streak dedicated the victory to Madondo.

India

S. S. Das c A. Flower b Blignaut	57	– lbw b Streak	70
H. K. Badani lbw b Watambwa	2	– (7) not out	16
V. V. S. Laxman c Blignaut b Streak	15	– c Murphy b Friend	20
S. R. Tendulkar b Streak	20	– c G. W. Flower b Streak	69
*S. C. Ganguly c Blignaut b Streak	9	– (6) lbw b Blignaut	0
R. Dravid not out	68	– (5) c A. Flower b Blignaut	26
†S. S. Dighe c G. W. Flower b Friend	20	– (2) c A. Flower b Blignaut	4
A. B. Agarkar c Blignaut b Friend	6	– c A. Flower b Streak	0
Harbhajan Singh b Murphy	31	– c Ebrahim b Blignaut	5
J. Srinath run out	0	– c A. Flower b Streak	3
A. Nehra c sub (P. A. Strang) b Murphy	0	– b Blignaut	0
L-b 2, w 6, n-b 1	9	L-b 9, w 12	21
	237		234

1/7 (2) 2/45 (3) 3/90 (4) 4/103 (1)
5/122 (5) 6/165 (7) 7/172 (8)
8/228 (9) 9/237 (10) 10/237 (11)

1/8 (2) 2/32 (3) 3/150 (4)
4/197 (5) 5/199 (6) 6/202 (1)
7/202 (8) 8/207 (9) 9/226 (10) 10/234 (11)

Watambwa 3.4–0–14–1; Streak 20–4–69–3; Friend 20.2–4–48–2; Blignaut 20–1–84–1; Murphy 9.2–3–17–2; G. W. Flower 1–0–3–0. *Second Innings*—Streak 27–12–46–4; Blignaut 31.5–14–74–5; Friend 22–4–47–1; Whittall 7–4–15–0; Murphy 10–1–42–0; G. W. Flower 1–0–1–0.

Zimbabwe

G. J. Whittall c Dravid b Nehra	0	– c Dravid b Srinath	10
D. D. Ebrahim lbw b Harbhajan Singh	49	– c Badani b Harbhajan Singh	20
S. V. Carlisle c Badani b Nehra	3	– not out	62
A. D. R. Campbell b Nehra	8	– lbw b Nehra	13
†A. Flower c Das b Harbhajan Singh	45	– (8) not out	8
G. W. Flower c Laxman b Srinath	86	– (5) c Laxman b Agarkar	3
*H. H. Streak b Tendulkar	40	– (6) c Dighe b Srinath	8
A. M. Blignaut st Dighe b Harbhajan Singh	35	– (7) b Nehra	16
T. J. Friend b Nehra	15		
B. A. Murphy b Harbhajan Singh	17		
B. T. Watambwa not out	2		
B 4, l-b 5, w 2, n-b 4	15	B 1, l-b 11, n-b 5	17
	315	(6 wkts)	157

1/5 (1) 2/9 (3) 3/18 (4) 4/105 (5)
5/110 (2) 6/175 (7) 7/242 (8)
8/271 (9) 9/301 (10) 10/315 (6)

1/25 (1) 2/45 (2)
3/71 (4) 4/89 (5)
5/119 (6) 6/144 (7)

Srinath 29.3–7–82–1; Nehra 24–6–72–4; Agarkar 24–7–62–0; Harbhajan Singh 26–5–71–4; Tendulkar 4–0–19–1. *Second Innings*—Nehra 13–0–45–2; Srinath 13–1–46–2; Harbhajan Singh 19–6–25–1; Agarkar 8–3–22–1; Tendulkar 1–0–7–0.

Umpires: E. A. R. de Silva (Sri Lanka) (3) and I. D. Robinson (Zimbabwe) (25).
Third umpire: G. R. Evans (Zimbabwe).   Referee: D. T. Lindsay (South Africa) (2).

Close of play: First day, Zimbabwe 31-3 (Ebrahim 13*, A. Flower 5*); Second day, Zimbabwe 301-8 (G. W. Flower 80*, Murphy 17*); Third day, India 197-4 (Das 68*).

ENGLAND v AUSTRALIA 2001 (1st Test)

At Edgbaston, Birmingham, on 5, 6, 7, 8 July.
Toss: Australia.　　Result: AUSTRALIA won by an innings and 118 runs.
Debuts: England – U. Afzaal.
Man of the Match: A. C. Gilchrist.

One session was all Australia needed to settle into their defence of the Ashes. England were 106 for one with an over to lunch, but then on came Warne. Butcher gloved his second ball to Ponting, diving forward from short cover: it was the beginning of the end. The opening day featured 427 runs, 236 of them after tea. Century stands topped and tailed England's innings: Caddick's 49 not out had been bettered by an England No. 11 only by John Snow's unbeaten 59 against West Indies in 1966. In between, though, it was an old story. In seven overs either side of tea, four wickets fell for 21. Slater then crashed Gough's first two deliveries behind point for four, and collected another two fours in an opening over that cost 18. Afterwards Steve Waugh's 26th Test hundred (during which he passed 9,000 runs) and Martyn's first cemented Australia's advantage. Butcher's part-time swing briefly seemed unplayable – three wickets in five balls – but Gilchrist (93 when the No. 11 entered) reached his hundred in 118 balls by scooping Caddick's bouncer inventively over the wicketkeeper. Then he went into overdrive, ending with 152 from 143 balls with 20 fours and five sixes, and 22 off Butcher to equal the most expensive over in Ashes history. McGrath's contribution to a stand of 63 was a single; and he completed his day by dismissing Atherton yet again, for the 14th time in 26 innings. Gillespie broke Hussain's little finger as England's woes continued.

England

M. A. Atherton c M. E. Waugh b Gillespie	57	– c M. E. Waugh b McGrath	4
M. E. Trescothick c Warne b Gillespie	0	– c M. E. Waugh b Warne	76
M. A. Butcher c Ponting b Warne	38	– c Gilchrist b Lee	41
*N. Hussain lbw b McGrath	13	– retired hurt	9
I. J. Ward b McGrath	23	– b Lee	3
†A. J. Stewart lbw b McGrath	65	– c Warne b Gillespie	5
U. Afzaal b Warne	4	– lbw b Gillespie	2
C. White lbw b Warne	4	– b Gillespie	0
A. F. Giles c Gilchrist b Warne	7	– c M. E. Waugh b Warne	0
D. Gough c Gillespie b Warne	0	– lbw b Warne	0
A. R. Caddick not out	49	– not out	6
B 10, l-b 8, n-b 16	34	B 1, l-b 5, n-b 12	18

1/2 (2) 2/106 (3) 3/123 (1) 4/136 (4) 　　　294　　1/4 (1) 2/99 (3) 3/142 (5) 　　　164
5/159 (5) 6/170 (7) 7/174 (8) 　　　　　　　　　　4/148 (6) 5/150 (7) 6/154 (8)
8/191 (9) 9/191 (10) 10/294 (6) 　　　　　　　　　7/155 (2) 8/155 (10) 9/164 (9)

In the second innings Hussain retired hurt at 117.

McGrath 17.3–2–67–3; Gillespie 17–3–67–2; Lee 12–2–71–0; Warne 19–4–71–5. *Second Innings*—McGrath 13–5–34–1; Gillespie 11–2–52–3; Warne 10.1–4–29–3; M. E. Waugh 1–0–6–0; Lee 7–0–37–2.

Australia

M. J. Slater b Gough	77	J. N. Gillespie lbw b Butcher	0
M. L. Hayden c White b Giles	35	G. D. McGrath not out	1
R. T. Ponting lbw b Gough	11		
M. E. Waugh c Stewart b Caddick	49	B 3, l-b 7, n-b 23	33
*S. R. Waugh lbw b Gough	105		
D. R. Martyn c Trescothick b Butcher	105	1/98 (2) 2/130 (3) 3/134 (1)	576
†A. C. Gilchrist c Caddick b White	152	4/267 (4) 5/336 (5) 6/496 (6)	
S. K. Warne c Atherton b Butcher	8	7/511 (8) 8/513 (9)	
B. Lee c Atherton b Butcher	0	9/513 (10) 10/576 (7)	

Gough 33–6–152–3; Caddick 36–0–163–1; White 26.4–5–101–1; Giles 25–0–108–1; Butcher 9–3–42–4.

Umpires: S. A. Bucknor *(West Indies)* (57) and G. Sharp *(England)* (14).
Third umpire: K. E. Palmer *(England)*.　　Referee: Talat Ali *(Pakistan)* (6).

Close of play: First day, Australia 133-2 (Slater 76*, M. E. Waugh 0*); Second day, Australia 332-4 (S. R. Waugh 101*, Martyn 34*); Third day, England 48-1 (Trescothick 21*, Butcher 15*).

ENGLAND v AUSTRALIA 2001 (2nd Test)

At Lord's, London, on 19, 20, 21, 22 July.
Toss: Australia.   Result: AUSTRALIA won by eight wickets.
Debuts: none.
Man of the Match: G. D. McGrath.

Australia ended England's run of three Lord's victories with a display of all-round brilliance. For the home side, events had a depressing familiarity. At Edgbaston, Hussain had broken a finger (Atherton returned for a record 53rd match as captain); now Thorpe broke a bone in his right hand. Once again, only the weather dragged play into a fourth day, and for the fifth time in seven Ashes series, England were 2–0 down after two Tests. After a rain-affected first day, they withered in the face of a devastating McGrath onslaught on the second. He took three for one in 20 pitch-perfect deliveries, starting with Stewart's first Lord's duck in 29 Test innings. Gough and Caddick briefly fostered hopes that 187 was not quite so feeble, but the Waughs added 107 for the fourth wicket before Mark eventually went for a cultured 108. England were desperate for an early breakthrough next morning, but when Gilchrist (13) edged Gough's first ball to second slip Butcher dropped it, and four more reprieves allowed Gilchrist to make a typically aggressive 90. Later Warne bowled Atherton (who had just crawled to tenth in the list of Test runscorers), one ahead of Colin Cowdrey's 7,624) round his legs, then Lee had Thorpe lbw shortly after injuring him. Butcher and Ramprakash added 96, but on the fourth morning McGrath took three for four in 11 balls. The *coup de grâce* came when Mark Waugh held a Test-record 158th catch to dismiss Gough.

England

*M. A. Atherton lbw b McGrath	37	– b Warne	20
M. E. Trescothick c Gilchrist b Gillespie	15	– c Gilchrist b Gillespie	3
M. A. Butcher c M. E. Waugh b McGrath	21	– c Gilchrist b Gillespie	83
G. P. Thorpe c Gilchrist b McGrath	20	– lbw b Lee	2
M. R. Ramprakash b Lee	14	– lbw b Gillespie	40
†A. J. Stewart c Gilchrist b McGrath	0	– lbw b McGrath	28
I. J. Ward not out	23	– c Ponting b McGrath	0
C. White c Hayden b McGrath	0	– not out	27
D. G. Cork c Ponting b Gillespie	24	– c Warne b McGrath	2
A. R. Caddick b Warne	0	– c Gilchrist b Gillespie	7
D. Gough b Warne	5	– c M. E. Waugh b Gillespie	1
B 7, l-b 8, w 2, n-b 11	28	L-b 3, w 2, n-b 9	14

1/33 (2) 2/75 (3) 3/96 (1) 4/121 (5)   187   1/8 (2) 2/47 (1) 3/50 (4)   227
5/126 (6) 6/129 (4) 7/131 (8)   4/146 (5) 5/188 (6) 6/188 (7)
8/178 (9) 9/181 (10) 10/187 (11)   7/188 (3) 8/193 (9) 9/225 (10) 10/227 (11)

McGrath 24–9–54–5; Gillespie 18–6–56–2; Lee 16–3–46–1; Warne 5.3–0–16–2. *Second Innings*—McGrath 19–4–60–3; Gillespie 16–4–53–5; Lee 9–1–41–1; Warne 20–4–58–1; M. E. Waugh 2–1–12–0.

Australia

M. J. Slater c Stewart b Caddick	25	– (2) c Butcher b Caddick	4
M. L. Hayden c Butcher b Caddick	0	– (1) not out	6
R. T. Ponting c Thorpe b Gough	14	– lbw b Gough	4
M. E. Waugh run out	108	– not out	0
*S. R. Waugh c Stewart b Cork	45		
D. R. Martyn c Stewart b Caddick	52		
†A. C. Gilchrist c Stewart b Gough	90		
S. K. Warne c Stewart b Caddick	5		
B. Lee b Caddick	20		
J. N. Gillespie b Gough	9		
G. D. McGrath not out	0		
L-b 9, w 1, n-b 23	33		

1/5 (2) 2/27 (3) 3/105 (1) 4/212 (4)   401   1/6 (2) 2/13 (3)   (2 wkts) 14
5/230 (5) 6/308 (6) 7/322 (8)
8/387 (7) 9/401 (10) 10/401 (9)

Gough 25–3–115–3; Caddick 32.1–4–101–5; White 18–1–80–0; Cork 23–3–84–1; Butcher 3–1–12–0. *Second Innings*—Gough 2–0–5–1; Caddick 1.1–0–9–1.

Umpires: S. A. Bucknor *(West Indies)* (58) and J. W. Holder *(England)* (11).
Third umpire: J. W. Lloyds *(England)*.   Referee: Talat Ali *(Pakistan)* (7).

Close of play: First day, England 121-4 (Thorpe 16*, Stewart 0*); Second day, Australia 255-5 (Martyn 24*, Gilchrist 10*); Third day, England 163-4 (Butcher 73*, Stewart 13*).

ENGLAND v AUSTRALIA 2001 (3rd Test)

At Trent Bridge, Nottingham, on 2, 3, 4 August.
Toss: England.   Result: AUSTRALIA won by seven wickets.
Debuts: none.
Man of the Match: S. K. Warne.

Australia won their seventh consecutive Ashes series, courtesy of a Caddick no-ball, at 4pm on the third day, their successful defence having taken just over a week in actual playing time. England twice held the upper hand, but both times the visitors regrouped in dynamic fashion, led first by Gilchrist, then by Warne. England, meanwhile, experienced their usual quota of misfortunes. First was the loss of their captain, moments after winning England's first toss in ten attempts. McGrath's second ball looped from forearm guard to second slip, and umpire Hampshire upheld the appeal to complete Atherton's 20th Test duck, an England record. The pitch, recently relaid, offered discomfiting bounce and sideways movement, and England might have been out before lunch but for Trescothick. Warne claimed his 100th Ashes wicket, Croft caught at silly point. Australia's openers eased to 48 in 55 minutes, but then Tudor, in his first Test for two years, trapped Hayden lbw. Seven wickets followed for 54 before Gilchrist bolted to a 47-ball fifty. England's reply was derailed when Trescothick's well-struck sweep rebounded from short leg's ankle to Gilchrist, then Warne struck. Atherton was adjudged caught behind, but there was no doubt about the careless dismissal of Stewart, and Ramprakash, who squandered 75 minutes' application by charging down the track. Gillespie claimed three quick wickets on Saturday morning, including his 100th in Tests (Caddick). Australia needed 158, and their only major inconvenience came when Steve Waugh tore his left calf in setting off for his first run.

England

*M. A. Atherton c M. E. Waugh b McGrath	0	– c Gilchrist b Warne	51
M. E. Trescothick c Gilchrist b Gillespie	69	– c Gilchrist b Warne	32
M. A. Butcher c Ponting b McGrath	13	– lbw b Lee	1
M. R. Ramprakash c Gilchrist b Gillespie	14	– st Gilchrist b Warne	26
†A. J. Stewart c M. E. Waugh b McGrath	46	– b Warne	0
I. J. Ward c Gilchrist b McGrath	6	– lbw b Gillespie	13
C. White c Hayden b McGrath	0	– c S. R. Waugh b Warne	7
A. J. Tudor lbw b Warne	3	– c Ponting b Warne	9
R. D. B. Croft c Ponting b Warne	3	– b Gillespie	0
A. R. Caddick b Lee	13	– c Gilchrist b Gillespie	4
D. Gough not out	0	– not out	5
B 1, l-b 9, w 1, n-b 7	18	B 4, l-b 3, n-b 7	14

1/0 (1) 2/30 (3) 3/63 (4) 4/117 (2)   185   1/57 (2) 2/59 (3) 3/115 (1)   162
5/142 (6) 6/147 (7) 7/158 (8)   4/115 (5) 5/126 (4) 6/144 (7)
8/168 (9) 9/180 (5) 10/185 (10)   7/144 (6) 8/146 (9) 9/156 (10) 10/162 (8)

McGrath 18–4–49–5; Lee 6.5–0–30–1; Gillespie 12–1–59–2; Warne 16–4–37–2. *Second Innings*—McGrath 11–3–31–0; Gillespie 20–8–61–3; Lee 8–1–30–1; Warne 18–5–33–6.

Australia

M. J. Slater b Gough	15	– (2) c Trescothick b Caddick	12
M. L. Hayden lbw b Tudor	33	– (1) lbw b Tudor	42
R. T. Ponting c Stewart b Gough	14	– c Stewart b Croft	17
M. E. Waugh c Atherton b Tudor	15	– not out	42
*S. R. Waugh c Atherton b Caddick	13	– retired hurt	1
D. R. Martyn c Stewart b Caddick	4	– not out	33
†A. C. Gilchrist c Atherton b Tudor	54		
S. K. Warne lbw b Caddick	0		
B. Lee c Butcher b Tudor	4		
J. N. Gillespie not out	27		
G. D. McGrath c Butcher b Tudor	2		
L-b 3, w 1, n-b 5	9	L-b 4, n-b 7	11

1/48 (2) 2/56 (1) 3/69 (3) 4/82 (5)   190   1/36 (2) 2/72 (3)   (3 wkts) 158
5/94 (4) 6/102 (6) 7/102 (8)   3/88 (1)
8/122 (9) 9/188 (7) 10/190 (11)

In the second innings S. R. Waugh retired hurt at 89.

Gough 15–3–63–2; Caddick 20–4–70–3; Tudor 15.5–5–44–5; White 2–1–8–0; Croft 2–0–2–0. *Second Innings*—Gough 9–1–38–0; Caddick 12.2–1–71–1; Tudor 7–0–37–1; Croft 1–0–8–1.

Umpires: J. H. Hampshire *(England)* (17) and S. Venkataraghavan *(India)* (46).
Third umpire: D. J. Constant *(England)*.   Referee: Talat Ali *(Pakistan)* (8).

Close of play: First day, Australia 105-7 (Gilchrist 4*, Lee 3*); Second day, England 144-6 (Ward 13*).

ENGLAND v AUSTRALIA 2001 (4th Test)

At Headingley, Leeds, on 16, 17, 18, 19, 20 August.
Toss: Australia.   Result: ENGLAND won by six wickets.
Debuts: Australia – S. M. Katich.
Man of the Match: M. A. Butcher.

Few cricketers play an innings that will become an Ashes legend. Mark Butcher joined this elite to show that, for a day at least, McGrath, Gillespie and Warne could be tamed. Butcher's exhilarating display was out of character with the rest of a one-sided Ashes contest: he cut anything short of a length with exquisite power and timing, stepped forward to drive McGrath, and clipped sweet boundaries off his legs. Australia's stand-in captain hardly expected this when he declared 314 ahead with 110 overs still to play. Rain had disrupted Gilchrist's plans, stealing around two sessions of Australian batting time. Still, only once (Melbourne in 1928-29) had England scored as many in the fourth innings to win. When the openers fell cheaply, it seemed that a routine humbling would follow. But Butcher and the restored Hussain added 181, and after tea the outcome was not in doubt. Finally Butcher carved Gillespie for a crackerjack six behind point, then steered Warne away for three: England were home with 20 overs to spare. Butcher faced 227 balls and hit 23 fours as well as that six. Australia, though, had dominated the first four days. On the first, they scorched to 288 for 4 after rain delayed the start until 2.15. Ponting's superb 144 from just 154 balls included three sixes and 20 fours, while Martyn hit 18 fours before being last out. England responded competently, the top six all starting well but failing to reach 50. Stewart, unhappy at his demotion to No. 7 for the first time in 114 Tests, responded by throwing the bat with daredevil irresponsibility.

Australia

M. J. Slater lbw b Caddick	21	– (2) b Gough	16
M. L. Hayden lbw b Caddick	15	– (1) c Stewart b Mullally	35
R. T. Ponting c Stewart b Tudor	144	– lbw b Gough	72
M. E. Waugh c Ramprakash b Caddick	72	– not out	24
D. R. Martyn c Stewart b Gough	118	– lbw b Caddick	6
S. M. Katich b Gough	15	– not out	0
*†A. C. Gilchrist c Trescothick b Gough	19		
S. K. Warne c Stewart b Gough	0		
B. Lee c Ramprakash b Mullally	0		
J. N. Gillespie c Atherton b Gough	5		
G. D. McGrath not out	8		
B 5, l-b 15, w 1, n-b 9	30	B 5, l-b 7, n-b 11	23

1/39 (1) 2/42 (2) 3/263 (3) 4/288 (4)   447   1/25 (2) 2/129 (3)   (4 wkts dec.) 176
5/355 (6) 6/396 (7) 7/412 (8)   3/141 (1) 4/171 (5)
8/422 (9) 9/438 (10) 10/447 (5)

Gough 25.1–4–103–5; Caddick 29–4–143–3; Mullally 23–8–65–1; Tudor 18–1–97–1; Butcher 1–0–7–0; Ramprakash 4–0–12–0. *Second Innings*—Gough 17–3–68–2; Caddick 11–2–45–1; Tudor 4–1–17–0; Mullally 7.3–2–34–1.

England

M. A. Atherton c Gilchrist b McGrath	22	– c Gilchrist b McGrath	8
M. E. Trescothick c Gilchrist b McGrath	37	– c Hayden b Gillespie	10
M. A. Butcher run out	47	– not out	173
*N. Hussain lbw b McGrath	46	– c Gilchrist b Gillespie	55
M. R. Ramprakash c Gilchrist b Lee	40	– c Waugh b Warne	32
U. Afzaal c Warne b McGrath	14	– not out	4
†A. J. Stewart not out	76		
A. J. Tudor c Gilchrist b McGrath	2		
A. R. Caddick c Gilchrist b Lee	5		
D. Gough c Slater b McGrath	8		
A. D. Mullally c Katich b McGrath	0		
B 2, l-b 3, n-b 7	12	B 14, l-b 16, n-b 3	33

1/50 (1) 2/67 (2) 3/158 (4) 4/158 (3)   309   1/8 (1) 2/33 (2)   (4 wkts) 315
5/174 (6) 6/252 (5) 7/267 (8)   3/214 (4) 4/289 (5)
8/289 (9) 9/299 (10) 10/309 (11)

McGrath 30.2–9–76–7; Gillespie 26–6–76–0; Lee 22–3–103–2; Warne 16–2–49–0. *Second Innings*—McGrath 16–3–61–1; Gillespie 22–4–94–2; Warne 18.2–3–58–1; Lee 16–4–65–0; Waugh 1–0–7–0.

Umpires: D. R. Shepherd *(England)* (57) and S. Venkataraghavan *(India)* (47).
Third umpire: N. A. Mallender *(England)*.   Referee: Talat Ali *(Pakistan)* (9).

Close of play: First day, Australia 288-4 (Martyn 19*); Second day, England 155-2 (Butcher 47*, Hussain 45*); Third day, Australia 69-1 (Hayden 12*, Ponting 30*); Fourth day, England 4-0 (Atherton 4*, Trescothick 0*).

ENGLAND v AUSTRALIA 2001 (5th Test)

At Kennington Oval, London, on 23, 24, 25, 26, 27 August.
Toss: Australia.   Result: AUSTRALIA won by an innings and 25 runs.
Debuts: England – J. Ormond.
Man of the Match: S. K. Warne.   Men of the Series: M. A. Butcher and G. D. McGrath.

Normally, the glow from a sensational Test victory lasts for weeks or months; in the case of Headingley '81 it lasted 20 years and more. But any home joy from Headingley '01 was snuffed out inside 72 hours, thanks to the first back-to-back Tests in England in 89 years. The last time Australia won at The Oval, in 1972, both Chappell brothers both scored centuries: this time, the Waughs did the same. Mark Waugh's 20th Test hundred was a thing of beauty, while Steve – who was not what anyone else would have called fit after his leg injury – winced his way to his 27th. Before the opening day was gone, the only question was whether England might save the game. Butcher, the Headingley hero, was loudly applauded to the crease twice by his home crowd – and back again. Australia's new opening pair put on 158: after a patchy start, Langer reached his eighth Test century before retiring hurt on being hit on the helmet trying to hook Caddick. Ramprakash responded with his second Test century, but no-one ever truly mastered McGrath or Warne, who became the first Australian to take 400 Test wickets during his best overseas analysis. Gilchrist ended the innings with his 100th dismissal in his 22nd Test, beating Mark Boucher's record of 23. England just failed to avert the follow-on, heralding the final episode in the McGrath–Atherton saga, which ended in the bowler's 19th personal victory. Australia's 4–1 series victory was completed before tea.

Australia

M. L. Hayden c Trescothick b Tufnell	68	D. R. Martyn not out 64
J. L. Langer retired hurt	102	
R. T. Ponting c Atherton b Ormond	62	B 10, l-b 13, w 1, n-b 19 43
M. E. Waugh b Gough	120	
*S. R. Waugh not out	157	1/158 (1) 2/292 (3) (4 wkts dec.) 641
†A. C. Gilchrist c Ramprakash b Afzaal	25	3/489 (4) 4/534 (6)

S. K. Warne, B. Lee, J. N. Gillespie and G. D. McGrath did not bat.

Langer retired hurt at 236.

Gough 29–4–113–1; Caddick 36–9–146–0; Ormond 34–4–115–1; Tufnell 39–2–174–1; Butcher 1–0–2–0; Ramprakash 4–0–19–0; Afzaal 9–0–49–1.

England

M. A. Atherton b Warne	13	– c Warne b McGrath	9
M. E. Trescothick b Warne	55	– c and b McGrath	24
M. A. Butcher c Langer b Warne	25	– c S. R. Waugh b Warne	14
*N. Hussain b M. E. Waugh	52	– lbw b Warne	2
M. R. Ramprakash c Gilchrist b McGrath	133	– c Hayden b Warne	19
U. Afzaal c Gillespie b McGrath	54	– c Ponting b McGrath	5
†A. J. Stewart c Gilchrist b Warne	29	– b Warne	34
A. R. Caddick lbw b Warne	0	– b Lee	17
J. Ormond b Warne	18	– c Gilchrist b McGrath	17
D. Gough st Gilchrist b Warne	24	– not out	39
P. C. R. Tufnell not out	7	– c Warne b McGrath	0
B 3, l-b 13, w 1, n-b 5	22	L-b 2, n-b 2	4

1/58 (1) 2/85 (2) 3/104 (3) 4/166 (4)	432	1/17 (1) 2/46 (3) 3/48 (2) 184
5/255 (6) 6/313 (7) 7/313 (8)		4/50 (4) 5/55 (6) 6/95 (5)
8/350 (9) 9/424 (5) 10/432 (10)		7/126 (7) 8/126 (8) 9/184 (9) 10/184 (11)

McGrath 30–11–67–2; Gillespie 20–3–96–0; Warne 44.2–7–165–7; Lee 14–1–43–0; Ponting 2–0–5–0; M. E. Waugh 8–0–40–1. *Second Innings*—Lee 10–3–30–1; McGrath 15.3–6–43–5; Warne 28–8–64–4; Ponting 2–0–3–0; Gillespie 12–5–38–0; M. E. Waugh 1–0–4–0.

Umpires: R. E. Koertzen *(South Africa)* (26) and P. Willey *(England)* (24).
Third umpire: M. J. Kitchen *(England)*.   Referee: Talat Ali *(Pakistan)* (10).

Close of play: First day, Australia 324-2 (M. E. Waugh 48*, S. R. Waugh 12*); Second day, England 80-1 (Trescothick 55*, Butcher 10*); Third day, England 409-8 (Ramprakash 124*, Gough 17*); Fourth day, England 40-1 (Trescothick 20*, Butcher 11*).

ZIMBABWE v WEST INDIES 2001 (1st Test)

At Queens Sports Club, Bulawayo, on 19, 20, 21, 22 July.
Toss: Zimbabwe.   Result: WEST INDIES won by an innings and 176 runs.
Debuts: Zimbabwe – T. Taibu.
Man of the Match: C. H. Gayle.

West Indies were in control throughout this match, apart from a four-hour period while Ebrahim and Campbell put on 164 in the second innings. Campbell, opening for the first time in his (and Zimbabwe's) 53rd Test, went on to reach his second century, but all nine wickets (Carlisle was absent after breaking a finger in the field) fell for 64 after that fine start. It had been a similar story in the first innings: West Indies' fast bowlers shared the wickets around as no-one managed a half-century. West Indies, though, had no such problems: Ganga and Gayle hoisted them into the lead without being separated, and eventually added 214. Gayle reached his first Test century, although he was lucky that umpire Riazuddin missed a nick behind off Streak when he had 96. Hooper advanced smoothly to his tenth Test hundred, striking 18 fours and a six all round the wicket. Zimbabwe were without Andy Flower, who had torn tendons in his thumb during the previous series in India. He had played in all his country's previous 52 Tests, but now left Campbell as the only ever-present. Flower's absence meant a first cap for the 18-year-old wicketkeeper (and future captain) Tatenda Taibu. The pitch played well throughout, seemingly unaffected by the layer of ice that formed nightly on the covers during a match played in the African winter. The first day's play was delayed by five minutes, however, as King had trouble starting his run-up over the sponsor's logo on the outfield.

Zimbabwe

D. D. Ebrahim lbw b Collins	0	– lbw b Stuart	71
A. D. R. Campbell c Jacobs b King	21	– lbw b McGarrell	103
S. V. Carlisle c Hooper b Collins	10	– absent hurt	
C. B. Wishart c Chanderpaul b Stuart	36	– lbw b Stuart	4
G. J. Whittall c Gayle b Stuart	42	– not out	10
G. W. Flower c Jacobs b King	6	– c Gayle b McGarrell	2
*H. H. Streak c Chanderpaul b McGarrell	5	– c Sarwan b McGarrell	2
A. M. Blignaut c Gayle b King	21	– c and b McGarrell	9
†T. Taibu c Sarwan b Stuart	6	– (3) lbw b Stuart	4
B. C. Strang not out	0	– (9) c sub (L. V. Garrick) b King	7
R. W. Price lbw b King	0	– (10) c sub (L. V. Garrick) b King	4
L-b 3, n-b 5	8	L-b 8, n-b 4	12

1/1 (1) 2/31 (3) 3/31 (2) 4/80 (4)   155   1/164 (1) 2/170 (3) 3/187 (4)   228
5/105 (6) 6/119 (7) 7/139 (5)   4/193 (2) 5/195 (6) 6/197 (7)
8/155 (9) 9/155 (8) 10/155 (11)   7/211 (8) 8/218 (9) 9/228 (10)

King 17–4–51–4; Collins 13.3–4–29–2; Stuart 15.3–3–45–3; McGarrell 12–5–22–1; Hooper 1–0–5–0. *Second Innings*—King 23.4–9–47–2; Collins 13–1–47–0; McGarrell 24–9–38–4; Stuart 19–5–45–3; Hooper 21–6–38–0; Samuels 1–0–5–0.

West Indies

D. Ganga c and b Price	89	N. C. McGarrell not out	8
C. H. Gayle c Price b Streak	175		
S. Chanderpaul c Whittall b Streak	7	B 1, l-b 10, n-b 1	12
R. R. Sarwan c Blignaut b Strang	58		
*C. L. Hooper c Taibu b Strang	149	1/214 (1) 2/261 (3) (6 wkts dec.) 559
M. N. Samuels b Price	42	3/289 (2) 4/420 (4)
†R. D. Jacobs not out	19	5/520 (6) 6/538 (5)

C. E. L. Stuart, P. T. Collins and R. D. King did not bat.

Streak 35–8–110–2; Blignaut 30–6–116–0; Strang 45–15–111–2; Price 44–6–157–2; Flower 13–1–52–0; Whittall 1–0–2–0.

Umpires: Riazuddin *(Pakistan)* (10) and I. D. Robinson *(Zimbabwe)* (26).
Third umpire: C. K. Coventry *(Zimbabwe)*.   Referee: D. T. Lindsay *(South Africa)* (3).

Close of play: First day, West Indies 100-0 (Ganga 44*, Gayle 52*); Second day, West Indies 393-3 (Sarwan 47*, Hooper 66*); Third day, Zimbabwe 112-0 (Ebrahim 51*, Campbell 58*).

ZIMBABWE v WEST INDIES 2001 (2nd Test)

At Harare Sports Club on 27, 28, 29, 30, 31 July.
Toss: West Indies.   Result: MATCH DRAWN.
Debuts: Zimbabwe – H. Masakadza.
Man of the Match: H. Masakadza.   Man of the Series: C. H. Gayle.

Eleven days short of his 18th birthday, schoolboy Hamilton Masakadza became the youngest batsman to score a century on Test debut (a record later claimed by Bangladesh's Mohammad Ashraful). Masakadza, the first black African to score a Test hundred, inspired a remarkable recovery from a first-innings deficit of 216, and it was ironic that Zimbabwe's chances of an extraordinary victory were washed away by the first significant rain of the winter, which allowed only 31 overs on the final day. It had looked like business as usual at the start, when Zimbabwe were bowled out before tea on the first day: slow left-armer McGarrell took four wickets for one run in 18 balls immediately after lunch, and the collapse was only briefly halted by Whittall. Ganga and Chanderpaul put on 100 at a run a minute, then Sarwan came within touching distance of a maiden Test century before being run out by Masakadza's direct hit from mid-off. Zimbabwe then shocked the tourists by making what remains their highest Test total. Masakadza, tall, upright and strong on the leg side, put on 91 with Campbell and 169 with Wishart, and later the big-hitting allrounders Streak and Blignaut shared a national seventh-wicket record of 154. Ganga departed in the fifth over, but the weather was already closing in, presenting West Indies with the draw that gave them the series, and also made them the first holders of the new Clive Lloyd Trophy for matches between these two sides.

Zimbabwe

D. D. Ebrahim c Browne b King	19	– c Browne b Stuart	12
A. D. R. Campbell lbw b Stuart	13	– c Gayle b Hooper	65
H. Masakadza b Stuart	9	– c Hooper b McGarrell	119
C. B. Wishart lbw b McGarrell	8	– run out	93
G. J. Whittall c Ganga b Black	43	– lbw b McGarrell	12
G. W. Flower c Browne b McGarrell	0	– c Chanderpaul b King	15
*H. H. Streak lbw b McGarrell	6	– not out	83
A. M. Blignaut c Browne b McGarrell	0	– b Stuart	92
†T. Taibu c King b Stuart	9	– b Stuart	10
B. C. Strang c Sarwan b Black	20	– c Gayle b McGarrell	13
R. W. Price not out	0		
L-b 1, w 2, n-b 1	4	B 11, l-b 21, n-b 17	49

1/20 (1) 2/42 (2) 3/43 (3) 4/62 (4)   131
5/62 (6) 6/68 (7) 7/72 (8)
8/95 (9) 9/116 (5) 10/131 (10)

1/27 (1) 2/118 (2)   (9 wkts dec.) 563
3/287 (4) 4/324 (5)
5/333 (3) 6/367 (6) 7/521 (8) 8/535 (9) 9/563 (10)

King 16–6–39–1; Black 11.1–2–35–2; Stuart 13–2–33–3; McGarrell 17–7–23–4. *Second Innings*—King 27–7–80–1; Black 17–1–93–0; McGarrell 60–19–162–3; Stuart 32–9–99–3; Hooper 28–7–86–1; Samuels 3–0–11–0.

West Indies

D. Ganga c Taibu b Blignaut	43	– c Strang b Streak	5
C. H. Gayle lbw b Strang	6	– not out	52
S. Chanderpaul c Taibu b Streak	74		
R. R. Sarwan run out	86	– (3) not out	31
*C. L. Hooper c Streak b Strang	39		
M. N. Samuels c Campbell b Price	39		
†C. O. Browne c Taibu b Blignaut	13		
N. C. McGarrell c sub (T. J. Friend) b Strang	33		
C. E. L. Stuart lbw b Strang	1		
M. I. Black b Price	6		
R. D. King not out	2		
L-b 2, w 2, n-b 1	5	B 4, l-b 5, w 1	10

1/14 (2) 2/114 (1) 3/126 (3) 4/180 (5)   347
5/259 (6) 6/283 (7) 7/333 (4)
8/338 (9) 9/345 (8) 10/347 (10)

1/25 (1)   (1 wkt) 98

Streak 22–6–75–1; Strang 32–13–83–4; Blignaut 16–2–92–2; Price 35.2–13–81–2; Flower 6–3–14–0. *Second Innings*—Streak 15.2–4–34–1; Blignaut 8–3–24–0; Strang 14–8–19–0; Price 8–3–9–0; Masakadza 1–0–3–0.

Umpires: K. C. Barbour *(Zimbabwe)* (3) and A. V. Jayaprakash *(India)* (10).
Third umpire: Q. J. Goosen *(Zimbabwe)*.   Referee: D. T. Lindsay *(South Africa)* (4).

Close of play: First day, West Indies 126-2 (Chanderpaul 74*, Sarwan 2*); Second day, Zimbabwe 27-1 (Campbell 9*); Third day, Zimbabwe 324-4 (Masakadza 115*); Fourth day, West Indies 42-1 (Gayle 17*, Sarwan 11*).

SRI LANKA v INDIA 2001 (1st Test)

At Galle International Stadium on 14, 15, 16, 17 August.
Toss: Sri Lanka.   Result: SRI LANKA won by ten wickets.
Debuts: none.
Man of the Match: S. T. Jayasuriya.

The series began, like the two preceding ones in Sri Lanka, with a home win at Galle. India's only consolation was that a defiant half-century from Dravid ensured that, unlike South Africa and England, they did not suffer an innings defeat. Even so, Jayasuriya needed only two scoring shots to complete a ten-wicket victory on the fourth morning, having already played a major role in his team's first win over India for 15 years with a stroke-filled century (he also won the toss for the 18th time in 22 Tests). India, without Sachin Tendulkar (toe injury) for the first time since April 1989, recorded their lowest total against Sri Lanka in the first innings, then did even worse in the second. The first-innings destroyer was Fernando, who completed a fiery five-over spell of five for 18 and also injured Srinath's left-hand little finger. India surrendered their last six wickets for 32, then Jayasuriya blazed away, unleashing a stunning square cut for six over point off Srinath in addition to 16 fours. Sangakkara, dropped by Dravid at slip when 8, batted for six hours. Earlier in the year, he had twice narrowly missed a maiden Test hundred, and had 93 here when last man Muralitharan came in – but Murali saw him to the 100th century by a wicketkeeper in Tests. India slumped to 81 for six. Dravid alone held out, for 219 minutes. Sri Lanka's Suresh Perera was reported for a suspect bowling action.

India

S. S. Das c Jayasuriya b Vaas	40	– c A. S. A. Perera b P. D. R. L. Perera		23
S. Ramesh c Jayasuriya b Muralitharan	42	– b P. D. R. L. Perera		2
M. Kaif b Fernando	37	– c Tillekeratne b Muralitharan		14
R. Dravid c Arnold b Muralitharan	12	– not out		61
*S. C. Ganguly c Sangakkara b Fernando	15	– b Fernando		4
H. K. Badani c Sangakkara b Fernando	6	– c Sangakkara b Muralitharan		5
†S. S. Dighe c Sangakkara b Fernando	9	– c Arnold b Muralitharan		3
J. Srinath retired hurt	0	– absent hurt		
Harbhajan Singh b Fernando	4	– (8) c and b Muralitharan		12
Zaheer Khan not out	0	– (9) c Arnold b Jayasuriya		3
B. K. V. Prasad b Muralitharan	0	– (10) lbw b Muralitharan		20
B 4, l-b 3, w 2, n-b 13	22	B 12, l-b 8, n-b 13		33

1/79 (2) 2/105 (1) 3/124 (4)   187   1/15 (2) 2/37 (1) 3/53 (3)   180
4/155 (3) 5/161 (6) 6/176 (5)   4/64 (5) 5/73 (6) 6/81 (7)
7/181 (9) 8/185 (7) 9/187 (11)   7/104 (8) 8/120 (9) 9/180 (10)

In the first innings Srinath retired hurt at 177.

Vaas 22–10–38–1; Fernando 25–9–42–5; P. D. R. L. Perera 12–4–25–0; Muralitharan 24.3–8–41–3; A. S. A. Perera 12–0–34–0. *Second Innings*—Vaas 16–2–45–0; Fernando 17–4–35–1; P. D. R. L. Perera 8–1–21–2; Muralitharan 26.5–10–49–5; Jayasuriya 7–3–10–1.

Sri Lanka

M. S. Atapattu c Badani b Harbhajan Singh	33	– not out	0
*S. T. Jayasuriya c Dravid b Zaheer Khan	111	– not out	6
†K. C. Sangakkara not out	105		
D. P. M. D. Jayawardene c Dighe b Srinath	28		
R. P. Arnold c Ramesh b Prasad	20		
H. P. Tillekeratne lbw b Srinath	11		
A. S. A. Perera lbw b Srinath	1		
W. P. U. J. C. Vaas c Ramesh b Zaheer Khan	13		
C. R. D. Fernando c Srinath b Zaheer Khan	3		
P. D. R. L. Perera c Dighe b Srinath	0		
M. Muralitharan c Kaif b Srinath	8		
B 1, l-b 6, w 8, n-b 14	29		

1/101 (1) 2/171 (2) 3/211 (4) 4/274 (5)   362   (no wkt)   6
5/292 (6) 6/296 (7) 7/316 (8)
8/340 (9) 9/342 (10) 10/362 (11)

Srinath 24.5–5–114–5; Prasad 24–4–83–1; Zaheer Khan 26–3–89–3; Harbhajan Singh 33–12–69–1. *Second Innings*—Srinath 1–1–0–0; Zaheer Khan 0.5–0–6–0.

Umpires: S. A. Bucknor *(West Indies)* (59) and E. A. R. de Silva *(Sri Lanka)* (4).
Third umpire: P. T. Manuel *(Sri Lanka)*.   Referee: C. W. Smith *(West Indies)* (34).

Close of play: First day, India 163-5 (Ganguly 10*, Dighe 2*); Second day, Sri Lanka 264-3 (Sangakkara 54*, Arnold 19*); Third day, India 130-8 (Dravid 37*, Prasad 5*).

SRI LANKA v INDIA 2001 (2nd Test)

At Asgiriya Stadium, Kandy, on 22, 23, 24, 25 August.
Toss: India.   Result: INDIA won by seven wickets.
Debuts: none.
Man of the Match: S. C. Ganguly.

Sri Lanka let slip a golden opportunity to go 2–0 up with an uncharacteristic collapse on the third morning, when their top order threw away the advantage of a useful lead. Only a last-ditch stand raised the target to 264, which India had more than two days to chase. Dravid was once again in the thick of things, winning his duel with Muralitharan through some audacious back-foot play square of the wicket, while Ganguly, without a half-century in his previous 13 Test innings, made a timely return to form. Jayasuriya lost the toss for once, then ran himself out in the fifth over. Jayawardene tidied things up with a diligent century, backed up by 42 from Vaas, who followed that with some penetrative seam bowling. India's eventual total owed much to a face-saving seventh-wicket stand between Dighe and Harbhajan Singh, whose 32-ball cameo included nine fours, four off successive deliveries from Fernando. Sri Lanka's main batsmen then succumbed to some excellent seam bowling from Prasad and Zaheer Khan, and when the ninth wicket fell the overall lead was just 199. Muralitharan unexpectedly gave Sri Lanka a chance, smashing a maiden Test fifty to the delight of his home crowd; Ruchira Perera contributed just six to their stand of 64. Ganguly finally turned to Harbhajan, who had Murali caught going for another six. But Muralitharan posed fewer problems with the ball, as India squared the series with a day to spare.

Sri Lanka

M. S. Atapattu	b Zaheer Khan	39	– c Dighe b Prasad		45
*S. T. Jayasuriya	run out	3	– b Zaheer Khan		6
†K. C. Sangakkara	c Ramesh b Ganguly	31	– c Dighe b Zaheer Khan		13
D. P. M. D. Jayawardene	c Dighe b Prasad	104	– c Badani b Zaheer Khan		25
R. P. Arnold	c Dravid b Zaheer Khan	5	– (6) lbw b Zaheer Khan		4
H. P. Tillekeratne	c Dighe b Prasad	10	– (5) lbw b Prasad		16
A. S. A. Perera	lbw b Ganguly	18	– c Badani b Prasad		15
W. P. U. J. C. Vaas	b Harvinder Singh	42	– lbw b Prasad		4
M. Muralitharan	b Harvinder Singh	5	– c Ramesh b Harbhajan Singh		67
C. R. D. Fernando	c Dighe b Zaheer Khan	4	– b Prasad		4
P. D. R. L. Perera	not out	0	– not out		6
	L-b 7, w 1, n-b 5	13	B 4, l-b 7, n-b 5		16

1/18 (2) 2/78 (3) 3/82 (1) 4/101 (5)   **274**   1/20 (2) 2/52 (3) 3/84 (1)   **221**
5/138 (6) 6/189 (7) 7/232 (4)   4/108 (4) 5/116 (6) 6/137 (7)
8/245 (9) 9/274 (10) 10/274 (8)   7/140 (5) 8/153 (8) 9/157 (10) 10/221 (9)

Zaheer Khan 22–6–62–3; Harvinder Singh 14.3–1–62–2; Prasad 18–4–52–2; Ganguly 17–5–69–2; Harbhajan Singh 7–1–22–0. *Second Innings*—Zaheer Khan 23–4–76–4; Harvinder Singh 8–1–25–0; Prasad 21–7–72–5; Ganguly 10–4–21–0; Harbhajan Singh 4.3–2–16–1.

India

S. S. Das	lbw b Vaas	8	– b Muralitharan		19
S. Ramesh	c Sangakkara b Fernando	47	– c Jayasuriya b Fernando		31
R. Dravid	lbw b Vaas	15	– c Arnold b Muralitharan		75
*S. C. Ganguly	c Tillekeratne b P. D. R. L. Perera	18	– not out		98
M. Kaif	c Atapattu b Fernando	17	– not out		19
H. K. Badani	c Fernando b P. D. R. L. Perera	16			
†S. S. Dighe	lbw b Vaas	28			
Harbhajan Singh	b Vaas	44			
Zaheer Khan	c Tillekeratne b Muralitharan	0			
B. K. V. Prasad	not out	1			
Harvinder Singh	b Muralitharan	6			
	L-b 7, w 2, n-b 23	32	B 4, l-b 2, n-b 16		22

1/11 (1) 2/36 (3) 3/68 (4) 4/120 (5)   **232**   1/42 (1) 2/103 (2)   (3 wkts)   **264**
5/123 (2) 6/154 (6) 7/218 (7)   3/194 (3)
8/223 (9) 9/223 (8) 10/232 (11)

Vaas 21–3–65–4; Fernando 14–2–66–2; P. D. R. L. Perera 7–2–23–2; Muralitharan 20.1–5–62–2; A. S. A. Perera 2–0–9–0. *Second Innings*—Vaas 20.4–9–42–0; Fernando 16–4–64–1; P. D. R. L. Perera 9–2–26–0; Muralitharan 25–2–96–2; Jayasuriya 3–0–12–0; A. S. A. Perera 3–0–11–0; Arnold 2–0–7–0.

Umpires: S. A. Bucknor *(West Indies)* (60) and T. H. Wijewardene *(Sri Lanka)* (1).
Third umpire: G. Silva *(Sri Lanka)*.   Referee: C. W. Smith *(West Indies)* (35).

Close of play: First day, Sri Lanka 274-9 (Vaas 42*, P. D. R. L. Perera 0*); Second day, Sri Lanka 52-1 (Atapattu 30*, Sangakkara 13*); Third day, India 55-1 (Ramesh 15*, Dravid 11*).

SRI LANKA v INDIA 2001 (3rd Test)

At Sinhalese Sports Club, Colombo, on 29, 30, 31 August, 1, 2 September.
Toss: India.   Result: SRI LANKA won by an innings and 77 runs.
Debuts: Sri Lanka – T. T. Samaraweera.
Man of the Match: M. Muralitharan.   Man of the Series: M. Muralitharan.

Sri Lanka took the series by equalling their then-biggest winning margin in Tests (against Zimbabwe in September 1996). After Muralitharan had claimed eight wickets on the first day, a phenomenal achievement for a spinner, the home side simply batted India out of the game. For the first time four batsmen scored hundreds for Sri Lanka, as they ran up their second-highest Test total. However, at first it had been India who seemed on course for a big score. Das and Ramesh opened with 97, but before the close India were dismissed for 234, spun out by Muralitharan, who exploited some bounce to take 8 for 87 in a single spell. The two wickets that eluded him went to Vaas, who became the second Sri Lankan to take 150 Test wickets. Then the home batsmen began their feast: Atapattu and Jayawardene put on 133, but the stand that finally knocked India out came from Tillekeratne, who made his seventh Test century, and Thilan Samaraweera, only the third Sri Lankan to make a hundred on Test debut. India's openers started well once more, despite a massive deficit, but Muralitharan again removed them both. Dravid and Ganguly took India to a promising 186 for 2, but two run-outs swung the scales back Sri Lanka's way. First Dravid, after passing 4,000 runs in his 48th Test, was beaten by Atapattu's direct hit from mid-on, then Kaif failed to make his ground after being sent back by Ganguly.

India

S. S. Das b Muralitharan	59	– c Tillekeratne b Muralitharan		68
S. Ramesh c Jayawardene b Muralitharan	46	– b Muralitharan		55
R. Dravid c Tillekeratne b Muralitharan	36	– run out		36
*S. C. Ganguly lbw b Muralitharan	1	– c Jayawardene b Samaraweera		30
M. Kaif c Sangakkara b Vaas	14	– run out		5
H. K. Badani c Tillekeratne b Muralitharan	38	– lbw b Vaas		11
†S. S. Dighe lbw b Muralitharan	0	– (8) run out		4
S. V. Bahutule st Sangakkara b Muralitharan	18	– (7) b Jayasuriya		0
Harbhajan Singh lbw b Vaas	2	– c Atapattu b Vaas		17
Zaheer Khan c Jayawardene b Muralitharan	0	– c Atapattu b Muralitharan		45
B. K. V. Prasad not out	10	– not out		4
B 2, l-b 3, w 2, n-b 3	10	B 8, l-b 5, w 2, n-b 9		24

1/97 (1) 2/115 (2) 3/119 (4) 4/146 (5)   234   1/107 (1) 2/147 (2) 3/186 (3)   299
5/192 (3) 6/192 (7) 7/207 (6)   4/196 (5) 5/210 (4) 6/211 (7)
8/210 (9) 9/213 (10) 10/234 (8)   7/221 (6) 8/221 (8) 9/269 (9) 10/299 (10)

Vaas 24–7–60–2; Liyanage 9–2–32–0; Fernando 12–2–38–0; Muralitharan 34.1–9–87–8; Samaraweera 2–0–12–0.
Second Innings—Vaas 27–9–62–2; Fernando 17–3–59–0; Muralitharan 46.5–17–109–3; Jayasuriya 21–10–34–1; Liyanage 5–0–12–0; Samaraweera 8–4–10–1.

Sri Lanka

M. S. Atapattu c Das b Harbhajan Singh	108	H. P. Tillekeratne not out		136
*S. T. Jayasuriya b Prasad	30	T. T. Samaraweera not out		103
†K. C. Sangakkara c Badani b Prasad	47	L-b 4, w 4, n-b 5		13
D. P. M. D. Jayawardene lbw b Bahutule	139			
R. P. Arnold b Prasad	31	1/48 (2) 2/119 (3)	(6 wkts dec.)	610
D. K. Liyanage c Dighe b Harbhajan Singh	3	3/252 (1) 4/310 (5)		
		5/321 (6) 6/416 (4)		

W. P. U. J. C. Vaas, M. Muralitharan and C. R. D. Fernando did not bat.

Zaheer Khan 27–3–134–0; Prasad 34–8–101–3; Harbhajan Singh 53.3–6–185–2; Ganguly 12.3–3–44–0; Bahutule 31–5–101–1; Badani 8–2–17–0; Ramesh 5–0–24–0.

Umpires: E. A. R. de Silva *(Sri Lanka)* (5) and D. L. Orchard *(South Africa)* (24).
Third umpire: T. H. Wijewardene *(Sri Lanka)*.   Referee: C. W. Smith *(West Indies)* (36).

Close of play: First day, Sri Lanka 13-0 (Atapattu 2*, Jayasuriya 10*); Second day, Sri Lanka 323-5 (Jayawardene 95*, Tillekeratne 0*); Third day, India 28-0 (Das 22*, Ramesh 4*); Fourth day, India 217-6 (Badani 8*, Dighe 4*).

PAKISTAN v BANGLADESH 2001–02
(Asian Test Championship – 1st Match)

At Multan Cricket Stadium on 29, 30, 31 August.
Toss: Bangladesh.   Result: PAKISTAN (24 pts) won by an innings and 264 runs.
Debuts: Pakistan – Shoaib Malik, Taufeeq Umar.
Man of the Match: Danish Kaneria.

India's withdrawal a week beforehand (their government forbade sport with Pakistan until relations were "normalised") spoiled this second Asian Test Championship, reducing it to three matches – this one and the next, and a final, played at Lahore in March 2002 *(Test No. 1594)*. The first match at the 81st Test venue (Multan's Ibn-e-Qasim Bagh Stadium also staged one Test against West Indies in 1980-81) was all over before lunch on the third day. The scale of Bangladesh's defeat raised serious questions about the ICC's decision to grant them Test status. Their batting, apart from Habibul Bashar, was cavalier throughout – both innings lasted 41.1 overs. Pakistan, by contrast, amassed 546 for 3: five batsmen scored centuries, only the second such instance in Tests, after Australia against West Indies at Kingston in 1954-55. Saeed Anwar (who passed 4,000 Test runs) rattled up 168 for the first wicket in 33 overs with Taufeeq Umar, who became the eighth Pakistani (the fifth since 1996) to score a century on debut. Inzamam-ul-Haq realised a childhood dream by hitting a hundred on his home ground, before promptly retiring hurt, apparently dehydrated. Pakistan's bowlers enjoyed themselves too. Danish Kaneria scooped up six wickets in each innings, ten of them caught close to the bat, four by Younis Khan, who set an innings record for a substitute. However, the celebrations for Pakistan's biggest victory in Tests were overshadowed when a tearful Saeed Anwar announced that his three-year-old daughter had died that afternoon.

Bangladesh

Javed Omar c Shoaib Malik b Waqar Younis	12	– c Abdul Razzaq b Waqar Younis	4
Mehrab Hossain, sen. c Faisal Iqbal b Danish Kaneria	19	– c Rashid Latif b Waqar Younis	9
Habibul Bashar c Rashid Latif b Waqar Younis	13	– not out	56
Aminul Islam b Shoaib Malik	10	– c sub (Younis Khan) b Danish Kaneria	18
Akram Khan c Yousuf Youhana b Danish Kaneria	12	– c sub (Younis Khan) b Danish Kaneria	8
*Naimur Rahman c Faisal Iqbal b Danish Kaneria	8	– c sub (Younis Khan) b Danish Kaneria	4
†Khaled Mashud lbw b Danish Kaneria	4	– c and b Danish Kaneria	0
Enamul Haque, sen. c Waqar Younis b Danish Kaneria	14	– c Yousuf Youhana b Danish Kaneria	7
Hasibul Hossain c Taufeeq Umar b Danish Kaneria	18	– c sub (Younis Khan) b Danish Kaneria	31
Mohammad Sharif b Shoaib Malik	13	– c Rashid Latif b Waqar Younis	3
Manjurul Islam not out	0	– b Waqar Younis	2
L-b 5, w 1, n-b 5	11	L-b 3, n-b 3	6

1/20 (1) 2/50 (3) 3/55 (2) 4/67 (4)   134   1/5 (1) 2/22 (2) 3/52 (4)   148
5/76 (6) 6/83 (5) 7/101 (8)   4/72 (5) 5/84 (6) 6/84 (7) 7/96 (8)
8/107 (7) 9/134 (9) 10/134 (10)   8/141 (9) 9/144 (10) 10/148 (11)

Bonus points – Pakistan 4.

Wasim Akram 10–2–17–0; Waqar Younis 6–0–25–2; Abdul Razzaq 8–1–27–0; Danish Kaneria 13–3–42–6; Shoaib Malik 4.1–0–18–2. *Second Innings*—Wasim Akram 9–1–32–0; Waqar Younis 7.1–1–19–4; Abdul Razzaq 8–0–34–0; Danish Kaneria 15–3–52–6; Shoaib Malik 2–0–8–0.

Pakistan

Saeed Anwar c Hasibul Hossain b Mohammad Sharif	101	Abdul Razzaq not out ... 110
Taufeeq Umar c Khaled Mashud b Hasibul Hossain	104	B 1, l-b 3, w 3, n-b 8 ... 15
Faisal Iqbal b Mohammad Sharif	9	
Inzamam-ul-Haq retired hurt	105	1/168 (1) 2/178 (3) (3 wkts dec.) 546
Yousuf Youhana not out	102	3/258 (2)

†Rashid Latif, Wasim Akram, *Waqar Younis, Shoaib Malik and Danish Kaneria did not bat.

Bonus points – Pakistan 4 (100 overs: 443-3).

Inzamam-ul-Haq retired hurt at 381.

Manjurul Islam 19–2–103–0; Mohammad Sharif 24.5–4–110–2; Hasibul Hossain 31–5–145–1; Naimur Rahman 19–1–77–0; Enamul Haque 16–1–78–0; Aminul Islam 4–0–17–0; Javed Omar 1–0–12–0.

Umpires: D. B. Hair *(Australia)* (39) and P. T. Manuel *(Sri Lanka)* (9).
Third umpire: Riazuddin *(Pakistan)*.   Referee: J. R. Reid *(New Zealand)* (47).

Close of play: First day, Pakistan 219-2 (Taufeeq Umar 77, Inzamam-ul-Haq 25); Second day, Bangladesh 55-3 (Habibul Bashar 19, Akram Khan 1).

SRI LANKA v BANGLADESH 2001–02
(Asian Test Championship – 2nd Match)

At Sinhalese Sports Club Ground, Colombo, on 6, 7, 8 September.

Toss: Sri Lanka.　　Result: SRI LANKA (24 pts) won by an innings and 137 runs.

Debuts: Sri Lanka – M. G. Vandort. Bangladesh – Mohammad Ashraful.

Men of the Match: Mohammad Ashraful and M. Muralitharan.

A week after their demolition by Pakistan, Bangladesh took on Sri Lanka, who had just beaten India by an innings. Another hopeless mismatch resulted, though not before some pride was restored: Mohammad Ashraful, on debut, became the youngest Test century-maker (at 17 years 63 days, beating Mushtaq Mohammad's old mark by 20 days). Jayasuriya's decision to bowl first on a superb batting track, variously interpreted as confident or condescending, was certainly successful. Bangladesh crumpled for 90 – their lowest total so far, and the lowest by anyone against Sri Lanka. Then Jayasuriya looked set for the fastest Test century before losing momentum. Still, his 89 came from only 56 balls, and included 68 in boundaries. Atapattu cruised to his fifth Test double-century before his captain called him in – the first "retired out" scorecard entry in Test history. The same fate befell Jayawardene after he had smashed 150 off 115 balls. Some claimed this devalued Test cricket, but on the field it made little difference, as Sri Lanka sailed to 555 at 5.36 an over. With a bone-dry pitch offering increasing turn Bangladesh – trailing by 465 – were always up against it, but Ashraful provided a memorable distraction. He crashed a series of Vaas bouncers through midwicket, and danced down the track to loft Muralitharan over the top. Sri Lanka nonetheless retained control, taking the last five wickets for 25. Five more wickets for Murali took his career total to 350 from 66 Tests: no other bowler had reached this landmark so quickly.

Bangladesh

Javed Omar c Jayasuriya b Vaas	7	– lbw b Muralitharan	40
Mehrab Hossain, sen. run out	23	– lbw b Muralitharan	4
Habibul Bashar b Vaas	4	– (5) c Jayawardene b Muralitharan	19
Aminul Islam c Sangakkara b Perera	6	– b Jayasuriya	56
Al Sahariar c Sangakkara b Muralitharan	16	– (3) lbw b Samaraweera	7
*Naimur Rahman b Muralitharan	0	– (7) c Atapattu b Perera	48
Mohammad Ashraful c Jayasuriya b Muralitharan	26	– (6) c and b Perera	114
†Khaled Mashud b Muralitharan	0	– lbw b Muralitharan	3
Hasibul Hossain b Muralitharan	2	– c Sangakkara b Perera	0
Mohammad Sharif c Vandort b Vaas	1	– c and b Muralitharan	19
Manjural Islam not out	3	– not out	1
L-b 1, n-b 1	2	B 5, l-b 5, n-b 7	17

1/10 (1) 2/16 (3) 3/29 (4) 4/57 (5)　　　　　　90　　1/31 (2) 2/54 (1) 3/54 (3)　　　　　　328
5/58 (2) 6/61 (6) 7/61 (8)　　　　　　　　　　　　4/81 (5) 5/207 (4) 6/303 (7)
8/67 (9) 9/72 (10) 10/90 (7)　　　　　　　　　　　7/308 (6) 8/308 (8) 9/314 (9) 10/328 (10)

Bonus points – Sri Lanka 4.

Vaas 14–2–47–3; Pushpakumara 7–4–9–0; Perera 5–1–17–1; Muralitharan 9.4–4–13–5; Samaraweera 1–0–3–0. *Second Innings*—Vaas 16–2–71–0; Pushpakumara 8–5–15–0; Muralitharan 35.3–6–98–5; Perera 13–3–40–3; Samaraweera 13–2–42–1; Jayasuriya 16–2–52–1.

Sri Lanka

M. S. Atapattu retired out	201	H. P. Tillekeratne not out	10
*S. T. Jayasuriya lbw b Naimur Rahman	89		
†K. C. Sangakkara c Aminul Islam b Hasibul Hossain	54	L-b 5, w 2, n-b 8	15
D. P. M. D. Jayawardene retired out	150		
M. G. Vandort c Manjural Islam b Naimur Rahman	36	1/144 (2) 2/269 (3)　　　(5 wkts dec.) 555	

3/440 (1) 4/530 (4) 5/555 (5)

T. T. Samaraweera, W. P. U. J. C. Vaas, K. R. Pushpakumara, P. D. R. L. Perera and M. Muralitharan did not bat.

Bonus points – Sri Lanka 4 (100 overs: 539-4).

Manjurul Islam 18–1–94–0; Mohammad Sharif 17–0–120–0; Hasibul Hussain 23–6–122–1; Naimur Rahman 30.3–8–117–2; Mohammad Ashraful 10–0–63–0; Habibul Bashar 5–0–34–0.

Umpires: R. E. Koertzen *(South Africa)* (27) and Mian Aslam *(Pakistan)* (7).
Third umpire: Riazuddin *(Pakistan)*.　　Referee: J. R. Reid *(New Zealand)* (48).

Close of play: First day, Sri Lanka 246-1 (Atapattu 99, Sangakkara 49); Second day, Bangladesh 100-4 (Aminul Islam 19, Mohammad Ashraful 4).

ZIMBABWE v SOUTH AFRICA 2001–02 (1st Test)

At Harare Sports Club on 7, 8, 9, 10, 11 September.
Toss: South Africa.   Result: SOUTH AFRICA won by nine wickets.
Debuts: Zimbabwe – D. T. Hondo. South Africa – C. W. Henderson, A. Nel.
Man of the Match: A. Flower.

This match will be remembered for the exploits of Andy Flower, who batted for 879 minutes and scored 341 runs, the most for anyone on the losing side until surpassed by Brian Lara *(Test No. 1573)*. Kirsten and Gibbs got South Africa off to a flyer, reaching 142 by lunch. Gibbs's century included 86 in boundaries. Kirsten studiously completed his set of hundreds against the eight countries he had faced. He went on to his third double-century (shortly after becoming the first South African to score 5,000 runs), latterly in concert with Kallis, who accumulated runs like an automaton. Pollock rather surprisingly declared at 600 – only 22 shy of South Africa's Test-best – and probably expected to win by an innings. He would have done, but for Flower. Campbell hooked Nel's fourth ball in Test cricket and was caught behind, but Ebrahim made a gritty 71. After that, it was Flower all the way, a giant among pygmies. He passed 4,000 Test runs en route to his 10th Test century. Three quick wickets in the follow-on meant he was soon in again. This time, he found an ally in 18-year-old Masakadza, and they added 186. Flower became the first wicketkeeper to make two hundreds in the same Test, and would surely have turned this one into a double had he not run out of partners, finally being stranded one short. He was only the second man, after South Africa's Jimmy Sinclair against England in 1898-99, to score more than half his team's aggregate over two innings in a Test.

South Africa

H. H. Gibbs b Friend	147		
G. Kirsten c A. Flower b Hondo	220	– not out	31
J. H. Kallis not out	157	– not out	42
N. D. McKenzie c Hondo b Friend	52		
L. Klusener not out	8		
H. H. Dippenaar (did not bat)		– (1) lbw b Friend	0
L-b 2, w 6, n-b 8	16	B 5, l-b 1	6

1/256 (1) 2/455 (2) 3/582 (4)   (3 wkts dec.) 600   1/0 (1)   (1 wkt) 79

†M. V. Boucher, *S. M. Pollock, C. W. Henderson, M. Ntini and A. Nel did not bat.

Streak 34–4–120–0; Friend 27–2–147–2; Hondo 18–0–87–1; Price 42–2–192–0; Whittall 12–2–34–0; G. W. Flower 6–0–18–0. *Second Innings*—Friend 7–0–44–1; Streak 4–2–10–0; Price 3.2–0–19–0; Hondo 1–1–0–0.

Zimbabwe

D. D. Ebrahim st Boucher b Henderson	71	– lbw b Pollock	0
A. D. R. Campbell c Boucher b Nel	0	– b Kallis	7
H. Masakadza run out	13	– c Dippenaar b Henderson	85
C. B. Wishart c Klusener b Kallis	0	– c Klusener b Pollock	6
†A. Flower lbw b Pollock	142	– not out	199
R. W. Price c Kirsten b Nel	0	– (10) c McKenzie b Klusener	4
G. W. Flower c Dippenaar b Nel	0	– (6) c Dippenaar b Ntini	16
G. J. Whittall b Kallis	16	– (7) lbw b Henderson	3
*H. H. Streak lbw b Henderson	7	– (8) c Kallis b Pollock	19
T. J. Friend c Pollock b Nel	30	– (9) b Klusener	17
D. T. Hondo not out	1	– lbw b Nel	6
B 4, n-b 2	6	B 10, l-b 9, n-b 10	29

1/2 (2) 2/43 (3) 3/51 (4) 4/133 (1)   286   1/0 (1) 2/18 (2) 3/25 (4)   391
5/143 (6) 6/143 (7) 7/188 (8)   4/211 (3) 5/243 (6) 6/260 (7)
8/207 (9) 9/282 (10) 10/286 (5)   7/287 (8) 8/326 (9) 9/344 (10) 10/391 (11)

Pollock 22.3–5–62–1; Nel 16–6–53–4; Ntini 13–2–60–0; Kallis 12–1–39–2; Henderson 24–5–55–2; Klusener 3–0–13–0. *Second Innings*—Pollock 29–5–67–3; Nel 14.5–5–33–1; Kallis 21–5–52–1; Henderson 55–16–122–2; Ntini 23–10–48–1; Klusener 29–9–50–2.

Umpires: D. B. Hair *(Australia)* (40) and R. B. Tiffin *(Zimbabwe)* (21).
Third umpire: Q. J. Goosen *(Zimbabwe)*.   Referee: Naushad Ali *(Pakistan)* (4).

Close of play: First day, South Africa 414-1 (Kirsten 202, Kallis 56); Second day, Zimbabwe 143-4 (A. Flower 54, Price 0); Third day, Zimbabwe 97-3 (Masakadza 37, A. Flower 43); Fourth day, Zimbabwe 304-7 (A. Flower 138, Friend 10)

ZIMBABWE v SOUTH AFRICA 2001–02 (2nd Test)

At Queens Sports Club, Bulawayo, on 14, 15 *(no play)*, 16, 17, 18 September.
Toss: Zimbabwe.   Result: MATCH DRAWN.
Debuts: none.
Man of the Match: J. H. Kallis.   Man of the Series: J. H. Kallis.

Zimbabwe avoided defeat for the first time in their five Tests against South Africa, thanks partly to the loss of a full day's play, but also to the visitors' reluctance to take risks and a much-improved showing from Andy Flower's team-mates. Openers Campbell and Ebrahim put on 152 in almost five hours, only to fall in quick succession. The weather was cold and blustery (very rare for Bulawayo in September), and, even more surprisingly, this gave way to rain which washed out the second day. It was not until late on the third that South Africa began their innings, and they batted slowly on a placid pitch against a toothless attack, which was handicapped when Paul Strang damaged his right hand in a valiant attempt to catch Gibbs in his first over. Gibbs earned praise for walking when he edged Price to the keeper; Kallis earned brickbats for his laboriousness. He lumbered towards the double-century he never reached, despite batting for 580 minutes in the cushiest conditions he could have wished for. His total for the series was a record 1,028 minutes without dismissal. After their eventual declaration the South Africans began to apply pressure ... too late. Henderson obtained considerable turn, but lacked support. Even so, the batsmen had a difficult time before Masakadza, assisted by the calm presence of Flower, secured the draw. Had Zimbabwe been required to bat for a full day on the wearing pitch, they would have struggled to survive.

Zimbabwe

A. D. R. Campbell c Gibbs b Klusener	77	– c Dippenaar b Henderson	20
D. D. Ebrahim c Pollock b Henderson	71	– b Henderson	4
H. Masakadza c Boucher b Nel	13	– not out	42
S. V. Carlisle lbw b Pollock	49	– c Ntini b Henderson	4
†A. Flower c McKenzie b Henderson	67	– not out	14
G. W. Flower run out	44		
G. J. Whittall c Pollock b Henderson	16		
*H. H. Streak c Klusener b Henderson	31		
P. A. Strang not out	38		
T. J. Friend b Pollock	4		
R. W. Price not out	0		
L-b 8, n-b 1	9	B 4, l-b 4, n-b 4	12

1/152 (1) 2/154 (2) 3/175 (3)   (9 wkts dec.) 419   1/21 (2) 2/38 (1)   (3 wkts) 96
4/261 (5) 5/327 (6) 6/330 (4)   3/58 (4)
7/377 (8) 8/377 (7) 9/406 (10)

Pollock 28–14–40–2; Nel 21–3–73–1; Ntini 25–9–68–0; Klusener 37–10–87–1; Henderson 67–24–143–4. *Second Innings*—Pollock 4–1–8–0; Nel 3–0–9–0; Henderson 18–11–33–3; Ntini 3–0–11–0; Klusener 12–7–21–0; Kirsten 2–1–6–0.

South Africa

H. H. Gibbs c A. Flower b Price	74	C. W. Henderson b Friend	0
G. Kirsten st A. Flower b Price	65		
J. H. Kallis not out	189	B 3, l-b 7	10
N. D. McKenzie lbw b Friend	88		
H. H. Dippenaar c G. W. Flower b Price	11	1/117 (1) 2/162 (2) (8 wkts dec.) 519
L. Klusener c Campbell b Price	27	3/343 (4) 4/368 (5)
*S. M. Pollock c Carlisle b Price	41	5/418 (6) 6/490 (7)
†M. V. Boucher b Friend	14	7/513 (8) 8/519 (9)

M. Ntini and A. Nel did not bat.

Streak 25–9–64–0; Friend 30.2–9–87–3; Strang 14.2–2–52–0; Price 79–19–181–5; Whittall 29.4–6–80–0; G. W. Flower 8–0–45–0.

Umpires: K. C. Barbour *(Zimbabwe)* (4) and J. H. Hampshire *(England)* (18).
Third umpire: G. R. Evans *(Zimbabwe)*.   Referee: Naushad Ali *(Pakistan)* (5).

Close of play: First day, Zimbabwe 154-2 (Masakadza 2, Carlisle 0); Second day, No play; Third day, South Africa 26-0 (Gibbs 15, Kirsten 11); Fourth day, South Africa 300-2 (Kallis 81, McKenzie 74).

SOUTH AFRICA v INDIA 2001–02 (1st Test)

At Springbok Park, Bloemfontein, on 3, 4, 5, 6 November.
Toss: South Africa.   Result: SOUTH AFRICA won by nine wickets.
Debuts: India – D. Dasgupta, V. Sehwag.
Man of the Match: S. M. Pollock.

Pollock's decision to bowl first earned good returns in the short term – four wickets in 90 minutes – but South Africa's advance was halted by Tendulkar, who scored a masterly 26th Test hundred, and his partnership of 220 with Virender Sehwag, who made a flawless century in his first Test innings. Sehwag might not have played had Harbhajan Singh not been taken ill on the eve of the match. Tendulkar became comfortably the youngest player to reach 7,000 Test runs, at 28 years 193 days in his 85th Test, beating David Gower (who was 31). South Africa replied with their highest total against India (previously 529 for seven at Cape Town in 1996-97), a score founded on a third consecutive century opening stand between Gibbs and Kirsten. India fought back: when Kallis was caught at second slip, it was his first dismissal in 1,241 minutes of batting (spread over three matches), then a Test record. Srinath accounted for the next two with consecutive balls to reach 200 wickets in his 54th Test. With four wickets left, South Africa were still two behind, but then they took decisive control, thanks to a stand of 121 between Boucher and Klusener, who overcame an edgy start to bludgeon 18 fours and a six. India lost only one wicket on the third day, but on the fourth nine tumbled for 129, as the probing Pollock completed ten wickets in a Test for the first time.

India

S. S. Das b Hayward	9	– c Boucher b Hayward	62
R. Dravid c Kallis b Pollock	2	– c Kirsten b Pollock	11
V. V. S. Laxman c Boucher b Hayward	32	– c Kallis b Pollock	29
S. R. Tendulkar c McKenzie b Ntini	155	– c Gibbs b Kallis	15
*S. C. Ganguly c Kirsten b Kallis	14	– c Boucher b Ntini	30
V. Sehwag b Pollock	105	– b Pollock	31
†D. Dasgupta c Boucher b Pollock	34	– c Boucher b Pollock	4
A. Kumble c Boucher b Kallis	6	– lbw b Hayward	4
J. Srinath c Gibbs b Hayward	1	– c McKenzie b Pollock	16
Zaheer Khan c Boucher b Pollock	0	– c Boucher b Pollock	0
A. Nehra not out	0	– not out	17
L-b 7, w 7, n-b 7	21	B 4, l-b 8, n-b 6	18

1/7 (2) 2/43 (1) 3/51 (3) 4/68 (5)   379   1/29 (2) 2/108 (3) 3/108 (1)   237
5/288 (4) 6/351 (6) 7/372 (8)   4/154 (4) 5/188 (5) 6/195 (6)
8/378 (7) 9/379 (10) 10/379 (9)   7/202 (8) 8/206 (7) 9/206 (10) 10/237 (9)

Pollock 27–8–91–4; Hayward 20.3–5–70–3; Kallis 22–6–87–2; Ntini 14.4–2–71–1; Klusener 6–1–32–0; Boje 5–1–21–0. *Second Innings*—Pollock 21.4–10–56–6; Hayward 23–8–74–2; Kallis 15–3–56–1; Ntini 10–3–39–1.

South Africa

H. H. Gibbs c Zaheer Khan b Srinath	107	– lbw b Kumble	1
G. Kirsten b Kumble	73	– not out	30
J. H. Kallis c Laxman b Nehra	68	– not out	21
N. D. McKenzie lbw b Kumble	68		
H. H. Dippenaar b Srinath	20		
L. Klusener c and b Kumble	108		
*S. M. Pollock c Das b Srinath	0		
†M. V. Boucher c Dravid b Srinath	47		
N. Boje c Dasgupta b Nehra	6		
M. Ntini c Dasgupta b Srinath	23		
M. Hayward not out	0		
B 7, l-b 11, w 4, n-b 16, p 5	43	N-b 2	2

1/189 (2) 2/197 (1) 3/327 (4) 4/359 (3)   563   1/6 (1)   (1 wkt) 54
5/377 (5) 6/377 (7) 7/498 (8)
8/517 (9) 9/548 (6) 10/563 (10)

Srinath 33–6–140–5; Nehra 22–3–121–2; Zaheer Khan 26–7–98–0; Kumble 50–12–132–3; Tendulkar 7–0–27–0; Sehwag 5–0–22–0. *Second Innings*—Srinath 5–1–13–0; Kumble 4–0–23–1; Nehra 3–0–9–0; Zaheer Khan 2.4–0–9–0.

Umpires: E. A. R. de Silva *(Sri Lanka)* (6) and D. L. Orchard *(South Africa)* (25).
Third umpire: I. L. Howell *(South Africa)*.   Referee: M. H. Denness *(England)* (11).

Close of play: First day, India 372-7 (Dasgupta 29); Second day, South Africa 327-3 (Kallis 49); Third day, India 96-1 (Das 54, Laxman 25).

SOUTH AFRICA v INDIA 2001–02 (2nd Test)

At St George's Park, Port Elizabeth, on 16, 17, 18, 19, 20 November.
Toss: India.   Result: MATCH DRAWN.
Debuts: none.
Man of the Match: H. H. Gibbs.   Man of the Series: H. H. Gibbs.

Achievements on the field were overshadowed by a furore triggered by the last-day announcement of penalties imposed by the referee, Mike Denness, on six Indian players for alleged disciplinary breaches. India started the final day in some peril – 366 behind with one wicket down. But they resisted gallantly and, helped by the weather, secured a comfortable draw. Without Gibbs, who batted with fluent authority, the opening day would have been desperately tedious. Kallis took 70 balls over 24 runs and Dippenaar 138 over 29. Gibbs was finally caught at gully in Tendulkar's first over as he tried to reach 200. Despite the benign pitch, India contrived to lose half their wickets for 69 before Laxman, ninth out for 89, led a revival. South Africa dipped to 26 for 3, but Kallis and Pollock shared an unbroken stand of 94 which stretched into the fourth day, when rain permitted only 25 overs. It was during the early stages of this partnership, when fieldsmen were clustered round the bat, that Harbhajan, Das, Dasgupta and Sehwag allegedly violated the Code of Conduct by charging at the umpire. The third day was also when Tendulkar supposedly "interfered with the match ball", after failing to obtain the umpires' permission to clean mud from the seam. India survived the final day, but the diplomatic drama was only just beginning: the third Test at Centurion (South Africa won it by an innings and 73 runs) was deemed unofficial by the ICC after India refused to play if Denness officiated.

South Africa

H. H. Gibbs c Sehwag b Tendulkar	196	– b Agarkar		12
G. Kirsten c Laxman b Srinath	4	– c Laxman b Srinath		5
J. H. Kallis b Srinath	24	– not out		89
N. D. McKenzie b Harbhajan Singh	12	– c Dasgupta b Srinath		2
H. H. Dippenaar c Dasgupta b Agarkar	29	– c Sehwag b Harbhajan Singh		28
L. Klusener c Laxman b Srinath	9	– c Sehwag b Harbhajan Singh		29
*S. M. Pollock c Harbhajan Singh b Srinath	3	– not out		55
†M. V. Boucher not out	68			
N. Boje lbw b Kumble	1			
M. Ntini c Das b Srinath	10			
M. Hayward b Srinath	0			
L-b 2, n-b 4	6	B 3, l-b 3, n-b 7		13

1/17 (2) 2/87 (3) 3/116 (4) 4/221 (5)   362   1/14 (2) 2/22 (1)   (5 wkts dec.) 233
5/230 (6) 6/244 (7) 7/324 (1)   3/26 (4) 4/91 (5)
8/325 (9) 9/353 (10) 10/362 (11)   5/139 (6)

Srinath 30–6–76–6; Agarkar 22–2–85–1; Ganguly 2–0–21–0; Kumble 29–10–67–1; Harbhajan Singh 34–6–89–1; Tendulkar 4–0–22–1. *Second Innings*—Srinath 17–9–28–2; Agarkar 23–3–71–1; Ganguly 5–0–17–0; Tendulkar 4–0–10–0; Harbhajan Singh 20–2–79–2; Kumble 9–0–22–0.

India

S. S. Das lbw b Pollock	1	– c Boucher b Pollock		0
†D. Dasgupta b Ntini	13	– c Kallis b Hayward		63
R. Dravid b Pollock	2	– c Boucher b Hayward		87
S. R. Tendulkar c Klusener b Pollock	1	– not out		22
*S. C. Ganguly b Pollock	42	– not out		4
V. V. S. Laxman lbw b Pollock	89			
V. Sehwag c Kirsten b Kallis	13			
A. B. Agarkar c Boucher b Kallis	1			
Harbhajan Singh run out	0			
A. Kumble c Kirsten b Hayward	28			
J. Srinath not out	0			
L-b 3, w 2, n-b 6	11	B 10, l-b 7, w 1, n-b 12		30

1/5 (1) 2/13 (3) 3/15 (4) 4/47 (2)   201   1/0 (1) 2/171 (3)   (3 wkts) 206
5/69 (5) 6/111 (7) 7/119 (8)   3/184 (2)
8/119 (9) 9/199 (6) 10/201 (10)

Pollock 16–3–40–5; Hayward 17–5–45–1; Ntini 14–3–49–1; Kallis 10–2–50–2; Boje 4–2–8–0; Klusener 1–0–6–0. *Second Innings*—Pollock 26–11–39–1; Hayward 25–6–58–2; Kallis 11.2–5–15–0; Ntini 12–4–25–0; Boje 14–4–33–0; Klusener 7–3–15–0; McKenzie 1–0–4–0.

Umpires: I. L. Howell *(South Africa)* (2) and R. B. Tiffin *(Zimbabwe)* (22).
Third umpire: R. E. Koertzen *(South Africa)*.   Referee: M. H. Denness *(England)* (12).

Close of play: First day, South Africa 237-5 (Gibbs 155, Pollock 0); Second day, India 182-8 (Laxman 77, Kumble 21); Third day, South Africa 211-5 (Kallis 84, Pollock 38); Fourth day, India 28-1 (Dasgupta 22, Dravid 3).

AUSTRALIA v NEW ZEALAND 2001–02 (1st Test)

At Woolloongabba, Brisbane, on 8, 9, 10, 11, 12 November.
Toss: New Zealand.   Result: MATCH DRAWN.
Debuts: none.
Man of the Match: B. Lee.

A cluster of declarations transformed this from a weather-doomed grind into a hair-raising cliffhanger. An explosive innings from Cairns, in his 50th Test, almost carried New Zealand to an astonishing victory before he perished on the long-on boundary with ten balls remaining and 20 needed. The draw – Australia's first since October 1999, after 20 wins and three defeats – appeared likely after rain allowed only 98 overs during the middle three days, but a remarkably generous declaration (284 from 57 overs) presented New Zealand with their opportunity. Fleming put on 100 with Astle in 19 overs, but it was Cairns who scared the Australians with a whirlwind 43 in 38 balls, including two mighty sixes off Warne. The gallant chase ended only ten short. Before this Australia had dominated: Hayden and Langer led off with a partnership of 224 – a first-wicket record in Australia–New Zealand Tests, and also the highest Test opening stand by two left-handers. While Langer crawled to 9, Hayden raced to 50 with three successive fours off O'Connor, then struck his next ball, Vettori's first, for six. New Zealand were back in leather-chasing mode between showers on the second and third days, with Gilchrist, who put on 135 with Lee, making his fourth Test century. Lee then produced a fiery spell of pace, including Parore to Steve Waugh's 100th Test catch. New Zealand crept past the follow-on mark just before lunch on the last day. Fleming declared immediately ... and it very nearly paid off.

Australia

J. L. Langer c Vettori b McMillan	104	– (4) not out		18
M. L. Hayden c Richardson b Cairns	136	– run out		13
R. T. Ponting c Vettori b Cairns	5	– not out		32
M. E. Waugh lbw b Astle	0			
*S. R. Waugh c Parore b McMillan	3			
D. R. Martyn c Vettori b McMillan	4			
†A. C. Gilchrist c sub (L. Vincent) b Cairns	118	– (1) b Cairns		20
S. K. Warne c Sinclair b Cairns	22			
B. Lee c Parore b Cairns	61			
J. N. Gillespie not out	20			
L-b 4, w 1, n-b 8	13	N-b 1		1

1/224 (2) 2/233 (3) 3/235 (4)   (9 wkts dec.) 486   1/30 (1) 2/39 (2)   (2 wkts dec.) 84
4/256 (5) 5/260 (6) 6/263 (1)
7/302 (8) 8/437 (9) 9/486 (7)

G. D. McGrath did not bat.

Cairns 37–8–146–5; Nash 30–6–93–0; O'Connor 17.2–4–67–0; Vettori 13.4–0–65–0; Astle 19–7–46–1; McMillan 14–1–65–3. *Second Innings*—Cairns 5–1–29–1; McMillan 7–0–47–0; Vettori 2–0–8–0.

New Zealand

M. H. Richardson lbw b Gillespie	26	– lbw b Warne		57
M. D. Bell c Ponting b Gillespie	6	– lbw b McGrath		5
M. S. Sinclair c Ponting b Lee	3	– st Gilchrist b Warne		23
*S. P. Fleming c Gilchrist b Gillespie	0	– run out		57
N. J. Astle c Gillespie b Lee	66	– c Gillespie b Warne		49
C. D. McMillan c Warne b Lee	45	– (7) not out		23
C. L. Cairns c S. R. Waugh b Lee	61	– (6) c Ponting b Lee		43
†A. C. Parore c S. R. Waugh b Lee	11	– not out		3
D. J. Nash not out	25			
D. L. Vettori not out	3			
L-b 15, n-b 26	41	B 1, l-b 9, w 1, n-b 3		14

1/36 (2) 2/51 (1) 3/51 (4)   (8 wkts dec.) 287   1/33 (2) 2/89 (1)   (6 wkts) 274
4/55 (3) 5/147 (6) 6/242 (5)   3/90 (3) 4/190 (5)
7/243 (7) 8/271 (8)   5/213 (4) 6/264 (6)

S. B. O'Connor did not bat.

McGrath 26–6–80–0; Gillespie 18.4–6–56–3; Lee 23–6–67–5; Warne 18–2–61–0; Ponting 3–0–8–0. *Second Innings*—Lee 10–0–53–1; Gillespie 8–0–48–0; McGrath 20–4–66–1; Warne 18–2–89–3; M. E. Waugh 1–0–8–0.

Umpires: S. A. Bucknor *(West Indies)* (61) and D. J. Harper *(Australia)* (14).
Third umpire: P. D. Parker *(Australia)*.   Referee: J. L. Hendriks *(West Indies)* (14).

Close of play: First day, Australia 294-6 (Gilchrist 13, Warne 18); Second day, Australia 435-7 (Gilchrist 88, Lee 60); Third day, New Zealand 29-0 (Richardson 10, Bell 6); Fourth day, New Zealand 186-5 (Astle 51, Cairns 25).

AUSTRALIA v NEW ZEALAND 2001–02 (2nd Test)

At Bellerive Oval, Hobart, on 22, 23, 24, 25, 26 November.
Toss: New Zealand.   Result: MATCH DRAWN.
Debuts: New Zealand – S. E. Bond.
Man of the Match: R. T. Ponting.

A hopeful dawn soon became a calamitous morning for New Zealand as their bowling was demolished again by Langer and Hayden. The last time Fleming had invited them to bat, they had piled on 224; this time it was 223, their third consecutive century partnership. Australia, no longer settling for a mere 300 in a day, marched through to a commanding 411 for 6. A touch of magic from Vettori, who obtained just enough purchase for his left-arm spin to make his arm-ball effective, dragged New Zealand back from hopelessness. Langer brought up his tenth Test century, becoming the first Australian since David Boon in England in 1993 to score three in three Tests. On the second day, Australia added 147 in the 34 overs permitted by the weather before declaring. Ponting required only eight deliveries to convert his overnight 92 into his ninth Test century, the first in his native Tasmania: like Langer, he hit 20 fours, and added a six off the debutant Shane Bond. Just 35 overs were possible on the third day as New Zealand started cautiously; only 51 were squeezed in on the fourth and 20 on the last. Fleming had helped to ensure his team's safety by stroking 71. Over the last three days the third umpire, John Smeaton, stood with Steve Bucknor, after Steve Davis injured his knee.

Australia

J. L. Langer c Vettori b Cairns	123	B. Lee c McMillan b Vettori	41
M. L. Hayden c Bond b Vettori	91		
R. T. Ponting not out	157	B 3, l-b 5, w 2, n-b 15	25
M. E. Waugh b Vettori	12		
*S. R. Waugh lbw b Bond	0	1/223 (1) 2/238 (2)	(8 wkts dec.) 558
D. R. Martyn lbw b Vettori	0	3/253 (4) 4/266 (5)	
†A. C. Gilchrist b Vettori	39	5/267 (6) 6/336 (7)	
S. K. Warne b Astle	70	7/481 (8) 8/558 (9)	

J. N. Gillespie and G. D. McGrath did not bat.

Cairns 28–3–122–1; Tuffey 15–1–74–0; Bond 28–0–135–1; Vettori 36–5–138–5; McMillan 8–0–51–0; Astle 9–0–30–1.

New Zealand

M. H. Richardson lbw b Gillespie	30	†A. C. Parore not out	10
M. D. Bell c Gilchrist b Warne	4	D. L. Vettori not out	10
M. S. Sinclair b Gillespie	23	L-b 1, n-b 8	9
*S. P. Fleming lbw b McGrath	71		
N. J. Astle c Warne b M. E. Waugh	11	1/11 (2) 2/53 (3) 3/76 (1)	(7 wkts) 243
C. D. McMillan b Gillespie	55	4/100 (5) 5/197 (4)	
C. L. Cairns c Gilchrist b McGrath	20	6/219 (6) 7/223 (7)	

D. R. Tuffey and S. E. Bond did not bat.

McGrath 27–12–46–2; Gillespie 28–14–45–3; Warne 24.2–3–70–1; Lee 19–5–51–0; M. E. Waugh 7–1–30–1.

Umpires: S. A. Bucknor *(West Indies)* (62) and S. J. Davis *(Australia)* (5).
Third umpire: J. H. Smeaton *(Australia)* and B. W. Jackman *(Australia)*.   Referee: J. L. Hendriks *(West Indies)* (15).

Close of play: First day, Australia 411-6 (Ponting 92, Warne 31); Second day, Australia 558-8 dec.; Third day, New Zealand 71-2 (Richardson 25, Fleming 16); Fourth day, New Zealand 197-4 (Fleming 71, McMillan 51).

AUSTRALIA v NEW ZEALAND 2001–02 (3rd Test)

At W. A. C. A. Ground, Perth, on 30 November, 1, 2, 3, 4 December.
Toss: New Zealand.   Result: MATCH DRAWN.
Debuts: New Zealand – L. Vincent.
Man of the Match: D. L. Vettori.   Man of the Series: J. L. Langer.

New Zealand almost snatched an outrageous series victory after challenging their hosts to score the highest fourth-innings total to win a Test. Even more outrageously, Australia came close to doing it, but the series finally ended with its third draw after a thrilling match. Fleming this time chose to bat, whereupon Lou Vincent made a fairy-tale debut, cracking 104 in the first innings and a run-a-ball 54 in the second. He was the sixth New Zealander to score a Test-debut century, and only the fourth tourist to do it in Australia. The last was the senior Nawab of Pataudi in the 1932-33 Bodyline series, following "Tip" Foster (1903-04) and George Gunn (1907-08), all for England at Sydney. Vincent added 199 with Fleming, who scored his first Test hundred for 3½ years. Then Astle and Parore put on 253, the second-highest eighth-wicket stand in Tests after 313 by Wasim Akram and Saqlain Mushtaq against Zimbabwe in 1996-97. It was the first time four New Zealanders had scored centuries in the same innings, and Australia had conceded four only once before, to England at Nottingham in 1938. Australia seemed likely to follow on at 192 for 6, but Warne saved them with his Test-best 99 as the last four wickets added 159. Fleming eventually set the uphill task of 440 in 107 overs. It seemed even steeper when Australia soon lost Langer and Ponting by the close, but in fact they finished only 59 short with three wickets left.

New Zealand

M. H. Richardson b Gillespie	9	– run out	30
L. Vincent c M. E. Waugh b Warne	104	– c M. E. Waugh b Lee	54
M. S. Sinclair lbw b McGrath	2	– c Gilchrist b McGrath	29
*S. P. Fleming lbw b Lee	105	– (5) b Warne	4
N. J. Astle not out	156	– (6) c Langer b Gillespie	40
C. D. McMillan lbw b Gillespie	4	– (7) c Warne b Gillespie	19
D. L. Vettori c Martyn b Gillespie	2	– (9) c S. R. Waugh b Lee	3
C. L. Cairns c Gilchrist b Lee	8	– (4) c Warne b Lee	42
†A. C. Parore c McGrath b Lee	110	– (8) not out	16
S. E. Bond b Lee	0	– b Lee	8
B 4, l-b 15, w 2, n-b 13	34	B 1, l-b 6, n-b 4	11

1/12 (1) 2/19 (3) 3/218 (2)   (9 wkts dec.) 534   1/77 (2) 2/90 (1)   (9 wkts dec.) 256
4/264 (4) 5/269 (6) 6/272 (7)   3/128 (3) 4/151 (5)
7/281 (8) 8/534 (9) 9/534 (10)   5/199 (4) 6/208 (6) 7/241 (7) 8/246 (9) 9/256 (10)

C. S. Martin did not bat.

McGrath 27–11–72–1; Gillespie 40–7–112–3; Lee 32.5–5–125–4; Warne 43–9–135–1; Martyn 10–0–44–0; M. E. Waugh 6–1–26–0; Ponting 4–3–1–0. *Second Innings*—McGrath 17–4–63–1; Gillespie 17–0–55–2; Lee 16–3–56–4; Warne 21–3–75–1.

Australia

J. L. Langer c Parore b Cairns	75	– c Vettori b Bond	0
M. L. Hayden c Vincent b Bond	0	– c Sinclair b Vettori	57
R. T. Ponting c Parore b Martin	31	– b Cairns	26
M. E. Waugh c Bond b Vettori	42	– b McMillan	86
*S. R. Waugh c Parore b Vettori	8	– run out	67
D. R. Martyn c Fleming b Cairns	60	– b Vettori	30
†A. C. Gilchrist c Richardson b Vettori	0	– not out	83
S. K. Warne c Richardson b Vettori	99	– run out	10
B. Lee c McMillan b Vettori	17		
J. N. Gillespie c Parore b Vettori	0	– (9) not out	1
G. D. McGrath not out	0		
L-b 2, w 1, n-b 16	19	L-b 3, w 2, n-b 16	21

1/3 (2) 2/61 (3) 3/122 (4) 4/137 (5)   351   1/1 (1) 2/52 (3)   (7 wkts) 381
5/191 (1) 6/192 (7) 7/270 (6)   3/130 (2) 4/195 (4)
8/342 (9) 9/346 (10) 10/351 (8)   5/244 (6) 6/339 (5) 7/355 (8)

Cairns 23–5–86–2; Bond 18–2–74–1; Martin 23–4–88–1; Vettori 34.4–7–87–6; Astle 5–1–14–0. *Second Innings*—Bond 21–3–80–1; Martin 12–0–51–0; Vettori 45–11–142–2; Cairns 15–2–72–1; Astle 12–5–18–0; McMillan 5–2–15–1.

Umpires: D. B. Hair *(Australia)* (41) and I. D. Robinson *(Zimbabwe)* (27).
Third umpire: D. J. Harper *(Australia)*.   Referee: J. L. Hendriks *(West Indies)* (16).

Close of play: First day, New Zealand 293-7 (Astle 28, Parore 5); Second day, Australia 75-2 (Langer 34, M. E. Waugh 5); Third day, Australia 351; Fourth day, Australia 69-2 (Hayden 31, M. E. Waugh 8).

BANGLADESH v ZIMBABWE 2001–02 (1st Test)

At Bangabandhu National Stadium, Dhaka, on 8, 9, 10, 11 *(no play)*, 12 *(no play)* November 2001.
Toss: Zimbabwe.   Result: MATCH DRAWN.
Debuts: Bangladesh – Khaled Mahmud, Mashrafe bin Mortaza.
Man of the Match: T. J. Friend.

After five consecutive defeats since gaining Test status, Bangladesh finally achieved a draw. But they were helped by rain: not a single ball was bowled on the last two days. Murphy, in what turned out to be his only Test as captain, had put the home side in, and the first afternoon's overcast conditions seemed to transform Bangladesh's own backyard into an alien environment. All the batsmen struggled against the seamers, and it was left to the No. 10, Enamul Haque to help inch the total past 100 as the last two wickets added 51. Manjural Islam countered with a wicket in each of his first two overs, and the bowlers continued their good work next morning, despite what seemed perfect batting conditions, under a blazing sun. When Enamul bowled Andy Flower, Zimbabwe were an unprepossessing 89 for 5 – but they still amassed a huge lead. Wishart and Marillier put on 137, then Streak added 108 with Friend, who followed up his first Test five-for with a maiden fifty. Mashrafe bin Mortaza generated good pace and took four wickets on debut (first-class as well as Test). Bangladesh batted much better in their second innings. Habibul Bashar built a determined partnership with Javed Omar, although both fell before the close, leaving their side with little chance of saving the game. But next day, the heavens opened, and Bangladesh escaped. Zimbabwe's bad luck was compounded when Murphy fractured a finger in the nets and was forced to go home.

Bangladesh

Javed Omar b Streak	3	– c Olonga b Marillier		35
Al Sahariar lbw b Friend	4	– c G. W. Flower b Friend		5
Habibul Bashar c A. Flower b Friend	0	– c Murphy b Friend		65
Aminul Islam lbw b Olonga	12	– not out		6
Mohammad Ashraful c Wishart b Olonga	0	– not out		0
Khaled Mahmud c Gripper b Friend	6			
*Naimur Rahman b Friend	13			
†Khaled Mashud c Carlisle b Friend	6			
Mashrafe bin Mortaza c A. Flower b Streak	8			
Enamul Haque, sen. not out	24			
Manjural Islam c Gripper b Olonga	9			
B 3, l-b 3, w 1, n-b 15	22	B 3, l-b 1, n-b 10		14

1/6 (2) 2/6 (3) 3/11 (1) 4/13 (5) 107   1/6 (2) 2/108 (1)   (3 wkts) 125
5/30 (6) 6/38 (4) 7/49 (7)   3/120 (3)
8/56 (8) 9/84 (9) 10/107 (11)

Streak 18–8–30–2; Friend 18–7–31–5; Olonga 6.2–0–18–3; Murphy 6–1–22–0. *Second Innings*—Streak 11–4–25–0; Friend 11.4–2–26–2; Olonga 5–1–17–0; Murphy 12–4–37–0; Marillier 7–2–16–1.

Zimbabwe

D. D. Ebrahim lbw b Manjural Islam	3	T. J. Friend b Enamul Haque		81
T. R. Gripper c Javed Omar b Manjural Islam	0	*B. A. Murphy c Habibul Bashar		
S. V. Carlisle c Khaled Mashud		b Mashrafe bin Mortaza		25
b Mashrafe bin Mortaza	33	H. K. Olonga not out		2
G. W. Flower c Al Sahariar				
b Mashrafe bin Mortaza	10	B 4, l-b 7, w 4, n-b 2		17
†A. Flower b Enamul Haque	28			
C. B. Wishart run out	94	1/3 (2) 2/4 (1) 3/31 (4)		431
D. A. Marillier lbw b Enamul Haque	73	4/60 (3) 5/89 (5) 6/226 (6)		
H. H. Streak c Khaled Mashud		7/259 (7) 8/367 (8)		
b Mashrafe bin Mortaza	65	9/417 (9) 10/431 (10)		

Manjural Islam 26–5–74–2; Mashrafe bin Mortaza 32–8–106–4; Khaled Mahmud 15–2–59–0; Enamul Haque 43–13–74–3; Naimur Rahman 18–1–56–0; Mohammad Ashraful 15–3–49–0; Aminul Islam 1–0–2–0.

Umpires: A. F. M. Akhtaruddin *(Bangladesh)* (1) and Mian Aslam *(Pakistan)* (8).
Third umpire: Sailab Hossain *(Bangladesh)*.   Referee: Hanumant Singh *(India)* (8).

Close of play: First day, Zimbabwe 20-2 (Carlisle 10, G. W. Flower 6); Second day, Zimbabwe 348-7 (Streak 57, Friend 38); Third day, Bangladesh 125-3 (Aminul Islam 6, Mohammad Ashraful 0); Fourth day, No play.

BANGLADESH v ZIMBABWE 2001–02 (2nd Test)

At M. A. Aziz Stadium, Chittagong, on 15, 16, 17, 18, 19 November.
Toss: Bangladesh.   Result: ZIMBABWE won by eight wickets.
Debuts: none.
Man of the Match: G. W. Flower.

Although Zimbabwe won comfortably to take the series, there was a hint of improvement by Bangladesh: they took the game into a fifth day for only the second time (excluding the rain-affected draw at Dhaka) in their seven Tests. The M. A. Aziz Stadium became Bangladesh's second Test venue, and the world's 82nd. Carlisle took over as Zimbabwe's captain from the injured Murphy. Naimur Rahman surprised everyone by bowling first, probably influenced by his side's three preceding Tests, in each of which they batted first and were bundled out for under 140. Zimbabwe's batsmen responded gleefully: Gripper batted nearly six hours and reached a maiden Test century, as did Wishart, after two near-misses. Andy Flower, who had retired hurt after colliding with Enamul Haque, returned to complete his 12th Test hundred as Zimbabwe passed 500 for the third time in 12 months. Avoiding the follow-on looked an uphill task, and Bangladesh never got near it. Apart from Habibul Bashar, with yet another maiden century, only Mohammad Ashraful showed application, with 33 in 140 minutes. In the follow-on, he showed even greater self-denial – 10 in 146 minutes. Javed Omar featured in partnerships of 73 and 122, and Habibul proved his class again, until a rash shot triggered a mini-collapse of three for eight, all to Grant Flower's slow left-armers. Bangladesh entered the last day with a faint hope of saving the match. That disappeared with the first ball: Friend trapped Omar in front after 416 minutes' defiance.

Zimbabwe

D. D. Ebrahim b Mashrafe bin Mortaza	41	– b Mashrafe bin Mortaza		0
T. R. Gripper run out	112	– not out		11
*S. V. Carlisle lbw b Enamul Haque	14	– c Akram Khan b Mashrafe bin Mortaza		0
G. W. Flower c Naimur Rahman b Enamul Haque	33	– not out		0
†A. Flower not out	114			
G. B. Brent c Habibul Bashar b Mashrafe bin Mortaza	25			
C. B. Wishart c Mohammad Sharif b Mohammad Ashraful	114			
D. A. Marillier c Habibul Bashar b Aminul Islam	52			
H. H. Streak not out	16			
B 2, l-b 5, w 2, n-b 12	21			

1/108 (1) 2/145 (3) 3/210 (4)   (7 wkts dec.) 542   1/0 (1) 2/0 (3)   (2 wkts) 11
4/214 (2) 5/280 (6)
6/469 (7) 7/496 (8)

T. J. Friend and H. K. Olonga did not bat.

In the first innings A. Flower, when 66, retired hurt at 346 and resumed at 469.

Mashrafe bin Mortaza 28–4–101–2; Mohammad Sharif 29–7–118–0; Enamul Haque 54–12–134–2; Naimur Rahman 15–2–54–0; Mohammad Ashraful 17–0–62–1; Aminul Islam 17–1–66–1. *Second Innings*—Mashrafe bin Mortaza 1.4–1–10–2; Enamul Haque 1–0–1–0.

Bangladesh

Javed Omar c A. Flower b Streak	8	– lbw b Friend		80
Al Sahariar lbw b Olonga	29	– lbw b Olonga		40
Habibul Bashar b G. W. Flower	108	– c sub (S. M. Ervine) b G. W. Flower		76
Aminul Islam c and b Marillier	21	– c Gripper b G. W. Flower		1
Akram Khan lbw b Marillier	6	– b G. W. Flower		2
Mohammad Ashraful c Ebrahim b G. W. Flower	33	– c sub (P. A. Strang) b Marillier		10
*Naimur Rahman lbw b Streak	5	– lbw b Marillier		28
†Khaled Mashud b G. W. Flower	8	– c Ebrahim b G. W. Flower		12
Enamul Haque, sen. not out	12	– c and b Marillier		0
Mashrafe bin Mortaza lbw b Brent	1	– st A. Flower b Marillier		0
Mohammad Sharif c Brent b G. W. Flower	3	– not out		24
B 3, l-b 3, w 2, n-b 9	17	B 2, l-b 16, w 1, n-b 9		28

1/15 (1) 2/80 (2) 3/135 (4) 4/146 (5)   251   1/73 (2) 2/195 (3) 3/201 (4)   301
5/204 (3) 6/217 (7) 7/226 (8)   4/203 (5) 5/227 (1) 6/264 (6)
8/235 (6) 9/244 (10) 10/251 (11)   7/267 (7) 8/267 (9) 9/267 (10) 10/301 (8)

Friend 16–3–63–0; Streak 19–6–32–2; Olonga 12–0–40–1; Marillier 15–6–39–2; Brent 17–9–30–1; G. W. Flower 15.3–3–41–4; Gripper 1–1–0–0. *Second Innings*—Friend 25–7–53–1; Brent 25–6–58–0; G. W. Flower 38.4–18–63–4; Olonga 15–5–31–1; Marillier 19–4–57–4; Gripper 4–2–21–0.

Umpires: E. A. R. de Silva *(Sri Lanka)* (7) and Showkatur Rahman *(Bangladesh)* (1).
Third umpire: Jahangir Alam *(Bangladesh)*.   Referee: Hanumant Singh *(India)* (9).

Close of play: First day, Zimbabwe 236-4 (A. Flower 15, Brent 9); Second day, Bangladesh 57-1 (Al Sahariar 25, Habibul Bashar 21); Third day, Bangladesh 15-0 (Javed Omar 2, Al Sahariar 11); Fourth day, Bangladesh 227-4 (Javed Omar 80, Mohammad Ashraful 1).

SRI LANKA v WEST INDIES 2001–02 (1st Test)

At Galle International Stadium on 13, 14, 15, 16, 17 November.
Toss: West Indies.   Result: SRI LANKA won by ten wickets.
Debuts: Sri Lanka – T. C. B. Fernando *(also known as Charitha Buddhika)*.
Man of the Match: M. Muralitharan.

At lunch on the second day, West Indies were 409 for 4, with Lara motoring; by tea on the fifth, their last man, Stuart, was sending a gentle catch to mid-off to give Muralitharan his 11th wicket of the match. Sixteen West Indians had departed for 169, and Sri Lanka required only three runs for their first victory in four Tests against them. Galle, overlooked by its 17th-century Dutch fort, had become a cricket fortress for Sri Lanka, with Muralitharan its commander. He had taken 39 wickets in his last four Tests there, all emphatic home wins. On the opening day Murali toiled through 40 overs in sweltering heat for a solitary wicket. But he turned the game dramatically on the second afternoon, with four for nine in 40 balls, starting with Lara for a splendid 178, to trigger a collapse in which the last six wickets tumbled for 25. Sri Lanka's batsmen quickly put the pitch and an inexperienced attack into proper perspective. Sangakkara shared successive stands of 109 and 162 with Atapattu and the bubbly Jayawardene, who was run out by Samuels's direct hit from midwicket one short of his fourth hundred in four Tests. Tillekeratne and Samaraweera extended the lead in a 154-run partnership that included only two fours. Ganga and Sarwan raised West Indian hopes of a draw, but when they were dismissed within seven balls on the last morning, only Lara delayed the inevitable for long as Muralitharan completed his 30th Test five-for.

West Indies

D. Ganga c Jayawardene b Vaas	47	– c Tillekeratne b Bandaratilleke	33
C. H. Gayle c Sangakkara b Vaas	9	– c Muralitharan b Vaas	1
R. R. Sarwan b Muralitharan	88	– c Arnold b Muralitharan	30
B. C. Lara c Sangakkara b Muralitharan	178	– c Muralitharan b Samaraweera	40
*C. L. Hooper c and b Muralitharan	69	– c Jayasuriya b Bandaratilleke	6
M. N. Samuels b Muralitharan	16	– lbw b Muralitharan	2
†R. D. Jacobs c Sangakkara b Vaas	8	– b Muralitharan	9
N. C. McGarrell c Arnold b Muralitharan	4	– not out	10
M. Dillon c Jayasuriya b Vaas	5	– lbw b Muralitharan	0
D. Ramnarine not out	0	– b Vaas	0
C. E. L. Stuart b Muralitharan	0	– c Vaas b Muralitharan	2
B 8, l-b 6, n-b 5, p 5	24	B 2, l-b 2, n-b 7	11

1/15 (2) 2/95 (1) 3/240 (3) 4/393 (5)   448   1/3 (2) 2/70 (1) 3/70 (3)   144
5/423 (4) 6/434 (6) 7/440 (7)   4/83 (5) 5/93 (6) 6/131 (4)
8/448 (9) 9/448 (8) 10/448 (11)   7/135 (7) 8/138 (9) 9/139 (10) 10/144 (11)

Vaas 31–6–95–4; Fernando 18–2–80–0; Muralitharan 53.4–11–126–6; Bandaratilleke 22–3–76–0; Jayasuriya 9–2–24–0; Samaraweera 6–0–24–0; Arnold 2–1–4–0. *Second Innings*—Vaas 17–8–20–2; Bandaratilleke 19–6–46–2; Muralitharan 31.3–10–44–5; Fernando 2–0–10–0; Jayasuriya 5–0–13–0; Samaraweera 4–1–7–1.

Sri Lanka

M. S. Atapattu c Lara b Ramnarine	61	– (2) not out	0
*S. T. Jayasuriya c McGarrell b Dillon	25	– (1) not out	6
†K. C. Sangakkara run out	140		
D. P. M. D. Jayawardene run out	99		
R. P. Arnold lbw b Ramnarine	33		
H. P. Tillekeratne not out	105		
T. T. Samaraweera c Jacobs b Stuart	77		
W. P. U. J. C. Vaas c Samuels b Dillon	7		
M. R. C. N. Bandaratilleke c Jacobs b Ramnarine	4		
M. Muralitharan lbw b Stuart	14		
B 1, l-b 13, w 4, n-b 7	25		

1/37 (2) 2/146 (1) 3/308 (4)   (9 wkts dec.) 590   (no wkt) 6
4/358 (5) 5/395 (3) 6/549 (7)
7/562 (8) 8/567 (9) 9/590 (10)

T. C. B. Fernando did not bat.

Dillon 51–11–121–2; Stuart 37.4–7–138–2; McGarrell 31–3–95–0; Ramnarine 58–12–158–3; Hooper 24–3–59–0; Samuels 1–0–5–0. *Second Innings*—Stuart 0.4–0–6–0.

Umpires: J. H. Hampshire *(England)* (19) and P. T. Manuel *(Sri Lanka)* (10).
Third umpire: T.H. Wijewardene *(Sri Lanka)*.   Referee: R. Subba Row *(England)* (39).

Close of play: First day, West Indies 316-3 (Lara 117, Hooper 34); Second day, Sri Lanka 103-1 (Atapattu 45, Sangakkara 27); Third day, Sri Lanka 343-3 (Sangakkara 126, Arnold 18); Fourth day, West Indies 9-1 (Ganga 3, Sarwan 5).

SRI LANKA v WEST INDIES 2001–02 (2nd Test)

At Asgiriya Stadium, Kandy, on 21, 22, 23, 24, 25 November.
Toss: Sri Lanka.   Result: SRI LANKA won by 131 runs.
Debuts: none.
Man of the Match: M. Muralitharan.

West Indies came agonisingly close to saving the match before Muralitharan hurried out the last four wickets for four runs in 21 balls to secure the series with just 16 minutes to spare. It was another one-sided affair, despite the loss of 130 overs to rain. Yet luck did not go West Indies' way. They had reinforced their pace attack, but were soon down to two pacemen again. The fifth over featured three bowlers: Dillon had trapped Atapattu in his first over, but then went off ill after two balls of his third. Stuart stepped in, but two unintentional head-high full-tosses in three balls to Jayasuriya gave umpire Hampshire no option but to ban him for the rest of the innings, the first such instance in Tests. Gayle then delivered the last three balls of the over. West Indies' surviving bowlers prospered during the next hour, reducing Sri Lanka to 53 for 4, but their shortcomings were exposed by a stand of 116 between Jayawardene and Tillekeratne, who put on a further 80 with Samaraweera before he was bowled – his first dismissal in 975 minutes spread over four Tests. Later, when Lara looked capable of saving the game, he was given out caught at short leg off a shot he clearly played into the ground. Muralitharan took ten wickets in a Test for the ninth time, equalling Richard Hadlee's record, and for the fourth Test in succession, breaking Clarrie Grimmett's record of three for Australia against South Africa in 1935-36.

Sri Lanka

M. S. Atapattu lbw b Dillon	0	– st Jacobs b Ramnarine		84
*S. T. Jayasuriya c Gayle b Collins	16	– c Gayle b Ramnarine		55
†K. C. Sangakkara b Ramnarine	15	– c Ramnarine b Dillon		45
D. P. M. D. Jayawardene c and b Ramnarine	88	– c Stuart b Dillon		16
R. P. Arnold b Ramnarine	4	– c Dillon b Ramnarine		1
H. P. Tillekeratne b Collins	87	– not out		7
T. T. Samaraweera c Jacobs b Dillon	29	– (8) not out		3
W. P. U. J. C. Vaas c Hooper b Collins	0	– (7) c Ganga b Ramnarine		0
M. R. C. N. Bandaratilleke not out	12			
D. N. T. Zoysa b Collins	23			
M. Muralitharan c Stuart b Dillon	4			
L-b 6, n-b 4	10	B 3, l-b 6, w 2, n-b 2		13

1/1 (1) 2/27 (2) 3/49 (3) 4/53 (5)   288   1/89 (2) 2/176 (3)   (6 wkts dec.) 224
5/169 (4) 6/249 (6) 7/249 (7)   3/204 (4) 4/206 (5)
8/249 (8) 9/281 (10) 10/288 (11)   5/215 (1) 6/215 (7)

Dillon 20–4–55–3; Collins 27–7–78–4; Stuart 0.1–0–2–0; Gayle 0.3–0–4–0; Hooper 21–6–44–0; Ramnarine 25–6–81–3; Samuels 3–0–18–0. *Second Innings*—Dillon 19–2–60–2; Collins 11–0–52–0; Ramnarine 16–2–66–4; Stuart 8–1–21–0; Hooper 13–4–16–0.

West Indies

C. H. Gayle b Zoysa	44	– (2) c Sangakkara b Vaas		0
D. Ganga c Jayawardene b Zoysa	0	– (1) b Muralitharan		8
R. R. Sarwan b Muralitharan	17	– c Arnold b Muralitharan		48
B. C. Lara lbw b Muralitharan	74	– c Tillekeratne b Bandaratilleke		45
*C. L. Hooper lbw b Muralitharan	23	– lbw b Bandaratilleke		4
M. N. Samuels c Sangakkara b Muralitharan	0	– lbw b Muralitharan		54
†R. D. Jacobs b Vaas	24	– c Sangakkara b Vaas		5
M. Dillon c Sangakkara b Vaas	0	– b Muralitharan		19
D. Ramnarine lbw b Vaas	0	– not out		0
P. T. Collins lbw b Vaas	0	– b Muralitharan		0
C. E. L. Stuart not out	0	– b Muralitharan		0
L-b 5, n-b 4	9	B 3, l-b 2, n-b 2		7

1/8 (2) 2/51 (3) 3/72 (1) 4/126 (5)   191   1/3 (2) 2/25 (1) 3/83 (3)   190
5/126 (6) 6/167 (7) 7/173 (8)   4/126 (5) 5/110 (4) 6/126 (7)
8/173 (9) 9/181 (10) 10/191 (4)   7/185 (8) 8/190 (6) 9/190 (10) 10/190 (11)

Vaas 22–8–56–4; Zoysa 13–3–34–2; Muralitharan 23.4–5–54–4; Bandaratilleke 4–0–25–0; Samaraweera 4–1–17–0. *Second Innings*—Vaas 13–2–39–2; Zoysa 8–4–13–0; Muralitharan 35.5–16–81–6; Bandaratilleke 15–7–29–2; Samaraweera 5–2–9–0; Jayasuriya 5–2–13–0; Tillekeratne 2–1–1–0.

Umpires: J. H. Hampshire *(England)* (20) and M. G. Silva *(Sri Lanka)* (2).
Third umpire: P. T. Manuel *(Sri Lanka)*.   Referee: R. Subba Row *(England)* (40).

Close of play: First day, Sri Lanka 193-5 (Tillekeratne 60, Samaraweera 4); Second day, Sri Lanka 273-8 (Bandaratilleke 9, Zoysa 15); Third day, West Indies 39-1 (Gayle 25, Sarwan 12); Fourth day, Sri Lanka 128-1 (Atapattu 58, Sangakkara 10).

SRI LANKA v WEST INDIES 2001–02 (3rd Test)

At Sinhalese Sports Club, Colombo, on 29, 30 November, 1, 2, 3 December.
Toss: West Indies.   Result: SRI LANKA won by ten wickets.
Debuts: none.
Men of the Match: B. C. Lara and W. P. U. J. C. Vaas.   Man of the Series: B. C. Lara.

Sri Lanka completed a clean sweep in a game of two giant performances. Vaas took 14 wickets, twice improving his career-best analysis, swinging new ball and old, in and out. And Lara completed a phenomenal series – 688 runs in all – with scores of 221 and 130, batting for over 11½ hours. Only five others had combined a double and a single hundred in the same Test, and none had ended up losing. He also broke Andy Flower's recent record *(Test No. 1562)* for the most runs by anyone on the losing side. West Indies were in a strong position after the first day, only to fold yet again, losing seven wickets for 43, five to Vaas. In reply, Sri Lanka amassed their second-highest total, led by Tillekeratne, whose first Test double-century lasted nine hours Then, despite Lara's second hundred, West Indies capitulated again after passing 200 with only three wickets down: this time, the last seven tumbled for 59. Lara passed 7,000 runs in Tests during his fourth double-century, while his captain, Hooper, collected his 100th wicket – no-one had previously needed as many balls (12,073) or Tests (90). Going into the last day, the deficit was only 92, with eight wickets standing. Most other teams would have escaped with a draw, but West Indies were never far away from collapse, and another followed once Sarwan was caught behind. Appropriately, Vaas – who had earlier inflicted a third consecutive duck on Gayle – finished off the innings with four wickets in nine balls.

West Indies

D. Ganga lbw b Vaas	6	– lbw b Vaas	10
C. H. Gayle c Sangakkara b Vaas	0	– c Jayawardene b Vaas	0
R. R. Sarwan run out	69	– c Sangakkara b Vaas	66
B. C. Lara b Vaas	221	– b Zoysa	130
*C. L. Hooper lbw b Vaas	56	– st Sangakkara b Muralitharan	9
M. N. Samuels lbw b Vaas	4	– c Jayawardene b Muralitharan	0
†R. D. Jacobs b Zoysa	2	– not out	31
M. Dillon lbw b Vaas	2	– c sub (U. D. U. Chandana) b Vaas	8
D. Ramnarine c Jayawardene b Muralitharan	0	– lbw b Vaas	0
P. T. Collins c Samaraweera b Vaas	4	– lbw b Vaas	0
M. I. Black not out	0	– lbw b Vaas	0
B 5, l-b 7, n-b 14	26	B 4, l-b 1, n-b 3	8

1/2 (2) 2/17 (1) 3/211 (3) 4/347 (5)   **390**
5/359 (6) 6/368 (7) 7/376 (8)
8/385 (4) 9/389 (9) 10/390 (10)

1/1 (2) 2/20 (1) 3/161 (3)   **262**
4/203 (5) 5/203 (6) 6/240 (4)
7/258 (8) 8/258 (9) 9/262 (10) 10/262 (11)

Vaas 32.2–5–120–7; Zoysa 20–4–55–1; Samaraweera 8–0–31–0; Bandaratilleke 9–2–37–0; Muralitharan 37–6–115–1; Jayasuriya 3–0–11–0; Arnold 3–0–8–0; Tillekeratne 1–0–1–0. *Second Innings*—Vaas 25–3–71–7; Zoysa 11–1–45–1; Muralitharan 36–5–116–2; Samaraweera 8–2–23–0; Bandaratilleke 2–0–2–0.

Sri Lanka

M. S. Atapattu c Gayle b Collins	4	– not out	19
*S. T. Jayasuriya c Ramnarine b Black	85	– not out	8
†K. C. Sangakkara c Gayle b Dillon	55		
D. P. M. D. Jayawardene lbw b Dillon	39		
R. P. Arnold c Jacobs b Hooper	65		
H. P. Tillekeratne not out	204		
T. T. Samaraweera run out	87		
W. P. U. J. C. Vaas c Samuels b Collins	23		
D. N. T. Zoysa b Hooper	10		
M. R. C. N. Bandaratilleke c Jacobs b Collins	25		
M. Muralitharan not out	4		
B 5, l-b 14, w 2, n-b 5	26		

1/5 (1) 2/104 (3) 3/179 (2)   (9 wkts dec.) **627**
4/204 (4) 5/345 (5) 6/510 (7)
7/550 (8) 8/569 (9) 9/611 (10)

(no wkt) **27**

Dillon 46–9–131–2; Collins 47–4–156–3; Black 32–6–123–1; Ramnarine 17–3–51–0; Hooper 43–7–112–2; Gayle 10–1–28–0; Sarwan 2–0–7–0. *Second Innings*—Dillon 3–0–12–0; Collins 2.3–0–15–0.

Umpires: E. A. R. de Silva *(Sri Lanka)* (8) and R. B. Tiffin *(Zimbabwe)* (23).
Third umpire: M. G. Silva *(Sri Lanka)*.   Referee: R. Subba Row *(England)* (41).

Close of play: First day, West Indies 327-3 (Lara 178, Hooper 52); Second day, Sri Lanka 193-3 (Jayawardene 32, Arnold 10); Third day, Sri Lanka 477-5 (Tillekeratne 143, Samaraweera 68); Fourth day, West Indies 145-2 (Sarwan 57, Lara 76).

INDIA v ENGLAND 2001–02 (1st Test)

At Punjab C. A. Stadium, Mohali, Chandigarh, on 3, 4, 5, 6 December.
Toss: India.   Result: INDIA won by ten wickets.
Debuts: India – S. B. Bangar, I. R. Siddiqui, T. Yohannan. England – R. K. J. Dawson, J. S. Foster.
Man of the Match: A. Kumble.

When they raced to 200 for 3 inside two sessions, with Hussain eyeing a century in the first Test innings in the land of his birth, England seemed to be in charge, even though Butcher had been dismissed by the fourth ball of the series. But when Hussain was caught at silly point England's well-being departed, and Kumble and Harbhajan Singh took control. In 25 overs, the last seven wickets were surrendered for 38: Harbhajan's final spell of 7.3 overs brought five wickets for six runs. England's bowlers responded manfully, but for scant reward. Their only victims on the second day were the nightwatchman, Kumble (a first Test wicket with his 12th ball for offspinner Richard Dawson) and Dasgupta, India's sixth wicketkeeper in a year, whose maiden Test hundred in his third match was a masterpiece of self-denial. India didn't waste their advantage. Tendulkar's unflustered 88 brought gasps of admiration from the bowlers, as well as the usual idolatry from the stands. His on-driving, in particular, was exquisite. India's 469 took the best part of two days. On the third evening, England survived their first taste of Test batting under floodlights, if only for seven overs. Next day they were dazzled by Kumble, whose six wickets removed fears that a recent shoulder operation had reduced his powers. Once Ganguly belatedly bowled them in tandem his spinners tore England apart: the last seven wickets clattered in 22 overs. Kumble and Harbhajan finished with 15 wickets between them.

England

M. A. Butcher c Laxman b Yohannan	4	– c sub (J. J. Martin) b Yohannan	18
M. E. Trescothick b Yohannan	66	– c Siddiqui b Yohannan	46
*N. Hussain c Laxman b Kumble	85	– b Kumble	12
G. P. Thorpe c Laxman b Siddiqui	23	– c and b Kumble	62
M. R. Ramprakash c Das b Harbhajan Singh	17	– lbw b Kumble	28
A. Flintoff c Kumble b Harbhajan Singh	18	– c Ganguly b Kumble	4
C. White c Dravid b Kumble	5	– c Dasgupta b Harbhajan Singh	22
†J. S. Foster lbw b Harbhajan Singh	0	– lbw b Harbhajan Singh	5
J. Ormond not out	3	– b Kumble	0
R. K. J. Dawson c Laxman b Harbhajan Singh	5	– b Kumble	11
M. J. Hoggard c sub (C. C. Williams) b Harbhajan Singh	0	– not out	0
L-b 7, n-b 5	12	B 10, l-b 13, w 1, n-b 3	27

1/4 (1) 2/129 (2) 3/172 (4) 4/200 (3)   238   1/68 (1) 2/82 (2) 3/87 (3)   235
5/224 (5) 6/227 (6) 7/229 (8)   4/159 (5) 5/163 (6) 6/196 (7)
8/229 (7) 9/238 (10) 10/238 (11)   7/206 (8) 8/207 (9) 9/224 (4) 10/235 (10)

Yohannan 18–3–75–2; Siddiqui 11–2–32–1; Bangar 5–2–17–0; Kumble 19–6–52–2; Tendulkar 4–3–4–0; Harbhajan Singh 19.3–4–51–5. *Second Innings*—Yohannan 17–3–56–2; Siddiqui 8–3–16–0; Kumble 28.4–6–81–6; Harbhajan Singh 24–9–59–2.

India

S. S. Das b Butcher	2		
†D. Dasgupta b White	100	– not out	0
A. Kumble c Foster b Dawson	37		
R. Dravid lbw b Ormond	86		
S. R. Tendulkar c Foster b Hoggard	88		
*S. C. Ganguly c Thorpe b Hoggard	47		
V. V. S. Laxman c Hussain b Dawson	28		
S. B. Bangar c and b Dawson	36		
Harbhajan Singh lbw b Dawson	1		
I.R. Siddiqui b Hoggard	24	– (1) not out	5
T. Yohannan not out	2		
L-b 12, w 2, n-b 4	18		

1/23 (1) 2/76 (3) 3/212 (2) 4/290 (4)   469   (no wkt) 5
5/370 (5) 6/378 (6) 7/430 (7)
8/436 (9) 9/449 (8) 10/469 (10)

Hoggard 32–9–98–3; Ormond 28–8–70–1; Butcher 7–1–19–1; Flintoff 34–11–80–0; White 25–8–56–1; Dawson 43–6–134–4. *Second Innings*—Hoggard 0.2–0–5–0.

Umpires: S. A. Bucknor *(West Indies)* (63) and S. Venkataraghavan *(India)* (48).
Third umpire: K. Murali *(India).*   Referee: D. T. Lindsay *(South Africa)* (5).

Close of play: First day, India 24-1 (Dasgupta 19, Kumble 1); Second day, India 262-3 (Dravid 78, Tendulkar 31); Third day, England 34-0 (Butcher 11, Trescothick 16).

INDIA v ENGLAND 2001–02 (2nd Test)

At Sardar Patel Stadium, Motera, Ahmedabad, on 11, 12, 13, 14, 15 December.
Toss: England.   Result: MATCH DRAWN.
Debuts: none.
Man of the Match: C. White.

Even without Thorpe, who decided only hours before the start to fly home for family reasons, England dominated large tracts of the match, but ultimately lacked the firepower to force the victory that would have levelled the series. Hussain, wary of the damage that Tendulkar, in particular, might inflict on his inexperienced attack, did not chance a declaration, leaving India's batsmen just over a day to negotiate. On a comatose pitch that had failed to offer the expected sharp turn, they did so with ease. Hussain had won the toss for the first time since the Lahore Test, 13 months before, and Trescothick and Butcher celebrated with a positive opening stand of 124. Butcher's eventual dismissal was the first of ten in the match for Kumble, which took him to 299 Test wickets. Hussain, lbw to a ball snaking down leg, and Vaughan, given out caught off bat and pad, were both left cursing umpire Robinson. With Flintoff's technique against spin proving hopelessly unsubtle, England needed a maiden century from White – in his 23rd Test 7½ years after his debut – to pass 400. They then claimed a lead of 116, largely thanks to Giles who, beset by heel and Achilles problems, trundled up to the crease like an old wheelie bin, but claimed a Test-best 5 for 67 from 43.3 overs in sapping heat. He had bowled only 17 overs since July. Earlier, the crowd had hero-worshipped Tendulkar towards an impressive hundred, his 27th in Tests.

England

M. A. Butcher c Dasgupta b Kumble	51	– c Dravid b Harbhajan Singh	92
M. E. Trescothick c Dasgupta b Kumble	99	– c Das b Srinath	12
*N. Hussain lbw b Kumble	1	– c Sehwag b Harbhajan Singh	50
M. P. Vaughan c Sehwag b Kumble	11	– (7) not out	31
M. R. Ramprakash b Tendulkar	37	– (4) c Tendulkar b Harbhajan Singh	19
A. Flintoff c Laxman b Kumble	0	– (5) b Kumble	4
C. White b Harbhajan Singh	121	– (6) run out	18
†J. S. Foster c Tendulkar b Kumble	40	– c Yohannan b Kumble	3
A. F. Giles b Kumble	7	– c Das b Harbhajan Singh	8
R. K. J. Dawson c Dasgupta b Srinath	9	– c Tendulkar b Kumble	2
M. J. Hoggard not out	4	– c Das b Harbhajan Singh	1
B 6, l-b 15; w 1, n-b 5	27	B 6, l-b 8, n-b 3	17

1/124 (1) 2/144 (3) 3/172 (4) 4/176 (2)   407   1/21 (2) 2/133 (3) 3/178 (4)   257
5/180 (6) 6/239 (5) 7/344 (8)   4/183 (5) 5/183 (1) 6/225 (6)
8/360 (9) 9/391 (10) 10/407 (7)   7/231 (8) 8/247 (9) 9/253 (10) 10/257 (11)

Srinath 29–7–105–1; Yohannan 17–2–57–0; Harbhajan Singh 35.3–9–78–1; Kumble 51–13–115–7; Tendulkar 10–0–27–1; Sehwag 2–1–4–0. *Second Innings*—Srinath 9–2–24–1; Yohannan 4–0–25–0; Kumble 38–5–118–3; Harbhajan Singh 30.2–6–71–5; Sehwag 2–0–5–0.

India

S. S. Das c Butcher b Flintoff	41	– run out	58
†D. Dasgupta c Hussain b Giles	17	– c Butcher b Dawson	60
R. Dravid c Foster b Hoggard	7	– not out	26
S. R. Tendulkar c Hussain b Hoggard	103	– c Vaughan b Dawson	26
*S. C. Ganguly c sub (M. C. J. Ball) b Flintoff	5	– not out	16
V. V. S. Laxman c Butcher b Giles	75		
V. Sehwag lbw b White	20		
A. Kumble b Giles	5		
Harbhajan Singh c Flintoff b Giles	0		
J. Srinath c Butcher b Giles	0		
T. Yohannan not out	3		
B 6, l-b 5, w 1, n-b 3	15	B 12	12

1/54 (2) 2/64 (1) 3/86 (3) 4/93 (5)   291   1/119 (1) 2/124 (2)   (3 wkts)   198
5/211 (4) 6/248 (7) 7/268 (8)   3/168 (4)
8/272 (9) 9/274 (10) 10/291 (6)

Hoggard 28–7–65–2; Flintoff 22–7–42–2; Giles 43.3–16–67–5; Dawson 15–0–73–0; White 12–2–33–1. *Second Innings*—Hoggard 17–6–33–0; Giles 31–12–57–0; Dawson 32–9–72–2; Flintoff 8–4–17–0; White 9–5–7–0.

Umpires: A. V. Jayaprakash *(India)* (11) and I. D. Robinson *(Zimbabwe)* (28).
Third umpire: Jasbir Singh *(India)*.   Referee: D. T. Lindsay *(South Africa)* (6).

Close of play: First day, England 277-6 (White 42, Foster 15); Second day, India 71-2 (Dravid 5, Tendulkar 2); Third day, England 15-0 (Butcher 5, Trescothick 10); Fourth day, India 17-0 (Das 11, Dasgupta 6).

INDIA v ENGLAND 2001–02 (3rd Test)

At M. Chinnaswamy Stadium, Bangalore, on 19, 20, 21, 22, 23 *(no play)* December.
Toss: England.   Result: MATCH DRAWN.
Debuts: none.
Man of the Match: A. Flintoff.   Man of the Series: S. R. Tendulkar.

Dank weather more Manchester than Bangalore initially encouraged England to think that they could still level the series. But overcast skies – floodlights were in use throughout – increasingly bore unseasonal rain. Hussain came in for much criticism for his negative bowling tactics against Tendulkar. He complained that an inexperienced team's attempts to compete in alien conditions deserved more support, but the spectacle of Flintoff (who conjured up memories of Bodyline by banging the ball in short from round the wicket) and Giles aiming outside Tendulkar's leg stump was not edifying. On the third morning, 90% of Giles's deliveries pitched outside leg, and Tendulkar padded away more than half. An ICC meeting in March agreed that such tactics should be discouraged, although they did eventually work here: Tendulkar was stumped for the first time in his 89 Tests. But his 90 had used up 263 minutes, time which England could ill afford. Earlier Kumble, in his 66th Test, had become the second Indian and the fourth spinner to reach 300 wickets, when he dismissed Hoggard. Vaughan was the seventh batsman to be out "handled the ball" in a Test, brushing the ball away when he missed a sweep at the off-spinner Sarandeep Singh. Flintoff slogged his fourth ball to midwicket, extending his miserable sequence to 26 runs in five innings, and it took another plucky innings from the improving Foster to lift England to 336. But then the rain, which allowed less than 16 overs during the last two days, ruined everything.

England

M. A. Butcher run out	27	– not out	23
M. E. Trescothick c Laxman b Srinath	8	– not out	9
*N. Hussain c Dasgupta b Srinath	43		
M. P. Vaughan handled the ball	64		
M. R. Ramprakash c Dravid b Sarandeep Singh	58		
A. Flintoff c Tendulkar b Sarandeep Singh	0		
C. White c Das b Srinath	39		
†J. S. Foster c Dasgupta b Srinath	48		
A. F. Giles lbw b Sarandeep Singh	28		
R. K. J. Dawson not out	0		
M. J. Hoggard lbw b Kumble	1		
B 8, l-b 9, n-b 3	20	B 1	1

1/21 (2) 2/68 (1) 3/93 (3) 4/206 (4)   **336**   (no wkt) **33**
5/206 (6) 6/219 (5) 7/271 (7)
8/334 (8) 9/334 (9) 10/336 (11)

Srinath 29–9–73–4; Ganguly 13–3–39–0; Kumble 29.3–6–74–1; Harbhajan Singh 27–7–59–0; Sarandeep Singh 21–5–54–3; Tendulkar 3–0–19–0; Sehwag 1–0–1–0. *Second Innings*—Srinath 4–0–19–0; Ganguly 3–0–12–0; Harbhajan Singh 0.1–0–1–0.

India

S. S. Das b Flintoff	28	Harbhajan Singh c Hussain b Hoggard	8
†D. Dasgupta c Trescothick b Flintoff	0	Sarandeep Singh run out	4
V. V. S. Laxman b Flintoff	12	J. Srinath not out	2
S. R. Tendulkar st Foster b Giles	90	B 4, l-b 4, n-b 3	11
R. Dravid c Foster b Hoggard	3		
*S. C. Ganguly c Butcher b Hoggard	0	1/8 (2) 2/22 (3) 3/88 (1) 4/121 (5)	**238**
V. Sehwag c Foster b Hoggard	66	5/121 (6) 6/173 (4) 7/218 (7)	
A. Kumble c Trescothick b Flintoff	14	8/228 (8) 9/235 (9) 10/238 (10)	

Hoggard 24.3–7–80–4; Flintoff 28–9–50–4; Giles 34–18–74–1; White 8–2–26–0.

Umpires: E. A. R. de Silva *(Sri Lanka)* (9) and A. V. Jayaprakash *(India)* (12).
Third umpire: F. Gomes *(India)*.   Referee: D. T. Lindsay *(South Africa)* (7).

Close of play: First day, England 255-6 (White 30, Foster 14); Second day, India 99-3 (Tendulkar 50, Dravid 1); Third day, India 218-7 (Kumble 10, Harbhajan Singh 0); Fourth day, England 33-0 (Butcher 23, Trescothick 9).

AUSTRALIA v SOUTH AFRICA 2001–02 (1st Test)

At Adelaide Oval on 14, 15, 16, 17, 18 December.
Toss: Australia.   Result: AUSTRALIA won by 246 runs.
Debuts: none.
Man of the Match: S. K. Warne.

After a drawn series against New Zealand, Steve Waugh entered this match with the objective of proving Australia were "still a very good cricket side". They accomplished it with ease and a session to spare, although South Africa's final capitulation made it look a little too easy. Langer made his fourth century in five Tests, reaching it with a six off Henderson, but was then becalmed, spending 100 minutes over his last 14 runs. Both Waughs failed in their 100th Test together, but Martyn's first home Test century set up a total of 439. Without a three-hour stand of 141 between McKenzie and Boucher, South Africa's innings would have been a ragged affair, and the deficit far greater than 65. Batting became more difficult from the fourth morning, but Hayden was allowed to put on 181 at better than a run a minute with Mark Waugh. Steve Waugh gave South Africa 12 overs plus the last day to score 375. His men crowded the bat and attacked the stumps, hassling and hustling for a breakthrough. Both openers prodded anxiously to short leg, Kirsten from the fourth day's final delivery. The last morning was a rout. The tourists' doubts about the bounce showed in their diffident shots and non-shots. Kallis alone suggested permanence, steering his side from the ignominy of 74 for 8 to finish unbeaten after almost four hours. Warne's first-innings figures were the best by a legspinner at Adelaide since Richie Benaud's 5 for 96 against West Indies in 1960-61.

Australia

J. L. Langer c Pollock b Henderson	116	– c Boucher b Pollock		1
M. L. Hayden c Ntini b Klusener	31	– b Kallis		131
R. T. Ponting run out	54	– lbw b Kallis		25
M. E. Waugh c Boucher b Hayward	2	– c Boucher b Henderson		74
*S. R. Waugh c McKenzie b Henderson	8	– (6) c Pollock b Henderson		13
D. R. Martyn not out	124	– (7) not out		6
†A. C. Gilchrist c Hayward b Henderson	7	– (5) c McKenzie b Kallis		22
S. K. Warne b Klusener	41	– b Henderson		6
B. Lee c McKenzie b Hayward	32			
J. N. Gillespie c Boucher b Henderson	3			
G. D. McGrath b Hayward	5			
L-b 6, n-b 10	16	B 8, l-b 16, n-b 7		31

1/80 (2) 2/182 (3) 3/199 (4) 4/211 (5)   439   1/8 (1) 2/66 (3)   (7 wkts dec.) 309
5/238 (1) 6/248 (7) 7/332 (8)   3/247 (2) 4/273 (4)
8/409 (9) 9/434 (10) 10/439 (11)   5/291 (5) 6/303 (6) 7/309 (8)

Pollock 28–8–64–0; Hayward 31–5–108–3; Ntini 19–7–64–0; Kallis 16–1–37–0; Klusener 14–4–44–2; Henderson 33–4–116–4. *Second Innings*—Pollock 12–4–38–1; Hayward 10–0–32–0; Henderson 29.1–1–130–3; Kallis 15–2–45–3; Ntini 8–3–13–0; Klusener 4–0–27–0.

South Africa

H. H. Gibbs st Gilchrist b Warne	78	– c Langer b McGrath		9
G. Kirsten lbw b McGrath	47	– c Ponting b Warne		7
H. H. Dippenaar c Ponting b McGrath	4	– c Warne b McGrath		0
C. W. Henderson run out	30	– (9) c Ponting b Warne		3
J. H. Kallis lbw b McGrath	5	– (4) not out		65
N. D. McKenzie lbw b Martyn	87	– (5) lbw b McGrath		0
L. Klusener b Warne	22	– (6) c Warne b Gillespie		18
†M. V. Boucher c Langer b Warne	64	– (7) c Gilchrist b Gillespie		0
*S. M. Pollock c Gilchrist b Warne	0	– (8) c Ponting b Warne		1
M. Ntini c Ponting b Warne	9	– b Lee		4
M. Hayward not out	0	– c Gilchrist b Lee		12
B 8, l-b 9, n-b 11	28	B 4, l-b 1, w 1, n-b 3		9

1/87 (2) 2/93 (3) 3/155 (4) 4/178 (1)   374   1/12 (1) 2/17 (2) 3/21 (3) 4/21 (5)   128
5/178 (5) 6/214 (7) 7/355 (6)   5/54 (6) 6/58 (7) 7/67 (8) 8/74 (9)
8/356 (9) 9/365 (8) 10/374 (10)   9/113 (10) 10/128 (11)

McGrath 33–10–94–3; Gillespie 23–7–57–0; Warne 39.4–9–113–5; Lee 19–2–81–0; M. E. Waugh 3–0–9–0; Martyn 4–2–3–1. *Second Innings*—McGrath 14–8–13–3; Gillespie 11–4–23–2; Warne 29–7–57–3; Lee 12–3–29–2; Martyn 1–0–1–0.

Umpires: S. J. A. Taufel *(Australia)* (2) and S. Venkataraghavan *(India)* (49).
Third umpire: S. J. Davis *(Australia)*.   Referee: R. S. Madugalle *(Sri Lanka)* (36).

Close of play: First day, Australia 272-6 (Martyn 37, Warne 7); Second day, South Africa 101-2 (Gibbs 42, Henderson 3); Third day, Australia 3-0 (Langer 0, Hayden 3); Fourth day, South Africa 17-2 (Dippenaar 0).

AUSTRALIA v SOUTH AFRICA 2001–02 (2nd Test)

At Melbourne Cricket Ground on 26, 27, 28, 29 December.
Toss: Australia.   Result: AUSTRALIA won by nine wickets.
Debuts: none.
Man of the Match: M. L. Hayden.

The South Africans were not merely beaten, but beaten into submission. Their grim, regimented cricket was brittle beside Australia's confident ebullience, and above all the indefatigable openers, Hayden and Langer. Kallis, dropped twice off Bichel, needed almost three hours to score 38, and was then adjudged caught behind, off Bichel again, from a ball he clearly missed; umpire Nicholls was deceived by the outswing once it passed the bat. Hayden and Langer were more positive in reply. Their first 50 materialised in 11 overs, and they marched to their third double-century stand of the season. Hayden's flawless 138 took him past Bob Simpson's Australian calendar-year record of 1,381 Test runs in 1964; Hayden finished 2001 with 1,391 at 63.22, including five centuries. Steve Waugh was out in the nineties for the tenth time in Tests, a record. Beaten by Gibbs's direct hit, he did not see umpire Hair's raised finger, and was awaiting a replay when informed. He stayed for almost 20 seconds, apparently suggesting consulting the third umpire; the referee docked half his match fee. When McGrath fell in the first over of the fourth day, Australia had lost their last six wickets for 58 in 23 overs. But again only Kallis stood firm, despite an excellent pitch and sapping heat. Mark Waugh, in his 100th consecutive Test, took two slick catches at slip. Kallis batted more than 7½ hours in the match: a feat splendid in its defiance and disappointing in its loneliness.

South Africa

H. H. Gibbs c Ponting b McGrath	14	– c Gilchrist b Lee	21
G. Kirsten b McGrath	10	– c Ponting b Lee	10
H. H. Dippenaar c Hayden b Lee	26	– c Hayden b Warne	23
J. H. Kallis c Gilchrist b Bichel	38	– run out	99
N. D. McKenzie lbw b Lee	67	– c Gilchrist b Warne	12
L. Klusener c and b Bichel	0	– lbw b McGrath	7
†M. V. Boucher c Bichel b M. E. Waugh	43	– c M. E. Waugh b Warne	0
*S. M. Pollock not out	42	– run out	18
C. W. Henderson run out	5	– c M. E. Waugh b McGrath	16
A. A. Donald c Ponting b Lee	0	– b Bichel	7
M. Hayward c M. E. Waugh b Bichel	14	– not out	0
B 1, l-b 10, n-b 7	18	B 4, n-b 2	6

1/24 (1) 2/36 (2) 3/59 (3) 4/131 (4)   277   1/24 (2) 2/37 (1) 3/74 (3)   219
5/131 (6) 6/198 (7) 7/220 (5)   4/107 (5) 5/120 (6) 6/121 (7)
8/225 (9) 9/233 (10) 10/277 (11)   7/157 (8) 8/192 (9) 9/215 (10) 10/219 (4)

McGrath 26–8–70–2; Lee 31–10–77–3; Bichel 19.5–6–44–3; Warne 19–3–56–0; M. E. Waugh 8–1–19–1. *Second Innings*—McGrath 21–6–43–2; Lee 18–5–52–2; Warne 24–3–68–3; Bichel 12.1–0–52–1.

Australia

J. L. Langer c Klusener b Donald	85	– c Henderson b Pollock	7
M. L. Hayden c Donald b Henderson	138	– not out	3
R. T. Ponting c Kallis b Hayward	22	– not out	0
M. E. Waugh b Donald	34		
*S. R. Waugh run out	90		
D. R. Martyn c Kallis b Pollock	52		
†A. C. Gilchrist not out	30		
S. K. Warne c Kirsten b Donald	1		
B. Lee c McKenzie b Hayward	3		
A. J. Bichel c Boucher b Pollock	5		
G. D. McGrath lbw b Pollock	0		
L-b 17, w 1, n-b 9	27		

1/202 (1) 2/267 (3) 3/267 (2) 4/348 (4)   487   1/7 (1)   (1 wkt) 10
5/429 (5) 6/462 (6) 7/463 (8)
8/470 (9) 9/475 (10) 10/487 (11)

Donald 29–5–103–3; Pollock 31–3–84–3; Hayward 26–1–109–2; Kallis 17–3–55–0; Henderson 29–3–108–1; Klusener 7–1–11–0. *Second Innings*—Donald 2–0–4–0; Pollock 1–0–6–1.

Umpires: D. B. Hair *(Australia)* (42) and E. A. Nicholls *(West Indies)* (17).
Third umpire: R. L. Parry *(Australia)*.   Referee: R. S. Madugalle *(Sri Lanka)* (37).

Close of play: First day, South Africa 89-3 (Kallis 22, McKenzie 14); Second day, Australia 126-0 (Langer 67, Hayden 55); Third day, Australia 487-9 (Gilchrist 30, McGrath 0).

AUSTRALIA v SOUTH AFRICA 2001–02 (3rd Test)

At Sydney Cricket Ground on 2, 3, 4, 5 January.

Toss: Australia.   Result: AUSTRALIA won by ten wickets.

Debuts: South Africa – J. L. Ontong.

Men of the Match: M. L. Hayden and J. L. Langer.   Man of the Series: M. L. Hayden.

One of the most anticlimactic rubbers in memory ended in a whitewash. The result had been in little doubt since tea on the first day, when Australia were 215 without loss, with Hayden and Langer again set like concrete in their fourth double-century partnership in ten starts. Only Gordon Greenidge and Desmond Haynes had shared so many opening doubles in Tests, and they had taken 134 innings. Although five wickets fell in the final session, next day Martyn made 117 as the last four wickets added 198. South Africa's reply lasted only five balls longer than the Hayden–Langer stand, Australia benefiting from picking two spinners for the first time in the series. South Africa followed on, and looked like losing in three days when Lee whisked Gibbs's off stump away four overs after lunch – but then Kirsten and Dippenaar added 149 in 42 overs, which at least made Australia bat again. After the match Steve Waugh announced that his side would donate their prizemoney to victims of bushfires, which had burned out half a million hectares of forest around New South Wales during the Test. A selection row had dominated the preliminaries. Jacques Rudolph was lined up for his debut, but the day before the match Percy Sonn, South Africa's board president, insisted the place should go to a "player of colour", in accordance with a stated policy of promoting non-whites when opportunities arose. Justin Ontong did not disgrace himself, making some useful runs and running out Ponting.

Australia

J. L. Langer c McKenzie b Boje	126	– not out		30
M. L. Hayden c Kallis b Pollock	105	– not out		21
R. T. Ponting run out	14			
M. E. Waugh c Boucher b Donald	19			
*S. R. Waugh b Pollock	30			
D. R. Martyn c McKenzie b Boje	117			
†A. C. Gilchrist c Boucher b Kallis	34			
S. K. Warne b Pollock	37			
B. Lee b Boje	29			
S. C. G. MacGill c Henderson b Boje	20			
G. D. McGrath not out	1			
B 4, l-b 8, w 1, n-b 9	22	L-b 2, n-b 1		3

1/219 (2) 2/247 (3) 3/253 (1) 4/302 (5)   554   (no wkt) 54
5/308 (4) 6/356 (7) 7/439 (8)
8/502 (9) 9/542 (10) 10/554 (6)

Donald 31–6–119–1; Pollock 37–11–109–3; Kallis 22–1–129–1; Henderson 27–3–112–0; Boje 25.2–6–63–4; Ontong 2–0–10–0. *Second Innings*—Donald 3–0–12–0; Pollock 3–1–11–0; Boje 2.1–0–15–0; Henderson 2–0–14–0.

South Africa

H. H. Gibbs c M. E. Waugh b MacGill	32	– b Lee		10
G. Kirsten c Ponting b McGrath	18	– b MacGill		153
H. H. Dippenaar b McGrath	3	– c Ponting b MacGill		74
J. H. Kallis c Gilchrist b MacGill	4	– c Gilchrist b Warne		34
N. D. McKenzie b Warne	20	– c MacGill b Lee		38
J. L. Ontong lbw b Warne	9	– lbw b Warne		32
†M. V. Boucher c Ponting b Warne	35	– c Gilchrist b McGrath		27
*S. M. Pollock c Martyn b McGrath	6	– not out		61
N. Boje run out	7	– b MacGill		1
C. W. Henderson c McGrath b MacGill	9	– b MacGill		2
A. A. Donald not out	2	– c Lee b Warne		2
L-b 8, n-b 1	9	B 8, l-b 7, n-b 3		18

1/37 (2) 2/43 (3) 3/56 (4) 4/77 (1)   154   1/17 (1) 2/166 (3) 3/211 (4)   452
5/93 (5) 6/98 (6) 7/111 (8)   4/282 (5) 5/356 (6) 6/372 (2)
8/121 (9) 9/148 (7) 10/154 (10)   7/392 (7) 8/393 (9) 9/403 (10) 10/452 (11)

McGrath 17–6–35–3; Lee 6–2–13–0; MacGill 20.2–6–51–3; Warne 19–5–47–3. *Second Innings*—McGrath 28–5–95–1; Warne 42.5–8–132–3; Lee 19–5–62–2; MacGill 45–13–123–4; M. E. Waugh 6–1–14–0; Ponting 1–0–11–0.

Umpires: D. J. Harper *(Australia)* (16) and D. R. Shepherd *(England)* (58).
Third umpire: S. J. A. Taufel *(Australia)*.   Referee: R. S. Madugalle *(Sri Lanka)* (38).

Close of play: First day, Australia 308-5 (Martyn 1); Second day, South Africa 93-4 (McKenzie 20, Ontong 8); Third day, South Africa 209-2 (Kirsten 82, Kallis 32).

NEW ZEALAND v BANGLADESH 2001–02 (1st Test)

At Seddon Park, Hamilton, on 18 *(no play)*, 19 *(no play)*, 20, 21, 22 December.
Toss: Bangladesh.   Result: NEW ZEALAND won by an innings and 52 runs.
Debuts: Bangladesh – Sanwar Hossain.
Man of the Match: M. H. Richardson.

Rain washed out the first day and, just as Khaled Mashud was winning the toss, it returned to blight the second. However, each of the remaining days could be extended from 90 to 105 overs, and New Zealand still managed a comfortable victory in that time. They started badly, though, losing four quick wickets, including Vincent to the third ball of the match. Richardson and McMillan restored order with a stand of 190, watchful at first before accelerating. McMillan hit 18 fours and two sixes in a three-hour hundred, despite having damaged a hand in a taxi accident two days earlier. Once Fleming declared on the fourth morning, the critical question was whether Bangladesh would avoid the follow-on (which was 216 rather than 166 after the loss of the first two days). They made brisk progress, but the clatter of falling wickets was a constant accompaniment. Habibul Bashar and Sanwar Hossain made sprightly contributions, and Khaled Mahmud launched a belated onslaught, yet soon after tea Bangladesh fell 11 short. By the close, they were four wickets down again. On the last morning, Cairns, who had been bowling without conviction, returned to his best. Two years before, he had taken 7 for 27 here to set up victory over West Indies; this time, he claimed five wickets in 38 balls. Bangladesh lost their last six wickets for 18, Cairns finished with 7 for 53, and New Zealand had won inside seven sessions.

New Zealand

M. H. Richardsone c and b Mohammad Sharif 143	†A. C. Parore b Mohammad Sharif	20
L. Vincent c and b Mashrafe bin Mortaza 0	D. L. Vettori lbw b Khaled Mahmud	0
M. S. Sinclair c Khaled Mashud b Manjural Islam 7	S. E. Bond not out.	4

*S. P. Fleming c Khaled Mashud
            b Mashrafe bin Mortaza 4

B 2, l-b 18, w 5, n-b 328

N. J. Astle c Al Sahariar b Manjural Islam 5
C. D. McMillan c Manjural Islam
            b Mashrafe bin Mortaza 106
C. L. Cairns b Mohammad Sharif 48

1/1 (2) 2/19 (3) 3/29 (4)   (9 wkts dec.) 365
4/51 (5) 5/241 (6)
6/330 (7) 7/357 (1) 8/359 (9) 9/365 (8)

C. S. Martin did not bat.

Mashrafe bin Mortaza 27–3–100–3; Manjural Islam 18–5–66–2; Mohammad Sharif 20.1–2–114–3; Khaled Mahmud 9–0–40–1; Mohammad Ashraful 3–0–25–0.

Bangladesh

Javed Omar c Richardson b Cairns.	9	– lbw b Martin.	15
Al Sahariar c Sinclair b Bond.	15	– c Parore b Cairns	53
Habibul Bashar c Martin b Vettori	61	– c Parore b Cairns	1
Aminul Islam c Parore b Bond	14	– b Cairns	0
Mohammad Ashraful c Sinclair b Vettori.	1	– c sub (C. J. Drum) b Bond	6
Sanwar Hossain c Vincent b McMillan	45	– b Bond	12
*†Khaled Mashud c Bond b McMillan	6	– c Fleming b Cairns.	6
Khaled Mahmud c Richardson b Bond.	45	– c Sinclair b Cairns	6
Mohammad Sharif b Martin	0	– not out.	4
Mashrafe bin Mortaza lbw b Bond.	3	– c Vincent b Cairns	2
Manjural Islam not out	0	– c Fleming b Cairns.	1
L-b 1, n-b 5	6	L-b 4, n-b 4	8

1/24 (1) 2/32 (2) 3/92 (4) 4/95 (5)   205   1/39 (1) 2/42 (3) 3/42 (4)   108
5/121 (3) 6/146 (7) 7/155 (6)   4/68 (5) 5/90 (2) 6/98 (7)
8/156 (9) 9/204 (10) 10/205 (8)   7/98 (8) 8/104 (6) 9/107 (10) 10/108 (11)

Cairns 11–0–55–1; Bond 13.1–2–47–4; Martin 11–4–38–1; McMillan 8–1–39–2; Vettori 15–4–25–2. *Second Innings*—Cairns 18.2–2–53–7; Bond 15–4–28–2; Martin 4–1–6–1; Vettori 9–4–17–0.

Umpires: A. L. Hill *(New Zealand)* (1) and D. L. Orchard *(South Africa)* (26).
Third umpire: D. B. Cowie *(New Zealand)*.   Referee: B. N. Jarman *(Australia)* (24).

Close of play: First day, No play; Second day, No play; Third day, New Zealand 306-5 (Richardson 124, Cairns 40); Fourth day, Bangladesh 90-4 (Al Sahariar 53, Sanwar Hossain 7).

NEW ZEALAND v BANGLADESH 2001–02 (2nd Test)

At Basin Reserve, Wellington, on 26, 27 *(no play)*, 28, 29 December.
Toss: New Zealand.   Result: NEW ZEALAND won by an innings and 74 runs.
Debuts: none.
Man of the Match: C. D. McMillan.

Once again, rain made significant inroads, yet New Zealand still had time to win in style. After downpours so heavy that the groundstaff had to prepare the pitch under a tent, it was little surprise that it was sluggish. Fleming predictably inserted Bangladesh, whose batsmen had been instructed by their coach, Trevor Chappell, to occupy the crease for longer, and to measure success in terms of time rather than runs. He would not have been pleased to see his top three still playing as if late for an urgent engagement; all fell to rash shots as Bangladesh folded again for 132. Yet more rain meant no play on the second day, and a delayed start to the third, which brought about eccentric playing hours of one o'clock till eight. By lunch (at 3 pm), New Zealand were 117 for one; after that, the runs flowed, allowing Fleming to declare 209 ahead and invite his bowlers to make a quick kill before the sun dipped on a midsummer's evening. By the close, 24 overs later, the top order had already been ripped out. Resuming at 67 for 5, Bangladesh lasted just over an hour. Bond soon took his fourth wicket, and Fleming gave him plenty of time to take five for the first time in Tests, but Mashrafe bin Mortaza responded by giving him plenty of hammer, including a straight six. It fell to Cairns to mop up. Again, New Zealand's comprehensive victory had taken less than seven sessions.

Bangladesh

Javed Omar c Vincent b Cairns	0	– lbw b Bond	12
Al Sahariar c Bond b Vettori	18	– c Horne b Bond	0
Habibul Bashar c Sinclair b Cairns	6	– lbw b Drum	32
Aminul Islam c Vincent b Bond	42	– c Vettori b Bond	4
Mohammad Ashraful c Fleming b Cairns	11	– lbw b Vettori	10
Sanwar Hossain run out	10	– b Bond	7
Khaled Mahmud c Parore b Drum	10	– run out	4
*†Khaled Mashud not out	10	– not out	19
Hasibul Hossain c Vincent b Drum	4	– c Parore b Vettori	7
Manjural Islam b Vettori	0	– (11) c Sinclair b Cairns	0
Mashrafe bin Mortaza run out	8	– (10) b Cairns	29
L-b 4, w 1, n-b 8	13	L-b 7, w 1, n-b 3	11

1/0 (1) 2/6 (3) 3/49 (2) 4/81 (5)   132   1/5 (2) 2/28 (1) 3/41 (4)   135
5/92 (4) 6/108 (6) 7/114 (7)   4/62 (3) 5/64 (5) 6/75 (7)
8/118 (9) 9/119 (10) 10/132 (11)   7/79 (6) 8/86 (9) 9/135 (10) 10/135 (11)

Cairns 15–7–24–3; Bond 13–4–21–1; Drum 11–1–26–2; Vettori 25–6–57–2. *Second Innings*—Cairns 6–1–27–2; Bond 15–5–54–4; Vettori 17–8–38–2; Drum 3–0–9–1.

New Zealand

M. H. Richardson c Mashrafe bin Mortaza b Hasibul Hossain	83	C. L. Cairns c Habibul Bashar b Manjural Islam	36
M. J. Horne c Khaled Mashud b Manjural Islam	38	B 1, l-b 6, w 1, n-b 3	11
L. Vincent c Khaled Mashud b Mashrafe bin Mortaza	23		
*S. P. Fleming c Khaled Mashud b Manjural Islam	61	1/104 (2) 2/148 (1) (6 wkts dec.) 341	
C. D. McMillan run out	70	3/153 (3) 4/283 (5)	
M. S. Sinclair not out	19	5/285 (4) 6/341 (7)	

†A. C. Parore, D. L. Vettori, S. E. Bond and C. J. Drum did not bat.

Mashrafe bin Mortaza 16–1–57–1; Manjural Islam 29–5–99–3; Hasibul Hossain 21–3–88–1; Aminul Islam 7–0–37–0; Khaled Mahmud 12–2–42–0; Mohammad Ashraful 3–0–11–0.

Umpires: B. F. Bowden *(New Zealand)* (2) and D. J. Harper *(Australia)* (15).
Third umpire: D. M. Quested *(New Zealand)*.   Referee: B. N. Jarman *(Australia)* (25).

Close of play: First day, New Zealand 72-0 (Richardson 38, Horne 30); Second day, No play; Third day, Bangladesh 67-5 (Sanwar Hossain 4, Khaled Mahmud 0).

SRI LANKA v ZIMBABWE 2001–02 (1st Test)

At Sinhalese Sports Club, Colombo, on 27, 28, 29, 31 December.
Toss: Zimbabwe.   Result: SRI LANKA won by an innings and 166 runs.
Debuts: none.
Man of the Match: K. C. Sangakkara.

On a bone-dry pitch which belied the ground's usual reputation for encouraging fast bowlers early on, Sri Lanka initially took their time on their way to a big score. Jayasuriya made an uncharacteristically watchful four-hour 92, and his side had pottered to 211 for 3 when bad light intervened after 74 overs. Zimbabwe's bowlers were less disciplined next day: 127 runs were plundered in the first session, 123 in the second. Sangakkara, who began on 62, struck seven fours to complete his century in 30 balls. Then Samaraweera took over, the next two wickets adding 266 at a run a minute before the declaration. By contrast, no Zimbabwean managed a half-century. In the first innings, they were bowled out inside 80 overs, with only Andy Flower approaching two hours at the crease. Following on 402 behind, they closed at 64 for 2 before a rest day, the first in a Test since West Indies and India paused for Good Friday at Bridgetown in 1997. The cause this time was a full moon, observed as a poya day (public holiday) by Buddhists. On resumption, Zimbabwe improved their performance slightly, thanks to a three-hour innings from Friend, the nightwatchman. An hour's rain merely delayed Sri Lanka's sixth successive victory, the margin being their then-biggest in Tests. Muralitharan finished with eight wickets in the match, which took him to 80 from 12 Tests in 2001; only Dennis Lillee, with 85 from 13 Tests in 1981, had taken more in a calendar year.

Sri Lanka

M. S. Atapattu c A. Flower b Streak	25	T. T. Samaraweera not out	123
*S. T. Jayasuriya c A. Flower b Gripper	92	W. P. U. J. C. Vaas not out	74
†K. C. Sangakkara c Wishart b Brent	128	B 2, l-b 4, w 3, n-b 8	17
D. P. M. D. Jayawardene c Carlisle b Gripper	18		
R. P. Arnold lbw b Streak	13	1/78 (1) 2/150 (2) (6 wkts dec.)	586
H. P. Tillekeratne c A. Flower b Streak	96	3/170 (4) 4/249 (5)	
		5/320 (3) 6/450 (6)	

D. N. T. Zoysa, T. C. B. Fernando and M. Muralitharan did not bat.

Streak 34–5–113–3; Friend 27–5–102–0; Olonga 23–3–103–0; Brent 33–5–82–1; Gripper 22–3–91–2; G. W. Flower 22–3–89–0.

Zimbabwe

H. Masakadza c Tillekeratne b Zoysa	3	– c Atapattu b Muralitharan	28
T. R. Gripper c Jayawardene b Muralitharan	30	– c Sangakkara b Muralitharan	10
*S. V. Carlisle c Jayasuriya b Vaas	10	– c Sangakkara b Fernando	32
G. J. Rennie lbw b Muralitharan	35	– c Jayawardene b Fernando	4
†A. Flower b Samaraweera	42	– (6) lbw b Zoysa	10
G. W. Flower c Tillekeratne b Muralitharan	0	– (7) c Tillekeratne b Muralitharan	18
C. B. Wishart c Tillekeratne b Zoysa	21	– (8) c Tillekeratne b Samaraweera	27
H. H. Streak not out	26	– (9) not out	36
T. J. Friend lbw b Vaas	6	– (4) b Muralitharan	44
G. B. Brent b Muralitharan	0	– c Jayasuriya b Zoysa	7
H. K. Olonga lbw b Fernando	4	– c Sangakkara b Vaas	0
L-b 1, n-b 6	7	B 4, l-b 7, n-b 9	20

1/3 (1) 2/29 (3) 3/60 (2) 4/89 (4)	184	1/40 (1) 2/58 (2) 3/93 (3)	236
5/105 (6) 6/146 (7) 7/146 (5)		4/105 (5) 5/127 (6) 6/145 (4)	
8/166 (9) 9/167 (10) 10/184 (11)		7/165 (7) 8/197 (8) 9/235 (10) 10/236 (11)	

Vaas 24–6–63–2; Zoysa 14–6–24–2; Muralitharan 26–8–53–4; Jayasuriya 1–0–4–0; Fernando 9.5–0–32–1; Samaraweera 5–1–7–1. *Second Innings*—Vaas 21.2–6–76–1; Zoysa 15–4–34–2; Fernando 15–3–48–2; Muralitharan 36–17–35–4; Jayasuriya 7–3–22–0; Samaraweera 7–2–10–1.

Umpires: P. T. Manuel *(Sri Lanka)* (11) and Riazuddin *(Pakistan)* (11).
Third umpire: T. H. Wijewardene *(Sri Lanka)*.   Referee: C. W. Smith *(West Indies)* (37).

Close of play: First day, Sri Lanka 211-3 (Sangakkara 62, Arnold 4); Second day, Zimbabwe 14-1 (Gripper 4, Carlisle 6); Third day, Zimbabwe 64-2 (Carlisle 22, Friend 0).

SRI LANKA v ZIMBABWE 2001–02 (2nd Test)

At Asgiriya Stadium, Kandy, on 4, 5, 6, 7 January.
Toss: Zimbabwe. Result: SRI LANKA won by an innings and 94 runs.
Debuts: none.
Man of the Match: M. Muralitharan.

Muttiah Muralitharan came agonisingly close to the best innings figures in Test history. By the first evening he had taken 9 for 51 from 39 overs, with one wicket to fall. Next morning, Friend offered a regulation bat-pad catch off Murali's first ball, only for Arnold to drop it; then an lbw appeal was turned down. At the other end, Vaas bowled wide of off stump to Olonga, but could not stop him nicking one, which Sangakkara could not bring himself to drop. If Murali had taken that wicket, he would have beaten Jim Laker's 10 for 53 against Australia in 1956. As it was, he had to be content with the fifth-best analysis in Test cricket. Zimbabwe had claimed first use of a true pitch, but Murali was soon whisking through their line-up in front of his home crowd. He came on in the ninth over, and Gripper edged his second ball to slip. He bowled Masakadza in his third over, had Rennie stumped in his fifth, and Andy Flower caught behind in his seventh. Sri Lanka put the disappointment behind them, rattling along at four an over as Jayasuriya raced to his ninth Test hundred. Zimbabwe started again 269 behind and, by the end of the third day, had lost three more wickets – one of them, almost inevitably, to Muralitharan, who thus took ten in a match for the tenth time, beating Richard Hadlee's Test record of nine – and Sri Lanka glided to another innings victory next day.

Zimbabwe

H. Masakadza b Muralitharan	10	– b Vaas	0
T. R. Gripper c Jayawardene b Muralitharan	20	– lbw b Muralitharan	21
*S. V. Carlisle lbw b Muralitharan	20	– c Atapattu b Vaas	9
G. J. Rennie st Sangakkara b Muralitharan	0	– lbw b Fernando	68
†A. Flower c Sangakkara b Muralitharan	8	– lbw b Fernando	11
G. W. Flower b Muralitharan	72	– c Sangakkara b Fernando	21
C. B. Wishart lbw b Muralitharan	26	– c Jayasuriya b Muralitharan	3
H. H. Streak b Muralitharan	1	– not out	14
D. A. Marillier b Muralitharan	8	– lbw b Muralitharan	9
T. J. Friend not out	29	– b Fernando	0
H. K. Olonga c Sangakkara b Vaas	18	– c Samaraweera b Muralitharan	1
B 3, l-b 7, n-b 14	24	L-b 6, n-b 12	18

1/39 (2) 2/45 (1) 3/51 (4) 4/67 (5)　236　1/0 (1) 2/16 (3) 3/51 (2)　175
5/83 (3) 6/137 (7) 7/140 (8)　4/109 (5) 5/134 (4) 6/138 (7)
8/166 (9) 9/201 (6) 10/236 (11)　7/160 (6) 8/173 (9) 9/174 (10) 10/175 (11)

Vaas 17–4–58–1; Zoysa 15–2–44–0; Muralitharan 40–19–51–9; Fernando 5–2–13–0; Samaraweera 8–2–33–0; Jayasuriya 12–3–27–0. *Second Innings*—Vaas 18–5–35–2; Zoysa 10–1–30–0; Muralitharan 26.4–7–64–4; Samaraweera 4–2–2–0; Tillekeratne 1–0–8–0; Jayasuriya 1–0–3–0; Fernando 12–2–27–4.

Sri Lanka

M. S. Atapattu lbw b Friend	9	T. C. B. Fernando c Friend b Masakadza	45
*S. T. Jayasuriya c Gripper b G. W. Flower	139	D. N. T. Zoysa run out	4
†K. C. Sangakkara hit wkt b Friend	42	M. Muralitharan b Streak	1
D. P. M. D. Jayawardene lbw b G. W. Flower	56		
R. P. Arnold c Wishart b G. W. Flower	71	B 3, l-b 1, w 1, n-b 7	12
H. P. Tillekeratne lbw b Streak	37		
T. T. Samaraweera c A. Flower b Friend	17	1/11 (1) 2/82 (3) 3/202 (4)	505
W. P. U. J. C. Vaas not out	72	4/273 (2) 5/336 (6) 6/365 (7) 7/388 (5)	
		8/499 (9) 9/503 (10) 10/505 (11)	

Streak 32.5–7–85–2; Friend 26–4–97–3; Olonga 24–2–131–0; Marillier 21–4–75–0; G. W. Flower 28–4–66–3; Gripper 14–3–38–0; Masakadza 3–0–9–1.

Umpires: E. A. R. de Silva *(Sri Lanka)* (10) and S. Venkataraghavan *(India)* (50).
Third umpire: P. T. Manuel *(Sri Lanka).*　Referee: C. W. Smith *(West Indies)* (38).

Close of play: First day, Zimbabwe 234-9 (Friend 28, Olonga 17); Second day, Sri Lanka 334-4 (Arnold 44, Tillekeratne 35); Third day, Zimbabwe 68-3 (Rennie 26, A. Flower 6).

SRI LANKA v ZIMBABWE 2001–02 (3rd Test)

At Galle International Stadium on 12, 13, 14, 15 January.
Toss: Sri Lanka.   Result: SRI LANKA won by 315 runs.
Debuts: none.
Man of the Match: S. T. Jayasuriya.   Man of the Series: M. Muralitharan.

Muralitharan entered the match needing five wickets to become the seventh bowler– and the second spinner, after Shane Warne – to reach 400 Test wickets. But he had to wait until the fourth morning, as Zimbabwe played their best cricket of the series during the first three days. At first, they seemed to have the measure of the home batsmen; when Streak trapped Vaas on the second morning, they had captured the first seven wickets for 254, with part-time spinners Grant Flower and Marillier doing much of the damage. But Samaraweera and Chandana added 146, an eighth-wicket record for Sri Lanka in Tests at the time. Samaraweera took his average after eight Tests to 103.00 – not bad for a player selected largely for his bowling. Zimbabwe's batsmen also showed more resolve. Carlisle and Gripper put on 153 in 81 overs, patiently demonstrating that Murali could be played off the front foot. On the fourth day, however, they fell apart spectacularly. The last five wickets added only four runs: Jayasuriya claimed his first five-for, but the crowd got what they really wanted when Murali reached 400 by bowling Friend and Olonga with successive balls. He had got there in 72 Tests, trimming eight off Richard Hadlee's record, and at 29 years 273 days was also the youngest to do so (Warne was almost 32). Zimbabwe collapsed again in their second innings. Jayasuriya and Muralitharan continued to share the spoils, shooting them out for their second-lowest total in Tests inside 44 overs.

Sri Lanka

M. S. Atapattu c Rennie b G. W. Flower	50	– not out		100
*S. T. Jayasuriya b Friend	28	– c Wishart b Olonga		36
†K. C. Sangakkara b Marillier	29	– c Gripper b Friend		56
D. P. M. D. Jayawardene c and b G. W. Flower	76	– not out		17
R. P. Arnold c A. Flower b Streak	40			
H. P. Tillekeratne c A. Flower b Marillier	3			
T. T. Samaraweera run out	76			
W. P. U. J. C. Vaas lbw b Streak	8			
U. D. U. Chandana c Carlisle b Marillier	92			
T. C. B. Fernando b Marillier	1			
M. Muralitharan not out	5			
B 2, l-b 5, n-b 3	10	L-b 1, n-b 2		3

1/50 (2) 2/107 (1) 3/125 (3) 4/222 (4)   418   1/75 (2) 2/170 (3)   (2 wkts dec.) 212
5/229 (6) 6/236 (5) 7/254 (8)
8/400 (9) 9/413 (7) 10/418 (10)

Streak 32–11–70–2; Friend 26–7–58–1; Olonga 18–6–52–0; G. W. Flower 39–7–89–2; Marillier 34.4–5–101–4; Gripper 9–0–41–0. *Second Innings*—Streak 11–1–35–0; Friend 7–0–39–1; G. W. Flower 9–0–38–0; Marillier 6–0–34–0; Olonga 7–0–56–1; Rennie 1–0–9–0.

Zimbabwe

*S. V. Carlisle lbw b Muralitharan	64	– lbw b Jayasuriya		28
T. R. Gripper st Sangakkara b Jayasuriya	83	– lbw b Jayasuriya		3
C. B. Wishart lbw b Jayasuriya	1	– c Samaraweera b Muralitharan		7
G. J. Rennie c Sangakkara b Jayasuriya	7	– c Arnold b Muralitharan		6
†A. Flower c Tillekeratne b Muralitharan	6	– c Jayawardene b Jayasuriya		3
G. W. Flower lbw b Muralitharan	19	– lbw b Jayasuriya		0
H. H. Streak b Jayasuriya	33	– c Jayasuriya b Muralitharan		7
D. D. Ebrahim c Arnold b Jayasuriya	1	– not out		5
D. A. Marillier not out	0	– c and b Muralitharan		15
T. J. Friend b Muralitharan	1	– lbw b Vaas		3
H. K. Olonga b Muralitharan	0	– c Fernando b Vaas		0
B 11, l-b 8, n-b 2	21	L-b 1, n-b 1		2

1/153 (2) 2/155 (3) 3/161 (1) 4/171 (4)   236   1/17 (2) 2/30 (3) 3/38 (4)   79
5/171 (5) 6/232 (6) 7/234 (7)   4/45 (5) 5/45 (6) 6/54 (1)
8/235 (8) 9/236 (10) 10/236 (11)   7/56 (7) 8/72 (9) 9/79 (10) 10/79 (11)

Vaas 19–7–36–0; Fernando 11–1–33–0; Muralitharan 58.3–26–67–5; Jayasuriya 29–10–43–5; Chandana 12–4–24–0; Samaraweera 5–1–14–0. *Second Innings*—Vaas 7.3–2–17–2; Fernando 2–0–6–0; Jayasuriya 18–5–31–4; Muralitharan 16–7–24–4.

Umpires: D. R. Shepherd *(England)* (59) and T. H. Wijewardene *(Sri Lanka)* (2).
Third umpire: M. G. Silva *(Sri Lanka)*.   Referee: C. W. Smith *(West Indies)* (39).

Close of play: First day, Sri Lanka 243-6 (Samaraweera 8, Vaas 2); Second day, Zimbabwe 18-0 (Carlisle 13, Gripper 3); Third day, Zimbabwe 230-5 (G. W. Flower 19, Streak 29).

BANGLADESH v PAKISTAN 2001–02 (1st Test)

At Bangabandhu National Stadium, Dhaka, on 9, 10, 11 January.
Toss: Pakistan.   Result: PAKISTAN won by an innings and 178 runs.
Debuts: Bangladesh – Fahim Muntasir.
Man of the Match: Abdul Razzaq.

From the first ball to the last, 25 minutes after tea on the third afternoon, Pakistan were firmly in control. The postponement of New Zealand's visit after the New York terrorist attacks of September 11 had meant a four-month break from Test cricket, but Pakistan looked refreshed rather than rusty. They picked up where they had left off, with another emphatic win over Bangladesh. Then, as now, Abdul Razzaq hit a rasping hundred and Danish Kaneria caused problems with his leg-spin. Bangladesh started well enough, reaching 140 for 3 – but then came the deluge. Waqar Younis blasted out the last six wickets for seven runs in 29 balls, his first five-for for almost four years. Pakistan's new opening pair, Taufeeq Umar and Shadab Kabir, raced to 100 in the 23rd over. Yousuf Youhana contributed a classy 72 but, at 221 for 5, there was a chance Bangladesh could steal back into the match. Instead, Razzaq and Rashid Latif put on 175. Needing a daunting 330 to avoid an innings defeat, Bangladesh enjoyed another encouraging start. The arrival of Kaneria, who bowled continuously from the sixth over, brought it to an abrupt end. He completely mesmerised the batsmen and finished with his best Test figures; in two matches against Bangladesh, he had taken 21 wickets at 9.85. Only the debutant Fahim Muntasir passed 22 – he hit Kaneria over long-on for six – but his spirited swing of the bat ultimately counted for little.

Bangladesh

Al Sahariar lbw b Abdul Razzaq	18	– (7) lbw b Waqar Younis		21
Mehrab Hossain, sen. c Shadab Kabir b Abdul Razzaq	11	– (1) c Inzamam-ul-Haq b Danish Kaneria		19
Mohammad Ashraful c Yousuf Youhana b Danish Kaneria	27	– (2) c Younis Khan b Abdul Razzaq		22
Habibul Bashar c Danish Kaneria b Waqar Younis	53	– (3) c Waqar Younis b Danish Kaneria		0
Aminul Islam lbw b Danish Kaneria	25	– (4) lbw b Abdul Razzaq		11
Sanwar Hossain c Inzamam-ul-Haq b Waqar Younis	3	– (5) c Shadab Kabir b Danish Kaneria		1
*†Khaled Mashud lbw b Waqar Younis	0	– (6) c Waqar Younis b Danish Kaneria		5
Enamul Haque, sen. c Inzamam-ul-Haq b Waqar Younis	12	– b Danish Kaneria		19
Fahim Muntasir b Waqar Younis	0	– c sub (Mohammad Sami) b Danish Kaneria		33
Mohammad Sharif b Waqar Younis	0	– c Waqar Younis b Danish Kaneria		11
Manjural Islam not out	0	– not out		2
L-b 8, w 1, n-b 2	11	L-b 5, n-b 3		8
	160			**152**

1/30 (2) 2/45 (1) 3/77 (3) 4/140 (5)   160   1/38 (1) 2/38 (3) 3/49 (2)   152
5/146 (4) 6/146 (7) 7/147 (6)   4/52 (5) 5/64 (4) 6/86 (6)
8/147 (9) 9/151 (10) 10/160 (8)   7/90 (7) 8/112 (8) 9/139 (10) 10/152 (9)

Wasim Akram 2.4–1–5–0; Waqar Younis 16.2–2–55–6; Abdul Razzaq 8.2–2–42–2; Danish Kaneria 19–5–36–2; Saqlain Mushtaq 7–2–14–0. *Second Innings*—Waqar Younis 9–3–27–1; Abdul Razzaq 10–2–29–2; Danish Kaneria 19.4–4–77–1; Saqlain Mushtaq 5–1–14–0.

Pakistan

Taufeeq Umar lbw b Mohammad Sharif	53
Shadab Kabir b Enamul Haque	55
Younis Khan c Khaled Mashud b Enamul Haque	0
Yousuf Youhana run out	72
Saqlain Mushtaq lbw b Enamul Haque	9
Abdul Razzaq c Aminul Islam b Manjural Islam	134
†Rashid Latif c Al Sahariar b Mohammad Sharif	94
Inzamam-ul-Haq c Mehrab Hossain b Enamul Haque	43
*Waqar Younis c Al Sahariar b Manjural Islam	8
Danish Kaneria not out	3
L-b 13, w 2, n-b 4	19
(9 wkts dec.)	**490**

1/100 (2) 2/100 (3)   (9 wkts dec.) 490
3/116 (1) 4/162 (5) 5/221 (4)
6/396 (7) 7/463 (6) 8/471 (9) 9/490 (8)

Wasim Akram did not bat.

Manjural Islam 33–4–124–2; Mohammad Sharif 35–9–95–2; Fahim Muntasir 32–6–109–0; Enamul Haque 39.4–9–136–4; Mohammad Ashraful 1–0–13–0.

Umpires: A. F. M. Akhtaruddin *(Bangladesh)* (2) and J. H. Hampshire *(England)* (21).
Third umpire: Mesbahuddin Ahmed *(Bangladesh)*.   Referee: B. F. Hastings *(New Zealand)* (9).

Close of play: First day, Pakistan 126-3 (Yousuf Youhana 14, Saqlain Mushtaq 1); Second day, Pakistan 436-6 (Abdul Razzaq 114, Inzamam-ul-Haq 22).

BANGLADESH v PAKISTAN 2001–02 (2nd Test)

At M. A. Aziz Stadium, Chittagong, on 16, 17, 18 January.
Toss: Bangladesh.   Result: PAKISTAN won by an innings and 169 runs.
Debuts: none.
Man of the Match: Yousuf Youhana.   Man of the Series: Danish Kaneria.

Play echoed the pattern of the previous Test, with Bangladesh subsiding inside two sessions, and Pakistan batting throughout the second day before declaring, over 300 ahead, on the third morning. Bangladesh's batsmen failed again, and they slumped to a fourth consecutive innings defeat, all of them within three days' cricket. After a confident start, Bangladesh lost wickets as the spinners proved difficult to read: Danish Kaneria claimed four scalps, while Saqlain Mushtaq, wicketless at Dhaka, took five. Bangladesh missed Mohammad Ashraful, one of their three Test centurions, who was in New Zealand for the Under-19 World Cup. By the close, Pakistan were just 49 behind. Next day belonged initially to Younis Khan, with a sparkling century, but he was eclipsed by Yousuf Youhana, who cut, drove and pulled to perfection, and reached his second Test double-century with a six off Mohammad Sharif. Bangladesh's deficit was still a shiver-inducing 317. The result was hardly in doubt, but they could have made Pakistan work for their wickets. Instead, their cavalier approach gave them away again: by the 12th over, they were 41 for 4. Habibul Bashar struck 51 in 49 balls to ward off abject humiliation, but the second innings lasted just three hours. Shoaib Akhtar made hay with four wickets, the last three coming in one over. Bangladesh made the same score in both innings, the seventh such instance in Tests, and the first since Sri Lanka made 306 twice against South Africa at Cape Town in 1997-98.

Bangladesh

Javed Omar c Shadab Kabir b Saqlain Mushtaq	17	– c Rashid Latif b Waqar Younis	0
Al Sahariar c Rashid Latif b Waqar Younis	13	– c Rashid Latif b Waqar Younis	8
Mehrab Hossain, sen. b Danish Kaneria	16	– c Rashid Latif b Waqar Younis	14
Habibul Bashar c Shadab Kabir b Saqlain Mushtaq	2	– (5) c Shadab Kabir b Saqlain Mushtaq	51
Aminul Islam c Yousuf Youhana b Danish Kaneria	25	– (4) b Shoaib Akhtar	2
Sanwar Hossain lbw b Saqlain Mushtaq	11	– c Younis Khan b Saqlain Mushtaq	30
Enamul Haque, sen. c Shadab Kabir b Danish Kaneria	0	– (8) b Shoaib Akhtar	9
*†Khaled Mashud c Taufeeq Umar b Saqlain Mushtaq	28		
Fahim Muntasir c Inzamam-ul-Haq b Danish Kaneria	9	– (7) not out	15
Mohammad Sharif st Rashid Latif b Saqlain Mushtaq	0	– b Shoaib Akhtar	2
Manjural Islam not out	4	– b Shoaib Akhtar	0
		– c Shadab Kabir b Waqar Younis	0
B 5, l-b 9, n-b 9	23	B 8, l-b 1, n-b 8	17
	148		**148**

1/21 (2) 2/57 (1) 3/60 (4) 4/65 (3)
5/84 (6) 6/85 (7) 7/112 (5)
8/126 (9) 9/127 (10) 10/148 (8)

1/0 (1) 2/23 (3) 3/24 (2)
4/41 (4) 5/110 (5) 6/128 (6)
7/144 (8) 8/147 (9) 9/147 (10) 10/148 (11)

Waqar Younis 7–2–19–1; Shoaib Akhtar 6–2–15–0; Danish Kaneria 22–6–62–4; Abdul Razzaq 5–2–3–0; Saqlain Mushtaq 16.4–3–35–5. *Second Innings*—Waqar Younis 8.5–0–36–4; Shoaib Akhtar 11–1–48–4; Saqlain Mushtaq 11–3–34–2; Abdul Razzaq 2–0–12–0; Danish Kaneria 6–3–9–0.

Pakistan

Taufeeq Umar c Aminul Islam b Mohammad Sharif	47	Shoaib Akhtar c Sanwar Hossain	
Shadab Kabir c Khaled Mashud b Mohammad Sharif	4	b Manjural Islam	2
Younis Khan c Mehrab Hossain b Fahim Muntasir	119	Danish Kaneria not out	4
Inzamam-ul-Haq c Aminul Islam b Fahim Muntasir	30	W 1, n-b 4	5
Yousuf Youhana not out	204		
Abdul Razzaq b Mohammad Sharif	18	1/12 (2) 2/99 (1) (9 wkts dec.)	**465**
†Rashid Latif lbw b Manjural Islam	15	3/166 (4) 4/236 (3) 5/274 (6)	
*Waqar Younis c Mehrab Hossain b Fahim Muntasir	10	6/315 (7) 7/339 (8) 8/438	
Saqlain Mushtaq c Aminul Islam b Mohammad Sharif	7	(9) 9/447 (10)	

Manjural Islam 35–9–95–2; Mohammad Sharif 35.5–10–98–4; Enamul Haque 33–6–114–0; Fahim Muntasir 27–3–131–3; Aminul Islam 4–0–27–0.

Umpires: Mahbubur Rahman *(Bangladesh)* (1) and R. B. Tiffin *(Zimbabwe)* (24).
Third umpire: Manzur Rahman *(Bangladesh)*.   Referee: B. F. Hastings *(New Zealand)* (10).

Close of play: First day, Pakistan 99-1 (Taufeeq Umar 47, Younis Khan 47); Second day, Pakistan 429-7 (Yousuf Youhana 174, Saqlain Mushtaq 7).

PAKISTAN v WEST INDIES 2001–02 (1st Test)

At Sharjah C. A. Stadium on 31 January, 1, 2, 3, 4 February.
Toss: Pakistan.   Result: PAKISTAN won by 170 runs.
Debuts: Pakistan – Naved Latif. West Indies – R. O. Hinds.
Man of the Match: Shoaib Akhtar.

After West Indies voiced concerns about playing in Pakistan, this series was relocated to Sharjah, which thus staged its first Test matches after 181 one-day internationals. These were the first Tests on neutral territory since the Triangular Tournament in England in 1912, apart from the final of the Asian Test Championship between Pakistan and Sri Lanka at Dhaka in 1998-99. The original itinerary included three Tests, but one was dropped because 15 days on the same ground was deemed impractical. There were also doubts about the durability of the pitches, but as it happened they played reasonably well. Although the bounce was slow and low, it was pace bowling of exceptional quality that proved decisive in the first match. Waqar Younis was outstanding, shooting out West Indies' lower half for 41 on the fourth morning, while Shoaib Akhtar and Abdul Razzaq wrecked them on the final day. West Indies, who dropped several chances, held the advantage when Pakistan were 178 for 5 late on the first day, but Yousuf Youhana and Rashid Latif (who made his maiden Test century; he later completed a century of dismissals) steadied the innings and went on to a matchwinning stand of 204 in just 57 overs. West Indies saved the follow-on with some ease, but collapsed in their second innings as Razzaq, repeatedly finding reverse swing, struck three times in an over. The last nine wickets tumbled for 56 runs in less than 23 overs.

Pakistan

Taufeeq Umar b Hooper	24	– run out	23
Naved Latif lbw b Dillon	0	– c Jacobs b Dillon	20
Younis Khan c Gayle b Hooper	53	– c Jacobs b Cuffy	32
Inzamam-ul-Haq c Jacobs b Dillon	10	– c Hooper b Dillon	48
Yousuf Youhana b Cuffy	146	– c Dillon b Cuffy	12
Abdul Razzaq c Jacobs b W. W. Hinds	34	– c Ganga b Collins	29
†Rashid Latif b Gayle	150	– not out	47
Saqlain Mushtaq c and b Dillon	17		
*Waqar Younis not out	25		
Shoaib Akhtar b Gayle	20		
Danish Kaneria c and b Gayle	0		
B 6, l-b 7, w 1	14	N-b 3	3

1/3 (2) 2/45 (1) 3/80 (4) 4/94 (3)   493   1/35 (2) 2/54 (1)   (6 wkts dec.) 214
5/178 (6) 6/382 (5) 7/438 (8)   3/101 (3) 4/134 (5)
8/457 (7) 9/493 (10) 10/493 (11)   5/146 (4) 6/214 (6)

Dillon 42–10–140–3; Collins 33–3–96–0; Cuffy 35–10–75–1; Hooper 32–7–85–2; R. O. Hinds 4–0–31–0; W. W. Hinds 8–1–26–1; Gayle 7.5–0–27–3. *Second Innings*—Dillon 17–3–46–2; Cuffy 19–3–78–2; Collins 14.4–1–56–1; Hooper 5–0–23–0; W. W. Hinds 2–0–11–0.

West Indies

D. Ganga lbw b Saqlain Mushtaq	20	– b Shoaib Akhtar	34
C. H. Gayle b Saqlain Mushtaq	68	– b Shoaib Akhtar	66
S. L. Campbell lbw b Danish Kaneria	6	– run out	20
W. W. Hinds st Rashid Latif b Danish Kaneria	59	– c Rashid Latif b Shoaib Akhtar	8
*C. L. Hooper lbw b Abdul Razzaq	56	– lbw b Abdul Razzaq	13
S. Chanderpaul b Waqar Younis	66	– c Rashid Latif b Abdul Razzaq	0
R. O. Hinds c Rashid Latif b Waqar Younis	62	– not out	9
†R. D. Jacobs c Danish Kaneria b Waqar Younis	6	– lbw b Abdul Razzaq	0
M. Dillon run out	5	– b Shoaib Akhtar	0
C. E. Cuffy b Waqar Younis	0	– b Shoaib Akhtar	0
P. T. Collins not out	1	– b Abdul Razzaq	12
B 1, l-b 3, w 1, n-b 12	17	B 1, l-b 1, n-b 7	9

1/88 (1) 2/96 (2) 3/126 (3) 4/180 (4)   366   1/76 (1) 2/115 (2) 3/125 (4)   171
5/231 (5) 6/352 (6) 7/353 (7)   4/146 (3) 5/149 (6) 6/150 (5)
8/362 (9) 9/363 (10) 10/366 (8)   7/150 (8) 8/155 (9) 9/155 (10) 10/171 (11)

Waqar Younis 25.3–4–93–4; Shoaib Akhtar 18–4–68–0; Abdul Razzaq 18–2–49–1; Danish Kaneria 26–5–75–2; Saqlain Mushtaq 36–12–71–2; Taufeeq Umar 2–0–6–0. *Second Innings*—Waqar Younis 9–2–35–0; Saqlain Mushtaq 11–5–30–0; Danish Kaneria 19–7–55–0; Shoaib Akhtar 16–7–24–5; Abdul Razzaq 7.5–1–25–4.

Umpires: Riazuddin *(Pakistan)* (12) and G. Sharp *(England)* (15).
Third umpire: Athar Zaidi *(Pakistan)*.   Referee: M. H. Denness *(England)* (13).

Close of play: First day, Pakistan 230-5 (Yousuf Youhana 78, Rashid Latif 27); Second day, West Indies 54-0 (Ganga 11, Gayle 41); Third day, West Indies 325-5 (Chanderpaul 45, R. O. Hinds 55); Fourth day, West Indies 24-0 (Ganga 19, Gayle 5).

PAKISTAN v WEST INDIES 2001–02 (2nd Test)

At Sharjah C. A. Stadium on 7, 8, 9, 10 February.
Toss: West Indies.   Result: PAKISTAN won by 244 runs.
Debuts: none.
Man of the Match: Younis Khan.   Men of the Series: Abdul Razzaq and M. Dillon.

West Indies went down to their fifth consecutive defeat, their 23rd in 27 overseas Tests, with a day to spare. Their batting and fielding let them down again, although they had no luck with injuries and umpiring decisions. Hooper chose to bowl first solely because West Indies had taken early wickets in the previous Test. The move proved a blunder, and was compounded by more fluffed catches, four of them offered by Shahid Afridi, who made an aggressive 107, with 16 fours and three sixes from 150 balls. He put on 190 with Younis Khan, who proceeded to 153 in nearly seven hours. Cuffy, on his 32nd birthday, was the main wicket-taker, but the luckless Dillon was the pick of the attack. West Indies then stumbled to 164 for 4, and would have been worse off had Hooper not been dropped twice at slip by Younis off the spinners. He survived to pass 5,000 Test runs next day, but only Jacobs lent him any support. Pakistan did not enforce the follow-on, preferring to add quick runs. They left themselves 150 overs to dismiss West Indies, but 61 sufficed as they completed their sixth consecutive win the same evening. Though the ball turned viciously from the rough, only two wickets fell to spin. Instead, the damage was done by Waqar Younis, whose four wickets took him past 350 in Tests, and Abdul Razzaq, still finding reverse swing at will to capture three in one deadly spell.

Pakistan

Taufeeq Umar c Ganga b Dillon	8	– (2) lbw b Dillon	69
Shahid Afridi b Cuffy	107	– (1) c Jacobs b Dillon	0
Younis Khan c Ganga b Collins	153	– c Ganga b Dillon	71
Inzamam-ul-Haq c Hooper b Ramnarine	36	– c sub (D. Brown) b Collins	6
Yousuf Youhana b Dillon	60	– not out	52
Abdul Razzaq not out	64	– run out	16
†Rashid Latif c Hooper b Ramnarine	16	– not out	2
Saqlain Mushtaq b Cuffy	50		
*Waqar Younis lbw b Ramnarine	2		
Shoaib Akhtar c and b Cuffy	4		
Danish Kaneria c Gayle b Cuffy	0		
B 12, l-b 2, n-b 3	17	L-b 6, w 1, n-b 2	9

1/12 (1) 2/202 (2) 3/272 (4) 4/364 (5)   472   1/0 (1) 2/144 (3)   (5 wkts dec.) 225
5/393 (3) 6/416 (7) 7/447 (8)   3/145 (2) 4/175 (4)
8/454 (9) 9/463 (10) 10/472 (11)   5/216 (6)

Dillon 27–6–63–2; Collins 30–5–99–1; Cuffy 29–4–82–4; Ramnarine 36–5–137–3; Hooper 7–0–41–0; R. O. Hinds 5–1–24–0; Gayle 1–0–12–0. *Second Innings*—Dillon 18–2–57–3; Cuffy 20–4–52–0; Collins 14–2–56–1; R. O. Hinds 12–3–15–0; Ramnarine 12–1–39–0.

West Indies

D. Ganga b Shahid Afridi	65	– lbw b Shoaib Akhtar	21
C. H. Gayle b Shoaib Akhtar	6	– lbw b Waqar Younis	4
W. W. Hinds b Saqlain Mushtaq	25	– c Taufeeq Umar b Saqlain Mushtaq	34
*C. L. Hooper not out	84	– lbw b Saqlain Mushtaq	1
S. Chanderpaul c Yousuf Youhana b Danish Kaneria	16	– lbw b Abdul Razzaq	19
M. Dillon c Taufeeq Umar b Shoaib Akhtar	0	– (8) lbw b Abdul Razzaq	0
R. O. Hinds lbw b Abdul Razzaq	11	– (6) lbw b Waqar Younis	46
†R. D. Jacobs b Saqlain Mushtaq	31	– (7) not out	35
D. Ramnarine b Shoaib Akhtar	0	– b Abdul Razzaq	0
C. E. Cuffy b Shoaib Akhtar	4	– b Waqar Younis	15
P. T. Collins c Inzamam-ul-Haq b Saqlain Mushtaq	1	– b Waqar Younis	0
B 6, l-b 9, n-b 6	21	B 2, l-b 6, n-b 6	14

1/19 (2) 2/88 (3) 3/116 (1) 4/159 (5)   264   1/19 (2) 2/46 (1) 3/47 (4)   189
5/170 (6) 6/189 (7) 7/236 (8)   4/84 (3) 5/114 (5) 6/161 (6)
8/237 (9) 9/247 (10) 10/264 (11)   7/162 (8) 8/162 (9) 9/189 (10) 10/189 (11)

Waqar Younis 9–1–24–0; Shoaib Akhtar 18–4–63–4; Danish Kaneria 13–2–34–1; Saqlain Mushtaq 21.5–4–75–3; Shahid Afridi 15–0–34–1; Abdul Razzaq 8–1–19–1. *Second Innings*—Waqar Younis 10–2–44–4; Shoaib Akhtar 8–3–23–1; Abdul Razzaq 11–2–33–3; Saqlain Mushtaq 19–8–42–2; Shahid Afridi 2–0–14–0; Danish Kaneria 11–2–25–0.

Umpires: D. B. Hair *(Australia)* (43) and Shakeel Khan *(Pakistan)* (6).
Third umpire: Mian Aslam *(Pakistan)*.   Referee: M. H. Denness *(England)* (14).

Close of play: First day, Pakistan 344-3 (Younis Khan 131, Yousuf Youhana 47); Second day, West Indies 164-4 (Hooper 40, Dillon 0); Third day, Pakistan 130-1 (Taufeeq Umar 64, Younis Khan 61).

INDIA v ZIMBABWE 2001–02 (1st Test)

At Vidarbha C. A. Ground, Nagpur, on 21, 22, 23, 24, 25 February.
Toss: Zimbabwe.   Result: INDIA won by an innings and 101 runs.
Debuts: none.
Man of the Match: A. Kumble.

Zimbabwe returned to the Orange City, the venue of their previous Test in India, and again conceded three hundreds in an innings. Das and Tendulkar re-enacted their feats of 15 months earlier, and the third century came from Sanjay Bangar, in only his second Test. In November 2000 Zimbabwe had responded in kind on a placid pitch, Andy Flower making 232. This time, he totalled just 11 runs on a dusty, crumbling surface, as Kumble and Harbhajan Singh bowled India to an overwhelming victory. Friend's late flourish prolonged Zimbabwe's innings into the second morning, but Das then compiled his second Test century (both against Zimbabwe at Nagpur), batting for five hours until he edged to slip in the final over. In came Tendulkar: even he was slowed down by the pitch, but he cruised to his 28th Test hundred, one behind Don Bradman. Friend was barred from the attack by umpire Venkataraghavan on the third evening after a beamer to Tendulkar – he had been no-balled and warned the previous day for a similar offence against Das. By then, Bangar had joined Tendulkar, and next morning they piled on 110 in 16 overs. Needing 283 to make India bat again, or to survive for just over five sessions, Zimbabwe soon wilted against some clinical spin. By the close, the cream of their batting had already been skimmed, with only Gripper stubbornly hanging on. On the final day, Kumble and Harbhajan completed the last rites in little more than an hour.

Zimbabwe

*S. V. Carlisle run out	77	– lbw b Zaheer Khan	28
T. R. Gripper c Dasgupta b Zaheer Khan	5	– c sub (V. Sehwag) b Harbhajan Singh	60
A. D. R. Campbell c Laxman b Kumble	57	– c Laxman b Kumble	30
A. Flower b Zaheer Khan	3	– c Dravid b Kumble	8
G. J. Rennie c sub (V. Sehwag) b Srinath	9	– c Laxman b Kumble	25
G. W. Flower c Dravid b Kumble	14	– (7) lbw b Kumble	1
H. H. Streak c Das b Zaheer Khan	24	– (8) c Ganguly b Kumble	8
†T. Taibu b Kumble	1	– (9) c sub (V. Sehwag) b Harbhajan Singh	0
T. J. Friend not out	60	– (10) not out	6
R. W. Price run out	18	– (6) c Dravid b Harbhajan Singh	4
B. T. Watambwa lbw b Kumble	0	– c Tendulkar b Harbhajan Singh	1
B 6, l-b 11, n-b 2	19	B 1, l-b 8, n-b 2	11

1/12 (2) 2/118 (3) 3/125 (4) 4/151 (5)   287   1/32 (1) 2/80 (3) 3/103 (4)   182
5/175 (1) 6/182 (6) 7/194 (8)   4/147 (5) 5/156 (6) 6/159 (7)
8/227 (7) 9/286 (10) 10/287 (11)   7/161 (2) 8/167 (9) 9/181 (8) 10/182 (11)

Srinath 22–6–65–1; Zaheer Khan 14–2–45–3; Bangar 8–3–20–0; Kumble 33.5–12–82–4; Harbhajan Singh 26–8–58–0. *Second Innings*—Srinath 6–3–20–0; Kumble 37–15–63–5; Zaheer Khan 8–1–33–1; Harbhajan Singh 31.4–9–46–4; Tendulkar 6–2–11–0.

India

S. S. Das c Campbell b Price	105	Zaheer Khan b Watambwa	0
†D. Dasgupta b Price	33	A. Kumble not out	13
R. Dravid b Streak	65	B 16, l-b 2, w 3, n-b 6	27
S. R. Tendulkar c A. Flower b Price	176		
*S. C. Ganguly c G. W. Flower b Price	38	1/79 (2) 2/209 (1) (7 wkts dec.) 570	
V. V. S. Laxman c Rennie b Price	13	3/247 (3) 4/344 (5)	
S. B. Bangar not out	100	5/376 (6) 6/547 (4) 7/547 (8)	

J. Srinath and Harbhajan Singh did not bat.

Streak 34–9–108–1; Watambwa 25.5–6–87–1; Price 68–18–182–5; Friend 22–3–61–0; G. W. Flower 30–8–96–0; Gripper 5–0–18–0.

Umpires: D. R. Shepherd *(England)* (60) and S. Venkataraghavan *(India)* (51).
Third umpire: Jasbir Singh *(India)*.   Referee: J. R. Reid *(New Zealand)* (49).

Close of play: First day, Zimbabwe 248-8 (Friend 33, Price 6); Second day, India 209-2 (Dravid 57, Tendulkar 0); Third day, India 437-5 (Tendulkar 137, Bangar 22); Fourth day, Zimbabwe 152-4 (Gripper 52, Price 4).

INDIA v ZIMBABWE 2001–02 (2nd Test)

At Feroz Shah Kotla, Delhi, on 28 February, 1, 2, 3, 4 March.
Toss: Zimbabwe.   Result: INDIA won by four wickets.
Debuts: none.
Man of the Match: Harbhajan Singh.   Man of the Series: A. Kumble.

India whitewashed the short series, but Zimbabwe put up much more of a fight, giving the Indians a nasty scare chasing 122. Their improvement unsurprisingly coincided with Andy Flower's only half-century of the Tests. In his previous 60 matches, he had reached 90 a dozen times and always made a hundred; this was 13th time unlucky. Ebrahim narrowly missed a maiden Test century, and Friend saw Zimbabwe past 300. Ganguly dominated India's reply with his first Test hundred as captain, in his 18th match. He was supported by Sehwag, who scored all but ten of his 74 runs in fours. On an eroding pitch, 17 wickets tumbled on the fourth day. India managed a lead of 25, which looked plenty when Zimbabwe fizzled out for 146. Harbhajan grabbed three for one in 17 balls, and had Andy Flower caught at short leg again, for a four-ball duck. Last out was Grant Flower, who was soon back in the action, dismissing Ganguly and Kumble with consecutive deliveries: India were 36 for 3, with Sehwag unlikely to bat, after injuring his shoulder attempting a catch. Friend was warned for bowling a beamer, as Zaheer Khan had been earlier in the match. Tendulkar calmed home nerves with a breezy 42, but tension rose again when Price removed him for the third time running. Two more quick wickets left India effectively seven down, with 17 required. But four leg-byes, four overthrows from a missed run-out, and a four and a six from Harbhajan settled the issue.

Zimbabwe

*S. V. Carlisle b Srinath	0	– c and b Harbhajan Singh	37
T. R. Gripper c Dravid b Zaheer Khan	8	– c Dravid b Harbhajan Singh	10
A. D. R. Campbell c Dravid b Zaheer Khan	16	– c Dravid b Harbhajan Singh	2
A. Flower c Das b Harbhajan Singh	92	– c Das b Harbhajan Singh	0
D. D. Ebrahim lbw b Srinath	94	– lbw b Kumble	22
G. W. Flower run out	30	– c Harbhajan Singh b Kumble	49
H. H. Streak b Kumble	0	– lbw b Kumble	9
T. J. Friend c Tendulkar b Harbhajan Singh	43	– b Harbhajan Singh	0
†T. Taibu lbw b Kumble	13	– c Bangar b Kumble	10
R. W. Price b Kumble	0	– c Das b Harbhajan Singh	3
B. T. Watambwa not out	3	– not out	1
B 5, l-b 16, n-b 9	30	B 2, n-b 1	3

1/0 (1) 2/11 (2) 3/65 (3) 4/181 (4)   329   1/23 (2) 2/31 (3) 3/31 (4)   146
5/246 (6) 6/246 (7) 7/289 (5)   4/69 (1) 5/95 (5) 6/113 (7)
8/310 (9) 9/310 (10) 10/329 (8)   7/114 (8) 8/129 (9) 9/142 (10) 10/146 (6)

Srinath 18–4–37–2; Zaheer Khan 22–4–76–2; Bangar 7–1–25–0; Kumble 34–13–88–3; Harbhajan Singh 27.5–5–70–2; Sehwag 1–0–6–0; Tendulkar 1–0–6–0. *Second Innings*—Srinath 4–0–12–0; Zaheer Khan 3–0–12–0; Harbhajan Singh 31–5–62–6; Kumble 29.3–8–58–4.

India

S. S. Das c Taibu b Streak	13	– lbw b Streak	31
†D. Dasgupta lbw b Friend	19	– run out	1
*S. C. Ganguly c Gripper b Price	136	– lbw b G. W. Flower	20
S. R. Tendulkar lbw b Price	36	– (5) lbw b Price	42
R. Dravid run out	1	– (6) c A. Flower b Price	6
V. Sehwag lbw b Streak	74		
S. B. Bangar run out	4	– not out	3
A. Kumble not out	34	– (4) c Gripper b G. W. Flower	0
J. Srinath c Gripper b Price	0		
Harbhajan Singh lbw b Streak	9	– (8) not out	14
Zaheer Khan b Streak	8		
B 9, l-b 6, w 1, n-b 4	20	L-b 4, n-b 5	9

1/24 (1) 2/58 (2) 3/142 (4) 4/144 (5)   354   1/3 (2) 2/36 (3)   (6 wkts) 126
5/264 (6) 6/280 (7) 7/321 (3)   3/36 (4) 4/93 (5)
8/331 (9) 9/340 (10) 10/354 (11)   5/103 (1) 6/105 (6)

Streak 37.2–11–92–4; Watambwa 18–5–47–0; Friend 19–2–75–1; Price 50–16–108–3; G. W. Flower 5–0–17–0. *Second Innings*—Streak 16.5–4–53–1; Friend 3–0–17–0; Price 19–9–24–2; G. W. Flower 6–3–22–2; Gripper 1–0–6–0.

Umpires: E. A. R. de Silva *(Sri Lanka)* (11) and A. V. Jayaprakash *(India)* (13).
Third umpire: N. N. Menon *(India)*.   Referee: J. R. Reid *(New Zealand)* (50).

Close of play: First day, Zimbabwe 260-6 (Ebrahim 82, Friend 7); Second day, India 171-4 (Ganguly 78, Sehwag 16); Third day, India 319-6 (Ganguly 135, Kumble 19); Fourth day, India 36-3 (Das 10, Tendulkar 0).

SOUTH AFRICA v AUSTRALIA 2001–02 (1st Test)

At The Wanderers, Johannesburg, on 22, 23, 24 February.
Toss: Australia.　　Result: AUSTRALIA won by an innings and 360 runs.
Debuts: South Africa – A. G. Prince.
Man of the Match: A. C. Gilchrist.

After three savage beatings in Australia, South Africa came home to something worse – the second-heaviest defeat in Test history after England's innings-and-579-run hammering of Australia at The Oval in 1938. A single moment summed up Australia's crushing superiority: Gilchrist took a pot-shot at an advertisement around 100 yards away at deep midwicket, offering a bar of gold, worth 1.3million rand (over £80,000), for a direct hit. Gilchrist had 169, and had butchered the entire front-line attack, which badly missed the injured Pollock. He scooped a length delivery from McKenzie towards the hoarding – and started to jump up and down as he realised how close it would be. He missed by a couple of feet, but what remained of South Africa's spirit was broken. The carnage had started the day before, with Hayden's fourth century in as many Tests. A torn hamstring forced Donald off the field, and he retired from Test cricket after the match. Gilchrist reached 200 with his 19th four from his 212th delivery. It was the quickest Test double in terms of balls ... for three weeks (see *Test No. 1595*). He also smashed eight sixes before Australia declared at their highest total against a shell-shocked South Africa, who were dismissed in 48 overs and followed on 493 behind (there had been only three higher first-innings leads in Tests at the time). The second innings was even shorter: during the third day, South Africa lost 16 wickets in 54.3 overs. McGrath wound things up with four wickets in nine balls.

Australia

J. L. Langer lbw b Donald	28	S. K. Warne c McKenzie b Boje	12
M. L. Hayden c Boucher b Nel	122	B. Lee not out	4
R. T. Ponting c Boucher b Nel	39	B 2, l-b 14, w 4, n-b 5	25
M. E. Waugh c Boucher b Ntini	53		
*S. R. Waugh c Gibbs b Kallis	32	1/46 (1) 2/113 (3)　(7 wkts dec.)	652
D. R. Martyn c Kirsten b Kallis	133	3/224 (4) 4/272 (2)	
†A. C. Gilchrist not out	204	5/293 (5) 6/610 (6) 7/643 (8)	

J. N. Gillespie and G. D. McGrath did not bat.

Donald 15.2–2–72–1; Ntini 33–8–124–1; Kallis 24–1–116–2; Nel 30.4–6–121–2; Boje 35–4–153–1; McKenzie 8–0–50–0.

South Africa

H. H. Gibbs lbw b Warne	34	– st Gilchrist b Warne	47
G. Kirsten c Warne b McGrath	1	– c Martyn b Gillespie	12
A. G. Prince c Hayden b Gillespie	49	– b Warne	28
J. H. Kallis c Warne b Lee	3	– c Gilchrist b McGrath	8
N. D. McKenzie c Gillespie b McGrath	16	– not out	27
H. H. Dippenaar c Gilchrist b McGrath	2	– lbw b Warne	1
*†M. V. Boucher c Gilchrist b Lee	23	– b Warne	1
N. Boje c M. E. Waugh b Gillespie	0	– c Ponting b McGrath	5
M. Ntini c S. R. Waugh b Lee	9	– b McGrath	0
A. Nel lbw b Warne	7	– c Langer b McGrath	0
A. A. Donald not out	3	– c Hayden b McGrath	0
B 4, l-b 3, n-b 5	12	W 1, n-b 3	4

1/11 (2) 2/51 (1) 3/55 (4) 4/108 (5)	159	1/20 (2) 2/89 (3) 3/98 (1)　133
5/113 (3) 6/113 (6) 7/114 (8)		4/98 (4) 5/107 (6) 6/109 (7)
8/146 (9) 9/155 (5) 10/159 (10)		7/122 (8) 8/122 (9) 9/122 (10) 10/133 (11)

McGrath 14–6–28–3; Gillespie 15–5–58–2; Warne 9–0–26–2; Lee 10–1–40–3. *Second Innings*—McGrath 12.3–4–21–5; Lee 10–2–55–0; Gillespie 4–1–13–1; Warne 12–3–44–4.

　　　Umpires: S. A. Bucknor *(West Indies)* (64) and R. E. Koertzen *(South Africa)* (28).
　　Third umpire: I. L. Howell *(South Africa)*.　　Referee: C. W. Smith *(West Indies)* (40).

Close of play: First day, Australia 331-5 (Martyn 21, Gilchrist 25); Second day, South Africa 111-4 (Prince 47, Dippenaar 2).

SOUTH AFRICA v AUSTRALIA 2001–02 (2nd Test)

At Newlands, Cape Town, on 8, 9, 10, 11, 12 March.
Toss: South Africa.   Result: AUSTRALIA won by four wickets.
Debuts: South Africa – A. J. Hall, D. Pretorius, G. C. Smith.
Man of the Match: S. K. Warne.

Shane Warne flew in 16 friends and relatives for his 100th Test, and they saw him bowl 98 overs, take eight wickets, score 63, win the match award – and propel his team to yet another series triumph. In the end, it was a memorable battle. But that hardly looked likely when South Africa crashed to 92 for 6 on the first day. They clawed their way back, mainly thanks to Hall, with 70 on debut. Australia cruised to 130 for 1, but when Hayden top-edged a hook to fine leg, the innings took a dramatic turn. Four wickets in the next 20 overs made it 185 for 6 – still 54 behind. Then came Gilchrist. Again. It was impossible to imagine he could equal his feats at Johannesburg, but he did. Within five minutes, he was charging down the track at Adams, and after his first 26 balls had 42, with nine blazing fours. His second fifty needed 38 balls, and his final 38 runs just 17; he hit Adams's last two overs for 36. South Africa's top five fired at last second time round, collecting 366 between them – no centuries, but McKenzie was only one short when beaten by Martyn's direct hit from cover. Langer and Hayden launched the hunt for 331 with their sixth century stand in 14 starts. Some welcome tension entered the chase when Ntini removed Mark Waugh. Then Adams's googlies removed Steve Waugh and Martyn in successive overs – but Gilchrist effectively finished the job with a run-a-ball 24.

South Africa

H. H. Gibbs c M. E. Waugh b Gillespie	12	– c Ponting b Warne		39
G. Kirsten c M. E. Waugh b Lee	7	– lbw b Lee		87
G. C. Smith c Ponting b McGrath	3	– c Gilchrist b Warne		68
J. H. Kallis c Gilchrist b McGrath	23	– lbw b Warne		73
N. D. McKenzie b Warne	20	– run out		99
A. G. Prince c Gilchrist b McGrath	10	– c Ponting b Warne		20
*†M. V. Boucher c Gilchrist b Lee	26	– lbw b Gillespie		37
A. J. Hall c Gilchrist b Gillespie	70	– run out		0
P. R. Adams c Warne b Gillespie	35	– not out		23
M. Ntini c M. E. Waugh b Warne	14	– c Langer b Warne		11
D. Pretorius not out	5	– c M. E. Waugh b Warne		0
B 4, l-b 5, n-b 5	14	B 8, l-b 3, w 2, n-b 3		16

1/15 (1) 2/18 (3) 3/25 (2) 4/70 (5)   239   1/84 (1) 2/183 (2) 3/254 (3)   473
5/73 (4) 6/92 (6) 7/147 (7)   4/284 (4) 5/350 (6) 6/431 (7)
8/216 (9) 9/229 (8) 10/239 (10)   7/433 (8) 8/440 (5) 9/464 (10) 10/473 (11)

McGrath 20–4–42–3; Gillespie 15–4–52–3; Lee 16–1–65–2; Warne 28–10–70–2; M. E. Waugh 1–0–1–0.
Second Innings—McGrath 25–7–56–0; Gillespie 29–10–81–1; Warne 70–15–161–6; Lee 22–3–99–1; M. E. Waugh 9–3–34–0; Martyn 4–0–15–0; S. R. Waugh 3–0–16–0.

Australia

J. L. Langer b Ntini	37	– b Pretorius		58
M. L. Hayden c Hall b Kallis	63	– c Boucher b Kallis		96
R. T. Ponting c Boucher b Adams	47	– not out		100
M. E. Waugh c Gibbs b Ntini	25	– c Boucher b Ntini		16
*S. R. Waugh b Adams	0	– b Adams		14
D. R. Martyn c Boucher b Ntini	2	– lbw b Adams		0
†A. C. Gilchrist not out	138	– c McKenzie b Kallis		24
S. K. Warne c Kallis b Adams	63	– not out		15
B. Lee c Prince b Kallis	0			
J. N. Gillespie c Kallis b Adams	0			
G. D. McGrath lbw b Ntini	2			
B 2, l-b 1, w 2	5	L-b 6, n-b 5		11

1/67 (1) 2/130 (2) 3/162 (3) 4/168 (5)   382   1/102 (1) 2/201 (2)   (6 wkts) 334
5/176 (4) 6/185 (6) 7/317 (8)   3/251 (4) 4/268 (5)
8/338 (9) 9/343 (10) 10/382 (11)   5/268 (6) 6/305 (7)

Ntini 22.5–5–93–4; Pretorius 11–1–72–0; Kallis 16–1–65–2; Hall 11–1–47–0; Adams 20–1–102–4. *Second Innings*—Ntini 24–4–90–1; Pretorius 14–5–60–1; Adams 21.1–0–104–2; Hall 3–0–6–0; Kallis 17–2–68–2.

Umpires: S. A. Bucknor *(West Indies)* (65) and R. E. Koertzen *(South Africa)* (29).
Third umpire: D. L. Orchard *(South Africa)*.   Referee: C. W. Smith *(West Indies)* (41).

Close of play: First day, Australia 46-0 (Langer 28, Hayden 17); Second day, South Africa 7-0 (Gibbs 5, Kirsten 2); Third day, South Africa 307-4 (McKenzie 28, Prince 5); Fourth day, Australia 131-1 (Hayden 50, Ponting 17).

SOUTH AFRICA v AUSTRALIA 2001–02 (3rd Test)

At Kingsmead, Durban, on 15, 16, 17, 18 March.
Toss: South Africa.   Result: SOUTH AFRICA won by five wickets.
Debuts: none.
Man of the Match: H. H. Gibbs.   Man of the Series: A. C. Gilchrist.

Australia found themselves on the back foot for the first time in six Tests when South Africa put them in and reduced them to 182 for 5. They still seemed more than capable of retrieving the situation, and claimed a large first-innings lead, but five successive victories had left little in the tank. Gilchrist was, once again, the star. He was nearing his third century in consecutive Tests when he decided he could not rely on Gillespie and slogged Adams to deep midwicket: his series average tumbled from 366 to 228.50. Despite a good start, South Africa collapsed for 167. Australia's second innings featured over-confidence and lack of concentration. Five of the top seven made starts, but the top score was only 42. Martyn's outside edge made Boucher the fastest wicketkeeper to reach 200 Test dismissals, in terms of both matches (52) and age (25 years 103 days). Australia subsided for 186 – the first time in 11 Tests that they had been out for less than 300. Even so, South Africa needed 335, four more than Australia at Cape Town, and 38 more than their own highest winning fourth-innings total, at Melbourne in 1952-53. The openers set the tone with a stand of 142, and the third day ended with another 71 needed with six wickets left. Kallis was the key, and he saw the job through. When Warne had Prince caught at slip, his 450th Test wicket, with four runs required, Boucher came in to end the game with a six.

Australia

J. L. Langer c Kirsten b Terbrugge	11	– c Boucher b Terbrugge	18
M. L. Hayden c McKenzie b Kallis	28	– c Prince b Terbrugge	0
R. T. Ponting run out	89	– c Terbrugge b Ntini	34
M. E. Waugh c Smith b Kallis	45	– b Kallis	30
*S. R. Waugh c Boucher b Adams	7	– c Kallis b Ntini	42
D. R. Martyn b Terbrugge	11	– c Boucher b Kallis	0
†A. C. Gilchrist c Smith b Adams	91	– c Boucher b Kallis	16
S. K. Warne c Boucher b Ntini	26	– c McKenzie b Adams	13
B. Lee b Ntini	0	– (10) not out	23
J. N. Gillespie c Boucher b Hall	1	– (9) c Kallis b Adams	3
G. D. McGrath not out	4	– b Ntini	0
W 2	2	B 1, l-b 3, w 1, n-b 2	7

1/11 (1) 2/61 (2) 3/169 (3) 4/178 (4)   **315**   1/4 (2) 2/19 (1) 3/77 (3)   **186**
5/182 (5) 6/230 (6) 7/287 (8)   4/90 (4) 5/90 (6) 6/114 (7)
8/289 (9) 9/311 (7) 10/315 (10)   7/129 (8) 8/150 (9) 9/186 (5) 10/186 (11)

Ntini 20–3–87–2; Terbrugge 16–2–61–2; Kallis 20–3–95–2; Hall 9.1–2–35–1; Adams 9–0–37–2. *Second Innings*— Ntini 17–2–65–3; Terbrugge 4–1–21–2; Hall 4–1–20–0; Adams 13–0–47–2; Kallis 11–2–29–3.

South Africa

H. H. Gibbs c Gilchrist b Gillespie	51	– c Martyn b M. E. Waugh	104
G. Kirsten c Gilchrist b Lee	21	– run out	64
P. R. Adams c Hayden b Lee	6		
G. C. Smith c Gilchrist b McGrath	1	– (3) c Gilchrist b M. E. Waugh	42
J. H. Kallis c and b Warne	16	– (4) not out	61
N. D. McKenzie c Martyn b Lee	25	– (5) c Hayden b Warne	4
A. G. Prince c Lee b Warne	0	– (6) c M. E. Waugh b Warne	48
*†M. V. Boucher c and b Warne	0	– (7) not out	8
A. J. Hall not out	27		
M. Ntini c McGrath b Warne	14		
D. J. Terbrugge c Gilchrist b Lee	0		
L-b 1, w 1, n-b 4	6	L-b 2, w 2, n-b 5	9

1/48 (2) 2/74 (3) 3/75 (4) 4/85 (1)   **167**   1/142 (2) 2/216 (3)   **(5 wkts) 340**
5/109 (5) 6/119 (7) 7/119 (8)   3/218 (1) 4/232 (5)
8/148 (6) 9/167 (10) 10/167 (11)   5/331 (6)

McGrath 11–4–26–1; Lee 17.2–1–82–4; Gillespie 14–6–25–1; Warne 13–4–33–4. *Second Innings*—McGrath 28–11–54–0; Lee 20–2–75–0; Gillespie 15–2–58–0; Warne 30–6–108–2; M. E. Waugh 11.5–1–43–2.

Umpires: D. L. Orchard *(South Africa)* (27) and S. Venkataraghavan *(India)* (52).
Third umpire: I. L. Howell *(South Africa)*.   Referee: C. W. Smith *(West Indies)* (42).

Close of play: First day, South Africa 48-1 (Gibbs 24, Adams 0); Second day, Australia 159-8 (S. R. Waugh 34, Lee 5); Third day, South Africa 264-4 (Kallis 35, Prince 8).

PAKISTAN v SRI LANKA 2001–02
(Asian Test Championship – Final)

At Gaddafi Stadium, Lahore, on 6, 7, 8, 9, 10 March.
Toss: Sri Lanka.   Result: SRI LANKA won by eight wickets.
Debuts: none.
Man of the Match: K. C. Sangakkara.

After Sri Lanka and Pakistan had both swatted Bangladesh aside in the preliminaries *(Tests Nos. 1560-1)*, this match at last promised a contest. But it proved just as one-sided as when these teams met in the first Asian Test Championship final in March 1999. Then, Pakistan won by an innings; this time, it was Sri Lanka's party. Put in on a hard, even pitch, both Pakistan's openers perished within six overs, before Younis Khan and Inzamam-ul-Haq added 86 in as many minutes before another collapse. In reply, Sri Lanka were as steadfast as Pakistan had been shaky: Sangakkara batted three hours longer than his opponents' entire innings. His eight-hour 230 featured partnerships of 203 with Jayasuriya and 173 with Jayawardene. In the first 123 years of Test cricket there were only three double-centuries by wicketkeepers; Sangakkara's was the third in 16 months, and the second-highest of any of them behind Andy Flower's 232. Mohammad Sami finally ended the innings with a hat-trick that straddled lunch on the third day. But the fireworks came too late (Wasim Akram had been omitted, ostensibly on fitness grounds). Pakistan, 294 behind, needed to bat well into the fifth day to stand a chance of salvaging a draw, but by the third evening, they were already five down. Only 32 overs were possible on the fourth day, but blue skies next morning dashed their first hope, and the dismissal of Inzamam for a five-hour 99 extinguished their last. The remaining batsmen lasted less than 12 overs.

Pakistan

Shahid Afridi run out	9	– st Sangakkara b Muralitharan	70
Taufeeq Umar c Samaraweera b Vaas	6	– b Vaas	19
Younis Khan b Muralitharan	46	– c Samaraweera b Zoysa	19
Inzamam-ul-Haq c Jayasuriya b Fernando	29	– lbw b Vaas	99
Yousuf Youhana c Sangakkara b Fernando	6	– c Atapattu b Muralitharan	7
Abdul Razzaq lbw b Vaas	24	– lbw b Muralitharan	5
Shoaib Malik c Sangakkara b Fernando	13	– c Samaraweera b Zoysa	21
†Rashid Latif c Sangakkara b Muralitharan	36	– c Muralitharan b Vaas	2
*Waqar Younis b Muralitharan	19	– c Tillekeratne b Muralitharan	25
Shoaib Akhtar lbw b Muralitharan	15	– not out	4
Mohammad Sami not out	0	– c Sangakkara b Vaas	0
L-b 4, w 1, n-b 26	31	B 12, l-b 2, w 1, n-b 39	54

1/18 (2) 2/18 (1) 3/104 (3) 4/108 (4)   234   1/31 (2) 2/66 (3) 3/150 (1)   325
5/127 (5) 6/147 (6) 7/176 (7)   4/166 (5) 5/181 (6) 6/281 (4)
8/216 (9) 9/219 (8) 10/234 (10)   7/285 (8) 8/291 (7) 9/321 (9) 10/325 (11)

Vaas 17–2–62–2; Zoysa 9–2–29–0; Fernando 16–1–84–3; Muralitharan 25–9–55–4. *Second Innings*—Vaas 22.5–3–85–4; Zoysa 21–3–54–2; Fernando 14–2–68–0; Muralitharan 34–8–72–4; Jayasuriya 1–0–7–0; Samaraweera 9–1–25–0.

Sri Lanka

M. S. Atapattu c Shoaib Akhtar b Waqar Younis	0	– c Rashid Latif b Mohammad Sami	1
*S. T. Jayasuriya c Rashid Latif b Abdul Razzaq	88	– c Yousuf Youhana b Shoaib Akhtar	1
†K. C. Sangakkara c Younis Khan b Abdul Razzaq	230	– not out	14
D. P. M. D. Jayawardene c Inzamam-ul-Haq b Mohammad Sami	68	– not out	12
R. P. Arnold b Shoaib Akhtar	44		
W. P. U. J. C. Vaas c Taufeeq Umar b Abdul Razzaq	43		
H. P. Tillekeratne not out	19		
T. T. Samaraweera c Rashid Latif b Shoaib Akhtar	8		
T. C. B. Fernando lbw b Mohammad Sami	7		
D. N. T. Zoysa lbw b Mohammad Sami	0		
M. Muralitharan b Mohammad Sami	0		
B 1, l-b 7, w 5, n-b 8	21	L-b 1, w 2, n-b 2	5

1/0 (1) 2/203 (2) 3/376 (4) 4/447 (3)   528   1/1 (1) 2/14 (2)   (2 wkts) 33
5/447 (5) 6/501 (6) 7/519 (8)
8/528 (9) 9/528 (10) 10/528 (11)

Waqar Younis 30–4–123–1; Shoaib Akhtar 27–4–114–2; Mohammad Sami 36.5–4–120–4; Abdul Razzaq 29–5–82–3; Shoaib Malik 14–3–55–0; Shahid Afridi 3–0–26–0. *Second Innings*—Shoaib Akhtar 3.2–0–17–1; Mohammad Sami 3–0–15–1.

Umpires: Athar Zaidi *(Pakistan)* (8) and D. J. Harper *(Australia)* (17).
Third umpire: Salim Badar *(Pakistan)*.   Referee: A. M. Ebrahim *(Zimbabwe)* (4).

Close of play: First day, Sri Lanka 94-1 (Jayasuriya 47, Sangakkara 39); Second day, Sri Lanka 447-5 (Vaas 0, Tillekeratne 0); Third day, Pakistan 193-5 (Inzamam-ul-Haq 38, Shoaib Malik 6); Fourth day, Pakistan 248-5 (Inzamam-ul-Haq 72, Shoaib Malik 19).

NEW ZEALAND v ENGLAND 2001–02 (1st Test)

At Lancaster Park, Christchurch, on 13, 14, 15, 16 March.
Toss: New Zealand.   Result: ENGLAND won by 98 runs.
Debuts: New Zealand – I. G. Butler.
Man of the Match: G. P. Thorpe.

This match will be remembered for perhaps the most glorious failure in Test history. When the injured Cairns walked out to join Astle, New Zealand were 333 for 9, still 217 short of a wildly improbable victory. But Astle, who then had 134, smashed his way to easily the fastest Test double-century, briefly threatening a jaw-dropping win. The carnage began in earnest when Hussain took the second new ball: the next four overs yielded 61 runs. Hoggard, unplayable on the second day when he took the first seven wickets to fall, went for 41 in two overs. Astle raced from 101 to 200 in just 39 balls, reaching his maiden Test double-century in 153, smashing Adam Gilchrist's record (set only three weeks earlier) by 59 deliveries. It took 217 minutes, three more than Don Bradman at Headingley in 1930, when the balls were not totted up. The relief England felt when he was caught behind was palpable. New Zealand's 451 was the second-highest fourth-innings total in any Test, bettered only by England's 654 for 5 against South Africa at Durban in 1938-39. Earlier Thorpe had made his own maiden Test double-century, in 330 minutes with 28 fours and four sixes, piling on a national-record 281 for the sixth wicket with Flintoff, who improved his previous-highest score by 95. The final two days, when 856 runs were scored at almost five an over, provided a violent counterpoint to the first two, when 438 came at under three on a drop-in pitch.

England

M. E. Trescothick c Parore b Cairns	0	– c Vettori b Butler	33
M. P. Vaughan c Parore b Cairns	27	– b Butler	0
M. A. Butcher c Butler b Cairns	0	– hit wkt b Butler	34
*N. Hussain lbw b Drum	106	– c Parore b Drum	11
G. P. Thorpe c Fleming b Drum	17	– not out	200
M. R. Ramprakash c Parore b Astle	31	– b Drum	11
A. Flintoff lbw b Astle	0	– c sub (M. N. McKenzie) b Astle	137
†J. S. Foster lbw b Drum	19	– not out	22
A. F. Giles c Drum b Butler	8		
A. R. Caddick lbw b Butler	0		
M. J. Hoggard not out	0		
B 1, l-b 10, n-b 9	20	B 6, l-b 4, n-b 10	20

1/0 (1) 2/0 (3) 3/46 (2) 4/83 (5)   228   1/11 (2) 2/50 (1)   (6 wkts dec.) 468
5/139 (6) 6/151 (7) 7/196 (8)   3/81 (4) 4/85 (3)
8/214 (9) 9/226 (10) 10/228 (4)   5/106 (6) 6/387 (7)

Cairns 15–4–58–3; Drum 20.2–8–36–3; Butler 16–2–59–2; Astle 18–10–32–2; Vettori 9–1–26–0; McMillan 3–1–6–0. *Second Innings*—Drum 32–6–130–2; Butler 23–2–137–3; Cairns 4–0–8–0; McMillan 10–0–66–0; Astle 5.4–0–20–1; Vettori 22–3–97–0.

New Zealand

M. H. Richardson lbw b Hoggard	2	– c Foster b Caddick	76
M. J. Horne c Thorpe b Hoggard	14	– c Foster b Caddick	4
D. L. Vettori c Foster b Hoggard	42	– (8) c Flintoff b Giles	12
L. Vincent b Hoggard	12	– (3) c Butcher b Caddick	0
*S. P. Fleming c Giles b Caddick	12	– (4) c Foster b Flintoff	48
N. J. Astle lbw b Hoggard	10	– (5) c Foster b Hoggard	222
C. D. McMillan c Vaughan b Hoggard	40	– (6) c and b Caddick	24
C. L. Cairns c Flintoff b Caddick	0	– (11) not out	23
†A. C. Parore lbw b Caddick	0	– (7) b Caddick	1
C. J. Drum not out	2	– (9) lbw b Flintoff	0
I. G. Butler c Hussain b Hoggard	0	– (10) c Foster b Caddick	4
L-b 5, n-b 8	13	B 9, l-b 11, w 1, n-b 16	37

1/4 (1) 2/50 (2) 3/65 (3) 4/79 (4)   147   1/42 (2) 2/53 (3) 3/119 (1)   451
5/93 (6) 6/117 (5) 7/117 (8)   4/189 (4) 5/242 (6) 6/252 (7)
8/117 (9) 9/146 (7) 10/147 (11)   7/300 (8) 8/301 (9) 9/333 (10) 10/451 (5)

Caddick 18–8–50–3; Hoggard 21.2–7–63–7; Flintoff 12–2–29–0. *Second Innings*—Caddick 25–8–122–6; Hoggard 24.3–5–142–1; Giles 28–6–73–1; Flintoff 16–1–94–2.

Umpires: B. F. Bowden *(New Zealand)* (3) and E. A. R. de Silva *(Sri Lanka)* (12).
Third umpire: D. M. Quested *(New Zealand)*.   Referee: J. L. Hendriks *(West Indies)* (17).

Close of play: First day, New Zealand 9-1 (Horne 0, Vettori 4); Second day, England 63-2 (Butcher 22, Hussain 6); Third day, New Zealand 28-0 (Richardson 20, Horne 3).

NEW ZEALAND v ENGLAND 2001–02 (2nd Test)

At Basin Reserve, Wellington, on 21 *(no play)*, 22, 23, 24, 25 March.
Toss: New Zealand.   Result: MATCH DRAWN.
Debuts: none.
Man of the Match: A. R. Caddick.

Cricket shrivelled into insignificance during the third morning, as news filtered through that Ben Hollioake, England's 24-year-old all-rounder, had been killed in a car crash in Australia. The players found out at lunch: they emerged afterwards wearing black armbands. It would have taken a heart of steel to condemn England for slumping from 199 for 4 to 280. The Test, already blighted by a bad weather and poor pitch-covering, felt like an irrelevant sideshow. But the sideshow had to go on and, after a minute's silence on the fourth morning, it did. England were understandably subdued, and New Zealand took advantage. After 57 careful overs, Richardson and Vincent had taken them to 135 for 1, from where they should have dictated terms. Instead, England who took charge. On a pitch with little to offer the seamers, Caddick summoned up real fire, while Giles, aiming into the rough, found turn and bounce. They grabbed five wickets for 14 in nine overs as New Zealand slumped to 149 for 6. McMillan counter-attacked, but the eventual collapse of nine for 83 spoke volumes for England's spirit. Caddick became the first England bowler to take consecutive six-fors since Ian Botham at Bombay in 1979-80. England went for quick runs against a weakened attack – Flintoff smacked 75 off 44 balls – and New Zealand were left 356 in 88 overs. Neither side came close to victory; Fleming (dropped behind when one) ground out 11 in 142 minutes, one of the slowest Test innings.

England

M. E. Trescothick	c Vincent b Vettori	37	– c Richardson b Vettori		88
M. P. Vaughan	c Fleming b Drum	7	– c Drum b Vettori		34
M. A. Butcher	c Astle b Drum	47	– c Martin b Drum		60
*N. Hussain	c Astle b Vettori	66	– (5) not out		13
G. P. Thorpe	c Fleming b Martin	11	– (6) not out		1
M. R. Ramprakash	b Butler	24			
A. Flintoff	c Drum b Butler	2	– (4) c and b Vettori		75
†J. S. Foster	not out	25			
A. F. Giles	c McMillan b Butler	10			
A. R. Caddick	c Richardson b Martin	10			
M. J. Hoggard	c Parore b Butler	7			
	B 4, l-b 2, w 6, n-b 22	34	B 5, l-b 13, n-b 4		22

1/26 (2) 2/63 (1) 3/133 (3) 4/163 (5)   280   1/79 (2) 2/194 (3)   (4 wkts dec.) 293
5/221 (6) 6/221 (4) 7/223 (7)   3/209 (1) 4/291 (4)
8/238 (9) 9/250 (10) 10/280 (11)

Butler 18.3–2–60–4; Drum 24–6–85–2; Martin 17–3–58–2; Vettori 25–3–62–2; Astle 1–0–1–0; McMillan 3–0–8–0. *Second Innings*—Butler 6–0–32–0; Drum 16–2–78–1; Vettori 24–1–90–3; Astle 9–4–18–0; Martin 7–1–40–0; McMillan 3–0–17–0.

New Zealand

M. H. Richardson	c Giles b Caddick	60	– c Thorpe b Giles		4
M. J. Horne	b Caddick	8	– c Foster b Flintoff		38
L. Vincent	c Thorpe b Giles	57	– lbw b Hoggard		71
*S. P. Fleming	c Thorpe b Caddick	3	– b Hoggard		11
N. J. Astle	c Hussain b Giles	4	– not out		11
C. D. McMillan	lbw b Caddick	41	– not out		17
†A. C. Parore	c Ramprakash b Giles	0			
D. L. Vettori	c Thorpe b Caddick	11			
C. J. Drum	c Trescothick b Giles	2			
I. G. Butler	c Foster b Caddick	12			
C. S. Martin	not out	0			
	B 2, l-b 9, n-b 9	20	B 3, l-b 1, n-b 2		6

1/16 (2) 2/135 (3) 3/138 (4) 4/143 (1)   218   1/28 (1) 2/65 (2)   (4 wkts) 158
5/147 (5) 6/149 (7) 7/178 (8)   3/128 (3) 4/131 (4)
8/201 (6) 9/207 (9) 10/218 (10)

Caddick 28.3–8–63–6; Hoggard 13–5–32–0; Giles 37–3–103–4; Flintoff 10–4–9–0. *Second Innings*—Caddick 17–6–31–0; Hoggard 13–4–31–2; Giles 33–11–53–1; Flintoff 16–6–24–1; Vaughan 5–1–15–0.

Umpires: R. S. Dunne *(New Zealand)* (39) and D. B. Hair *(Australia)* (44).
Third umpire: E. A. Watkin *(New Zealand)*.   Referee: J. L. Hendriks *(West Indies)* (18).

Close of play: First day, No play; Second day, England 92-2 (Butcher 24, Hussain 16); Third day, New Zealand 70-1 (Richardson 29, Vincent 30); Fourth day, England 184-1 (Trescothick 77, Butcher 57).

NEW ZEALAND v ENGLAND 2001–02 (3rd Test)

At Eden Park, Auckland, on 30, 31 *(no play)* March, 1, 2, 3 April.
Toss: New Zealand.   Result: NEW ZEALAND won by 78 runs.
Debuts: New Zealand – A. R. Adams.
Man of the Match: D. R. Tuffey.

New Zealand dramatically squared the series with their first home Test win over England for 18 years. They were given room to manoeuvre by the floodlights, switched on at 5.50 on the fourth afternoon. Play continued until shortly before eight, by which time the moon was shining and New Zealand were beaming, having scored 216 in a manic session of 41.2 overs. Hussain complained that his players were unable to see the ball clearly, but England – who the previous winter had been happy to pursue victory in the gloom at Karachi – had to get on with it. A New Zealand victory had looked a distant prospect on the first morning. Fleming chose to bat on a damp pitch, only for Caddick and Hoggard to reduce his side to 19 for 4. Harris led a revival, although Caddick took his 200th Test wicket (McMillan). Amid the showers, New Zealand reached 202, and then made inroads with the new ball, reprising England's 0 for 2 at Christchurch. The following morning, the giant Tuffey made the ball misbehave to claim a Test-best six wickets. When Fleming held his 100th Test catch to dismiss Hoggard, England's 160 was their lowest for 22 Tests. After the floodlit frenzy, an overnight declaration set England 312 in 105 overs, and at 122 for 2 anything seemed possible. But the pitch was worsening. Astle got one to pop at Butcher, while Parore, in his final Test, made his 200th dismissal as a wicketkeeper when he caught Thorpe.

New Zealand

M. H. Richardson b Caddick	5	– c sub (U. Afzaal) b Butcher	25
L. Vincent b Caddick	10	– (9) c Giles b Hoggard	10
*S. P. Fleming c Ramprakash b Hoggard	1	– b Hoggard	1
C. Z. Harris lbw b Flintoff	71	– lbw b Butcher	43
N. J. Astle c Thorpe b Caddick	2	– c Butcher b Flintoff	65
C. D. McMillan lbw b Caddick	41	– not out	50
†A. C. Parore c sub (U. Afzaal) b Flintoff	45	– (2) c Thorpe b Hoggard	36
D. L. Vettori lbw b Hoggard	3	– c Foster b Flintoff	0
A. R. Adams c Giles b Flintoff	7	– (7) b Flintoff	11
D. R. Tuffey c Butcher b Hoggard	0	– b Hoggard	5
C. J. Drum not out	2		
L-b 10, n-b 5	15	B 3, l-b 9, w 1, n-b 10	23

1/12 (1) 2/17 (3) 3/17 (2) 4/19 (5)   202
5/86 (6) 6/172 (4) 7/191 (8)
8/198 (7) 9/200 (9) 10/202 (10)

1/53 (2) 2/55 (3)   (9 wkts dec.) 269
3/91 (1) 4/166 (4)
5/217 (5) 6/232 (7) 7/235 (8) 8/262 (9) 9/269 (10)

Caddick 25–5–70–4; Hoggard 28.2–10–66–3; Flintoff 16–6–49–3; Butcher 5–3–6–0; Giles 1–0–1–0. *Second Innings*—Caddick 11–3–41–0; Hoggard 19.1–3–68–4; Flintoff 23–1–108–3; Butcher 9–2–34–2; Giles 1–0–6–0.

England

M. E. Trescothick lbw b Tuffey	0	– b Drum	14
M. P. Vaughan c Parore b Adams	27	– c Fleming b Drum	36
M. A. Butcher c Richardson b Tuffey	0	– c sub (B. G. K. Walker) b Astle	35
*N. Hussain c Fleming b Drum	2	– c and b Adams	82
G. P. Thorpe b Tuffey	42	– c Parore b Tuffey	3
M. R. Ramprakash c Parore b Tuffey	9	– (7) b Tuffey	2
A. Flintoff c Parore b Adams	29	– (6) b Tuffey	0
†J. S. Foster not out	16	– c Parore b Adams	23
A. F. Giles lbw b Tuffey	0	– not out	21
A. R. Caddick b Tuffey	20	– c Vettori b Drum	4
M. J. Hoggard c Fleming b Adams	0	– c Astle b Adams	2
B 1, l-b 11, n-b 3	15	B 1, l-b 8, n-b 2	11

1/0 (1) 2/0 (3) 3/11 (4) 4/60 (2)   160
5/75 (6) 6/118 (7) 7/122 (5)
8/124 (9) 9/159 (10) 10/160 (11)

1/23 (1) 2/73 (2) 3/122 (3)   233
4/125 (5) 5/125 (6) 6/155 (7)
7/204 (8) 8/207 (4) 9/230 (10) 10/233 (11)

Tuffey 19–6–54–6; Drum 10–3–45–1; Adams 15.4–2–44–3; McMillan 1–0–5–0. *Second Innings*—Tuffey 16–3–62–3; Drum 10–0–52–3; Adams 16–3–61–3; Astle 19–6–44–1; Vettori 2–0–5–0.

Umpires: D. B. Cowie *(New Zealand)* (22) and S. Venkataraghavan *(India)* (53).
Third umpire: A. L. Hill *(New Zealand)*.   Referee: J. L. Hendriks *(West Indies)* (19).

Close of play: First day, New Zealand 151-5 (Harris 55, Parore 24); Second day, No play; Third day, England 12-3 (Vaughan 8, Thorpe 0); Fourth day, New Zealand 269-9 (McMillan 50).

WEST INDIES v INDIA 2001–02 (1st Test)

At Bourda, Georgetown, Guyana, 11, 12, 13, 14, 15 *(no play)* April.
Toss: West Indies.   Result: MATCH DRAWN.
Debuts: West Indies – A. Sanford.
Man of the Match: C. L. Hooper.

Bourda's Test followed a familiar pattern. An easy-paced pitch produced high scores, before rain washed away the last day and a half. At least the sizeable Guyanese crowds had the satisfaction of witnessing a partnership of 293 – three short of West Indies' all-wicket record against India – between two local heroes, Hooper and Chanderpaul. West Indies reached 500 for only the second time in 39 Tests stretching back over four years, and then India were made to fight to avoid the follow-on. When Laxman was the first of three wickets to fall within five overs on the fourth morning, they were still 226 behind, but Dravid dug in, shrugging off a blow to the helmet to complete his tenth Test hundred. Soon after the start West Indies had been 44 for 3 (all to Srinath) after Lara, with no competitive cricket since fracturing his left elbow in Sri Lanka four months earlier, was given out for nought by umpire Harper, caught behind when even the bowler seemed unconvinced that he had touched it. Hooper might have been caught by the diving Dasgupta next ball, and edged between first and second slip when 10. But once settled Hooper batted with increasing authority. He put on 113 with Sarwan (another Guyanese), then batted with Chanderpaul for 361 minutes. Hooper converted his first Test hundred on his home ground into 233, his maiden double, with three sixes and 29 fours in 635 minutes and 402 balls, before he finally top-edged to long leg.

West Indies

C. H. Gayle c Dasgupta b Srinath	12	M. Dillon lbw b Bangar	0
S. C. Williams lbw b Srinath	13	A. Sanford lbw b Kumble	1
R. R. Sarwan c Zaheer Khan b Sarandeep Singh	53	C. E. Cuffy run out	0
B. C. Lara c Dasgupta b Srinath	0	B 1, l-b 4, w 3, n-b 26	34
*C. L. Hooper c Sarandeep Singh b Kumble	233		
S. Chanderpaul lbw b Zaheer Khan	140	1/21 (1) 2/37 (2) 3/44 (4) 4/157 (3)	501
†J. R. Murray lbw b Zaheer Khan	0	5/450 (6) 6/454 (7) 7/494 (5)	
M. V. Nagamootoo not out	15	8/494 (9) 9/499 (10) 10/501 (11)	

Srinath 33–8–91–3; Zaheer Khan 32–9–97–2; Bangar 27–6–63–1; Kumble 45.1–7–145–2; Ganguly 2–1–2–0; Sarandeep Singh 21–5–80–1; Tendulkar 3–0–18–0.

India

S. S. Das b Sanford	33	A. Kumble c Nagamootoo b Sanford	3
†D. Dasgupta lbw b Cuffy	0	Sarandeep Singh not out	39
*S. C. Ganguly c Nagamootoo b Dillon	5	B 4, l-b 12, w 2, n-b 5	23
S. R. Tendulkar lbw b Nagamootoo	79		
R. Dravid not out	144	1/6 (2) 2/21 (3) 3/99 (1) (7 wkts)	395
V. V. S. Laxman c Gayle b Cuffy	69	4/144 (4) 5/263 (6)	
S. B. Bangar lbw b Cuffy	0	6/270 (7) 7/275 (8)	

Zaheer Khan and J. Srinath did not bat.

Dillon 32.3–5–115–1; Cuffy 27–6–57–3; Sanford 25–5–81–2; Nagamootoo 40–13–103–1; Hooper 12–4–16–0; Gayle 4–2–7–0.

Umpires: E. A. R. de Silva *(Sri Lanka)* (13) and D. J. Harper *(Australia)* (18).
Third umpire: B. R. Doctrove *(West Indies)*.   Referee: R. S. Madugalle *(Sri Lanka)* (39).

Close of play: First day, West Indies 270-4 (Hooper 108, Chanderpaul 57); Second day, West Indies 494-7 (Nagamootoo 9, Dillon 0); Third day, India 237-4 (Dravid 57, Laxman 46); Fourth day, India 395-7 (Dravid 144, Sarandeep Singh 39).

WEST INDIES v INDIA 2001–02 (2nd Test)

At Queen's Park Oval, Port-of-Spain, Trinidad, 19, 20, 21, 22, 23 April.
Toss: West Indies.   Result: INDIA won by 37 runs.
Debuts: India – A. Ratra.
Man of the Match: V. V. S. Laxman.

A year earlier, West Indies had wanted 200 on the final day in Trinidad to beat South Africa, with nine wickets left; this time, they needed 182, with Lara and Hooper together. Again, they fell short, as India completed their third Test victory in the Caribbean at the same venue as their earlier two, in 1970-71 and 1975-76. The groundwork was laid after India were put in. Following a difficult start Tendulkar settled into his 29th Test hundred, which put him level with Don Bradman (only Sunil Gavaskar, with 34, had more at the time). West Indies were well placed at 179 for 3 but, as the shadows lengthened, three wickets fell for one inside ten balls, then Hooper had little support next morning as India gained a lead of 94. They were ebbing again at 56 for 4 – Sanford dismissed Tendulkar fourth ball – before Ganguly and Laxman added 149 to restore the balance. The new ball tilted it yet again: Laxman chopped on, and the last six wickets crashed for 13. Gayle retired with cramp as the quest for 313 began, but the stage was set for Lara to convert his overnight 40 into a first home Test hundred in front of a final-day crowd of 10,000. But, after an uncertain hour, Nehra's fourth ball induced a slip catch. The returning Gayle kept India waiting more than two hours, but when he drove loosely to cover West Indies needed 76 more – and Chanderpaul could find no-one to help him.

India

S. S. Das lbw b Dillon	10	– lbw b Dillon		0
S. B. Bangar c Murray b Sanford	9	– c Hooper b Sanford		16
R. Dravid b Black	67	– c Murray b Cuffy		36
S. R. Tendulkar lbw b Cuffy	117	– lbw b Sanford		0
*S. C. Ganguly c Dillon b Hooper	25	– not out		75
V. V. S. Laxman not out	69	– b Dillon		74
†A. Ratra c Murray b Cuffy	0	– lbw b Cuffy		2
Harbhajan Singh c Cuffy b Sanford	0	– c Gayle b Cuffy		0
Zaheer Khan b Sanford	5	– (10) run out		4
J. Srinath lbw b Black	18	– (9) c Williams b Dillon		2
A. Nehra c Hooper b Black	0	– b Dillon		0
B 4, l-b 13, n-b 2	19	B 5, l-b 2, n-b 2		9

1/18 (1) 2/38 (2) 3/162 (3) 4/218 (5)　　339　　1/6 (1) 2/54 (2) 3/54 (3)　　218
5/276 (4) 6/282 (7) 7/287 (8)　　　　　　　　4/56 (4) 5/205 (6) 6/210 (7)
8/298 (9) 9/339 (10) 10/339 (11)　　　　　　7/210 (8) 8/213 (9) 9/218 (10) 10/218 (11)

Dillon 28–7–82–1; Cuffy 30–12–49–2; Sanford 29–5–111–3; Black 17.5–7–53–3; Hooper 11–4–27–1. *Second Innings*—Dillon 21.1–7–42–4; Cuffy 20–6–53–3; Black 14–3–36–0; Sanford 17–5–46–2; Hooper 17–4–28–0; Sarwan 3–0–6–0.

West Indies

C. H. Gayle c Das b Srinath	13	– (2) c Harbhajan Singh b Zaheer Khan		52
S. C. Williams c Das b Harbhajan Singh	43	– (1) c Dravid b Srinath		13
R. R. Sarwan c Dravid b Nehra	35	– c Dravid b Harbhajan Singh		41
B. C. Lara c Ratra b Zaheer Khan	52	– c Dravid b Nehra		47
*C. L. Hooper c Ganguly b Zaheer Khan	50	– c Das b Nehra		22
S. Chanderpaul lbw b Srinath	1	– not out		67
†J. R. Murray lbw b Srinath	0	– run out		1
M. Dillon lbw b Nehra	9	– b Srinath		0
M. I. Black run out	6	– c Das b Srinath		3
A. Sanford c Tendulkar b Harbhajan Singh	12	– b Nehra		1
C. E. Cuffy not out	1	– c Bangar b Zaheer Khan		4
B 5, l-b 8, w 3, n-b 7	23	B 2, l-b 5, w 4, n-b 13		24

1/50 (1) 2/80 (2) 3/136 (3) 4/179 (4)　　245　　1/27 (1) 2/125 (3) 3/157 (4)　　275
5/180 (6) 6/180 (7) 7/201 (8)　　　　　　　　4/164 (5) 5/237 (2) 6/238 (7)
8/217 (9) 9/232 (5) 10/245 (10)　　　　　　　7/238 (8) 8/254 (9) 9/263 (10) 10/275 (11)

In the second innings Gayle, when 21, retired hurt at 68 and resumed at 164.

Srinath 22–4–71–3; Nehra 20–4–52–2; Zaheer Khan 14–2–47–2; Harbhajan Singh 19.5–3–51–2; Bangar 2–0–11–0. *Second Innings*—Srinath 32–9–69–3; Nehra 31–8–72–3; Harbhajan Singh 30–8–66–1; Zaheer Khan 21.1–5–55–2; Tendulkar 1–0–6–0.

Umpires: E. A. R. de Silva *(Sri Lanka)* (14) and D. J. Harper *(Australia)* (19).
Third umpire: E. A. Nicholls *(West Indies)*.   Referee: R. S. Madugalle *(Sri Lanka)* (40).

Close of play: First day, India 262-4 (Tendulkar 113, Laxman 21); Second day, West Indies 197-6 (Hooper 30, Dillon 6); Third day, India 165-4 (Ganguly 48, Laxman 60); Fourth day, West Indies 131-2 (Lara 40, Hooper 1).

WEST INDIES v INDIA 2001–02 (3rd Test)

At Kensington Oval, Bridgetown, Barbados, 2, 3, 4, 5 May.

Toss: West Indies.   Result: WEST INDIES won by ten wickets.

Debuts: none.

Man of the Match: M. Dillon.

If Port-of-Spain had proved itself India's lucky venue, Bridgetown was the precise opposite. They had never won a match of any kind at Kensington Oval, and had lost six of their seven Tests there. The aversion was confirmed with the first ball, with which Dillon bowled Das, and India were shot out for 102. Once Hooper and Chanderpaul reprised their Georgetown hundreds, there was no realistic way back. Tendulkar was out to his second ball, which was also Collins's second on his return after injury. The only fight came from Ganguly, last out when Dillon followed up his four wickets with a breathtaking catch on the third-man boundary. A century partnership between Lara and Sarwan took West Indies into the lead, but Nehra accounted for both in eight deliveries. Hooper and Chanderpaul rebuilt, and were not separated until they had completed their second double-century stand of the series. Chanderpaul had 91 when he lost Hooper, and just managed to beat the usual lower-order collapse – six for 18 – to reach his hundred, which took just over six hours. Das and his third opening partner in as many Tests, Wasim Jaffer, put on 80, India's best start of the series. It took a direct hit by Chanderpaul from point to part them, just before tea. But three more wickets were down by the end of the third day. Defiant innings from Ganguly and Zaheer Khan forced West Indies to bat again, but they needed only five runs to level the series.

India

S. S. Das b Dillon	0	– c Sarwan b Dillon	35
Wasim Jaffer c Jacobs b Dillon	12	– run out	51
R. Dravid run out	17	– c Jacobs b Sanford	14
S. R. Tendulkar c Jacobs b Collins	0	– lbw b Dillon	8
*S. C. Ganguly c Dillon b Sanford	48	– not out	60
V. V. S. Laxman b Cuffy	1	– c Hooper b Collins	43
†A. Ratra c Jacobs b Dillon	1	– lbw b Dillon	13
Harbhajan Singh c Dillon b Sanford	13	– b Cuffy	3
Zaheer Khan c Sarwan b Sanford	4	– c Jacobs b Sarwan	46
J. Srinath lbw b Dillon	0	– c Gayle b Sarwan	0
A. Nehra not out	0	– c Collins b Dillon	3
W 2, n-b 4	6	L-b 6, n-b 14	20

1/0 (1) 2/26 (2) 3/27 (4) 4/50 (3)   **102**   1/80 (2) 2/101 (1) 3/117 (3)   **296**
5/51 (6) 6/61 (7) 7/78 (8)   4/118 (4) 5/183 (6) 6/208 (7)
8/86 (9) 9/101 (10) 10/102 (5)   7/211 (8) 8/285 (9) 9/285 (10) 10/296 (11)

Dillon 11–1–41–4; Cuffy 9–4–17–1; Collins 8–0–24–1; Sanford 5.4–0–20–3. *Second Innings*—Dillon 31.2–8–82–4; Cuffy 24–16–26–1; Collins 22–1–78–1; Sanford 15–3–78–1; Hooper 5–0–11–0; Gayle 3–0–14–0; Sarwan 1–0–1–2.

West Indies

S. C. Williams c Wasim Jaffer b Zaheer Khan	18	– (2) not out	4
C. H. Gayle lbw b Zaheer Khan	14	– (1) not out	0
R. R. Sarwan c Wasim Jaffer b Nehra	60		
B. C. Lara c and b Nehra	55		
*C. L. Hooper c Tendulkar b Harbhajan Singh	115		
S. Chanderpaul not out	101		
†R. D. Jacobs c Ratra b Nehra	0		
M. Dillon c Das b Nehra	6		
P. T. Collins b Harbhajan Singh	0		
A. Sanford lbw b Harbhajan Singh	0		
C. E. Cuffy run out	1		
B 3, l-b 8, n-b 13	24	N-b 1	1

1/30 (1) 2/35 (2) 3/154 (4) 4/161 (3)   **394**   (no wkt) **5**
5/376 (5) 6/376 (7) 7/392 (8)
8/393 (9) 9/393 (10) 10/394 (11)

Srinath 32–7–85–0; Nehra 32–9–112–4; Zaheer Khan 29–8–83–2; Ganguly 7–5–9–0; Harbhajan Singh 34.5–7–87–3; Tendulkar 1–0–7–0. *Second Innings*—Tendulkar 1–0–1–0; Harbhajan Singh 0.2–0–4–0.

Umpires: E. A. R. de Silva *(Sri Lanka)* (15) and D. J. Harper *(Australia)* (20).
Third umpire: B. R. Doctrove *(West Indies)*.   Referee: R. S. Madugalle *(Sri Lanka)* (41).

Close of play: First day, West Indies 33-1 (Gayle 14, Sarwan 0); Second day, West Indies 314-4 (Hooper 70, Chanderpaul 75); Third day, India 169-4 (Ganguly 15, Laxman 30).

WEST INDIES v INDIA 2001–02 (4th Test)

At Antigua Recreation Ground, St John's, Antigua, 10, 11, 12, 13, 14 May.
Toss: West Indies.   Result: MATCH DRAWN.
Debuts: none.
Man of the Match: A. Ratra.

On a pitch so lifeless it yielded 1,142 runs for 18 wickets, India amassed their highest total in the Caribbean, and West Indies passed 600 for the first time in nearly seven years – yet the most prominent batsmen of their generation, Tendulkar and Lara, managed only four runs between them. Ratra, in his third Test, and Jacobs contributed an odd record: it was the first time in 125 years of Test cricket that opposing wicketkeepers had scored hundreds in the same match. At 20 years 150 days, Ratra was also the youngest keeper to make one. Later, he sent down what became the game's penultimate over as all 11 Indians bowled, only the third such instance in Tests. But the most memorable image of a batsman's match was provided by a bowler, Kumble. Sheathed in head bandages like some battle-front survivor after being hit by Dillon when batting, he returned on the third evening with a broken jaw. When he saw Tendulkar turning the ball he hurried out and bowled 14 consecutive overs, dismissing Lara and having Hooper caught off a no-ball. He flew home next day, and was sorely missed. The home batsmen spent the remainder of the match cashing in. On the meaningless last day, while Jacobs entertained a small home-town crowd with the quickest hundred of the match – completed in 172 balls, with his fifth six – while Chanderpaul scored 56 off 242 balls, crawling past Jacques Kallis's recent record of 1,241 minutes without dismissal in Tests.

India

S. S. Das b Collins	3	J. Srinath c Lara b Cuffy		15
Wasim Jaffer c Jacobs b Collins	86	A. Nehra not out		1
R. Dravid b Dillon	91			
S. R. Tendulkar c Jacobs b Collins	0	L-b 6, w 1, n-b 10		17
*S. C. Ganguly c Hinds b Cuffy	45			
V. V. S. Laxman hit wkt b Dillon	130	1/13 (1) 2/168 (2)	(9 wkts dec.)	513
A. Kumble c Chanderpaul b Dillon	6	3/168 (4) 4/233 (5)		
†A. Ratra not out	115	5/235 (3) 6/257 (7)		
Zaheer Khan c Jacobs b Cuffy	4	7/474 (6) 8/485 (9) 9/508 (10)		

Dillon 51–14–116–3; Cuffy 40–7–87–3; Collins 44–10–125–3; Sanford 32–6–113–0; Hooper 13–4–29–0; Hinds 2–0–9–0; Sarwan 9–3–23–0; Gayle 5–1–5–0.

West Indies

C. H. Gayle c Ratra b Zaheer Khan	32	A. Sanford c Zaheer Khan b Laxman		2
W. W. Hinds b Tendulkar	65	C. E. Cuffy not out		0
R. R. Sarwan lbw b Zaheer Khan	51			
B. C. Lara lbw b Kumble	4	B 10, l-b 9, w 6, n-b 6		31
*C. L. Hooper c Nehra b Tendulkar	136			
S. Chanderpaul not out	136	1/65 (1) 2/121 (2)	(9 wkts dec.)	629
†R. D. Jacobs c Laxman b Dravid	118	3/135 (4) 4/196 (3)		
M. Dillon b Wasim Jaffer	43	5/382 (5) 6/548 (7)		
P. T. Collins c sub (Harbhajan Singh) b Wasim Jaffer	11	7/607 (8) 8/625 (9) 9/628 (10)		

Srinath 45–19–82–0; Nehra 49–16–122–0; Zaheer Khan 48–14–129–2; Ganguly 12–0–44–0; Tendulkar 34–4–107–2; Kumble 14–5–29–1; Laxman 17–6–32–1; Dravid 9–3–18–1; Wasim Jaffer 11–3–18–2; Das 8–2–28–0; Ratra 1–0–1–0.

Umpires: D. R. Shepherd *(England)* (61) and R. B. Tiffin *(Zimbabwe)* (25).
Third umpire: E. A. Nicholls *(West Indies)*.   Referee: R. S. Madugalle *(Sri Lanka)* (42).

Close of play: First day, India 226-3 (Dravid 86, Ganguly 41); Second day, India 462-6 (Laxman 124, Ratra 93); Third day, West Indies 187-3 (Sarwan 50, Hooper 26); Fourth day, West Indies 405-5 (Chanderpaul 80, Jacobs 18).

WEST INDIES v INDIA 2001–02 (5th Test)

At Sabina Park, Kingston, Jamaica, 18, 19, 20, 21, 22 May.
Toss: India.   Result: WEST INDIES won by 155 runs.
Debuts: none.
Man of the Match: W. W. Hinds.   Man of the Series: S. Chanderpaul.

Drizzle delayed the start on the final morning, and the rain that would drench Kingston for the next 11 days was no more than 30 minutes away when Zaheer Khan slogged to extra cover, giving West Indies the victory that secured the series. They had needed only nine overs to extract India's last three wickets. Ganguly, who chose to bowl on the grassiest Sabina Park pitch anyone could remember, identified the opening stand of 111 between the two local left-handers, Gayle and Hinds, as decisive. India were better placed when Srinath dismissed Hooper, but the balance shifted again as Chanderpaul and Jacobs put on 109; even though the last five fell for 21, by then West Indies were back in control, and Chanderpaul had extended his record for batting without dismissal to 1,513 minutes, spread over four Tests. Once Dillon separated Ganguly and Laxman, the usual late-order collapse ensued: the last six tumbled for 44, Dillon returning Test-best figures. Hooper waived the follow-on, but some complacent batting meant West Indies were 122 for 7 before Chanderpaul and Collins built an overwhelming target – 408, two more than India's own record total to win, at Port-of-Spain in 1975-76. Collins removed both openers in his first two overs, but Tendulkar was in such commanding touch that India's task began to appear less daunting. He became the tenth player to reach 8,000 Test runs, but shortly after tea his nemesis Collins breached his defences again.

West Indies

C. H. Gayle	c Wasim Jaffer b Zaheer Khan	68	– c Ganguly b Srinath	15
W. W. Hinds	c Wasim Jaffer b Harbhajan Singh	113	– c Laxman b Srinath	6
R. R. Sarwan	c Das b Harbhajan Singh	65	– c Das b Zaheer Khan	12
B. C. Lara	c Ratra b Nehra	9	– b Zaheer Khan	35
*C. L. Hooper	c Dravid b Srinath	17	– c Ratra b Zaheer Khan	6
S. Chanderpaul	c Ratra b Srinath	58	– c and b Zaheer Khan	59
†R. D. Jacobs	b Harbhajan Singh	59	– c sub (D. Mongia) b Harbhajan Singh	16
M. Dillon	lbw b Harbhajan Singh	0	– b Nehra	4
P. T. Collins	c Laxman b Nehra	12	– b Harbhajan Singh	24
A. Sanford	c and b Harbhajan Singh	1	– c Ganguly b Harbhajan Singh	5
C. E. Cuffy	not out	0	– not out	3
	B 5, l-b 6, w 5, n-b 4	20	B 4, n-b 8	12

1/111 (1) 2/246 (2) 3/264 (4) 4/264 (3)   422   1/17 (2) 2/24 (1) 3/38 (3)   197
5/292 (5) 6/401 (7) 7/409 (8)   4/60 (5) 5/81 (4) 6/117 (7)
8/411 (6) 9/422 (10) 10/422 (9)   7/122 (8) 8/170 (6) 9/187 (10) 10/197 (9)

Srinath 32–9–111–2; Nehra 30–14–72–2; Zaheer Khan 24–4–78–1; Ganguly 8–4–12–0; Harbhajan Singh 38–3–138–5. *Second Innings*—Srinath 16–3–49–2; Nehra 9–2–23–1; Zaheer Khan 20–2–79–4; Harbhajan Singh 17.2–2–42–3.

India

S. S. Das	lbw b Cuffy	33	– lbw b Collins	10
Wasim Jaffer	c Jacobs b Dillon	0	– c Hinds b Collins	7
R. Dravid	lbw b Dillon	5	– lbw b Sanford	30
S. R. Tendulkar	b Sanford	41	– b Collins	86
*S. C. Ganguly	c Jacobs b Dillon	36	– c Sarwan b Sanford	28
V. V. S. Laxman	not out	65	– c Dillon b Sanford	23
†A. Ratra	c Hinds b Dillon	3	– lbw b Cuffy	19
Harbhajan Singh	c Hinds b Dillon	4	– c Cuffy b Gayle	17
Zaheer Khan	c Lara b Cuffy	6	– c Collins b Dillon	12
J. Srinath	c Gayle b Collins	2	– b Cuffy	4
A. Nehra	run out	0	– not out	0
	L-b 6, n-b 11	17	B 5, l-b 1, w 1, n-b 9	16

1/5 (2) 2/15 (3) 3/84 (4) 4/86 (1)   212   1/19 (2) 2/25 (1) 3/77 (3)   252
5/168 (5) 6/178 (7) 7/184 (8)   4/170 (4) 5/176 (5) 6/209 (6)
8/194 (9) 9/197 (10) 10/212 (11)   7/228 (8) 8/242 (7) 9/252 (10) 10/252 (9)

Dillon 24–4–71–5; Cuffy 22–5–49–2; Collins 19–2–54–1; Sanford 9–1–27–1; Hooper 1–0–5–0. *Second Innings*—Dillon 22.3–6–77–1; Cuffy 18–6–34–2; Collins 17–4–60–3; Sanford 19–8–48–3; Hooper 5–1–15–0; Gayle 4–2–7–1; Sarwan 3–0–5–0.

Umpires: D. R. Shepherd *(England)* (62) and R. B. Tiffin *(Zimbabwe)* (26).
Third umpire: B. R. Doctrove *(West Indies)*.   Referee: R. S. Madugalle *(Sri Lanka)* (43).

Close of play: First day, West Indies 287-4 (Hooper 14, Chanderpaul 4); Second day, India 141-4 (Ganguly 22, Laxman 27); Third day, West Indies 165-7 (Chanderpaul 55, Collins 4); Fourth day, India 237-7 (Ratra 16, Zaheer Khan 4).

PAKISTAN v NEW ZEALAND 2002 (1st Test)

At Gaddafi Stadium, Lahore, on 1, 2, 3 May.
Toss: Pakistan.   Result: PAKISTAN won by an innings and 324 runs.
Debuts: New Zealand – R. G. Hart.
Man of the Match: Inzamam-ul-Haq.

Pakistan recorded the fifth-biggest victory in Test cricket – their own largest, and New Zealand's heaviest defeat. On the first day Imran Nazir, in his first Test for 17 months, passed 100 with his third six. Inzamam-ul-Haq completed his 16th Test hundred next over with a crisp four off Vettori. His only blemish came at 110, when he drove Vettori uppishly but was dropped by Vincent. Inzamam passed 200 shortly before lunch on the second day. He had begun to suffer from cramp, and was allowed a runner for three overs before the interval; afterwards, the privilege was withdrawn. Struggling to run, he made up for it by hitting boundaries. He pushed a single after tea to reach Pakistan's second triple-century, following Hanif Mohammad's 337 in Barbados in 1957-58. In all, he smashed 38 fours and nine sixes. Now it was Shoaib Akhtar's turn. His lethal yorkers claimed four for four in 25 balls – all bowled – to leave New Zealand reeling. Shoaib sprained an ankle, but limped back on for two more wickets in eight runless deliveries, for a career-best 6 for 11. The tourists sank to the lowest Test total at Lahore, and followed on a massive 570 behind. In Shoaib's absence, they reached a respectable 186 for 3, but the last seven wickets tumbled for 60. The Second Test (and the rest of the tour) in Karachi was called off two hours before the start, after a car bomb in front of the teams' hotel killed 14 people.

Pakistan

Imran Nazir c Richardson b McMillan	127	Shoaib Akhtar st Hart b Walker 37
Shahid Afridi c Hart b Tuffey	0	Danish Kaneria not out 4
Younis Khan c Fleming b Vettori	27	
Inzamam-ul-Haq c Tuffey b Walker	329	B 1, l-b 8, w 1, n-b 8 18
Yousuf Youhana c Fleming b Martin	29	
Abdul Razzaq lbw b Tuffey	25	1/1 (2) 2/57 (3) 3/261 (1) 643
†Rashid Latif c and b Harris	7	4/355 (5) 5/384 (6) 6/399 (7)
Saqlain Mushtaq b McMillan	30	7/510 (8) 8/534 (9)
*Waqar Younis c and b McMillan	10	9/612 (10) 10/643 (4)

Tuffey 25–7–94–2; Martin 31–12–108–1; Vettori 40–4–178–1; Walker 14.5–3–97–2; Harris 29–3–109–1; McMillan 18–1–48–3.

New Zealand

M. H. Richardson b Shoaib Akhtar	8	– c Rashid Latif b Saqlain Mushtaq	32
M. J. Horne b Shoaib Akhtar	4	– c Rashid Latif b Waqar Younis	0
L. Vincent c Rashid Latif b Danish Kaneria	21	– c Rashid Latif b Danish Kaneria	57
*S. P. Fleming b Shoaib Akhtar	2	– c sub (Mohammad Sami) b Danish Kaneria	66
C. Z. Harris b Shoaib Akhtar	2	– lbw b Abdul Razzaq	43
C. D. McMillan c Shahid Afridi b Saqlain Mushtaq	15	– lbw b Danish Kaneria	2
†R. G. Hart lbw b Waqar Younis	4	– b Danish Kaneria	0
D. L. Vettori c Waqar Younis b Saqlain Mushtaq	7	– c sub (Shoaib Malik) b Abdul Razzaq	5
B. G. K. Walker lbw b Shoaib Akhtar	0	– not out	15
D. R. Tuffey not out	6	– c Younis Khan b Danish Kaneria	12
C. S. Martin b Shoaib Akhtar	0	– c sub (Shoaib Malik) b Saqlain Mushtaq	0
L-b 1, n-b 3	4	B 4, l-b 6, n-b 4	14

1/12 (2) 2/17 (1) 3/19 (4) 4/21 (5)	73	1/3 (2) 2/69 (1) 3/101 (3) 246
5/53 (6) 6/57 (3) 7/66 (8)		4/186 (5) 5/193 (6) 6/193 (7)
8/67 (7) 9/73 (9) 10/73 (11)		7/204 (8) 8/227 (4) 9/245 (10) 10/246 (11)

Waqar Younis 10–6–21–1; Shoaib Akhtar 8.2–4–11–6; Danish Kaneria 6–1–19–1; Saqlain Mushtaq 6–1–21–2. *Second Innings*—Waqar Younis 9–1–38–1; Abdul Razzaq 14–2–47–2; Danish Kaneria 32–3–110–5; Saqlain Mushtaq 17.3–3–38–2; Shahid Afridi 4–1–3–0.

Umpires: S. A. Bucknor *(West Indies)* (66) and R. E. Koertzen *(South Africa)* (30).
Third umpire: Aleem Dar *(Pakistan)*.   Referee: M. J. Procter *(South Africa)* (1).

Close of play: First day, Pakistan 355-4 (Inzamam-ul-Haq 159); Second day, New Zealand 58-6 (Hart 2, Vettori 0).

ENGLAND v SRI LANKA 2002 (1st Test)

At Lord's, London, on 16, 17, 18, 19, 20 May.
Toss: Sri Lanka.   Result: MATCH DRAWN.
Debuts: none.
Man of the Match: M. S. Atapattu.

Sri Lanka had won nine straight Tests when they took the field here, but were without Muttiah Muralitharan, being treated for a dislocated shoulder after a bad fall in an inconsequential one-day game in Sharjah. Hussain lost the toss for the 19th time in 22, but Sri Lanka lost two quick wickets before Atapattu and Jayawardene batted sumptuously, displaying style and finesse in a stand of 206. Jayawardene was a revelation. He already had eight Test centuries to his name, but this was statistical excellence made flesh. When he was on 47, a ball from Flintoff badly bruised his left hip. A runner was called for, but his power and precision did not desert him. Atapattu, meanwhile, failed by only 15 to make his sixth Test double-century. England collapsed abysmally, and failed by 81 to avoid the follow-on. The result may well have been decided in the first 20 minutes of the bright, fine fourth morning: Jayasuriya, at first slip, dropped Vaughan twice, both easy chances. Vaughan added 168 for the first wicket with Trescothick and made a fluent, upright second Test century. Early wickets on the last morning might still have set off a panic, but in the second over Jayasuriya sent four men to the boundary; three more patrolled the covers, and there was just one slip: Sri Lanka had accepted the draw. Left-armer Ruchira Perera's action was referred to the ICC after the match, but his three wickets came from poor shots rather than illegal deliveries.

Sri Lanka

M. S. Atapattu c Trescothick b Cork	185	– c Butcher b Caddick	7
*S. T. Jayasuriya run out	18		
†K. C. Sangakkara c Flintoff b Hoggard	10	– (2) not out	6
D. P. M. D. Jayawardene c Trescothick b Flintoff	107	– (3) not out	14
P. A. de Silva c Stewart b Cork	88		
R. P. Arnold c Trescothick b Hoggard	50		
H. P. Tillekeratne not out	17		
W. P. U. J. C. Vaas c Trescothick b Cork	6		
D. N. T. Zoysa c Stewart b Flintoff	28		
T. C. B. Fernando not out	6		
B 1, l-b 13, w 1, n-b 25	40	B 5, l-b 2, n-b 8	15

1/38 (2) 2/55 (3) 3/261 (4)   (8 wkts dec.) 555   1/16 (1)   (1 wkt) 42
4/407 (1) 5/492 (6) 6/492 (5)
7/505 (8) 8/540 (9)

P. D. R. L. Perera did not bat.

Caddick 38.3–8–135–0; Hoggard 39–4–160–2; Cork 35.3–11–93–3; Flintoff 39–8–101–2; Butcher 3–0–17–0; Vaughan 14–2–35–0. *Second Innings*—Caddick 7–2–10–1; Flintoff 5–0–18–0; Hoggard 1–0–7–0.

England

M. E. Trescothick c Jayasuriya b Zoysa	13	– lbw b Zoysa	76
M. P. Vaughan c Zoysa b Perera	64	– c Sangakkara b Perera	115
M. A. Butcher c Jayawardene b Fernando	17	– run out	105
*N. Hussain c Sangakkara b Zoysa	57	– lbw b Perera	68
G. P. Thorpe lbw b Perera	27	– c Fernando b de Silva	65
J. P. Crawley c Sangakkara b Vaas	31	– not out	41
†A. J. Stewart run out	7	– not out	26
A. Flintoff c Sangakkara b Fernando	12		
D. G. Cork c Sangakkara b Fernando	0		
A. R. Caddick c Sangakkara b Perera	13		
M. J. Hoggard not out	0		
B 4, l-b 7, w 9, n-b 14	34	B 1, l-b 9, w 1, n-b 22	33

1/17 (1) 2/43 (3) 3/149 (4) 4/203 (2)   275   1/168 (1) 2/213 (2)   (5 wkts dec.) 529
5/203 (5) 6/214 (7) 7/237 (8)   3/372 (4) 4/432 (3)
8/237 (9) 9/267 (10) 10/275 (6)   5/483 (5)

Vaas 21.1–4–51–1; Zoysa 19–3–82–2; Fernando 22–5–83–3; Perera 11–0–48–3. *Second Innings*—Vaas 44–8–113–0; Zoysa 34–6–84–1; Perera 30–4–90–2; de Silva 27–7–63–1; Fernando 26–1–96–0; Jayasuriya 25–6–66–0; Arnold 4–1–7–0; Tillekeratne 1–1–0–0.

Umpires: D. J. Harper *(Australia)* (21) and S. Venkataraghavan *(India)* (54).
Third umpire: J. W. Lloyds *(England)*.   Referee: G. R. Viswanath *(India)* (3).

Close of play: First day, Sri Lanka 314-3 (Atapattu 133, de Silva 24); Second day, England 27-1 (Vaughan 4, Butcher 7); Third day, England 53-0 (Trescothick 31, Vaughan 20); Fourth day, England 321-2 (Butcher 55, Hussain 51).

ENGLAND v SRI LANKA 2002 (2nd Test)

At Edgbaston, Birmingham, on 30, 31 May, 1, 2 June.
Toss: England.　　Result: ENGLAND won by an innings and 111 runs.
Debuts: none.
Man of the Match: M. J. Hoggard.

England dictated terms throughout, barely suffering so much as a bad session. Their victory was as clinical as it was crushing. For Sri Lanka, there was just one selection issue: would Muralitharan be fit to play? He wasn't, but played anyway, increasing the burden on his injured shoulder. Sri Lanka had won none of the 12 Tests he had missed since his 1992-93 debut, and ached to have him back. Given the chance to exploit a dampish pitch after Hussain won the toss for a change, Caddick did so. Sangakkara chased one from Flintoff so wide it seemed to be hurtling towards gully, and Stewart somehow clung on to his 200th Test dismissal as a wicketkeeper. Jayawardene was undone by a Caddick classic, and Sri Lanka were hustled out for 162. Next day, under a warm summer sun and on an impeccable pitch, runs flowed. Trescothick and Butcher added 202, a record for any English wicket against Sri Lanka. Murali's injured left shoulder hurt so much that each appeal turned his winsome grin into a wince of pain, yet on the second day he still totted up 42 overs, and 64 in all. England dipped to 454 for 9, but Hoggard helped Thorpe (who had already passed 5,000 runs in Tests) from 61 to a canny 11th century during a stand of 91. When Sri Lanka batted again Hoggard, brimful of confidence, castled Jayasuriya then despatched Sangakkara. Next morning, there was little resistance once Atapattu played on.

Sri Lanka

M. S. Atapattu c Stewart b Hoggard	13	– b Hoggard	56
*S. T. Jayasuriya c Stewart b Caddick	8	– b Hoggard	12
†K. C. Sangakkara c Stewart b Flintoff	16	– lbw b Hoggard	1
D. P. M. D. Jayawardene c Flintoff b Caddick	47	– c Thorpe b Caddick	59
P. A. de Silva c Trescothick b Hoggard	10	– c Thorpe b Caddick	47
H. P. Tillekeratne lbw b Tudor	20	– b Caddick	39
R. P. Arnold c Flintoff b Caddick	1	– c Giles b Hoggard	4
W. P. U. J. C. Vaas b Flintoff	23	– st Stewart b Giles	28
D. N. T. Zoysa c Hoggard b Tudor	0	– (10) not out	1
T. C. B. Fernando run out	13	– (9) b Hoggard	0
M. Muralitharan not out	0	– absent hurt	
B 1, n-b 10	11	B 4, l-b 4, n-b 17	25

1/23 (1) 2/23 (2) 3/76 (3) 4/96 (5)　　162　　1/28 (2) 2/30 (3) 3/135 (1)　　272
5/100 (4) 6/108 (7) 7/141 (6)　　　　　　　4/156 (4) 5/233 (6) 6/238 (5)
8/141 (9) 9/159 (8) 10/162 (10)　　　　　　7/247 (7) 8/247 (9) 9/272 (8)

Caddick 17–4–47–3; Hoggard 17–4–55–2; Giles 4–1–7–0; Tudor 9.5–3–25–2; Flintoff 5–0–27–2. *Second Innings—* Caddick 25–4–67–3; Hoggard 23–2–92–5; Flintoff 6–0–23–0; Giles 26.1–3–57–1; Tudor 9–1–25–0.

England

M. E. Trescothick c Tillekeratne b Vaas	161	A. F. Giles c Sangakkara b Zoysa	0
M. P. Vaughan c Jayasuriya b Muralitharan	46	A. R. Caddick c Sangakkara b Zoysa	3
M. A. Butcher b Muralitharan	94	M. J. Hoggard not out	17
*N. Hussain b Muralitharan	22	L-b 19, w 6, n-b 15	40
G. P. Thorpe c Vaas b Fernando	123		
†A. J. Stewart c Tillekeratne b Muralitharan	7	1/92 (2) 2/294 (1) 3/338 (3) 4/341 (4)	545
A. Flintoff c Tillekeratne b Muralitharan	29	5/368 (6) 6/426 (7) 7/436 (8)	
A. J. Tudor c Tillekeratne b Zoysa	3	8/444 (9) 9/454 (10) 10/545 (5)	

Vaas 41–3–141–1; Zoysa 24–3–93–3; Muralitharan 64–12–143–5; Fernando 21.5–2–92–1; Jayasuriya 6–2–27–0; de Silva 7–0–30–0.

Umpires: D. J. Harper *(Australia)* (22) and S. Venkataraghavan *(India)* (55).
Third umpire: P. Willey *(England)*.　　Referee: G. R. Viswanath *(India)* (4).

Close of play: First day, England 24-0 (Trescothick 9, Vaughan 14); Second day, England 401-5 (Thorpe 30, Flintoff 14); Third day, Sri Lanka 132-2 (Atapattu 56, Jayawardene 45).

ENGLAND v SRI LANKA 2002 (3rd Test)

At Old Trafford, Manchester, on 13, 14, 15, 16, 17 June.
Toss: England.   Result: ENGLAND won by ten wickets.
Debuts: none.
Man of the Match: A. J. Tudor.   Men of the Series: M. A. Butcher and D. P. M. D. Jayawardene.

A Test that had crept along in the shadow of football's World Cup sprang to life in the equivalent of extra time. As darkness began to fall on the final evening, Giles removed Sri Lanka's last two wickets in two balls to leave England needing 50 in six overs. Vaughan and Trescothick attacked, and sealed a 2–0 series win with an over to spare. England's victory was a triumph of patience and timing. For an unprecedented third innings running they racked up 500, then bowled Sri Lanka out twice. Trescothick motored to 81 before edging to slip, the first time he had fallen to Muralitharan in 350 balls in Tests. Stewart, under pressure for his place despite equalling Graham Gooch's record of 118 caps, was dropped in the gully on nought – and went on to his 15th Test century, reaching it with four consecutive fours off Fernando soon after Tudor had become Vaas's 200th wicket. Sri Lanka reached 219 for 4, but then lost their last five for 34, and followed on against England for the first time. Luck seemed to be on their side when Jayawardene flicked Flintoff to Hoggard at deep backward square, only for umpire Orchard to signal no-ball after spotting that Hoggard had accidentally become the third leg-side fielder behind square. Orchard's colleague Steve Bucknor was standing in his 67th Test, surpassing Dickie Bird's record of 66. At tea, with Sri Lanka 253 for 4, a draw seemed certain: but the second new ball proved crucial.

England

M. E. Trescothick c Jayawardene b Muralitharan	81	– not out	23
M. P. Vaughan c Vaas b Fernando	36	– not out	24
M. A. Butcher lbw b Vaas	123		
*N. Hussain c Muralitharan b Fernando	16		
G. P. Thorpe c Sangakkara b Upashantha	32		
†A. J. Stewart c Tillekeratne b Muralitharan	123		
A. Flintoff run out	1		
A. J. Tudor c Arnold b Vaas	19		
A. F. Giles c Sangakkara b Muralitharan	45		
A. R. Caddick not out	2		
M. J. Hoggard lbw b Fernando	7		
B 5, l-b 10, n-b 12	27	L-b 2, n-b 1	3

1/66 (2) 2/192 (1) 3/219 (4) 4/262 (5)   512   (no wkt) 50
5/354 (3) 6/361 (7) 7/400 (8)
8/502 (9) 9/503 (6) 10/512 (11)

Vaas 38–8–121–2; Upashantha 8–0–65–1; Fernando 29.2–2–154–3; Muralitharan 60–20–137–3; de Silva 2–0–5–0; Jayasuriya 8–2–15–0. *Second Innings*—Vaas 1–0–8–0; Fernando 2–0–23–0; Muralitharan 2–0–17–0.

Sri Lanka

M. S. Atapattu retired hurt	10	– (10) lbw b Giles	6
R. P. Arnold c Vaughan b Tudor	62	– (1) c Stewart b Tudor	109
†K. C. Sangakkara c Thorpe b Hoggard	40	– lbw b Tudor	32
D. P. M. D. Jayawardene c and b Tudor	17	– c Hussain b Giles	28
P. A. de Silva c Hussain b Flintoff	18	– c Vaughan b Tudor	40
*S. T. Jayasuriya lbw b Hoggard	35	– (2) b Hoggard	26
H. P. Tillekeratne c Flintoff b Giles	20	– (6) not out	32
W. P. U. J. C. Vaas lbw b Hoggard	14	– (7) lbw b Hoggard	1
K. E. A. Upashantha c Stewart b Tudor	1	– (8) c Stewart b Flintoff	3
C. R. D. Fernando not out	6	– (9) lbw b Giles	4
M. Muralitharan c Stewart b Tudor	6	– c sub (M. J. Powell) b Giles	0
B 1, l-b 3, n-b 20	24	B 9, l-b 9, w 2, n-b 7	27

1/107 (2) 2/142 (4) 3/149 (3)   253   1/44 (2) 2/110 (3) 3/170 (4)   308
4/171 (5) 5/219 (7) 6/227 (6)   4/233 (5) 5/263 (1) 6/264 (7)
7/228 (9) 8/240 (8) 9/253 (11)   7/270 (8) 8/285 (9) 9/308 (10) 10/308 (11)

In the first innings, Atapattu retired hurt at 48.

Caddick 5.3–2–17–0; Hoggard 16–4–38–3; Flintoff 23–5–65–1; Tudor 25–8–65–4; Giles 23–3–64–1. *Second Innings*—Hoggard 37–8–97–2; Flintoff 29–7–78–1; Giles 24.2–4–62–4; Tudor 21–6–44–3; Vaughan 2–0–9–0.

Umpires: S. A. Bucknor *(West Indies)* (67) and D. L. Orchard *(South Africa)* (28).
Third umpire: N. A. Mallender *(England)*.   Referee: G. R. Viswanath *(India)* (5).

Close of play: First day, England 273-4 (Butcher 85, Stewart 7); Second day, England 377-6 (Stewart 57, Tudor 6); Third day, Sri Lanka 130-1 (Sangakkara 33, Jayawardene 11); Fourth day, Sri Lanka 63-1 (Arnold 26, Sangakkara 9).

WEST INDIES v NEW ZEALAND 2002 (1st Test)

At Kensington Oval, Bridgetown, Barbados, on 21, 22, 23, 24 June.
Toss: West Indies.   Result: NEW ZEALAND won by 204 runs.
Debuts: West Indies – D. B. Powell.
Man of the Match: S. P. Fleming.

New Zealand's first Test victory in the Caribbean, in their 12th match, was a comprehensive one, completed inside four days. It was particularly satisfying for Fleming, whose century underpinned his 17th Test win as captain – exactly one third of New Zealand's 51 victories. The defeat was only West Indies' fourth in 39 Tests at Kensington Oval. The outcome was all but settled on the second afternoon when West Indies collapsed for 107, their lowest at Bridgetown since their 102 against England on an uncovered, rain-affected pitch in 1934-35. With time on his side, Fleming did not opt to enforce the follow-on despite a lead of 230. He had already completed his fourth Test hundred to lead New Zealand out of their own middle-order slump, well supported by Hart, in only his second Test. When West Indies batted, only Chanderpaul put up a fight, lasting for just over two hours before running out of partners. Apart from Lara, who played on to Vettori, all the wickets were caught, most of them from attacking shots. At 88 for 5, New Zealand seemed likely to fall some way short of the unassailable target they wanted, and it took a counter-attack by Astle to put them back on track; when Collins wound up the innings, the lead was 473. Once Bond broke through in a pacy second spell only Lara's flailing 73 delayed matters unduly, and Bond rounded things off with three wickets, including Lara's, in 12 deliveries with the second new ball.

New Zealand

M. H. Richardson b Sanford	41	– c Lara b Collins	0
L. Vincent c Jacobs b Dillon	14	– lbw b Collins	2
*S. P. Fleming c Gayle b Hooper	130	– (7) c Hinds b Sanford	34
C. Z. Harris c Lara b Collins	0	– lbw b Powell	19
N. J. Astle c Lara b Dillon	2	– c Lara b Dillon	77
C. D. McMillan lbw b Sanford	6	– c Hooper b Collins	1
†R. G. Hart not out	57	– (8) c Hinds b Collins	24
D. L. Vettori c Hinds b Collins	39	– (9) b Sanford	11
D. R. Tuffey lbw b Powell	28	– (3) c Gayle b Hooper	31
S. E. Bond b Powell	5	– not out	6
I. G. Butler run out	3	– c Jacobs b Collins	26
L-b 8, n-b 4	12	L-b 8, w 1, n-b 3	12

1/38 (2) 2/88 (1) 3/89 (4) 4/106 (5)   337   1/0 (1) 2/11 (2) 3/48 (4) 4/69 (3)   243
5/117 (6) 6/225 (3) 7/278 (8)   5/88 (6) 6/164 (5) 7/181 (7)
8/323 (9) 9/333 (10) 10/337 (11)   8/205 (9) 9/213 (8) 10/243 (11)

Dillon 28–6–73–2; Collins 24–5–80–2; Powell 21–6–41–2; Sanford 28.4–7–101–2; Hooper 13–5–21–1; Gayle 10–3–12–0; Sarwan 1–0–1–0. *Second Innings*—Collins 30.4–8–76–6; Powell 20–4–61–1; Dillon 6–3–11–0; Sanford 17–5–68–2; Hooper 17–8–19–1.

West Indies

C. H. Gayle c Vettori b Bond	3	– lbw b Bond	73
W. W. Hinds c McMillan b Tuffey	10	– c Richardson b Vettori	37
R. R. Sarwan c Butler b Bond	0	– c Vettori b Bond	18
B. C. Lara b Vettori	28	– b Bond	73
*C. L. Hooper c Tuffey b Butler	6	– c Fleming b Tuffey	16
S. Chanderpaul not out	35	– c Fleming b Vettori	17
†R. D. Jacobs c Astle b Vettori	4	– c Astle b Vettori	6
P. T. Collins c Vincent b Butler	8	– (9) lbw b Bond	8
A. Sanford c Hart b Butler	1	– (10) not out	0
D. B. Powell c Harris b Vettori	0	– (8) c Astle b Butler	2
M. Dillon c Fleming b Vettori	0	– c Vincent b Bond	0
L-b 4, n-b 8	12	B 5, l-b 11, w 2, n-b 1	19

1/6 (1) 2/6 (3) 3/31 (2) 4/47 (5)   107   1/68 (2) 2/133 (3) 3/142 (1)   269
5/62 (4) 6/73 (7) 7/90 (8)   4/179 (5) 5/204 (6) 6/216 (7)
8/93 (9) 9/103 (10) 10/107 (11)   7/222 (8) 8/252 (9) 9/269 (4) 10/269 (11)

Bond 12–1–34–2; Tuffey 7–3–16–1; Butler 11–2–26–3; Vettori 12.1–2–27–4. *Second Innings*—Bond 21–7–78–5; Tuffey 15–5–43–1; Butler 14–0–58–1; Vettori 19–3–53–3; Astle 5–4–4–0; Harris 9–3–17–0.

Umpires: R. E. Koertzen *(South Africa)* (31) and S. Venkataraghavan *(India)* (56).
Third umpire: B. R. Doctrove *(West Indies)*.   Referee: Wasim Raja *(Pakistan)* (1).

Close of play: First day, New Zealand 257-6 (Hart 34, Vettori 21); Second day, New Zealand 4-1 (Vincent 1, Tuffey 1); Third day, West Indies 5-0 (Gayle 0, Hinds 4).

WEST INDIES v NEW ZEALAND 2002 (2nd Test)

At Queen's Park, St George's, Grenada, on 28, 29, 30 June, 1, 2 July.
Toss: West Indies.   Result: MATCH DRAWN.
Debuts: New Zealand – S. B. Styris.
Man of the Match: C. H. Gayle.   Man of the Series: S. E. Bond.

In the first match at Test cricket's 84th venue, New Zealand were made to fight for the draw that gave them the series. Their hero was Scott Styris, who marked his Test debut with 107 – from No. 8 – to rescue them on the second day, and an unbeaten 69 on the last which helped stave off a late West Indian charge. Hooper won his sixth toss of the home season's seven Tests and, for the fifth time, chose to bowl; for the fourth time, the opposition responded by passing 300. But they were an uncertain 208 for 6 when Styris entered in the first over of the second day; when he was last out he had become the seventh New Zealander to score a debut century. The West Indian response was based on Gayle's belligerent double-hundred, which included huge sixes off Butler and Bond, and four consecutive fours, of 29 all told, in Butler's first over with the second new ball. Bond finished with his second five-for of the week, but the tail carried the lead to 97. Richardson and Vincent, missed twice in the slips off Collins when two, erased the deficit. Then the spinners claimed five for 40 on a wearing pitch to give West Indies a scent of victory. New Zealand were only 60 ahead with half the side out and McMillan nursing a sore hand, but Styris and Hart calmed nerves in a stand of 99, helped by rain, which permitted only 23 overs after lunch.

New Zealand

M. H. Richardson c Gayle b Collins	95	– c Jacobs b Nagamootoo	71
L. Vincent b Cuffy	24	– b Sarwan	54
*S. P. Fleming c Lara b Collins	6	– c Lara b Hooper	5
C. Z. Harris c Jacobs b Hooper	0	– c Sarwan b Nagamootoo	17
N. J. Astle lbw b Collins	69	– c Hinds b Hooper	0
D. L. Vettori c Jacobs b Collins	1		
C. D. McMillan c Lara b Cuffy	14		
S. B. Styris b Sanford	107	– (6) not out	69
†R. G. Hart c Hinds b Hooper	20	– (7) not out	28
S. E. Bond lbw b Chanderpaul	17		
I. G. Butler not out	5		
L-b 6, w 2, n-b 7	15	L-b 7, n-b 5	12

1/61 (2) 2/81 (3) 3/82 (4) 4/205 (1)   373
5/206 (6) 6/208 (5) 7/256 (7)
8/312 (9) 9/361 (10) 10/373 (8)

1/117 (2) 2/132 (3)   (5 wkts) 256
3/148 (1) 4/149 (5)
5/157 (4)

Collins 30–9–68–4; Cuffy 35–12–76–2; Sanford 22.5–4–74–1; Nagamootoo 33–9–88–0; Hooper 25–3–44–2; Gayle 3–1–5–0; Chanderpaul 4–0–12–1. *Second Innings*—Collins 17–7–28–0; Cuffy 10–3–20–0; Nagamootoo 42–16–75–2; Sanford 14–3–27–0; Hooper 34–10–66–2; Gayle 6–2–7–0; Sarwan 6–0–26–1; Chanderpaul 2–2–0–0.

West Indies

C. H. Gayle c Hart b Bond	204	A. Sanford c Butler b Bond	12
W. W. Hinds b Bond	10	C. E. Cuffy not out	0
R. R. Sarwan run out	39		
B. C. Lara c Hart b Styris	48	B 4, l-b 2, w 5, n-b 15	26
*C. L. Hooper lbw b Bond	17		
S. Chanderpaul c Fleming b Bond	51	1/28 (2) 2/128 (3) 3/204 (4)	470
†R. D. Jacobs c Styris b Butler	17	4/242 (5) 5/385 (1) 6/394 (6)	
M. V. Nagamootoo c Hart b Styris	32	7/441 (7) 8/448 (8)	
P. T. Collins lbw b Vettori	14	9/470 (9) 10/470 (10)	

Bond 30.1–7–104–5; Butler 21–4–83–1; Styris 25–3–88–2; Vettori 41–9–134–1; Astle 6–2–15–0; Harris 15–4–40–0.

Umpires: R. E. Koertzen *(South Africa)* (32) and S. Venkataraghavan *(India)* (57).
Third umpire: B. R. Doctrove *(West Indies)*.   Referee: Wasim Raja *(Pakistan)* (2).

Close of play: First day, New Zealand 208-5 (Astle 69, McMillan 1); Second day, West Indies 63-1 (Gayle 23, Sarwan 22); Third day, West Indies 394-5 (Chanderpaul 51, Jacobs 2); Fourth day, New Zealand 139-2 (Richardson 69, Harris 6).

SRI LANKA v BANGLADESH 2002 (1st Test)

At P. Saravanamuttu Stadium, Colombo, on 21, 22, 23 July.

Toss: Sri Lanka.   Result: SRI LANKA won by an innings and 196 runs.

Debuts: Sri Lanka – W. R. S. de Silva. Bangladesh – Alamgir Kabir, Ehsanul Haque, Hannan Sarkar, Talha Jubair.

Man of the Match: M. Muralitharan.

Inspired by Aravinda de Silva, who became the fourth batsman after Andy Sandham, Bill Ponsford and Seymour Nurse to score a double-century in his final Test, Sri Lanka improved on their biggest Test victory for the third time in 11 months. de Silva led the onslaught, extending his 20th century to the fourth-quickest double in Tests (229 balls). It turned out to be his swansong; he did not play in the next game, and retired from Test cricket afterwards. He was helped by Muralitharan who, returning after a shoulder injury, took five wickets in each innings to equal Richard Hadlee's record of 36 five-fors. Hannan Sarkar, one of four debutants, and Habibul Bashar took Bangladesh to 107 for 2 just before lunch, but Sarkar was trapped by Jayasuriya's first delivery, and Murali deceived Habibul in the next over. After a lengthy rain-break, Bangladesh were shot out for 161. Because of the time lost, an extra hour was added to the second day. Sri Lanka made full use of it, scoring 509 in 104 overs, a Test record for a single side in a day. Only England had previously managed it, with 503 in 111 overs against South Africa at Lord's in 1924. Trailing by 380, Bangladesh fared slightly better, but yet again Muralitharan proved too much, brilliantly supported in the field: Sangakkara held four catches at silly point. de Silva claimed the final wicket before tea on the third day in the Saravanamuttu Stadium's first Test for almost eight years.

Bangladesh

Hannan Sarkar lbw b Jayasuriya	55	– lbw b W. R. S. de Silva		1
Al Sahariar lbw b W. R. S. de Silva	13	– c Sangakkara b Muralitharan		67
Ehsanul Haque b C. R. D. Fernando	2	– c T. C. B. Fernando b C. R. D. Fernando	...	5
Habibul Bashar lbw b Muralitharan	24	– b Muralitharan		34
Akram Khan c H. A. P. W. Jayawardene b T. C. B. Fernando	20	– c Sangakkara b Muralitharan		5
Aminul Islam c Arnold b Muralitharan	0	– c Sangakkara b Muralitharan		0
*†Khaled Mashud c Jayasuriya b Muralitharan	23	– c T. C. B. Fernando b P. A. de Silva		26
Enamul Haque, sen. st H. A. P. W. Jayawardene b Muralitharan	1	– b C. R. D. Fernando		22
Manjural Islam b T. C. B. Fernando	0	– c Sangakkara b Muralitharan		2
Alamgir Kabir b Muralitharan	0	– b W. R. S. de Silva		0
Talha Jubair not out	0	– not out		5
B 8, l-b 4, w 1, n-b 10	23	L-b 5, w 1, n-b 11		17

1/32 (2) 2/50 (3) 3/107 (1) 4/111 (4)   161   1/2 (1) 2/14 (3) 3/91 (4)   184
5/111 (6) 6/148 (7) 7/151 (8)   4/113 (5) 5/113 (6) 6/124 (2)
8/156 (9) 9/161 (5) 10/161 (10)   7/158 (8) 8/161 (9) 9/166 (10) 10/184 (7)

T. C. B. Fernando 10–3–38–2; W. R. S. de Silva 13–3–31–1; C. R. D. Fernando 10–3–40–1; Muralitharan 19.4–6–39–5; Jayasuriya 1–0–1–1. *Second Innings*—C. R. D. Fernando 11–4–24–2; W. R. S. de Silva 11–1–35–2; T. C. B. Fernando 7–2–34–0; Muralitharan 25–6–59–5; Jayasuriya 10–2–20–0; P. A. de Silva 2.3–1–7–1.

Sri Lanka

M. S. Atapattu b Talha Jubair	20
R. P. Arnold c sub (Fahim Muntasir) b Manjural Islam	25
K. C. Sangakkara run out	75
D. P. M. D. Jayawardene b Talha Jubair	0
P. A. de Silva lbw b Enamul Haque	206
*S. T. Jayasuriya c sub (Mohammad Ashraful) b Enamul Haque	145
†H. A. P. W. Jayawardene c Al Sahariar b Manjural Islam	5
T. C. B. Fernando not out	31

M. Muralitharan c Al Sahariar b Enamul Haque	0
C. R. D. Fernando c Habibul Bashar b Enamul Haque	15
W. R. S. de Silva not out	5
L-b 6, w 2, n-b 6	14

1/35 (1) 2/49 (2)   (9 wkts. dec.) 541
3/56 (4) 4/206 (3)
55/440 (5) 6/447 (7)
7/491 (6) 8/491 (9) 9/524 (10)

Manjural Islam 25–1–128–2; Talha Jubair 21–0–120–2; Alamgir Kabir 15–1–82–0; Enamul Haque 38–6–144–4; Habibul Bashar 9–0–43–0; Ehsanul Haque 3–0–18–0.

Umpires: S. A. Bucknor *(West Indies)* (68) and D. R. Shepherd *(England)* (63).
Third umpire: T. H. Wijewardene *(Sri Lanka)*.   Referee: Wasim Raja *(Pakistan)* (3).

Close of play: First day, Sri Lanka 32-0 (Atapattu 20, Arnold 10); Second day, Sri Lanka 541-9 (T. C. B. Fernando 31, W. R. S. de Silva 5).

SRI LANKA v BANGLADESH 2002 (2nd Test)

At Sinhalese Sports Club Ground, Colombo, on 28, 29, 30, 31 July.
Toss: Bangladesh.   Result: SRI LANKA won by 288 runs.
Debuts: Sri Lanka – M. K. G. C. P. Lakshitha *(also known as Chamila Gamage)*, J. Mubarak, M. N. Nawaz. Bangladesh – Alok Kapali, Tapash Baisya, Tushar Imran.
Man of the Match: M. G. Vandort.

Bangladesh's batsmen showed little improvement, but at least their bowlers had the satisfaction of bowling out an inexperienced Sri Lankan side (the selectors made seven changes, including some players Jayasuriya said he had never seen play before) for 373 – only the third time in their last ten home Tests that they had not reached 500. The new openers provided a solid start, Jayasuriya plundered 85, and Lakshitha clouted 40 in 46 balls at No. 11. Then Lakshitha, a lean bowler from the Air Force club, became the first Sri Lankan – the 13th from all countries – to claim a wicket with his maiden delivery in Test cricket, when he bowled Mohammad Ashraful with an inswinger in the ninth over. Tapash Baisya's unbeaten 52 in his first Test innings almost spirited Bangladesh past the follow-on target, but Jayasuriya chose not to enforce it anyway, enabling Vandort, a tall left-hander who had played one previous Test (also against Bangladesh), to make a maiden century. His controlled 140 featured 17 fours and a six, and he added 172 with Nawaz, who ended his only Test with an average of 99. Bangladesh were left the unlikely task of chasing 473, or surviving seven sessions. Ashraful reached 75, but the end came swiftly after that. Sujeewa de Silva, a left-arm seamer in his second Test, and offspinner Samaraweera sent the last six wickets tumbling for 17. It was the first time Sri Lanka had won a Test without Muttiah Muralitharan since his debut in August 1992.

Sri Lanka

M. G. Vandort lbw b Alok Kapali		61	– b Talha Jubair	140
J. Mubarak lbw b Tapash Baisya		24	– run out	31
M. N. Nawaz c Khaled Mashud b Fahim Muntasir		21	– not out	78
H. P. Tillekeratne c and b Fahim Muntasir		18	– not out	5
*S. T. Jayasuriya c Khaled Mashud b Manjural Islam		85		
T. T. Samaraweera c Habibul Bashar b Manjural Islam		58		
†H. A. P. W. Jayawardene c Khaled Mashud b Manjural Islam		0		
U. D. U. Chandana c Habibul Bashar b Alok Kapali		20		
T. C. B. Fernando not out		29		
W. R. S. de Silva c Khaled Mashud b Talha Jubair		5		
M. K. G. C. P. Lakshitha c Alok Kapali b Talha Jubair		40		
B 1, l-b 5, n-b 6		12	B 4, l-b 1, w 1, n-b 3	9

1/60 (2) 2/90 (3) 3/131 (1) 4/133 (4)   373   1/80 (2) 2/252 (1)   (2 wkts dec.) 263
5/260 (5) 6/260 (7) 7/298 (8)
8/298 (6) 9/309 (10) 10/373 (11)

Manjural Islam 23–4–46–3; Talha Jubair 21.4–3–74–2; Tapash Baisya 12–1–69–1; Fahim Muntasir 18–3–46–2; Alok Kapali 29–2–122–2; Habibul Bashar 3–1–10–0. *Second Innings*—Manjural Islam 9–0–28–0; Talha Jubair 14–1–52–1; Alok Kapali 11–0–54–0; Tapash Baisya 8–0–40–0; Fahim Muntasir 19–3–56–0; Habibul Bashar 5–0–28–0.

Bangladesh

Hannan Sarkar lbw b Fernando		5	– c Jayawardene b de Silva	30
Al Sahariar c Jayawardene b Jayasuriya		12	– b de Silva	6
Habibul Bashar lbw b Fernando		11	– c Jayawardene b Lakshitha	3
Mohammad Ashraful c Lakshitha		1	– c Mubarak b Samaraweera	75
Tushar Imran lbw b Lakshitha		8	– st Jayawardene b Chandana	28
*†Khaled Mashud c Tillekeratne b Samaraweera		15	– (7) not out	13
Alok Kapali lbw b Jayasuriya		39	– (6) c Mubarak b Samaraweera	23
Fahim Muntasir c and b Samaraweera		7	– (9) lbw b de Silva	1
Tapash Baisya not out		52	– (8) c Chandana b de Silva	3
Manjural Islam c Jayawardene b Jayasuriya		0	– c Tillekeratne b Samaraweera	0
Talha Jubair c Jayasuriya b Chandana		0	– c Mubarak b Samaraweera	0
L-b 4, n-b 10		14	L-b 1, n-b 1	2

1/20 (1) 2/28 (2) 3/31 (4) 4/43 (3)   164   1/27 (2) 2/36 (3) 3/40 (1)   184
5/51 (5) 6/72 (6) 7/86 (8)   4/99 (5) 5/167 (6) 6/168 (4)
8/123 (7) 9/163 (10) 10/164 (11)   7/171 (8) 8/175 (9) 9/184 (10) 10/184 (11)

Fernando 15–3–36–2; de Silva 11–2–45–0; Jayasuriya 7–2–17–3; Lakshitha 12–5–33–2; Samaraweera 12–3–18–2; Chandana 5–1–11–1. *Second Innings*—Fernando 5–2–12–0; de Silva 13–5–35–4; Lakshitha 12–2–48–1; Jayasuriya 9–4–14–0; Samaraweera 11.4–1–49–4; Chandana 10–3–25–1.

Umpires: S. A. Bucknor *(West Indies)* (69) and D. R. Shepherd *(England)* (64).
Third umpire: P. T. Manuel *(Sri Lanka).*   Referee: Wasim Raja *(Pakistan)* (4).

Close of play: First day, Sri Lanka 301-8 (Fernando 2, de Silva 1); Second day, Sri Lanka 25-0 (Vandort 18, Mubarak 2); Third day, Bangladesh 103-4 (Mohammad Ashraful 31, Alok Kapali 3).

ENGLAND v INDIA 2002 (1st Test)

At Lord's, London, on 25, 26, 27, 28, 29 July.
Toss: England.   Result: ENGLAND won by 170 runs.
Debuts: England – S. P. Jones.
Man of the Match: N. Hussain.

In the 12 years since Graham Gooch's 333 at Lord's, England had beaten India only once, home or away. But you would never have known it from this match, a personal triumph for Hussain: he won his third Test running, made his highest score for five years, and spiked India's big guns with rigorous game-plans. India, by contrast, were tentative. Ganguly made one crucial error, leaving out Harbhajan Singh in favour of a third seamer. The match was not as one-sided as the result suggests. Zaheer Khan was superb early on, as England stuttered to 78 for 3. Hussain's first 60 runs took 50 overs before, bothered by cramp, he went for his shots and reached his hundred in another 12 overs. When Zaheer removed Stewart, England (263 for 5) might have crumpled, but Flintoff showed the effortless power of his driving, White played the spinners with panache and Jones slogged like the village blacksmith. Sehwag, opening for the first time in a Test, rattled up 84 from 96 balls before falling to Giles. Tendulkar tried to knuckle down, but after Dravid got a lifter, he could resist temptation no longer. Hussain waived the follow-on, and Vaughan and Crawley collected centuries before a cautious declaration set India 568. They reached 110 for 1, but only Dravid threatened the big salvage act that was needed, and eventually he picked the wrong ball to cut. On the final day, Agarkar (previous batting average 7.47) became one of Test cricket's more improbable centurions.

England

M. A. Butcher c Wasim Jaffer b Kumble	29	– lbw b Kumble	18
M. P. Vaughan lbw b Zaheer Khan	0	– c Wasim Jaffer b Nehra	100
*N. Hussain c Ratra b Agarkar	155	– c Ratra b Agarkar	12
G. P. Thorpe b Zaheer Khan	4	– c Ganguly b Kumble	1
J. P. Crawley c Dravid b Sehwag	64	– not out	100
†A. J. Stewart lbw b Zaheer Khan	19	– (7) st Ratra b Kumble	33
A. Flintoff c Ratra b Agarkar	59	– (6) c Tendulkar b Nehra	7
C. White st Ratra b Kumble	53	– not out	6
A. F. Giles b Nehra	19		
S. P. Jones c Dravid b Kumble	44		
M. J. Hoggard not out	10		
B 11, l-b 11, w 2, n-b 7	31	B 5, l-b 14, n-b 5	24

1/0 (2) 2/71 (1) 3/78 (4) 4/223 (5)   487   1/32 (1) 2/65 (3)   (6 wkts dec.) 301
5/263 (6) 6/356 (7) 7/357 (3)   3/76 (4) 4/213 (2)
8/390 (9) 9/452 (10) 10/487 (8)   5/228 (6) 6/287 (7)

Nehra 30–4–101–1; Zaheer Khan 36–13–90–3; Agarkar 21–3–98–2; Kumble 42.2–9–128–3; Ganguly 3–1–16–0; Sehwag 10–0–32–1. *Second Innings*—Nehra 14–1–80–2; Zaheer Khan 11–1–41–0; Kumble 24–1–84–3; Agarkar 11.4–1–53–1; Tendulkar 2–0–14–0; Sehwag 2–0–10–0.

India

Wasim Jaffer b Hoggard	1	– c Hussain b Vaughan	53
V. Sehwag b Giles	84	– b Jones	27
R. Dravid c Vaughan b Hoggard	46	– b Giles	63
A. Nehra lbw b Flintoff	0	– (11) c Thorpe b White	19
S. R. Tendulkar c Stewart b White	16	– (4) b Hoggard	12
*S. C. Ganguly c Vaughan b Flintoff	5	– (5) lbw b Hoggard	0
V. V. S. Laxman not out	43	– (6) c Vaughan b Jones	74
†A. Ratra c Stewart b Jones	1	– (7) c Butcher b Hoggard	1
A. B. Agarkar c Flintoff b Jones	2	– (8) not out	109
A. Kumble b White	0	– (9) c and b Hoggard	15
Zaheer Khan c Thorpe b Hoggard	3	– (10) c Stewart b White	7
B 4, l-b 8, n-b 8	20	B 4, l-b 3, w 2, n-b 8	17

1/2 (1) 2/128 (2) 3/130 (4) 4/162 (3)   221   1/61 (2) 2/110 (1) 3/140 (4)   397
5/168 (5) 6/177 (6) 7/191 (8)   4/140 (5) 5/165 (3) 6/170 (7)
8/196 (9) 9/209 (10) 10/221 (11)   7/296 (6) 8/320 (9) 9/334 (10) 10/397 (11)

Hoggard 16.5–4–33–3; Flintoff 19–9–22–2; Giles 9–1–47–1; Jones 21–2–61–2; White 16–3–46–2. *Second Innings*—Hoggard 24–7–87–4; Flintoff 17–2–87–0; White 16.4–2–61–2; Jones 17–1–68–2; Giles 29–7–75–1; Vaughan 6–2–12–1.

Umpires: R. E. Koertzen *(South Africa)* (33) and R. B. Tiffin *(Zimbabwe)* (27).
Third umpire: P. Willey *(England)*.   Referee: M. J. Procter *(South Africa)* (2).

Close of play: First day, England 257-4 (Hussain 120, Stewart 19); Second day, India 130-3 (Dravid 33); Third day, England 184-3 (Vaughan 81, Crawley 56); Fourth day, India 232-6 (Laxman 38, Agarkar 28).

ENGLAND v INDIA 2002 (2nd Test)

At Trent Bridge, Nottingham, on 8, 9, 10, 11, 12 August.
Toss: India.   Result: MATCH DRAWN.
Debuts: England – S. J. Harmison, R. W. T. Key. India – P. A. Patel.
Man of the Match: M. P. Vaughan.

India forced a draw in front of a Test rarity – a final-day full house. England were denied by bad light and rain – which cost the equivalent of a day's play over the first four days – and some disappointing bowling on the first day, when India made 210 for 4 in conditions ideal for seam and swing. Ganguly fought his way back to form, while Agarkar and Harbhajan Singh made handy contributions. With the debutant Steve Harmison producing bounce and hostility, England might still have won but for the weather – or, possibly, the umpires' interpretation of its suitability. For the most part, their myriad bad-light offers were hopelessly out of synch with the clause requiring physical danger to be part of the equation, and it reached laughable proportions when, despite being well placed, England's batsmen left the field on Saturday evening in what most people would have considered bright sunshine. A handsome century from Sehwag underpinned India's 357, but a majestic 197 from Vaughan – his third century of the summer – provided England with the launch pad to a lead of 260. Stewart's frisky 87 took him past Mike Atherton's 7,728 Test runs, to fourth on England's list. India needed at least three of their big four to come good, especially after both openers went cheaply, and they did: Tendulkar, Dravid and Ganguly made the game virtually safe, although it still required an unbeaten 19 in 84 minutes from the 17-year-old wicketkeeper Parthiv Patel to eliminate any chance of an England victory.

India

Wasim Jaffer b Hoggard	0	– (2) lbw b Flintoff	5
V. Sehwag b White	106	– (1) lbw b Hoggard	0
R. Dravid c Key b Hoggard	13	– lbw b Cork	115
S. R. Tendulkar b Cork	34	– b Vaughan	92
*S. C. Ganguly c Stewart b Hoggard	68	– b Harmison	99
V. V. S. Laxman c Key b Flintoff	22	– c White b Cork	14
A. B. Agarkar c Butcher b Harmison	34	– lbw b Vaughan	32
†P. A. Patel c Flintoff b Harmison	0	– not out	19
Harbhajan Singh c Hussain b Harmison	54	– b Harmison	1
Zaheer Khan not out	14	– not out	14
A. Nehra c Stewart b Hoggard	0		
B 1, l-b 8, w 2, n-b 1	12	B 5, l-b 12, w 4, n-b 12	33
	357	(8 wkts dec.)	424

1/6 (1) 2/34 (3) 3/108 (4) 4/179 (2)   357
5/218 (6) 6/285 (7) 7/287 (8)
8/295 (5) 9/356 (9) 10/357 (11)

1/0 (1) 2/11 (2)   (8 wkts dec.) 424
3/174 (4) 4/309 (3)
5/339 (6) 6/378 (5) 7/395 (7) 8/396 (9)

Hoggard 35.1–10–105–4; Cork 11–3–45–1; Harmison 20–7–57–3; Flintoff 27–6–85–1; White 8–0–56–1. *Second Innings*—Hoggard 23–0–109–1; Flintoff 22–2–95–1; Harmison 29–5–63–2; Cork 12–1–54–2; Vaughan 21–5–71–2; White 8–2–15–0.

England

R. W. T. Key b Nehra	17	D. G. Cork c Wasim Jaffer b Harbhajan Singh	31
M. P. Vaughan c Patel b Agarkar	197	M. J. Hoggard c Dravid b Nehra	32
M. A. Butcher c Dravid b Harbhajan Singh	53	S. J. Harmison c Wasim Jaffer b Agarkar	3
*N. Hussain c Patel b Harbhajan Singh	3		
J. P. Crawley c Wasim Jaffer b Zaheer Khan	22	B 9, l-b 17, w 4, n-b 15	45
†A. J. Stewart b Zaheer Khan	87		
A. Flintoff b Zaheer Khan	33		617
C. White not out	94		

1/56 (1) 2/221 (3) 3/228 (4) 4/272 (5)   617
5/335 (2) 6/432 (7) 7/433 (6)
8/493 (9) 9/596 (10) 10/617 (11)

Nehra 32–3–138–2; Zaheer Khan 26–4–110–3; Agarkar 24.5–3–93–2; Harbhajan Singh 45–3–175–3; Ganguly 5–0–42–0; Tendulkar 6–0–15–0; Sehwag 6–1–18–0.

Umpires: R. E. Koertzen *(South Africa)* (34) and R. B. Tiffin *(Zimbabwe)* (28).
Third umpire: J. W. Lloyds *(England)*.   Referee: C. H. Lloyd *(West Indies)* (14).

Close of play: First day, India 210-4 (Ganguly 29, Laxman 22); Second day, India 302-8 (Harbhajan Singh 13, Zaheer Khan 1); Third day, England 341-5 (Stewart 30, Flintoff 2); Fourth day, India 99-2 (Dravid 34, Tendulkar 56).

ENGLAND v INDIA 2002 (3rd Test)

At Headingley, Leeds, on 22, 23, 24, 25, 26 August.
Toss: India.   Result: INDIA won by an innings and 46 runs.
Debuts: none.
Man of the Match: R. Dravid.

England can usually rely on Headingley for home comforts. So it was a nasty shock that this year the old girl turned against them, embracing instead India – it was they who looked up at the furious age-old leaden skies, mastered the demons in the pitch, and served up a win by an innings, something they hadn't achieved overseas since routing a Packer-scarred Australia at Sydney in 1977-78. It was a magnificent performance, built on a sublime first-day century by Dravid. That enabled Tendulkar, in his 99th Test, to play freely for his 30th century, while Ganguly produced a knockabout hundred in a fourth-wicket stand of 249, an Indian record against England on the way to their highest score against them. It was the first time all three had made a century in the same innings. This excellent batting was matched by wise bowling from Kumble, who merrily spun his buoyant legbreaks for seven wickets and thoroughly deserved his first Test victory outside the subcontinent in 12 years. For England, there were more runs from Vaughan, though not on the heroic scale that he was increasingly favouring, valiant efforts from Stewart and an innings of angry defiance from Hussain on the final afternoon, but it was not enough after the initiative had been lost so clearly on the first two days. England also dropped several catches – four in 35 minutes on a slapdash Saturday morning, including Parthiv Patel three times in his 11-ball innings.

India

S. B. Bangar c Stewart b Flintoff	68	Harbhajan Singh c Hoggard b Caddick .. 18
V. Sehwag c Flintoff b Hoggard	8	
R. Dravid st Stewart b Giles	148	B 14, l-b 13, w 5, n-b 18.... 50
S. R. Tendulkar lbw b Caddick	193	
*S. C. Ganguly b Tudor	128	1/15 (2) 2/185 (1) (8 wkts dec.) 628
V. V. S. Laxman c Hussain b Tudor	6	3/335 (3) 4/584 (5)
A. B. Agarkar b Caddick	2	5/596 (4) 6/602 (7)
†P. A. Patel not out	7	7/604 (6) 8/628 (9)

Zaheer Khan and A. Kumble did not bat.

Hoggard 36–12–102–1; Caddick 40.1–5–150–3; Tudor 36–10–146–2; Flintoff 27–6–68–1; Giles 39–3–134–1; Butcher 1–1–0–0; Vaughan 1–0–1–0.

England

R. W. T. Key c Laxman b Zaheer Khan	30	– lbw b Kumble	34
M. P. Vaughan c Sehwag b Agarkar	61	– lbw b Agarkar	15
M. A. Butcher lbw b Kumble	16	– c Dravid b Bangar	42
*N. Hussain lbw b Zaheer Khan	25	– c Sehwag b Kumble	110
J. P. Crawley c Laxman b Harbhajan Singh	13	– c Sehwag b Bangar	12
†A. J. Stewart not out	78	– c Dravid b Kumble	47
A. Flintoff lbw b Harbhajan Singh	0	– c Dravid b Zaheer Khan	0
A. J. Tudor c Sehwag b Agarkar	1	– c Sehwag b Harbhajan Singh	21
A. F. Giles lbw b Kumble	25	– run out	10
A. R. Caddick b Harbhajan Singh	1	– c Ganguly b Kumble	3
M. J. Hoggard c Sehwag b Kumble	0	– not out	1
B 1, l-b 12, n-b 10	23	B 3, l-b 5, n-b 6	14

1/67 (1) 2/109 (3) 3/130 (2) 4/140 (4)   273   1/28 (2) 2/76 (1) 3/116 (3)   309
5/164 (5) 6/164 (7) 7/185 (8)   4/148 (5) 5/265 (4) 6/267 (7)
8/255 (9) 9/258 (10) 10/273 (11)   7/267 (6) 8/299 (9) 9/307 (8) 10/309 (10)

Zaheer Khan 19–3–59–2; Agarkar 15–4–59–2; Bangar 4–1–9–0; Kumble 33–7–93–3; Harbhajan Singh 18–6–40–3.
Second Innings—Zaheer Khan 22–7–63–1; Agarkar 18–5–59–1; Bangar 13–2–54–2; Kumble 29.5–12–66–4; Harbhajan Singh 27–7–56–1; Sehwag 1–0–3–0.

Umpires: E. A. R. de Silva *(Sri Lanka)* (16) and D. L. Orchard *(South Africa)* (29).
Third umpire: P. Willey *(England)*.   Referee: C. H. Lloyd *(West Indies)* (15).

Close of play: First day, India 236-2 (Dravid 110, Tendulkar 18); Second day, India 584-4 (Tendulkar 185); Third day, England 264-9 (Stewart 71, Hoggard 0); Fourth day, England 239-4 (Hussain 90, Stewart 40).

ENGLAND v INDIA 2002 (4th Test)

At Kennington Oval, London, on 5, 6, 7, 8, 9 *(no play)* September.
Toss: England.   Result: MATCH DRAWN.
Debuts: none.
Man of the Match: R. Dravid.   Men of the Series: R. Dravid and M. P. Vaughan.

Before this match few people expected a draw, but a tranquil pitch ensured there was never much danger of anything but. Vaughan and Dravid again played epic innings, sharing almost 19 hours at the crease in a match where nobody else lasted four. Only 20 wickets fell in 353 overs, before a last-day washout. It was the first Oval draw since 1995, when another series decider, against West Indies, proved similarly unproductive. After Hussain had won an apparently critical toss, another Vaughan masterclass helped England storm to 336 for 2. Vaughan had made 182 of those, mostly with drives that were both pristine and urgent, becoming the sixth man to make four Test hundreds in an English summer. Finally he fished at Zaheer Khan and was caught behind for 195, his second attack of the nervous 190s in three Tests. England blundered through the rest of the second day: only 179 runs came off 65 overs for eight wickets, only Cork showing much gumption. Harbhajan Singh took his ninth Test five-for, all of those them having come when India fielded first. Then Dravid settled in. He took his crease occupation for the series past 30 hours, and eventually made his highest first-class score, in 10½ hours, before he was finally run out. The enchantment came from Tendulkar, who at 29 became the youngest man to play a century of Tests. He received a standing ovation as he came in to bat, and breezed to a boundary-laden 54.

England

M. E. Trescothick c Bangar b Zaheer Khan	57	– not out	58
M. P. Vaughan c Ratra b Zaheer Khan	195	– not out	47
M. A. Butcher c Dravid b Harbhajan Singh	54		
J. P. Crawley lbw b Bangar	26		
*N. Hussain c Laxman b Bangar	10		
†A. J. Stewart c Ratra b Harbhajan Singh	23		
D. G. Cork lbw b Harbhajan Singh	52		
A. J. Tudor c Dravid b Harbhajan Singh	2		
A. F. Giles c Dravid b Kumble	31		
A. R. Caddick not out	14		
M. J. Hoggard lbw b Harbhajan Singh	0		
B 12, l-b 31, w 1, n-b 7	51	B 4, n-b 5	9

1/98 (1) 2/272 (3) 3/349 (2) 4/367 (4)   515
5/372 (5) 6/434 (6) 7/446 (8)
8/477 (7) 9/514 (9) 10/515 (11)

(no wkt) 114

Zaheer Khan 28–4–83–2; Agarkar 24–4–111–0; Bangar 24–8–48–2; Harbhajan Singh 38.4–6–115–5; Kumble 35–11–105–1; Ganguly 4–1–6–0; Tendulkar 2–0–4–0. *Second Innings*—Zaheer Khan 5–0–37–0; Bangar 2–0–6–0; Kumble 10–2–28–0; Harbhajan Singh 7–1–24–0; Agarkar 4–0–15–0.

India

S. B. Bangar c Butcher b Hoggard	21	A. Kumble c Hussain b Giles	7
V. Sehwag c Cork b Caddick	12	Harbhajan Singh b Giles	17
R. Dravid run out	217	Zaheer Khan not out	6
S. R. Tendulkar lbw b Caddick	54	B 10, l-b 6, n-b 28	44
*S. C. Ganguly c Stewart b Cork	51		
V. V. S. Laxman c Giles b Caddick	40	1/18 (2) 2/87 (1) 3/178 (4) 4/283 (5) 508
A. B. Agarkar b Vaughan	31	5/396 (6) 6/465 (7) 7/473 (3)
†A. Ratra c Butcher b Caddick	8	8/477 (8) 9/493 (9) 10/508 (10)

Hoggard 25–2–97–1; Caddick 43–11–114–4; Giles 49–12–98–2; Tudor 19–2–80–0; Cork 22–5–67–1; Vaughan 12–1–36–1.

Umpires: E. A. R. de Silva *(Sri Lanka)* (17) and D. L. Orchard *(South Africa)* (30).
Third umpire: N. A. Mallender *(England)*.   Referee: C. H. Lloyd *(West Indies)* (16).

Close of play: First day, England 336-2 (Vaughan 182, Crawley 16); Second day, India 66-1 (Bangar 17, Dravid 31); Third day, India 315-4 (Dravid 131, Laxman 14); Fourth day, England 114-0 (Trescothick 58, Vaughan 47).

PAKISTAN v AUSTRALIA 2002–03 (1st Test)

At P. Saravanamuttu Stadium, Colombo, on 3, 4, 5, 6, 7 October.
Toss: Australia.   Result: AUSTRALIA won by 41 runs.
Debuts: none.
Man of the Match: S. K. Warne.

Pakistan's proximity to trouble-torn Afghanistan, and the aftermath of the Karachi bomb that cut short New Zealand's recent tour, meant that Australia refused to go there. Pakistan's board instead arranged an eccentric series on neutral territory, starting in Sri Lanka and concluding in Sharjah. Pakistan had several leading players out injured, but nonetheless competed in the first match, which finally fell Australia's way. They had dominated until Shoaib Akhtar's breathtaking second-innings spell of five wickets in 15 balls. Set 316, Pakistan were within striking distance, but finally fell short. Australia had collected a formidable 467 after a chanceless 141 from Ponting. Only Shoaib's old-ball assault prevented a much higher total; against reverse swing at nearly 100mph, the last five wickets fell for ten. In reply, with Warne showing the benefits of his new fitness regime in the heat, Pakistan only just avoided the follow-on. Next day Australia seemingly had the match in hand, but Shoaib returned to rip the heart out of the innings, removing Ponting and the Waughs in four balls, then in his next over a yorker from round the wicket castled Gilchrist. Australia were routed for 127. On the final day Pakistan – helped by uncharacteristically shoddy fielding – needed only 137 more; at 230 for 4, wanting just 86, they were within sight of triumph. But Australia piled on the pressure; the pivotal moment was Warne's dismissal of Younis Khan for an elegant 51, then five wickets tumbled for 26 to McGrath and Gillespie with the new ball.

Australia

J. L. Langer	c Rashid Latif b Abdul Razzaq	72	– c Taufeeq Umar b Saqlain Mushtaq	25
M. L. Hayden	c Imran Nazir b Waqar Younis	4	– c Taufeeq Umar b Saqlain Mushtaq	34
R. T. Ponting	c Younis Khan b Waqar Younis	141	– b Shoaib Akhtar	7
M. E. Waugh	c and b Saqlain Mushtaq	55	– b Shoaib Akhtar	0
*S. R. Waugh	c Younis Khan b Saqlain Mushtaq	31	– lbw b Shoaib Akhtar	0
D. R. Martyn	c Younis Khan b Saqlain Mushtaq	67	– c Imran Nazir b Saqlain Mushtaq	20
†A. C. Gilchrist	not out	66	– b Shoaib Akhtar	5
S. K. Warne	c Faisal Iqbal b Shoaib Akhtar	0	– lbw b Shoaib Akhtar	0
B. Lee	b Shoaib Akhtar	2	– c Misbah-ul-Haq b Saqlain Mushtaq	12
J. N. Gillespie	lbw b Shoaib Akhtar	0	– lbw b Mohammad Sami	1
G. D. McGrath	lbw b Saqlain Mushtaq	4	– not out	5
	B 4, l-b 16, n-b 5	25	B 4, l-b 12, n-b 2	18

1/5 (2) 2/188 (1) 3/272 (3) 4/302 (4)   467   1/61 (1) 2/74 (3) 3/74 (4)   127
5/329 (5) 6/457 (6) 7/458 (8)   4/74 (5) 5/74 (2) 6/85 (7)
8/462 (9) 9/462 (10) 10/467 (11)   7/89 (8) 8/107 (9) 9/112 (10) 10/127 (6)

Waqar Younis 16–2–86–2; Shoaib Akhtar 21–5–51–3; Mohammad Sami 20–3–93–0; Abdul Razzaq 17–0–78–1; Saqlain Mushtaq 40.5–6–136–4; Taufeeq Umar 2–1–3–0. *Second Innings*—Waqar Younis 8–1–23–0; Shoaib Akhtar 8–2–21–5; Saqlain Mushtaq 15.5–0–46–4; Taufeeq Umar 2–0–8–0; Mohammad Sami 6–0–13–1.

Pakistan

Imran Nazir	lbw b McGrath	0	– c McGrath b Warne	40
Taufeeq Umar	c Ponting b Gillespie	0	– c M. E. Waugh b Lee	88
Abdul Razzaq	c Gilchrist b Warne	11	– lbw b Warne	4
Younis Khan	c Langer b Lee	58	– lbw b Warne	51
Misbah-ul-Haq	c M. E. Waugh b Warne	17	– c S. R. Waugh b Warne	10
Faisal Iqbal	c M. E. Waugh b Warne	83	– c Ponting b McGrath	39
†Rashid Latif	c Martyn b Warne	66	– c Gilchrist b Gillespie	11
Saqlain Mushtaq	lbw b Warne	1	– c S. R. Waugh b McGrath	1
*Waqar Younis	lbw b Warne	14	– c Gilchrist b Gillespie	1
Shoaib Akhtar	c McGrath b Warne	5	– lbw b McGrath	6
Mohammad Sami	not out	0	– not out	6
	B 11, l-b 10, n-b 3	24	B 3, l-b 6, n-b 8	17

1/2 (1) 2/4 (2) 3/45 (3) 4/75 (4)   279   1/91 (1) 2/117 (3) 3/173 (2)   274
5/116 (5) 6/219 (6) 7/239 (8)   4/187 (5) 5/230 (4) 6/248 (7)
8/267 (9) 9/274 (7) 10/279 (10)   7/251 (8) 8/252 (9) 9/259 (10) 10/274 (6)

McGrath 15–3–40–1; Gillespie 12–2–55–1; Lee 11–3–49–1; Warne 24.3–7–94–7; M. E. Waugh 3–0–20–0. *Second Innings*—McGrath 24.2–12–38–3; Gillespie 23.3–8–62–2; Lee 14–1–63–1; Warne 30.3–3–94–4; M. E. Waugh 2–1–8–0.

Umpires: S. A. Bucknor *(West Indies)* (70) and S. Venkataraghavan *(India)* (58).
Third umpire: Aleem Dar *(Pakistan)*.   Referee: C. H. Lloyd *(West Indies)* (17).

Close of play: First day, Australia 330-5 (Martyn 6, Gilchrist 1); Second day, Pakistan 210-5 (Faisal Iqbal 78, Rashid Latif 30); Third day, Australia 127; Fourth day, Pakistan 179-3 (Younis Khan 32, Misbah-ul-Haq 4).

PAKISTAN v AUSTRALIA 2002–03 (2nd Test)

At Sharjah C. A. Stadium on 11, 12 October.
Toss: Pakistan.   Result: AUSTRALIA won by an innings and 198 runs.
Debuts: none.
Man of the Match: M. L. Hayden.

Pakistan slumped to a display that, even allowing for their mercurial reputation, could only be described as a shocker. In 125 years, Test cricket had produced only 16 two-day defeats; here, on a slow, flat pitch, Pakistan subsided to the 17th. First they were rolled over for their lowest total, three below their 62 at Perth in 1981-82. The openers repeated their pair of ducks from the first innings in Colombo, and only Abdul Razzaq, who endured almost two hours for 21, reached double figures. Warne caused the damage again, bewitching the batsmen with his new "slider". Pushing forward, they found themselves trapped lbw by deliveries doing precisely nothing. Two balls after tea on the first day, the Australians were already in front. With the temperature pushing 50°C, Hayden likened it to batting in an oven – but ground his way relentlessly to 119. Dropped twice, he never truly dominated – though he reached three figures with a six off Danish Kaneria – but the seven-hour vigil was exactly what Australia needed. His innings proved to be only the fifth instance of one batsman outscoring the entire opposition in a Test. After Imran Nazir turned his back on Taufeeq Umar as he charged through for a run in the first over of the second innings, and Razzaq's wrist was broken by Lee in the sixth, Pakistan's resolve fractured too. Warne again imposed his authority, and the quick bowlers mopped up. Pakistan were routed for 53: their record low had lasted only one day.

Pakistan

Imran Nazir c Warne b McGrath	0	– c Gilchrist b Warne	16
Taufeeq Umar b Lee	0	– run out	0
Abdul Razzaq c Martyn b Warne	21	– retired hurt	4
Younis Khan c Bichel b McGrath	5	– lbw b McGrath	0
Misbah-ul-Haq c M. E. Waugh b Bichel	2	– c S. R. Waugh b Bichel	12
Faisal Iqbal lbw b Warne	4	– c M. E. Waugh b Warne	7
†Rashid Latif not out	4	– c M. E. Waugh b Bichel	0
Saqlain Mushtaq lbw b Warne	0	– c Warne b Lee	9
Shoaib Akhtar c Gilchrist b Bichel	1	– c S. R. Waugh b Warne	2
*Waqar Younis lbw b Warne	0	– lbw b Warne	0
Danish Kaneria b Lee	8	– not out	1
B 8, l-b 2, n-b 4	14	N-b 2	2

1/0 (1) 2/1 (2) 3/8 (4) 4/23 (5)   59   1/0 (2) 2/13 (4) 3/32 (1)   53
5/41 (6) 6/46 (3) 7/46 (8)   4/34 (5) 5/36 (7) 6/50 (6)
8/49 (9) 9/50 (10) 10/59 (11)   7/52 (8) 8/52 (9) 9/53 (10)

In the second innings Abdul Razzaq retired hurt at 11.

McGrath 7–4–10–2; Lee 7.5–1–15–2; Bichel 6–2–13–2; Warne 11–4–11–4. *Second Innings*—McGrath 6–2–5–1; Lee 5–2–16–1; Bichel 7–1–19–2; Warne 6.5–2–13–4.

Australia

J. L. Langer run out	37	
M. L. Hayden c Imran Nazir b Saqlain Mushtaq	119	
R. T. Ponting lbw b Danish Kaneria	44	
M. E. Waugh lbw b Saqlain Mushtaq	2	
*S. R. Waugh c sub (Imran Farhat) b Saqlain Mushtaq	0	
D. R. Martyn c Taufeeq Umar b Abdul Razzaq	34	
†A. C. Gilchrist c Taufeeq Umar b Shoaib Akhtar	17	
S. K. Warne c Younis Khan		
b Saqlain Mushtaq	19	

B. Lee lbw b Abdul Razzaq	12
A. J. Bichel not out	2
G. D. McGrath lbw b Abdul Razzaq	0
B 15, l-b 7, n-b 2	24

1/55 (1) 2/145 (3) 3/148 (4) 4/148 (5)   310
5/224 (6) 6/252 (7) 7/285 (8)
8/304 (9) 9/310 (2) 10/310 (11)

Waqar Younis 8–2–25–0; Shoaib Akhtar 14–3–42–1; Danish Kaneria 26–2–116–1; Abdul Razzaq 10.1–3–22–3; Saqlain Mushtaq 34–2–83–4.

Umpires: S. A. Bucknor *(West Indies)* (71) and S. Venkataraghavan *(India)* (59).
Third umpire: Nadeem Ghauri *(Pakistan)*.   Referee: C. H. Lloyd *(West Indies)* (18).

Close of play: First day, Australia 191-4 (Hayden 74, Martyn 19).

PAKISTAN v AUSTRALIA 2002–03 (3rd Test)

At Sharjah C. A. Stadium on 19, 20, 21, 22 October.
Toss: Australia.   Result: AUSTRALIA won by an innings and 20 runs.
Debuts: none.
Man of the Match: S. K. Warne.   Man of the Series: S. K. Warne.

This was a triumphant match for the Australians, collectively and individually, as they completed a clean sweep early on the fourth day. McGrath became the eighth bowler to reach 400 Test wickets when he trapped Waqar Younis in the first innings, and Steve Waugh returned to form (and possibly saved his career) with a thrilling century. It took a brilliant bat-pad catch to deny Hayden a hundred, but Ponting completed his, despite battling heat exhaustion. He also suffered a gashed jaw from a Mohammad Sami bouncer – he was wearing only a cap because his helmet was too hot – but remained in charge during a chanceless 150, dancing down to the spinners and punishing a pace attack diluted by a back injury to Shoaib Akhtar. Meanwhile, Mark Waugh's dismissal for 23, stumbling forward and caught behind off Saqlain Mushtaq, proved to be the ungainly last chapter of a graceful Test career. His twin brother was another matter. He had 82 when the No. 11, McGrath, trudged in. Waugh was not about to dither. He promptly smashed 20 off a Danish Kaneria over, slogging consecutive sixes to leg and celebrating his first century in 12 Tests. In reply, Pakistan soon fell under Warne's spell again. He took five wickets with his mesmerising combination of sharp spin and disguised straighter balls. When Pakistan followed on, only a second half-century from Hasan Raza – and bad light, which forced the match into the fourth morning – held up Australia's march to victory for long.

Australia

J. L. Langer b Waqar Younis	4	A. J. Bichel c Taufeeq Umar b Danish Kaneria	9
M. L. Hayden c Faisal Iqbal b Saqlain Mushtaq	89	G. D. McGrath c Rashid Latif b Waqar Younis	3
R. T. Ponting b Waqar Younis	150	B 4, l-b 10, n-b 3	17
M. E. Waugh c Rashid Latif b Saqlain Mushtaq	23		
*S. R. Waugh not out	103	1/4 (1) 2/188 (2) 3/233 (4)	444
D. R. Martyn lbw b Waqar Younis	0	4/308 (3) 5/308 (6)	
†A. C. Gilchrist c Rashid Latif b Danish Kaneria	34	6/363 (7) 7/403 (8)	
S. K. Warne lbw b Danish Kaneria	11	8/404 (9) 9/418 (10) 10/444 (11)	
B. Lee run out	1		

Waqar Younis 17.3–5–55–4; Mohammad Sami 28–6–81–0; Saqlain Mushtaq 45–5–159–2; Danish Kaneria 36–8–128–3; Taufeeq Umar 2–0–7–0.

Pakistan

Taufeeq Umar lbw b McGrath	5	– c Gilchrist b McGrath	1
Imran Farhat lbw b Warne	29	– c Gilchrist b Bichel	18
Younis Khan c Gilchrist b McGrath	5	– lbw b McGrath	4
Faisal Iqbal c Gilchrist b Warne	9	– run out	2
Misbah-ul-Haq lbw b Bichel	11	– lbw b Warne	17
Hasan Raza not out	54	– c Gilchrist b Bichel	68
†Rashid Latif c M. E. Waugh b Warne	17	– lbw b Warne	17
Saqlain Mushtaq b McGrath	44	– lbw b Warne	10
*Waqar Younis lbw b McGrath	6	– c M. E. Waugh b McGrath	24
Mohammad Sami lbw b Warne	0	– c Martyn b Bichel	22
Danish Kaneria st Gilchrist b Warne	15	– not out	2
B 3, l-b 10, w 2, n-b 11	26	L-b 9, n-b 9	18

1/22 (1) 2/50 (3) 3/50 (2) 4/70 (5)   221   1/6 (1) 2/12 (3) 3/18 (4)   203
5/76 (4) 6/100 (7) 7/191 (8)   4/30 (2) 5/58 (5) 6/86 (7)
8/198 (9) 9/199 (10) 10/221 (11)   7/102 (8) 8/157 (9) 9/197 (6) 10/203 (10)

McGrath 16–4–41–4; Lee 11–1–47–0; Warne 30.1–10–74–5; Bichel 9–0–31–1; M. E. Waugh 4–0–10–0; Ponting 1–0–5–0. *Second Innings*—McGrath 7–2–18–3; Lee 18–5–44–0; Bichel 11.2–1–43–3; Warne 21–3–56–3; M. E. Waugh 10–3–33–0.

Umpires: S. A. Bucknor *(West Indies)* (72) and S. Venkataraghavan *(India)* (60).
Third umpire: Asad Rauf *(Pakistan)*.   Referee: C. H. Lloyd *(West Indies)* (19).

Close of play: First day, Australia 298-3 (Ponting 142, S. R. Waugh 33); Second day, Pakistan 163-6 (Hasan Raza 37, Saqlain Mushtaq 27); Third day, Pakistan 176-8 (Hasan Raza 56, Mohammad Sami 12).

INDIA v WEST INDIES 2002–03 (1st Test)

At Wankhede Stadium, Mumbai, on 9, 10, 11, 12 October.
Toss: India. Result: INDIA won by an innings and 112 runs.
Debuts: none.
Man of the Match: V. Sehwag.

A newly relaid surface had none of its predecessor's liveliness, and was underprepared – the match had been brought forward by two weeks so that Tendulkar could play his 101st Test on his home ground, where a stand was renamed in his honour. The new pitch harked back to the 1990s, when India repeatedly won on dustbowls that never gave visitors a chance: West Indies duly crumbled as India banished the demons of losing in the Caribbean five months earlier with their first innings victory against these opponents. Sehwag and Bangar shared India's first double-century opening partnership since Sunil Gavaskar's final series in 1986-87, and their best opening stand against West Indies. On the second day Laxman added a dour 105 in 53 overs with Dravid, who completed his fourth consecutive Test century, one behind Everton Weekes's record, despite cramping up during his 99th run (he limped back for the vital one). Srinath, back after a short-lived retirement, helped lift the score to 457. After West Indies slid to 59 for 4, Hooper, in his 100th Test, and Chanderpaul threatened a recovery, but Zaheer Khan wrenched out three crucial wickets in 21 balls. Following on, West Indies had no chance on the fourth morning, when the pitch appeared more suited to beach cricket than a Test match. The spinners took all ten wickets, seven of them to Harbhajan Singh, who flighted the ball beautifully. Chanderpaul, last man out in the first innings, was last man standing in the second.

India

S. B. Bangar c Sarwan b Dillon	55
V. Sehwag c Jacobs b Dillon	147
R. Dravid retired hurt	100
S. R. Tendulkar c Jacobs b Dillon	35
*S. C. Ganguly lbw b Cuffy	4
V. V. S. Laxman st Jacobs b Nagamootoo	45
†P. A. Patel not out	21
Harbhajan Singh c Jacobs b Cuffy	0
A. Kumble c Hooper b Nagamootoo	0
Zaheer Khan lbw b Nagamootoo	0
J. Srinath c Jacobs b Hooper	31
L-b 7, w 3, n-b 9	19
	457

1/201 (1) 2/213 (2) 3/281 (4)
4/296 (5) 5/401 (6) 6/407 (8)
7/408 (9) 8/408 (10) 9/457 (11)

Dravid retired hurt at 407-5.

Dillon 31.2–9–54–3; Collins 28–7–76–0; Cuffy 28.4–6–88–2; Nagamootoo 47–12–132–3; Hooper 11.5–3–40–1; W. W. Hinds 4–0–11–0; R. O. Hinds 10–0–40–0; Gayle 2–1–3–0; Sarwan 1–0–6–0.

West Indies

C. H. Gayle lbw b Zaheer Khan	7	– c Ganguly b Harbhajan Singh	42
W. W. Hinds c sub (S. S. Das) b Harbhajan Singh	1	– b Harbhajan Singh	40
R. R. Sarwan lbw b Kumble	22	– c Tendulkar b Kumble	17
M. Dillon b Srinath	21	– (9) c Dravid b Harbhajan Singh	0
S. Chanderpaul c and b Kumble	54	– (4) not out	36
*C. L. Hooper c Bangar b Zaheer Khan	23	– (5) c and b Harbhajan Singh	1
R. O. Hinds lbw b Zaheer Khan	9	– (6) c Sehwag b Kumble	2
†R. D. Jacobs c Ganguly b Zaheer Khan	0	– (7) c Ganguly b Kumble	0
M. V. Nagamootoo c Harbhajan Singh b Kumble	9	– (8) c Ganguly b Harbhajan Singh	18
P. T. Collins lbw b Kumble	0	– c Dravid b Harbhajan Singh	8
C. E. Cuffy not out	4	– c and b Harbhajan Singh	0
L-b 5, n-b 2	7	B 8, l-b 15, n-b 1	24
	157		188

1/7 (1) 2/27 (2) 3/43 (3) 4/59 (4) 157
5/103 (6) 6/119 (7) 7/123 (8)
8/145 (9) 9/146 (10) 10/157 (5)

1/60 (2) 2/105 (1) 3/107 (3) 188
4/110 (5) 5/117 (6) 6/117 (7)
7/158 (8) 8/158 (9) 9/184 (10) 10/188 (11)

Srinath 11–5–16–1; Zaheer Khan 16–4–41–4; Harbhajan Singh 21–8–37–1; Kumble 24.5–5–51–4; Sehwag 2–0–7–0. *Second Innings*—Srinath 4–2–19–0; Zaheer Khan 4–0–26–0; Bangar 6–1–20–0; Harbhajan Singh 28.3–12–48–7; Kumble 25–8–50–3; Tendulkar 1–0–2–0.

Umpires: E. A. R. de Silva *(Sri Lanka)* (18) and D. R. Shepherd *(England)* (65).
Third umpire: I. Shivram *(India)*. Referee: M. J. Procter *(South Africa)* (3).

Close of play: First day, India 278-2 (Dravid 28, Tendulkar 35); Second day, West Indies 33-2 (Sarwan 20, Dillon 4); Third day, West Indies 91-1 (Gayle 34, Sarwan 9).

INDIA v WEST INDIES 2002–03 (2nd Test)

At M. A. Chidambaram Stadium, Chennai, on 17, 18, 19, 20 October.
Toss: West Indies.   Result: INDIA won by eight wickets.
Debuts: West Indies – G. R. Breese, J. J. C. Lawson.
Man of the Match: Harbhajan Singh.

The saga of relaid-pitches-gone-wrong continued here. The fast bowlers got little assistance and not much bounce, while the spinners extracted plenty of turn and often made the ball rear up viciously. On the first day, West Indies ground to 45 for 1 by lunch, but that was one of their best sessions. Uncharacteristically, too many batsmen tried to bat out time rather than score runs – Hinds's 18 occupied 97 balls and 125 minutes. The pitch did deteriorate, but it wasn't quite that bad yet. Only Hooper counter-attacked, and Kumble, on his 32nd birthday, picked up four for ten in 8.3 overs after tea to finish with five in a Test innings for the 20th time. The openers gave India another solid start, but once Sehwag was out they lost their way. Ganguly got a doubtful decision first ball, and Dravid was beaten by sheer pace – Jermaine Lawson's first Test wicket thus protecting Everton Weekes's record of five successive Test centuries. However, India's tail wagged viciously to create a lead of 149. Sarwan took West Indies past 200 for the first time in this series but, once he went, they lost their last six wickets for 21. Harbhajan took three in a single over. Sehwag celebrated his 24th birthday with a 30-ball blast, and India reached their target of 81 in light drizzle just before the clouds opened. In less than seven days' playing time India had completed their first series victory over West Indies in nearly 24 years

West Indies

C. H. Gayle	c Tendulkar b Harbhajan Singh	23	– c Kumble b Srinath	0
W. W. Hinds	lbw b Kumble	18	– c Ganguly b Harbhajan Singh	61
R. R. Sarwan	b Srinath	19	– lbw b Zaheer Khan	78
S. Chanderpaul	c Patel b Kumble	27	– c Harbhajan Singh b Srinath	3
*C. L. Hooper	c Ganguly b Zaheer Khan	35	– c Patel b Kumble	46
R. O. Hinds	lbw b Kumble	16	– c Kumble b Harbhajan Singh	7
†R. D. Jacobs	c Sehwag b Harbhajan Singh	9	– c Patel b Zaheer Khan	3
G. R. Breese	c Sehwag b Harbhajan Singh	5	– c Ganguly b Harbhajan Singh	0
M. Dillon	b Kumble	4	– lbw b Harbhajan Singh	4
P. T. Collins	not out	1	– not out	6
J. J. C. Lawson	c Ganguly b Kumble	0	– b Zaheer Khan	2
	B 8, l-b 1, n-b 1	10	B 12, l-b 3, w 1, n-b 3	19

1/40 (1) 2/46 (2) 3/62 (3) 4/117 (5)   167   1/0 (1) 2/96 (2) 3/107 (4)   229
5/135 (4) 6/142 (6) 7/161 (8)   4/179 (5) 5/208 (3) 6/210 (6)
8/166 (9) 9/166 (7) 10/167 (11)   7/210 (8) 8/214 (9) 9/222 (7) 10/229 (11)

Srinath 10–5–14–1; Zaheer Khan 10–3–21–1; Bangar 6–3–29–0; Harbhajan Singh 29–13–56–3; Kumble 23.3–10–30–5; Sehwag 1–0–8–0. *Second Innings*—Srinath 9–4–16–2; Zaheer Khan 12.4–5–23–3; Harbhajan Singh 30–6–79–4; Kumble 26–3–87–1; Sehwag 2–0–9–0.

India

S. B. Bangar	c Hooper b Dillon	40	– c Gayle b Hooper	20
V. Sehwag	b Collins	61	– st Jacobs b Hooper	33
R. Dravid	b Lawson	11	– not out	6
S. R. Tendulkar	b Lawson	43	– not out	16
*S. C. Ganguly	lbw b Dillon	0		
V. V. S. Laxman	c and b Breese	24		
†P. A. Patel	st Jacobs b Breese	23		
Harbhajan Singh	b Dillon	37		
J. Srinath	run out	39		
A. Kumble	not out	12		
Zaheer Khan	run out	4		
	B 4, l-b 10, w 1, n-b 7	22	L-b 3, n-b 3	6

1/93 (2) 2/109 (3) 3/155 (1) 4/155 (5)   316   1/50 (2) 2/61 (1)   (2 wkts) 81
5/180 (4) 6/204 (6) 7/255 (8)
8/281 (7) 9/305 (9) 10/316 (11)

Dillon 26–11–44–3; Collins 23–5–59–1; Lawson 20–4–63–2; Breese 26.1–3–108–2; Hooper 6–2–19–0; R. O. Hinds 5–1–9–0. *Second Innings*—Dillon 5–1–10–0; Collins 2–0–7–0; Lawson 2–0–2–0; Breese 5.1–0–27–0; Hooper 7–1–32–2.

Umpires: E. A. R. de Silva *(Sri Lanka)* (19) and D. R. Shepherd *(England)* (66).
Third umpire: K. Hariharan *(India)*.   Referee: M. J. Procter *(South Africa)* (4).

Close of play: First day, India 31-0 (Bangar 6, Sehwag 24); Second day, India 190-5 (Laxman 18, Patel 1); Third day, West Indies 186-4 (Sarwan 62, R. O. Hinds 1).

INDIA v WEST INDIES 2002–03 (3rd Test)

At Eden Gardens, Kolkata, on 30, 31 October, 1, 2, 3 November.
Toss: India.   Result: MATCH DRAWN.
Debuts: none.
Man of the Match: S. R. Tendulkar.   Man of the Series: Harbhajan Singh.

West Indies sprung a surprise even before the toss: they included no specialist spinner, unprecedented in almost 70 years of Tests at Eden Gardens. This was followed by spirited cricket, and they might have won but for a match-saving partnership between Tendulkar and Laxman, back at the scene of his magnificent 281 against Australia the previous year. At first India batted as the West Indians had been doing. Eight got starts, but only Bangar passed 50, and it took a brisk 46 from Srinath to propel India past 300. Gayle and Hinds responded with grim determination and an opening stand of 172. But the partnership of the innings belonged to Chanderpaul and Samuels, who put West Indies in front while adding 195. Samuels had almost been sent home after breaking a curfew at a disco, but now he danced to his maiden Test century, his effortless flair evoking Caribbean batting of an earlier era. The last five wickets tumbled in an hour on the fourth morning, and a lead of 139 did not look much on a good pitch – until India slid to 49 for 3. Dravid was given out leg-before off an inside edge for the second time in the match, and later Ganguly got his third doubtful decision in four innings. An upset was in the offing – but Tendulkar stepped up, settling all nerves with an imperious 176, his first Test century at Kolkata. Laxman was the perfect support act in a stand of 214 spanning 70 overs.

India

S. B. Bangar c Hinds b Cuffy	77	– c Chanderpaul b Dillon		0
V. Sehwag lbw b Dillon	35	– c Chanderpaul b Dillon		10
R. Dravid lbw b Powell	14	– lbw b Powell		17
S. R. Tendulkar c Gayle b Lawson	36	– c Gayle b Cuffy		176
*S. C. Ganguly c Jacobs b Hooper	29	– lbw b Cuffy		16
V. V. S. Laxman c Gayle b Dillon	48	– not out		154
†P. A. Patel c Chanderpaul b Lawson	47	– run out		27
Harbhajan Singh b Cuffy	6	– c Hooper b Samuels		26
J. Srinath c Hooper b Dillon	46	– c Hooper b Chanderpaul		21
A. Kumble lbw b Powell	4	– not out		8
A. Nehra not out	0			
L-b 7, w 1, n-b 8	16	B 8, l-b 7, n-b 1		16

1/49 (2) 2/72 (3) 3/116 (4) 4/165 (5)   358   1/0 (1) 2/11 (2)   (8 wkts dec.) 471
5/242 (1) 6/271 (6) 7/280 (8)   3/49 (3) 4/87 (5)
8/353 (7) 9/358 (9) 10/358 (10)   5/301 (4) 6/373 (7) 7/407 (8) 8/458 (9)

Dillon 22–3–82–3; Cuffy 25–4–84–2; Lawson 20–3–76–2; Powell 16.2–4–62–2; Hooper 15–5–36–1; Gayle 2–0–6–0; Sarwan 1–0–5–0. *Second Innings*—Dillon 25–6–85–2; Cuffy 17–3–52–2; Lawson 22–3–65–0; Powell 25–4–53–1; Hooper 20–1–63–0; Gayle 23–5–70–0; Sarwan 8–1–38–0; Samuels 16–3–21–1; Chanderpaul 3–0–9–1.

West Indies

C. H. Gayle c Sehwag b Kumble	88	J. J. C. Lawson lbw b Kumble	5
W. W. Hinds c Ganguly b Harbhajan Singh	100	C. E. Cuffy c Laxman b Harbhajan Singh	0
R. R. Sarwan st Patel b Harbhajan Singh	2	B 4, l-b 7, n-b 6	17
M. Dillon b Harbhajan Singh	0		
S. Chanderpaul c Harbhajan Singh b Sehwag	140	1/172 (2) 2/186 (3) 3/186 (4)	497
*C. L. Hooper c Patel b Nehra	19	4/213 (1) 5/255 (6) 6/450 (5)	
M. N. Samuels c Sehwag b Harbhajan Singh	104	7/469 (7) 8/470 (9)	
†R. D. Jacobs not out	22	9/496 (10) 10/497 (11)	
D. B. Powell lbw b Kumble	0		

Srinath 19–3–62–0; Nehra 23–9–66–1; Harbhajan Singh 57.3–15–115–5; Kumble 54–9–169–3; Bangar 6–3–14–0; Tendulkar 7–0–33–0; Sehwag 5–0–27–1.

Umpires: E. A. R. de Silva *(Sri Lanka)* (20) and D. R. Shepherd *(England)* (67).
Third umpire: A. V. Jayaprakash *(India)*.   Referee: M. J. Procter *(South Africa)* (5).

Close of play: First day, India 275-6 (Patel 18, Harbhajan Singh 3); Second day, West Indies 189-3 (Gayle 80, Chanderpaul 1); Third day, West Indies 446-5 (Chanderpaul 136, Samuels 89); Fourth day, India 195-4 (Tendulkar 114, Laxman 30).

SOUTH AFRICA v BANGLADESH 2002–03 (1st Test)

At Buffalo Park, East London, on 18, 19, 20, 21 October.
Toss: Bangladesh.   Result: SOUTH AFRICA won by an innings and 107 runs.
Debuts: South Africa – M. van Jaarsveld.
Man of the Match: G. C. Smith.

Given Bangladesh's dire Test record – one draw and 12 defeats before this – it was probably unkind of one local journalist to claim they won the toss and "refused to bat". Even so, Khaled Mashud's timid insertion spoke volumes about their frame of mind. In his defence, Buffalo Park, the 85th Test venue, had served up a green pitch for its first match. However, the visiting bowlers struggled to exploit helpful conditions and, by the first-day close, South Africa were in complete command. Graeme Smith had just converted his first Test hundred into a double when, having hit precisely half his runs in fours, he lofted to mid-on. By then, Kirsten – Smith's partner in a stand of 272 – had become the first to score centuries against nine Test opponents. Next day Boucher, standing in on his home ground for the injured Shaun Pollock, declared at 529 for 4. Ntini, also at home, then precipitated Bangladesh's rapid spiral towards defeat. He produced a fiery spell, taking three for 13 in ten overs. Bangladesh's second innings was a grittier effort, and they succeeded in taking the match into a fourth day. Al Sahariar hit a career-best 71, and Sanwar Hossain also made the bowlers work before falling one short of a maiden fifty. But the frustrater-in-chief was Mashud, who held out for nearly 3½ hours. He departed as soon as the flame-haired Terbrugge took the second new ball on the fourth morning, on his way to his only Test five-for.

South Africa

G. C. Smith c Manjural Islam b Sanwar Hossain	. . . . .	200
H. H. Gibbs c Tushar Imran b Tapash Baisya	. . . .	41
G. Kirsten c Alok Kapali b Talha Jubair	. . . .	150
J. H. Kallis not out	. . . .	75
A. G. Prince c Alok Kapali b Talha Jubair	. . . .	2

M. van Jaarsveld not out	 39
B 2, l-b 1, w 4, n-b 15	 22
1/87 (2) 2/359 (1)	(4 wkts dec.) 529
3/440 (3) 4/448 (5)	

*†M. V. Boucher, D. J. Terbrugge, C. W. Henderson, M. Ntini and M. Hayward did not bat.

Manjural Islam 29–3–104–0; Tapash Baisya 30–3–148–1; Talha Jubair 26–5–108–2; Mohammad Rafique 23–2–85–0; Alok Kapali 18–0–72–0; Sanwar Hossain 3–0–9–1.

Bangladesh

Javed Omar lbw b Terbrugge	 7	– c Gibbs b Hayward	10
Al Sahariar b Hayward	 18	– b Ntini.	71
Habibul Bashar c Boucher b Ntini	 38	– c Terbrugge b Hayward	21
Sanwar Hossain c Boucher b Ntini	 31	– lbw b Terbrugge	49
Tushar Imran b Ntini	 0	– (6) c van Jaarsveld b Henderson	8
Alok Kapali c Kallis b Henderson	 35	– (7) lbw b Terbrugge	10
*†Khaled Mashud c van Jaarsveld b Hayward	 4	– (5) lbw b Terbrugge	33
Mohammad Rafique not out	 17	– b Terbrugge.	19
Tapash Baisya c Boucher b Ntini	 2	– c Kirsten b Terbrugge	10
Manjural Islam b Ntini	 4	– c sub (A. C. Thomas) b Ntini	8
Talha Jubair c Boucher b Terbrugge	 3	– not out.	4
L-b 9, w 1, n-b 1	 11	B 3, l-b 3, n-b 3	9

1/21 (1) 2/25 (2) 3/91 (4) 4/97 (5)	170	1/22 (1) 2/78 (3) 3/121 (2)
5/100 (3) 6/130 (7) 7/149 (6)		4/158 (4) 5/176 (6) 6/211 (7)
8/155 (9) 9/161 (10) 10/170 (11)		7/212 (5) 8/231 (8) 9/244 (9) 10/252 (10)

And the second innings total: **252**

Hayward 15–3–50–2; Terbrugge 11.4–3–43–2; Henderson 9–2–23–1; Ntini 15–9–19–5; Kallis 8–2–26–0. *Second Innings*—Ntini 18.5–6–55–2; Terbrugge 15–1–46–5; Hayward 16–2–65–2; Kallis 10–3–22–0; Henderson 28–8–58–1.

Umpires: D. J. Harper *(Australia)* (23) and R. B. Tiffin *(Zimbabwe)* (29).
Third umpire: S. Wadvalla *(South Africa)*.   Referee: R. S. Madugalle *(Sri Lanka)* (44).

Close of play: First day, South Africa 369-2 (Kirsten 113, Kallis 1); Second day, Bangladesh 153-7 (Mohammad Rafique 10, Tapash Baisya 1); Third day, Bangladesh 209-5 (Khaled Mashud 32, Alok Kapali 9).

SOUTH AFRICA v BANGLADESH 2002–03 (2nd Test)

At North West Cricket Stadium, Potchefstroom, on 25, 26, 27 October.
Toss: Bangladesh.   Result: SOUTH AFRICA won by an innings and 160 runs.
Debuts: Bangladesh – Rafiqul Islam.
Man of the Match: J. H. Kallis.   Man of the Series: J. H. Kallis.

For the second time in a fortnight Bangladesh won the toss – and were steamrollered. A desperately one-sided contest came to a merciful close on the third afternoon with South Africa completing an entirely predictable 2–0 rout. Bangladesh did punch above their weight for an entire session: after deciding to bat on a flat track at another ground making its Test debut (the 86th), they went to lunch at 124 for 1. The rollicking start was provided by Al Sahariar and Hannan Sarkar, who struck a Test-best 65, and continued by Habibul Bashar, perhaps their only batsman of genuine class. It was stirring stuff; as boundaries blazed, South Africa's bowling and fielding dropped well below their usual standards. Lunch changed everything. Pollock, back as captain, led the resurgence, but the wickets were shared around as Bangladesh succumbed for 215. Kirsten provided the backbone of the reply with his 16th Test century, but Gibbs laid the foundations in flamboyant style. Kallis became the third centurion before the third-morning declaration, five down and 267 ahead. Pollock set his bowlers the target of finishing the game off that day, and they obliged in less than 31 overs, thanks largely to Kallis, who careered through the lower order with five wickets in 12 balls. His figures were impressive in themselves, but what turned the eye was his ability to conjure sharp lift from a pitch that appeared to have breathed its last on the first day.

Bangladesh

Hannan Sarkar c Kallis b Ntini	65	– b Ntini		17
Al Sahariar c Smith b Hayward	30	– c Kallis b Hayward		27
Habibul Bashar c Boucher b Pollock	40	– c Boucher b Ntini		7
Sanwar Hossain lbw b Ntini	0	– c Kallis b Ntini		6
*†Khaled Mashud c van Jaarsveld b Kallis	20	– (6) c Boucher b Kallis		9
Rafiqul Islam c Gibbs b Kallis	6	– (8) c Kirsten b Kallis		1
Tushar Imran c Boucher b Pollock	8	– (5) c Prince b Hayward		0
Alok Kapali not out	38	– (7) c Boucher b Kallis		23
Tapash Baisya c van Jaarsveld b Hayward	2	– c Gibbs b Kallis		0
Manjural Islam c Smith b Henderson	0	– c Gibbs b Kallis		5
Talha Jubair run out	0	– not out		1
B 4, n-b 2	6	L-b 8, n-b 3		11

1/52 (2) 2/136 (1) 3/136 (4) 4/140 (3)   215   1/33 (1) 2/43 (3) 3/52 (4) 4/60 (2)   107
5/162 (6) 6/169 (5) 7/184 (7)   5/61 (5) 6/95 (7) 7/101 (8)
8/197 (9) 9/202 (10) 10/215 (11)   8/101 (6) 9/104 (9) 10/107 (10)

Pollock 16–6–38–2; Ntini 21–4–69–2; Hayward 14–3–64–2; Kallis 13–4–26–2; Henderson 5.5–2–14–1.
Second Innings—Pollock 6–0–25–0; Ntini 12–1–37–3; Hayward 8–3–16–2; Kallis 4.3–1–21–5.

South Africa

G. C. Smith c Khaled Mashud b Sanwar Hossain	24	M. van Jaarsveld lbw b Tapash Baisya	11
H. H. Gibbs run out	114	†M. V. Boucher not out	14
G. Kirsten c Khaled Mashud b Talha Jubair	160	B 13, l-b 2, n-b 5	20
J. H. Kallis not out	139		
A. G. Prince c Khaled Mashud b Talha Jubair	0	1/61 (1) 2/202 (2) (5 wkts dec.) 482	
		3/436 (3) 4/436 (5) 5/452 (6)	

*S. M. Pollock, C. W. Henderson, M. Ntini and M. Hayward did not bat.

Manjural Islam 26–7–80–0; Tapash Baisya 28–3–103–1; Talha Jubair 26–3–109–2; Alok Kapali 20–2–75–0; Sanwar Hossain 20–1–98–1; Habibul Bashar 1–0–2–0.

Umpires: D. J. Harper *(Australia)* (24) and R. B. Tiffin *(Zimbabwe)* (30).
Third umpire: S. Wadvalla *(South Africa)*.   Referee: R. S. Madugalle *(Sri Lanka)* (45).

Close of play: First day, South Africa 61-1 (Gibbs 36); Second day, South Africa 414-2 (Kirsten 154, Kallis 107).

AUSTRALIA v ENGLAND 2002–03 (1st Test)

At Woolloongabba, Brisbane, 7, 8, 9, 10 November.
Toss: England.   Result: AUSTRALIA won by 384 runs.
Debuts: none.
Man of the Match: M. L. Hayden.

It will go down as one of the costliest decisions in Test history. Although his openers were clearly his most potent weapons, Hussain sent Australia in. By the end of the first day, they were 364 for 2. He had expected some early life in a green-tinged pitch, but it quickly dried out into the proverbial belter, and Hayden and Ponting piled on 272. By then, Jones had tumbled out of the attack – and the series – after rupturing knee ligaments in the field. Hayden, dropped four times, moved to 197 before gloving a leg-side catch as four wickets tumbled for 37: it was left to Warne to scramble a total of 492. England began well, also helped by poor catching, but once Hussain fell, a familiar collapse ensued – from 268 for 3 to 325. Hussain's aggressive fields were rewarded when Langer and Ponting departed quickly, but Hayden motored on to become the seventh batsman to score two hundreds in an Ashes Test. It was his seventh century in ten Tests, and his sixth in seven on his home ground. Now came England's darkest hour. Needing a fanciful 464 to win or to bat for a day and a half to avert defeat, they lost Vaughan third ball, and went on to capitulate pathetically in just 28.2 overs in little more than two hours. The final result was their fourth-heaviest defeat by runs; it was also a 50th defeat in 123 Tests for Stewart, who completed his first pair.

Australia

J. L. Langer c Stewart b Jones	32	– c Stewart b Caddick	22
M. L. Hayden c Stewart b Caddick	197	– c and b Giles	103
R. T. Ponting b Giles	123	– c Trescothick b Caddick	3
D. R. Martyn c Trescothick b White	26	– c Hussain b Giles	64
*S. R. Waugh c Crawley b Caddick	7	– (6) c Trescothick b Caddick	12
D. S. Lehmann c Butcher b Giles	30	– (7) not out	20
†A. C. Gilchrist c Giles b White	0	– (5) not out	60
S. K. Warne c Butcher b Caddick	57		
A. J. Bichel lbw b Giles	0		
J. N. Gillespie not out	0		
G. D. McGrath lbw b Giles	0		
B 1, l-b 11, w 1, n-b 7	20	B 3, l-b 5, n-b 4	12

1/67 (1) 2/339 (3) 3/378 (2) 4/399 (4)   492
5/408 (5) 6/415 (7) 7/478 (6)
8/478 (9) 9/492 (8) 10/492 (11)

1/30 (1) 2/39 (3)   (5 wkts dec.) 296
3/192 (2) 4/213 (4)
5/242 (6)

Caddick 35–9–108–3; Hoggard 30–4–122–0; Jones 7–0–32–1; White 27–4–105–2; Giles 29.2–3–101–4; Butcher 2–0–12–0. *Second Innings*—Caddick 23–2–95–3; Hoggard 13–2–42–0; White 11–0–61–0; Giles 24–2–90–2.

England

M. E. Trescothick c Ponting b McGrath	72	– c Gilchrist b Gillespie	1
M. P. Vaughan c Gilchrist b McGrath	33	– lbw b McGrath	0
M. A. Butcher c Hayden b McGrath	54	– c Ponting b Warne	40
*N. Hussain c Gilchrist b Gillespie	51	– c Ponting b McGrath	11
J. P. Crawley not out	69	– run out	0
†A. J. Stewart b Gillespie	0	– c Hayden b Warne	0
C. White b McGrath	12	– c Hayden b McGrath	13
A. F. Giles c Gilchrist b Bichel	13	– c Gilchrist b McGrath	4
A. R. Caddick c Ponting b Bichel	0	– c Lehmann b Warne	4
M. J. Hoggard c Hayden b Warne	4	– not out	1
S. P. Jones absent hurt		– absent hurt	
B 2, l-b 8, n-b 7	17	L-b 1, n-b 4	5

1/49 (2) 2/170 (3) 3/171 (1) 4/268 (4)   325
5/270 (6) 6/283 (7) 7/308 (8)
8/308 (9) 9/325 (10)

1/1 (2) 2/3 (1) 3/33 (4)   79
4/34 (5) 5/35 (6) 6/66 (7)
7/74 (8) 8/74 (3) 9/79 (9)

McGrath 30–9–87–4; Gillespie 18–4–51–2; Bichel 23–4–74–2; Warne 26.5–4–87–1; Waugh 4–2–5–0; Lehmann 5–0–11–0. *Second Innings*—McGrath 12–3–36–4; Gillespie 6–1–13–1; Warne 10.2–3–29–3.

Umpires: S. A. Bucknor *(West Indies)* (73) and R. E. Koertzen *(South Africa)* (35).
Third umpire: S. J. A. Taufel *(Australia)*.   Referee: Wasim Raja *(Pakistan)* (5).

Close of play: First day, Australia 364-2 (Hayden 186, Martyn 9); Second day, England 158-1 (Trescothick 63, Butcher 51); Third day, Australia 111-2 (Hayden 40, Martyn 40).

AUSTRALIA v ENGLAND 2002–03 (2nd Test)

At Adelaide Oval on 21, 22, 23, 24 November.
Toss: England.   Result: AUSTRALIA won by an innings and 51 runs.
Debuts: none.
Man of the Match: R. T. Ponting.

When England reached 295 for 3 with four balls of the first day remaining, they appeared for once to be offering a genuine challenge to Australia. Then, however, Vaughan's magnificent if controversial 177 (at 19 he seemed to have been caught at point by Langer, but stood his ground, and TV replays were inconclusive) was ended and, in little more than seven further sessions, England descended to a crushing defeat. Despite Hussain's insistence to the contrary, the Australians dominated mentally as well as technically. Vaughan's dismissal in the 90th over of the opening day was a fine example: Steve Waugh brought back Bichel, an honest toiler alongside three wonderful craftsmen, for a single over. He ran in as hard as if it was his first spell, nudged one away from the bat and Warne held the catch at slip. It was the turning point of the match. Bichel did it again when called up for the final over of the third evening, breaching Hussain's defences. Equally revealing, and even more spectacular, was Vaughan's second-innings dismissal: a running, diving, stunning catch by McGrath at deep square leg. In between, Hayden and Langer shared their seventh century opening stand in Tests, then Ponting made his second hundred of the series, putting on 242 with Martyn. England lost three wickets inside 12 overs on the third evening, and although Vaughan and Stewart (who reached 8,000 Test runs when 52) added 74, Australia's victory march was not long delayed.

England

M. E. Trescothick b McGrath	35	– lbw b Gillespie	0
M. P. Vaughan c Warne b Bichel	177	– c McGrath b Warne	41
R. W. T. Key c Ponting b Warne	1	– (5) c Lehmann b Bichel	1
*N. Hussain c Gilchrist b Warne	47	– b Bichel	10
M. A. Butcher c Gilchrist b Gillespie	22	– (3) lbw b McGrath	4
†A. J. Stewart lbw b Gillespie	29	– lbw b Warne	57
C. White c Bichel b Gillespie	1	– c sub (B. Lee) b McGrath	5
R. K. J. Dawson lbw b Warne	6	– c Gilchrist b McGrath	19
A. R. Caddick b Warne	0	– (11) not out	6
M. J. Hoggard c Gilchrist b Gillespie	6	– (9) b McGrath	1
S. J. Harmison not out	3	– (10) lbw b Warne	0
L-b 7, n-b 8	15	B 3, l-b 4, n-b 8	15

1/88 (1) 2/106 (3) 3/246 (4) 4/295 (2)   342   1/5 (1) 2/17 (3) 3/36 (4)   159
5/295 (5) 6/308 (7) 7/325 (8)   4/40 (5) 5/114 (2) 6/130 (7)
8/325 (9) 9/337 (6) 10/342 (10)   7/130 (6) 8/132 (9) 9/134 (10) 10/159 (8)

McGrath 30–11–77–1; Gillespie 26.5–8–78–4; Bichel 20–2–78–1; Warne 34–10–93–4; Waugh 5–1–9–0.
Second Innings—McGrath 17.2–6–41–4; Gillespie 12–1–44–1; Warne 25–7–36–3; Bichel 5–0–31–2.

Australia

J. L. Langer c Stewart b Dawson	48	A. J. Bichel b Hoggard	48
M. L. Hayden c Caddick b White	46	J. N. Gillespie not out	0
R. T. Ponting c Dawson b White	154		
D. R. Martyn c Hussain b Harmison	95	B 1, l-b 17, w 7, n-b 18	43
*S. R. Waugh c Butcher b White	34		
D. S. Lehmann c sub (A. Flintoff) b White	5	1/101 (2) 2/114 (1) (9 wkts dec.) 552
†A. C. Gilchrist c Stewart b Harmison	54	3/356 (4) 4/397 (3)
S. K. Warne c and b Dawson	25	5/414 (6) 6/423 (5)
		7/471 (8) 8/548 (9) 9/552 (7)

G. D. McGrath did not bat.

Caddick 20–2–95–0; Hoggard 26–4–84–1; Harmison 28.2–8–106–2; White 28–2–106–4; Dawson 37–2–143–2.

Umpires: S. A. Bucknor *(West Indies)* (74) and R. E. Koertzen *(South Africa)* (36).
Third umpire: S. J. Davis *(Australia)*.   Referee: Wasim Raja *(Pakistan)* (6).

Close of play: First day, England 295-4 (Butcher 22); Second day, Australia 247-2 (Ponting 83, Martyn 48); Third day, England 36-3 (Vaughan 17).

AUSTRALIA v ENGLAND 2002–03 (3rd Test)

At W. A. C. A. Ground, Perth, on 29, 30 November, 1 December.
Toss: England.   Result: AUSTRALIA won by an innings and 48 runs.
Debuts: none.
Man of the Match: D. R. Martyn.

England's quest for the Ashes came to an end on December 1, the earliest ever. It had taken just 11 playing days for the Australians to dismantle a team reeling from two thumping defeats and a catalogue of injuries which had reached ridiculous proportions. Silverwood, who had not bowled in the middle after being summoned when Jones was injured, was surprisingly preferred to Hoggard ... and almost inevitably broke down with an ankle injury after only four overs. At 69 for 1, England had seemed to be competing well on a pacy track, but then came the first of two catastrophic mix-ups between Vaughan and Butcher. Waugh, from cover, unerringly hit the non-striker's stumps with Butcher yards adrift, a self-inflicted blow from which England never recovered. Only Key resisted for long, and he was duped by Martyn's gentle medium-pacers just before tea. Australia found run-scoring a more straightforward occupation, although no-one managed a major innings. Ponting, in sublime form, looked set for his third century of the series until he played on, one of five victims for White. Then England folded again after a masochistic run-out. This time Vaughan was the victim, but Butcher was so ruffled that he missed his next ball, was patently lbw, and swiped the bails off to earn a fine. Just before the end, Tudor ducked into a Lee bouncer and received a sickening blow to the head. He briefly feared he had lost an eye, but fortunately suffered nothing worse than a nasty gash.

England

M. E. Trescothick c Gilchrist b Lee	34	– c Gilchrist b Lee		4
M. P. Vaughan c Gilchrist b McGrath	34	– run out		9
M. A. Butcher run out	9	– (4) lbw b McGrath		0
*N. Hussain c Gilchrist b Lee	8	– (5) c Gilchrist b Warne		61
R. W. T. Key b Martyn	47	– (6) lbw b McGrath		23
†A. J. Stewart c Gilchrist b McGrath	7	– (7) not out		66
C. White c Martyn b Lee	2	– (8) st Gilchrist b Warne		15
A. J. Tudor c Martyn b Warne	0	– (9) retired hurt		3
R. K. J. Dawson not out	19	– (3) c Waugh b Gillespie		8
C. E. W. Silverwood c Hayden b Gillespie	10	– absent hurt		
S. J. Harmison b Gillespie	6	– (10) b Lee		5
L-b 2, n-b 7	9	B 8, l-b 5, w 1, n-b 15		29

1/47 (1) 2/69 (3) 3/83 (4) 4/101 (2)   185   1/13 (1) 2/33 (3) 3/34 (2)   223
5/111 (6) 6/121 (7) 7/135 (8)   4/34 (4) 5/102 (6) 6/169 (5)
8/156 (5) 9/173 (10) 10/185 (11)   7/208 (8) 8/223 (10)

In the second innings Tudor retired hurt at 214.

McGrath 17–5–30–2; Gillespie 17.2–8–43–2; Lee 20–1–78–3; Warne 9–0–32–1; Martyn 1–1–0–1. *Second Innings*—Lee 18.1–3–72–2; McGrath 21–9–24–2; Gillespie 15–4–35–1; Warne 26–5–70–2; Martyn 2–0–9–0.

Australia

J. L. Langer run out	19	B. Lee c Key b White		41
M. L. Hayden c Tudor b Harmison	30	J. N. Gillespie b White		27
R. T. Ponting b White	68	G. D. McGrath not out		8
D. R. Martyn c Stewart b Tudor	71	B 4, l-b 5, n-b 15		24
D. S. Lehmann c Harmison b White	42			
*S. R. Waugh b Tudor	53	1/31 (1) 2/85 (2) 3/159 (3) 4/226 (5)		456
†A. C. Gilchrist c Tudor b White	38	5/264 (4) 6/316 (7) 7/348 (6)		
S. K. Warne run out	35	8/416 (8) 9/423 (9) 10/456 (10)		

Silverwood 4–0–29–0; Tudor 29–2–144–2; Harmison 28–7–86–1; White 23.1–3–127–5; Butcher 10–1–40–0; Dawson 5–0–21–0.

Umpires: S. A. Bucknor *(West Indies)* (75) and R. E. Koertzen *(South Africa)* (37).
Third umpire: D. J. Harper *(Australia)*.   Referee: Wasim Raja *(Pakistan)* (7).

Close of play: First day, Australia 126-2 (Ponting 43, Martyn 20); Second day, England 33-1 (Vaughan 8, Dawson 8).

AUSTRALIA v ENGLAND 2002–03 (4th Test)

At Melbourne Cricket Ground on 26, 27, 28, 29, 30 December.
Toss: Australia.   Result: AUSTRALIA won by five wickets.
Debuts: Australia – M. L. Love.
Man of the Match: J. L. Langer.

Australia showed signs of their old fallibility when chasing small targets, but finally made it 4–0 with five wickets to spare. It might have been closer: after Harmison had grabbed two wickets, Waugh somehow survived a manic over in which he was beaten, caught behind (but no-one appealed), then caught off a no-ball. The spell was broken with a four and, although Waugh really was out a few overs later, the moment had passed. All this drama had seemed unthinkable as Australia racked up 551 before declaring. Hayden clattered his 12th Test hundred, the ninth in the last 14 months, while Langer rolled on to his highest Test score, which included 30 fours, plus a six off Dawson to reach three figures. White rescued England from 118 for 6, but they still had to follow on, even though Warne was missing, having injured his shoulder in a one-day game. Vaughan then emulated Hayden by gliding to his sixth century of 2002, and eclipsed Dennis Amiss's England record of 1,379 runs in a calendar year, finishing with 1,481. But the last five wickets added only 45, and Australia's target was a seemingly simple 107; England's feisty final-day display suggested that a few more might have been interesting. This was Waugh's 33rd win in just 44 Tests as captain, passing Allan Border's 32 in 93, and closing in on the overall record of 36 in 74 by Clive Lloyd. Martin Love made his Test debut after an Australian-record 129 first-class matches.

Australia

J. L. Langer c Caddick b Dawson	250	– lbw b Caddick		24
M. L. Hayden c Crawley b Caddick	102	– c sub (A. J. Tudor) b Caddick		1
R. T. Ponting b White	21	– c Foster b Harmison		30
D. R. Martyn c Trescothick b White	17	– c Foster b Harmison		0
*S. R. Waugh c Foster b White	77	– c Butcher b Caddick		14
M. L. Love not out	62	– not out		6
†A. C. Gilchrist b Dawson	1	– not out		10
L-b 11, w 5, n-b 5	21	B 8, l-b 5, n-b 9		22

1/195 (2) 2/235 (3) 3/265 (4)   (6 wkts dec.) 551   1/8 (2) 2/58 (3) 3/58 (4)   (5 wkts) 107
4/394 (5) 5/545 (1) 6/551 (7)   4/83 (5) 5/90 (1)

B. Lee, J. N. Gillespie, S. C. G. MacGill and G. D. McGrath did not bat.

Caddick 36–6–126–1; Harmison 36–7–108–0; White 33–5–133–3; Dawson 28–1–121–2; Butcher 13–2–52–0. *Second Innings*—Caddick 12–1–51–3; Harmison 11.1–1–43–2.

England

M. E. Trescothick c Gilchrist b Lee	37	– lbw b MacGill		37
M. P. Vaughan b McGrath	11	– c Love b MacGill		145
M. A. Butcher lbw b Gillespie	25	– c Love b Gillespie		6
*N. Hussain c Hayden b MacGill	24	– c and b McGrath		23
R. K. J. Dawson c Love b McGrath	6	– (9) not out		15
R. W. T. Key lbw b Lee	0	– (5) c Ponting b Gillespie		52
J. P. Crawley c Langer b Gillespie	17	– (6) b Lee		33
C. White not out	85	– (7) c Gilchrist b MacGill		21
†J. S. Foster lbw b Waugh	19	– (8) c Love b MacGill		6
A. R. Caddick b Gillespie	17	– c Waugh b MacGill		10
S. J. Harmison c Gilchrist b Gillespie	2	– b Gillespie		7
B 3, l-b 10, n-b 14	27	B 3, l-b 21, w 2, n-b 6		32

1/13 (2) 2/73 (1) 3/94 (3) 4/111 (5)   270   1/67 (1) 2/89 (3) 3/169 (4)   387
5/113 (6) 6/118 (4) 7/172 (7)   4/236 (2) 5/287 (5) 6/342 (6)
8/227 (9) 9/264 (10) 10/270 (11)   7/342 (7) 8/356 (8) 9/378 (10) 10/387 (11)

McGrath 16–5–41–1; Gillespie 16.3–7–25–4; MacGill 36–10–108–2; Lee 17–4–70–2; Waugh 4–0–13–1. *Second Innings*—McGrath 19–5–44–1; Gillespie 24.4–6–71–3; MacGill 48–10–152–5; Lee 27–4–87–1; Waugh 2–0–9–0.

Umpires: D. L. Orchard *(South Africa)* (31) and R. B. Tiffin *(Zimbabwe)* (31).
Third umpire: D. B. Hair *(Australia)*.   Referee: Wasim Raja *(Pakistan)* (8).

Close of play: First day, Australia 356-3 (Langer 146, Waugh 62); Second day, England 97-3 (Hussain 17, Dawson 0); Third day, England 111-2 (Vaughan 55, Hussain 8); Fourth day, Australia 8-0 (Langer 4, Hayden 1).

AUSTRALIA v ENGLAND 2002–03 (5th Test)

At Sydney Cricket Ground on 2, 3, 4, 5, 6 January.
Toss: England.   Result: ENGLAND won by 225 runs.
Debuts: none.
Man of the Match: M. P. Vaughan.   Man of the Series: M. P. Vaughan.

England built on their Melbourne momentum to inflict Australia's first home defeat in four years. It was tempting to blame it on dead-rubber syndrome, but this was a hard-fought victory. England's two previous wins over Australia hinged on a miraculous spell by Dean Headley and an even more miraculous innings by Mark Butcher. This time they played grinding cricket for five days, under a hot sun and an unflinching leader. For the first time since November 1992, Australia went into a Test without either McGrath (side strain) or Warne (shoulder). The match was witnessed by the second-biggest Sydney crowd in history, and a further 2.1 million – one in nine Australians – watched the gripping second evening on TV as Steve Waugh, who had entered his 156th Test (equalling Allan Border's record) knowing that it might be his last, cracked Dawson's last ball for four to reach his 29th century, equalling Don Bradman's Australian record. Gilchrist's 133 from 121 balls, and his stand of 82 with Gillespie, helped Australia take the lead by one; but after Trescothick became Lee's 100th Test victim, Vaughan – who added 189 with Hussain – produced another superb innings, taking his series aggregate to 633, England's best in Australia since Geoff Boycott's 657 in 1970-71. Australia needed 452, but Langer, Hayden and Ponting were despatched lbw on a tense fourth evening, and Caddick, making use of uneven bounce and undisciplined batting, finished with ten wickets for the only time in what turned out to be his final Test.

England

M. E. Trescothick c Gilchrist b Bichel	19	– b Lee	22
M. P. Vaughan c Gilchrist b Lee	0	– lbw b Bichel	183
M. A. Butcher b Lee	124	– c Hayden b MacGill	34
*N. Hussain c Gilchrist b Gillespie	75	– c Gilchrist b Lee	72
R. W. T. Key lbw b Waugh	3	– c Hayden b Lee	14
J. P. Crawley not out	35	– lbw b Gillespie	8
†A. J. Stewart b Bichel	71	– not out	38
R. K. J. Dawson c Gilchrist b Bichel	2	– c and b Bichel	12
A. R. Caddick b MacGill	7	– c Langer b MacGill	8
M. J. Hoggard st Gilchrist b MacGill	0	– b MacGill	0
S. J. Harmison run out	4	– not out	20
B 6, l-b 3, n-b 13	22	B 9, l-b 20, w 2, n-b 10	41

1/4 (2) 2/32 (1) 3/198 (4) 4/210 (5)   362   1/37 (1) 2/124 (3)   (9 wkts dec.) 452
5/240 (3) 6/332 (7) 7/337 (8)   3/313 (4) 4/344 (5)
8/348 (9) 9/350 (10) 10/362 (11)   5/345 (2) 6/356 (6) 7/378 (8) 8/407 (9) 9/409 (10)

Gillespie 27–10–62–1; Lee 31–9–97–2; Bichel 21–5–86–3; MacGill 44–8–106–2; Waugh 4–3–2–1. *Second Innings*—Gillespie 18.3–4–70–1; Lee 31.3–5–132–3; MacGill 41–8–120–3; Bichel 25.3–3–82–2; Martyn 3–1–14–0; Waugh 6–2–5–0.

Australia

J. L. Langer c Hoggard b Caddick	25	– lbw b Caddick	3
M. L. Hayden lbw b Caddick	15	– lbw b Hoggard	2
R. T. Ponting c Stewart b Caddick	7	– (4) lbw b Caddick	11
D. R. Martyn c Caddick b Harmison	26	– (5) c Stewart b Dawson	21
*S. R. Waugh c Butcher b Hoggard	102	– (6) b Caddick	6
M. L. Love c Trescothick b Harmison	0	– (7) b Harmison	27
†A. C. Gilchrist c Stewart b Harmison	133	– (8) c Butcher b Caddick	37
A. J. Bichel c Crawley b Hoggard	4	– (3) lbw b Caddick	49
B. Lee c Stewart b Hoggard	0	– c Stewart b Caddick	46
J. N. Gillespie not out	31	– not out	3
S. C. G. MacGill c Hussain b Hoggard	1	– b Caddick	1
B 2, l-b 6, w 2, n-b 9	19	B 6, l-b 8, w 3, n-b 3	20

1/36 (2) 2/45 (3) 3/56 (1) 4/146 (4)   363   1/5 (1) 2/5 (2) 3/25 (4)   226
5/150 (6) 6/241 (5) 7/267 (8)   4/93 (3) 5/99 (6) 6/109 (5)
8/267 (9) 9/349 (7) 10/363 (11)   7/139 (7) 8/181 (8) 9/224 (9) 10/226 (11)

Hoggard 21.3–4–92–4; Caddick 23–3–121–3; Harmison 20–4–70–3; Dawson 16–0–72–0. *Second Innings*—Hoggard 13–3–35–1; Caddick 22–5–94–7; Harmison 9–1–42–1; Dawson 10–2–41–1.

Umpires: D. L. Orchard *(South Africa)* (32) and R. B. Tiffin *(Zimbabwe)* (32).
Third umpire: S. J. A. Taufel *(Australia)*.   Referee: Wasim Raja *(Pakistan)* (9).

Close of play: First day, England 264-5 (Crawley 6, Stewart 20); Second day, Australia 237-5 (Waugh 102, Gilchrist 45); Third day, England 218-2 (Vaughan 113, Hussain 34); Fourth day, Australia 91-3 (Bichel 49, Martyn 19).

SOUTH AFRICA v SRI LANKA 2002–03 (1st Test)

At The Wanderers, Johannesburg, on 8, 9, 10 November.
Toss: Sri Lanka.   Result: SOUTH AFRICA won by an innings and 64 runs.
Debuts: Sri Lanka – K. H. R. K. Fernando.
Man of the Match: J. H. Kallis.

The Sri Lankans were brimming with optimism before the start; their coach, Dav Whatmore, thought his side better prepared than ever before during his tenure. Eight sessions later, they had been routed – overawed and over-powered by a five-pronged pace attack on a trampoline-like pitch. But the game did not begin smoothly for South Africa. Herschelle Gibbs developed back spasms during the warm-up and, as the captains tossed, his replacement Martin van Jaarsveld was still in Pretoria. Jayasuriya boldly chose to bat on a green-tinged surface, which allowed South Africa to regroup. Sri Lanka's top six all made starts only to waste them, and the eventual 192 was well below par. Kirsten and Smith cruised to 133, relishing the width offered by the seamers. Dilhara Fernando repeatedly overstepped, delivering 17 no-balls, while Ruchira Perera, back after remedial work on his action, was banned from bowling after repeatedly running down the pitch. Even Muralitharan was treated harshly, especially by Smith, who kept drilling him through the off side. But South Africa were derailed by a triple strike from Hasantha Fernando, starting with his second delivery in a Test, which removed Smith. Kallis glued things together with a painstaking five-hour 75, before Sri Lanka crumbled against Ntini and Pollock. Arnold lasted one ball, completing a pair, as did Hasantha Fernando; by the 13th over, it was 25 for 4. Atapattu and Tillekeratne both survived for two hours, but the game ended in a rush as the last four wickets fell for just eight runs.

Sri Lanka

M. S. Atapattu b Pollock	34	– c Smith b Elworthy		43
R. P. Arnold c Smith b Ntini	0	– c Kallis b Ntini		0
†K. C. Sangakkara c Smith b Elworthy	26	– c Boucher b Ntini		7
D. P. M. D. Jayawardene c Boucher b Kallis	39	– c Kirsten b Pollock		1
*S. T. Jayasuriya c Smith b Kallis	32	– b Pollock		0
H. P. Tillekeratne run out	24	– c Elworthy b Hall		27
K. H. R. K. Fernando c Kirsten b Kallis	0	– lbw b Elworthy		0
W. P. U. J. C. Vaas c Kallis b Hall	1	– c Kirsten b Ntini		32
C. R. D. Fernando b Pollock	7	– not out		4
M. Muralitharan c Ntini b Hall	10	– b Hall		0
P. D. R. L. Perera not out	11	– b Hall		4
B 4, l-b 2, w 1, n-b 1	8	B 4, l-b 7, w 1		12

1/2 (2) 2/46 (3) 3/86 (1) 4/137 (4)   192   1/2 (2) 2/16 (3) 3/21 (4) 4/25 (5)   130
5/140 (5) 6/140 (7) 7/141 (8)   5/77 (1) 6/81 (7) 7/122 (8)
8/152 (9) 9/165 (10) 10/192 (6)   8/122 (6) 9/122 (10) 10/130 (11)

Pollock 18–8–45–2; Ntini 14–5–45–1; Elworthy 15.3–3–42–1; Kallis 17–8–35–3; Hall 11–6–19–2. *Second Innings*—Pollock 8–3–17–2; Ntini 10–4–22–3; Kallis 11–3–40–0; Elworthy 10–3–39–2; Hall 2–1–1–3.

South Africa

G. C. Smith c Tillekeratne b K. H. R. K. Fernando	73	A. J. Hall lbw b Muralitharan	31
G. Kirsten c Muralitharan b K. H. R. K. Fernando	55	S. Elworthy lbw b Muralitharan	6
M. van Jaarsveld b K. H. R. K. Fernando	3	M. Ntini not out	2
J. H. Kallis c Sangakkara b Vaas	75	B 16, l-b 10, w 5, n-b 31	62
A. G. Prince c Perera b Vaas	3		
N. D. McKenzie lbw b Vaas	0	1/133 (1) 2/148 (3) 3/175 (2) 4/179 (5) . . 386
†M. V. Boucher c Sangakkara b Muralitharan	38	5/180 (6) 6/249 (7) 7/329 (8)
*S. M. Pollock c Sangakkara		8/378 (9) 9/378 (4) 10/386 (10)
b C. R. D. Fernando	38	

Vaas 22–2–79–3; Perera 10.2–2–40–0; C. R. D. Fernando 20–2–95–1; Muralitharan 31.2–8–83–3; K. H. R. K. Fernando 21–2–63–3.

Umpires: D. J. Harper *(Australia)* (25) and R. B. Tiffin *(Zimbabwe)* (33).
Third umpire: S. Wadvalla *(South Africa)*.   Referee: G. R. Viswanath *(India)* (6).

Close of play: First day, South Africa 51-0 (Smith 15, Kirsten 21); Second day, South Africa 378-7 (Kallis 75, Hall 31).

SOUTH AFRICA v SRI LANKA 2002–03 (2nd Test)

At Centurion Park, Pretoria, on 15, 16, 17, 18, 19 November.
Toss: South Africa.   Result: SOUTH AFRICA won by three wickets.
Debuts: none.
Man of the Match: S. M. Pollock.   Man of the Series: J. H. Kallis.

Sri Lanka bounced back well from heavy defeat in the previous match. They started solidly, despite lacking Jaya-suriya (injured ankle), reaching 263 for 5 against a one-dimensional attack – but Ntini tore in with the second new ball like an Olympic sprinter, and it was soon 281 for 9. Tillekeratne, then 91, did manage to complete Sri Lanka's first Test century in South Africa during a comical last-wicket stand with Muralitharan, who slogged Ntini for six. Dilhara Fernando plucked out two wickets before Gibbs and Kallis plodded soporifically through the second afternoon, but next morning the game burst back into life as the score slid to 264 for 6. However, Pollock extended the lead to 125 before Ntini's wild slog marooned him on 99, the fourth such instance in Tests. Ntini took two quick wickets to appease his captain, but Sri Lanka looked to build a lead. They were rattling along so fluently that they declined two bad-light offers. The floodlit cricket was exhilarating – Ntini surging in as light-ning flashed – but foolhardy: Sangakkara was out moments before the heavens opened. Next day a shocking deci-sion by umpire Tiffin despatched Jayawardene lbw first ball, and four more tumbled for 29. The ninth wicket stretched the lead: 120 hardly looked enough but, far from fizzling out, the contest intensified. Vaas pinned Smith first ball, then Dilhara Fernando created panic as South Africa dipped to 44 for 5. Murali bowled McKenzie with nine needed, but that was the final twist in a fascinating match.

Sri Lanka

*M. S. Atapattu c Kirsten b Kallis	17	– c Boucher b Kallis	22
J. Mubarak c Smith b Pollock	48	– c Boucher b Ntini	15
†K. C. Sangakkara c Pollock b Hall	35	– c Boucher b Ntini	89
D. P. M. D. Jayawardene b Pollock	44	– lbw b Ntini	40
H. P. Tillekeratne not out	104	– c Boucher b Kallis	6
R. P. Arnold c Boucher b Kallis	2	– lbw b Pollock	4
K. H. R. K. Fernando c Kallis b Ntini	24	– c Hall b Ntini	14
W. P. U. J. C. Vaas c Boucher b Ntini	7	– lbw b Kallis	17
M. K. G. C. P. Lakshitha c Kirsten b Ntini	2	– c Pollock b Kallis	0
C. R. D. Fernando c Boucher b Ntini	0	– c Boucher b Elworthy	14
M. Muralitharan b Kallis	27	– not out	0
L-b 10, w 1, n-b 2	13	B 13, l-b 1, w 7, n-b 3	24
	323		**245**

1/34 (1) 2/90 (3) 3/108 (2) 4/189 (4)   323
5/207 (6) 6/263 (7) 7/277 (8)
8/281 (9) 9/281 (10) 10/323 (11)

1/23 (2) 2/60 (1) 3/179 (3)   245
4/180 (4) 5/185 (6) 6/205 (7)
7/209 (5) 8/209 (9) 9/245 (10) 10/245 (8)

Pollock 29–11–51–2; Ntini 29–6–86–4; Elworthy 21–4–71–0; Kallis 15.5–2–71–3; Hall 14–3–34–1. *Second Innings*—Pollock 17–7–45–1; Ntini 22–5–52–4; Elworthy 12–1–54–1; Hall 8–0–29–0; Kallis 14.2–5–39–4; Smith 4–2–12–0.

South Africa

G. C. Smith lbw b C. R. D. Fernando	15	– lbw b Vaas	0
H. H. Gibbs run out	92	– c Sangakkara b C. R. D. Fernando	7
G. Kirsten c K. H. R. K. Fernando b C. R. D. Fernando	11	– c Mubarak b C. R. D. Fernando	11
J. H. Kallis b K. H. R. K. Fernando	84	– b C. R. D. Fernando	6
A. G. Prince c Sangakkara b Vaas	20	– c Sangakkara b C. R. D. Fernando	5
N. D. McKenzie lbw b Lakshitha	28	– (7) b Muralitharan	39
†M. V. Boucher c and b Lakshitha	63	– (8) not out	22
*S. M. Pollock not out	99	– (9) not out	6
A. J. Hall lbw b Muralitharan	0	– (6) c Arnold b Muralitharan	16
S. Elworthy c Tillekeratne b Muralitharan	5		
M. Ntini c Arnold b Vaas	8		
B 4, l-b 10, w 4, n-b 5	23	B 5, l-b 1, n-b 6	12
	448	(7 wkts)	**124**

1/45 (1) 2/71 (3) 3/211 (2) 4/219 (4)   448
5/258 (5) 6/264 (6) 7/396 (7)
8/400 (9) 9/408 (10) 10/448 (11)

1/0 (1) 2/13 (2) 3/23 (3)   (7 wkts) 124
4/31 (4) 5/44 (5)
6/73 (6) 7/112 (7)

Vaas 33.3–7–81–2; Lakshitha 22–2–71–2; C. R. D. Fernando 27–0–91–2; Muralitharan 57–10–133–2; K. H. R. K. Fernando 18–5–45–1; Mubarak 2–0–6–0; Jayawardene 2–1–2–0; Arnold 5–2–5–0. *Second Innings*—Vaas 8–2–28–1; C. R. D. Fernando 12–0–49–4; Muralitharan 13.3–1–35–2; Lakshitha 2–1–6–0.

Umpires: D. J. Harper *(Australia)* (26) and R. B. Tiffin *(Zimbabwe)* (34).
Third umpire: S. Wadvalla *(South Africa)*.   Referee: G. R. Viswanath *(India)* (7).

Close of play: First day, Sri Lanka 263-6 (Tillekeratne 82, Vaas 0); Second day, South Africa 183-2 (Gibbs 76, Kallis 69); Third day, South Africa 421-9 (Pollock 78, Ntini 3); Fourth day, Sri Lanka 180-3 (Jayawardene 40, Tillekeratne 0).

ZIMBABWE v PAKISTAN 2002–03 (1st Test)

At Harare Sports Club on 9, 10, 11, 12 November.
Toss: Zimbabwe. Result: PAKISTAN won by 119 runs.
Debuts: Zimbabwe – N. B. Mahwire. Pakistan – Kamran Akmal.
Man of the Match: Taufeeq Umar.

Pakistan overcame some early nerves to emerge as convincing winners in the end. Campbell, deputising as captain for Streak (injured in an auto-rickshaw crash in Sri Lanka), optimistically bowled first, but if there was any early life the bowlers failed to exploit it. The best was Blignaut – also recovering from a road accident – who took the first three wickets. The middle order all contributed, but when Inzamam skyed a pull on the stroke of tea, Zimbabwe fought back, taking the last six wickets for only 39. The Flower brothers were rescuing the reply after an indifferent start when Andy was given out by umpire Venkataraghavan, caught behind down the leg side off his thigh-pad. But Taibu held out for three hours and a maiden Test fifty, and Blignaut bludgeoned 50 in 38 balls to keep the lead down to 60 before Olonga grabbed two early wickets. Pakistan roared back, Inzamam achieving a rare century before lunch (admittedly in an extended 150-minute session after bad light shortened the previous day), plundering 112 from 107 balls with 20 fours, and becoming the second Pakistani to reach 6,000 Test runs in the process. Taufeeq, who helped him add 180, batted six hours in his second responsible innings of the match, and Zimbabwe were eventually set 430. They did exceed their previous-best fourth-innings total of 246, but still did not make it into the fifth day. It later emerged that Shoaib Akhtar had been severely reprimanded for ball-tampering, although no fine was imposed.

Pakistan

Taufeeq Umar c A. Flower b Blignaut	75	– c Taibu b Blignaut	111
Salim Elahi c Campbell b Blignaut	2	– c Campbell b Olonga	0
Younis Khan c Ebrahim b Blignaut	40	– c Campbell b Olonga	8
Inzamam-ul-Haq c sub (M. A. Vermeulen) b Olonga	39	– c G. W. Flower b Olonga	112
Yousuf Youhana lbw b Price	63	– c Taibu b Blignaut	0
Hasan Raza c Campbell b Mahwire	46	– c Blignaut b Price	11
†Kamran Akmal b Price	0	– b Price	38
Saqlain Mushtaq c A. Flower b Whittall	2	– not out	29
*Waqar Younis lbw b Blignaut	2	– b Blignaut	0
Shoaib Akhtar c G. W. Flower b Blignaut	1	– c Taibu b Olonga	16
Mohammad Sami not out	0	– c G. W. Flower b Olonga	17
L-b 2, w 4, n-b 9	15	B 4, l-b 3, w 11, n-b 9	27

1/7 (2) 2/122 (3) 3/125 (1) 4/217 (4)   285
5/246 (5) 6/251 (7) 7/262 (8)
8/271 (9) 9/274 (10) 10/285 (6)

1/10 (2) 2/25 (3) 3/205 (4)   369
4/207 (5) 5/238 (6) 6/292 (7)
7/318 (1) 8/318 (9) 9/339 (10) 10/369 (11)

Blignaut 21–4–79–5; Olonga 16–2–46–1; Mahwire 14.5–2–58–1; Price 16–4–56–2; Whittall 22–10–44–1. *Second Innings—* Blignaut 20–1–81–3; Olonga 17.5–1–93–5; Mahwire 14–4–60–0; Whittall 14–5–62–0; Price 24–5–66–2.

Zimbabwe

D. D. Ebrahim c Inzamam-ul-Haq b Mohammad Sami	31	– b Shoaib Akhtar	69
H. Masakadza c Kamran Akmal b Mohammad Sami	9	– c Salim Elahi b Shoaib Akhtar	0
*A. D. R. Campbell b Shoaib Akhtar	2	– c Kamran Akmal b Mohammad Sami	30
G. W. Flower lbw b Waqar Younis	31	– c Kamran Akmal b Saqlain Mushtaq	69
A. Flower c Kamran Akmal b Mohammad Sami	29	– c and b Shoaib Akhtar	67
G. J. Whittall b Shoaib Akhtar	7	– c Younis Khan b Saqlain Mushtaq	2
†T. Taibu not out	51	– lbw b Waqar Younis	28
A. M. Blignaut c Hasan Raza b Mohammad Sami	50	– c Younis Khan b Saqlain Mushtaq	12
N. B. Mahwire c Younis Khan b Saqlain Mushtaq	4	– lbw b Waqar Younis	3
R. W. Price c Younis Khan b Saqlain Mushtaq	2	– not out	5
H. K. Olonga b Shoaib Akhtar	3	– b Shoaib Akhtar	5
L-b 1, w 2, n-b 3	6	B 8, l-b 6, w 1, n-b 5	20

1/36 (2) 2/41 (3) 3/43 (1) 4/76 (5)   225
5/93 (6) 6/136 (4) 7/199 (8)
8/203 (9) 9/209 (10) 10/225 (11)

1/4 (2) 2/51 (3) 3/162 (1)   310
4/201 (5) 5/203 (6) 6/256 (7)
7/280 (8) 8/291 (9) 9/301 (5) 10/310 (11)

Waqar Younis 14–3–58–1; Shoaib Akhtar 14.5–1–43–3; Mohammad Sami 19–3–53–4; Saqlain Mushtaq 19–5–70–2. *Second Innings—* Waqar Younis 16–1–73–2; Shoaib Akhtar 18.3–4–75–4; Mohammad Sami 15–3–50–1; Saqlain Mushtaq 31–5–98–3; Taufeeq Umar 1–1–0–0.

Umpires: D. L. Orchard *(South Africa)* (33) and S. Venkataraghavan *(India)* (61).
Third umpire: I. D. Robinson *(Zimbabwe).* Referee: C. H. Lloyd *(West Indies)* (20).

Close of play: First day, Pakistan 285; Second day, Pakistan 14-1 (Taufeeq Umar 14, Younis Khan 0); Third day, Zimbabwe 19-1 (Ebrahim 9, Campbell 9).

ZIMBABWE v PAKISTAN 2002–03 (2nd Test)

At Queens Sports Club, Bulawayo, on 16, 17, 18, 19 November.

Toss: Zimbabwe.   Result: PAKISTAN won by ten wickets.

Debuts: Zimbabwe – M. A. Vermeulen.

Man of the Match: Yousuf Youhana.   Man of the Series: Saqlain Mushtaq.

Pakistan became only the second touring team to win both Tests of a two-match series in Zimbabwe, and they did it in eight days, to New Zealand's ten in 2000-01. They swiftly seized the initiative on a lifeless pitch, and never relinquished it. Both home openers were gone by the fifth over: a determined partnership between Campbell and Grant Flower temporarily stemmed the tide, but Saqlain Mushtaq was finding spin by the first afternoon. Once he had despatched these two, Zimbabwe never looked like saving the match. They lost their last five wickets for 23 after tea: Shoaib Akhtar produced a superb spell at one end, while Saqlain bamboozled them from the other to finish with seven wickets. The following day, Yousuf Youhana cruised to 159 off 282 balls; he batted just over six hours and hit 21 fours, surviving four chances. He shared century partnerships with Younis Khan and the new wicketkeeper Kamran Akmal, who showed pleasing fluency in a maiden Test fifty, and also impressed behind the stumps. Nine Zimbabweans reached double figures in the second innings, but none made the major contribution needed. The debutant Mark Vermeulen played a brief cameo, striking five fours off nine balls from Shoaib Akhtar, but Campbell alone reached fifty. Saqlain had to toil harder for his wickets second time round, but deservedly finished with ten in the match. Pakistan raced to their target of 57 in only 8.3 overs, with all but nine of their runs coming in boundaries.

Zimbabwe

D. D. Ebrahim lbw b Waqar Younis	5	– lbw b Waqar Younis		7
M. A. Vermeulen lbw b Shoaib Akhtar	2	– lbw b Waqar Younis		26
*A. D. R. Campbell c Kamran Akmal b Saqlain Mushtaq	46	– b Mohammad Sami		62
G. W. Flower lbw b Saqlain Mushtaq	54	– b Shoaib Akhtar		43
A. Flower c Inzamam-ul-Haq b Shoaib Akhtar	30	– lbw b Waqar Younis		13
H. Masakadza c Kamran Akmal b Saqlain Mushtaq	0	– c Yousuf Youhana b Saqlain Mushtaq		16
†T. Taibu c Kamran Akmal b Saqlain Mushtaq	15	– c Yousuf Youhana b Waqar Younis		37
A. M. Blignaut c Taufeeq Umar b Saqlain Mushtaq	0	– st Kamran Akmal b Saqlain Mushtaq		41
M. L. Nkala not out	10	– c Kamran Akmal b Saqlain Mushtaq		14
R. W. Price b Saqlain Mushtaq	1	– b Mohammad Sami		12
H. K. Olonga b Saqlain Mushtaq	8	– not out		3
L-b 3, w 1, n-b 3	7	L-b 5, n-b 2		7

1/4 (2) 2/8 (1) 3/94 (3) 4/119 (4)   **178**   1/28 (1) 2/37 (2) 3/125 (4)   **281**
5/119 (6) 6/155 (7) 7/159 (8)   4/146 (3) 5/171 (6) 6/171 (5)
8/161 (5) 9/170 (10) 10/178 (11)   7/226 (8) 8/248 (9) 9/265 (10) 10/281 (7)

Waqar Younis 13–6–20–1; Shoaib Akhtar 16–3–39–2; Mohammad Sami 15–3–38–0; Saqlain Mushtaq 25.5–2–66–7; Taufeeq Umar 2–0–12–0. *Second Innings*—Waqar Younis 21.2–4–78–4; Saqlain Mushtaq 38–9–89–3; Shoaib Akhtar 12–4–61–1; Mohammad Sami 19–6–47–2; Hasan Raza 1–0–1–0.

Pakistan

Taufeeq Umar c Taibu b Olonga	34	– not out		21
Salim Elahi b Olonga	27	– not out		30
Younis Khan lbw b Blignaut	52			
Inzamam-ul-Haq b Price	11			
Yousuf Youhana b Price	159			
Hasan Raza b Olonga	4			
†Kamran Akmal lbw b Nkala	56			
Saqlain Mushtaq c sub (C. K. Coventry) b Price	14			
Mohammad Sami c Campbell b Blignaut	1			
*Waqar Younis c Ebrahim b Price	6			
Shoaib Akhtar not out	9			
B 10, l-b 5, w 2, n-b 8, p 5	30	B 1, w 1, n-b 4		6

1/63 (2) 2/64 (1) 3/82 (4) 4/209 (3)   **403**   (no wkt) **57**
5/225 (6) 6/346 (7) 7/374 (5)
8/387 (8) 9/387 (9) 10/403 (10)

Blignaut 22.4–5–75–2; Olonga 20–4–69–3; Price 51.3–14–116–4; Nkala 25–5–93–1; G. W. Flower 12–4–26–0; A. Flower 0.2–0–4–0. *Second Innings*—Olonga 4.3–0–35–0; Price 4–1–21–0.

Umpires: D. L. Orchard *(South Africa)* (34) and S. Venkataraghavan *(India)* (62).
Third umpire: M. A. Esat *(Zimbabwe)*.   Referee: C. H. Lloyd *(West Indies)* (21).

Close of play: First day, Pakistan 29-0 (Taufeeq Umar 16, Salim Elahi 13); Second day, Pakistan 295-5 (Yousuf Youhana 116, Kamran Akmal 27); Third day, Zimbabwe 171-5 (A. Flower 13).

BANGLADESH v WEST INDIES 2002–03 (1st Test)

At Bangabandhu National Stadium, Dhaka, on 8, 9, 10 December.
Toss: West Indies.   Result: WEST INDIES won by an innings and 310 runs.
Debuts: Bangladesh – Anwar Hossain Piju. West Indies – V. C. Drakes.
Man of the Match: J. J. C. Lawson.

Bangladesh hit several new lows on the third day: their lowest total, their lowest match aggregate, and their biggest defeat in 16 Tests so far. Their destroyer was Jermaine Lawson, the 20-year-old Jamaican fast bowler, who returned scarcely believable figures of 6.5–4–3–6, the most economical six-wicket haul in Test history. All his wickets came in a devastating 15-ball spell, in which he did not concede a run. Bangladesh lost their final seven wickets for as many runs, the last five all failing to score (only two previous Test innings had contained six ducks: Pakistan v West Indies at Karachi in 1980-81, and South Africa v India at Ahmedabad in 1996-97). Things started to go wrong when Hannan Sarkar fell to the first ball of the match, a perfect yorker from Collins, who proved too hot to handle along withVasbert Drakes, making his debut at 33. By the 16th over it was 44 for 5, although Habibul Bashar had become the first Bangladeshi to reach 1,000 Test runs. Alok Kapali and Khaled Mashud added 73, but the innings folded for 139. West Indies' openers almost matched that, putting on 131 before both fell in the same over. Sarwan finally scored his first Test hundred, after passing fifty 14 times in his previous 48 innings. Jacobs, captaining as Hooper had returned home for knee surgery, was stranded on 91 as West Indies were finally bowled out 397 ahead. Thanks to Lawson, they completed the seventh-largest victory in Tests on the third evening.

Bangladesh

Hannan Sarkar b Collins	0	– c Ganga b Drakes	25
Anwar Hossain Piju c Jacobs b Drakes	2	– b Drakes	12
Mohammad Ashraful c Jacobs b Collins	6	– b Drakes	0
Habibul Bashar c Ganga b Collins	24	– lbw b Collins	22
Aminul Islam lbw b Lawson	5	– lbw b Lawson	12
Alok Kapali lbw b Drakes	52	– lbw b Lawson	0
*†Khaled Mashud b Drakes	22	– lbw b Lawson	0
Naimur Rahman c Gayle b Collins	1	– not out	5
Enamul Haque, sen. b Collins	6	– c Jacobs b Lawson	0
Tapash Baisya c Jacobs b Drakes	7	– b Lawson	0
Talha Jubair not out	4	– b Lawson	0
L-b 6, w 1, n-b 3	10	B 4, l-b 3, n-b 4	11

1/0 (1) 2/4 (2) 3/25 (3) 4/40 (4)   **139**   1/30 (1) 2/30 (3) 3/44 (2)   **87**
5/44 (5) 6/117 (7) 7/118 (6)   4/80 (4) 5/80 (5) 6/80 (7)
8/124 (8) 9/135 (10) 10/139 (9)   7/81 (6) 8/83 (9) 9/87 (10) 10/87 (11)

Collins 17.1–7–26–5; Drakes 18–2–61–4; Lawson 9–2–24–1; Powell 10–2–22–0. *Second Innings*—Collins 9–2–30–1; Drakes 9–3–19–3; Powell 7–1–28–0; Lawson 6.5–4–3–6.

West Indies

C. H. Gayle c Khaled Mashud b Tapash Baisya	51	P. T. Collins c Habibul Bashar b Mohammad Ashraful	13
W. W. Hinds c Naimur Rahman b Tapash Baisya	75	J. J. C. Lawson lbw b Talha Jubair	1
R. R. Sarwan c Naimur Rahman b Talha Jubair	119		
S. Chanderpaul c Khaled Mashud b Enamul Haque	4		
M. N. Samuels lbw b Talha Jubair	91	L-b 8, w 3, n-b 9	20
D. Ganga run out	40		
*†R. D. Jacobs not out	91	1/131 (1) 2/132 (2) 3/150 (4)	536
V. C. Drakes c sub (Al Sahariar) b Naimur Rahman	15	4/326 (5) 5/377 (3) 6/417 (6)	
D. B. Powell st Khaled Mashud b Mohammad Ashraful	16	7/453 (8) 8/493 (9) 9/527 (10) 10/536 (11)	

Tapash Baisya 34–3–117–2; Talha Jubair 31–3–135–3; Naimur Rahman 36–5–118–1; Enamul Haque 46–13–101–1; Mohammad Ashraful 13–0–57–2.

Umpires: D. L. Orchard *(South Africa)* (35) and D. R. Shepherd *(England)* (68).
Third umpire: A. F. M. Akhtaruddin *(Bangladesh)*.   Referee: R. S. Madugalle *(Sri Lanka)* (46).

Close of play: First day, West Indies 118-0 (Gayle 44, Hinds 73); Second day, West Indies 400-5 (Ganga 34, Jacobs 14).

BANGLADESH v WEST INDIES 2002–03 (2nd Test)

At M. A. Aziz Stadium, Chittagong, on 16, 17, 18 December.
Toss: Bangladesh.   Result: WEST INDIES won by seven wickets.
Debuts: none.
Man of the Match: Alok Kapali.   Man of the Series: J. J. C. Lawson.

Bangladesh suffered their eighth three-day defeat in 17 Tests – but this was actually one of their better perform-ances. They put up a brave fight, displaying an intensity rarely seen before. As usual, however, they had too few runs to defend: they had made very little of winning the toss in perfect batting conditions, going under for 194. The rot really began when Mohammad Ashraful fell to an outstanding one-handed catch by a leaping Powell at mid-off. To date, the average first-innings total against Bangladesh had been 468, the average lead 282. But the home seamers decided to write a different script, removing the top five for only 127. It took a stand of 99 between Ganga and Jacobs to tug the tourists into the lead, and they were eventually restricted to 296, the lowest all-out total against Bangladesh thus far. The deficit was 102, and the openers started promisingly - but both were victims of the vagaries of the pitch. Hannan Sarkar was bowled by a straight, low ball, and Al Sahariar was pinned in front when Powell cut one back from a crack outside off. Before long, Bangladesh were 137 for 6. They were salvaged by Alok Kapali, pulling and flicking gracefully while finding an ally in Enamul Haque, who contributed just nine to their 73-run rearguard before the last four wickets crashed in 21 deliveries. Needing 111, West Indies romped home inside 22 overs, thanks to Gayle (37 in 31 balls), although the seamers did grab three wickets.

Bangladesh

Hannan Sarkar c Gayle b Powell	15	– b Drakes	13
Al Sahariar lbw b Drakes	25	– lbw b Powell	34
Habibul Bashar c Jacobs b Powell	3	– c Jacobs b Collins	0
Sanwar Hossain c Jacobs b Lawson	36	– c Gayle b Lawson	24
Mohammad Ashraful c Powell b Collins	28	– c Sarwan b Lawson	15
Alok Kapali c Gayle b Collins	2	– c Jacobs b Powell	85
*†Khaled Mashud c Sarwan b Drakes	32	– lbw b Drakes	5
Enamul Haque, sen c Samuels b Lawson	8	– not out	11
Tapash Baisya hit wkt b Powell	5	– c Chanderpaul b Powell	0
Manjural Islam b Collins	21	– b Collins	0
Talha Jubair not out	4	– c Jacobs b Collins	0
L-b 5, n-b 10	15	B 1, l-b 12, w 3, n-b 9	25

1/43 (2) 2/43 (1) 3/48 (3) 4/112 (5)   **194**   1/44 (1) 2/45 (3) 3/76 (2)   **212**
5/116 (4) 6/125 (6) 7/144 (8)   4/100 (4) 5/126 (5) 6/137 (7)
8/153 (9) 9/189 (7) 10/194 (10)   7/210 (6) 8/210 (9) 9/210 (10) 10/212 (11)

Collins 16.1–3–60–3; Drakes 9–3–23–2; Powell 16–4–51–3; Lawson 22–9–55–2. *Second Innings*—Collins 23–8–58–3; Drakes 18–6–52–2; Lawson 18–5–53–2; Powell 13–2–36–3.

West Indies

C. H. Gayle b Talha Jubair	38	– b Tapash Baisya	37
W. W. Hinds c Khaled Mashud b Tapash Baisya	14	– lbw b Tapash Baisya	26
R. R. Sarwan c Khaled Mashud b Manjural Islam	17	– c Enamul Haque b Manjural Islam	13
S. Chanderpaul c Khaled Mashud b Enamul Haque	16	– not out	19
M. N. Samuels c Al Sahariar b Talha Jubair	31	– not out	15
D. Ganga c Tapash Baisya b Sanwar Hossain	63		
*†R. D. Jacobs c Khaled Mashud b Tapash Baisya	59		
V. C. Drakes run out	26		
D. B. Powell b Tapash Baisya	1		
P. T. Collins not out	12		
J. J. C. Lawson c Habibul Bashar b Tapash Baisya	6		
B 8, l-b 4, n-b 1	13	L-b 1	1

1/16 (2) 2/53 (3) 3/74 (1) 4/99 (4)   **296**   1/52 (1) 2/77 (2) 3/81 (3)   (3 wkts) **111**
5/127 (5) 6/226 (6) 7/264 (7)
8/278 (9) 9/279 (8) 10/296 (11)

Manjural Islam 21–11–34–1; Tapash Baisya 21.3–2–72–4; Talha Jubair 20–5–58–2; Enamul Haque 19–3–62–1; Mohammad Ashraful 5–0–29–0; Sanwar Hossain 7–1–29–1. *Second Innings*—Manjural Islam 8–2–38–1; Tapash Baisya 9–0–45–2; Talha Jubair 3–0–20–0; Mohammad Ashraful 1–0–3–0; Alok Kapali 0.3–0–4–0.

Umpires: D. L. Orchard *(South Africa)* (36) and D. R. Shepherd *(England)* (69).
Third umpire: Mahbubur Rahman *(Bangladesh)*.   Referee: R. S. Madugalle *(Sri Lanka)* (47).

Close of play: First day, West Indies 38-1 (Gayle 10, Sarwan 14); Second day, Bangladesh 40-0 (Hannan Sarkar 12, Al Sahariar 21).

NEW ZEALAND v INDIA 2002–03 (1st Test)

At Basin Reserve, Wellington, on 12, 13, 14 December.
Toss: New Zealand.   Result: NEW ZEALAND won by ten wickets.
Debuts: New Zealand – J. D. P. Oram.
Man of the Match: M. H. Richardson.

New Zealand's 300th Test match was all over by 4.30 on the third afternoon, but rain meant it actually lasted little more than two days' actual play. Fleming admitted that the toss was crucial. The pitch changed from green to brown, yet never lost its spongy quality, with seam movement and bounce throughout. Batsmen needed to graft rather than glitter but, with the exception of Dravid and Tendulkar, India's did neither. Tuffey quickly removed the openers, then the debutant Jacob Oram cut one back at Tendulkar, who perished lbw playing no stroke to a delivery heading over the stumps. Bond hurried out Ganguly, already dropped twice in the slips, and Laxman to leave India in disarray at 55 for 5. They were saved by the wristy Dravid, who took his chances before he was ninth out. In reply, New Zealand were grateful for the unfussy application of Richardson, who shouldered arms like an automaton and forced the bowlers to aim straighter. At 181 for 3, a big lead looked likely, but the last seven wickets fell for 66 as Zaheer Khan collected his first Test five-for. Richardson, dropped twice, finally fell to the first delivery with the second new ball after 405 minutes and 245 balls. Tearing in with the wind behind him, Bond blew away Sehwag, Dravid and Ganguly, then bowled Tendulkar with a no-ball. It didn't matter: Tuffey chipped away at the lower order, then Bond bowled Tendulkar off the inside edge again, this time legitimately.

India

S. B. Bangar c Styris b Tuffey	1	– lbw b Oram		12
V. Sehwag b Tuffey	2	– lbw b Bond		12
R. Dravid b Styris	76	– b Bond		7
S. R. Tendulkar lbw b Oram	8	– b Bond		51
*S. C. Ganguly c Vincent b Bond	17	– c Hart b Bond		2
V. V. S. Laxman c Hart b Bond	0	– c Fleming b Oram		0
†P. A. Patel c Vincent b Oram	8	– c Fleming b Tuffey		10
A. B. Agarkar c Astle b Styris	12	– c McMillan b Tuffey		9
Harbhajan Singh c McMillan b Styris	0	– c Styris b Tuffey		1
Zaheer Khan c Oram b Bond	19	– c Styris b Oram		9
A. Nehra not out	10	– not out		0
L-b 1, w 1, n-b 6	8	L-b 1, n-b 7		8

1/2 (2) 2/9 (1) 3/29 (4) 4/51 (5)   161   1/23 (2) 2/31 (1) 3/31 (3)   121
5/55 (6) 6/92 (7) 7/118 (8)   4/33 (5) 5/36 (6) 6/76 (7)
8/118 (9) 9/147 (3) 10/161 (10)   7/88 (8) 8/96 (9) 9/121 (10) 10/121 (4)

Bond 18.4–4–66–3; Tuffey 16–7–25–2; Oram 15–4–31–2; Styris 6–0–28–3; Astle 3–1–10–0. *Second Innings*—Bond 13.1–5–33–4; Tuffey 9–3–35–3; Oram 12–3–36–3; Styris 4–0–16–0.

New Zealand

M. H. Richardson lbw b Zaheer Khan	89	– not out		14
L. Vincent c Patel b Bangar	12	– not out		21
*S. P. Fleming b Zaheer Khan	25			
C. D. McMillan lbw b Bangar	9			
N. J. Astle c Harbhajan Singh b Zaheer Khan	41			
S. B. Styris st Patel b Harbhajan Singh	0			
J. D. P. Oram lbw b Harbhajan Singh	0			
†R. G. Hart lbw b Zaheer Khan	6			
D. L. Vettori c Patel b Zaheer Khan	21			
D. R. Tuffey not out	9			
S. E. Bond b Agarkar	2			
B 6, l-b 12, w 2, n-b 8, p 5	33	W 1		1

1/30 (2) 2/96 (3) 3/111 (4) 4/181 (5)   247   (no wkt) 36
5/182 (6) 6/186 (7) 7/201 (8)
8/228 (1) 9/237 (9) 10/247 (11)

Zaheer Khan 25–8–53–5; Nehra 19–4–50–0; Agarkar 13.1–1–54–1; Bangar 15–4–23–2; Harbhajan Singh 17–4–33–2; Ganguly 2–0–11–0. *Second Innings*—Zaheer Khan 3–0–13–0; Nehra 4.3–0–21–0; Harbhajan Singh 2–1–2–0.

Umpires: E. A. R. de Silva *(Sri Lanka)* (21) and D. J. Harper *(Australia)* (27).
Third umpire: B. F. Bowden *(New Zealand)*.   Referee: M. J. Procter *(South Africa)* (6).

Close of play: First day, New Zealand 53-1 (Richardson 27, Fleming 11); Second day, New Zealand 201-7 (Richardson 83, Vettori 0).

NEW ZEALAND v INDIA 2002–03 (2nd Test)

At Seddon Park, Hamilton, on 19 *(no play)*, 20, 21, 22 December.
Toss: New Zealand.   Result: NEW ZEALAND won by four wickets.
Debuts: none.
Man of the Match: D. R. Tuffey.

By the time New Zealand scraped home on the fourth afternoon there had been just 176 overs – nearly 21 fewer than in the previous Test. Torrential rain played havoc with the preparation, and when play finally started, at 4.30 on the second day, excessive sideways movement turned run-making into Russian roulette. Never before in a Test had both sides been dismissed for under 100 in their first innings. By the time Tuffey conceded his first run, from his 39th delivery, he had already removed Bangar and Tendulkar. India staggered to 92 for 8 by the close, but the next day was even more remarkable: there were 22 wickets, and it featured part of all four innings (only the second instance in a Test, after England v West Indies at Lord's in 2000). New Zealand were chugging along at 39 for 1 before the wheels came off: the last nine tumbled for 55, four to Zaheer Khan, while Nehra and Harbhajan Singh both took two in an over. India fared a little better second time around, Dravid making 39, the highest score of the 13th Test in history not to include a half-century, but Tuffey and Oram again exploited the conditions well. New Zealand needed 160, and somehow survived unscathed to the close. Next day batting was slightly easier, and they reached 89 for 2 before two quick wickets from Nehra set the nerves jangling again. Finally Hart shovelled the winning single to fine leg to seal a 2–0 series victory.

India

S. B. Bangar	c Oram b Tuffey	1	– c and b Tuffey	7
V. Sehwag	c Richardson b Bond	1	– (7) c Tuffey b Bond	25
R. Dravid	c Hart b Tuffey	9	– c sub (M. J. Mason) b Oram	39
S. R. Tendulkar	c Styris b Tuffey	9	– b Tuffey	32
*S. C. Ganguly	c Fleming b Tuffey	5	– c Hart b Oram	5
V. V. S. Laxman	b Bond	23	– b Astle	4
†P. A. Patel	c Hart b Oram	8	– (2) b Tuffey	0
Harbhajan Singh	b Bond	20	– c Hart b Tuffey	18
Zaheer Khan	b Oram	0	– c Astle b Oram	0
A. Nehra	c Fleming b Bond	7	– c Hart b Oram	10
T. Yohannan	not out	0	– not out	8
	L-b 12, n-b 4	16	L-b 1, w 2, n-b 3	6

1/1 (1) 2/11 (2) 3/26 (4) 4/34 (5)   99   1/2 (2) 2/8 (1) 3/57 (4)   154
5/40 (3) 6/70 (6) 7/91 (8)   4/64 (5) 5/85 (6) 6/110 (7)
8/92 (9) 9/93 (7) 10/99 (10)   7/130 (3) 8/131 (9) 9/136 (8) 10/154 (10)

Bond 14.2–7–39–4; Tuffey 9–6–12–4; Oram 10–1–22–2; Styris 2–0–10–0; Astle 3–2–4–0. *Second Innings*—Bond 10–0–58–1; Tuffey 16–3–41–4; Oram 12.5–2–41–4; Astle 5–1–13–1.

New Zealand

M. H. Richardson	lbw b Zaheer Khan	13	– c Patel b Nehra	28
L. Vincent	c Dravid b Zaheer Khan	3	– c Patel b Yohannan	9
*S. P. Fleming	c and b Zaheer Khan	21	– c Zaheer Khan b Nehra	32
C. D. McMillan	c Dravid b Nehra	4	– lbw b Nehra	18
N. J. Astle	c Harbhajan Singh b Nehra	0	– c Patel b Zaheer Khan	14
S. B. Styris	lbw b Harbhajan Singh	13	– c Patel b Harbhajan Singh	17
J. D. P. Oram	c Tendulkar b Harbhajan Singh	3	– not out	26
†R. G. Hart	lbw b Zaheer Khan	3	– not out	11
D. L. Vettori	c Laxman b Zaheer Khan	6		
D. R. Tuffey	run out	13		
S. E. Bond	not out	0		
	B 1, l-b 4, n-b 10	15	L-b 4, n-b 1	5

1/7 (2) 2/39 (1) 3/47 (4) 4/48 (5)   94   1/30 (2) 2/52 (1)   (6 wkts) 160
5/60 (3) 6/64 (7) 7/69 (6)   3/89 (3) 4/90 (4)
8/79 (8) 9/94 (10) 10/94 (9)   5/105 (5) 6/136 (6)

Zaheer Khan 13.2–4–29–5; Yohannan 9–4–16–0; Nehra 8–3–20–2; Bangar 2–1–4–0; Harbhajan Singh 6–0–20–2. *Second Innings*—Zaheer Khan 13–0–56–1; Yohannan 16–5–27–1; Nehra 16.2–4–34–3; Harbhajan Singh 11–0–39–1.

Umpires: E. A. R. de Silva *(Sri Lanka)* (22) and D. J. Harper *(Australia)* (28).
Third umpire: D. B. Cowie *(New Zealand)*.   Referee: M. J. Procter *(South Africa)* (7).

Close of play: First day, No play; Second day, India 92-8 (Patel 8); Third day, New Zealand 24-0 (Richardson 18, Vincent 6).

SOUTH AFRICA v PAKISTAN 2002–03 (1st Test)

At Kingsmead, Durban, on 26, 27, 28, 29 December.
Toss: Pakistan.   Result: SOUTH AFRICA won by ten wickets.
Debuts: none.
Man of the Match: J. H. Kallis.

On the first afternoon, Pakistan's hopes were raised when South Africa were 214 for 5 – but it was their only moment of optimism before the home side's depth and resilience proved decisive. The first morning was typically hard work for batsmen on the country's greenest wicket, but Pakistan's three seamers wasted the bounce and seam movement with some wide, harmless deliveries. Even their early successes owed something to good fortune: Smith flapped at a wide half-volley swinging wider still, while Gibbs slapped a long-hop to backward point. A couple more edges and a classic Waqar Younis inswinger later, and South Africa were nervous. But Kallis was in stubborn mood: long periods of dishearteningly solid defence drained the bowlers, and he completed a 205-ball hundred shortly before bad light ended play. Next morning, South Africa reached 368. In reply, the openers were unworried in adding 77 – but after Taufeeq Umar edged a Hayward lifter, the rest whimpered like scolded dogs. In between many dreadful deliveries, Hayward filched five wickets inside 11 eventful overs. Waqar hit 28 in 19 balls, but was last out just eight short of saving the follow-on. Pakistan again batted without much application. Although Taufeeq again tried to weld things together, four of his colleagues wafted catches to the keeper, and their collective approach was best summed up when Yousuf Youhana flailed yet another Hayward bouncer straight to third man. Gibbs and Smith completed a ten-wicket win before lunch on the fourth day.

South Africa

G. C. Smith c Kamran Akmal b Mohammad Sami	16	– not out		13
H. H. Gibbs c Faisal Iqbal b Waqar Younis	11	– not out		25
G. Kirsten c Younis Khan b Saqlain Mushtaq	56			
J. H. Kallis b Mohammad Sami	105			
H. H. Dippenaar c Kamran Akmal b Saqlain Mushtaq	1			
N. D. McKenzie b Waqar Younis	24			
†M. V. Boucher c Faisal Iqbal b Saqlain Mushtaq	55			
*S. M. Pollock c Kamran Akmal b Waqar Younis	21			
N. Boje not out	37			
M. Ntini c Taufeeq Umar b Saqlain Mushtaq	0			
M. Hayward b Mohammad Sami	10			
B 4, l-b 5, n-b 23	32	L-b 1, n-b 6		7

1/27 (1) 2/33 (2) 3/155 (3) 4/159 (5)   368   (no wkt) 45
5/214 (6) 6/252 (4) 7/286 (8)
8/344 (7) 9/344 (10) 10/368 (11)

Waqar Younis 25–3–91–3; Mohammad Sami 26–5–92–3; Abdul Razzaq 19–3–57–0; Saqlain Mushtaq 37–4–119–4. *Second Innings*—Mohammad Sami 5–0–36–0; Saqlain Mushtaq 4–2–8–0.

Pakistan

Taufeeq Umar c Smith b Hayward	39	– lbw b Boje		39
Salim Elahi c McKenzie b Ntini	39	– c Smith b Ntini		18
Younis Khan lbw b Pollock	1	– c Boucher b Kallis		30
Inzamam-ul-Haq c and b Ntini	18	– c Gibbs b Boje		13
Yousuf Youhana c Smith b Ntini	12	– c McKenzie b Hayward		42
Faisal Iqbal run out	6	– b Kallis		17
Abdul Razzaq c McKenzie b Hayward	1	– c Boucher b Hayward		22
†Kamran Akmal c Pollock b Hayward	12	– c Boucher b Ntini		29
Saqlain Mushtaq b Hayward	0	– c Boucher b Pollock		4
*Waqar Younis b Hayward	28	– c Kirsten b Pollock		15
Mohammad Sami not out	0	– not out		11
L-b 1, w 1, n-b 3	5	L-b 2, w 1, n-b 7		10

1/77 (1) 2/83 (3) 3/83 (2) 4/107 (4)   161   1/50 (2) 2/64 (1) 3/88 (4)   250
5/119 (6) 6/120 (5) 7/120 (7)   4/132 (3) 5/156 (6) 6/184 (5)
8/120 (9) 9/145 (8) 10/161 (10)   7/199 (7) 8/216 (9) 9/226 (8) 10/250 (10)

Pollock 14–5–23–1; Ntini 18–4–59–3; Hayward 10.4–1–56–5; Kallis 6–0–22–0. *Second Innings*—Ntini 21–2–73–2; Pollock 17.3–4–29–2; Kallis 17–5–30–2; Hayward 13–1–63–2; Boje 19–2–53–2.

Umpires: S. A. Bucknor *(West Indies)* (76) and S. Venkataraghavan *(India)* (63).
Third umpire: I. L. Howell *(South Africa)*.   Referee: G. R. Viswanath *(India)* (8).

Close of play: First day, South Africa 250-5 (Kallis 104, Boucher 13); Second day, Pakistan 120-8 (Kamran Akmal 0, Waqar Younis 0); Third day, Pakistan 218-8 (Kamran Akmal 21, Waqar Younis 2).

SOUTH AFRICA v PAKISTAN 2002–03 (2nd Test)

At Newlands, Cape Town, on 2, 3, 4, 5 January.

Toss: South Africa.   Result: SOUTH AFRICA won by an innings and 142 runs.

Debuts: none.

Man of the Match: H. H. Gibbs.   Man of the Series: M. Ntini.

Another comprehensive victory pushed South Africa past Australia atop the ICC world rankings. This win was set up by Gibbs and Smith, who demoralised Pakistan's bowlers with an opening stand of 368. South Africa had 445 by the first-day close, more than they had managed in a single day before. Gibbs skipped down to hit everyone, inside out, over extra cover, while Smith hooked, pulled and hooked again. Eddie Barlow and Graeme Pollock's 341 for the third wicket at Adelaide in 1963-64 was erased as South Africa's highest partnership: soon afterwards, Gibbs reached his second Test double-century, from 211 deliveries, the second-fastest Test double-century in terms of balls (211), and his eventual 228, the highest Test score at Newlands, included 29 fours and six sixes. Next day, Pollock declared just two short of South Africa's then-highest total, 622 for 9 against Australia at Durban in 1969-70 (Graeme Pollock, Shaun's uncle, made 274). By now, most of the Pakistanis seemed to have lost hope, and they would later be fined their entire match fee for a funereal over-rate. The exception was the left-hander Taufeeq Umar, who led them to 152 for 1, eventually batting for nearly six hours. On the third morning, though, nine wickets fell for 100. Taufeeq showed more guts in the follow-on, top-scoring again. Yousuf Youhana rampaged to 50 in 27 balls – only Ian Botham (26 balls against India at Delhi in 1981-82) had made a faster Test half-century at the time – but the rest folded next day.

South Africa

G. C. Smith b Mohammad Zahid	151	*S. M. Pollock not out	36
H. H. Gibbs c Younis Khan b Saqlain Mushtaq	228	N. Boje not out	7
G. Kirsten c Younis Khan b Waqar Younis	19	B 1, l-b 5, w 1, n-b 21	28
J. H. Kallis lbw b Mohammad Sami	31		
H. H. Dippenaar c Kamran Akmal b Saqlain Mushtaq	62	1/368 (1) 2/413 (2) (7 wkts dec.)	620
N. D. McKenzie c Kamran Akmal b Mohammad Zahid	51	3/414 (3) 4/463 (4)	
†M. V. Boucher b Saqlain Mushtaq	7	5/548 (6) 6/557 (7) 7/594 (5)	

M. Ntini and M. Hayward did not bat.

Waqar Younis 28–4–121–1; Mohammad Sami 28–2–124–1; Mohammad Zahid 25–3–108–2; Saqlain Mushtaq 50–3–237–3; Younis Khan 4–0–24–0.

Pakistan

Taufeeq Umar c Kallis b Ntini	135	– c Boucher b Pollock	67
Salim Elahi c Smith b Pollock	10	– c Dippenaar b Ntini	0
Younis Khan lbw b Pollock	46	– c McKenzie b Kallis	2
Inzamam-ul-Haq c Dippenaar b Hayward	32	– st Boucher b Boje	60
Yousuf Youhana c Boucher b Hayward	0	– c Kallis b Boje	50
Faisal Iqbal b Ntini	24	– c Pollock b Ntini	11
†Kamran Akmal lbw b Pollock	0	– lbw b Ntini	4
Saqlain Mushtaq c Boucher b Ntini	1	– run out	9
*Waqar Younis c Kallis b Pollock	0	– lbw b Hayward	9
Mohammad Sami not out	0	– not out	9
Mohammad Zahid c Smith b Ntini	0	– c Pollock b Ntini	0
L-b 1, n-b 3	4	L-b 1, w 1, n-b 3	5

1/36 (2) 2/152 (3) 3/208 (4) 4/208 (5)	252	1/0 (2) 2/9 (3) 3/130 (4)	226
5/240 (1) 6/247 (7) 7/251 (6)		4/130 (1) 5/184 (5) 6/190 (7)	
8/252 (9) 9/252 (8) 10/252 (11)		7/203 (6) 8/216 (9) 9/221 (8) 10/226 (11)	

Pollock 23–6–45–4; Ntini 20.4–7–62–4; Kallis 12–2–35–0; Hayward 15–2–56–2; Boje 17–2–53–0. *Second Innings*—Pollock 12–5–32–1; Ntini 15.1–2–33–4; Kallis 6–1–34–1; Hayward 11–3–44–1; Boje 15–0–82–2.

Umpires: S. A. Bucknor *(West Indies)* (77) and S. Venkataraghavan *(India)* (64).
Third umpire: B. G. Jerling *(South Africa)*.   Referee: G. R. Viswanath *(India)* (9).

Close of play: First day, South Africa 445-3 (Kallis 19, Dippenaar 8); Second day, Pakistan 141-1 (Taufeeq Umar 85, Younis Khan 44); Third day, Pakistan 184-5 (Faisal Iqbal 2).

WEST INDIES v AUSTRALIA 2002–03 (1st Test)

At Bourda, Georgetown, Guyana, on 10, 11, 12, 13 April.
Toss: West Indies.   Result: AUSTRALIA won by nine wickets.
Debuts: West Indies – D. S. Smith.
Man of the Match: J. L. Langer.

Test cricket resumed after the one-day World Cup. Australia, who had retained their title in Johannesburg, showed that they were still the masters of the long game too, securing victory in Steve Waugh's record 157th Test after an initial blast from Chanderpaul, whose 69-ball century was the third-fastest in Tests. Just after he came in, his team were 53 for 5, even though Glenn McGrath was missing, at home with his sick wife. In 108 minutes Chanderpaul proved the calypso spirit was far from dead, launching himself at the bowling and ensuring a respectable total. He was well supported by Jacobs, who battled courageously after yanking a thigh muscle, which required Hinds to keep wicket. The Australians then showed how to bat on a flat, slow pitch. Langer and Ponting bettered West Indies' total in a single partnership of 248, before Gilchrist's robust 77 stretched the lead to 252. But Lara completed his 19th Test century on his return to the captaincy (Carl Hooper was absent, apparently sulking after being sacked), and West Indies sniffed safety, only to be undone. First Hogg removed Lara when he lost his grip on the bat trying a sweep, and it came down on his leg stump, then, after Ganga had finally made his maiden century, in his 18th Test, he drove lazily at Lehmann's occasional spin and was caught at short midwicket. West Indies' last hopes vanished on the fourth morning, as the last five wickets crumbled for 16 in just 45 balls.

West Indies

W. W. Hinds c Langer b Hogg	10	– lbw b MacGill	7
D. S. Smith lbw b Lee	3	– c Gilchrist b Gillespie	62
D. Ganga b Gillespie	0	– c Lee b Lehmann	113
*B. C. Lara lbw b Bichel	26	– hit wkt b Hogg	110
M. N. Samuels c Hayden b Hogg	0	– c Ponting b MacGill	7
S. Chanderpaul lbw b Bichel	100	– c Gilchrist b Gillespie	31
†R. D. Jacobs not out	54	– (9) c Lehmann b MacGill	11
V. C. Drakes c Gilchrist b Bichel	0	– (7) lbw b Gillespie	14
M. Dillon lbw b MacGill	20	– (8) lbw b Gillespie	0
P. T. Collins st Gilchrist b MacGill	3	– not out	1
J. J. C. Lawson b Lee	0	– lbw b Gillespie	0
B 10, l-b 2, w 3, n-b 6	21	B 6, l-b 13, w 1, n-b 22	42

1/9 (2) 2/10 (3) 3/47 (1) 4/47 (5)   237   1/52 (1) 2/110 (2) 3/295 (4)   398
5/53 (4) 6/184 (6) 7/184 (8)   4/303 (5) 5/354 (3) 6/382 (7)
8/222 (9) 9/236 (10) 10/237 (11)   7/384 (8) 8/391 (6) 9/397 (9) 10/398 (11)

Lee 10.3–1–41–2; Gillespie 12–3–40–1; Bichel 8–1–55–3; Hogg 8–1–40–2; MacGill 12–4–49–2. *Second Innings—* MacGill 31–5–140–3; Hogg 15–0–68–1; Lee 14–4–57–0; Gillespie 20.2–5–39–5; Bichel 13–4–40–0; Waugh 8–1–29–0; Lehmann 4–0–6–1.

Australia

J. L. Langer c Hinds b Drakes	146	– not out	78
M. L. Hayden run out	10	– c sub (N. Deonarine) b Lawson	19
R. T. Ponting c Samuels b Drakes	117	– not out	42
D. S. Lehmann c sub (D. E. Bernard) b Drakes	6		
*S. R. Waugh lbw b Dillon	25		
†A. C. Gilchrist c and b Lawson	77		
G. B. Hogg lbw b Collins	3		
A. J. Bichel c Hinds b Drakes	39		
B. Lee c Dillon b Drakes	20		
J. N. Gillespie b Lawson	7		
S. C. G. MacGill not out	4		
B 18, l-b 5, w 2, n-b 10	35	B 1, l-b 2, w 2, n-b 3	8

1/37 (2) 2/285 (3) 3/300 (4) 4/319 (1)   489   1/77 (2)   (1 wkt) 147
5/349 (5) 6/362 (7) 7/447 (8)
8/473 (6) 9/485 (10) 10/489 (9)

Dillon 23–1–116–1; Collins 23–1–96–1; Lawson 21–0–111–2; Drakes 26.1–5–93–5; Samuels 21–6–49–0; Ganga 1–0–1–0. *Second Innings—*Dillon 6–0–21–0; Drakes 8–0–28–0; Collins 6–2–14–0; Lawson 9–2–31–1; Samuels 9.1–1–41–0; Ganga 4–0–9–0.

Umpires: E. A. R. de Silva *(Sri Lanka)* (23) and R. E. Koertzen *(South Africa)* (38).
Third umpire: E. A. Nicholls *(West Indies)*.   Referee: M. J. Procter *(South Africa)* (8).

Close of play: First day, Australia 120-1 (Langer 55, Ponting 46); Second day, West Indies 16-0 (Hinds 2, Smith 13); Third day, West Indies 381-5 (Chanderpaul 26, Drakes 14).

WEST INDIES v AUSTRALIA 2002-03 (2nd Test)

At Queen's Park Oval, Port-of-Spain, Trinidad, on 19, 20, 21, 22, 23 April.

Toss: Australia.   Result: AUSTRALIA won by 118 runs.

Debuts: West Indies – C. S. Baugh, D. E. Bernard.

Man of the Match: R. T. Ponting.

Helped by injuries to Chanderpaul (knee) and Jacobs (thigh), Australia sailed to another victory, and retained the Frank Worrell Trophy. The die was cast on the first day, when Australia took advantage of a threadbare attack to make 391 for 3 – and two of those wickets came from lamentable lbw decisions from umpire de Silva, who seemed to have trouble with the law about balls pitching outside leg. Ponting shared an Australian-record third-wicket stand of 315 with Lehmann, who made an overdue maiden century in his tenth Test. Next morning Ponting scorched to his first Test double-hundred, and Gilchrist celebrated his promotion to No. 5 with another century. Waugh declared at 576 for 4, and grabbed three wickets before the second-day close, including the key one of Lara, bowled around his legs within sight of a first Test hundred on his home ground. Ganga's second successive hundred narrowed the gap to 168, but with Hayden becoming their fourth century-maker of the match Australia soon stretched that to 406. By lunch on the last day, local hopes were rising after Lara and Sarwan batted through the morning session to narrow the deficit to 197 with seven wickets left. Lara had reached a breakthrough home-town century despite an inspired spell of brutish fast bowling from Lee. But that was followed by something almost as quick: West Indies went into free-fall, losing their last seven wickets for 75 in 23 overs. Australia, by contrast, lost only seven wickets in the whole match.

Australia

J. L. Langer lbw b Dillon	25	– lbw b Drakes	3
M. L. Hayden lbw b Dillon	30	– not out	100
R. T. Ponting st Baugh b Samuels	206	– c Baugh b Dillon	45
D. S. Lehmann c Baugh b Drakes	160	– b Dillon	66
†A. C. Gilchrist not out	101		
G. B. Hogg not out	17		
B 11, l-b 7, w 7, n-b 12	37	B 13, l-b 5, w 1, n-b 5	24

1/49 (1) 2/56 (2)   (4 wkts dec.) 576   1/12 (1) 2/118 (3)   (3 wkts dec.) 238
3/371 (4) 4/542 (3)   3/238 (4)

*S. R. Waugh, A. J. Bichel, B. Lee, J. N. Gillespie and S. C. G. MacGill did not bat.

Dillon 28.5–1–124–2; Collins 25–2–123–0; Drakes 33–3–112–1; Samuels 26–2–111–1; Bernard 11–1–61–0; Sarwan 2–0–7–0; Hinds 7–0–20–0. *Second Innings*—Dillon 18.2–0–64–2; Drakes 20–4–61–1; Samuels 21–1–65–0; Collins 7–1–30–0.

West Indies

W. W. Hinds c Hayden b Lee	20	– b MacGill	35
D. S. Smith c Gilchrist b Gillespie	0	– lbw b Gillespie	0
D. Ganga c Hayden b Lee	117	– c Hayden b Gillespie	2
*B. C. Lara b Hogg	91	– c Hayden b MacGill	122
R. R. Sarwan b Lee	26	– c Lehmann b Bichel	34
M. N. Samuels c Bichel b MacGill	68	– lbw b Bichel	1
D. E. Bernard b Gillespie	7	– c Hayden b Bichel	4
†C. S. Baugh hit wkt b MacGill	19	– c Langer b Hogg	1
V. C. Drakes lbw b Lee	24	– not out	26
M. Dillon lbw b Gillespie	0	– c Bichel b Lee	13
P. T. Collins not out	7	– lbw b Gillespie	5
B 4, l-b 15, w 2, n-b 8	29	B 25, l-b 7, w 3, n-b 10	45

1/4 (2) 2/25 (1) 3/183 (4) 4/258 (5)   408   1/2 (2) 2/12 (3) 3/107 (1)   288
5/279 (3) 6/300 (7) 7/367 (8)   4/213 (5) 5/222 (6) 6/228 (7)
8/376 (6) 9/384 (10) 10/408 (9)   7/238 (4) 8/238 (8) 9/270 (10) 10/288 (11)

Lee 23–4–69–4; Gillespie 28–9–50–3; Bichel 12–1–58–0; MacGill 27–4–98–2; Hogg 22–3–98–1; Waugh 7–2–16–0. *Second Innings*—Lee 19–4–68–1; Gillespie 17.2–3–36–3; Bichel 13–3–21–3; Lehmann 7–0–20–0; MacGill 20–6–53–2; Hogg 13–1–58–1.

Umpires: E. A. R. de Silva *(Sri Lanka)* (24) and R. E. Koertzen *(South Africa)* (39).
Third umpire: B. R. Doctrove *(West Indies)*.   Referee: M. J. Procter *(South Africa)* (9).

Close of play: First day, Australia 391-3 (Ponting 146, Gilchrist 14); Second day, West Indies 186-3 (Ganga 69, Sarwan 1); Third day, Australia 31-1 (Hayden 15, Ponting 10); Fourth day, West Indies 107-3 (Lara 52, Sarwan 0).

WEST INDIES v AUSTRALIA 2002–03 (3rd Test)

At Kensington Oval, Bridgetown, Barbados, on 1, 2, 3, 4, 5 May.
Toss: West Indies.   Result: AUSTRALIA won by nine wickets.
Debuts: West Indies – O. A. C. Banks, T. L. Best.
Man of the Match: S. C. G. MacGill.

Despite rating the pitch as the slowest and flattest he had come across, Waugh managed to wring out of it his 30th century, another Test win – his 36th as captain, equalling the record held by Clive Lloyd – and yet another series success, his tenth as captain. It also restored his side to the top of the ICC Test Championship. His opposite number's memories were less happy. Lara went down with a mystery virus on the second day, his 34th birthday, and was too ill to bat in his usual spot. Some wondered whether he had been feverish at the start, when – 2–0 down and with a seam attack boasting nine previous caps between them – he put the world's most relentless batting team in: they responded with 605, Waugh and Ponting making hundreds. The off-spinner Omari Banks, the first Test player from Anguilla, took 3 for 204, the most runs conceded in an innings on debut at the time. West Indies had to follow on, 277 behind, but with the pitch still a featherbed they had a chance of saving the match. They began the final day just 90 adrift, only for Lara and Sarwan to fall during the first few minutes. MacGill worked his way through the rest; McGrath, who had missed the first two Tests, went wicketless for the first time in 26 Tests. There was some local cheer, though: by dismissing Langer first ball Lawson became the first West Indian to take a Test hat-trick at home.

Australia

J. L. Langer c Chanderpaul b Banks	78	– lbw b Lawson	0
M. L. Hayden c Gayle b Drakes	27	– not out	2
R. T. Ponting run out	113		
D. S. Lehmann lbw b Drakes	96	– (3) not out	4
*S. R. Waugh b Lawson	115		
†A. C. Gilchrist c Smith b Banks	65		
A. J. Bichel c Lara b Banks	71		
B. Lee b Lawson	11		
J. N. Gillespie not out	18		
S. C. G. MacGill b Lawson	0		
B 3, l-b 3, w 3, n-b 2	11	B 2	2

1/43 (2) 2/151 (1) 3/292 (3)   (9 wkts dec.) 605   1/0 (1)   (1 wkt) 8
4/331 (4) 5/444 (6) 6/568 (7)
7/580 (5) 8/605 (8) 9/605 (10)

G. D. McGrath did not bat.

Lawson 32.3–2–131–3; Best 20–1–99–0; Drakes 30–2–85–2; Banks 40–2–204–3; Gayle 31–5–79–0; Sarwan 1–0–1–0. *Second Innings*—Lawson 1–0–2–1; Banks 1–0–2–0; Gayle 0.3–0–2–0.

West Indies

C. H. Gayle b Gillespie	71	– st Gilchrist b MacGill	56
D. S. Smith c Gilchrist b Gillespie	59	– lbw b Lee	5
D. Ganga c Bichel b Lehmann	26	– lbw b Lee	6
R. R. Sarwan c Gilchrist b Lee	40	– lbw b MacGill	58
S. Chanderpaul c Lee b MacGill	0	– (6) c Gilchrist b Gillespie	21
O. A. C. Banks c Ponting b Gillespie	24	– (7) c Hayden b MacGill	32
†C. S. Baugh c Ponting b MacGill	24	– (8) run out	18
*B. C. Lara lbw b Bichel	14	– (5) lbw b Bichel	42
V. C. Drakes c Lee b MacGill	11	– b MacGill	0
T. L. Best not out	20	– c Bichel b MacGill	0
J. J. C. Lawson st Gilchrist b MacGill	1	– not out	5
B 11, l-b 16, n-b 11	38	B 13, l-b 25, w 1, n-b 2	41

1/139 (1) 2/142 (2) 3/205 (3) 4/206 (5)   328   1/14 (2) 2/31 (3) 3/94 (1)   284
5/245 (4) 6/245 (6) 7/281 (8)   4/187 (4) 5/195 (5) 6/256 (7)
8/291 (7) 9/324 (9) 10/328 (11)   7/256 (6) 8/261 (9) 9/265 (10) 10/284 (8)

McGrath 18–7–25–0; Gillespie 21–9–31–3; Lee 25–8–77–1; MacGill 39.5–8–107–4; Lehmann 9–2–26–1; Bichel 16–3–35–1. *Second Innings*—McGrath 18–4–39–0; Gillespie 28–11–37–1; MacGill 36–11–75–5; Lee 15–6–44–2; Bichel 12–2–35–1; Ponting 2–0–6–0; Waugh 4–1–6–0; Lehmann 1–0–4–0.

Umpires: D. R. Shepherd *(England)* (70) and S. Venkataraghavan *(India)* (65).
Third umpire: E. A. Nicholls *(West Indies)*.   Referee: M. J. Procter *(South Africa)* (10).

Close of play: First day, Australia 320-3 (Lehmann 89, Waugh 7); Second day, West Indies 89-0 (Gayle 47, Smith 34); Third day, West Indies 291-8 (Drakes 4); Fourth day, West Indies 187-3 (Sarwan 58, Lara 41).

WEST INDIES v AUSTRALIA 2002–03 (4th Test)

At Antigua Recreation Ground, St John's, Antigua, on 9, 10, 11, 12, 13 May.
Toss: Australia.   Result: WEST INDIES won by three wickets.
Debuts: none.
Man of the Match: S. Chanderpaul.   Man of the Series: R. T. Ponting.

After three defeats, few expected West Indies to win, let alone pull off the largest successful run-chase in Test history, surpassing India's 406 in Trinidad in 1975-76. The target of 418, while unlikely, was not impossible as the pitch had lost its juice. But when Lara was fourth out at 165, trying to belt MacGill for a fourth huge six, prospects looked bleak. However, Sarwan and Chanderpaul, nursing a broken finger, patiently added 123 before Sarwan's mis-hook left things delicately poised at 288 for 5. The first-ball dismissal of Jacobs, adjudged caught behind off his elbow, tilted things back Australia's way. Chanderpaul grafted to a magnificent hundred, but he added only one on the final morning. Finally Banks and Drakes – neither really an all-rounder – coolly took care of the 46 needed to reach a stunning, unparalleled victory. The talking-point on the opening day was the bowling action of Lawson, who was reported to ICC by the umpires. Later there were confrontations between Lara and some of the Australians, including a toe-to-toe discussion with Waugh – in between Lara smashed his first ball, from Lee, over point for six – and later Sarwan and McGrath had a public on-field argument. The play was equally dramatic. After the sides tied on first innings – the seventh instance in Tests – Australia looked to have taken charge through Langer and Hayden's fifth double-century opening stand, a Test record. But Australia were restricted to 417 – about 150 fewer than Waugh had envisaged – which, remarkably, was not quite enough.

Australia

J. L. Langer c Banks b Lawson	42	– c Lara b Gayle	111
M. L. Hayden c Drakes b Lawson	14	– run out	177
M. L. Love b Banks	36	– (4) c sub (M. N. Samuels) b Banks	2
D. S. Lehmann c Jacobs b Lawson	7	– (5) b Dillon	14
*S. R. Waugh c Jacobs b Dillon	41	– (6) not out	45
†A. C. Gilchrist c Chanderpaul b Dillon	33	– (3) c sub (M. N. Samuels) b Banks	6
A. J. Bichel c sub (M. N. Samuels) b Lawson	34	– c Smith b Dillon	0
B. Lee c Jacobs b Lawson	9	– c sub (S. C. Joseph) b Dillon	18
J. N. Gillespie c Jacobs b Lawson	6	– c Lara b Drakes	5
S. C. G. MacGill c Sarwan b Lawson	2	– c Lara b Dillon	0
G. D. McGrath not out	5	– c Ganga b Drakes	14
B 2, l-b 3, w 2, n-b 4	11	B 4, l-b 9, n-b 12	25
	240		**417**

1/27 (2) 2/80 (1) 3/93 (4) 4/128 (3)   240   1/242 (1) 2/273 (3) 3/285 (4)   417
5/181 (5) 6/194 (6) 7/224 (7)   4/330 (5) 5/338 (2) 6/343 (7)
8/231 (8) 9/233 (10) 10/240 (9)   7/373 (8) 8/385 (9) 9/388 (10) 10/417 (11)

Dillon 18–2–53–2; Lawson 19.1–3–78–7; Drakes 15–2–42–0; Banks 20–2–62–1. *Second Innings*—Lawson 6–1–17–0; Dillon 29–3–112–4; Banks 37–5–153–2; Drakes 19–1–92–2; Gayle 13–1–30–1.

West Indies

C. H. Gayle b McGrath	0	– c Waugh b Lee	19
D. S. Smith c Gilchrist b Lee	37	– c Gilchrist b Gillespie	23
D. Ganga c Gilchrist b Bichel	6	– lbw b McGrath	8
V. C. Drakes lbw b Lee	21	– (9) not out	27
*B. C. Lara c Langer b Bichel	68	– (4) b MacGill	60
R. R. Sarwan c and b Bichel	24	– (5) c and b Lee	105
S. Chanderpaul b McGrath	1	– (6) c Gilchrist b Lee	104
†R. D. Jacobs run out	26	– (7) c Gilchrist b Lee	0
O. A. C. Banks not out	16	– (8) not out	47
M. Dillon b Lee	9		
J. J. C. Lawson c Love b MacGill	14		
L-b 8, w 3, n-b 7	18	B 9, l-b 9, w 1, n-b 6	25
	240	(7 wkts)	**418**

1/1 (1) 2/30 (3) 3/73 (2) 4/80 (4)   240   1/48 (1) 2/50 (2) 3/74 (3)   (7 wkts) 418
5/137 (6) 6/140 (7) 7/185 (8)   4/165 (4) 5/288 (5)
8/197 (5) 9/224 (10) 10/240 (11)   6/288 (7) 7/372 (6)

McGrath 17–6–44–2; Gillespie 17–3–56–0; Bichel 14–4–53–3; Lee 15–2–71–3; MacGill 2.3–0–8–1. *Second Innings*—McGrath 25–10–50–1; Gillespie 25–10–64–1; Lee 23–4–63–4; MacGill 35.5–8–149–1; Bichel 15–3–49–0; Waugh 5–0–25–0.

Umpires: D. R. Shepherd *(England)* (71) and S. Venkataraghavan *(India)* (66).
Third umpire: B. R. Doctrove *(West Indies)*.   Referee: M. J. Procter *(South Africa)* (11).

Close of play: First day, West Indies 47-2 (Smith 22, Drakes 12); Second day, Australia 171-0 (Langer 80, Hayden 79); Third day, West Indies 47-0 (Gayle 19, Smith 21); Fourth day, West Indies 371-6 (Chanderpaul 103, Banks 28).

BANGLADESH v SOUTH AFRICA 2003 (1st Test)

At M. A. Aziz Stadium, Chittagong, on 24, 25, 26, 27 April.

Toss: Bangladesh.   Result: SOUTH AFRICA won by an innings and 60 runs.

Debuts: Bangladesh – Mohammad Salim. South Africa – A. C. Dawson, J. A. Rudolph, C. M. Willoughby.

Man of the Match: J. A. Rudolph.

Fifteen months earlier, Jacques Rudolph was selected to make his Test debut at Sydney, then left out because of South Africa's racial-quota system. Now, he finally got his cap ... and made quite an impression, becoming only the fifth batsman to score a debut double-century – a brilliant 222 not out – and putting on 429 (the sixth-largest partnership in Tests) with Dippenaar. South Africa lost only two wickets in storming to victory, only the fourth such instance in Tests. Bangladesh had started reasonably, but a familiar procession followed, and they were all out for 173, undone by a resurgent Adams, whose 5 for 37 included a characteristic mix of long-hops, full-tosses and unplayable deliveries. The early wickets of Smith (who had become the third-youngest captain in Test history, after the junior Nawab of Pataudi in 1961-62 and Waqar Younis in 1993-94) and Gibbs gave Bangladesh some encouragement, but they toiled unrewarded in the heat for a further 123 overs as Rudolph and Dippenaar surpassed their country's highest stand for any wicket, Smith and Gibbs's 368 against Pakistan just four months previously. At 98 Rudolph survived a stumping chance off Mohammad Ashraful; unperturbed, he stroked the next delivery through the covers to become only the second South African debut centurion after Andrew Hudson. When Bangladesh batted again Omar (who batted for 260 minutes) and Bashar again showed admirable resilience, but South Africa wrapped things up early on the fourth day, with Adams taking ten wickets in a Test for the only time.

Bangladesh

Javed Omar lbw b Dawson	28	– c Boucher b Ntini	71
Mehrab Hossain, sen. c Boucher b Pollock	6	– lbw b Pollock	5
Habibul Bashar c Gibbs b Dawson	60	– c Boucher b Pollock	75
Mohammad Ashraful c Dippenaar b Adams	12	– c Smith b Willoughby	28
Akram Khan c Rudolph b Adams	13	– (7) c Dippenaar b Adams	16
Alok Kapali c Boucher b Adams	0	– (5) c Boucher b Adams	7
*Khaled Mahmud b Ntini	6	– (8) st Boucher b Smith	1
†Mohammad Salim not out	16	– (6) lbw b Adams	0
Tapash Baisya c Dippenaar b Ntini	4	– (10) not out	0
Enamul Haque, sen. b Adams	1	– (11) c and b Adams	11
Mashrafe bin Mortaza st Boucher b Adams	20	– (9) c Pollock b Adams	0
W 1, n-b 6	7	B 5, l-b 10, w 6, n-b 2	23

1/14 (2) 2/97 (1) 3/100 (3) 4/124 (5)   **173**   1/7 (2) 2/138 (3) 3/173 (1)   **237**
5/124 (6) 6/126 (4) 7/136 (7)   4/183 (5) 5/185 (6) 6/213 (4)
8/144 (9) 9/147 (10) 10/173 (11)   7/224 (7) 8/224 (9) 9/224 (8) 10/237 (11)

Pollock 11–2–22–1; Ntini 17–4–45–2; Dawson 13–3–37–2; Willoughby 12–5–32–0; Adams 12.3–3–37–5. *Second Innings*—Pollock 13–9–12–2; Willoughby 18–6–47–1; Ntini 16–4–37–1; Dawson 12–4–48–0; Adams 18.4–5–69–5; Smith 5–2–9–1.

South Africa

*G. C. Smith c Mohammad Salim b Tapash Baisya	16	H. H. Dippenaar not out	177
H. H. Gibbs c Mohammad Salim b Mashrafe bin Mortaza	17	B 9, l-b 6, w 2, n-b 21	38
J. A. Rudolph not out	222	1/38 (1) 2/41 (2) (2 wkts dec.) 470	

N. D. McKenzie, †M. V. Boucher, S. M. Pollock, P. R. Adams, A. C. Dawson, C. M. Willoughby and M. Ntini did not bat.

Mashrafe bin Mortaza 24–3–108–1; Khaled Mahmud 17–5–56–0; Tapash Baisya 23–8–70–1; Enamul Haque 33–10–81–0; Alok Kapali 18.5–2–71–0; Mohammad Ashraful 8–0–31–0; Habibul Bashar 7–0–38–0.

Umpires: B. F. Bowden *(New Zealand)* (4) and S. A. Bucknor *(West Indies)* (78).
Third umpire: Mahbubur Rahman *(Bangladesh)*.   Referee: C. H. Lloyd *(West Indies)* (22).

Close of play: First day, South Africa 84-2 (Rudolph 15, Dippenaar 16); Second day, South Africa 364-2 (Rudolph 170, Dippenaar 131); Third day, Bangladesh 185-5 (Mohammad Ashraful 12).

BANGLADESH v SOUTH AFRICA 2003 (2nd Test)

At Bangabandhu National Stadium, Dhaka, on 1, 2, 3, 4 May.
Toss: South Africa.   Result: SOUTH AFRICA won by an innings and 18 runs.
Debuts: South Africa – R. J. Peterson.
Man of the Match: Mohammad Rafique.   Man of the Series: J. A. Rudolph.

Only rain on the second day prevented a three-day finish, yet, despite the lop-sided result, Bangladesh had much to encourage them. They reduced South Africa to 63 for 4 on the first day, and might have caused more embarrassment if slow left-armer Mohammad Rafique had had more support. Rudolph again stroked the ball around with ease, while Boucher used his feet to good effect during a fifth-wicket stand of 107. Later Robin Peterson, a left-arm spinner making his Test debut, dragged the innings to respectability with a gutsy half-century. Rafique finished with 6 for 77, Bangladesh's best Test figures at the time, but sadly their batsmen again capitulated without resolve or resistance. Pollock and Ntini exploited the moist conditions to strike four times between them in the opening stages, then only Khaled Mahmud stood firm as Peterson and Dawson swept the tail away in eight overs. Mehrab Hossain's run-out in the follow-on hinted at further panic and frustration: five of the top six got starts only to squander their hard work. Habibul Bashar battled for two hours in making 33, then Alok Kapali and Mohammad Salim applied themselves bravely as the bowlers showed signs of wilting in the heat: by the close Bangladesh needed only 24 to avoid yet another defeat, their 13th by an innings out of 18. But the task proved too much. With rain threatening, Pollock removed Salim and Mashrafe bin Mortaza in the third over of the day.

South Africa

*G. C. Smith c Mohammad Ashraful b Tapash Baisya ..	15	
H. H. Gibbs c Tapash Baisya b Mohammad Rafique ...	21	
J. A. Rudolph st Mohammad Salim		
b Mohammad Ashraful	71	
H. H. Dippenaar c Mehrab Hossain		
b Mohammad Rafique...................	1	
N. D. McKenzie lbw b Mohammad Rafique	7	
†M. V. Boucher b Mohammad Rafique	71	
S. M. Pollock lbw b Mashrafe bin Mortaza..........	41	
R. J. Peterson c Akram Khan		
b Mohammad Ashraful	61	

A. C. Dawson c Mohammad Salim	
b Mohammad Rafique	10
P. R. Adams b Mohammad Rafique	9
M. Ntini not out.......................	0
B 6, l-b 6, w 1, n-b 5, p 5	23
	330

1/30 (1) 2/49 (2) 3/51 (4)
4/63 (5) 5/170 (3) 6/219 (6)
7/264 (7) 8/294 (9)
9/330 (8) 10/330 (10)

Tapash Baisya 19–5–67–1; Mashrafe bin Mortaza 20–3–53–1; Khaled Mahmud 14–6–36–0; Mohammad Rafique 37.2–7–77–6; Alok Kapali 11–2–33–0; Mohammad Ashraful 10–0–42–2; Mehrab Hossain 2–0–5–0.

Bangladesh

Javed Omar c sub (A. J. Hall) b Ntini	11	– c Pollock b Adams................	27
Mehrab Hossain, sen. c Smith b Pollock	8	– run out	14
Habibul Bashar lbw b Pollock	14	– c Boucher b Peterson............	33
Mohammad Ashraful c Pollock b Ntini	15	– c Pollock b Peterson............	23
Akram Khan c Boucher b Ntini	13	– c Rudolph b Ntini	23
Alok Kapali run out........................	1	– c Ntini b Dawson	23
*Khaled Mahmud not out	20	– c sub (A. J. Hall) b Peterson...........	0
†Mohammad Salim c Boucher b Peterson	7	– c Smith b Pollock..............	26
Mohammad Rafiq c Pollock b Dawson	0	– c Boucher b Adams	18
Tapash Baisya b Dawson.....................	4	– not out........................	8
Mashrafe bin Mortaza c Dippenaar b Peterson	1	– b Pollock......................	4
L-b 4, w 1, n-b 3	8	B 5, w 2, n-b 4	11

1/22 (2) 2/22 (1) 3/37 (3) 4/53 (5)	102
5/62 (6) 6/66 (4) 7/73 (8)	
8/77 (9) 9/85 (10) 10/102 (11)	

1/46 (2) 2/46 (1) 3/93 (4)	210
4/119 (5) 5/131 (3) 6/139 (7)	
7/163 (6) 8/190 (9) 9/206 (8) 10/210 (11)	

Pollock 8–3–21–2; Ntini 11–4–32–3; Dawson 7–2–20–2; Peterson 8.5–1–22–2; Adams 1–0–3–0. *Second Innings*—Pollock 8–1–21–2; Ntini 12–2–37–1; Peterson 27–13–46–3; Dawson 10–5–12–1; Adams 19–3–70–2; Smith 7–0–19–0.

Umpires: B. F. Bowden *(New Zealand)* (5) and S. A. Bucknor *(West Indies)* (79).
Third umpire: A. F. M. Akhtaruddin *(Bangladesh)*.   Referee: C. H. Lloyd *(West Indies)* (23).

Close of play: First day, South Africa 264-6 (Pollock 41, Peterson 15); Second day, Bangladesh 4-0 (Javed Omar 3, Mehrab Hossain 0); Third day, Bangladesh 204-8 (Mohammad Salim 24, Tapash Baisya 8).

SRI LANKA v NEW ZEALAND 2003 (1st Test)

At P. Saravanamuttu Stadium, Colombo, on 25, 26, 27, 28, 29 April.
Toss: New Zealand.   Result: MATCH DRAWN.
Debuts: Sri Lanka – K. S. Lokuarachchi, R. A. P. Nissanka.
Man of the Match: no award.

This otherwise dreary match will be remembered for the amazing tenacity of Stephen Fleming. In ferocious heat, he showed great stamina and unwavering concentration – and almost single-handedly earned his side a draw. Fleming was on the field for all but the first 44 minutes of the match; in total, he defied the bowlers for 956 minutes. His 343 runs was the highest Test aggregate by a New Zealander, passing Martin Crowe's 329 at Wellington in 1990-91, also against Sri Lanka. But the numbers did not tell the whole story. Fleming's unbeaten first-innings 274 saved the game psychologically as well as statistically by calming his team-mates' fears that they would be torn apart by Muralitharan and his three fellow spinners. That didn't happen – partly because the pitch turned out to be a little too good, partly because more than 40 overs were lost to the weather, and partly because Tillekeratne, Sri Lanka's new captain, was more concerned with avoiding defeat than pursuing victory. Sri Lanka had reached 424 for 6 by the close of the fourth day, with Kaluwitharana, in his first Test for more than two years, hitting 14 fours from 90 balls. Tillekeratne (who himself had scored 55 in 53 overs) could have declared behind and let his spinners loose – but instead chose to let the innings drift aimlessly into the fifth day, after which Fleming booked in for five more hours. Murali still created enough trouble on the last afternoon to leave spectators wondering what might have been.

New Zealand

M. H. Richardson b Vaas	85	– (7) not out	6
M. J. Horne c Dharmasena b Nissanka	4	– (1) lbw b Lokuarachchi	42
*S. P. Fleming not out	274	– (2) not out	69
M. S. Sinclair c Sangakkara b Dharmasena	17	– (3) c sub (T. M. Dilshan) b Muralitharan	1
S. B. Styris c Vaas b Dharmasena	63	– (4) lbw b Lokuarachchi	16
J. D. P. Oram c Lokuarachchi b Muralitharan	33	– (5) c Kaluwitharana b Muralitharan	19
†R. G. Hart c Jayawardene b Muralitharan	9	– (6) c Sangakkara b Muralitharan	0
D. L. Vettori lbw b Dharmasena	7		
P. J. Wiseman not out	16		
B 2, l-b 3, w 1, n-b 1	7	B 2, l-b 5, n-b 1	8

1/20 (2) 2/192 (1) 3/235 (4)   (7 wkts dec.) 515
4/392 (5) 5/471 (6)
6/486 (7) 7/499 (8)

1/71 (1) 2/76 (3)   (5 wkts dec.) 161
3/108 (4) 4/133 (5)
5/133 (6)

D. R. Tuffey and S. E. Bond did not bat.

Vaas 29–8–73–1; Nissanka 23–9–53–1; Dharmasena 40–7–132–3; Muralitharan 58.5–16–140–2; Lokuarachchi 18–2–83–0; Jayasuriya 6–0–29–0. *Second Innings*—Vaas 7–2–27–0; Nissanka 6–1–18–0; Muralitharan 30–15–41–3; Lokuarachchi 19–2–47–2; Dharmasena 16–7–21–0.

Sri Lanka

M. S. Atapattu lbw b Tuffey	0	K. S. Lokuarachchi not out	28
S. T. Jayasuriya b Bond	50	R. A. P. Nissanka lbw b Vettori	0
W. P. U. J. C. Vaas c Fleming b Bond	4	M. Muralitharan lbw b Vettori	0
K. C. Sangakkara c Oram b Wiseman	67	L-b 21, w 1, n-b 3	25
D. P. M. D. Jayawardene c Hart b Oram	58		
*H. P. Tillekeratne b Bond	144		483
†R. S. Kaluwitharana c Sinclair b Wiseman	76		
H. D. P. K. Dharmasena lbw b Vettori	31		

1/0 (1) 2/11 (3) 3/114 (2)   483
4/134 (4) 5/267 (5) 6/374 (7)
7/444 (6) 8/483 (8)
9/483 (10) 10/483 (11)

Tuffey 17–5–54–1; Bond 28–6–97–3; Oram 30–13–62–1; Vettori 33–8–94–3; Wiseman 41–13–127–2; Styris 3–0–28–0.

Umpires: D. J. Harper (Australia) (29) and S. J. A. Taufel (Australia) (3).
Third umpire: T. H. Wijewardene (Sri Lanka).   Referee: G. R. Viswanath (India) (10).

Close of play: First day, New Zealand 207-2 (Fleming 112, Sinclair 4); Second day, Sri Lanka 4-1 (Jayasuriya 2, Vaas 2); Third day, Sri Lanka 267-4 (Jayawardene 58, Tillekeratne 71); Fourth day, Sri Lanka 424-6 (Tillekeratne 126, Dharmasena 19).

SRI LANKA v NEW ZEALAND 2003 (2nd Test)

At Asgiriya Stadium, Kandy, on 3 *(no play)*, 4, 5, 6, 7 May.
Toss: New Zealand.   Result: MATCH DRAWN.
Debuts: none.
Man of the Match: no award.

Sri Lanka's crushingly negative approach condemned a rain-affected match to a draw, just when it seemed that a thrilling finish was possible. After losing six wickets before lunch on the last day, New Zealand were only 151 ahead, with seven wickets down. But instead of attacking, Tillekeratne posted three fielders on the boundary. As a result, Hart and Wiseman were able to survive largely untroubled for 28 overs, and New Zealand lasted until tea. Even then, 191 in 38 overs to win the series was stiff but by no means impossible: Sri Lanka had plenty of talented strokemakers, the pitch was still sound, and Vettori only half-fit. When Jayasuriya blazed two early fours it looked as if the chase was on, but when he was deceived by a slower ball the shutters came down. The match had begun on a flat note too. No play was possible until late on the second day after heavy rain turned parts of the outfield into a bog, one of the problems of playing at a rainy time of year. New Zealand then made a disastrous start, slumping to 11 for 3 before Oram and Vettori led a recovery. Jayasuriya launched the reply in positive style, but when he edged to slip the innings slipped into a self-induced coma. New Zealand tried to set up a run-chase, with Richardson scoring his third half-century in three completed innings. Muralitharan took his 450th wicket (Tuffey), and completed his 37th five-for, passing Richard Hadlee's Test record of 36.

New Zealand

M. H. Richardson c Sangakkara b Lokuarachchi	55	– c Kaluwitharana b Nissanka	55
M. J. Horne c Kaluwitharana b Vaas	1	– c Tillekeratne b Muralitharan	27
*S. P. Fleming lbw b Nissanka	0	– c Kaluwitharana b Dharmasena	33
M. S. Sinclair lbw b Vaas	3	– st Kaluwitharana b Muralitharan	0
S. B. Styris c Tillekeratne b Muralitharan	32	– c Muralitharan b Vaas	1
J. D. P. Oram c Kaluwitharana b Lokuarachchi	74	– lbw b Muralitharan	16
†R. G. Hart lbw b Muralitharan	31	– c Kaluwitharana b Vaas	12
D. L. Vettori run out	55	– b Muralitharan	0
P. J. Wiseman b Muralitharan	7	– c Tillekeratne b Vaas	29
D. R. Tuffey c Jayawardene b Nissanka	15	– c Jayasuriya b Muralitharan	1
S. E. Bond not out	10	– not out	1
B 3, l-b 7, w 5, n-b 7	22	B 1, l-b 6, n-b 1	8

1/6 (2) 2/7 (3) 3/11 (4) 4/71 (5)   305
5/109 (1) 6/189 (7) 7/222 (6)
8/237 (9) 9/271 (10) 10/305 (8)

1/65 (2) 2/109 (1) 3/110 (4)   183
4/115 (5) 5/136 (3) 6/139 (6)
7/139 (8) 8/179 (7) 9/182 (10) 10/183 (9)

Vaas 22–8–48–2; Nissanka 16.5–5–41–2; Muralitharan 34–10–90–3; Jayasuriya 8–0–24–0; Dharmasena 15–5–40–0; Lokuarachchi 16–5–52–2. *Second Innings*—Vaas 15.3–6–31–3; Nissanka 10–4–18–1; Dharmasena 12–2–32–1; Lokuarachchi 14–3–26–0; Muralitharan 39–18–49–5; Jayasuriya 7–0–20–0.

Sri Lanka

K. C. Sangakkara c Hart b Tuffey	10	– not out	27
S. T. Jayasuriya c Fleming b Wiseman	82	– c Richardson b Bond	9
D. P. M. D. Jayawardene c Hart b Oram	15	– not out	32
*H. P. Tillekeratne b Wiseman	93		
†R. S. Kaluwitharana c Tuffey b Bond	20		
H. D. P. K. Dharmasena c Fleming b Wiseman	5		
K. S. Lokuarachchi c Tuffey b Oram	20		
W. P. U. J. C. Vaas b Oram	22		
M. S. Atapattu retired hurt	2		
R. A. P. Nissanka b Wiseman	6		
M. Muralitharan not out	2		
B 6, l-b 11, n-b 4	21	L-b 4	4

1/30 (1) 2/69 (3) 3/126 (2) 4/169 (5)   298
5/189 (6) 6/234 (7) 7/264 (8)
8/285 (10) 9/298 (4)

1/14 (2)   (1 wkt) 72

In the first innings Atapattu retired hurt at 267.

Tuffey 20–6–45–1; Bond 25–6–78–1; Oram 20–2–54–3; Wiseman 32.3–4–104–4. *Second Innings*—Tuffey 9–3–18–0; Bond 6–1–19–1; Wiseman 9–4–20–0; Vettori 6–1–11–0.

Umpires: D. J. Harper *(Australia)* (30) and S. J. A. Taufel *(Australia)* (4).
Third umpire: P. T. Manuel *(Sri Lanka)*.   Referee: G. R. Viswanath *(India)* (11).

Close of play: First day, No play; Second day, New Zealand 75-4 (Richardson 32, Oram 0); Third day, Sri Lanka 94-2 (Jayasuriya 53, Tillekeratne 10); Fourth day, New Zealand 92-1 (Richardson 51, Fleming 10).

ENGLAND v ZIMBABWE 2003 (1st Test)

At Lord's, London, on 22, 23, 24 May.
Toss: Zimbabwe.   Result: ENGLAND won by an innings and 92 runs.
Debuts: England – J. M. Anderson, A. McGrath. Zimbabwe – S. M. Ervine.
Man of the Match: M. A. Butcher.

Zimbabwe, now without Andy Flower – like Henry Olonga, effectively in exile after their black-armband protest at the "death of democracy" in the country during the World Cup – slumped to their eighth successive Test defeat, this one inside three days. Flower had missed only two of Zimbabwe's previous 65 Tests. England's crushing win was competent rather than compelling: the exception was a dazzling spell from James Anderson, who became the first England bowler since Dominic Cork in 1995 to take a five-for on debut, taking the last four first-innings wickets in 14 balls in a deadly afternoon spell after looking relatively unthreatening in the morning.. Early-morning rain delayed the start, providing ideal conditions for Zimbabwe's seamers. Vaughan made a painful 42-ball eight, and for one deceptive hour England were not on top. But Zimbabwe bowled too wide. It might have been different had Butcher not survived a convincing lbw shout from Hondo on ten, and a chance at slip at 36. On the second day the pitch eased, Butcher went on to 137, and the last four wickets added a spirit-sapping 130. The third day was one of the longest in Test history (seven hours 39 minutes), and 19 wickets fell, but it was a hollow sort of epic: Zimbabwe simply rolled over. In the follow-on, they lost nine wickets in 42 overs in the best batting conditions of the match, seven to the unsung military-medium swingers of Butcher and Anthony McGrath, who had earlier made a composed 69 on debut.

England

M. E. Trescothick c Ervine b Blignaut	59	M. J. Hoggard c Ebrahim b Blignaut 19
M. P. Vaughan b Streak	8	J. M. Anderson not out 4
M. A. Butcher c Vermeulen b Price	137	
*N. Hussain c Hondo b Friend	19	B 14, l-b 27, w 3, n-b 17 61
R. W. T. Key c Taibu b Streak	18	
†A. J. Stewart c Taibu b Streak	26	1/45 (2) 2/121 (1) 3/165 (4) 472
A. McGrath b Ervine	69	4/204 (5) 5/274 (6) 6/342 (3)
A. F. Giles b Blignaut	52	7/408 (7) 8/408 (9)
S. J. Harmison c Ebrahim b Ervine	0	9/465 (10) 10/472 (8)

Streak 37–9–99–3; Blignaut 26.1–4–96–3; Hondo 14–4–45–0; Ervine 22–5–95–2; Friend 13–2–49–1; Price 20–6–44–1; Flower 1–0–3–0.

Zimbabwe

D. D. Ebrahim c McGrath b Butcher	68	– c Key b Harmison	6
M. A. Vermeulen b Anderson	1	– c Trescothick b Butcher	61
S. V. Carlisle c Trescothick b Hoggard	11	– lbw b Butcher	24
G. W. Flower c Key b Hoggard	3	– c Trescothick b Harmison	26
†T. Taibu c Hoggard b Harmison	25	– c Butcher b McGrath	16
S. M. Ervine lbw b Hoggard	4	– c Trescothick b McGrath	4
*H. H. Streak b Anderson	10	– lbw b McGrath	11
A. M. Blignaut c Butcher b Anderson	3	– b Butcher	6
T. J. Friend b Anderson	0	– c Giles b Butcher	43
R. W. Price not out	7	– c Trescothick b Giles	26
D. T. Hondo b Anderson	0	– not out	0
B 5, l-b 1, w 1, n-b 8	15	B 1, l-b 6, w 3	10

1/20 (2) 2/64 (3) 3/79 (4) 4/104 (1)	147	1/11 (1) 2/91 (2) 3/95 (3)	233
5/109 (6) 6/129 (5) 7/133 (7)		4/128 (5) 5/132 (6) 6/150 (7)	
8/133 (9) 9/147 (8) 10/147 (11)		7/158 (8) 8/168 (4) 9/219 (10) 10/233 (9)	

Hoggard 18–8–24–3; Anderson 16–4–73–5; Harmison 16–5–36–1; Butcher 5–2–8–1. *Second Innings*—Anderson 15–4–65–0; Hoggard 15–5–35–0; Harmison 12–4–35–2; Giles 8–2–15–1; Butcher 12.5–0–60–4; McGrath 6–1–16–3.

Umpires: S. A. Bucknor *(West Indies)* (80) and D. L. Orchard *(South Africa)* (37).
Third umpire: N. A. Mallender *(England)*.   Referee: C. H. Lloyd *(West Indies)* (24).

Close of play: First day, England 184-3 (Butcher 52, Key 11); Second day, Zimbabwe 48-1 (Ebrahim 40, Carlisle 4).

ENGLAND v ZIMBABWE 2003 (2nd Test)

At Riverside Ground, Chester-le-Street, on 5, 6, 7 June.
Toss: England.   Result: ENGLAND won by an innings and 69 runs.
Debuts: England – R. L. Johnson.
Man of the Match: R. L. Johnson.   Men of the Series: M. A. Butcher and H. H. Streak.

England's first new Test venue for 101 years – the 87th worldwide – produced an occasion that the contest failed to match. Streak bowled with admirable control, and there was some belated resistance late on, but too many of the tourists lacked method or gumption, or both, as they slipped to their ninth consecutive defeat. When Hondo took three wickets in 11 balls England were in a spot of bother at 156 for 5, but they were rescued by Stewart (who passed David Gower's aggregate of 8,231 runs) and McGrath: the last five wickets contributed 260. England's bowling star was Richard Johnson (who had replaced the injured Matthew Hoggard), nine years after taking ten wickets in an innings for Middlesex. He instantly found a good length and accurate inswing: helped by two wickets in his first over (a first in Tests, emulated since only by Graeme Swann in Test No. 1899 in 2008-09), Johnson followed Anderson at Lord's in taking a five-for in his first Test; his eventual figures were the sixth-best by an England debutant. All out in 32.1 overs with a Test-record seven lbws – only Taibu showed much fight – Zimbabwe could hardly do worse in the follow-on, and in the event survived for most of the third day, pleasing the match's only capacity crowd. Ebrahim made a dogged half-century, while Friend hit out towards the end. Local boy Harmison finished off the match as, for the first time since the 1985 Ashes, England won successive Tests by an innings.

England

M. E. Trescothick c Taibu b Price	43	
M. P. Vaughan c Ervine b Streak	20	
M. A. Butcher b Hondo	47	
*N. Hussain c Taibu b Hondo	18	
R. W. T. Key c Flower b Hondo	4	
†A. J. Stewart lbw b Streak	68	
A. McGrath c Taibu b Blignaut	81	
A. F. Giles c Ervine b Streak	50	
R. L. Johnson c Streak b Blignaut	24	

S. J. Harmison c Vermeulen b Streak ..., .. 11
J. M. Anderson not out 12

B 1, l-b 5, w 7, n-b 25 38

1/49 (2) 2/109 (1) 3/146 (3)   416
4/152 (5) 5/156 (4) 6/305 (6)
7/324 (7) 8/356 (9)
9/390 (10) 10/416 (8)

Streak 34.1–11–64–4; Blignaut 23–4–95–2; Hondo 22–1–98–3; Ervine 3–0–17–0; Price 40–9–105–1; Friend 4–0–26–0; Flower 1–0–5–0.

Zimbabwe

D. D. Ebrahim lbw b Anderson	6	– lbw b Harmison	55
M. A. Vermeulen lbw b Johnson	0	– c McGrath b Anderson	0
S. V. Carlisle lbw b Johnson	0	– c Key b Anderson	28
G. W. Flower c Trescothick b Anderson	8	– b Anderson	16
†T. Taibu lbw b Johnson	31	– c Butcher b Giles	14
S. M. Ervine c Stewart b Johnson	0	– b Harmison	34
T. J. Friend lbw b Johnson	0	– not out	65
*H. H. Streak lbw b Johnson	4	– run out	3
A. M. Blignaut c Anderson b Harmison	13	– c Hussain b Anderson	12
R. W. Price lbw b Harmison	17	– c Stewart b Harmison	6
D. T. Hondo not out	5	– b Harmison	4
B 5, l-b 3, n-b 2	10	B 6, l-b 10	16

1/3 (2) 2/3 (3) 3/11 (1) 4/18 (4)   94
5/23 (6) 6/31 (7) 7/35 (8)
8/48 (9) 9/73 (5) 10/94 (10)

1/5 (2) 2/65 (3) 3/102 (1)   253
4/113 (4) 5/131 (5) 6/185 (6)
7/202 (8) 8/223 (9) 9/244 (10) 10/253 (11)

Anderson 10–2–30–2; Johnson 12–4–33–6; Harmison 9.1–3–22–2; Giles 1–0–1–0. *Second Innings*—Anderson 23–8–55–4; Johnson 22–7–67–0; Harmison 21.4–4–55–4; Giles 25–9–51–1; Butcher 2–0–9–0.

Umpires: D. B. Hair *(Australia)* (45) and D. L. Orchard *(South Africa)* (38).
Third umpire: P. Willey *(England)*.   Referee: C. H. Lloyd *(West Indies)* (25).

Close of play: First day, England 298-5 (Stewart 67, McGrath 68); Second day, Zimbabwe 41-1 (Ebrahim 22, Carlisle 19).

WEST INDIES v SRI LANKA 2003 (1st Test)

At Beausejour Stadium, Gros Islet, St Lucia, on 20, 21, 22, 23 *(no play)*, 24 June.
Toss: Sri Lanka.   Result: MATCH DRAWN.
Debuts: West Indies – J. E. Taylor.
Man of the Match: B. C. Lara.

The wisdom of scheduling cricket at the start of the Caribbean rainy season was questioned again after the loss of more than half the third day and all of the fourth to the weather. The rain dampened the spectators' already lukewarm response to St Lucia's first Test match. The president of the West Indian board, Wes Hall, compared it with trying to play in the English winter. Despite being located in supposedly the driest part of the island, the Beausejour Stadium – the 88th Test venue – did not escape the showers for long. Atapattu had batted serenely through the opening day: next morning, his dismissal by part-time seamer Hinds triggered a collapse. Four wickets tumbled for 22, the other three to Collymore, who had lost pace but gained an outswinger since his only previous Test four years earlier. Sri Lanka pottered to 354 before Lara and Hinds belted anything remotely off line, eventually adding 174. Always mindful of an occasion, Lara had hoped he would reach his 21st century on the fourth day, which marked exactly 75 years since West Indies' first Test, in England in 1928. But the weather meant he had to wait until the final morning to complete his fifth century in as many Tests against Sri Lanka. He then stepped up the pace, reaching his second hundred in 151 minutes, and celebrating with a huge six over long-on; but his dismissal slowed things down, delaying a declaration, and Sri Lanka had no problems batting out time.

Sri Lanka

M. S. Atapattu c Lara b Hinds	118	– not out		50
S. T. Jayasuriya c Banks b Collymore	8	– not out		72
K. C. Sangakkara lbw b Gayle	56			
D. P. M. D. Jayawardene c Lara b Banks	45			
*H. P. Tillekeratne b Collymore	13			
T. T. Samaraweera c Jacobs b Collymore	11			
†R. S. Kaluwitharana lbw b Collymore	2			
K. S. Lokuarachchi c Lara b Collymore	15			
W. P. U. J. C. Vaas c Jacobs b Gayle	38			
M. Muralitharan lbw b Hinds	14			
R. A. P. Nissanka not out	12			
B 4, l-b 5, w 5, n-b 8	22	B 1, l-b 2, n-b 1		4

1/19 (2) 2/127 (3) 3/195 (4) 4/228 (5)   **354**   (no wkt) **126**
5/266 (1) 6/269 (7) 7/285 (8)
8/288 (6) 9/326 (10) 10/354 (9)

Dillon 29–7–48–0; Collymore 29–5–66–5; Taylor 27–3–97–0; Hinds 11–4–28–2; Banks 33–8–74–1; Gayle 9.2–1–22–2; Samuels 3–0–9–0; Sarwan 2–1–1–0. *Second Innings*—Dillon 5–1–24–0; Collymore 3–0–8–0; Hinds 4–0–25–0; Taylor 6–1–19–0; Banks 10–0–28–0; Samuels 3–1–15–0; Sarwan 3–0–4–0.

West Indies

C. H. Gayle lbw b Muralitharan	27	M. Dillon c Atapattu b Lokuarachchi		2
D. Ganga lbw b Vaas	12	C. D. Collymore c and b Muralitharan		0
W. W. Hinds run out	113	J. E. Taylor not out		9
*B. C. Lara c Kaluwitharana b Nissanka	209	B 4, l-b 4, w 2, n-b 17		27
R. R. Sarwan c Atapattu b Muralitharan	7			
M. N. Samuels st Kaluwitharana b Muralitharan	8	1/18 (2) 2/66 (1)	(9 wkts dec.)	477
†R. D. Jacobs lbw b Muralitharan	13	3/240 (3) 4/262 (5)		
O. A. C. Banks not out	50	5/279 (6) 6/305 (7)		
		7/441 (4) 8/447 (9) 9/448 (10)		

Vaas 39–5–116–1; Nissanka 21.3–1–108–1; Samaraweera 8–0–53–0; Muralitharan 50–10–138–5; Lokuarachchi 20–6–54–1.

Umpires: B. F. Bowden *(New Zealand)* (6) and D. J. Harper *(Australia)* (31).
Third umpire: B. R. Doctrove *(West Indies)*.   Referee: Wasim Raja *(Pakistan)* (10).

Close of play: First day, Sri Lanka 250-4 (Atapattu 108, Samaraweera 7); Second day, West Indies 161-2 (Hinds 74, Lara 36); Third day, West Indies 272-4 (Lara 93, Samuels 5); Fourth day, No play.

WEST INDIES v SRI LANKA 2003 (2nd Test)

At Sabina Park, Kingston, Jamaica, on 27, 28, 29 June.
Toss: West Indies.   Result: WEST INDIES won by seven wickets.
Debuts: West Indies – F. H. Edwards. Sri Lanka – M. T. T. Mirando *(also known as Thilan Thushara)*.
Man of the Match: C. D. Collymore.   Man of the Series: C. D. Collymore.

A rare Kingston pitch offering help to the bowlers provided the stage for a spectacular Test debut by Fidel Edwards. He and his fellow Barbadian Collymore took 15 wickets as ball dominated bat, before a dramatic reversal on the third afternoon, when ultra-aggressive innings by Lara and Sarwan made a target of 212 – the highest total of the match – look easy. Edwards, 21, was selected by Lara on the basis of a few net sessions, a move criticised by some as a reckless gamble ... but Edwards's performance made it look like inspired genius. No giant at 5ft 8ins, and playing only his second first-class game, he became the seventh West Indian to take a five-for on debut, carving through Sri Lanka's first innings with a slingy, roundarm action. A skimpy total was made to look more competitive by Nissanka, who took five wickets inside 13 overs in his fourth Test, while Lara was soon trapped on the back foot by Muralitharan's straight one. Some lower-order resistance lifted West Indies to within 17, which grew in significance as Taylor and Collymore worked through Sri Lanka's top order: 15 wickets fell on the long second day. Collymore took the last five next morning, but the target nonetheless looked tricky until Lara's brilliant counter-attack. He cracked Murali's first ball for four for the third innings running, but also survived several close lbw appeals. The last 92 runs came in less than 12 overs after tea, though Sarwan fell one short of victory.

Sri Lanka

M. S. Atapattu c Gayle b Drakes	15	– c Jacobs b Taylor	28
S. T. Jayasuriya c Jacobs b Collymore	26	– lbw b Collymore	13
K. C. Sangakkara lbw b Edwards	75	– c Jacobs b Collymore	12
D. P. M. D. Jayawardene c Gayle b Edwards	10	– c Jacobs b Edwards	32
*H. P. Tillekeratne c Lara b Banks	13	– (6) b Collymore	7
†R. S. Kaluwitharana c Samuels b Banks	10	– (5) b Taylor	23
H. D. P. K. Dharmasena c Samuels b Collymore	6	– c Lara b Collymore	20
W. P. U. J. C. Vaas not out	12	– c Lara b Collymore	21
M. T. T. Mirando c Lara b Edwards	11	– c Lara b Collymore	13
M. Muralitharan b Edwards	0	– c Sarwan b Collymore	6
R. A. P. Nissanka c Gayle b Edwards	0	– not out	0
B 1, l-b 17, w 2, n-b 10	30	B 4, l-b 6, w 2, n-b 7	19
	208		**194**

1/38 (2) 2/48 (1) 3/77 (4) 4/109 (5)   208
5/129 (6) 6/140 (7) 7/192 (3)
8/204 (9) 9/208 (10) 10/208 (11)

1/25 (2) 2/43 (3) 3/80 (1)   194
4/118 (4) 5/118 (5) 6/138 (6)
7/173 (7) 8/176 (8) 9/184 (10) 10/194 (9)

Collymore 15–6–28–2; Taylor 11–1–40–0; Drakes 18–3–54–1; Edwards 15.4–1–36–5; Banks 22–6–31–2; Gayle 4–3–1–0. *Second Innings*—Edwards 15–2–54–1; Collymore 16–2–57–7; Drakes 11–3–29–0; Taylor 10–1–38–2; Banks 2–0–6–0.

West Indies

C. H. Gayle c Sangakkara b Nissanka	31	– lbw b Vaas	0
W. W. Hinds c Kaluwitharana b Nissanka	19	– b Muralitharan	29
R. R. Sarwan b Vaas	31	– c Jayasuriya b Vaas	82
*B. C. Lara lbw b Muralitharan	10	– not out	80
M. N. Samuels c Tillekeratne b Nissanka	14	– not out	0
O. A. C. Banks c Tillekeratne b Nissanka	2		
†R. D. Jacobs lbw b Muralitharan	16		
V. C. Drakes b Muralitharan	30		
J. E. Taylor c Muralitharan b Dharmasena	1		
C. D. Collymore c Sangakkara b Nissanka	13		
F. H. Edwards not out	5		
B 5, l-b 3, w 6, n-b 5	19	B 8, l-b 3, w 4, n-b 6	21
	191	(3 wkts)	**212**

1/54 (1) 2/59 (2) 3/85 (4) 4/107 (3)   191
5/110 (6) 6/123 (5) 7/162 (7)
8/163 (9) 9/175 (8) 10/191 (10)

1/1 (1) 2/50 (2) 3/211 (3)   (3 wkts) 212

Vaas 15–4–33–1; Mirando 10–1–36–0; Nissanka 12.3–0–64–5; Muralitharan 11–3–23–3; Dharmasena 5–0–27–1. *Second Innings*—Vaas 12–2–54–2; Mirando 5–0–23–0; Nissanka 8–1–64–0; Muralitharan 15.4–1–48–1; Dharmasena 2–0–12–0.

Umpires: D. B. Hair *(Australia)* (46) and R. B. Tiffin *(Zimbabwe)* (35).
Third umpire: E. A. Nicholls *(West Indies)*.   Referee: Wasim Raja *(Pakistan)* (11).

Close of play: First day, West Indies 4-0 (Gayle 3, Hinds 1); Second day, Sri Lanka 129-5 (Tillekeratne 2, Dharmasena 9).

AUSTRALIA v BANGLADESH 2003 (1st Test)

At Marrara Cricket Ground, Darwin, on 18, 19, 20 July.
Toss: Australia.   Result: AUSTRALIA won by an innings and 132 runs.
Debuts: none.
Man of the Match: S. R. Waugh.

Australia's first winter Test, played at Darwin in the Northern Territory (the 89th Test venue), was done and dusted in less than half the scheduled playing time. Bangladesh's fate was sealed on the first day when they collapsed for 97 on a drop-in pitch (prepared in Melbourne and airlifted to Darwin a month before the match), which proved to be slow and low. Only Javed Omar was beaten by the bounce, but no-one other than Mohammad Ashraful, who pulled straight to deep square just before lunch for 23, and Khaled Mashud batted for longer than an hour. The Australians also found scoring difficult, at least until Gilchrist joined Waugh and upped the tempo. By then Lehmann had completed Darwin's first Test century; Waugh's own was just over an hour quicker at 177 minutes, and completed his nap hand against all nine possible Test opponents, matching the feat of Gary Kirsten. Bangladesh started their second innings brightly, reaching 89 for the loss of Javed Omar. But, still prone to losing wickets in batches, they collapsed on the third morning as MacGill continued to turn the ball sharply. Alok Kapali completed a pair, and only a sensible innings from Al Sahariar – who was singled out for praise by Waugh after the match, then dropped for the next Test – delayed the inevitable. Finally, he skyed a return catch, and the match was over at 12.41 on the third day (half an hour after lunch, as play up in the Tropics started at 9.30).

Bangladesh

Hannan Sarkar lbw b McGrath	0	– c Gilchrist b Gillespie		35
Javed Omar c Gilchrist b Gillespie	5	– lbw b McGrath		5
Habibul Bashar b Lee	16	– b MacGill		54
Mohammad Ashraful c MacGill b McGrath	23	– c Gilchrist b Lee		7
Al Sahariar b Lee	0	– c and b MacGill		36
Alok Kapali lbw b MacGill	0	– lbw b MacGill		0
†Khaled Mashud lbw b McGrath	11	– c Gilchrist b MacGill		6
*Khaled Mahmud c Gilchrist b MacGill	21	– b Gillespie		5
Mashrafe bin Mortaza c Gilchrist b Gillespie	3	– (10) run out		15
Tapash Baisya not out	2	– (9) lbw b MacGill		4
Manjural Islam c Langer b Lee	1	– not out		0
B 1, l-b 5, w 6, n-b 3	15	L-b 6, w 2, n-b 3		11

1/4 (1) 2/26 (2) 3/36 (3) 4/39 (5)   97   1/8 (2) 2/89 (1) 3/112 (4)   178
5/40 (6) 6/60 (4) 7/87 (7)   4/112 (3) 5/112 (6) 6/122 (7)
8/91 (8) 9/94 (9) 10/97 (11)   7/143 (8) 8/152 (9) 9/171 (10) 10/178 (5)

McGrath 13–6–20–3; Gillespie 8–1–27–2; Lee 8.2–2–23–3; MacGill 13–4–21–2. *Second Innings*—McGrath 10–0–25–1; Gillespie 16–3–48–2; Lee 12–5–34–1; MacGill 13.1–1–65–5.

Australia

J. L. Langer lbw b Alok Kapali	71	B. Lee run out	23
M. L. Hayden b Mashrafe bin Mortaza	11	J. N. Gillespie not out	16
R. T. Ponting c Javed Omar b Tapash Baisya	10	B 5, l-b 8, w 7, n-b 3	23
D. S. Lehmann c Javed Omar b Mashrafe bin Mortaza	110		
*S. R. Waugh not out	100	1/13 (2) 2/43 (3) (7 wkts dec.)	407
M. L. Love b Mashrafe bin Mortaza	0	3/184 (1) 4/243 (4)	
†A. C. Gilchrist b Manjural Islam	43	5/244 (6) 6/313 (7) 7/377 (8)	

S. C. G. MacGill and G. D. McGrath did not bat.

Manjural Islam 24–4–78–1; Mashrafe bin Mortaza 23–7–74–3; Tapash Baisya 21.5–4–69–1; Khaled Mahmud 28–2–98–0; Alok Kapali 18–2–65–1; Mohammad Ashraful 2–0–9–0; Habibul Bashar 1–0–1–0.

Umpires: R. E. Koertzen *(South Africa)* (40) and D. R. Shepherd *(England)* (72).
Third umpire: S. J. A. Taufel *(Australia)*.   Referee: M. J. Procter *(South Africa)* (12).

Close of play: First day, Australia 121-2 (Langer 40, Lehmann 51); Second day, Bangladesh 70-1 (Hannan Sarkar 29, Habibul Bashar 26).

AUSTRALIA v BANGLADESH 2003 (2nd Test)

At Bundaberg Rum Stadium (Cazaly's Oval), Cairns, on 25, 26, 27, 28 July.
Toss: Australia.   Result: AUSTRALIA won by an innings and 98 runs.
Debuts: Bangladesh – Anwar Hossain Monir.
Man of the Match: S. C. G. MacGill.   Man of the Series: S. C. G. MacGill.

Australia predictably swept the short Top End series 2–0. Rain had left question-marks about the pitch at Test cricket's 90th venue, which looked green and enticing for the fast men – but it played better than expected, and Bangladesh's batsmen applied themselves well at first. Hannan Sarkar made a wristy 76 before losing concentration after Mohammad Ashraful departed for the first half of a sorry pair. Khaled Mashud and Sanwar Hossain, whose forthright 46 included eight fours, three in succession off Lee, lifted their side to a competitive 289 for 8 by the close – but that was as good as it got for Bangladesh. They lasted only 13 balls next morning, and although the bowlers started brightly, Australia's batsmen proved tough to shift. Lehmann's 177 – his highest Test score – included 105 between tea and the end of the second day, then Love put a first-ball duck at Darwin behind him and compiled a neat maiden century in what turned out to be his final Test. There was also time for Waugh to stretch his record to a score of 150 or more against all nine opponents, and for Sanwar's jerky offspinning action to be reported to the ICC. Bangladesh began brightly again, but three quick wickets just before the third-day close sealed their fate. Next morning MacGill completed his third successive five-for, while Gillespie finally adjusted his radar, pitched the ball up, and took three wickets in eight balls as Bangladesh subsided to their 20th defeat in 21 Tests.

Bangladesh

Hannan Sarkar lbw b MacGill	76	– c Hayden b MacGill	55
Javed Omar c Gilchrist b Lee	26	– lbw b Gillespie	8
Habibul Bashar c and b MacGill	46	– c Langer b Lee	25
Mohammad Ashraful c Gilchrist b Gillespie	0	– c Ponting b MacGill	0
Sanwar Hossain b MacGill	46	– c Ponting b MacGill	16
Alok Kapali c Love b MacGill	5	– c Langer b MacGill	17
†Khaled Mashud c Love b Gillespie	44	– lbw b Gillespie	14
*Khaled Mahmud lbw b MacGill	0	– c Lee b MacGill	17
Tapash Baisya c Gilchrist b McGrath	25	– lbw b Gillespie	0
Mashrafe bin Mortaza c Lee b Gillespie	8	– not out	3
Anwar Hossain Monir not out	0	– b Gillespie	4
L-b 8, n-b 11	19	L-b 2, n-b 2	4

1/47 (2) 2/155 (3) 3/156 (4) 4/156 (1)   295   1/12 (2) 2/87 (1) 3/90 (4)   163
5/170 (6) 6/230 (5) 7/230 (8)   4/90 (3) 5/123 (6) 6/136 (5)
8/281 (7) 9/295 (10) 10/295 (9)   7/156 (7) 8/156 (9) 9/156 (8) 10/163 (11)

McGrath 17.1–2–57–1; Gillespie 25–7–57–3; Lee 18–1–88–1; MacGill 24–9–77–5; Waugh 5–3–4–0; Lehmann 3–1–4–0. *Second Innings*—McGrath 15–9–22–0; Gillespie 12.4–3–38–4; MacGill 20–3–56–5; Lee 11–2–45–1.

Australia

J. L. Langer c Javed Omar b Mashrafe bin Mortaza	1	M. L. Love not out	100
M. L. Hayden b Sanwar Hossain	50	L-b 11, w 1, n-b 1	13
R. T. Ponting c Mohammad Ashraful b Sanwar Hossain	59		
D. S. Lehmann c Mohammad Ashraful b Tapash Baisya	177	1/14 (1) 2/105 (2) (4 wkts dec.) 556	
*S. R. Waugh not out	156	3/132 (3) 4/382 (4)	

†A. C. Gilchrist, B. Lee, J. N. Gillespie, S. C. G. MacGill and G. D. McGrath did not bat.

Mashrafe bin Mortaza 25–7–60–1; Tapash Baisya 26–5–96–1; Anwar Hossain Monir 21–4–95–0; Khaled Mahmud 19–3–75–0; Sanwar Hossain 30–2–128–2; Alok Kapali 14.2–0–69–0; Mohammad Ashraful 4–0–22–0.

Umpires: R. E. Koertzen *(South Africa)* (41) and D. R. Shepherd *(England)* (73).
Third umpire: S. J. Davis *(Australia)*.   Referee: M. J. Procter *(South Africa)* (13);
R. G. Archer *(Australia)* deputised when Procter flew home after a family bereavement.

Close of play: First day, Bangladesh 289-8 (Tapash Baisya 21, Mashrafe bin Mortaza 7); Second day, Australia 351-3 (Lehmann 156, Waugh 74); Third day, Bangladesh 106-4 (Sanwar Hossain 6, Alok Kapali 10).

ENGLAND v SOUTH AFRICA 2003 (1st Test)

At Edgbaston, Birmingham, on 24, 25 (no play), 26, 27, 28 July.
Toss: South Africa.   Result: MATCH DRAWN.
Debuts: none.
Man of the Match: G. C. Smith.

The dominant figure in a game of three captains was Graeme Smith, who hit 35 fours in his 277. Hussain felt so powerless that he resigned afterwards; Vaughan, having struck his eighth Test hundred in 14 months, was installed as his successor. Smith's innings, spanning 373 balls and 541 minutes, was the highest individual score for his country. He and Gibbs became the second pair to share two triple-century stands in Tests: Bradman and Ponsford managed it twice against England in 1934. And Smith's match aggregate of 362 runs was South Africa's biggest, passing Bruce Mitchell's 309 at The Oval in 1947. Gough, in his first Test for nearly two years, endured a torrid return; it was Vaughan who finally broke through, with a cunning long-hop, just after the previous-best opening partnership against England – 329 by Mark Taylor and Geoff Marsh for Australia at Trent Bridge in 1989 – had been surpassed. South Africa scored so quickly the loss of the second day to rain was not fatal to their hopes. Smith sailed past his second double-century, in his 11th Test, before finally perishing on the leg-side boundary. England avoided the follow-on, but only just, thanks largely to Vaughan. Becalmed on 12 for 62 minutes (41 balls) during a compelling battle with Pollock, he finished with 156 in 415 minutes. There was little urgency in South Africa's second innings, except from Smith – 85 from 70 balls – and England were never likely to attempt a nominal target of 321 from 65 overs.

South Africa

*G. C. Smith c Anderson b Giles	277	– b Giles	85
H. H. Gibbs c Butcher b Vaughan	179	– b Anderson	9
G. Kirsten c Stewart b Giles	44	– c McGrath b Harmison	1
H. H. Dippenaar c Butcher b Gough	22	– not out	28
J. A. Rudolph c Gough b Harmison	10	– st Stewart b Giles	8
†M. V. Boucher not out	15		
S. M. Pollock not out	24		
B 8, l-b 11, n-b 4	23	L-b 2, n-b 1	3

1/338 (2) 2/438 (3) 3/514 (4)   (5 wkts dec.) 594   1/30 (2) 2/32 (3)   (4 wkts dec.) 134
4/552 (5) 5/556 (1)   3/114 (1) 4/134 (5)

R. J. Peterson, D. Pretorius, C. M. Willoughby and M. Ntini did not bat.

Anderson 16–2–92–0; Gough 25–6–88–1; Flintoff 25–6–97–0; Harmison 27–2–104–1; Giles 42–2–153–2; Butcher 2–0–15–0; Vaughan 8–0–26–1. *Second Innings*—Harmison 6–0–34–1; Anderson 10–1–37–1; Giles 8–0–45–2; Flintoff 2–0–16–0.

England

M. E. Trescothick b Ntini	31	– not out	52
M. P. Vaughan c Boucher b Pretorius	156	– c Pollock b Peterson	22
M. A. Butcher lbw b Ntini	13		
*N. Hussain lbw b Pollock	1	– (3) not out	23
A. McGrath c Rudolph b Pretorius	34		
†A. J. Stewart b Pretorius	38		
A. Flintoff lbw b Pretorius	40		
A. F. Giles b Pollock	41		
D. Gough c Rudolph b Ntini	1		
S. J. Harmison b Ntini	0		
J. M. Anderson not out	0		
B 19, l-b 6, w 11, n-b 17	53	B 8, l-b 5	13

1/66 (1) 2/132 (3) 3/133 (4) 4/222 (5)   408   1/72 (2)   (1 wkt) 110
5/306 (2) 6/311 (6) 7/374 (7)
8/398 (9) 9/398 (10) 10/408 (8)

Pollock 27.4–10–51–2; Ntini 28–8–114–4; Willoughby 20–7–46–0; Pretorius 25–2–115–4; Peterson 22–9–57–0. *Second Innings*—Pollock 7–3–6–0; Ntini 4–0–38–0; Peterson 13–3–33–1; Pretorius 10–6–20–0.

Umpires: D. J. Harper *(Australia)* (32) and S. Venkataraghavan *(India)* (67).
Third umpire: J. W. Lloyds *(England)*.   Referee: R. S. Madugalle *(Sri Lanka)* (48).

Close of play: First day, South Africa 398-1 (Smith 178, Kirsten 26); Second day, No play; Third day, England 25-0 (Trescothick 14, Vaughan 4); Fourth day, England 374-7 (Giles 9).

ENGLAND v SOUTH AFRICA 2003 (2nd Test)

At Lord's, London, on 31 July, 1, 2, 3 August.
Toss: South Africa.   Result: SOUTH AFRICA won by an innings and 92 runs.
Debuts: none.
Men of the Match: M. Ntini and G. C. Smith.

Vaughan's "honeymoon period" as England captain lasted only about 65 hours. He was appointed on Monday night, but by Thursday lunchtime England were again in crisis – and this time there was no escape. South Africa bettered their highest total for the second match running, and their captain made 259. Not helped by having to play back-to-back Tests, England were too distracted to combat Smith's relentless, but not infallible, batting. Soon a man being patronised ten days earlier as a young inadequate was being compared to Bradman – indeed he bettered The Don's 73-year-old record 254 by an overseas player in a Lord's Test. England's batting after being put in was gormless. The batsmen nearly all looked set but got out needlessly, the mood typified by Vaughan's top-edged hook on 33. The last pair shared the highest stand of the innings, an oddity last achieved for England 133 Tests earlier, by Phillip DeFreitas and David Lawrence against West Indies in 1991. Smith was badly dropped by Hussain at cover on eight, and that was it: he batted for nine more hours, hitting 34 fours. England batted far better in their second innings: after Butcher and Hussain put on 126, Flintoff smashed 142, with 18 fours and five sixes, the highest by a No. 7 in a Lord's Test, beating Les Ames's 137 against New Zealand in 1931. Ntini was the standout bowler, becoming the first South African to take ten wickets in a Lord's Test. Gough retired from Tests after the match.

England

M. E. Trescothick b Ntini	6	– c Adams b Ntini	23
*M. P. Vaughan c sub (N. D. McKenzie) b Ntini	33	– c Pollock b Hall	29
M. A. Butcher c Hall b Pollock	19	– c Kirsten b Hall	70
N. Hussain b Hall	14	– c Boucher b Ntini	61
A. McGrath c Kirsten b Hall	4	– c Boucher b Pollock	13
†A. J. Stewart c Adams b Ntini	7	– c Hall b Ntini	0
A. Flintoff c Adams b Ntini	11	– st Boucher b Adams	142
A. F. Giles c Pollock b Hall	7	– c Pollock b Ntini	23
D. Gough c Adams b Pollock	34	– c Adams b Pollock	14
S. J. Harmison b Ntini	0	– c Hall b Ntini	7
J. M. Anderson not out	21	– not out	4
B 5, l-b 3, w 1, n-b 3, p 5	17	B 6, l-b 5, w 3, n-b 17	31

1/11 (1) 2/35 (3) 3/73 (4) 4/77 (5)   173   1/52 (2) 2/60 (1) 3/186 (3)   417
5/85 (2) 6/96 (6) 7/109 (8)   4/208 (4) 5/208 (6) 6/208 (5)
8/112 (7) 9/118 (10) 10/173 (9)   7/297 (8) 8/344 (9) 9/371 (10) 10/417 (7)

Pollock 14.4–5–28–2; Ntini 17–3–75–5; Pretorius 4–0–20–0; Hall 10–4–18–3; Adams 3–0–19–0. *Second Innings—* Pollock 29–7–105–2; Ntini 31–5–145–5; Hall 24–6–66–2; Adams 20.1–1–74–1; Pretorius 3–0–16–0.

South Africa

*G. C. Smith b Anderson	259	A. J. Hall not out	6
H. H. Gibbs b Harmison	49		
G. Kirsten b McGrath	108	B 25, l-b 21, w 5, n-b 13	64
H. H. Dippenaar c Butcher b Giles	92		
J. A. Rudolph c Stewart b Flintoff	26	1/133 (2) 2/390 (3)	(6 wkts dec.) 682
†M. V. Boucher b Anderson	68	3/513 (1) 4/580 (5)	
S. M. Pollock not out	10	5/630 (4) 6/672 (6)	

P. R. Adams, D. Pretorius and M. Ntini did not bat.

Gough 28–3–127–0; Anderson 27–6–90–2; Harmison 22–3–103–1; Flintoff 40–10–115–1; Giles 43–5–142–1; Butcher 6–1–19–0; McGrath 11–0–40–1.

Umpires: S. A. Bucknor *(West Indies)* (81) and D. B. Hair *(Australia)* (47).
Third umpire: P. Willey *(England)*.   Referee: R. S. Madugalle *(Sri Lanka)* (49).

Close of play: First day, South Africa 151-1 (Smith 80, Kirsten 9); Second day, South Africa 412-2 (Smith 214, Dippenaar 11); Third day, England 129-2 (Butcher 33, Hussain 36).

ENGLAND v SOUTH AFRICA 2003 (3rd Test)

At Trent Bridge, Nottingham, on 14, 15, 16, 17, 18 August.
Toss: England.   Result: ENGLAND won by 70 runs.
Debuts: England – R. J. Kirtley, E. T. Smith.
Man of the Match: R. J. Kirtley.

Having been roundly outplayed in the opening two Tests, losing a captain in the process, England bounced back to level the series. After Vaughan won an important toss, Butcher was fortunate to survive a convincing lbw appeal from Pollock before he had scored but, applying himself well, he went on to his third century in six Tests: the timing of his driving was remarkable on a pitch showing early signs of treachery. But it was Hussain's cathartic 189-ball hundred that received the more moving ovation from the packed stands. England's satisfaction was compounded when Smith went back to a good-length ball and trod on his stumps for 35 (his series average plummeted to 164). South Africa recovered well from 88 for 4 to restrict the lead to 83, but at 44 for 5 on the fourth morning England were losing, even though the pitch was misbehaving more frequently. However, Hussain again proved his skill on dodgy pitches and a violent cameo from Flintoff helped stretch the advantage to 201. As South Africa began their pursuit the match was delicately and dramatically poised. That soon changed. The debutant James Kirtley gave England the impetus of winners: first Smith tried to work an inswinger to leg, getting more bat on it than umpire Harper suspected when he upheld the lbw appeal, then Rudolph fell quickly. Swinging the ball both ways and bowling the odd shooter, Kirtley wrapped things up next morning, finishing with 6 for 34 and a beaming smile.

England

M. E. Trescothick c Boucher b Hall	24	– c Adams b Pollock	0
*M. P. Vaughan c Gibbs b Pollock	1	– c Boucher b Pollock	5
M. A. Butcher c Boucher b Ntini	106	– b Hall	8
N. Hussain lbw b Pollock	116	– lbw b Pollock	30
E. T. Smith c Boucher b Kallis	64	– lbw b Hall	0
†A. J. Stewart c Smith b Adams	72	– c Boucher b Kallis	5
A. Flintoff c Pollock b Hall	0	– c Gibbs b Pollock	30
A. F. Giles b Hall	22	– c Boucher b Pollock	21
R. J. Kirtley c Smith b Ntini	1	– c Boucher b Ntini	3
S. J. Harmison c Pollock b Adams	14	– not out	2
J. M. Anderson not out	0	– lbw b Pollock	2
B 9, l-b 8, w 4, n-b 4	25	B 4, l-b 5, n-b 3	12

1/7 (2) 2/29 (1) 3/218 (3) 4/322 (4) 445   1/0 (1) 2/17 (2) 3/39 (3) 118
5/334 (5) 6/347 (7) 7/388 (8)   4/39 (5) 5/44 (6) 6/76 (4)
8/408 (9) 9/440 (6) 10/445 (10)   7/91 (7) 8/114 (9) 9/114 (8) 10/118 (11)

Pollock 36–18–65–2; Ntini 33–3–137–2; Hall 24–6–88–3; Kallis 27–7–92–1; Adams 26.3–7–46–2. *Second Innings*—Pollock 17.4–4–39–6; Ntini 13–5–28–1; Kallis 10–2–36–1; Hall 6–2–6–2.

South Africa

*G. C. Smith hit wkt b Flintoff	35	– lbw b Kirtley	5
H. H. Gibbs b Harmison	19	– c Giles b Harmison	28
J. A. Rudolph c Stewart b Kirtley	15	– lbw b Kirtley	0
J. H. Kallis b Anderson	27	– b Anderson	13
H. H. Dippenaar lbw b Kirtley	0	– c Smith b Anderson	1
N. D. McKenzie c Trescothick b Anderson	90	– b Kirtley	11
†M. V. Boucher lbw b Flintoff	48	– c Stewart b Kirtley	52
S. M. Pollock c Kirtley b Anderson	62	– b Flintoff	0
A. J. Hall b Anderson	15	– c Trescothick b Kirtley	0
P. R. Adams b Anderson	13	– c and b Kirtley	15
M. Ntini not out	4	– not out	3
B 4, l-b 19, w 3, n-b 8	34	L-b 2, n-b 1	3

1/56 (2) 2/66 (1) 3/88 (3) 4/88 (5) 362   1/22 (1) 2/28 (3) 3/40 (2) 131
5/132 (4) 6/261 (6) 7/284 (7)   4/41 (5) 5/50 (4) 6/71 (6)
8/309 (9) 9/337 (10) 10/362 (8)   7/80 (8) 8/81 (9) 9/126 (10) 10/131 (7)

Anderson 27.5–4–102–5; Kirtley 31–8–80–2; Flintoff 33–8–91–2; Harmison 17–3–42–1; Giles 10–3–24–0; Vaughan 1–1–0–0. *Second Innings*—Kirtley 16.2–7–34–6; Flintoff 17–4–54–1; Harmison 11–2–24–1; Anderson 12–4–17–2.

Umpires: D. B. Hair *(Australia)* (48) and D. J. Harper *(Australia)* (33).
Third umpire: N. A. Mallender *(England)*.   Referee: R. S. Madugalle *(Sri Lanka)* (50).

Close of play: First day, England 296-3 (Hussain 108, Smith 40); Second day, South Africa 84-2 (Rudolph 11, Kallis 11); Third day, England 0-1 (Vaughan 0); Fourth day, South Africa 63-5 (McKenzie 6, Boucher 9).

ENGLAND v SOUTH AFRICA 2003 (4th Test)

At Headingley, Leeds, on 21, 22, 23, 24, 25 August.
Toss: South Africa.   Result: SOUTH AFRICA won by 191 runs.
Debuts: England – Kabir Ali. South Africa – M. Zondeki.
Man of the Match: G. Kirsten.

At 21 for 4 after choosing to bat, South Africa were in disarray – but somehow regrouped to win. Smith played a nasty swat fourth ball, and Martin Bicknell, playing his third Test ten years (and a record 115 matches) after his second, bowled a metronomic line and length for two early victims. Despite a fifth-wicket stand of 95 it was soon 142 for 7. But Monde Zondeki, on debut with no previous batting form to speak of, made a heroic 59, while Kirsten chiselled his way to an 18th Test century. They equalled South Africa's eighth-wicket record of 150 (set by Neil McKenzie and Shaun Pollock against Sri Lanka at Centurion in 2000-01), as the last three wickets contributed 200 to a healthy 342. Not long afterwards England were motoring at 164 for 1, when the umpires surprisingly offered the rampant batsmen the light – and Trescothick and Butcher marched off. Predictably, when play resumed 30 minutes later, both previously well-set batsmen were soon out. Next day Rudolph took a key maiden Test wicket by deceiving Hussain with his legspin, and the last five wickets added only 68. Kirsten battled hard to boost the narrow lead, but Hall put the match beyond doubt: when the last man was torpedoed by a shooter, he was only the fifth man to be stranded on 99 in Tests, having faced just 87 balls. Kallis completed a crushing victory with classic, fast awayswingers that earned him career-best figures for both an innings and a match.

South Africa

*G. C. Smith c Stewart b Kirtley	2	– lbw b Bicknell	14
H. H. Gibbs c Stewart b Bicknell	0	– lbw b Kirtley	2
G. Kirsten c Bicknell b Ali	130	– lbw b Ali	60
J. H. Kallis c Vaughan b Bicknell	6	– c Stewart b Kirtley	41
N. D. McKenzie c Stewart b Ali	4	– c Bicknell b Flintoff	38
J. A. Rudolph lbw b Ali	55	– c Smith b Anderson	10
†M. V. Boucher c Vaughan b Flintoff	16	– c Stewart b Flintoff	39
A. J. Hall c Smith b Flintoff	0	– not out	99
M. Zondeki c Butcher b Anderson	59	– b Bicknell	7
M. Ntini not out	32	– lbw b Ali	8
D. Pretorius c Stewart b Kirtley	9	– b Kirtley	8
L-b 20, w 2, n-b 7	29	B 7, l-b 24, n-b 8	39

1/2 (1) 2/2 (2) 3/16 (4) 4/21 (5)   342   1/9 (2) 2/31 (1) 3/128 (4)   365
5/116 (6) 6/142 (7) 7/142 (8)   4/139 (3) 5/160 (6) 6/219 (5)
8/292 (9) 9/316 (3) 10/342 (11)   7/232 (7) 8/281 (9) 9/311 (10) 10/365 (11)

Kirtley 29.4–10–74–2; Bicknell 27–11–50–2; Ali 22–3–80–3; Anderson 18–7–63–1; Flintoff 18–5–55–2. *Second Innings*—Kirtley 21.5–7–71–3; Bicknell 22–3–75–2; Flintoff 22–5–63–2; Anderson 16–4–56–1; Ali 14–2–56–2; Vaughan 5–1–13–0.

England

M. E. Trescothick c and b Kallis	59	– c Gibbs b Ntini	4
*M. P. Vaughan b Ntini	15	– c Gibbs b Kallis	21
M. A. Butcher c Boucher b Kallis	77	– c Hall b Kallis	61
N. Hussain c and b Rudolph	42	– lbw b Kallis	6
E. T. Smith c Boucher b Kallis	0	– c Smith b Hall	7
†A. J. Stewart c Hall b Pretorius	15	– c Boucher b Ntini	7
A. Flintoff b Ntini	55	– c Hall b Kallis	50
M. P. Bicknell b Ntini	4	– c Boucher b Kallis	15
Kabir Ali c Boucher b Hall	1	– c Kirsten b Kallis	9
R. J. Kirtley c Boucher b Hall	1	– c Kirsten b Hall	11
J. M. Anderson not out	0	– not out	0
B 2, l-b 17, w 6, n-b 13	38	L-b 9, w 2, n-b 7	18

1/27 (2) 2/169 (1) 3/193 (3) 4/197 (5)   307   1/11 (1) 2/44 (2) 3/62 (4)   209
5/239 (6) 6/261 (4) 7/289 (8)   4/81 (5) 5/95 (6) 6/169 (3)
8/293 (9) 9/307 (10) 10/307 (7)   7/182 (7) 8/189 (8) 9/206 (9) 10/209 (10)

Pretorius 19–1–100–1; Ntini 20.2–4–62–3; Hall 24–3–77–2; Zondeki 1.5–0–10–0; Kallis 20.1–7–38–3; Rudolph 2–1–1–1. *Second Innings*—Ntini 11–2–40–2; Hall 21.4–3–64–2; Pretorius 9–3–27–0; Kallis 17–4–54–6; Zondeki 3–0–15–0.

Umpires: B. F. Bowden *(New Zealand)* (7) and S. J. A. Taufel *(Australia)* (5).
Third umpire: P. Willey *(England)*.   Referee: R. S. Madugalle *(Sri Lanka)* (51).

Close of play: First day, South Africa 260-7 (Kirsten 109, Zondeki 50); Second day, England 197-3 (Hussain 14, Smith 0); Third day, South Africa 164-5 (McKenzie 17, Boucher 2); Fourth day, England 165-5 (Butcher 57, Flintoff 45).

ENGLAND v SOUTH AFRICA 2003 (5th Test)

At Kennington Oval, London, on 4, 5, 6, 7, 8 September.
Toss: South Africa.   Result: ENGLAND won by nine wickets.
Debuts: none.
Man of the Match: M. E. Trescothick.   Men of the Series: A. Flintoff and G. C. Smith.

At the start of the second day, bookies were offering 40/1 against an England win – not quite the 500/1 that tempted Rod Marsh and Dennis Lillee at Headingley in 1981, but an indication of the mountain England went on to climb. Gibbs had sprinted to his tenth Test century with 20 fours and a six: only Flintoff, 18 months earlier in Christchurch, had hit more in boundaries in a Test century. At 362 for 4, a huge score (and victory in the series) beckoned for South Africa. But from then on England produced much the better cricket. On a sublime pitch, 484 simply wasn't enough. Only once before in England, when Arthur Morris and Don Bradman triumphed at Headingley in 1948, had a first-innings total above 450 led to defeat. England stuttered early on – Vaughan became Pollock's 300th Test wicket (at 20.45, cheaper than anyone else) – but then Trescothick crunched his way to a maiden double-century, and Thorpe, returning to Test cricket after a 14-month exile only because Hussain had broken another finger, grafted to his 12th hundred during a stand of 268. Flintoff's power-packed 95 – Harmison contributed only three to their stand of 99 – stretched the lead to 120, and suddenly England could dream of a series-levelling victory. By the end of the fourth day South Africa were effectively 65 for 6 – and next morning England tore home at nearly five an over, allowing Stewart to end his Test career, after a national-record 133 caps, on the winning side.

South Africa

*G. C. Smith run out	18	– lbw b Bicknell	19
H. H. Gibbs b Giles	183	– c Stewart b Anderson	9
G. Kirsten lbw b Giles	90	– c Trescothick b Harmison	29
J. H. Kallis run out	66	– lbw b Harmison	35
N. D. McKenzie c Stewart b Anderson	9	– lbw b Flintoff	38
J. A. Rudolph lbw b Bicknell	0	– b Bicknell	8
†M. V. Boucher c Stewart b Bicknell	8	– c Stewart b Bicknell	25
S. M. Pollock not out	66	– c Thorpe b Harmison	43
A. J. Hall lbw b Flintoff	1	– c Smith b Bicknell	0
P. R. Adams run out	1	– not out	13
M. Ntini b Anderson	11	– c Smith b Harmison	1
B 12, l-b 10, w 4, n-b 5	31	B 1, l-b 7, n-b 1	9

1/63 (1) 2/290 (3) 3/345 (2) 4/362 (5)   484   1/24 (2) 2/34 (1) 3/92 (3)   229
5/365 (6) 6/385 (7) 7/419 (4)   4/93 (4) 5/118 (6) 6/150 (5)
8/421 (9) 9/432 (10) 10/484 (11)   7/193 (7) 8/193 (9) 9/215 (8) 10/229 (11)

Bicknell 20–3–71–2; Anderson 25–6–86–2; Harmison 27–8–73–0; Giles 29–3–102–2; Flintoff 19–4–88–1; Vaughan 5–0–24–0; Butcher 3–0–18–0. *Second Innings*—Bicknell 24–5–84–4; Anderson 10–1–55–1; Harmison 19.2–8–33–4; Giles 10–2–36–0; Flintoff 6–2–13–1.

England

M. E. Trescothick c Rudolph b Ntini	219	– not out	69
*M. P. Vaughan c Gibbs b Pollock	23	– c Boucher b Kallis	13
M. A. Butcher lbw b Hall	32	– not out	20
G. P. Thorpe b Kallis	124		
E. T. Smith lbw b Hall	16		
†A. J. Stewart lbw b Pollock	38		
A. Flintoff b Adams	95		
A. F. Giles c Hall b Kallis	2		
M. P. Bicknell lbw b Pollock	0		
S. J. Harmison not out	6		
J. M. Anderson not out	0		
B 11, l-b 18, w 9, n-b 11	49	L-b 4, n-b 4	8

1/28 (2) 2/78 (3) 3/346 (4)   (9 wkts dec.) 604   1/47 (2)   (1 wkt) 110
4/379 (5) 5/480 (6) 6/489 (1)
7/502 (8) 8/502 (9) 9/601 (7)

Pollock 39–10–111–3; Ntini 31–4–129–1; Hall 35–5–111–2; Kallis 34–5–117–2; Adams 17–2–79–1; Rudolph 6–1–28–0. *Second Innings*—Pollock 6–0–15–0; Ntini 8–0–46–0; Kallis 5.2–0–25–1; Adams 3–0–20–0.

Umpires: S. J. A. Taufel *(Australia)* (6) and S. Venkataraghavan *(India)* (68).
Third umpire: J. W. Lloyds *(England)*.   Referee: R. S. Madugalle *(Sri Lanka)* (52).

Close of play: First day, South Africa 362-4 (Kallis 32); Second day, England 165-2 (Trescothick 64, Thorpe 28); Third day, England 502-7 (Flintoff 10, Bicknell 0); Fourth day, South Africa 185-6 (Boucher 22, Pollock 19).

PAKISTAN v BANGLADESH 2003 (1st Test)

At National Stadium, Karachi, on 20, 21, 22, 23, 24 August.

Toss: Pakistan.   Result: PAKISTAN won by seven wickets.

Debuts: Pakistan – Mohammad Hafeez, Shabbir Ahmed, Umar Gul, Yasir Hameed. Bangladesh – Rajin Saleh.

Man of the Match: Yasir Hameed.

Test cricket returned to Pakistan after a gap of nearly 16 months, but the spectators still stayed away. On each of the five days police and security men outnumbered the spectators. Those who turned up saw cricket which was generally competitive and sometimes riveting. Bangladesh showed remarkable tenacity, initially making 288 after being put in, and the eventual margin of their defeat did not reflect the real picture. At the end of the third day, the underdogs were 105 ahead with seven second-innings wickets in hand: Rashid Latif, Pakistan's captain, admitted it was the worst sleepless night of his career. But Bangladesh's inexperience showed next day. As the lead grew to 193, with five wickets left, an upset was still on the cards, but that soon changed as the last five wickets fell for only 23. Pakistan were left needing 217, which they achieved without fuss. Along the way, Yasir Hameed, one of four Pakistan debutants, wrote his name in the record books by scoring his second century of the match. It was a pivotal performance. In the first innings, Yasir saved Pakistan by scoring 170 – almost half the total. And, by taking his side to the brink of victory with 105 in the second, he joined Lawrence Rowe of West Indies (who hit 214 and 100 not out against New Zealand at Kingston in 1971-72) with two centuries on Test debut. On his first-class debut, on this same ground in 1996-97, Yasir had bagged a pair.

Bangladesh

Hannan Sarkar c Rashid Latif b Shabbir Ahmed	41	– lbw b Mohammad Hafeez	30
Javed Omar b Umar Gul	1	– lbw b Shoaib Akhtar	13
Habibul Bashar c Mohammad Hafeez b Shoaib Akhtar	71	– c Shabbir Ahmed b Danish Kaneria	108
Sanwar Hossain lbw b Shoaib Akhtar	15	– lbw b Shabbir Ahmed	3
Rajin Saleh c Umar Gul b Danish Kaneria	26	– c Rashid Latif b Shabbir Ahmed	60
Alok Kapali c Shabbir Ahmed b Danish Kaneria	46	– b Danish Kaneria	1
†Khaled Mashud lbw b Umar Gul	19	– st Rashid Latif b Danish Kaneria	22
*Khaled Mahmud c Yasir Hameed b Danish Kaneria	14	– lbw b Shabbir Ahmed	0
Tapash Baisya c Taufeeq Umar b Shabbir Ahmed	10	– c Rashid Latif b Shabbir Ahmed	5
Mohammad Rafique c Rashid Latif b Shabbir Ahmed	14	– lbw b Shabbir Ahmed	6
Mashrafe bin Mortaza not out	9	– not out	10
B 3, l-b 5, n-b 14	22	L-b 11, w 1, n-b 4	16

1/9 (2) 2/123 (1) 3/123 (3) 4/146 (4)   **288**   1/19 (2) 2/73 (1) 3/83 (4)   **274**
5/176 (5) 6/231 (6) 7/251 (8)   4/194 (3) 5/195 (6) 6/251 (5)
8/252 (7) 9/273 (9) 10/288 (10)   7/251 (8) 8/254 (7) 9/262 (9) 10/274 (10)

Shoaib Akhtar 18–4–56–2; Umar Gul 20–5–91–2; Shabbir Ahmed 20.3–3–61–3; Danish Kaneria 21–6–58–3; Mohammad Hafeez 7–2–14–0. *Second Innings*—Shoaib Akhtar 25–8–59–1; Umar Gul 19–3–57–0; Danish Kaneria 38–12–85–3; Shabbir Ahmed 18.1–2–48–5; Mohammad Hafeez 14–8–14–1.

Pakistan

Mohammad Hafeez c Javed Omar b Mashrafe bin Mortaza	2	– b Mohammad Rafique	50
Taufeeq Umar c Javed Omar b Mohammad Rafique	38	– c Rajin Saleh b Tapash Baisya	4
Yasir Hameed c Mohammad Rafique b Mashrafe bin Mortaza	170	– b Mohammad Rafique	105
Inzamam-ul-Haq c Rajin Saleh b Tapash Baisya	0	– not out	35
Yousuf Youhana c and b Rajin Saleh	46	– not out	15
Misbah-ul-Haq lbw b Mashrafe bin Mortaza	13		
*†Rashid Latif not out	54		
Shoaib Akhtar b Mohammad Rafique	1		
Shabbir Ahmed c Rajin Saleh b Mohammad Rafique	6		
Danish Kaneria c and b Khaled Mahmud	8		
Umar Gul run out	0		
L-b 4, n-b 4	8	L-b 7, w 1	8

1/5 (1) 2/102 (2) 3/103 (4) 4/234 (5)   **346**   1/10 (2) 2/144 (1)   (3 wkts) **217**
5/270 (3) 6/304 (6) 7/307 (8)   3/170 (3)
8/323 (9) 9/338 (10) 10/346 (11)

Mashrafe bin Mortaza 19–3–68–3; Tapash Baisya 17–6–42–1; Khaled Mahmud 17–2–74–1; Mohammad Rafique 32–9–76–3; Sanwar Hossain 9–0–23–0; Alok Kapali 18–3–50–0; Rajin Saleh 5–0–9–1. *Second Innings*—Mashrafe bin Mortaza 18–4–62–0; Tapash Baisya 11–1–34–1; Khaled Mahmud 6–3–8–0; Mohammad Rafique 26–6–61–2; Alok Kapali 2–0–10–0; Rajin Saleh 2–0–12–0; Sanwar Hossain 5–1–23–0.

Umpires: S. A. Bucknor *(West Indies)* (82) and T. H. Wijewardene *(Sri Lanka)* (3).
Third umpire: Nadeem Ghauri *(Pakistan)*.   Referee: M. J. Procter *(South Africa)* (14).

Close of play: First day, Bangladesh 278-9 (Mohammad Rafique 10, Mashrafe bin Mortaza 4); Second day, Pakistan 301-5 (Misbah-ul-Haq 12, Rashid Latif 27); Third day, Bangladesh 163-3 (Habibul Bashar 82, Rajin Saleh 27); Fourth day, Pakistan 112-1 (Mohammad Hafeez 36, Yasir Hameed 68).

PAKISTAN v BANGLADESH 2003 (2nd Test)

At Arbab Niaz Stadium, Peshawar, on 27, 28, 29, 30 August.
Toss: Bangladesh.   Result: PAKISTAN won by nine wickets.
Debuts: none.
Man of the Match: Shoaib Akhtar.

For the second Test running, Bangladesh dominated long periods, but left empty-handed. They even took their maiden first-innings lead in Tests. In the end it took two devastating spells from Shoaib Akhtar to sink them. Conditions were extreme throughout, with temperatures hovering around 40°C and high humidity. Umpire Tiffin suffered heat exhaustion on the second afternoon and was temporarily replaced by the TV official Asad Rauf. Bangladesh made good use of an ideal batting pitch, threatening their highest total of 400, made in their inaugural Test: thanks to Shoaib, they had to settle for 361. That included a national-record second-wicket partnership of 167 between Habibul Bashar, and Javed Omar, who batted in all for eight hours 13 minutes. Just after lunch on the second day, Bangladesh were 310 for 2. Then lightning struck, in the form of Shoaib, who suddenly found rhythm, extreme pace and reverse swing. He started by bowling Omar with a full-length thunderbolt: 16 balls later, he had taken five wickets for five runs. Bangladesh still earned a handy lead, with Alok Kapali docking the tail by taking his country's first hat-trick, just after tea on the third day. They batted again looking to set a stiff target ... but failed. Shoaib had removed both openers by the fifth over, and next day another two victims gave him ten in a Test for the first time. A target of 163 was not testing enough and Mohammad Hafeez made it look easy with a maiden Test century.

Bangladesh

Hannan Sarkar c Rashid Latif b Umar Gul	6	– c Mohammad Hafeez b Shoaib Akhtar	7
Javed Omar b Shoaib Akhtar	119	– c Rashid Latif b Shoaib Akhtar	0
Habibul Bashar lbw b Shabbir Ahmed	97	– lbw b Umar Gul	28
Mohammad Ashraful c Rashid Latif b Shoaib Akhtar	77	– c Taufeeq Umar b Danish Kaneria	7
Rajin Saleh c Rashid Latif b Danish Kaneria	3	– lbw b Shoaib Akhtar	6
Alok Kapali c Rashid Latif b Shoaib Akhtar	4	– c Rashid Latif b Shabbir Ahmed	16
†Khaled Mashud lbw b Shoaib Akhtar	0	– lbw b Shoaib Akhtar	0
*Khaled Mahmud c Shabbir Ahmed b Shoaib Akhtar	25	– lbw b Danish Kaneria	1
Mohammad Rafiq b Shoaib Akhtar	0	– not out	9
Mashrafe bin Mortaza b Umar Gul	10	– b Umar Gul	14
Alamgir Kabir not out	1	– b Umar Gul	4
B 4, l-b 4, w 1, n-b 10	19	L-b 2, n-b 2	4

1/13 (1) 2/180 (3) 3/310 (2) 4/315 (5)   361   1/7 (2) 2/20 (1) 3/43 (4)   96
5/315 (4) 6/315 (7) 7/320 (6)   4/43 (3) 5/64 (5) 6/64 (7)
8/320 (9) 9/341 (10) 10/361 (8)   7/65 (8) 8/75 (6) 9/90 (10) 10/96 (11)

Shoaib Akhtar 22.5–4–50–6; Umar Gul 27–3–67–2; Shabbir Ahmed 25–7–73–1; Danish Kaneria 41–11–110–1; Shoaib Malik 12–4–27–0; Mohammad Hafeez 10–4–26–0. *Second Innings*—Shoaib Akhtar 12–2–30–4; Shabbir Ahmed 7–2–21–1; Umar Gul 4.5–1–16–3; Danish Kaneria 10–3–27–2.

Pakistan

Mohammad Hafeez c Khaled Mashud b Khaled Mahmud	21	– not out	102
Taufeeq Umar c Khaled Mashud b Mohammad Rafique	75	– c Mashrafe bin Mortaza b Khaled Mahmud	43
Yasir Hameed b Mohammad Rafique	23	– not out	18
Inzamam-ul-Haq lbw b Mohammad Rafique	43		
Yousuf Youhana not out	64		
*†Rashid Latif st Khaled Masud b Mohammad Rafique	40		
Shoaib Malik lbw b Mohammad Rafique	0		
Shoaib Akhtar b Khaled Mahmud	15		
Shabbir Ahmed c Mashrafe bin Mortaza b Alok Kapali	8		
Danish Kaneria lbw b Alok Kapali	0		
Umar Gul lbw b Alok Kapali	0		
L-b 1, n-b 5	6	L-b 1, w 1	2

1/51 (1) 2/84 (3) 3/159 (2) 4/178 (4)   295   1/140 (2)   (1 wkt) 165
5/242 (6) 6/250 (7) 7/265 (8)
8/289 (9) 9/289 (10) 10/295 (11)

Mashrafe bin Mortaza 18–6–48–0; Alamgir Kabir 13–3–61–0; Khaled Mahmud 21–6–42–2; Mohammad Rafique 45–13–118–5; Rajin Saleh 7–2–13–0; Mohammad Ashraful 2–0–9–0; Alok Kapali 2.1–1–3–3. *Second Innings*— Mashrafe bin Mortaza 7–1–26–0; Alamgir Kabir 7.3–1–39–0; Khaled Mahmud 14–5–28–1; Mohammad Rafique 12–2–34–0; Alok Kapali 6–0–30–0; Mohammad Ashraful 1–0–7–0.

Umpires: S. A. Bucknor *(West Indies)* (83) and R. B. Tiffin *(Zimbabwe)* (36).
Third umpire: Asad Rauf *(Pakistan)*.   Referee: M. J. Procter *(South Africa)* (15).

Close of play: First day, Bangladesh 240-2 (Javed Omar 96, Mohammad Ashraful 34); Second day, Pakistan 134-2 (Taufeeq Umar 60, Inzamam-ul-Haq 24); Third day, Bangladesh 52-4 (Rajin Saleh 5, Alok Kapali 4).

PAKISTAN v BANGLADESH 2003 (3rd Test)

At Multan Cricket Stadium on 3, 4, 5, 6 September.

Toss: Bangladesh.   Result: PAKISTAN won by one wicket.

Debuts: Pakistan – Farhan Adil, Salman Butt, Yasir Ali.

Man of the Match: Inzamam-ul-Haq.

Inzamam-ul-Haq played perhaps the innings of his life to save Pakistan from humiliation. On the third afternoon, Bangladesh's first Test win, so desperately longed for during three years of demoralising defeat, was within touching distance. On a well-grassed pitch helping seamers, Pakistan were 132 for 6 – still 129 short of victory. But Inzamam stood firm for 317 minutes to orchestrate only the tenth one-wicket win in Test history: he had been at the crease for two of them. While the 1994-95 victory over Australia came at Karachi, this was in front of Inzamam's home crowd, which showered him in rose petals afterwards. It was cruel for Bangladesh, who dominated from the start. But Hannan Sarkar at second slip dropped Shabbir Ahmed on nought: he went on to help add 41 for the eighth wicket. Later, with 49 needed, the No. 10 Umar Gul narrowly survived a run-out then, in the same over, Mohammad Rafique sportingly chose not to run him out when he was backing up too far. By the time Gul was finally run out they had added 52. Four runs were now needed, but the last batsman was Yasir Ali, 17 and making his first-class debut. But he kept out three balls then tickled a single, before Inzamam flicked the winning boundary. Earlier Bangladesh had batted well then restricted Pakistan to 175, with Khaled Mahmud (previously five Test wickets at 111.60) taking the first four before Rafique took over. But Pakistan fought back, despite two delays for sandstorms.

Bangladesh

Hannan Sarkar c Rashid Latif b Umar Gul	13	– c Rashid Latif b Umar Gul 3
Javed Omar c Younis Khan b Umar Gul	38	– c Inzamam-ul-Haq b Shabbir Ahmed 16
Habibul Bashar c Rashid Latif b Yasir Ali	72	– c Rashid Latif b Umar Gul 3
Mohammad Ashraful lbw b Saqlain Mushtaq	12	– c Salman Butt b Shabbir Ahmed......... 3
Rajin Saleh run out	49	– c Rashid Latif b Umar Gul 42
Alok Kapali b Umar Gul	11	– c Rashid Latif b Yasir Ali 22
†Khaled Mashud c Rashid Latif b Umar Gul	29	– (8) lbw b Shabbir Ahmed 28
*Khaled Mahmud lbw b Shabbir Ahmed	19	– (7) lbw b Shabbir Ahmed 2
Mohammad Rafique b Shabbir Ahmed	11	– lbw b Umar Gul..................... 4
Tapash Baisya lbw b Shabbir Ahmed	0	– not out........................ 14
Manjural Islam not out	0	– c Younis Khan b Saqlain Mushtaq 5
B 4, l-b 10, n-b 13	27	B 5, l-b 2, w 2, n-b 3 12

1/28 (1) 2/102 (2) 3/136 (4) 4/166 (3)   281   1/4 (1) 2/9 (3) 3/23 (4)   154
5/179 (6) 6/241 (5) 7/248 (7)   4/41 (2) 5/77 (7) 6/91 (6)
8/278 (9) 9/278 (10) 10/281 (8)   7/111 (5) 8/127 (9) 9/137 (8) 10/154 (11)

In the second innings Alok Kapali, when 17, retired hurt at 71 and resumed at 77.

Shabbir Ahmed 25.2–3–70–3; Umar Gul 32–7–86–4; Yasir Ali 14–4–43–1; Saqlain Mushtaq 25–5–61–1; Mohammad Hafeez 3–1–7–0. *Second Innings*—Umar Gul 15–2–58–4; Shabbir Ahmed 23–6–68–4; Yasir Ali 6–1–12–1; Saqlain Mushtaq 2.3–0–9–1.

Pakistan

Mohammad Hafeez lbw b Khaled Mahmud	21	– (2) c sub (Mashrafe bin Mortaza) b Manjural Islam 18
Salman Butt c Khaled Mashud b Khaled Mahmud	12	– (1) c sub (Mashrafe bin Mortaza) b Manjural Islam 37
Yasir Hameed b Mohammad Rafique	39	– c sub (Mashrafe bin Mortaza) b Khaled Mahmud 18
Inzamam-ul-Haq c Hannan Sarkar b Khaled Mahmud	10	– not out............................... 138
Younis Khan c Khaled Mashud b Khaled Mahmud	34	– run out 0
Farhan Adil lbw b Mohammad Rafique	25	– c Habibul Bashar b Mohammad Rafique ... 8
*†Rashid Latif c Alok Kapali b Tapash Baisya	5	– lbw b Khaled Mahmud 5
Saqlain Mushtaq b Mohammad Rafique	9	– c Khaled Mashud b Khaled Mahmud...... 11
Shabbir Ahmed lbw b Mohammad Rafique	4	– lbw b Mohammad Rafique 13
Umar Gul b Mohammad Rafique	5	– run out 5
Yasir Ali not out	0	– not out.......................... 1
B 1, l-b 5, n-b 5	11	L-b 4, w 4 8

1/27 (2) 2/36 (1) 3/50 (4) 4/121 (5)   175   1/45 (1) 2/62 (2) 3/78 (3)   (9 wkts) 262
5/135 (3) 6/152 (7) 7/154 (6)   4/81 (5) 5/99 (6) 6/132 (7)
8/166 (9) 9/170 (8) 10/175 (10)   7/164 (8) 8/205 (9) 9/257 (10)

Manjural Islam 13–3–42–0; Tapash Baisya 11–2–54–1; Khaled Mahmud 13–1–37–4; Mohammad Rafiq 17.4–7–36–5. *Second Innings*—Manjural Islam 21–2–64–2; Tapash Baisya 12–0–46–0; Khaled Mahmud 28–9–68–3; Mohammad Rafique 30–6–80–2.

Umpires: E. A. R. de Silva *(Sri Lanka)* (25) and R. B. Tiffin *(Zimbabwe)* (37).
Third umpire: Aleem Dar *(Pakistan)*.   Referee: M. J. Procter *(South Africa)* (16).

Close of play: First day, Bangladesh 248-6 (Khaled Mashud 29, Khaled Mahmud 1); Second day, Bangladesh 77-4 (Rajin Saleh 29, Khaled Mahmud 2); Third day, Pakistan 148-6 (Inzamam-ul-Haq 53, Saqlain Mushtaq 3).

INDIA v NEW ZEALAND 2003-04 (1st Test)

At Sardar Patel Stadium, Motera, Ahmedabad, on 8, 9, 10, 11, 12 October.
Toss: India.   Result: MATCH DRAWN.
Debuts: India – L. Balaji, A. Chopra.
Man of the Match: R. Dravid.

New Zealand inched to safety in the end, despite gifting India the initiative from the start with some peculiar tactics. Despite having no genuinely fast bowlers, they worked on the theory that Indian batsmen struggle against the bouncing ball. The approach was not exactly a success: Dravid grafted to a high-class 222 off 387 balls, while Ganguly added an unbeaten hundred before declaring. New Zealand needed 301 to avoid the follow-on, and were soon in trouble as the lively Zaheer Khan took three quick wickets. Next morning Astle led a fightback with an accomplished hundred, the first by a New Zealander in India since Glenn Turner at Kanpur in 1976-77, but the follow-on was still a real danger, particularly when Oram poked to slip to give Kumble his 350th wicket, in his 77th Test. At that stage 74 were needed with three wickets in hand, but one of those was Vettori, whose crucial 60, in baking temperatures against two of the world's best spinners, made him only the fourth New Zealander (after Richard Hadlee, Chris Cairns and John Bracewell) to complete the Test double of 1,000 runs and 100 wickets. India used up 45 overs in extending their advantage to 369. New Zealand never seriously threatened the target, but earned credit for their never-say-die approach in temperatures topping 40°C, digging in for 107 overs of rugged defiance. McMillan and Vincent, both recalled after being dumped for the series against Sri Lanka, repaid the selectors with matchsaving half-centuries.

India

A. Chopra c and b Vettori	42	– c Styris b Vettori		31
V. Sehwag lbw b Tuffey	29	– c Hart b Oram		17
R. Dravid c Hart b Oram	222	– c Vincent b Wiseman		73
S. R. Tendulkar c Astle b Styris	8	– c Vettori b Wiseman		7
V. V. S. Laxman c Wiseman b Vettori	64	– c Vettori b Wiseman		44
*S. C. Ganguly not out	100	– b Wiseman		25
†P. A. Patel not out	29	– not out		5
B 2, l-b 3, n-b 1	6	B 4, l-b 3		7

1/35 (2) 2/107 (1) 3/134 (4)   (5 wkts dec.) 500   1/20 (2) 2/97 (1)   (6 wkts dec.) 209
4/264 (5) 5/446 (3)   3/118 (4) 4/166 (3)
                                                       5/177 (5) 6/209 (6)

A. Kumble, Harbhajan Singh, L. Balaji and Zaheer Khan did not bat.

Tuffey 31–6–103–1; Oram 33–8–95–1; Styris 26–5–83–1; Vettori 44–9–128–2; McMillan 4–1–6–0; Wiseman 21–0–80–0. *Second Innings*—Tuffey 9–2–18–0; Oram 8–0–39–1; Vettori 16–0–81–1; Wiseman 11.5–0–64–4.

New Zealand

M. H. Richardson b Zaheer Khan	6	– c Chopra b Kumble		21
L. Vincent c Patel b Zaheer Khan	7	– b Kumble		67
*S. P. Fleming b Zaheer Khan	1	– (4) c Laxman b Harbhajan Singh		8
S. B. Styris c Chopra b Harbhajan Singh	34	– (5) lbw b Kumble		0
N. J. Astle st Patel b Harbhajan Singh	103	– (8) not out		51
C. D. McMillan c Chopra b Sehwag	54	– not out		83
J. D. P. Oram c Dravid b Kumble	5	– c Dravid b Harbhajan Singh		7
†R. G. Hart lbw b Balaji	15			
D. L. Vettori c Dravid b Kumble	60			
P. J. Wiseman c Laxman b Zaheer Khan	27			
D. R. Tuffey not out	2	– (3) b Kumble		8
B 4, l-b 18, n-b 4	26	B 4, l-b 11, n-b 12		27

1/11 (1) 2/16 (2) 3/17 (3) 4/108 (4)   340   1/44 (1) 2/68 (3)   (6 wkts) 272
5/199 (6) 6/223 (5) 7/227 (7)   3/85 (4) 4/86 (5)
8/265 (8) 9/332 (10) 10/340 (9)   5/150 (2) 6/169 (7)

Zaheer Khan 23–3–68–4; Balaji 26–7–84–1; Kumble 35.1–11–58–2; Harbhajan Singh 36–8–86–2; Sehwag 8–2–17–1; Tendulkar 3–2–5–0. *Second Innings*—Zaheer Khan 10–1–36–0; Balaji 11–4–21–0; Harbhajan Singh 38–9–65–2; Kumble 39–12–95–4; Tendulkar 7–0–40–0; Sehwag 2–2–0–0.

Umpires: R. E. Koertzen *(South Africa)* (42) and D. R. Shepherd *(England)* (74).
Third umpire: K. Hariharan *(India)*.   Referee: R. S. Madugalle *(Sri Lanka)* (53).

Close of play: First day, India 249-3 (Dravid 110, Laxman 56); Second day, New Zealand 41-3 (Styris 10, Astle 13); Third day, New Zealand 282-8 (Vettori 28, Wiseman 8); Fourth day, New Zealand 48-1 (Vincent 21, Tuffey 0).

INDIA v NEW ZEALAND 2003-04 (2nd Test)

At Punjab C. A. Stadium, Mohali, Chandigarh, on 16, 17, 18, 19, 20 October.
Toss: New Zealand.   Result: MATCH DRAWN.
Debuts: India – Yuvraj Singh.
Man of the Match: D. R. Tuffey.   Man of the Series: V. V. S. Laxman.

In a complete turnaround this time it was India who hung on to save this Test, mainly thanks to Laxman, who followed his first-innings century by batting for most of the final day to ensure the series ended in an honourable draw. New Zealand's bowling hero was Tuffey, who produced by far his best performance away from home: four first-innings wickets, a brilliant run-out, then three quick strikes on the final morning. He had Sehwag and Dravid caught behind, then produced a peach of an offcutter to bowl Tendulkar, reducing India to a shaky 18 for 3. At that stage they were still 188 behind, but then Laxman and Aakash Chopra settled in. Chopra, in only his second Test, hit his second half-century of the match off 159 balls. New Zealand's 630 for 6, their highest total overseas, was studded with four centuries, only the second time they had achieved this in a Test, following Perth in 2001-02 (when Vincent was again one of the quartet). Sehwag also romped to a century before stumps on the third day, at which stage more than 800 runs had been scored for the loss of just seven wickets. The bowlers upped the ante after that, but the batsmen – and the pitch – had the final say. Dravid led India in a Test for the first time because Ganguly needed minor surgery for an abscess on his thigh; his place went to Yuvraj Singh, making his Test debut on his home ground.

New Zealand

M. H. Richardson c Kumble b Harbhajan Singh		145
L. Vincent lbw b Kumble		106
S. B. Styris lbw b Kumble		119
*S. P. Fleming b Tendulkar		30
N. J. Astle c Patel b Harbhajan Singh		18
C. D. McMillan not out		100
†R. G. Hart b Kumble		11
D. L. Vettori not out		48
B 21, l-b 28, w 1, n-b 3		53
		630

1/231 (2) 2/382 (1) 3/433 (4)   (6 wkts dec.)   630
4/447 (3) 5/507 (5) 6/540 (7)

P. J. Wiseman, D. R. Tuffey and I. G. Butler did not bat.

Zaheer Khan 26–8–95–0; Balaji 30–10–78–0; Tendulkar 22–3–55–1; Kumble 66–18–181–3; Harbhajan Singh 48–7–149–2; Sehwag 5.3–1–22–0; Yuvraj Singh 1–0–1–0.

India

A. Chopra c Astle b Tuffey	60	– c Richardson b Wiseman		52
V. Sehwag b Styris	130	– c Fleming b Tuffey		1
*R. Dravid c Hart b Butler	13	– c Fleming b Tuffey		5
S. R. Tendulkar c Richardson b Vettori	55	– b Tuffey		1
V. V. S. Laxman not out	104	– not out		67
Yuvraj Singh c Hart b Tuffey	20	– not out		5
†P. A. Patel c Richardson b Vettori	18			
A. Kumble run out	5			
Harbhajan Singh run out	8			
L. Balaji c Hart b Tuffey	4			
Zaheer Khan c Hart b Tuffey	0			
B 2, l-b 1, w 2, n-b 2	7	L-b 4, w 1		5
	424		(4 wkts)	136

1/164 (1) 2/208 (3) 3/218 (2) 4/330 (4)   424   1/6 (2) 2/12 (3)   (4 wkts) 136
5/364 (6) 6/388 (7) 7/396 (8)   3/18 (4) 4/128 (1)
8/408 (9) 9/424 (10) 10/424 (11)

Tuffey 29–5–80–4; Butler 35–7–116–1; Styris 19–7–40–1; Vettori 56–24–84–2; Wiseman 32–7–95–0; McMillan 1–0–6–0. *Second Innings*—Tuffey 14–4–30–3; Butler 5–1–12–0; Vettori 23–8–40–0; Styris 4–2–4–0; Wiseman 17–6–37–1; McMillan 6–3–9–0.

Umpires: R. E. Koertzen *(South Africa)* (43) and D. R. Shepherd *(England)* (75).
Third umpire: I. Shivram *(India)*.   Referee: R. S. Madugalle *(Sri Lanka)* (54).

Close of play: First day, New Zealand 247-1 (Richardson 102, Styris 7); Second day, New Zealand 536-5 (McMillan 58, Hart 10); Third day, India 203-1 (Sehwag 128, Dravid 9); Fourth day, India 390-6 (Laxman 86, Kumble 1).

AUSTRALIA v ZIMBABWE 2003-04 (1st Test)

At W. A. C. A. Ground, Perth, on 9, 10, 11, 12, 13 October.
Toss: Zimbabwe.   Result: AUSTRALIA won by an innings and 175 runs.
Debuts: none.
Man of the Match: M. L. Hayden.

Matthew Hayden went to work with a sore back. He wore a heavy vest to keep it warm, and hardly indulged in the sweeps that had previously served him so well. Instead he played blissfully, ruthlessly straight. He started after Streak invited Australia to bat ... and bat. Hayden tucked in for 622 minutes, and ended up by breaking Brian Lara's record for the highest Test score, with a monumental 380. He started slowly: 76 by tea on the first day, it took him 210 balls, and just over five hours, to reach 100 – but then he cut loose. His next 50 came in just 35 minutes and 32 balls, and on the way from 200 to 300 he unleashed five enormous sixes. His concentration did not waver until he had passed the revered Australian number of 334, set by Don Bradman and equalled by Mark Taylor. At 335 Gripper fumbled a catch at deep midwicket, allowing Hayden to cruise on towards Lara's 375, which he passed three balls before tea on the second day. In all he batted for 437 balls, and hit 38 fours and 11 sixes as Australia reached their second-highest Test total, behind 758 for 8 at Kingston in 1954-55. Gilchrist's 84-ball hundred was hardly noticed in the excitement. Zimbabwe were then bowled out twice: a crushing victory was only threatened by rainstorms on the fourth afternoon and fifth morning, as a last-wicket partnership of 74 between Streak and the stubborn Price delayed the inevitable.

Australia

J. L. Langer b Ervine	26	†A. C. Gilchrist not out		113
M. L. Hayden c Carlisle b Gripper	380	B 4, l-b 10, w 1, n-b 3		18
R. T. Ponting lbw b Ervine	37			
D. R. Martyn c Wishart b Gripper	53	1/43 (1) 2/102 (3)	(6 wkts dec.)	735
*S. R. Waugh c and b Ervine	78	3/199 (4) 4/406 (5)		
D. S. Lehmann c and b Ervine	30	5/502 (6) 6/735 (2)		

A. J. Bichel, B. Lee, J. N. Gillespie and S. C. G. MacGill did not bat.

Streak 26–6–131–0; Blignaut 28–4–115–0; Ervine 31–4–146–4; Price 36–5–187–0; Gripper 25.3–0–142–2.

Zimbabwe

D. D Ebrahim b Gillespie	29	– b Gillespie	4
T. R. Gripper c Lehmann b Lee	53	– c Gilchrist b Gillespie	0
M. A. Vermeulen c Hayden b MacGill	38	– c Gilchrist b Lee	63
S. V. Carlisle c Hayden b MacGill	2	– c Hayden b Lehmann	35
C. B. Wishart c Gilchrist b Bichel	46	– lbw b Bichel	8
C. N. Evans b Bichel	22	– b Lehmann	5
†T. Taibu lbw b Gillespie	15	– c Gilchrist b Bichel	3
*H. H. Streak b Lee	9	– (9) not out	71
S. M. Ervine c Waugh b Gillespie	6	– (8) b Bichel	53
A. M. Blignaut lbw b Lee	0	– st Gilchrist b Lehmann	22
R. W. Price not out	2	– c Waugh b Bichel	36
L-b 10, w 2, n-b 5	17	B 4, l-b 6, w 5, n-b 6	21

1/61 (1) 2/105 (2) 3/120 (4) 4/131 (3)   239   1/2 (2) 2/11 (1) 3/110 (3)   321
5/199 (5) 6/200 (6) 7/231 (7)   4/112 (4) 5/118 (5) 6/126 (7)
8/231 (8) 9/231 (10) 10/239 (9)   7/126 (6) 8/209 (8) 9/247 (10) 10/321 (11)

Lee 15–4–48–3; Gillespie 25.3–9–52–3; Bichel 21–2–62–2; MacGill 21–4–54–2; Lehmann 2–1–3–0; Waugh 5–1–10–0. *Second Innings*—Lee 35–8–96–1; Gillespie 3–0–6–2; MacGill 3.4–1–10–0; Bichel 28.2–15–63–4; Lehmann 31.2–15–61–3; Martyn 13–5–34–0; Waugh 8–2–26–0; Ponting 5–1–15–0.

Umpires: S. Venkataraghavan *(India)* (69) and P. Willey *(England)* (25).
Third umpire: S. J. Davis *(Australia)*.   Referee: G. R. Viswanath *(India)* (12).

Close of play: First day, Australia 368-3 (Hayden 183, Waugh 61); Second day, Zimbabwe 79-1 (Gripper 37, Vermeulen 9); Third day, Zimbabwe 87-2 (Vermeulen 50, Carlisle 26); Fourth day, Zimbabwe 272-9 (Streak 42, Price 17).

AUSTRALIA v ZIMBABWE 2003-04 (2nd Test)

At Sydney Cricket Ground on 17, 18, 19, 20 October.

Toss: Zimbabwe.   Result: AUSTRALIA won by nine wickets.

Debuts: Australia – B. A. Williams. Zimbabwe – G. M. Ewing.

Man of the Match: R. T. Ponting.   Man of the Series: M. L. Hayden.

This was a more even contest than the First Test, with Australia weakened by the absence of the injured Gillespie, MacGill, Lehmann and, by the end of the second day, Lee. The whole stadium felt eerily vacant, as Sydney demonstrated its ambivalence towards Test cricket in October – Waugh was uncertain whether such an experiment should be repeated. But it was a worthwhile experience for some. Brad Williams, a hearty and brutally fast bowler, made his Test debut at 28, while Hogg and Katich, each armed with left-arm wrist-spin that was almost entirely alien to Zimbabwe's batsmen, played their first Tests on Australian soil. The loss of so many experienced bowlers did not seem much of a problem by lunch on the first day, with Zimbabwe's top three batsmen all gone, but Carlisle was well set. The fielders helpfully reminded him that he had never made a Test century, but he let this spur him on to his first one. Ponting trumped that with his 18th, pulling, driving and cutting with abandon before Price carved out the heart of Australia's middle order with his thoughtful left-arm spin. Katich, though, rattled up his maiden Test half-century to stretch the lead then, although a late developer as a bowler, extracted six second-innings wickets. Ponting and Hayden easily devoured the 172 needed for victory, giving Waugh his ninth clean sweep in 16 series as captain. Zimbabwe might have suffered their 11th consecutive defeat, but nonetheless took some satisfaction from this match

Zimbabwe

D. D Ebrahim b Lee	9	– c Katich b Williams	0
T. R. Gripper c Gilchrist b Bichel	15	– c Hayden b Katich	47
M. A. Vermeulen lbw b Williams	17	– c Waugh b Williams	48
S. V. Carlisle c Ponting b Bichel	118	– c Williams b Katich	5
C. B. Wishart c Gilchrist b Williams	14	– st Gilchrist b Katich	45
†T. Taibu c Gilchrist b Hogg	27	– c Ponting b Katich	35
*H. H. Streak lbw b Hogg	14	– run out	25
G. M. Ewing c Martyn b Lee	2	– c Gilchrist b Hogg	0
A. M. Blignaut not out	38	– c Williams b Katich	44
R. W. Price c Williams b Bichel	20	– lbw b Katich	0
N. B. Mahwire c Gilchrist b Bichel	6	– not out	1
B 4, l-b 12, w 3, n-b 9	28	B 6, l-b 5, w 1, n-b 4	16

1/15 (1) 2/45 (2) 3/47 (3) 4/95 (5)   308   1/0 (1) 2/93 (3) 3/103 (4)   266
5/151 (6) 6/218 (7) 7/222 (8)   4/114 (2) 5/176 (5) 6/212 (7)
8/243 (4) 9/296 (10) 10/308 (11)   7/216 (8) 8/230 (6) 9/244 (10) 10/266 (9)

Lee 23–5–78–2; Williams 23–6–58–2; Bichel 24.2–7–66–4; Hogg 23–8–49–2; Waugh 4–0–7–0; Katich 7–0–25–0; Martyn 3–1–9–0. *Second Innings*—Williams 16–8–56–2; Bichel 19–5–64–0; Hogg 31–9–70–1; Katich 25.5–3–65–6.

Australia

J. L. Langer c Streak b Blignaut	2	– c Taibu b Streak	8
M. L. Hayden c Carlisle b Blignaut	20	– not out	101
R. T. Ponting b Price	169	– not out	53
D. R. Martyn lbw b Price	32		
*S. R. Waugh c Carlisle b Price	61		
S. M. Katich b Price	52		
†A. C. Gilchrist b Streak	20		
G. B. Hogg c Ebrahim b Price	13		
A. J. Bichel c Wishart b Blignaut	5		
B. Lee not out	6		
B. A. Williams c and b Price	7		
L-b 2, w 1, n-b 13	16	B 3, l-b 3, n-b 4	10

1/7 (1) 2/51 (2) 3/148 (4) 4/283 (5)   403   1/21 (1)   (1 wkt) 172
5/306 (3) 6/347 (7) 7/375 (8)
8/384 (6) 9/394 (9) 10/403 (11)

Streak 21–3–83–1; Blignaut 20–2–83–3; Mahwire 10–1–61–0; Price 41.3–6–121–6; Ewing 11–1–53–0. *Second Innings*—Streak 9–1–46–1; Blignaut 4–0–35–0; Price 12.1–0–63–0; Gripper 1–0–2–0; Ewing 3–0–20–0.

Umpires: B. F. Bowden *(New Zealand)* (8) and S. Venkataraghavan *(India)* (70). Third umpire: P. D. Parker *(Australia)*.   Referee: G. R. Viswanath *(India)* (13).

Close of play: First day, Zimbabwe 256-8 (Blignaut 9, Price 7); Second day, Australia 245-3 (Ponting 137, Waugh 43); Third day, Zimbabwe 151-4 (Wishart 32, Taibu 13).

PAKISTAN v SOUTH AFRICA 2003-04 (1st Test)

At Gaddafi Stadium, Lahore, on 17, 18, 19, 20, 21 October.
Toss: South Africa.   Result: PAKISTAN won by eight wickets.
Debuts: Pakistan – Asim Kamal.
Men of the Match: Danish Kaneria and Taufeeq Umar.

South Africa were cruising at 159 for 3 when Kirsten was struck by a Shoaib Akhtar bouncer. After that they were never again in control and Pakistan – missing the injured Inzamam-ul-Haq and with only one player (Yasir Hameed) remaining from their previous Test against Bangladesh six weeks earlier – slowly took charge. Kirsten sustained a broken nose and left eye socket – but amazingly he was batting again on the fourth morning. "The pitches here are too good to go home," he said afterwards. When Pakistan batted Taufeeq Umar had a huge slice of luck on 17, playing Pollock on to his stumps without dislodging the bails (one of three occasions this happened in the match): he continued to his fourth Test century. Asim Kamal, who survived a massive lbw appeal from Nel first ball, edged on to his stumps to become only the third player to make 99 on debut, after Australia's Arthur Chipperfield in 1934 and Robert Christiani of West Indies in 1947-48. With Adams returning Test-best figures, the lead was restricted to 81. On the fourth day, though, Shoaib took three key wickets before injuring his hamstring, then Danish Kaneria – who bowled unchanged for 28.3 overs from the University End – removed Kirsten, caught off a leading edge as he tried to work a wrong'un to leg, starting a collapse in which the last four wickets went down for four in 13 balls. Shoaib was banned from the next Test after being found guilty of abusing Adams while he batted.

South Africa

*G. C. Smith c Asim Kamal b Mohammad Sami	33	– c Taufeeq Umar b Shoaib Akhtar	12
H. H. Gibbs c Taufeeq Umar b Danish Kaneria	27	– c Taufeeq Umar b Shoaib Akhtar	59
G. Kirsten retired hurt	53	– (6) c Yousuf Youhana b Danish Kaneria	46
J. H. Kallis c Moin Khan b Danish Kaneria	29	– c Moin Khan b Shoaib Akhtar	18
H. H. Dippenaar c Imran Farhat b Shoaib Malik	24	– (3) c Yousuf Youhana b Shoaib Akhtar	27
N. D. McKenzie lbw b Shoaib Akhtar	0	– (5) b Danish Kaneria	14
†M. V. Boucher c Imran Farhat b Shoaib Malik	72	– c Imran Farhat b Danish Kaneria	15
S. M. Pollock b Shoaib Malik	28	– b Danish Kaneria	18
P. R. Adams not out	18	– lbw b Danish Kaneria	0
A. Nel lbw b Shoaib Akhtar	0	– b Mushtaq Ahmed	0
M. Ntini c Asim Kamal b Shoaib Malik	8	– not out	0
L-b 5, n-b 23	28	B 1, l-b 11, n-b 20	32

1/52 (1) 2/84 (2) 3/154 (4)   320   1/43 (1) 2/104 (3) 3/108 (2)   241
4/159 (6) 5/229 (5) 6/282 (7)   4/149 (4) 5/149 (5) 6/192 (7)
7/302 (8) 8/307 (10) 9/320 (11)   7/237 (6) 8/238 (9) 9/241 (10) 10/241 (8)

Kirsten retired hurt at 159-3.

Shoaib Akhtar 14–1–62–2; Mohammad Sami 13–2–66–1; Mushtaq Ahmed 18–1–80–0; Danish Kaneria 21–2–65–2; Shoaib Malik 17–4–42–4. *Second Innings*—Shoaib Akhtar 14.3–2–36–4; Mohammad Sami 19.3–0–77–0; Mushtaq Ahmed 8–1–18–1; Shoaib Malik 14–0–52–0; Danish Kaneria 28.3–8–46–5.

Pakistan

Taufeeq Umar c and b Adams	111	– b Adams	63
Imran Farhat b Adams	41	– c Gibbs b Smith	58
Yasir Hameed c Boucher b Pollock	16	– not out	20
*Yousuf Youhana c Boucher b Nel	8		
Asim Kamal b Nel	99		
Shoaib Malik b Adams	47	– (4) not out	8
†Moin Khan lbw b Adams	37		
Shoaib Akhtar st Boucher b Adams	1		
Mohammad Sami b Adams	0		
Mushtaq Ahmed not out	14		
Danish Kaneria c Smith b Adams	0		
B 2, l-b 17, w 2, n-b 6	27	L-b 6, w 5, n-b 4	15

1/109 (2) 2/151 (3) 3/160 (4)   401   1/134 (2) 2/141 (1)   (2 wkts) 164
4/223 (1) 5/322 (6) 6/363 (5) 7/366 (8)
8/366 (9) 9/401 (7) 10/401 (11)

Pollock 22–7–48–1; Ntini 28–4–88–0; Adams 45–11–128–7; Nel 27–5–67–2; Kallis 18–3–37–0; Smith 8–1–14–0. *Second Innings*—Pollock 7–2–21–0; Ntini 6–0–24–0; Nel 5–1–13–0; Kallis 6–1–30–0; Adams 11–1–57–1; Smith 5.1–2–13–1.

Umpires: D. B. Hair *(Australia)* (49) and N. A. Mallender *(England)* (1).
Third umpire: Nadeem Ghauri *(Pakistan)*.   Referee: C. H. Lloyd *(West Indies)* (26).

Close of play: First day, South Africa 320; Second day, Pakistan 275-4 (Asim Kamal 49, Shoaib Malik 27); Third day, South Africa 99-1 (Gibbs 56, Dippenaar 25); Fourth day, Pakistan 137-1 (Taufeeq Umar 61, Yasir Hameed 3).

PAKISTAN v SOUTH AFRICA 2003-04 (2nd Test)

At Iqbal Stadium, Faisalabad, on 24, 25, 26, 27, 28 October.
Toss: South Africa.   Result: MATCH DRAWN.
Debuts: none.
Men of the Match: G. Kirsten and Taufeeq Umar.   Man of the Series: Taufeeq Umar.

Poor fielding cost South Africa the chance of squaring the series. Four catches went down as they pressed for victory on the final afternoon, and one of them proved fatal. Ntini and Pollock had struck with successive deliveries with the second new ball' and were rampant. There was more than an hour left, with the last recognised batsmen at the crease. Twice Shoaib Malik involuntarily fenced Ntini through the slips then, surprised by a lifting ball that cut back sharply, he fended it to fine leg, where Kirsten – whose batting had helped set up this winning position – moved to his right but grassed a waist-high chance. With it went South Africa's hopes of victory. Pakistan themselves briefly had visions of victory on the last afternoon as, after a painfully slow start to the day, their batsmen suddenly realised the pitch was still good. Earlier, after South Africa batted indiscreetly on the first day, Taufeeq Umar and Imran Farhat looked largely untroubled except when a toy kite, fluttering over deepish mid-off, briefly stopped play. Farhat, strong square of the wicket and unafraid to use his feet, completed his maiden hundred in his sixth Test. Ntini and Pollock restricted the lead to 70, but three wickets kept Pakistan on top. On the fourth day, however, Kirsten's dogged-ness – and Pakistan's slow over-rate and defensive fields – gave his side the edge. Kirsten eventually fell the same way as the first innings, cutting to give Taufeeq his sixth catch of the match, a Pakistan record.

South Africa

*G. C. Smith c Inzamam-ul-Haq b Shabbir Ahmed ...	2	– lbw b Shabbir Ahmed		65
H. H. Gibbs lbw b Mushtaq Ahmed	98	– lbw b Danish Kaneria		20
H. H. Dippenaar c Taufeeq Umar b Shabbir Ahmed ...	4	– lbw b Shoaib Malik		21
J. H. Kallis c Taufeeq Umar b Danish Kaneria	10	– (6) lbw b Abdul Razzaq		43
G. Kirsten c Taufeeq Umar b Abdul Razzaq	54	– (4) c Taufeeq Umar b Abdul Razzaq		118
N. D. McKenzie c Mushtaq Ahmed b Shabbir Ahmed ...	27	– (5) c Taufeeq Umar b Danish Kaneria		35
†M. V. Boucher b Abdul Razzaq	27	– b Abdul Razzaq		0
S. M. Pollock run out	16	– not out		30
R. J. Peterson c sub (Misbah-ul-Haq) b Shabbir Ahmed	4	– c Inzamam–ul–Haq b Shabbir Ahmed		17
P. R. Adams c Taufeeq Umar b Danish Kaneria	14	– not out		9
M. Ntini not out	16			
L-b 1, w 1, n-b 4	6	B 1, l-b 7, w 2, n-b 3		13

1/6 (1) 2/20 (3) 3/40 (4) 4/148 (5)   278   1/42 (2) 2/93 (3)   (8 wkts dec.) 371
5/195 (2) 6/212 (6) 7/236 (7)   3/128 (1) 4/213 (5)
8/247 (8) 9/250 (9) 10/278 (10)   5/303 (4) 6/303 (7) 7/325 (6) 8/358 (9)

Shabbir Ahmed 26–8–74–4; Abdul Razzaq 22–4–68–2; Danish Kaneria 33.1–10–68–2; Shoaib Malik 5–0–19–0; Mushtaq Ahmed 13–1–48–1. *Second Innings*—Shabbir Ahmed 34.3–10–70–2; Abdul Razzaq 18–3–70–3; Danish Kaneria 37–6–100–2; Shoaib Malik 26–5–70–1; Mushtaq Ahmed 12–3–53–0.

Pakistan

Taufeeq Umar c Gibbs b Adams	68	– c Smith b Peterson		71
Imran Farhat c Peterson b Pollock	128	– lbw b Kallis		8
Yasir Hameed c Gibbs b Pollock	21	– c Dippenaar b Ntini		17
*Inzamam-ul-Haq lbw b Pollock	23	– lbw b Ntini		60
Asim Kamal c Pollock b Ntini	1	– c Boucher b Adams		38
Shoaib Malik c Smith b Pollock	9	– (7) not out		23
Abdul Razzaq c sub (J. A. Rudolph) b Ntini	37	– (6) b Pollock		10
†Moin Khan c Gibbs b Kallis	18	– not out		9
Mushtaq Ahmed lbw b Pollock	6			
Shabbir Ahmed not out	24			
Danish Kaneria c Smith b Pollock	0			
B 3, l-b 8, w 1, n-b 1	13	B 1, l-b 1, n-b 4		6

1/137 (1) 2/178 (3) 3/248 (4) 4/251 (2)   348   1/18 (2) 2/46 (3)   (6 wkts) 242
5/257 (5) 6/261 (6) 7/293 (8)   3/125 (1) 4/187 (5)
8/309 (9) 9/339 (7) 10/348 (11)   5/209 (4) 6/209 (6)

Pollock 29.2–9–78–6; Ntini 29–9–64–2; Kallis 22–4–57–1; Peterson 8–1–40–0; Adams 25–5–82–1; Smith 3–0–16–0. *Second Innings*—Pollock 22–12–27–1; Ntini 20–7–45–2; Kallis 19–6–51–1; Adams 20–2–75–1; Peterson 15–6–21–1; Smith 2–0–21–0.

Umpires: D. J. Harper *(Australia)* (34) and S. J. A. Taufel *(Australia)* (7).
Third umpire: Asad Rauf *(Pakistan)*.   Referee: C. H. Lloyd *(West Indies)* (27).

Close of play: First day, South Africa 256-9 (Adams 3, Ntini 5); Second day, Pakistan 237-2 (Imran Farhat 123, Inzamam-ul-Haq 16); Third day, South Africa 140-3 (Kirsten 27, McKenzie 0); Fourth day, Pakistan 8-0 (Taufeeq Umar 6, Imran Farhat 1).

BANGLADESH v ENGLAND 2003-04 (1st Test)

At Bangabandhu National Stadium, Dhaka, on 21, 22, 23, 24, 25 October.
Toss: Bangladesh.   Result: ENGLAND won by seven wickets.
Debuts: Bangladesh – Enamul Haque, jun. England – G. J. Batty, R. Clarke.
Man of the Match: S. J. Harmison.

The inaugural Test between Bangladesh and England – the last unplayed fixture between any of the ten full members of ICC – came close to surpassing any of England's embarrassments down the years. With a day to go, Bangladesh (previous Test record P24 L23 D1) had a distinct chance of victory. After the first day was almost entirely washed out (the actual rain only lasted 15 minutes, but it stair-rodded, and the outfield turned to mush), England soon made up for lost time. Harmison mopped up with the new ball, then Trescothick blazed away, while Vaughan hinted at allaying doubts about whether the captaincy was harming his batting. But next morning, sweeping, he played on, and England contrived to collapse from 137 without loss to 295 all out, despite Trescothick's 113. Most of the batsmen struggled against the left-arm spinners, Mohammad Rafique and Enamul Haque (no relation to the player of the same name who had also played for Bangladesh). This Enamul was officially listed as 16; he said on TV he was 17; local sources suggested he was 18 at least. He looked about 12 – and bowled like a mature and confident cricketer. England still hoped to make inroads on the third evening but, after only 3.4 overs, the floodlights failed. Next morning Habibul Bashar and Hannan Sarkar eased Bangladesh into the lead; by the close, they were 153 ahead, their hopes sky-high. But Harmison and Hoggard whipped out the last four wickets in nine overs next morning, then Vaughan led England's victory charge.

Bangladesh

Hannan Sarkar b Hoggard	20	– c Trescothick b Hoggard	59
Javed Omar c Clarke b Harmison	3	– (7) lbw b Hoggard	27
Habibul Bashar c Trescothick b Harmison	2	– c Trescothick b Batty	58
Rajin Saleh c Read b Harmison	11	– (2) c Read b Harmison	8
Alok Kapali b Batty	28	– (4) c Butcher b Harmison	12
Mushfiqur Rahman lbw b Hoggard	34	– (5) not out	46
†Khaled Mashud lbw b Clarke	51	– (6) c Hussain b Giles	7
*Khaled Mahmud lbw b Hoggard	4	– lbw b Harmison	18
Mohammad Rafique b Harmison	32	– c Read b Harmison	1
Mashrafe bin Mortaza b Harmison	11	– c Trescothick b Hoggard	1
Enamul Haque, jun. not out	0	– lbw b Hoggard	0
B 2, l-b 3, n-b 2	7	L-b 10, n-b 3, p 5	18

1/12 (2) 2/24 (3) 3/38 (1) 4/40 (4)   203   1/12 (2) 2/120 (3) 3/140 (4)   255
5/72 (5) 6/132 (6) 7/148 (8)   4/148 (1) 5/176 (6) 6/219 (7)
8/182 (7) 9/198 (9) 10/203 (10)   7/248 (8) 8/254 (9) 9/255 (10) 10/255 (11)

Hoggard 23–6–55–3; Harmison 21.5–9–35–5; Clarke 6–1–18–1; Batty 21–6–43–1; Giles 12–1–47–0. *Second Innings*—Hoggard 27–11–48–4; Harmison 25–8–44–4; Batty 20–2–65–1; Giles 20–4–52–1; Clarke 15–6–31–0.

England

M. E. Trescothick c Khaled Mahmud b Enamul Haque	113	– st Khaled Mashud b Mohammad Rafique	32
*M. P. Vaughan b Mohammad Rafique	48	– not out	81
M. A. Butcher lbw b Mushfiqur Rahman	0	– lbw b Mohammad Rafique	8
N. Hussain c Khaled Mashud b Mushfiqur Rahman	0	– lbw b Mashrafe bin Mortaza	17
G. P. Thorpe c Rajin Saleh b Mashrafe bin Mortaza	64	– not out	18
R. Clarke b Mohammad Rafique	14		
†C. M. W. Read c Khaled Mashud b Enamul Haque	1		
G. J. Batty c Khaled Mashud b Mashrafe bin Mortaza	19		
A. F. Giles c sub (Aftab Ahmed) b Mohammad Rafique	19		
S. J. Harmison lbw b Mashrafe bin Mortaza	0		
M. J. Hoggard not out	6		
L-b 4, w 2, n-b 5	11	B 1, l-b 1, w 1, n-b 5	8

1/137 (2) 2/140 (3) 3/140 (4) 4/175 (1)   295   1/64 (1) 2/86 (3)   (3 wkts) 164
5/224 (6) 6/225 (7) 7/266 (8)   3/128 (4)
8/267 (5) 9/267 (10) 10/295 (9)

Mashrafe bin Mortaza 23–6–41–3; Mushfiqur Rahman 17–6–55–2; Khaled Mahmud 17–7–45–0; Mohammad Rafique 35.3–9–84–3; Enamul Haque 23–8–53–2; Rajin Saleh 2–0–9–0; Alok Kapali 3–1–4–0. *Second Innings*—Mashrafe bin Mortaza 11–2–46–1; Mushfiqur Rahman 3–1–16–0; Khaled Mahmud 3–1–14–0; Mohammad Rafique 13.2–0–57–2; Enamul Haque 7–0–27–0; Rajin Saleh 2–0–2–0.

Umpires: Aleem Dar *(Pakistan)* (1) and E. A. R. de Silva *(Sri Lanka)* (26).
Third umpire: A. F. M. Akhtaruddin *(Bangladesh)*.   Referee: Wasim Raja *(Pakistan)* (12).

Close of play: First day, Bangladesh 24-2 (Hannan Sarkar 18, Rajin Saleh 0); Second day, England 111-0 (Trescothick 77, Vaughan 30); Third day, Bangladesh 12-1 (Hannan Sarkar 4, Habibul Bashar 0); Fourth day, Bangladesh 245-6 (Mushfiqur Rahman 43, Khaled Mahmud 17).

BANGLADESH v ENGLAND 2003-04 (2nd Test)

At M. A. Aziz Stadium, Chittagong, on 29, 30, 31 October, 1 November.
Toss: Bangladesh.   Result: ENGLAND won by 329 runs.
Debuts: England – M. J. Saggers.
Man of the Match: R. L. Johnson.   Man of the Series: M. J. Hoggard.

For six consecutive Tests, coinciding with coach Dav Whatmore's appointment, Bangladesh had displayed slow but steady improvement. Here, though, they were sent scurrying back to the drawing board as England wrapped up a 2–0 clean sweep. It was not the heaviest defeat of Whatmore's brief reign, but it was the most dispiriting. Bangladesh had competed eagerly for seven of the nine days in the series, including the first half of this match, but fell away badly in the end. Johnson, playing only his second Test, buzzed the ball around the Bangladeshis' midriffs and took nine wickets. He was helped by a green and tufty pitch quite unlike any other encountered on tour. It gave ample assistance to the seamers and no end of problems to Bangladesh's brittle batsmen, who mustered only 290 all told. When the openers eased to another century stand, Khaled Mahmud's decision to bowl first looked debatable; but then four wickets tumbled in five overs. However, Hussain dropped anchor for nearly six hours, adding 116 with the inexperienced Clarke, before another collapse. Clarke then grabbed two wickets in two balls as Bangladesh tottered to 93 for 4 by the second-day close. That marked the end of their resistance; the last six wickets folded in 24 overs, four for Johnson and his alarming bounce, and a brace for the debutant Martin Saggers, who later pulled off an astonishing one-handed back-pedalling catch at fine leg. England romped to a lead of 467, then two early run-outs sealed Bangladesh's fate.

England

M. E. Trescothick c Mushfiqur Rahman			
b Khaled Mahmud	60	– (7) not out	1
*M. P. Vaughan c Khaled Mashud			
b Mashrafe bin Mortaza	54	– run out	25
M. A. Butcher b Mohammad Rafique	6	– (1) c Khaled Mashud b Mohammad Rafique	42
N. Hussain c Khaled Mashud b Mashrafe bin Mortaza	76	– (3) c and b Mohammad Rafique	95
G. P. Thorpe b Mashrafe bin Mortaza	0	– (4) lbw b Mohammad Rafique	54
R. Clarke c Hannan Sarkar b Mashrafe bin Mortaza	55	– lbw b Enamul Haque	27
†C. M. W. Read c Rajin Saleh b Enamul Haque	37	– (5) not out	38
A. F. Giles lbw b Mushfiqur Rahman	6		
R. L. Johnson c Khaled Mashud b Mushfiqur Rahman	6		
M. J. Saggers lbw b Mohammad Rafique	1		
M. J. Hoggard not out	0		
B 8, l-b 5, w 7, n-b 5	25	B 4, w 1, n-b 6	11

1/126 (1) 2/133 (3) 3/134 (2) 4/134 (5)   326   1/66 (1) 2/70 (2)   (5 wkts dec.) 293
5/250 (6) 6/313 (7) 7/313 (4)   3/208 (4) 4/231 (3)
8/321 (9) 9/326 (10) 10/326 (8)   5/290 (6)

Mashrafe bin Mortaza 28–11–60–4; Mushfiqur Rahman 18.3–6–50–2; Khaled Mahmud 23–8–46–1; Mohammad Rafique 37–15–63–2; Enamul Haque 23–4–81–1; Alok Kapali 4–0–12–0; Rajin Saleh 2–1–1–0. *Second Innings*—Mashrafe bin Mortaza 4–0–23–0; Mushfiqur Rahman 5–0–41–0; Mohammad Rafique 29–3–106–3; Khaled Mahmud 14–3–64–0; Enamul Haque 14–5–40–1; Rajin Saleh 1–0–15–0.

Bangladesh

Hannan Sarkar lbw b Clarke	28	– c Read b Johnson	4
Javed Omar c Vaughan b Johnson	2	– c Read b Saggers	18
Habibul Bashar c Butcher b Hoggard	18	– run out	21
Rajin Saleh c Read b Johnson	32	– c Read b Clarke	9
Alok Kapali c Butcher b Clarke	0	– (6) c Saggers b Johnson	19
Mushfiqur Rahman c Read b Saggers	28	– (5) run out	6
†Khaled Mashud c sub (P. D. Collingwood) b Johnson	0	– c Read b Johnson	15
*Khaled Mahmud c sub (P. D. Collingwood) b Johnson	15	– c Vaughan b Johnson	33
Mohammad Rafique not out	12	– c Read b Hoggard	0
Mashrafe bin Mortaza b Johnson	1	– absent hurt	
Enamul Haque, jun. c Hoggard b Saggers	9	– (10) not out	1
L-b 1, n-b 6	7	B 4, l-b 5, w 1, n-b 2	12

1/6 (2) 2/44 (3) 3/61 (1)   152   1/5 (1) 2/33 (3) 3/51 (2)   138
4/63 (5) 5/107 (4) 6/110 (7) 7/126 (8)   4/58 (5) 5/70 (4) 6/91 (6) 7/108 (7)
8/138 (6) 9/139 (10) 10/152 (11)   8/126 (9) 9/138 (8)

Hoggard 20–3–64–1; Johnson 21–6–49–5; Clarke 7–4–7–2; Saggers 12.1–3–29–2; Giles 2–1–2–0. *Second Innings*—Hoggard 12–3–37–1; Johnson 12.1–1–44–4; Giles 5–1–11–0; Saggers 7–1–33–1; Clarke 1–0–4–1.

Umpires: Aleem Dar *(Pakistan)* (2) and E. A. R. de Silva *(Sri Lanka)* (27).
Third umpire: Mahbubur Rahman *(Bangladesh)*.   Referee: Wasim Raja *(Pakistan)* (13).

Close of play: First day, England 237-4 (Hussain 47, Clarke 53); Second day, Bangladesh 93-4 (Rajin Saleh 24, Mushfiqur Rahman 16); Third day, England 293-5 (Read 38, Trescothick 1).

ZIMBABWE v WEST INDIES 2003-04 (1st Test)

At Harare Sports Club on 4, 5, 6, 7, 8 November.
Toss: Zimbabwe.   Result: MATCH DRAWN.
Debuts: Zimbabwe – S. Matsikenyeri, V. Sibanda.
Man of the Match: H. H. Streak.

Against all expectations, Zimbabwe dominated an enthralling match to end a run of 11 consecutive defeats, and came heartbreakingly close to their first victory over a senior Test team since June 2001. It took a gallant last-wicket partnership between Jacobs and the inexperienced Edwards to save West Indies from humiliation in their 400th Test: they played out the final 32 minutes and 71 deliveries. Any thoughts of a West Indies victory had ended when a debatable decision against Lara reduced them to 38 for 3. After that only Streak and Price looked threatening until Blignaut suddenly produced an inspired spell. Price followed up with his tenth wicket of the match, but when deteriorating light forced Streak to remove Blignaut, the last pair were able to play out the spinners in the gloaming. On an excellent batting pitch, Zimbabwe had recovered after an indifferent start. Taibu was distraught to fall for 83, but Streak completed a determined maiden century, in his 56th Test, a record at the time. He added 168 with Blignaut, Zimbabwe's best for the eighth wicket. West Indies passed 200 with only three out, but then lost three quick wickets: they finally saved the follow-on with eight wickets down. A freak incident delayed the third day's play. As the pitch was being rolled while the players warmed up, a ball went under the roller, leaving a deep indentation just short of a fast bowler's length to a left-hander. Repairs were carried out and play started 90 minutes late.

Zimbabwe

V. Sibanda c Jacobs b Edwards	18	– c Ganga b Collymore	16
T. R. Gripper c Lara b Taylor	41	– lbw b Drakes	26
M. A. Vermeulen c Hinds b Edwards	8	– c Chanderpaul b Edwards	2
S. V. Carlisle c Lara b Collymore	8	– lbw b Drakes	10
C. B. Wishart c Jacobs b Hinds	47	– b Drakes	34
S. Matsikenyeri c Jacobs b Edwards	57	– not out	46
†T. Taibu b Edwards	83	– b Drakes	21
*H. H. Streak not out	127	– (9) not out	7
A. M. Blignaut c Gayle b Drakes	91	– (8) c Jacobs b Collymore	13
R. W. Price lbw b Edwards	2		
N. B. Mahwire not out	1		
B 1, l-b 5, w 3, n-b 15	24	B 8, l-b 2, w 2, n-b 13	25

1/26 (1) 2/35 (3) 3/58 (4)   (9 wkts dec.) 507   1/21 (1) 2/27 (3)   (7 wkts dec.) 200
4/112 (2) 5/154 (5) 6/233 (6)   3/60 (4) 4/90 (2)
7/314 (7) 8/482 (9) 9/495 (10)   5/107 (5) 6/152 (7) 7/175 (8)

Collymore 29–6–131–1; Edwards 34.3–3–133–5; Hinds 15–6–40–1; Drakes 34–4–85–1; Taylor 9.4–4–32–1; Gayle 19.2–6–38–0; Sarwan 9–0–35–0; Chanderpaul 1–0–7–0; Ganga 1–1–0–0. *Second Innings*—Collymore 15–2–59–2; Edwards 16–5–52–1; Drakes 20–2–67–4; Sarwan 1–0–12–0.

West Indies

C. H. Gayle lbw b Streak	14	– c Taibu b Price	13
W. W. Hinds c Blignaut b Mahwire	79	– c Carlisle b Streak	24
D. Ganga b Mahwire	73	– b Price	16
*B. C. Lara c Mahwire b Price	29	– lbw b Streak	1
R. R. Sarwan lbw b Price	9	– st Taibu b Gripper	39
S. Chanderpaul lbw b Streak	36	– c Sibanda b Price	39
†R. D. Jacobs c Vermeulen b Price	5	– not out	60
V. C. Drakes c Streak b Price	31	– c Taibu b Blignaut	4
J. E. Taylor c Wishart b Price	9	– c Matsikenyeri b Blignaut	3
C. D. Collymore not out	11	– c Vermeulen b Price	1
F. H. Edwards c Matsikenyeri b Price	18	– not out	1
B 7, l-b 7, w 3, n-b 4	21	B 1, l-b 1, w 1, n-b 3	6

1/50 (1) 2/127 (2) 3/179 (4) 4/211 (5)   335   1/37 (2) 2/37 (1)   (9 wkts) 207
5/215 (3) 6/240 (7) 7/290 (6)   3/38 (4) 4/73 (3)
8/294 (8) 9/309 (9) 10/335 (11)   5/103 (5) 6/171 (6) 7/184 (8) 8/194 (9) 9/204 (10)

Blignaut 14–3–68–0; Streak 28–9–74–2; Mahwire 25–7–75–2; Price 37.2–13–73–6; Matsikenyeri 2–0–10–0; Gripper 8–1–21–0. *Second Innings*—Streak 15–7–28–2; Blignaut 14–2–50–2; Price 38–11–88–4; Mahwire 2–0–10–0; Gripper 12–5–23–1; Matsikenyeri 2–0–6–0.

Umpires: B. F. Bowden *(New Zealand)* (9) and S. J. A. Taufel *(Australia)* (8).
Third umpire: K. C. Barbour *(Zimbabwe)*.   Referee: G. R. Viswanath *(India)* (14).

Close of play: First day, Zimbabwe 284-6 (Taibu 75, Streak 16); Second day, West Indies 11-0 (Gayle 6, Hinds 0); Third day, West Indies 241-6 (Chanderpaul 19, Drakes 0); Fourth day, Zimbabwe 94-4 (Wishart 25, Matsikenyeri 1).

ZIMBABWE v WEST INDIES 2003-04 (2nd Test)

At Queens Sports Club, Bulawayo, on 12, 13, 14, 15, 16 November.
Toss: West Indies.   Result: WEST INDIES won by 128 runs.
Debuts: none.
Man of the Match: B. C. Lara.

Lara's fine innings, his 22nd Test century, ultimately proved the difference between the sides in a match notable for abysmal batting on the fourth day, when 18 wickets fell for 205 runs. After an opening burst from Gayle, Lara raced to 50 in 53 balls. On the second day, he seemed deliberately to play the ball straighter, gaining many runs with drives between mid-on and mid-off. Lara overtook Vivian Richards's aggregate of 8,540 to become West Indies' leading Test runscorer, before being caught at second slip. Zimbabwe lost three wickets by the 14th over before Vermeulen – who completed his maiden Test century despite a thigh injury – and Wishart added 154. Gayle then fell lbw first ball in the second innings, presaging the remarkable events of the fourth day on a crumbling pitch: Zimbabwe began it with little hope of victory, but by mid-afternoon faced an attainable target. Streak and Blignaut cut through the West Indian top order: among the victims was Lara, bowled for a single by a wicked inswinging yorker which pierced his high backlift and knocked middle stump out of the ground. But Zimbabwe never looked like chasing 233. With Edwards unfit, Hinds showed how to succeed with simple line and length against batsmen all too ready to make mistakes. Nine wickets tumbled for 75 before Streak (who came in far too low at No. 9) and Mahwire dug in to suggest what might have been, batting 40 minutes into the final day.

West Indies

C. H. Gayle c Taibu b Blignaut	47	– lbw b Streak	0
W. W. Hinds st Taibu b Price	81	– c Carlisle b Price	28
D. Ganga c Matsikenyeri b Price	23	– c Carlisle b Blignaut	8
*B. C. Lara c Wishart b Blignaut	191	– b Streak	1
R. R. Sarwan c Vermeulen b Price	65	– c Wishart b Blignaut	9
S. Chanderpaul c Wishart b Price	15	– lbw b Streak	15
†R. D. Jacobs c Gripper b Streak	1	– c Blignaut b Price	10
O. A. C. Banks lbw b Blignaut	3	– c Vermeulen b Price	16
M. Dillon c Matsikenyeri b Price	19	– not out	27
C. D. Collymore not out	16	– b Price	0
F. H. Edwards c Taibu b Blignaut	0	– b Blignaut	0
B 1, l-b 12, w 2, n-b 5	20	B 5, l-b 3, w 4, n-b 2	14

1/73 (1) 2/146 (3) 3/161 (2) 4/351 (5)   481   1/0 (1) 2/17 (3) 3/21 (4) 4/51 (5)   128
5/389 (6) 6/394 (7) 7/422 (8)   5/51 (2) 6/82 (6) 7/82 (7)
8/449 (4) 9/475 (9) 10/481 (11)   8/127 (8) 9/127 (10) 10/128 (11)

Streak 24–4–87–1; Blignaut 20–4–86–4; Mahwire 15–3–79–0; Price 43–1–199–5; Gripper 5–1–17–0. *Second Innings*—Streak 15–2–39–3; Blignaut 14.4–6–29–3; Price 21–7–36–4; Mahwire 2–0–16–0.

Zimbabwe

V. Sibanda c and b Edwards	2	– c Lara b Dillon	0
T. R. Gripper b Dillon	1	– c Ganga b Banks	8
M. A. Vermeulen b Banks	118	– b Hinds	24
S. V. Carlisle b Edwards	11	– c Jacobs b Banks	9
C. B. Wishart lbw b Collymore	96	– c Jacobs b Hinds	13
S. Matsikenyeri b Collymore	8	– (7) run out	5
†T. Taibu c Gayle b Collymore	27	– (8) lbw b Collymore	1
*H. H. Streak lbw b Dillon	3	– (9) not out	33
A. M. Blignaut lbw b Collymore	31	– (6) lbw b Banks	3
R. W. Price c Ganga b Banks	35	– b Collymore	4
N. B. Mahwire not out	8	– b Dillon	4
B 17, l-b 4, w 1, n-b 15	37		

1/5 (1) 2/10 (2) 3/31 (4) 4/185 (5)   377   1/0 (1) 2/32 (3) 3/33 (2) 4/54 (5)   104
5/201 (6) 6/279 (7) 7/289 (8)   5/56 (4) 6/62 (7) 7/63 (6)
8/302 (3) 9/336 (9) 10/377 (10)   8/67 (8) 9/75 (10) 10/104 (11)

Hinds 6–2–18–0; Edwards 15–3–48–2; Dillon 34–13–57–2; Collymore 24–5–70–4; Banks 41.1–13–106–2; Gayle 6–1–23–0; Sarwan 7–0–34–0. *Second Innings*—Dillon 8–2–17–2; Collymore 15–7–29–2; Hinds 9–2–20–2; Banks 15–2–35–3; Sarwan 2–1–3–0.

Umpires: R. E. Koertzen *(South Africa)* (44) and S. J. A. Taufel *(Australia)* (9).
Third umpire: I. D. Robinson *(Zimbabwe)*.   Referee: G. R. Viswanath *(India)* (15).

Close of play: First day, West Indies 282-3 (Lara 77, Sarwan 46); Second day, Zimbabwe 173-3 (Vermeulen 60, Wishart 86); Third day, West Indies 13-1 (Hinds 5, Ganga 8); Fourth day, Zimbabwe 90-9 (Streak 19, Mahwire 4).

SRI LANKA v ENGLAND 2003-04 (1st Test)

At Galle International Stadium on 2, 3, 4, 5, 6 December.
Toss: Sri Lanka.   Result: MATCH DRAWN.
Debuts: Sri Lanka – K. A. D. M. Fernando. England – P. D. Collingwood.
Man of the Match: M. Muralitharan.

Drawn Tests rarely set the pulse racing: this one nearly induced several coronaries. At tea on the final day, Sri Lanka were three wickets away from their sixth successive victory at Galle, but England's tail launched one of Test cricket's most improbable rearguards. The umpires finally offered the light to the last pair (who had kept out 19 balls) at 5.42pm. The Sri Lankans were devastated. They had enjoyed the best of the game, but the worst of the umpiring; one home estimate made the error count 10-2 against them. England had made the early running with three early wickets, then two strikes from Flintoff made it 239 for 7 after Sangakkara's classy 71. But the tail wagged: Muralitharan made hay with an agricultural run-a-ball 38. Next day England's last eight wickets added only 93 as Murali embarrassed the inexperienced middle order. Sri Lanka slipped to 85 for 5 – only 181 ahead – before Jayawardene shared several useful stands, including 46 with Murali, whose two Keystone Kops innings helped swell the eventual target by 86. Rain curtailed the fourth day, allowing England to start the final morning with all ten wickets intact, but Vaughan edged a leaden-footed drive, then Trescothick and Thorpe fell to inappropriate slogs. The debutant Collingwood frustrated Sri Lanka for nearly three hours after surviving a referred appeal for a close catch. Batty hung around for an hour, and although he spoiled things by heaving across the line, Sri Lanka's bowlers were fading, as was the light.

Sri Lanka

M. S. Atapattu c Read b Flintoff	29	– st Read b Batty		35
S. T. Jayasuriya c Collingwood b Giles	48	– c Trescothick b Giles		17
†K. C. Sangakkara lbw b Johnson	71	– run out		19
D. P. M. D. Jayawardene c Collingwood b Giles	17	– not out		86
*H. P. Tillekeratne c Read b Giles	0	– lbw b Batty		1
T. T. Samaraweera c Read b Flintoff	45	– c Trescothick b Giles		1
U. D. U. Chandana lbw b Flintoff	21	– (8) lbw b Giles		19
H. D. P. K. Dharmasena lbw b Batty	27	– (9) lbw b Hoggard		2
W. P. U. J. C. Vaas not out	22	– (7) c Collingwood b Giles		19
K. A. D. M. Fernando c Collingwood b Batty	4	– c Trescothick b Flintoff		1
M. Muralitharan c Read b Giles	38	– c Collingwood b Batty		13
B 5, l-b 2, w 1, n-b 1	9	B 4, l-b 9		13
	331			**226**

1/76 (2) 2/88 (1) 3/132 (4) 4/132 (5)   331
5/202 (3) 6/238 (6) 7/239 (7)
8/279 (8) 9/291 (10) 10/331 (11)

1/26 (2) 2/72 (3) 3/72 (1)   226
4/78 (5) 5/85 (6) 6/123 (7)
7/163 (8) 8/179 (9) 9/180 (10) 10/226 (11)

Hoggard 20–4–49–0; Johnson 17–5–54–1; Flintoff 23–7–42–3; Collingwood 4–0–12–0; Batty 31–5–98–2; Giles 32.5–9–69–4. *Second Innings*—Hoggard 9–2–33–1; Johnson 7–2–28–0; Flintoff 17–5–32–1; Giles 40–14–63–4; Batty 23.2–7–55–3; Vaughan 1–0–2–0.

England

M. E. Trescothick c Sangakkara b Muralitharan	23	– b Jayasuriya		24
*M. P. Vaughan b Muralitharan	24	– c Tillekeratne b Fernando		8
M. A. Butcher c Sangakkara b Jayasuriya	51	– c Sangakkara b Vaas		54
G. P. Thorpe lbw b Vaas	43	– c Vaas b Muralitharan		10
P. D. Collingwood c Jayasuriya b Muralitharan	1	– c Tillekeratne b Dharmasena		36
A. Flintoff lbw b Muralitharan	1	– c Tillekeratne b Vaas		0
†C. M. W. Read c Tillekeratne b Muralitharan	0	– c Jayawardene b Muralitharan		14
G. J. Batty c Jayasuriya b Dharmasena	14	– b Muralitharan		26
A. F. Giles c Atapattu b Muralitharan	18	– not out		17
R. L. Johnson c Atapattu b Muralitharan	26	– b Muralitharan		3
M. J. Hoggard not out	6	– not out		0
B 12, l-b 8, n-b 8	28	B 10, l-b 1, n-b 7		18
	235	(9 wkts)		**210**

1/56 (1) 2/67 (2) 3/142 (4) 4/143 (5)   235
5/151 (6) 6/155 (7) 7/177 (3)
8/183 (8) 9/208 (9) 10/235 (10)

1/16 (2) 2/62 (1) 3/73 (4)   (9 wkts) 210
4/125 (3) 5/125 (6)
6/148 (7) 7/170 (5) 8/204 (8) 9/208 (10)

Vaas 12–2–25–1; Fernando 3–1–21–0; Dharmasena 24–6–55–1; Muralitharan 31.4–15–46–7; Chandana 13–2–24–0; Jayasuriya 17–2–44–1. *Second Innings*—Vaas 14–4–23–2; Fernando 4–0–29–1; Samaraweera 3–1–9–0; Jayasuriya 21–5–31–1; Muralitharan 37–18–47–4; Chandana 11–2–24–0; Dharmasena 18–8–36–1.

Umpires: D. J. Harper *(Australia)* (35) and S. Venkataraghavan *(India)* (71).
Third umpire: M. G. Silva *(Sri Lanka)*.   Referee: C. H. Lloyd *(West Indies)* (28).

Close of play: First day, Sri Lanka 138-4 (Sangakkara 39, Samaraweera 1); Second day, England 97-2 (Butcher 15, Thorpe 20); Third day, Sri Lanka 99-5 (Jayawardene 14, Vaas 6); Fourth day, England 4-0 (Trescothick 4, Vaughan 0).

SRI LANKA v ENGLAND 2003-04 (2nd Test)

At Asgiriya Stadium, Kandy, on 10, 11, 12, 13, 14 December.
Toss: Sri Lanka.   Result: MATCH DRAWN.
Debuts: none.
Man of the Match: M. P. Vaughan.

England's second successive great escape owed much to Vaughan, who exuded such calmness in compiling his first century as captain that he made it all look too easy. He had gone 15 innings as skipper without adding to his tally of nine centuries, but here evoked memories of Mike Atherton's epic match-saving 185 not out at Johannesburg in 1995-96. England's hopes of victory had ended on the second day, and they were eventually left with four sessions to survive. From the start, a draw had been the limit of England's ambitions. Kirtley buzzed and Flintoff bulldozed with the new ball, and Sri Lanka slid to 206 for 6 before the seventh wicket put on 64 and the ninth 76. Vaughan and Trescothick launched England's reply with panache, but Muralitharan accounted for both before pinning Thorpe with a deliciously disguised doosra. Sri Lanka finished with a potentially decisive lead of 88. Dilshan helped boost the advantage to 367 with a superb century, full of furious cuts and free-flowing drives. An England victory looked fanciful, but with Vaughan playing well Tillekeratne stayed on the defensive: even when Hussain fell fourth ball on the final morning, he persisted with a solitary slip and five men on the boundary. It still took a fine effort by England – Batty and Read saw through the last 87 minutes – to overcome Murali, who finished with 8 for 124 from 96 overs in the match. Butcher was stumped in both innings, the eighth such occurrence in Test cricket.

Sri Lanka

M. S. Atapattu lbw b Kirtley	11	– lbw b Giles	8
S. T. Jayasuriya c Read b Giles	32	– b Kirtley	27
†K. C. Sangakkara run out	34	– c Collingwood b Giles	10
D. P. M. D. Jayawardene c Kirtley b Giles	45	– b Flintoff	52
T. M. Dilshan c Trescothick b Flintoff	63	– st Read b Batty	100
*H. P. Tillekeratne c Butcher b Flintoff	45	– c Thorpe b Giles	20
T. T. Samaraweera lbw b Giles	3	– not out	23
W. P. U. J. C. Vaas lbw b Kirtley	32	– c Vaughan b Kirtley	20
H. D. P. K. Dharmasena lbw b Giles	29	– not out	7
K. A. D. M. Fernando not out	51		
M. Muralitharan b Giles	19		
B 1, l-b 15, n-b 2	18	L-b 6, w 1, n-b 5	12

1/20 (1) 2/76 (3) 3/84 (2)   382   1/33 (1) 2/41 (2)   (7 wkts dec.) 279
4/187 (4) 5/201 (5) 6/206 (7) 7/270 (8)   3/53 (3) 4/206 (5)
8/278 (6) 9/354 (9) 10/382 (11)   5/212 (4) 6/243 (6) 7/272 (8)

Kirtley 33–10–109–2; Flintoff 24–5–60–2; Giles 37.4–7–116–5; Collingwood 9–3–13–0; Batty 18–3–59–0; Vaughan 5–0–9–0. *Second Innings*—Kirtley 17–4–62–2; Flintoff 15–3–40–1; Giles 22–3–101–3; Batty 11–1–47–1; Vaughan 3–0–11–0; Collingwood 3–0–12–0.

England

M. E. Trescothick c Dilshan b Muralitharan	36	– c Jayawardene b Vaas	14
*M. P. Vaughan c Jayawardene b Muralitharan	52	– c Dilshan b Muralitharan	105
M. A. Butcher st Sangakkara b Dharmasena	4	– st Sangakkara b Muralitharan	6
N. Hussain lbw b Vaas	10	– c Sangakkara b Vaas	17
G. P. Thorpe lbw b Muralitharan	57	– c Sangakkara b Muralitharan	41
P. D. Collingwood c Sangakkara b Vaas	28	– c Jayawardene b Dharmasena	24
A. Flintoff b Muralitharan	16	– lbw b Muralitharan	19
†C. M. W. Read lbw b Jayasuriya	0	– not out	18
G. J. Batty c Dilshan b Vaas	38	– not out	25
A. F. Giles c Jayawardene b Vaas	16		
R. J. Kirtley not out	3		
B 16, l-b 10, n-b 8	34	B 5, l-b 6, n-b 5	16

1/89 (1) 2/100 (3) 3/119 (2) 4/119 (4)   294   1/24 (1) 2/50 (3) 3/90 (4)   (7 wkts) 285
5/177 (6) 6/202 (7) 7/205 (8)   4/167 (5) 5/208 (6) 6/233 (7)
8/256 (5) 9/279 (10) 10/294 (9)   7/239 (2)

Vaas 24.2–4–77–4; Fernando 7–0–36–0; Dharmasena 19–3–63–1; Muralitharan 40–18–60–4; Jayasuriya 24–6–32–1. *Second Innings*—Vaas 29–7–59–2; Fernando 7–1–21–0; Dharmasena 26–2–74–1; Muralitharan 56–28–64–4; Jayasuriya 17–2–45–0; Tillekeratne 1–0–1–0; Samaraweera 1–1–0–0; Dilshan 3–1–10–0.

Umpires: Aleem Dar *(Pakistan)* (3) and D. J. Harper *(Australia)* (36).
Third umpire: P. T. Manuel *(Sri Lanka)*.   Referee: C. H. Lloyd *(West Indies)* (29).

Close of play: First day, Sri Lanka 277-7 (Tillekeratne 45, Dharmasena 1); Second day, England 163-4 (Thorpe 20, Collingwood 19); Third day, Sri Lanka 39-1 (Jayasuriya 25, Sangakkara 1); Fourth day, England 89-2 (Vaughan 50, Hussain 17).

SRI LANKA v ENGLAND 2003-04 (3rd Test)

At Sinhalese Sports Club, Colombo, on 18, 19, 20, 21 December.
Toss: England.   Result: SRI LANKA won by an innings and 215 runs.
Debuts: none.
Man of the Match: T. T. Samaraweera.   Man of the Series: M. Muralitharan.

After two energy-sapping escape acts, England played with as much edge as a lump of plasticine, and crashed to their third-heaviest Test defeat. For Sri Lanka it was a delightful surprise. After failing to beat anyone but Bangladesh since March 2002, they pulled off the most crushing win in their history. There was little sign of the eventual rout when England reached 50 in only the ninth over, but then Vaughan nicked a legbreak, and Trescothick, who had crashed 11 fours in a 39-ball half-century, edged the last ball before lunch to slip. Under an hour later England were an eye-watering 139 for 5 on a superb pitch; Flintoff and Batty added 87 before the last five clattered for 39. England's total was quickly put into perspective. Sri Lanka's openers waltzed to 71 in 12 overs, then Jayawardene compiled his tenth Test century, putting on 262 with Samaraweera, who was dropped three times by Trescothick en route to his third, all of them scored at his home club ground. The declaration left England 5½ sessions to survive: they held out for just over two. Trescothick steered Vaas's sixth ball to point, and it was 44 for 3 when Hussain was caught behind, making Muralitharan the first bowler to take 100 wickets on a single Test ground. Thorpe and Batty were stumped off successive balls from Murali, who would have had a hat-trick had Flintoff's inside edge not cannoned off his pad over the head of silly point.

England

M. E. Trescothick c Jayawardene b Muralitharan	70	–	c sub (M. G. Vandort) b Vaas	0
*M. P. Vaughan c Jayawardene b Chandana	18	–	c Jayasuriya b Fernando	14
M. A. Butcher c Sangakkara b Fernando	23	–	b Jayasuriya	37
N. Hussain lbw b Vaas	8	–	c Sangakkara b Muralitharan	11
G. P. Thorpe lbw b Muralitharan	13	–	st Sangakkara b Muralitharan	19
A. Flintoff c and b Muralitharan	77	–	(7) c Sangakkara b Fernando	30
G. J. Batty c Atapattu b Chandana	14	–	(6) st Sangakkara b Muralitharan	0
†C. M. W. Read not out	17	–	lbw b Jayasuriya	0
A. F. Giles run out	10	–	b Fernando	13
R. J. Kirtley lbw b Vaas	1	–	b Muralitharan	12
J. M. Anderson lbw b Vaas	1	–	not out	1
B 4, l-b 8, n-b 1	13		B 2, l-b 8, n-b 1	11

1/78 (2) 2/108 (1) 3/114 (3) 4/135 (4)   265   1/0 (1) 2/22 (2) 3/44 (4)   148
5/139 (5) 6/226 (7) 7/236 (6)   4/82 (5) 5/82 (6) 6/84 (3)
8/258 (9) 9/259 (10) 10/265 (11)   7/84 (8) 8/124 (9) 9/137 (7) 10/148 (10)

Vaas 17–5–64–3; Fernando 12–3–55–1; Samaraweera 4–1–11–0; Chandana 26–7–82–2; Muralitharan 40–21–40–3; Jayasuriya 2–1–1–0. *Second Innings*—Vaas 7–2–25–1; Fernando 12–4–27–3; Chandana 13–7–18–0; Muralitharan 27–9–63–4; Jayasuriya 9–6–5–2.

Sri Lanka

†K. C. Sangakkara c Trescothick b Kirtley	31	M. Muralitharan not out		21
S. T. Jayasuriya c Trescothick b Flintoff	85	C. R. D. Fernando not out		1
T. T. Samaraweera run out	142			
D. P. M. D. Jayawardene		B 7, l-b 16, w 5, n-b 6		34
c sub (P. D. Collingwood) b Flintoff	134			
T. M. Dilshan b Giles	83	1/71 (1) 2/138 (2)	(8 wkts dec.)	628
*H. P. Tillekeratne b Giles	12	3/400 (4) 4/428 (3)		
U. D. U. Chandana c Vaughan b Kirtley	76	5/456 (6) 6/582 (5)		
W. P. U. J. C. Vaas run out	9	7/605 (8) 8/606 (7)		

M. S. Atapattu did not bat.

Kirtley 31–4–131–2; Anderson 24–5–85–0; Flintoff 18–0–47–2; Giles 65–16–190–2; Batty 41–4–137–0; Vaughan 1–0–5–0; Trescothick 2–0–10–0.

Umpires: Aleem Dar *(Pakistan)* (4) and S. A. Bucknor *(West Indies)* (85).
Third umpire: T. H. Wijewardene *(Sri Lanka)*.   Referee: C. H. Lloyd *(West Indies)* (30).

Close of play: First day, England 259-8 (Read 13, Kirtley 1); Second day, Sri Lanka 264-2 (Samaraweera 68, Jayawardene 60); Third day, Sri Lanka 563-5 (Dilshan 72, Chandana 54).

AUSTRALIA v INDIA 2003-04 (1st Test)

At Woolloongabba, Brisbane, on 4, 5, 6, 7, 8 December.
Toss: India.   Result: MATCH DRAWN.
Debuts: Australia – N. W. Bracken.
Man of the Match: S. C. Ganguly.

Rarely do three days of play contain as much drama without a conclusion. Despite the action being limited to 16 overs on the second day and just 38 balls on the third, the cricket was rarely uneventful. India's swing bowlers rocked Australia on the fragmented second day, triggering a sensational collapse – from 262 for 2 to 323 for 9 – but an hour into the fourth the home side seemed set for victory. After a resolute start, India lost three wickets, including Dravid and Tendulkar in the space of four balls from Gillespie, and suddenly the follow-on, a mere 62 away, seemed miles distant. Ganguly's first scoring shot was an edged three, and he swished and missed against Gillespie shortly afterwards . . . but for the next few hours he lorded it with a majesty that seemed to have deserted him in recent years. Ganguly added 65 with the steadfast Chopra, playing his first Test abroad, 146 at more than a run a minute with Laxman, and a further 56 with Patel. On the first morning, Ganguly had put Australia in on a greenish pitch under overcast conditions, but his bowlers let him down. The strokemakers had fun, but it was Langer who ground out a hundred. Less than six overs were possible before lunch on the second day; sensationally, Australia lost three wickets in the last eight balls. Still, 323 looked like a winning score until Ganguly and Laxman made the match safe.

Australia

J. L. Langer lbw b Agarkar	121	– (2) c Patel b Agarkar		0
M. L. Hayden c Laxman b Zaheer Khan	37	– (1) c Sehwag b Harbhajan Singh		99
R. T. Ponting c Patel b Zaheer Khan	54	– c Sehwag b Nehra		50
D. R. Martyn run out	42	– not out		66
*S. R. Waugh hit wkt b Zaheer Khan	0	– not out		56
S. M. Katich c Patel b Zaheer Khan	16			
†A. C. Gilchrist c Laxman b Zaheer Khan	0			
A. J. Bichel c Laxman b Agarkar	11			
J. N. Gillespie run out	8			
N. W. Bracken not out	6			
S. C. G. MacGill c Chopra b Agarkar	1			
B 4, l-b 7, w 2, n-b 14	27	B 4, n-b 9		13

1/73 (2) 2/162 (3) 3/268 (1) 4/275 (4)   323   1/6 (2) 2/146 (3)   (3 wkts dec.) 284
5/275 (5) 6/276 (7) 7/302 (8)   3/156 (1)
8/310 (6) 9/317 (9) 10/323 (11)

Zaheer Khan 23–2–95–5; Nehra 15–4–51–0; Agarkar 25.1–5–90–3; Harbhajan Singh 14–1–68–0; Ganguly 1–0–8–0. *Second Innings*—Zaheer Khan 3–0–15–0; Agarkar 12–3–45–1; Nehra 19–1–89–1; Harbhajan Singh 21–1–101–1; Tendulkar 2–0–9–0; Sehwag 5–1–21–0.

India

A. Chopra c Hayden b Gillespie	36	– c Langer b Bracken		4
V. Sehwag c Hayden b Bracken	45	– c Martyn b Bracken		0
R. Dravid c Hayden b Gillespie	1	– not out		43
S. R. Tendulkar lbw b Gillespie	0			
*S. C. Ganguly c Gillespie b MacGill	144			
V. V. S. Laxman c Katich b MacGill	75	– (4) not out		24
†P. A. Patel c Bichel b Gillespie	37			
A. B. Agarkar c Hayden b Bichel	12			
Harbhajan Singh not out	19			
Zaheer Khan b MacGill	27			
A. Nehra lbw b MacGill	0			
L-b 6, w 1, n-b 6	13	N-b 2		2

1/61 (2) 2/62 (3) 3/62 (4) 4/127 (1)   409   1/4 (2) 2/4 (1)   (2 wkts) 73
5/273 (6) 6/329 (5) 7/362 (8)
8/362 (7) 9/403 (10) 10/409 (11)

Gillespie 31–12–65–4; Bracken 26–5–90–1; Bichel 28–6–130–1; MacGill 26.1–4–86–4; Waugh 7–3–16–0; Katich 2–0–16–0. *Second Innings*—Gillespie 5–1–17–0; Bracken 4–1–12–2; MacGill 4–0–32–0; Bichel 3–0–12–0.

Umpires: S.A. Bucknor *(West Indies)* (84) and R. E. Koertzen *(South Africa)* (45).
Third umpire: P. D. Parker *(Australia)*.   Referee: M. J. Procter *(South Africa)* (17).

Close of play: First day, Australia 262-2 (Langer 115, Martyn 36); Second day, Australia 323-9 (Bracken 6, MacGill 1); Third day, India 11-0 (Chopra 5, Sehwag 5); Fourth day, India 362-6 (Patel 37, Agarkar 12).

AUSTRALIA v INDIA 2003-04 (2nd Test)

At Adelaide Oval on 12, 13, 14, 15, 16 December.
Toss: Australia.   Result: INDIA won by four wickets.
Debuts: India – I. K. Pathan.
Man of the Match: R. Dravid.

After five breathless days it was difficult to decide what was more confounding. Just how had Australia managed to lose after scoring 556? Or how had India managed to win after being 85 for 4 in reply? Only one higher first-innings total in a Test had resulted in defeat, and that 109-year-old record belonged to Australia too (586 against England at Sydney in 1894-95). India's spirit was exemplified by Dravid, who was on the field almost throughout, batting 835 minutes and scoring 305 runs. He was last out in the first innings and there at the end. India had not won in Australia for 23 years, while Australia had not lost a home Test of consequence in five – and they had scored 400 on the first day. Ponting made 176 of those, and extended that to 242, the highest score by anyone on the losing side in a Test. India were soon in trouble, Bichel taking three wickets as 66 for 0 became 85 for 4. But the next wicket was 94 overs away: Laxman and Dravid, who put on 376 in India's famous Kolkata fightback in 2000-01, this time added 303. Only 33 ahead, Australia collapsed dramatically: Agarkar's swing accounted for Langer and Ponting, then every top-order batsman fell trying aggressive strokes on a pitch that had slowed down. India were left 230 in 100 overs. There was a hiccough when the fourth wicket fell at 170, but Dravid sealed victory by cutting MacGill to the cover boundary.

Australia

J. L. Langer c Sehwag b Kumble	58	– lbw b Agarkar	10
M. L. Hayden c Patel b Pathan	12	– c Sehwag b Nehra	17
R. T. Ponting c Dravid b Kumble	242	– c Chopra b Agarkar	0
D. R. Martyn c Laxman b Nehra	30	– c Dravid b Tendulkar	38
*S. R. Waugh b Nehra	30	– c Dravid b Tendulkar	42
S. M. Katich c Sehwag b Agarkar	75	– c Nehra b Agarkar	31
†A. C. Gilchrist c Sehwag b Agarkar	29	– b Kumble	43
A. J. Bichel c Chopra b Kumble	19	– b Agarkar	1
J. N. Gillespie not out	48	– c Patel b Agarkar	3
B. A. Williams b Kumble	0	– not out	4
S. C. G. MacGill lbw b Kumble	0	– b Agarkar	1
B 1, l-b 7, w 1, n-b 4	13	B 2, l-b 2, w 1, n-b 1	6

1/22 (2) 2/135 (1) 3/200 (4) 4/252 (5)   556   1/10 (1) 2/18 (3) 3/44 (2)   196
5/390 (6) 6/426 (7) 7/473 (8)   4/109 (4) 5/112 (5) 6/183 (7)
8/556 (3) 9/556 (10) 10/556 (11)   7/184 (8) 8/188 (6) 9/192 (9) 10/196 (11)

Agarkar 26–1–119–2; Pathan 27–3–136–1; Nehra 25–3–115–2; Kumble 43–3–154–5; Sehwag 5–0–21–0; Tendulkar 1–0–3–0. *Second Innings*—Agarkar 16.2–2–41–6; Pathan 7–0–24–0; Nehra 7–2–21–1; Kumble 17–2–58–1; Tendulkar 6–0–36–2; Sehwag 3–0–12–0.

India

A. Chopra c and b Bichel	27	– lbw b Gillespie	20
V. Sehwag c Hayden b Bichel	47	– st Gilchrist b MacGill	47
R. Dravid c Bichel b Gillespie	233	– not out	72
S. R. Tendulkar c Gilchrist b Bichel	1	– lbw b MacGill	37
*S. C. Ganguly run out	2	– c Katich b Bichel	12
V. V. S. Laxman c Gilchrist b Bichel	148	– c Bichel b Katich	32
†P. A. Patel c Ponting b Katich	31	– b Katich	3
A. B. Agarkar c MacGill b Katich	11	– not out	0
A. Kumble lbw b MacGill	12		
I. K. Pathan c and b MacGill	1		
A. Nehra not out	0		
B 4, l-b 2, w 2, n-b 2	10	B 3, l-b 6, w 1	10

1/66 (1) 2/81 (2) 3/83 (4) 4/85 (5)   523   1/48 (1) 2/79 (2)   (6 wkts) 233
5/388 (6) 6/447 (7) 7/469 (8)   3/149 (4) 4/170 (5)
8/510 (9) 9/518 (10) 10/523 (3)   5/221 (6) 6/229 (7)

Gillespie 40.5–13–106–1; Williams 23–7–72–0; Bichel 28–3–118–4; MacGill 44–8–143–2; Katich 16–3–59–2; Waugh 9–2–15–0; Ponting 1–0–4–0. *Second Innings*—Gillespie 10.2–2–22–1; Williams 14–6–34–0; MacGill 24.4–3–101–2; Bichel 11.4–1–35–1; Katich 8–1–22–2; Waugh 4–0–10–0.

Umpires: R. E. Koertzen *(South Africa)* (46) and D. R. Shepherd *(England)* (76).
Third umpire: S. J. Davis *(Australia)*.   Referee: M. J. Procter *(South Africa)* (18).

Close of play: First day, Australia 400-5 (Ponting 176, Gilchrist 9); Second day, India 180-4 (Dravid 43, Laxman 55); Third day, India 477-7 (Dravid 199, Kumble 1); Fourth day, India 37-0 (Chopra 10, Sehwag 25).

AUSTRALIA v INDIA 2003-04 (3rd Test)

At Melbourne Cricket Ground on 26, 27, 28, 29, 30 December.
Toss: India.   Result: AUSTRALIA won by nine wickets.
Debuts: none.
Man of the Match: R. T. Ponting.

At 329 for 4 after a rollicking Boxing Day, India were poised to press home the advantage seized at Adelaide, but their abject batting on the second morning – the last six fell for 16 – was an affront to Sehwag, who had given them a stunning start, and cleared the way for a spectacular rally by the Australians. Sehwag had enthralled a first-day crowd of 62,613 – a record for India in Australia – with his bold strokeplay, which produced 25 fours and five sixes. His stand of 141 with Chopra was India's first century opening partnership outside the subcontinent for nearly ten years. But India collapsed next morning, then Hayden and Ponting added 234 for the second wicket. Ponting extended his 20th Test century to 257, his third double (all in 2003, equalling Don Bradman's 1930 record) and his second in successive Tests, something achieved only seven times before (three times by Bradman, twice by Wally Hammond, and once by Vinod Kambli and Graeme Smith). Ponting batted for ten minutes shy of ten hours to take the match away from India. Dravid lasted 332 minutes for 92, while Ganguly selflessly promoted himself ahead of Tendulkar (out first ball in the first innings) and compiled a neat 73. But the tail's meek capitulation undid this good work, and Australia needed only 95. Fittingly, Ponting had the last word, sweeping the winning four to take his total for 2003 to 1,503 Test runs, a calendar-year total exceeded only by Viv Richards and Sunil Gavaskar.

India

A. Chopra c Katich b MacGill	48	– c Gilchrist b Bracken	4
V. Sehwag c Bracken b Katich	195	– c Williams b Lee	11
R. Dravid c Martyn b Waugh	49	– c Gilchrist b Lee	92
S. R. Tendulkar c Gilchrist b Lee	0	– (5) c Gilchrist b Williams	44
*S. C. Ganguly c Langer b Lee	37	– (4) b Bracken	73
V. V. S. Laxman c Hayden b MacGill	19	– c Hayden b MacGill	18
†P. A. Patel c Gilchrist b Bracken	0	– not out	27
A. B. Agarkar run out	0	– b Williams	1
A. Kumble c Langer b Williams	3	– lbw b Williams	0
Zaheer Khan not out	0	– c Hayden b Williams	1
A. Nehra c Gilchrist b MacGill	0	– c Hayden b MacGill	0
L-b 3, w 1, n-b 11	15	B 4, l-b 3, w 1, n-b 7	15

1/141 (1) 2/278 (3) 3/286 (4) 4/311 (2) 366   1/5 (1) 2/19 (2) 3/126 (5) 286
5/350 (5) 6/353 (7) 7/353 (8) 4/160 (6) 5/253 (3) 6/258 (4)
8/366 (9) 9/366 (6) 10/366 (11) 7/271 (8) 8/271 (9) 9/277 (10) 10/286 (11)

In the second innings Ganguly, when 16, retired hurt at 39 and resumed at 160.

Lee 27–7–103–2; Bracken 28–6–71–1; Williams 20–6–66–1; MacGill 15–3–70–3; Katich 4–0–18–1; Waugh 9–0–35–1. *Second Innings*—Lee 22–3–97–2; Bracken 25–13–45–2; Williams 22–5–53–4; MacGill 26.5–5–68–2; Katich 4–0–16–0.

Australia

J. L. Langer c Tendulkar b Agarkar	14	– lbw b Agarkar	2
M. L. Hayden lbw b Kumble	136	– not out	53
R. T. Ponting st Patel b Kumble	257	– not out	31
†A. C. Gilchrist c Nehra b Kumble	14		
D. R. Martyn c Patel b Agarkar	31		
*S. R. Waugh lbw b Kumble	19		
S. M. Katich c Chopra b Kumble	29		
B. Lee c Laxman b Kumble	8		
N. W. Bracken c and b Tendulkar	1		
B. A. Williams not out	10		
S. C. G. MacGill lbw b Agarkar	0		
B 4, l-b 8, w 5, n-b 17, p 5	39	B 4, l-b 2, w 1, n-b 4	11

1/30 (1) 2/264 (2) 3/295 (4) 4/373 (5) 558   1/9 (1) (1 wkt) 97
5/437 (7) 6/502 (6) 7/535 (8)
8/542 (9) 9/555 (3) 10/558 (11)

In the first innings Waugh, when 0, retired hurt at 373-4 and resumed at 437.

Agarkar 33.2–5–115–3; Zaheer Khan 25–4–103–0; Nehra 29–3–90–0; Kumble 51–8–176–6; Tendulkar 13–0–57–1. *Second Innings*—Agarkar 7–2–25–1; Nehra 6–3–16–0; Kumble 6.2–0–43–0; Sehwag 3–0–7–0.

Umpires: B. F. Bowden *(New Zealand)* (10) and D. R. Shepherd *(England)* (77).
Third umpire: R. L. Parry *(Australia)*.   Referee: M. J. Procter *(South Africa)* (19).

Close of play: First day, India 329-4 (Ganguly 20, Laxman 6); Second day, Australia 317-3 (Ponting 120, Martyn 7); Third day, India 27-2 (Dravid 6, Ganguly 6); Fourth day, India 286.

AUSTRALIA v INDIA 2003-04 (4th Test)

At Sydney Cricket Ground on 2, 3, 4, 5, 6 January.
Toss: India.   Result: MATCH DRAWN.
Debuts: none.
Man of the Match: S. R. Tendulkar.   Man of the Series: R. Dravid.

Much of the cricket in this game became a sideshow as Australia bade farewell to Steve Waugh, playing his 168th and final Test. The hullaballoo surrounding his departure helped attract an overall crowd of 181,063, one surpassed at Sydney only by the 1946-47 Ashes Test, which lasted six days. On the field, though, the script was torn up: India batted Australia out of the game and ensured they would retain the Border-Gavaskar Trophy. Ganguly did his bit by winning the toss, Sehwag spanked a feisty 72, then the previously out-of-sorts Tendulkar took over. He cut out the cover-drive and waited for the chance to hit to leg: he did this for 613 minutes, collecting 188 of his runs – and 28 of his 33 fours – on the leg side. He was the fourth man to reach 9,000 Test runs, two days ahead of Brian Lara at Cape Town, and put on 353, an Indian fourth-wicket record, with Laxman. Ganguly batted on, and on, into the third day, finally closing at India's highest Test total. At 214 for 1, Australia looked safe, but Kumble varied his pace and was rewarded with eight wickets. Ganguly decided not to enforce the follow-on, and the lead was stretched to 442 before Kumble set to work again. At 196 for 4 there was some danger of an Aussie defeat – but Waugh stymied that, hitting 15 fours in an innings recalling his best years. By the time he was caught at deep square, attempting a six, Australia were safe.

India

A. Chopra b Lee	45	– c Martyn b Gillespie		2
V. Sehwag c Gilchrist b Gillespie	72	– c Gillespie b MacGill		47
R. Dravid lbw b Gillespie	38	– not out		91
S. R. Tendulkar not out	241	– not out		60
V. V. S. Laxman b Gillespie	178			
*S. C. Ganguly b Lee	16			
†P. A. Patel c Gilchrist b Lee	62			
A. B. Agarkar b Lee	2			
I. K. Pathan not out	13			
B 4, l-b 5, w 4, n-b 25	38	L-b 3, w 1, n-b 7		11

1/123 (2) 2/128 (1) 3/194 (3)   (7 wkts dec.) 705   1/11 (1) 2/73 (2)   (2 wkts dec.) 211
4/547 (5) 5/570 (6)
6/671 (7) 7/678 (8)

A. Kumble and M. Kartik did not bat.

Lee 39.3–5–201–4; Gillespie 45–11–135–3; Bracken 37–13–97–0; MacGill 38–5–146–0; Waugh 2–0–6–0; Katich 17–1–84–0; Martyn 9–1–27–0. *Second Innings*—Lee 12.2–2–75–0; Gillespie 7–2–32–1; MacGill 16–1–65–1; Bracken 8–0–36–0.

Australia

J. L. Langer c Patel b Kumble	117	– c Sehwag b Kartik		47
M. L. Hayden b Ganguly b Kumble	67	– c Dravid b Kumble		30
R. T. Ponting lbw b Kumble	25	– c and b Pathan		47
D. R. Martyn c and b Kumble	7	– c sub (Yuvraj Singh) b Kumble		40
*S. R. Waugh c Patel b Pathan	40	– c Tendulkar b Kumble		80
S. M. Katich c Sehwag b Kumble	125	– not out		77
†A. C. Gilchrist b Pathan	6	– st Patel b Kumble		4
B. Lee c Chopra b Kumble	0			
J. N. Gillespie st Patel b Kumble	47	– (8) not out		4
N. W. Bracken c Agarkar b Kumble	2			
S. C. G. MacGill not out	0			
B 6, l-b 9, w 3, n-b 20	38	B 6, l-b 7, w 2, n-b 13		28

1/147 (2) 2/214 (1) 3/229 (3) 4/261 (4)   474   1/75 (2) 2/92 (1)   (6 wkts) 357
5/311 (5) 6/341 (7) 7/350 (8)   3/170 (4) 4/196 (3)
8/467 (6) 9/473 (9) 10/474 (10)   5/338 (5) 6/342 (7)

Agarkar 25–3–116–0; Pathan 26–3–80–2; Kumble 46.5–7–141–8; Kartik 19–1–122–0; Ganguly 1–1–0–0. *Second Innings*—Agarkar 10–2–45–0; Kumble 42–8–138–4; Pathan 8–1–26–1; Kartik 26–5–89–1; Tendulkar 6–0–36–0; Sehwag 2–0–10–0.

Umpires: B. F. Bowden *(New Zealand)* (11) and S. A. Bucknor *(West Indies)* (86).
Third umpire: P. D. Parker *(Australia)*.   Referee: M. J. Procter *(South Africa)* (20).

Close of play: First day, India 284-3 (Tendulkar 73, Laxman 29); Second day, India 650-5 (Tendulkar 220, Patel 45); Third day, Australia 342-6 (Katich 51, Lee 0); Fourth day, Australia 10-0 (Langer 4, Hayden 1).

SOUTH AFRICA v WEST INDIES 2003-04 (1st Test)

At The Wanderers, Johannesburg, on 12, 13, 14, 15, 16 December.
Toss: South Africa.   Result: SOUTH AFRICA won by 189 runs.
Debuts: none.
Man of the Match: M. Ntini.

In spite of Lara's sixth Test double-century (the second in a losing cause), South Africa completed victory 20 minutes before tea on the last day. Smith and Gibbs set them on the way with an opening stand of 149, then Kallis put on 132 with van Jaarsveld, playing only because Gary Kirsten was attending the birth of his son. West Indies did take the last seven wickets for 189, despite losing Gayle with a torn hamstring (he needed a runner in both innings). Lara started hesitantly, offering a low chance to Pollock at first slip off Ntini when 15, but gradually found his customary timing and placement. His century was West Indies' first in South Africa, and his fusillade of two straight sixes and four fours in the third day's penultimate over, from Peterson, broke the New Zealander Craig McMillan's record for the most runs in a Test over. South Africa's lead was 151 and, although Gibbs broke his nose when an edged hook off Drakes burst through his grille, Smith eventually declared 377 ahead with 100 overs left. Ntini took three quick wickets, and Pollock followed up by removing Sarwan and Lara within the first seven overs next morning to make it 43 for 5. Chanderpaul abandoned his usual defence, stroking 13 fours to score 74 from 91 balls before perishing at long leg. Gayle thumped six fours in eight balls from Nel before the ninth had him taken at slip, and soon South Africa were home and dry.

South Africa

*G. C. Smith	c Lara b Edwards	132	– c sub (D. R. Smith) b Drakes		44
H. H. Gibbs	b Collymore	60	– retired hurt		6
J. A. Rudolph	c Lara b Drakes	2	– c Sarwan b Hinds		44
J. H. Kallis	b Dillon	158	– lbw b Hinds		44
M. van Jaarsveld	lbw b Dillon	73	– (6) run out		15
N. D. McKenzie	c Jacobs b Edwards	8	– (8) not out		9
†M. V. Boucher	c Ganga b Collymore	27	– (5) st Jacobs b Sarwan		18
S. M. Pollock	c Jacobs b Hinds	30	– (7) b Collymore		10
R. J. Peterson	c Jacobs b Hinds	25	– not out		18
A. Nel	b Hinds	0			
M. Ntini	not out	22			
	B 4, l-b 7, w 4, n-b 9	24	B 2, l-b 3, w 6, n-b 7		18

1/149 (2) 2/160 (3) 3/240 (1) 4/372 (5)   561   1/72 (1) 2/145 (4)   (6 wkts dec.) 226
5/398 (6) 6/456 (7) 7/510 (4)   3/158 (3) 4/180 (5)
8/520 (8) 9/520 (10) 10/561 (9)   5/188 (6) 6/206 (7)

In the second innings Gibbs retired hurt at 42.

Edwards 27–3–102–2; Dillon 36–7–96–2; Collymore 26–2–118–2; Drakes 29–5–92–1; Ganga 4–0–26–0; Sarwan 9–0–37–0; Hinds 17.4–3–79–3. *Second Innings*—Edwards 13–0–60–0; Dillon 10–0–26–0; Drakes 10–2–21–1; Collymore 9–3–19–1; Sarwan 10–0–40–1; Hinds 11–0–55–2.

West Indies

W. W. Hinds	c Peterson b Nel	10	– b Ntini		0
D. Ganga	c Peterson b Ntini	60	– lbw b Ntini		10
R. R. Sarwan	c Boucher b Pollock	21	– (4) lbw b Pollock		8
*B. C. Lara	c van Jaarsveld b Nel	202	– (5) b Pollock		5
S. Chanderpaul	b Ntini	34	– (6) c Nel b Pollock		74
†R. D. Jacobs	c Boucher b Ntini	4	– (7) b Nel		25
V. C. Drakes	lbw b Kallis	21	– (3) b Ntini		6
M. Dillon	b Ntini	13	– (9) b Ntini		7
C. H. Gayle	c Kallis b Ntini	8	– (8) c Boucher b Nel		26
F. H. Edwards	c McKenzie b Nel	0	– (11) not out		0
C. D. Collymore	not out	1	– (10) lbw b Pollock		0
	B 12, l-b 15, w 4, n-b 5	36	B 10, l-b 6, n-b 11		27

1/43 (1) 2/94 (3) 3/141 (2) 4/266 (5)   410   1/5 (1) 2/18 (3) 3/25 (2)   188
5/278 (6) 6/314 (7) 7/380 (8)   4/41 (4) 5/43 (5) 6/141 (7)
8/405 (9) 9/409 (4) 10/410 (10)   7/168 (6) 8/176 (8) 9/188 (9) 10/188 (10)

Pollock 30–7–65–1; Ntini 32–9–94–5; Nel 32.5–11–78–3; Kallis 22–6–53–1; Peterson 13–2–76–0; Smith 4–0–17–0. *Second Innings*—Pollock 17–6–31–4; Ntini 14–4–53–4; Nel 13–3–49–2; Kallis 4–0–21–0; Peterson 3–0–18–0.

Umpires: D. B. Hair *(Australia)* (50) and S. J. A. Taufel *(Australia)* (10).
Third umpire: B. G. Jerling *(South Africa)*.   Referee: R. S. Madugalle *(Sri Lanka)* (55).

Close of play: First day, South Africa 368-3 (Kallis 87, van Jaarsveld 69); Second day, West Indies 87-1 (Ganga 49, Sarwan 20); Third day, West Indies 363-6 (Lara 178, Dillon 6); Fourth day, West Indies 31-3 (Sarwan 6, Lara 0).

SOUTH AFRICA v WEST INDIES 2003-04 (2nd Test)

At Kingsmead, Durban, on 26, 27, 28, 29 December.
Toss: South Africa. Result: SOUTH AFRICA won by an innings and 65 runs.
Debuts: none.
Man of the Match: J. H. Kallis.

Lara's first disappointment in his 100th Test was losing the toss on a drizzly, overcast opening day which required floodlights throughout. The grassy pitch did not provide quite the movement expected at first, but it was still 57 for 5 by lunch. As the pitch and weather improved, there was no way back. West Indies were further undermined by their atrocious fielding, missing six chances, including two off Kirsten and one off Kallis, who both made centuries. Lara again found himself mounting a rearguard action after the pacemen swept aside the top order, all to catches off the outside edge. He and Jacobs checked the collapse by adding 98, then Drakes prolonged the innings with an entertaining maiden Test fifty. The match slipped away from West Indies while Kirsten and Kallis – who both hit 20 fours – were overturning their country's 74-year-old fourth-wicket record, the 214 of Herbie Taylor and "Nummy" Deane at The Oval in 1929, before Kirsten top-edged a sweep just after becoming the first South African to 7,000 Test runs. West Indies were facing a massive defeat at 130 for 5 when Sarwan was joined by Chanderpaul, who was unable to bat until No. 7 as he had been off the field with a strained leg muscle. They mounted an exciting but ultimately irrelevant counterattack, adding 113 in 35 overs – but West Indies still went down by an innings with more than a day to spare. It was their seventh defeat in seven Tests in South Africa.

West Indies

W. W. Hinds c Boucher b Pollock	0	– b Nel	11
D. Ganga c Pollock b Ntini	6	– lbw b Pollock	12
R. R. Sarwan c Kallis b Pollock	4	– b Ntini	114
*B. C. Lara c Pollock b Ntini	72	– c McKenzie b Hall	11
S. Chanderpaul c Hall b Ntini	0	– (7) c McKenzie b Ntini	109
C. S. Baugh c Kallis b Nel	21	– (5) c Ntini b Kallis	2
†R. D. Jacobs lbw b Nel	58	– (6) c Kirsten b Rudolph	15
V. C. Drakes c Boucher b Nel	67	– c Rudolph b Nel	4
M. Dillon b Ntini	6	– c Gibbs b Nel	0
A. Sanford c Hall b Ntini	15	– not out	18
F. H. Edwards not out	1	– c Boucher b Ntini	5
L-b 6, n-b 8	14	L-b 16, w 1, n-b 11	28
	264		**329**

1/0 (1) 2/4 (3) 3/15 (2) 4/17 (5)   264   1/31 (1) 2/32 (2) 3/78 (4)   329
5/50 (6) 6/148 (7) 7/172 (4)   4/95 (5) 5/130 (6) 6/243 (3)
8/191 (9) 9/261 (8) 10/264 (10)   7/271 (8) 8/271 (9) 9/317 (7) 10/329 (11)

Pollock 23–3–59–2; Ntini 25.5–8–66–5; Hall 10–2–51–0; Nel 13–4–43–3; Kallis 4–0–30–0; Rudolph 2–0–9–0. *Second Innings*—Pollock 22–9–42–1; Ntini 26–8–72–3; Nel 18–3–68–3; Hall 13–3–20–1; Kallis 11–3–20–1; Rudolph 23–3–91–1.

South Africa

*G. C. Smith c Sarwan b Edwards	14	A. J. Hall c sub (D. R. Smith) b Sarwan	32
H. H. Gibbs b Sanford	142	M. Ntini c Lara b Sanford	0
J. A. Rudolph c Ganga b Sanford	36	B 1, l-b 8, w 6, n-b 23	38
J. H. Kallis c Sarwan b Dillon	177		
G. Kirsten c Drakes b Sarwan	137	(9 wkts dec.)	**658**
N. D. McKenzie c Jacobs b Drakes	32	1/38 (1) 2/99 (3)	
†M. V. Boucher lbw b Drakes	12	3/267 (2) 4/516 (5)	
S. M. Pollock not out	38	5/562 (4) 6/572 (6)	
		7/599 (7) 8/649 (9) 9/658 (10)	

A. Nel did not bat.

Dillon 33–5–111–1; Edwards 25–1–115–1; Sanford 38.2–4–170–3; Sarwan 21–2–65–2; Drakes 30–3–113–2; Hinds 13–2–50–0; Ganga 6–1–25–0.

Umpires: D. B. Hair *(Australia)* (51) and S. J. A. Taufel *(Australia)* (11).
Third umpire: I. L. Howell *(South Africa)*.   Referee: R. S. Madugalle *(Sri Lanka)* (56).

Close of play: First day, West Indies 232-8 (Drakes 40, Sanford 13); Second day, South Africa 303-3 (Kallis 74, Kirsten 16); Third day, West Indies 18-0 (Hinds 7, Ganga 4).

SOUTH AFRICA v WEST INDIES 2003-04 (3rd Test)

At Newlands, Cape Town, on 2, 3, 4, 5, 6 January.
Toss: South Africa.   Result: MATCH DRAWN.
Debuts: West Indies – D. Mohammed, D. R. Smith.
Man of the Match: J. H. Kallis.

The pitch yielded 1,648 runs for only 28 wickets, and there were seven individual hundreds, only the third instance in Test cricket (the first since 1954-55). Gayle's came from only 79 balls – the ninth-fastest recorded in Tests – while Kallis thumped five sixes in his third century in successive matches as South Africa sped towards a declaration. Yet none was more spectacular than Dwayne Smith's run-a-ball 105 on debut, which not only ensured West Indies avoided their eighth defeat in eight Tests in South Africa, but briefly raised the possibility of an incredible victory. Smith, 20, was playing only because Chanderpaul had a leg strain. Another beating looked likely as he entered; Lara and Sarwan had both gone after a patient stand of 156, and more than 37 overs remained. But Smith rushed to 100 from 93 balls; his partners, Hinds and Jacobs, made 18 between them. Earlier, Rudolph made his second Test century, then Boucher and Kallis (resuming after a blow to the forearm from Edwards) added 146 as South Africa passed 500 for the third match running. Then came Gayle, back after injury. He slapped 19 fours and a six in reaching 100 out of 125 in the 23rd over. Next day Lara passed 9,000 runs in his 177th innings, two fewer than Sachin Tendulkar, who had got there at Sydney two days earlier, as the follow-on was avoided. Gibbs and Kallis made merry under the floodlights, adding 251 in 59 overs, including seven sixes in the final session, when West Indies spilled four catches.

South Africa

*G. C. Smith c Lara b Sanford	42	– b Edwards	24
H. H. Gibbs c Jacobs b Sanford	33	– c Gayle b Sarwan	142
J. A. Rudolph lbw b Mohammed	101	– c Jacobs b Drakes	0
J. H. Kallis lbw b Sanford	73	– not out	130
G. Kirsten c Sanford b Edwards	16	– not out	10
N. D. McKenzie b Mohammed	76		
P. R. Adams b Edwards	0		
†M. V. Boucher not out	122		
S. M. Pollock c Jacobs b Edwards	9		
M. Ntini c Jacobs b Mohammed	18		
A. Nel c Jacobs b Sanford	4		
B 6, l-b 12, w 2, n-b 18	38	B 3, l-b 7, w 8, n-b 11	29

1/70 (2) 2/90 (1) 3/162 (5) 4/304 (3)   532   1/48 (1) 2/50 (3)   (3 wkts dec.) 335
5/305 (7) 6/305 (6) 7/315 (9)   3/301 (2)
8/461 (4) 9/513 (10) 10/532 (11)

In the first innings Kallis, when 23, retired hurt at 120 and resumed at 315.

Drakes 26–7–64–0; Edwards 30–3–132–3; Sanford 37–4–132–4; Smith 2–0–4–0; Mohammed 33–5–112–3; Gayle 10–0–39–0; Hinds 7–2–31–0. *Second Innings*—Edwards 14–0–86–1; Sanford 8–1–38–0; Gayle 9–3–34–0; Drakes 20–0–68–1; Mohammed 6–0–30–0; Sarwan 19–1–69–1.

West Indies

C. H. Gayle lbw b Pollock	116	– c Gibbs b Ntini	32
D. Ganga b Nel	17	– c Boucher b Ntini	10
R. R. Sarwan c McKenzie b Nel	44	– c Gibbs b Ntini	69
*B. C. Lara b Nel	115	– c Boucher b Nel	86
W. W. Hinds c Boucher b Kallis	13	– b Pollock	25
D. R. Smith c Kallis b Nel	20	– not out	105
†R. D. Jacobs c Pollock b Ntini	23	– not out	9
V. C. Drakes c Boucher b Nel	20		
D. Mohammed c Kallis b Pollock	36		
A. Sanford run out	0		
F. H. Edwards not out	0		
B 6, l-b 7, n-b 10	23	B 2, l-b 7, w 2, n-b 7	18

1/126 (2) 2/183 (1) 3/187 (3) 4/224 (5)   427   1/28 (2) 2/47 (1)   (5 wkts) 354
5/252 (6) 6/306 (7) 7/361 (8)   3/203 (4) 4/224 (3)
8/409 (9) 9/426 (10) 10/427 (4)   5/296 (5)

Pollock 24–6–88–2; Ntini 20–1–105–1; Nel 28.1–8–87–5; Kallis 21–8–64–1; Adams 19–1–70–0. *Second Innings*—Pollock 17–3–64–1; Ntini 21–4–82–3; Nel 21–5–57–1; Kallis 16–3–38–0; Adams 22–3–103–0; Rudolph 1–1–0–0; Kirsten 2–1–1–0.

Umpires: D. J. Harper *(Australia)* (37) and S. Venkataraghavan *(India)* (72).
Third umpire: I. L. Howell *(South Africa).*   Referee: R. S. Madugalle *(Sri Lanka)* (57).

Close of play: First day, South Africa 308-6 (Boucher 0, Pollock 2); Second day, West Indies 178-1 (Gayle 112, Sarwan 39); Third day, South Africa 38-0 (Smith 18, Gibbs 19); Fourth day, South Africa 335-3 (Kallis 130, Kirsten 10).

SOUTH AFRICA v WEST INDIES 2003-04 (4th Test)

At Centurion Park, Pretoria, on 16, 17, 18, 19, 20 January.
Toss: West Indies.   Result: SOUTH AFRICA won by ten wickets.
Debuts: none.
Man of the Match: H. H. Gibbs.   Man of the Series: M. Ntini.

Lara won the toss and, encouraged by a grassy pitch and overcast conditions, chose to bowl. It made no difference. West Indies were overwhelmed by another huge total, almost half of it from Smith and Gibbs, who became
the first pair to share three 300-plus stands in Tests – all inside 13 months. Only Rahul Dravid and VVS Laxman
for India, and the Australians Bill Ponsford and Don Bradman 70 years earlier, had shared two. Kallis scored his
fourth hundred of the series, South Africa led by 303 and had West Indies back in on the third evening. Hopes that
they could salvage a draw, prompted by spirited hundreds from Sarwan and Gayle and the unsettled weather, swiftly
disappeared as the last seven wickets tumbled for 75. The 3.4 overs it took Smith and Gibbs to complete victory
were a précis of the indiscipline that marked West Indies' cricket throughout the series. There were ten wides from
Edwards – only two deliveries, but each went for four, the second to end the match – shoddy ground fielding and
a remarkable catch by Dwayne Smith at long-on that became a six when he stepped on the rope. Andre Nel was
relieved when play on the second evening was ended by bad light. He just had time to be whisked off by heli-
copter to his wedding, arranged long before, at nearby Benoni. Nel was back next morning to join Ntini in harassing
the West Indians with persistent pace. This was Srinivasaraghavan Venkataraghavan's last Test as an umpire.

South Africa

*G. C. Smith c Jacobs b Collymore	139	– not out	23
H. H. Gibbs c Ganga b Sarwan	192	– not out	8
J. A. Rudolph b Edwards	37		
J. H. Kallis not out	130		
G. Kirsten c and b Sarwan	10		
N. D. McKenzie c Lara b Dillon	40		
†M. V. Boucher c Edwards b Smith	13		
S. M. Pollock not out	1		
B 1, l-b 17, w 12, n-b 12	42	B 4, w 10, n-b 1	15

1/301 (1) 2/373 (3) 3/422 (2)   (6 wkts dec.) 604
4/446 (5) 5/532 (6) 6/567 (7)

(no wkt) 46

A. J. Hall, M. Ntini and A. Nel did not bat.

Dillon 31–5–109–1; Edwards 24–2–128–1; Drakes 33–5–101–0; Collymore 26–5–91–1; Gayle 7–0–39–0; Sarwan
14–0–55–2; Smith 13–1–42–1; Ganga 10–0–21–0. *Second Innings*—Dillon 2–0–17–0; Edwards 1.4–0–25–0.

West Indies

C. H. Gayle c McKenzie b Ntini	77	– c McKenzie b Ntini	107
D. Ganga c Kallis b Ntini	7	– b Ntini	0
R. R. Sarwan b Ntini	13	– lbw b Pollock	119
*B. C. Lara c Boucher b Nel	34	– lbw b Nel	6
S. Chanderpaul c Pollock b Nel	42	– c Gibbs b Kallis	27
D. R. Smith c Boucher b Kallis	39	– b Ntini	0
†R. D. Jacobs c Boucher b Nel	8	– lbw b Pollock	3
V. C. Drakes b Ntini	35	– c Gibbs b Pollock	4
M. Dillon b Ntini	30	– c Smith b Pollock	29
C. D. Collymore b Pollock	4	– not out	13
F. H. Edwards not out	0	– b Nel	10
L-b 7, n-b 5	12	B 4, l-b 11, w 7, n-b 8	30

1/22 (2) 2/37 (3) 3/139 (4) 4/142 (1)   301   1/18 (2) 2/32 (4) 3/99 (5)   348
5/195 (6) 6/224 (7) 7/241 (5)   4/273 (1) 5/277 (3) 6/278 (6)
8/280 (8) 9/301 (9) 10/301 (10)   7/284 (8) 8/309 (7) 9/322 (9) 10/348 (11)

In the second innings Gayle, when 14, retired hurt at 18-0 and resumed at 99.

Pollock 16.2–6–46–1; Ntini 20–7–49–5; Nel 18–6–64–3; Hall 11–0–65–0; Kallis 12–4–46–1; Smith 3–1–7–0;
Rudolph 2–0–17–0. *Second Innings*—Pollock 32–10–69–4; Ntini 28–4–99–3; Nel 15.4–2–64–2; Kallis
16–4–49–1; Hall 0.2–0–4–0; Smith 8.4–1–24–0; Rudolph 6–0–24–0.

Umpires: D. R. Shepherd *(England)* (78) and S. Venkataraghavan *(India)* (73).
Third umpire: B. G. Jerling *(South Africa)*.   Referee: R. S. Madugalle *(Sri Lanka)* (58).

Close of play: First day, South Africa 302-1 (Gibbs 139, Rudolph 1); Second day, West Indies 7-0 (Gayle 4, Ganga 2);
Third day, West Indies 44-2 (Sarwan 7, Chanderpaul 12); Fourth day, West Indies 263-3 (Gayle 106, Sarwan 107).

NEW ZEALAND v PAKISTAN 2003-04 (1st Test)

At Seddon Park, Hamilton, on 19, 20, 21, 22, 23 December.
Toss: Pakistan.   Result: MATCH DRAWN.
Debuts: none.
Man of the Match: S. P. Fleming.

At Adelaide a week earlier, Australia lost to India after scoring 556. And by the end of this Test, despite making 563 in their first innings New Zealand were grateful for the bad light that confirmed the draw. Inzamam-ul-Haq bowled first, perhaps thinking of the previous season's seaming Hamilton pitch on which both India and New Zealand managed less than 100. But the watchful New Zealanders soon blunted the bowling (lacking Shoaib Akhtar with a leg injury) and the pitch. Fleming added 101 with Richardson before four wickets tumbled after tea, but next day Vettori produced a fine maiden century. They put on 125 before Fleming was lbw for 192 after eight hours, his sixth Test century. Rain shortened the third day to 38.2 overs, and the fourth to 82, but Tuffey's unflagging off-stump line gave his side the edge and, at 285 for 6, a follow-on still looked likely. Then Moin Khan raced to a two-hour century, reaching it with four, six and four from consecutive balls from Vettori. Mohammad Sami defended stolidly for 25 in a stand of 152. New Zealand began the last day 104 ahead, but ended it shaken by a nerve-wracking collapse as Sami, clocked at nearly 96mph, showed the benefits of pace on a true pitch. When Umar Gul struck twice in two balls New Zealand were 42 for 5 and sliding, and there was further concern when McMillan ran himself out. However, rain had pinched too much time for a result.

New Zealand

M. H. Richardson run out	44	– c Moin Khan b Umar Gul	15
L. Vincent c Inzamam-ul-Haq b Shabbir Ahmed	8	– c Imran Farhat b Mohammad Sami	4
*S. P. Fleming lbw b Umar Gul	192	– c Moin Khan b Mohammad Sami	0
S. B. Styris c Taufeeq Umar b Danish Kaneria	33	– c Taufeeq Umar b Mohammad Sami	20
C. D. McMillan c Taufeeq Umar b Danish Kaneria	22	– run out	2
C. L. Cairns c Moin Khan b Shabbir Ahmed	11	– b Umar Gul	0
J. D. P. Oram b Shabbir Ahmed	6	– not out	23
†R. G. Hart c Yousuf Youhana b Shabbir Ahmed	10	– b Mohammad Sami	0
D. L. Vettori not out	137	– c Taufeeq Umar b Mohammad Sami	20
D. R. Tuffey b Umar Gul	35	– not out	1
I. G. Butler c Imran Farhat b Shabbir Ahmed	7		
B 4, l-b 12, w 9, n-b 33	58	L-b 4, w 1, n-b 6	11

1/16 (2) 2/117 (1) 3/217 (4) 4/249 (5)   563
5/266 (6) 6/274 (7) 7/314 (8)
8/439 (3) 9/538 (10) 10/563 (11)

1/13 (2) 2/13 (3) 3/42 (4)   (8 wkts) 96
4/42 (1) 5/42 (6) 6/47 (5)
7/52 (8) 8/95 (9)

Mohammad Sami 27–2–126–0; Shabbir Ahmed 43.2–9–117–5; Umar Gul 31–5–118–2; Abdul Razzaq 18–2–74–0; Danish Kaneria 32–6–112–2. *Second Innings*—Mohammad Sami 16–4–44–5; Shabbir Ahmed 10–7–10–0; Umar Gul 8.1–2–25–2; Danish Kaneria 4–2–6–0; Abdul Razzaq 3–1–7–0.

Pakistan

Imran Farhat c Hart b Oram	20	Shabbir Ahmed c Hart b Butler	8
Taufeeq Umar c Butler b Tuffey	27	Umar Gul c Vettori b Butler	3
Yasir Hameed lbw b Tuffey	80	Danish Kaneria not out	0
Yousuf Youhana c Vincent b Tuffey	28	L-b 4, w 11, n-b 21	36
*Inzamam-ul-Haq lbw b Tuffey	51		
Abdul Razzaq c Hart b Tuffey	48	1/47 (1) 2/55 (2) 3/134 (4) 4/209 (3)	463
†Moin Khan lbw b Oram	137	5/256 (5) 6/285 (6) 7/437 (8)	
Mohammad Sami c Hart b Vettori	25	8/453 (7) 9/462 (9) 10/463 (10)	

Tuffey 33–8–87–5; Butler 23.4–6–113–2; Oram 23–7–55–2; Cairns 17–0–60–0; Vettori 36–3–117–1; Styris 12–4–27–0.

Umpires: S. J. Davis *(Australia)* (6) and D. L. Orchard *(South Africa)* (39).
Third umpire: A. L. Hill *(New Zealand)*.   Referee: B. C. Broad *(England)* (1).

Close of play: First day, New Zealand 295-6 (Fleming 125, Hart 7); Second day, Pakistan 118-2 (Yasir Hameed 36, Yousuf Youhana 24); Third day, Pakistan 227-4 (Inzamam-ul-Haq 38, Abdul Razzaq 12); Fourth day, New Zealand 4-0 (Richardson 4, Vincent 0).

NEW ZEALAND v PAKISTAN 2003-04 (2nd Test)

At Basin Reserve, Wellington, on 26, 27, 28, 29, 30 December.
Toss: New Zealand.   Result: PAKISTAN won by seven wickets.
Debuts: New Zealand – R. A. Jones.
Man of the Match: Shoaib Akhtar.

This Test, like the First, produced a huge and improbable comeback – and this time there was no escape for New Zealand, as Pakistan overturned a first-innings deficit of 170 to win comfortably. The fightback was sparked by a devastating spell of fast bowling from Shoaib Akhtar on the fourth morning, when New Zealand lost seven wickets for eight runs. Shoaib had already made an impact at the start, bowling Vincent with his eighth ball and (after a long break for bad light) trapping Fleming with his 12th. Richardson held firm for more than seven hours, but no-one matched his resolution until Oram belatedly showed some batting form. New Zealand reached 366, then Butler removed five batsmen in five overs in a fiery spell as Pakistan lost their last six wickets for 28. But that collapse would soon pale into insignificance. As midday approached on the fourth morning, New Zealand were 265 ahead with seven wickets left: before 12.30 they were all out, Shoaib blowing away four of them. After fine innings from Yousuf Youhana and Inzamam-ul-Haq Pakistan needed only 28 more by the scheduled close, but they walked off in fine weather without claiming the extra half-hour. With an iffy final-day forecast, Inzamam was so mortified by his mistake that he could not face breakfast next morning. Bad weather delayed the start, then more rain interrupted. When play restarted shortly before midday Pakistan took no chances, surging home in less than four overs, enabling Inzamam to rediscover his appetite.

New Zealand

M. H. Richardson c Yousuf Youhana b Shabbir Ahmed ...	82	– c Moin Khan b Shoaib Akhtar	41
L. Vincent b Shoaib Akhtar........................	0	– lbw b Shoaib Akhtar	4
*S. P. Fleming lbw b Shoaib Akhtar...............	0	– lbw b Danish Kaneria	24
R. A. Jones b Abdul Razzaq....................	16	– c Moin Khan b Shoaib Akhtar	7
S. B. Styris c Moin Khan b Shoaib Akhtar	36	– (6) b Shoaib Akhtar....................	0
C. D. McMillan lbw b Shabbir Ahmed.............	26	– (7) not out............................	3
†R. G. Hart c Imran Farhat b Shoaib Akhtar........	19	– (10) b Shoaib Akhtar	0
J. D. P. Oram c Moin Khan b Shabbir Ahmed........	97	– lbw b Shabbir Ahmed	3
D. L. Vettori c Yasir Hameed b Mohammad Sami.....	44	– lbw b Shabbir Ahmed	0
D. R. Tuffey not out............................	9	– (5) run out	13
I. G. Butler c Moin Khan b Shoaib Akhtar	4	– b Shoaib Akhtar.......................	0
B 5, l-b 14, w 3, n-b 11	33	L-b 4, w 1, n-b 3..............	8

1/1 (2) 2/1 (3) 3/41 (4) 4/94 (5) **366**   1/8 (2) 2/43 (3) 3/73 (4) 4/95 (1) **103**
5/145 (6) 6/171 (7) 7/247 (1)   5/95 (6) 6/96 (5) 7/101 (8)
8/327 (8) 9/361 (9) 10/366 (11)   8/102 (9) 9/103 (10) 10/103 (11)

Shoaib Akhtar 20.3–5–48–5; Mohammad Sami 30–12–64–1; Shabbir Ahmed 37–8–87–3; Danish Kaneria 32–5–86–0; Abdul Razzaq 23–6–62–1. *Second Innings*—Shoaib Akhtar 18–3–30–6; Shabbir Ahmed 17–5–20–2; Mohammad Sami 4–1–12–0; Danish Kaneria 9–2–18–1; Abdul Razzaq 5–1–19–0.

Pakistan

Imran Farhat c Hart b Oram	20	– c Hart b Oram	14
Taufeeq Umar c Oram b Tuffey	16	– lbw b Vettori........................	34
Yasir Hameed b Butler	3	– c Hart b Butler......................	59
Yousuf Youhana c Fleming b Vettori.............	60	– not out..............................	88
*Inzamam-ul-Haq lbw b Oram	34	– not out..............................	72
Abdul Razzaq b Butler	26		
†Moin Khan c Vettori b Butler.................	19		
Mohammad Sami c Hart b Butler.................	4		
Shoaib Akhtar not out	0		
Shabbir Ahmed b Butler	0		
Danish Kaneria lbw b Butler....................	0		
B 4, l-b 3, w 1, n-b 6	14	B 4, l-b 2, n-b 4	10

1/27 (1) 2/30 (3) 3/60 (2) 4/112 (5) **196**   1/37 (1) 2/75 (2) (3 wkts) **277**
5/168 (4) 6/171 (6) 7/194 (8)   3/156 (3)
8/195 (9) 9/196 (7) 10/196 (11)

Tuffey 24–9–46–1; Butler 20–6–46–6; Oram 22–5–49–2; Vettori 22–6–47–1; Styris 2–1–1–0. *Second Innings*—Tuffey 14–5–41–0; Butler 18.5–1–100–1; Oram 9–1–34–1; Styris 6–1–26–0; Vettori 23–5–59–1; McMillan 4–0–11–0.

Umpires: E. A. R. de Silva *(Sri Lanka)* (28) and D. L. Orchard *(South Africa)* (40).
    Third umpire: D. B. Cowie *(New Zealand)*.   Referee: B. C. Broad *(England)* (2).

Close of play: First day, New Zealand 151-5 (Richardson 53, Hart 3); Second day, Pakistan 52-2 (Taufeeq Umar 13, Yousuf Youhana 11); Third day, New Zealand 75-3 (Richardson 35, Tuffey 0); Fourth day, Pakistan 246-3 (Yousuf Youhana 73, Inzamam-ul-Haq 57).

ZIMBABWE v BANGLADESH 2003-04 (1st Test)

At Harare Sports Club on 19, 20, 21, 22, 23 February.
Toss: Zimbabwe.   Result: ZIMBABWE won by 183 runs.
Debuts: Bangladesh – Manjural Islam Rana.
Man of the Match: S. M. Ervine.

There was little between the sides until the fourth evening, when Zimbabwe's batsmen tore into the bowling, and their attack shattered the Bangladeshi batting, as Blignaut took his country's first Test hat-trick. Zimbabwe had started slowly, though. Gripper was caught at slip first ball as he attempted a cut, but then Ebrahim and Carlisle ground out a century partnership, and the whole innings occupied most of the first two days. In reply, Shahriar Hossain and the middle order showed a determined response to three quick wickets. Mohammad Ashraful played beautifully for 98, looking confident until he dragged on a wide one from Streak, his 200th Test wicket (almost three times as many as any other Zimbabwean). Building on their lead, Zimbabwe again batted slowly before finally Taibu and Ervine decided it was safe to attack. Bangladesh were left to make 353, or bat out a day and 14 overs – but in those 14 overs, they collapsed to 14 for 5. Streak was unable to bowl because of back spasms, but Blignaut did the damage: he trapped Hannan Sarkar lbw with an inswinger, had Ashraful caught in the gully and then ripped one back off the pitch to Mushfiqur Rahman for a catch behind and the hat-trick. Blignaut managed just one more over before suffering a thigh injury, which kept him out of the next Test. It took Zimbabwe until midway through the last day to winkle out the final five wickets, with Khaled Mashud playing a fine defiant innings.

Zimbabwe

D. D. Ebrahim st Khaled Mashud b Mohammad Rafique .	65	– c Hannan Sarkar b Tapash Baisya		31
T. R. Gripper c Habibul Bashar b Tapash Baisya	0	– c Khaled Mashud b Manjural Islam		5
S. V. Carlisle c and b Tapash Baisya	58	– run out		33
G. W. Flower c Hannan Sarkar b Mohammad Rafique	5	– c Khaled Mashud b Tapash Baisya		3
†T. Taibu lbw b Mohammad Rafique	59	– c Habibul Bashar b Mohammad Rafique		58
S. M. Ervine c Hannan Sarkar b Tapash Baisya	86	– c Tapash Baisya b Manjural Islam Rana		74
*H. H. Streak c Khaled Mashud b Mushfiqur Rahman	68			
A. M. Blignaut st Khaled Mashud b Mohammad Rafique	7	– (7) b Manjural Islam Rana		32
G. M. Ewing c Khaled Mashud b Mushfiqur Rahman	71	– (8) c Khaled Mashud b Mohammad Rafique .		1
R. W. Price c Rajin Saleh b Mushfiqur Rahman	9	– (9) not out		1
D. T. Hondo not out	0			
B 1, l-b 7, w 3, n-b 2	13	L-b 2, w 2		4

1/0 (2) 2/107 (3) 3/130 (1) 4/133 (4)   441
5/258 (5) 6/299 (6) 7/306 (8)
8/412 (7) 9/433 (10) 10/441 (9)

1/12 (2) 2/50 (1)   (8 wkts dec.) 242
3/54 (4) 4/90 (3)
5/180 (5) 6/232 (6) 7/234 (8) 8/242 (7)

Manjural Islam 28–8–69–0; Tapash Baisya 36–6–133–3; Mushfiqur Rahman 24.2–8–75–3; Mohammad Rafique 57–11–121–4; Manjural Islam Rana 13–4–26–0; Mohammad Ashraful 2–1–9–0. *Second Innings*—Tapash Baisya 16–1–65–2; Manjural Islam 12–4–24–1; Mushfiqur Rahman 9–0–49–0; Mohammad Rafique 20–3–62–2; Manjural Islam Rana 7.2–0–40–2.

Bangladesh

Hannan Sarkar lbw b Streak	4	– lbw b Blignaut		10
Shahriar Hossain lbw b Hondo	48	– lbw b Hondo		1
Tapash Baisya c Taibu b Streak	4	– (9) lbw b Price		2
*Habibul Bashar c Taibu b Blignaut	0	– (3) lbw b Hondo		0
Rajin Saleh b Price	49	– (4) st Taibu b Price		47
Mohammad Ashraful b Streak	98	– (5) c sub (T. J. Friend) b Blignaut		0
Mushfiqur Rahman b Streak	44	– (6) c Taibu b Blignaut		0
Manjural Islam Rana not out	35	– (7) c Gripper b Price		31
†Khaled Mashud c Taibu b Hondo	6	– (8) st Taibu b Price		61
Mohammad Rafique c Ervine b Hondo	3	– c and b Ewing		5
Manjural Islam c Taibu b Blignaut	5	– not out		1
B 1, l-b 11, w 8, n-b 15	35	B 5, l-b 1, n-b 5		11

1/13 (1) 2/34 (3) 3/35 (4) 4/77 (2)   331
5/162 (5) 6/259 (6) 7/265 (7)
8/278 (9) 9/288 (10) 10/331 (11)

1/12 (2) 2/14 (3) 3/14 (1)   169
4/14 (5) 5/14 (6) 6/81 (4)
7/110 (7) 8/112 (9) 9/123 (10) 10/169 (8)

Streak 26.2–11–44–4; Blignaut 22.4–6–73–2; Ervine 12–2–52–0; Hondo 19.4–5–49–3; Price 25–4–79–1; Ewing 7–2–19–0; Gripper 3–2–3–0. *Second Innings*—Blignaut 4–1–12–3; Hondo 12–3–24–2; Ervine 12–3–34–0; Price 20.5–3–61–4; Ewing 8–3–27–1; Gripper 1–0–5–0.

Umpires: N. A. Mallender *(England)* (2) and D. L. Orchard *(South Africa)* (41).
Third umpire: I. D. Robinson *(Zimbabwe)*.   Referee: Wasim Raja *(Pakistan)* (14).

Close of play: First day, Zimbabwe 175-4 (Taibu 18, Ervine 25); Second day, Bangladesh 14-1 (Shahriar Hossain 8, Tapash Baisya 0); Third day, Bangladesh 313-9 (Manjural Islam Rana 30, Manjural Islam 3); Fourth day, Bangladesh 25-5 (Rajin Saleh 6, Manjural Islam Rana 4).

ZIMBABWE v BANGLADESH 2003-04 (2nd Test)

At Queens Sports Club, Bulawayo, on 26 (no play), 27 (*no play*), 28, 29 (*no play*) February, 1 March.
Toss: Zimbabwe.   Result: MATCH DRAWN.
Debuts: none.
Man of the Match: no award.

Bangladesh avoided defeat for only the second time in their 28 Tests, persistent rain gifting them a draw. Their only previous escape, against Zimbabwe at Dhaka in 2001-02, had also been rain-assisted. In the three weeks before this match, nearly a year's worth of rain soaked Bulawayo. After tireless work by the groundstaff, play was scheduled for the first afternoon, but another storm put paid to that and the second day. The game finally began an hour before lunch on the third day, after umpteen inspections. Streak put Bangladesh in, hoping a crash of wickets might make a result possible. But the opening batsmen began with great determination: the first runs off the bat came after 37 minutes. During the afternoon they opened up and were looking good until Shahriar Hossain slashed at Ervine and was caught behind. That was virtually the end of Bangladesh's resistance. Wickets tumbled against a backdrop of approaching rain, which finally interrupted at 88 for 5. The downpour was heavy, and more followed overnight, washing out the fourth day. More hard work by the groundstaff meant the last day started on time, but a result was virtually out of the question. Bangladesh subsided to 168: had Zimbabwe held their chances they could have been batting before lunch. Carlisle hit his second Test hundred, nine years after his debut, and four months after making 118 against Australia at Sydney.

Bangladesh

Hannan Sarkar b Ervine	25	Tapash Baisya c Flower b Price		2
Shahriar Hossain c Taibu b Ervine	31	Mohammad Rafique not out		26
*Habibul Bashar c Friend b Streak	4	Alamgir Kabir c Ebrahim b Price		3
Rajin Saleh c Ervine b Hondo	6	L-b 4, w 6, n-b 12		22
Mohammad Ashraful c Carlisle b Friend	1			
Manjural Islam Rana c Taibu b Price	39	1/64 (2) 2/73 (3) 3/73 (1) 4/81 (5)		168
Mushfiqur Rahman lbw b Hondo	0	5/87 (4) 6/89 (7) 7/126 (8)		
†Khaled Mashud lbw b Ervine	9	8/137 (9) 9/144 (6) 10/168 (11)		

Streak 15–9–19–1; Hondo 18–5–25–2; Ervine 15–4–44–3; Mahwire 10–2–36–0; Friend 9–2–20–1; Price 8.5–2–20–3.

Zimbabwe

D. D. Ebrahim c Hannan Sarkar b Tapash Baisya	2	G. W. Flower not out	37
T. R. Gripper c Khaled Mashud b Tapash Baisya	65	N-b 3	3
S. V. Carlisle not out	103		
		1/5 (1) 2/134 (2)	(2 wkts) 210

†T. Taibu, S. M. Ervine, *H. H. Streak, T. J. Friend, R. W. Price, N. B. Mahwire and D. T. Hondo did not bat.

Tapash Baisya 15–3–43–2; Alamgir Kabir 8–1–39–0; Mushfiqur Rahman 10–1–36–0; Mohammad Rafique 20–7–53–0; Manjural Islam Rana 6–0–33–0; Mohammad Ashraful 1.2–0–6–0.

Umpires: N. A. Mallender *(England)* (3) and D. L. Orchard *(South Africa)* (42).
Third umpire: I. D. Robinson *(Zimbabwe)*.   Referee: Wasim Raja *(Pakistan)* (15).

Close of play: First day, No play; Second day, No play; Third day, Bangladesh 88-5 (Manjural Islam Rana 5, Mushfiqur Rahman 0); Fourth day, No play.

SRI LANKA v AUSTRALIA 2003-04 (1st Test)

At Galle International Stadium on 8, 9, 10, 11, 12 March.
Toss: Australia.   Result: AUSTRALIA won by 197 runs.
Debuts: Australia – A. Symonds.
Man of the Match: M. L. Hayden.

After the first innings of this fabulous Test, Sri Lanka led by 161, with Muralitharan itching to bowl on an arid pitch, and history overwhelmingly in their favour – only nine Test sides since 1900 had overcome such a deficit and won. But Australia did it, through hard cricket and self-belief: Hayden hit a century of little style but match-changing substance, and the middle order ground Sri Lanka down before Warne and MacGill bowled them out on the last afternoon. Sri Lanka had packed their side with five spinners, but although the pitch turned only slowly at first, too many of the Australians were over-keen to make an attacking statement in the first innings, and Murali took six wickets in a paltry-looking total. In reply, Sri Lanka showed the patience Australia lacked. Then, in blazing heat on a wearing pitch, Hayden led Australia to safety, battling more than five hours, using little more than the sweep and iron willpower, with Martyn (with his first Test hundred in two years) and Lehmann following suit. Ponting – in his first Test as captain – was able to declare 351 ahead. Sri Lanka's demoralised batsmen fell to a masterly display from Warne. In his first Test since his 2003 drug ban, he found Tillekeratne's top edge to become only the second man to 500 Test wickets, after Courtney Walsh (Murali had 496 at this point). Later Dharmasena provided not only Warne's tenth victim of the match but Hayden's seventh catch, equalling the Test record.

Australia

J. L. Langer c Sangakkara b Dharmasena	12	– lbw b Jayasuriya	32
M. L. Hayden c Chandana b Muralitharan	41	– c Jayawardene b Muralitharan	130
*R. T. Ponting st Sangakkara b Chandana	21	– run out	28
D. R. Martyn c Jayawardene b Dharmasena	42	– c sub (K. S. Lokuarachchi) b Muralitharan	110
D. S. Lehmann b Muralitharan	63	– c and b Muralitharan	129
A. Symonds c Jayawardene b Muralitharan	0	– st Sangakkara b Muralitharan	24
†A. C. Gilchrist c Dharmasena b Muralitharan	4	– lbw b Chandana	0
S. K. Warne c Sangakkara b Vaas	23	– st Sangakkara b Muralitharan	0
J. N. Gillespie not out	4	– not out	11
M. S. Kasprowicz b Muralitharan	1	– not out	3
S. C. G. MacGill lbw b Muralitharan	0		
B 3, l-b 6	9	B 15, l-b 28, n-b 2	45

1/31 (1) 2/62 (2) 3/76 (3) 4/148 (4)   220
5/153 (6) 6/163 (7) 7/215 (5)
8/219 (8) 9/220 (10) 10/220 (11)

1/91 (1) 2/175 (3)   (8 wkts dec.) 512
3/245 (2) 4/451 (4)
5/480 (5) 6/498 (6) 7/498 (7) 8/498 (8)

Vaas 12–2–39–1; Dharmasena 20–4–52–2; Muralitharan 21.3–5–59–6; Chandana 14–1–59–1; Jayasuriya 1–0–2–0. *Second Innings*—Vaas 27–3–67–0; Dharmasena 24–1–100–0; Muralitharan 56–9–153–5; Dilshan 6–3–9–0; Jayasuriya 14.3–2–38–1; Chandana 24.3–2–102–1.

Sri Lanka

M. S. Atapattu b Gillespie	47	– c Hayden b Warne	16
S. T. Jayasuriya lbw b Warne	35	– (5) c Hayden b MacGill	5
†K. C. Sangakkara c and b Kasprowicz	22	– (2) lbw b Kasprowicz	7
D. P. M. D. Jayawardene c Hayden b Symonds	68	– (3) c Hayden b Warne	21
T. M. Dilshan c Langer b Kasprowicz	104	– (4) lbw b Warne	6
*H. P. Tillekeratne lbw b Warne	33	– c Symonds b Warne	25
T. T. Samaraweera not out	36	– b MacGill	15
U. D. U. Chandana c Gilchrist b Warne	27	– c Langer b MacGill	43
W. P. U. J. C. Vaas c Hayden b MacGill	0	– not out	10
H. D. P. K. Dharmasena c Hayden b Warne	6	– c Hayden b Warne	0
M. Muralitharan c and b Warne	0	– st Gilchrist b MacGill	0
B 2, n-b 1	3	B 4, w 1, n-b 1	6

1/53 (2) 2/92 (3) 3/123 (1) 4/198 (4)   381
5/298 (6) 6/323 (5) 7/369 (8)
8/372 (9) 9/381 (10) 10/381 (11)

1/14 (2) 2/41 (1) 3/49 (4)   154
4/56 (3) 5/56 (5) 6/89 (7)
7/119 (6) 8/153 (8) 9/153 (10) 10/154 (11)

Gillespie 28–9–61–1; Kasprowicz 23–3–56–2; Warne 42.4–9–116–5; Symonds 19–3–68–1; MacGill 22–4–69–1; Lehmann 2–0–9–0. *Second Innings*—Warne 15–5–43–5; Gillespie 9–2–20–0; Kasprowicz 5–1–13–1; MacGill 16.2–2–74–4.

Umpires: R. E. Koertzen *(South Africa)* (47) and D. R. Shepherd *(England)* (79).
Third umpire: M. G. Silva *(Sri Lanka)*.   Referee: B. C. Broad *(England)* (3).

Close of play: First day, Sri Lanka 81-1 (Atapattu 29, Sangakkara 16); Second day, Sri Lanka 352-6 (Samaraweera 21, Chandana 20); Third day, Australia 193-2 (Hayden 106, Martyn 10); Fourth day, Sri Lanka 3-0 (Atapattu 0, Sangakkara 3).

SRI LANKA v AUSTRALIA 2003-04 (2nd Test)

At Asgiriya Stadium, Kandy, on 16, 17, 18, 19, 20 March.
Toss: Australia.   Result: AUSTRALIA won by 27 runs.
Debuts: none.
Man of the Match: S. K. Warne.

Australia won a thriller to clinch the series, but it could easily have been 1–1. By lunch on the second day, both first innings were over. The pitch was not perfect, offering some seam movement, but the batting was horrid. Only Hayden managed more than 18 as Australia made their lowest total against Sri Lanka, and their worst anywhere since 104 on a crumbling Oval pitch in 1997. Local smiles were doubly broad because Muralitharan took his 500th Test wicket when he bowled Kasprowicz. But it proved a bittersweet game for Murali, partly because Warne had beaten him to 500 (and claimed another ten here), and also because fleet-footed second-innings batting forced him into a containing round-the-wicket line. Sri Lanka then crashed to 92 for 7, but Vaas and Murali collected 79 for the last wicket, a national record, for a lead of 91. Gilchrist, in terrible form, volunteered to replace Ponting (who had ricked his back) at No. 3 and hit ruthlessly straight. He put on 200 with Martyn, who continued to a career-best 161 and oversaw the addition of 416. For the second Test running, Sri Lanka needed 352. Jayasuriya bullied MacGill in a shot-a-ball hundred, but eventually cut to the keeper, then Warne bowled Dilshan, the last recognised batsman. Next morning Sri Lanka needed 51, Australia three wickets. Ponting gambled that Sri Lanka would crack under pressure: they did. The real tension lasted just three overs, before Vaas tried to hit Warne into the jungle past midwicket.

Australia

J. L. Langer lbw b Zoysa	3	– c Sangakkara b Zoysa	9
M. L. Hayden lbw b Muralitharan	54	– c and b Vaas	5
*R. T. Ponting lbw b Vaas	10	– (6) c Sangakkara b Vaas	27
D. R. Martyn lbw b Muralitharan	1	– st Sangakkara b Muralitharan	161
D. S. Lehmann b Zoysa	8	– lbw b Vaas	21
A. Symonds c Tillekeratne b Zoysa	6	– (7) lbw b Muralitharan	23
†A. C. Gilchrist c Sangakkara b Zoysa	0	– (3) lbw b Muralitharan	144
S. K. Warne c Muralitharan b Vaas	18	– c Zoysa b Muralitharan	6
J. N. Gillespie c Jayawardene b Muralitharan	8	– c Atapattu b Muralitharan	11
M. S. Kasprowicz b Muralitharan	0	– c Jayawardene b Zoysa	8
S. C. G. MacGill not out	8	– not out	17
B 1, l-b 3	4	B 2, l-b 7, n-b 1	10

1/25 (1) 2/47 (3) 3/50 (4) 4/60 (5)   120   1/11 (2) 2/26 (1) 3/226 (3)   442
5/84 (6) 6/84 (7) 7/86 (2)   4/255 (5) 5/304 (6) 6/360 (7)
8/100 (9) 9/106 (10) 10/120 (8)   7/376 (8) 8/393 (9) 9/408 (10) 10/442 (4)

Vaas 11.2–5–14–2; Zoysa 16–3–54–4; Muralitharan 15–4–48–4. *Second Innings*—Vaas 33–6–103–3; Muralitharan 50.3–8–173–5; Zoysa 33–11–102–2; Lokuarachchi 12–2–33–0; Jayasuriya 5–0–16–0; Dilshan 1–0–6–0.

Sri Lanka

M. S. Atapattu c Gilchrist b Kasprowicz	9	– lbw b Gillespie	8
S. T. Jayasuriya lbw b Kasprowicz	1	– c Gilchrist b Gillespie	131
D. A. Gunawardene lbw b Kasprowicz	13	– lbw b Kasprowicz	9
†K. C. Sangakkara c Symonds b Gillespie	5	– c and b Warne	29
D. P. M. D. Jayawardene c Symonds b Warne	17	– c Gilchrist b Gillespie	13
*H. P. Tillekeratne c Gilchrist b Warne	16	– (7) c Ponting b Warne	7
T. M. Dilshan lbw b Warne	0	– (6) b Warne	43
W. P. U. J. C. Vaas not out	68	– c Langer b Warne	45
D. N. T. Zoysa c Gilchrist b Kasprowicz	4	– (10) c Gilchrist b Gillespie	0
K. S. Lokuarachchi c Kasprowicz b Warne	15	– (9) lbw b Warne	16
M. Muralitharan c Symonds b Warne	43	– not out	4
B 8, l-b 9, n-b 3	20	B 4, l-b 14, n-b 1	19

1/6 (2) 2/34 (3) 3/39 (1) 4/49 (4)   211   1/17 (1) 2/36 (3) 3/98 (4)   324
5/67 (5) 6/67 (7) 7/88 (6)   4/174 (5) 5/218 (2) 6/239 (7)
8/111 (9) 9/132 (10) 10/211 (11)   7/274 (6) 8/319 (8) 9/320 (10) 10/324 (9)

Gillespie 12–4–25–1; Kasprowicz 24–5–83–4; Warne 20.1–3–65–5; Symonds 2–1–1–0; MacGill 5–1–20–0. *Second Innings*—Kasprowicz 17–1–55–1; Gillespie 20–1–76–4; Warne 21.1–2–90–5; Symonds 3–0–16–0; MacGill 12–0–69–0.

Umpires: S. A. Bucknor *(West Indies)* (87) and D. L. Orchard *(South Africa)* (43).
Third umpire: T. H. Wijewardene *(Sri Lanka)*.   Referee: B. C. Broad *(England)* (4).

Close of play: First day, Sri Lanka 92-7 (Vaas 16, Zoysa 0); Second day, Australia 221-2 (Gilchrist 140, Martyn 64); Third day, Australia 320-5 (Martyn 104, Symonds 6); Fourth day, Sri Lanka 301-7 (Vaas 30, Lokuarachchi 13).

SRI LANKA v AUSTRALIA 2003-04 (3rd Test)

At Sinhalese Sports Club, Colombo, on 24, 25, 26, 27, 28 March.
Toss: Australia.   Result: AUSTRALIA won by 121 runs.
Debuts: none.
Man of the Match: D. S. Lehmann.   Man of the Series: S. K. Warne.

For the third Test running, Australia overturned a first-innings lead to win, thus completing the least one-sided of series whitewashes. They were again in deep trouble in the second innings, but by now they had proved their mental superiority under pressure. Langer and Katich built a do-or-die stand, and the bowlers cut down the last Sri Lankan wicket in the penultimate over. "We need to show a bit of character when the going gets tough," said Tillekeratne, before resigning as captain. Lehmann's nonchalant first-day century gave Australia control. The humidity was appalling, and he used his bat as a walking stick as well as a weapon. Sri Lanka then cancelled out Australia's 401 and took a lead of six. On the fourth morning, Australia's second innings was on the verge of collapse at 98 for 5, but once again they recovered. Langer and Katich, in his first Test of the series, were immovable and added 218 in 65 overs. Australia set a target of 370 just before the end of the fourth day. With 40 overs left, Samaraweera and Jayawardene had defied the dusting pitch and reached 156 for 2, and a draw seemed likely. But as if Warne wasn't enough to cope with, Jayawardene, like Jayasuriya before him, got a bad decision. After tea Warne finally broke through with four wickets. Afterwards, referee Chris Broad stated his suspicion that Muralitharan's wrong'un was a throw, and the game itself was almost forgotten in the roar of the reignited chucking debate.

Australia

J. L. Langer c Dilshan b Vaas	19	– b Vaas	166
M. L. Hayden c sub (U. D. U. Chandana) b Samaraweera	25	– lbw b Vaas	28
*R. T. Ponting c Muralitharan b Vaas	92	– c Samaraweera b Herath	20
D. R. Martyn c Sangakkara b Vaas	14	– (5) lbw b Herath	5
D. S. Lehmann c Jayasuriya b Muralitharan	153	– (6) c Sangakkara b Muralitharan	1
S. M. Katich c and b Muralitharan	14	– (7) lbw b Muralitharan	86
†A. C. Gilchrist c Jayasuriya b Muralitharan	22	– (8) not out	31
S. K. Warne lbw b Muralitharan	32	– (9) c Samaraweera b Herath	0
J. N. Gillespie c Tillekeratne b Muralitharan	0	– (4) c Jayawardene b Muralitharan	1
M. S. Kasprowicz b Jayasuriya	4	– run out	3
B. A. Williams not out	0	– c and b Herath	2
B 13, l-b 9, n-b 4	26	B 11, l-b 11, w 4, n-b 6	32
	401		**375**

1/43 (1) 2/60 (2) 3/96 (4) 4/217 (3)   **401**
5/244 (6) 6/299 (7) 7/376 (8)
8/380 (9) 9/387 (10) 10/401 (5)

1/40 (2) 2/79 (3) 3/80 (4)   **375**
4/89 (5) 5/98 (6) 6/316 (1)
7/341 (7) 8/346 (9) 9/368 (10) 10/375 (11)

Vaas 26–3–93–3; Zoysa 3.3–1–23–0; Samaraweera 14.3–1–38–1; Muralitharan 37.1–6–123–5; Herath 23–5–75–0; Jayasuriya 11–1–27–1. *Second Innings*—Vaas 21–3–61–2; Zoysa 12–0–54–0; Muralitharan 29–5–93–3; Herath 24.2–1–92–4; Samaraweera 15–4–40–0; Jayasuriya 4–0–13–0; Dilshan 1–1–0–0.

Sri Lanka

M. S. Atapattu b Kasprowicz	118	– b Kasprowicz	14
S. T. Jayasuriya c Gillespie b Lehmann	71	– c Katich b Lehmann	51
†K. C. Sangakkara c Gilchrist b Lehmann	22	– (5) b Warne	27
D. P. M. D. Jayawardene c Gilchrist b Gillespie	29	– c Gilchrist b Lehmann	37
T. M. Dilshan b Gillespie	0	– (6) c Martyn b Warne	31
*H. P. Tillekeratne not out	74	– (7) lbw b Gillespie	17
T. T. Samaraweera c Gilchrist b Gillespie	41	– (3) st Gilchrist b Lehmann	53
W. P. U. J. C. Vaas b Warne	24	– lbw b Warne	9
D. N. T. Zoysa st Gilchrist b Lehmann	3	– b Warne	1
H. M. R. K. B. Herath c Martyn b Warne	3	– lbw b Kasprowicz	0
M. Muralitharan c Warne b Kasprowicz	8	– not out	0
B 4, l-b 7, w 1, n-b 2	14	B 4, l-b 1, w 1, n-b 2	8
	407		**248**

1/134 (2) 2/175 (3) 3/240 (4) 4/240 (5)   **407**
5/256 (1) 6/327 (7) 7/378 (8)
8/381 (9) 9/390 (10) 10/407 (11)

1/45 (1) 2/92 (2) 3/156 (3)   **248**
4/181 (4) 5/191 (5) 6/232 (6)
7/245 (7) 8/247 (9) 9/248 (8) 10/248 (10)

Gillespie 23–3–96–3; Kasprowicz 22.1–5–58–2; Williams 19–5–48–0; Warne 36–7–115–2; Lehmann 19–2–50–3; Katich 8–0–29–0. *Second Innings*—Gillespie 18–6–38–1; Kasprowicz 16.4–5–37–2; Warne 33–11–92–4; Williams 5–0–19–0; Lehmann 17–2–42–3; Katich 4–1–15–0.

Umpires: S. A. Bucknor *(West Indies)* (88) and D. L. Orchard *(South Africa)* (44).
Third umpire: P. T. Manuel *(Sri Lanka)*.   Referee: B. C. Broad *(England)* (5).

Close of play: First day, Australia 314-6 (Lehmann 104, Warne 7); Second day, Sri Lanka 239-2 (Atapattu 109, Jayawardene 29); Third day, Australia 80-3 (Langer 29); Fourth day, Sri Lanka 18-0 (Atapattu 5, Jayasuriya 13).

NEW ZEALAND v SOUTH AFRICA 2003-04 (1st Test)

At Seddon Park, Hamilton, on 10, 11, 12, 13, 14 March.
Toss: South Africa.   Result: MATCH DRAWN.
Debuts: New Zealand – B. B. McCullum, M. H. W. Papps.
Man of the Match: J. H. Kallis.

Speculation about the pitch dominated the build-up: the ground was waterlogged during floods that hit North Island the previous month, and algae had destroyed most of the grass on the square. The surface proved slow and low, and a high-scoring draw ensued. Kallis just missed a century in the first innings, chafing after Tuffey and Oram becalmed him on 90 for 20 balls, but Kirsten made no mistake, batting for 307 minutes. He had 98 when the last man came in, but calmly reached three figures then clattered another 37 from 21 balls. After an uncertain start Michael Papps settled down for a debut half-century, but New Zealand slipped to 225 for 6 before Oram dropped anchor for five hours and a maiden Test hundred. He hit 19 fours, and shared big stands with Brendon McCullum (another debutant), Vettori and Wiseman as New Zealand reached their highest score against South Africa and pulled out an unexpected lead of 50. On such a sluggish pitch South Africa had little trouble making the game safe. Kallis batted for 406 minutes and 312 balls: his 16th Test century was his fifth in successive matches, a sequence bettered only by Don Bradman, who made hundreds in six successive Tests in 1936-37 and 1938. The South Africans complained before the third day's play that the pitch had been illegally repaired: the groundsman had plugged a damaged area on a length outside the right-hander's leg stump with cement, but was ordered to remove the filling by the referee.

South Africa

*G. C. Smith c Oram b Vettori	25	– c McCullum b Tuffey	5
H. H. Gibbs c Styris b Vettori	40	– c McCullum b Wiseman	47
J. A. Rudolph c McCullum b Styris	72	– b Cairns	0
J. H. Kallis c Tuffey b Oram	92	– not out	150
G. Kirsten c Papps b Vettori	137	– (6) not out	34
P. R. Adams b Oram	7		
N. D. McKenzie lbw b Vettori	10	– (5) c Richardson b Wiseman	52
†M. V. Boucher lbw b Styris	22		
S. M. Pollock run out	10		
M. Ntini run out	21		
A. Nel not out	4		
B 1, l-b 5, w 1, n-b 12	19	B 12, l-b 5, n-b 8	25

1/51 (1) 2/79 (2) 3/211 (3) 4/271 (4)   459   1/15 (1) 2/16 (3)   (4 wkts dec.) 313
5/281 (6) 6/305 (7) 7/364 (8)   3/108 (2) 4/215 (5)
8/379 (9) 9/415 (10) 10/459 (5)

Tuffey 26–11–62–0; Oram 27–7–76–2; Cairns 18–2–52–0; Vettori 39.2–2–158–4; Wiseman 12–1–54–0; Styris 16–4–46–2; McMillan 1–0–5–0. *Second Innings*—Tuffey 15–3–28–1; Oram 15–4–29–0; Cairns 15–3–48–1; Vettori 34–11–79–0; Wiseman 19–4–68–2; Styris 13–4–29–0; McMillan 5.1–0–15–0.

New Zealand

M. H. Richardson lbw b Pollock	4		
M. H. W. Papps lbw b Kallis	59	– (1) c Boucher b Nel	12
*S. P. Fleming lbw b Adams	27		
S. B. Styris b Pollock	74	– (3) not out	3
C. D. McMillan lbw b Kallis	19		
C. L. Cairns c Boucher b Ntini	28		
J. D. P. Oram not out	119		
†B. B. McCullum c Boucher b Kallis	57	– (2) not out	19
D. L. Vettori b Adams	53		
P. J. Wiseman b Pollock	36		
D. R. Tuffey c Boucher b Pollock	0		
B 12, l-b 11, n-b 10	33	L-b 1, w 1, n-b 3	5

1/20 (1) 2/75 (3) 3/127 (2) 4/172 (5)   509   1/34 (1)   (1 wkt) 39
5/223 (4) 6/225 (6) 7/309 (8)
8/422 (9) 9/509 (10) 10/509 (11)

Pollock 30.4–4–98–4; Ntini 29–9–74–1; Kallis 26–7–71–3; Nel 27–8–91–0; Adams 45–11–118–2; Rudolph 5–0–20–0; Smith 2–0–14–0. *Second Innings*—Pollock 4–2–5–0; Ntini 4–0–15–0; Nel 4–0–15–1; Adams 3–1–2–0; McKenzie 1–0–1–0.

Umpires: S. J. Davis *(Australia)* (7) and R. B. Tiffin *(Zimbabwe)* (38).
Third umpire: A. L. Hill *(New Zealand)*.   Referee: C. H. Lloyd *(West Indies)* (31).

Close of play: First day, South Africa 279-4 (Kirsten 31, Adams 7); Second day, New Zealand 102-2 (Papps 50, Styris 16); Third day, New Zealand 361-7 (Oram 49, Vettori 21); Fourth day, South Africa 134-3 (Kallis 56, McKenzie 11).

NEW ZEALAND v SOUTH AFRICA 2003-04 (2nd Test)

At Eden Park, Auckland, on 18, 19, 20, 21, 22 March.
Toss: New Zealand.   Result: NEW ZEALAND won by nine wickets.
Debuts: none.
Man of the Match: C. S. Martin.

New Zealand gained their first victory in 13 home Tests against South Africa, the only country they had never beaten on their own soil. A win seemed improbable after Fleming put South Africa in only to watch the openers put on 177 – but that proved to be 60% of the eventual total. Martin, recalled after two years, proved to be the match-winner, claiming 11 for 180, New Zealand's best against South Africa. The openers played skilfully for their sixth century stand in Tests before Gibbs fell to the ball before tea and Smith to the first afterwards. Next day Martin took full advantage of cloudy conditions as eight wickets fell for 65. New Zealand lost Papps – taking Pollock past Allan Donald's South African-record 330 wickets – and Fleming inside eight overs. Stability was restored by Richardson and Styris, who struck the ball crisply. But South Africa were still in the game . . . until a magnificent display from Cairns (who blasted seven sixes) and Oram, whose stand of 225 was New Zealand's best for any wicket against South Africa. Rather less productive was Martin, who became the first player to fail to score in nine consecutive Test innings – but he did produce a splendid first ball, bowling Smith. Rudolph shared century stands with Gibbs and Kallis, but McMillan trapped Kallis leg-before, ending his chance of equalling Don Bradman's record of a century in six successive Tests. Next over Martin dismissed Kirsten – enduring a wretched 100th Test – and McKenzie with successive deliveries.

South Africa

*G. C. Smith lbw b Martin	88	– b Martin		0
H. H. Gibbs b Cairns	80	– lbw b Oram		61
J. A. Rudolph c Papps b Martin	17	– not out		154
J. H. Kallis c McCullum b Martin	40	– lbw b McMillan		71
G. Kirsten b Oram	1	– lbw b Martin		1
N. D. McKenzie c Papps b Martin	27	– c Papps b Martin		0
†M. V. Boucher c McMillan b Martin	4	– c Fleming b Martin		10
S. M. Pollock b Tuffey	10	– c Fleming b Martin		10
N. Boje not out	12	– c McCullum b Cairns		24
M. Ntini c McCullum b Martin	0	– c McMillan b Cairns		6
D. J. Terbrugge lbw b Oram	0	– c sub (J. A. H. Marshall) b Cairns		2
L-b 13, w 1, n-b 3	17	B 6, l-b 1, n-b 3		10

1/177 (2) 2/177 (1) 3/235 (3) 4/236 (5)   296   1/0 (1) 2/103 (2) 3/249 (4)   349
5/240 (4) 6/246 (7) 7/273 (8)   4/250 (5) 5/250 (6) 6/272 (7)
8/289 (6) 9/289 (10) 10/296 (11)   7/290 (8) 8/327 (9) 9/337 (10) 10/349 (11)

Tuffey 24–7–41–1; Martin 31–7–76–6; Oram 28.3–6–60–2; Cairns 21–6–54–1; Styris 14–5–37–0; Vettori 5–1–15–0. *Second Innings*—Martin 23–5–104–5; Oram 27–13–47–1; Tuffey 4–1–13–0; Cairns 13.3–1–63–3; Vettori 24–4–73–0; Styris 13–5–39–0; McMillan 4–1–3–1.

New Zealand

M. H. Richardson c Gibbs b Kallis	45	– (2) c Boje b Ntini		10
M. H. W. Papps c Boje b Pollock	0	– (1) not out		8
*S. P. Fleming c Kallis b Ntini	4	– not out		31
S. B. Styris c Pollock b Boje	170			
C. D. McMillan b Pollock	82			
†B. B. McCullum b Ntini	13			
C. L. Cairns c Kallis b Smith	158			
J. D. P. Oram b Ntini	90			
D. L. Vettori not out	4			
D. R. Tuffey b Pollock	13			
C. S. Martin b Pollock	0			
L-b 10, n-b 6	16	N-b 4		4

1/5 (2) 2/12 (3) 3/137 (1) 4/285 (4)   595   1/20 (2)   (1 wkt) 53
5/314 (5) 6/349 (6) 7/574 (7)
8/578 (8) 9/595 (10) 10/595 (11)

Pollock 32.5–6–113–4; Ntini 36–7–110–3; Terbrugge 22–4–93–0; Kallis 23–1–108–1; Boje 22–2–108–1; McKenzie 2–0–8–0; Rudolph 6–0–26–0; Smith 5–0–19–1. *Second Innings*—Pollock 5–1–16–0; Ntini 5–0–31–1; Boje 0.2–0–6–0.

Umpires: Aleem Dar *(Pakistan)* (5) and E. A. R. de Silva *(Sri Lanka)* (29).
Third umpire: D. B. Cowie *(New Zealand)*.   Referee: C. H. Lloyd *(West Indies)* (32).

Close of play: First day, South Africa 231-2 (Rudolph 14, Kallis 39); Second day, New Zealand 201-3 (Styris 118, McMillan 31); Third day, New Zealand 584-8 (Vettori 2, Tuffey 5); Fourth day, South Africa 277-6 (Rudolph 121, Pollock 5).

NEW ZEALAND v SOUTH AFRICA 2003-04 (3rd Test)

At Basin Reserve, Wellington, on 26, 27, 28, 29, 30 March.
Toss: South Africa.   Result: SOUTH AFRICA won by six wickets.
Debuts: New Zealand – M. J. Mason.
Man of the Match: G. C. Smith.

A crucial stand between Smith and Kirsten, playing his 101st and last Test, enabled South Africa to hit straight back and tie the series. The match started in a typical Wellington gale, a strong northerly that forced those bowling upwind to shorten their run-ups. New Zealand slipped to 97 for 4, but the recalled Sinclair struck 74 before Cairns batted with freedom. The new ball left Oram exposed: he hit out, and last man Martin managed a single, ending his record sequence of scoreless innings. South Africa looked set to take command as Smith and Gibbs started with their seventh century stand, a national record, then Rudolph and van Jaarsveld put on 115. Martin wrecked hopes of a big lead with three wickets in 16 balls with the second new ball, and the last seven wickets fell for 65. Pollock immediately struck back, removing Papps in the first over. By the third-day close, New Zealand were five down and only 109 ahead. Styris and Cairns scored freely, adding 70 in 15 overs, but Oram again found himself with only Martin for company, and again he hit effectively, taking his two last-ditch stands for the match to 61. South Africa needed 234: Kirsten arrived with his side in crisis at 36 for 3, but he then added 171 with Smith before falling lbw for 76. The formalities remained, but Kirsten had made a final, successful contribution – and South Africa had still not lost a Test series to New Zealand.

New Zealand

M. H. Richardson c Boucher b Kallis	14	– (2) c Smith b Boje	37
M. H. W. Papps lbw b Ntini	7	– (1) lbw b Pollock	0
*S. P. Fleming c Pollock b Boje	30	– c Boucher b Nel	9
M. S. Sinclair lbw b Boje	74	– lbw b Pollock	21
S. B. Styris b Boje	1	– c and b Nel	73
†B. B. McCullum lbw b Pollock	55	– b Boje	3
C. L. Cairns b Pollock	69	– c van Jaarsveld b Boje	41
J. D. P. Oram st Boucher b Boje	34	– lbw b Boje	40
D. L. Vettori c Boucher b Pollock	0	– c van Jaarsveld b Ntini	9
M. J. Mason c van Jaarsveld b Nel	3	– run out	0
C. S. Martin not out	1	– not out	1
B 2, l-b 1, w 1, n-b 5	9	B 1, l-b 9, w 3, n-b 5	18

1/23 (2) 2/23 (1) 3/90 (3) 4/97 (5)   297
5/163 (4) 6/248 (6) 7/257 (7)
8/257 (9) 9/264 (10) 10/297 (8)

1/1 (1) 2/42 (3) 3/73 (4)   252
4/107 (2) 5/111 (6) 6/198 (7)
7/201 (5) 8/220 (9) 9/224 (10) 10/252 (8)

Pollock 29–2–85–3; Ntini 21–6–63–1; Kallis 7–5–4–1; Nel 27–9–77–1; Boje 20–2–65–4. *Second Innings*—Pollock 22–10–65–2; Ntini 20–6–50–1; Nel 21–5–58–2; Boje 33.2–7–69–4.

South Africa

*G. C. Smith b Cairns	47	– not out	125
H. H. Gibbs c sub (J. A. H. Marshall) b Martin	77	– c Fleming b Martin	16
J. A. Rudolph not out	93	– b Martin	0
G. Kirsten c McCullum b Martin	1	– (5) lbw b Styris	76
M. van Jaarsveld c Oram b Martin	59	– (6) not out	13
J. H. Kallis c McCullum b Martin	0	– (4) lbw b Oram	1
†M. V. Boucher c Papps b Martin	0		
S. M. Pollock c Fleming b Oram	5		
N. Boje b Cairns	25		
M. Ntini c McCullum b Cairns	4		
A. Nel c Oram b Cairns	0		
L-b 1, n-b 4	5	L-b 2, n-b 1	3

1/103 (1) 2/130 (2) 3/136 (4) 4/251 (5)   316
5/265 (6) 6/265 (7) 7/270 (8)
8/304 (9) 9/308 (10) 10/316 (11)

1/29 (2) 2/31 (3)   (4 wkts) 234
3/36 (4) 4/207 (5)

Martin 20–6–55–5; Mason 16–4–73–0; Oram 11–3–21–1; Vettori 26–6–76–0; Cairns 16.5–2–60–4; Styris 10–4–30–0. *Second Innings*—Martin 18.2–2–65–2; Mason 6–1–32–0; Oram 11–3–23–1; Cairns 10–2–19–0; Vettori 18–2–53–0; Styris 9–1–40–1.

Umpires: Aleem Dar *(Pakistan)* (6) and E. A. R. de Silva *(Sri Lanka)* (30).
Third umpire: G. A. V. Baxter *(New Zealand)*.   Referee: C. H. Lloyd *(West Indies)* (33).

Close of play: First day, New Zealand 248-6 (Cairns 60); Second day, South Africa 237-3 (Rudolph 60, van Jaarsveld 48); Third day, New Zealand 128-5 (Styris 41, Cairns 7); Fourth day, South Africa 82-3 (Smith 46, Kirsten 19).

WEST INDIES v ENGLAND 2003-04 (1st Test)

At Sabina Park, Kingston, Jamaica, on 11, 12, 13, 14 March.
Toss: West Indies.   Result: ENGLAND won by ten wickets.
Debuts: none.
Man of the Match: S. J. Harmison.

For three days this was a gritty arm-wrestle; then, on the fourth morning, West Indies collapsed for 47, their lowest total ever. Harmison took the cheapest seven-wicket haul in Test history: after getting carried away and under-pitching in the first innings, he increased his length, cut his pace a fraction, and concentrated on the basics. It worked, probably beyond his wildest dreams. Only two bowlers have taken more wickets in an innings more cheaply: George Lohmann (8 for 7) and Johnny Briggs (8 for 11), both for England in South Africa in the 19th century. England were on top at the start, when Jones snared Lara with his 13th ball back in Test cricket, but Hinds put on 122 with Devon Smith, who reached his maiden Test century. Giles eventually accounted for both – his only wickets of the series – and West Indies' 311 felt like par. Then England's openers were swept aside by Edwards, and Butcher and Hussain could both have been out first ball before putting on 119. England filched a lead of 28, helped by wayward bowling: 339 was the highest Test total in which extras top-scored. But 28 was almost enough. Thorpe held a hot slip catch from Gayle, a borderline lbw completed Sarwan's pair, Chanderpaul nutmegged himself, an uncomfortable Lara (he had dislocated a finger dropping Butcher) lasted only five balls, and Hoggard clutched a scorching return catch from Smith: not long afterwards the second wave of five wickets went down for six runs in three overs.

West Indies

C. H. Gayle b Harmison	5	– c Thorpe b Harmison	9
D. S. Smith st Read b Giles	108	– c and b Hoggard	12
R. R. Sarwan lbw b Hoggard	0	– lbw b Harmison	0
*B. C. Lara c Flintoff b Jones	23	– (5) c Flintoff b Hoggard	0
S. Chanderpaul b Hoggard	7	– (4) b Harmison	0
R. O. Hinds c Butcher b Giles	84	– c Read b Jones	3
†R. D. Jacobs c Vaughan b Jones	38	– c Hussain b Harmison	15
T. L. Best lbw b Harmison	20	– c Read b Harmison	0
A. Sanford c Trescothick b Flintoff	1	– c Trescothick b Harmison	1
C. D. Collymore not out	3	– not out	2
F. H. Edwards c Flintoff b Hoggard	1	– c Trescothick b Harmison	0
L-b 6, w 1, n-b 14	21	L-b 4, n-b 1	5

1/17 (1) 2/22 (3) 3/73 (4) 4/101 (5)   311   1/13 (1) 2/13 (3) 3/15 (4)   47
5/223 (2) 6/281 (6) 7/289 (7)   4/16 (5) 5/21 (2) 6/41 (7)
8/300 (9) 9/307 (8) 10/311 (11)   7/41 (8) 8/43 (6) 9/43 (9) 10/47 (11)

Hoggard 18.4–3–68–3; Harmison 21–6–61–2; Flintoff 16–3–45–1; Jones 18–2–62–2; Giles 12–0–67–2; Vaughan 1–0–2–0. *Second Innings*—Hoggard 9–2–21–2; Harmison 12.3–8–12–7; Jones 4–1–10–1.

England

M. E. Trescothick b Edwards	7	– not out	6
*M. P. Vaughan c Lara b Edwards	15	– not out	11
M. A. Butcher c Jacobs b Edwards	58		
N. Hussain c sub (D. E. Bernard) b Best	58		
G. P. Thorpe c Sanford b Best	19		
A. Flintoff c Hinds b Sarwan	46		
†C. M. W. Read c Hinds b Best	20		
A. F. Giles b Sanford	27		
M. J. Hoggard not out	9		
S. P. Jones c Sanford b Hinds	7		
S. J. Harmison run out	13		
B 7, l-b 28, w 7, n-b 18	60	B 1, n-b 2	3

1/28 (1) 2/33 (2) 3/152 (3) 4/194 (5)   339   (no wkt) 20
5/209 (4) 6/268 (6) 7/278 (7)
8/313 (8) 9/325 (10) 10/339 (11)

Collymore 26–7–55–0; Edwards 19.3–3–72–3; Best 19–1–57–3; Sanford 22–1–90–1; Hinds 11.5–2–18–1; Gayle 1–0–6–0; Sarwan 4–1–6–1. *Second Innings*—Best 1.3–0–8–0; Hinds 1–0–11–0.

Umpires: B. F. Bowden *(New Zealand)* (12) and D. J. Harper *(Australia)* (38).
Third umpire: E. A. Nicholls *(West Indies)*.   Referee: M. J. Procter *(South Africa)* (21).

Close of play: First day, West Indies 311-9 (Collymore 3, Edwards 1); Second day, England 154-3 (Hussain 41, Thorpe 1); Third day, West Indies 8-0 (Gayle 8, Smith 0).

Test No. 1692/128 (WI407/E818)

WEST INDIES v ENGLAND 2003-04 (2nd Test)

At Queen's Park Oval, Port-of-Spain, Trinidad, on 19, 20, 21, 22, 23 March.
Toss: West Indies. Result: ENGLAND won by seven wickets.
Debuts: none.
Man of the Match: S. J. Harmison.

Less than a fortnight after the start of the series, England retained the Wisden Trophy, a prize they had barely sniffed for 27 years until 2000. Once again Harmison was the dominant figure: West Indies had made an excellent start, with Gayle leading the charge on a slow pitch. His century partnership with Devon Smith, containing 82 in boundaries, came up in the 25th over. But then clouds filled the blue sky and light rain started to fall. Harmison, whose first six-over spell had gone for 27, had just changed ends, and he got immediate results, dismissing both openers. He made it three in eight balls when Lara fended a short one to gully, the first time he had made successive Test ducks. England again lost both openers cheaply, leaving Butcher and Hussain to repair the damage. Later Thorpe pulled and hooked majestically, even with two men back, as the lead was stretched to 111. Jones now took centre-stage, ripping out the top three in his first four overs. Lara dropped himself to No. 6, promoting Jacobs. While hardly sending out a message of confident defiance, the ploy worked to a degree, Jacobs and Chanderpaul adding 102 in 32 overs before Jones removed Jacobs en route to his first Test five-for. Lara emerged on a pair, and made eight before Harmison pinned him to his crease with the first ball of a new spell. Umpire Harper took his time before giving a marginal – and momentous – lbw decision in England's favour.

West Indies

C. H. Gayle c Read b Harmison	62	– b Jones	16
D. S. Smith lbw b Harmison	35	– c Hoggard b Jones	17
R. R. Sarwan c Flintoff b Harmison	21	– lbw b Jones	13
*B. C. Lara c Giles b Harmison	0	– (6) lbw b Harmison	8
S. Chanderpaul c Read b Jones	2	– c Hussain b Flintoff	42
D. R. Smith c Hussain b Harmison	16	– (7) c sub (P. D. Collingwood) b Flintoff	14
†R. D. Jacobs run out	40	– (4) c Flintoff b Jones	70
T. L. Best c Read b Hoggard	1	– lbw b Hoggard	2
A. Sanford run out	1	– c Trescothick b Hoggard	1
P. T. Collins b Harmison	10	– b Jones	7
C. D. Collymore not out	3	– not out	0
L-b 7, w 6, n-b 4	17	B 1, l-b 3, w 5, n-b 10	19

1/100 (1) 2/110 (2) 3/110 (4) 4/113 (5)　　　208　　1/34 (1) 2/45 (2) 3/56 (3)　　　209
5/142 (6) 6/143 (3) 7/148 (8)　　　　　　　　　　4/158 (4) 5/171 (6) 6/194 (7)
8/165 (9) 9/202 (7) 10/208 (10)　　　　　　　　　7/195 (5) 8/200 (8) 9/205 (9) 10/209 (10)

Hoggard 15–3–38–1; Harmison 20.1–5–61–6; Flintoff 10–3–38–0; Giles 3–0–20–0; Jones 12–2–44–1. *Second Innings*—Hoggard 16–5–48–2; Harmison 16–5–40–1; Jones 15–2–57–5; Flintoff 12–1–27–2; Giles 7–1–29–0; Trescothick 1–0–4–0.

England

M. E. Trescothick c Sanford b Best	1	– b Best	4
*M. P. Vaughan lbw b Collins	0	– lbw b Sanford	23
M. A. Butcher c Jacobs b Best	61	– not out	46
N. Hussain b Best	58	– c Jacobs b Sanford	5
G. P. Thorpe c Gayle b Collins	90	– not out	13
A. Flintoff c and b D. R. Smith	23		
†C. M. W. Read lbw b Collins	3		
A. F. Giles c D. S. Smith b Collins	37		
M. J. Hoggard not out	0		
S. P. Jones b Gayle	1		
S. J. Harmison b Gayle	0		
B 5, l-b 20, w 3, n-b 17	45	B 4, l-b 3, n-b 1	8

1/2 (2) 2/8 (1) 3/128 (3) 4/186 (4)　　　319　　1/8 (1) 2/59 (2) 3/71 (4)　　(3 wkts) 99
5/218 (6) 6/230 (7) 7/315 (8)
8/318 (5) 9/319 (10) 10/319 (11)

Collins 29–8–71–4; Best 28–5–71–3; Sanford 26–6–60–0; Collymore 24–7–39–0; D. R. Smith 9–0–30–1; Gayle 16.5–6–20–2; Sarwan 1–0–3–0. *Second Innings*—Best 4–0–27–1; Collins 4–0–25–0; Sanford 4–1–32–2; Collymore 3–1–8–0.

Umpires: B. F. Bowden *(New Zealand)* (13) and D. J. Harper *(Australia)* (39).
Third umpire: E. A. Nicholls *(West Indies)*.   Referee: M. J. Procter *(South Africa)* (22).

Close of play: First day, West Indies 189-8 (Jacobs 29, Collins 6); Second day, England 54-2 (Butcher 25, Hussain 20); Third day, England 300-6 (Thorpe 81, Giles 28); Fourth day, England 71-2 (Butcher 32, Hussain 5).

WEST INDIES v ENGLAND 2003-04 (3rd Test)

At Kensington Oval, Bridgetown, Barbados, on 1, 2, 3 April.
Toss: England.   Result: ENGLAND won by eight wickets.
Debuts: none.
Man of the Match: G. P. Thorpe.

For much of this brief but compelling Test, the two teams looked evenly matched. But England's bowling was effective, disciplined and occasionally touched by magic, notably when Hoggard became the tenth England bowler to take a Test hat-trick – their third against West Indies, following Peter Loader and Dominic Cork – dismissing an impressive trio in Sarwan, Chanderpaul and Hinds. The West Indian batting, by contrast, was prone to outbreaks of wretchedness. England not only clinched the series but made sure of their most successful Caribbean tour ever. Yet they did not start well: three slip catches went down on the first day. Harmison found his length after tea, having Sarwan caught at second slip, but it was Flintoff's turn to shine, with his first Test five-for (including Lara caught in the gully) as the last seven tumbled for 57. The return of Edwards gave West Indies' bowling an old-fashioned feel: four fast bowlers, all Barbadian, three of them coming from the same small village, Boscobel, and two – Edwards and Collins – being half-brothers. Edwards's skiddy pace removed England's top three for only 33, and the rest of the batting succumbed too – apart from Thorpe, who reached an outstandingly determined century moments after the new ball was taken at 189 for 9. Last man Harmison helped him add 39, which inched England into a psychologically vital two-run lead. Next morning, in familiar cloudy conditions Hoggard settled matters as, for the fourth time in seven Tests, England bowled West Indies out in two figures.

West Indies

C. H. Gayle lbw b Hoggard	6	– b Harmison		15
D. Ganga lbw b Harmison	11	– c Thorpe b Hoggard		11
*B. C. Lara c Butcher b Flintoff	36	– c Vaughan b Harmison		33
R. R. Sarwan c Flintoff b Harmison	63	– c Giles b Hoggard		5
S. Chanderpaul c Thorpe b Flintoff	50	– lbw b Hoggard		0
R. O. Hinds c Jones b Harmison	5	– c Flintoff b Hoggard		0
†R. D. Jacobs c sub (P. D. Collingwood) b Flintoff	6	– c Butcher b Flintoff		1
T. L. Best c Butcher b Flintoff	17	– c Trescothick b Flintoff		12
P. T. Collins c Trescothick b Jones	7	– run out		1
C. D. Collymore not out	1	– not out		6
F. H. Edwards c Read b Flintoff	0	– c Hussain b Harmison		2
L-b 14, w 1, n-b 7	22	L-b 5, n-b 3		8
	224			**94**

1/6 (1) 2/20 (2) 3/88 (3) 4/167 (4)   **224**
5/179 (6) 6/197 (7) 7/198 (5)
8/208 (9) 9/224 (8) 10/224 (11)

1/19 (1) 2/34 (2) 3/45 (4)   **94**
4/45 (5) 5/45 (6) 6/48 (7)
7/80 (8) 8/81 (9) 9/85 (3) 10/94 (11)

Hoggard 16–5–34–1; Harmison 18–6–42–3; Flintoff 16.2–2–58–5; Jones 16–1–55–1; Giles 9–1–21–0. *Second Innings*—Hoggard 14–4–35–4; Harmison 15.1–5–34–3; Flintoff 13–4–20–2.

England

M. E. Trescothick b Edwards	2	– c Jacobs b Collymore		42
*M. P. Vaughan c Jacobs b Edwards	17	– c Jacobs b Collymore		32
M. A. Butcher c Gayle b Edwards	5	– not out		13
N. Hussain b Collymore	17	– not out		0
G. P. Thorpe not out	119			
A. Flintoff c Collymore b Best	15			
†C. M. W. Read lbw b Edwards	13			
A. F. Giles c sub (A. N. Mayers) b Collins	11			
M. J. Hoggard lbw b Collins	0			
S. P. Jones c Sarwan b Best	4			
S. J. Harmison b Collins	3			
L-b 5, w 3, n-b 12	20	L-b 3, w 1, n-b 2		6
	226	(2 wkts)		**93**

1/8 (1) 2/24 (3) 3/33 (2) 4/65 (4)   **226**
5/90 (6) 6/119 (7) 7/147 (8)
8/155 (9) 9/187 (10) 10/226 (11)

1/57 (2) 2/91 (1)   (2 wkts) **93**

Edwards 20–4–70–4; Collins 23–6–60–3; Collymore 16–3–26–1; Hinds 4–1–7–0; Best 14–4–26–2; Gayle 13–3–32–0. *Second Innings*—Edwards 6–0–32–0; Best 3–0–18–0; Collymore 7–2–24–2; Collins 4–0–16–0.

Umpires: D. B. Hair *(Australia)* (52) and R. E. Koertzen *(South Africa)* (48).
Third umpire: B. R. Doctrove *(West Indies)*.   Referee: M. J. Procter *(South Africa)* (23).

Close of play: First day, England 20-1 (Vaughan 12, Butcher 3); Second day, West Indies 21-1 (Ganga 5, Lara 1).

WEST INDIES v ENGLAND 2003-04 (4th Test)

At Antigua Recreation Ground, St John's, Antigua, on 10, 11, 12, 13, 14 April.
Toss: West Indies.   Result: MATCH DRAWN.
Debuts: England – G. O. Jones.
Man of the Match: B. C. Lara.   Man of the Series: S. J. Harmison.

Just 185 days after Matthew Hayden took his record for the highest Test innings, Brian Lara grabbed it back. Twenty-five minutes before lunch on the third day, he danced down to hoist Batty's off-break over long-on for the six that lifted him past his own 375 and level with Hayden at 380. He swept the next ball to fine leg for four to reclaim the record he had taken from Garry Sobers on the same ground ten years earlier. It was the tenth time the record had changed hands; no-one had previously recovered it. Lara swept Batty again for the single that raised Test cricket's first 400, the tenth in all first-class cricket. Next ball Jacobs's four made it 751, and Lara declared at the end of the over with the highest total ever conceded by England. He had batted two minutes short of 13 hours, faced 582 balls, and hit four sixes and 43 fours. Graham Thorpe and umpire Darrell Hair were on the field throughout both Lara's record innings: had Hair been persuaded by a convincing caught-behind appeal off Harmison, Lara would not have scored a run. Lara was not the only one to appreciate a return to a benign pitch: Gayle and Sarwan compensated for meagre series before Jacobs shared a stand of 282 with Lara, a West Indian sixth-wicket record. England did follow on but, without a genuine spinner, West Indies could make little impression on a wearing pitch as Vaughan compiled a fluent 11th Test century.

West Indies

C. H. Gayle c and b Batty	69	†R. D. Jacobs not out	107
D. Ganga lbw b Flintoff	10	B 4, l-b 5, w 2, n-b 5	16
*B. C. Lara not out	400		
R. R. Sarwan c Trescothick b Harmison	90	1/33 (2) 2/98 (1)	(5 wkts dec.) 751
R. L. Powell c Hussain b S. P. Jones	23	3/330 (4) 4/380 (5)	
R. O. Hinds c and b Batty	36	5/469 (6)	

T. L. Best, P. T. Collins, C. D. Collymore and F. H. Edwards did not bat.

Hoggard 18–2–82–0; Harmison 37–6–92–1; Flintoff 35–8–109–1; S. P. Jones 29–0–146–1; Batty 52–4–185–2; Vaughan 13–0–60–0; Trescothick 18–3–68–0.

England

M. E. Trescothick c Jacobs b Best	16	– c Sarwan b Edwards	88
*M. P. Vaughan c Jacobs b Collins	7	– c Jacobs b Sarwan	140
M. A. Butcher b Collins	52	– c Gayle b Hinds	61
N. Hussain b Best	3	– b Hinds	56
G. P. Thorpe c Collins b Edwards	10	– not out	23
A. Flintoff not out	102	– c Lara b Sarwan	14
†G. O. Jones b Edwards	38	– not out	10
G. J. Batty c Gayle b Collins	8		
M. J. Hoggard c Jacobs b Collins	1		
S. P. Jones lbw b Hinds	11		
S. J. Harmison b Best	5		
B 1, l-b 5, w 4, n-b 22	32	B 4, l-b 7, w 3, n-b 16	30

1/8 (2) 2/45 (1) 3/54 (4) 4/98 (3)	285	1/182 (1) 2/274 (2)	(5 wkts) 422
5/98 (5) 6/182 (7) 7/205 (8)		3/366 (3) 4/387 (4)	
8/229 (9) 9/283 (11) 10/285 (10)		5/408 (6)	

In the first innings S. P. Jones, when 11, retired hurt at 277 and resumed at 283.

Collins 26–4–76–4; Edwards 18–3–70–2; Collymore 19–5–45–0; Best 10.3–3–37–3; Hinds 17.3–7–29–1; Sarwan 7–0–18–0; Gayle 1–0–4–0. *Second Innings*—Best 16–1–57–0; Edwards 20–2–81–1; Collymore 18–3–58–0; Powell 8–0–36–0; Hinds 38–8–83–2; Gayle 17–6–36–0; Sarwan 12–2–26–2; Collins 8–2–34–0.

Umpires: Aleem Dar *(Pakistan)* (7) and D. B. Hair *(Australia)* (53).
Third umpire: B. R. Doctrove *(West Indies)*.   Referee: M. J. Procter *(South Africa)* (24);
J. J. Crowe *(New Zealand)* deputised for Procter on the fourth day.

Close of play: First day, West Indies 208-2 (Lara 86, Sarwan 41); Second day, West Indies 595-5 (Lara 313, Jacobs 47); Third day, England 171-5 (Flintoff 37, G. O. Jones 32); Fourth day, England 145-0 (Trescothick 74, Vaughan 61).

PAKISTAN v INDIA 2003-04 (1st Test)

At Multan Cricket Stadium on 28, 29, 30, 31 March, 1 April.
Toss: India.   Result: INDIA won by an innings and 52 runs.
Debuts: none.
Man of the Match: V. Sehwag.

It might have been Pakistan's 300th Test, but the main feature was India's first triple-century, which laid the foundation of their first victory in Pakistan in 21 Tests spanning 49 years. It was also, briefly, their most substantial win in 72 years of Tests away from home. Sehwag's innings, and his partnership of 336 with Tendulkar, a national third-wicket record, carried India to their third-highest total, and second-highest away (the highest had come in their previous Test, on a similar pitch at Sydney). Sehwag's glitzy epic was not faultless: dropped on 68 and 77 during his third century partnership with Chopra in as many Tests, he later offered two chances behind the wicket off Shabbir Ahmed, one ball either side of the four that took him past VVS Laxman's Indian-record 281. Nonetheless it was an innings of sustained and versatile violence. He thrashed six sixes and 39 fours in 531 minutes and 375 balls; he went from 99 to 105 by gliding Shoaib Akhtar for six over third man, and from 295 to 301 with a roundhouse blast over wide long-on off Saqlain Mushtaq. Despite this, Dravid (acting-captain for the injured Ganguly) said that bowling Pakistan out twice on a grassless, crumble-proof surface was arguably a better achievement. Dravid had stunned observers by declaring when Yuvraj Singh fell an hour before the second-day close, with Tendulkar on 194. Tendulkar did not take the field that evening, claiming a sprained ankle; at a press conference, he made clear his disappointment and surprise.

India

A. Chopra c Imran Farhat b Saqlain Mushtaq	42	Yuvraj Singh c and b Imran Farhat		59
V. Sehwag c Taufeeq Umar b Mohammad Sami	309	B 8, l-b 20, w 1, n-b 7		36
*R. Dravid c Yasir Hameed b Mohammad Sami	6			
S. R. Tendulkar not out	194	1/160 (1) 2/173 (3)	(5 wkts dec.)	675
V. V. S. Laxman run out	29	3/509 (2) 4/565 (5) 5/675 (6)		

†P. A. Patel, I. K. Pathan, A. Kumble, L. Balaji and Zaheer Khan did not bat.

Shoaib Akhtar 32–4–119–0; Mohammad Sami 34–4–110–2; Shabbir Ahmed 31–6–122–0; Saqlain Mushtaq 43–4–204–1; Abdul Razzaq 15–3–61–0; Imran Farhat 6.5–0–31–1.

Pakistan

Imran Farhat lbw b Balaji	38	– c Patel b Kumble	24
Taufeeq Umar c Dravid b Pathan	23	– lbw b Kumble	9
Yasir Hameed c Patel b Pathan	91	– c Sehwag b Yuvraj Singh	23
*Inzamam-ul-Haq c Chopra b Kumble	77	– run out	0
Yousuf Youhana c Patel b Zaheer Khan	35	– c Dravid b Pathan	112
Abdul Razzaq c Patel b Pathan	47	– c Chopra b Kumble	22
†Moin Khan b Tendulkar	17	– lbw b Pathan	5
Saqlain Mushtaq c Zaheer Khan b Pathan	5	– (9) lbw b Kumble	0
Mohammad Sami b Kumble	15	– (8) lbw b Kumble	0
Shoaib Akhtar c and b Tendulkar	0	– c Laxman b Kumble	4
Shabbir Ahmed not out	19	– not out	0
B 4, l-b 26, n-b 10	40	B 4, l-b 5, w 1, n-b 2, p 5	17

1/58 (2) 2/73 (1) 3/233 (4) 4/243 (3)	407	1/33 (1) 2/44 (2) 3/44 (4)	216
5/321 (5) 6/364 (7) 7/364 (6)		4/75 (3) 5/106 (6) 6/113 (7)
8/371 (8) 9/371 (10) 10/407 (9)		7/124 (8) 8/136 (9) 9/206 (10) 10/216 (5)

Zaheer Khan 23–6–76–1; Pathan 28–5–100–4; Kumble 39.3–12–100–2; Balaji 20–4–54–1; Sehwag 2–0–11–0; Tendulkar 14–1–36–2. *Second Innings*—Pathan 21–12–26–2; Balaji 11–3–48–0; Kumble 30–10–72–6; Sehwag 3–0–8–0; Yuvraj Singh 6–1–25–1; Tendulkar 6–2–23–0.

Umpires: D. R. Shepherd *(England)* (80) and S. J. A. Taufel *(Australia)* (12).
Third umpire: Asad Rauf *(Pakistan)*.   Referee: R. S. Madugalle *(Sri Lanka)* (59).

Close of play: First day, India 356-2 (Sehwag 228, Tendulkar 60); Second day, Pakistan 42-0 (Imran Farhat 17, Taufeeq Umar 20); Third day, Pakistan 364-6 (Abdul Razzaq 47); Fourth day, Pakistan 207-9 (Yousuf Youhana 107, Shabbir Ahmed 0).

PAKISTAN v INDIA 2003-04 (2nd Test)

At Gaddafi Stadium, Lahore, on 5, 6, 7, 8 April.
Toss: India.   Result: PAKISTAN won by nine wickets.
Debuts: none.
Man of the Match: Umar Gul.

Pakistan levelled the series, with seamer Umar Gul, 20 and matchstick-thin, playing a major role. Shoaib Akhtar's first ball took Chopra's edge and squirted through for four; the last ball of the first over hit him on the shoulder. It was obvious that justifying Dravid's decision to bat would be hard work, particularly during the first session. When Gul came on in the 11th over, India were rattling along at six an over, but in a 12-over spell either side of lunch he took five wickets, including Tendulkar, out for the first time in four innings in 2004, in which he had amassed a record 497 runs. Gul bowled no more in the first innings because of cramp, and later picked up a back injury that made him miss the Third Test. Yuvraj Singh took the chance to make an attacking maiden Test century in 110 balls. Pakistan went after a big lead: Inzamam-ul-Haq anchored the innings, while Imran Farhat made his second Test hundred, then Asim Kamal and the tail extended the advantage to 202. The game was soon up for India: Chopra, Tendulkar and Laxman, bowled by a marvellous leg-cutter from Gul, all went cheaply again, while Dravid was run out before facing a ball by Farhat's direct hit, only his third duck in 77 Tests. A raucous stand between Patel and Agarkar averted the innings defeat: when the final wicket fell Gul raced off, stumps in hand, before being reminded that Pakistan still had to bat again.

India

A. Chopra lbw b Mohammad Sami	4	– lbw b Shoaib Akhtar	5
V. Sehwag c Kamran Akmal b Umar Gul	39	– c Kamran Akmal b Shoaib Akhtar	90
*R. Dravid c Inzamam-ul-Haq b Umar Gul	33	– run out	0
S. R. Tendulkar lbw b Umar Gul	2	– lbw b Mohammad Sami	8
V. V. S. Laxman c Taufeeq Umar b Umar Gul	11	– b Umar Gul	13
Yuvraj Singh c Imran Farhat b Danish Kaneria	112	– c Kamran Akmal b Mohammad Sami	12
†P. A. Patel lbw b Umar Gul	0	– not out	62
A. B. Agarkar c Kamran Akmal b Shoaib Akhtar	2	– (9) c Taufeeq Umar b Danish Kaneria	36
I. K. Pathan c and b Danish Kaneria	49	– (8) c Taufeeq Umar b Shoaib Akhtar	0
L. Balaji c Kamran Akmal b Mohammad Sami	0	– (11) lbw b Danish Kaneria	0
A. Kumble not out	6	– (10) st Kamran Akmal b Danish Kaneria	0
B 6, l-b 8, w 6, n-b 9	29	L-b 8, w 1, n-b 6	15

1/5 (1) 2/69 (2) 3/75 (4) 4/94 (5)   287   1/15 (1) 2/15 (3) 3/43 (4)   241
5/125 (3) 6/127 (7) 7/147 (8)   4/88 (5) 5/105 (6) 6/160 (2)
8/264 (9) 9/265 (10) 10/287 (6)   7/160 (8) 8/235 (9) 9/241 (10) 10/241 (11)

Shoaib Akhtar 16–1–69–1; Mohammad Sami 23–1–117–2; Umar Gul 12–2–31–5; Danish Kaneria 13.1–1–56–2. *Second Innings*—Shoaib Akhtar 17–4–62–3; Mohammad Sami 26–6–92–2; Umar Gul 13–1–65–1; Danish Kaneria 6.4–2–14–3.

Pakistan

Imran Farhat c Patel b Balaji	101	– c Yuvraj Singh b Balaji	9
Taufeeq Umar b Balaji	24	– not out	14
Yasir Hameed c Dravid b Agarkar	19	– not out	16
*Inzamam-ul-Haq lbw b Pathan	118		
Yousuf Youhana c Patel b Balaji	72		
Asim Kamal c Patel b Kumble	73		
†Kamran Akmal lbw b Pathan	5		
Mohammad Sami b Pathan	2		
Shoaib Akhtar c Yuvraj Singh b Kumble	19		
Umar Gul hit wkt b Tendulkar	14		
Danish Kaneria not out	0		
B 4, l-b 18, w 4, n-b 16	42	N-b 1	1

1/47 (2) 2/95 (3) 3/205 (1) 4/356 (4)   489   1/15 (1)   (1 wkt) 40
5/366 (5) 6/379 (7) 7/386 (8)
8/432 (9) 9/470 (10) 10/489 (6)

Pathan 44–14–107–3; Balaji 33–11–81–3; Agarkar 23–5–80–1; Kumble 44.1–5–146–2; Tendulkar 12–1–38–1; Yuvraj Singh 3–0–7–0; Sehwag 1–0–8–0. *Second Innings*—Pathan 4–0–25–0; Balaji 3–0–15–1.

Umpires: S. A. Bucknor *(West Indies)* (89) and S. J. A. Taufel *(Australia)* (13).
Third umpire: Nadeem Ghauri *(Pakistan)*.   Referee: R. S. Madugalle *(Sri Lanka)* (60).

Close of play: First day, Pakistan 61-1 (Imran Farhat 25, Yasir Hameed 4); Second day, Pakistan 355-3 (Inzamam-ul-Haq 118, Yousuf Youhana 62); Third day, India 149-5 (Sehwag 86, Patel 13).

PAKISTAN v INDIA 2003-04 (3rd Test)

At Rawalpindi Cricket Stadium on 13, 14, 15, 16 April.
Toss: India.   Result: INDIA won by an innings and 131 runs.
Debuts: none.
Man of the Match: R. Dravid.   Man of the Series: V. Sehwag.

India not only bettered their thundering Multan victory for magnitude, but won their first away Test series for a decade. Ganguly, back from injury, chose to field, and went on to his 15th win as captain, beating Mohammad Azharuddin's Indian record. In the previous Test, India were 107 for 4 at lunch on the first day; here, Pakistan were 96 for 4. Then Balaji, bending the ball away, took three wickets in nine overs, making it 137 for 8, although Mohammad Sami and a comical innings from Fazl-e-Akbar lifted the total to 224. Then 270 from Dravid put the series beyond Pakistan. Scratchy on the first day, he blossomed on the second. It was a remarkable effort: between his 73 overs in the field and 175 overs' batting there was just a ten-minute break (Sehwag fell first ball). India's longest Test innings lasted 740 minutes and included 34 fours and a six. Dravid's fifth Test double-century was an Indian record, one ahead of Sunil Gavaskar. His task was eased when, late on the second afternoon, Shoaib Akhtar fell and injured his left thumb and a rib. He went off after six further balls and did not return except to bat. After India made a round 600, Pakistan's openers again fell in consecutive overs, leaving the rest to battle through the last two days. They did not come close, despite the best efforts of India's fielders, who dropped six catches in the first hour next morning, four of them off Balaji.

Pakistan

Imran Farhat lbw b Nehra	16	– c Sehwag b Balaji	3
Taufeeq Umar lbw b Balaji	9	– lbw b Pathan	13
Yasir Hameed c Laxman b Pathan	26	– c Patel b Nehra	20
*Inzamam-ul-Haq c Patel b Nehra	15	– (5) c Patel b Balaji	9
Yousuf Youhana b Pathan	13	– (6) c and b Kumble	48
Asim Kamal lbw b Balaji	21	– (7) not out	60
†Kamran Akmal c Laxman b Balaji	17	– (4) b Balaji	23
Mohammad Sami run out	49	– c Dravid b Kumble	0
Shoaib Akhtar b Balaji	0	– c Nehra b Kumble	28
Fazl-e-Akbar lbw b Kumble	25	– c Pathan b Kumble	12
Danish Kaneria not out	4	– c Ganguly b Tendulkar	0
B 14, l-b 5, w 7, n-b 3	29	B 5, l-b 11, w 2, n-b 11	29

1/34 (2) 2/34 (1) 3/77 (3) 4/77 (4)   224   1/30 (1) 2/34 (2) 3/64 (4)   245
5/110 (5) 6/120 (6) 7/137 (7)   4/90 (3) 5/94 (5) 6/175 (6)
8/137 (9) 9/207 (10) 10/224 (8)   7/179 (8) 8/221 (9) 9/244 (10) 10/245 (11)

Pathan 22–7–49–2; Balaji 19–4–63–4; Nehra 21–4–60–2; Ganguly 2–0–9–0; Kumble 8.5–2–24–1. *Second Innings*—Pathan 15–6–35–1; Balaji 20–2–108–3; Kumble 8–2–47–4; Nehra 6–2–20–1; Ganguly 4–0–18–0; Tendulkar 1–0–1–1.

India

V. Sehwag c Yasir Hameed b Shoaib Akhtar	0	A. Kumble st Kamran Akmal b Danish Kaneria	9
†P. A. Patel c Kamran Akmal b Fazl-e-Akbar	69	L. Balaji c sub (Shoaib Malik)	
R. Dravid b Imran Farhat	270	b Imran Farhat	11
S. R. Tendulkar c Kamran Akmal b Shoaib Akhtar	1	A. Nehra not out	1
V. V. S. Laxman b Shoaib Akhtar	71	B 11, l-b 12, w 6	29
*S. C. Ganguly run out	77		
Yuvraj Singh lbw b Mohammad Sami	47	1/0 (1) 2/129 (2) 3/130 (4)	600
I. K. Pathan c Fazl-e-Akbar b Danish Kaneria	15	4/261 (5) 5/392 (6) 6/490 (7)	
		7/537 (8) 8/572 (9) 9/593 (3) 10/600 (10)	

Shoaib Akhtar 21.2–7–47–3; Fazl-e-Akbar 40.4–3–162–1; Danish Kaneria 62–4–178–2; Mohammad Sami 40–11–116–1; Imran Farhat 12.2–1–69–2; Yasir Hameed 1–0–5–0.

Umpires: R. E. Koertzen *(South Africa)* (49) and D. R. Shepherd *(England)* (81).
Third umpire: Zamir Haider *(Pakistan)*.   Referee: R. S. Madugalle *(Sri Lanka)* (61).

Close of play: First day, India 23-1 (Patel 13, Dravid 10); Second day, India 342-4 (Dravid 134, Ganguly 53); Third day, Pakistan 49-2 (Yasir Hameed 8, Kamran Akmal 10).

ZIMBABWE v SRI LANKA 2003-04 (1st Test)

At Harare Sports Club on 6, 7, 8 May.
Toss: Sri Lanka.   Result: SRI LANKA won by an innings and 240 runs.
Debuts: Zimbabwe – E. Chigumbura, A. Maregwede, T. Panyangara, B. R. M. Taylor, P. Utseya. Sri Lanka – M. F. Maharoof.
Man of the Match: M. Muralitharan.

A dispute between the Zimbabwean board and 15 mainly white dissident players led to five debutants in a team sharing only 53 previous Test caps between them. Tatenda Taibu became the youngest-ever Test captain at 20 years 358 days. The predictable result was Zimbabwe's heaviest Test defeat, a record that lasted for nine days. Atapattu bowled first, despite a benign pitch. Taibu scored a determined 40 before walking for a bat-pad catch, and Utseya made 45, but Muralitharan mopped up the last six, drawing level with Courtney Walsh on 519 Test wickets. Zimbabwe's bowlers then toiled as Atapattu and Jayasuriya put on 281. The breakthrough finally came when Taibu took off his pads to bowl his skiddy medium-pacers; his third delivery bounced unexpectedly from the pitch, off Jayasuriya's gloves and into the gully. It was the first time a designated wicketkeeper had taken the first wicket in a Test. Atapattu was bowled by the second new ball for 170 during a middle-order slump, but the tail swelled the lead to 342. Zimbabwe then crashed to 18 for 5, Zoysa grabbing four for one in 21 balls, but Maregwede and Nkala had just equalled Zimbabwe's lowest Test score (63) when Nkala played forward and was caught pad-bat at silly mid-off, to become Murali's 520th Test wicket. As in the first innings, some courageous hitting by the last pair sneaked Zimbabwe into three figures, but they could not disguise the gulf between the sides.

Zimbabwe

S. Matsikenyeri c D. P. M. D. Jayawardene b Zoysa ...	10	– c D. P. M. D. Jayawardene b Zoysa........		11
B. R. M. Taylor c and b Maharoof................	19	– c Muralitharan b Vaas		4
D. D Ebrahim lbw b Zoysa.....................	1	– c H. A. P. W. Jayawardene b Zoysa........		2
*†T. Taibu c D. P. M. D. Jayawardene b Muralitharan ...	40	– lbw b Zoysa		0
E. Chigumbura c Muralitharan b Zoysa	14	– c H. A. P. W. Jayawardene b Zoysa........		0
A. Maregwede lbw b Muralitharan................	0	– c and b Muralitharan		22
M. L. Nkala lbw b Muralitharan..................	2	– c D. P. M. D. Jayawardene b Muralitharan ..		24
P. Utseya b Muralitharan	45	– b Maharoof............................		0
N. B. Mahwire b Muralitharan	0	– c D. P. M. D. Jayawardene b Zoysa........		2
D. T. Hondo b Muralitharan	19	– not out...............................		15
T. Panyangara not out	32	– c D. P. M. D. Jayawardene b Jayasuriya		18
B 4, l-b 6, n-b 7................	17	L-b 2, n-b 2		4

1/30 (2) 2/32 (3) 3/35 (1) 4/57 (5)   199 1/13 (1) 2/15 (3) 3/17 (2)   102
5/69 (6) 6/85 (7) 7/118 (4)   4/17 (4) 5/18 (5) 6/63 (7)
8/118 (9) 9/149 (8) 10/199 (10)   7/64 (8) 8/64 (6) 9/72 (9) 10/102 (11)

Vaas 19–6–39–0; Zoysa 17–6–53–3; Maharoof 10–3–45–1; Muralitharan 24.2–10–45–6; Jayasuriya 1–0–7–0. *Second Innings*—Vaas 8–2–24–1; Zoysa 9.5–2–20–5; Muralitharan 9.1–1–37–2; Maharoof 4–0–18–1; Jayasuriya 1–0–1–1.

Sri Lanka

*M. S. Atapattu b Hondo	170	M. F. Maharoof lbw b Mahwire	40
S. T. Jayasuriya c Hondo b Taibu	157	D. N. T. Zoysa not out..................	28
K. C. Sangakkara c Taibu b Matsikenyeri	11	M. Muralitharan c Maregwede b Panyangara ..	26
D. P. M. D. Jayawardene c Utseya b Chigumbura	37	B 2, l-b 13, w 3, n-b 6	24
T. M. Dilshan c Utseya b Mahwire................	10		
T. T. Samaraweera c Taibu b Panyangara	6	1/281 (2) 2/312 (3) 3/369 (4)	541
†H. A. P. W. Jayawardene b Panyangara.............	4	4/387 (1) 5/399 (6) 6/403 (7)	
W. P. U. J. C. Vaas c Matsikenyeri b Mahwire	28	7/414 (5) 8/457 (8)	
		9/496 (9) 10/541 (11)	

Hondo 27–6–103–1; Panyangara 26.1–2–101–3; Mahwire 18–1–97–3; Nkala 7–1–41–0; Utseya 12–2–55–0; Matsikenyeri 15–2–58–1; Taibu 8–1–27–1; Chigumbura 12–2–44–1.

Umpires: B. F. Bowden *(New Zealand)* (14) and R. E. Koertzen *(South Africa)* (50).
Third umpire: R. B. Tiffin *(Zimbabwe).*   Referee: M. J. Procter *(South Africa)* (25).

Close of play: First day, Sri Lanka 67-0 (Atapattu 21, Jayasuriya 43); Second day, Sri Lanka 456-7 (Vaas 28, Maharoof 16).

ZIMBABWE v SRI LANKA 2003-04 (2nd Test)

At Queens Sports Club, Bulawayo, on 14, 15, 16, 17 May.
Toss: Sri Lanka.   Result: SRI LANKA won by an innings and 254 runs.
Debuts: Zimbabwe – T. Mupariwa.
Man of the Match: K. C. Sangakkara.   Man of the Series: M. S. Atapattu.

Zimbabwe suffered the heaviest defeat in their history for the second match running, and this time managed just three Sri Lankan wickets. Another total mismatch finally persuaded the ICC that something had to be done to preserve the integrity of Test cricket. Zimbabwe included Vermeulen, the only contracted white player not to join the dissidents, but he contributed little. Matsikenyeri batted like a millionaire at the start, hitting 45 off 64 balls, while Ebrahim grafted. But Taibu and Maregwede were cut off in their prime, and Zimbabwe just failed to last the day. The second day was one for records, none favourable to Zimbabwe: Sri Lanka amassed 425 runs for a single wicket. The bowlers did keep Jayasuriya quiet, but had no answer to Atapattu or Sangakkara, who piled up 438, the sixth-highest stand for any Test wicket. Atapattu reached his sixth Test double-century – his third against Zimbabwe and his second in two Tests at Bulawayo – and Sangakkara followed him past 200 next day. Several hard chances were missed before Atapattu, trying to push a single for 250, edged to the keeper, then Sangakkara, who had just beaten the ground record (Dave Houghton's 266 against Sri Lanka almost ten years earlier), was well held by the diving Taibu (who did not bowl in this match but did catch the three batsmen who were out). There was one final unwelcome record: it was the first time six bowlers had conceded a century apiece in a Test innings.

Zimbabwe

S. Matsikenyeri run out	45	– c H. A. P. W. Jayawardene b Zoysa	14
B. R. M. Taylor c H. A. P. W. Jayawardene b Vaas	5	– c D. P. M. D. Jayawardene b Muralitharan	61
M. A. Vermeulen c Muralitharan b Vaas	0	– c Muralitharan b Zoysa	6
D. D Ebrahim c Dilshan b Maharoof	70	– c Atapattu b Jayasuriya	42
*†T. Taibu c Samaraweera b Maharoof	27	– c Dilshan b Muralitharan	0
A. Maregwede run out	24	– lbw b Vaas	28
E. Chigumbura c D. P. M. D. Jayawardene b Vaas	0	– lbw b Muralitharan	12
M. L. Nkala c Sangakkara b Muralitharan	19	– c Dilshan b Vaas	0
T. Panyangara c Vaas b Zoysa	11	– not out	40
T. Mupariwa not out	1	– c Vaas b Jayasuriya	14
D. T. Hondo b Muralitharan	11	– c Atapattu b Muralitharan	3
L-b 2, w 3, n-b 10	15	L-b 7, w 1, n-b 3	11

1/24 (2) 2/31 (3) 3/82 (1) 4/134 (5)   228   1/22 (1) 2/40 (3) 3/125 (2)   231
5/176 (6) 6/176 (7) 7/193 (4)   4/127 (5) 5/143 (4) 6/173 (6)
8/211 (9) 9/216 (8) 10/228 (11)   7/173 (8) 8/173 (7) 9/204 (10) 10/231 (11)

Vaas 19–8–41–3; Zoysa 14–0–50–1; Maharoof 16–2–62–2; Muralitharan 22–3–58–2; Jayasuriya 4–0–15–0. *Second Innings*—Vaas 18–6–53–2; Zoysa 13–4–27–2; Muralitharan 28.1–6–79–4; Maharoof 6–0–32–0; Jayasuriya 10–0–33–2.

Sri Lanka

*M. S. Atapattu c Taibu b Chigumbura	249
S. T. Jayasuriya c Taibu b Nkala	48
K. C. Sangakkara c Taibu b Panyangara	270
D. P. M. D. Jayawardene not out	100
T. T. Samaraweera not out	32
L-b 5, w 4, n-b 5	14

1/100 (2) 2/538 (1)   (3 wkts dec.) 713
3/627 (3)

T. M. Dilshan, †H. A. P. W. Jayawardene, W. P. U. J. C. Vaas, M. F. Maharoof, D. N. T. Zoysa and M. Muralitharan did not bat.

Hondo 29–5–116–0; Panyangara 25–4–120–1; Mupariwa 34–1–136–0; Nkala 32–3–111–1; Chigumbura 1–2–108–1; Matsikenyeri 23.3–1–112–0; Vermeulen 1–0–5–0.

Umpires: B. F. Bowden *(New Zealand)* (15) and R. E. Koertzen *(South Africa)* (51).
Third umpire: R. B. Tiffin *(Zimbabwe)*.   Referee: M. J. Procter *(South Africa)* (26).

Close of play: First day, Sri Lanka 18-0 (Atapattu 7, Jayasuriya 11); Second day, Sri Lanka 443-1 (Atapattu 202, Sangakkara 186); Third day, Zimbabwe 44-2 (Taylor 19, Ebrahim 3).

ENGLAND v NEW ZEALAND 2004 (1st Test)

At Lord's, London, on 20, 21, 22, 23, 24 May.
Toss: New Zealand.   Result: ENGLAND won by seven wickets.
Debuts: England – A. J. Strauss.
Man of the Match: A. J. Strauss.

Three days before the match, Michael Vaughan attempted an innocuous sweep, collapsed, and was counted out with a twisted right knee. Trescothick captained for the first time, and Andrew Strauss, not in the original 13-man squad, became only the fourth player – after Australian Harry Graham (1893), England's John Hampshire (1969) and India's Sourav Ganguly (1996) – to launch his Test career with a century at Lord's. Strauss was not the only adhesive left-handed opener on view: Richardson was a model of obduracy, batting more than 13½ hours in all. Astle and Oram upped the tempo before Cairns launched four sixes in ten balls, surpassing Viv Richards's Test-record 84 sixes. England's openers then made merry in a fluent stand, Strauss becoming England's first debut centurion since Graham Thorpe in 1993, then Flintoff and Geraint Jones set up a useful lead. After Richardson's defiance England needed 282 to win – 64 more than they had ever managed in 105 previous Lord's Tests. At a worrying 35 for 2, Hussain marched out. He steadied the ship with Strauss, who was close to becoming only the third to score two centuries on debut when he sacrificed himself after a mix-up. England were still 139 short, but Hussain scrambled to a 158-ball fifty before a rush of adrenalin carried him to the final curtain. His next fifty took only 45 balls, and he reached his hundred just before driving the winning run into the covers. Shortly afterwards, he announced his retirement after 96 Tests spanning 14 years.

New Zealand

M. H. Richardson lbw b Harmison	93	– c G. O. Jones b Harmison	101
*S. P. Fleming c Strauss b S. P. Jones	34	– c Hussain b Harmison	4
N. J. Astle c G. O. Jones b Flintoff	64	– (7) c G. O. Jones b Harmison	49
S. B. Styris c G. O. Jones b S. P. Jones	0	– c Hussain b Giles	4
C. D. McMillan lbw b Hoggard	6	– c Hussain b Giles	0
J. D. P. Oram c G. O. Jones b Harmison	67	– run out	4
D. R. Tuffey b Harmison	8	– (10) not out	14
C. L. Cairns c Harmison b Flintoff	82	– c Butcher b Giles	14
†B. B. McCullum b S. P. Jones	5	– (3) c G. O. Jones b S. P. Jones	96
D. L. Vettori b Harmison	2	– (9) c G. O. Jones b Harmison	5
C. S. Martin not out	1	– b Flintoff	7
B 9, l-b 6, w 2, n-b 7	24	B 14, l-b 16, n-b 8	38

1/58 (2) 2/161 (3) 3/162 (4) 4/174 (5)   386
5/280 (1) 6/287 (6) 7/324 (7)
8/329 (9) 9/338 (10) 10/386 (8)

1/7 (2) 2/180 (3) 3/187 (4)   336
4/187 (5) 5/203 (6) 6/287 (1)
7/290 (7) 8/304 (9) 9/310 (8) 10/336 (11)

Hoggard 22–7–68–1; Harmison 31–7–126–4; Flintoff 21.4–7–63–2; S. P. Jones 23–8–82–3; Giles 5–0–32–0. *Second Innings*—Harmison 29–8–76–4; Flintoff 16.1–5–40–1; Hoggard 14–3–39–0; S. P. Jones 23–5–64–1; Giles 39–8–87–3.

England

*M. E. Trescothick c McCullum b Oram	86	– c and b Tuffey	2
A. J. Strauss c Richardson b Vettori	112	– run out	83
M. A. Butcher c McCullum b Vettori	26	– c Fleming b Martin	6
M. J. Hoggard c McCullum b Oram	15		
N. Hussain b Martin	34	– (4) not out	103
G. P. Thorpe b Cairns	3	– (5) not out	51
A. Flintoff c Richardson b Martin	63		
†G. O. Jones c Oram b Styris	46		
A. F. Giles c Oram b Styris	11		
S. P. Jones b Martin	4		
S. J. Harmison not out	0		
B 4, l-b 18, n-b 19	41	B 7, l-b 12, w 5, n-b 13	37

1/190 (1) 2/239 (2) 3/254 (3) 4/288 (4)   441
5/297 (6) 6/311 (5) 7/416 (8)
8/428 (7) 9/441 (10) 10/441 (9)

1/18 (1) 2/35 (3)   (3 wkts) 282
3/143 (2)

Tuffey 26–4–98–0; Martin 27–6–94–3; Oram 30–8–76–2; Cairns 16–2–71–1; Vettori 21–1–69–2; Styris 4.3–0–11–2. *Second Innings*—Oram 15–4–39–0; Tuffey 10–3–32–1; Vettori 25–5–53–0; Martin 18–2–75–1; Styris 13–5–37–0; Cairns 6–0–27–0.

Umpires: D. B. Hair *(Australia)* (54) and R. E. Koertzen *(South Africa)* (52).
Third umpire: M. R. Benson *(England)*.   Referee: C. H. Lloyd *(West Indies)* (34).

Close of play: First day, New Zealand 284-5 (Oram 64, Tuffey 2); Second day, England 246-2 (Butcher 22, Hoggard 0); Third day, New Zealand 134-1 (Richardson 46, McCullum 72); Fourth day, England 8-0 (Trescothick 1, Strauss 6).

ENGLAND v NEW ZEALAND 2004 (2nd Test)

At Headingley, Leeds, on 3, 4, 5, 6, 7 June.
Toss: England.   Result: ENGLAND won by nine wickets.
Debuts: none.
Man of the Match: G. O. Jones.

Vaughan returned after injury (and Hussain's retirement) to oversee another victory, although his traditionalists' eyebrows were raised by his decision to drive to Sheffield, where his wife was about to give birth to their daughter, during Friday's elongated final session. On a wicket whose bounce was wholly unpredictable by the end, England's fast bowlers were, literally, dangerous. Rain allowed only 19 overs on Thursday, but Saggers dismissed Richardson, immovable at Lord's, with his first delivery. Next day Fleming, who reached his 41st Test fifty and for the 35th time failed to convert it to a hundred, put on 169 with Papps – included after McMillan broke a finger but soon to break a knuckle himself – helped by poor catching. McCullum raised New Zealand to 409, but England trumped them. Trescothick made a magnificently aggressive 132 and shared another century opening stand with Strauss. On Sunday morning, when the ball was doing plenty, Thorpe and Flintoff built on this, but the most eye-catching contribution came from Jones, who helped Flintoff add 118 on his way to a maiden Test hundred. New Zealand's injury list mounted: Papps could not field, Vettori went off (pulled hamstring) and Oram could not bowl (side strain). Having expected a first-innings lead, they conceded a deficit of 117 on a wicket getting steadily worse. By the fourth-day close, they were 15 behind with five wickets down, but Hoggard removed Styris with the 12th ball on Monday and the batting quickly unravelled despite some brutal hitting from Oram.

New Zealand

M. H. Richardson b Saggers	13	– c Jones b Hoggard	40
M. H. W. Papps lbw b Flintoff	86	– (9) c Vaughan b Harmison	0
*S. P. Fleming c Vaughan b Harmison	97	– (2) c Strauss b Flintoff	11
N. J. Astle c Butcher b Saggers	2	– lbw b Hoggard	8
S. B. Styris c Jones b Harmison	21	– c Jones b Hoggard	19
J. D. P. Oram c Thorpe b Flintoff	39	– (7) not out	36
C. L. Cairns c Strauss b Harmison	41	– (8) lbw b Hoggard	10
†B. B. McCullum b Hoggard	54	– (3) c Trescothick b Harmison	20
D. L. Vettori b Harmison	35	– absent hurt	
D. R. Tuffey lbw b Hoggard	0	– (6) c Jones b Harmison	7
C. S. Martin not out	0	– (10) run out	0
B 5, l-b 14, w 2	21	B 4, l-b 4, n-b 2	10

1/33 (1) 2/202 (2) 3/215 (3) 4/215 (4)   409   1/39 (2) 2/75 (1) 3/77 (3)   161
5/263 (5) 6/293 (6) 7/355 (7)   4/84 (4) 5/91 (6) 6/118 (5)
8/409 (8) 9/409 (10) 10/409 (9)   7/144 (8) 8/149 (9) 9/161 (10)

Hoggard 27–6–93–2; Harmison 36.2–8–74–4; Flintoff 27–7–64–2; Saggers 30–6–86–2; Trescothick 2–0–3–0; Giles 19–1–67–0; Vaughan 2–0–3–0. *Second Innings*—Hoggard 15–4–75–4; Harmison 16–5–57–3; Flintoff 6–0–16–1; Saggers 5–3–5–0.

England

M. E. Trescothick b Styris	132	– not out	30
A. J. Strauss c Tuffey b Vettori	62	– c Astle b Tuffey	10
M. A. Butcher lbw b Vettori	4	– not out	5
*M. P. Vaughan c Fleming b Styris	13		
G. P. Thorpe b Martin	34		
A. Flintoff c Martin b Styris	94		
†G. O. Jones c Fleming b Cairns	100		
A. F. Giles c Fleming b Martin	21		
M. J. Hoggard c McCullum b Tuffey	4		
M. J. Saggers c sub (S. E. Bond) b Cairns	0		
S. J. Harmison not out	0		
B 25, l-b 21, w 3, n-b 13	62		

1/153 (2) 2/174 (3) 3/229 (4) 4/240 (1)   526   1/18 (2)   (1 wkt) 45
5/339 (5) 6/457 (6) 7/491 (8)
8/526 (7) 9/526 (10) 10/526 (9)

Tuffey 26.1–7–88–1; Martin 30–9–127–2; Styris 27–5–88–3; Cairns 27–6–94–2; Vettori 23–2–83–2. *Second Innings*—Martin 4–1–17–0; Tuffey 4–0–28–1.

Umpires: S. A. Bucknor *(West Indies)* (90) and S. J. A. Taufel *(Australia)* (14).
Third umpire: N. J. Llong *(England)*.   Referee: C. H. Lloyd *(West Indies)* (35).

Close of play: First day, New Zealand 41-1 (Papps 24, Fleming 3); Second day, New Zealand 351-6 (Cairns 41, McCullum 31); Third day, England 248-4 (Thorpe 7, Flintoff 4); Fourth day, New Zealand 102-5 (Styris 7, Oram 4).

ENGLAND v NEW ZEALAND 2004 (3rd Test)

At Trent Bridge, Nottingham, on 10, 11, 12, 13 June.
Toss: New Zealand.   Result: ENGLAND won by four wickets.
Debuts: New Zealand – K. D. Mills.
Man of the Match: G. P. Thorpe.   Men of the Series: S. J. Harmison and M. H. Richardson.

New Zealand again began strongly and held the advantage at various stages, only for England to complete their first clean sweep in a three-match series for 26 years. New Zealand were unlucky that injuries sidelined two of their seamers – Martin (hamstring) and debutant Kyle Mills (side) – although Cairns, who turned 34 on the last day, marked his Test farewell with a valiant effort at his old county home ground. New Zealand's attack was already unbalanced, as they had no second spinner to replace the injured Vettori. England had to wait until the 52nd over for a breakthrough, when Giles ended yet another obdurate Richardson effort. Fleming completed his seventh Test hundred, but England made better use of the second new ball: despite Styris's hundred the total was kept to 384. Mills became Hoggard's 100th Test wicket and, four balls later, Martin his 101st. England dipped to 18 for 2, but Trescothick and Vaughan added 110, then Giles restricted the lead to 65. New Zealand were soon effectively 159 without loss – but once Giles deceived Richardson the collapse began. Fleming and Styris received questionable decisions, and the last five wickets added only 20. That still meant a target of 284, 37 more than had ever been made to win a Test at Trent Bridge. Three wickets fell in the first 15 overs, but Butcher hit 12 fours despite a broken finger, while Thorpe embarked on a 163-ball hundred. England claimed the extra half-hour on Sunday evening, with 25 needed: it took 21 balls.

New Zealand

M. H. Richardson c Vaughan b Giles	73	– lbw b Giles	49
*S. P. Fleming c Thorpe b Flintoff	117	– lbw b Flintoff	45
S. B. Styris c sub (B. M. Shafayat) b Giles	108	– (4) c Jones b Harmison	39
N. J. Astle b Harmison	15	– (5) lbw b Flintoff	0
C. D. McMillan lbw b Harmison	0	– (6) lbw b Harmison	30
J. D. P. Oram c Strauss b Saggers	14	– (8) c Flintoff b Harmison	0
C. L. Cairns c Thorpe b Saggers	12	– (9) b Giles	1
†B. B. McCullum c Hoggard b Harmison	21	– (3) c Flintoff b Giles	4
J. E. C. Franklin not out	4	– (7) c Jones b Flintoff	17
K. D. Mills c Jones b Hoggard	0	– c Harmison b Giles	8
C. S. Martin c Vaughan b Hoggard	2	– not out	0
B 2, l-b 14, n-b 2	18	B 1, l-b 21, n-b 3	25

1/163 (1) 2/225 (2) 3/272 (4) 4/272 (5)   **384**   1/94 (1) 2/106 (3) 3/126 (2)   **218**
5/308 (6) 6/331 (7) 7/366 (3)   4/134 (5) 5/185 (4) 6/198 (6)
8/377 (8) 9/382 (10) 10/384 (11)   7/198 (8) 8/208 (9) 9/210 (7) 10/218 (10)

Hoggard 25–6–85–2; Harmison 32–9–80–3; Flintoff 14–2–48–1; Saggers 22–5–80–2; Giles 27–6–70–2; Vaughan 1–0–5–0. *Second Innings*—Hoggard 6–2–25–0; Harmison 25–7–51–3; Saggers 6–2–14–0; Flintoff 20–3–60–3; Giles 24–6–46–4.

England

M. E. Trescothick c Styris b Franklin	63	– c and b Franklin	9
A. J. Strauss c McCullum b Cairns	0	– lbw b Cairns	6
M. A. Butcher c Styris b Franklin	5	– lbw b Cairns	59
*M. P. Vaughan lbw b Cairns	61	– lbw b Cairns	10
G. P. Thorpe c McCullum b Franklin	45	– not out	104
A. Flintoff lbw b Cairns	54	– c sub (H. J. H. Marshall) b Cairns	5
M. J. Hoggard c Styris b Franklin	5		
†G. O. Jones lbw b Styris	22	– (7) c Oram b Franklin	27
A. F. Giles not out	45	– (8) not out	36
M. J. Saggers b Cairns	0		
S. J. Harmison b Cairns	0		
B 2, l-b 5, n-b 12	19	B 4, l-b 16, n-b 8	28

1/1 (2) 2/18 (3) 3/128 (4) 4/140 (1)   **319**   1/12 (2) 2/16 (1)   (6 wkts) **284**
5/221 (6) 6/244 (7) 7/255 (5)   3/46 (4) 4/134 (3)
8/295 (8) 9/301 (10) 10/319 (11)   5/162 (6) 6/214 (7)

Martin 1.5–0–1–0; Cairns 23.3–5–79–5; Franklin 26.1–4–104–4; Mills 6–2–31–0; Oram 15–0–47–0; Styris 11–1–45–1; McMillan 2–1–5–0. *Second Innings*—Cairns 25–2–108–4; Franklin 17–2–59–2; Richardson 1–0–4–0; Oram 14.3–1–50–0; Styris 14–1–43–0.

Umpires: D. J. Harper *(Australia)* (41) and S. J. A. Taufel *(Australia)* (15).
Third umpire: M. R. Benson *(England)*.   Referee: C. H. Lloyd *(West Indies)* (36).

Close of play: First day, New Zealand 295-4 (Styris 68, Oram 10); Second day, England 225-5 (Thorpe 30, Hoggard 0); Third day, New Zealand 190-5 (McMillan 28, Franklin 2).

WEST INDIES v BANGLADESH 2004 (1st Test)

At Beausejour Stadium, Gros Islet, St Lucia, on 28, 29, 30, 31 May, 1 June.
Toss: Bangladesh.   Result: MATCH DRAWN.
Debuts: Bangladesh – Faisal Hossain, Tareq Aziz.
Man of the Match: C. H. Gayle.

Bangladesh showed gutsy resilience to force a deserved draw, only their third in 29 Tests – and both the previous ones owed much to the weather. There was more rain here: only 41.1 overs were bowled on the second day and 62.4 on the fourth, but this time Bangladesh did not need it. From a shaky 79 for 6 on the fourth evening, only 143 ahead, they rallied so strongly that Habibul Bashar could enjoy the luxury of their first-ever declaration. Hannan Sarkar fell first ball, but Habibul himself pulled and hooked merrily en route to a third Test century, hitting 15 fours in all. Bangladesh capitalised on dropped chances, eventually reaching 416, their highest in Tests (beating 400 in their maiden innings, against India in 2000-01). Mohammad Rafique, at No. 9, surged to a maiden first-class hundred, hitting 11 fours and three sixes in all. Bangladeshi spirits soared even higher when Devon Smith was run out without scoring, but then they also suffered from bad catching. Chance after embarrassingly easy chance was put down, with Gayle the chief beneficiary in his fifth Test century, but Bangladesh still took a lead of 64. A second-innings collapse put them in danger: Sarwan's usually innocuous leg-spin claimed three wickets in two overs, leaving Bangladesh tottering at 94 for 6, only for Khaled Mashud to defy every challenge Lara threw at him. By the time he reached his own maiden Test century the match had long since been saved.

Bangladesh

Hannan Sarkar lbw b Collins	0	– b Edwards	9
Javed Omar c D. S. Smith b Collins	32	– c Jacobs b Collins	7
*Habibul Bashar c D. R. Smith b Lawson	113	– b Best	25
Rajin Saleh c Jacobs b Sarwan	26	– lbw b Edwards	51
Mohammad Ashraful lbw b Lawson	81	– c and b Sarwan	1
Faisal Hossain c Best b Collins	5	– c Gayle b Sarwan	2
Mushfiqur Rahman c Jacobs b Sarwan	1	– lbw b Sarwan	0
†Khaled Mashud st Jacobs b Gayle	2	– not out	103
Mohammad Rafique b Collins	111	– c Jacobs b Sarwan	29
Tapash Baisya c and b Sarwan	9	– c and b Gayle	26
Tareq Aziz not out	6	– not out	1
L-b 10, w 1, n-b 19	30	L-b 5, n-b 12	17
	416	**(9 wkts dec.)**	**271**

1/0 (1) 2/121 (2) 3/171 (3) 4/227 (4)   **416**   1/17 (1) 2/21 (2)   (9 wkts dec.) **271**
5/238 (6) 6/241 (7) 7/250 (8)   3/70 (3) 4/73 (5)
8/337 (5) 9/370 (10) 10/416 (9)   5/79 (6) 6/79 (7) 7/123 (4) 8/179 (9) 9/253 (10)

Collins 27.3–8–83–4; Edwards 21–2–78–0; Lawson 16–2–66–2; Best 20–4–64–0; D. R. Smith 4–1–5–0; Gayle 24–3–51–1; Sarwan 23–7–59–3. *Second Innings*—Collins 17–5–42–1; Edwards 19–1–61–2; Lawson 16–0–60–0; Sarwan 20–9–37–4; Best 13–1–33–1; Gayle 19.2–7–33–1; Chanderpaul 1–1–0–0.

West Indies

D. S. Smith run out	0	– (2) not out	40
C. H. Gayle c Habibul Bashar b Tapash Baisya	141	– (1) not out	66
R. R. Sarwan c Mohammad Rafique b Tapash Baisya	40		
*B. C. Lara c Khaled Mashud b Mushfiqur Rahman	53		
S. Chanderpaul c Khaled Mashud b Mohammad Rafique	7		
D. R. Smith c Tareq Aziz b Mohammad Rafique	42		
†R. D. Jacobs not out	46		
T. L. Best b Mohammad Rafique	3		
P. T. Collins c Habibul Bashar b Mushfiqur Rahman	4		
J. J. C. Lawson c Hannan Sarkar b Mushfiqur Rahman	0		
F. H. Edwards lbw b Mushfiqur Rahman	5		
L-b 3, n-b 8	11	B 4, l-b 1, n-b 2	7
	352	**(no wkt)**	**113**

1/2 (1) 2/89 (3) 3/162 (4) 4/183 (5)   **352**   (no wkt) **113**
5/253 (6) 6/312 (2) 7/321 (8)
8/336 (9) 9/342 (10) 10/352 (11)

Tapash Baisya 26–5–87–2; Tareq Aziz 23–3–95–0; Mushfiqur Rahman 25.4–8–65–4; Mohammad Rafique 36–12–90–3; Rajin Saleh 6–0–12–0. *Second Innings*—Tapash Baisya 3–0–26–0; Tareq Aziz 6–1–31–0; Mushfiqur Rahman 6–0–25–0; Mohammad Rafique 5–1–7–0; Mohammad Ashraful 3–0–19–0.

Umpires: D. J. Harper *(Australia)* (40) and J. W. Lloyds *(England)* (1).
Third umpire: B. E. W. Morgan *(West Indies)*.   Referee: R. S. Mahanama *(Sri Lanka)* (1).

Close of play: First day, Bangladesh 278-7 (Mohammad Ashraful 65, Mohammad Rafique 17); Second day, Bangladesh 406-9 (Mohammad Rafique 103, Tareq Aziz 4); Third day, West Indies 262-5 (Gayle 110, Jacobs 1); Fourth day, Bangladesh 94-6 (Rajin Saleh 34, Khaled Mashud 8).

WEST INDIES v BANGLADESH 2004 (2nd Test)

At Sabina Park, Kingston, Jamaica, on 4, 5, 6, 7 June.
Toss: Bangladesh.   Result: WEST INDIES won by an innings and 99 runs.
Debuts: none.
Man of the Match: R. R. Sarwan.   Man of the Series: R. R. Sarwan.

Before the game, Lara dramatically raised the stakes by promising to step down as captain if West Indies failed to win. However, his pledge was never really in danger of being tested, even on a placid Sabina Park pitch. In their second innings Bangladesh's lower order failed to produce another gutsy fightback, and they collapsed spectacularly to defeat early on the fourth afternoon. West Indies' commanding first-innings lead of 275 was based on a monumental 261 not out from Sarwan – the highest score by a Guyanese batsman in Tests, beating Rohan Kanhai's 256 against India at Calcutta in 1958-59 – and fluent centuries by Lara (his 26th, to equal Garry Sobers's tally) and Chanderpaul. Bangladesh were surviving on the fourth day as Habibul Bashar and Manjural Islam Rana added 120, but Rana cut to backward point to start a sensational collapse. Habibul was lbw next ball, and in all the last seven wickets fell for 22. They were scattered primarily by Collins, who finished with six for 53 in the innings, nine for 117 in the match, including Hannan Sarkar to the very first ball – the third time he had fallen in this way to Collins (Sunil Gavaskar is the only other man to fall three times to the opening delivery of a Test, but the bowlers were different). Bangladesh's tail had done better in that first innings, stretching the score from 97 for 5 to 284, with Tapash Baisya top-scoring from No. 10.

Bangladesh

Hannan Sarkar lbw b Collins	0	– (2) lbw b Collins	10
Javed Omar c Jacobs b Edwards	20	– (1) c D. R. Smith b Best	5
*Habibul Bashar c Banks b Collins	20	– lbw b Collins	77
Rajin Saleh c and b Banks	47	– c D. R. Smith b Collins	0
Mohammad Ashraful c Sarwan b Banks	16	– (6) c Lara b Sarwan	9
Manjural Islam Rana c Jacobs b Best	7	– (5) c Lara b Banks	35
Mushfiqur Rahman st Jacobs b Banks	22	– c D. R. Smith b Collins	0
†Khaled Mashud c Banks b Edwards	39	– c Sarwan b Banks	0
Mohammad Rafique c Collins b Banks	30	– b Collins	2
Tapash Baisya c D. S. Smith b Collins	48	– c Sarwan b Collins	3
Tareq Aziz not out	10	– not out	5
B 4, l-b 7, w 2, n-b 12	25	B 8, l-b 6, w 8, n-b 8	30
	284		**176**

1/0 (1) 2/37 (3) 3/54 (2) 4/88 (5)
5/97 (6) 6/145 (7) 7/152 (4)
8/192 (9) 9/238 (8) 10/284 (10)

1/16 (2) 2/24 (1) 3/34 (4)
4/154 (5) 5/154 (3) 6/154 (7)
7/155 (8) 8/160 (9) 9/164 (10) 10/176 (6)

Collins 19–2–64–3; Edwards 20–5–66–2; Best 20–4–53–1; Banks 31–5–87–4; Sarwan 2–2–0–0; D. R. Smith 3–1–3–0. *Second Innings*—Collins 18–3–53–6; Best 10–0–32–1; Banks 13–2–40–2; Gayle 2–0–9–0; D. R. Smith 5–1–19–0; Sarwan 3–1–9–1.

West Indies

C. H. Gayle c Khaled Mashud b Tareq Aziz	14	S. Chanderpaul not out	101
D. S. Smith run out	44		
R. R. Sarwan not out	261	B 4, l-b 5, w 1, n-b 5	15
*B. C. Lara c Khaled Mashud b Mohammad Rafique	120		
T. L. Best c Khaled Mashud b Tapash Baisya	4	1/26 (1) 2/109 (2) (4 wkts dec.)	559
		3/288 (4) 4/297 (5)	

D. R. Smith, †R. D. Jacobs, O. A. C. Banks, P. T. Collins and F. H. Edwards did not bat.

Tapash Baisya 25–5–99–1; Tareq Aziz 19–2–76–1; Mushfiqur Rahman 33–3–127–0; Mohammad Rafique 38–2–124–1; Manjural Islam Rana 28–2–100–0; Mohammad Ashraful 1–1–0–0; Rajin Saleh 7–1–24–0.

Umpires: R. E. Koertzen *(South Africa)* (53) and J. W. Lloyds *(England)* (2).
Third umpire: B. R. Doctrove *(West Indies)*.   Referee: R. S. Mahanama *(Sri Lanka)* (2).

Close of play: First day, Bangladesh 264-9 (Tapash Baisya 36, Tareq Aziz 4); Second day, West Indies 294-3 (Sarwan 106, Best 1); Third day, Bangladesh 66-3 (Habibul Bashar 28, Manjural Islam Rana 7).

AUSTRALIA v SRI LANKA 2004 (1st Test)

At Marrara Cricket Ground, Darwin, on 1, 2, 3 July.
Toss: Sri Lanka.   Result: AUSTRALIA won by 149 runs.
Debuts: Sri Lanka – S. L. Malinga.
Man of the Match: G. D. McGrath.

Four months earlier Sri Lanka had failed to beat Australia at home on purpose-built raging turners, so they always seemed likely to struggle on a soft seamer in Darwin. Vaas and the explosive newcomer Lasith Malinga did well to restrict Australia to barely 200 in either innings, but the difficulties of batting on a slow, seaming pitch put even that well out of reach. Gilchrist was leading Australia for the third time, after Ponting remained in Tasmania for his aunt's funeral. He was replaced by Elliott, five years after his previous Test (it was an unhappy recall: he made a solitary run and was never picked again). This gave Australia their oldest Test team in more than 71 years, since the Adelaide Bodyline Test of 1932-33. Australia lost their last seven wickets for 30 on the opening day, but then McGrath, in his first Test for almost a year, found rhythm to take five wickets. Warne moved ahead of Courtney Walsh into second place on the Test wicket-takers' list, and Gillespie took his 200th wicket as Sri Lanka made their lowest total against Australia, who then wobbled to 77 for 5 before Gilchrist ensured a target of 312. Now it was Kasprowicz's turn: finding reverse-swing, he picked up seven wickets, five of them caught by Gilchrist, equalling the Test record for a bowler-keeper combination (shared by Ian Botham and Bob Taylor, for England in Bombay in 1979-80, and Allan Donald and Mark Boucher, for South Africa at Lord's in 1998).

Australia

J. L. Langer c Chandana b Samaraweera	30	– c Sangakkara b Vaas		10
M. L. Hayden c Jayasuriya b Vaas	37	– c Sangakkara b Zoysa		2
M. T. G. Elliott c Arnold b Vaas	1	– c Dilshan b Vaas		0
D. R. Martyn c Arnold b Jayasuriya	47	– c Sangakkara b Malinga		7
D. S. Lehmann lbw b Malinga	57	– c Sangakkara b Malinga		51
S. M. Katich c Sangakkara b Vaas	9	– c Dilshan b Chandana		15
*†A. C. Gilchrist c Sangakkara b Malinga	0	– run out		80
S. K. Warne run out	2	– lbw b Malinga		1
J. N. Gillespie lbw b Vaas	4	– c Samaraweera b Chandana		16
M. S. Kasprowicz not out	2	– c and b Malinga		15
G. D. McGrath c Samaraweera b Vaas	0	– not out		0
B 2, l-b 6, w 2, n-b 8	18	L-b 3, n-b 1		4

1/72 (1) 2/73 (3) 3/80 (2) 4/177 (4)   207   1/12 (1) 2/12 (2) 3/14 (3)   201
5/189 (5) 6/189 (7) 7/201 (8)   4/64 (4) 5/77 (5) 6/114 (6)
8/202 (6) 9/207 (9) 10/207 (11)   7/127 (8) 8/154 (9) 9/201 (7) 10/201 (10)

Vaas 18.3–6–31–5; Malinga 14–3–50–2; Zoysa 13–4–24–0; Samaraweera 9–1–43–1; Chandana 6–0–30–0; Jayasuriya 11–4–21–1. *Second Innings*—Vaas 14–4–51–2; Zoysa 16–3–57–1; Malinga 15.1–3–42–4; Jayasuriya 6–3–9–0; Chandana 11–1–30–2; Arnold 1–0–9–0.

Sri Lanka

*M. S. Atapattu b McGrath	4	– c Warne b Kasprowicz		10
S. T. Jayasuriya lbw b McGrath	8	– lbw b McGrath		16
†K. C. Sangakkara lbw b Gillespie	2	– run out		0
D. P. M. D. Jayawardene c Langer b Gillespie	14	– b McGrath		44
D. N. T. Zoysa c Gilchrist b McGrath	12	– (10) c Gilchrist b Kasprowicz		1
T. T. Samaraweera c Gilchrist b McGrath	1	– (5) c Gilchrist b Kasprowicz		32
T. M. Dilshan not out	17	– (6) c Gilchrist b Kasprowicz		14
R. P. Arnold c Elliott b McGrath	6	– (7) c Gilchrist b Kasprowicz		11
U. D. U. Chandana c Gilchrist b Warne	14	– (8) b Kasprowicz		17
W. P. U. J. C. Vaas c Hayden b Warne	5	– (9) not out		10
S. L. Malinga c Gillespie b Warne	0	– c Gilchrist b Kasprowicz		0
L-b 7, n-b 7	14	L-b 1, w 2, n-b 4		7

1/10 (1) 2/20 (3) 3/33 (2) 4/47 (4)   97   1/23 (1) 2/23 (3) 3/30 (2)   162
5/50 (6) 6/51 (5) 7/59 (8)   4/109 (5) 5/113 (4) 6/132 (7)
8/85 (9) 9/91 (10) 10/97 (11)   7/141 (6) 8/152 (8) 9/162 (10) 10/162 (11)

McGrath 15–4–37–5; Gillespie 13–4–18–2; Kasprowicz 7–1–15–0; Warne 6.5–1–20–3. *Second Innings*—McGrath 16–9–24–2; Gillespie 13–2–37–0; Kasprowicz 17.4–3–39–7; Warne 19–2–61–0.

Umpires: Aleem Dar *(Pakistan)* (8) and B. F. Bowden *(New Zealand)* (16).
Third umpire: S. J. A. Taufel *(Australia)*.   Referee: B. C. Broad *(England)* (6).

Close of play: First day, Sri Lanka 43-3 (Jayawardene 12, Zoysa 8); Second day, Australia 201.

AUSTRALIA v SRI LANKA 2004 (2nd Test)

At Bundaberg Rum Stadium (Cazaly's Oval), Cairns, on 9, 10, 11, 12, 13 July.
Toss: Sri Lanka.   Result: MATCH DRAWN.
Debuts: none.
Man of the Match: M. L. Hayden.   Man of the Series: M. L. Hayden.

Shane Warne started this match needing eight wickets to beat the Test record of Muttiah Muralitharan, who missed the series for "personal reasons", widely believed to be his disaffection with Australian crowds which persistently yelled "No-ball" when he bowled. Warne managed seven, but Sri Lanka held on to avoid defeat for only the second time in eight Tests in Australia. Put in, Langer and Hayden hurtled towards their sixth and biggest double-century stand: it was also the fifth time both had scored hundreds in the same innings, another record. Hayden followed up with 132 in the second innings, his 20th Test century in 95 innings, a strike-rate bettered (among batsmen with more than 20 innings) only by Don Bradman and George Headley. Australia had 370 for 2 at the end of the first day, but lost seven wickets in 15 overs either side of lunch on the second. Chandana took the first of two five-fors, an admirable effort on a pitch that hardly suited his unpretentious leg-spin. Sri Lanka's batsmen then fought hard. Atapattu batted for 5½ hours, while Sangakkara, relieved of keeping duties, survived nearly three on the second day, and 4½ more on the last to bankroll his side's escape. On the final morning Ponting's declaration left a target of 355 in 85 overs. That never entered Sri Lanka's sights, as Warne, in a marathon five-hour spell, almost got himself and his country over the line before both contests ended all square.

Australia

J. L. Langer c Jayawardene b Malinga	162	– c Kaluwitharana b Zoysa	8
M. L. Hayden c Jayasuriya b Samaraweera	117	– b Chandana	132
*R. T. Ponting c Atapattu b Malinga	22	– c Jayasuriya b Zoysa	45
D. R. Martyn lbw b Chandana	97	– st Kaluwitharana b Chandana	52
D. S. Lehmann c Sangakkara b Chandana	50	– c Jayawardene b Chandana	21
S. M. Katich b Chandana	1	– st Kaluwitharana b Dilshan	1
†A. C. Gilchrist c Kaluwitharana b Malinga	35	– b Dilshan	0
S. K. Warne c Samaraweera b Chandana	2	– c Samaraweera b Chandana	4
J. N. Gillespie c Kaluwitharana b Malinga	1	– st Kaluwitharana b Chandana	1
M. S. Kasprowicz c Atapattu b Chandana	9	– not out	3
G. D. McGrath not out	0		
B 7, l-b 3, w 4, n-b 7	21	L-b 20, w 1, n-b 4	25

1/255 (2) 2/291 (3) 3/392 (1) 4/454 (4)   517   1/10 (1) 2/105 (3)   (9 wkts dec.) 292
5/462 (6) 6/469 (5) 7/474 (8)   3/195 (4) 4/261 (5)
8/476 (9) 9/485 (10) 10/517 (7)   5/284 (6) 6/284 (2) 7/288 (8) 8/288 (7) 9/292 (9)

Vaas 27–2–102–0; Zoysa 19–5–72–0; Samaraweera 17–2–55–1; Malinga 29.2–2–149–4; Chandana 26–2–109–5; Jayasuriya 6–0–20–0. *Second Innings*—Vaas 13–3–52–0; Zoysa 14–6–34–2; Malinga 5–0–23–0; Samaraweera 11–0–50–0; Chandana 18.4–1–101–5; Jayasuriya 3–0–8–0; Dilshan 2–0–4–2.

Sri Lanka

*M. S. Atapattu c Hayden b McGrath	133	– c Warne b Gillespie	9
S. T. Jayasuriya c Gilchrist b Gillespie	13	– c Gilchrist b Warne	22
K. C. Sangakkara c Gillespie b Warne	74	– b Warne	66
D. P. M. D. Jayawardene c and b Kasprowicz	43	– c Gilchrist b McGrath	6
T. T. Samaraweera c Ponting b Gillespie	70	– run out	0
T. M. Dilshan c Kasprowicz b Warne	35	– c Warne b Gillespie	21
†R. S. Kaluwitharana c Warne b McGrath	34	– c Lehmann b Warne	14
U. D. U. Chandana st Gilchrist b Warne	19	– st Gilchrist b Warne	14
W. P. U. J. C. Vaas c Ponting b Gillespie	2	– not out	11
D. N. T. Zoysa not out	0	– not out	3
S. L. Malinga run out	0		
B 3, l-b 10, w 2, n-b 17	32	B 5, l-b 3, n-b 9	17

1/18 (2) 2/156 (3) 3/280 (1) 4/280 (4)   455   1/15 (1) 2/49 (2)   (8 wkts) 183
5/345 (6) 6/420 (7) 7/445 (5)   3/58 (4) 4/64 (5)
8/455 (9) 9/455 (8) 10/455 (11)   5/107 (6) 6/136 (7) 7/159 (3) 8/174 (8)

McGrath 34–10–79–2; Gillespie 37.4–6–116–3; Kasprowicz 32–5–113–1; Warne 38–7–129–3; Lehmann 3–0–5–0. *Second Innings*—McGrath 16–7–31–1; Gillespie 18–6–39–2; Warne 37–14–70–4; Kasprowicz 11–4–34–0; Lehmann 3–2–1–0.

Umpires: Aleem Dar *(Pakistan)* (9) and B. F. Bowden *(New Zealand)* (17).
Third umpire: R. L. Parry *(Australia)*.   Referee: B. C. Broad *(England)* (7).

Close of play: First day, Australia 370-2 (Langer 159, Martyn 56); Second day, Sri Lanka 184-2 (Atapattu 75, Jayawardene 9); Third day, Sri Lanka 411-5 (Samaraweera 53, Kaluwitharana 30); Fourth day, Australia 194-2 (Hayden 68, Martyn 52).

ENGLAND v WEST INDIES 2004 (1st Test)

At Lord's, London, on 22, 23, 24, 25, 26 July.
Toss: West Indies.   Result: ENGLAND won by 210 runs.
Debuts: West Indies – D. J. Bravo.
Man of the Match: A. F. Giles.

England's victory was not sealed until the last morning, when Giles turned a ball past the advancing Lara and into middle stump, his 100th Test wicket and one of nine in this match. England's other hero was Key, playing only because Butcher was injured, ending a run of 42 consecutive Tests. Unfazed by meeting the Queen when he had 90, Key converted his maiden Test century into 221. He put on 291 for the second wicket with Strauss, an England record against West Indies, and 165 with Vaughan, who completed his 12th Test hundred. Although next day the last seven wickets tumbled for 41, it mattered little: England were 527 for 3 when the slide started. West Indies began brightly, Gayle and Smith putting on 118. Then Lara was given out caught behind by umpire Harper when replays suggested the ball had only brushed pad, but Chanderpaul, back to his crustacean best after an indifferent run, nudged and nurdled to his 11th Test century: in all he would bat for 614 minutes in the match without being dismissed. England built quickly on their lead, with Vaughan joining George Headley and Graham Gooch in scoring two centuries in a Lord's Test, then Flintoff's 38-ball fifty set up an improbable target of 478. Gayle flashed 13 fours and a six in hurtling to 81 out of 102, but after that England's main concerns were drizzle, which briefly delayed the fifth day's play, and Lara, who batted confidently before Giles unfurled that killer ball.

England

M. E. Trescothick	c Sarwan b Best	16	– b Collins		45
A. J. Strauss	c Jacobs b Banks	137	– c Sarwan b Collins		35
R. W. T. Key	c Lara b Bravo	221	– run out		15
*M. P. Vaughan	c Smith b Collins	103	– not out		101
G. P. Thorpe	c Jacobs b Bravo	19	– c and b Gayle		38
A. Flintoff	b Banks	6	– c Jacobs b Collins		58
†G. O. Jones	c Jacobs b Collins	4			
A. F. Giles	c Smith b Collins	5			
M. J. Hoggard	not out	1			
S. P. Jones	lbw b Collins	4			
S. J. Harmison	b Bravo	4			
	B 2, l-b 20, w 13, n-b 13	48	B 3, l-b 14, n-b 16		33

1/29 (1) 2/320 (2) 3/485 (3) 4/527 (5)   568   1/86 (1) 2/104 (2)   (5 wkts dec.) 325
5/534 (6) 6/541 (7) 7/551 (8)   3/117 (3) 4/233 (5)
8/557 (4) 9/563 (10) 10/568 (11)   5/325 (6)

Collins 24–2–113–4; Best 21–1–104–1; Edwards 21–2–96–0; Bravo 24.4–5–74–3; Banks 22–3–131–2; Sarwan 9–0–28–0. *Second Innings*—Best 3–1–14–0; Collins 14.4–1–62–3; Banks 26–1–92–0; Edwards 13–0–47–0; Bravo 7–0–28–0; Gayle 9–0–45–1; Sarwan 4–0–20–0.

West Indies

C. H. Gayle	lbw b Giles	66	– b Harmison		81
D. S. Smith	b Giles	45	– lbw b Giles		6
R. R. Sarwan	lbw b Hoggard	1	– lbw b Hoggard		4
*B. C. Lara	c G. O. Jones b Giles	11	– b Giles		44
S. Chanderpaul	not out	128	– not out		97
D. J. Bravo	c G. O. Jones b S. P. Jones	44	– c and b Giles		10
†R. D. Jacobs	c G. O. Jones b Hoggard	32	– c Thorpe b Hoggard		1
O. A. C. Banks	b Flintoff	45	– b Harmison		0
T. L. Best	b Flintoff	0	– st G. O. Jones b Giles		3
P. T. Collins	b Flintoff	0	– st G. O. Jones b Giles		2
F. H. Edwards	b Giles	5	– c G. O. Jones b Flintoff		2
	B 20, l-b 11, w 5, n-b 3	39	B 5, l-b 9, n-b 3		17

1/118 (2) 2/119 (1) 3/127 (3) 4/139 (4)   416   1/24 (2) 2/35 (3) 3/102 (1)   267
5/264 (6) 6/327 (7) 7/399 (8)   4/172 (4) 5/194 (6) 6/195 (7)
8/399 (9) 9/401 (10) 10/416 (11)   7/200 (8) 8/203 (9) 9/247 (10) 10/267 (11)

Hoggard 28–7–89–2; Harmison 21–6–72–0; S. P. Jones 17–3–70–1; Giles 40.4–5–129–4; Flintoff 10–4–25–3. *Second Innings*—Hoggard 14–2–65–2; Harmison 21–2–78–2; Giles 35–9–81–5; S. P. Jones 8–3–29–0; Flintoff 1.3–1–0–1.

Umpires: D. J. Harper *(Australia)* (42) and R. E. Koertzen *(South Africa)* (54).
Third umpire: N. J. Llong *(England)*.   Referee: R. S. Madugalle *(Sri Lanka)* (62).

Close of play: First day, England 391-2 (Key 167, Vaughan 36); Second day, West Indies 208-4 (Chanderpaul 41, Bravo 30); Third day, England 71-0 (Trescothick 34, Strauss 27); Fourth day, West Indies 114-3 (Lara 11, Chanderpaul 4).

ENGLAND v WEST INDIES 2004 (2nd Test)

At Edgbaston, Birmingham, on 29, 30, 31 July, 1 August.
Toss: England.   Result: ENGLAND won by 256 runs.
Debuts: none.
Man of the Match: A. Flintoff.

England recorded another crushing victory, only their second over West Indies at Edgbaston, the other coming in 1963. Flintoff typified England's effervescence, steaming in at nearly 90mph, sweeping up sharp slip catches and swatting the ball to every corner, all with a cheeky grin. By Sunday, only ten days after the series began, the Wisden Trophy had been retained. At the start, Trescothick made an efficient century, England's first against West Indies at Edgbaston since the famous Peter May-Colin Cowdrey stand in 1957. Next morning, however, Flintoff and Jones broke loose in a stand worth 170. Flintoff smashed Banks over long-on for six to bring up 150; the next ball whizzed over midwicket for six more; the fifth ball of the over went the same way for the six (Flintoff's seventh, to go with 17 fours) that took him past his highest first-class score. Hoggard soon removed West Indies' openers, leaving Sarwan and Lara to pick up the pieces in a stand of 209. Almost inevitably, Flintoff broke through: Lara slashed to second slip, after which seven wickets cascaded for 39. England waived the follow-on, and rather unconvincingly built a lead of 478. Gayle briefly looked as if he would earn immortality by snatching five wickets, hitting a century and carrying his bat – not just in the same Test, but on the same day – before he was the fifth victim of the resurgent Giles, who took nine wickets for the second match running. Other than that, there was little resistance.

England

M. E. Trescothick c Lara b Bravo	105	– run out	107
A. J. Strauss c Jacobs b Lawson	24	– c Jacobs b Lawson	5
R. W. T. Key c Lara b Collins	29	– c Gayle b Lawson	4
*M. P. Vaughan c and b Bravo	12	– c Gayle b Lawson	3
G. P. Thorpe c Jacobs b Collymore	61	– st Jacobs b Gayle	54
A. Flintoff lbw b Bravo	167	– c Bravo b Gayle	20
†G. O. Jones c Jacobs b Collymore	74	– b Lawson	4
A. F. Giles c Chanderpaul b Bravo	24	– b Gayle	15
M. J. Hoggard not out	15	– c Smith b Gayle	6
J. M. Anderson b Banks	2	– (11) not out	8
S. J. Harmison not out	31	– (10) lbw b Gayle	1
L-b 6, w 1, n-b 15	22	B 8, l-b 2, w 5, n-b 6	21

1/77 (2) 2/125 (3) 3/150 (4)   (9 wkts dec.) 566   1/24 (2) 2/37 (3) 3/52 (4)   248
4/210 (1) 5/262 (5) 6/432 (7)   4/184 (1) 5/195 (5) 6/214 (7)
7/478 (8) 8/522 (6) 9/525 (10)   7/226 (6) 8/234 (8) 9/239 (10) 10/248 (9)

Collins 18–1–90–1; Collymore 30–6–126–2; Lawson 23–4–111–1; Bravo 24–6–76–4; Banks 27–3–108–1; Sarwan 12–0–49–0. *Second Innings*—Collins 9–1–29–0; Collymore 9–2–33–0; Lawson 21–2–94–4; Bravo 6–1–28–0; Banks 5–1–20–0; Gayle 15.1–4–34–5.

West Indies

C. H. Gayle b Hoggard	7	– c Strauss b Giles	82
D. S. Smith c Giles b Hoggard	4	– c Trescothick b Hoggard	11
R. R. Sarwan b Flintoff	139	– c Strauss b Giles	14
*B. C. Lara c Thorpe b Flintoff	95	– c Flintoff b Giles	13
S. Chanderpaul c Key b Giles	45	– lbw b Giles	43
D. J. Bravo b Giles	13	– b Giles	0
†R. D. Jacobs c Trescothick b Hoggard	0	– c Anderson b Hoggard	0
O. A. C. Banks c Jones b Harmison	4	– not out	25
P. T. Collins c Flintoff b Giles	6	– lbw b Hoggard	0
C. D. Collymore lbw b Giles	2	– b Anderson	10
J. J. C. Lawson not out	0	– b Anderson	2
B 9, l-b 5, w 1, n-b 6	21	B 17, l-b 4, n-b 1	22

1/5 (2) 2/12 (1) 3/221 (4) 4/297 (3)   336   1/15 (2) 2/54 (1) 3/101 (4)   222
5/323 (6) 6/324 (7) 7/324 (5)   4/172 (5) 5/172 (6) 6/177 (1)
8/334 (9) 9/336 (8) 10/336 (10)   7/177 (7) 8/182 (9) 9/210 (10) 10/222 (11)

Hoggard 18–0–89–3; Harmison 14–1–64–1; Anderson 11–3–37–0; Giles 30.3–7–65–4; Flintoff 15–1–52–2; Vaughan 1–0–8–0; Trescothick 2–0–7–0. *Second Innings*—Hoggard 16–5–64–3; Harmison 5–1–29–0; Flintoff 5–1–19–0; Giles 21–9–57–5; Anderson 5.3–1–23–2; Vaughan 3–0–9–0.

Umpires: D. B. Hair *(Australia)* (55) and S. J. A. Taufel *(Australia)* (16).
Third umpire: J. W. Lloyds *(England)*.   Referee: R. S. Madugalle *(Sri Lanka)* (63).

Close of play: First day, England 313-5 (Flintoff 42, Jones 27); Second day, West Indies 184-2 (Sarwan 87, Lara 74); Third day, England 148-3 (Trescothick 88, Thorpe 28).

ENGLAND v WEST INDIES 2004 (3rd Test)

At Old Trafford, Manchester, on 12, 13 (no play), 14, 15, 16 August.
Toss: West Indies.   Result: ENGLAND won by seven wickets.
Debuts: West Indies – S. C. Joseph.
Man of the Match: G. P. Thorpe.

England won their sixth successive Test, the winning run coming with 27 overs remaining, shortly before the long-forecast rain returned. By the fourth evening, Lara's side had built a strong position – 153 ahead with nine wickets left – only to collapse again. Lara, so often West Indies' crutch, made just seven runs, although he did win an important toss. Helped by rain, which washed out Friday's play, West Indies batted into the third day, with Chanderpaul and Bravo adding 157 on a surface where the occasional ball was already starting to leap or scuttle. Trescothick fell second ball, and soon England were 40 for 3, but Strauss and Thorpe calmed nerves in a stand of 177. When 58, Thorpe lobbed a catch to point, where Sarwan handled it like soap in a bath: the match pivoted round that miss. Thorpe reached 114, despite Edwards breaking his hand at 91. England's innings included 18 wides, a Test record. West Indies still led by 65, but after reaching 88 for 1 they crumbled again. A four off Flintoff made Lara the fourth to score 10,000 Test runs, in his 111th match and 195th innings, fewer than the other three (Sunil Gavaskar, Allan Border and Steve Waugh), but two balls later he fended a nasty lifter to slip. England now had to make a record score to win an Old Trafford Test, while dodging the predicted showers. Their luck held. Key, all puffed-chest defiance in an unbeaten 93, led them home as the dark clouds loomed.

West Indies

C. H. Gayle c Strauss b Hoggard	5	– c Hoggard b Giles	42
S. C. Joseph c Thorpe b Harmison	45	– c Vaughan b Flintoff	15
R. R. Sarwan b Flintoff	40	– c Trescothick b Harmison	60
*B. C. Lara b Flintoff	0	– c Strauss b Flintoff	7
S. Chanderpaul c Jones b Hoggard	76	– c Vaughan b Flintoff	2
D. J. Bravo c Jones b Hoggard	77	– c Flintoff b Giles	6
†C. S. Baugh c Vaughan b Anderson	68	– c sub (A. N. Bressington) b Harmison	3
D. Mohammed c Strauss b Flintoff	23	– c Key b Giles	9
P. T. Collins not out	19	– b Harmison	8
C. D. Collymore b Hoggard	5	– not out	5
F. H. Edwards not out	4	– c Flintoff b Harmison	0
B 9, l-b 14, w 6, n-b 4	33	B 2, l-b 4, w 1, n-b 1	8

1/10 (1) 2/85 (3) 3/97 (4)   (9 wkts dec.) 395
4/108 (2) 5/265 (6) 6/267 (5)
7/308 (8) 8/383 (10) 9/395 (7)

1/41 (2) 2/88 (1) 3/95 (4)   165
4/99 (5) 5/110 (6) 6/121 (7)
7/146 (8) 8/152 (3) 9/161 (9) 10/165 (11)

In the first innings Collins retired hurt at 358.

Hoggard 22–3–83–4; Harmison 26–5–94–1; Flintoff 20–5–79–3; Anderson 11.3–1–49–1; Giles 15–0–67–0. *Second Innings*—Hoggard 7–0–21–0; Harmison 13.4–3–44–4; Flintoff 12–1–26–3; Giles 22–6–46–3; Anderson 5–1–22–0.

England

M. E. Trescothick c Sarwan b Edwards	0	– b Collymore	12
A. J. Strauss b Bravo	90	– c Chanderpaul b Collins	12
R. W. T. Key b Collymore	6	– not out	93
*M. P. Vaughan b Bravo	12	– c Lara b Gayle	33
G. P. Thorpe c Lara b Bravo	114		
A. Flintoff lbw b Bravo	7	– (5) not out	57
M. J. Hoggard c Sarwan b Collymore	23		
†G. O. Jones b Bravo	12		
A. F. Giles c and b Bravo	10		
S. J. Harmison lbw b Collins	8		
J. M. Anderson not out	1		
B 10, l-b 10, w 18, n-b 9	47	B 7, l-b 3, n-b 14	24

1/0 (1) 2/13 (3) 3/40 (4) 4/217 (2)   330
5/227 (6) 6/283 (7) 7/310 (5)
8/321 (8) 9/322 (9) 10/330 (10)

1/15 (1) 2/27 (2)   (3 wkts) 231
3/111 (4)

Edwards 18–2–68–1; Collymore 26–6–66–2; Bravo 26–6–55–6; Joseph 2–0–8–0; Gayle 4–1–7–0; Mohammed 26–2–77–0; Collins 10.2–1–29–1. *Second Innings*—Edwards 11–0–51–0; Collymore 16–7–33–1; Collins 8–2–24–1; Bravo 12–3–41–0; Mohammed 6–0–25–0; Gayle 8.4–0–32–1; Sarwan 4–0–15–0.

Umpires: Aleem Dar *(Pakistan)* (10) and S. J. A. Taufel *(Australia)* (17).
Third umpire: M. R. Benson *(England)*.   Referee: R. S. Madugalle *(Sri Lanka)* (64).

Close of play: First day, West Indies 275-6 (Baugh 9, Mohammed 0); Second day, No play; Third day, England 233-5 (Thorpe 89, Hoggard 3); Fourth day, West Indies 161-9 (Collymore 2, Edwards 0).

ENGLAND v WEST INDIES 2004 (4th Test)

At Kennington Oval, London, on 19, 20, 21 August.
Toss: England.   Result: ENGLAND won by ten wickets.
Debuts: England – I. R. Bell.
Man of the Match: S. J. Harmison.   Men of the Series: S. Chanderpaul and A. Flintoff.

Four years after reclaiming the Wisden Trophy here, England administered a three-day whipping (only the fourth in 54 Tests at The Oval since five-day Tests became the norm in 1950) that sealed a clean sweep. Vaughan's men were determined to claim their own piece of history: a perfect record through the summer. Seven successive wins equalled England's best-ever runs, in 1885–1888 and 1928–1929. Harmison capitalised on a pitch offering reasonable bounce with nine wickets, including a devastating first-innings burst which ensured that West Indies followed on. England struggled early on the first day, but Vaughan and the debutant Ian Bell put on 146, before Flintoff passed fifty for the eighth time in eight Tests and shared another productive partnership with Jones: the innings finished as only the tenth in Tests in which all 11 made double figures. Crashing 14 fours in 93 balls, Lara gave glimpses of his best, but the capitulation he witnessed at the other end was bewildering: the entire innings lasted less than 37 overs. All eight wickets that fell to bowlers went to catches behind square, and a farcical run-out ended the innings. Gayle hammered all six deliveries of Hoggard's second over in the follow-on for fours – a unique occurrence in Tests – and sped past 50 before Joseph became Harmison's 100th Test victim. Lara's demise, caught at first slip, signalled the beginning of the end. This was his 23rd defeat in 40 Tests in charge, beating Allan Border's record of 22 losses (from 93 matches).

England

M. E. Trescothick c Sarwan b Edwards	30	– not out		4
A. J. Strauss c Edwards b Lawson	14	– not out		0
R. W. T. Key c Baugh b Bravo	10			
*M. P. Vaughan c Lara b Bravo	66			
I. R. Bell c Baugh b Lawson	70			
A. Flintoff c Lawson b Edwards	72			
†G. O. Jones c Sarwan b Collymore	22			
A. F. Giles c Lara b Bravo	52			
M. J. Hoggard c Joseph b Lawson	38			
S. J. Harmison not out	36			
J. M. Anderson b Gayle	12			
B 5, l-b 21, w 5, n-b 17	48			

1/51 (2) 2/64 (1) 3/64 (3) 4/210 (5)   470   (no wkt) 4
5/236 (4) 6/313 (7) 7/321 (6)
8/408 (8) 9/410 (9) 10/470 (11)

Edwards 19–4–64–2; Collymore 23–8–58–1; Lawson 24–4–115–3; Bravo 29–4–117–3; Smith 14–4–50–0; Gayle 7.2–2–18–1; Sarwan 7–0–22–0. *Second Innings*—Edwards 0.3–0–4–0.

West Indies

C. H. Gayle c Jones b Harmison	12	– c Flintoff b Anderson		105
S. C. Joseph c Giles b Harmison	9	– c Jones b Harmison		16
R. R. Sarwan c Strauss b Flintoff	2	– c Bell b Harmison		7
*B. C. Lara c Bell b Harmison	79	– c Trescothick b Anderson		15
S. Chanderpaul c Key b Hoggard	14	– (6) c Jones b Giles		32
D. J. Bravo c Jones b Harmison	16	– (5) lbw b Hoggard		54
†C. S. Baugh c Strauss b Harmison	6	– (8) c Jones b Harmison		34
C. D. Collymore c Trescothick b Harmison	4	– (9) c Jones b Anderson		7
F. H. Edwards run out	0	– (10) b Anderson		2
J. J. C. Lawson not out	3	– (11) not out		4
D. R. Smith absent hurt		– (7) c Anderson b Flintoff		28
L-b 7	7	B 1, l-b 12, n-b 1		14

1/19 (1) 2/22 (2) 3/26 (3)   152   1/73 (2) 2/81 (3) 3/126 (4)   318
4/54 (5) 5/101 (6) 6/118 (7)   4/155 (1) 5/237 (5) 6/265 (6)
7/136 (8) 8/149 (4) 9/152 (9)   7/285 (7) 8/312 (9) 9/314 (8) 10/318 (10)

Hoggard 9–2–31–1; Harmison 13–1–46–6; Flintoff 8–1–32–1; Anderson 6.5–0–36–0. *Second Innings*—Hoggard 12–5–50–1; Harmison 18–1–75–3; Giles 22–5–64–1; Flintoff 17–3–64–1; Anderson 15.2–2–52–4.

Umpires: D. B. Hair *(Australia)* (56) and R. E. Koertzen *(South Africa)* (55).
Third umpire: M. R. Benson *(England)*.   Referee: R. S. Madugalle *(Sri Lanka)* (65).

Close of play: First day, England 313-5 (Flintoff 72, Jones 22); Second day, West Indies 84-2 (Gayle 59, Lara 1).

SRI LANKA v SOUTH AFRICA 2004 (1st Test)

At Galle International Stadium on 4, 5, 6, 7, 8 August.
Toss: Sri Lanka.   Result: MATCH DRAWN.
Debuts: none.
Man of the Match: D. P. M. D. Jayawardene.

A combination of a pitch that did not deteriorate as much as expected and South African conservatism – they ignored a target of 325 in 93 overs – condemned this match to a tame finish. South Africa's approach was disappointing but not altogether surprising; they were without Gary Kirsten (retired) and Herschelle Gibbs (injured), and there was an underlying fear that their traditional weakness against spin would be exposed by Muralitharan, back after opting out of the tour of Australia. But that fear proved groundless as Rudolph led them to safety with a painstaking but worthy hundred. For Sri Lanka, Jayawardene's second Test double-century – and his stand of 170 with Vaas, a Sri Lankan eighth-wicket record – led his side from 279 for 7 at the end of the first day to 486. Muralitharan, in only his second Test since the ICC banned his *doosra*, regained sole possession of the record for most Test wickets – Shane Warne had drawn level with him on 527 in July – when he had van Jaarsveld caught at slip off bat and pad. With Smith suffering from a virus, the makeshift opening pair of van Jaarsveld and Dippenaar had eased concerns, and although both fell quickly on the third morning, Rudolph (last out after 413 minutes) ensured the follow-on was saved with ease. Sri Lanka needed to score quickly, but that was easier said than done as Pollock and Klusener (in his first Test for more than two years) proved adept at taking the pace off the ball.

Sri Lanka

*M. S. Atapattu c Boucher b Pollock	9	– lbw b Klusener	25
S. T. Jayasuriya c Klusener b Pollock	12	– c Boucher b Pollock	74
K. C. Sangakkara c Boucher b Boje	58	– c Hayward b Boje	13
D. P. M. D. Jayawardene lbw b Hayward	237	– c Rudolph b Boje	5
T. T. Samaraweera lbw b Pollock	13	– b Klusener	19
T. M. Dilshan b Hayward	25	– lbw b Pollock	1
†R. S. Kaluwitharana b Pollock	33	– c Pollock b Boje	19
U. D. U. Chandana b Ntini	5	– c Dippenaar b Boje	29
W. P. U. J. C. Vaas c Hayward b Boje	69	– not out	13
M. F. Maharoof not out	6	– (11) not out	3
M. Muralitharan b Hayward	0	– (10) c Dippenaar b Boje	2
B 8, l-b 3, w 2, n-b 6	19	B 4, l-b 1, w 2, n-b 4	11

1/13 (2) 2/22 (1) 3/108 (3) 4/145 (5)   486   1/62 (1) 2/89 (3) 3/103 (4)   (9 wkts dec.) 214
5/189 (6) 6/274 (7) 7/279 (8)   4/140 (2) 5/142 (6) 6/166 (5) 7/172
8/449 (9) 9/486 (4) 10/486 (11)   (7) 8/199 (8) 9/209 (10)

Pollock 23–5–48–4; Ntini 20–1–61–1; Hayward 16.4–0–81–3; Kallis 16–3–52–0; Klusener 19–0–69–0; Boje 42–3–148–2; Rudolph 9–2–16–0. *Second Innings*—Pollock 12–2–19–2; Hayward 6–1–21–0; Klusener 14–2–40–2; Ntini 5–0–19–0; Boje 22–0–88–5; Kallis 8–1–22–0.

South Africa

H. H. Dippenaar run out	46	– (2) c Jayawardene b Muralitharan	11
M. van Jaarsveld c Samaraweera b Muralitharan	37	– (3) lbw b Dilshan	29
J. A. Rudolph c Kaluwitharana b Muralitharan	102	– (5) not out	27
J. H. Kallis c Sangakkara b Muralitharan	59	– not out	52
*G. C. Smith lbw b Jayasuriya	23	– (1) b Chandana	74
†M. V. Boucher c Kaluwitharana b Jayasuriya	6		
S. M. Pollock c Sangakkara b Vaas	25		
L. Klusener c Jayawardene b Dilshan	2		
N. Boje c Kaluwitharana b Vaas	31		
M. Ntini c Chandana b Muralitharan	10		
M. Hayward not out	2		
B 14, l-b 8, w 1, n-b 10	33	B 1, l-b 4, w 2, n-b 3	10

1/84 (1) 2/96 (2) 3/168 (4) 4/213 (5)   376   1/34 (2) 2/98 (3)   (3 wkts) 203
5/225 (6) 6/287 (7) 7/295 (8)   3/135 (1)
8/348 (9) 9/363 (10) 10/376 (3)

Vaas 25–10–50–2; Maharoof 19–9–42–0; Muralitharan 46.4–9–130–4; Chandana 18–0–68–0; Jayasuriya 25–9–40–2; Dilshan 6–0–24–1. *Second Innings*—Vaas 10–3–20–0; Jayasuriya 17–7–30–0; Dilshan 16–5–30–1; Maharoof 5–2–4–0; Muralitharan 20–5–37–1; Chandana 18–1–60–1; Samaraweera 3–0–13–0; Sangakkara 1–0–4–0.

Umpires: D. J. Harper *(Australia)* (43) and D. R. Shepherd *(England)* (82).
Third umpire: T. H. Wijewardene *(Sri Lanka)*.   Referee: C. H. Lloyd *(West Indies)* (37).

Close of play: First day, Sri Lanka 279-7 (Jayawardene 116); Second day, South Africa 82-0 (Dippenaar 46, van Jaarsveld 30); Third day, South Africa 347-7 (Rudolph 85, Boje 31); Fourth day, South Africa 7-0 (Smith 5, Dippenaar 0).

SRI LANKA v SOUTH AFRICA 2004 (2nd Test)

At Sinhalese Sports Club, Colombo, on 11, 12, 13, 14, 15 August.
Toss: Sri Lanka.   Result: SRI LANKA won by 313 runs.
Debuts: none.
Man of the Match: K. C. Sangakkara.   Man of the Series: W. P. U. J. C. Vaas.

Sri Lanka recorded their first series win over South Africa after a comprehensive thrashing. After surviving on a slow turner in Galle, the South Africans believed they would be well placed to compete at a ground which usually helps the faster bowlers. But, after Sangakkara made 232 and Jayasuriya shredded some paper-thin batting with his best Test figures, it was Sri Lanka's quick bowlers who exploited conditions far better. In the fourth innings Vaas and Malinga terrorised the batsmen: a delicious irony after previous series when Sri Lanka's batsmen suffered continually against South Africa's quicks. Sangakkara's third Test double-century was a superb effort, although he was badly missed on 57 when Kallis grassed a regulation slip catch off Pollock. South Africa had a brief spell of dominance, taking the last six wickets for 78. The fightback continued as Smith and van Jaarsveld added 108 after Gibbs's return lasted just one ball. But once van Jaarsveld drove lazily to short extra, it was all downhill for them. On the third morning Jayasuriya and Herath ran through some ill-disciplined batting. Rather than risk batting last, Atapattu waived the follow-on, and the lead grew to 492 by the close. When it rained next morning the wisdom of his decision looked dubious. Only eight overs were possible that day, but during them Malinga had Gibbs caught fending off his ribcage, and Vaas bowled van Jaarsveld with a superb inswinging yorker. Vaas removed Kallis third ball next day, and the rest soon followed.

Sri Lanka

*M. S. Atapattu c Boucher b Pollock	4	– b Rudolph	72
S. T. Jayasuriya lbw b Boje	43	– st Boucher b Boje	19
K. C. Sangakkara c Kallis b Pollock	232	– c Ntini b Kallis	64
D. P. M. D. Jayawardene b Ntini	82	– c Boucher b Kallis	3
W. P. U. J. C. Vaas c van Jaarsveld b Pollock	10		
T. T. Samaraweera c Ntini b Kallis	21	– (5) not out	21
T. M. Dilshan c Kallis b Pollock	3	– (6) not out	23
†R. S. Kaluwitharana c Boucher b Hayward	7		
U. D. U. Chandana st Boucher b Boje	40		
H. M. R. K. B. Herath b Ntini	7		
S. L. Malinga not out	6		
L-b 6, w 1, n-b 8	15	B 6, l-b 1, w 2	9

1/4 (1) 2/99 (2) 3/291 (4) 4/316 (5)   470   1/46 (2) 2/142 (3)   (4 wkts dec.) 211
5/392 (6) 6/399 (7) 7/416 (8)   3/149 (4) 4/179 (1)
8/418 (3) 9/437 (10) 10/470 (9)

Pollock 30–8–81–4; Ntini 33–6–108–2; Hayward 17–4–75–1; Kallis 17–6–54–1; Boje 34.3–5–102–2; Rudolph 4–0–16–0; van Jaarsveld 7–0–28–0. *Second Innings*—Pollock 8–0–46–0; Ntini 4–0–19–0; Boje 23–6–81–1; Hayward 3–1–15–0; Smith 4–0–15–0; Kallis 6–4–6–2; Rudolph 7–2–22–1.

South Africa

*G. C. Smith c and b Jayasuriya	65	– c Samaraweera b Malinga	17
H. H. Gibbs lbw b Vaas	0	– c Samaraweera b Malinga	4
M. van Jaarsveld c Sangakkara b Jayasuriya	51	– b Vaas	2
N. Boje b Jayasuriya	0	– (9) lbw b Vaas	16
J. H. Kallis b Jayasuriya	13	– (4) c Dilshan b Vaas	3
J. A. Rudolph c Kaluwitharana b Malinga	6	– (5) c Malinga b Vaas	1
H. H. Dippenaar c Dilshan b Herath	25	– (6) not out	59
†M. V. Boucher not out	10	– (7) c Kaluwitharana b Vaas	51
S. M. Pollock lbw b Herath	1	– (8) c Atapattu b Dilshan	3
M. Ntini b Herath	0	– c Kaluwitharana b Vaas	0
M. Hayward b Jayasuriya	1	– c and b Malinga	1
B 1, l-b 8, n-b 8	17	B 6, l-b 3, w 1, n-b 12	22

1/1 (2) 2/109 (3) 3/109 (4) 4/140 (1)   189   1/4 (2) 2/18 (3) 3/24 (4)   179
5/141 (5) 6/166 (6) 7/186 (7)   4/36 (1) 5/36 (5) 6/137 (7)
8/188 (9) 9/188 (10) 10/189 (11)   7/140 (8) 8/163 (9) 9/163 (10) 10/179 (11)

Vaas 7–3–10–1; Malinga 13–1–51–1; Herath 25–6–60–3; Chandana 6–0–21–0; Dilshan 4–1–4–0; Jayasuriya 14.1–4–34–5. *Second Innings*—Vaas 18–8–29–6; Malinga 13–1–54–3; Jayasuriya 9–3–22–0; Herath 8–5–13–0; Chandana 7–1–26–0; Dilshan 12–6–26–1.

Umpires: B. F. Bowden *(New Zealand)* (18) and S. A. Bucknor *(West Indies)* (91).
Third umpire: E. A. R. de Silva *(Sri Lanka)*.   Referee: C. H. Lloyd *(West Indies)* (38).

Close of play: First day, Sri Lanka 303-3 (Sangakkara 157, Vaas 4); Second day, South Africa 116-3 (Smith 49, Kallis 4); Third day, Sri Lanka 211-4 (Samaraweera 21, Dilshan 23); Fourth day, South Africa 21-2 (Smith 9, Kallis 1).

INDIA v AUSTRALIA 2004-05 (1st Test)

At Chinnaswamy Stadium, Bangalore, on 6, 7, 8, 9, 10 October.
Toss: Australia.   Result: AUSTRALIA won by 217 runs.
Debuts: Australia – M. J. Clarke.
Man of the Match: M. J. Clarke.

Gilchrist, captaining while Ponting recovered from a broken thumb, called heads: the coin was going to fall tails but hit one of the pitch's larger cracks and flipped over the other way. The luck remained with Australia throughout. Michael Clarke became the 17th Australian to score a century on Test debut, the first since Greg Blewett in 1994-95, playing with great audacity, particularly against the spinners. When he reached 98 he replaced helmet with baggy green cap, which he kissed emotionally when he reached his century. Then he became even more aggressive, striking Kumble for two sixes. Kumble will prefer to remember becoming the ninth bowler to reach 400 Test wickets, on his home ground too, when he dismissed Katich to end a stand of 107 with Clarke. Gilchrist then demoralised India: his 11th Test hundred came from just 103 balls. India looked out of it at 150 for 6, but despite an obdurate 46 by Patel they fell only 29 short of the follow-on target. Perhaps spooked by the ghosts of Kolkata 2001, Gilchrist did not enforce it. Despite Harbhajan Singh bowling well again, the eventual target was 457, a remote prospect even if the pitch had not crumbled as anticipated. India started badly when umpire Bowden despatched Sehwag lbw despite a thick inside edge. Pathan, 87 minutes on seven, went on to his maiden Test fifty before being given out caught behind – another dubious decision – and India were bowled out shortly after lunch on the final day.

Australia

J. L. Langer b Pathan	52	– lbw b Pathan	0
M. L. Hayden c Yuvraj Singh b Harbhajan Singh	26	– run out	30
S. M. Katich b Kumble	81	– c Dravid b Kumble	39
D. R. Martyn c Chopra b Kumble	3	– c sub (M. Kaif) b Harbhajan Singh	45
D. S. Lehmann c Dravid b Kumble	17	– c Chopra b Harbhajan Singh	14
M. J. Clarke c Patel b Zaheer Khan	151	– c Chopra b Harbhajan Singh	17
*†A. C. Gilchrist c and b Harbhajan Singh	104	– c Chopra b Kumble	26
S. K. Warne c Dravid b Harbhajan Singh	1	– c Yuvraj Singh b Harbhajan Singh	31
J. N. Gillespie not out	7	– c Yuvraj Singh b Harbhajan Singh	8
M. S. Kasprowicz c Yuvraj Singh b Harbhajan Singh	3	– c Dravid b Harbhajan Singh	8
G. D. McGrath lbw b Harbhajan Singh	0	– not out	3
B 5, l-b 15, w 1, n-b 8	29	B 2, l-b 1, w 1, n-b 3	7

1/50 (2) 2/124 (1) 3/129 (4) 4/149 (5)   474   1/0 (1) 2/65 (2) 3/86 (3)   228
5/256 (3) 6/423 (7) 7/427 (8)   4/104 (5) 5/146 (6) 6/167 (4)
8/471 (6) 9/474 (10) 10/474 (11)   7/204 (7) 8/216 (8) 9/217 (9) 10/228 (10)

Pathan 21–6–62–1; Zaheer Khan 22–2–60–1; Harbhajan Singh 41–7–146–5; Kumble 39–4–157–3; Sehwag 5–0–26–0; Yuvraj Singh 2–0–3–0. *Second Innings*—Pathan 12–2–38–1; Zaheer Khan 13–1–45–0; Harbhajan Singh 30.1–5–78–6; Kumble 23–4–64–2.

India

A. Chopra lbw b McGrath	0	– lbw b Gillespie	5
V. Sehwag c Langer b Kasprowicz	39	– lbw b McGrath	0
R. Dravid b McGrath	0	– lbw b Kasprowicz	60
*S. C. Ganguly c Gilchrist b Kasprowicz	45	– run out	5
V. V. S. Laxman b Warne	31	– lbw b Warne	3
Yuvraj Singh c Gilchrist b McGrath	5	– c Gilchrist b McGrath	27
†P. A. Patel b Gillespie	46	– lbw b Warne	4
I. K. Pathan c Gilchrist b Warne	31	– c Gilchrist b Gillespie	55
A. Kumble b Gillespie	26	– b Kasprowicz	2
Harbhajan Singh c Lehmann b McGrath	8	– c McGrath b Gillespie	42
Zaheer Khan not out	0	– not out	22
B 5, l-b 2, w 5, n-b 3	15	B 6, l-b 5, n-b 3	14

1/0 (1) 2/4 (3) 3/87 (2) 4/98 (4)   246   1/1 (2) 2/7 (1) 3/12 (4)   239
5/124 (6) 6/136 (5) 7/196 (8)   4/19 (5) 5/81 (6) 6/86 (7) 7/118 (3)
8/227 (7) 9/244 (10) 10/246 (9)   8/125 (9) 9/214 (8) 10/239 (10)

McGrath 25–8–55–4; Gillespie 16.2–3–63–2; Warne 28–4–78–2; Kasprowicz 20–4–43–2. *Second Innings*—McGrath 20–10–39–2; Gillespie 14.4–4–33–3; Kasprowicz 14–7–23–2; Warne 32–8–115–2; Lehmann 6–3–14–0; Clarke 1–0–4–0.

Umpires: B. F. Bowden *(New Zealand)* (19) and S. A. Bucknor *(West Indies)* (92).
Third umpire: A. V. Jayaprakash *(India)*.   Referee: R. S. Madugalle *(Sri Lanka)* (66).

Close of play: First day, Australia 316-5 (Clarke 76, Gilchrist 35); Second day, India 150-6 (Patel 18, Pathan 1); Third day, Australia 127-4 (Martyn 29, Clarke 11); Fourth day, India 105-6 (Dravid 47, Pathan 7).

INDIA v AUSTRALIA 2004-05 (2nd Test)

At M. A. Chidambaram Stadium, Chennai, on 14, 15, 16, 17, 18 *(no play)* October.
Toss: Australia.   Result: MATCH DRAWN.
Debuts: none.
Man of the Match: A. Kumble.

Despite the batting of Sehwag and Martyn and the bowling of Kumble, this match will be remembered chiefly for its soggy ending. The fifth day's play was washed out entirely, with the match tantalisingly poised. India would probably have knocked off the 210 they required to level the series: they certainly thought so, and Gilchrist sheepishly admitted as much. But McGrath and Warne were still confident the game could be won, even though McGrath had already been lashed for 18 off two overs. Australia had started well: Langer and Hayden added 136 for the first wicket before all ten wickets tumbled for 99, the last eight contributing just 46. Kumble took seven wickets for 25 in 61 balls, and finished with 13 in the match. Warne bowled almost as well. His record in India had been poor – 24 wickets at 51 before this – but now he took 6 for 125. His second wicket – Pathan caught at slip – was his 533rd: for the first time in his wonderful career, Warne was Test cricket's outright leading wicket-taker, one ahead of Muttiah Muralitharan. Another of his victims was Sehwag, who slammed 155 out of 233, with 21 fours. India, leading by 141, might have won inside four days but for a fine century from Martyn, although he was dropped behind the wicket before he had scored. His four-hour stand with the nightwatchman Gillespie enabled Australia to take the match into the fifth day, when the unexpected arrival of the north-east monsoon confirmed their safety.

Australia

J. L. Langer c Dravid b Harbhajan Singh	71	– c Dravid b Kumble	19
M. L. Hayden c Laxman b Harbhajan Singh	58	– c Laxman b Kumble	39
S. M. Katich not out	36	– (4) lbw b Zaheer Khan	9
D. R. Martyn c Yuvraj Singh b Kumble	26	– (5) c Dravid b Harbhajan Singh	104
D. S. Lehmann c Patel b Kumble	0	– (8) c Patel b Kumble	31
M. J. Clarke lbw b Kumble	5	– (7) not out	39
*†A. C. Gilchrist c Yuvraj Singh b Kumble	3	– (3) b Kumble	49
S. K. Warne c and b Kumble	4	– (9) c Laxman b Kumble	0
J. N. Gillespie c Kaif b Kumble	5	– (6) c Dravid b Harbhajan Singh	26
M. S. Kasprowicz c Laxman b Kumble	4	– lbw b Kumble	5
G. D. McGrath run out	2	– b Harbhajan Singh	2
B 7, l-b 4, w 1, n-b 4, p 5	21	B 19, l-b 15, w 3, n-b 4, p 5	46

1/136 (2) 2/136 (1) 3/189 (4) 4/191 (5)   235
5/204 (6) 6/210 (7) 7/216 (8)
8/224 (9) 9/228 (10) 10/235 (11)

1/53 (1) 2/76 (2) 3/121 (4)   369
4/145 (3) 5/284 (5) 6/285 (6)
7/347 (8) 8/347 (9) 9/364 (10) 10/369 (11)

Pathan 12–3–29–0; Zaheer Khan 11–2–44–0; Harbhajan Singh 29–2–90–2; Kumble 17.3–4–48–7; Sehwag 2–1–8–0. *Second Innings*—Pathan 12–3–39–0; Zaheer Khan 22–6–36–1; Harbhajan Singh 46.5–12–108–3; Kumble 47–8–133–6; Sehwag 1–0–5–0; Yuvraj Singh 2–0–7–0; Ganguly 3–1–2–0.

India

Yuvraj Singh c Gilchrist b Warne	8	– not out	7
V. Sehwag c Clarke b Warne	155	– not out	12
I. K. Pathan c Hayden b Warne	14		
R. Dravid b Kasprowicz	26		
*S. C. Ganguly c Gilchrist b Gillespie	9		
V. V. S. Laxman b Gillespie	4		
M. Kaif run out	64		
†P. A. Patel c Gilchrist b Warne	54		
A. Kumble b Warne	20		
Harbhajan Singh c and b Warne	5		
Zaheer Khan not out	0		
B 6, l-b 3, w 2, n-b 6	17		

1/28 (1) 2/83 (3) 3/178 (4) 4/203 (5)   376
5/213 (6) 6/233 (2) 7/335 (8)
8/369 (9) 9/372 (10) 10/376 (7)

(no wkt) 19

In the first innings Kaif, when 60, retired hurt at 363 and resumed at 372.

McGrath 25–4–74–0; Gillespie 35–8–70–2; Warne 42.3–5–125–6; Kasprowicz 25–5–65–1; Lehmann 5–0–26–0; Katich 2–0–7–0. *Second Innings*—McGrath 2–0–18–0; Gillespie 1–0–1–0.

Umpires: R. E. Koertzen *(South Africa)* (56) and D. R. Shepherd *(England)* (83).
Third umpire: A. V. Jayaprakash *(India)*.   Referee: R. S. Madugalle *(Sri Lanka)* (67).

Close of play: First day, India 28-1 (Sehwag 20, Pathan 0); Second day, India 291-6 (Kaif 34, Patel 27); Third day, Australia 150-4 (Martyn 19, Gillespie 0); Fourth day, India 19-0 (Yuvraj Singh 7, Sehwag 12).

INDIA v AUSTRALIA 2004-05 (3rd Test)

At Vidarbha C. A. Stadium, Nagpur, on 26, 27, 28, 29 October.
Toss: Australia.   Result: AUSTRALIA won by 342 runs.
Debuts: none.
Man of the Match: D. R. Martyn.

As Australia sought to win their first series in India for 35 years, even the return of Tendulkar, out for two months with tennis elbow, was overshadowed by the preparation of the pitch, which looked like a typical English green seamer. India, already lacking Harbhajan Singh (gastro-enteritis), were further dispirited when Ganguly withdrew injured just before the start. The pitch suited tall fast bowlers: Australia had three, India none. McGrath, who became the first Australian fast bowler to win 100 Test caps, bowled with astonishing accuracy, but even he was upstaged by Gillespie, who bowled superbly throughout. Langer and Hayden got Australia off to a good start, but it was left to Martyn to score a handsome century. When India batted they were outclassed not just by McGrath and Gillespie but by Australia's thoughtful field placements, while Tendulkar's return yielded just eight diffident runs from 36 balls. Australia again declined to enforce the follow-on and added 329 for 5 before declaring just before lunch on the fourth day. Katich was unlucky to fall one short of his century, though he was probably lucky not to be given out lbw before he had scored. India required 543 to win, but they were soon 37 for 5, and only a late rally took them to 200. Tendulkar (McGrath's 450th Test victim), Dravid and Laxman made just six runs between them. Australia, two up with one to play, had won in India for the first time since Bill Lawry's side triumphed in 1969-70.

Australia

J. L. Langer c Dravid b Zaheer Khan	44	– c Laxman b Kartik	30
M. L. Hayden c Patel b Zaheer Khan	23	– b Zaheer Khan	9
S. M. Katich c Chopra b Kumble	4	– lbw b Kartik	99
D. R. Martyn c Agarkar b Kumble	114	– c Patel b Zaheer Khan	97
D. S. Lehmann c Dravid b Kartik	70		
M. J. Clarke c Patel b Zaheer Khan	91	– (5) c Kaif b Kumble	73
*†A. C. Gilchrist c and b Kartik	2	– (6) not out	3
S. K. Warne st Patel b Kartik	2		
J. N. Gillespie lbw b Zaheer Khan	9		
M. S. Kasprowicz c Patel b Agarkar	0		
G. D. McGrath not out	11		
B 6, l-b 13, w 1, n-b 8	28	B 1, l-b 15, w 2	18

1/67 (2) 2/79 (1) 3/86 (3) 4/234 (5)   398   1/19 (2) 2/99 (1)   (5 wkts dec.) 329
5/314 (4) 6/323 (7) 7/337 (8)   3/171 (3) 4/319 (5)
8/376 (9) 9/377 (10) 10/398 (6)   5/329 (4)

Agarkar 23–2–99–1; Zaheer Khan 26.2–6–95–4; Kumble 25–6–99–2; Kartik 20–1–57–3; Tendulkar 6–1–29–0.
Second Innings—Zaheer Khan 21.1–5–64–2; Agarkar 21–7–68–0; Kumble 21–1–89–1; Tendulkar 8–1–12–0;
Kartik 26–5–74–2; Sehwag 1–0–6–0.

India

A. Chopra c Warne b Gillespie	9	– b Gillespie	1
V. Sehwag c Gilchrist b McGrath	22	– c Clarke b Warne	58
*R. Dravid c Warne b McGrath	21	– b Gillespie	2
S. R. Tendulkar lbw b Gillespie	8	– c Martyn b McGrath	2
V. V. S. Laxman c Clarke b Warne	13	– c McGrath b Kasprowicz	2
M. Kaif c Warne b McGrath	55	– c Gilchrist b Kasprowicz	7
†P. A. Patel c Hayden b Warne	20	– c Gilchrist b Gillespie	32
A. B. Agarkar c Clarke b Gillespie	15	– not out	44
A. Kumble not out	7	– b Gillespie	2
M. Kartik c Clarke b Gillespie	3	– c Gilchrist b McGrath	22
Zaheer Khan b Gillespie	0	– c Martyn b Warne	25
L-b 10, w 1, n-b 1	12	L-b 2, n-b 1	3

1/31 (2) 2/34 (1) 3/49 (4) 4/75 (5)   185   1/1 (1) 2/9 (3) 3/20 (4) 4/29 (5)   200
5/103 (3) 6/150 (7) 7/173 (8)   5/37 (6) 6/102 (2) 7/114 (7)
8/178 (6) 9/181 (10) 10/185 (11)   8/122 (9) 9/148 (10) 10/200 (11)

McGrath 25–13–27–3; Gillespie 22.5–8–56–5; Kasprowicz 21–4–45–0; Warne 23–8–47–2. *Second Innings*—
McGrath 16–1–79–2; Gillespie 16–7–24–4; Kasprowicz 7–1–39–2; Warne 14.3–2–56–2.

Umpires: Aleem Dar *(Pakistan)* (11) and D. R. Shepherd *(England)* (84).
Third umpire: K. Hariharan *(India)*.   Referee: R. S. Madugalle *(Sri Lanka)* (68).

Close of play: First day, Australia 362-7 (Clarke 73, Gillespie 4); Second day, India 146-5 (Kaif 47, Patel 16);
Third day, Australia 202-3 (Martyn 41, Clarke 10).

INDIA v AUSTRALIA 2004-05 (4th Test)

At Wankhede Stadium, Mumbai, on 3, 4, 5 November.
Toss: India.　　Result: INDIA won by 13 runs.
Debuts: India – G. Gambhir, K. D. Karthik. Australia – N. M. Hauritz.
Man of the Match: M. Kartik.　　Man of the Series: D. R. Martyn.

India won a thrilling match, though the circumstances surrounding their narrow victory detracted from the cele-brations. It was achieved on a pitch which turned square from the start: 20 wickets fell on the third day after 18 had tumbled on the second. "The wicket was no way near to being Test standard," said Ponting, back after injury. "It's been a fantastic series but this has left a sour taste." Australia badly missed Warne, who broke his right thumb batting in the nets the day before the match. Stuart MacGill was on standby at home, but the injury came too late for him: although the debutant off-spinner Nathan Hauritz bowled tidily, it was not enough on a pitch so conducive to spin that part-time left-armer Clarke took 6 for 9 in the second innings. Only 11 overs were possible on the first day, but on the second India were bundled out for 104. Australia took the upper hand with 203, although only Martyn played the spinners with any assurance. Tendulkar briefly found his form and prospered with Laxman: 205 gave India's bowlers an outside chance, and they grabbed it. Set 107, Australia subsided for 93. Langer fell second ball, then after a brief stand Ponting was caught at slip, and Martyn was lbw in the same over. Australia still appeared to be favourites, but at 48 Hayden was bowled off his pads and Clarke deceived by the arm-ball, then Gilchrist, almost the last hope, swept to deep square leg at 58.

India

G. Gambhir lbw b Gillespie	3	– c Clarke b McGrath	1
V. Sehwag b McGrath	8	– lbw b McGrath	5
*R. Dravid not out	31	– (5) c Gilchrist b Clarke	27
S. R. Tendulkar c Gilchrist b Gillespie	5	– c Clarke b Hauritz	55
V. V. S. Laxman c Gilchrist b Gillespie	1	– (3) c and b Hauritz	69
M. Kaif lbw b Gillespie	2	– lbw b Clarke	25
†K. D. Karthik b Kasprowicz	10	– c Ponting b Clarke	4
A. Kumble c Ponting b Hauritz	16	– not out	13
Harbhajan Singh c Katich b Hauritz	14	– c Hayden b Clarke	0
M. Kartik c Gilchrist b Hauritz	0	– b Clarke	2
Zaheer Khan b Kasprowicz	0	– lbw b Clarke	0
B 6, l-b 7, n-b 1	14	B 4	4

1/11 (2) 2/11 (1) 3/29 (4) 4/31 (5)　　　104　　1/5 (1) 2/14 (2) 3/105 (4)　　　205
5/33 (6) 6/46 (7) 7/68 (8)　　　　　　　　　　　4/153 (3) 5/182 (5) 6/188 (7)
8/100 (9) 9/102 (10) 10/104 (11)　　　　　　　7/195 (6) 8/195 (9) 9/199 (10) 10/205 (11)

McGrath 16–9–35–1; Gillespie 12–2–29–4; Kasprowicz 8.3–3–11–2; Hauritz 5–0–16–3. *Second Innings—*Gillespie 15–1–47–0; Hauritz 22–4–87–2; McGrath 12–6–29–2; Kasprowicz 13–5–29–0; Clarke 6.2–0–9–6.

Australia

J. L. Langer c Dravid b Zaheer Khan	12	– c Karthik b Zaheer Khan	0
M. L. Hayden c Kaif b Kartik	35	– b Harbhajan Singh	24
*R. T. Ponting lbw b Kumble	11	– c Laxman b Kartik	12
D. R. Martyn b Kartik	55	– lbw b Kartik	0
S. M. Katich c Kaif b Kumble	7	– c Dravid b Harbhajan Singh	1
M. J. Clarke st Karthik b Kumble	17	– b Kartik	7
†A. C. Gilchrist c Kaif b Kartik	26	– c Tendulkar b Harbhajan Singh	5
J. N. Gillespie c Kaif b Kumble	2	– not out	9
N. M. Hauritz c Harbhajan Singh b Kumble	0	– lbw b Kumble	15
M. S. Kasprowicz c Kumble b Kartik	19	– c Dravid b Harbhajan Singh	7
G. D. McGrath not out	9	– c Laxman b Harbhajan Singh	0
B 2, l-b 4, n-b 4	10	B 8, l-b 5	13

1/17 (1) 2/37 (3) 3/81 (2) 4/101 (5)　　　203　　1/0 (1) 2/24 (3) 3/24 (4)　　　93
5/121 (6) 6/157 (7) 7/167 (8)　　　　　　　　　4/33 (5) 5/48 (2) 6/48 (6)
8/171 (9) 9/184 (4) 10/203 (10)　　　　　　　　7/58 (7) 8/78 (9) 9/93 (10) 10/93 (11)

Zaheer Khan 6–0–10–1; Harbhajan Singh 21–4–53–0; Kumble 19–0–90–5; Kartik 15.3–1–44–4. *Second Innings—*Zaheer Khan 2–0–14–1; Harbhajan Singh 10.5–2–29–5; Kartik 12–3–32–3; Kumble 6–3–5–1.

Umpires: Aleem Dar *(Pakistan)* (12) and R. E. Koertzen *(South Africa)* (57).
Third umpire: K. Hariharan *(India).*　　Referee: R. S. Madugalle *(Sri Lanka)* (69).

Close of play: First day, India 22-2 (Dravid 9, Tendulkar 2); Second day, India 5-0 (Gambhir 1, Sehwag 4).

BANGLADESH v NEW ZEALAND 2004-05 (1st Test)

At Bangabandhu National Stadium, Dhaka, on 19, 20, 21, 22 October.
Toss: Bangladesh.   Result: NEW ZEALAND won by an innings and 99 runs.
Debuts: Bangladesh – Nafis Iqbal.
Man of the Match: B. B. McCullum.

The first seven overs set the tone for the match, and the series. After opting to bat in ideal conditions, Bangladesh lost their first three wickets for five runs in the space of 39 deliveries, handing New Zealand an initiative they never relinquished. Hannan Sarkar, who shares with Sunil Gavaskar the dubious distinction of being dismissed by the first ball of a Test three times, narrowly missed claiming the record outright, edging the third ball to first slip. Rajin Saleh and Mohammad Ashraful added 115, but any hope of sustained late-order resistance evaporated when the left-arm seamer Franklin took a hat-trick, only the second for New Zealand after off-spinner Peter Petherick on debut at Lahore in 1976-77. Franklin dismissed Manjural Islam Rana and Mohammad Rafique with the last two deliveries of his 14th over and Tapash Baisya with the first ball of his 15th. At first New Zealand fared little better. Only Sinclair (76 from 173 balls) looked at ease against the left-arm spinners Rafique and Manjural. When he was fifth out, at 139, Bangladesh entertained reasonable hopes of restricting the lead, only for McCullum to rattle up his maiden Test century: the last five wickets contributed 263 decisive runs. Vettori then wasted little time in exploiting the conditions. He had taken only 16 wickets in his last nine Tests, but now claimed his first five-for since December 2001. Bangladesh's top order failed again. Nafis and Ashraful briefly stemmed the tide, but then the last seven wickets clattered for 39.

Bangladesh

Hannan Sarkar c Fleming b Oram	0	– (3) c and b Vettori	1
Javed Omar b Franklin	1	– c McCullum b Vettori	14
Nafis Iqbal c McCullum b Oram	1	– (1) run out	49
Rajin Saleh c Oram b Franklin	41	– c McCullum b Vettori	0
Mohammad Ashraful c Astle b Vettori	67	– c Styris b Vettori	26
Alok Kapali c McCullum b Vettori	14	– c McCullum b Wiseman	0
*†Khaled Mashud not out	23	– c Styris b Wiseman	2
Manjural Islam Rana c McCullum b Franklin	16	– c Richardson b Vettori	1
Mohammad Rafique c Styris b Franklin	0	– c Fleming b Wiseman	24
Tapash Baisya b Franklin	0	– (11) not out	0
Tareq Aziz c Astle b Oram	0	– (10) lbw b Vettori	0
L-b 7, w 1, n-b 6	14	B 6, n-b 3	9

1/0 (1) 2/5 (2) 3/5 (3) 4/120 (4)   177   1/27 (2) 2/33 (3) 3/41 (4)   126
5/124 (5) 6/136 (6) 7/165 (8)   4/87 (1) 5/88 (6) 6/92 (7) 7/101 (8)
8/165 (9) 9/165 (10) 10/177 (11)   8/112 (5) 9/122 (10) 10/126 (9)

Oram 22.5–9–36–3; Franklin 17–7–28–5; Styris 2–1–4–0; Butler 12–3–34–0; Vettori 29–15–26–2; Wiseman 16–5–42–0. *Second Innings*—Oram 7–4–6–0; Franklin 5–1–14–0; Butler 4–1–8–0; Vettori 22–13–28–6; Wiseman 16.5–1–64–3.

New Zealand

M. H. Richardson c Khaled Mashud b Mohammad Rafique	15	D. L. Vettori c Nafis Iqbal b Manjural Islam Rana ... 23
M. S. Sinclair lbw b Mohammad Rafique	76	J. E. C. Franklin c Rajin Saleh b Tapash Baisya ... 23
*S. P. Fleming c Khaled Mashud b Manjural Islam Rana	29	P. J. Wiseman b Mohammad Rafique ... 28
S. B. Styris c Rajin Saleh b Manjural Islam Rana	2	I. G. Butler not out ... 15
N. J. Astle c Manjural Islam Rana b Mohammad Rafique	11	B 3, l-b 5, w 4, n-b 2 ... 14
J. D. P. Oram c Manjural Islam Rana b Mohammad Rafique	23	402
†B. B. McCullum c Alok Kapali b Mohammad Rafique	143	

1/34 (1) 2/97 (3) 3/99 (4)
4/122 (5) 5/139 (2) 6/223 (6)
7/294 (8) 8/351 (9)
9/371 (7) 10/402 (10)

Tapash Baisya 28–4–112–1; Tareq Aziz 12–1–59–0; Mohammad Rafique 59.1–18–122–6; Manjural Islam Rana 42–12–84–3; Rajin Saleh 1–0–4–0; Alok Kapali 2–0–6–0; Mohammad Ashraful 1–0–7–0.

Umpires: M. R. Benson *(England)* (1) and D. J. Harper *(Australia)* (44).
Third umpire: Mahbubur Rahman *(Bangladesh)*.   Referee: A. G. Hurst *(Australia)* (1).

Close of play: First day, Bangladesh 165-6 (Khaled Mashud 12, Manjural Islam Rana 16); Second day, New Zealand 207-5 (Oram 18, McCullum 48); Third day, Bangladesh 41-2 (Nafis Iqbal 24, Rajin Saleh 0).

BANGLADESH v NEW ZEALAND 2004-05 (2nd Test)

At M. A. Aziz Stadium, Chittagong, on 26, 27, 28, 29 October.
Toss: New Zealand.   Result: NEW ZEALAND won by an innings and 101 runs.
Debuts: Bangladesh – Aftab Ahmed.
Man of the Match: S. P. Fleming.   Man of the Series: D. L. Vettori.

Bangladesh suffered another humiliating defeat, their 18th by an innings in 32 Tests: like the previous match, this one ended five sessions early. Vettori played a crucial role again, with 12 wickets in the match, and 20 in the short series. But even he was upstaged by Fleming, who celebrated his 87th Test appearance, surpassing the New Zealand record held by Richard Hadlee, with a double-century. He also passed Martin Crowe's national record of 5,444 Test runs. Fleming chose to bat first on another typically low, slow subcontinental pitch, and was soon in the action: after both openers went cheaply, he and Styris put on 204. Requiring 346 just to make New Zealand bat again, Bangladesh desperately needed a solid start but, despite an early flurry of boundaries, they were soon in disarray. Vettori made the breakthrough, having Nafis Iqbal well caught in the gully, and after that Javed Omar (who became only the second Bangladeshi after Habibul Bashar to score 1,000 runs) offered sustained resistance. They fared little better second time around, losing their first five wickets for 74. Mohammad Ashraful collected the second pair of his Test career in the space of three hours. A surprisingly large crowd of around 2,000 turned up for the last rites, and they were rewarded by some enterprising play from No. 10 Tapash Baisya, who raced to his half-century from just 36 balls. It was fun while it lasted, but could not disguise the grim reality that, once again, Bangladesh had been completely outplayed.

New Zealand

M. H. Richardson c Mushfiqur Rahman			H. J. H. Marshall c Tapash Baisya	
b Enamul Haque	28		b Enamul Haque	69
M. S. Sinclair b Mohammad Rafique	23		J. D. P. Oram not out	38
*S. P. Fleming c Mushfiqur Rahman b Rajin Saleh	202		†B. B. McCullum not out	17
S. B. Styris c and b Mohammad Rafique	89		B 9, l-b 11, w 2, n-b 18	40
N. J. Astle lbw b Mohammad Rafique	39			

1/49 (2) 2/61 (1) 3/265 (4)   (6 wkts dec.) 545
4/364 (5) 5/447 (3) 6/517 (6)

D. L. Vettori, J. E. C. Franklin and P. J. Wiseman did not bat.

Tapash Baisya 17–0–82–0; Mushfiqur Rahman 15–1–68–0; Mohammad Rafique 55–12–130–3; Enamul Haque 42–4–142–2; Rajin Saleh 19–0–81–1; Mohammad Ashraful 1–0–5–0; Alok Kapali 3–0–17–0.

Bangladesh

Nafis Iqbal c Styris b Vettori	13	– b Wiseman		9
Javed Omar c Sinclair b Wiseman	58	– c and b Franklin		1
Aftab Ahmed lbw b Vettori	20	– b Vettori		28
Rajin Saleh c Sinclair b Wiseman	2	– c Sinclair b Vettori		35
Mohammad Ashraful c Astle b Wiseman	0	– c Styris b Vettori		0
Alok Kapali c Fleming b Vettori	13	– c Astle b Wiseman		13
*†Khaled Mashud lbw b Vettori	18	– b Oram		51
Mushfiqur Rahman c McCullum b Franklin	15	– b Vettori		20
Mohammad Rafique c Wiseman b Vettori	32	– c Sinclair b Vettori		31
Tapash Baisya c Sinclair b Vettori	0	– st McCullum b Vettori		66
Enamul Haque, jun. not out	0	– not out		0
B 4, l-b 2, w 2, n-b 3	11	B 4, l-b 3, w 1		8

1/34 (1) 2/66 (3) 3/82 (4) 4/82 (5)   182   1/9 (2) 2/25 (1) 3/47 (3)   262
5/108 (6) 6/128 (2) 7/142 (7)   4/51 (5) 5/74 (6) 6/123 (4)
8/181 (9) 9/182 (8) 10/182 (10)   7/161 (8) 8/183 (7) 9/217 (9) 10/262 (10)

Oram 5–0–20–0; Franklin 5–0–17–1; Vettori 32.2–12–70–6; Wiseman 27–5–68–3; Astle 2–1–1–0. *Second Innings*— Oram 10–4–33–1; Franklin 8–3–16–1; Wiseman 24–4–106–2; Vettori 28.2–9–100–6.

Umpires: M. R. Benson *(England)* (2) and D. J. Harper *(Australia)* (45).
Third umpire: A. F. M. Akhtaruddin *(Bangladesh)*.   Referee: A. G. Hurst *(Australia)* (2).

Close of play: First day, New Zealand 338-3 (Fleming 137, Astle 34); Second day, Bangladesh 82-3 (Javed Omar 45); Third day, Bangladesh 210-8 (Mohammad Rafique 30, Tapash Baisya 15).

PAKISTAN v SRI LANKA 2004-05 (1st Test)

At Iqbal Stadium, Faisalabad, on 20, 21, 22, 23, 24 October.
Toss: Sri Lanka.   Result: SRI LANKA won by 201 runs.
Debuts: none.
Man of the Match: S. T. Jayasuriya.

If ever a Test could be said to have turned on one delivery, this was it. At 15 for 1 in their second innings, Sri Lanka still trailed by six when Jayasuriya (nine) was caught behind off Shoaib Akhtar. But it was a no-ball, and Jayasuriya went on to a wonderfully authoritative 253. It would be wrong, however, to put Sri Lanka's success simply down to one man. Samaraweera scored his first overseas Test hundred to help rescue them from 9 for 3 on the first morning; Herath excelled with ball and, more surprisingly, bat; Sangakkara and Jayawardene played important innings; and Fernando produced an outstanding spell of fast bowling. By the time Pakistan went in the pitch appeared benign, but disciplined bowling and careless batting ensured the match remained evenly poised. Only Yasir Hameed passed 50, and the last five wickets tumbled for 37. Atapattu completed his fourth Test pair, then came Akhtar's crucial no-ball ... after which Sri Lanka galloped along. Jayasuriya reached his 13th Test hundred with a six over midwicket off Danish Kaneria, and next day brought up his third double-century by pulling Shoaib for six. He added 101 with Fernando – a Sri Lankan ninth-wicket record – shielding his partner so well that he faced just 23 balls out of 102. Pakistan needed to bat for four sessions to save the match: they started positively enough, but then Fernando grabbed four for nine in 36 balls, and it was all over 40 minutes after lunch on the final day.

Sri Lanka

*M. S. Atapattu lbw b Shoaib Akhtar	0	– lbw b Shoaib Akhtar	0
S. T. Jayasuriya c Asim Kamal b Mohammad Sami	38	– lbw b Danish Kaneria	253
K. C. Sangakkara c Imran Farhat b Shoaib Akhtar	2	– c Moin Khan b Shoaib Akhtar	59
D. P. M. D. Jayawardene c Moin Khan b Mohammad Sami	0	– c Moin Khan b Danish Kaneria	57
T. T. Samaraweera c Mohammad Sami b Shoaib Akhtar	100	– run out	21
J. Mubarak c Inzamam-ul-Haq b Mohammad Sami	34	– c Moin Khan b Shoaib Akhtar	0
†R. S. Kaluwitharana c and b Danish Kaneria	4	– c sub (Naved-ul-Hasan) b Danish Kaneria	1
W. P. U. J. C. Vaas c Yousuf Youhana b Shoaib Akhtar	22	– b Shoaib Malik	4
H. M. R. K. B. Herath not out	33	– lbw b Danish Kaneria	5
C. R. D. Fernando b Shoaib Akhtar	0	– run out	1
S. L. Malinga b Mohammad Sami	1	– not out	0
L-b 3, n-b 6	9	B 12, l-b 5, w 3, n-b 12, p 5	37

1/0 (1) 2/6 (3) 3/9 (4) 4/77 (2)   243   1/0 (1) 2/98 (3) 3/216 (4)   438
5/142 (6) 6/147 (7) 7/180 (8)   4/309 (5) 5/314 (6) 6/319 (7)
8/237 (5) 9/242 (10) 10/243 (11)   7/330 (8) 8/337 (9) 9/438 (10) 10/438 (2)

Shoaib Akhtar 19–3–60–5; Mohammad Sami 21.4–5–71–4; Abdul Razzaq 15–5–33–0; Danish Kaneria 18–3–53–1; Shoaib Malik 8–1–23–0. *Second Innings*—Shoaib Akhtar 25–1–115–3; Mohammad Sami 12–1–48–0; Abdul Razzaq 22–7–78–0; Danish Kaneria 38.2–4–117–4; Shoaib Malik 12–1–58–1.

Pakistan

Yasir Hameed c Mubarak b Fernando	58	– lbw b Fernando	17
Imran Farhat c Mubarak b Malinga	11	– lbw b Fernando	53
Asim Kamal c Jayawardene b Fernando	17	– b Fernando	1
*Inzamam-ul-Haq c Malinga b Herath	32	– b Fernando	3
Yousuf Youhana c Kaluwitharana b Herath	17	– lbw b Herath	44
Shoaib Malik run out	48	– c and b Herath	59
Abdul Razzaq c Jayawardene b Vaas	39	– lbw b Herath	0
†Moin Khan b Jayasuriya	5	– c Kaluwitharana b Vaas	1
Mohammad Sami not out	5	– run out	6
Shoaib Akhtar lbw b Herath	9	– st Kaluwitharana b Herath	12
Danish Kaneria run out	1	– not out	0
B 6, l-b 4, n-b 12	22	B 4, l-b 1, w 6, n-b 9	20

1/28 (2) 2/94 (3) 3/109 (1) 4/134 (5)   264   1/59 (1) 2/65 (3) 3/86 (2)   216
5/188 (4) 6/227 (6) 7/246 (8)   4/91 (4) 5/154 (5) 6/158 (7)
8/248 (7) 9/262 (10) 10/264 (11)   7/159 (8) 8/187 (9) 9/215 (6) 10/216 (10)

Vaas 26–5–62–1; Malinga 10–1–50–1; Fernando 16–0–65–2; Herath 27.1–6–68–3; Samaraweera 1–0–5–0; Jayasuriya 4–1–4–1. *Second Innings*—Vaas 16–4–54–1; Malinga 6–2–13–0; Herath 32.2–10–64–4; Fernando 20–4–77–4; Jayasuriya 4–2–2–0; Mubarak 1–0–1–0.

Umpires: B. F. Bowden *(New Zealand)* (20) and S. A. Bucknor *(West Indies)* (93).
Third umpire: Nadeem Ghauri *(Pakistan)*.   Referee: J. J. Crowe *(New Zealand)* (1).

Close of play: First day, Sri Lanka 233-7 (Samaraweera 97, Herath 28); Second day, Pakistan 256-8 (Mohammad Sami 2, Shoaib Akhtar 6); Third day, Sri Lanka 285-3 (Jayasuriya 131, Samaraweera 15); Fourth day, Pakistan 114-4 (Yousuf Youhana 23, Shoaib Malik 3).

PAKISTAN v SRI LANKA 2004-05 (2nd Test)

At National Stadium, Karachi, on 28, 29, 30, 31 October, 1 November.
Toss: Pakistan.   Result: PAKISTAN won by six wickets.
Debuts: Pakistan – Naved-ul-Hasan, Riaz Afridi.
Man of the Match: Danish Kaneria.   Man of the Series: S. T. Jayasuriya.

This was a fantastic Test that could have gone either way. Pakistan won to square the series, but Sri Lanka – 270 behind on first innings – showed real fighting spirit and might have pulled off an astonishing victory had Sangakkara held an edge from Abdul Razzaq when Pakistan were 57 for 4, chasing 137. Inzamam-ul-Haq's brave decision to bowl first – without the injured Mohammad Sami (groin) and Shoaib Akhtar (shoulder), his new-ball pair were both debutants – set the ball rolling. Sri Lanka started well: Jayasuriya and Atapattu became only the second opening pair, after Gordon Greenidge and Desmond Haynes, to add 4,000 runs together in Tests. But Pakistan chipped away with some disciplined bowling, especially from Razzaq, who completed a maiden five-for and also injured Kaluwitharana's right hand, forcing him to pass the wicketkeeping gloves to Sangakkara. Younis Khan and Inzamam both made hundreds to ensure a big lead, not that that fazed Jayasuriya: his first ball disappeared through midwicket for four, and by the close (28 overs) he had 97, and had passed Aravinda de Silva's Sri Lankan record of 6,361 Test runs, in the same match in which he beat de Silva's 93 caps (a national record held jointly with Arjuna Ranatunga). The others dropped anchor in the face of a marathon spell from Danish Kaneria. Sloppy fielding by Pakistan on the final morning meant they had to chase 137 in around two sessions. It proved ticklish, but Shoaib Malik eventually ensured victory by hammering 22 in an over off Herath.

Sri Lanka

S. T. Jayasuriya lbw b Danish Kaneria	26	– c Shoaib Malik b Danish Kaneria	107
*M. S. Atapattu c Younis Khan b Danish Kaneria	44	– c Yasir Hameed b Danish Kaneria	25
K. C. Sangakkara c Danish Kaneria b Riaz Afridi	13	– c Kamran Akmal b Naved-ul-Hasan	138
D. P. M. D. Jayawardene c Inzamam-ul-Haq b Riaz Afridi	16	– c Yasir Hameed b Danish Kaneria	32
T. T. Samaraweera c Imran Farhat b Abdul Razzaq	13	– c Younis Khan b Danish Kaneria	22
J. Mubarak c Yasir Hameed b Abdul Razzaq	13	– c Imran Farhat b Danish Kaneria	2
†R. S. Kaluwitharana c Kamran Akmal b Danish Kaneria	54	– b Danish Kaneria	7
W. P. U. J. C. Vaas c Imran Farhat b Abdul Razzaq	7	– not out	32
M. F. Maharoof c Kamran Akmal b Abdul Razzaq	2	– b Danish Kaneria	3
H. M. R. K. B. Herath c Kamran Akmal b Abdul Razzaq	12	– c and b Naved-ul-Hasan	6
C. R. D. Fernando not out	0	– c Kamran Akmal b Naved-ul-Hasan	4
B 4, l-b 3, w 1	8	B 6, l-b 10, n-b 12	28

1/66 (1) 2/79 (2) 3/97 (3) 4/106 (4)   208
5/126 (5) 6/140 (6) 7/158 (8)
8/164 (9) 9/208 (7) 10/208 (10)

1/117 (2) 2/170 (1) 3/253 (4)   406
4/333 (5) 5/351 (3) 6/359 (6)
7/360 (7) 8/364 (9) 9/387 (10) 10/406 (11)

Naved-ul-Hasan 17–2–52–0; Riaz Afridi 19–7–42–2; Abdul Razzaq 23.1–9–35–5; Danish Kaneria 23–3–72–3. *Second Innings*—Naved-ul-Hasan 24.5–4–83–3; Riaz Afridi 12–3–45–0; Abdul Razzaq 29–8–99–0; Danish Kaneria 60–20–118–7; Shoaib Malik 16–5–45–0.

Pakistan

Yasir Hameed c Sangakkara b Maharoof	3	– c Atapattu b Herath	15
Imran Farhat lbw b Vaas	72	– c Jayawardene b Vaas	19
Younis Khan c Samaraweera b Herath	124	– c Atapattu b Vaas	14
*Inzamam-ul-Haq c Jayawardene b Vaas	117		
Riaz Afridi b Vaas	9		
Yousuf Youhana c Sangakkara b Fernando	46	– (4) lbw b Herath	1
Shoaib Malik lbw b Fernando	44	– (5) not out	53
Abdul Razzaq c Fernando b Jayasuriya	16	– (6) not out	35
†Kamran Akmal c Jayawardene b Herath	15		
Naved-ul-Hasan b Fernando	11		
Danish Kaneria not out	5		
L-b 9, n-b 7	16	L-b 1, n-b 1	2

1/13 (1) 2/135 (2) 3/284 (3) 4/298 (5)   478
5/372 (6) 6/387 (4) 7/437 (8)
8/462 (7) 9/464 (9) 10/478 (10)

1/31 (2) 2/43 (1)   (4 wkts) 139
3/47 (4) 4/57 (3)

Vaas 33–5–106–3; Maharoof 23–4–62–1; Fernando 22.1–1–96–3; Herath 33–3–125–2; Mubarak 9–2–33–0; Jayasuriya 11–3–35–1; Samaraweera 6–0–12–0. *Second Innings*—Vaas 14–0–45–2; Maharoof 2–0–13–0; Herath 15–2–63–2; Jayasuriya 3–1–6–0; Fernando 3–0–11–0.

Umpires: B. F. Bowden *(New Zealand)* (21) and S. A. Bucknor *(West Indies)* (94).
Asad Rauf deputised for Bowden on the third day.
Third umpire: Asad Rauf *(Pakistan).*   Referee: J. J. Crowe *(New Zealand)* (2).

Close of play: First day, Sri Lanka 208; Second day, Pakistan 298-4 (Inzamam-ul-Haq 79); Third day, Sri Lanka 134-1 (Jayasuriya 97, Sangakkara 3); Fourth day, Sri Lanka 361-7 (Vaas 2, Maharoof 0).

AUSTRALIA v NEW ZEALAND 2004-05 (1st Test)

At Woolloongabba, Brisbane, on 18, 19, 20, 21 November.
Toss: New Zealand.   Result: AUSTRALIA won by an innings and 156 runs.
Debuts: none.
Man of the Match: M. J. Clarke.

By the end of the second day, Fleming had much to smile about. After a preparation hampered by a mystery illness and the late withdrawal of Franklin with a groin injury, he had four Australian wickets and a lead of 156. Oram had rescued the side with his second Test century, while the bowlers had bitten into Australia's top order. Oram had 92 when Martin (the ultimate No. 11) arrived, but he reached three figures, then opened up with three sixes, including two in a row off Kasprowicz. However, by lunch next day Fleming's control had been loosened by a spectacular innings from Clarke, who added a memorable home debut to his stunning first Test at Bangalore a month earlier. Clarke, who put on 216 with Gilchrist, had 89 when Martin started the last over before lunch, but reached 100 with a four off the final delivery. Worse was to follow for New Zealand when Gillespie and McGrath both collected half-centuries in a frolicking partnership that was just 13 short of Australia's highest last-wicket stand. McGrath's 61, including a hooked six, was the highest by an Australian No. 11, beating Rodney Hogg's 52 at Georgetown in 1983-84, one record no-one ever expected McGrath to break. In just three sessions, Fleming had gone from plotting a target to contemplating an almost impossible match-saving assignment: as it turned out, New Zealand surrendered meekly in 165 minutes, for their lowest total against Australia since their first meeting at Wellington in 1945-46.

New Zealand

M. H. Richardson c Ponting b Kasprowicz	19	– c Gilchrist b McGrath	4
M. S. Sinclair c Ponting b Gillespie	69	– lbw b McGrath	0
*S. P. Fleming c Warne b Kasprowicz	0	– c Langer b McGrath	11
S. B. Styris c Gilchrist b Kasprowicz	27	– lbw b Warne	7
N. J. Astle run out	19	– c Warne b Kasprowicz	17
C. D. McMillan c Gilchrist b Warne	23	– lbw b Gillespie	9
J. D. P. Oram not out	126	– c Hayden b Warne	8
†B. B. McCullum st Gilchrist b Warne	10	– c Gilchrist b Gillespie	8
D. L. Vettori c Warne b Kasprowicz	21	– c Hayden b Warne	2
K. D. Mills c Hayden b Warne	29	– not out	4
C. S. Martin c Ponting b Warne	0	– lbw b Warne	0
B 1, l-b 2, w 3, n-b 4	10	L-b 2, n-b 4	6

1/26 (1) 2/26 (3) 3/77 (4) 4/138 (5)   353   1/6 (1) 2/7 (2) 3/19 (3) 4/42 (4)   76
5/138 (2) 6/180 (6) 7/206 (8)   5/44 (5) 6/55 (7) 7/69 (8)
8/264 (9) 9/317 (10) 10/353 (11)   8/72 (6) 9/72 (9) 10/76 (11)

McGrath 27–4–67–0; Gillespie 29–7–84–1; Kasprowicz 28–5–90–4; Warne 29.3–3–97–4; Lehmann 4–0–12–0.
Second Innings—McGrath 8–1–19–3; Gillespie 10–5–19–2; Kasprowicz 8–2–21–1; Warne 10.2–3–15–4.

Australia

J. L. Langer lbw b Vettori	34	M. S. Kasprowicz c Mills b Martin	5
M. L. Hayden lbw b Mills	8	G. D. McGrath c Astle b Martin	61
*R. T. Ponting c Astle b Martin	51		
D. R. Martyn c McMillan b Martin	70	B 1, l-b 7, w 1, n-b 8	17
D. S. Lehmann c McCullum b Vettori	8		
M. J. Clarke c Vettori	141	1/16 (2) 2/85 (1) 3/109 (3)	585
†A. C. Gilchrist c Styris b Martin	126	4/128 (5) 5/222 (4) 6/438 (6)	
S. K. Warne lbw b Vettori	10	7/450 (7) 8/464 (8)	
J. N. Gillespie not out	54	9/471 (10) 10/585 (11)	

Martin 39.5–7–152–5; Mills 26–8–99–1; Styris 8–1–33–0; Oram 25–4–116–0; Vettori 50–9–154–4; McMillan 5–1–23–0.

Umpires: Aleem Dar *(Pakistan)* (13) and S. A. Bucknor *(West Indies)* (95).
Third umpire: P. D. Parker *(Australia)*.   Referee: M. J. Procter *(South Africa)* (27).

Close of play: First day, New Zealand 250-7 (Oram 63, Vettori 13); Second day, Australia 197-4 (Martyn 59, Clarke 31); Third day, Australia 564-9 (Gillespie 44, McGrath 54).

AUSTRALIA v NEW ZEALAND 2004-05 (2nd Test)

At Adelaide Oval on 26, 27, 28, 29, 30 November.
Toss: Australia.   Result: AUSTRALIA won by 213 runs.
Debuts: none.
Man of the Match: J. L. Langer.   Man of the Series: G. D. McGrath.

New Zealand had enjoyed some moments of supremacy at Brisbane, but there were to be none here. Langer began with a boundary off Martin, and collected four more in Franklin's next over, something he repeated when Franklin later took the new ball. Langer and Hayden took their combined opening partnerships past 4,000 runs (the third pair to achieve this; see Test No. 1720) with their 13th century stand, and the batting almost became a carnival. Vettori took five wickets, but his second only came when Langer, who brought up his double-century with one of three sixes to go with 25 crashed fours, departed at 445. New Zealand immediately struggled: the crucial wicket came when Fleming was caught behind off McGrath, but all the front-line bowlers made telling contributions, Warne breaking the untrodden ground of 550 Test wickets when Franklin was lbw playing back. Leading by 324, Ponting decided against the follow-on: the top four plodded to 139 from 56 overs, sparking unusual hurry-ups from the crowd to a home captain. Australia did then turn it on: within 21 overs New Zealand were 34 for 4, Fleming again falling to McGrath. Vettori's half-century dragged the match into the second session of the final day, but. Australia took only six balls after lunch to capture the final wicket. New Zealand's fast bowlers failed to strike in the match: the ten Australian wickets to fall were shared by Vettori and Wiseman, although Warne took only three of the 20 New Zealand wickets.

Australia

J. L. Langer c Oram b Vettori	215	– lbw b Wiseman	46
M. L. Hayden c and b Wiseman	70	– c McCullum b Vettori	54
*R. T. Ponting st McCullum b Vettori	68	– not out	26
D. R. Martyn c Fleming b Wiseman	7	– not out	6
D. S. Lehmann b Wiseman	81		
M. J. Clarke lbw b Vettori	7		
†A. C. Gilchrist c and b Vettori	50		
S. K. Warne not out	53		
J. N. Gillespie c Richardson b Vettori	12		
B 4, l-b 4, n-b 4	12	L-b 6, n-b 1	7

1/137 (2) 2/240 (3) 3/261 (4)   (8 wkts dec.) 575   1/93 (1) 2/119 (2)   (2 wkts dec.) 139
4/445 (1) 5/457 (6) 6/465 (5)
7/543 (7) 8/575 (9)

M. S. Kasprowicz and G. D. McGrath did not bat.

Martin 27–4–118–0; Franklin 17–2–102–0; Oram 24–7–55–0; Vettori 55.2–10–152–5; Wiseman 32–7–140–3. *Second Innings*—Martin 6–1–11–0; Oram 5–1–17–0; Franklin 5–0–18–0; Wiseman 22–3–52–1; Vettori 18–2–35–1.

New Zealand

M. H. Richardson b Kasprowicz	9	– c Langer b Kasprowicz	16
M. S. Sinclair c Warne b Gillespie	0	– lbw b Gillespie	2
*S. P. Fleming c Gilchrist b McGrath	83	– b McGrath	3
P. J. Wiseman lbw b Kasprowicz	11	– (10) not out	15
N. J. Astle c Langer b McGrath	52	– c Langer b Lehmann	38
J. D. P. Oram c Gilchrist b Gillespie	12	– c Gilchrist b McGrath	40
†B. B. McCullum lbw b Gillespie	10	– lbw b Gillespie	36
D. L. Vettori lbw b McGrath	20	– c Gillespie b Lehmann	59
J. E. C. Franklin lbw b Warne	7	– c Gilchrist b Kasprowicz	13
S. B. Styris c Clarke b McGrath	28	– (4) c Clarke b Warne	8
C. S. Martin not out	2	– c Ponting b Warne	2
B 3, l-b 5, n-b 9	17	B 1, l-b 12, n-b 5	18

1/2 (2) 2/44 (1) 3/80 (4) 4/153 (3)   251   1/11 (2) 2/18 (3) 3/34 (1)   250
5/178 (5) 6/183 (6) 7/190 (7)   4/34 (4) 5/97 (5) 6/150 (6)
8/213 (9) 9/242 (8) 10/251 (10)   7/160 (7) 8/206 (9) 9/243 (8) 10/250 (11)

McGrath 20.1–3–66–4; Gillespie 19–4–37–3; Warne 28–5–65–1; Kasprowicz 16–3–66–2; Lehmann 5–2–9–0. *Second Innings*—McGrath 12–2–32–2; Gillespie 16–5–41–2; Kasprowicz 14–4–39–2; Warne 27.3–6–79–2; Lehmann 13–0–46–2.

Umpires: S. A. Bucknor *(West Indies)* (96) and D. R. Shepherd *(England)* (85).
Third umpire: S. J. Davis *(Australia)*.   Referee: M. J. Procter *(South Africa)* (28).

Close of play: First day, Australia 327-3 (Langer 144, Lehmann 28); Second day, New Zealand 56-2 (Fleming 38, Wiseman 4); Third day, Australia 57-0 (Langer 31, Hayden 21); Fourth day, New Zealand 149-5 (Oram 40, McCullum 34).

INDIA v SOUTH AFRICA 2004-05 (1st Test)

At Green Park, Kanpur, on 20, 21, 22, 23, 24 November.
Toss: South Africa.   Result: MATCH DRAWN.
Debuts: South Africa – Z. de Bruyn, T. L. Tsolekile.
Man of the Match: A. J. Hall.

Two very different innings dominated a match that meandered to a draw. Sehwag careered past 1,000 runs for the year, while Hall eked out a painstaking 163. In the absence of Herschelle Gibbs, Hall – who had never opened even at provincial level – was expected to provide a similarly cavalier approach at the top of the order. He did anything but, exterminating any trace of flair to construct an innings remarkable for its patience and discipline. By the time he was finally bowled behind his pads, Hall had stonewalled for 588 minutes: only three South Africans had played longer innings in Tests. Zander de Bruyn also produced a stolid and composed innings on debut, and even the indefatigable Kumble could only make intermittent inroads on a surface that gave few signs of life. When India batted, Sehwag tucked in to the bowling, and his Delhi team-mate Gambhir, in only his second Test, matched him shot for shot, which unnerved even the usually metronomic Pollock. They put on 218, India's best opening stand for 49 years. It didn't help that Thami Tsolekile, picked instead of Mark Boucher, missed a stumping off Peterson when Sehwag had just 29. Once Sehwag departed for 164 off 228 balls (Hall faced 454 for one fewer run), the momentum was lost. A fiery burst from Ntini restricted the last six wickets to 65 runs, giving South Africa the satisfaction of a slender lead. By then, though, it was already the fifth morning, so it meant nothing.

South Africa

*G. C. Smith b Kumble	37	– c Gambhir b Kartik	47
A. J. Hall b Kumble	163	– c Karthik b Harbhajan Singh	26
M. van Jaarsveld lbw b Kumble	2	– lbw b Kartik	13
J. H. Kallis lbw b Kumble	37	– not out	28
J. A. Rudolph b Kumble	0	– c Karthik b Harbhajan Singh	2
H. H. Dippenaar c Karthik b Ganguly	48	– not out	31
Z. de Bruyn c Dravid b Harbhajan Singh	83		
S. M. Pollock not out	44		
†T. L. Tsolekile lbw b Kumble	9		
R. J. Peterson b Harbhajan Singh	34		
B 9, l-b 22, w 1, n-b 16, p 5	53	B 12, l-b 5, n-b 5	22

1/61 (1) 2/69 (3) 3/154 (4)	(9 wkts dec.) 510	1/67 (2) 2/100 (3) (4 wkts) 169
4/154 (5) 5/241 (6) 6/385 (2)		3/110 (1) 4/115 (5)
7/445 (7) 8/467 (9) 9/510 (10)		

M. Ntini did not bat.

Zaheer Khan 29–7–59–0; Ganguly 12–2–45–1; Kumble 54–13–131–6; Harbhajan Singh 44.4–9–127–2; Kartik 42–12–76–0; Tendulkar 9–0–36–0. *Second Innings*—Zaheer Khan 8–2–26–0; Kumble 21–8–52–0; Harbhajan Singh 16–5–39–2; Kartik 14–6–17–2; Tendulkar 5–0–18–0.

India

V. Sehwag lbw b Hall	164	Zaheer Khan b Hall	30
G. Gambhir c Tsolekile b Pollock	96	M. Kartik not out	0
R. Dravid c Tsolekile b Ntini	54		
S. R. Tendulkar b Hall	3	B 10, l-b 9, n-b 7	26
*S. C. Ganguly c Peterson b de Bruyn	57		
V. V. S. Laxman b Ntini	9	1/218 (2) 2/294 (1) 3/298 (4)	466
†K. D. Karthik lbw b Pollock	1	4/394 (5) 5/407 (3) 6/408 (7)	
A. Kumble c Tsolekile b Ntini	9	7/419 (8) 8/420 (6)	
Harbhajan Singh c Dippenaar b Peterson	17	9/456 (9) 10/466 (10)	

Pollock 38–11–100–2; Ntini 39–0–135–3; Peterson 21–2–90–1; Hall 25.4–7–93–3; de Bruyn 11–3–29–1.

Umpires: D. J. Harper *(Australia)* (46) and S. J. A. Taufel *(Australia)* (18).
Third umpire: A. V. Jayaprakash *(India)*.   Referee: J. J. Crowe *(New Zealand)* (3).

Close of play: First day, South Africa 230-4 (Hall 78, Dippenaar 46); Second day, South Africa 459-7 (Pollock 31, Tsolekile 5); Third day, India 185-0 (Sehwag 85, Gambhir 85); Fourth day, India 401-4 (Dravid 52, Laxman 4).

INDIA v SOUTH AFRICA 2004-05 (2nd Test)

At Eden Gardens, Kolkata, on 28, 29, 30 November, 1, 2 December.
Toss: South Africa.   Result: INDIA won by eight wickets.
Debuts: South Africa – H. M. Amla.
Man of the Match: Harbhajan Singh.   Man of the Series: V. Sehwag.

Harbhajan Singh revisited the scene of his greatest triumph to inspire India to victory, but they were made to toil. In March 2001, Harbhajan had taken 13 Australian wickets in a match remembered more for Laxman's glorious 281; this time, his 7 for 87 snuffed out the last resistance. South Africa started the final day with a lead of 66, and five wickets in hand – but once Harbhajan deceived Kallis in the flight for a simple return catch hopes faded, not helped by a dubious bat-pad decision against Pollock, after the ball struck his ribcage and then appeared to be caught on the bounce. Demolition job complete, Harbhajan handed over to Kumble, who joined Kapil Dev as India's highest Test wicket-taker with 434. India were left just 117 and eased home with time to spare. South Africa's problems arose from a below-par first innings on a placid track. Both Smith – passed fit at the last minute after his chauffeur drove over his foot – and Hall had given the keeper catching practice: Kallis motored to his 17th Test century, but it was a lone battle. For India, Sehwag kicked off with a dazzling 88, before the impressive Ntini had him caught at slip off a snorter that was shooting straight for the nose. Dravid chiselled out a valuable if scarcely fluent 80, and the middle order ensured a healthy lead. Although Smith played quite beautifully before Harbhajan snaffled him with a magnificent off-break, India never relinquished their grip.

South Africa

*G. C. Smith c Karthik b Pathan	0	– c Laxman b Harbhajan Singh	71
A. J. Hall c Karthik b Zaheer Khan	7	– c Karthik b Harbhajan Singh	21
J. A. Rudolph b Zaheer Khan	61	– lbw b Harbhajan Singh	3
J. H. Kallis b Ganguly	121	– c and b Harbhajan Singh	55
H. M. Amla b Pathan	24	– c Laxman b Harbhajan Singh	2
H. H. Dippenaar c Karthik b Pathan	1	– c Sehwag b Kumble	2
Z. de Bruyn c Karthik b Zaheer Khan	15	– not out	32
S. M. Pollock c Dravid b Kumble	18	– c Gambhir b Harbhajan Singh	6
J. L. Ontong not out	16	– c Karthik b Harbhajan Singh	0
†T. L. Tsolekile c and b Harbhajan Singh	15	– b Kumble	1
M. Ntini c Pathan b Harbhajan Singh	0	– c Dravid b Kumble	12
L-b 17, n-b 10	27	B 12, l-b 2, n-b 3	17

1/0 (1) 2/21 (2) 3/130 (3) 4/176 (5)   305   1/77 (2) 2/81 (3) 3/126 (1)   222
5/182 (6) 6/230 (7) 7/261 (4)   4/138 (5) 5/147 (6) 6/183 (4)
8/273 (8) 9/305 (10) 10/305 (11)   7/193 (8) 8/193 (9) 9/194 (10) 10/222 (11)

Pathan 31–7–72–3; Zaheer Khan 27–7–64–3; Kumble 30–6–76–1; Ganguly 9–3–14–1; Harbhajan Singh 21.3–6–54–2; Tendulkar 3–0–8–0. *Second Innings*—Pathan 5–1–17–0; Zaheer Khan 5–0–22–0; Kumble 34.4–7–82–3; Harbhajan Singh 30–3–87–7.

India

V. Sehwag c Smith b Ntini	88	– c Smith b Ntini	10
G. Gambhir lbw b Pollock	7	– lbw b Rudolph	26
R. Dravid b Hall	80	– not out	47
S. R. Tendulkar b de Bruyn	20	– not out	32
*S. C. Ganguly lbw b de Bruyn	40		
V. V. S. Laxman c Ontong b Ntini	38		
†K. D. Karthik lbw b Pollock	46		
I. K. Pathan c Smith b Ntini	24		
A. Kumble c Kallis b Ntini	8		
Harbhajan Singh c Dippenaar b Ontong	14		
Zaheer Khan not out	11		
L-b 19, w 6, n-b 10	35	L-b 1, n-b 4	5

1/17 (2) 2/144 (1) 3/189 (4) 4/238 (3)   411   1/15 (1) 2/60 (2)   (2 wkts) 120
5/267 (5) 6/308 (6) 7/366 (8)
8/382 (9) 9/387 (7) 10/411 (10)

Pollock 45–13–101–2; Ntini 44–9–112–4; Ontong 18.1–1–79–1; Hall 27–5–68–1; de Bruyn 16–4–32–2. *Second Innings*—Pollock 7–1–22–0; Ntini 4–0–11–1; Ontong 10.4–1–44–0; Rudolph 8–1–24–1; Smith 7–1–16–0; Hall 3–2–2–0.

Umpires: D. J. Harper *(Australia)* (47) and S. J. A. Taufel *(Australia)* (19).
Third umpire: I. Shivram *(India)*.   Referee: J. J. Crowe *(New Zealand)* (4).

Close of play: First day, South Africa 227-5 (Kallis 103, de Bruyn 15); Second day, India 129-1 (Sehwag 82, Dravid 33); Third day, India 359-6 (Karthik 35, Pathan 21); Fourth day, South Africa 172-5 (Kallis 52, de Bruyn 9).

BANGLADESH v INDIA 2004-05 (1st Test)

At Bangabandhu National Stadium, Dhaka, on 10, 11, 12, 13 December.

Toss: India.   Result: INDIA won by an innings and 140 runs.

Debuts: none.

Man of the Match: I. K. Pathan.

That India would win, and easily, was never in doubt. India put Bangladesh in on a pitch with a bit of bounce in it, and Pathan immediately hit his stride, scything through the top order and claiming his first Test five-for. Before the batsmen could come to terms with what was swerving at them, they were 50 for 5. Mohammad Ashraful helped that to 171 before Kumble claimed a slice of history, trapping Mohammad Rafique in front with a typical fizzing slider to give him his 435th Test wicket – one more than Kapil Dev, India's previous record-holder, but in 40 fewer matches. Bangladesh had recovered to some extent, but 184 was never going to be enough. Predictably, the second day was a roaring Indian bat-fest, even if seven wickets did fall. Tendulkar drew level with Sunil Gavaskar as Test cricket's most prolific centurion. His 34th hundred was not the toughest test of his career, yet he was dropped three times – including two sitters – before he reached 50. On the third day, India romped to 526. Tendulkar's final contribution was a Test-best 248 not out, while Zaheer Khan rollicked his way to 75, the highest score by a Test No. 11, beating Richard Collinge's 68 not out for New Zealand against Pakistan at Auckland in 1972-73. When India's bowlers were unleashed again, Pathan just needed to run in and bowl with a strong wrist position – the swinging ball took care of the rest, and he finished the match with 11 wickets.

Bangladesh

Javed Omar lbw b Pathan	4	– lbw b Pathan	4
Nafis Iqbal lbw b Pathan	20	– lbw b Kumble	54
*Habibul Bashar c Tendulkar b Zaheer Khan	8	– c Zaheer Khan b Pathan	12
Rajin Saleh lbw b Pathan	0	– lbw b Pathan	0
Mohammad Ashraful not out	60	– lbw b Pathan	0
†Khaled Mashud c Karthik b Zaheer Khan	8	– c Karthik b Pathan	5
Manjural Islam Rana c Karthik b Pathan	24	– c Karthik b Zaheer Khan	69
Mushfiqur Rahman lbw b Pathan	0	– c Dravid b Harbhajan Singh	6
Mohammad Rafique lbw b Kumble	47	– c Sehwag b Kumble	11
Tapash Baisya c Dravid b Kumble	0	– c Tendulkar b Pathan	29
Mashrafe bin Mortaza run out	7	– not out	0
L-b 4, n-b 2	6	L-b 5, w 2, n-b 5	12

1/8 (1) 2/29 (2) 3/29 (4) 4/35 (3)	184
5/50 (6) 6/106 (7) 7/106 (8)	
8/171 (9) 9/171 (10) 10/184 (11)	

1/4 (1) 2/24 (3) 3/24 (4)	202
4/24 (5) 5/36 (6) 6/100 (2) 7/117 (8)	
8/133 (9) 9/202 (10) 10/202 (7)	

Pathan 16–5–45–5; Zaheer Khan 15–2–51–2; Ganguly 4–2–16–0; Kumble 13.5–2–45–2; Harbhajan Singh 9–1–23–0. *Second Innings*—Pathan 15–5–51–6; Zaheer Khan 13.2–2–60–1; Kumble 13–4–42–2; Harbhajan Singh 12–3–44–1.

India

G. Gambhir run out	35	A. Kumble b Mashrafe bin Mortaza	1
V. Sehwag lbw b Tapash Baisya	13	Harbhajan Singh c Habibul Bashar	
R. Dravid b Mashrafe bin Mortaza	0	b Mushfiqur Rahman	8
S. R. Tendulkar not out	248	Zaheer Khan st Khaled Mashud	
*S. C. Ganguly b Tapash Baisya	71	b Mohammad Ashraful	75
V. V. S. Laxman lbw b Mohammad Rafique	32	B 2, l-b 11	13
†K. D. Karthik c Mashrafe bin Mortaza			
b Mushfiqur Rahman	25	1/19 (2) 2/24 (3) 3/68 (1)	526
I. K. Pathan c Mushfiqur Rahman		4/232 (5) 5/291 (6) 6/339 (7)	
b Mohammad Rafique	5	7/348 (8) 8/368 (9) 9/393 (10) 10/526 (11)	

Tapash Baisya 29–4–114–2; Mashrafe bin Mortaza 31–8–125–2; Mushfiqur Rahman 24–4–104–2; Mohammad Rafique 40–9–113–2; Manjural Islam Rana 12–1–55–0; Mohammad Ashraful 0.4–0–2–1.

Umpires: Aleem Dar *(Pakistan)* (14) and J. W. Lloyds *(England)* (3).
Third umpire: A. F. M. Akhtaruddin *(Bangladesh)*.   Referee: B. C. Broad *(England)* (8).

Close of play: First day, Bangladesh 184; Second day, India 348-7 (Tendulkar 159, Kumble 0); Third day, Bangladesh 170-8 (Manjural Islam Rana 50, Tapash Baisya 17).

BANGLADESH v INDIA 2004-05 (2nd Test)

At M. A. Aziz Stadium, Chittagong, on 17, 18, 19, 20 December.
Toss: India.   Result: INDIA won by an innings and 83 runs.
Debuts: Bangladesh – Nazmul Hossain.
Man of the Match: Mohammad Ashraful.   Man of the Series: I. K. Pathan.

India's victory did not quite come as easily as expected on a pitch that had none of the pace or bounce of Dhaka. The ball did not come on to the bat, and big shots did not fetch their reward – at least not until Mohammad Ashraful eased the pain of yet another defeat. Mashrafe bin Mortaza was back after more than a year out with a knee injury, and immediately dismissed Sehwag. But then India dug deep. Gambhir, with his maiden hundred, and Dravid, the first man to score centuries in all ten Test-playing countries, put on 259. Tendulkar was trapped in front by the first ball of the second day, but India still racked up 540. Bangladesh dipped to 54 for 3 before Ashraful got going. His forthright biffing of the pacemen – hooking while hopping on one leg *à la* Gordon Greenidge – and his effervescent thwacking of the spinners got the crowd to its feet. He grafted to 50 from 70 balls, but needed just 55 more to reach his second Test century, racing from 76 to three figures with seven consecutive scoring shots. His eventual score was Bangladesh's highest, beating Aminul Islam's 145 in their inaugural Test, also against India, in 2000-01. But he ran out of partners; the last man departed eight runs short of the follow-on mark. India's bowlers regrouped for the kill. Pathan found his rhythm, and India needed only four balls on the fourth morning. Talha Jubair became only the sixth No. 11 to top-score in a Test innings.

India

V. Sehwag c Habibul Bashar b Mashrafe bin Mortaza	10	Harbhajan Singh c Manjural Islam Rana	
G. Gambhir b Nazmul Hossain	139	b Nazmul Hossain	47
R. Dravid c Khaled Mashud b Mashrafe bin Mortaza	160	Zaheer Khan not out	0
S. R. Tendulkar lbw b Mashrafe bin Mortaza	36	B 5, l-b 4, w 2, n-b 2	13
*S. C. Ganguly c Talha Jubair b Mohammad Rafique	88		
V. V. S. Laxman c and b Mohammad Rafique	9	1/14 (1) 2/273 (2) 3/334 (4)	540
†K. D. Karthik c Khaled Mashud b Mohammad Rafique	11	4/371 (3) 5/384 (6) 6/402 (7)	
I. K. Pathan c Khaled Mashud b Mohammad Rafique	4	7/412 (8) 8/465 (9)	
A. Kumble st Khaled Mashud		9/540 (5) 10/540 (10)	
b Mohammad Ashraful	23		

Masrafe bin Mortaza 26–5–60–3; Nazmul Hossain 25.5–4–114–2; Talha Jubair 19–1–95–0; Mohammad Rafique 50–2–156–4; Manjural Islam Rana 16.3–0–63–0; Aftab Ahmed 4–0–14–0; Mohammad Ashraful 7–0–29–1.

Bangladesh

Nafis Iqbal c Gambhir b Harbhajan Singh	31	– lbw b Pathan	0
Javed Omar c Dravid b Kumble	10	– c Karthik b Pathan	6
Mashrafe bin Mortaza lbw b Kumble	4	– (9) c Harbhajan Singh b Tendulkar	6
*Habibul Bashar st Karthik b Kumble	22	– (3) lbw b Pathan	17
Mohammad Ashraful not out	158	– (6) lbw b Kumble	3
Aftab Ahmed lbw b Kumble	43	– (4) c Karthik b Pathan	4
Manjural Islam Rana lbw b Zaheer Khan	0	– c Gambhir b Kumble	0
†Khaled Mashud c Karthik b Zaheer Khan	22	– c Dravid b Harbhajan Singh	0
Mohammad Rafique c Dravid b Pathan	4	– (5) c Sehwag b Pathan	22
Talha Jubair b Pathan	0	– (11) c Pathan b Harbhajan Singh	31
Nazmul Hossain run out	0	– (10) not out	8
B 17, l-b 8, w 3, n-b 11	39	B 9, l-b 7, w 7, n-b 4	27

1/48 (2) 2/54 (1) 3/54 (3) 4/124 (4)	333	1/0 (1) 2/30 (2) 3/34 (4)	124
5/239 (6) 6/240 (7) 7/300 (8)		4/75 (5) 5/76 (3) 6/77 (7)	
8/312 (9) 9/312 (10) 10/333 (11)		7/78 (6) 8/80 (8) 9/84 (9) 10/124 (11)	

Pathan 23–7–86–2; Zaheer Khan 18–3–76–2; Kumble 26–9–55–4; Harbhajan Singh 22–5–79–1; Tendulkar 2–0–12–0. *Second Innings*—Pathan 9–2–32–5; Zaheer Khan 6–1–28–0; Kumble 4–2–2–2; Harbhajan Singh 4.4–0–19–2; Tendulkar 3–0–27–1.

Umpires: Aleem Dar *(Pakistan)* (15) and M. R. Benson *(England)* (3).
Third umpire: Mahbubur Rahman *(Bangladesh)*.   Referee: B. C. Broad *(England)* (9).

Close of play: First day, India 334-2 (Dravid 145, Tendulkar 36); Second day, Bangladesh 54-3 (Habibul Bashar 0); Third day, Bangladesh 118-9 (Nazmul Hossain 8, Talha Jubair 25).

AUSTRALIA v PAKISTAN 2004-05 (1st Test)

At W. A. C. A. Ground, Perth, on 16, 17, 18, 19 December.
Toss: Pakistan.   Result: AUSTRALIA won by 491 runs.
Debuts: Pakistan – Mohammad Khalil.
Man of the Match: J. L. Langer.

Australia's largest victory in terms of runs for over 70 years was achieved on the stroke of lunch on the fourth day after McGrath returned career-best figures. Pakistan lost their last nine wickets in 21 overs for just 38 in a display their coach Bob Woolmer described as disgraceful. Against outstanding fast bowling on a quick, bouncy pitch, most failed to move their feet and played with bats well away from bodies. It was the first time McGrath had taken more than four wickets in an innings in ten Tests at Perth; six of his victims were caught in the cordon from wicketkeeper to gully. Shoaib Akhtar and Mohammad Sami had also caused problems on the first day, but the supporting seamers were ineffective. At 78 for 5 Pakistan were perhaps one wicket away from dismissing Australia cheaply, but then bowled poorly: Langer put on 152 in 29 overs with Gilchrist, then 80 with the improved Gillespie. Last out after 280 balls, Langer narrowly missed carrying his bat. Pakistan's fate was sealed by abject first-innings batting. Only Younis Khan seemed to have much stomach for a fight, and he was one of three to fall to ugly slog-sweeps at Warne. Ponting decided to waive the follow-on after it took 30 overs to claim the last two wickets, and Australia's second innings became something of a run-feast. After bowling at a funereal pace in the first innings, Pakistan hustled through 43 overs of spin in the second, precluding any possibility of over-rate fines.

Australia

J. L. Langer c Younis Khan b Mohammad Sami	191	– b Abdul Razzaq	97
M. L. Hayden lbw b Shoaib Akhtar	4	– b Shoaib Akhtar	10
*R. T. Ponting b Mohammad Sami	25	– st Kamran Akmal b Danish Kaneria	98
D. R. Martyn c Kamran Akmal b Mohammad Sami	1	– not out	100
D. S. Lehmann b Shoaib Akhtar	12	– b Danish Kaneria	5
M. J. Clarke c Inzamam-ul-Haq b Shoaib Akhtar	1	– c Inzamam-ul-Haq b Mohammad Sami	27
†A. C. Gilchrist b Abdul Razzaq	69	– not out	0
S. K. Warne c Yousuf Youhana b Abdul Razzaq	12		
J. N. Gillespie c Kamran Akmal b Shoaib Akhtar	24		
M. S. Kasprowicz lbw b Shoaib Akhtar	4		
G. D. McGrath not out	8		
B 1, l-b 14, w 5, n-b 10	30	L-b 15, w 2, n-b 7	24

1/6 (2) 2/56 (3) 3/58 (4) 4/71 (5)	381	1/28 (2) 2/191 (1) (5 wkts dec.) 361
5/78 (6) 6/230 (7) 7/253 (8)		3/271 (3) 4/281 (5)
8/333 (9) 9/362 (10) 10/381 (1)		5/360 (6)

Shoaib Akhtar 22–1–99–5; Mohammad Sami 25.5–3–104–3; Mohammad Khalil 16–0–59–0; Abdul Razzaq 12–0–55–2; Danish Kaneria 15–2–49–0. *Second Innings*—Shoaib Akhtar 6.3–1–22–1; Mohammad Sami 14–1–55–1; Abdul Razzaq 12.3–1–48–1; Mohammad Khalil 9.2–0–38–0; Danish Kaneria 32–3–130–2; Imran Farhat 11–0–53–0.

Pakistan

Salman Butt c Gilchrist b Kasprowicz	17	– c Hayden b McGrath	9
Imran Farhat c Gilchrist b Gillespie	18	– lbw b McGrath	1
Younis Khan c Gillespie b Warne	42	– c Warne b McGrath	17
*Inzamam-ul-Haq b Kasprowicz	1	– (6) c Gilchrist b McGrath	0
Yousuf Youhana c Gilchrist b Kasprowicz	1	– (4) c Gilchrist b McGrath	27
Abdul Razzaq b Warne	21	– (5) c Gilchrist b McGrath	1
†Kamran Akmal b Kasprowicz	2	– c Clarke b McGrath	0
Mohammad Sami c Clarke b Kasprowicz	29	– b Kasprowicz	2
Mohammad Khalil b Warne	0	– (10) c and b Kasprowicz	5
Shoaib Akhtar c Warne b McGrath	27	– (9) c Lehmann b McGrath	1
Danish Kaneria not out	6	– not out	0
B 1, l-b 3, w 7, n-b 4	15	L-b 7, w 2	9

1/32 (2) 2/45 (1) 3/55 (4) 4/60 (5)	179	1/5 (2) 2/34 (1) 3/43 (3)	72
5/108 (3) 6/110 (6) 7/110 (7)		4/49 (5) 5/49 (6) 6/61 (7)
8/111 (9) 9/171 (10) 10/179 (8)		7/64 (4) 8/66 (8) 9/72 (9) 10/72 (10)

McGrath 19–7–44–1; Gillespie 14–2–43–1; Kasprowicz 16.3–6–30–5; Warne 21–9–38–3; Lehmann 4–2–5–0; Ponting 3–1–15–0. *Second Innings*—McGrath 16–8–24–8; Gillespie 12–3–37–0; Kasprowicz 3.3–2–4–2.

Umpires: B. F. Bowden *(New Zealand)* (22) and R. E. Koertzen *(South Africa)* (58).
Third umpire: S. J. Davis *(Australia)*.   Referee: R. S. Madugalle *(Sri Lanka)* (70).

Close of play: First day, Australia 357-8 (Langer 181, Kasprowicz 4); Second day, Australia 15-0 (Langer 3, Hayden 7); Third day, Pakistan 18-1 (Salman Butt 8, Younis Khan 7).

AUSTRALIA v PAKISTAN 2004-05 (2nd Test)

At Melbourne Cricket Ground on 26, 27, 28, 29 December.
Toss: Pakistan.   Result: AUSTRALIA won by nine wickets.
Debuts: none.
Man of the Match: D. R. Martyn.

Australia's ability to extricate themselves from tight corners was well illustrated by a victory that clinched their fifth successive series win over Pakistan. When Clarke was fifth out, they faced the likelihood of a first-innings deficit, possibly a large one, and the prospect of a difficult run-chase. Barely five sessions later, they had won the series. Inzamam-ul-Haq was ruled out by a back injury, so Yousuf Youhana became Pakistan's first Christian captain, and responded with a brilliant 111 off 134 balls, putting on 192 with Younis Khan. Both played Warne particularly well, mainly off the back foot: Youhana hit him for three of his four sixes. But Pakistan lost their last seven wickets for 55. Abdul Razzaq's strokeless stay played completely into Australia's hands, his unbeaten four spanning 110 minutes and 76 balls. Australia also batted indifferently, save for Martyn, who was almost flawless during his 370-minute vigil. His fourth hundred in seven Tests – and Gillespie's second fifty – shepherded Australia to an unlikely lead. Shoaib Akhtar and Danish Kaneria fully deserved their five-fors, but they lacked support: Razzaq, suffering from dizziness, managed only seven overs. Pakistan then again succumbed to pressure on a drop-in pitch still playing well. Many perished to ill-advised shots, although Youhana was unlucky to be given out caught against Warne. From 68 for 5, there was no way back, although Shoaib Malik resisted stoutly after earlier retiring hurt with split webbing. Australia made short work of their target, and Ponting sealed victory with a straight six.

Pakistan

Salman Butt run out	70	– c Kasprowicz b McGrath	0
Imran Farhat c Ponting b Kasprowicz	20	– c Martyn b Gillespie	5
Yasir Hameed lbw b Gillespie	2	– c Gilchrist b McGrath	23
Younis Khan c Gilchrist b Gillespie	87	– c Hayden b Kasprowicz	23
*Yousuf Youhana st Gilchrist b Warne	111	– c Ponting b Warne	12
Shoaib Malik c Ponting b Gillespie	6	– c Gillespie b Warne	41
Abdul Razzaq not out	4	– (8) c Gilchrist b McGrath	19
†Kamran Akmal c Gilchrist b McGrath	24	– (9) lbw b Warne	0
Mohammad Sami lbw b Warne	12	– (7) lbw b Gillespie	11
Shoaib Akhtar st Gilchrist b Warne	0	– b McGrath	14
Danish Kaneria run out	0	– not out	9
L-b 4, w 1	5	B 4, l-b 1, n-b 1	6

1/85 (2) 2/93 (3) 3/94 (1) 4/286 (5)   341
5/298 (4) 6/301 (6) 7/326 (8)
8/341 (9) 9/341 (10) 10/341 (11)

1/0 (1) 2/13 (2) 3/35 (3)   163
4/60 (5) 5/68 (4) 6/98 (7) 7/101 (9)
8/140 (6) 9/140 (8) 10/163 (10)

In the second innings Shoaib Malik, when 15, retired hurt at 91 and resumed at 101.

McGrath 28–12–54–1; Gillespie 26–7–77–3; Kasprowicz 20–6–66–1; Warne 28.3–2–103–3; Clarke 3–0–24–0; Lehmann 2–0–13–0. *Second Innings*—McGrath 11.2–1–35–4; Gillespie 12–7–15–2; Kasprowicz 16–3–42–1; Warne 25–7–66–3.

Australia

J. L. Langer c Imran Farhat b Danish Kaneria	50	– c Kamran Akmal b Mohammad Sami	5
M. L. Hayden c Shoaib Malik b Shoaib Akhtar	9	– not out	56
*R. T. Ponting c Shoaib Malik b Shoaib Akhtar	7	– not out	62
D. R. Martyn lbw b Danish Kaneria	142		
D. S. Lehmann c Yasir Hameed b Shoaib Akhtar	11		
M. J. Clarke c Shoaib Akhtar b Danish Kaneria	20		
†A. C. Gilchrist c Mohammad Sami b Danish Kaneria	48		
S. K. Warne c and b Shoaib Akhtar	10		
J. N. Gillespie not out	50		
M. S. Kasprowicz c sub b Shoaib Akhtar	4		
G. D. McGrath lbw b Danish Kaneria	1		
B 1, l-b 2, w 5, n-b 19	27	L-b 2, n-b 2	4

1/13 (2) 2/32 (3) 3/122 (1) 4/135 (5)   379   1/11 (1)   (1 wkt) 127
5/171 (6) 6/230 (7) 7/254 (8)
8/347 (4) 9/368 (10) 10/379 (11)

Shoaib Akhtar 27–4–109–5; Mohammad Sami 23–2–102–0; Abdul Razzaq 7–0–27–0; Danish Kaneria 39.3–5–125–5; Imran Farhat 3–0–13–0. *Second Innings*—Shoaib Akhtar 7–0–35–0; Mohammad Sami 5–0–22–1; Danish Kaneria 10.5–1–52–0; Imran Farhat 5–2–16–0.

Umpires: R. E. Koertzen *(South Africa)* (59) and J. W. Lloyds *(England)* (4).
Third umpire: R. L. Parry *(Australia)*.   Referee: R. S. Madugalle *(Sri Lanka)* (71).

Close of play: First day, Pakistan 318-6 (Abdul Razzaq 1, Kamran Akmal 16); Second day, Australia 203-5 (Martyn 67, Gilchrist 26); Third day, Pakistan 85-5 (Shoaib Malik 11, Mohammad Sami 8).

AUSTRALIA v PAKISTAN 2004-05 (3rd Test)

At Sydney Cricket Ground on 2, 3, 4, 5 January.
Toss: Pakistan.   Result: AUSTRALIA won by nine wickets.
Debuts: Australia – S. R. Watson. Pakistan – Mohammad Asif.
Man of the Match: S. C. G. MacGill.   Man of the Series: D. R. Martyn.

Pakistan began with their first century opening stand against Australia for 22 years before fading away yet again for another whitewash. From 193 for 1 they subsided to 304 on a slowish pitch, despite Salman Butt's fine maiden Test hundred. MacGill took his record at Sydney to 40 wickets in six Tests, but no less decisive were outstanding innings from Ponting (only the third Australian, after Don Bradman and Greg Chappell, to score four Test double-hundreds) and Gilchrist, whose 13th century passed Andy Flower's Test record for a wicketkeeper. Yasir Hameed was dropped off successive balls – by Warne at first slip, and Gilchrist – in Gillespie's opening over, and it was not until the 32nd that Warne finally broke through. Later McGrath unearthed a fine legcutter with the third ball of a new spell after tea to get rid of Butt, whose dismissal kick-started a collapse. An Australian lead was never in doubt once Ponting and Martyn added 174. Favouring the leg side, Ponting completed his first Test hundred for 13 months, and his eventual 207 contained 30 fours. Gilchrist then gave a scintillating display, surging from 82 to 94 with successive pulled sixes off the debutant seamer Mohammad Asif, and reached a 109-ball hundred two overs later with a straight six off Shahid Afridi. Trailing by 264, Pakistan again made a hash of a promising beginning. The top six all got starts, but none apart from Asim Kamal, last out for a doughty 87, went on to a major innings.

Pakistan

Salman Butt c Gilchrist b McGrath	108	– c Warne b MacGill	21
Yasir Hameed c Clarke b Warne	58	– lbw b Warne	63
Younis Khan c McGrath b MacGill	46	– lbw b Watson	44
*Yousuf Youhana c Warne b MacGill	8	– b MacGill	30
Asim Kamal c Gillespie b MacGill	10	– c Ponting b Gillespie	87
Shahid Afridi c McGrath b MacGill	12	– run out	46
†Kamran Akmal c Warne b McGrath	47	– c Hayden b Warne	4
Naved-ul-Hasan lbw b McGrath	0	– lbw b Warne	9
Shoaib Akhtar b McGrath	0	– c Martyn b Warne	0
Danish Kaneria c Gilchrist b MacGill	3	– b MacGill	0
Mohammad Asif not out	0	– not out	12
B 6, l-b 2, w 1, n-b 3	12	B 4, l-b 3, n-b 2	9

1/102 (2) 2/193 (3) 3/209 (4) 4/241 (1)   304   1/46 (1) 2/104 (2) 3/164 (4)   325
5/241 (5) 6/261 (6) 7/261 (8)   4/164 (3) 5/238 (6) 6/243 (7)
8/261 (9) 9/280 (10) 10/304 (7)   7/261 (8) 8/269 (9) 9/270 (10) 10/325 (5)

McGrath 16.4–5–50–4; Gillespie 14–3–47–0; Watson 10–3–28–0; Warne 24–4–84–1; MacGill 22–4–87–5. *Second Innings*—McGrath 16–2–53–0; Gillespie 13.2–2–39–1; Warne 26–2–111–4; MacGill 25–3–83–3; Watson 9–2–32–1.

Australia

J. L. Langer b Naved-ul-Hasan	13	– b Danish Kaneria	34
M. L. Hayden b Danish Kaneria	26	– not out	23
*R. T. Ponting b Naved-ul-Hasan	207	– not out	4
D. R. Martyn st Kamran Akmal b Danish Kaneria	67		
M. J. Clarke st Kamran Akmal b Danish Kaneria	35		
†A. C. Gilchrist st Kamran Akmal b Danish Kaneria	113		
S. R. Watson c Mohammad Asif b Danish Kaneria	31		
S. K. Warne c Younis Khan b Danish Kaneria	16		
J. N. Gillespie lbw b Naved-ul-Hasan	0		
G. D. McGrath c Yousuf Youhana b Danish Kaneria	9		
S. C. G. MacGill not out	9		
B 6, l-b 13, w 3, n-b 20	42	N-b 1	1

1/26 (1) 2/83 (2) 3/257 (4) 4/318 (5)   568   1/58 (1)   (1 wkt) 62
5/471 (6) 6/529 (3) 7/535 (7)
8/537 (9) 9/556 (10) 10/568 (8)

Shoaib Akhtar 15–2–69–0; Naved-ul-Hasan 26–3–107–3; Mohammad Asif 16–3–72–0; Danish Kaneria 49.3–7–188–7; Shahid Afridi 27–3–113–0. *Second Innings*—Naved-ul-Hasan 3–0–28–0; Mohammad Asif 2–0–16–0; Danish Kaneria 2.3–0–16–1; Shahid Afridi 2–0–2–0.

Umpires: B. F. Bowden *(New Zealand)* (23) and D. R. Shepherd *(England)* (86).
Third umpire: S. J. Davis *(Australia)*.   Referee: R. S. Madugalle *(Sri Lanka)* (72).

Close of play: First day, Pakistan 292-9 (Kamran Akmal 35, Mohammad Asif 0); Second day, Australia 340-4 (Ponting 155, Gilchrist 17); Third day, Pakistan 67-1 (Yasir Hameed 40, Younis Khan 5).

Test No. 1730/126 (SA293/E828)

SOUTH AFRICA v ENGLAND 2004-05 (1st Test)

At St George's Park, Port Elizabeth, on 17, 18, 19, 20, 21 December.
Toss: South Africa.   Result: ENGLAND won by seven wickets.
Debuts: South Africa – A. B. de Villiers, D. W. Steyn.
Man of the Match: A. J. Strauss.

Two fine innings from Strauss carried England to an unprecedented eighth consecutive Test victory, eclipsing the seven last achieved in 1928-29. Strauss, in his first Test overseas, became the first to score debut centuries against three consecutive opponents. In England in 2003, Graeme Smith had started the series with 277, 85 and 259. This time he was caught second ball, then Kallis was bowled by a low Harmison full-toss, both without scoring. Rudolph and Dippenaar put on 112, but the eventual total was well below par. England's openers added 152 before Trescothick whipped across the line, a memorable maiden wicket for Steyn. Raw, rapid and only 21, Steyn looked to have a big future – but he also delivered 16 of South Africa's 35 no-balls. Ntini wrecked the middle order with three wickets in four balls, and England's 425 was a dominant position squandered. South African hopes rose when Kallis was badly dropped on 28 by Butcher at cover, but the match lurched decisively back England's way after Simon Jones's inspirational sprawling catch at fine leg. He then rediscovered his natural length – full, fast and reverse-swinging – and the last six wickets folded for 28. England lost Trescothick (first ball) and Butcher for ducks, but a feature of 2004 was England's superb fourth-innings batting – this was their ninth successful run-chase in 11 victories. Once the menace of the new ball had passed, South Africa's lack of a genuine spinner proved costly, and Strauss hit the winning runs under rain-bearing skies.

South Africa

*G. C. Smith c Strauss b Hoggard	0	– (2) c S. P. Jones b Flintoff	55
A. B. de Villiers lbw b Flintoff	28	– (1) c and b Hoggard	14
J. A. Rudolph c G. O. Jones b Flintoff	93	– c Trescothick b Giles	28
J. H. Kallis b Harmison	0	– lbw b S. P. Jones	61
H. H. Dippenaar c Trescothick b S. P. Jones	110	– b Giles	10
Z. de Bruyn b Flintoff	6	– c Trescothick b Flintoff	19
S. M. Pollock c Trescothick b Hoggard	31	– c G. O. Jones b S. P. Jones	0
A. J. Hall b Hoggard	6	– run out	17
†T. L. Tsolekile c Flintoff b Giles	22	– b S. P. Jones	0
M. Ntini not out	2	– lbw b S. P. Jones	4
D. W. Steyn c Strauss b Giles	8	– not out	2
L-b 13, w 4, n-b 14	31	B 4, l-b 3, w 1, n-b 6, p 5	19

1/0 (1) 2/63 (2) 3/66 (4) 4/178 (3)   337   1/26 (1) 2/64 (3) 3/152 (2)   229
5/192 (6) 6/253 (7) 7/261 (8)   4/168 (5) 5/201 (4) 6/201 (7)
8/324 (5) 9/327 (9) 10/337 (11)   7/217 (6) 8/218 (9) 9/224 (10) 10/229 (8)

Hoggard 20–4–56–3; Harmison 25–2–88–1; S. P. Jones 16–4–39–1; Flintoff 22–4–72–3; Giles 27.4–8–69–2. *Second Innings*—Hoggard 12–2–38–1; Harmison 14–1–54–0; Giles 15–2–39–2; Flintoff 15–2–47–2; S. P. Jones 13.1–3–39–4.

England

M. E. Trescothick b Steyn	47	– c Tsolekile b Pollock	0
A. J. Strauss c de Villiers b Pollock	126	– not out	94
M. A. Butcher c Tsolekile b Ntini	79	– c Smith b Ntini	0
*M. P. Vaughan c Smith b Hall	10	– b Steyn	15
G. P. Thorpe b Smith	4	– not out	31
A. Flintoff c Rudolph b Ntini	35		
†G. O. Jones c Dippenaar b Ntini	2		
A. F. Giles c Hall b Pollock	26		
M. J. Hoggard c Tsolekile b Hall	0		
S. P. Jones c and b Steyn	24		
S. J. Harmison not out	15		
L-b 21, w 1, n-b 35	57	L-b 3, n-b 2	5

1/152 (1) 2/238 (2) 3/249 (4) 4/267 (5)   425   1/0 (1) 2/11 (3) 3/50 (4)   (3 wkts) 145
5/346 (3) 6/353 (6) 7/353 (7)
8/358 (9) 9/394 (8) 10/425 (10)

Pollock 32–14–61–2; Ntini 28–6–75–3; Steyn 25.5–2–117–2; Hall 22–1–95–2; de Bruyn 9–1–31–0; Smith 10–3–25–1. *Second Innings*—Pollock 11–2–36–1; Ntini 6.4–1–24–1; Hall 9–1–14–0; Steyn 6–1–29–1; Smith 8–0–39–0.

Umpires: D. B. Hair *(Australia)* (57) and S. J. A. Taufel *(Australia)* (20).
Third umpire: I. L. Howell *(South Africa)*.   Referee: C. H. Lloyd *(West Indies)* (39).

Close of play: First day, South Africa 273-7 (Dippenaar 79, Tsolekile 6); Second day, England 227-1 (Strauss 120, Butcher 24); Third day, South Africa 99-2 (Smith 33, Kallis 10); Fourth day, England 93-3 (Strauss 51, Thorpe 23).

SOUTH AFRICA v ENGLAND 2004-05 (2nd Test)

At Kingsmead, Durban, on 26, 27, 28, 29, 30 December.
Toss: South Africa.   Result: MATCH DRAWN.
Debuts: none.
Man of the Match: J. H. Kallis.

This Test breathed fresh life into the cliché about cricket's glorious uncertainty. After two days, a South African victory seemed inevitable – but by tea on the fifth, England were favourites. For darkness to close in – with South Africa eight down and England itching to finish them off in the 15 overs that theoretically remained – was the final twist. The draw ended England's record run of eight wins, but preserved their unbeaten record in 2004 (played 13, won 11). When van Jaarsveld fell, South Africa were 183 for 7, but Pollock joined de Villiers in a fighting 27-over stand, taking the match deep into the final session. Simon Jones rekindled English hopes with a direct hit from mid-on to run out Pollock, but 11 balls later the umpires consulted – and that was that. When England, put in, were bundled out for 139 they would have gladly accepted a draw. Three quick wickets gave them a glimmer: South Africa dipped to 118 for 6, but Kallis battled on, supervising the addition of 214 for the last four wickets. Strauss and Trescothick set about one of Test cricket's most vivacious fightbacks, wiping out the deficit without being parted: they put on 273, England's highest opening stand since Colin Cowdrey and Geoff Pullar added 290 against South Africa at The Oval in 1960. Still the game remained up for grabs. England began the fourth day just 88 ahead, lost three quick wickets, and could easily have folded – but Thorpe chipped and chivvied South Africa out of the game.

England

M. E. Trescothick c de Villiers b Ntini	18	– c de Villiers b Pollock	132
A. J. Strauss c Ntini b Boje	25	– c van Jaarsveld b Ntini	136
M. A. Butcher b Steyn	5	– c van Jaarsveld b Kallis	13
*M. P. Vaughan lbw b Ntini	18	– c de Villiers b Ntini	10
G. P. Thorpe lbw b Pollock	1	– not out	118
A. Flintoff c Amla b Pollock	0	– c de Villiers b Smith	60
†G. O. Jones c Rudolph b Ntini	24	– c Ntini b Boje	73
A. F. Giles c Rudolph b Steyn	10	– c de Villiers b Steyn	0
M. J. Hoggard not out	6		
S. P. Jones b Pollock	21		
S. J. Harmison b Pollock	0		
L-b 9, n-b 2	11	B 3, l-b 8, w 2, n-b 15	28

1/21 (1) 2/32 (3) 3/53 (2) 4/62 (5)	**139**	1/273 (1) 2/293 (2) (7 wkts dec.) **570**
5/64 (6) 6/80 (4) 7/93 (7)		3/306 (4) 4/314 (3)
8/113 (8) 9/139 (10) 10/139 (11)		5/428 (6) 6/560 (7) 7/570 (8)

Pollock 15.1–7–32–4; Ntini 13–2–41–3; Steyn 13–4–26–2; Kallis 7–4–10–0; Boje 9–2–21–1. *Second Innings*— Pollock 36–16–79–1; Ntini 37–4–111–2; Steyn 25.3–2–122–1; Boje 44–5–163–1; Kallis 25–4–57–1; Smith 5–1–27–1.

South Africa

*G. C. Smith c Flintoff b Harmison	9	– lbw b Hoggard	5
H. H. Gibbs b Hoggard	15	– c Giles b Harmison	36
J. A. Rudolph c Thorpe b Harmison	32	– (4) c Strauss b Giles	61
J. H. Kallis c sub (P. D. Collingwood) b Hoggard	162	– (5) c G. O. Jones b Harmison	10
M. van Jaarsveld b Flintoff	1	– (6) c Trescothick b Hoggard	49
H. M. Amla c G. O. Jones b Harmison	1	– (7) lbw b S. P. Jones	0
†A. B. de Villiers c Thorpe b S. P. Jones	14	– (8) not out	52
S. M. Pollock c G. O. Jones b Vaughan	43	– (9) run out	35
N. Boje c sub (P. D. Collingwood) b Hoggard	15	– (3) c Thorpe b Flintoff	10
M. Ntini c S. P. Jones b Flintoff	22	– not out	16
D. W. Steyn not out	7		
L-b 7, n-b 4	11	B 8, l-b 4, w 1, n-b 3	16

1/17 (1) 2/48 (2) 3/70 (3) 4/80 (5)	**332**	1/12 (1) 2/33 (3) 3/87 (2) (8 wkts) **290**
5/90 (6) 6/118 (7) 7/205 (8)		4/103 (5) 5/172 (4)
8/243 (9) 9/293 (10) 10/332 (4)		6/173 (7) 7/183 (6) 8/268 (9)

Hoggard 23–8–58–3; Harmison 28–3–91–3; Flintoff 23–5–66–2; S. P. Jones 18–1–81–1; Vaughan 10–2–29–1. *Second Innings*—Hoggard 19–3–58–2; Harmison 19–4–62–2; Flintoff 14–5–38–1; S. P. Jones 14–4–36–1; Giles 19–1–84–1; Vaughan 1–1–0–0.

Umpires: D. B. Hair *(Australia)* (58) and S. J. A. Taufel *(Australia)* (21).
Third umpire: K. H. Hurter *(South Africa)*.   Referee: C. H. Lloyd *(West Indies)* (40).

Close of play: First day, South Africa 70-3 (Kallis 13); Second day, England 30-0 (Trescothick 7, Strauss 21); Third day, England 281-1 (Strauss 132, Butcher 1); Fourth day, South Africa 21-1 (Gibbs 11, Boje 4).

SOUTH AFRICA v ENGLAND 2004-05 (3rd Test)

At Newlands, Cape Town, on 2, 3, 4, 5, 6 January.
Toss: South Africa.   Result: SOUTH AFRICA won by 196 runs.
Debuts: South Africa – C. K. Langeveldt.
Man of the Match: J. H. Kallis.

South Africa levelled the series, mainly thanks to the immovable Kallis, who contributed another century of stultifying application, his eighth in 14 Tests and his seventh in nine at home. He drew the sting from an England attack already weary after their exertions in the Second Test. Vaughan called incorrectly for the 16th time in 22 Tests, and South Africa sensed a shift in momentum. They took tenacious advantage, slowly initially but finishing with an imposing total after Boje injected some urgency. Strauss brought up his 1,000th run in just ten Tests and 19 innings, but the innings unravelled dismally as Charl Langeveldt – pumped with adrenalin and anaesthetics after breaking his left hand when batting – became the first South African since Lance Klusener in 1996-97 to take a five-for on debut. The only resistance came from Giles, whose unbeaten 31 enabled him to become the ninth Englishman to achieve the Test double of 1,000 runs and 100 wickets, a feat Flintoff would emulate later in the match. With a big lead and time to spare, Smith waived the follow-on, instead condemning England to another frazzling in the outfield, eventually declaring 500 ahead. England needed to survive for more than five sessions but, once Trescothick had fallen second ball, escape never seemed likely. It was left to Harmison to apply some gloss to a tatty performance; he became only the seventh No. 11 to top-score in a Test innings (but the second in three weeks: see also Test No. 1726).

South Africa

*G. C. Smith c Trescothick b Giles	74	– lbw b Hoggard	2
H. H. Gibbs b Hoggard	4	– c G. O. Jones b Flintoff	24
J. A. Rudolph c G. O. Jones b S. P. Jones	26	– c Key b S. P. Jones	23
J. H. Kallis c G. O. Jones b Flintoff	149	– run out	66
H. H. Dippenaar b Giles	29	– c Vaughan b Flintoff	44
H. M. Amla lbw b Hoggard	25	– (7) c G. O. Jones b S. P. Jones	10
†A. B. de Villiers b Giles	21	– (8) c Giles b Harmison	10
S. M. Pollock c G. O. Jones b Flintoff	4	– (9) not out	3
N. Boje c G. O. Jones b Flintoff	76	– (6) run out	4
M. Ntini c Vaughan b Flintoff	0	– not out	0
C. K. Langeveldt not out	5		
B 4, l-b 15, w 3, n-b 6	28	B 7, l-b 12, w 10, n-b 7	36

1/9 (2) 2/70 (3) 3/145 (1) 4/213 (5)   441   1/2 (1) 2/62 (2)   (8 wkts dec.) 222
5/261 (6) 6/308 (7) 7/313 (8)   3/101 (3) 4/184 (5)
8/417 (4) 9/417 (10) 10/441 (9)   5/190 (6) 6/203 (4) 7/215 (8) 8/219 (7)

Hoggard 32–7–87–2; Harmison 26–6–82–0; Flintoff 31.1–7–79–4; S. P. Jones 18–0–69–1; Giles 35–3–105–3.
Second Innings—Hoggard 10–0–46–1; Harmison 19–3–55–1; Flintoff 18–1–46–2; Giles 13–2–41–0; S. P. Jones 9.3–4–15–2.

England

M. E. Trescothick c Gibbs b Ntini	28	– c Amla b Pollock	0
A. J. Strauss b Ntini	45	– lbw b Boje	39
R. W. T. Key c de Villiers b Pollock	0	– st de Villiers b Boje	41
*M. P. Vaughan c de Villiers b Langeveldt	11	– c Rudolph b Ntini	20
G. P. Thorpe c Rudolph b Langeveldt	12	– c de Villiers b Pollock	26
M. J. Hoggard c Smith b Ntini	1	– (9) not out	7
A. Flintoff c Gibbs b Ntini	12	– (6) c de Villiers b Pollock	20
†G. O. Jones c Smith b Langeveldt	13	– (7) c Kallis b Boje	38
A. F. Giles not out	31	– (8) c Kallis b Boje	25
S. P. Jones b Langeveldt	0	– c Kallis b Pollock	19
S. J. Harmison c Smith b Langeveldt	0	– c Dippenaar b Ntini	42
B 4, l-b 6	10	B 6, l-b 3, w 6, n-b 12	27

1/52 (1) 2/55 (3) 3/70 (4) 4/95 (2)   163   1/0 (1) 2/68 (2) 3/103 (3)   304
5/97 (6) 6/109 (7) 7/128 (8)   4/105 (4) 5/146 (6) 6/158 (5)
8/141 (5) 9/149 (10) 10/163 (11)   7/220 (8) 8/225 (7) 9/253 (10) 10/304 (11)

Pollock 17–5–36–1; Ntini 19–6–50–4; Langeveldt 16–4–46–5; Boje 4–1–15–0; Kallis 2–1–6–0. *Second Innings*—Pollock 31–11–65–4; Ntini 24.4–6–49–2; Langeveldt 17–3–50–0; Boje 34–13–71–4; Kallis 15–4–49–0; Smith 2–0–11–0.

Umpires: S. A. Bucknor *(West Indies)* (97) and D. J. Harper *(Australia)* (48).
Third umpire: B. G. Jerling *(South Africa)*.   Referee: C. H. Lloyd *(West Indies)* (41).

Close of play: First day, South Africa 247-4 (Kallis 81, Amla 21); Second day, England 95-4 (Thorpe 6, Hoggard 0); Third day, South Africa 184-3 (Kallis 60, Dippenaar 44); Fourth day, England 151-5 (Thorpe 22, G. O. Jones 2).

SOUTH AFRICA v ENGLAND 2004-05 (4th Test)

At The Wanderers, Johannesburg, on 13, 14, 15, 16, 17 January.

Toss: England.   Result: ENGLAND won by 77 runs.

Debuts: none.

Man of the Match: M. J. Hoggard.

This match was proceeding towards the draw most expected when Hoggard turned the game with a classical display of swing bowling. As at Durban, England were hamstrung by the onset of darkness, but this time they just managed to win, and went 2–1 up with their 12th Test victory in ten months. It was their first win at the Wanderers in 48 years, one to rank among their most remarkable anywhere. Several bowlers were injured or off form, so it was left to Hoggard to return England's best match figures for 25 years. Strauss's third century of the series propelled England to 262 for 2, but Ntini started a collapse with the new ball before Vaughan and Harmison injected some oomph late on. South Africa were wobbling at 184 for 5, but Gibbs and the lower order turned a probable deficit into a narrow lead. England were still behind when Strauss finally failed, and on the last morning they were only 189 on with half the side out. But Trescothick charged to 180, and South Africa were set 325 in what seemed a notional 68 overs, because of the likelihood of bad light. Now Hoggard found the perfect length: soon it was 18 for 3, with Kallis nicking a slip catch first ball. Gibbs, though, galloped to 98, and Smith (concussed after being hit at fielding practice) shrugged off doctor's orders to hold firm at No. 8. England were anxiously scanning the clouds, but at 5.53pm Hoggard removed last man Steyn.

England

M. E. Trescothick c Boucher b Steyn	16	– c Boucher b Ntini	180
A. J. Strauss c Kallis b Pollock	147	– c de Villiers b Ntini	0
R. W. T. Key c Smith b Ntini	83	– c Kallis b Ntini	19
*M. P. Vaughan not out	82	– c Boucher b Pollock	54
G. P. Thorpe c Dippenaar b Ntini	0	– c and b Kallis	1
M. J. Hoggard c de Villiers b Ntini	5	– (9) c Boucher b Kallis	0
A. Flintoff c Smith b Ntini	2	– (6) c Boucher b Pollock	7
†G. O. Jones c Smith b Pollock	2	– (7) c de Villiers b Pollock	13
A. F. Giles c Gibbs b Steyn	26	– (8) c Gibbs b Kallis	31
S. J. Harmison not out	30	– not out	3
L-b 13, n-b 5	18	L-b 7, w 6, n-b 11	24

1/45 (1) 2/227 (3) 3/262 (2)   (8 wkts dec.) 411
4/263 (5) 5/273 (6) 6/275 (7)
7/278 (8) 8/329 (9)

1/2 (2) 2/51 (3)   (9 wkts dec.) 332
3/175 (4) 4/176 (5) 5/186 (6)
6/222 (7) 7/272 (8) 8/274 (9) 9/332 (1)

J. M. Anderson did not bat.

Pollock 33–12–81–2; Ntini 34–8–111–4; Steyn 21–7–75–2; Kallis 22–2–79–0; Boje 14–2–52–0. *Second Innings—* Pollock 19–2–74–3; Ntini 20.1–2–62–3; Kallis 21–5–93–3; Steyn 9–0–47–0; Boje 12–0–49–0.

South Africa

*G. C. Smith lbw b Hoggard	29	– (8) not out	67
H. H. Gibbs c Hoggard b Anderson	161	– lbw b Giles	98
J. A. Rudolph c Giles b Hoggard	4	– b Hoggard	2
J. H. Kallis b Hoggard	33	– c Trescothick b Hoggard	0
H. H. Dippenaar c Trescothick b Flintoff	0	– c Giles b Hoggard	14
A. B. de Villiers c Giles b Hoggard	19	– (1) lbw b Hoggard	3
†M. V. Boucher c Strauss b Anderson	64	– (6) c Jones b Hoggard	0
S. M. Pollock lbw b Hoggard	0	– (9) c Jones b Flintoff	4
N. Boje run out	48	– (7) c and b Hoggard	18
M. Ntini b Giles	26	– lbw b Flintoff	13
D. W. Steyn not out	0	– c Jones b Hoggard	8
B 9, l-b 11, w 6, n-b 9	35	B 2, l-b 5, w 1, n-b 12	20

1/64 (1) 2/75 (3) 3/138 (4) 4/149 (5)   419
5/184 (6) 6/304 (7) 7/306 (8)
8/358 (2) 9/399 (9) 10/419 (10)

1/10 (1) 2/18 (3) 3/18 (4)   247
4/80 (5) 5/86 (6) 6/118 (7)
7/163 (2) 8/172 (9) 9/216 (10) 10/247 (11)

Hoggard 34–2–144–5; Harmison 12.5–4–25–0; Anderson 28–3–117–2; Flintoff 30.1–8–77–1; Giles 8.1–0–25–1; Trescothick 5–1–11–0. *Second Innings—*Hoggard 18.3–5–61–7; Harmison 14–1–64–0; Flintoff 16–2–59–2; Anderson 6–1–32–0; Giles 5–0–24–1.

Umpires: Aleem Dar *(Pakistan)* (16) and S. A. Bucknor *(West Indies)* (98).
Third umpire: K. H. Hurter *(South Africa).*   Referee: C. H. Lloyd *(West Indies)* (42).

Close of play: First day, England 263-4 (Vaughan 9, Hoggard 0); Second day, England 411-8 (Vaughan 82, Harmison 30); Third day, South Africa 306-6 (Gibbs 136, Pollock 0); Fourth day, England 197-5 (Trescothick 101, Jones 1).

SOUTH AFRICA v ENGLAND 2004-05 (5th Test)

At Centurion Park, Pretoria, on 21 *(no play)*, 22, 23, 24, 25 January.
Toss: England.   Result: MATCH DRAWN.
Debuts: none.
Man of the Match: A. B. de Villiers.   Man of the Series: A. J. Strauss.

For the second time at Centurion, a rain-affected match involving England was given a fresh lease of life by a tempting late declaration. But whereas Hansie Cronje's 1999-2000 gamble was motivated by greed, Smith's was born purely of desperation. South Africa's hopes of levelling the series had not been helped by a first-day washout (or by two thunderstorms which reduced the third day to 46 overs), but, after dallying on the final morning, they allowed themselves just 44 overs to pull off a miracle. As if to highlight the missed opportunity, England then slumped to 20 for 3. But Vaughan stood firm for over two hours to secure England's fourth successive series win, his fifth in seven as captain, and their first in South Africa since 1964-65. They thus became the first custodians of the new Basil D'Oliveira Trophy. The blame for South Africa's reticence was pinned on Kallis – perhaps unfairly, as he had carried their batting all series. His third century took his series tally to 625 runs (over 250 more than any of his team-mates) but he seemed not to share Smith's optimism that a result was still attainable on the last day. After reaching three figures, he added only 34 more in 16 overs before the declaration. If Kallis was South Africa's scapegoat, then de Villiers was their silver lining. Back opening after his dalliance with the wicketkeeping gloves, he just missed a maiden hundred in the first innings, but made amends in the second. At 20 years 11 months, he was South Africa's third-youngest centurion, behind Graeme Pollock and Tuppy Owen-Smith.

South Africa

A. B. de Villiers lbw b Giles	92	– c Hoggard b S. P. Jones	109
H. H. Gibbs c G. O. Jones b Flintoff	14	– c G. O. Jones b Flintoff	4
J. A. Rudolph b Key b Hoggard	33	– (6) b Harmison	2
J. H. Kallis b Flintoff	8	– not out	136
*G. C. Smith c Trescothick b Flintoff	25	– c sub (P. D. Collingwood) b Harmison	3
†M. V. Boucher c Trescothick b S. P. Jones	25	– (7) c Trescothick b Hoggard	6
S. M. Pollock b Flintoff	0		
N. Boje c Thorpe b S. P. Jones	9		
A. J. Hall c Strauss b S. P. Jones	11	– (3) b Flintoff	9
M. Ntini c Hoggard b S. P. Jones	6		
A. Nel not out	1		
L-b 1, w 3, n-b 19	23	B 2, l-b 14, w 2, n-b 9	27

1/27 (2) 2/114 (3) 3/144 (4) 4/187 (1)   247   1/17 (2) 2/29 (3)   (6 wkts dec.) 296
5/200 (5) 6/200 (7) 7/222 (6)   3/256 (1) 4/267 (5)
8/237 (8) 9/245 (10) 10/247 (9)   5/277 (6) 6/296 (7)

Hoggard 18–4–64–1; Harmison 17–2–79–0; Flintoff 19–6–44–4; S. P. Jones 15.3–3–47–4; Giles 6–1–12–1. *Second Innings*—Hoggard 14–2–51–1; Flintoff 13–2–46–2; Giles 11–1–50–0; S. P. Jones 19–2–74–1; Harmison 16–2–59–2.

England

M. E. Trescothick run out	20	– b Ntini	7
A. J. Strauss c Boucher b Nel	44	– c Kallis b Ntini	0
R. W. T. Key c Boucher b Pollock	1	– lbw b Pollock	9
*M. P. Vaughan c Rudolph b Pollock	0	– not out	26
G. P. Thorpe b Nel	86	– c Gibbs b Ntini	8
A. Flintoff c Boucher b Hall	77	– not out	14
†G. O. Jones c Smith b Nel	50		
A. F. Giles b Nel	39		
M. J. Hoggard c Kallis b Nel	1		
S. P. Jones not out	0		
S. J. Harmison lbw b Nel	6		
B 1, l-b 22, w 8, n-b 4	35	L-b 7, n-b 2	9

1/27 (1) 2/29 (3) 3/29 (4) 4/114 (2)   359   1/0 (2) 2/16 (3)   (4 wkts) 73
5/255 (5) 6/257 (6) 7/335 (7)   3/20 (1) 4/45 (5)
8/351 (8) 9/352 (9) 10/359 (11)

Pollock 21–11–30–2; Ntini 28–8–92–0; Nel 29–7–81–6; Hall 16–3–58–1; Boje 19–7–59–0; Kallis 2–0–5–0; Smith 8–2–11–0. *Second Innings*—Nel 12–5–24–0; Ntini 11–6–12–3; Pollock 7–3–9–1; Smith 3–1–8–0; Hall 5.2–2–9–0; Boje 1–1–0–0; Kallis 2–0–4–0.

Umpires: Aleem Dar *(Pakistan)* (17) and S. A. Bucknor *(West Indies)* (99).
Third umpire: K. H. Hurter *(South Africa)*.   Referee: C. H. Lloyd *(West Indies)* (43).

Close of play: First day, No play; Second day, South Africa 247-9 (Hall 11, Nel 1); Third day, England 114-4 (Thorpe 32, Flintoff 0); Fourth day, South Africa 59-2 (de Villiers 20, Kallis 19).

BANGLADESH v ZIMBABWE 2004-05 (1st Test)

At M. A. Aziz Stadium, Chittagong, on 6, 7, 8, 9, 10 January.
Toss: Bangladesh.　　Result: BANGLADESH won by 226 runs.
Debuts: Zimbabwe – A. G. Cremer, C. B. Mpofu, B. G. Rogers.
Man of the Match: Enamul Haque, jun.

The moment all Bangladesh had been waiting for finally arrived, as they recorded their maiden victory in their 35th Test. They had been dreaming of this since gaining Test status in 2000, but first had to endure 31 defeats, three draws and innumerable sleepless nights. Bangladesh were on top throughout. They amassed their highest Test total, took a sizeable lead, scored quickly to earn ample time to dismiss Zimbabwe again, and completed their historic victory at 12.53 p.m. on the final day. Habibul Bashar and Rajin Saleh were unlucky to miss out on centuries on the opening day, and Zimbabwe's misery grew as the last four wickets added 147, carrying Bangladesh past their 416 against West Indies in St Lucia in May 2004. Zimbabwe dipped to 152 for 6, but Taibu and Chigumbura fought back, and the follow-on was averted by the time Taibu finally fell, eight short of a maiden century. Bangladesh went for quick runs, eventually declaring for only the second time in Tests. Zimbabwe needed 381, but Tapash Baisya soon reduced them to 2 for 2. Taylor and Masakadza, in his first Test since November 2002, added 70 attractively, but when Taylor was lbw offering no shot the floodgates opened. Slow left-armer Enamul Haque had bowled beautifully in the first innings without reward; this time, luck was on his side. Dismissing the last man gave him the best Test figures for Bangladesh, before cartwheels and a lap of honour kicked off the national celebrations.

Bangladesh

Javed Omar c Taibu b Chigumbura	33	– (7) c Masakadza b Chigumbura	15
Nafis Iqbal c Sibanda b Nkala	56	– c Taylor b Hondo	0
*Habibul Bashar c Taibu b Mpofu	94	– c Masakadza b Chigumbura	55
Mohammad Ashraful c Masakadza b Nkala	19	– c Taibu b Mpofu	22
Rajin Saleh c and b Matsikenyeri	89	– (1) c and b Hondo	26
Aftab Ahmed lbw b Mpofu	6	– (5) c Cremer b Chigumbura	11
†Khaled Mashud c Nkala b Cremer	49	– (6) c Cremer b Hondo	23
Mohammad Rafique c Taibu b Mpofu	69	– not out	14
Mashrafe bin Mortaza c Sibanda b Cremer	48	– c Hondo b Chigumbura	19
Tapash Baisya b Mpofu	6	– c Sibanda b Chigumbura	1
Enamul Haque, jun. not out	0		
B 7, l-b 3, w 6, n-b 3	19	B 1, l-b 8, n-b 4, p 5	18

1/91 (1) 2/93 (2) 3/153 (4) 4/272 (3)　　　　488
5/283 (6) 6/341 (5) 7/410 (7)
8/472 (8) 9/480 (10) 10/488 (9)

1/7 (2) 2/47 (1)　　　　　　　(9 wkts dec.) 204
3/83 (4) 4/114 (5) 5/145 (3) 6/156
(6) 7/176 (7) 8/202 (9) 9/204 (10)

Mpofu 29–3–109–4; Hondo 27–6–70–0; Chigumbura 28–6–79–1; Nkala 26–10–50–2; Cremer 16.3–1–86–2; Matsikenyeri 23–3–84–1. *Second Innings*—Mpofu 12–1–47–1; Hondo 17–0–61–3; Chigumbura 16.1–3–54–5; Matsikenyeri 6–0–28–0.

Zimbabwe

S. Matsikenyeri c Habibul Bashar b Tapash Baisya	28	– b Enamul Haque	20
B. G. Rogers run out	5	– c sub (Manjural Islam Rana) b Tapash Baisya	0
V. Sibanda lbw b Mohammad Rafique	12	– lbw b Tapash Baisya	0
H. Masakadza b Mashrafe bin Mortaza	29	– c and b Enamul Haque	56
A. G. Cremer lbw b Mohammad Rafique	0	– (9) c Rajin Saleh b Enamul Haque	2
B. R. M. Taylor lbw b Mashrafe bin Mortaza	39	– (5) lbw b Enamul Haque	44
*†T. Taibu lbw b Mohammad Rafique	92	– (6) c Aftab Ahmed b Enamul Haque	0
E. Chigumbura c Khaled Mashud b Mohammad Rafique	71	– (7) c Khaled Mashud b Mashrafe bin Mortaza	10
M. L. Nkala c Khaled Mashud b Mohammad Rafique	23	– (8) b Mashrafe bin Mortaza	5
D. T. Hondo c Khaled Mashud b Mashrafe bin Mortaza	1	– not out	6
C. B. Mpofu not out	0	– c Mohammad Ashraful b Enamul Haque	5
B 1, l-b 1, w 1, n-b 9	12	L-b 1, w 1, n-b 4	6

1/31 (1) 2/48 (3) 3/59 (2) 4/59 (5)　　　　312
5/86 (4) 6/152 (6) 7/271 (8)
8/308 (7) 9/312 (10) 10/312 (9)

1/2 (2) 2/2 (3) 3/42 (1) 4/112 (5)　　　　154
5/115 (6) 6/126 (4) 7/138 (7)
8/143 (9) 9/145 (8) 10/154 (11)

Mashrafe bin Mortaza 31–12–59–3; Tapash Baisya 24–5–87–1; Mohammad Rafique 41.4–19–65–5; Enamul Haque 26–9–55–0; Mohammad Ashraful 5–0–19–0; Rajin Saleh 4–0–25–0. *Second Innings*—Mashrafe bin Mortaza 17–4–45–2; Tapash Baisya 10–6–20–2; Enamul Haque 22.2–5–45–6; Mohammad Rafique 15–6–43–0.

Umpires: Asad Rauf *(Pakistan)* (1) and T. H. Wijewardene *(Sri Lanka)* (4).
Third umpire: A. F. M. Akhtaruddin *(Bangladesh)*.　　Referee: R. S. Mahanama *(Sri Lanka)* (3).

Close of play: First day, Bangladesh 280-4 (Rajin Saleh 60, Aftab Ahmed 6); Second day, Zimbabwe 84-4 (Masakadza 28, Taylor 8); Third day, Zimbabwe 308-8 (Nkala 20, Hondo 0); Fourth day, Zimbabwe 46-3 (Masakadza 26, Taylor 0).

BANGLADESH v ZIMBABWE 2004-05 (2nd Test)

At Bangabandhu National Stadium, Dhaka, on 14, 15, 16, 17, 18 January.
Toss: Zimbabwe.   Result: MATCH DRAWN.
Debuts: none.
Man of the Match: T. Taibu.   Man of the Series: Enamul Haque, jun.

At the end of the third day, Zimbabwe were 290 ahead with four second-innings wickets left; Bangladesh eventually needed 374 to win, or to survive five sessions to ensure their first series victory. When they batted out time, their delighted coach Dav Whatmore announced that this draw was better than a win: it proved Bangladesh could occupy the crease when required. A dramatic Test showcased two young talents. Taibu, 21, batted brilliantly to accumulate 238 runs for once out, while Enamul Haque, just 18, rewrote his own national record, from the previous game, with 7 for 95 and 12 in the match (no Bangladeshi had previously taken more than seven). Taibu was stranded on 85 in the first innings, as Zimbabwe were pegged back by Enamul. Bangladesh's reply started strongly, before Hondo, finding un-expected reverse swing, took the first six wickets in an unbroken 17-over spell. A resolute fifty from Mohammad Rafique, fighting a hamstring injury, took Bangladesh past 200 before Mashrafe bin Mortaza reduced Zimbabwe to 37 for 4. Taylor then put on 150 with Taibu, who carried on to his maiden Test hundred. Last out, he added 67 for the ninth wicket with Hondo, whose contribution was three. Zimbabwe had a real chance of levelling the series, but Javed Omar and Nafis Iqbal dug in, bringing up Bangladesh's first century opening partnership. They were finally separated after 83 overs, but Nafis completed his first Test century to ensure the draw and a historic series win.

Zimbabwe

S. Matsikenyeri b Enamul Haque	51	– lbw b Mashrafe bin Mortaza		14
B. G. Rogers b Enamul Haque	29	– lbw b Mashrafe bin Mortaza		20
D. D Ebrahim lbw b Enamul Haque	12	– lbw b Mashrafe bin Mortaza		1
H. Masakadza c Aftab Ahmed b Tapash Baisya	43	– c Rajin Saleh b Mohammad Rafique		1
B. R. M. Taylor lbw b Enamul Haque	2	– b Enamul Haque		78
*†T. Taibu not out	85	– c Tapash Baisya b Enamul Haque		153
E. Chigumbura c Mohammad Ashraful b Tapash Baisya	34	– c Khaled Mashud b Mohammad Ashraful		0
T. Panyangara c Khaled Mashud b Mashrafe bin Mortaza	21	– st Khaled Mashud b Enamul Haque		6
A. G. Cremer b Enamul Haque	1	– lbw b Enamul Haque		0
D. T. Hondo b Enamul Haque	9	– c Aftab Ahmed b Enamul Haque		3
C. B. Mpofu c Mohammad Ashraful b Enamul Haque	0	– not out		1
B 4, l-b 6, n-b 1	11	L-b 2, n-b 7		9

1/65 (2) 2/96 (1) 3/107 (3) 4/111 (5)   298   1/30 (1) 2/36 (3) 3/37 (4)   286
5/171 (4) 6/221 (7) 7/257 (8)   4/37 (2) 5/187 (5) 6/196 (7)
8/262 (9) 9/298 (10) 10/298 (11)   7/212 (8) 8/218 (9) 9/285 (10) 10/286 (6)

Tapash Baisya 22–7–67–2; Mashrafe bin Mortaza 23–5–69–1; Mohammad Rafique 38–14–57–0; Enamul Haque 35–9–95–7. *Second Innings*—Mashrafe bin Mortaza 19.4–7–51–3; Tapash Baisya 13.2–2–50–0; Mohammad Rafique 24–9–56–1; Enamul Haque 37–8–105–5; Mohammad Ashraful 9–2–22–1.

Bangladesh

Javed Omar c Taibu b Hondo	34	– c Taylor b Cremer		43
Nafis Iqbal c Taibu b Hondo	28	– c Taylor b Panyangara		121
*Habibul Bashar b Hondo	10	– c Masakadza b Panyangara		2
Mohammad Ashraful lbw b Hondo	5	– c Ebrahim b Cremer		3
Rajin Saleh c Masakadza b Cremer	24	– not out		56
Aftab Ahmed c Matsikenyeri b Hondo	0	– c Taibu b Panyangara		5
†Khaled Mashud b Hondo	0	– not out		28
Mohammad Rafique c Ebrahim b Masakadza	56			
Mashrafe bin Mortaza c Chigumbura b Panyangara	26			
Tapash Baisya c Chigumbura b Cremer	13			
Enamul Haque, jun. not out	3			
L-b 7, n-b 5	12	B 13, l-b 6, n-b 8		27

1/58 (1) 2/71 (2) 3/84 (4) 4/85 (3)   211   1/133 (1) 2/148 (3)   (5 wkts) 285
5/103 (6) 6/107 (7) 7/132 (5)   3/153 (4) 4/196 (2)
8/168 (8) 9/203 (9) 10/211 (10)   5/206 (6)

Panyangara 17–5–37–1; Mpofu 11–3–28–0; Hondo 22–7–59–6; Chigumbura 9–1–32–0; Cremer 12.4–1–32–2; Masakadza 7–1–16–1. *Second Innings*—Panyangara 21–10–28–3; Mpofu 22–10–29–0; Hondo 21–7–37–0; Chigumbura 19–7–31–0; Cremer 34–9–61–2; Matsikenyeri 8–0–41–0; Masakadza 10–3–11–0; Taylor 4–0–11–0; Rogers 3–0–17–0.

Umpires: Nadeem Ghauri *(Pakistan)* (1) and M. G. Silva *(Sri Lanka)* (3).
Third umpire: Mahbubur Rahman *(Bangladesh)*.   Referee: R. S. Mahanama *(Sri Lanka)* (4).

Close of play: First day, Zimbabwe 244-6 (Taibu 49, Panyangara 14); Second day, Bangladesh 169-8 (Mashrafe bin Mortaza 4, Tapash Baisya 0); Third day, Zimbabwe 203-6 (Taibu 81, Panyangara 2); Fourth day, Bangladesh 98-0 (Javed Omar 36, Nafis Iqbal 55).

SOUTH AFRICA v ZIMBABWE 2004-05 (1st Test)

At Newlands, Cape Town, on 4, 5 March.
Toss: Zimbabwe.   Result: SOUTH AFRICA won by an innings and 21 runs.
Debuts: none.
Man of the Match: J. H. Kallis.

Zimbabwe, with seasoned allrounders Streak and Blignaut back in the fold, were expected to prove a tougher proposition – but instead folded to an embarrassing two-day defeat. They lurched to lunch on the first day at 37 for 7 and were dismissed for their lowest Test total barely five overs later. Only Matsikenyeri reached double figures, and only Masakadza displayed much technique, surviving longer than anyone else – 38 balls. Eight men were caught in the arc between keeper and gully, unable to cope with Ntini's pace and the outswing of Kallis and Pollock. It took Smith and de Villiers only 33 overs to reach 200, then Kallis hit the fastest Test fifty in terms of balls, in 24, two quicker than Ian Botham at Delhi in 1981-82, helped by three consecutive sixes off Cremer. South Africa's scoring rate (6.80 an over) was the highest for any Test innings of 150 for more. Smith declared overnight 286 ahead, a record lead for the first day of any Test. Blignaut hit Boje for six sixes, reaching his own fifty in 39 balls, before the sorry spectacle came to an end. Boucher became only the third wicketkeeper to make 300 Test dismissals, after Australians Ian Healy and Rod Marsh, while Ntini was the third South African after Shaun Pollock and Allan Donald to reach 200 wickets. At 940 deliveries, this was the 11th-shortest completed Test of all but, given that conditions were faultless and there were no injuries, surely it was the most one-sided of all.

Zimbabwe

S. Matsikenyeri c de Villiers b Ntini	12	– c Rudolph b Ntini	13
B. G. Rogers c Boucher b Pollock	1	– c Boucher b Ntini	28
D. D. Ebrahim b Ntini	3	– lbw b Langeveldt	72
H. Masakadza lbw b Kallis	6	– c Gibbs b Boje	46
B. R. M. Taylor c Boucher b Ntini	2	– c Langeveldt b Boje	9
*†T. Taibu c de Villiers b Kallis	7	– c sub (W. E. September) b Langeveldt	9
E. Chigumbura c Smith b Kallis	2	– b Boje	0
H. H. Streak c Boucher b Pollock	9	– c Gibbs b Kallis	12
A. M. Blignaut c Boje b Kallis	8	– st Boucher b Boje	61
A. G. Cremer c Kallis b Pollock	0	– run out	2
C. B. Mpofu not out	0	– not out	0
N-b 4	4	B 2, l-b 7, w 2, n-b 2	13
	54		265

1/2 (2) 2/13 (3) 3/20 (1) 4/22 (5)   1/25 (1) 2/59 (2) 3/157 (4)
5/33 (4) 6/36 (6) 7/37 (7)   4/173 (5) 5/183 (6) 6/186 (7)
8/50 (8) 9/50 (10) 10/54 (9)   7/186 (3) 8/214 (8) 9/247 (10) 10/265 (9)

Pollock 8–4–9–3; Ntini 10–2–23–3; Langeveldt 6–2–9–0; Kallis 7.2–3–13–4. *Second Innings*—Pollock 5–1–14–0; Ntini 16–2–68–2; Langeveldt 9.3–3–27–2; Kallis 17.3–7–40–1; Boje 26.2–5–106–4; Rudolph 1–0–1–0.

South Africa

*G. C. Smith c Masakadza b Cremer	121
A. B. de Villiers c Blignaut b Cremer	98
J. A. Rudolph not out	49
J. H. Kallis c Blignaut b Cremer	54
H. H. Gibbs not out	8
L-b 1, w 1, n-b 8	10

1/217 (1) 2/234 (2)   (3 wkts dec.) 340
3/328 (4)

A. G. Prince, †M. V. Boucher, S. M. Pollock, N. Boje, M. Ntini and C. K. Langeveldt did not bat.

Streak 13–0–90–0; Mpofu 12–2–53–0; Blignaut 6–0–44–0; Chigumbura 8–0–53–0; Cremer 9–0–86–3; Matsikenyeri 1–0–6–0; Taylor 1–0–7–0.

Umpires: B. F. Bowden *(New Zealand)* (24) and B. R. Doctrove *(West Indies)* (3).
Third umpire: B. G. Jerling *(South Africa)*.   Referee: A. G. Hurst *(Australia)* (3).

Close of play: First day, South Africa 340-3 (Rudolph 49, Gibbs 8).

SOUTH AFRICA v ZIMBABWE 2004-05 (2nd Test)

At Centurion Park, Pretoria, on 11, 12, 13 March.
Toss: South Africa.   Result: SOUTH AFRICA won by an innings and 62 runs.
Debuts: none.
Man of the Match: M. Zondeki.   Man of the Series: J. H. Kallis.

Everything appeared to be following the expected script when Zimbabwe, put in, collapsed to 115 for 7, an improvement on the previous week but predictably feeble. Then Nel pulled a hamstring and hobbled off. Langeveldt twisted a muscle in his back and hobbled off. Kallis wrenched his hip and . . . hobbled off. The fourth seamer, Zondeki, had just completed a lengthy second spell, so South Africa, who had rested Pollock and Ntini, were down to slow left-armer Boje and not much else. Smith resorted to his own off-spin, and called up de Villiers, who had never bowled in first-class cricket, while Adrian le Roux, the fitness trainer who had last played cricket at university five years previously, fielded as a substitute. All this allowed Streak and Blignaut to complete half-centuries, taking Zimbabwe to a semi-respectable total. When South Africa batted Prince, recalled after more than two years, cautiously earned his first Test century. South Africa added exactly 100 runs in 18.5 overs on the third morning, before Boje's quest for a maiden century was cut short. Zimbabwe were soon in trouble again, stumbling to 29 for 4 as Zondeki, in his first Test since injury ended his debut in England in 2003, cashed in. His performance, like every South African's in this series, had to be measured against one of the weakest teams ever to have played Test cricket. With their two best bowlers rested and three more injured, South Africa still won inside three days.

Zimbabwe

S. Matsikenyeri c Smith b Langeveldt	12	– b Zondeki		5
B. G. Rogers c Boucher b Nel	7	– c Boucher b Zondeki		0
D. D. Ebrahim b Kallis	37	– c Smith b Nel		1
H. Masakadza c Smith b Zondeki	26	– c Boucher b Zondeki		47
B. R. M. Taylor b Kallis	4	– lbw b Zondeki		6
*†T. Taibu c Gibbs b Zondeki	14	– c Boucher b Zondeki		13
E. Chigumbura c sub (A. M. Phangiso) b Kallis	0	– (8) c Boucher b Boje		44
H. H. Streak b Kallis	85	– (7) c Gibbs b Kallis		16
A. M. Blignaut c Smith b Zondeki	52	– c Boucher b Kallis		0
A. G. Cremer c Boucher b Nel	12	– c Boucher b Zondeki		0
C. B. Mpofu not out	1	– not out		0
B 4, l-b 8, w 4, n-b 3	19	B 4, l-b 10, n-b 3		17

1/15 (2) 2/22 (1) 3/71 (4) 4/80 (5)   269   1/6 (2) 2/13 (3) 3/18 (1)   149
5/115 (3) 6/115 (6) 7/115 (7)   4/29 (5) 5/76 (6) 6/85 (4) 7/143 (7) 8/147
8/191 (9) 9/264 (8) 10/269 (10)   (8) 9/149 (9) 10/149 (10)

Nel 12–7–17–2; Zondeki 21–7–66–3; Langeveldt 5–1–19–1; Kallis 13–4–33–4; Smith 7–2–39–0; Boje 18–1–62–0; de Villiers 7–0–16–0; Rudolph 2–0–5–0. *Second Innings*—Nel 16–6–42–1; Zondeki 14.3–2–39–6; Kallis 12–5–20–2; Boje 15–7–25–1; Rudolph 2–1–9–0.

South Africa

A. B. de Villiers c Masakadza b Mpofu	47	N. Boje b Cremer		82
*G. C. Smith c Rogers b Chigumbura	41			
J. A. Rudolph b Cremer	12	B 4, l-b 5, w 5, n-b 22		36
H. H. Gibbs c Taibu b Streak	47			
A. G. Prince not out	139	1/93 (2) 2/106 (1)	(7 wkts dec.)	480
†M. V. Boucher c Masakadza b Cremer	18	3/133 (3) 4/197 (4)		
J. H. Kallis b Streak	58	5/219 (6) 6/338 (7) 7/480 (8)		

M. Zondeki, C. K. Langeveldt and A. Nel did not bat.

Streak 20–1–78–2; Mpofu 21–1–110–1; Chigumbura 25–1–97–1; Cremer 26.5–4–106–3; Blignaut 16–0–74–0; Taylor 1–0–6–0.

Umpires: B. R. Doctrove *(West Indies)* (4) and D. J. Harper *(Australia)* (49).
Third umpire: I. L. Howell *(South Africa)*.   Referee: A. G. Hurst *(Australia)* (4).

Close of play: First day, South Africa 13-0 (de Villiers 9, Smith 3); Second day, South Africa 380-6 (Prince 101, Boje 24).

INDIA v PAKISTAN 2004-05 (1st Test)

At Punjab C. A. Stadium, Mohali, Chandigarh, on 8, 9, 10, 11, 12 March.
Toss: India.   Result: MATCH DRAWN.
Debuts: none.
Man of the Match: Kamran Akmal.

Pakistan struggled against Balaji's full length and late swing in the first innings, then poor catching allowed India to assume control and build a 204-run lead. And when Pakistan slumped to 10 for 3 on the fourth morning, defeat seemed certain, but India relaxed their grip. Pakistan closed on 257 for 6, 53 ahead, and the overnight pair saved them. Kamran Akmal, the wicketkeeper, made his maiden Test century and put on 184 with Abdul Razzaq, a seventh-wicket record for Pakistan against India, to ensure the draw. India's lack of a second spinner probably cost them the match. They had opted for an extra seamer, assuming the pitch would help the quick bowlers but, despite a sprinkling of grass, the seam attack faltered apart from Balaji, returning after a serious side injury. Sehwag then punished anything off line or short: in all he batted nearly six hours for 173, and shared century partnerships for the first three wickets, a feat never achieved by an Indian before. After he was out the spotlight turned to Tendulkar's quest for a record 35th Test century: he fell just short, caught in the gully playing away from his body. Pakistan lost three wickets in the first five overs before Inzamam-ul-Haq put on 139 with Yousuf Youhana. Next day Ganguly became negative with his fields, and Akmal was able to play his shots. He and Razzaq were not parted for 56 overs, and the tail advanced to 496, briefly Pakistan's highest total in India.

Pakistan

Salman Butt b Pathan	5	– c Karthik b Pathan	5
Taufeeq Umar b Balaji	44	– c and b Balaji	4
Younis Khan lbw b Zaheer Khan	9	– b Balaji	1
*Inzamam-ul-Haq lbw b Kumble	57	– (5) lbw b Kumble	86
Yousuf Youhana c Karthik b Pathan	6	– (4) b Kumble	68
Asim Kamal b Balaji	91	– lbw b Balaji	48
Abdul Razzaq c Karthik b Balaji	26	– c Dravid b Kumble	71
†Kamran Akmal c Dravid b Kumble	15	– c sub (Harbhajan Singh) b Balaji	109
Mohammad Sami b Balaji	20	– c and b Kumble	10
Naved-ul-Hasan lbw b Balaji	11	– not out	38
Danish Kaneria not out	8	– not out	4
B 11, l-b 5, w 1, n-b 3	20	B 17, l-b 20, w 13, n-b 2	52

1/11 (1) 2/30 (3) 3/89 (2) 4/104 (5)   312   1/6 (2) 2/10 (3)   (9 wkts dec.) 496
5/156 (4) 6/191 (7) 7/239 (8)   3/10 (1) 4/149 (5) 5/193 (4)
8/282 (9) 9/303 (6) 10/312 (10)   6/243 (6) 7/427 (8) 8/436 (7) 9/467 (9)

Pathan 23–5–68–2; Zaheer Khan 17–2–70–1; Balaji 20.4–5–76–5; Kumble 22–6–76–2; Ganguly 2–0–3–0; Sehwag 2–1–3–0. *Second Innings*—Pathan 27–7–70–1; Balaji 30–5–95–4; Kumble 54–16–160–4; Zaheer Khan 22–0–93–0; Tendulkar 8–0–30–0; Sehwag 3–1–11–0.

India

G. Gambhir c Naved-ul-Hasan b Danish Kaneria	41	– not out	32
V. Sehwag c Yousuf Youhana b Abdul Razzaq	173	– st Kamran Akmal b Younis Khan	36
R. Dravid c Asim Kamal b Mohammad Sami	50		
S. R. Tendulkar c Asim Kamal b Naved-ul-Hasan	94		
*S. C. Ganguly c Salman Butt b Danish Kaneria	21		
V. V. S. Laxman b Danish Kaneria	58		
†K. D. Karthik c Naved-ul-Hasan b Mohammad Sami	6		
I. K. Pathan st Kamran Akmal b Danish Kaneria	13		
L. Balaji c Kamran Akmal b Danish Kaneria	31		
A. Kumble not out	1		
Zaheer Khan c and b Danish Kaneria	0		
B 1, l-b 5, w 1, n-b 21	28	B 5, l-b 8, n-b 4	17

1/113 (1) 2/216 (3) 3/334 (2) 4/381 (5)   516   1/85 (2)   (1 wkt) 85
5/417 (4) 6/444 (7) 7/465 (8)
8/507 (9) 9/516 (6) 10/516 (11)

Mohammad Sami 36–6–120–2; Naved-ul-Hasan 32–1–133–1; Abdul Razzaq 26–1–107–1; Danish Kaneria 53.4–12–150–6. *Second Innings*—Mohammad Sami 7–0–25–0; Naved-ul-Hasan 2–0–6–0; Danish Kaneria 6–2–17–0; Younis Khan 2–0–24–1.

Umpires: D. B. Hair *(Australia)* (59) and R. E. Koertzen *(South Africa)* (60).
Third umpire: K. Hariharan *(India)*.   Referee: B. C. Broad *(England)* (10).

Close of play: First day, Pakistan 312; Second day, India 184-1 (Sehwag 95, Dravid 39); Third day, India 447-6 (Laxman 33, Pathan 1); Fourth day, Pakistan 257-6 (Abdul Razzaq 22, Kamran Akmal 9).

INDIA v PAKISTAN 2004-05 (2nd Test)

At Eden Gardens, Kolkata, on 16, 17, 18, 19, 20 March.
Toss: India.   Result: INDIA won by 195 runs.
Debuts: none.
Man of the Match: R. Dravid.

Rahul Dravid enjoyed an epic Test, scoring two brilliant centuries and delivering India from a hazardous position to the threshold of victory. India's other hero was Kumble, who took ten wickets, including 7 for 63 in the second innings, displaying excellent control. Dravid spent most of the first day establishing India's dominance, while Pakistan's captain, Inzamam-ul-Haq, spent most of it off the field suffering from dehydration. Dravid's biggest partnership was 122 with Tendulkar, who followed Sunil Gavaskar, Allan Border, Steve Waugh and Brian Lara in completing 10,000 Test runs, matching Lara's record of 195 innings. When Dravid was finally caught behind, India already had 344, and the tail took them past 400. Pakistan closed to within 14, mainly thanks to Younis Khan and Yousuf Youhana, who put on 211. India were batting again by the third afternoon. Mohammad Sami bowled both openers in his first two overs, then Steve Bucknor, the first umpire to stand in 100 Tests, controversially gave Tendulkar out caught behind. But, as a crisis loomed, Dravid was calm and collected. He reached two hundreds in a Test for the second time; the second was even better than the first, and was his 20th in all. India recovered to equal their first innings exactly. Pakistan's fears of a final-day collapse soon came true, as Younis fell to a leg-side stumping first ball. Everyone struggled against Kumble's variety and accuracy, and eventually Harbhajan Singh's *doosra* bowled Danish Kaneria to complete India's first victory over Pakistan in six Tests at Eden Gardens.

India

V. Sehwag c Inzamam-ul-Haq b Shahid Afridi	81	– b Mohammad Sami		15
G. Gambhir lbw b Danish Kaneria	29	– b Mohammad Sami		1
R. Dravid c Kamran Akmal b Danish Kaneria	110	– c Asim Kamal b Danish Kaneria		135
S. R. Tendulkar c Kamran Akmal b Shahid Afridi	52	– c Kamran Akmal b Abdul Razzaq		52
*S. C. Ganguly c Kamran Akmal b Abdul Razzaq	12	– c and b Mohammad Sami		12
V. V. S. Laxman lbw b Abdul Razzaq	0	– st Kamran Akmal b Danish Kaneria		24
†K. D. Karthik run out	28	– b Danish Kaneria		93
I. K. Pathan c Younis Khan b Danish Kaneria	8	– not out		38
L. Balaji b Shahid Afridi	3	– (10) c Kamran Akmal b Abdul Razzaq		0
Harbhajan Singh lbw b Abdul Razzaq	27	– (9) b Abdul Razzaq		0
A. Kumble not out	21	– not out		14
B 2, l-b 12, w 6, n-b 16	36	B 5, l-b 5, w 1, n-b 12		23

1/80 (2) 2/156 (1) 3/278 (4) 4/298 (5)   407   1/14 (2) 2/23 (1)   (9 wkts dec.) 407
5/298 (6) 6/344 (3) 7/345 (7)   3/121 (4) 4/154 (5) 5/321 (3)
8/357 (9) 9/363 (8) 10/407 (10)   6/331 (7) 7/377 (6) 8/378 (9) 9/378 (10)

In the second innings Laxman, when 2, retired hurt at 156 and resumed at 331.

Mohammad Sami 22–3–76–0; Mohammad Khalil 11–3–39–0; Danish Kaneria 35–1–136–3; Abdul Razzaq 22.1–4–62–3; Shahid Afridi 21–0–80–3. *Second Innings*—Mohammad Khalil 12–0–64–0; Mohammad Sami 23–5–82–3; Danish Kaneria 34–7–123–3; Shahid Afridi 15–2–47–0; Abdul Razzaq 19–3–80–3; Younis Khan 1–0–1–0.

Pakistan

Taufeeq Umar c Harbhajan Singh b Balaji	18	– c Sehwag b Balaji		35
Shahid Afridi c Tendulkar b Pathan	29	– c Ganguly b Kumble		59
Younis Khan c Laxman b Kumble	147	– st Karthik b Kumble		0
Yousuf Youhana lbw b Balaji	104	– (5) c Gambhir b Kumble		22
*Inzamam-ul-Haq c Karthik b Pathan	30	– (4) b Kumble		13
Asim Kamal run out	6	– c sub (M. Kaif) b Kumble		50
Abdul Razzaq c Dravid b Kumble	17	– b Kumble		6
†Kamran Akmal c Tendulkar b Harbhajan Singh	0	– b Harbhajan Singh		7
Mohammad Sami c Ganguly b Harbhajan Singh	7	– lbw b Kumble		9
Mohammad Khalil c Sehwag b Kumble	4	– not out		0
Danish Kaneria not out	3	– b Harbhajan Singh		3
B 5, l-b 13, w 2, n-b 8	28	B 17, l-b 3, w 1, n-b 1		22

1/35 (2) 2/70 (1) 3/281 (4) 4/331 (5)   393   1/93 (2) 2/95 (3) 3/115 (4)   226
5/347 (6) 6/361 (3) 7/362 (8)   4/115 (1) 5/178 (5) 6/188 (7)
8/378 (7) 9/378 (9) 10/393 (10)   7/203 (8) 8/214 (6) 9/223 (9) 10/226 (11)

Pathan 23–6–90–2; Balaji 21–1–81–2; Kumble 37.1–11–98–3; Ganguly 2–0–12–0; Harbhajan Singh 30–6–94–2. *Second Innings*—Pathan 7–1–32–0; Balaji 16–4–60–1; Kumble 38–16–63–7; Harbhajan Singh 30.3–16–51–2.

Umpires: S. A. Bucknor *(West Indies)* (100) and D. B. Hair *(Australia)* (60).
Third umpire: A. V. Jayaprakash *(India)*.   Referee: B. C. Broad *(England)* (11).

Close of play: First day, India 344-6 (Karthik 28); Second day, Pakistan 273-2 (Younis Khan 108, Yousuf Youhana 101); Third day, India 133-3 (Dravid 54, Ganguly 4); Fourth day, Pakistan 95-1 (Taufeeq Umar 29, Younis Khan 0).

INDIA v PAKISTAN 2004-05 (3rd Test)

At Chinnaswamy Stadium, Bangalore, on 24, 25, 26, 27, 28 March.
Toss: Pakistan.   Result: PAKISTAN won by 168 runs.
Debuts: none.
Man of the Match: Younis Khan.   Man of the Series: V. Sehwag.

A charged-up Pakistan somehow levelled a series in which they had largely been outplayed. India reached lunch on the final day with only one wicket down, but were bowled out with six overs to go. The toss was crucial: Inzamam-ul-Haq called correctly, and batted on an easy-paced pitch. Pakistan's fifth opening pair in as many Tests went by the third over, but over the next six hours Inzamam and Younis Khan built the third-highest stand ever conceded by India, whose bowling lost its purpose and drive: 7 for 2 became 331 for 2. Inzamam pounded some delightful strokes off the front foot, and followed Colin Cowdrey, Gordon Greenidge, Javed Miandad and Alec Stewart in scoring a century in his 100th Test. Younis powered to 267, the highest Test score by any batsman visiting India. Sehwag responded in kind, storming to a double-century of his own and passing 3,000 runs in his 55th innings, an Indian record. But Laxman was the only other man to reach 50, and Pakistan claimed a handy lead. Shahid Afridi quickly extended it on the fourth afternoon. He battered 58 off 34 balls – reaching 50 in 26, only two balls slower than the new Test record set three weeks previously by Jacques Kallis (see Test No. 1737). Inzamam declared 382 ahead. Afridi took three quick wickets, including Tendulkar, who had just overtaken Sunil Gavaskar as India's leading run-scorer. Kumble was at his blocking best but, when Balaji padded up to Danish Kaneria, it was all over.

Pakistan

Yasir Hameed c Karthik b Pathan	6	– lbw b Kumble	76
Shahid Afridi c Dravid b Balaji	0	– st Karthik b Tendulkar	58
Younis Khan c Pathan b Harbhajan Singh	267	– not out	84
*Inzamam-ul-Haq lbw b Balaji	184	– not out	31
Yousuf Youhana c Karthik b Harbhajan Singh	37		
Asim Kamal c Ganguly b Harbhajan Singh	4		
Abdul Razzaq c and b Harbhajan Singh	5		
†Kamran Akmal b Harbhajan Singh	28		
Mohammad Sami run out	17		
Arshad Khan not out	1		
Danish Kaneria c Laxman b Harbhajan Singh	0		
B 8, l-b 5, w 4, n-b 4	21	B 4, l-b 1, w 5, n-b 2	12

1/4 (2) 2/7 (1) 3/331 (4) 4/415 (5)   570   1/91 (2) 2/183 (1)   (2 wkts dec.) 261
5/428 (6) 6/446 (7) 7/504 (8)
8/565 (9) 9/569 (3) 10/570 (11)

Pathan 34–4–105–1; Balaji 29–4–114–2; Kumble 46–8–159–0; Harbhajan Singh 51.5–9–152–6; Tendulkar 3–0–14–0; Ganguly 4–0–13–0. *Second Innings*—Pathan 5–0–45–0; Balaji 3–0–26–0; Kumble 21–1–88–1; Tendulkar 15–1–62–1; Harbhajan Singh 6–0–35–0.

India

G. Gambhir c Younis Khan b Mohammad Sami	24	– lbw b Mohammad Sami	52
V. Sehwag c and b Danish Kaneria	201	– run out	38
R. Dravid lbw b Danish Kaneria	22	– c Younis Khan b Arshad Khan	16
S. R. Tendulkar c Younis Khan b Shahid Afridi	41	– c Asim Kamal b Shahid Afridi	16
V. V. S. Laxman not out	79	– lbw b Shahid Afridi	5
*S. C. Ganguly st Kamran Akmal b Danish Kaneria	1	– b Shahid Afridi	2
†K. D. Karthik c Asim Kamal b Mohammad Sami	10	– b Mohammad Sami	9
I. K. Pathan c Yousuf Youhana b Mohammad Sami	5	– (9) c Yousuf Youhana b Arshad Khan	0
Harbhajan Singh c Abdul Razzaq b Danish Kaneria	1	– (10) c Younis Khan b Danish Kaneria	8
L. Balaji c Kamran Akmal b Danish Kaneria	2	– (11) lbw b Danish Kaneria	0
A. Kumble b Shahid Afridi	22	– (8) not out	37
B 9, l-b 13, w 1, n-b 18	41	B 8, l-b 8, w 10, n-b 5	31

1/98 (1) 2/172 (3) 3/257 (4) 4/337 (2)   449   1/87 (2) 2/108 (1) 3/118 (3) 4/127 (5)   214
5/343 (6) 6/374 (7) 7/386 (8)   5/135 (6) 6/164 (7) 7/164 (4)
8/388 (9) 9/396 (10) 10/449 (11)   8/189 (9) 9/210 (10) 10/214 (11)

Mohammad Sami 34–5–106–3; Abdul Razzaq 17–0–77–0; Danish Kaneria 39–7–127–5; Arshad Khan 28–3–87–0; Shahid Afridi 10.4–3–30–2. *Second Innings*—Mohammad Sami 21–5–84–2; Abdul Razzaq 13–3–34–0; Danish Kaneria 25–11–46–2; Shahid Afridi 17–7–13–3; Arshad Khan 14–8–21–2.

Umpires: B. F. Bowden *(New Zealand)* (25) and S. J. A. Taufel *(Australia)* (22).
Third umpire: I. Shivram *(India)*.   Referee: B. C. Broad *(England)* (12).

Close of play: First day, Pakistan 323-2 (Younis Khan 127, Inzamam-ul-Haq 184); Second day, India 55-0 (Gambhir 13, Sehwag 39); Third day, India 379-6 (Laxman 51, Pathan 0); Fourth day, India 25-0 (Gambhir 19, Sehwag 6).

NEW ZEALAND v AUSTRALIA 2004-05 (1st Test)

At Lancaster Park, Christchurch, on 10, 11, 12, 13 March.
Toss: Australia.   Result: AUSTRALIA won by nine wickets.
Debuts: New Zealand – C. D. Cumming, I. E. O'Brien.
Man of the Match: A. C. Gilchrist.

For two days it looked as though New Zealand might get the better of Australia, who were fleetingly in danger of following on. But it was all an illusion. On the third afternoon, normal service was resumed and by next evening Australia had romped home. Sent in on an even-paced pitch, New Zealand's batsmen prospered: Marshall's maiden Test century took them to 330 for 3 on the second morning. But McGrath then ran through the batting in electrifying fashion, taking 6 for 40 in his last ten overs. Immediately, Australia's openers went on the attack: 15 came from Martin's opening over, but Vettori quelled the scoring, and wickets began to fall. At 160 for 5, Australia were still 74 short of the follow-on target. But after nightwatchman Gillespie fell at 201, Katich and Gilchrist added 212, just five shy of Australia's seventh-wicket record, set by Doug Walters and Gary Gilmour on the same ground 28 years earlier. Gilchrist's hundred came from 105 balls, and his 121 contained six stunning sixes, five off Vettori. New Zealand had a lead ... of one run. They looked demoralised, and duly capitulated. Warne bowled round the wicket into the fast bowlers' footmarks, and finished with his 29th Test five-for as New Zealand were rolled for 131, with seven lbws, equalling the Test record from Zimbabwe's first innings at Chester-le-Street in 2003. Langer and Ponting helped themselves to a steady diet of 19 fours and two sixes, and victory, in the end, was very easy.

New Zealand

C. D. Cumming c Gillespie b Kasprowicz	74	– lbw b Gillespie	7
*S. P. Fleming lbw b Warne	18	– lbw b McGrath	17
H. J. H. Marshall b Warne	146	– b Warne	22
L. Vincent lbw b Clarke	27	– lbw b Gillespie	4
N. J. Astle lbw b McGrath	74	– b Kasprowicz	21
C. D. McMillan c Gilchrist b McGrath	13	– c Katich b Warne	5
†B. B. McCullum c Langer b McGrath	29	– lbw b Gillespie	24
D. L. Vettori not out	24	– lbw b Warne	23
J. E. C. Franklin lbw b McGrath	0	– not out	5
I. E. O'Brien c Gilchrist b McGrath	5	– lbw b Warne	0
C. S. Martin c Gilchrist b McGrath	1	– lbw b Warne	0
B 4, l-b 14, w 2, n-b 2	22	B 1, l-b 1, n-b 1	3

1/56 (2) 2/153 (1) 3/199 (4) 4/330 (3)   433   1/20 (2) 2/30 (1) 3/34 (4) 4/71 (5)   131
5/355 (6) 6/388 (5) 7/403 (7)   5/78 (6) 6/87 (3)7/121 (7)
8/403 (9) 9/415 (10) 10/433 (11)   8/127 (8) 9/131 (10) 10/131 (11)

McGrath 42–9–115–6; Gillespie 29–5–87–0; Kasprowicz 25–6–85–1; Warne 40–6–112–2; Clarke 5–0–16–1. *Second Innings*—McGrath 14–7–19–1; Gillespie 12–2–38–3; Kasprowicz 10–3–33–1; Warne 14–3–39–5.

Australia

J. L. Langer b Franklin	23	– not out	72
M. L. Hayden c Astle b O'Brien	35	– c Cumming b Vettori	15
*R. T. Ponting c McCullum b Martin	46	– not out	47
D. R. Martyn lbw b Vettori	32		
J. N. Gillespie c Cumming b Vettori	12		
M. J. Clarke c McCullum b Franklin	8		
S. M. Katich c Vincent b Astle	118		
†A. C. Gilchrist c O'Brien b Vettori	121		
S. K. Warne c Astle b Vettori	2		
M. S. Kasprowicz not out	13		
G. D. McGrath lbw b Vettori	0		
B 2, l-b 13, w 3, n-b 4	22	N-b 1	1

1/48 (1) 2/75 (2) 3/140 (4) 4/147 (3)   432   1/25 (2)   (1 wkt) 135
5/160 (6) 6/201 (5) 7/413 (8)
8/418 (7) 9/426 (9) 10/432 (11)

Martin 29–6–104–1; Franklin 26–5–102–2; O'Brien 14–3–73–1; Vettori 40.2–13–106–5; Astle 14–6–32–1. *Second Innings*—Martin 8–0–27–0; Franklin 5–1–26–0; Vettori 13.3–0–55–1; O'Brien 5–0–27–0.

Umpires: Aleem Dar *(Pakistan)* (18) and D. R. Shepherd *(England)* (87).
Third umpire: A. L. Hill *(New Zealand).*   Referee: C. H. Lloyd *(West Indies)* (44).

Close of play: First day, New Zealand 265-3 (Marshall 103, Astle 29); Second day, Australia 141-3 (Ponting 41, Gillespie 0); Third day, New Zealand 9-0 (Cumming 2, Fleming 7).

NEW ZEALAND v AUSTRALIA 2004-05 (2nd Test)

At Basin Reserve, Wellington, on 18 *(no play)*, 19, 20, 21, 22 March.
Toss: New Zealand.   Result: MATCH DRAWN.
Debuts: none.
Man of the Match: A. C. Gilchrist.

Low cloud and drizzle hung over the ground for much of the match, allowing New Zealand to escape with a draw. After rain and fog wiped out the opening day, Fleming put Australia in, and at 163 for 4 shortly before tea on the extended second day, it looked a fruitful decision. But once again the sting in Australia's batting lay just before the tail. This time it was Martyn who joined forces with Gilchrist to take the game away from New Zealand with a partnership of 256, a sixth-wicket record between the two nations. While Martyn's highest Test score was typically graceful and classical, Gilchrist again stole the accolades with his clinically brutal hitting, reaching his third hundred in five innings from 86 balls. He struck 22 fours and five sixes in all, one of which (off Vettori) smashed a nearby window, and passed Ian Healy's 4,356 Test runs – from 86 fewer innings – to become Australia's most prolific wicketkeeper-batsman. New Zealand made the worst possible start when Fleming shouldered arms to his first ball from McGrath and was lbw, and under gloomy skies next morning they lost a clatter of wickets to be dismissed 326 runs behind. The only blessing for Fleming's team was that the weather closed in again and denied the Australians any opportunity to make further inroads in the follow-on. Only 42.1 overs were possible on the fourth day, and 17.3 on the last, although that was time for Kasprowicz to claim his 100th Test wicket.

Australia

J. L. Langer c McCullum b Vettori	46		J. N. Gillespie b Franklin	2	
M. L. Hayden c Vincent b Franklin	61		M. S. Kasprowicz not out	2	
*R. T. Ponting lbw b Vettori	9		B 4, l-b 8, w 2, n-b 16	30	
D. R. Martyn c McCullum b O'Brien	165				
M. J. Clarke c Fleming b Astle	8		1/82 (1) 2/100 (3)	(8 wkts dec.)	570
S. M. Katich c McCullum b Franklin	35		3/146 (2) 4/163 (5)		
†A. C. Gilchrist c and b Franklin	162		5/247 (6) 6/503 (4)		
S. K. Warne not out	50		7/557 (7) 8/559 (9)		

G. D. McGrath did not bat.

Martin 28–6–123–0; Franklin 28–4–128–4; O'Brien 24–4–97–1; Vettori 47–5–170–2; Astle 13–2–40–1.

New Zealand

C. D. Cumming b Kasprowicz	37		– not out	10	
*S. P. Fleming lbw b McGrath	0		– lbw b McGrath	1	
H. J. H. Marshall c Gillespie b McGrath	18		– lbw b McGrath	0	
L. Vincent c Gilchrist b Kasprowicz	63		– b Kasprowicz	24	
N. J. Astle c Warne b Clarke	9		– not out	4	
J. E. C. Franklin c Gilchrist b Kasprowicz	26				
C. D. McMillan b Warne	20				
†B. B. McCullum c Clarke b Warne	3				
D. L. Vettori c Martyn b Warne	45				
I. E. O'Brien b Gillespie	5				
C. S. Martin not out	0				
B 4, l-b 8, w 1, n-b 5	18		B 3, l-b 5, n-b 1	9	

1/9 (2) 2/55 (3) 3/78 (1) 4/108 (5)	244		1/3 (2) 2/3 (3) 3/37 (4)	(3 wkts) 48
5/166 (6) 6/180 (4) 7/184 (8)				
8/201 (7) 9/212 (10) 10/244 (9)				

McGrath 14–3–50–2; Gillespie 20–4–63–1; Kasprowicz 16–2–42–3; Warne 28.1–7–69–3; Clarke 3–1–8–1. *Second Innings*—McGrath 6–3–10–2; Gillespie 5–2–5–0; Warne 3.2–0–14–0; Kasprowicz 3–0–11–1.

Umpires: R. E. Koertzen *(South Africa)* (61) and D. R. Shepherd *(England)* (88).
Third umpire: E. A. Watkin *(New Zealand)*.   Referee: C. H. Lloyd *(West Indies)* (45).

Close of play: First day, No play; Second day, Australia 337-5 (Martyn 106, Gilchrist 45); Third day, New Zealand 122-4 (Vincent 38, Franklin 6); Fourth day, New Zealand 244.

NEW ZEALAND v AUSTRALIA 2004-05 (3rd Test)

At Eden Park, Auckland, on 26, 27, 28, 29 March.
Toss: New Zealand.   Result: AUSTRALIA won by nine wickets.
Debuts: New Zealand – J. A. H. Marshall.
Man of the Match: R. T. Ponting.   Man of the Series: A. C. Gilchrist.

Australia completed a 2–0 series win without much trouble, starting by restricting the batsmen to such effect that McGrath's first-day figures were 24–17–20–1. New Zealand reached 292 next day, but then Ponting scotched suggestions that the pitch was the cause of the dawdling. He blasted a century at almost a run a ball, with four imperious sixes, and by lunch on the third day Australia were ahead – with Gilchrist yet to bat. When he did, his unbeaten 60 from 62 balls lifted his series return to 343 in three innings (from 334 balls, with 12 sixes and 44 fours). Australia's lead was hardly emphatic, though it quickly seemed so once both openers fell to McGrath in failing light on the third evening. Two more wickets fell quickly next day, one a freakish one-handed reaction catch by Gillespie to end Fleming's wretched series. Astle and Vincent added 70, but even so the lead was just two when the sixth wicket fell. Vettori hit out, extending the advantage to 163. With 33 overs remaining on the fourth day and showers forecast for the fifth, the New Zealanders opted for stalling tactics, but Ponting carried Australia to victory that night, hitting 86 from 84 balls in what, save for the glare of the rugby stadium's floodlights, would have been almost complete darkness. James Marshall joined his brother Hamish in New Zealand's side for this match, Test cricket's second set of twins after the Waugh brothers, but the first identical pair.

New Zealand

C. D. Cumming lbw b Gillespie	5	– lbw b McGrath	0
J. A. H. Marshall c Hayden b McGrath	29	– c Langer b McGrath	3
H. J. H. Marshall c Ponting b Warne	76	– c Gilchrist b McGrath	7
*S. P. Fleming b Kasprowicz	65	– c and b Gillespie	3
N. J. Astle c Langer b McGrath	19	– c Katich b Warne	69
L. Vincent b Gillespie	2	– run out	40
†B. B. McCullum c Gilchrist b McGrath	25	– lbw b Warne	0
D. L. Vettori not out	41	– c McGrath b Warne	65
J. E. C. Franklin c Katich b Warne	3	– c Ponting b Warne	23
P. J. Wiseman c Gillespie b Warne	8	– b McGrath	23
C. S. Martin c Clarke b Kasprowicz	0	– not out	4
B 4, l-b 13, n-b 2	19	B 1, l-b 14, n-b 2	17

1/15 (1) 2/53 (2) 3/179 (3) 4/183 (4)   292
5/194 (6) 6/228 (5) 7/247 (7)
8/262 (9) 9/288 (10) 10/292 (11)

1/0 (1) 2/9 (2) 3/15 (4)   254
4/23 (3) 5/93 (6) 6/93 (7)
7/174 (5) 8/220 (9) 9/227 (8) 10/254 (10)

McGrath 34–20–49–3; Gillespie 25–8–64–2; Kasprowicz 30.2–7–89–2; Warne 23–4–63–3; Ponting 4–1–10–0. *Second Innings*—McGrath 16.2–5–40–4; Gillespie 16–4–63–1; Kasprowicz 14–2–59–0; Warne 23–5–77–4.

Australia

J. L. Langer b Franklin	6	– not out	59
M. L. Hayden lbw b Franklin	38	– run out	9
*R. T. Ponting c McCullum b Astle	105	– not out	86
D. R. Martyn b Wiseman	38		
M. J. Clarke run out	22		
J. N. Gillespie c McCullum b Martin	35		
S. M. Katich c Wiseman b Franklin	35		
†A. C. Gilchrist not out	60		
S. K. Warne c Fleming b Franklin	1		
M. S. Kasprowicz b Franklin	23		
G. D. McGrath c McCullum b Franklin	0		
B 4, l-b 7, n-b 9	20	L-b 10, n-b 2	12

1/8 (1) 2/84 (2) 3/187 (3) 4/215 (4)   383
5/226 (5) 6/297 (6) 7/297 (7)
8/303 (9) 9/377 (10) 10/383 (11)

1/18 (2)   (1 wkt) 166

Martin 21–4–92–1; Franklin 26.1–3–119–6; Astle 21–7–50–1; Vettori 19–4–47–0; Wiseman 31–7–64–1. *Second Innings*—Martin 8–1–51–0; Franklin 7–0–40–0; Vettori 4–0–19–0; Astle 7–0–33–0; Wiseman 3.3–0–13–0.

Umpires: R. E. Koertzen (*South Africa*) (62) and J. W. Lloyds (*England*) (5).
Third umpire: D. B. Cowie (*New Zealand*).   Referee: C. H. Lloyd (*West Indies*) (46).

Close of play: First day, New Zealand 199-5 (Astle 7, McCullum 1); Second day, Australia 219-4 (Clarke 18, Gillespie 1); Third day, New Zealand 11-2 (H. J. H. Marshall 3, Fleming 1).

WEST INDIES v SOUTH AFRICA 2004-05 (1st Test)

At Bourda, Georgetown, Guyana, on 31 March, 1, 2, 3, 4 April.
Toss: West Indies.   Result: MATCH DRAWN.
Debuts: West Indies – N. Deonarine, D. J. Pagon.
Man of the Match: S. Chanderpaul.

West Indies went into the match with only one survivor (Chanderpaul) from their last Test, at The Oval in August, as a result of a prolonged sponsorship dispute which kept Brian Lara and several others on the sidelines. In the circumstances, West Indies were expected to lose heavily – but in fact they were only denied victory by one of Test cricket's most resolute defensive innings. Kallis guided South Africa to safety in their 300th Test after an innings defeat had seemed inevitable. He batted almost seven hours and faced 346 balls after his side had followed on 355 behind. West Indies' big total owed almost everything to Hinds, whose maiden double-century was briefly the highest score for West Indies against South Africa, and Chanderpaul, a rather reluctant first-time captain. After their partnership of 284, "Brian Who?" was the question in the stands. West Indies' total was then their biggest against South Africa. The visitors replied aimlessly, slumping to 130 for 6 in the 37 overs possible on the third day after overnight rain. Following on, South Africa inched to 85 for 2 from 63 overs by the close. The West Indians knew what they had to do on the final day: remove Kallis. But that proved a bridge too far. He was helped by an uncharacteristically restrained Gibbs, who batted four hours for 49. South Africa lost just two wickets on the last day, and batted out 161 overs – and looked capable of lasting another 161, had time allowed.

West Indies

W. W. Hinds c Boucher b Langeveldt	213	N. Deonarine not out		15
D. S. Smith c Boucher b Nel	11	L-b 8, w 2, n-b 8		18
D. Ganga c Boucher b Nel	0			
D. J. Pagon c Kallis b Nel	35	1/24 (2) 2/24 (3)	(5 wkts dec.)	543
*S. Chanderpaul not out	203	3/106 (4) 4/390 (1)		
R. O. Hinds c Kallis b Boje	48	5/506 (6)		

†C. O. Browne, D. B. Powell, P. T. Collins and R. D. King did not bat.

Ntini 23–5–98–0; Nel 33–8–93–3; Langeveldt 27–5–65–1; Hall 16–4–53–0; Kallis 14–3–70–0; Boje 29.1–2–106–1; Smith 10–0–50–0.

South Africa

*G. C. Smith c Browne b Collins	2	– (2) b Collins		34
A. B. de Villiers c Browne b King	41	– (1) b King		20
J. A. Rudolph c R. O. Hinds b Powell	0	– lbw b Deonarine		24
J. H. Kallis b Powell	0	– not out		109
H. H. Gibbs lbw b Collins	5	– b R. O. Hinds		49
†M. V. Boucher c Chanderpaul b Collins	41	– not out		4
A. J. Hall c Collins b King	2			
N. Boje b King	34			
M. Ntini lbw b Powell	8			
C. K. Langeveldt c R. O. Hinds b Deonarine	10			
A. Nel not out	6			
L-b 6, w 2, n-b 31	39	B 16, l-b 2, w 2, n-b 9		29
	188	1/46 (1) 2/68 (2)	(4 wkts)	269

1/15 (1) 2/16 (3) 3/16 (4) 4/30 (5)   188   1/46 (1) 2/68 (2)   (4 wkts) 269
5/71 (2) 6/95 (7) 7/158 (8)   3/119 (3) 4/258 (5)
8/169 (9) 9/172 (6) 10/188 (10)

Collins 18–5–39–3; Powell 18–2–61–3; King 16–2–48–3; R. O. Hinds 13–5–29–0; Deonarine 1.5–0–5–1. *Second Innings*—Collins 24–10–44–1; Powell 28–15–46–0; King 24–5–54–1; W. W. Hinds 14–5–16–0; R. O. Hinds 27–13–27–1; Deonarine 30–15–35–1; Chanderpaul 13–6–25–0; Ganga 1–0–4–0.

Umpires: Aleem Dar *(Pakistan)* (19) and D. R. Shepherd *(England)* (89).
Third umpire: E. A. Nicholls *(West Indies)*.   Referee: J. J. Crowe *(New Zealand)* (5).

Close of play: First day, West Indies 347-3 (W. W. Hinds 188, Chanderpaul 102); Second day, South Africa 2-0 (Smith 1, de Villiers 0); Third day, South Africa 130-6 (Boucher 32, Boje 21); Fourth day, South Africa 85-2 (Rudolph 19, Kallis 1).

WEST INDIES v SOUTH AFRICA 2004-05 (2nd Test)

At Queen's Park Oval, Port-of-Spain, Trinidad, on 8, 9, 10, 11, 12 April.
Toss: West Indies.   Result: SOUTH AFRICA won by eight wickets.
Debuts: none.
Man of the Match: M. Ntini.

Ntini's relentlessness outweighed Lara's genius, and South Africa claimed victory in a match harder-fought than the result might suggest. Lara's 196 was batting at its most beautiful, but Ntini ran in, and ran in, and ran in some more. He finished with 13 for 132, the best figures for South Africa in a Test, beating Hugh Tayfield's 13 for 165 at Melbourne in 1952-53. The match began amid intense anticipation at Lara's return to the team, though not the captaincy, after the temporary settlement of the sponsorship dispute, and he did not disappoint, going past Garry Sobers's West Indian record with his 27th Test century. There was general astonishment when Nel came round the wicket and, with Lara just a boundary away from 200, produced an outswinger that clipped his off bail. Smith slowed the game down – so much so that 90 overs on the third day brought just 188 runs and three wickets. West Indies bounced back next day, when Gayle's innocuous-looking off-spin took four for nine in 29 balls, limiting the deficit to 51. By the close West Indies had turned that into a lead of 119, but they had lost five wickets, including Lara, bowled by a subterranean turner from Boje. The final day belonged to Ntini, starting when Bravo was caught behind off his third delivery: the last five wickets cascaded for 14. South Africa had a potentially tricky target of 144, but Smith and de Villiers guaranteed victory with a bristling opening stand.

West Indies

W. W. Hinds c Smith b Ntini	32	– lbw b Boje		22
C. H. Gayle c Boucher b Ntini	6	– c de Villiers b Ntini		1
R. R. Sarwan c Nel b Ntini	5	– not out		107
B. C. Lara b Nel	196	– b Boje		4
*S. Chanderpaul c and b Boje	35	– lbw b Ntini		1
D. J. Pagon b Ntini	0	– b Ntini		2
D. J. Bravo b Nel	5	– c Boucher b Ntini		33
†C. O. Browne c Rudolph b Ntini	26	– lbw b Ntini		2
D. B. Powell b Ntini	15	– c Kallis b Nel		1
P. T. Collins lbw b Nel	2	– b Ntini		0
R. D. King not out	1	– b Ntini		0
B 4, l-b 8, w 2, n-b 5, p 5	24	B 6, l-b 10, w 1, n-b 4		21

1/7 (2) 2/13 (3) 3/108 (1) 4/203 (5)   **347**   1/14 (2) 2/79 (1) 3/85 (4) 4/86 (5)   **194**
5/204 (6) 6/225 (7) 7/299 (8)   5/92 (6) 6/180 (7) 7/188 (8) 8/189
8/318 (9) 9/325 (10) 10/347 (4)   (9) 9/190 (10) 10/194 (11)

Nel 28.4–7–71–3; Ntini 28–3–95–6; Kallis 13–4–41–0; Zondeki 15–0–71–0; Boje 20–2–52–1. *Second Innings*—Nel 21–6–42–1; Ntini 19.5–7–37–7; Zondeki 11–4–24–0; Boje 20–6–37–2; Kallis 11–3–29–0; Smith 7–1–9–0.

South Africa

*G. C. Smith lbw b Hinds	148	– (2) c Gayle b Bravo		41
A. B. de Villiers c Chanderpaul b King	33	– (1) b Powell		62
J. A. Rudolph c Browne b Bravo	8	– not out		7
J. H. Kallis lbw b Bravo	39	– not out		19
M. Zondeki b Collins	14			
H. H. Gibbs b Collins	34			
A. G. Prince c Chanderpaul b Gayle	45			
†M. V. Boucher c and b Gayle	28			
N. Boje not out	13			
M. Ntini b Gayle	4			
A. Nel b Gayle	6			
B 2, l-b 2, w 2, n-b 20	26	B 5, l-b 2, w 3, n-b 7		17

1/70 (2) 2/86 (3) 3/181 (4) 4/222 (5)   **398**   1/117 (2) 2/119 (1)   (2 wkts) **146**
5/274 (1) 6/303 (6) 7/374 (8)
8/375 (7) 9/384 (10) 10/398 (11)

Collins 29–5–78–2; Powell 22–3–86–0; King 26–7–50–1; Bravo 37–8–98–2; Gayle 37.5–18–50–4; Chanderpaul 2–0–6–0; Hinds 8–5–9–1; Sarwan 5–0–17–0. *Second Innings*—Collins 4–0–27–0; Powell 10–2–27–1; Gayle 11–3–16–0; King 11.5–1–28–0; Bravo 6–2–27–1; Hinds 2–0–14–0.

Umpires: Aleem Dar *(Pakistan)* (20) and D. R. Shepherd *(England)* (90).
Third umpire: B. R. Doctrove *(West Indies)*.   Referee: J. J. Crowe *(New Zealand)* (6).

Close of play: First day, West Indies 281-6 (Lara 159, Browne 19); Second day, South Africa 182-3 (Smith 90, Zondeki 1); Third day, South Africa 370-6 (Prince 41, Boucher 28); Fourth day, West Indies 170-5 (Sarwan 93, Bravo 30).

WEST INDIES v SOUTH AFRICA 2004-05 (3rd Test)

At Kensington Oval, Bridgetown, Barbados, on 21, 22, 23, 24 April.
Toss: West Indies.   Result: SOUTH AFRICA won by an innings and 86 runs.
Debuts: none.
Man of the Match: A. Nel.

Lara again delivered an innings that will be remembered for ever by those who saw it; but again a South African fast bowler trumped him, and this time it secured the series. The bowler was the steadily maturing Andre Nel, who hissed, glared and bowled his way to a career-best ten for 88. But before the South Africans could savour their success, they had to endure another stupendous innings from Lara, whose 176 saved West Indies from ignominy. The score was 12 for 3 in the seventh over when Chanderpaul joined him, and their fightback endured until just before tea. The South Africans seemed resigned to granting Lara his runs, secure in the knowledge that they were masters of everyone else. It worked: Nel and Zondeki shared eight wickets. South Africa then responded with their own methodical approach. Smith reached his second hundred in successive Tests before slicing to extra cover, while de Villiers maintained his unusually subdued vigil into the third day. The declaration at last came in the sixth over of the fourth day, giving South Africa a lead of 252. The pitch was still sound, but the home batting was not. When West Indies lost three wickets in four balls the result seemed inevitable. Lara repelled the hat-trick ball from Ntini, but Nel trapped both him and Chanderpaul not long afterwards. From 71 for 6, Browne saved some blushes with a carefree 68 off 75 balls, but it was too little too late.

West Indies

W. W. Hinds c Smith b Ntini	1	– (2) c Gibbs b Nel	11
C. H. Gayle c Boucher b Nel	0	– (1) c Smith b Ntini	5
R. R. Sarwan c Prince b Nel	10	– c Gibbs b Ntini	0
B. C. Lara b Nel	176	– lbw b Nel	13
*S. Chanderpaul c Boucher b Zondeki	53	– lbw b Nel	31
R. O. Hinds c Boucher b Kallis	10	– (7) c Kallis b Boje	15
D. J. Bravo c Smith b Zondeki	26	– (6) c Boucher b Kallis	6
†C. O. Browne c Zondeki b Nel	5	– c Dippenaar b Nel	68
D. B. Powell c Boucher b Zondeki	3	– lbw b Nel	5
F. H. Edwards c Dippenaar b Zondeki	2	– c Ntini b Nel	2
R. D. King not out	0	– not out	3
B 1, l-b 3, w 1, n-b 5	10	B 1, l-b 2, n-b 4	7

1/2 (2) 2/12 (1) 3/12 (3) 4/150 (5) — 296
5/171 (6) 6/286 (4) 7/288 (7)
8/292 (9) 9/296 (10) 10/296 (8)

1/17 (1) 2/17 (3) 3/17 (2) — 166
4/54 (4) 5/63 (5) 6/71 (6)
7/107 (7) 8/130 (9) 9/143 (10) 10/166 (8)

Nel 21.2–3–56–4; Ntini 17–2–61–1; Kallis 14–6–37–1; Zondeki 16–1–50–4; Smith 8–1–23–0; Boje 16–2–65–0. *Second Innings*—Nel 16.2–3–32–6; Ntini 11–2–40–2; Zondeki 8–3–43–0; Boje 11–1–33–1; Kallis 6–3–7–1; Smith 2–0–8–0.

South Africa

*G. C. Smith c W. W. Hinds b Gayle	104	M. Zondeki c Chanderpaul b Powell	2
A. B. de Villiers c Browne b King	178	M. Ntini c Bravo b Powell	16
H. H. Dippenaar run out	71	A. Nel not out	4
J. H. Kallis c sub (D. R. Smith) b W. W. Hinds	78	B 1, l-b 2, n-b 13	16
H. H. Gibbs c Bravo b Gayle	8		
A. G. Prince c Bravo b Gayle	23	1/191 (1) 2/334 (3) (9 wkts dec.) 548
†M. V. Boucher b Powell	28	3/392 (2) 4/410 (5)
N. Boje not out	20	5/450 (6) 6/496 (4)
		7/502 (7) 8/504 (9) 9/542 (10)

Edwards 32.5–3–112–0; King 30–5–80–1; Powell 31–2–103–3; Bravo 29–3–73–0; R. O. Hinds 18–1–67–0; Gayle 27–3–85–3; W. W. Hinds 9–2–18–1; Sarwan 1–0–7–0.

Umpires: B. F. Bowden *(New Zealand)* (26) and S. J. A. Taufel *(Australia)* (23).
Third umpire: B. R. Doctrove *(West Indies)*.   Referee: J. J. Crowe *(New Zealand)* (7).

Close of play: First day, West Indies 292-7 (Browne 3, Powell 3); Second day, South Africa 253-1 (de Villiers 122, Dippenaar 23); Third day, South Africa 521-8 (Boje 8, Ntini 7).

WEST INDIES v SOUTH AFRICA 2004-05 (4th Test)

At Antigua Recreation Ground, St John's, Antigua, on 29, 30 April, 1, 2, 3 May.
Toss: South Africa.   Result: MATCH DRAWN.
Debuts: West Indies – D. M. Washington.
Man of the Match: C. H. Gayle.   Man of the Series: G. C. Smith.

The ARG continued to be a bowlers' graveyard. After Lara's quadruple-century a year earlier, the highest individual contribution this time was a mere 317 by Gayle, the 14th-highest score in Test history and the highest against South Africa, beating Don Bradman's 299 not out at Adelaide in 1931-32. There were eight centuries in all, a Test record. The most eager participants were probably Pollock, in his 94th Test after missing the last four with an inflamed ankle, and Dwight Washington, a 22-year-old Jamaican fast bowler in his first. Neither experience nor youth could take a wicket. The lasting memory will be Gayle's innings. Previously out of form, he batted with a wonderful eye, a lack of fear, and a lust for hard hitting, and less foot movement than it would take to nudge a lemming off a cliff. The match had begun with South Africa's batsmen holding sway. Smith and de Villiers started by putting on 245 for the first wicket, then Kallis and Prince added 267, a national fifth-wicket record. Kallis displaced Gary Kirsten as South Africa's most prolific Test batsman both in terms of runs – ending the match with 7,337 – and hundreds (22). Gayle and Sarwan put on 331 as West Indies reached 747, their third-highest total and the biggest against South Africa at the time. All 11 South Africans bowled: Bravo, after completing his maiden Test century, was dismissed by Boucher, who bowled for the first time in a Test after passing the gloves to de Villiers.

South Africa

A. B. de Villiers c Browne b Best	114	– (2) c Washington b Best	12
*G. C. Smith c Washington b Powell	126	– (1) not out	50
H. H. Dippenaar run out	5	– not out	56
J. H. Kallis c Washington b Powell	147		
H. H. Gibbs c Deonarine b Gayle	23		
A. G. Prince c Browne b Bravo	131		
†M. V. Boucher not out	11		
S. M. Pollock not out	13		
B 4, l-b 1, w 5, n-b 8	18	W 3, n-b 6	9

1/245 (1) 2/245 (2) 3/251 (3)   (6 wkts dec.) 588   1/14 (2)   (1 wkt) 127
4/295 (5) 5/562 (4) 6/563 (6)

N. Boje, M. Zondeki and M. Ntini did not bat.

Powell 32–3–137–2; Best 26–4–116–1; Washington 22–3–73–0; Bravo 27–4–97–1; Gayle 31–11–65–1; Hinds 6–0–24–0; Deonarine 18–1–69–0; Sarwan 1–0–2–0. *Second Innings*—Best 5–0–32–1; Powell 6–2–15–0; Washington 7–1–20–0; Bravo 5–0–24–0; Hinds 3–1–10–0; Deonarine 3–1–20–0; Sarwan 1–0–3–0; Gayle 1–0–3–0.

West Indies

C. H. Gayle c Smith b Zondeki	317	T. L. Best c Gibbs b de Villiers	5
W. W. Hinds c and b Ntini	0	D. M. Washington not out	7
R. R. Sarwan c Prince b Zondeki	127		
B. C. Lara c Boucher b Zondeki	4	B 2, l-b 9, w 3, n-b 23	37
*S. Chanderpaul run out	127		
N. Deonarine c Boucher b Smith	4	1/14 (2) 2/345 (3) 3/363 (4)	747
D. J. Bravo c Prince b Boucher	107	4/512 (1) 5/535 (6) 6/665 (5)	
†C. O. Browne lbw b Smith	0	7/665 (8) 8/700 (9)	
D. B. Powell b de Villiers	12	9/712 (10) 10/747 (7)	

Pollock 34–5–111–0; Ntini 33–3–106–1; Zondeki 25–4–120–3; Kallis 36–6–96–0; Boje 30–6–76–0; Smith 43–3–145–2; de Villiers 21–6–49–2; Prince 9–1–22–0; Dippenaar 2–1–1–0; Boucher 1.2–0–6–1; Gibbs 1–0–4–0.

Umpires: B. F. Bowden *(New Zealand)* (27) and S. J. A. Taufel *(Australia)* (24).
Third umpire: B. E. W. Morgan *(West Indies)*.   Referee: J. J. Crowe *(New Zealand)* (8).

Close of play: First day, South Africa 214-0 (de Villiers 103, Smith 106); Second day, South Africa 525-4 (Kallis 127, Prince 114); Third day, West Indies 299-1 (Gayle 184, Sarwan 103); Fourth day, West Indies 565-5 (Chanderpaul 82, Bravo 10).

NEW ZEALAND v SRI LANKA 2004-05 (1st Test)

At McLean Park, Napier, on 4, 5, 6, 7, 8 April.
Toss: New Zealand.   Result: MATCH DRAWN.
Debuts: Sri Lanka – K. M. D. N. Kulasekara.
Man of the Match: S. L. Malinga.

Sri Lanka's coach John Dyson described the pitch at Napier – being used because of concerns about the surface at Hamilton, the original venue – as "a belter", and although initially it was the opposition doing the belting, in the end Sri Lanka did their fair share, and came closer to victory. Vaas removed Cumming an hour into the first morning, allowing the Marshall twins to add 107 in perfect conditions; in his second Test, James reached his first half-century. Fleming continued his run of low scores – just one 50 in eight Test innings – but Hamish Marshall seemed set for his maiden double-century when he chipped a simple catch to mid-on. Astle hit a cultured 114, his first Test century in 18 months and his tenth in all, McCullum fell one short of his second, and Franklin strode elegantly to his first international fifty as New Zealand reached 561. Atapattu and Jayasuriya were untroubled at first then, after a hiccough, Atapattu and Jayawardene recovered brilliantly, taking the score to 285. Jayawardene went on to a fine 141, but the last six wickets fell for 46 just as Sri Lanka were contemplating a lead. A draw seemed certain, but Malinga had other ideas. In fading light, he grabbed two wickets before the fourth-day close, and kept going next morning, helped by the batsmen having trouble picking up his low-slung skimmers. At lunch, New Zealand were 148 for 7, a precarious 211 ahead, before Vincent dug in grimly and guaranteed the draw.

New Zealand

C. D. Cumming lbw b Vaas	12	– lbw b Malinga	16
J. A. H. Marshall c Samaraweera b Chandana	52	– lbw b Jayasuriya	39
H. J. H. Marshall c Vaas b Malinga	160	– lbw b Malinga	6
*S. P. Fleming b Malinga	16	– (5) c Kulasekara b Malinga	41
N. J. Astle c Jayasuriya b Vaas	114	– (6) run out	19
L. Vincent c Dilshan b Kulasekara	0	– (7) b Chandana	52
†B. B. McCullum lbw b Malinga	99	– (8) c Samaraweera b Jayasuriya	7
J. E. C. Franklin c Malinga b Herath	55	– (9) b Malinga	7
K. D. Mills b Malinga	4	– (10) c Jayasuriya b Herath	22
P. J. Wiseman c Atapattu b Herath	27	– (4) lbw b Malinga	0
C. S. Martin not out	1	– not out	4
B 5, l-b 4, w 2, n-b 10	21	B 6, l-b 7, w 2, n-b 10	25

1/35 (1) 2/142 (2) 3/187 (4) 4/312 (3)   561   1/51 (1) 2/64 (3) 3/69 (4)   238
5/317 (6) 6/446 (5) 7/487 (7)   4/85 (2) 5/115 (6) 6/128 (8)
8/497 (9) 9/540 (10) 10/561 (8)   7/148 (9) 8/181 (7) 9/222 (10) 10/238 (5)

In the second innings Fleming, when 6, retired hurt at 77 and resumed at 148.

Vaas 33–5–125–2; Malinga 34–5–130–4; Kulasekara 25–7–70–1; Herath 30.1–5–91–2; Chandana 33–4–123–1; Jayasuriya 3–1–8–0; Dilshan 1–0–5–0. *Second Innings*—Vaas 17–4–38–0; Malinga 24.4–4–80–5; Kulasekara 11–2–19–0; Herath 11–4–29–1; Jayasuriya 21–8–41–2; Samaraweera 1–0–6–0; Chandana 7–2–12–1.

Sri Lanka

*M. S. Atapattu c Fleming b Astle	127	– not out	2
S. T. Jayasuriya lbw b Martin	48	– not out	5
†K. C. Sangakkara b Martin	5		
D. P. M. D. Jayawardene c McCullum b Franklin	141		
T. T. Samaraweera c Fleming b Martin	88		
T. M. Dilshan c Vincent b Martin	28		
W. P. U. J. C. Vaas c Astle b Wiseman	17		
U. D. U. Chandana c Martin b Franklin	19		
H. M. R. K. B. Herath b Franklin	0		
K. M. D. N. Kulasekara c Fleming b Franklin	0		
S. L. Malinga not out	0		
B 1, l-b 6, w 6, n-b 12	25		

1/95 (2) 2/101 (3) 3/285 (1) 4/407 (4)   498   (no wkt) 7
5/452 (6) 6/463 (5) 7/488 (7)
8/491 (9) 9/497 (10) 10/498 (8)

Martin 37–9–132–4; Franklin 32.1–8–126–4; Wiseman 38–7–128–1; Mills 23–6–59–0; Astle 18–6–46–1. Second Innings—Martin 1–0–1–0; Franklin 0.3–0–6–0.

Umpires: S. A. Bucknor *(West Indies)* (101) and D. B. Hair *(Australia)* (61).
Third umpire: D. B. Cowie *(New Zealand)*.   Referee: M. J. Procter *(South Africa)* (29).

Close of play: First day, New Zealand 267-3 (H. J. H. Marshall 133, Astle 37); Second day, Sri Lanka 48-0 (Atapattu 14, Jayasuriya 31); Third day, Sri Lanka 351-3 (Jayawardene 118, Samaraweera 34); Fourth day, New Zealand 64-2 (J. A. H. Marshall 33, Wiseman 0).

NEW ZEALAND v SRI LANKA 2004-05 (2nd Test)

At Basin Reserve, Wellington, on 11, 12, 13, 14 April.
Toss: New Zealand.   Result: NEW ZEALAND won by an innings and 38 runs.
Debuts: Sri Lanka – S. Kalavitigoda.
Man of the Match: L. Vincent.

Victory was enough for New Zealand's first series victory (a facile 2–0 success in Bangladesh aside) since beating India at the end of 2002, a sequence which included just one win in 18 front-line Tests. Now, though, they enjoyed an emphatic innings victory on the back of some sharp bowling from Martin and a dogged 224 from Vincent. Fleming inserted Sri Lanka on a green-tinged pitch, and Martin roared in downwind. He had Atapattu held at point third ball, and had four more wickets by the end of his 11-over opening spell. Shortly after lunch Martin made it six out of six when the debutant Shantha Kalavitigoda edged to third slip, but Samaraweera dropped anchor, and with the fielding losing its razor-sharp edge he shared an eighth-wicket stand of 89 with Chandana before being last out for a precious 73. Vaas also found menacing swing and was a persistent problem; like Martin, he seized the first six wickets, including Fleming for 88, his highest score in 13 Test innings. Vaas was twice on a hat-trick, but Vincent dug in, dominating valuable stands for the seventh, eighth and ninth wickets which together added 205. Dropped on 193 by Jayasuriya, Vincent sailed on to his maiden double-hundred before he was run out. New Zealand needed less than one of the two days available to bowl Sri Lanka out a second time, despite two-hour rearguards from Sangakkara and Dilshan, while the nightwatchman Maharoof survived longer than any of his team-mates.

Sri Lanka

*M. S. Atapattu c Vincent b Martin	0	– (2) c Fleming b Franklin	16
S. T. Jayasuriya c Astle b Martin	22	– (1) c Vincent b Martin	2
†K. C. Sangakkara c J. A. H. Marshall b Martin	16	– (4) b Franklin	45
D. P. M. D. Jayawardene lbw b Martin	1	– (5) c McCullum b Franklin	13
T. T. Samaraweera lbw b Astle	73	– (6) c Fleming b Astle	17
T. M. Dilshan c McCullum b Martin	9	– (7) b Astle	73
S. Kalavitigoda c Vincent b Martin	7	– (8) c McCullum b Mills	1
W. P. U. J. C. Vaas b Franklin	5	– (9) b Franklin	38
U. D. U. Chandana lbw b Astle	41	– (10) b Astle	8
M. F. Maharoof c sub (J. M. How) b Astle	12	– (3) c Astle b Mills	36
S. L. Malinga not out	4	– not out	0
B 4, l-b 5, w 1, n-b 11	21	B 4, l-b 10, w 2, n-b 8	24

1/0 (1) 2/34 (3) 3/36 (4) 4/41 (2)   **211**   1/6 (1) 2/47 (2) 3/95 (3)   **273**
5/60 (6) 6/80 (7) 7/86 (8)   4/117 (5) 5/137 (4) 6/164 (6)
8/175 (9) 9/200 (10) 10/211 (5)   7/177 (8) 8/255 (7) 9/267 (10) 10/273 (9)

Martin 20–7–54–6; Franklin 11–1–51–1; Mills 20–6–50–0; Astle 12.1–2–35–3; Wiseman 2–0–12–0. *Second Innings*—Martin 18–4–50–1; Mills 11–4–34–2; Vincent 1–0–2–0; Astle 13–4–27–3; Wiseman 26–7–75–0; Franklin 23.5–4–71–4.

New Zealand

C. D. Cumming lbw b Vaas	47	P. J. Wiseman not out	32
J. A. H. Marshall lbw b Vaas	28	C. S. Martin not out	4
H. J. H. Marshall c Jayawardene b Vaas	6		
L. Vincent run out	224	B 11, l-b 23, w 1, n-b 12	47
N. J. Astle c Kalavitigoda b Vaas	0		
*S. P. Fleming c Kalavitigoda b Vaas	88	1/61 (2) 2/70 (3) (9 wkts dec.)	522
†B. B. McCullum c and b Vaas	0	3/153 (1) 4/153 (5)	
J. E. C. Franklin lbw b Malinga	15	5/294 (6) 6/294 (7)	
K. D. Mills c Jayawardene b Malinga	31	7/342 (8) 8/440 (9) 9/499 (4)	

Vaas 40–12–108–6; Malinga 34–2–124–2; Maharoof 28–10–96–0; Jayawardene 6–2–14–0; Chandana 28–4–97–0; Jayasuriya 9–2–34–0; Dilshan 1–0–15–0.

Umpires: S. A. Bucknor *(West Indies)* (102) and D. B. Hair *(Australia)* (62).
Third umpire: A. L. Hill *(New Zealand)*.   Referee: M. J. Procter *(South Africa)* (30).

Close of play: First day, New Zealand 52-0 (Cumming 14, J. A. H. Marshall 24); Second day, New Zealand 253-4 (Vincent 80, Fleming 60); Third day, Sri Lanka 10-1 (Atapattu 5, Maharoof 1).

ENGLAND v BANGLADESH 2005 (1st Test)

At Lord's, London, on 26, 27, 28 May.

Toss: England.   Result: ENGLAND won by an innings and 261 runs.

Debuts: Bangladesh – Mushfiqur Rahim, Shahadat Hossain.

Man of the Match: M. E. Trescothick.

Hoggard and Harmison started slowly, donating nine no-balls in as many overs, but once they got going it became perfectly obvious that Bangladesh's batsmen were completely out of their depth in their first Test in English conditions. Vaughan said diplomatically: "The players don't set out the schedules. We can only beat what's put in front of us." And beat them they duly did, by noon on the third day, forcing MCC to give the deprived spectators a 50% refund. They were lucky that the match lasted that long, because it was effectively decided inside a session and a half. Javed Omar applied himself diligently to top-score with 22, Aftab Ahmed blazed five fours in a defiant 14-ball 20, and the diminutive Mushfiqur Rahim, making his debut at 16 – the youngest player ever to appear in a Lord's Test – battled it out for 85 minutes, but Bangladesh were still rolled for 108 inside 39 overs. The only question then was how long England wanted to bat against an attack offering little more than glorified practice. The answer turned out to be 112 overs, from which they scored 528 for 3. Trescothick and Vaughan helped themselves to centuries; Vaughan's was his third in successive Test innings at Lord's. The prospect of a two-day Test was looming when Bangladesh resumed, but Omar's defence and Aftab's flashing blade got them into a third day. England still completed the second-biggest victory in any Lord's Test, behind their innings and 285-run win over India in 1974.

Bangladesh

Javed Omar c Trescothick b S. P. Jones	22	– c Thorpe b S. P. Jones	25
Nafis Iqbal c Trescothick b Harmison	8	– c Flintoff b Hoggard	3
*Habibul Bashar c G. O. Jones b Hoggard	3	– c Hoggard b S. P. Jones	16
Aftab Ahmed c Strauss b Flintoff	20	– lbw b Hoggard	32
Mohammad Ashraful lbw b Flintoff	6	– c Harmison b Flintoff	2
Mushfiqur Rahim b Hoggard	19	– c G. O. Jones b Flintoff	3
†Khaled Mashud lbw b Hoggard	6	– c Thorpe b Flintoff	44
Mohammad Rafique run out	1	– c G. O. Jones b Harmison	0
Mashrafe bin Mortaza b Harmison	0	– b Harmison	0
Anwar Hossain Monir not out	5	– c Trescothick b S. P. Jones	13
Shahadat Hossain c G. O. Jones b Hoggard	4	– not out	2
B 1, l-b 1, n-b 12	14	B 1, l-b 4, n-b 14	19
	108		**159**

1/31 (2) 2/34 (3) 3/65 (4) 4/65 (1)   108
5/71 (5) 6/89 (7) 7/94 (8)
8/98 (9) 9/98 (6) 10/108 (11)

1/15 (2) 2/47 (3) 3/57 (1)   159
4/60 (5) 5/65 (6) 6/96 (4)
7/97 (8) 8/97 (9) 9/155 (10) 10/159 (7)

Hoggard 13.2–5–42–4; Harmison 14–3–38–2; Flintoff 5–0–22–2; S. P. Jones 6–4–4–1. *Second Innings*—Hoggard 9–1–42–2; Harmison 10–0–39–2; Flintoff 9.5–0–44–3; S. P. Jones 11–3–29–3.

England

M. E. Trescothick c Khaled Mashud b Mohammad Rafique	194	G. P. Thorpe not out	42
A. J. Strauss lbw b Mashrafe bin Mortaza	69	B 4, l-b 11, w 3, n-b 20	38
*M. P. Vaughan c Khaled Mashud b Mashrafe bin Mortaza	120	1/148 (2) 2/403 (3) (3 wkts dec.)	528
I. R. Bell not out	65	3/415 (1)	

A. Flintoff, †G. O. Jones, G. J. Batty, M. J. Hoggard, S. J. Harmison and S. P. Jones did not bat.

Mashrafe bin Mortaza 29–6–107–2; Shahadat Hossain 12–0–101–0; Anwar Hossain Monir 22–0–110–0; Mohammad Rafique 41–3–150–1; Aftab Ahmed 8–1–45–0.

Umpires: K. Hariharan *(India)* (1) and D. J. Harper *(Australia)* (50).
Third umpire: J. W. Lloyds *(England)*.   Referee: A. G. Hurst *(Australia)* (5).

Close of play: First day, England 188-1 (Trescothick 78, Vaughan 22); Second day, Bangladesh 90-5 (Aftab Ahmed 26, Khaled Mashud 6).

ENGLAND v BANGLADESH 2005 (2nd Test)

At Riverside Ground, Chester-le-Street, on 3, 4, 5 June.
Toss: England.   Result: ENGLAND won by an innings and 27 runs.
Debuts: none.
Man of the Match: M. J. Hoggard.   Men of the Series: Javed Omar and M. E. Trescothick.

This Test stuck uncannily to the script of the previous one: Vaughan won the toss, England bowled out Bangladesh in half a day and completed victory so early on the third day that spectators were entitled to a refund, leading to further muttering about Bangladesh's Test status. The game began on a Friday, the first non-Thursday scheduled start for a Test in England in 50 years. On a blameless pitch, England's four-pronged pace attack barely broke sweat, dismissing Bangladesh in 40 overs. The batsmen showed little idea of how to handle the moving ball or one bouncing above waist height; Geraint Jones collected six routine catches in the innings, nine in the match. By the end of the first day, Trescothick had his second century of the series and England led by 165. Bell, who added 178 with Thorpe (in his 100th and, as it turned out, last Test) on Saturday before the lunchtime declaration, scored 105 in the session, completing a maiden century in his third Test. Bangladesh's batsmen decided the best form of survival was attack, which at least made for some entertainment: Habibul Bashar lashed Simon Jones for four fours in an over, and Aftab Ahmed lifted Flintoff for an enormous six over long leg. Three overs from the scheduled close, they were 235 for 5, but Hoggard struck twice in four balls, and again after England claimed the extra half-hour, though they could not quite finish the job. Instead, they completed it in four overs next morning.

Bangladesh

Javed Omar c G. O. Jones b Hoggard	37	– c G. O. Jones b Harmison	71
Nafis Iqbal c Strauss b Harmison	7	– c G. O. Jones b Flintoff	15
*Habibul Bashar b Harmison	6	– (5) lbw b Flintoff	63
Mohammad Ashraful c G. O. Jones b S. P. Jones	3	– c Hoggard b Batty	12
Rajin Saleh c Thorpe b Flintoff	2	– (3) c Strauss b Flintoff	7
Aftab Ahmed c G. O. Jones b Harmison	6	– (7) not out	82
†Khaled Mashud c G. O. Jones b Harmison	22	– (6) lbw b Hoggard	25
Mohammad Rafique c Batty b Hoggard	9	– b Hoggard	2
Tapash Baisya c G. O. Jones b Hoggard	0	– (10) c G. O. Jones b Hoggard	18
Mashrafe bin Mortaza c G. O. Jones b Harmison	1	– (11) c Trescothick b Hoggard	0
Anwar Hossain Monir not out	0	– (9) c Thorpe b Hoggard	0
L-b 2, w 5, n-b 4	11	L-b 6, w 1, n-b 14	21

1/17 (2) 2/27 (3) 3/34 (4) 4/42 (5)   104
5/59 (1) 6/69 (6) 7/87 (8)
8/87 (9) 9/93 (10) 10/104 (7)

1/50 (2) 2/75 (3) 3/101 (4)   316
4/125 (1) 5/195 (5) 6/235 (6)
7/245 (8) 8/251 (9) 9/311 (10) 10/316 (11)

Hoggard 12–6–24–3; Harmison 12.5–2–38–5; S. P. Jones 8–2–26–1; Flintoff 7–3–14–1. *Second Innings*—Hoggard 15.5–3–73–5; Harmison 17–1–86–1; S. P. Jones 10–1–49–0; Flintoff 15–2–58–3; Batty 15–2–44–1.

England

M. E. Trescothick c Mohammad Ashraful b Aftab Ahmed	151	G. P. Thorpe not out	66
A. J. Strauss lbw b Mashrafe bin Mortaza	8	B 1, l-b 10, w 2, n-b 3	16
*M. P. Vaughan c Khaled Mashud b Mashrafe bin Mortaza	44	1/18 (2) 2/105 (3) (3 wkts dec.) 447	
I. R. Bell not out	162	3/260 (1)	

A. Flintoff, †G. O. Jones, G. J. Batty, M. J. Hoggard, S. J. Harmison and S. P. Jones did not bat.

Mashrafe bin Mortaza 22–4–91–2; Tapash Baisya 15–2–80–0; Mohammad Rafique 18–0–107–0; Anwar Hossain Monir 15–1–102–0; Aftab Ahmed 8–0–56–1.

Umpires: D. J. Harper *(Australia)* (51) and A. L. Hill *(New Zealand)* (2).
Third umpire: N. J. Llong *(England)*.   Referee: A. G. Hurst *(Australia)* (6).

Close of play: First day, England 269-3 (Bell 57, Thorpe 2); Second day, Bangladesh 297-8 (Aftab Ahmed 67, Tapash Baisya 18).

WEST INDIES v PAKISTAN 2005 (1st Test)

At Kensington Oval, Bridgetown, Barbados, on 26, 27, 28, 29 May.
Toss: West Indies.   Result: WEST INDIES won by 276 runs.
Debuts: Pakistan – Bazid Khan.
Man of the Match: S. Chanderpaul.

West Indies recorded their first Test win in almost a year, and halted a humiliating run of four consecutive defeats at a venue previously synonymous with Caribbean domination. Fearsome fast bowling from Edwards wrecked Pakistan's first innings after another majestic Lara hundred, which made him the sixth to score a Test century against all nine possible opponents. Pakistan were without Inzamam-ul-Haq (serving a one-match ban for dissent in his previous Test, against India) and Yousuf Youhana, who had returned home as his father was ill. Despite this, Pakistan started well, reducing West Indies to 45 for 3 in the first hour. But Lara unfurled a masterful 130, reaching his 29th Test century in just 88 balls with consecutive straight sixes off Danish Kaneria. Chanderpaul added 92 before he was caught at cover by Bazid Khan, following his father Majid Khan and grandfather Jahangir Khan into Test cricket (he was only the second third-generation Test player, after Dean Headley, son of Ron and grandson of George). Pakistan crumbled to Edwards on the second afternoon. Chanderpaul waived the follow-on, and his unbeaten 153 stretched the lead to 572 before Pakistan capitulated again. Edwards promptly removed Salman Butt, but then strained a hamstring, ending his involvement in the match and the series. His absence gave Pakistan some breathing space, and Shahid Afridi smashed his third Test hundred off just 78 balls; in all, he clubbed nine fours and six sixes, but his dismissal, going for yet another big hit, triggered the final slide.

West Indies

C. H. Gayle c Abdul Razzaq b Shabbir Ahmed	4	– c Asim Kamal b Danish Kaneria 50
D. S. Smith c Yasir Hameed b Abdul Razzaq	19	– c Kamran Akmal b Abdul Razzaq 10
R. R. Sarwan c Bazid Khan b Shabbir Ahmed	6	– c Kamran Akmal b Shahid Afridi 1
B. C. Lara b Danish Kaneria	130	– st Kamran Akmal b Shahid Afridi 48
*S. Chanderpaul c Bazid Khan b Danish Kaneria	92	– not out................................ 153
W. W. Hinds run out	28	– b Danish Kaneria 52
†C. O. Browne c Kamran Akmal b Shabbir Ahmed	12	– c Kamran Akmal b Shahid Afridi 1
D. B. Powell b Abdul Razzaq	10	– b Naved-ul-Hasan 5
F. H. Edwards c Yasir Hameed b Danish Kaneria	3	– c Kamran Akmal b Shabbir Ahmed. 20
R. D. King c Kamran Akmal b Abdul Razzaq	3	– b Shabbir Ahmed 5
C. D. Collymore not out	0	– lbw b Abdul Razzaq.................... 0
B 3, l-b 6, w 2, n-b 27	38	B 4, l-b 9, w 2, n-b 11 26

1/12 (1) 2/25 (3) 3/45 (2) 4/214 (4)   **345**   1/59 (2) 2/64 (3) 3/65 (1)   **371**
5/263 (6) 6/287 (7) 7/336 (8)   4/137 (4) 5/271 (6) 6/274 (7)
8/336 (5) 9/343 (10) 10/345 (9)   7/307 (8) 8/353 (9) 9/367 (10) 10/371 (11)

Naved-ul-Hasan 18–2–66–0; Shabbir Ahmed 18–4–66–3; Abdul Razzaq 17–3–58–3; Danish Kaneria 24.3–1–114–3; Shahid Afridi 6–0–32–0. *Second Innings*—Naved-ul-Hasan 24–7–88–1; Shabbir Ahmed 20–2–70–2; Danish Kaneria 26–4–115–2; Abdul Razzaq 15–4–36–2; Shahid Afridi 17–3–49–3.

Pakistan

Salman Butt c Browne b Collymore	27	– c Gayle b Edwards 0
Shahid Afridi c Smith b Edwards	16	– (6) c Chanderpaul b Powell............ 122
Yasir Hameed b Edwards	12	– (2) c Browne b Powell 11
*Younis Khan c Collymore b Edwards	31	– (3) run out............................ 0
Bazid Khan c Browne b Collymore	9	– (4) lbw b Collymore.................... 23
Asim Kamal c Sarwan b King	0	– (5) c Smith b Gayle 55
Abdul Razzaq lbw b Edwards	10	– st Browne b Gayle 41
†Kamran Akmal c Hinds b King	4	– b Gayle 21
Naved-ul-Hasan c Sarwan b Collymore	17	– c Lara b Gayle 6
Shabbir Ahmed b Edwards	6	– not out............................... 0
Danish Kaneria not out	4	– c Browne b Gayle...................... 0
B 4, n-b 4	8	L-b 7, n-b 10................... 17

1/26 (2) 2/54 (3) 3/76 (1) 4/96 (5)   **144**   1/0 (1) 2/1 (3) 3/16 (2)   **296**
5/96 (6) 6/100 (4) 7/113 (8)   4/47 (4) 5/162 (5) 6/257 (6)
8/120 (7) 9/132 (10) 10/144 (9)   7/277 (7) 8/295 (9) 9/296 (8) 10/296 (11)

Edwards 14–1–38–5; Powell 10–4–36–0; King 11–1–46–2; Collymore 8.4–3–20–3. *Second Innings*—Edwards 1.2–1–0–1; Powell 11–1–47–2; King 11.4–0–70–0; Collymore 19–2–80–1; Gayle 18.3–3–91–5; Hinds 1–0–1–0.

Umpires: D. B. Hair *(Australia)* (63) and D. R. Shepherd *(England)* (91).
Third umpire: B. E. W. Morgan *(West Indies)*.   Referee: R. S. Madugalle *(Sri Lanka)* (73).

Close of play: First day, Pakistan 22-0 (Salman Butt 5, Shahid Afridi 12); Second day, West Indies 168-4 (Chanderpaul 37, Hinds 14); Third day, Pakistan 113-4 (Asim Kamal 38, Shahid Afridi 32).

WEST INDIES v PAKISTAN 2005 (2nd Test)

At Sabina Park, Kingston, Jamaica, on 3, 4, 5, 6, 7 June.
Toss: Pakistan.   Result: PAKISTAN won by 136 runs.
Debuts: none.
Man of the Match: Danish Kaneria.   Man of the Series: B. C. Lara.

Pakistan completed their first Test victory in the Caribbean for 17 years to share the honours in this brief series. Inzamam-ul-Haq led the way with two crucial innings, yet the turning-point was Courtney Browne's error on the third afternoon. With Pakistan unsteady at 119 for 3 – only 89 in front – he put down a straightforward catch from Inzamam's first ball: he made the most of his luck (he was also caught behind off a no-ball when 92) to grind out a century. The game started calmly enough, Younis Khan's entertaining hundred underpinning a solid total, although Pakistan seemed set for more before Collymore, nagging at off stump, snared six of the last seven wickets. Lara crafted his 30th Test hundred – his fourth in five matches – taking him past Don Bradman's 29. Danish Kaneria removed Chanderpaul with the second day's final ball, but was banned for the rest of the innings next morning for following through down the pitch by umpire Hair, whose partner David Shepherd was over-seeing his 92nd and last Test. After Browne gave Inzamam his lifeline, Pakistan extended their lead to 279, despite losing their last six for 42 as Collymore took his match figures to 11 for 134, the best in any Kingston Test, surpassing Hines Johnson's 10 for 96 against England in 1947-48. Soon West Indies were floundering at 114 for 6. It was Kaneria's time to shine: Sarwan trod on his stumps, Lara touched a leg-side catch, Chanderpaul was lbw to a shooter, and West Indies were in tatters.

Pakistan

Shoaib Malik c Browne b Collymore	13	– c Browne b Collymore	64
Yasir Hameed c Gayle b Powell	14	– c Smith b Collymore	26
Younis Khan c Hinds b Collymore	106	– c and b Gayle	43
*Inzamam-ul-Haq c Smith b Gayle	50	– (5) not out	117
Asim Kamal b Collymore	51	– (4) lbw b Collymore	0
Shahid Afridi c Browne b Collymore	33	– c Smith b Best	43
Abdul Razzaq lbw b Collymore	19	– b Best	2
†Kamran Akmal lbw b Powell	49	– c Browne b Best	1
Naved-ul-Hasan not out	7	– b King	0
Shabbir Ahmed c Browne b Collymore	0	– c Browne b Best	0
Danish Kaneria b Collymore	6	– c and b Collymore	0
B 4, l-b 3, w 2, n-b 17	26	L-b 2, w 3, n-b 8	13

1/16 (2) 2/43 (1) 3/130 (4) 4/247 (3)   374   1/66 (2) 2/119 (1) 3/119 (4)   309
5/260 (5) 6/298 (6) 7/336 (7)   4/194 (3) 5/267 (6) 6/273 (7)
8/360 (10) 9/374 (8) 10/374 (11)   7/279 (8) 8/280 (9) 9/295 (10) 10/309 (11)

Powell 21–4–69–2; Best 12–1–59–0; Collymore 27.3–5–78–7; King 13–1–65–0; Gayle 25–1–85–1; Sarwan 2–0–11–0. *Second Innings*—Powell 22–0–100–0; Best 13–1–46–4; King 16–1–70–1; Collymore 16.5–2–56–4; Gayle 10–2–35–1.

West Indies

C. H. Gayle c Kamran Akmal b Abdul Razzaq	33	– c Yasir Hameed b Shabbir Ahmed	15
D. S. Smith b Abdul Razzaq	25	– c Kamran Akmal b Danish Kaneria	49
R. R. Sarwan c Danish Kaneria b Shabbir Ahmed	55	– hit wkt b Danish Kaneria	8
B. C. Lara c Kamran Akmal b Shabbir Ahmed	153	– c Kamran Akmal b Danish Kaneria	0
*S. Chanderpaul c Kamran Akmal b Danish Kaneria	28	– lbw b Danish Kaneria	0
W. W. Hinds c Yasir Hameed b Shahid Afridi	63	– c Younis Khan b Abdul Razzaq	19
†C. O. Browne c Kamran Akmal b Shabbir Ahmed	0	– c Kamran Akmal b Shabbir Ahmed	10
D. B. Powell c Kamran Akmal b Shabbir Ahmed	14	– c Yasir Hameed b Danish Kaneria	12
T. L. Best b Shahid Afridi	18	– c Shahid Afridi b Shabbir Ahmed	4
R. D. King lbw b Shahid Afridi	0	– c Kamran Akmal b Shabbir Ahmed	4
C. D. Collymore not out	2	– not out	7
B 3, l-b 7, w 1, n-b 2	13	L-b 5, n-b 10	15

1/48 (1) 2/59 (2) 3/205 (3) 4/275 (5)   404   1/27 (1) 2/48 (3) 3/48 (4)   143
5/326 (4) 6/326 (7) 7/356 (8)   4/56 (5) 5/94 (2) 6/100 (6)
8/385 (9) 9/393 (10) 10/404 (6)   7/126 (8) 8/126 (7) 9/130 (10) 10/143 (9)

Naved-ul-Hasan 6–0–50–0; Shabbir Ahmed 22–4–64–4; Abdul Razzaq 23–4–83–2; Danish Kaneria 28.5–7–94–1; Shahid Afridi 13.1–3–51–3; Shoaib Malik 19–2–52–0. *Second Innings*—Shabbir Ahmed 18.5–4–55–4; Abdul Razzaq 14–5–37–1; Danish Kaneria 20–8–46–5.

Umpires: D. B. Hair *(Australia)* (64) and D. R. Shepherd *(England)* (92).
Third umpire: B. R. Doctrove *(West Indies)*.   Referee: R. S. Madugalle *(Sri Lanka)* (74).

Close of play: First day, Pakistan 336-6 (Abdul Razzaq 19, Kamran Akmal 24); Second day, West Indies 275-4 (Lara 125); Third day, Pakistan 223-4 (Inzamam-ul-Haq 64, Shahid Afridi 16); Fourth day, West Indies 114-6 (Browne 9, Powell 4).

245

SRI LANKA v WEST INDIES 2005 (1st Test)

At Sinhalese Sports Club, Colombo, on 13, 14, 15, 16 July.

Toss: West Indies.   Result: SRI LANKA won by six wickets.

Debuts: Sri Lanka – W. M. G. Ramyakumara (*also known as Gayan Wijekoon*). West Indies – X. M. Marshall, R. S. Morton, D. Ramdin.

Man of the Match: W. P. U. J. C. Vaas.

Despite fielding an inexperienced team after several players refused to tour after a long-running sponsorship dispute, West Indies repeatedly gained favourable positions. Each time, though, maturity counted, and Sri Lanka eventually won an hour after tea on the fourth day. Vaas and Muralitharan were yet again the key men, while the West Indian fast bowlers, led by Lawson, exposed weaknesses in the home batting. West Indies recovered from the loss of three cheap wickets either side of lunch on the opening day to end it satisfactorily. Chanderpaul led the recovery, sharing partnerships of 79 with Ramdin and 81 with Banks, but he was out next morning without addition, as the last four wickets were swept aside by the new ball. Sri Lanka were down 113 for 7, but Vaas held firm for 140 minutes while Muralitharan's hit-and-miss slogging exasperated the fieldsmen. The big two were soon back to persecute West Indies with the ball: three wickets tumbled for 17 in near-darkness at the end of the second day, and next morning it was 21 for 5. Chanderpaul repaired the damage between stoppages, but it was left to Best to take the total past 100. Sri Lanka had only once scored as many as 172 to win a home Test, and when Jayasuriya and Sangakkara fell to spectacular catches off successive balls, and Atapattu fell to a tumbling leg-side catch, they were faltering at 49 for 3 – but Jayawardene and Samaraweera gradually took charge, all but settling the issue by adding 86.

West Indies

S. C. Joseph lbw b Ramyakumara	28	– c Jayawardene b Muralitharan	2
X. M. Marshall lbw b Vaas	10	– lbw b Vaas	2
R. S. Morton b Muralitharan	43	– lbw b Vaas	0
N. Deonarine c Sangakkara b Malinga	12	– lbw b Vaas	7
*S. Chanderpaul lbw b Vaas	69	– not out	48
D. R. Smith lbw b Malinga	4	– lbw b Vaas	0
†D. Ramdin b Ramyakumara	56	– lbw b Muralitharan	11
O. A. C. Banks b Malinga	32	– c Dilshan b Muralitharan	7
D. B. Powell c Jayawardene b Malinga	3	– c Jayawardene b Muralitharan	0
T. L. Best b Vaas	4	– st Sangakkara b Muralitharan	27
J. J. C. Lawson not out	4	– c sub (U. D. U. Chandana) b Muralitharan	0
L-b 7, n-b 13	20	B 8, n-b 1	9

1/14 (2) 2/72 (1) 3/95 (3) 4/109 (4) **285**   1/3 (2) 2/3 (3) 3/15 (1) **113**
5/113 (6) 6/192 (7) 7/273 (5)   4/21 (4) 5/21 (6) 6/48 (7)
8/276 (9) 9/281 (8) 10/285 (10)   7/69 (8) 8/69 (9) 9/113 (10) 10/113 (11)

Vaas 16.4–4–35–3; Malinga 14–1–71–4; Ramyakumara 10–1–49–2; Muralitharan 29–8–56–1; Herath 14–1–52–0; Jayasuriya 5–1–15–0. *Second Innings*—Vaas 18–9–15–4; Malinga 12–5–22–0; Muralitharan 21–8–36–6; Jayasuriya 6–1–20–0; Herath 3–0–12–0.

Sri Lanka

*M. S. Atapattu b Powell	1	– (2) c Ramdin b Lawson	28
S. T. Jayasuriya c Smith b Lawson	3	– (1) c Marshall b Lawson	15
†K. C. Sangakkara c Ramdin b Banks	34	– c Joseph b Lawson	0
D. P. M. D. Jayawardene c Morton b Powell	3	– not out	41
T. T. Samaraweera c and b Lawson	11	– lbw b Lawson	51
T. M. Dilshan c Smith b Banks	32	– not out	27
W. P. U. J. C. Vaas b Smith	49		
W. M. G. Ramyakumara c Joseph b Best	12		
H. M. R. K. B. Herath c Ramdin b Lawson	24		
M. Muralitharan b Lawson	36		
S. L. Malinga not out	5		
L-b 6, n-b 11	17	L-b 6, w 2, n-b 2	10

1/4 (1) 2/7 (2) 3/32 (4) 4/47 (3) **227**   1/34 (1) 2/34 (3) (4 wkts) **172**
5/91 (6) 6/93 (5) 7/113 (8)   3/49 (2) 4/135 (5)
8/149 (9) 9/215 (7) 10/227 (10)

Powell 13–4–31–2; Lawson 14.3–3–59–4; Best 11–1–47–1; Banks 16–3–70–2; Deonarine 1–0–9–0; Smith 2–0–5–1. *Second Innings*—Powell 8–0–44–0; Lawson 12–1–43–4; Best 8.3–1–37–0; Banks 7–0–31–0; Smith 3–1–11–0.

Umpires: Nadeem Ghauri *(Pakistan)* (2) and S. J. A. Taufel *(Australia)* (25).
Third umpire: P. T. Manuel *(Sri Lanka)*.   Referee: M. J. Procter *(South Africa)* (31).

Close of play: First day, West Indies 271-6 (Chanderpaul 69, Banks 30); Second day, West Indies 17-3 (Deonarine 5, Chanderpaul 0); Third day, West Indies 59-6 (Chanderpaul 29, Banks 0).

SRI LANKA v WEST INDIES 2005 (2nd Test)

At Asgiriya Stadium, Kandy, on 22, 23, 24, 25 July.
Toss: West Indies.   Result: SRI LANKA won by 240 runs.
Debuts: West Indies – R. R. Ramdass.
Man of the Match: K. C. Sangakkara.   Man of the Series: W. P. U. J. C. Vaas.

After two low-scoring first innings, Sri Lanka asserted their superiority through two Kandy men. Sangakkara's unbeaten 157 was his eighth Test hundred, but his first at his old school ground (Trinity College). It set up a spell of typically perplexing spin bowling by Muralitharan, another local boy, whose 8 for 46 hurried Sri Lanka to their second successive victory with more than a day to spare. It was the 46th time Murali, who finished the match with 549 Test wickets, had claimed a Test five-for, and the 14th occasion he had taken ten in a match, both records by a distance. Sri Lanka were shot out for their lowest total against West Indies after being sent in. Powell claimed his first five-for, while Best flattened Atapattu's off stump with his first ball. West Indies were again bothered by Vaas, who took four of the first five wickets. Sangakkara and Jayawardene stabilised things, putting on 98, then, after Lawson struck twice, Dilshan joined Sangakkara to put the match out of reach. Best was banned from bowling by umpire Tony Hill after his third fast full-pitch, even though Herath smacked it to the boundary. Vaas, who had torn his right hamstring, was not around to torment West Indies when they batted again – but that was a mixed blessing, as it simply meant that they had to confront Murali earlier than usual, after just nine overs. Jayawardene pouched four close catches, one that accounted for Chanderpaul off Herath's left-arm spin interrupting Murali's sequence.

Sri Lanka

*M. S. Atapattu b Best	17	– (2) c Banks b Powell	19
S. T. Jayasuriya c Ramdin b Powell	2	– (1) c Morton b Lawson	36
†K. C. Sangakkara c Morton b Powell	6	– not out	157
D. P. M. D. Jayawardene c Morton b Best	6	– b Lawson	43
T. T. Samaraweera c Deonarine b Banks	37	– c Ramdin b Lawson	0
T. M. Dilshan run out	36	– c Morton b Banks	49
W. P. U. J. C. Vaas c Ramdass b Best	6	– (8) b Banks	19
W. M. G. Ramyakumara c Ramdass b Powell	14	– (7) b Powell	12
H. M. R. K. B. Herath c Ramdin b Powell	1	– not out	15
M. Muralitharan not out	18		
S. L. Malinga c Ramdin b Powell	0		
L-b 6, n-b 1	7	B 4, l-b 6, w 6, n-b 9	25

1/3 (2) 2/17 (3) 3/35 (1) 4/42 (4)   150   1/55 (2) 2/57 (1)   (7 wkts dec.) 375
5/98 (6) 6/107 (7) 7/127 (5)   3/155 (4) 4/155 (5)
8/130 (9) 9/143 (8) 10/150 (11)   5/264 (6) 6/278 (7) 7/321 (8)

Powell 13.1–4–25–5; Lawson 10–0–29–0; Best 10–1–50–3; Banks 13–1–40–1. *Second Innings*—Powell 28–4–89–2; Lawson 29–1–104–3; Best 20–3–84–0; Banks 19–5–47–2; Deonarine 3–0–13–0; Morton 5–0–15–0; Chanderpaul 3–1–13–0.

West Indies

X. M. Marshall c Atapattu b Vaas	4	– lbw b Malinga	1
R. R. Ramdass run out	3	– c Jayawardene b Muralitharan	23
R. S. Morton b Vaas	1	– lbw b Muralitharan	9
*S. Chanderpaul lbw b Vaas	13	– c Jayawardene b Herath	24
S. C. Joseph c Dilshan b Vaas	18	– c Jayawardene b Muralitharan	0
N. Deonarine c and b Jayasuriya	40	– b Muralitharan	29
†D. Ramdin lbw b Vaas	13	– b Muralitharan	28
O. A. C. Banks c Dilshan b Muralitharan	17	– c Sangakkara b Muralitharan	1
D. B. Powell b Vaas	0	– c Jayawardene b Muralitharan	0
T. L. Best not out	26	– b Muralitharan	8
J. J. C. Lawson b Muralitharan	3	– not out	1
B 4, l-b 2, n-b 4	10	B 4, l-b 2, w 2, n-b 5	13

1/9 (1) 2/9 (2) 3/12 (3) 4/27 (4)   148   1/2 (1) 2/38 (3) 3/49 (2) 4/49 (5)   137
5/75 (5) 6/97 (6) 7/101 (7)   5/77 (4) 6/105 (6) 7/111 (8)
8/101 (9) 9/122 (8) 10/148 (11)   8/119 (9) 9/131 (7) 10/137 (10)

Vaas 15–6–22–6; Malinga 9–3–22–0; Ramyakumara 5–2–9–0; Muralitharan 9.1–0–37–2; Herath 9–0–26–0; Jayasuriya 11–3–26–1. *Second Innings*—Malinga 12–2–48–1; Ramyakumara 4–1–8–0; Muralitharan 16.2–4–46–8; Herath 9–2–29–1.

Umpires: A. L. Hill *(New Zealand)* (3) and S. J. A. Taufel *(Australia)* (26).
Third umpire: T. H. Wijewardene *(Sri Lanka)*.   Referee: M. J. Procter *(South Africa)* (32).

Close of play: First day, West Indies 92-5 (Deonarine 36, Ramdin 8); Second day, Sri Lanka 146-2 (Sangakkara 46, Jayawardene 38); Third day, Sri Lanka 340-7 (Sangakkara 135, Herath 4).

ENGLAND v AUSTRALIA 2005 (1st Test)

At Lord's, London, on 21, 22, 23, 24 July.

Toss: Australia.   Result: AUSTRALIA won by 239 runs.

Debuts: England – K. P. Pietersen.

Man of the Match: G. D. McGrath.

Australia's bowling champions, McGrath and Warne, proved as effective as ever in exploiting the conditions and batsmen's nerves. Further swaying the outcome was England's failure to hold catches. The upshot was that Australia's unbeaten sequence in Lord's Tests was extended to at least three-quarters of a century (England's only win in the 20th century was in 1934). England started in uncompromising fashion, Harmison hitting each of the top three. By lunch, Australia were 97 for 5, and although Gilchrist collected six fours Harmison returned to dock the tail with four wickets in 14 balls. Australia's 190 looked paltry – until McGrath got to work. His first ball after tea brought him his 50th Test wicket (Trescothick), beginning a spell which brought him five for two in 31 deliveries. Pietersen, making a seemingly nerveless debut, dragged the total to within 35, but later he was responsible for the most crucial of England's seven dropped catches. Clarke – 21 when put down at cover – went on to 91, and Australia stretched their lead to 419. England were half out by the end of the third day, despite an encouraging opening stand of 80. Although Pietersen continued to counter-attack – he was the first to top-score in both innings of his England debut since another South African-born batsman, Tony Greig, against Australia in 1972 – Australia needed just 61 balls to wrap things up after a delayed start on the fourth day. For the first time in 51 Tests, England had been bowled out twice for under 200.

Australia

J. L. Langer c Harmison b Flintoff	40	– run out	6
M. L. Hayden b Hoggard	12	– b Flintoff	34
*R. T. Ponting c Strauss b Harmison	9	– c sub (J. C. Hildreth) b Hoggard	42
D. R. Martyn c G. O. Jones b S. P. Jones	2	– lbw b Harmison	65
M. J. Clarke lbw b S. P. Jones	11	– b Hoggard	91
S. M. Katich c G. O. Jones b Harmison	27	– c S. P. Jones b Harmison	67
†A. C. Gilchrist c G. O. Jones b Flintoff	26	– b Flintoff	10
S. K. Warne b Harmison	28	– c Giles b Harmison	2
B. Lee c G. O. Jones b Harmison	3	– run out	8
J. N. Gillespie lbw b Harmison	1	– b S. P. Jones	13
G. D. McGrath not out	10	– not out	20
B 5, l-b 4, w 1, n-b 11	21	B 10, l-b 8, n-b 8	26

1/35 (2) 2/55 (3) 3/66 (1) 4/66 (4)   190   1/18 (1) 2/54 (2) 3/100 (3)   384
5/87 (5) 6/126 (7) 7/175 (8)   4/255 (5) 5/255 (4) 6/274 (7)
8/178 (6) 9/178 (9) 10/190 (10)   7/279 (8) 8/289 (9) 9/341 (10) 10/384 (6)

Harmison 11.2–0–43–5; Hoggard 8–0–40–1; Flintoff 11–2–50–2; S. P. Jones 10–0–48–2. *Second Innings*—Harmison 27.4–6–54–3; Hoggard 16–1–56–2; Flintoff 27–4–123–2; S. P. Jones 18–1–69–1; Giles 11–1–56–0; Bell 1–0–8–0.

England

M. E. Trescothick c Langer b McGrath	4	– c Hayden b Warne	44
A. J. Strauss c Warne b McGrath	2	– c and b Lee	37
*M. P. Vaughan b McGrath	3	– b Lee	4
I. R. Bell b McGrath	6	– lbw b Warne	8
K. P. Pietersen c Martyn b Warne	57	– not out	64
A. Flintoff b McGrath	0	– c Gilchrist b Warne	3
†G. O. Jones c Gilchrist b Lee	30	– c Gillespie b McGrath	6
A. F. Giles c Gilchrist b Lee	11	– c Hayden b McGrath	0
M. J. Hoggard c Hayden b Warne	0	– lbw b McGrath	0
S. J. Harmison c Martyn b Lee	11	– lbw b Warne	0
S. P. Jones not out	20	– c Warne b McGrath	0
B 1, l-b 5, n-b 5	11	B 6, l-b 5, n-b 3	14

1/10 (1) 2/11 (2) 3/18 (3) 4/19 (4)   155   1/80 (2) 2/96 (1) 3/104 (4)   180
5/21 (6) 6/79 (7) 7/92 (8)   4/112 (3) 5/119 (6) 6/158 (7)
8/101 (9) 9/122 (5) 10/155 (10)   7/158 (8) 8/164 (9) 9/167 (10) 10/180 (11)

McGrath 18–5–53–5; Lee 15.1–5–47–3; Gillespie 8–1–30–0; Warne 7–2–19–2. *Second Innings*—McGrath 17.1–2–29–4; Lee 15–3–58–2; Gillespie 6–0–18–0; Warne 20–2–64–4.

Umpires: Aleem Dar *(Pakistan)* (21) and R. E. Koertzen *(South Africa)* (63).
Third umpire: M. R. Benson *(England)*.   Referee: R. S. Madugalle *(Sri Lanka)* (75).

Close of play: First day, England 92-7 (Pietersen 28); Second day, Australia 279-7 (Katich 10); Third day, England 156-5 (Pietersen 42, G. O. Jones 6).

ENGLAND v AUSTRALIA 2005 (2nd Test)

At Edgbaston, Birmingham, on 4, 5, 6, 7 August.
Toss: Australia.   Result: ENGLAND won by two runs.
Debuts: none.
Man of the Match: A. Flintoff.

One of the most riveting of all Test matches ended when Kasprowicz gloved down the leg side and was adjudged caught behind. The final margin was the closest in England-Australia Tests, edging the three-run thrillers of Manchester 1902 and Melbourne 1982-83. The drama began before the start, when McGrath tore ankle ligaments after treading on a ball. Ponting nonetheless bowled first, only for England to hurtle to 407, the highest score conceded by Australia on the first day of any Test since 1938. Flintoff carved five sixes and six fours before becoming Gillespie's 250th Test victim. Australia started badly when Hayden drove his first ball straight to cover, his first Test duck for 40 months (68 innings). Langer dropped anchor, but the later order misfired, conceding a handy lead of 99. Warne became the first overseas bowler to take 100 Test wickets in England when his second ball fizzed across Strauss into the stumps, then, after a burst from Lee, Warne reduced England to 131 for 9. However, Flintoff slammed four more sixes (his nine in the match was an Ashes record) as the last wicket stretched the lead by 51 and then, when Australia started their quest for 282, he dismissed Langer and Ponting in the same over. At 140 for 7, England claimed the extra half-hour, but the only casualty was Clarke, bamboozled by Harmison's rare slower ball. It seemed all over bar the shouting – but there was a lot of that still to come on an unforgettable Sunday morning.

England

M. E. Trescothick c Gilchrist b Kasprowicz	90	– c Gilchrist b Lee	21
A. J. Strauss b Warne	48	– b Warne	6
*M. P. Vaughan c Lee b Gillespie	24	– (4) b Lee	1
I. R. Bell c Gilchrist b Kasprowicz	6	– (5) c Gilchrist b Warne	21
K. P. Pietersen c Katich b Lee	71	– (6) c Gilchrist b Warne	20
A. Flintoff c Gilchrist b Gillespie	68	– (7) b Warne	73
†G. O. Jones c Gilchrist b Kasprowicz	1	– (8) c Ponting b Lee	9
A. F. Giles lbw b Warne	23	– (9) c Hayden b Warne	8
M. J. Hoggard lbw b Warne	16	– (3) c Hayden b Lee	1
S. J. Harmison b Warne	17	– c Ponting b Warne	0
S. P. Jones not out	19	– not out	12
L-b 9, w 1, n-b 14	24	L-b 1, n-b 9	10

1/112 (2) 2/164 (1) 3/170 (4) 4/187 (3) **407**   1/25 (2) 2/27 (1) 3/29 (4) **182**
5/290 (6) 6/293 (7) 7/342 (8)   4/31 (3) 5/72 (6) 6/75 (5)
8/348 (5) 9/375 (10) 10/407 (9)   7/101 (8) 8/131 (9) 9/131 (10) 10/182 (7)

Lee 17–1–111–1; Gillespie 22–3–91–2; Kasprowicz 15–3–80–3; Warne 25.2–4–116–4. *Second Innings*—Lee 18–1–82–4; Gillespie 8–0–24–0; Kasprowicz 3–0–29–0; Warne 23.1–7–46–6.

Australia

J. L. Langer lbw b S. P. Jones	82	– b Flintoff	28
M. L. Hayden c Strauss b Hoggard	0	– c Trescothick b S. P. Jones	31
*R. T. Ponting c Vaughan b Giles	61	– c G. O. Jones b Flintoff	0
D. R. Martyn run out	20	– c Bell b Hoggard	28
M. J. Clarke c G. O. Jones b Giles	40	– b Harmison	30
S. M. Katich c G. O. Jones b Flintoff	4	– c Trescothick b Giles	16
†A. C. Gilchrist not out	49	– c Flintoff b Giles	1
S. K. Warne b Giles	8	– (9) hit wkt b Flintoff	42
B. Lee c Flintoff b S. P. Jones	6	– (10) not out	43
J. N. Gillespie lbw b Flintoff	7	– (8) lbw b Flintoff	0
M. S. Kasprowicz lbw b Flintoff	0	– c G. O. Jones b Harmison	20
B 13, l-b 7, w 1, n-b 10	31	B 13, l-b 8, w 1, n-b 18	40

1/0 (2) 2/88 (3) 3/118 (4) 4/194 (5) **308**   1/47 (1) 2/48 (3) 3/82 (2) **279**
5/208 (6) 6/262 (1) 7/273 (8)   4/107 (4) 5/134 (6) 6/136 (7)
8/282 (9) 9/308 (10) 10/308 (11)   7/137 (8) 8/175 (5) 9/220 (9) 10/279 (11)

Harmison 11–1–48–0; Hoggard 8–0–41–1; S. P. Jones 16–2–69–2; Flintoff 15–1–52–3; Giles 26–2–78–3. *Second Innings*—Harmison 17.3–3–62–2; Hoggard 5–0–26–1; Giles 15–3–68–2; Flintoff 22–3–79–4; S. P. Jones 5–1–23–1.

Umpires: B. F. Bowden *(New Zealand)* (28) and R. E. Koertzen *(South Africa)* (64).
Third umpire: J. W. Lloyds *(England)*.   Referee: R. S. Madugalle *(Sri Lanka)* (76).

Close of play: First day, England 407; Second day, England 25-1 (Trescothick 19, Hoggard 0); Third day, Australia 175-8 (Warne 20).

ENGLAND v AUSTRALIA 2005 (3rd Test)

At Old Trafford, Manchester, on 11, 12, 13, 14, 15 August.
Toss: England.   Result: MATCH DRAWN.
Debuts: none.
Man of the Match: R. T. Ponting.

The bald result was the first draw in 17 Ashes Tests. But an estimated 10,000 had to be turned away on the final morning, while those who made it inside the ground were rewarded with another nail-biting finish: Australia's last pair kept out the last 24 balls to save the game. This followed an inspirational innings from Ponting, who batted nearly seven hours. When he was ninth out, with four overs remaining, he thought he had blown it. It was a good match for the captains: Ponting's 156 was preceded by 166 from Vaughan, who rode his luck; he was missed at 41 by Gilchrist, bowled by a McGrath no-ball next ball, and dropped again on 141. Warne became the first bowler to take 600 Test wickets when Trescothick tried to sweep and was caught behind. Flintoff and Geraint Jones lifted England to 444, and Australia struggled uncharacteristically – the highest scorer in their first innings was Warne, who combated the reverse swing of Simon Jones (who returned Test-best figures) and reduced the deficit to 142. Strauss, struck by a Lee bouncer early on, scored his first Ashes century with a piece of white plaster stuck to his ear, as England took their lead to 422. Ponting came to the crease in the final day's second over, and saw Hayden worked over magnificently by Flintoff before being bowled behind his legs. But, despite the regular fall of wickets at the other end, Ponting did just enough to ensure the draw.

England

M. E. Trescothick c Gilchrist b Warne	63	– b McGrath	41
A. J. Strauss b Lee	6	– c Martyn b McGrath	106
*M. P. Vaughan c McGrath b Katich	166	– c sub (B. J. Hodge) b Lee	14
I. R. Bell c Gilchrist b Lee	59	– c Katich b McGrath	65
K. P. Pietersen c sub (B. J. Hodge) b Lee	21	– lbw b McGrath	0
M. J. Hoggard b Lee	4		
A. Flintoff c Langer b Warne	46	– (6) b McGrath	4
†G. O. Jones b Gillespie	42	– (7) not out	27
A. F. Giles c Hayden b Warne	0	– (8) not out	0
S. J. Harmison not out	10		
S. P. Jones b Warne	0		
B 4, l-b 5, w 3, n-b 15	27	B 5, l-b 3, w 1, n-b 14	23

1/26 (2) 2/163 (1) 3/290 (3) 4/333 (5) **444**   1/64 (1) 2/97 (3)   (6 wkts dec.) **280**
5/341 (6) 6/346 (4) 7/433 (7)   3/224 (2) 4/225 (5)
8/434 (8) 9/438 (9) 10/444 (11)   5/248 (6) 6/264 (4)

McGrath 25–6–86–0; Lee 27–6–100–4; Gillespie 19–2–114–1; Warne 33.2–5–99–4; Katich 9–1–36–1. *Second Innings*—McGrath 20.5–1–115–5; Lee 12–0–60–1; Warne 25–3–74–0; Gillespie 4–0–23–0.

Australia

J. L. Langer c Bell b Giles	31	– c G. O. Jones b Hoggard	14
M. L. Hayden lbw b Giles	34	– b Flintoff	36
*R. T. Ponting c Bell b S. P. Jones	7	– c G. O. Jones b Harmison	156
D. R. Martyn b Giles	20	– lbw b Harmison	19
S. M. Katich b Flintoff	17	– c Giles b Flintoff	12
†A. C. Gilchrist c G. O. Jones b S. P. Jones	30	– c Bell b Flintoff	4
S. K. Warne c Giles b S. P. Jones	90	– (9) c G. O. Jones b Flintoff	34
M. J. Clarke c Flintoff b S. P. Jones	7	– (7) b S. P. Jones	39
J. N. Gillespie lbw b S. P. Jones	26	– (8) lbw b Hoggard	0
B. Lee c Trescothick b S. P. Jones	1	– not out	18
G. D. McGrath not out	1	– not out	5
B 8, l-b 7, w 8, n-b 15	38	B 5, l-b 8, w 2, n-b 19	34

1/58 (1) 2/73 (3) 3/86 (2) 4/119 (5) **302**   1/25 (1) 2/96 (2) 3/129 (4)   (9 wkts) **371**
5/133 (4) 6/186 (6) 7/201 (8)   4/165 (5) 5/182 (6) 6/263 (7)
8/287 (7) 9/293 (10) 10/302 (9)   7/264 (8) 8/340 (9) 9/354 (3)

Harmison 10–0–47–0; Hoggard 6–2–22–0; Flintoff 20–1–65–1; S. P. Jones 17.5–6–53–6; Giles 31–4–100–3. *Second Innings*—Harmison 22–4–67–2; Hoggard 13–0–49–2; Giles 26–4–93–0; Vaughan 5–0–21–0; Flintoff 25–6–71–4; S. P. Jones 17–3–57–1.

Umpires: B. F. Bowden *(New Zealand)* (29) and S. A. Bucknor *(West Indies)* (103).
Third umpire: N. J. Llong *(England)*.   Referee: R. S. Madugalle *(Sri Lanka)* (77).

Close of play: First day, England 341-5 (Bell 59); Second day, Australia 214-7 (Warne 45, Gillespie 4); Third day, Australia 264-7 (Warne 78, Gillespie 7); Fourth day, Australia 24-0 (Langer 14, Hayden 5).

ENGLAND v AUSTRALIA 2005 (4th Test)

At Trent Bridge, Nottingham, on 25, 26, 27, 28 August.
Toss: England.   Result: ENGLAND won by three wickets.
Debuts: Australia – S. W. Tait.
Man of the Match: A. Flintoff.

England took the lead in the series after another stomach-churning climax. Unchanged for the fourth Test running, England had made a good start, but after a rain delay Trescothick's fluent 65 was ended by a rapid inswinger from the debutant Shaun Tait (included as McGrath was missing again, this time with elbow trouble) who also had Bell caught behind, Gilchrist's 300th Test dismissal. Flintoff and Geraint Jones then piled on 177, ensuring England again passed 400. Hoggard relocated his awayswinger in an 11-over burst of three for 32, Harmison undid Clarke in the last over of the day, as he had at Edgbaston, then Strauss dived full stretch at second slip to catch Gilchrist, before Simon Jones cleaned up. Lee thumped 47, but could not prevent Australia following on for the first time since Karachi 1988-89. Still, at 155 for 2 second time round, they were progressing smoothly before Ponting, to his evident disgust, was beaten by a direct hit from the substitute, Gary Pratt, in the covers. Clarke and Katich added 100 to wipe out the lead, and England eventually needed 129. They seemed to be coasting at 32 without loss after five overs, but Warne grabbed three quick wickets. Pietersen and Flintoff put on 46 before Lee removed both, and with 13 still needed, Geraint Jones spooned to deep extra cover, and England were 116 for 7. Catharsis arrived when Hoggard drove a Lee full-toss to the cover fence, and victory was secured next over when Giles clipped Warne through midwicket.

England

M. E. Trescothick b Tait	65	– c Ponting b Warne		27
A. J. Strauss c Hayden b Warne	35	– c Clarke b Warne		23
*M. P. Vaughan c Gilchrist b Ponting	58	– c Hayden b Warne		0
I. R. Bell c Gilchrist b Tait	3	– c Kasprowicz b Lee		3
K. P. Pietersen c Gilchrist b Lee	45	– c Gilchrist b Lee		23
A. Flintoff lbw b Tait	102	– b Lee		26
†G. O. Jones c and b Kasprowicz	85	– c Kasprowicz b Warne		3
A. F. Giles lbw b Warne	15	– not out		7
M. J. Hoggard c Gilchrist b Warne	10	– not out		8
S. J. Harmison st Gilchrist b Warne	2			
S. P. Jones not out	15			
B 1, l-b 15, w 1, n-b 25	42	L-b 4, n-b 5		9

1/105 (2) 2/137 (1) 3/146 (4) 4/213 (3)   477   1/32 (1) 2/36 (3) 3/57 (2)   (7 wkts) 129
5/241 (5) 6/418 (6) 7/450 (7)   4/57 (4) 5/103 (5)
8/450 (8) 9/454 (10) 10/477 (9)   6/111 (6) 7/116 (7)

Lee 32–2–131–1; Kasprowicz 32–3–122–1; Tait 24–4–97–3; Warne 29.1–4–102–4; Ponting 6–2–9–1. *Second Innings*—Lee 12–0–51–3; Kasprowicz 2–0–19–0; Warne 13.5–2–31–4; Tait 4–0–24–0.

Australia

J. L. Langer c Bell b Hoggard	27	– c Bell b Giles		61
M. L. Hayden lbw b Hoggard	7	– c Giles b Flintoff		26
*R. T. Ponting lbw b S. P. Jones	1	– run out		48
D. R. Martyn lbw b Hoggard	1	– c G. O. Jones b Flintoff		13
M. J. Clarke lbw b Harmison	36	– c G. O. Jones b Hoggard		56
S. M. Katich c Strauss b S. P. Jones	45	– lbw b Harmison		59
†A. C. Gilchrist c Strauss b Flintoff	27	– lbw b Hoggard		11
S. K. Warne c Bell b S. P. Jones	0	– st G. O. Jones b Giles		45
B. Lee c Bell b S. P. Jones	47	– not out		26
M. S. Kasprowicz b S. P. Jones	5	– c G. O. Jones b Harmison		19
S. W. Tait not out	3	– b Harmison		4
L-b 2, w 1, n-b 16	19	B 1, l-b 4, n-b 14		19

1/20 (2) 2/21 (3) 3/22 (4) 4/58 (1)   218   1/50 (2) 2/129 (1) 3/155 (3)   387
5/99 (5) 6/157 (6) 7/157 (8)   4/161 (4) 5/261 (5) 6/277 (7)
8/163 (7) 9/175 (10) 10/218 (9)   7/314 (6) 8/342 (8) 9/373 (10) 10/387 (11)

Harmison 9–1–48–1; Hoggard 15–3–70–3; S. P. Jones 14.1–4–44–5; Flintoff 11–1–54–1. *Second Innings*—Hoggard 27–7–72–2; S. P. Jones 4–0–15–0; Harmison 30–5–93–3; Flintoff 29–4–83–2; Giles 28–3–107–2; Bell 6–2–12–0.

Umpires: Aleem Dar *(Pakistan)* (22) and S. A. Bucknor *(West Indies)* (104).
Third umpire: M. R. Benson *(England)*.   Referee: R. S. Madugalle *(Sri Lanka)* (78).

Close of play: First day, England 229-4 (Pietersen 33, Flintoff 8); Second day, Australia 99-5 (Katich 20); Third day, Australia 222-4 (Clarke 39, Katich 24).

ENGLAND v AUSTRALIA 2005 (5th Test)

At Kennington Oval, London, on 8, 9, 10, 11, 12 September.
Toss: England.   Result: MATCH DRAWN.
Debuts: none.
Man of the Match: K. P. Pietersen.   Men of the Series: A. Flintoff and S. K. Warne.

The series ended in the sort of obscure anticlimax which baffled outsiders were inclined to associate with cricket before 2005. As England moved towards the draw they needed to reclaim the Ashes after 16 years and 42 days, the roads went quiet as the nation headed for the TV. Next day, the noise was on the streets as the replica trophy was paraded from an open-top bus, and the game's new fans jumped into the Trafalgar Square fountains. This was the climax of what *Wisden* was to call the Greatest Series Ever, and it matched expectations in all but its very end. Australia might still have won – and squared the series and retained the Ashes – had Pietersen been taken throat-high at first slip when he had scored just 15 on the final day. The culprit, cruelly, was Warne, who otherwise bowled superbly, taking his series tally to 40 wickets. Other important innings came from Strauss, whose 129 (and stand of 143 with Flintoff) buttressed England's first innings, and Hayden, who saved his career with a gritty century, his first in Tests for 14 months. He and Langer, who passed 7,000 runs during his own century, added 185 before superb spells from Flintoff and Hoggard turned a probable deficit into a narrow lead. But Pietersen's 158, which included seven sixes, ensured the Ashes changed hands on a surreal final day when the crowd even applauded the umpires for taking the players off, as that increased England's chances of reclaiming the urn.

England

M. E. Trescothick c Hayden b Warne	43	– lbw b Warne	33
A. J. Strauss c Katich b Warne	129	– c Katich b Warne	1
*M. P. Vaughan c Clarke b Warne	11	– c Gilchrist b McGrath	45
I. R. Bell lbw b Warne	0	– c Warne b McGrath	0
K. P. Pietersen b Warne	14	– b McGrath	158
A. Flintoff c Warne b McGrath	72	– c and b Warne	8
P. D. Collingwood lbw b Tait	7	– c Ponting b Warne	10
†G. O. Jones b Lee	25	– b Tait	1
A. F. Giles lbw b Warne	32	– b Warne	59
M. J. Hoggard c Martyn b McGrath	2	– not out	4
S. J. Harmison not out	20	– c Hayden b Warne	0
B 4, l-b 6, w 1, n-b 7	18	B 4, w 7, n-b 5	16

1/82 (1) 2/102 (3) 3/104 (4) 4/131 (5)   373   1/2 (2) 2/67 (3) 3/67 (4)   335
5/274 (6) 6/289 (7) 7/297 (2)   4/109 (1) 5/126 (6) 6/186 (7)
8/325 (8) 9/345 (10) 10/373 (9)   7/199 (8) 8/308 (5) 9/335 (9) 10/335 (11)

McGrath 27–5–72–2; Lee 23–3–94–1; Tait 15–1–61–1; Warne 37.3–5–122–6; Katich 3–0–14–0. *Second Innings*— McGrath 26–3–85–3; Lee 20–4–88–0; Warne 38.3–3–124–6; Clarke 2–0–6–0; Tait 5–0–28–1.

Australia

J. L. Langer b Harmison	105	– not out	0
M. L. Hayden lbw b Flintoff	138	– not out	0
*R. T. Ponting c Strauss b Flintoff	35		
D. R. Martyn c Collingwood b Flintoff	10		
M. J. Clarke lbw b Hoggard	25		
S. M. Katich lbw b Flintoff	1		
†A. C. Gilchrist lbw b Hoggard	23		
S. K. Warne c Vaughan b Flintoff	0		
B. Lee c Giles b Hoggard	6		
G. D. McGrath c Strauss b Hoggard	0		
S. W. Tait not out	1		
B 4, l-b 8, w 2, n-b 9	23	L-b 4	4

1/185 (1) 2/264 (3) 3/281 (4) 4/323 (2)   367   (no wkt)   4
5/329 (6) 6/356 (7) 7/359 (5)
8/363 (8) 9/363 (10) 10/367 (9)

Harmison 22–2–87–1; Hoggard 24.1–2–97–4; Flintoff 34–10–78–5; Giles 23–1–76–0; Collingwood 4–0–17–0. *Second Innings*—Harmison 0.4–0–0–0.

Umpires: B. F. Bowden *(New Zealand)* (30) and R. E. Koertzen *(South Africa)* (65).
Third umpire: J. W. Lloyds *(England)*.   Referee: R. S. Madugalle *(Sri Lanka)* (79).

Close of play: First day, England 319-7 (Jones 21, Giles 5); Second day, Australia 112-0 (Langer 75, Hayden 32); Third day, Australia 277-2 (Hayden 110, Martyn 9); Fourth day, England 34-1 (Trescothick 14, Vaughan 19).

ZIMBABWE v NEW ZEALAND 2005 (1st Test)

At Harare Sports Club on 7, 8 August.
Toss: Zimbabwe.   Result: NEW ZEALAND won by an innings and 294 runs.
Debuts: Zimbabwe – N. R. Ferreira.
Man of the Match: D. L. Vettori.

Zimbabwe's results had been disastrous since the 2004 player rebellion, but with several ex-rebels back in harness they hoped for a better showing. Instead, they suffered their heaviest defeat, losing inside two days for the second time in three Tests, and became only the second team in Test history, after India at Old Trafford in 1952, to be dismissed twice in a day. All this after dominating the first session: Streak and Mahwire bowled superbly, and shortly after lunch New Zealand were 113 for 5. McCullum started the revival with his second Test century before Vettori, coming in straight after tea, hit New Zealand's fastest Test hundred, off 82 balls, after a freakish escape on 67: he played a ball from Streak on to his wicket, and the leg bail flipped, only to land back on top of the stump at right angles, miraculously retaining its balance. New Zealand's 452 for 9 was their best for a single day's play. Zimbabwe were soon 11 for 4, Franklin taking three wickets in four deliveries, the other being a no-ball. Taylor was run out by an accidental deflection off the bowler, and the innings folded for 59 four overs after lunch. The follow-on was little better, as the last eight wickets tumbled for 62 after tea. Bond, in his first international since May 2003 after persistent back trouble, took only two wickets, but started with six straight maidens. The match ended when Mpofu was stumped for the second time in the match.

New Zealand

J. A. H. Marshall c Taibu b Mahwire	5	S. E. Bond not out		41
L. Vincent c Carlisle b Mahwire	13	C. S. Martin not out		4
H. J. H. Marshall lbw b Mpofu	20			
*S. P. Fleming c Carlisle b Mpofu	73	B 3, l-b 5, w 2, n-b 5		15
N. J. Astle c Taylor b Streak	23			
S. B. Styris run out	7	1/21 (2) 2/24 (1)	(9 wkts dec.)	452
†B. B. McCullum c Cremer b Mahwire	111	3/63 (3) 4/104 (5)		
D. L. Vettori b Streak	127	5/113 (6) 6/233 (4)		
J. E. C. Franklin b Cremer	13	7/309 (7) 8/369 (9) 9/432 (8)		

Streak 23.4–5–102–2; Mahwire 26–4–115–3; Mpofu 16.2–1–100–2; Cremer 22–0–113–1; Taylor 1–0–14–0.

Zimbabwe

N. R. Ferreira c McCullum b Franklin	5	– c Fleming b Franklin	16
B. R. M. Taylor run out	10	– c Vettori b Franklin	0
D. D. Ebrahim lbw b Franklin	0	– b Martin	8
H. Masakadza lbw b Franklin	0	– c and b Vettori	42
C. B. Wishart b Bond	0	– c Fleming b Bond	5
S. V. Carlisle not out	20	– c Fleming b Bond	0
*†T. Taibu lbw b Martin	5	– c Fleming b Martin	4
H. H. Streak c McCullum b Martin	0	– lbw b Vettori	3
N. B. Mahwire lbw b Martin	4	– not out	4
A. G. Cremer c Martin b Vettori	1	– c J. A. H. Marshall b Vettori	3
C. B. Mpofu st McCullum b Vettori	0	– st McCullum b Vettori	0
B 4, l-b 2, w 1, n-b 7	14	L-b 8, n-b 6	14

1/9 (1) 2/9 (3) 3/10 (4) 4/11 (5)	59	1/5 (2) 2/14 (3) 3/53 (1)	99
5/28 (2) 6/46 (7) 7/46 (8)		4/76 (5) 5/80 (6) 6/84 (4)	
8/51 (9) 9/53 (10) 10/59 (11)		7/90 (8) 8/90 (7) 9/99 (10) 10/99 (11)	

Bond 5–1–11–1; Franklin 5–0–11–3; Martin 10–1–21–3; Styris 7–4–9–0; Vettori 2.4–2–1–2. *Second Innings—* Bond 11–8–10–2; Franklin 10–3–19–2; Styris 2–0–3–0; Martin 8–5–16–2; Vettori 13.5–4–28–4; Astle 5–0–15–0.

Umpires: M. R. Benson *(England)* (4) and D. B. Hair *(Australia)* (65).
Third umpire: K. C. Barbour *(Zimbabwe)*.   Referee: B. C. Broad *(England)* (13).

Close of play: First day, New Zealand 452-9 (Bond 41, Martin 4).

ZIMBABWE v NEW ZEALAND 2005 (2nd Test)

At Queens Sports Club, Bulawayo, on 15, 16, 17 August.
Toss: Zimbabwe.   Result: NEW ZEALAND won by an innings and 46 runs.
Debuts: Zimbabwe – K. M. Dabengwa.
Man of the Match: S. E. Bond.   Man of the Series: S. E. Bond.

On one of the world's friendliest pitches, Zimbabwe twice passed 200, and also bowled New Zealand out – but were still totally outclassed as they went down to their fourth successive innings defeat. Bond reaped the reward for some outstanding pace bowling, starting with wickets in each of his first three overs. Six were out by lunch – five to Bond – before Taibu and Mahwire added 88 for the eighth wicket. Zimbabwe removed the Marshall twins early on, but the bowlers struggled on the second day, although only Astle applied himself sufficiently to reach three figures. The last three wickets fell in 11 overs next morning, but Zimbabwe's batting problems continued: two wickets were gone before lunch in an innings in which fine strokeplay sat alongside naive dismissals – there were three foolish run-outs – and big hitting, including six sixes on a large ground. Taylor looked well entrenched at tea (134 for 4), but the wheels came off quickly once Bond's slower ball deceived him into giving a simple catch to mid-on. The exception was Mahwire, who hammered eight fours and two sixes for a maiden Test fifty in 34 balls, Zimbabwe's fastest ever. However, this sped the match to a bizarre conclusion. Mahwire reached 50 with a leg-side single; Mpofu completed the run and then, without waiting for the ball to be returned from the field, jogged back down the pitch to congratulate his partner, and was easily run out. It was a farcical end to a farcical series.

Zimbabwe

D. D. Ebrahim lbw b Bond	0	– c Styris b Bond	2
B. R. M. Taylor c McCullum b Bond	37	– c Vettori b Bond	77
S. V. Carlisle lbw b Bond	1	– run out	10
H. Masakadza c Martin b Bond	0	– b Vettori	28
C. B. Wishart c Astle b Franklin	30	– run out	0
*†T. Taibu c Vettori b Bond	76	– lbw b Vettori	25
H. H. Streak c McCullum b Bond	0	– c McCullum b Bond	2
K. M. Dabengwa b Martin	17	– c McCullum b Bond	4
N. B. Mahwire c Astle b Vettori	42	– not out	50
A. G. Cremer not out	7	– lbw b Vettori	1
C. B. Mpofu c J. A. H. Marshall b Vettori	7	– run out	3
L-b 4, n-b 10	14	L-b 2, n-b 3	5

1/0 (1) 2/3 (3) 3/7 (4) 4/65 (5)   231   1/4 (1) 2/19 (3) 3/69 (4)   207
5/74 (2) 6/74 (7) 7/123 (8)   4/69 (5) 5/146 (2) 6/146 (6)
8/211 (6) 9/217 (9) 10/231 (11)   7/153 (7) 8/164 (8) 9/173 (10) 10/207 (11)

Bond 17–5–51–6; Franklin 12–3–43–1; Martin 13–4–42–1; Styris 4–2–9–0; Vettori 27–9–56–2; Astle 6–2–26–0.
Second Innings—Bond 14–1–48–4; Franklin 10–3–24–0; Martin 12–2–47–0; Vettori 22.1–8–66–3; Styris 3–0–20–0.

New Zealand

J. A. H. Marshall c Carlisle b Streak	10	S. E. Bond b Mahwire	8
L. Vincent b Streak	92	C. S. Martin not out	0
H. J. H. Marshall run out	13		
*S. P. Fleming c Taibu b Mahwire	65	B 6, l-b 6, w 2, n-b 18	32
N. J. Astle b Streak	128		
S. B. Styris c Taibu b Mahwire	45	1/34 (1) 2/48 (3) 3/185 (4)	484
†B. B. McCullum c Taylor b Dabengwa	24	4/205 (2) 5/292 (6) 6/346 (7)	
D. L. Vettori c Taibu b Dabengwa	48	7/439 (8) 8/475 (5)	
J. E. C. Franklin lbw b Streak	19	9/484 (9) 10/484 (10)	

Streak 22–6–73–4; Mahwire 25.1–2–121–3; Mpofu 15–1–80–0; Cremer 24–1–111–0; Dabengwa 25–2–87–2.

Umpires: M. R. Benson *(England)* (5) and D. B. Hair *(Australia)* (66).
Third umpire: K. C. Barbour *(Zimbabwe)*.   Referee: B. C. Broad *(England)* (14).

Close of play: First day, New Zealand 48-2 (Vincent 20); Second day, New Zealand 454-7 (Astle 116, Franklin 9).

SRI LANKA v BANGLADESH 2005-06 (1st Test)

At R. Premadasa Stadium, Colombo, on 12, 13, 14 September.
Toss: Sri Lanka.   Result: SRI LANKA won by an innings and 96 runs.
Debuts: Bangladesh – Shahriar Nafees, Syed Rasel.
Man of the Match: M. Muralitharan.

The Premadasa Stadium's first Test for more than seven years was a one-sided, unmemorable contest. There were more groundstaff than spectators, and it was all over within seven sessions. Bangladesh did at least begin positively, after being inserted in overcast conditions. Habibul Bashar guided his team into a position of strength with a determined 84, but, after playing with uncharacteristic care for 74 minutes for 17, Mohammad Ashraful had a rush of blood; shortly afterwards, Habibul was run out by a brilliant reflex stop-and-flick by Dilshan from short leg. The spinners ran through the middle order – five wickets fell in 20 balls – and Bangladesh slumped to 188. Jayasuriya blasted a quick 46 to leave Sri Lanka only 28 behind by the close, but next day the middle order had to graft hard on a fast-deteriorating pitch. Samaraweera dropped anchor for a four-hour 78, while Dilshan provided more entertainment with a flamboyant 86 before Atapattu declared, 182 ahead. Muralitharan bowled just one over on the second evening, embarrassing both Shahriar Nafees and Ashraful with his *doosra*. His double-wicket maiden left Bangladesh floundering at 36 for 3 when a storm cut short the final session. Their only hope was the early arrival of the October monsoon – but the third day dawned bright and sunny. Murali soon grabbed centre stage, spinning the ball viciously both ways. Victory was completed an hour before lunch as Bangladesh slumped to 86 all out, by one their lowest total in Test cricket at the time.

Bangladesh

Javed Omar c Sangakkara b Fernando	30	– c Sangakkara b Malinga		9
Shahriar Nafees b Malinga	3	– b Muralitharan		13
*Habibul Bashar run out	84	– c Sangakkara b Vaas		15
Mohammad Ashraful c Fernando b Herath	17	– lbw b Muralitharan		0
Tushar Imran b Herath	0	– b Muralitharan		3
Aftab Ahmed c Samaraweera b Herath	0	– c Samaraweera b Muralitharan		8
†Khaled Mashud c Samaraweera b Muralitharan	2	– b Malinga		15
Mohammad Rafique lbw b Muralitharan	9	– c Samaraweera b Muralitharan		4
Syed Rasel st Sangakkara b Herath	19	– b Malinga		1
Shahadat Hossain lbw b Muralitharan	2	– not out		5
Enamul Haque, jun. not out	0	– st Sangakkara b Muralitharan		2
B 8, l-b 2, w 1, n-b 11	22	B 4, w 5, n-b 2		11

1/4 (2) 2/63 (1) 3/155 (4) 4/156 (5)　　　188　　1/9 (1) 2/35 (2) 3/35 (4)　　　　　86
5/156 (3) 6/158 (7) 7/158 (6)　　　　　　　　4/39 (3) 5/47 (5) 6/50 (6)
8/170 (8) 9/176 (10) 10/188 (9)　　　　　　7/59 (8) 8/73 (9) 9/83 (7) 10/86 (11)

Vaas 6–1–25–0; Malinga 8–1–44–1; Fernando 4–0–29–1; Muralitharan 14–1–42–3; Herath 12–4–38–4. *Second Innings*—Vaas 10–4–31–1; Malinga 6–1–32–3; Muralitharan 10.4–4–18–6; Herath 1–0–1–0.

Sri Lanka

S. T. Jayasuriya c Aftab Ahmed b Shahadat Hossain	46	H. M. R. K. B. Herath c Khaled Mashud b Mohammad Rafique 13
*M. S. Atapattu lbw b Syed Rasel	18	M. Muralitharan c Khaled Mashud b Mohammad Rafique 3
†K. C. Sangakkara c Mohammad Ashraful b Mohammad Rafique	30	C. R. D. Fernando not out 1
T. T. Samaraweera c Khaled Mashud b Shahadat Hossain	78	L-b 6, w 1, n-b 20 27
D. P. M. D. Jayawardene c Khaled Mashud b Mohammad Rafique	63	1/41 (2) 2/97 (1)　　　(9 wkts dec.) 370
T. M. Dilshan b Syed Rasel	86	3/130 (3) 4/231 (5) 5/295 (4)
W. P. U. J. C. Vaas lbw b Mohammad Rafique	5	6/306 (7) 7/337 (8) 8/345 (9) 9/370 (6)

S. L. Malinga did not bat.

Syed Rasel 19.2–2–67–2; Shahadat Hossain 20–0–75–2; Mohammad Rafique 37–9–114–5; Enamul Haque 33–8–106–0; Mohammad Ashraful 1–0–2–0.

Umpires: Asad Rauf *(Pakistan)* (2) and S. A. Bucknor *(West Indies)* (105).
Third umpire: P. T. Manuel *(Sri Lanka)*.   Referee: C. H. Lloyd *(West Indies)* (47).

Close of play: First day, Sri Lanka 160-3 (Samaraweera 33, Jayawardene 17); Second day, Bangladesh 36-3 (Habibul Bashar 13, Tushar Imran 0).

SRI LANKA v BANGLADESH 2005-06 (2nd Test)

At P. Saravanamuttu Stadium, Colombo, on 20, 21, 22 September.
Toss: Sri Lanka.   Result: SRI LANKA won by an innings and 69 runs.
Debuts: none.
Man of the Match: T. T. Samaraweera.   Man of the Series: T. M. Dilshan.

This match followed a depressingly familiar pattern: Bangladesh started promisingly, before being thoroughly outplayed. Sri Lanka wrapped up the match (and the series) before lunch on the third day, as Bangladesh slipped to their fourth consecutive three-day innings defeat. Jayasuriya became the first Sri Lankan to play in 100 Tests, but was not able to celebrate with a century, falling for 13 as Bangladesh's young fast bowlers exploited first-morning juice in the pitch, reducing Sri Lanka to 48 for 4. But the new-ball pair (the only seamers selected) tired, and a hot sun deadened the pitch. Dilshan shrugged off a painful elbow to make 103 in the afternoon session alone: in all he spanked a superb 168 from 179 balls, while Samaraweera collected 138 from 217 balls. Vaas breezed to a half-century, and there was time for Muralitharan to complete 1,000 runs, in his 95th Test. Next day Sri Lanka's bowlers grabbed control, collecting 14 more wickets. The only sustained resistance came from Shahriar Nafees, who made a plucky maiden Test half-century. The impressive Fernando nipped the ball off the seam and bowled with sustained hostility. Mohammad Ashraful dented his figures slightly with a swashbuckling 41-ball 42, before he miscued a cleverly disguised slower delivery. Murali broke the fourth-wicket stand just before the second day ended, and Sri Lanka quickly finished things off next morning. Vaas started the procession, dismissing Ashraful with a legcutter and bowling nightwatchman Shahadat with an in-dipper, then Murali and Herath disposed of the tail.

Sri Lanka

S. T. Jayasuriya lbw b Syed Rasel	13	M. Muralitharan b Shahadat Hossain	24
*M. S. Atapattu c Khaled Mashud b Shahadat Hossain	11	C. R. D. Fernando not out	4
†K. C. Sangakkara b Syed Rasel	5	B 4, l-b 10, w 1, n-b 11	26
D. P. M. D. Jayawardene b Shahadat Hossain	2		
T. T. Samaraweera c Shahriar Nafees b Syed Rasel	138	1/28 (2) 2/28 (1) 3/33 (4) (9 wkts dec.)	457
T. M. Dilshan c Khaled Mashud b Aftab Ahmed	168	4/48 (3) 5/328 (6)	
W. P. U. J. C. Vaas b Syed Rasel	65	6/397 (5) 7/400 (8)	
H. M. R. K. B. Herath		8/453 (9) 9/457 (7)	
lbw b Shahadat Hossain	1		

S. L. Malinga did not bat.

Syed Rasel 21.3–2–129–4; Shahadat Hossain 20–3–108–4; Aftab Ahmed 8–2–33–1; Mohammad Rafique 23–1–92–0; Enamul Haque 18–2–70–0; Mohammad Ashraful 2–0–11–0.

Bangladesh

Javed Omar b Fernando	18	– (2) c Atapattu b Vaas	9
Shahriar Nafees c Sangakkara b Malinga	5	– (4) c Samaraweera b Muralitharan	51
*Habibul Bashar c Vaas b Fernando	18	– c Muralitharan b Fernando	10
Nafis Iqbal c Sangakkara b Fernando	5	– (1) c Sangakkara b Fernando	30
Mohammad Ashraful c Atapattu b Fernando	42	– c Samaraweera b Vaas	26
Aftab Ahmed c Sangakkara b Fernando	23	– (7) c Samaraweera b Herath	25
†Khaled Mashud st Sangakkara b Muralitharan	26	– (8) lbw b Muralitharan	18
Mohammad Rafique c Dilshan b Muralitharan	6	– (9) b Herath	9
Syed Rasel c Vaas b Muralitharan	5	– (10) c Jayasuriya b Herath	1
Shahadat Hossain c Sangakkara b Malinga	7	– (6) b Vaas	1
Enamul Haque, jun. not out	2	– not out	1
B 8, l-b 9, w 1, n-b 16	34	B 7, l-b 3, n-b 6	16

1/16 (2) 2/46 (3) 3/52 (1) 4/72 (4)	191	1/22 (2) 2/44 (3) 3/56 (1)	197
5/115 (5) 6/135 (6) 7/143 (8)		4/131 (4) 5/136 (5) 6/139 (6)	
8/157 (9) 9/166 (10) 10/191 (7)		7/172 (7) 8/194 (8) 9/196 (9) 10/197 (10)	

Vaas 10–0–31–0; Malinga 9–1–32–2; Fernando 11–2–60–5; Muralitharan 14.4–2–47–3; Herath 1–0–4–0. *Second Innings*—Vaas 13–1–36–3; Malinga 7–0–31–0; Fernando 10–0–35–2; Herath 15.4–3–52–3; Muralitharan 14–6–28–2; Dilshan 1–0–5–0.

Umpires: B. F. Bowden *(New Zealand)* (31) and S. A. Bucknor *(West Indies)* (106).
Third umpire: E. A. R. de Silva *(Sri Lanka)*.   Referee: C. H. Lloyd *(West Indies)* (48).

Close of play: First day, Sri Lanka 449-7 (Vaas 61, Muralitharan 24); Second day, Bangladesh 131-4 (Mohammad Ashraful 21, Shahadat Hossain 0).

ZIMBABWE v INDIA 2005-06 (1st Test)

At Queens Sports Club, Bulawayo, on 13, 14, 15, 16 September.
Toss: Zimbabwe.   Result: INDIA won by an innings and 90 runs.
Debuts: Zimbabwe – C. K. Coventry, T. Duffin.
Man of the Match: I. K. Pathan.

Zimbabwe crashed to their seventh successive innings defeat against the senior Test nations. Only in Bangladesh had they avoided this humiliation, losing by a mere 226 runs. They started well enough, reaching their highest total of those seven Tests: left-hander Terry Duffin made a solid 56 on debut, but Taibu was again the backbone of the innings. Next morning, however, Pathan was too good for the tail, then India's openers made a flying start. After lunch, umpire Harper was unwell and had to retire for the rest of the day; he made the "supersub" signal as he handed over to Russell Tiffin. Laxman reached a fine century, looking invulnerable until Ganguly refused his call for a quick single. In his 48th Test as captain – beating the Indian record shared by Sunil Gavaskar and Mohammad Azharuddin – but under fire for poor batting form, Ganguly was taking no chances. He compiled a laborious but determined century in 261 balls, his first in 14 Tests since December 2003. On the way, he passed 5,000 Test runs and spent an hour in the nineties. There were 18 overs left before the close: after 8.1, Zimbabwe were reeling at 18 for 5, four of them to Pathan, swinging the ball superbly again, in 22 balls. In the final over Charles Coventry, another debutant, became Harbhajan Singh's 200th wicket in 46 Tests, an Indian record. He claimed three more next morning, though the remaining four wickets did add 118, with Taibu reaching another fighting fifty.

Zimbabwe

B. R. M. Taylor c Gambhir b Zaheer Khan	13	– lbw b Pathan	4
T. Duffin lbw b Pathan	56	– b Zaheer Khan	2
H. Masakadza c Karthik b Zaheer Khan	14	– c Kumble b Pathan	2
D. D. Ebrahim c and b Pathan	24	– b Pathan	1
*†T. Taibu not out	71	– c Karthik b Kumble	52
H. H. Streak c Dravid b Kumble	27	– lbw b Pathan	0
C. K. Coventry lbw b Kumble	2	– c Gambhir b Harbhajan Singh	24
A. M. Blignaut lbw b Zaheer Khan	4	– b Harbhajan Singh	26
K. M. Dabengwa c Laxman b Pathan	35	– lbw b Harbhajan Singh	16
G. M. Ewing lbw b Pathan	0	– lbw b Harbhajan Singh	34
N. B. Mahwire b Pathan	4	– not out	13
B 1, l-b 7, w 1, n-b 20	29	B 2, w 2, n-b 7	11

1/25 (1) 2/45 (3) 3/119 (2) 4/124 (4)   279
5/193 (6) 6/197 (7) 7/210 (8)
8/269 (9) 9/269 (10) 10/279 (11)

1/4 (1) 2/9 (3) 3/9 (2)   185
4/16 (4) 5/18 (6) 6/67 (7)
7/110 (8) 8/130 (5) 9/138 (9) 10/185 (10)

Pathan 18.5–3–58–5; Zaheer Khan 22–5–74–3; Ganguly 1–1–0–0; Kumble 26–7–71–2; Harbhajan Singh 26–5–55–0; Sehwag 5–1–13–0. *Second Innings*—Pathan 12–4–53–4; Zaheer Khan 8–1–28–1; Harbhajan Singh 15.5–1–59–4; Kumble 12–2–43–1.

India

G. Gambhir c Taylor b Mahwire	46	Harbhajan Singh c Coventry b Mahwire	37
V. Sehwag b Mahwire	44	Zaheer Khan not out	13
R. Dravid c Taylor b Mahwire	77		
V. V. S. Laxman run out	140	L-b 7, w 3, n-b 4	14
*S. C. Ganguly c Duffin b Ewing	101		
Yuvraj Singh b Dabengwa	12	1/88 (2) 2/98 (1) 3/228 (3)	554
†K. D. Karthik c Taibu b Blignaut	1	4/356 (4) 5/372 (6) 6/379 (7)	
I. K. Pathan c and b Dabengwa	52	7/476 (8) 8/502 (5)	
A. Kumble c Coventry b Dabengwa	17	9/522 (9) 10/554 (10)	

Streak 26–3–91–0; Mahwire 25.3–4–92–4; Blignaut 19–2–96–1; Dabengwa 39–7–127–3; Ewing 42–5–141–1.

Umpires: Aleem Dar *(Pakistan)* (23) and D. J. Harper *(Australia)* (52).
R. B. Tiffin deputised for Harper on the second day.
Third umpire: R. B. Tiffin *(Zimbabwe)*.   Referee: M. J. Procter *(South Africa)* (33).

Close of play: First day, Zimbabwe 265-7 (Taibu 61, Dabengwa 35); Second day, India 325-3 (Laxman 125, Ganguly 23); Third day, Zimbabwe 67-6 (Taibu 30).

ZIMBABWE v INDIA 2005-06 (2nd Test)

At Harare Sports Club on 20, 21, 22 September.
Toss: India.   Result: INDIA won by ten wickets.
Debuts: Zimbabwe – W. Mwayenga.
Man of the Match: I. K. Pathan.   Man of the Series: I. K. Pathan.

Zimbabwe finally broke their run of innings defeats, although India still won – their first victory in four Tests at Harare – by ten wickets. When Ganguly chose to bowl first on a grassy pitch, locals feared the worst. Zimbabwe made a predictably poor start: after driving the match's second ball handsomely to the cover boundary, Taylor edged the third to slip. Taibu lasted only two balls, as everyone struggled against Pathan, who used the old ball just as well as the new and finished with career-best figures. Sehwag and Gambhir raced away at a run a ball, and by the close India already led by 34. However, the second day wandered from the script. Tight bowling and fielding kept India down to two an over. Only Pathan and Harbhajan Singh seemed able to handle this unexpectedly controlled bowling and, with Streak taking Test-best figures, the eventual lead was 205. But Zimbabwe collapsed again, and another innings defeat looked inevitable before India's catching suddenly went to pieces. Blignaut, who had taken Zimbabwe's first Test hat-trick in February 2004, enjoyed another sort of hat-trick: he survived three chances in three balls from Zaheer Khan. Pathan finished with 12 for 126, a record for an Indian seamer overseas. After this match Zimbabwe voluntarily withdrew from Test cricket, heading off probable similar action by ICC. By late 2009 there was no immediate prospect of Zimbabwe returning to Test cricket, although they retained full membership of ICC, and all the funding that went with it.

Zimbabwe

B. R. M. Taylor c Dravid b Pathan	4	– lbw b Pathan	4
T. Duffin c Laxman b Pathan	12	– c Dravid b Pathan	10
D. D. Ebrahim c Karthik b Zaheer Khan	14	– c Yuvraj Singh b Zaheer Khan	3
*†T. Taibu c Karthik b Pathan	0	– (5) c Kumble b Zaheer Khan	1
H. Masakadza lbw b Pathan	27	– (4) lbw b Pathan	71
H. H. Streak c Gambhir b Harbhajan Singh	14	– c Laxman b Zaheer Khan	8
C. K. Coventry c Dravid b Harbhajan Singh	37	– c Ganguly b Pathan	25
A. M. Blignaut c Karthik b Pathan	13	– not out	84
K. M. Dabengwa c Laxman b Pathan	18	– c Karthik b Pathan	0
N. B. Mahwire lbw b Pathan	1	– b Kumble	0
W. Mwayenga not out	14	– lbw b Zaheer Khan	1
B 1, l-b 3, w 1, n-b 2	7	B 5, l-b 6, w 2, n-b 3	16

1/4 (1) 2/31 (2) 3/31 (4) 4/31 (3)   **161**   1/13 (2) 2/18 (1) 3/18 (3)   **223**
5/75 (6) 6/83 (5) 7/122 (8)   4/21 (5) 5/42 (6) 6/85 (7)
8/136 (7) 9/138 (10) 10/161 (9)   7/201 (4) 8/201 (9) 9/202 (10) 10/223 (11)

Pathan 15.2–4–59–7; Zaheer Khan 7–1–24–1; Ganguly 4–2–10–0; Kumble 7–1–19–0; Harbhajan Singh 11–3–45–2. *Second Innings*—Pathan 19–3–67–5; Zaheer Khan 19–4–58–4; Harbhajan Singh 5–0–27–0; Kumble 11–3–52–1; Ganguly 1–0–8–0.

India

G. Gambhir c Taibu b Mahwire	97	– not out	1
V. Sehwag c Taibu b Streak	44	– not out	14
R. Dravid b Mahwire	98		
V. V. S. Laxman lbw b Streak	8		
*S. C. Ganguly c Taibu b Mwayenga	16		
Yuvraj Singh b Streak	25		
†K. D. Karthik b Streak	1		
I. K. Pathan c Coventry b Streak	32		
A. Kumble c Ebrahim b Streak	8		
Harbhajan Singh not out	13		
Zaheer Khan c Taibu b Blignaut	3		
B 2, l-b 11, n-b 8	21	B 4	4

1/75 (2) 2/198 (1) 3/219 (4) 4/245 (5)   **366**   (no wkt) **19**
5/306 (6) 6/306 (3) 7/318 (7)
8/342 (9) 9/361 (8) 10/366 (11)

Streak 32–10–73–6; Mahwire 26–5–86–2; Blignaut 19.3–1–80–1; Mwayenga 21–6–79–1; Dabengwa 9–1–35–0. *Second Innings*—Blignaut 1.2–0–6–0; Mahwire 1–0–9–0.

Umpires: Aleem Dar *(Pakistan)* (24) and D. J. Harper *(Australia)* (53).
Third umpire: R. B. Tiffin *(Zimbabwe)*.   Referee: M. J. Procter *(South Africa)* (34).

Close of play: First day, India 195-1 (Gambhir 95, Dravid 49); Second day, Zimbabwe 39-4 (Masakadza 11, Streak 6).

AUSTRALIA v ICC WORLD XI 2005-06 (Only Test)

At Sydney Cricket Ground on 14, 15, 16, 17 October.
Toss: Australia.   Result: AUSTRALIA won by 210 runs.
Debuts: none.
Man of the Match: M. L. Hayden.

The idea was sound enough: match up the world's top-ranked team with the best of the rest. But, short of practice or motivation (or possibly both), the World XI lost all three one-day games of the ICC's so-called "Super Series", then lost the six-day showpiece Test with more than two days to spare against an Australian side itching to prove that their recent Ashes defeat was just a blip. Some statisticians refused to accept this as a Test match (the ICC's own regulations at the time described Tests as contests between nations), but *Wisden*, while not enthused by the idea, accepted the governing body's right to rule on its status. However, the ICC soon went cold on the concept: it was initially trumpeted as a quadrennial jamboree, but there seems no prospect of a repeat. On the field, MacGill took nine wickets to his fellow leg-spinner Warne's six (although Warne was the crucial partnership-breaker in both innings). The World XI, with five of the top six batsmen in the world rankings, survived only 97.1 overs in the match: Hayden batted longer on his own. Clarke became the first man to fall to a bat/pad catch on referral in a Test match (any disputed decisions could be referred to the third umpire). McGrath overtook Courtney Walsh's record of 519 Test wickets by a fast bowler when he removed Lara, who was on the way to a less-welcome record of his own – this was his 55th Test defeat, eclipsing Alec Stewart's old mark.

Australia

J. L. Langer b Harmison	0	– c Smith b Kallis	22
M. L. Hayden c Kallis b Muralitharan	111	– b Harmison	77
*R. T. Ponting c Kallis b Flintoff	46	– c Boucher b Flintoff	54
M. J. Clarke c Sehwag b Vettori	39	– b Harmison	5
S. M. Katich run out	0	– c and b Muralitharan	2
†A. C. Gilchrist lbw b Flintoff	94	– c Kallis b Muralitharan	1
S. R. Watson lbw b Muralitharan	24	– c Boucher b Flintoff	10
S. K. Warne c Kallis b Flintoff	5	– c Dravid b Flintoff	7
B. Lee c Smith b Flintoff	1	– c Muralitharan b Harmison	3
G. D. McGrath run out	0	– c Smith b Muralitharan	2
S. C. G. MacGill not out	0	– not out	0
B 5, l-b 11, w 3, n-b 6	25	B 7, l-b 7, n-b 2	16

1/0 (1) 2/73 (3) 3/154 (4) 4/163 (5)   345   1/30 (1) 2/152 (2) 3/160 (4)   199
5/260 (2) 6/323 (7) 7/331 (6)   4/167 (3) 5/167 (5) 6/170 (6)
8/339 (8) 9/344 (9) 10/345 (10)   7/177 (8) 8/192 (7) 9/195 (10) 10/199 (9)

Harmison 18–3–60–1; Flintoff 18–3–59–4; Kallis 7–1–35–0; Muralitharan 30–3–102–2; Vettori 17–3–73–1. *Second Innings*—Harmison 12.3–2–41–3; Flintoff 16–2–48–3; Kallis 3–1–3–1; Muralitharan 24–5–55–3; Vettori 10–0–38–0.

ICC World XI

*G. C. Smith c Gilchrist b Lee	12	– b McGrath	0
V. Sehwag c Katich b Warne	76	– c Gilchrist b MacGill	7
R. Dravid c Gilchrist b McGrath	0	– c Hayden b Warne	23
B. C. Lara lbw b McGrath	5	– c Gilchrist b Warne	36
J. H. Kallis c Hayden b Warne	44	– not out	39
Inzamam-ul-Haq st Gilchrist b MacGill	1	– lbw b Lee	0
A. Flintoff c Lee b MacGill	35	– c sub (B. J. Hodge) b MacGill	15
†M. V. Boucher c Gilchrist b Warne	0	– c Hayden b Warne	17
D. L. Vettori not out	8	– c Ponting b MacGill	0
S. J. Harmison c Clarke b MacGill	1	– lbw b MacGill	0
M. Muralitharan c Langer b MacGill	2	– st Gilchrist b MacGill	0
B 1, l-b 1, w 1, n-b 3	6	B 1, l-b 2, n-b 4	7

1/27 (1) 2/31 (3) 3/43 (4) 4/134 (2)   190   1/0 (1) 2/18 (2) 3/56 (3)   144
5/135 (6) 6/147 (5) 7/151 (8)   4/69 (4) 5/70 (6) 6/122 (7)
8/183 (7) 9/184 (10) 10/190 (11)   7/143 (8) 8/144 (9) 9/144 (10) 10/144 (11)

McGrath 12–4–34–2; Lee 8–1–54–1; Watson 6–0–38–0; Warne 12–3–23–3; MacGill 9.1–0–39–4. *Second Innings*—McGrath 6–3–8–1; Lee 10–2–42–1; Warne 19–4–48–3; MacGill 15–4–43–5.

Umpires: R. E. Koertzen *(South Africa)* (66) and S. J. A. Taufel *(Australia)* (27).
Third umpire: D. B. Hair *(Australia)*.   Referee: R. S. Madugalle *(Sri Lanka)* (80).

Close of play: First day, Australia 331-6 (Gilchrist 94, Warne 1); Second day, Australia 66-1 (Hayden 27, Ponting 17); Third day, ICC World XI 25-2 (Dravid 17, Lara 0).

AUSTRALIA v WEST INDIES 2005-06 (1st Test)

At Woolloongabba, Brisbane, on 3, 4, 5, 6 November.
Toss: West Indies.   Result: AUSTRALIA won by 379 runs.
Debuts: Australia – M. E. K. Hussey.
Man of the Match: R. T. Ponting.

Australia had few problems in completing a ruthless victory (their 46th, against 32 defeats) in their 100th Test against West Indies. Ponting, criticised during the Ashes defeat, recaptured his authority by scoring twin centuries, covering the cracks forming in an uncertain middle order in the first innings. Chanderpaul had gambled by sending in Australia's first new opening partnership since The Oval 2001: with Justin Langer injured (broken rib), Michael Hussey won his first cap after 15,313 first-class runs, an Australian record. Collymore took three wickets in three overs after lunch, but Ponting calmly rescued his side from 111 for 4, putting on 104 with Gilchrist, then healthy contributions from the lower order pushed Australia to 435, a comfortable position reinforced when West Indies lost their last eight wickets for 76 after Smith's defiant four-hour rearguard; McGrath became the first bowler to take 100 wickets against West Indies. Australia's aversion to enforcing the follow-on, dating from the 2000-01 Kolkata defeat, persuaded Ponting to demand an unassailable buffer, and Hayden squeezed his third century in as many matches, against sloppy fielding and even sloppier bowling. Ponting eventually declared before the fourth day started, having passed Greg Chappell's 24 Test hundreds. Set a notional 509 for victory – or two days of obduracy for a draw – West Indies succumbed to Lee's first five-for in four years, and the swing of Bracken: they kept McGrath and Warne both wicketless for the first time in the 157 completed innings in which they had bowled together.

Australia

M. L. Hayden lbw b Collymore	37	– (2) c Sarwan b Gayle	118
M. E. K. Hussey c Ramdin b Powell	1	– (1) c Collymore b Gayle	29
*R. T. Ponting c Sarwan b Lawson	149	– not out	104
M. J. Clarke c Ramdin b Collymore	5	– not out	14
S. M. Katich c Gayle b Collymore	0		
†A. C. Gilchrist lbw b Collymore	44		
S. R. Watson lbw b Edwards	16		
S. K. Warne c Ramdin b Powell	47		
B. Lee c Collymore b Powell	47		
N. W. Bracken c Sarwan b Edwards	37		
G. D. McGrath not out	6		
B 5, l-b 13, w 6, n-b 22	46	B 6, l-b 3, w 1, n-b 8	18

1/9 (2) 2/101 (1) 3/108 (4) 4/111 (5)   435   1/71 (1) 2/258 (2)   (2 wkts dec.) 283
5/215 (6) 6/273 (7) 7/294 (3)
8/369 (8) 9/417 (9) 10/435 (10)

Edwards 21.3–1–94–2; Powell 20–1–100–3; Collymore 26–4–72–4; Lawson 14–0–73–1; Samuels 4–0–29–0; Gayle 20–3–49–0. *Second Innings*—Edwards 5–0–27–0; Powell 5–1–24–0; Lawson 6–0–47–0; Collymore 11–0–56–0; Gayle 27–4–74–2; Samuels 12–1–46–0.

West Indies

C. H. Gayle c Gilchrist b McGrath	10	– c Warne b Watson	33
D. S. Smith b McGrath	88	– c Warne b Lee	3
R. R. Sarwan c Gilchrist b McGrath	21	– c Gilchrist b Lee	31
B. C. Lara lbw b Lee	30	– c Hayden b Bracken	14
*S. Chanderpaul c Bracken b Warne	2	– lbw b Bracken	7
M. N. Samuels c Gilchrist b McGrath	5	– not out	17
†D. Ramdin not out	37	– c Gilchrist b Lee	6
D. B. Powell c Gilchrist b Warne	4	– lbw b Bracken	0
F. H. Edwards b Warne	2	– b Bracken	0
C. D. Collymore c Clarke b Warne	0	– lbw b Lee	4
J. J. C. Lawson lbw b Warne	0	– b Lee	1
L-b 7, w 1, n-b 3	11	L-b 3, n-b 10	13

1/20 (1) 2/74 (3) 3/134 (4) 4/149 (5)   210   1/11 (2) 2/53 (1) 3/85 (4)   129
5/161 (6) 6/174 (2) 7/187 (8)   4/99 (5) 5/99 (3) 6/105 (7)
8/204 (9) 9/210 (10) 10/210 (11)   7/106 (8) 8/106 (9) 9/114 (10) 10/129 (11)

McGrath 22–3–72–4; Lee 15–4–59–1; Bracken 10–4–23–0; Warne 28–9–48–5; Clarke 2–1–1–0. *Second Innings*—McGrath 11–3–22–0; Lee 14–4–30–5; Watson 6–0–25–1; Bracken 16–3–48–4; Warne 2–1–1–0.

Umpires: I. L. Howell *(South Africa)* (3) and R. E. Koertzen *(South Africa)* (67).
Third umpire: P. D. Parker *(Australia)*.   Referee: M. J. Procter *(South Africa)* (35).

Close of play: First day, Australia 340-7 (Warne 31, Lee 19); Second day, West Indies 182-6 (Ramdin 12, Powell 4); Third day, Australia 283-2 (Ponting 104, Clarke 14).

AUSTRALIA v WEST INDIES 2005-06 (2nd Test)

At Bellerive Oval, Hobart, on 17, 18, 19, 20, 21 November.
Toss: West Indies.   Result: AUSTRALIA won by nine wickets.
Debuts: Australia – B. J. Hodge.
Man of the Match: M. E. K. Hussey.

Australia seemed set for another comfortable victory before the Trinidadian pair of Bravo and Ramdin put on 182; the result did eventually go Australia's way, but they had to toil significantly harder than at Brisbane to seal the Frank Worrell Trophy for the sixth consecutive series. West Indies were still 117 from avoiding an innings defeat when Bravo and Ramdin came together, for a refreshing seventh-wicket stand that pushed the match into the fifth day. West Indies' performance over the first three days was less impressive. Chanderpaul won the toss, but his team crumbled for 149 on a friendly surface. Gayle top-scored, despite retiring at 18 for medical attention after dizzy spells caused by an irregular heartbeat. Australia's openers responded with 231 at more than four an over; Hussey made his maiden century in Tests, Hayden the fourth in his last four. West Indies fought back with six wickets in the third day's extended opening session, but Hodge settled the nerves with a composed debut half-century, and Australia ended up 257 ahead. The recovery gained by the West Indian bowlers was quickly wasted by their batsmen. Both openers failed to survive a niggardly opening spell from McGrath (whose 48 overs in the match cost him only 60 runs), and the only hope seemed to be a big innings from Lara. He became Test cricket's second-highest runscorer, passing Steve Waugh's 10,927 runs when 12, but at 45 umpire Koertzen gave him out caught behind when bat missed ball but brushed pad.

West Indies

C. H. Gayle lbw b McGrath	56	– b McGrath		4
D. S. Smith b Lee	4	– c Ponting b McGrath		8
R. R. Sarwan c Gilchrist b McGrath	2	– c Gilchrist b Lee		32
B. C. Lara lbw b Lee	13	– c Gilchrist b Warne		45
*S. Chanderpaul c Hodge b MacGill	39	– c Gilchrist b Lee		10
M. N. Samuels c Gilchrist b McGrath	5	– c Hodge b Warne		29
D. J. Bravo c Hodge b MacGill	3	– b Warne		113
†D. Ramdin c Warne b MacGill	2	– c Warne b MacGill		71
D. B. Powell c Gilchrist b Lee	15	– lbw b MacGill		0
F. H. Edwards c Symonds b McGrath	0	– not out		2
C. D. Collymore not out	3	– c Gilchrist b Warne		0
L-b 3, w 1, n-b 3	7	B 4, l-b 12, w 1, n-b 3		20

1/15 (2) 2/26 (3) 3/60 (4) 4/119 (5)   149   1/4 (1) 2/27 (2) 3/62 (3)   334
5/119 (1) 6/124 (7) 7/126 (8)   4/76 (5) 5/133 (4) 6/140 (6)
8/130 (6) 9/141 (10) 10/149 (9)   7/322 (8) 8/326 (9) 9/332 (7) 10/334 (11)

In the first innings Gayle, when 18, retired ill at 24 and resumed at 60.

McGrath 23–9–31–4; Lee 13.3–6–32–3; Symonds 10–4–17–0; Warne 11–2–48–0; MacGill 11–3–18–3. *Second Innings*—McGrath 25–13–29–2; Lee 27–4–99–2; Symonds 5–1–9–0; Warne 39–4–112–4; MacGill 26–4–69–2.

Australia

M. L. Hayden c Bravo b Collymore	110	– (2) c Smith b Gayle		46
M. E. K. Hussey c Sarwan b Bravo	137	– (1) not out		31
*R. T. Ponting b Edwards	17	– not out		0
M. J. Clarke c sub (D. R. Smith) b Edwards	5			
B. J. Hodge lbw b Collymore	60			
A. Symonds run out	1			
†A. C. Gilchrist c sub (D. R. Smith) b Bravo	2			
S. K. Warne c Sarwan b Powell	1			
B. Lee c Ramdin b Edwards	18			
S. C. G. MacGill not out	20			
G. D. McGrath run out	14			
L-b 6, w 3, n-b 12	21	N-b 1		1

1/231 (1) 2/257 (3) 3/271 (4) 4/306 (2)   406   1/77 (2)   (1 wkt) 78
5/315 (6) 6/317 (7) 7/324 (8)
8/362 (9) 9/377 (5) 10/406 (11)

Edwards 27.4–2–116–3; Powell 24–2–117–1; Collymore 28–11–54–2; Bravo 23–2–96–2; Gayle 7–0–17–0. *Second Innings*—Edwards 5–1–16–0; Powell 7–1–21–0; Bravo 7–1–21–0; Gayle 6–2–16–1; Sarwan 1.1–0–4–0.

Umpires: Aleem Dar *(Pakistan)* (25) and R. E. Koertzen *(South Africa)* (68).
Third umpire: S. J. Davis *(Australia)*.   Referee: M. J. Procter *(South Africa)* (36).

Close of play: First day, Australia 60-0 (Hayden 31, Hussey 26); Second day, Australia 256-1 (Hussey 116, Ponting 17); Third day, West Indies 82-4 (Lara 18, Samuels 2); Fourth day, West Indies 334.

AUSTRALIA v WEST INDIES 2005-06 (3rd Test)

At Adelaide Oval on 25, 26, 27, 28, 29 November.
Toss: West Indies.　　Result: AUSTRALIA won by seven wickets.
Debuts: none.
Man of the Match: B. C. Lara.　　Man of the Series: M. L. Hayden.

Brian Lara added yet another record to his bulging individual collection when he became the highest Test run-scorer. He overtook Allan Border's 11,174 runs at 11.22 a.m. on the second day, paddle-sweeping McGrath to fine leg for a single to take him to 214 of his eventual 226. His 405-minute 298-ball masterclass contained a mix of delightful swings between point and cover, clever innovation against the spinners, extended periods of resolute defence as he fought to repel the opposition, and occasional flinches to short ones from McGrath and Symonds. But still it wasn't enough: the next-best score was 34, and West Indies lost again. It was only the 14th time a Test double-century had not prevented defeat, and Lara was responsible for three of those. Only one higher score had been made in a losing cause, Ponting's 242 against India at Adelaide two seasons earlier. It was Lara's 31st Test century, and his eighth double: only Don Bradman (12) made more. Australia were indebted to Hussey, who rescued them from 295 for 8 (110 behind) with a superb century, despite having only 35 when joined by No. 10 MacGill. A probable deficit became a narrow lead, then Lee and Warne – helped by contentious decisions against Sarwan and Dwayne Smith – shot West Indies out for 204. Australia needed 182 to complete West Indies' 35th defeat in their last 39 overseas Tests, excluding six in Bangladesh and Zimbabwe – and were made to work through three sessions to seal their series clean sweep.

West Indies

W. W. Hinds c Hayden b Lee	10	– st Gilchrist b Warne	15
D. S. Smith c Hayden b Lee	7	– c Ponting b Lee	0
R. R. Sarwan c Symonds b Lee	16	– lbw b Lee	62
B. C. Lara b McGrath	226	– (5) c Hayden b Warne	17
*S. Chanderpaul c Gilchrist b Symonds	25	– (6) c Hodge b Warne	4
D. J. Bravo c Ponting b MacGill	34	– (7) b Lee	64
D. R. Smith c Symonds b MacGill	14	– (8) lbw b Warne	0
†D. Ramdin lbw b McGrath	27	– (9) c Gilchrist b Warne	28
D. B. Powell lbw b McGrath	14	– (4) b Warne	2
F. H. Edwards c Hayden b Warne	10	– c Warne b Lee	9
C. D. Collymore not out	5	– not out	1
B 2, l-b 5, w 1, n-b 9	17	L-b 2	2

1/16 (1) 2/19 (2) 3/53 (3) 4/121 (5)　　　405　　1/2 (2) 2/60 (1) 3/72 (4)　　　204
5/237 (6) 6/263 (7) 7/333 (8)　　　　　　　　　4/96 (5) 5/96 (3) 6/106 (6)
8/381 (4) 9/388 (9) 10/405 (10)　　　　　　　　7/106 (8) 8/160 (9) 9/203 (7) 10/204 (10)

McGrath 30–3–106–3; Lee 28–3–111–3; Symonds 16–5–44–1; Warne 19.2–2–77–1; MacGill 18–3–60–2. *Second Innings*—McGrath 18–8–25–0; Lee 17–5–46–4; Symonds 2–0–9–0; Warne 33–9–80–6; MacGill 11–2–42–0.

Australia

J. L. Langer c Ramdin b Edwards	99	– c D. R. Smith b Collymore	20
M. L. Hayden c Chanderpaul b Bravo	47	– not out	87
*R. T. Ponting lbw b Bravo	56	– c Sarwan b Collymore	3
B. J. Hodge lbw b Edwards	18	– c D. R. Smith b Powell	23
M. E. K. Hussey not out	133	– not out	30
A. Symonds b Bravo	9		
†A. C. Gilchrist c Chanderpaul b Bravo	6		
S. K. Warne c and b Bravo	0		
B. Lee c Ramdin b Bravo	9		
S. C. G. MacGill b Edwards	22		
G. D. McGrath b D. R. Smith	5		
L-b 7, w 2, n-b 15	24	L-b 3, w 1, n-b 15	19

1/97 (2) 2/211 (3) 3/228 (1) 4/238 (4)　　　428　　1/51 (1) 2/55 (3)　　　(3 wkts)　182
5/271 (6) 6/277 (7) 7/277 (8)　　　　　　　　　3/110 (4)
8/295 (9) 9/388 (10) 10/428 (11)

Edwards 23–4–114–3; Powell 24–6–80–0; Collymore 23–1–59–0; Bravo 27–7–84–6; D. R. Smith 17.3–3–59–1; Hinds 9–1–25–0. *Second Innings*—Edwards 11–1–52–0; Powell 14–2–40–1; Collymore 20–6–51–2; Sarwan 12–2–35–0; D. R. Smith 1–0–1–0.

Umpires: Aleem Dar *(Pakistan)* (26) and B. F. Bowden *(New Zealand)* (32).
Third umpire: S. J. Davis *(Australia)*.　　Referee: M. J. Procter *(South Africa)* (37).

Close of play: First day, West Indies 352-7 (Lara 202, Powell 7); Second day, Australia 229-3 (Hodge 13, Hussey 0); Third day, West Indies 68-2 (Sarwan 53, Powell 0); Fourth day, Australia 76-2 (Hayden 38, Hodge 10).

PAKISTAN v ENGLAND 2005-06 (1st Test)

At Multan Cricket Stadium on 12, 13, 14, 15, 16 November.
Toss: Pakistan.   Result: PAKISTAN won by 22 runs.
Debuts: England – S. D. Udal. For Pakistan, Mohammad Yousuf played his first Test since changing his name from Yousuf Youhana on becoming a Muslim.
Man of the Match: Salman Butt.

England's 2005 Ashes campaign had suggested they had the mental strength to take on all comers, but it was Pakistan – supposedly more flaky – who came through under pressure, squeaking to victory early on the final afternoon. The pivotal passage of play came earlier that day, when England, chasing 198, lost five wickets in ten overs. Such a result looked far-fetched after England's pacemen combined well to dismiss Pakistan for 274 on a glorious batting surface, before Trescothick – captaining because Vaughan had damaged his right knee – made a superb 193. Salman Butt, who batted for 403 minutes, put Pakistan back in front, but Inzamam-ul-Haq fell to the second new ball as the last seven wickets added only 75. England should have overhauled their modest target on a benign surface, and looked like doing so at 64 for 1. Then three wickets fell in eight balls, starting with Bell, looking to be too aggressive against Danish Kaneria. Flintoff swiped straight to deep midwicket, while Pietersen flailed at a very wide delivery. Jones got England within 32 before he was bowled off bat and pad, and it was all over ten balls later. Pakistan's only disappointment was that the bowling actions of Shabbir Ahmed and Shoaib Malik were reported as suspect. Shaun Udal, at 36 years 239 days, was England's oldest debutant since John Childs in 1988. His first wicket was unusual: Butt's thick edge flew through Trescothick's hands at slip, pinged off his forehead and was well taken by the alert Jones.

Pakistan

Shoaib Malik lbw b Flintoff	39	– c Trescothick b Harmison	18
Salman Butt c Jones b Udal	74	– c Jones b Hoggard	122
Younis Khan lbw b Harmison	39	– c Trescothick b Flintoff	48
Mohammad Yousuf b Flintoff	5	– (6) c Bell b Flintoff	16
*Inzamam-ul-Haq c Strauss b Flintoff	53	– lbw b Hoggard	72
Hasan Raza b Harmison	0	– (7) c Trescothick b Flintoff	1
†Kamran Akmal c Trescothick b Hoggard	28	– (8) c Pietersen b Harmison	33
Mohammad Sami c Jones b Hoggard	1	– (4) c Jones b Flintoff	3
Shoaib Akhtar not out	10	– c Bell b Giles	11
Shabbir Ahmed b Flintoff	0	– c Jones b Harmison	0
Danish Kaneria c Giles b Harmison	6	– not out	1
B 1, l-b 7, n-b 11	19	L-b 6, n-b 10	16

1/80 (1) 2/161 (2) 3/166 (4) 4/181 (3)   274   1/31 (1) 2/124 (3) 3/131 (4)   341
5/183 (6) 6/238 (7) 7/244 (8)   4/266 (5) 5/285 (6) 6/291 (7)
8/260 (5) 9/260 (10) 10/274 (11)   7/295 (2) 8/331 (9) 9/332 (10) 10/341 (8)

Hoggard 22–4–55–2; Harmison 16.2–5–37–3; Flintoff 23–6–68–4; Collingwood 4–1–15–0; Giles 16–3–44–0; Udal 17–3–47–1. *Second Innings*—Hoggard 27–2–81–2; Flintoff 25–3–88–4; Harmison 19.5–3–52–3; Udal 12–1–47–0; Giles 22–2–67–1.

England

*M. E. Trescothick c Kamran Akmal b Shabbir Ahmed	193	– b Shabbir Ahmed	5
A. J. Strauss lbw b Mohammad Sami	9	– c Hasan Raza b Danish Kaneria	23
I. R. Bell c Salman Butt b Shoaib Malik	71	– c Kamran Akmal b Danish Kaneria	31
P. D. Collingwood c Kamran Akmal b Shabbir Ahmed	10	– lbw b Mohammad Sami	3
M. J. Hoggard c Kamran Akmal b Shoaib Akhtar	1	– (10) not out	0
K. P. Pietersen c Salman Butt b Danish Kaneria	5	– (5) c Kamran Akmal b Mohammad Sami	19
A. Flintoff c Shoaib Malik b Shoaib Akhtar	45	– (6) c Younis Khan b Danish Kaneria	11
†G. O. Jones b Shabbir Ahmed	22	– (7) b Shoaib Akhtar	33
A. F. Giles c Hasan Raza b Shabbir Ahmed	16	– (8) b Shoaib Akhtar	14
S. D. Udal lbw b Shoaib Akhtar	0	– (9) b Danish Kaneria	18
S. J. Harmison not out	4	– c Younis Khan b Shoaib Akhtar	9
B 8, l-b 11, w 1, n-b 22	42	B 6, l-b 1, n-b 2	9

1/18 (2) 2/198 (3) 3/251 (4) 4/266 (5)   418   1/7 (1) 2/64 (3) 3/67 (2)   175
5/271 (6) 6/364 (7) 7/388 (1)   4/67 (4) 5/93 (6) 6/101 (5)
8/399 (8) 9/400 (10) 10/418 (9)   7/117 (8) 8/166 (7) 9/166 (9) 10/175 (11)

Shoaib Akhtar 27–2–99–3; Mohammad Sami 16–1–76–1; Shabbir Ahmed 22.4–7–54–4; Danish Kaneria 27–4–106–1; Shoaib Malik 18–1–64–1. *Second Innings*—Shoaib Akhtar 12.4–1–49–3; Shabbir Ahmed 10–0–25–1; Danish Kaneria 20–0–62–4; Mohammad Sami 9–0–31–2; Shoaib Malik 1–0–1–0.

Umpires: B. F. Bowden *(New Zealand)* (33) and S. J. A. Taufel *(Australia)* (28).
Third umpire: Asad Rauf *(Pakistan)*.   Referee: R. S. Mahanama *(Sri Lanka)* (5).

Close of play: First day, Pakistan 244-6 (Inzamam-ul-Haq 41, Mohammad Sami 1); Second day, England 253-3 (Trescothick 135, Hoggard 0); Third day, Pakistan 125-2 (Salman Butt 53, Mohammad Sami 0); Fourth day, England 24-1 (Strauss 7, Bell 12).

PAKISTAN v ENGLAND 2005-06 (2nd Test)

At Iqbal Stadium, Faisalabad, on 20, 21, 22, 23, 24 November.
Toss: Pakistan.   Result: MATCH DRAWN.
Debuts: none.
Man of the Match: Inzamam-ul-Haq.

This was a mini-epic, offering incident, honest battle, and an occasionally electric ambience. Twenty-five minutes into the final afternoon, a result beckoned. Shoaib Akhtar and Naved-ul-Hasan dismissed England's top four in six overs, three of them for ducks. But, with bad light helping – it ended play early every day, costing 55 overs in all – the later batsmen bravely clawed their way to safety, ensuring that England's fourth Test at Faisalabad was, like the other three, drawn. Pakistan had made an uncertain start: Inzamam-ul-Haq crept to 38 in 37 overs by tea on the first day, while Mohammad Yousuf batted more than three hours. Shahid Afridi upped the tempo with 92 from 85 balls, with six sixes, while Inzamam completed his 23rd Test century – equalling Javed Miandad's Pakistan record – before he was erroneously given out while taking evasive action to avoid the bowler Harmison's reflex throw at the stumps. During a hold-up after a gas canister exploded in the stands, Afridi pirouetted on the pitch, trying to scuff it up for the spinners; but he was spotted, and banned from the next Test. Pietersen and Bell stabilised the reply by adding 154, and England finished only 16 behind. Pakistan dawdled to 108 for 3 in 42 overs, then a clatter of wickets endangered them before Inzamam compiled a masterful second century of the match before declaring, 284 ahead. He had removed defeat from the equation, and four quick wickets suggested that more urgency by his earlier batsmen might have brought victory.

Pakistan

Shoaib Malik c Flintoff b Hoggard	27	– c Bell b Flintoff	26
Salman Butt c Jones b Harmison	26	– lbw b Udal	50
Younis Khan c Pietersen b Flintoff	7	– lbw b Hoggard	27
Mohammad Yousuf c and b Bell	78	– b Flintoff	20
*Inzamam-ul-Haq run out	109	– not out	100
Shahid Afridi c Trescothick b Hoggard	92	– b Flintoff	0
†Kamran Akmal c Jones b Giles	41	– c Jones b Harmison	9
Naved-ul-Hasan b Harmison	25	– c Jones b Harmison	1
Mohammad Sami c and b Giles	18	– (10) lbw b Hoggard	5
Shoaib Akhtar c Flintoff b Harmison	12	– (9) c Jones b Hoggard	14
Danish Kaneria not out	4	– not out	2
B 5, l-b 3, n-b 15	23	B 4, l-b 5, w 2, n-b 3	14

1/53 (2) 2/63 (3) 3/73 (1) 4/201 (4)   462   1/54 (1) 2/104 (3)   (9 wkts dec.) 268
5/346 (6) 6/369 (5) 7/403 (8)   3/108 (2) 4/164 (4)
8/431 (9) 9/446 (7) 10/462 (10)   5/164 (6) 6/183 (7) 7/187 (8) 8/234 (9) 9/244 (10)

Hoggard 22–0–115–2; Flintoff 29–2–76–1; Giles 20–1–85–2; Harmison 24.4–5–85–3; Udal 13–1–60–0; Bell 7–1–33–1. *Second Innings*—Hoggard 16–1–50–3; Flintoff 27.1–2–66–3; Harmison 19–2–61–2; Giles 17–3–51–0; Udal 14–2–31–1.

England

M. E. Trescothick c Kamran Akmal b Mohammad Sami	48	– b Shoaib Akhtar	0
A. J. Strauss b Naved-ul-Hasan	12	– b Naved-ul-Hasan	0
*M. P. Vaughan b Naved-ul-Hasan	2	– lbw b Naved-ul-Hasan	9
I. R. Bell c Kamran Akmal b Shahid Afridi	115	– c Kamran Akmal b Shoaib Akhtar	0
K. P. Pietersen c Mohammad Yousuf b Shoaib Akhtar	100	– c sub (Asim Kamal) b Naved-ul-Hasan	42
A. Flintoff b Shoaib Akhtar	1	– c sub (Hasan Raza) b Shoaib Akhtar	56
†G. O. Jones lbw b Shahid Afridi	55	– not out	30
A. F. Giles b Shahid Afridi	26	– not out	13
S. D. Udal not out	33		
M. J. Hoggard b Shahid Afridi	2		
S. J. Harmison run out	16		
B 1, l-b 12, w 1, n-b 22	36	B 4, l-b 8, n-b 2	14

1/33 (2) 2/39 (3) 3/107 (1) 4/261 (5)   446   1/1 (1) 2/5 (2)   (6 wkts) 164
5/272 (6) 6/327 (4) 7/378 (7)   3/10 (4) 4/20 (3)
8/395 (8) 9/399 (10) 10/446 (11)   5/100 (5) 6/138 (6)

Shoaib Akhtar 27–4–93–2; Naved-ul-Hasan 20–2–63–2; Mohammad Sami 19–4–51–1; Shahid Afridi 30.3–3–95–4; Danish Kaneria 32–3–102–0; Shoaib Malik 4–0–29–0. *Second Innings*—Shoaib Akhtar 11–2–61–3; Naved-ul-Hasan 12–3–30–3; Mohammad Sami 6–1–18–0; Danish Kaneria 12–4–27–0; Shahid Afridi 7–2–16–0.

Umpires: D. B. Hair *(Australia)* (67) and S. J. A. Taufel *(Australia)* (29).
Third umpire: Nadeem Ghauri *(Pakistan)*.   Referee: R. S. Mahanama *(Sri Lanka)* (6).

Close of play: First day, Pakistan 300-4 (Inzamam-ul-Haq 80, Shahid Afridi 67); Second day, England 113-3 (Bell 36, Pietersen 4); Third day, England 391-7 (Giles 23, Udal 6); Fourth day, Pakistan 183-6 (Inzamam-ul-Haq 41, Naved-ul-Hasan 0).

PAKISTAN v ENGLAND 2005-06 (3rd Test)

At Gaddafi Stadium, Lahore, on 29, 30 November, 1, 2, 3 December.
Toss: England.   Result: PAKISTAN won by an innings and 100 runs.
Debuts: England – L. E. Plunkett.
Man of the Match: Mohammad Yousuf.   Man of the Series: Inzamam-ul-Haq.

England were inching towards a draw on the final day – but then, after lunch, eight wickets tumbled for 43 in just 70 minutes, so their Ashes-winning year ended on a low note. The win was concocted by Shoaib Akhtar, who combined extreme pace and a near-unreadable slower ball, and the legspinner Danish Kaneria. England's batting at the end was abject, but not especially incompetent. Their real disaster had come on the first day, when they squandered a good start after winning the toss at last, and were bowled out for 288. For a while, it seemed this might be a passable score, but it gradually became clear that a series-levelling victory was unattainable; in the end, a draw proved elusive too. Vaughan and Trescothick had to endure a difficult opening session on a juicy pitch. They came through it, putting on 101, but the later batsmen wasted that foundation. The exception was Collingwood, with the first of two four-hour vigils, neither of which quite brought him a maiden century. Hoggard reduced Pakistan to 12 for 2, but Mohammad Yousuf grafted 602 minutes for 223, his first Test century as a Muslim. He put on 269, a Pakistan sixth-wicket record, with Kamran Akmal, before Inzamam-ul-Haq, returning after being hit on the forearm, threatened a third successive century. England had around five sessions to survive, but lost two quick wickets. Bell and Collingwood dug in for another four-hour rearguard, before the sudden torrent of wickets gave Pakistan the series 2–0.

England

M. E. Trescothick c Kamran Akmal b Shoaib Malik	50	– lbw b Shoaib Akhtar	0
*M. P. Vaughan c Mohammad Yousuf b Shoaib Malik	58	– c and b Shoaib Akhtar	13
I. R. Bell c Mohammad Yousuf b Shoaib Malik	4	– lbw b Shoaib Akhtar	92
P. D. Collingwood c Danish Kaneria b Shoaib Akhtar	96	– c Hasan Raza b Danish Kaneria	80
K. P. Pietersen c Kamran Akmal b Naved-ul-Hasan	34	– c Hasan Raza b Danish Kaneria	1
A. Flintoff c Shoaib Akhtar b Naved-ul-Hasan	12	– b Danish Kaneria	0
†G. O. Jones b Danish Kaneria	4	– lbw b Shoaib Akhtar	5
S. D. Udal c Asim Kamal b Danish Kaneria	10	– c Salman Butt b Mohammad Sami	25
L. E. Plunkett b Mohammad Sami	9	– lbw b Shoaib Akhtar	0
M. J. Hoggard not out	1	– b Danish Kaneria	0
S. J. Harmison c Kamran Akmal b Mohammad Sami	0	– not out	0
L-b 5, n-b 5	10	B 13, l-b 9, w 1, n-b 9	32

1/101 (2) 2/114 (3) 3/115 (1) 4/183 (5)   288   1/0 (1) 2/30 (2) 3/205 (4)   248
5/201 (6) 6/225 (7) 7/249 (8)   4/212 (5) 5/212 (6) 6/212 (3)
8/280 (4) 9/288 (9) 10/288 (11)   7/227 (7) 8/227 (9) 9/248 (8) 10/248 (10)

Shoaib Akhtar 22–6–45–1; Naved-ul-Hasan 20–3–76–2; Mohammad Sami 18–2–57–2; Shoaib Malik 14–1–58–3; Danish Kaneria 20–2–47–2. *Second Innings*—Shoaib Akhtar 19–3–71–5; Naved-ul-Hasan 16–3–55–0; Mohammad Sami 16–4–39–1; Shoaib Malik 4–2–9–0; Danish Kaneria 22.1–8–52–4.

Pakistan

Shoaib Malik c Plunkett b Hoggard	0	Naved-ul-Hasan not out	42
Salman Butt c Jones b Plunkett	28		
Asim Kamal lbw b Hoggard	5	B 5, l-b 12, w 4, n-b 7	28
Mohammad Yousuf c Pietersen b Udal	223		
*Inzamam-ul-Haq run out	97	1/0 (1) 2/12 (3) (8 wkts dec.)	636
Hasan Raza c Flintoff b Harmison	21	3/68 (2) 4/180 (6)	
Shoaib Akhtar c Udal b Plunkett	38	5/247 (7) 6/516 (4)	
†Kamran Akmal c Vaughan b Flintoff	154	7/546 (8) 8/636 (5)	

Mohammad Sami and Danish Kaneria did not bat.

Inzamam-ul-Haq, when 35, retired hurt at 148 and resumed at 516.

Hoggard 23–4–106–2; Flintoff 36–8–111–1; Harmison 43–3–154–1; Plunkett 28.2–1–125–2; Udal 18–1–92–1; Collingwood 6–0–22–0; Bell 2–0–9–0.

Umpires: D. B. Hair *(Australia)* (68) and R. E. Koertzen *(South Africa)* (69).
Third umpire: Zamir Haider *(Pakistan)*.   Referee: R. S. Mahanama *(Sri Lanka)* (7).

Close of play: First day, England 248-6 (Collingwood 71, Udal 10); Second day, Pakistan 185-4 (Mohammad Yousuf 84, Shoaib Akhtar 0); Third day, Pakistan 446-5 (Mohammad Yousuf 183, Kamran Akmal 115); Fourth day, England 121-2 (Bell 60, Collingwood 37).

INDIA v SRI LANKA 2005-06 (1st Test)

At M. A. Chidambaram Stadium, Chennai, on 2 *(no play)*, 3 *(no play)*, 4 *(no play)*, 5, 6 December.
Toss: India.   Result: MATCH DRAWN.
Debuts: India – M. S. Dhoni.
Man of the Match: W. P. U. J. C. Vaas.

Cyclone Baaz reduced this Test to a non-event. Chennai had suffered record rains in the month before the match, and the wisdom of scheduling it in a city historically wet at this time of year has to be questioned. There was no play on the first three days, despite the efforts of the groundstaff, and only 32.3 overs on the fourth. It was a pity, as the match had been eagerly awaited, particularly in India, whose deposed captain Ganguly was making a come-back after being left out by coach Greg Chappell. It was also Sri Lanka's first Test in India for eight years, and even in the short amount of play that was possible, Muralitharan – whose wife comes from Chennai – proved a handful. India batted diffidently after winning the toss, scoring at little more than two an over in stumbling to 167 on the undercooked surface, where ankles were in more danger than ribs. The sluggish track made stroke-making almost impossible on the fourth evening, although Sehwag typically hurtled to 36 from just 28 balls. Vaas sent down 11 successive maidens, most of them on the final morning, to India's prime batsmen. He finished with four for 20 from 21 overs, 14 of them maidens. As the sun came out, the pitch eased on the last day, and Sri Lanka hurried to the minor satisfaction of a first-innings lead. They were helped by five penalty runs when an under-edge from Jayawardene eluded Dhoni and hit the helmet behind him.

India

G. Gambhir b Vaas	0	A. Kumble c and b Vaas		9
V. Sehwag c Atapattu b Vaas	36	Harbhajan Singh not out		4
*R. Dravid c Sangakkara b Vaas	32			
S. R. Tendulkar lbw b Muralitharan	22	B 12, l-b 2, n-b 6		20
V. V. S. Laxman run out	5			
S. C. Ganguly c Dilshan b Fernando	5	1/13 (1) 2/45 (2) 3/97 (3)		167
†M. S. Dhoni c Gunawardene b Bandara	30	4/108 (4) 5/109 (5) 6/117 (6)		
I. K. Pathan c and b Muralitharan	0	7/118 (8) 8/128 (9)		
A. B. Agarkar run out	4	9/159 (10) 10/167 (7)		

Vaas 21–14–20–4; Fernando 16–4–58–1; Muralitharan 25–6–60–2; Bandara 11.2–6–15–1.

Sri Lanka

D. A. Gunawardene c Dhoni b Pathan	4	T. M. Dilshan not out		8
†K. C. Sangakkara lbw b Kumble	30			
D. P. M. D. Jayawardene c Gambhir b Kumble	71	W 1, n-b 7, p 5		13
T. T. Samaraweera not out	35			
*M. S. Atapattu b Kumble	7	1/5 (1) 2/62 (2)	(4 wkts)	168
		3/124 (3) 4/158 (5)		

J. Mubarak, W. P. U. J. C. Vaas, C. M. Bandara, M. Muralitharan and C. R. D. Fernando did not bat.

Pathan 7–0–43–1; Agarkar 10–3–29–0; Ganguly 2–0–16–0; Harbhajan Singh 9–2–34–0; Kumble 15–3–41–3.

Umpires: M. R. Benson *(England)* (6) and D. J. Harper *(Australia)* (54).
Third umpire: K. Hariharan *(India)*.   Referee: C. H. Lloyd *(West Indies)* (49).

Close of play: First day, No play; Second day, No play; Third day, No play; Fourth day, India 90-2 (Dravid 30, Tendulkar 11).

INDIA v SRI LANKA 2005-06 (2nd Test)

At Feroz Shah Kotla, Delhi, on 10, 11, 12, 13, 14 December.
Toss: India.   Result: INDIA won by 188 runs.
Debuts: none.
Man of the Match: A. Kumble.

This match will be remembered for Sachin Tendulkar keeping his appointment with destiny, and passing Sunil Gavaskar as Test cricket's leading century-maker. Tendulkar's 35th hundred, in his 125th match – the same number Gavaskar played for his 34 – was his only Test century of 2005. The first half was a lesson in the art of innings-building, but his second fifty passed in a flash, filled with deft strokes, and a doting nation cheered when he turned Vaas to fine leg for the vital single from the last ball before bad light ended the first day's play. Sri Lanka had their moments: Muralitharan claimed five for 23 to send India tail-spinning from 254 for 3 to 290 all out, before Atapattu and Jayawardene took them to 175 for 2. Then, in 45 minutes of madness, Sri Lanka were spun out by Kumble. He sent down 15 overs before his first wicket, but then took three more in his next six. With Sehwag out with a throat infection, Pathan was promoted to open to build quickly on the lead of 60. He was unflustered when Murali shared the new ball with Vaas, who claimed Gambhir as his 300th wicket in his 90th Test. Dravid declared shortly after lunch on the fourth day, setting an unlikely target of 436. Atapattu and Jayawardene again provided most of the resistance, before Sri Lanka collapsed again: Kumble completed his eighth ten-wicket haul in a Test as India won with more than three hours to spare.

India

G. Gambhir lbw b Vaas	2	– lbw b Vaas	3
*R. Dravid c Mubarak b Muralitharan	24	– (5) run out	53
V. V. S. Laxman c Sangakkara b Muralitharan	69	– c Sangakkara b Vaas	11
S. R. Tendulkar lbw b Muralitharan	109	– lbw b Bandara	16
S. C. Ganguly lbw b Muralitharan	40	– (6) b Muralitharan	39
Yuvraj Singh c Mubarak b Bandara	0	– (7) not out	77
†M. S. Dhoni b Muralitharan	5	– (8) not out	51
I. K. Pathan c Mubarak b Muralitharan	0	– (2) c Sangakkara b Fernando	93
A. B. Agarkar not out	14		
A. Kumble b Bandara	8		
Harbhajan Singh b Muralitharan	7		
B 4, l-b 8	12	B 9, l-b 16, n-b 7	32

1/2 (1) 2/56 (2) 3/133 (3) 4/254 (5)   290   1/12 (1) 2/42 (3)   (6 wkts dec.) 375
5/255 (6) 6/255 (4) 7/255 (8)   3/86 (4) 4/178 (2)
8/260 (7) 9/271 (10) 10/290 (11)   5/190 (5) 6/271 (6)

Vaas 22–5–77–1; Fernando 18–5–43–0; Muralitharan 38.4–8–100–7; Bandara 17–1–54–2; Dilshan 1–0–4–0.
Second Innings—Vaas 21–4–65–2; Muralitharan 38–5–118–1; Fernando 22–5–75–1; Bandara 20–2–74–1; Dilshan 4–0–18–0.

Sri Lanka

D. A. Gunawardene lbw b Pathan	25	– lbw b Pathan	9
*M. S. Atapattu c Gambhir b Kumble	88	– c and b Kumble	67
†K. C. Sangakkara c Kumble b Pathan	3	– c Dhoni b Agarkar	33
D. P. M. D. Jayawardene lbw b Kumble	60	– c Gambhir b Harbhajan Singh	67
T. T. Samaraweera b Kumble	1	– (6) c Dravid b Harbhajan Singh	0
T. M. Dilshan lbw b Kumble	0	– (8) b Kumble	32
J. Mubarak not out	29	– lbw b Agarkar	3
W. P. U. J. C. Vaas c Harbhajan Singh b Kumble	2	– (9) c Harbhajan Singh b Kumble	17
C. M. Bandara b Pathan	1	– (5) lbw b Kumble	0
M. Muralitharan b Kumble	9	– c Dhoni b Harbhajan Singh	2
C. R. D. Fernando c Ganguly b Harbhajan Singh	0	– not out	2
B 4, l-b 2, n-b 1, p 5	12	B 2, l-b 7, n-b 6	15

1/54 (1) 2/62 (3) 3/175 (4) 4/179 (5)   230   1/30 (1) 2/109 (3) 3/119 (2)   247
5/179 (6) 6/198 (2) 7/200 (8)   4/119 (5) 5/123 (6) 6/131 (7)
8/204 (9) 9/219 (10) 10/230 (11)   7/199 (8) 8/243 (4) 9/243 (9) 10/247 (10)

Pathan 22–8–34–3; Agarkar 16–4–40–0; Kumble 28–6–72–6; Harbhajan Singh 15.3–0–67–1; Tendulkar 2–0–6–0.
Second Innings—Pathan 14–2–38–1; Agarkar 16–4–45–2; Kumble 36–7–85–4; Harbhajan Singh 25.2–5–70–3.

Umpires: Nadeem Ghauri *(Pakistan)* (3) and S. J. A. Taufel *(Australia)* (30).
Third umpire: A. V. Jayaprakash *(India)*.   Referee: C. H. Lloyd *(West Indies)* (50).

Close of play: First day, India 245-3 (Tendulkar 100, Ganguly 39); Second day, Sri Lanka 198-6 (Mubarak 10); Third day, India 237-5 (Ganguly 22, Yuvraj Singh 28); Fourth day, Sri Lanka 123-5 (Jayawardene 9).

INDIA v SRI LANKA 2005-06 (3rd Test)

At Sardar Patel Stadium, Motera, Ahmedabad, on 18, 19, 20, 21, 22 December.
Toss: India.   Result: INDIA won by 259 runs.
Debuts: Sri Lanka – W. U. Tharanga.
Man of the Match: Harbhajan Singh.   Man of the Series: A. Kumble.

India went into this match in some turmoil: a huge public outcry over the exclusion of Ganguly was followed by Dravid being hospitalised with gastroenteritis, ending a run of 93 consecutive Tests since his debut. But it all ended happily, a comprehensive victory hoisting India above England to second in the Test rankings (their highest position) behind Australia. Sri Lanka again had their moments, chiefly when India were 97 for 5 on the first day. But in his first Test as captain, Sehwag marshalled his resources admirably. Kumble, in his 100th Test, and Harbhajan Singh bowled persistently, taking 17 wickets between them, but the pitch was no dustbowl: if anything, batting became easier as the game progressed. After India won the toss Malinga, playing in place of Vaas who was ill, took two quick wickets, before a sharp catch at short leg accounted for Tendulkar. But then Laxman settled in, batting for more than 6½ hours for his ninth Test century. Sri Lanka were never in the game after collapsing again to concede a lead of 192. Only Dilshan held firm as Harbhajan put some indifferent form behind him to take seven wickets. Then it was India's turn to collapse against the spinners before Yuvraj Singh showed why he had been preferred to Ganguly, with a muscular half-century. Sehwag declared 508 ahead. Sri Lanka fought back, but the relentlessness of the Indian spinners – Kumble took five more wickets, to lift his overall tally 485 – made a difficult task impossible.

India

G. Gambhir c Tharanga b Malinga	19	– (2) c Sangakkara b Muralitharan	30
*V. Sehwag b Malinga	20	– (1) c Maharoof b Malinga	0
V. V. S. Laxman b Maharoof	104	– c Sangakkara b Maharoof	5
S. R. Tendulkar c Mubarak b Muralitharan	23	– lbw b Dilshan	19
Yuvraj Singh c Samaraweera b Muralitharan	0	– c Sangakkara b Bandara	75
M. Kaif c Atapattu b Bandara	4	– lbw b Bandara	9
†M. S. Dhoni lbw b Muralitharan	49	– lbw b Muralitharan	14
I. K. Pathan ibw b Maharoof	82	– b Muralitharan	27
A. B. Agarkar b Malinga	26	– c and b Bandara	48
A. Kumble c Jayawardene b Bandara	21	– not out	29
Harbhajan Singh not out	8	– not out	40
B 15, l-b 13, w 5, n-b 9	42	B 7, l-b 9, w 1, n-b 3	20

1/31 (1) 2/52 (2) 3/88 (4) 4/88 (5) 398   1/0 (1) 2/9 (3)   (9 wkts dec.) 316
5/97 (6) 6/183 (7) 7/308 (3)   3/34 (4) 4/81 (2) 5/100 (6) 6/134 (7)
8/345 (8) 9/384 (9) 10/398 (10)   7/174 (5) 8/198 (8) 9/247 (9)

Malinga 32–4–113–3; Maharoof 27–11–52–2; Muralitharan 36–4–128–3; Bandara 24.4–3–69–2; Dilshan 3–0–8–0. *Second Innings*—Malinga 12–2–63–1; Maharoof 6–0–25–1; Dilshan 12–2–36–1; Muralitharan 21–5–90–3; Bandara 19–2–84–3; Mubarak 1–0–2–0.

Sri Lanka

W. U. Tharanga c Dhoni b Pathan	2	– c Gambhir b Kumble	47
*M. S. Atapattu c Sehwag b Harbhajan Singh	40	– c Kaif b Harbhajan Singh	16
†K. C. Sangakkara b Harbhajan Singh	41	– lbw b Kumble	17
D. P. M. D. Jayawardene c Kaif b Harbhajan Singh	0	– c and b Agarkar	57
T. T. Samaraweera c Kaif b Harbhajan Singh	1	– c Kaif b Kumble	5
T. M. Dilshan c Kaif b Harbhajan Singh	65	– c Dhoni b Pathan	65
J. Mubarak b Kumble	13	– c Laxman b Harbhajan Singh	18
M. F. Maharoof c and b Harbhajan Singh	4	– lbw b Kumble	2
C. M. Bandara not out	28	– c Sehwag b Kumble	11
M. Muralitharan st Dhoni b Kumble	3	– b Harbhajan Singh	3
S. L. Malinga c Sehwag b Harbhajan Singh	0	– not out	0
B 1, l-b 2, n-b 6	9	B 1, n-b 7	8

1/14 (1) 2/74 (2) 3/74 (4) 4/82 (5) 206   1/39 (2) 2/84 (3) 3/89 (1)   249
5/105 (3) 6/144 (7) 7/155 (8)   4/96 (5) 5/201 (4) 6/229 (6)
8/198 (6) 9/201 (10) 10/206 (11)   7/235 (8) 8/235 (7) 9/245 (10) 10/249 (9)

Pathan 10–1–36–1; Agarkar 6–2–18–0; Kumble 25–3–87–2; Harbhajan Singh 22.2–3–62–7. *Second Innings*— Pathan 9–1–31–1; Harbhajan Singh 31–7–79–3; Agarkar 11–3–18–1; Kumble 34.3–9–89–5; Sehwag 3–0–18–0; Tendulkar 4–0–13–0.

Umpires: B. F. Bowden *(New Zealand)* (34) and Nadeem Ghauri *(Pakistan)* (4).
Third umpire: I. Shivram *(India)*.   Referee: C. H. Lloyd *(West Indies)* (51).

Close of play: First day, India 247-6 (Laxman 71, Pathan 39); Second day, Sri Lanka 131-5 (Dilshan 27, Mubarak 11); Third day, India 287-9 (Kumble 23, Harbhajan Singh 19); Fourth day, Sri Lanka 235-6 (Mubarak 18, Maharoof 2).

Test No. 1778/72 (A675/SA304)

AUSTRALIA v SOUTH AFRICA 2005-06 (1st Test)

At W. A. C. A. Ground, Perth, on 16, 17, 18, 19, 20 December.
Toss: Australia.   Result: MATCH DRAWN.
Debuts: none.
Man of the Match: B. J. Hodge.

Brad Hodge became only the fifth Australian to turn his maiden Test century into a double, but Ponting delaying his declaration to let him get there might have cost his side victory. It still took a monumental display of concentration from Rudolph (playing only because Kallis had tennis elbow) to save the match: he batted throughout the final day, and more than seven hours in total – but, on a pitch that had become uncharacteristically slow, an extra hour might have made the difference. At the start, Hayden mis-pulled his second ball to gully, and later Langer, Hussey and Symonds donated their wickets with pulls too. South Africa's batting also promised more than it delivered. The openers added 86, but when Warne trapped Prince – his 86th wicket of 2005, breaking Dennis Lillee's calendar-year record from 1981 – they were 187 for 6, still 71 adrift. Boucher's run-a-ball stand of 77 with Pollock ensured a lead, but a modest one. In Australia's second innings Kemp at second slip dropped Hodge off Langeveldt when he had only 13, and when the time came for the team-agreed declaration, 45 minutes before tea, Hodge had 176. Ponting allowed him to continue, easing South Africa's task: they had 132 overs to survive. By lunch on the final day it was 140 for 4, but Kemp used his long reach to smother the spin, while Rudolph played with nerveless patience. Their partnership of 112 lasted 52 overs before Warne had Kemp snaffled at silly point, but it was too late.

Australia

J. L. Langer c Smith b Ntini	37	– b Pollock	47
M. L. Hayden c Rudolph b Ntini	0	– c Boucher b Langeveldt	20
*R. T. Ponting lbw b Pollock	71	– (4) c Boucher b Ntini	53
B. J. Hodge c Boucher b Ntini	41	– (5) not out	203
M. E. K. Hussey c Langeveldt b Ntini	23	– (6) c Boucher b Pollock	58
A. Symonds b Nel	13	– (7) c Gibbs b Langeveldt	25
†A. C. Gilchrist c Gibbs b Ntini	6	– (8) c Rudolph b Nel	44
S. K. Warne lbw b Langeveldt	24	– (9) lbw b Kemp	5
B. Lee not out	19	– (3) lbw b Langeveldt	32
N. W. Bracken c Boucher b Nel	10	– not out	14
G. D. McGrath c Boucher b Nel	0		
B 4, l-b 2, w 2, n-b 6	14	B 5, l-b 4, w 1, n-b 17	27

1/0 (2) 2/111 (1) 3/117 (3) 4/180 (5)   258
5/185 (4) 6/199 (7) 7/210 (6)
8/243 (8) 9/258 (10) 10/258 (11)

1/37 (2) 2/86 (3)   (8 wkts dec.) 528
3/129 (1) 4/184 (4)
5/316 (6) 6/377 (7) 7/444 (8) 8/451 (9)

Pollock 19–6–46–1; Ntini 19–3–64–5; Langeveldt 17–1–100–1; Nel 17.2–3–29–3; Kemp 3–0–13–0. *Second Innings*—Pollock 36–6–98–2; Ntini 34–8–113–1; Langeveldt 31–3–117–3; Nel 28–2–104–1; Rudolph 6.4–1–29–0; Kemp 11–0–58–1.

South Africa

A. B. de Villiers b Warne	68	– (2) c Hodge b Warne	12
*G. C. Smith c Ponting b Bracken	34	– (1) lbw b Bracken	30
H. H. Gibbs b Lee	21	– c Warne b Lee	33
J. A. Rudolph c Langer b Lee	8	– not out	102
A. G. Prince lbw b Warne	28	– lbw b Warne	8
J. M. Kemp c Hodge b McGrath	7	– c Ponting b Warne	55
†M. V. Boucher c Hayden b Warne	62	– not out	13
S. M. Pollock b Lee	34		
A. Nel not out	4		
C. K. Langeveldt lbw b Lee	0		
M. Ntini c Hodge b Lee	12		
B 4, l-b 2, n-b 12	18	B 18, l-b 13, n-b 3	34

1/83 (2) 2/127 (3) 3/135 (1) 4/145 (4)   296
5/167 (6) 6/187 (5) 7/264 (8)
8/282 (7) 9/283 (10) 10/296 (11)

1/35 (2) 2/55 (1)   (5 wkts) 287
3/109 (3) 4/138 (5)
5/250 (6)

McGrath 18–3–59–1; Lee 22.2–1–93–5; Bracken 12–3–46–1; Warne 29–4–92–3. *Second Innings*—McGrath 24–11–39–0; Lee 31–9–83–1; Warne 47–21–83–3; Bracken 19–5–37–1; Symonds 3–0–6–0; Hodge 2–0–8–0.

Umpires: S. A. Bucknor *(West Indies)* (107) and B. R. Doctrove *(West Indies)* (5).
Third umpire: D. J. Harper *(Australia)*.   Referee: B. C. Broad *(England)* (15).

Close of play: First day, South Africa 38-0 (de Villiers 14, Smith 18); Second day, Australia 38-1 (Langer 15, Lee 0); Third day, Australia 310-4 (Hodge 91, Hussey 54); Fourth day, South Africa 85-2 (Gibbs 17, Rudolph 18).

AUSTRALIA v SOUTH AFRICA 2005-06 (2nd Test)

At Melbourne Cricket Ground on 26, 27, 28, 29, 30 December.
Toss: Australia.   Result: AUSTRALIA won by 184 runs.
Debuts: Australia – P. A. Jaques.
Man of the Match: M. E. K. Hussey.

Australia's eventual convincing victory owed much to Hussey, who scored an improbable hundred to transform the match. After Hayden spent almost four hours and 177 balls over 65 – he and Ponting added 152 – four wickets in 25 deliveries from Nel (who enjoyed the interaction with a first-day crowd of 72,000) helped reduce Australia to 248 for 9. Hussey had 27 then, but after being dropped by Kallis at second slip he blossomed, collecting successive sixes off Nel plus the singles on offer as the South Africans tried to get at the No. 11. However, McGrath faced only a third of the deliveries during his 28 overs at the crease, as he emulated New Zealand's Nathan Astle in sharing two last-wicket hundred partnerships in Tests. Gibbs played with unaccustomed restraint, but when he was seventh out after 347 minutes, South Africa began their slide to defeat. Hayden became the game's third centurion but, like the others, he was dropped before reaching 30. Symonds had started the match under pressure, with averages of 85 with ball and 12.62 with bat. He lofted his third ball back over Smith's head for six, and never looked back, clubbing six sixes and five fours in his 54-ball 72. Ponting declared shortly before tea on the fourth day. South Africa survived that awkward period, but Warne was not about to waste a scuffed, tired pitch with some inviting bowlers' footmarks. Three quick wickets, plus two from the rejuvenated Symonds, effectively ended the contest.

Australia

P. A. Jaques c Rudolph b Pollock	2	– (2) lbw b Nel	28
M. L. Hayden c Smith b Pollock	65	– (1) c Boucher b Kallis	137
*R. T. Ponting c Gibbs b Nel	117	– lbw b Pollock	11
B. J. Hodge c Smith b Pollock	7	– c Boucher b Nel	24
M. E. K. Hussey b Ntini	122	– c Kallis b Smith	31
A. Symonds c Boucher b Nel	0	– c Nel b Kallis	72
†A. C. Gilchrist c Gibbs b Nel	2	– c Prince b Kallis	0
S. K. Warne c Boje b Nel	9	– not out	0
B. Lee lbw b Ntini	4		
S. C. G. MacGill b Ntini	4		
G. D. McGrath not out	11		
B 2, l-b 4, w 2, n-b 4	12	B 6, l-b 3, n-b 9	18
	355	(7 wkts dec.)	321

1/2 (1) 2/154 (2) 3/176 (4) 4/207 (3)   355   1/53 (2) 2/82 (3)   (7 wkts dec.) 321
5/207 (6) 6/213 (7) 7/227 (8)   3/131 (4) 4/193 (5)
8/239 (9) 9/248 (10) 10/355 (5)   5/317 (1) 6/321 (6) 7/321 (7)

Pollock 26–5–67–3; Ntini 22.3–3–70–3; Kallis 21.5–4–69–0; Nel 31–6–84–4; Boje 18.1–3–59–0. *Second Innings—* Pollock 23–5–60–1; Ntini 8–2–17–0; Kallis 11–0–58–3; Nel 20–3–71–2; Boje 14–0–65–0; Smith 7–0–41–1.

South Africa

A. B. de Villiers lbw b McGrath	61	– (2) st Gilchrist b Warne	8
*G. C. Smith lbw b Lee	22	– (1) c Gilchrist b McGrath	25
H. H. Gibbs b Symonds	94	– b Warne	9
J. H. Kallis b Lee	23	– c Gilchrist b Symonds	9
A. G. Prince c Ponting b Warne	6	– c Hayden b Warne	26
J. A. Rudolph b Lee	13	– b Symonds	4
†M. V. Boucher lbw b Symonds	23	– c Ponting b Warne	5
S. M. Pollock lbw b Symonds	9	– not out	67
N. Boje b Warne	12	– b McGrath	13
A. Nel c Hussey b MacGill	14	– c Gilchrist b McGrath	2
M. Ntini not out	10	– b MacGill	2
B 2, l-b 7, n-b 15	24	L-b 6, w 1, n-b 4	11
	311		181

1/36 (2) 2/122 (1) 3/184 (4) 4/192 (5)   311   1/39 (2) 2/45 (1) 3/58 (3)   181
5/214 (6) 6/260 (7) 7/265 (3)   4/64 (4) 5/72 (6) 6/82 (7)
8/281 (8) 9/291 (9) 10/311 (10)   7/130 (5) 8/166 (8) 9/178 (10) 10/181 (11)

McGrath 27–13–57–1; Lee 28–5–92–3; Symonds 20–6–50–3; Warne 21–7–62–2; MacGill 15–3–41–1. *Second Innings*—McGrath 15–3–44–3; Lee 11–4–23–0; Warne 28–7–74–4; Symonds 4–2–6–2; MacGill 16–7–28–1.

Umpires: Asad Rauf *(Pakistan)* (3) and S. A. Bucknor *(West Indies)* (108).
Third umpire: R. L. Parry *(Australia)*.   Referee: B. C. Broad *(England)* (16).

Close of play: First day, Australia 239-8 (Hussey 23); Second day, South Africa 169-2 (Gibbs 54, Kallis 17); Third day, Australia 110-2 (Hayden 45, Hodge 17); Fourth day, South Africa 99-6 (Prince 16, Pollock 13).

AUSTRALIA v SOUTH AFRICA 2005-06 (3rd Test)

At Sydney Cricket Ground on 2, 3, 4, 5, 6 January.
Toss: South Africa.   Result: AUSTRALIA won by eight wickets.
Debuts: South Africa – J. Botha.
Man of the Match: R. T. Ponting.   Man of the Series: R. T. Ponting.

Ricky Ponting became the first man to score centuries in both innings of his 100th Test, to set up a stunning victory following a brave declaration. Australia needed 287 in 76 overs, but Ponting thundered his way to 143 from only 159 balls, putting on 182 with Hayden, and Australia romped home with 15.3 overs to spare. For the first two days, they had been under pressure, after a stand of 219 between Kallis, whose 23rd Test century was his first against Australia since his maiden hundred, at Melbourne eight years previously, and Prince, whose third was notable for his success in dealing with Warne after perishing in eight of ten previous innings against him. But they scored at under three an over, which used up valuable time. Nonetheless, Australia were struggling before Ponting got going for his first century. He passed 8,000 Test runs when 10, and put on 130 with Hussey. At 263 for 8, though, Australia were 188 behind, until Gilchrist put on 59 with MacGill and 37 with McGrath, who scored one. South Africa still had a handy lead, and sought the quick runs they had spurned in the first innings, only to be handicapped when persistent rain allowed only 20.3 overs on the fourth day. Smith declared early on the fifth morning in his search for a series-levelling victory, but Ponting made him only the second captain to lose a Test after declaring twice, following Garry Sobers for West Indies against England at Port-of-Spain in 1967-68.

South Africa

A. B. de Villiers c Gilchrist b Lee	2	– (2) lbw b Lee		1
*G. C. Smith lbw b Lee	39	– (1) lbw b McGrath		5
H. H. Gibbs b McGrath	27	– run out		67
J. H. Kallis c McGrath b Symonds	111	– not out		50
A. G. Prince lbw b Warne	119	– c Ponting b MacGill		18
J. A. Rudolph c Gilchrist b McGrath	38	– c McGrath b MacGill		4
†M. V. Boucher c Gilchrist b MacGill	5	– st Gilchrist b MacGill		11
S. M. Pollock c Hodge b Lee	46	– not out		26
J. Botha not out	20			
A. Nel c Hodge b Warne	12			
C. K. Langeveldt not out	1			
B 9, l-b 6, n-b 16	31	B 3, l-b 4, w 3, n-b 2		12

1/16 (1) 2/69 (3) 3/86 (2)   (9 wkts dec.) 451   1/4 (2) 2/6 (1)   (6 wkts dec.) 194
4/305 (4) 5/344 (5) 6/355 (7)   3/92 (3) 4/123 (5)
7/394 (6) 8/433 (8) 9/449 (10)   5/129 (6) 6/152 (7)

McGrath 34–17–65–2; Lee 30.4–7–82–3; Symonds 23–4–69–1; Warne 36–5–106–2; Hussey 2–0–12–0; MacGill 29–5–102–1. *Second Innings*—McGrath 15–2–61–1; Lee 10–3–48–1; Warne 11–1–45–0; MacGill 6–1–33–3.

Australia

J. L. Langer b Langeveldt	25	– b Langeveldt		20
M. L. Hayden b Langeveldt	4	– c Smith b Botha		90
*R. T. Ponting lbw b Kallis	120	– not out		143
B. J. Hodge c Rudolph b Nel	6	– not out		27
M. E. K. Hussey c Boucher b Botha	45			
A. Symonds lbw b Nel	12			
†A. C. Gilchrist c Boucher b Nel	86			
S. K. Warne c Boucher b Nel	0			
B. Lee c Smith b Kallis	17			
S. C. G. MacGill c Nel b Pollock	29			
G. D. McGrath not out	1			
L-b 10, w 2, n-b 2	14	L-b 1, w 3, n-b 4		8

1/22 (2) 2/35 (1) 3/54 (4) 4/184 (5)   359   1/30 (1) 2/212 (2)   (2 wkts) 288
5/222 (3) 6/226 (6) 7/226 (8)
8/263 (9) 9/322 (10) 10/359 (7)

Pollock 25–3–109–1; Langeveldt 24–4–108–2; Nel 24.1–3–81–4; Kallis 15–4–25–2; Botha 7–2–26–1. *Second Innings*—Pollock 14–2–55–0; Langeveldt 14–1–52–1; Nel 7–0–46–0; Botha 12.3–0–77–1; Kallis 2–0–8–0; Rudolph 11–0–49–0.

Umpires: Aleem Dar *(Pakistan)* (27) and B. F. Bowden *(New Zealand)* (35).
Third umpire: R. L. Parry *(Australia)*.   Referee: B. C. Broad *(England)* (17).

Close of play: First day, South Africa 230-3 (Kallis 80, Prince 62); Second day, Australia 54-3 (Ponting 13); Third day, South Africa 4-1 (Smith 3); Fourth day, South Africa 94-3 (Kallis 14, Prince 0).

PAKISTAN v INDIA 2005-06 (1st Test)

At Gaddafi Stadium, Lahore, on 13, 14, 15, 16, 17 January.
Toss: Pakistan.   Result: MATCH DRAWN.
Debuts: none.
Man of the Match: V. Sehwag.

There was never going to be a result: the pitch was as flat as a pancake, and the weather allowed only 15 overs on the third day, then just 14 balls on the fifth. There was time, though, to keep the statisticians busy. Dravid and Sehwag began India's reply with an opening stand of 410, just three short of the 50-year-old Test record, by their compatriots Vinoo Mankad and Pankaj Roy against New Zealand at Madras. Sehwag hit a six and 47 fours, only nine of them on the leg side; his double-century was the second-fastest by balls faced in a Test (182), after Nathan Astle's 153 balls against England in 2001-02. Ganguly's selection (widely thought to have been imposed on the management) ahead of a second specialist opener forced Dravid to do the job: he responded with his first Test hundred as captain. Earlier, Pakistan did their share of pillaging. Younis Khan became the sixth batsman to be dismissed for 199 in a Test, but the first to be run out, after Harbhajan Singh's direct hit. Younis and Mohammad Yousuf added 319, then Shahid Afridi and Kamran Akmal rollicked along at eight an over. Afridi started circumspectly, reaching lunch on the second day with 18 from 31 balls, but 47 balls later reached 100, including 27 (666621) off one Harbhajan over. Akmal kept pace, racing to an 81-ball century, then the fastest by a wicketkeeper in Tests, temporarily overhauling Adam Gilchrist. Each wicket cost an average of 136.13 runs, a record for any Test.

Pakistan

Shoaib Malik c Harbhajan Singh b Pathan	59	Naved-ul-Hasan c Ganguly b Agarkar	9
Salman Butt run out	6	Mohammad Sami not out	1
Younis Khan run out	199	B 4, l-b 12, w 2, n-b 8	26
Mohammad Yousuf st Dhoni b Kumble	173		
*Inzamam-ul-Haq lbw b Kumble	1	1/12 (2) 2/136 (1)	(7 wkts dec.) 679
Shahid Afridi c Harbhajan Singh b Agarkar	103	3/455 (4) 4/456 (5)	
†Kamran Akmal not out	102	5/477 (3) 6/647 (6) 7/668 (8)	

Shoaib Akhtar and Danish Kaneria did not bat.

Pathan 32–4–133–1; Agarkar 24–3–122–2; Ganguly 6–1–14–0; Harbhajan Singh 34–5–176–0; Kumble 39.3–2–178–2; Sehwag 6–0–24–0; Tendulkar 2–0–16–0.

India

V. Sehwag c Kamran Akmal b Naved-ul-Hasan	254
*R. Dravid not out	128
V. V. S. Laxman not out	0
B 2, l-b 7, w 2, n-b 17	28

1/410 (1)   (1 wkt) 410

S. C. Ganguly, S. R. Tendulkar, Yuvraj Singh, †M. S. Dhoni, I. K. Pathan, A. B. Agarkar, A. Kumble and Harbhajan Singh did not bat.

Shoaib Akhtar 16.2–6–46–0; Naved-ul-Hasan 16–1–94–1; Shahid Afridi 11–0–55–0; Mohammad Sami 12–1–67–0; Danish Kaneria 10–0–69–0; Shoaib Malik 12–1–70–0.

Umpires: D. B. Hair *(Australia)* (69) and R. E. Koertzen *(South Africa)* (70).
Third umpire: Nadeem Ghauri *(Pakistan)*.   Referee: R. S. Madugalle *(Sri Lanka)* (81).

Close of play: First day, Pakistan 326-2 (Younis Khan 147, Mohammad Yousuf 95); Second day, India 65-0 (Sehwag 36, Dravid 22); Third day, India 145-0 (Sehwag 96, Dravid 37); Fourth day, India 403-0 (Sehwag 247, Dravid 128).

PAKISTAN v INDIA 2005-06 (2nd Test)

At Iqbal Stadium, Faisalabad, on 21, 22, 23, 24, 25 January.
Toss: Pakistan.   Result: MATCH DRAWN.
Debuts: India – R. P. Singh.
Man of the Match: R. P. Singh.

This time there was no inclement weather to curtail the run-infested agony. There was a single hour, after lunch on the third day, when the fight between bat and ball became competitive as India tottered from 236 for 1 to 281 for 5. Laxman and Dravid had added 197, but then Shoaib Akhtar returned for his fourth spell, and suddenly found top gear for six overs, all terrifyingly quick. Dravid was run out, and Tendulkar, after being harried with short balls, walked after gloving one. Dhoni was also peppered, but hooked his seventh delivery from Shoaib for six. He later hit Danish Kaneria out of the ground; after a delay while the ball was retrieved, he did it again, to reach fifty in 34 balls. Dhoni calmed down for a 93-ball maiden Test century, and put on 210 with Pathan. There was time for Younis Khan to make his fourth hundred in successive Tests against India, while Mohammad Yousuf helped him add 242. The innings came to a surprisingly abrupt end, Zaheer Khan claiming four wickets in ten balls. In the first innings Pakistan had been an uncertain 216 for 4 before Shahid Afridi clattered 156, off only 128 balls, while Inzamam-ul-Haq made his 25th Test century. In all, Pakistan scored 1,078 runs, second only to England's 1,121 against West Indies in a nine-day Test in 1929-30. There were nine cases of bowlers conceding 100 in an innings, a record equalled by England and Pakistan at Headingley seven months later.

Pakistan

Shoaib Malik c Dravid b R. P. Singh	19			
Salman Butt c Dhoni b Zaheer Khan	37	– (1) c Tendulkar b Kumble	24	
Younis Khan c Yuvraj Singh b R. P. Singh	83	– lbw b R. P. Singh	194	
Mohammad Yousuf c Dhoni b R. P. Singh	65	– run out	126	
*Inzamam-ul-Haq c Dhoni b Zaheer Khan	119			
Shahid Afridi c Yuvraj Singh b Kumble	156	– c Dhoni b Zaheer Khan	1	
Abdul Razzaq c Dhoni b R. P. Singh	37	– (5) c Laxman b Zaheer Khan	32	
†Kamran Akmal c Sehwag b Kumble	0	– (2) c Kumble b Pathan	78	
Shoaib Akhtar c Harbhajan Singh b Zaheer Khan	47	– (8) not out	0	
Mohammad Asif not out	6	– (7) b Zaheer Khan	0	
Danish Kaneria b Kumble	0	– (9) b Zaheer Khan	0	
B 3, l-b 4, w 3, n-b 9	19	B 9, l-b 10, w 3, n-b 13	35	

1/49 (1) 2/65 (2) 3/207 (3) 4/216 (4)   **588**   1/52 (1) 2/181 (2)   (8 wkts dec.) **490**
5/467 (6) 6/469 (8) 7/509 (7)   3/423 (4) 4/488 (5)
8/567 (5) 9/584 (9) 10/588 (11)   5/490 (6) 6/490 (3) 7/490 (7) 8/490 (9)

In the first innings Inzamam-ul-Haq, when 79, retired hurt at 379 and resumed at 469.

Pathan 19–4–106–0; R. P. Singh 25–3–89–4; Zaheer Khan 32–7–135–3; Harbhajan Singh 25–1–101–0; Kumble 35.2–5–150–3. *Second Innings*—Pathan 22–2–80–1; R. P. Singh 22–3–75–1; Kumble 21–3–118–1; Zaheer Khan 19.4–4–61–4; Harbhajan Singh 22–2–78–0; Yuvraj Singh 9–0–46–0; Dhoni 1–0–13–0.

India

V. Sehwag c sub (Imran Farhat) b Abdul Razzaq	31		
*R. Dravid run out	103	– not out	5
V. V. S. Laxman c Kamran Akmal b Danish Kaneria	90	– (1) not out	8
S. R. Tendulkar c Kamran Akmal b Shoaib Akhtar	14		
Yuvraj Singh c Danish Kaneria b Mohammad Asif	4		
†M. S. Dhoni st Kamran Akmal b Danish Kaneria	148		
I. K. Pathan lbw b Abdul Razzaq	90		
A. Kumble st Kamran Akmal b Danish Kaneria	15		
Harbhajan Singh lbw b Shahid Afridi	38		
Zaheer Khan not out	20		
R. P. Singh c and b Shahid Afridi	6		
B 3, l-b 15, w 3, n-b 23	44	W 6, n-b 2	8

1/39 (1) 2/236 (3) 3/241 (2) 4/258 (5)   **603**   (no wkt) **21**
5/281 (4) 6/491 (6) 7/529 (7)
8/553 (8) 9/587 (9) 10/603 (11)

Shoaib Akhtar 25–7–100–1; Mohammad Asif 34–6–103–1; Abdul Razzaq 28–1–126–2; Danish Kaneria 54–6–165–3; Shahid Afridi 24.4–0–91–2. *Second Innings*—Shahid Afridi 4–0–16–0; Younis Khan 4–0–5–0.

Umpires: R. E. Koertzen *(South Africa)* (71) and S. J. A. Taufel *(Australia)* (31).
Third umpire: Zamir Haider *(Pakistan)*.   Referee: R. S. Madugalle *(Sri Lanka)* (82).

Close of play: First day, Pakistan 379-4 (Inzamam-ul-Haq 79, Shahid Afridi 85); Second day, India 110-1 (Dravid 46, Laxman 28); Third day, India 441-5 (Dhoni 116, Pathan 49); Fourth day, Pakistan 152-1 (Kamran Akmal 59, Younis Khan 64).

PAKISTAN v INDIA 2005-06 (3rd Test)

At National Stadium, Karachi, on 29, 30, 31 January, 1 February.
Toss: India.   Result: PAKISTAN won by 341 runs.
Debuts: none.
Man of the Match: Kamran Akmal.   Man of the Series: Younis Khan.

The imbalance between bat and ball of the first two Tests was redressed abruptly: Pathan (two for 319 in the series) took a hat-trick with the last three balls of the first over, the earliest ever in a Test. His pace – or the lack of it – mattered less than movement in the air and from a green and lively pitch. Zaheer Khan followed up with two wickets, and Pakistan were 39 for 6 in the 11th over – and yet they went on to win easily. Kamran Akmal made by far the most meaningful century of the series, lifting his side to 245. India lost four wickets by the first-day close, and conceded a narrow lead next day. Then Pakistan's batsmen cut loose: only once before had seven batsmen reached 50 in a Test innings (England against Australia at Manchester in 1934; Sri Lanka would do it at Lord's less than four months later). Younis Khan and Mohammad Yousuf shared their fourth century stand of the series, while Faisal Iqbal, recalled after three years because of Inzamam-ul-Haq's bad back, scored a punchy maiden hundred. Younis eventually set India 607 in 5½ sessions ... they lasted 4½ hours. Shoaib struck in the first over, Mohammad Asif bowled three of the top four, and Razzaq worked through the middle. Yuvraj Singh blazed a final act of defiance, the 15th hundred of the series to equal the record for a three-Test rubber, by England and India in 1990.

Pakistan

Salman Butt c Dravid b Pathan	0	– lbw b Ganguly	53
Imran Farhat c Dhoni b R. P. Singh	22	– c Tendulkar b Pathan	57
*Younis Khan lbw b Pathan	0	– lbw b Kumble	77
Mohammad Yousuf b Pathan	0	– lbw b Kumble	97
Faisal Iqbal lbw b Zaheer Khan	5	– c Tendulkar b Zaheer Khan	139
Shahid Afridi b Zaheer Khan	10	– c Tendulkar b R. P. Singh	60
Abdul Razzaq lbw b R. P. Singh	45	– c Yuvraj Singh b Kumble	90
†Kamran Akmal c Dhoni b Pathan	113	– not out	0
Shoaib Akhtar c Yuvraj Singh b Pathan	45		
Mohammad Asif c Laxman b R. P. Singh	0		
Danish Kaneria not out	0		
L-b 2, w 2, n-b 1	5	B 7, l-b 7, w 1, n-b 11	26

1/0 (1) 2/0 (3) 3/0 (4) 4/13 (5)   245   1/109 (1) 2/122 (2)   (7 wkts dec.) 599
5/37 (6) 6/39 (2) 7/154 (7)   3/280 (3) 4/318 (4)
8/236 (8) 9/245 (10) 10/245 (9)   5/402 (6) 6/598 (5) 7/599 (7)

Pathan 17.1–4–61–5; Zaheer Khan 15–2–75–2; R. P. Singh 16–1–66–3; Ganguly 2–0–9–0; Kumble 10–1–32–0.
Second Innings—Pathan 25–3–106–1; Zaheer Khan 28–4–103–1; R. P. Singh 24–1–115–1; Kumble 37.1–3–151–3; Ganguly 16–1–68–1; Sehwag 1–0–2–0; Tendulkar 9–0–40–0.

India

V. V. S. Laxman b Mohammad Asif	19	– (3) b Mohammad Asif	21
*R. Dravid c Kamran Akmal b Mohammad Asif	3	– c Kamran Akmal b Shoaib Akhtar	2
V. Sehwag c Kamran Akmal b Shoaib Akhtar	5	– (1) b Mohammad Asif	4
S. R. Tendulkar b Abdul Razzaq	23	– b Mohammad Asif	26
S. C. Ganguly c Mohammad Asif b Abdul Razzaq	34	– lbw b Abdul Razzaq	37
Yuvraj Singh lbw b Mohammad Asif	45	– c Kamran Akmal b Abdul Razzaq	122
†M. S. Dhoni c Kamran Akmal b Abdul Razzaq	13	– c Imran Farhat b Abdul Razzaq	18
I. K. Pathan c Mohammad Yousuf b Shahid Afridi	40	– c Faisal Iqbal b Abdul Razzaq	4
A. Kumble lbw b Shoaib Akhtar	7	– c Imran Farhat b Danish Kaneria	5
Zaheer Khan c Kamran Akmal b Mohammad Asif	21	– b Danish Kaneria	10
R. P. Singh not out	0	– not out	0
B 8, l-b 3, n-b 17	28	B 7, w 5, n-b 4	16

1/9 (2) 2/14 (3) 3/56 (1) 4/56 (4)   238   1/8 (2) 2/8 (1) 3/63 (3)   265
5/137 (5) 6/165 (6) 7/165 (7)   4/74 (4) 5/177 (5) 6/208 (7)
8/181 (9) 9/237 (8) 10/238 (10)   7/216 (8) 8/231 (9) 9/251 (10) 10/265 (6)

Shoaib Akhtar 16–3–70–2; Mohammad Asif 19.1–1–78–4; Abdul Razzaq 16–3–67–3; Shahid Afridi 3–0–12–1.
Second Innings—Shoaib Akhtar 8–1–37–1; Mohammad Asif 12–1–48–3; Abdul Razzaq 18.4–0–88–4; Danish Kaneria 18–0–75–2; Shahid Afridi 2–0–10–0.

Umpires: D. J. Harper *(Australia)* (55) and S. J. A. Taufel *(Australia)* (32).
Third umpire: Asad Rauf *(Pakistan)*.   Referee: R. S. Madugalle *(Sri Lanka)* (83).

Close of play: First day, India 74-4 (Ganguly 9, Yuvraj Singh 7); Second day, Pakistan 173-2 (Younis Khan 25, Mohammad Yousuf 30); Third day, Pakistan 511-5 (Faisal Iqbal 103, Abdul Razzaq 44).

BANGLADESH v SRI LANKA 2005-06 (1st Test)

At Bir Shrestha Shahid Ruhul Amin Stadium, Chittagong, on 28 February, 1, 2, 3 March.
Toss: Bangladesh.   Result: SRI LANKA won by eight wickets.
Debuts: none.
Man of the Match: Mohammad Ashraful.

Muttiah Muralitharan marked his 100th Test match with a vintage display, grabbing six wickets in the second innings as Bangladesh crumbled for 181, leaving Sri Lanka a modest target of 163. Until Murali's decisive intervention, this was a close-run affair, with Sri Lanka managing a slender first-innings lead of 19 after Bangladesh had made 319. It was the first Test at a venue also known as the Chittagong Divisional Stadium, a cricket-only ground which had superseded the city's multipurpose M. A. Aziz Stadium and became the 91st to stage a Test. Mohammad Ashraful struck 15 fours and three sixes in a memorable 136, his third Test century. Sri Lanka lost wickets at regular intervals, and were in some trouble at 178 for 5 before Samaraweera, who resisted for exactly four hours, and the more adventurous Maharoof put on 117. Then Murali took centre-stage. His 1,000th wicket in international cricket (by the end of this match he had 593 in Tests and 411 in one-day internationals) came when Khaled Mashud was given out caught close in by Dilshan, although replays appeared to show the ball running up his body without touching the bat. Mohammad Rafique extended the lead with an uncompromising late 40, but the eventual target held few terrors for Sri Lanka. Vandort anchored his side to victory with an unbeaten 64 in his first Test for 3½ years, after making 61 and 140 in his previous one, also against Bangladesh, in Colombo in July 2002.

Bangladesh

Javed Omar c Samaraweera b Malinga	4	– lbw b Fernando	31
Nafis Iqbal b Bandara	34	– c Sangakkara b Fernando	6
*Habibul Bashar lbw b Bandara	29	– lbw b Bandara	12
Shahriar Nafees b Maharoof	27	– c Fernando b Muralitharan	38
Mohammad Ashraful c Tharanga b Muralitharan	136	– c Tharanga b Muralitharan	1
†Khaled Mashud lbw b Muralitharan	6	– c Dilshan b Muralitharan	15
Alok Kapali c Tharanga b Muralitharan	16	– lbw b Muralitharan	9
Mohammad Rafique b Malinga	17	– st Sangakkara b Muralitharan	40
Shahadat Hossain c Tharanga b Malinga	13	– c Malinga b Bandara	0
Syed Rasel b Malinga	1	– (11) not out	2
Enamul Haque, jun. not out	3	– (10) lbw b Muralitharan	1
B 11, l-b 4, w 3, n-b 15	33	B 13, l-b 3, w 3, n-b 7	26

1/4 (1) 2/76 (2) 3/81 (3) 4/146 (4)   319   1/47 (2) 2/56 (1) 3/68 (3)   181
5/210 (6) 6/248 (7) 7/293 (8)   4/69 (5) 5/122 (6) 6/131 (4)
8/308 (5) 9/314 (10) 10/319 (9)   7/135 (7) 8/150 (9) 9/168 (10) 10/181 (8)

Malinga 16.5–3–57–4; Maharoof 11–3–37–1; Fernando 17–4–50–0; Muralitharan 32–8–87–3; Bandara 13–0–61–2; Dilshan 2–0–12–0. *Second Innings*—Malinga 13–2–41–0; Maharoof 2–0–5–0; Bandara 20–2–55–2; Muralitharan 19.5–6–54–6; Fernando 4–1–10–2.

Sri Lanka

M. G. Vandort c Khaled Mashud b Syed Rasel	0	– not out	64
W. U. Tharanga c Mohammad Ashraful b Mohammad Rafique	42	– c Shahriar Nafees b Syed Rasel	19
†K. C. Sangakkara c Mohammad Ashraful b Enamul Haque	69	– c and b Enamul Haque	46
*D. P. M. D. Jayawardene c Shahadat Hossain b Mohammad Rafique	30	– not out	23
T. T. Samaraweera c Javed Omar b Shahadat Hossain	58		
T. M. Dilshan lbw b Enamul Haque	22		
M. F. Maharoof b Shahadat Hossain	72		
C. M. Bandara not out	19		
C. R. D. Fernando c Shahriar Nafees b Shahadat Hossain	6		
M. Muralitharan c Shahriar Nafees b Shahadat Hossain	5		
S. L. Malinga run out	0		
L-b 2, w 2, n-b 11	15	B 4, l-b 5, n-b 2	11

1/0 (1) 2/86 (2) 3/149 (4) 4/149 (3)   338   1/25 (2) 2/115 (3)   (2 wkts) 163
5/178 (6) 6/295 (7) 7/316 (5)
8/330 (9) 9/338 (10) 10/338 (11)

Syed Rasel 18–1–75–1; Shahadat Hossain 22–3–83–4; Mohammad Rafique 29–6–76–2; Enamul Haque 24.1–5–76–2; Alok Kapali 1–0–6–0; Mohammad Ashraful 3–0–20–0. *Second Innings*—Syed Rasel 8–4–18–1; Shahadat Hossain 8–1–39–0; Enamul Haque 9–1–50–1; Mohammad Rafique 8–0–28–0; Alok Kapali 2–0–6–0; Mohammad Ashraful 2–0–13–0.

Umpires: Asad Rauf *(Pakistan)* (4) and S. A. Bucknor *(West Indies)* (109).
Third umpire: A. F. M. Akhtaruddin *(Bangladesh)*.   Referee: C. H. Lloyd *(West Indies)* (52).

Close of play: First day, Bangladesh 315-9 (Shahadat Hossain 11, Enamul Haque 1); Second day, Sri Lanka 313-6 (Samaraweera 57, Bandara 8); Third day, Sri Lanka 25-0 (Vandort 6, Tharanga 19).

BANGLADESH v SRI LANKA 2005-06 (2nd Test)

At Shaheed Chandu Stadium, Bogra, on 8, 9, 10, 11 March.
Toss: Bangladesh.   Result: SRI LANKA won by ten wickets.
Debuts: none.
Man of the Match: W. U. Tharanga.   Man of the Series: M. Muralitharan.

Sri Lanka clinched the series after scenes reminiscent of The Oval 1968, when England's players joined the ground-staff to dry the ground after a downpour in an Ashes Test. This time it was the tourists helping the groundsmen: Tom Moody, Sri Lanka's coach, was the busiest man around, manning the super-sopper. Sri Lanka had needed only 43 more when bad light stopped play with seven overs remaining on the third day, and were not inclined to hang around any longer than necessary. It paid off: play finally resumed at 4.30, and only eight overs were required to finish things off. The first Test at Bogra (the 92nd ground to stage one) was closer than the victory margin suggests. Bangladesh struggled at first against Muralitharan, but then reduced Sri Lanka to 43 for 4, before a superb maiden century from Upul Tharanga spared their blushes. He was last out after 442 minutes, a fifth wicket for Shahadat Hossain, who had earlier removed Samaraweera and Sangakkara (to a debatable lbw decision by Asad Rauf) with successive balls. Bangladesh's second-innings batting let them down again, although three dubious decisions, this time from Hariharan, didn't help. Murali, after his 50th Test five-for in the first innings, contented himself with the two victims he needed for 600 in Tests. The landmark wicket was Khaled Mashud, who had also been Murali's 550th scalp, and (in the previous Test) his 1,000th international victim. Sri Lanka needed just 120 to win, and only the weather threatened to stop them.

Bangladesh

Javed Omar lbw b Muralitharan	35	– c Sangakkara b Fernando	13
Nafis Iqbal lbw b Muralitharan	26	– c Sangakkara b Malinga	2
*Habibul Bashar c Tharanga b Muralitharan	69	– lbw b Malinga	73
Shahriar Nafees c Sangakkara b Malinga	9	– c Maharoof b Muralitharan	6
Mohammad Ashraful b Bandara	24	– c Jayawardene b Bandara	13
Mushfiqur Rahim lbw b Muralitharan	2	– c Sangakkara b Bandara	0
†Khaled Mashud c Sangakkara b Malinga	12	– c Malinga b Muralitharan	6
Mohammad Rafique c Muralitharan b Fernando	32	– c Muralitharan b Malinga	64
Shahadat Hossain c Muralitharan b Fernando	6	– b Fernando	8
Enamul Haque, jun. not out	3	– c Sangakkara b Fernando	3
Syed Rasel c Bandara b Muralitharan	0	– not out	1
B 3, l-b 5, n-b 8	16	B 1, l-b 4, w 2, n-b 5	12

1/52 (2) 2/85 (1) 3/106 (4) 4/157 (5)   **234**   1/15 (2) 2/29 (1) 3/46 (4)   **201**
5/172 (6) 6/186 (3) 7/208 (7)   4/95 (5) 5/95 (6) 6/110 (7)
8/231 (8) 9/233 (9) 10/234 (11)   7/162 (3) 8/187 (9) 9/198 (10) 10/201 (8)

Malinga 20–1–73–2; Maharoof 4–0–22–0; Fernando 9–4–24–2; Muralitharan 30.5–8–79–5; Bandara 13–1–28–1.
Second Innings—Malinga 14.1–1–51–3; Fernando 19–4–51–3; Muralitharan 13–1–62–2; Bandara 10–4–32–2.

Sri Lanka

M. G. Vandort lbw b Syed Rasel	0	– not out	40
W. U. Tharanga c Khaled Mashud b Shahadat Hossain	165	– not out	71
C. M. Bandara c Nafis Iqbal b Shahadat Hossain	2		
T. T. Samaraweera c Khaled Mashud b Shahadat Hossain	20		
†K. C. Sangakkara lbw b Shahadat Hossain	0		
*D. P. M. D. Jayawardene c Mushfiqur Rahim b Mohammad Ashraful	49		
T. M. Dilshan b Mohammad Rafique	33		
M. F. Maharoof c Khaled Mashud b Enamul Haque	7		
C. R. D. Fernando lbw b Enamul Haque	5		
S. L. Malinga c Shahriar Nafees b Shahadat Hossain	12		
M. Muralitharan not out	8		
B 5, l-b 4, w 2, n-b 4	15	L-b 5, w 3, n-b 1	9

1/4 (1) 2/13 (3) 3/43 (4) 4/43 (5)   **316**   **(no wkt) 120**
5/167 (6) 6/232 (7) 7/251 (8)
8/263 (9) 9/305 (10) 10/316 (2)

Syed Rasel 20–8–50–1; Shahadat Hossain 21.3–2–86–5; Mohammad Rafique 32–9–84–1; Enamul Haque 26–3–71–2; Mohammad Ashraful 4–1–16–1. *Second Innings*—Syed Rasel 5–0–21–0; Shahadat Hossain 8–2–43–0; Mohammad Rafique 9–2–32–0; Enamul Haque 6–0–19–0.

Umpires: Asad Rauf *(Pakistan)* (5) and K. Hariharan *(India)* (2).
Third umpire: Mahbubur Rahman *(Bangladesh)*.   Referee: C. H. Lloyd *(West Indies)* (53).

Close of play: First day, Sri Lanka 25-2 (Tharanga 12, Samaraweera 7); Second day, Sri Lanka 302-8 (Tharanga 160, Malinga 12); Third day, Sri Lanka 77-0 (Vandort 22, Tharanga 48).

INDIA v ENGLAND 2005-06 (1st Test)

At Vidarbha C. A. Ground, Nagpur, on 1, 2, 3, 4, 5 March.
Toss: England.   Result: MATCH DRAWN.
Debuts: India – S. Sreesanth. England – I. D. Blackwell, A. N. Cook, M. S. Panesar.
Man of the Match: M. J. Hoggard.

A final-session run-flurry roused India's supporters, but failed to hide that they had been second-best for much of the game in conditions supposedly to their advantage. England had scrapped tenaciously to set India 368, a startling achievement given that fielding a full XI had once appeared beyond them. Marcus Trescothick had departed in tears, followed by Michael Vaughan and Simon Jones, both with knee trouble. First-time captain Flintoff's side included three debutants. One of them, Alastair Cook, had just left England's A-team in the Caribbean, and unveiled a compact technique and tremendous temperament in scoring 60 and 104 not out to become England's youngest Test centurion for 67 years. India's newcomer, Sreesanth, castled Pietersen to set England wobbling, but Collingwood's tenacious maiden century helped the last three wickets add 149. Hoggard showed his mastery of swing with three for five in 11 balls, while Tendulkar was the first Test victim of Monty Panesar, who could scarcely believe what his arm-ball had accomplished. India were 190 for 7, but Kaif scored 91 and Kumble made his first international fifty for nearly nine years. With England needing to press on, Cook dropped anchor while Pietersen galloped to 87, before Kumble had the final word. Chasing the target never looked a realistic option for India once Hoggard cleaned up Sehwag, whose form was becoming a concern. Jaffer and Dravid made the game safe with some ease, which said much about the placid nature of the pitch, and the inexperience of England's spinners.

England

A. J. Strauss c Laxman b Sreesanth	28	– c Dhoni b Pathan	46
A. N. Cook b Pathan	60	– not out	104
I. R. Bell c Dravid b Harbhajan Singh	9	– c Dhoni b Pathan	1
K. P. Pietersen b Sreesanth	15	– c Dravid b Kumble	87
P. D. Collingwood not out	134	– not out	36
*A. Flintoff lbw b Kumble	43		
†G. O. Jones lbw b Pathan	14		
I. D. Blackwell b Pathan	4		
M. J. Hoggard c Dhoni b Sreesanth	11		
S. J. Harmison st Dhoni b Harbhajan Singh	39		
M. S. Panesar lbw b Sreesanth	9		
B 7, l-b 7, w 1, n-b 12	27	B 12, l-b 7, w 2, n-b 2	23

1/56 (1) 2/81 (3) 3/110 (4) 4/136 (2)   393   1/95 (1) 2/97 (3)   (3 wkts dec.) 297
5/203 (6) 6/225 (7) 7/244 (8)   3/221 (4)
8/267 (9) 9/327 (10) 10/393 (11)

Pathan 23–5–92–3; Sreesanth 28.5–6–95–4; Harbhajan Singh 34–5–93–2; Kumble 40–13–88–1; Tendulkar 2–0–11–0. *Second Innings*—Pathan 14–2–48–2; Sreesanth 10–2–36–0; Kumble 32–8–101–1; Harbhajan Singh 30–6–79–0; Sehwag 1–0–14–0.

India

Wasim Jaffer c Flintoff b Hoggard	81	– c Strauss b Flintoff	100
V. Sehwag c Pietersen b Hoggard	2	– b Hoggard	0
*R. Dravid lbw b Hoggard	40	– b Panesar	71
S. R. Tendulkar lbw b Panesar	16	– (6) not out	28
V. V. S. Laxman lbw b Hoggard	0	– (8) not out	0
M. Kaif b Panesar	91		
†M. S. Dhoni c Jones b Flintoff	5	– (5) c Strauss b Harmison	16
I. K. Pathan c Flintoff b Hoggard	2	– (4) c Strauss b Flintoff	35
A. Kumble c Cook b Harmison	58		
Harbhajan Singh not out	0	– (7) b Harmison	7
S. Sreesanth lbw b Hoggard	1		
B 17, l-b 3, w 5, n-b 2	27	L-b 3	3

1/11 (2) 2/140 (3) 3/149 (1) 4/149 (5)   323   1/1 (2) 2/168 (3)   (6 wkts) 260
5/176 (4) 6/183 (7) 7/190 (8)   3/198 (1) 4/215 (4)
8/318 (9) 9/322 (6) 10/323 (11)   5/252 (5) 6/260 (7)

Hoggard 30.5–13–57–6; Harmison 27–5–75–1; Flintoff 29–10–68–1; Panesar 42–19–73–2; Blackwell 7–0–28–0; Bell 1–0–2–0. *Second Innings*—Hoggard 16–7–29–1; Harmison 17.2–4–48–2; Flintoff 17–2–79–2; Panesar 16–2–58–1; Blackwell 12–2–43–0.

Umpires: Aleem Dar *(Pakistan)* (28) and I. L. Howell *(South Africa)* (4).
Third umpire: I. Shivram *(India)*.   Referee: R. S. Madugalle *(Sri Lanka)* (84).

Close of play: First day, England 246-7 (Collingwood 53, Hoggard 0); Second day, India 136-1 (Wasim Jaffer 73, Dravid 40); Third day, India 322-9 (Harbhajan Singh 0); Fourth day, England 297-3 (Cook 104, Collingwood 36).

INDIA v ENGLAND 2005-06 (2nd Test)

At Punjab C. A. Stadium, Mohali, Chandigarh, on 9, 10, 11, 12, 13 March.
Toss: England.   Result: INDIA won by nine wickets.
Debuts: India – P. P. Chawla, M. M. Patel.
Man of the Match: A. Kumble.

England's weakened side finally slipped on the fourth morning, and eight days' hard work was undone in three sessions as they slithered towards their third defeat in five Tests since winning the Ashes. A draw seemed likelier after rain allowed only 65 overs on the first two days, leaving a bouncy pitch which favoured England's seamers. When Harmison removed Dhoni with a throat-bound bouncer India were unravelling at 153 for 5 – but then England's decline began. The damage was done by India's bowlers. First, they whacked 185 runs for the last five wickets, then Kumble took over: five top-order batsmen fell for 112 in 51 nightmarish and almost strokeless overs. For once, India had a quick bowler to finish the job: Munaf Patel demolished the lower order, and ended with the best match figures by a debutant Indian paceman. England had chosen to bat, but the regular interruptions did not make things easy. They eked out 300, but in sweeping away the last three in four balls Kumble reached 500 wickets in his 105th Test when his flipper deceived Harmison. England's quick bowlers again did well, but their batsmen struggled once more against Kumble, who took three of the five wickets to fall before the fourth-day close. Patel settled matters with a searing spell of reverse swing (9–2–16–3) on the final morning: Flintoff, England's top scorer and wicket-taker, was the last to fall, then Sehwag smashed 76 in 89 balls to make sure of victory by tea.

England

A. J. Strauss c Dhoni b Pathan	18	– c Dhoni b Kumble	13
A. N. Cook lbw b Pathan	17	– c Dhoni b Patel	2
I. R. Bell b Kumble	38	– c Dhoni b Kumble	57
K. P. Pietersen c and b Patel	64	– c Dravid b Harbhajan Singh	4
P. D. Collingwood b Kumble	25	– c Dravid b Kumble	14
*A. Flintoff c and b Patel	70	– c Patel b Chawla	51
†G. O. Jones b Kumble	52	– b Patel	5
L. E. Plunkett c Dhoni b Patel	0	– lbw b Patel	1
M. J. Hoggard not out	4	– b Patel	4
S. J. Harmison lbw b Kumble	0	– st Dhoni b Kumble	13
M. S. Panesar c Dravid b Kumble	0	– not out	0
L-b 5, w 1, n-b 6	12	L-b 10, w 1, n-b 6	17

1/35 (1) 2/36 (2) 3/117 (3) 4/157 (4)   300   1/7 (2) 2/50 (1) 3/55 (4) 4/88 (5)   181
5/180 (5) 6/283 (6) 7/290 (8)   5/109 (3) 6/116 (7) 7/124 (8)
8/300 (7) 9/300 (10) 10/300 (11)   8/139 (9) 9/181 (10) 10/181 (6)

Pathan 28–9–71–2; Patel 25–6–72–3; Harbhajan Singh 12–0–31–0; Chawla 9–1–45–0; Kumble 29.4–8–76–5. *Second Innings*—Pathan 6–1–16–0; Patel 13–4–25–4; Harbhajan Singh 23–5–52–1; Kumble 29–7–70–4; Chawla 5.1–2–8–1.

India

Wasim Jaffer c Flintoff b Panesar	31	– lbw b Hoggard	17
V. Sehwag c Jones b Harmison	11	– not out	76
*R. Dravid b Flintoff	95	– not out	42
S. R. Tendulkar c Strauss b Flintoff	4		
Yuvraj Singh c Bell b Hoggard	15		
†M. S. Dhoni c Jones b Harmison	16		
I. K. Pathan c Collingwood b Flintoff	52		
A. Kumble b Plunkett	32		
Harbhajan Singh c Jones b Flintoff	36		
P. P. Chawla c Collingwood b Hoggard	1		
M. M. Patel not out	11		
L-b 25, w 1, n-b 8	34	B 4, l-b 5	9

1/18 (2) 2/96 (1) 3/103 (4) 4/134 (5)   338   1/39 (1)   (1 wkt) 144
5/153 (6) 6/229 (3) 7/260 (7)
8/313 (9) 9/321 (10) 10/338 (8)

Hoggard 18–6–55–2; Harmison 28–9–60–2; Flintoff 22–3–96–4; Plunkett 9.2–1–37–1; Panesar 19–3–65–1. *Second Innings*—Harmison 4–1–10–0; Hoggard 8–2–24–1; Panesar 11–0–48–0; Flintoff 5–0–11–0; Plunkett 2–0–22–0; Collingwood 3–1–20–0.

Umpires: D. B. Hair *(Australia)* (70) and S. J. A. Taufel *(Australia)* (33).
Third umpire: A. V. Jayaprakash *(India)*.   Referee: R. S. Madugalle *(Sri Lanka)* (85).

Close of play: First day, England 163-4 (Collingwood 19, Flintoff 4); Second day, England 200-5 (Flintoff 26, Jones 7); Third day, India 149-4 (Dravid 60, Dhoni 12); Fourth day, England 112-5 (Flintoff 16, Jones 1).

INDIA v ENGLAND 2005-06 (3rd Test)

At Wankhede Stadium, Mumbai, on 18, 19, 20, 21, 22 March.
Toss: India.   Result: ENGLAND won by 212 runs.
Debuts: England – O. A. Shah.
Man of the Match: A. Flintoff.   Man of the Series: A. Flintoff.

Flintoff asked for a "monumental effort" from his team, and they delivered a monumental victory – England's first Test win in India for 21 years, and their biggest by runs on Indian soil. It squared the series, a marvellous achievement for a depleted side whose problems had grown even worse: Harmison had a shin injury and Cook a stomach bug. Dravid strangely chose to forego the opportunity of bowling fourth at a venue where no side had won a Test chasing more than 163. England countered with 400: Strauss broke his run of eight Test innings on the subcontinent without a fifty with an understated 128, while his Middlesex team-mate Owais Shah made 88 on his long-awaited debut despite suffering from hand cramps. Hoggard dismissed both openers with bouncers, while the recalled Anderson removed Dravid and Tendulkar, whose one in 21 balls extended a patchy run that was becoming a matter of national debate; in his 132nd Test (breaking Kapil Dev's Indian record) Mumbai's most famous son was even booed by a small section of his home crowd. England built on a lead of 121 with surprising caution, managing only 160 runs from 77.4 overs on the fourth day. Needing 313 from 98 overs, India reached lunch on the final day at 75 for 3, but crumbled to 100 all out in another 15 overs. Flintoff, hurling thunderbolts, finished with three wickets; Udal went one better after being recalled for his fourth (and final) Test on his 37th birthday.

England

A. J. Strauss c Dhoni b Harbhajan Singh	128	– c Dhoni b Patel	4
I. R. Bell c Harbhajan Singh b Sreesanth	18	– c Dhoni b Sreesanth	8
O. A. Shah c Dravid b Harbhajan Singh	88	– run out	38
K. P. Pietersen c Dhoni b Sreesanth	39	– (5) c and b Kumble	7
P. D. Collingwood c Dhoni b Sreesanth	31	– (6) c and b Harbhajan Singh	32
*A. Flintoff c Tendulkar b Kumble	50	– (7) st Dhoni b Kumble	50
†G. O. Jones c Kumble b Sreesanth	1	– (8) c Pathan b Harbhajan Singh	3
S. D. Udal lbw b Patel	9	– (4) c Wasim Jaffer b Pathan	14
M. J. Hoggard b Patel	0	– lbw b Kumble	6
J. M. Anderson c Yuvraj Singh b Harbhajan Singh	15	– c Dravid b Kumble	6
M. S. Panesar not out	3	– not out	0
B 5, l-b 7, w 3, n-b 3	18	B 1, l-b 8, w 4, n-b 10	23
	400		**191**

1/52 (2) 2/230 (1) 3/242 (4) 4/326 (5)   400   1/9 (1) 2/21 (2) 3/61 (4)   191
5/328 (6) 6/333 (7) 7/356 (8)   4/73 (5) 5/85 (3) 6/151 (6)
8/356 (9) 9/385 (3) 10/400 (10)   7/157 (8) 8/183 (9) 9/188 (7) 10/191 (10)

In the first innings Shah, when 50, retired hurt at 158 and resumed at 326.

Pathan 17–4–64–0; Sreesanth 22–5–70–4; Patel 29–4–81–2; Kumble 39–7–84–1; Harbhajan Singh 26.4–4–89–3. *Second Innings*—Pathan 13–2–24–1; Patel 13–2–39–1; Sreesanth 13–3–30–1; Kumble 30.4–13–49–4; Harbhajan Singh 23–9–40–2.

India

Wasim Jaffer c Jones b Hoggard	11	– lbw b Flintoff	10
V. Sehwag c Shah b Hoggard	6	– (7) lbw b Anderson	0
*R. Dravid c Jones b Anderson	52	– (4) c Jones b Flintoff	9
S. R. Tendulkar c Jones b Anderson	1	– (5) c Bell b Udal	34
Yuvraj Singh c Jones b Flintoff	37	– (6) c Collingwood b Flintoff	12
†M. S. Dhoni run out	64	– (8) c Panesar b Udal	5
I. K. Pathan c Hoggard b Udal	26	– (2) b Anderson	6
A. Kumble lbw b Panesar	30	– (3) lbw b Hoggard	8
Harbhajan Singh c Jones b Anderson	2	– c Hoggard b Udal	6
S. Sreesanth not out	29	– not out	0
M. M. Patel b Anderson	7	– c Hoggard b Udal	1
B 4, l-b 7, n-b 3	14	B 1, l-b 4, w 1, n-b 3	9
	279		**100**

1/9 (2) 2/24 (1) 3/28 (4) 4/94 (5)   279   1/6 (2) 2/21 (3) 3/33 (1)   100
5/142 (3) 6/186 (7) 7/212 (6)   4/75 (4) 5/76 (5) 6/77 (7)
8/217 (9) 9/272 (8) 10/279 (11)   7/92 (8) 8/99 (9) 9/99 (6) 10/100 (11)

Hoggard 22–6–54–2; Flintoff 21–4–68–1; Anderson 19.1–8–40–4; Panesar 26–7–53–1; Udal 16–2–53–1. *Second Innings*—Hoggard 12–6–13–1; Anderson 12–2–39–2; Panesar 4–1–15–0; Flintoff 11–4–14–3; Udal 9.2–3–14–4.

Umpires: D. B. Hair *(Australia)* (71) and S. J. A. Taufel *(Australia)* (34).
Third umpire: K. Hariharan *(India)*.   Referee: R. S. Madugalle *(Sri Lanka)* (86).

Close of play: First day, England 272-3 (Collingwood 11, Flintoff 17); Second day, India 89-3 (Dravid 37, Yuvraj Singh 32); Third day, England 31-2 (Shah 15, Udal 2); Fourth day, India 18-1 (Wasim Jaffer 4, Kumble 8).

NEW ZEALAND v WEST INDIES 2005-06 (1st Test)

At Eden Park, Auckland, on 9, 10, 11, 12, 13 March.
Toss: West Indies.   Result: NEW ZEALAND won by 27 runs.
Debuts: New Zealand – P. G. Fulton, J. M. How. West Indies – I. D. R. Bradshaw.
Man of the Match: S. E. Bond.

This was a fascinating match in which the advantage changed session by session: the vital turning-point came on the fourth day, as West Indies chased 291. Their opening stand reached three figures when Gayle drove Vettori for a six so huge the ball could not be found. Chanderpaul only accepted the replacement after it had been scraped and bounced on concrete, and soon wished Gayle had restrained himself: Bond had been unable to move the previous ball, but loved this one. At one point West Indies were 148 without loss, but slumped to 246 for 8, and lasted less than nine overs on the final morning – 50 years to the day after New Zealand's first-ever Test victory, also against West Indies here. There was little spite in the drop-in pitch, but New Zealand struggled after being put in before Styris's patient century. He caused further damage by dismissing nightwatchman Bradshaw and Gayle in three balls. Smith's breezy 38 ensured the deficit was only 18, and when Astle was run out by Ganga's direct hit from gully it was 146 for 7 – only 164 in front – and West Indies were clear favourites. But McCullum curbed his usual enthusiasm, putting on 64 with Vettori and 62 with Bond before Martin completed his fourth Test pair (equalling the record shared by Bhagwat Chandrasekhar, Merv Dillon, Courtney Walsh and Marvan Atapattu). Gayle and Ganga took West Indies halfway to their target – but then, led by Bond, New Zealand took all ten wickets for 115.

New Zealand

H. J. H. Marshall c Edwards b Taylor	11	–	c Ganga b Bradshaw	1
J. M. How run out	11	–	c Ramdin b Bradshaw	37
P. G. Fulton c Ganga b Bradshaw	17	–	b Edwards	28
*S. P. Fleming c Ramdin b Bradshaw	14	–	lbw b Bradshaw	33
N. J. Astle c Ramdin b Smith	51	–	(7) run out	13
S. B. Styris not out	103	–	(5) c Bradshaw b Edwards	5
†B. B. McCullum b Smith	19	–	(8) c Bravo b Gayle	74
D. L. Vettori c Gayle b Smith	6	–	(9) c sub (D. S. Smith) b Gayle	33
J. E. C. Franklin c sub (R. S. Morton) b Gayle	14	–	(6) b Gayle	20
S. E. Bond b Gayle	3	–	not out	18
C. S. Martin c Ramdin b Bradshaw	0	–	b Gayle	0
B 4, l-b 2, w 9, n-b 11	26		L-b 3, w 2, n-b 5	10

1/23 (2) 2/31 (1) 3/54 (3) 4/69 (4)   **275**   1/11 (1) 2/66 (2) 3/73 (3)   **272**
5/140 (5) 6/170 (7) 7/199 (8)   4/88 (5) 5/118 (4) 6/143 (6)
8/240 (9) 9/261 (10) 10/275 (11)   7/146 (7) 8/210 (9) 9/272 (8) 10/272 (11)

Edwards 15–1–76–0; Bradshaw 23.1–3–73–3; Taylor 8–2–39–1; Smith 18–2–71–3; Gayle 5–0–10–2. *Second Innings*—Edwards 21–3–65–2; Bradshaw 34–10–83–3; Taylor 1–0–6–0; Gayle 30.1–5–71–4; Smith 17–6–44–0.

West Indies

C. H. Gayle c McCullum b Styris	25	–	c Fleming b Astle	82
D. Ganga c How b Martin	20	–	c How b Astle	95
I. D. R. Bradshaw c How b Styris	0	–	(9) c Fleming b Vettori	10
R. R. Sarwan c Franklin b Bond	62	–	(3) c Styris b Bond	4
B. C. Lara c sub (C. Cachopa) b Bond	5	–	(4) b Bond	0
*S. Chanderpaul c McCullum b Franklin	13	–	(5) c Fulton b Vettori	15
D. J. Bravo c Bond b Martin	59	–	(6) lbw b Bond	17
D. R. Smith c McCullum b Martin	38	–	(7) c Fleming b Bond	0
†D. Ramdin c and b Vettori	9	–	(8) c Franklin b Vettori	15
F. H. Edwards c McCullum b Vettori	1	–	(11) not out	2
J. E. Taylor not out	4	–	(10) b Bond	13
L-b 7, w 1, n-b 13	21		B 1, l-b 3, w 1, n-b 5	10

1/47 (2) 2/48 (3) 3/49 (1) 4/60 (5)   **257**   1/148 (1) 2/157 (4) 3/182 (5)   **263**
5/90 (6) 6/179 (4) 7/237 (8)   4/211 (2) 5/216 (7) 6/218 (3)
8/248 (7) 9/252 (9) 10/257 (10)   7/221 (6) 8/246 (8) 9/251 (9) 10/263 (10)

In the second innings Sarwan, when 4, retired hurt at 157-1 and resumed at 216.

Bond 19–4–57–2; Franklin 21–4–83–1; Martin 17–1–80–3; Styris 7–1–23–2; Vettori 7.2–3–7–2. *Second Innings*—Bond 27.3–7–69–5; Franklin 14–1–46–0; Martin 16–5–39–0; Vettori 35–11–92–3; Astle 10–4–13–2.

Umpires: D. J. Harper *(Australia)* (56) and R. E. Koertzen *(South Africa)* (72).
Third umpire: G. A. V. Baxter *(New Zealand)*.   Referee: M. J. Procter *(South Africa)* (38).

Close of play: First day, West Indies 51-3 (Sarwan 3, Lara 0); Second day, New Zealand 98-4 (Fleming 19, Franklin 3); Third day, West Indies 48-0 (Gayle 28, Ganga 20); Fourth day, West Indies 246-8 (Bradshaw 8, Taylor 0).

NEW ZEALAND v WEST INDIES 2005-06 (2nd Test)

At Basin Reserve, Wellington, on 17, 18, 19, 20 March.
Toss: West Indies.   Result: NEW ZEALAND won by ten wickets.
Debuts: none.
Man of the Match: S. P. Fleming.

A sound batting display gave New Zealand victory in the series. West Indies crashed to their 12th consecutive away defeat, their 42nd in 54 Tests outside the Caribbean since 1996: there were only seven away wins in that time, four of those in Bangladesh and Zimbabwe. Batting first, the West Indians did not make good use of a lively pitch, against a ball that did not swing or seam noticeably. By the 14th over both openers had been caught behind and Lara had edged to slip for a single, and when Morton finally fell for a Test-best 63, 50 of them in boundaries, West Indies were 165 for 8. Franklin, moving the ball both ways, took five wickets. Mills (a late replacement for the injured Bond) mopped up quickly next morning, but New Zealand also started badly: Marshall and How fell to successive balls, leaving Fulton and Fleming to repair the damage. Astle batted for three hours, while Vettori underlined his batting credentials in extending the lead to 180. It was almost enough, with West Indies' batting again veering from the sublime to the ridiculous. The openers started solidly again, but then Morton and Lara went quickly. Despite a three-hour 36 from Chanderpaul, and 40 from the Grenadian Rawl Lewis, in his first Test for more than seven years (he was unable to claim a wicket with his leg-spin, and his bowling average reached 388.00 by the end of the game), the innings – and the match – were soon over.

West Indies

C. H. Gayle c McCullum b Franklin	30	– lbw b Vettori	68
D. Ganga c McCullum b Mills	15	– c McCullum b Martin	23
R. S. Morton lbw b Franklin	63	– c Fleming b Franklin	7
B. C. Lara c Fleming b Franklin	1	– c Marshall b Astle	1
*S. Chanderpaul c Fleming b Martin	8	– c Fleming b Mills	36
D. J. Bravo lbw b Franklin	9	– c Astle b Martin	7
†D. Ramdin b Franklin	2	– b Vettori	7
R. N. Lewis c Fleming b Martin	22	– c Astle b Mills	40
I. D. R. Bradshaw not out	20	– c Styris b Franklin	2
D. B. Powell c How b Mills	16	– c How b Mills	7
F. H. Edwards c Fleming b Mills	0	– not out	0
B 2, l-b 1, n-b 3	6	W 6, n-b 11	17

1/43 (1) 2/45 (2) 3/49 (4) 4/80 (5)   192   1/54 (2) 2/75 (3) 3/84 (4)   215
5/102 (6) 6/108 (7) 7/142 (8)   4/113 (1) 5/129 (6) 6/156 (7)
8/165 (3) 9/186 (10) 10/192 (11)   7/163 (5) 8/189 (9) 9/210 (10) 10/215 (8)

Martin 14–1–66–2; Franklin 20–7–53–5; Mills 19.4–7–53–3; Vettori 5–2–13–0; Astle 3–2–4–0. *Second Innings*—Martin 27–8–65–2; Franklin 21–8–64–2; Mills 9.5–2–29–3; Astle 13–4–17–1; Vettori 20–4–40–2.

New Zealand

H. J. H. Marshall c Chanderpaul b Bradshaw	3	– not out	23
J. M. How b Edwards	0	– not out	9
P. G. Fulton c Ramdin b Powell	75		
*S. P. Fleming c Bravo b Edwards	97		
N. J. Astle c Ramdin b Powell	65		
S. B. Styris c Morton b Powell	8		
†B. B. McCullum c Ramdin b Powell	23		
D. L. Vettori c Chanderpaul b Edwards	42		
J. E. C. Franklin not out	28		
K. D. Mills c Ramdin b Edwards	10		
C. S. Martin b Edwards	0		
L-b 4, w 2, n-b 15	21	N-b 5	5

1/3 (1) 2/3 (2) 3/168 (4) 4/207 (3)   372   (no wkt) 37
5/219 (6) 6/246 (7) 7/332 (8)
8/335 (5) 9/372 (10) 10/372 (11)

Edwards 15.3–2–65–5; Bradshaw 19–2–97–1; Powell 24–7–83–4; Gayle 18–4–46–0; Lewis 29–8–70–0; Morton 1–0–7–0. *Second Innings*—Powell 4.1–1–21–0; Bradshaw 4–0–16–0.

Umpires: M. R. Benson *(England)* (7) and D. J. Harper *(Australia)* (57).
Third umpire: A. L. Hill *(New Zealand)*.   Referee: M. J. Procter *(South Africa)* (39).

Close of play: First day, West Indies 182-8 (Bradshaw 10, Powell 16); Second day, New Zealand 335-7 (Astle 65, Franklin 2); Third day, West Indies 118-4 (Chanderpaul 13, Bravo 2).

NEW ZEALAND v WEST INDIES 2005-06 (3rd Test)

At McLean Park, Napier, on 25, 26, 27 *(no play)*, 28 *(no play)*, 29 *(no play)* March.
Toss: New Zealand.   Result: MATCH DRAWN.
Debuts: none.
Man of the Match: no award.

By the end of a chilly tour the West Indians were stoical about New Zealand's summer, adding more and more sweaters. The weather did help stop their run of defeats: less than 80 overs were possible on the first two days, and none at all on the last three. The match only got under way after a boundary rope was shifted to cordon off a particularly boggy strip of outfield. Fleming, in his 75th Test as captain, ahead of Clive Lloyd and behind only Allan Border (93), put West Indies in. There was time for 27.2 overs on the first afternoon before it got too dark, and roughly double that next day before the rain set in for good. There were two notable events amid the mist and murk. After four single-figure innings Lara moved back up to No. 3 on a difficult pitch, batted primly on the first afternoon, belted regally past 50 with 24442 from one Franklin over next day, but then fell unluckily when a bottom edge cannoned off his boot into his stumps. The second incident was a comical run-out muddle involving Morton and Chanderpaul. They both ended up at the bowlers' end after Morton's drive to Vettori at mid-on, and the question was who had been the first to reach the safety of the bowling crease as the keeper broke the stumps. The TV replay ruled that Morton had won by a whisker: he carefully avoided crossing Chanderpaul's path as his captain left the field.

West Indies

C. H. Gayle c Fulton b Martin	30	D. J. Bravo not out 22
D. Ganga b Bond	38	L-b 3, n-b 8 11
B. C. Lara b Astle	83	
R. S. Morton not out	70	1/37 (1) 2/111 (2) (4 wkts) 256
*S. Chanderpaul run out	2	3/171 (3) 4/189 (5)

D. R. Smith, †D. Ramdin, I. D. R. Bradshaw, D. B. Powell and F. H. Edwards did not bat.

Bond 18–2–87–1; Franklin 15–1–66–0; Martin 10–2–39–1; Astle 14–5–23–1; Styris 13.1–5–27–0; Vettori 8–4–11–0.

New Zealand

H. J. H. Marshall, J. M. How, P. G. Fulton, *S. P. Fleming, N. J. Astle, S. B. Styris, †B. B. McCullum, D. L. Vettori, J. E. C. Franklin, S. E. Bond and C. S. Martin.

Umpires: M. R. Benson *(England)* (8) and I. L. Howell *(South Africa)* (5).
Third umpire: G. A. V. Baxter *(New Zealand)*.   Referee: M. J. Procter *(South Africa)* (40).

Close of play: First day, West Indies 95-1 (Ganga 31, Lara 28); Second day, West Indies 256-4 (Morton 70, Bravo 22); Third day, No play; Fourth day, No play.

SOUTH AFRICA v AUSTRALIA 2005-06 (1st Test)

At Newlands, Cape Town, on 16, 17, 18 March.
Toss: South Africa.　　Result: AUSTRALIA won by seven wickets.
Debuts: Australia – S. R. Clark.
Man of the Match: S. R. Clark.

Australia were without Glenn McGrath, nursing his sick wife, but they found a ready-made replacement in Stuart Clark, an affable seamer from New South Wales making his Test debut at 30. Like McGrath, he had control, stamina and the ability to land the ball consistently on the seam. He grabbed three wickets in his opening spell and returned to complete a well-deserved five-for, relishing the conditions as South Africa declined to 205 all out. In reply, Hayden and Ponting added 154 superb runs for the second wicket, a stand that went a long way towards winning the Test. A first-innings lead of 103 looked telling, and so it proved. Clark, his control as constant as before, was again the pick of the bowlers; his nine for 89 in the match was the third-best return on debut for Australia. Warne also came back to life in the second innings, claiming the key wickets of Smith and Rudolph. Australia needed only 95: Ntini, bowling with his usual enthusiasm and sense of purpose, removed the top three, but a controversial episode left the South Africans seething. Hayden punched Boje powerfully to midwicket, where Hall dived forward for what seemed a good catch. When the batsman refused to walk, the umpires looked nonplussed, and conferred for several minutes before shrugging their shoulders and giving Hayden the benefit of the doubt. It made no difference to the result, though: the Australians had played the better cricket throughout, and ran out deserved winners inside three days.

South Africa

*G. C. Smith c Gilchrist b Clark	19	– (2) lbw b Warne ... 16
A. B. de Villiers b Kasprowicz	8	– (1) c Gilchrist b Lee ... 7
H. H. Gibbs b Clark	18	– b Lee ... 0
J. H. Kallis c Hayden b Clark	6	– c Gilchrist b Clark ... 36
A. G. Prince c Hayden b Lee	17	– c Gilchrist b Clark ... 27
J. A. Rudolph c Gilchrist b Kasprowicz	10	– b Warne ... 41
†M. V. Boucher c Gilchrist b Clark	16	– c Langer b Kasprowicz ... 2
A. J. Hall c Hayden b Lee	24	– not out ... 34
N. Boje lbw b Clark	31	– c and b Clark ... 14
A. Nel lbw b Lee	18	– b Clark ... 4
M. Ntini not out	17	– c Kasprowicz b Warne ... 6
L-b 6, n-b 15	21	W 3, n-b 7 ... 10

1/24 (2) 2/42 (1) 3/48 (4) 4/61 (3)　　　　　205　　1/20 (1) 2/20 (3) 3/37 (2)　　　　　197
5/76 (6) 6/104 (7) 7/124 (5)　　　　　　　　　　　　4/75 (4) 5/92 (5) 6/108 (7)
8/148 (8) 9/173 (9) 10/205 (10)　　　　　　　　　　7/158 (6) 8/179 (9) 9/183 (10) 10/197 (11)

Lee 14.5–2–37–3; Kasprowicz 13–0–44–2; Symonds 10–2–22–0; Clark 17–3–55–5; Warne 9–0–41–0. *Second Innings*—Lee 17–5–47–2; Kasprowicz 12–0–39–1; Clark 16–7–34–4; Warne 18.5–1–77–3.

Australia

J. L. Langer lbw b Nel	16	– b Ntini ... 34
M. L. Hayden c Rudolph b Ntini	94	– c Gibbs b Ntini ... 32
*R. T. Ponting c Hall b Kallis	74	– lbw b Ntini ... 1
D. R. Martyn c Boucher b Kallis	22	– not out ... 9
M. E. K. Hussey c Boucher b Hall	6	– not out ... 14
A. Symonds c Nel b Boje	55	
†A. C. Gilchrist c Smith b Kallis	12	
S. K. Warne c de Villiers b Boje	7	
B. Lee c Gibbs b Ntini	0	
M. S. Kasprowicz not out	6	
S. R. Clark c Gibbs b Nel	8	
L-b 7, w 1	8	L-b 5 ... 5

1/21 (1) 2/175 (3) 3/192 (2) 4/214 (5)　　　　308　　1/71 (2) 2/71 (1)　　　　(3 wkts) 95
5/236 (4) 6/272 (7) 7/294 (6)　　　　　　　　　　　3/76 (3)
8/294 (9) 9/296 (8) 10/308 (11)

Ntini 21–2–76–2; Nel 22.2–6–45–2; Hall 16–2–66–1; Boje 16–4–63–2; Kallis 12–0–51–3. *Second Innings*—Nel 7–1–25–0; Ntini 10–3–28–3; Hall 5–1–16–0; Boje 5.1–1–21–0.

Umpires: Aleem Dar *(Pakistan)* (29) and B. R. Doctrove *(West Indies)* (6).
Third umpire: K. H. Hurter *(South Africa)*.　　Referee: B. C. Broad *(England)* (18).

Close of play: First day, Australia 63-1 (Hayden 22, Ponting 20); Second day, South Africa 70-3 (Kallis 31, Prince 14).

SOUTH AFRICA v AUSTRALIA 2005-06 (2nd Test)

At Kingsmead, Durban, on 24, 25, 26, 27, 28 March.
Toss: Australia.   Result: AUSTRALIA won by 112 runs.
Debuts: none.
Man of the Match: S. K. Warne.

Under floodlights, with barely a suggestion of natural light, Australia wrapped up the series on the final evening. Bucknor, the senior umpire, steadfastly kept the players on the field as the match drew to its gripping climax, although on previous days, in far better conditions, both sides had been offered the light. Ponting underpinned Australia's success, hitting twin hundreds for the second time in three Tests against South Africa. He was uncharacteristically restrained for his first hundred, which took 224 balls; even more uncharacteristically, he drove the next ball straight to short extra. Only when Warne came in did the tempo rise: encouraged by the ease of his strokeplay, Hussey squeezed 110 from the last three wickets to turn a decent total into a formidable one. Kallis and de Villiers fought back, adding 134 in 38 overs, before Lee filleted the tail with four wickets in 15 balls. Hayden and Ponting put on 201 to swell the lead, and South Africa were eventually set 410. Warne grabbed four of the first six wickets; South Africa limped to 181 for 7 and seemingly certain defeat, but Boje exploited the attacking fields, while Boucher dug in for more than 50 overs. Nel also survived for over an hour as the rain threatened and the light deteriorated. And when No. 11 Ntini walked out, the scene was more like a day/nighter rather than a Test. Warne pinned Ntini with a perfect googly. He didn't pick it. But in that light, nobody could.

Australia

J. L. Langer c Boucher b Kallis	35	– c Pollock b Boje		37
M. L. Hayden c de Villiers b Ntini	0	– c Boucher b Ntini		102
*R. T. Ponting c Gibbs b Boje	103	– c Boje b Pollock		116
D. R. Martyn c Kallis b Ntini	57	– not out		15
M. E. K. Hussey lbw b Kallis	75			
B. Lee c Boucher b Ntini	0			
A. Symonds lbw b Nel	13			
†A. C. Gilchrist c Boucher b Nel	2	– (5) c Nel b Boje		24
S. K. Warne c de Villiers b Pollock	36			
M. S. Kasprowicz c de Villiers b Nel	7			
S. R. Clark not out	13			
B 9, l-b 10, w 2, n-b 7	28	L-b 5, w 1, n-b 7		13

1/0 (2) 2/97 (1) 3/198 (3) 4/218 (4)   369   1/49 (1) 2/250 (2)   (4 wkts dec.) 307
5/219 (6) 6/253 (7) 7/259 (8)   3/278 (3) 4/307 (5)
8/315 (9) 9/327 (10) 10/369 (5)

Pollock 32–11–73–1; Ntini 24–4–81–3; Nel 31–8–83–3; Kallis 21.1–8–52–2; Boje 19–1–61–1. *Second Innings—* Pollock 19–4–55–1; Ntini 15–2–62–1; Boje 26.4–4–87–2; Nel 14–3–58–0; Kallis 8–0–40–0.

South Africa

*G. C. Smith c Langer b Lee	0	– (2) c Langer b Warne		40
A. B. de Villiers c Hayden b Clark	50	– (1) st Gilchrist b Warne		46
H. H. Gibbs b Kasprowicz	9	– c Warne b Clark		17
J. H. Kallis c and b Clark	114	– lbw b Warne		7
A. G. Prince c Symonds b Warne	33	– c Hussey b Clark		7
J. A. Rudolph c Hussey b Warne	13	– c Langer b Warne		36
†M. V. Boucher b Lee	19	– not out		51
S. M. Pollock c Gilchrist b Lee	1	– b Lee		4
N. Boje not out	6	– c sub (M. J. Clarke) b Kasprowicz		48
A. Nel c Hayden b Lee	5	– c Hayden b Warne		14
M. Ntini c Ponting b Lee	0	– lbw b Warne		0
L-b 3, n-b 14	17	B 5, l-b 8, n-b 14		27

1/0 (1) 2/10 (3) 3/144 (2) 4/200 (5)   267   1/91 (1) 2/98 (2) 3/122 (4)   297
5/226 (6) 6/255 (4) 7/256 (8)   4/122 (3) 5/146 (5) 6/170 (6)
8/257 (7) 9/267 (10) 10/267 (11)   7/181 (8) 8/253 (9) 9/292 (10) 10/297 (11)

Lee 19.4–5–69–5; Kasprowicz 14–0–60–1; Warne 25–2–80–2; Symonds 11–3–16–0; Hussey 1–0–2–0; Clark 18–4–37–2. *Second Innings—* Lee 22–6–65–1; Clark 21–6–46–2; Symonds 8–0–32–0; Warne 35.5–9–86–6; Kasprowicz 12–2–51–1; Hussey 1–0–4–0.

Umpires: S. A. Bucknor *(West Indies)* (110) and B. R. Doctrove *(West Indies)* (7).
Third umpire: B. G. Jerling *(South Africa).*   Referee: B. C. Broad *(England)* (19).

Close of play: First day, Australia 228-5 (Hussey 10, Symonds 4); Second day, South Africa 140-2 (de Villiers 48, Kallis 72); Third day, Australia 125-1 (Hayden 36, Ponting 48); Fourth day, South Africa 29-0 (de Villiers 17, Smith 10).

SOUTH AFRICA v AUSTRALIA 2005-06 (3rd Test)

At The Wanderers, Johannesburg, on 31 March, 1, 2, 3, 4 April.
Toss: South Africa.   Result: AUSTRALIA won by two wickets.
Debuts: none.
Man of the Match: B. Lee.   Man of the Series: S. R. Clark.

Australia belied their reputation for losing dead matches by pulling off another thrilling victory, to complete South Africa's first home series whitewash since losing to England in 1895-96. Set comfortably the highest total to win at Johannesburg, Australia were carried to the brink by Martyn's high-class century, and over the line by Lee and Kasprowicz, something they had famously just failed to do eight months earlier at Edgbaston. Lee took five wickets – including Kallis, captain in place of Smith (injured finger) – and hit his highest Test score. South Africa reached 300 for the only time in the series, despite another seamer-friendly pitch. Then Langer, in his 100th Test, ducked into Ntini's first-ball bouncer and staggered off with concussion. Ntini grabbed four more wickets before Hussey and Warne added 68. In the end, South Africa had to settle for a lead of just 33, which they battled resolutely to increase. Australia needed 292, but Martyn justified his controversial selection for the tour ahead of Brad Hodge, who had just made a double-century against South Africa. Hussey's crafty 89 was also important, though he was fortunate to survive two early lbw shouts. The match still hung in the balance when Pollock nipped one back at Martyn with 34 required. Clark helped add 17 before becoming Ntini's tenth wicket, and as Lee and Kasprowicz reduced the target to single figures, a groggy Langer started to pad up. But Lee's cover-driven four ensured he could stay in the pavilion – and Australia could celebrate their clean sweep.

South Africa

A. B. de Villiers c Martyn b Clark	12	– b Clark	4
H. H. Gibbs b Kasprowicz	16	– c Martyn b Warne	53
H. H. Dippenaar c Gilchrist b Clark	32	– c Hayden b Clark	20
*J. H. Kallis b Lee	37	– lbw b Clark	27
A. G. Prince c Langer b Lee	93	– c Symonds b Warne	9
J. A. Rudolph c Hayden b Warne	25	– (7) c Gilchrist b Clark	0
†M. V. Boucher lbw b Symonds	24	– (8) c Gilchrist b Lee	63
S. M. Pollock c Ponting b Clark	8	– (6) c Gilchrist b Lee	44
N. Boje c Langer b Kasprowicz	43	– c Symonds b Warne	4
A. Nel c Martyn b Lee	0	– not out	18
M. Ntini not out	0	– b Lee	0
L-b 4, n-b 9	13	B 6, l-b 4, w 1, n-b 5	16

1/26 (1) 2/38 (2) 3/97 (3) 4/106 (4)   303   1/9 (1) 2/55 (3) 3/100 (2)   258
5/161 (6) 6/233 (7) 7/251 (8)   4/120 (5) 5/130 (4) 6/140 (7)
8/285 (5) 9/303 (10) 10/303 (9)   7/186 (6) 8/194 (9) 9/258 (8) 10/258 (11)

Lee 24–8–57–3; Clark 28–8–81–3; Kasprowicz 24.2–4–86–2; Warne 13–2–49–1; Symonds 8–2–26–1. *Second Innings*—Lee 18.3–3–57–3; Clark 18–4–64–4; Kasprowicz 2–0–12–0; Symonds 5–0–18–0; Ponting 2–1–7–0; Warne 26–5–90–3.

Australia

J. L. Langer retired hurt	0		
M. L. Hayden c Gibbs b Ntini	3	– (1) c de Villiers b Ntini	0
*R. T. Ponting c de Villiers b Ntini	34	– c Boucher b Kallis	20
D. R. Martyn c Nel b Ntini	21	– lbw b Pollock	101
M. E. K. Hussey lbw b Boje	73	– (2) lbw b Boje	89
A. Symonds lbw b Ntini	4	– (5) c Boucher b Kallis	29
†A. C. Gilchrist c Rudolph b Nel	12	– (6) c Boucher b Ntini	0
S. K. Warne c Pollock b Ntini	36	– (7) c Boucher b Ntini	3
B. Lee c Boje b Ntini	64	– (8) not out	24
M. S. Kasprowicz c Gibbs b Pollock	2	– not out	7
S. R. Clark not out	0	– (9) c Boucher b Ntini	10
B 5, l-b 14, w 2	21	B 1, l-b 9, n-b 1	11

1/12 (2) 2/68 (4) 3/73 (3) 4/89 (6)   270   1/0 (1) 2/33 (3)   (8 wkts) 294
5/106 (7) 6/174 (8) 7/242 (5)   3/198 (2) 4/228 (5)
8/260 (10) 9/270 (9)   5/229 (6) 6/237 (7) 7/258 (4) 8/275 (9)

In the first innings Langer retired hurt at 0.

Ntini 18.5–2–100–6; Nel 15–2–42–1; Pollock 15–2–56–1; Kallis 10–2–43–0; Boje 4–1–10–1. *Second Innings*—Ntini 26–4–78–4; Nel 2–1–4–0; Pollock 25.4–3–81–1; Kallis 18–6–44–2; Boje 19–5–65–1; de Villiers 1–0–12–0.

Umpires: S. A. Bucknor *(West Indies)* (111) and A. L. Hill *(New Zealand)* (4).
Third umpire: K. H. Hurter *(South Africa)*.   Referee: B. C. Broad *(England)* (20).

Close of play: First day, South Africa 238-6 (Prince 79, Pollock 4); Second day, Australia 246-7 (Lee 42, Kasprowicz 0); Third day, South Africa 250-8 (Boucher 55, Nel 18); Fourth day, Australia 248-6 (Martyn 93, Lee 9).

SRI LANKA v PAKISTAN 2005-06 (1st Test)

At Sinhalese Sports Club, Colombo, on 26 *(no play)*, 27, 28, 29, 30 March.
Toss: Pakistan.　　Result: MATCH DRAWN.
Debuts: none.
Man of the Match: K. C. Sangakkara.

An intriguing match, during which the pitch improved daily after being drenched on the washed-out first day, was eventually drawn after Shoaib Malik dug in for a maiden Test century. Put in when play finally started, Sri Lanka slumped to 32 for 5 as the new-ball pair extracted prodigious movement in the first hour. Both Sangakkara and Samaraweera were dismissed shouldering arms to devilish deliveries from Mohammad Asif which cut back after a series of outswingers. But Dilshan consolidated elegantly, adding 111 with Maharoof, and Sri Lanka eventually reached 185, a modest but respectable total in the circumstances. Maharoof followed up his valuable runs with a fine spell, moving the ball enough to pose problems before Muralitharan whirled through the lower order. Sri Lanka claimed a lead of nine, a remarkable turnaround. Tharanga stitched together useful stands with an out-of-sorts Jayasuriya and Sangakkara, who continued to an epic 185 in 7½ hours, a mature innings of unflagging patience. Jayawardene caressed a silky 82 himself before declaring midway through the fourth afternoon, setting a mountainous 458. Facing Murali in the fourth innings has proved too much for many sides, but Pakistan secured a draw quite comfortably in the end, helped by an 81-minute rain delay. Shoaib Malik, neither a regular opener nor a regular blocker, avoided his normal flamboyance for more than eight hours. Crucially, Sangakkara – not surprisingly exhausted after almost three whole days on the field – fumbled an edge off Malinga when Malik had made only 14.

Sri Lanka

W. U. Tharanga lbw b Mohammad Asif	0	– c Imran Farhat b Danish Kaneria		72
S. T. Jayasuriya b Umar Gul	6	– c Kamran Akmal b Mohammad Asif		13
†K. C. Sangakkara b Mohammad Asif	8	– c Inzamam-ul-Haq b Shoaib Malik		185
*D. P. M. D. Jayawardene c Kamran Akmal b Umar Gul .		1– c Abdul Razzaq b Mohammad Asif		82
T. T. Samaraweera b Mohammad Asif	4	– c Imran Farhat b Shahid Afridi		64
T. M. Dilshan c Younis Khan b Danish Kaneria	69	– not out		8
M. F. Maharoof c Younis Khan b Mohammad Asif	46	– not out		5
C. M. Bandara b Danish Kaneria	16			
C. R. D. Fernando c Inzamam-ul-Haq b Danish Kaneria .	16			
S. L. Malinga c Inzamam-ul-Haq b Shahid Afridi	8			
M. Muralitharan not out	0			
B 4, l-b 6, w 1	11	B 10, l-b 6, n-b 3		19

1/0 (1) 2/10 (2) 3/18 (3) 4/26 (4)　　　　185　1/53 (2) 2/127 (1)　　　(5 wkts dec.) 448
5/32 (5) 6/143 (7) 7/149 (6)　　　　　　　　　3/285 (4) 4/429 (3)
8/162 (8) 9/177 (10) 10/185 (9)　　　　　　　5/438 (5)

Mohammad Asif 16–5–41–4; Umar Gul 12–2–41–2; Abdul Razzaq 10–1–43–0; Danish Kaneria 17.5–3–44–3; Shahid Afridi 2–0–6–1. *Second Innings*—Mohammad Asif 23–4–71–2; Umar Gul 20–1–73–0; Danish Kaneria 36–5–138–1; Shoaib Malik 15–2–48–1; Shahid Afridi 21–0–57–1; Abdul Razzaq 12–1–43–0; Imran Farhat 1–0–2–0.

Pakistan

Shoaib Malik c Tharanga b Maharoof	13	– not out		148
Imran Farhat c Bandara b Malinga	69	– c Jayawardene b Muralitharan		34
Younis Khan c Sangakkara b Maharoof	0	– b Muralitharan		8
Faisal Iqbal c Maharoof b Malinga	2	– lbw b Maharoof		60
*Inzamam-ul-Haq c Sangakkara b Maharoof	31	– c Dilshan b Muralitharan		48
Abdul Razzaq b Maharoof	8	– not out		20
Shahid Afridi b Muralitharan	14			
†Kamran Akmal c Tharanga b Muralitharan	27			
Umar Gul lbw b Muralitharan	2			
Mohammad Asif b Malinga	0			
Danish Kaneria not out	0			
B 1, w 1, n-b 8	10	B 6, l-b 7, w 1, n-b 5		19

1/25 (1) 2/25 (3) 3/28 (4) 4/122 (2)　　　　176　1/59 (2) 2/71 (3)　　　　(4 wkts) 337
5/127 (5) 6/138 (6) 7/154 (7)　　　　　　　　3/186 (4) 4/267 (5)
8/160 (9) 9/172 (10) 10/176 (8)

Malinga 12–3–30–3; Maharoof 15–2–52–4; Fernando 3–0–20–0; Bandara 7–1–32–0; Muralitharan 17.4–4–41–3. *Second Innings*—Malinga 13–3–44–0; Maharoof 23–8–70–1; Muralitharan 42–13–94–3; Fernando 15–3–40–0; Bandara 14–4–35–0; Jayasuriya 13–3–37–0; Dilshan 1–0–4–0.

Umpires: S. J. Davis *(Australia)* (8) and R. E. Koertzen *(South Africa)* (73).
Third umpire: T. H. Wijewardene *(Sri Lanka)*.　　Referee: A. G. Hurst *(Australia)* (7).

Close of play: First day, No play; Second day, Pakistan 124-4 (Inzamam-ul-Haq 30, Abdul Razzaq 1); Third day, Sri Lanka 242-2 (Sangakkara 77, Jayawardene 69); Fourth day, Pakistan 89-2 (Shoaib Malik 30, Faisal Iqbal 9).

SRI LANKA v PAKISTAN 2005-06 (2nd Test)

At Asgiriya Stadium, Kandy, on 3, 4, 5 April.
Toss: Pakistan.   Result: PAKISTAN won by eight wickets.
Debuts: Pakistan – Iftikhar Anjum.
Man of the Match: Mohammad Asif.   Man of the Series: Mohammad Asif.

This was a classic contest, full of on-field drama and off-field distractions, chiefly the sideshow of Jayasuriya's short-lived Test retirement (a new selection panel persuaded him to return a few months later). Mohammad Asif was once more in the thick of things after Sri Lanka were put in again, claiming the first three wickets. But although there was a lot of lateral movement, the bounce was consistent, and batting was far from impossible. Sangakkara opted for aggression this time, and made a scintillating 79 from 98 balls, while Samaraweera bedded down for 65 in 4½ hours. The match seesawed during a dramatic second day. Sri Lanka's tail was mopped up by Asif, then Pakistan's openers started confidently. But Mohammad Yousuf's dismissal triggered a collapse: Muralitharan claimed five wickets as the last eight clattered for 49. Sri Lanka, 109 ahead, were firmly in the driving seat: but they self-destructed during a frenetic evening session, against more fine new-ball bowling from Asif. By the end of a day on which 20 wickets fell, Sri Lanka were 73 for 8. They lasted just one ball next morning (Jayasuriya could not bat after dislocating his thumb holding a catch at gully), leaving a potentially tricky target of 183. The momentum, though, had shifted emphatically Pakistan's way. When the new ball failed to work, everything rested on Murali's shoulders – but it was not to be his day. A series of marginal lbw appeals were turned down, and Younis Khan, after three low scores, took control.

Sri Lanka

W. U. Tharanga c Younis Khan b Mohammad Asif	....	10	– b Mohammad Asif	12
S. T. Jayasuriya b Mohammad Asif	....	14	– absent hurt	
†K. C. Sangakkara c Faisal Iqbal b Danish Kaneria	...	79	– (2) b Mohammad Asif	16
*D. P. M. D. Jayawardene c Imran Farhat				
b Mohammad Asif	....	4	– (3) b Abdul Razzaq	15
T. T. Samaraweera b Mohammad Asif	....	65	– (4) b Mohammad Asif	4
T. M. Dilshan c Kamran Akmal b Mohammad Asif	....	22	– (5) c Kamran Akmal b Mohammad Asif	...	11
M. F. Maharoof c Younis Khan b Danish Kaneria	....	7	– (6) lbw b Mohammad Asif.............	1
C. M. Bandara c Kamran Akmal b Mohammad Asif	..	43	– (7) c Kamran Akmal b Abdul Razzaq.......	4
K. M. D. N. Kulasekara b Mohammad Asif.	....	13	– (8) c Umar Gul b Abdul Razzaq	6
S. L. Malinga c Abdul Razzaq b Danish Kaneria	....	9	– (9) not out...........................	0
M. Muralitharan not out	....	1	– (10) c Umar Gul b Abdul Razzaq	0
L-b 4, w 1, n-b 2, p 5	....	12	L-b 3, w 1.....................	4

1/18 (1) 2/27 (2) 3/61 (4) 4/142 (3)   **279**   1/22 (1) 2/40 (2) 3/46 (4)   **73**
5/178 (6) 6/193 (7) 7/238 (5)   4/56 (3) 5/57 (6) 6/65 (5)
8/256 (8) 9/271 (9) 10/279 (10)   7/72 (8) 8/73 (7) 9/73 (10)

Mohammad Asif 23–7–44–6; Umar Gul 23–3–83–0; Iftikhar Anjum 11–1–54–0; Danish Kaneria 23.2–6–53–4; Abdul Razzaq 11–1–36–0. *Second Innings*—Mohammad Asif 12–6–27–5; Iftikhar Anjum 3–0–8–0; Umar Gul 3–0–15–0; Abdul Razzaq 6.5–1–20–4.

Pakistan

Imran Farhat c Jayasuriya b Kulasekara	....	23	– c Jayawardene b Kulasekara..............	65
†Kamran Akmal c Jayawardene b Muralitharan	......	33	– c Sangakkara b Malinga.................	24
Younis Khan c Samaraweera b Maharoof	....	35	– not out.............................	73
Mohammad Yousuf b Muralitharan	....	17	– not out.............................	14
*Inzamam-ul-Haq run out	....	15		
Faisal Iqbal lbw b Muralitharan	....	5		
Abdul Razzaq b Muralitharan	....	4		
Iftikhar Anjum not out.	....	9		
Umar Gul c Sangakkara b Kulasekara	....	4		
Mohammad Asif run out	....	0		
Danish Kaneria c Sangakkara b Muralitharan	....	4		
B 4, l-b 9, w 1, n-b 7	....	21	L-b 3, n-b 4	7

1/57 (1) 2/71 (2) 3/121 (4) 4/125 (3)   **170**   1/38 (2) 2/152 (1)   **(2 wkts) 183**
5/140 (6) 6/149 (7) 7/162 (5)
8/166 (9) 9/166 (10) 10/170 (11)

Malinga 6–2–19–0; Maharoof 14–2–54–1; Kulasekara 16–3–45–2; Muralitharan 16.4–4–39–5. *Second Innings*—Maharoof 10–0–52–0; Kulasekara 12–3–34–1; Malinga 6.2–0–33–1; Muralitharan 13–3–46–0; Bandara 2–0–15–0.

Umpires: S. J. Davis *(Australia)* (9) and D. J. Harper *(Australia)* (58).
Third umpire: E. A. R. de Silva *(Sri Lanka)*.   Referee: A. G. Hurst *(Australia)* (8).

Close of play: First day, Sri Lanka 267-8 (Kulasekara 11, Malinga 0); Second day, Sri Lanka 73-8 (Malinga 0).

BANGLADESH v AUSTRALIA 2005-06 (1st Test)

At Narayanganj Osmani Stadium, Fatullah, on 9, 10, 11, 12, 13 April.
Toss: Bangladesh.   Result: AUSTRALIA won by three wickets.
Debuts: none.
Man of the Match: A. C. Gilchrist.

Fatullah, on the southern outskirts of Dhaka, became the 93rd ground to stage a Test match – and it almost produced a bigger surprise than anything the other 92 ever produced. The top side in the world rankings visited the bottom one for the first time, and received the fright of their lives. Bangladesh claimed a first-innings lead for only the fifth time in Tests, and it was a big one. An entertaining 138 from 20-year-old left-hander Shahriar Nafees – he and Habibul Bashar put on 187, a Bangladesh record for any wicket in Tests at the time – lifted them to 427 (their only higher score was 488 against Zimbabwe), before Australia, a week after winning a Test in Johannesburg, slumped to 93 for 6. Even a superb 144 from Gilchrist only reduced the deficit to 158. He hit six sixes, the first taking him past Chris Cairns's Test record of 87, and also passed 5,000 runs. Bangladesh struggled in their second innings, managing only 148: Warne, wicketless in the first innings (while his fellow legspinner MacGill took a career-best 8 for 108), wrapped things up with three wickets in 11 balls. Australia needed 307, and although Hayden and Ponting took them to 173 for 1, a middle-order collapse left them 231 for 6. But Ponting stood firm for his 31st Test century, helped by Lee and also by being dropped by Mashrafe bin Mortaza at fine leg (that would have been 283 for 8), and inched his side over the line.

Bangladesh

Javed Omar lbw b Gillespie	27	– c Gilchrist b Gillespie	18
Shahriar Nafees b MacGill	138	– b Lee	33
*Habibul Bashar c Lee b MacGill	76	– run out	7
Rajin Saleh c sub (A. Symonds) b MacGill	67	– c Hayden b Gillespie	33
Mohammad Ashraful lbw b Gillespie	29	– lbw b Clark	4
Aftab Ahmed c Hayden b MacGill	29	– lbw b MacGill	17
†Khaled Mashud st Gilchrist b MacGill	17	– b Gillespie	0
Mohammad Rafique b MacGill	6	– lbw b Warne	14
Mashrafe bin Mortaza lbw b MacGill	6	– b Warne	0
Shahadat Hossain not out	3	– not out	1
Enamul Haque, jun. c Hayden b MacGill	0	– lbw b Warne	0
L-b 16, w 2, n-b 11	29	B 10, l-b 7, n-b 4	21

1/51 (1) 2/238 (3) 3/265 (2) 4/295 (5)   427   1/48 (2) 2/58 (1) 3/66 (3)   148
5/351 (6) 6/398 (7) 7/416 (8)   4/77 (5) 5/124 (6) 6/128 (7)
8/417 (4) 9/424 (9) 10/427 (11)   7/147 (8) 8/147 (9) 9/147 (4) 10/148 (11)

Lee 19–5–68–0; Clark 25–4–69–0; Gillespie 23–7–47–2; Warne 20–1–112–0; MacGill 33.3–2–108–8; Clarke 3–0–7–0. *Second Innings*—Lee 8–0–47–1; Gillespie 11–4–18–3; MacGill 13–4–30–1; Clark 4–2–8–1; Warne 13–4–28–3; Clarke 1–1–0–0.

Australia

M. L. Hayden lbw b Mashrafe bin Mortaza	6	– run out	72
M. E. K. Hussey b Mohammad Rafique	23	– b Enamul Haque	37
*R. T. Ponting lbw b Shahadat Hossain	21	– not out	118
D. R. Martyn b Mohammad Rafique	4	– b Mohammad Rafique	7
M. J. Clarke b Enamul Haque	19	– c Khaled Mashud b Mohammad Rafique	9
†A. C. Gilchrist c Shahadat Hossain b Mohammad Rafique	144	– b Mohammad Rafique	12
S. K. Warne c Khaled Mashud b Enamul Haque	6	– lbw b Mohammad Rafique	5
B. Lee lbw b Mashrafe bin Mortaza	15	– c Khaled Mashud b Mashrafe bin Mortaza	29
J. N. Gillespie b Mohammad Rafique	26	– not out	4
S. R. Clark lbw b Mohammad Rafique	0		
S. C. G. MacGill not out	0		
L-b 4, n-b 1	5	B 4, l-b 7, w 1, n-b 2	14

1/6 (1) 2/43 (3) 3/50 (4) 4/61 (2)   269   1/64 (2) 2/173 (1)   (7 wkts) 307
5/79 (5) 6/93 (7) 7/156 (8)   3/183 (4) 4/205 (5)
8/229 (9) 9/268 (10) 10/269 (6)   5/225 (6) 6/231 (7) 7/277 (8)

Mashrafe bin Mortaza 22–3–56–2; Shahadat Hossain 14–2–48–1; Mohammad Rafique 32.2–9–62–5; Enamul Haque 25–4–83–2; Mohammad Ashraful 1–0–11–0; Rajin Saleh 1–0–5–0. *Second Innings*—Mashrafe bin Mortaza 22–7–51–1; Shahadat Hossain 20–5–67–0; Mohammad Rafique 38–6–98–4; Enamul Haque 27–5–80–1.

Umpires: Aleem Dar *(Pakistan)* (30) and Nadeem Ghauri *(Pakistan)* (5).
Third umpire: A. F. M. Akhtaruddin *(Bangladesh)*.   Referee: J. J. Crowe *(New Zealand)* (9).

Close of play: First day, Bangladesh 355-5 (Rajin Saleh 35, Khaled Mashud 2); Second day, Australia 145-6 (Gilchrist 51, Lee 13); Third day, Bangladesh 124-5 (Rajin Saleh 29, Khaled Mashud 0); Fourth day, Australia 212-4 (Ponting 72, Gilchrist 6).

BANGLADESH v AUSTRALIA 2005-06 (2nd Test)

At Chittagong Divisional Stadium on 16, 17, 18, 19, 20 April.

Toss: Bangladesh.   Result: AUSTRALIA won by an innings and 80 runs.

Debuts: Bangladesh – Abdul Razzak. Australia – D. J. Cullen.

Man of the Match: J. N. Gillespie.   Man of the Series: J. N. Gillespie.

This time Australia were not surprised by the opposition, or by a media sit-in protesting at the alleged police assault of a photographer which delayed the start by ten minutes, or by the violent thunderstorms that blew the scoreboard down on the second day. No, the most unthinkable sight of all was Jason Gillespie tickling a ball down to fine leg and running ecstatically back towards the dressing-room with 201 against his name, in what turned out to be his final Test. When Ponting asked him to go in as nightwatchman, after Gillespie had dismissed Bangladesh's top three in his first four overs to send them lurching towards a paltry 197, he was focused only on guarding his stumps and staying in as long as possible. Three days later – his 31st birthday – Gillespie (previous-best first-class score: 58) was still there after nine hours 34 minutes at the crease, and brought up his double-century off 425 balls with his 26th four to go with two sixes. His feat overshadowed that of Hussey – they added 320 for the fourth wicket – who completed 1,000 Test runs just 166 days after his debut, knocking two months off Andrew Strauss's record. Equally shell-shocked, Bangladesh caved in again, despite 79 from Shahriar Nafees and some late defiance from Mohammad Rafique, whose 65 off 53 balls included three sixes in one Warne over and three more off MacGill. But the two legspinners could afford such largesse – they took 15 wickets between them to seal Australia's clean sweep.

Bangladesh

Javed Omar lbw b Gillespie	2	–	lbw b Lee	19
Shahriar Nafees c Lee b Gillespie	0	–	c Gilchrist b Warne	79
*Habibul Bashar c Jaques b Gillespie	9	–	c Hayden b Warne	49
Rajin Saleh b MacGill	71	–	c Ponting b Warne	5
Mohammad Ashraful c Hayden b Warne	6	–	b Warne	29
Aftab Ahmed c Gilchrist b Warne	18	–	c Gilchrist b MacGill	18
†Khaled Mashud not out	34	–	lbw b MacGill	11
Mohammad Rafique c Hayden b MacGill	19	–	c Warne b MacGill	65
Mashrafe bin Mortaza c Gilchrist b Cullen	4	–	c Gillespie b Warne	1
Abdul Razzak c Lee b MacGill	15	–	c Ponting b MacGill	0
Shahadat Hossain c Gillespie b Warne	0	–	not out	3
L-b 10, w 3, n-b 6	19		B 7, l-b 11, w 2, n-b 5	25

1/0 (2) 2/11 (3) 3/17 (1) 4/41 (5)   197   1/25 (1) 2/127 (3) 3/137 (4)   304
5/102 (6) 6/130 (4) 7/152 (8)   4/187 (5) 5/201 (2) 6/229 (6)
8/157 (9) 9/193 (10) 10/197 (11)   7/230 (7) 8/233 (9) 9/235 (10) 10/304 (8)

Lee 9–2–36–0; Gillespie 5–2–11–3; Warne 18.2–3–47–3; MacGill 22–4–68–3; Cullen 7–0–25–1. *Second Innings*—Lee 11–3–35–1; Gillespie 4–0–14–0; Warne 36–4–113–5; MacGill 22.2–3–95–4; Cullen 7–0–29–0.

Australia

M. L. Hayden c sub (Alok Kapali) b Mohammad Rafique	29	M. J. Clarke not out	23
P. A. Jaques c Shahriar Nafees b Mohammad Rafique	66	B 10, l-b 10, w 5, n-b 3	28
J. N. Gillespie not out	201		
*R. T. Ponting run out	52	1/67 (1) 2/120 (2) (4 wkts dec.)	581
M. E. K. Hussey c Shahadat Hossain b Aftab Ahmed	182	3/210 (4) 4/530 (5)	

†A. C. Gilchrist, S. K. Warne, B. Lee, D. J. Cullen and S. C. G. MacGill did not bat.

Mashrafe bin Mortaza 26–3–114–0; Shahadat Hossain 33–3–143–0; Mohammad Rafique 48.3–11–145–2; Abdul Razzak 30–5–99–0; Rajin Saleh 8–0–32–0; Aftab Ahmed 7–1–28–1.

Umpires: Aleem Dar *(Pakistan)* (31) and I. L. Howell *(South Africa)* (6).
Third umpire: Mahbubur Rahman *(Bangladesh)*.   Referee: J. J. Crowe *(New Zealand)* (10).

Close of play: First day, Australia 76-1 (Jaques 38, Gillespie 5); Second day, Australia 151-2 (Gillespie 28, Ponting 19); Third day, Australia 364-3 (Gillespie 102, Hussey 93); Fourth day, Bangladesh 195-4 (Shahriar Nafees 75, Aftab Ahmed 1).

SOUTH AFRICA v NEW ZEALAND 2005-06 (1st Test)

At Centurion Park, Pretoria, on 15, 16, 17, 18, 19 April.
Toss: South Africa.   Result: SOUTH AFRICA won by 128 runs.
Debuts: none.
Man of the Match: M. Ntini.

Makhaya Ntini celebrated his second consecutive ten-wicket haul, the fourth of his Test career (both national records), as he bowled South Africa to a convincing victory six overs into the fifth day. New Zealand could only wonder at what might have been had Shane Bond been fit to exploit the variable bounce and movement offered by the pitch, particularly in the mornings. Mills, Bond's replacement, shared eight wickets with Franklin as South Africa dawdled to 276. But then, presented with the opportunity to drive home the advantage their bowlers had won, New Zealand crashed to 45 for 5. They were steered away from ignominy by Oram, back in the Test team after struggling with injuries for 18 months: he put on 183 with Vettori to set up a lead of 51. South Africa lost three wickets before the deficit was cleared, but then forged ahead, led by controlled aggression from de Villiers. Bad light and rain restricted the fourth day to just 37.1 overs, but in that time New Zealand, chasing 249, collapsed again to 28 for 6, with Ntini once more the sharpest thorn in their side. Marshall stood firm for 165 minutes, while McCullum and Vettori offered some late-order sparkle. For the first time, three players reached a century of Test caps in the same match, appropriately enough at Centurion Park. Afterwards Kallis (whose total included his appearance for the World XI) and Pollock were happier than Fleming, the first New Zealander to reach 100 (76 as captain).

South Africa

*G. C. Smith lbw b Franklin	45	–	lbw b Martin		7
H. H. Gibbs b Mills	6	–	c Styris b Franklin		2
H. H. Dippenaar c Fulton b Mills	52	–	c Fleming b Oram		16
J. H. Kallis b Franklin	38	–	c Vettori b Styris		62
A. G. Prince c Styris b Mills	9	–	c McCullum b Franklin		11
A. B. de Villiers b Franklin	27	–	c Franklin b Oram		97
†M. V. Boucher c Fleming b Martin	18	–	b Mills		21
S. M. Pollock c Styris b Mills	24	–	lbw b Vettori		10
N. Boje lbw b Franklin	23	–	c McCullum b Astle		31
D. W. Steyn c Mills b Martin	13	–	not out		7
M. Ntini not out	1	–	lbw b Vettori		16
B 6, l-b 4, w 3, n-b 7	20		B 12, l-b 2, n-b 5		19
	276				299

1/16 (2) 2/95 (1) 3/119 (3) 4/130 (5)   276
5/177 (4) 6/197 (6) 7/229 (7)
8/233 (8) 9/274 (9) 10/276 (10)

1/8 (1) 2/19 (2) 3/42 (3)   299
4/73 (5) 5/140 (4) 6/194 (7)
7/205 (8) 8/270 (6) 9/276 (9) 10/299 (11)

Mills 18–7–43–4; Franklin 18–3–75–4; Martin 22.4–4–66–2; Oram 14–7–27–0; Vettori 18–2–44–0; Astle 5–2–11–0.
Second Innings—Franklin 14–2–60–2; Martin 24–6–64–1; Mills 21–5–57–1; Oram 17–3–44–2; Vettori 15.1–0–42–2; Astle 5–1–15–1; Styris 2–0–3–1.

New Zealand

H. J. H. Marshall b Ntini	6	–	c Boucher b Ntini		25
P. G. Fulton c Boucher b Pollock	14	–	c Boucher b Ntini		4
*S. P. Fleming c and b Ntini	0	–	(4) c Kallis b Steyn		6
S. B. Styris c Gibbs b Ntini	17	–	(5) c Boucher b Steyn		2
N. J. Astle c Boucher b Steyn	4	–	(6) c de Villiers b Ntini		2
J. D. P. Oram c Pollock b Steyn	133	–	(7) b Ntini		2
†B. B. McCullum c Boje b Kallis	31	–	(8) c Dippenaar b Steyn		33
D. L. Vettori c Prince b Ntini	81	–	(9) c Boucher b Steyn		38
J. E. C. Franklin c Boucher b Ntini	8	–	(10) not out		0
K. D. Mills c Boje b Pollock	12	–	(3) c Dippenaar b Ntini		0
C. S. Martin not out	1	–	b Steyn		0
L-b 12, n-b 8	20		L-b 2, n-b 6		8
	327				120

1/8 (1) 2/12 (3) 3/32 (4) 4/38 (2)   327
5/45 (5) 6/89 (7) 7/272 (8)
8/280 (9) 9/322 (10) 10/327 (6)

1/5 (2) 2/5 (3) 3/17 (4)   120
4/23 (5) 5/26 (6) 6/28 (7)
7/73 (8) 8/119 (1) 9/119 (9) 10/120 (11)

Ntini 19–2–94–5; Steyn 18.4–1–95–2; Pollock 15–4–45–2; Kallis 9–1–41–1; Boje 7–0–29–0; Smith 3–1–11–0.
Second Innings—Ntini 14–3–51–5; Steyn 17–4–47–5; Pollock 5–1–20–0.

Umpires: M. R. Benson *(England)* (9) and D. J. Harper *(Australia)* (59).
Third umpire: M. Erasmus *(South Africa)*.   Referee: R. S. Madugalle *(Sri Lanka)* (87).

Close of play: First day, South Africa 266-8 (Boje 20, Steyn 8); Second day, South Africa 4-0 (Smith 3, Gibbs 0); Third day, South Africa 280-9 (Steyn 5, Ntini 0); Fourth day, New Zealand 98-7 (Marshall 24, Vettori 18).

SOUTH AFRICA v NEW ZEALAND 2005-06 (2nd Test)

At Newlands, Cape Town, on 27, 28, 29, 30 April, 1 May.
Toss: South Africa.   Result: MATCH DRAWN.
Debuts: New Zealand – J. S. Patel.
Man of the Match: S. P. Fleming.

Stephen Fleming's 262 was the main reason to remember this match, but his side had the better of it in other ways too: Franklin's century from No. 9, and Jeetan Patel's assured debut with bat and ball. Fleming became the first New Zealander to make three double-centuries, while his partnership of 256 with Franklin was their highest against South Africa. The match also showed the pitfalls of playing in South Africa as winter approached. The first day's play was delayed by a damp outfield, and ended prematurely by bad light, while on the second morning, dense fog rendered Table Mountain about as visible as a polar bear in a blizzard. Smith was criticised for fielding first, but he had felt that his bowlers' best chance of success was on the first day. New Zealand did slip to 82 for 3 after lunch, and lost six wickets in all on that first day – but were not bowled out until an hour into the third day after scoring 593. When Fleming eventually fell to the occasional bowling of Prince, after 576 minutes, 423 balls, 31 fours and two sixes, Patel unveiled a steady bat to usher Franklin to his first Test century. He was only the fourth person to have achieved both a Test hundred and a hat-trick, following Johnny Briggs of England and the Pakistanis Abdul Razzaq and Wasim Akram. Amla, with a maiden hundred in his first Test for 15 months, and Prince made the game safe for South Africa.

New Zealand

M. H. W. Papps b Nel	22	– c Prince b Steyn		20
P. G. Fulton c Boucher b Steyn	36	– c Kallis b Ntini		11
*S. P. Fleming b Prince	262			
S. B. Styris c Dippenaar b Ntini	11	– (3) not out		54
N. J. Astle lbw b Ntini	50	– (4) c Smith b Kallis		14
J. D. P. Oram run out	13	– (5) not out		8
†B. B. McCullum lbw b Ntini	5			
D. L. Vettori c Nel b Ntini	11			
J. E. C. Franklin not out	122			
J. S. Patel not out	27			
B 3, l-b 15, w 1, n-b 15	34	B 1, l-b 9, n-b 4		14

1/50 (1) 2/62 (2) 3/82 (4)   (8 wkts dec.) 593   1/34 (1) 2/41 (2)   (3 wkts) 121
4/188 (5) 5/237 (6) 6/259 (7)   3/81 (4)
7/279 (8) 8/535 (3)

C. S. Martin did not bat.

Ntini 43–5–162–4; Steyn 31–4–114–1; Nel 27–3–98–1; Kallis 15–4–45–0; Boje 29–4–89–2; Smith 17–2–61–0; Amla 1–0–4–0; Prince 2–0–2–1. *Second Innings*—Steyn 9–3–26–1; Ntini 8–2–25–1; Nel 10–2–41–0; Kallis 5–3–5–1; Boje 5–1–14–0.

South Africa

*G. C. Smith c and b Patel	25	D. W. Steyn st McCullum b Vettori		13
H. H. Dippenaar b Patel	47	M. Ntini run out		11
H. M. Amla lbw b Vettori	149			
J. H. Kallis c Martin b Oram	71	B 15, l-b 10, n-b 5		30
A. G. Prince not out	108			
A. B. de Villiers c Papps b Patel	13	1/36 (1) 2/108 (2) 3/252 (4)		512
†M. V. Boucher c Fleming b Franklin	33	4/344 (3) 5/361 (6) 6/435 (7)		
N. Boje lbw b Franklin	0	7/435 (8) 8/462 (9)		
A. Nel lbw b Franklin	12	9/495 (10) 10/512 (11)		

Martin 20–7–62–0; Franklin 33–5–95–3; Vettori 63–10–147–2; Patel 42–8–117–3; Styris 10–2–33–0; Oram 18–10–24–1; Astle 2–0–9–0.

Umpires: M. R. Benson *(England)* (10) and E. A. R. de Silva *(Sri Lanka)* (31).
Third umpire: M. Erasmus *(South Africa)*.   Referee: R. S. Madugalle *(Sri Lanka)* (88).

Close of play: First day, New Zealand 265-6 (Fleming 114, Vettori 1); Second day, New Zealand 535-8 (Franklin 93); Third day, South Africa 155-2 (Amla 50, Kallis 25); Fourth day, South Africa 427-5 (Prince 70, Boucher 26).

SOUTH AFRICA v NEW ZEALAND 2005-06 (3rd Test)

At The Wanderers, Johannesburg, on 5, 6, 7 May.
Toss: South Africa.   Result: SOUTH AFRICA won by four wickets.
Debuts: none.
Man of the Match: G. C. Smith.   Man of the Series: M. Ntini.

Ntini took the chance to wrap up a fine home season (39 wickets in six Tests) with five victims in New Zealand's miserable first innings of 119, to set up a three-day victory and a series win. Both openers went before a run had been scored, and Styris soon followed for another duck. Six men fell to catches between wicketkeeper and third slip, while Papps played on. "I hope I'm not putting any of the South African bowlers down, but I don't think they knew which way it was going either," said Astle, who gritted out 20. Expectation of an early finish increased when South Africa managed a lead of only 67, despite resuming on the second morning at 133 for 4: 11 overs later they were all out. Kallis soon took his 200th wicket, when Fleming edged to third slip: he followed Garry Sobers in scoring 8,000 runs and taking 200 wickets in Tests. By the end of the second day, 26 wickets had fallen for 519 runs in 146 overs – and no-one blamed the pitch. New Zealand were steadied by a defiant 60 by Vettori before folding to leave a target of 217. The resolute Smith clipped his second half-century of the match – his first scores above 50 for a year – and victory seemed imminent when he was caught behind. But a marathon season wasn't quite ready to be consigned to the record books, and South Africa needed Prince's prosaic approach to take them home.

New Zealand

M. H. W. Papps b Ntini	0	– c Hall b Kallis	15
J. M. How c de Villiers b Steyn	0	– lbw b Steyn	4
*S. P. Fleming c Boucher b Ntini	46	– c de Villiers b Kallis	37
S. B. Styris c de Villiers b Ntini	0	– c and b Steyn	42
N. J. Astle c Kallis b Steyn	20	– c Boucher b Steyn	45
J. D. P. Oram lbw b Pollock	18	– c Dippenaar b Steyn	27
†B. B. McCullum c and b Ntini	0	– c Boucher b Pollock	5
D. L. Vettori lbw b Steyn	2	– c de Villiers b Hall	60
J. E. C. Franklin c Boucher b Hall	19	– b Pollock	19
K. D. Mills not out	0	– not out	0
C. S. Martin c Smith b Ntini	1	– c Amla b Hall	0
L-b 9, w 1, n-b 3	13	B 5, l-b 17, w 3, n-b 4	29
	119		**283**

1/0 (2) 2/0 (1) 3/2 (4) 4/57 (5)   119   1/9 (2) 2/40 (1) 3/82 (3)   283
5/78 (3) 6/78 (7) 7/82 (8)   4/158 (5) 5/177 (4) 6/190 (7)
8/118 (9) 9/118 (6) 10/119 (11)   7/239 (6) 8/283 (9) 9/283 (8) 10/283 (11)

Ntini 16–7–35–5; Steyn 12–3–43–3; Hall 9–2–21–1; Pollock 7–2–11–1. *Second Innings*—Steyn 22–3–91–4; Ntini 17–4–44–0; Kallis 14–1–40–2; Hall 12.5–1–50–2; Pollock 13–3–36–2.

South Africa

*G. C. Smith c McCullum b Franklin	63	– c McCullum b Franklin	68
H. H. Dippenaar b Martin	0	– c McCullum b Martin	37
H. M. Amla c Papps b Styris	56	– b Mills	28
J. H. Kallis b Martin	9	– c How b Mills	13
A. G. Prince c McCullum b Martin	4	– not out	43
A. B. de Villiers c Styris b Franklin	2	– b Franklin	5
†M. V. Boucher lbw b Franklin	0	– b Franklin	6
S. M. Pollock not out	32	– not out	6
A. J. Hall lbw b Martin	5		
D. W. Steyn b Martin	2		
M. Ntini c McCullum b Mills	8		
N-b 5	5	B 4, l-b 5, w 2, n-b 3	14
	186	(6 wkts)	**220**

1/1 (2) 2/99 (1) 3/131 (4) 4/131 (3)   186   1/69 (2) 2/130 (1)   (6 wkts) 220
5/139 (6) 6/139 (7) 7/139 (5)   3/156 (3) 4/167 (4)
8/145 (9) 9/161 (10) 10/186 (11)   5/180 (6) 6/202 (7)

Martin 15–2–37–5; Franklin 13–2–87–3; Oram 4–0–20–0; Mills 8–0–30–1; Astle 2–0–11–0; Styris 2–1–1–1. *Second Innings*—Martin 17–1–64–1; Franklin 13.3–0–67–3; Mills 11–3–49–2; Oram 2–0–8–0; Styris 3–0–12–0; Vettori 1–0–11–0.

Umpires: E. A. R. de Silva *(Sri Lanka)* (32) and D. B. Hair *(Australia)* (72).
Third umpire: I. L. Howell *(South Africa)*.   Referee: R. S. Madugalle *(Sri Lanka)* (89).

Close of play: First day, South Africa 133-4 (Prince 1, de Villiers 1); Second day, New Zealand 214-6 (Oram 19, Vettori 21).

ENGLAND v SRI LANKA 2006 (1st Test)

At Lord's, London, on 11, 12, 13, 14, 15 May.
Toss: England.   Result: MATCH DRAWN.
Debuts: England – S. I. Mahmood. Sri Lanka – C. K. Kapugedera.
Man of the Match: D. P. M. D. Jayawardene.

Patronised as mere fodder for England's seamers in early May, Sri Lanka's batsmen pulled off one of the finest acts of escapology since Clint Eastwood bust out of Alcatraz. Following on 359 behind, they survived 199 overs and three new balls – helped by six dropped catches – on a benign pitch. Flintoff's personal workload was 68.3 overs, although such hard labour looked unlikely when England cruised to 551 for 6 in five sessions of one-way traffic then skittled Sri Lanka for 192. Two close lbw shouts from Muralitharan apart, Trescothick's 14th Test century was a routine one, then Pietersen batted England over the horizon with his second successive 158 on home soil. He passed 1,000 Test runs, 295 days after his debut. Sajid Mahmood then found prodigious swing on his debut, ripping out three wickets in nine deliveries as Sri Lanka slipped to 85 for 6. But in the follow-on Jayawardene (dropped on 58) batted six hours to set the tone for a wonderful rearguard in which seven batsmen reached 50, for only the third time in Tests. When Cook missed Kulasekara seven overs after lunch, Sri Lanka (449 for 8) were only 90 ahead; when Kulasekara finally holed out, he and Vaas had survived 189 minutes and 45 overs, adding 105, a national ninth-wicket record. By 5.43, and the final bad-light stoppage, Sri Lanka had become only the tenth Test side to score 500 after following on, a list also including England against Sri Lanka at Lord's four years earlier.

England

M. E. Trescothick c Jayawardene b Muralitharan	106	*A. Flintoff not out	33
A. J. Strauss c Jayawardene b Muralitharan	48	†G. O. Jones not out.	11
A. N. Cook c Sangakkara b Maharoof	89	B 16, l-b 7, w 4, n-b 15	42
K. P. Pietersen lbw b Vaas	158		
M. J. Hoggard b Vaas	7	1/86 (2) 2/213 (1) (6 wkts dec.)	551
P. D. Collingwood b Muralitharan	57	3/312 (3) 4/329 (5) 5/502 (4) 6/502 (6)	

L. E. Plunkett, S. I. Mahmood and M. S. Panesar did not bat.

Vaas 36–2–124–2; Maharoof 28–4–125–1; Kulasekara 25–3–89–0; Muralitharan 48–10–158–3; Dilshan 6–0–32–0.

Sri Lanka

J. Mubarak lbw b Hoggard	0	– b Hoggard	6
W. U. Tharanga lbw b Hoggard	10	– c Jones b Panesar	52
†K. C. Sangakkara c Trescothick b Mahmood	21	– c Jones b Panesar	65
*D. P. M. D. Jayawardene c Jones b Flintoff	61	– c Jones b Flintoff	119
T. T. Samaraweera lbw b Mahmood	0	– (6) c Jones b Mahmood	6
T. M. Dilshan run out	0	– (7) c Trescothick b Plunkett	69
C. K. Kapugedera lbw b Mahmood	0	– (8) c Jones b Flintoff	10
M. F. Maharoof c and b Hoggard	22	– (5) c Pietersen b Mahmood	59
W. P. U. J. C. Vaas c Trescothick b Hoggard	31	– not out	50
K. M. D. N. Kulasekara c Strauss b Flintoff	29	– c Pietersen b Hoggard	64
M. Muralitharan not out	0	– not out	1
L-b 8, n-b 10	18	B 9, l-b 19, w 3, n-b 5	36

1/0 (1) 2/21 (2) 3/81 (3) 4/81 (5)   192   1/10 (1) 2/119 (2)   (9 wkts) 537
5/85 (6) 6/85 (7) 7/129 (8)   3/178 (3) 4/291 (5) 5/303 (6)
8/131 (4) 9/192 (9) 10/192 (10)   6/371 (4) 7/405 (8) 8/421 (7) 9/526 (10)

Hoggard 14–4–27–4; Flintoff 17.3–2–55–2; Plunkett 11–0–52–0; Mahmood 13–2–50–3. *Second Innings*—Hoggard 46–11–110–2; Flintoff 51–11–131–2; Mahmood 35–5–118–2; Plunkett 31–10–85–1; Collingwood 9–2–16–0; Panesar 27–10–49–2.

Umpires: Aleem Dar *(Pakistan)* (32) and R. E. Koertzen *(South Africa)* (74).
Third umpire: N. J. Llong *(England)*.   Referee: A. G. Hurst *(Australia)* (9).

Close of play: First day, England 318-3 (Pietersen 54, Hoggard 2); Second day, Sri Lanka 91-6 (Jayawardene 40, Maharoof 6); Third day, Sri Lanka 183-3 (Jayawardene 35, Maharoof 5); Fourth day, Sri Lanka 381-6 (Dilshan 39, Kapugedera 5).

ENGLAND v SRI LANKA 2006 (2nd Test)

At Edgbaston, Birmingham, on 25, 26, 27, 28 May.
Toss: Sri Lanka.   Result: ENGLAND won by six wickets.
Debuts: none.
Man of the Match: K. P. Pietersen.

One moment of genius lit up this otherwise moderate Test. Kevin Pietersen had already motored to 136 from 154 balls in England's first innings, while no-one else passed 30. His battle with Muralitharan had been engrossing, but now Pietersen did his own pirouette at the crease, changing his feet and his grip to turn himself into a left-hander. He then unleashed the ball into the crowd for six. Murali could no more believe it than anyone else: he said afterwards that Pietersen was now "on top of the world" as a batsman (although the official ICC rankings merely lifted him to No. 10). Pietersen fell attempting an orthodox sweep two balls later: perhaps he had become over-confident, but he had set up England's victory. The conditions again suited their combination of swing and seam, and Sri Lanka were 65 for 6 at lunch on the first day, and although Vaas again proved tenacious (he was to face more balls in the series than any of Sri Lanka's recognised batsmen) the eventual total of 141 was one fewer than Pietersen managed on his own. This time there was no Great Escape, despite the loss of much of the third day to rain and a diligent century from the tall Vandort, who batted for 6½ hours and put on 125 with Dilshan. England needed 78, but lost four wickets in getting there, all of them to Murali, who thus took ten in a match for the 15th time in Tests.

Sri Lanka

M. G. Vandort c Collingwood b Plunkett	9	– c Jones b Plunkett	105
W. U. Tharanga b Hoggard	0	– c Jones b Hoggard	0
†K. C. Sangakkara c Jones b Plunkett	25	– c Collingwood b Panesar	18
*D. P. M. D. Jayawardene c Jones b Plunkett	0	– lbw b Hoggard	5
T. T. Samaraweera c Collingwood b Hoggard	3	– st Jones b Panesar	8
T. M. Dilshan c Trescothick b Flintoff	27	– lbw b Hoggard	59
M. F. Maharoof c Jones b Mahmood	5	– c and b Flintoff	13
W. P. U. J. C. Vaas not out	30	– c Collingwood b Plunkett	1
K. M. D. N. Kulasekara c Trescothick b Mahmood	3	– c Collingwood b Plunkett	0
S. L. Malinga lbw b Panesar	26	– c Strauss b Flintoff	2
M. Muralitharan c Plunkett b Flintoff	1	– not out	0
L-b 6, n-b 6	12	L-b 8, w 1, n-b 11	20

1/3 (2) 2/16 (1) 3/16 (4) 4/25 (5)   141
5/46 (3) 6/65 (7) 7/79 (6)
8/82 (9) 9/132 (10) 10/141 (11)

1/2 (2) 2/38 (3) 3/43 (4)   231
4/56 (5) 5/181 (6) 6/219 (7)
7/223 (8) 8/223 (9) 9/231 (10) 10/231 (1)

Hoggard 15–4–32–2; Flintoff 13.2–4–28–2; Plunkett 12–1–43–3; Mahmood 9–1–25–2; Panesar 2–0–7–1. *Second Innings*—Hoggard 22–8–64–3; Flintoff 19–3–50–2; Plunkett 13.2–6–17–3; Panesar 28–6–73–2; Mahmood 9–2–19–0; Collingwood 2–2–0–0.

England

M. E. Trescothick c Sangakkara b Muralitharan	27	– lbw b Muralitharan	0
A. J. Strauss run out	30	– c Jayawardene b Muralitharan	16
A. N. Cook lbw b Muralitharan	23	– not out	34
K. P. Pietersen lbw b Muralitharan	142	– lbw b Muralitharan	13
M. J. Hoggard b Vaas	3		
P. D. Collingwood c Tharanga b Muralitharan	19	– (5) c Sangakkara b Muralitharan	3
*A. Flintoff b Malinga	9	– (6) not out	4
†G. O. Jones c Samaraweera b Muralitharan	4		
L. E. Plunkett c Vandort b Muralitharan	0		
S. I. Mahmood not out	0		
M. S. Panesar lbw b Malinga	0		
B 6, l-b 13, n-b 14, p 5	38	B 2, n-b 9	11

1/56 (1) 2/69 (2) 3/125 (3) 4/169 (5)   295
5/238 (6) 6/290 (4) 7/290 (7)
8/293 (9) 9/294 (8) 10/295 (11)

1/9 (1) 2/35 (2)   (4 wkts) 81
3/63 (4) 4/73 (5)

Vaas 16–6–30–1; Malinga 13.3–2–68–2; Maharoof 11–3–42–0; Muralitharan 25–2–86–6; Kulasekara 13–2–45–0. *Second Innings*—Vaas 7–2–12–0; Malinga 7–1–29–0; Muralitharan 12.2–3–29–4; Dilshan 1–0–9–0.

Umpires: Aleem Dar *(Pakistan)* (33) and D. B. Hair *(Australia)* (73).
Third umpire: I. J. Gould *(England)*.   Referee: A. G. Hurst *(Australia)* (10).

Close of play: First day, England 138-3 (Pietersen 30, Hoggard 2); Second day, Sri Lanka 86-4 (Vandort 30, Dilshan 21); Third day, Sri Lanka 194-5 (Vandort 89, Maharoof 0).

ENGLAND v SRI LANKA 2006 (3rd Test)

At Trent Bridge, Nottingham, on 2, 3, 4, 5 June.
Toss: Sri Lanka.   Result: SRI LANKA won by 134 runs.
Debuts: England – J. Lewis.
Man of the Match: M. Muralitharan.   Men of the Series: M. Muralitharan and K. P. Pietersen.

Sri Lanka were expected to roll over again – but instead levelled the series, only their third Test win outside the subcontinent or Zimbabwe, after Napier 1994-95 and The Oval 1998. Eight years after taking 16 wickets in that Oval game, and now armed with the *doosra*, Muralitharan wreaked havoc on a dry pitch. His second-innings 8 for 70 were the best figures in a Trent Bridge Test, beating B. J. T. Bosanquet's 8 for 107 against Australia 101 years previously. When he snaffled the first seven wickets on the fourth afternoon, Murali was eyeing all ten, a feat achieved in Tests only by Jim Laker and Anil Kumble – but Kapugedera kyboshed that by running out Hoggard, hitting a single stump from midwicket. Murali also contributed a robust 29-ball 33 to a last-wicket stand of 62 with Vaas, which lifted Sri Lanka to a respectable first-innings total after being 139 for 8, including Vandort to Jon Lewis's fourth delivery in a Test. But from then on, it was Sri Lanka calling the shots. England batted poorly, only Collingwood digging in (for nearly four hours). Sri Lanka's tail again proved troublesome: the last three wickets added 84 before Panesar completed his first Test five-for. England's eventual target was 325 – more than they had ever made to win at home. Even so, the openers started confidently, putting on 84 in 27 overs before Trescothick failed to pick the *doosra*. That began a sequence in which Murali took eight for 26 in 105 balls.

Sri Lanka

M. G. Vandort b Lewis		1	– b Hoggard		5
W. U. Tharanga c Jones b Hoggard		34	– c Cook b Panesar		46
†K. C. Sangakkara c Jones b Flintoff		36	– c Trescothick b Flintoff		66
*D. P. M. D. Jayawardene c Jones b Flintoff		0	– c Jones b Plunkett		45
T. M. Dilshan c Flintoff b Lewis		8	– (6) c Jones b Hoggard		32
S. T. Jayasuriya c Pietersen b Flintoff		4	– (5) lbw b Panesar		4
C. K. Kapugedera c Strauss b Plunkett		14	– c Cook b Plunkett		50
M. F. Maharoof c Flintoff b Hoggard		13	– b Panesar		6
W. P. U. J. C. Vaas not out		38	– not out		34
S. L. Malinga c Pietersen b Lewis		21	– b Panesar		22
M. Muralitharan c Flintoff b Plunkett		33	– c Strauss b Panesar		2
B 4, l-b 3, w 2, n-b 20		29	B 1, l-b 3, w 1, n-b 5		10

1/2 (1) 2/84 (3) 3/85 (2) 4/86 (4) 231   1/6 (1) 2/100 (2) 3/143 (3) 322
5/97 (5) 6/105 (6) 7/129 (8)   4/148 (5) 5/191 (4) 6/223 (6)
8/139 (7) 9/169 (10) 10/231 (11)   7/238 (8) 8/287 (7) 9/320 (10) 10/322 (11)

Hoggard 17–3–65–2; Lewis 21–3–68–3; Plunkett 8.2–1–36–2; Flintoff 15–2–52–3; Panesar 5–3–3–0. *Second Innings*—Hoggard 22–4–71–2; Lewis 20–6–54–0; Flintoff 13–1–38–1; Panesar 37.1–13–78–5; Plunkett 19–2–65–2; Pietersen 2–0–12–0.

England

M. E. Trescothick run out		24	– b Muralitharan		31
A. J. Strauss b Vaas		7	– c Jayawardene b Muralitharan		55
A. N. Cook b Malinga		24	– lbw b Muralitharan		5
K. P. Pietersen c Jayawardene b Muralitharan		41	– c Dilshan b Muralitharan		6
P. D. Collingwood lbw b Vaas		48	– c Dilshan b Muralitharan		9
*A. Flintoff c Jayawardene b Jayasuriya		1	– c Dilshan b Muralitharan		0
†G. O. Jones st Sangakkara b Muralitharan		19	– b Muralitharan		6
L. E. Plunkett b Jayasuriya		9	– not out		22
M. J. Hoggard c Jayawardene b Muralitharan		10	– run out		4
J. Lewis c Dilshan b Malinga		20	– lbw b Muralitharan		7
M. S. Panesar not out		0	– lbw b Jayasuriya		26
B 2, l-b 13, w 3, n-b 8		26	B 13, l-b 1, w 1, n-b 4		19

1/25 (2) 2/39 (1) 3/73 (3) 4/117 (4) 229   1/84 (1) 2/104 (3) 3/111 (2) 190
5/118 (6) 6/151 (7) 7/184 (8)   4/120 (4) 5/120 (6) 6/125 (5)
8/196 (5) 9/229 (9) 10/229 (10)   7/132 (7) 8/136 (9) 9/153 (10) 10/190 (11)

Vaas 26–5–71–2; Malinga 23.1–3–62–2; Muralitharan 31–10–62–3; Jayasuriya 11–4–19–2. *Second Innings*—Vaas 9–1–28–0; Malinga 7–0–24–0; Muralitharan 30–10–70–8; Jayasuriya 22.5–3–54–1.

Umpires: D. B. Hair *(Australia)* (74) and R. E. Koertzen *(South Africa)* (75).
Third umpire: P. J. Hartley *(England)*.   Referee: A. G. Hurst *(Australia)* (11).

Close of play: First day, England 53-2 (Cook 12, Pietersen 6); Second day, Sri Lanka 45-1 (Tharanga 17, Sangakkara 22); Third day, Sri Lanka 286-7 (Kapugedera 50, Vaas 24).

WEST INDIES v INDIA 2006 (1st Test)

At Antigua Recreation Ground, St John's, on 2, 3, 4, 5, 6 June.
Toss: India.   Result: MATCH DRAWN.
Debuts: India – V. R. Singh.
Man of the Match: Wasim Jaffer.

With the nearby Sir Vivian Richards Stadium under construction for the 2007 World Cup, this was expected to be the ARG's last big match. Almost inevitably, it ended in another run-banquet; more surprisingly, it also produced one of Test cricket's tensest finishes. On the first day, the usually benign pitch crackled with life, thanks to some grass on a good length, and India struggled after being inserted: six were caught behind the wicket off the outside edge, although Dravid lasted more than four hours. Then normal service resumed: Gayle provided the early propulsion before Sarwan and Bravo consolidated. By mid-morning on the third day, India were batting again, 130 behind. But the pitch was far easier now, and the batsmen were boosted when the fiery Edwards injured his hamstring. Wasim Jaffer cashed in, becoming only the fourth Indian, after Sunil Gavaskar, Dilip Sardesai and Navjot Sidhu, to make a Test double-century in the Caribbean. Bradshaw's heroic 25-over spell – he bowled unchanged for the equivalent of two sessions, conceding only 47 – helped delay the declaration, which finally came with India 391 ahead and 95 overs remaining. At lunch on the final day, with three wickets down including Lara for a duck, it seemed all over: Gayle and Chanderpaul resisted for more than a session, but India still entered the final hour needing only three wickets. Two of them fell . . . but Edwards and Collymore, childhood mates from the Barbadian village of Boscobelle, kept out the last 19 balls to salvage a draw.

India

Wasim Jaffer c Ramdin b Edwards	1	– b Bradshaw	212
V. Sehwag c Lara b Collymore	36	– c Gayle b Collymore	41
V. V. S. Laxman c Ramdin b Bravo	29	– c Bradshaw b Mohammed	31
*R. Dravid c Lara b Collymore	49	– c Bradshaw b Mohammed	62
Yuvraj Singh b Mohammed	23	– c Chanderpaul b Gayle	39
M. Kaif c Ramdin b Bravo	13	– not out	46
†M. S. Dhoni c Lara b Collymore	19	– c Ganga b Mohammed	69
A. Kumble b Bravo	21		
S. Sreesanth not out	29		
V. R. Singh c Sarwan b Bravo	2		
M. M. Patel b Edwards	0		
L-b 8, w 2, n-b 9	19	L-b 6, w 6, n-b 9	21

1/10 (1) 2/51 (2) 3/72 (3) 4/126 (5)   241   1/72 (2) 2/147 (3)   (6 wkts dec.) 521
5/155 (6) 6/179 (7) 7/180 (4)   3/350 (4) 4/375 (1)
8/227 (8) 9/231 (10) 10/241 (11)   5/419 (5) 6/521 (7)

Edwards 18.5–3–53–2; Bradshaw 24–3–83–0; Collymore 17–7–27–3; Gayle 4–0–6–0; Bravo 22–9–40–4; Mohammed 7–1–24–1. *Second Innings*—Edwards 5.4–2–16–0; Collymore 23–8–50–1; Bradshaw 40–9–108–1; Bravo 26.2–4–98–0; Mohammed 29.5–3–162–3; Gayle 22–5–66–1; Sarwan 4–0–15–0.

West Indies

C. H. Gayle c Dravid b Kumble	72	– lbw b Kumble	69
D. Ganga lbw b Patel	9	– c Yuvraj Singh b Kumble	36
R. R. Sarwan lbw b Kumble	58	– c Kumble b Sreesanth	1
*B. C. Lara c Yuvraj Singh b Patel	18	– lbw b Sreesanth	0
S. Chanderpaul c Dhoni b Sehwag	24	– c Dravid b Kumble	62
D. J. Bravo st Dhoni b Sehwag	68	– c Dhoni b Sehwag	28
†D. Ramdin c Dhoni b Patel	26	– c Dravid b Sehwag	8
I. D. R. Bradshaw c Yuvraj Singh b V. R. Singh	33	– c Dhoni b Patel	10
D. Mohammed not out	19	– b Kumble	52
F. H. Edwards c Dhoni b V. R. Singh	4	– not out	1
C. D. Collymore lbw b Kumble	0	– not out	1
B 2, l-b 14, w 2, n-b 22	40	B 5, l-b 8, n-b 17	30

1/18 (2) 2/137 (1) 3/159 (4) 4/182 (3)   371   1/67 (2) 2/68 (3)   (9 wkts) 298
5/255 (5) 6/282 (6) 7/331 (7)   3/72 (4) 4/171 (1)
8/359 (8) 9/370 (10) 10/371 (11)   5/202 (5) 6/220 (6) 7/226 (7) 8/277 (8) 9/297 (9)

Sreesanth 16–1–96–0; Patel 28–7–80–3; V. R. Singh 15–1–61–2; Kumble 27.3–6–86–3; Sehwag 12–2–32–2. *Second Innings*—Patel 20–4–55–1; Sreesanth 19–10–49–2; Kumble 34–8–107–4; V. R. Singh 11–3–35–0; Sehwag 11–2–39–2.

Umpires: Asad Rauf *(Pakistan)* (6) and S. J. A. Taufel *(Australia)* (35).
Third umpire: B. R. Doctrove *(West Indies)*.   Referee: J. J. Crowe *(New Zealand)* (11).

Close of play: First day, India 235-9 (Sreesanth 24, Patel 0); Second day, West Indies 318-6 (Ramdin 22, Bradshaw 15); Third day, India 215-2 (Wasim Jaffer 113, Dravid 21); Fourth day, West Indies 13-0 (Gayle 1, Ganga 10).

WEST INDIES v INDIA 2006 (2nd Test)

At Beausejour Stadium, Gros Islet, St Lucia, on 10, 11, 12, 13 *(no play)*, 14 June.
Toss: India.   Result: MATCH DRAWN.
Debuts: none.
Man of the Match: V. Sehwag.

Just when India seemed set for victory, rain washed out the entire fourth day, allowing West Indies a lifeline: Lara took it, and ensured the series remained all square. The match had started uncomfortably for him: West Indies had misread the greenish pitch and chosen five fast bowlers, then had to endure a 78-ball hundred (India's third-fastest) from Sehwag. He slashed his first ball for four, by the tenth over had spread the field, and came within one run of becoming the first Indian to score a hundred before lunch in a Test. He finally fell after tea, having hit 180 off 190 balls – his 12th Test century, the last eight all exceeding 150. At the other end Dravid cruised to his 23rd Test hundred, while Kaif brought up a memorable first one. Patel soon reduced West Indies to 36 for 2, then Lara padded up to one that straightened from Kumble, and the batting gradually disintegrated. Sehwag, filling in for the injured Harbhajan Singh, showed all the attributes of a genuine off-spinner. India led by 373: with two full days remaining, West Indies needed some divine intervention, and got it. "God is a West Indian," joked India's coach Greg Chappell during a fourth day of unrelenting gloom. The weather set up the stalemate, but Lara sealed it. Making amends for his recent second-innings failings – no fifties in 19 attempts over almost 2½ years – he grafted to three figures in 272 balls, the slowest of his 32 Test centuries.

India

Wasim Jaffer c Bravo b Collins	43	A. Kumble b Taylor	14
V. Sehwag c and b Collins	180		
V. V. S. Laxman c Ramdin b Collins	0	B 4, l-b 7, w 4, n-b 12	27
*R. Dravid c Lara b Sarwan	146		
Yuvraj Singh b Collins	2	1/159 (1) 2/161 (3)	(8 wkts dec.) 588
M. Kaif not out	148	3/300 (2) 4/306 (5)	
†M. S. Dhoni c Ganga b Bradshaw	9	5/485 (4) 6/517 (7)	
I. K. Pathan c Ganga b Gayle	19	7/555 (8) 8/588 (9)	

M. M. Patel and V. R. Singh did not bat.

Collins 28–5–116–4; Taylor 24.2–4–88–1; Bravo 10–0–66–0; Collymore 21–1–92–0; Bradshaw 26–6–80–1; Sarwan 18–0–83–1; Gayle 21–6–52–1.

West Indies

C. H. Gayle c Dhoni b Kumble	46	– c Dhoni b Pathan	2
D. Ganga lbw b Patel	16	– b Kumble	26
R. R. Sarwan lbw b Patel	0	– (4) c Dhoni b Patel	1
*B. C. Lara lbw b Kumble	7	– (3) lbw b Sehwag	120
S. Chanderpaul lbw b Pathan	30	– c Pathan b Kumble	54
D. J. Bravo c Dravid b Kumble	25	– c Yuvraj Singh b Kumble	47
†D. Ramdin c Dhoni b Patel	30	– not out	19
I. D. R. Bradshaw c and b Sehwag	20	– lbw b Patel	1
J. E. Taylor c Kaif b Sehwag	23	– not out	0
P. T. Collins c Dravid b Sehwag	0		
C. D. Collymore not out	2		
B 5, l-b 2, n-b 9	16	L-b 4, n-b 15, p 5	24
	215	(7 wkts)	294

1/36 (2) 2/36 (3) 3/55 (4) 4/106 (1)   215   1/2 (1) 2/51 (2)   (7 wkts) 294
5/106 (5) 6/167 (6) 7/178 (7)   3/52 (4) 4/181 (5)
8/209 (9) 9/210 (10) 10/215 (8)   5/252 (3) 6/277 (6) 7/291 (8)

Pathan 11–2–43–1; Patel 17–4–51–3; Kumble 30–12–57–3; V. R. Singh 10–3–23–0; Sehwag 16.1–5–33–3; Yuvraj Singh 1–0–1–0. *Second Innings*—Pathan 15–2–50–1; Patel 21–7–50–2; V. R. Singh 11–0–39–0; Kumble 42–10–98–3; Sehwag 30–9–48–1.

Umpires: Asad Rauf *(Pakistan)* (7) and S. J. A. Taufel *(Australia)* (36).
Third umpire: S. A. Bucknor *(West Indies)*.   Referee: J. J. Crowe *(New Zealand)* (12).

Close of play: First day, India 361-4 (Dravid 95, Kaif 18); Second day, West Indies 65-3 (Gayle 34, Chanderpaul 5); Third day, West Indies 43-1 (Ganga 24, Lara 15); Fourth day, No play.

WEST INDIES v INDIA 2006 (3rd Test)

At Warner Park, Basseterre, St Kitts, on 22, 23, 24, 25, 26 June.
Toss: West Indies.   Result: MATCH DRAWN.
Debuts: none.
Man of the Match: D. Ganga.

The first Test at Warner Park, the 94th ground to stage one, ended in a high-scoring draw – always the likely result on another shirt-front and with clouds hovering. The roles were reversed this time: West Indies piled up 581 – the first time in more than ten years they had passed 560 in the first innings outside Antigua – before it was their turn to be thwarted by rain and opposition grit. Lara's decision not to enforce the follow-on was controversial but justifiable, and probably made little difference to the outcome. Chasing 392, India briefly threatened an extraordinary victory: Sehwag started quickly, then Dhoni clattered his first ball, from Collins, for six over long-off. But with 134 needed from the last 20 overs, Lara turned to defence. Earlier Ganga had made a composed century, while Gayle attacked Harbhajan Singh before Sarwan raced to an aggressive hundred, hurrying from 75 to 99 with six successive boundaries off Patel, who joined Bob Willis and Matthew Hoggard in conceding six fours in a Test over. But West Indies managed only 20 runs in 14 overs as Chanderpaul neared his hundred before being stranded three short. India's reply began confidently, but was set back by Taylor's three wickets in six balls before the last five wickets added 203. Lara opted for caution and batted again. His batsmen did their bit, giving the bowlers 88 overs to do their stuff. But with the pitch still playing easily, it was India who ended up closer to victory.

West Indies

C. H. Gayle b Patel	83	– c Dhoni b Sreesanth	3
D. Ganga b Patel	135	– not out	66
R. R. Sarwan lbw b Sreesanth	116	– c Dravid b Sreesanth	23
*B. C. Lara lbw b Patel	10	– st Dhoni b Kumble	19
S. Chanderpaul not out	97	– c and b Kumble	11
D. J. Bravo c Dhoni b Harbhajan Singh	21	– c Sreesanth b Kumble	9
M. N. Samuels c Harbhajan Singh b Sehwag	87	– st Dhoni b Harbhajan Singh	20
†D. Ramdin c Wasim Jaffer b Harbhajan Singh	3	– not out	8
J. E. Taylor c Yuvraj Singh b Harbhajan Singh	2		
P. T. Collins c Dravid b Harbhajan Singh	1		
C. D. Collymore b Harbhajan Singh	0		
L-b 14, w 1, n-b 11	26	B 4, l-b 7, w 1, n-b 1	13

1/143 (1) 2/346 (2) 3/356 (4) 4/371 (3)　　　581　　1/3 (1) 2/46 (3)　　　　　(6 wkts dec.) 172
5/406 (6) 6/562 (7) 7/570 (8)　　　　　　　　　　3/81 (4) 4/102 (5)
8/576 (9) 9/581 (10) 10/581 (11)　　　　　　　　5/120 (6) 6/152 (7)

Patel 32–4–134–3; Sreesanth 31–8–99–1; Kumble 47–8–140–0; Harbhajan Singh 44–6–147–5; Sehwag 16–3–47–1. *Second Innings*—Patel 7–0–43–0; Sreesanth 6–1–19–2; Kumble 12–0–60–3; Harbhajan Singh 7–0–39–1.

India

Wasim Jaffer c Lara b Bravo	60	– c Gayle b Collins	54
V. Sehwag c Lara b Collymore	31	– lbw b Collymore	65
V. V. S. Laxman c Ramdin b Collins	100	– c Lara b Collins	63
*R. Dravid lbw b Taylor	22	– not out	68
Yuvraj Singh c Ramdin b Taylor	0	– (6) not out	8
M. Kaif lbw b Taylor	0		
†M. S. Dhoni lbw b Collymore	29	– (5) c Gayle b Taylor	20
A. Kumble c Collins b Collymore	43		
Harbhajan Singh not out	38		
S. Sreesanth c Lara b Collins	0		
M. M. Patel c Ganga b Bravo	13		
B 8, l-b 5, n-b 13	26	B 9, l-b 8, w 1, n-b 2	20

1/61 (2) 2/124 (1) 3/157 (4) 4/159 (5)　　　362　　1/109 (2) 2/143 (1)　　　　　(4 wkts) 298
5/159 (6) 6/220 (7) 7/297 (3)　　　　　　　　　　3/243 (3) 4/273 (5)
8/311 (8) 9/315 (10) 10/362 (11)

Taylor 26–3–118–3; Collins 29.3–4–117–2; Collymore 25–4–63–3; Bravo 17.3–6–38–2; Gayle 2–0–3–0; Samuels 7–1–10–0. *Second Innings*—Collins 18–1–66–2; Taylor 11–1–40–1; Collymore 15–3–40–1; Samuels 20–3–68–0; Bravo 7–1–36–0; Gayle 14–2–31–0.

Umpires: B. G. Jerling *(South Africa)* (1) and R. E. Koertzen *(South Africa)* (76).
Third umpire: C. E. Mack *(West Indies)*.   Referee: J. J. Crowe *(New Zealand)* (13).

Close of play: First day, West Indies 207-1 (Ganga 64, Sarwan 44); Second day, West Indies 420-5 (Chanderpaul 24, Samuels 8); Third day, India 150-2 (Laxman 28, Dravid 20); Fourth day, West Indies 113-4 (Ganga 41, Bravo 9).

WEST INDIES v INDIA 2006 (4th Test)

At Sabina Park, Kingston, Jamaica, on 30 June, 1, 2 July.
Toss: India.   Result: INDIA won by 49 runs.
Debuts: none.
Man of the Match: R. Dravid.   Man of the Series: R. Dravid.

India won their 400th Test match to beat serious opposition outside the subcontinent for the first time since 1986. A bouncy, unpredictable pitch demanded technique and application, and the batsmen all stood exposed – except one. Dravid showed that batting was not about bullying on featherbeds but footwork, skill and assurance in difficult conditions. Without his two masterful efforts the result would probably have been reversed. Taylor began with an incisive maiden five-for, but could not prevent Dravid and Kumble producing the crucial partnership, 93 for the seventh wicket. Statistics did not favour India – no team had won after making 200 or less in the opening innings of a Test at Kingston – but on this surface they had a distinct edge, emphasised when Harbhajan Singh took five wickets in 27 balls. Lara had hoped his side would bat for two days; they didn't manage two sessions. Taylor claimed four more wickets in the second innings, while Collymore carried on his affair with Sabina Park, taking his record to 27 wickets at 12.55 in four Tests there. Three batsmen, including Dravid, stood little chance against ankle-high shooters. India's 171 was their lowest of the series, but an overall lead of 268 was worth 100 more. Lara's dismissal, which made it 29 for 3 after Gayle bagged a pair, seemed to herald the end, before West Indies threatened an extraordinary comeback . . . but Kumble, the only Indian player born before April 1971, when India last won a series in the Caribbean, nailed the final wicket.

India

Wasim Jaffer b Taylor	1	– c sub (R. S. Morton) b Taylor	1
V. Sehwag c Sarwan b Collins	0	– lbw b Taylor	4
V. V. S. Laxman c sub (R. S. Morton) b Bravo	18	– c Lara b Collymore	16
*R. Dravid c Ramdin b Collymore	81	– b Collymore	68
Yuvraj Singh lbw b Taylor	19	– c Lara b Collymore	13
M. Kaif c Lara b Taylor	13	– b Collins	6
†M. S. Dhoni c Bravo b Collymore	3	– b Taylor	19
A. Kumble b Bravo	45	– c Bravo b Collymore	10
Harbhajan Singh not out	9	– c Lara b Collymore	9
S. Sreesanth b Taylor	0	– c Lara b Taylor	16
M. M. Patel c Ramdin b Taylor	0	– not out	0
B 2, l-b 2, w 5, n-b 2	11	B 4, l-b 3, w 1, n-b 1	9

1/1 (2) 2/3 (1) 3/34 (3) 4/58 (5)   **200**   1/1 (1) 2/6 (2) 3/49 (3)   **171**
5/78 (6) 6/91 (7) 7/184 (8)   4/63 (5) 5/76 (6) 6/122 (7)
8/197 (4) 9/200 (10) 10/200 (11)   7/141 (8) 8/154 (4) 9/171 (10) 10/171 (9)

Collins 19–7–34–1; Taylor 18.4–4–50–5; Bravo 24–3–68–2; Collymore 19–11–17–2; Chanderpaul 5–0–17–0; Gayle 2–0–10–0. *Second Innings*—Collins 22–8–61–1; Taylor 15–4–45–4; Collymore 24.1–9–48–5; Bravo 4–1–10–0.

West Indies

C. H. Gayle b Sreesanth	0	– c Laxman b Sreesanth	0
D. Ganga lbw b Harbhajan Singh	40	– b Sreesanth	16
*B. C. Lara c Wasim Jaffer b Sreesanth	26	– lbw b Patel	11
M. N. Samuels st Dhoni b Kumble	2	– (7) lbw b Kumble	5
S. Chanderpaul c Dhoni b Patel	10	– lbw b Kumble	13
D. J. Bravo c Yuvraj Singh b Harbhajan Singh	0	– b Kumble	33
R. R. Sarwan c Kaif b Harbhajan Singh	7	– (4) c Dravid b Sreesanth	51
†D. Ramdin c Yuvraj Singh b Harbhajan Singh	10	– not out	62
J. E. Taylor run out	6	– lbw b Kumble	20
P. T. Collins c Sehwag b Harbhajan Singh	0	– lbw b Kumble	3
C. D. Collymore not out	0	– c Dhoni b Kumble	0
W 1, n-b 1	2	L-b 2, n-b 3	5

1/0 (1) 2/42 (3) 3/53 (4) 4/72 (5)   **103**   1/0 (1) 2/27 (2) 3/29 (3)   **219**
5/80 (2) 6/81 (6) 7/88 (7)   4/56 (5) 5/126 (4) 6/128 (6)
8/99 (8) 9/103 (9) 10/103 (10)   7/144 (7) 8/180 (9) 9/219 (10) 10/219 (11)

Sreesanth 9–3–34–2; Patel 12–5–24–1; Kumble 8–3–32–1; Harbhajan Singh 4.3–0–13–5. *Second Innings*—Sreesanth 15–2–38–3; Patel 12–2–26–1; Harbhajan Singh 16–3–65–0; Kumble 22.4–3–78–6; Sehwag 4–0–10–0.

Umpires: B. G. Jerling *(South Africa)* (2) and R. E. Koertzen *(South Africa)* (77).
Third umpire: N. A. Malcolm *(West Indies)*.   Referee: J. J. Crowe *(New Zealand)* (14).

Close of play: First day, India 200; Second day, India 128-6 (Dravid 62, Kumble 2).

ENGLAND v PAKISTAN 2006 (1st Test)

At Lord's, London, on 13, 14, 15, 16, 17 July.
Toss: England.   Result: MATCH DRAWN.
Debuts: none.
Man of the Match: Mohammad Yousuf.

The final day might have turned into a classic, but Strauss, in his first Test as captain in the absence of the injured Vaughan and Flintoff, chose to bat on for half an hour, setting Pakistan an unlikely 380 in 80 overs. They never threatened the target, but neither did England ever look like taking ten wickets, even after Hoggard removed Salman Butt first ball. It did not help that two of England's four bowlers were not fully fit: Harmison was still struggling for rhythm after a shin injury, while Hoggard had stitches in his hand. Mohammad Yousuf rescued Pakistan from 68 for 4 in the first innings, batting 468 minutes for his second successive double-century against England. Then Inzamam-ul-Haq, unruffled as ever, hit a record ninth consecutive half-century against the same opposition to bring his side close to parity. England's big total was built around 186 from Collingwood – England's 700th Test century – and further hundreds from Cook (with whom Collingwood put on 233, a national fourth-wicket record against Pakistan, beating 188 by Ted Dexter and Peter Parfitt at Karachi in 1961-62) and Bell. England's hunt for quick runs in the second innings was hampered by losing wickets regularly: Pietersen, the man most likely to mount a matchwinning assault, took 14 balls to get off the mark before being outwitted by Shahid Afridi for 41 off 70 deliveries. Strauss did become the third England player to score a century on his Test-captaincy debut, following Archie MacLaren and Allan Lamb.

England

M. E. Trescothick c Kamran Akmal b Umar Gul	16	– b Umar Gul	18
*A. J. Strauss lbw b Abdul Razzaq	30	– c Imran Farhat b Danish Kaneria	128
A. N. Cook b Mohammad Sami	105	– c Mohammad Yousuf b Umar Gul	4
K. P. Pietersen lbw b Abdul Razzaq	21	– st Kamran Akmal b Shahid Afridi	41
P. D. Collingwood st Kamran Akmal b Danish Kaneria	186	– c Salman Butt b Danish Kaneria	3
I. R. Bell not out	100	– run out	28
†G. O. Jones lbw b Danish Kaneria	18	– c Kamran Akmal b Danish Kaneria	16
L. E. Plunkett c Imran Farhat b Danish Kaneria	0	– c Kamran Akmal b Abdul Razzaq	28
M. J. Hoggard lbw b Shahid Afridi	13	– not out	12
S. J. Harmison run out	2		
M. S. Panesar not out	0		
B 8, w 15, n-b 14	37	B 5, l-b 6, w 1, n-b 6	18

1/60 (1) 2/60 (2) 3/88 (4)   (9 wkts dec.) 528   1/38 (1) 2/64 (3)   (8 wkts dec.) 296
4/321 (3) 5/441 (5) 6/469 (7)   3/141 (4) 4/146 (5)
7/473 (8) 8/515 (9) 9/525 (10)   5/203 (6) 6/250 (7) 7/253 (2) 8/296 (8)

Mohammad Sami 28–4–116–1; Umar Gul 33–6–133–1; Abdul Razzaq 25–2–86–2; Danish Kaneria 52–6–119–3; Shahid Afridi 19.3–0–63–1; Imran Farhat 1–0–3–0. *Second Innings*—Mohammad Sami 6–1–23–0; Umar Gul 19–4–70–2; Danish Kaneria 30–4–77–3; Abdul Razzaq 9.5–0–45–1; Shahid Afridi 19–1–65–1; Imran Farhat 1–0–5–0.

Pakistan

Salman Butt c Strauss b Harmison	10	– lbw b Hoggard	0
Imran Farhat b Plunkett	33	– c Collingwood b Hoggard	18
Faisal Iqbal c Collingwood b Harmison	0	– c Cook b Panesar	48
Mohammad Yousuf c Jones b Harmison	202	– lbw b Panesar	48
Mohammad Sami c Jones b Hoggard	0		
*Inzamam-ul-Haq b Plunkett	69	– (5) not out	56
Abdul Razzaq c Jones b Harmison	22	– (6) not out	25
†Kamran Akmal c Jones b Pietersen	58		
Shahid Afridi c Bell b Hoggard	17		
Umar Gul c Jones b Hoggard	0		
Danish Kaneria not out	1		
B 7, l-b 14, w 7, n-b 5	33	B 1, l-b 8, w 6, n-b 4	19

1/28 (1) 2/28 (3) 3/65 (2) 4/68 (5)   445   1/0 (1) 2/33 (2)   (4 wkts) 214
5/241 (6) 6/300 (7) 7/399 (8)   3/116 (4) 4/141 (3)
8/435 (9) 9/436 (10) 10/445 (4)

Hoggard 33–3–117–3; Harmison 29.3–6–94–4; Panesar 27–3–93–0; Plunkett 21–3–78–2; Collingwood 7–1–31–0; Pietersen 2–0–11–1. *Second Innings*—Hoggard 12–3–31–2; Harmison 15–3–43–0; Plunkett 12–2–41–0; Panesar 27–7–60–2; Pietersen 5–1–19–0; Collingwood 2–0–11–0.

Umpires: S. A. Bucknor *(West Indies)* (112) and S. J. A. Taufel *(Australia)* (37).
Third umpire: P. J. Hartley *(England)*.   Referee: R. S. Madugalle *(Sri Lanka)* (90).

Close of play: First day, England 309-3 (Cook 101, Collingwood 109); Second day, Pakistan 66-3 (Mohammad Yousuf 20, Mohammad Sami 0); Third day, Pakistan 409-7 (Mohammad Yousuf 185, Shahid Afridi 0); Fourth day, England 258-7 (Plunkett 5, Hoggard 0).

ENGLAND v PAKISTAN 2006 (2nd Test)

At Old Trafford, Manchester, on 27, 28, 29 July.
Toss: Pakistan.   Result: ENGLAND won by an innings and 120 runs.
Debuts: none.
Man of the Match: S. J. Harmison.

Fifty years to the week after Jim Laker took 19 Australian wickets at Old Trafford, England produced their most effective display of the summer to go 1–0 up. Cook and Bell recorded hundreds for the second Test in a row, while Harmison, rhythm and confidence restored, claimed match figures of 11 for 76. He and Panesar, who further bolstered his growing reputation, finished up sharing 19 wickets, a feat achieved only once for England since Laker's day: by Phil Tufnell and Andrew Caddick in the 1997 Ashes win at The Oval. Little went right for Pakistan after Inzamam-ul-Haq won the toss. Early variations in bounce made batting awkward, but could not excuse a meagre first innings which was all over inside three hours, the last eight wickets adding only 29 after Mohammad Yousuf and Younis Khan put on 81. Inzamam, beaten for pace, was caught at gully off the splice, ending his record sequence of nine half-centuries against England. Cook then became the first England player since Ian Botham to score a third hundred in his first seven Tests, before Bell completed an attractive hundred as the lead stretched to 342. Pakistan made them work slightly harder second time around: eight players, rather than three, reached double figures. After Harmison bounced out Kamran Akmal, Panesar claimed the next five, including Yousuf, stumped first ball after lunch. A ruthless display was completed on the third evening when Jones held a skyer from Abdul Razzaq, his fifth dismissal of the innings.

Pakistan

†Kamran Akmal c Trescothick b Harmison	4	– c Jones b Harmison		4
Imran Farhat c Pietersen b Harmison	0	– c Bell b Panesar		34
Younis Khan c Collingwood b Harmison	44	– lbw b Panesar		62
Mohammad Yousuf c Jones b Panesar	38	– st Jones b Panesar		15
*Inzamam-ul-Haq c Pietersen b Harmison	0	– c Cook b Panesar		13
Faisal Iqbal c Jones b Panesar	3	– c Trescothick b Panesar		29
Abdul Razzaq b Harmison	9	– c Jones b Harmison		13
Shahid Afridi c Pietersen b Panesar	15	– c Strauss b Harmison		17
Mohammad Sami c Strauss b Harmison	1	– c Jones b Harmison		0
Umar Gul not out	1	– c Jones b Harmison		13
Danish Kaneria run out	0	– not out		4
L-b 2, w 2	4	B 4, l-b 4, w 6, n-b 4		18

1/4 (2) 2/9 (1) 3/90 (4) 4/90 (3)   119   1/21 (1) 2/60 (2) 3/101 (4)   222
5/93 (6) 6/93 (5) 7/112 (8)   4/117 (5) 5/161 (3) 6/174 (6)
8/113 (9) 9/118 (7) 10/119 (11)   7/194 (8) 8/194 (9) 9/208 (10) 10/222 (7)

Hoggard 9–1–30–0; Harmison 13–7–19–6; Mahmood 6–1–33–0; Collingwood 3–0–14–0; Panesar 7.4–3–21–3. *Second Innings*—Hoggard 14–2–52–0; Harmison 18.1–3–57–5; Mahmood 6–1–22–0; Panesar 27–4–72–5; Pietersen 2–0–11–0.

England

M. E. Trescothick c Kamran Akmal		M. J. Hoggard lbw b Shahid Afridi	6
b Mohammad Sami	5	S. J. Harmison c Kamran Akmal	
*A. J. Strauss c Kamran Akmal		b Danish Kaneria	26
b Abdul Razzaq	42	M. S. Panesar not out	3
A. N. Cook lbw b Umar Gul	127	B 9, l-b 10, w 7, n-b 14	40
K. P. Pietersen c Imran Farhat b Umar Gul	38		
P. D. Collingwood c Mohammad Sami b Umar Gul	48		
I. R. Bell not out	106		
†G. O. Jones lbw b Mohammad Sami	8		
S. I. Mahmood c and b Abdul Razzaq	12		

1/30 (1) 2/95 (2)   (9 wkts dec.) 461
3/169 (4) 4/288 (5)
5/304 (3) 6/321 (7)
7/357 (8) 8/384 (9) 9/457 (10)

Mohammad Sami 28–5–92–2; Umar Gul 28–2–96–3; Abdul Razzaq 19–4–72–2; Danish Kaneria 37–8–106–1; Shahid Afridi 21–0–76–1.

Umpires: S. A. Bucknor *(West Indies)* (113) and S. J. A. Taufel *(Australia)* (38).
Third umpire: I. J. Gould *(England)*.   Referee: R. S. Madugalle *(Sri Lanka)* (91).

Close of play: First day, England 168-2 (Cook 65, Pietersen 38); Second day, Pakistan 12-0 (Kamran Akmal 2, Imran Farhat 9).

ENGLAND v PAKISTAN 2006 (3rd Test)

At Headingley, Leeds, on 4, 5, 6, 7, 8 August.
Toss: England.   Result: ENGLAND won by 167 runs.
Debuts: none.
Man of the Match: Younis Khan.

The enduring image of the season came on the third afternoon, when Inzamam-ul-Haq tried to sweep Panesar, only to overbalance and knock off the bails as he belly-flopped to the ground, where he sat bewildered, his expression worthy of Oliver Hardy. If the sideshow was comical, the main event was clinical: England clinched their first series triumph since regaining the Ashes. They started by making 515, Pietersen returning to form and Bell becoming the first Englishman since Graham Gooch in 1990 to score hundreds in three successive Tests. Younis Khan and Mohammad Yousuf then put on 363 in 84 overs, Pakistan's highest stand against England, and the biggest in Tests in a losing cause. But from 447 for 3, three wickets tumbled for four in ten balls, including Collingwood's first Test victim with his 381st delivery. Trescothick and Strauss started the second innings bullishly, and after the recalled Read had punched a maiden Test fifty Pakistan were left requiring 323 on the last day. At 68 for 2, their supporters dared to dream – but then Yousuf was beaten by Collingwood's brilliant underarm shy from backward point. Younis was later undone by a beauty from Panesar that pitched on middle stump and shaved the top off. It was only the tenth instance of a team losing a Test after scoring 500, while the match aggregate of 1,553 was the highest for a five-day Test in which all 40 wickets fell, though four timeless Tests had beaten it over six or seven days.

England

M. E. Trescothick c and b Mohammad Sami	28	– c Salman Butt b Umar Gul	58
*A. J. Strauss c Younis Khan b Shahid Nazir	36	– c Kamran Akmal b Mohammad Sami	116
A. N. Cook c and b Umar Gul	23	– c Faisal Iqbal b Danish Kaneria	21
K. P. Pietersen c Shahid Nazir b Mohammad Sami	135	– b Danish Kaneria	16
P. D. Collingwood c Taufeeq Umar b Umar Gul	31	– b Shahid Nazir	25
I. R. Bell b Danish Kaneria	119	– c Kamran Akmal b Mohammad Sami	4
†C. M. W. Read lbw b Umar Gul	38	– b Mohammad Sami	55
M. J. Hoggard b Umar Gul	0	– (9) c Younis Khan b Shahid Nazir	8
S. I. Mahmood b Umar Gul	34	– (8) c Kamran Akmal b Shahid Nazir	2
S. J. Harmison c Mohammad Sami b Danish Kaneria	36	– c sub (Imran Farhat) b Umar Gul	4
M. S. Panesar not out	5	– not out	5
B 13, l-b 6, n-b 11	30	B 8, l-b 3, w 1, n-b 19	31

1/67 (1) 2/67 (2) 3/110 (3) 4/192 (5)   515
5/345 (7) 6/347 (8) 7/421 (4)
8/445 (6) 9/501 (10) 10/515 (9)

1/158 (1) 2/190 (3) 3/214 (4)   345
4/237 (2) 5/248 (6) 6/299 (5)
7/301 (8) 8/323 (9) 9/332 (10) 10/345 (7)

In the first innings Pietersen, when 104, retired hurt at 259 and resumed at 347.

Mohammad Sami 26–1–135–2; Umar Gul 29–4–123–5; Shahid Nazir 28–7–101–1; Danish Kaneria 34–4–111–2; Taufeeq Umar 2–0–8–0; Salman Butt 4–0–18–0. *Second Innings*—Mohammad Sami 21.3–4–100–3; Umar Gul 20–1–76–2; Shahid Nazir 14–4–32–3; Danish Kaneria 33–2–126–2.

Pakistan

Salman Butt run out	20	– c Trescothick b Hoggard	16
Taufeeq Umar c Read b Hoggard	7	– c Cook b Panesar	11
Younis Khan run out	173	– b Panesar	41
Mohammad Yousuf c Read b Harmison	192	– run out	8
*Inzamam-ul-Haq hit wkt b Panesar	26	– (7) st Read b Panesar	37
Faisal Iqbal lbw b Collingwood	0	– (5) c Read b Mahmood	11
†Kamran Akmal c Trescothick b Mahmood	20	– (6) c Read b Mahmood	0
Mohammad Sami c Harmison b Panesar	19	– run out	0
Shahid Nazir not out	13	– c Trescothick b Mahmood	17
Umar Gul c Panesar b Mahmood	7	– c Collingwood b Mahmood	0
Danish Kaneria c Trescothick b Panesar	29	– not out	0
B 1, l-b 20, w 5, n-b 6	32	L-b 6, w 5, n-b 3	14

1/34 (2) 2/36 (1) 3/399 (4) 4/447 (3)   538
5/447 (6) 6/451 (5) 7/481 (7)
8/489 (8) 9/496 (10) 10/538 (11)

1/23 (1) 2/52 (2) 3/68 (4)   155
4/80 (5) 5/80 (6) 6/112 (3)
7/113 (8) 8/148 (9) 9/149 (10) 10/155 (7)

Hoggard 29–4–93–1; Harmison 30–1–142–1; Mahmood 24–4–108–2; Panesar 47.4–13–127–3; Pietersen 1–0–14–0; Collingwood 10–1–33–1. *Second Innings*—Hoggard 7–3–26–1; Panesar 17.5–4–39–3; Harmison 15–3–62–0; Mahmood 8–2–22–4.

Umpires: B. R. Doctrove *(West Indies)* (8) and D. B. Hair *(Australia)* (75).
Third umpire: N. J. Llong *(England)*.   Referee: R. S. Madugalle *(Sri Lanka)* (92).

Close of play: First day, England 347-6 (Bell 66); Second day, Pakistan 202-2 (Younis Khan 64, Mohammad Yousuf 91); Third day, England 3-0 (Trescothick 0, Strauss 3); Fourth day, Pakistan 0-0 (Salman Butt 0, Taufeeq Umar 0).

ENGLAND v PAKISTAN 2006 (4th Test)

At Kennington Oval, London, on 17, 18, 19, 20 August.
Toss: Pakistan.   Result: ENGLAND won by forfeit.
Debuts: none.
Man of the Match: no award.   Men of the Series: Mohammad Yousuf and A. J. Strauss.

Late on the scheduled fourth day, cricket plunged into crisis. Outraged at being punished for ball-tampering, the Pakistan team refused to take the field after tea, and the umpires decided they had forfeited the match, the first such instance in 129 years of Test cricket. The fallout was immense: Darrell Hair, the senior umpire, was effectively hounded out of international cricket, and the ICC later changed the result (to a draw) before reconsidering and confirming the forfeiture under Law 21. The first signs of the impending turmoil had come when the umpires called for a replacement ball. It was assumed the original (56 overs old) had gone out of shape, but the batsmen, not the umpires, chose the new one – an indication the officials believed the ball had been doctored. Hair then signalled that five penalty runs should be added to England's total. Without warning, without opportunity to defend themselves and without apparent thought to the ramifications, Pakistan were very publicly found guilty of cheating. Play continued until bad light forced the players off, but when almost an hour later the umpires took the field again, Pakistan's players did not. Not until later that night was it clear that the Test really was over – and that an intriguing game of cricket had been lost. Another century from Mohammad Yousuf had made England's first-innings 173 look puny, and although Pietersen made a punchy 96, his dismissal shortly before the dramatic end still left England in the red.

England

M. E. Trescothick c Mohammad Hafeez b Umar Gul	...	6	– c Kamran Akmal b Mohammad Asif	....	4
*A. J. Strauss c Kamran Akmal b Mohammad Asif	...	38	– lbw b Danish Kaneria	....	54
A. N. Cook lbw b Shahid Nazir	....	40	– lbw b Umar Gul	....	83
K. P. Pietersen c Kamran Akmal b Mohammad Asif	..	0	– c Kamran Akmal b Shahid Nazir	....	96
P. D. Collingwood lbw b Mohammad Asif	....	5	– not out	....	26
I. R. Bell c Faisal Iqbal b Danish Kaneria	....	9	– not out	....	9
†C. M. W. Read b Umar Gul	....	33			
S. I. Mahmood b Umar Gul	....	15			
M. J. Hoggard c Kamran Akmal b Mohammad Asif	...	3			
S. J. Harmison not out	....	8			
M. S. Panesar b Umar Gul	....	0			
B 4, l-b 5, n-b 7	....	16	B 8, l-b 3, n-b 10, p 5	....	26

1/36 (1) 2/54 (2) 3/54 (4) 4/64 (5)   173   1/8 (1) 2/115 (2)   (4 wkts) 298
5/91 (6) 6/112 (3) 7/158 (8)   3/218 (3) 4/277 (4)
8/163 (9) 9/173 (7) 10/173 (11)

Mohammad Asif 19–6–56–4; Umar Gul 15.2–3–46–4; Shahid Nazir 11–1–44–1; Danish Kaneria 8–1–18–1. *Second Innings*—Mohammad Asif 17–1–79–1; Umar Gul 14–1–70–1; Mohammad Hafeez 4–1–13–0; Danish Kaneria 29–6–94–1; Shahid Nazir 8–1–26–1.

Pakistan

Mohammad Hafeez c Strauss b Hoggard	....	95	Umar Gul lbw b Panesar	13
Imran Farhat c Trescothick b Hoggard	....	91	Danish Kaneria c Trescothick b Harmison ..	15
Younis Khan c Read b Mahmood	....	9	Mohammad Asif c Cook b Harmison	0
Mohammad Yousuf c Read b Hoggard	....	128	B 4, l-b 9, w 11, n-b 8	32
*Inzamam-ul-Haq c Strauss b Harmison	....	31		
Faisal Iqbal not out	....	58	1/70 (3) 2/148 (2) 3/325 (1)	504
†Kamran Akmal c Collingwood b Harmison	....	15	4/379 (5) 5/381 (4) 6/398 (7)	
Shahid Nazir c Hoggard b Mahmood	....	17	7/444 (8) 8/475 (9)	
			9/504 (10) 10/504 (11)	

Mohammad Hafeez, when 8, retired hurt at 35 and resumed at 148.

Hoggard 34–2–124–3; Harmison 30.5–6–125–4; Mahmood 27–3–101–2; Panesar 30–6–103–1; Collingwood 6–0–29–0; Pietersen 2–0–9–0.

Umpires: B. R. Doctrove *(West Indies)* (9) and D. B. Hair *(Australia)* (76).
Third umpire: P. J. Hartley *(England)*.   Referee: M. J. Procter *(South Africa)* (41).

Close of play: First day, Pakistan 96-1 (Imran Farhat 56, Mohammad Yousuf 12); Second day, Pakistan 336-3 (Mohammad Yousuf 115, Inzamam-ul-Haq 2); Third day, England 78-1 (Strauss 37, Cook 33).

SRI LANKA v SOUTH AFRICA 2006 (1st Test)

At Sinhalese Sports Club, Colombo, on 27, 28, 29, 30, 31 July.
Toss: South Africa.   Result: SRI LANKA won by an innings and 153 runs.
Debuts: none.
Man of the Match: D. P. M. D. Jayawardene.

This match will forever be remembered for the batting of Mahela Jayawardene and Kumar Sangakkara, who rewrote *Wisden's* records section with a quite devastating third-wicket stand of 624, the highest in all first-class cricket, anywhere, ever. Sri Lanka were responding to a feeble 169, South Africa's lowest against them. Both openers were snared by Steyn, but then Sangakkara was dropped in the gully, and bowled by a no-ball. After that the pair batted with metronomic efficiency, waltzing through the second day . . . and into the third. The most resonant landmark, for the locals, was Sanath Jayasuriya and Roshan Mahanama's 576, the highest Test partnership, set against India at Colombo's Premadasa Stadium in 1997 on a similarly anodyne pitch. That was passed with four byes, which also took the pair past the 577 of Vijay Hazare and Gul Mahomed in 1946-47, the previous-highest partnership in all first-class cricket. Sangakkara finally chased a wide one, but Jayawardene, already past 300, carried on. He soon passed Jayasuriya's 340, the Sri Lankan record, and was closing in on Brian Lara's Test-best 400 when a devilish ball cut in, kept low, and knocked back his off stump. Muralitharan then set about bowling South Africa out again. They applied themselves much better than in the first innings: Rudolph and Hall started with a stubborn stand of 165, Prince gritted out 61 from 182 balls, and Boucher survived nearly four hours. But Murali twirled slowly but surely on, finishing with ten wickets for the third Test running.

South Africa

H. H. Gibbs b Fernando	19	– (7) c and b Muralitharan		18
A. J. Hall b Fernando	17	– lbw b Muralitharan		64
J. A. Rudolph c H. A. P. W. Jayawardene b Maharoof	29	– (1) c Kapugedera b Fernando		90
H. M. Amla st H. A. P. W. Jayawardene b Muralitharan	19	– (3) lbw b Fernando		2
*A. G. Prince c H. A. P. W. Jayawardene b Maharoof	1	– (4) c D. P. M. D. Jayawardene b Muralitharan		61
A. B. de Villiers c Kapugedera b Muralitharan	65	– (5) lbw b Muralitharan		24
†M. V. Boucher c Jayasuriya b Muralitharan	4	– (6) c and b Jayasuriya		85
N. Boje lbw b Muralitharan	5	– not out		33
A. Nel lbw b Fernando	0	– b Muralitharan		0
D. W. Steyn b Fernando	0	– b Muralitharan		4
M. Ntini not out	0	– b Malinga		16
B 4, l-b 6	10	B 11, l-b 4, w 2, n-b 20		37
	169			**434**

1/32 (2) 2/45 (1) 3/78 (3) 4/80 (5)   169   1/165 (1) 2/171 (3) 3/185 (2)   434
5/112 (4) 6/128 (7) 7/148 (8)   4/234 (5) 5/312 (4) 6/350 (7)
8/151 (9) 9/151 (10) 10/169 (6)   7/401 (6) 8/404 (9) 9/412 (10) 10/434 (11)

Malinga 10–2–38–0; Maharoof 9–1–32–2; Fernando 13–2–48–4; Muralitharan 18.2–6–41–4. *Second Innings*—Malinga 16.2–0–85–1; Maharoof 15–3–48–0; Fernando 24–6–69–2; Muralitharan 64–11–131–6; Dilshan 4–1–10–0; Jayasuriya 34–8–76–1.

Sri Lanka

W. U. Tharanga c Boucher b Steyn	7
S. T. Jayasuriya lbw b Steyn	4
K. C. Sangakkara c Boucher b Hall	287
*D. P. M. D. Jayawardene b Nel	374
T. M. Dilshan lbw b Steyn	45

C. K. Kapugedera not out	1
B 17, l-b 5, w 8, n-b 8	38

1/6 (2) 2/14 (1) 3/638 (3)   (5 wkts dec.) 756
4/751 (5) 5/756 (4)

†H. A. P. W. Jayawardene, M. F. Maharoof, S. L. Malinga, C. R. D. Fernando and M. Muralitharan did not bat.

Ntini 31–3–97–0; Steyn 26–1–129–3; Nel 25.1–2–114–1; Hall 25–2–99–1; Boje 65–5–221–0; Rudolph 7–0–45–0; Prince 2–0–7–0; de Villiers 4–0–22–0.

Umpires: M. R. Benson *(England)* (11) and B. F. Bowden *(New Zealand)* (36).
Third umpire: E. A. R. de Silva *(Sri Lanka)*.   Referee: J. Srinath *(India)* (1).

Close of play: First day, Sri Lanka 128-2 (Sangakkara 59, D. P. M. D. Jayawardene 55); Second day, Sri Lanka 485-2 (Sangakkara 229, D. P. M. D. Jayawardene 224); Third day, South Africa 43-0 (Rudolph 24, Hall 13); Fourth day, South Africa 311-4 (Prince 60, Boucher 38).

SRI LANKA v SOUTH AFRICA 2006 (2nd Test)

At P. Saravanamuttu Stadium, Colombo, on 4, 5, 6, 7, 8 August.
Toss: South Africa.   Result: SRI LANKA won by one wicket.
Debuts: none.
Man of the Match: D. P. M. D. Jayawardene.   Man of the Series: M. Muralitharan.

After the one-way traffic of the previous match, this was a classic, the winner uncertain until the final stroke. Malinga's single completed the sixth-highest successful Test run-chase – and sealed the series with the 11th one-wicket Test victory. South Africa had stormed back on a frenetic first day featuring 56 fours, two sixes and ten wickets. Their batsmen were more aggressive, especially against Muralitharan (who nonetheless took his customary ten wickets in the match), and raced to 361 despite both openers making ducks. A fiery new-ball burst from Ntini reduced Sri Lanka to 86 for 5, but the middle order rallied: Kapugedera and Prasanna Jayawardene (keeping wicket in this series after the selectors decided Sangakkara should focus on his batting) counter-attacked, smashing 105 for the sixth wicket. South Africa built slowly on their lead, Gibbs ending a barren run with a hard-working 92 before Boucher extended the advantage to 351. Jayawardene instructed his batsmen to attack: Jayasuriya needed no second invitation, and completed his first Test half-century since 2004. A mini-collapse left Sri Lanka wobbling at 201 for 5, but Jayawardene started carefully (crucially, he was dropped by Gibbs in the gully when two): considering the context, his six-hour 123 was probably a greater innings than his 374. He had taken his team to the brink of victory with only 11 more needed and four wickets left, when he tried his favourite inside-out cover-drive, but was caught at slip. Amid unbearable tension two more wickets fell before the last pair clinched it.

South Africa

H. H. Gibbs lbw b Vaas	0	– c Jayasuriya b Muralitharan	92
A. J. Hall c Dilshan b Malinga	0	– c H. A. P. W. Jayawardene b Maharoof	32
J. A. Rudolph b Malinga	13	– run out	15
H. M. Amla lbw b Muralitharan	40	– run out	8
*A. G. Prince c H. A. P. W. Jayawardene b Muralitharan	86	– c and b Muralitharan	17
A. B. de Villiers c H. A. P. W. Jayawardene b Malinga	95	– c Dilshan b Muralitharan	33
†M. V. Boucher b Muralitharan	32	– c Dilshan b Muralitharan	65
S. M. Pollock not out	57	– c Tharanga b Muralitharan	14
N. Boje c Sangakkara b Maharoof	11	– c H. A. P. W. Jayawardene b Muralitharan	15
D. W. Steyn c Jayasuriya b Muralitharan	6	– lbw b Muralitharan	0
M. Ntini c Maharoof b Muralitharan	13	– not out	5
N-b 8	8	B 9, l-b 4, w 1, n-b 1	15

1/0 (1) 2/4 (2) 3/31 (3) 4/70 (4)   361   1/76 (2) 2/119 (3) 3/131 (4)   311
5/231 (5) 6/256 (6) 7/273 (7)   4/161 (1) 5/206 (5) 6/207 (6)
8/307 (9) 9/327 (10) 10/361 (11)   7/235 (8) 8/280 (9) 9/282 (10) 10/311 (7)

Vaas 18–4–71–1; Malinga 18–4–81–3; Muralitharan 33.5–2–128–5; Maharoof 15–2–52–1; Jayasuriya 5–0–29–0. *Second Innings*—Vaas 19–4–53–0; Malinga 12–1–55–0; Maharoof 21–3–53–1; Muralitharan 46.5–12–97–7; Jayasuriya 9–0–40–0.

Sri Lanka

W. U. Tharanga c Boje b Ntini	2	– c Gibbs b Ntini	0
S. T. Jayasuriya c Gibbs b Ntini	47	– c Amla b Boje	73
K. C. Sangakkara c Amla b Ntini	14	– c Amla b Pollock	39
*D. P. M. D. Jayawardene c Boucher b Steyn	13	– c Gibbs b Boje	123
T. M. Dilshan b Ntini	4	– c Gibbs b Boje	18
C. K. Kapugedera b Boje	63	– c de Villiers b Boje	13
†H. A. P. W. Jayawardene b Steyn	42	– lbw b Hall	30
M. F. Maharoof b Steyn	56	– not out	29
W. P. U. J. C. Vaas c Boucher b Steyn	64	– c de Villiers b Hall	4
S. L. Malinga not out	8	– (11) not out	1
M. Muralitharan c Hall b Steyn	0	– (10) b Hall	2
L-b 1, w 2, n-b 5	8	B 4, l-b 8, w 4, n-b 4	20

1/16 (1) 2/43 (3) 3/74 (4) 4/85 (5)   321   1/12 (1) 2/94 (3) 3/121 (2)   (9 wkts) 352
5/86 (2) 6/191 (6) 7/191 (7) 8/308 (8)   4/164 (5) 5/201 (6)
9/317 (9) 10/321 (11)   6/279 (7) 7/341 (4) 8/348 (9) 9/350 (10)

Ntini 21–3–84–4; Steyn 13.1–1–82–5; Pollock 16–4–52–0; Hall 15–7–31–0; Boje 20–6–71–1. *Second Innings*— Ntini 7.2–2–13–1; Steyn 22.4–2–81–0; Boje 39.3–11–111–4; Pollock 19–2–60–1; Hall 25–3–75–3.

Umpires: Aleem Dar *(Pakistan)* (34) and B. F. Bowden *(New Zealand)* (37).
Third umpire: T. H. Wijewardene *(Sri Lanka)*.   Referee: J. Srinath *(India)* (2).

Close of play: First day, South Africa 361; Second day, South Africa 6-0 (Gibbs 4, Hall 2); Third day, South Africa 257-7 (Boucher 28, Boje 5); Fourth day, Sri Lanka 262-5 (D. P. M. D. Jayawardene 77, H. A. P. W. Jayawardene 27).

PAKISTAN v WEST INDIES 2006-07 (1st Test)

At Gaddafi Stadium, Lahore, on 19, 20, 21, 22, 23 November.
Toss: West Indies.   Result: PAKISTAN won by nine wickets.
Debuts: none.
Man of the Match: Umar Gul.

Pakistan overcame off-field worries about the forfeited Oval Test and drug bans on their two leading pacemen, Shoaib Akhtar and Mohammad Asif, to complete a convincing victory. The unsung new-ball pairing of Umar Gul and Shahid Nazir (playing only his 11th Test in ten years) shared 15 wickets against opponents whose batting was a letdown, apart from Lara's brilliance in both innings. West Indies were also undermined by some butter-fingered fielding, which let Mohammad Yousuf off three times, and by a shaky performance from umpire de Silva. Gayle blasted six fours off 28 balls before, struck high on the pad, he was despatched by de Silva, then the top order imploded: West Indies went to lunch at 122 for 6. Lara, slowly finding his touch, and the unorthodox Mohammed added 52, the highest stand of the innings, but then Gul found Lara's edge with a beauty. For a while, with Taylor bowling well, it looked as if the lead would be modest - but that reckoned without Yousuf, who extended his 20th Test century to 192 in 501 minutes, putting on 148 with Kamran Akmal. West Indies' second-innings resistance came from a predictable quarter: Lara's 33rd Test hundred, on the ground where he made his Test debut 16 years previously, was filled with breathtaking strokes, and Chanderpaul helped him put on 137. But when Lara was lbw sweeping an offbreak, the last six wickets folded for 53, and Pakistan cruised to victory as the sun set on the fourth day.

West Indies

C. H. Gayle lbw b Shahid Nazir	34	– c Kamran Akmal b Umar Gul	11
D. Ganga c Younis Khan b Umar Gul	3	– run out	5
R. R. Sarwan c Younis Khan b Shahid Nazir	3	– lbw b Umar Gul	23
*B. C. Lara c Kamran Akmal b Umar Gul	61	– lbw b Mohammad Hafeez	122
S. Chanderpaul lbw b Shahid Nazir	5	– (6) c Mohammad Yousuf b Shahid Nazir	81
D. J. Bravo c Shahid Nazir b Danish Kaneria	32	– (7) lbw b Umar Gul	2
†D. Ramdin c Mohammad Hafeez b Danish Kaneria	12	– (8) c Imran Farhat b Danish Kaneria	1
D. Mohammed c Kamran Akmal b Umar Gul	35	– (9) c Abdul Razzaq b Shahid Nazir	15
J. E. Taylor lbw b Umar Gul	8	– (10) c Kamran Akmal b Umar Gul	8
F. H. Edwards c Shoaib Malik b Umar Gul	2	– (5) c Younis Khan b Shahid Nazir	10
C. D. Collymore not out	1	– not out	1
L-b 8, n-b 2	10	L-b 7, n-b 5	12

1/41 (2) 2/41 (1) 3/46 (3) 4/52 (5)   206
5/96 (6) 6/122 (7) 7/174 (4)
8/202 (9) 9/203 (8) 10/206 (10)

1/16 (2) 2/20 (1) 3/56 (3)   291
4/101 (5) 5/238 (4) 6/248 (7)
7/251 (8) 8/278 (6) 9/288 (9) 10/291 (10)

Umar Gul 15.1–2–65–5; Shahid Nazir 14–4–42–3; Abdul Razzaq 7–2–22–0; Danish Kaneria 18–3–58–2; Shoaib Malik 2–0–11–0. *Second Innings*—Umar Gul 29–6–99–4; Shahid Nazir 20–8–63–3; Abdul Razzaq 7–2–19–0; Danish Kaneria 29–7–78–1; Shoaib Malik 5–1–14–0; Mohammad Hafeez 4–0–11–1.

Pakistan

Mohammad Hafeez lbw b Taylor	57	– lbw b Collymore	1
Imran Farhat lbw b Taylor	9	– not out	8
Younis Khan c Sarwan b Edwards	11	– not out	0
Mohammad Yousuf st Ramdin b Gayle	192		
*Inzamam-ul-Haq b Mohammed	0		
Shoaib Malik c Mohammed b Taylor	69		
Abdul Razzaq c Ramdin b Taylor	5		
†Kamran Akmal c Lara b Gayle	78		
Shahid Nazir c Collymore b Mohammed	0		
Umar Gul not out	16		
Danish Kaneria c Ramdin b Mohammed	23		
B 4, l-b 7, w 6, n-b 8	25	L-b 4	4

1/16 (2) 2/45 (3) 3/133 (1) 4/140 (5)   485   1/2 (1)   (1 wkt) 13
5/279 (6) 6/285 (7) 7/433 (8)
8/444 (4) 9/446 (9) 10/485 (11)

Edwards 26–3–109–1; Taylor 33–7–115–4; Collymore 25–6–63–0; Bravo 20–3–63–0; Mohammed 31–4–98–3; Gayle 10–3–24–2; Sarwan 1–0–2–0. *Second Innings*—Collymore 3–2–2–1; Edwards 2.1–1–7–0.

Umpires: E. A. R. de Silva *(Sri Lanka)* (33) and S. J. A. Taufel *(Australia)* (39).
Third umpire: Nadeem Ghauri *(Pakistan)*.   Referee: R. S. Mahanama *(Sri Lanka)* (8).

Close of play: First day, Pakistan 39-1 (Mohammad Hafeez 11, Younis Khan 10); Second day, Pakistan 265-4 (Mohammad Yousuf 107, Shoaib Malik 61); Third day, West Indies 74-3 (Lara 28, Edwards 5).

Test No. 1816/43 (P326/WI435)

PAKISTAN v WEST INDIES 2006-07 (2nd Test)

At Multan Cricket Stadium on 19, 20, 21, 22, 23 November.
Toss: Pakistan.   Result: MATCH DRAWN.
Debuts: none.
Man of the Match: Mohammad Yousuf.

West Indies bounced back with a robust performance: an awesome 216 from Lara, and some fine fast bowling from Taylor, gave them a sniff of a series-levelling victory. But dropped catches again cost them dear, and Mohammad Yousuf piloted Pakistan to a draw. Lara's memorable innings contained a century before lunch on the third day, off only 77 balls. The other batsmen – minus vice-captain Sarwan, who had been dropped – gave good support for once. Pakistan had been restricted to 357 in spite of meaningful contributions from all their top six: no-one exceeded Imran Farhat's 74. West Indies' openers began by putting on 162, then Bravo helped Lara add 200. Lara's epic assault began soberly, but after reaching 50 in 48 balls, he went into overdrive against Danish Kaneria: one over produced a sequence of 406664 from authentic strokes down the ground. Lara completed his ninth Test double-century – more than anyone except Don Bradman (12) – early on the fourth day. His 19th score of 150 or more, surpassing Bradman's record of 18, was adorned with 22 fours and seven sixes. The lead was 234, but that could not be converted into victory. Needing to bat for five sessions, Pakistan had several anxious moments, but a combination of Yousuf's broad bat, three other half-centuries and more faulty catching – six chances went down in all – took them comfortably to safety in the end. Yousuf hit 22 fours before falling in the 190s for an unprecedented third time, with the match already safe.

Pakistan

Mohammad Hafeez c Ramdin b Taylor	36	– b Taylor		18
Imran Farhat c Lara b Bravo	74	– run out		76
Younis Khan c Morton b Taylor	56	– c Ramdin b Mohammed		56
Mohammad Yousuf c Lara b Gayle	56	– c Chanderpaul b Mohammed		191
*Inzamam-ul-Haq c Ramdin b Taylor	31	– lbw b Taylor		10
Shoaib Malik c Bravo b Collymore	42	– b Powell		4
Abdul Razzaq not out	16	– c Chanderpaul b Mohammed		80
†Kamran Akmal c Bravo b Collymore	17	– not out		2
Shahid Nazir lbw b Taylor	7			
Umar Gul c Bravo b Taylor	7			
Danish Kaneria run out	0			
B 9, l-b 4, n-b 2	15	B 8, l-b 10, w 3, n-b 3		24

1/83 (1) 2/125 (2) 3/212 (3) 4/250 (4)   357   1/24 (1) 2/124 (3)   (7 wkts) 461
5/269 (5) 6/315 (6) 7/333 (8)   3/243 (2) 4/284 (5)
8/346 (9) 9/357 (10) 10/357 (11)   5/306 (6) 6/458 (7) 7/461 (4)

Taylor 26–6–91–5; Collymore 31–9–67–2; Powell 14–4–50–0; Gayle 22–6–52–1; Bravo 19–6–41–1; Mohammed 11–1–39–0; Morton 1–0–4–0. *Second Innings*—Taylor 25–4–75–2; Collymore 28–9–66–0; Gayle 29–5–85–0; Powell 20–6–47–1; Bravo 13–3–40–0; Mohammed 27.4–4–101–3; Chanderpaul 2–0–9–0; Morton 3–0–20–0.

West Indies

C. H. Gayle lbw b Danish Kaneria	93	
D. Ganga lbw b Danish Kaneria	82	
*B. C. Lara c Shoaib Malik b Danish Kaneria	216	
R. S. Morton lbw b Umar Gul	5	
S. Chanderpaul c Abdul Razzaq b Shahid Nazir	14	
D. J. Bravo c Younis Khan b Danish Kaneria	89	
†D. Ramdin c Kamran Akmal b Shahid Nazir	11	
D. Mohammed st Kamran Akmal b Danish Kaneria	36	

D. B. Powell lbw b Abdul Razzaq 9
J. E. Taylor lbw b Abdul Razzaq 1
C. D. Collymore not out 1
  B 9, l-b 18, n-b 7 34

1/162 (1) 2/220 (2) 3/281 (4)   591
4/302 (5) 5/502 (6) 6/523 (7)
7/563 (3) 8/583 (8) 9/590 (10) 10/591 (9)

Umar Gul 38–13–96–1; Shahid Nazir 29–2–103–2; Danish Kaneria 46–7–181–5; Abdul Razzaq 17.4–4–65–2; Mohammad Hafeez 24–2–72–0; Shoaib Malik 13–1–47–0.

Umpires: M. R. Benson *(England)* (12) and D. J. Harper *(Australia)* (60).
Third umpire: Zameer Haider *(Pakistan)*.   Referee: R. S. Mahanama *(Sri Lanka)* (9).

Close of play: First day, Pakistan 263-4 (Inzamam-ul-Haq 31, Shoaib Malik 4); Second day, West Indies 151-0 (Gayle 87, Ganga 59); Third day, West Indies 509-5 (Lara 196, Ramdin 4); Fourth day, Pakistan 213-2 (Imran Farhat 70, Mohammad Yousuf 56).

PAKISTAN v WEST INDIES 2006-07 (3rd Test)

At National Stadium, Karachi, on 27, 28, 29, 30 November, 1 December.
Toss: Pakistan.   Result: PAKISTAN won by 199 runs.
Debuts: none.
Man of the Match: Mohammad Yousuf.   Man of the Series: Mohammad Yousuf.

Mohammad Yousuf's record-breaking year culminated in a comprehensive Pakistan win, although they had to go an hour into the final session to seal the series 2–0. Twin centuries – his fifth and six in the last five Tests – boosted his aggregate for the calendar year to 1,788, eclipsing Viv Richards's previous record of 1,710 in 1976. Yousuf made an unprecedented nine centuries, beating seven by Richards and Aravinda de Silva (1997); Ricky Ponting would also make seven in 2006. After Inzamam-ul-Haq decided to bat on a grassless pitch, Yousuf's century seemed inevitable, although he was dropped by Ramdin off Gayle when 63. Umar Gul's spell, which included three for none in ten balls, probably decided the match: Gayle lofted to mid-off, Lara's off stump went cartwheeling, then the recalled Sarwan received a wicked yorker. Ganga managed an adhesive 81, but Pakistan still claimed an important lead. Yousuf then put on 149 with Mohammad Hafeez, who batted for just under seven hours. On the fourth day almost 20,000 turned up to see Richards's record broken, and they were not disappointed: Yousuf had the rare treat of raising his bat at 48, after on-driving Collymore for four to go past the old mark. Lara and Sarwan threatened to save their side, putting on 80 before Gul persuaded Lara to drive uppishly then thudded another yorker into Sarwan's right foot, breaking it. Chanderpaul fell to Kaneria shortly after tea, and Pakistan soon secured their 21st victory in 39 Tests at the National Stadium.

Pakistan

Mohammad Hafeez b Collymore	18	– c Ramdin b Taylor	104
Imran Farhat c Ramdin b Bravo	47	– c Ramdin b Powell	20
Younis Khan run out	20	– lbw b Gayle	38
Mohammad Yousuf lbw b Collymore	102	– b Sarwan	124
*Inzamam-ul-Haq c Chanderpaul b Ganga	18	– not out	58
Shoaib Malik lbw b Taylor	18	– b Collymore	10
Abdul Razzaq c Ramdin b Bravo	7	– c Gayle b Sarwan	10
†Kamran Akmal b Collymore	31		
Shahid Nazir b Powell	0		
Umar Gul b Powell	26		
Danish Kaneria not out	7		
B 1, l-b 7, n-b 2	10	B 13, l-b 21, w 1	35

1/26 (1) 2/72 (3) 3/112 (2) 4/178 (5)   304   1/43 (2) 2/122 (3)   (6 wkts dec.) 399
5/222 (6) 6/239 (4) 7/248 (7)   3/271 (1) 4/365 (4)
8/265 (9) 9/272 (8) 10/304 (10)   5/384 (6) 6/399 (7)

Taylor 22–3–76–1; Collymore 21–6–57–3; Gayle 16–3–27–0; Powell 23.5–5–83–2; Bravo 14–6–33–2; Ganga 4–0–20–1. *Second Innings*—Taylor 24–8–60–1; Collymore 22–10–52–1; Powell 24–6–70–1; Bravo 19–1–68–0; Gayle 15–2–38–1; Sarwan 17.5–0–70–2; Chanderpaul 2–0–7–0.

West Indies

C. H. Gayle c Abdul Razzaq b Umar Gul	40	– b Umar Gul	2
D. Ganga c Kamran Akmal b Abdul Razzaq	81	– lbw b Shahid Nazir	2
*B. C. Lara b Umar Gul	0	– c Shoaib Malik b Umar Gul	49
R. R. Sarwan b Umar Gul	0	– retired hurt	35
S. Chanderpaul c Imran Farhat b Danish Kaneria	36	– lbw b Danish Kaneria	69
R. S. Morton c Imran Farhat b Danish Kaneria	21	– c and b Danish Kaneria	16
D. J. Bravo c Kamran Akmal b Danish Kaneria	8	– c Younis Khan b Shahid Nazir	26
†D. Ramdin run out	50	– not out	25
D. B. Powell b Umar Gul	1	– c Younis Khan b Danish Kaneria	0
J. E. Taylor c Kamran Akmal b Shahid Nazir	1	– lbw b Abdul Razzaq	1
C. D. Collymore not out	8	– lbw b Abdul Razzaq	0
B 5, l-b 2, n-b 7	14	B 5, l-b 9, n-b 5	19

1/51 (1) 2/51 (3) 3/51 (4) 4/114 (5)   260   1/2 (1) 2/17 (2) 3/97 (3)   244
5/153 (6) 6/190 (7) 7/204 (2)   4/126 (6) 5/183 (7) 6/227 (5)
8/213 (9) 9/216 (10) 10/260 (8)   7/227 (9) 8/236 (10) 9/244 (11)

In the second innings, Sarwan retired hurt at 101.

Umar Gul 24–5–79–4; Shahid Nazir 17–3–58–1; Danish Kaneria 35–12–62–3; Abdul Razzaq 16–5–44–1; Mohammad Hafeez 4–1–10–0. *Second Innings*—Umar Gul 19–2–89–2; Shahid Nazir 18–6–49–2; Danish Kaneria 26–6–69–3; Shoaib Malik 1–1–0–0; Abdul Razzaq 12–5–23–2.

Umpires: M. R. Benson *(England)* (13) and D. J. Harper *(Australia)* (61).
Third umpire: Riazuddin *(Pakistan)*.   Referee: R. S. Mahanama *(Sri Lanka)* (10).

Close of play: First day, Pakistan 257-7 (Kamran Akmal 18, Shahid Nazir 0); Second day, West Indies 191-6 (Ganga 77, Ramdin 0); Third day, Pakistan 130-2 (Mohammad Hafeez 57, Mohammad Yousuf 1); Fourth day, West Indies 39-2 (Lara 18, Sarwan 11).

AUSTRALIA v ENGLAND 2006-07 (1st Test)

At Woolloongabba, Brisbane, on 23, 24, 25, 26, 27 November.
Toss: Australia.   Result: AUSTRALIA won by 277 runs.
Debuts: none.
Man of the Match: R. T. Ponting.

Harmison's opening delivery went straight to second slip and was signalled wide. A record Gabba crowd of nearly 40,000 roared with derision or disbelief, and the teams drew their own conclusions: Australia grinned quietly, England grimaced visibly, and Australia were soon well on their way to winning the opening match of an Ashes series for the eighth time out of ten. Ponting hit his ninth hundred in 12 Tests, equalling Steve Waugh's national record of 32, and added 209 with Hussey. Hoggard briefly demonstrated that a flat pitch need not preclude guile, trapping Ponting four short of 200 and then removing Gilchrist three balls later, but the eventual declaration left England 17 overs to survive before the second-day close. It was enough to decide the match. McGrath had predicted he would get Strauss on the pull and Cook from round the wicket: in the space of two balls, he was proved eerily correct. Leading by 445, Ponting waived the follow-on: Langer took advantage of some resigned bowling to hit his first Test hundred since The Oval 2005, and Ponting became the seventh to pass 9,000 Test runs. England were left 648 to win, or 172 overs to survive. Humiliation beckoned at 91 for 3, then Collingwood and Pietersen added 153. But Pietersen whipped Lee's fourth ball of the final day to short midwicket, and it was all over in 90 minutes. Clark's match figures of seven for 93 embarrassed England's collective effort of ten for 804, one of them a run-out.

Australia

J. L. Langer c Pietersen b Flintoff	82	– not out	100
M. L. Hayden c Collingwood b Flintoff	21	– run out	37
*R. T. Ponting lbw b Hoggard	196	– not out	60
D. R. Martyn c Collingwood b Giles	29		
M. E. K. Hussey b Flintoff	86		
M. J. Clarke c Strauss b Anderson	56		
†A. C. Gilchrist lbw b Hoggard	0		
S. K. Warne c Jones b Harmison	17		
B. Lee not out	43		
S. R. Clark b Flintoff	39		
G. D. McGrath not out	8		
B 2, l-b 8, w 8, n-b 7	25	L-b 4, n-b 1	5

1/79 (2) 2/141 (1) 3/198 (4)   (9 wkts dec.) 602   1/68 (2)   (1 wkt dec.) 202
4/407 (5) 5/467 (3) 6/467 (7)
7/500 (8) 8/528 (6) 9/578 (10)

Harmison 30–4–123–1; Hoggard 31–5–98–2; Anderson 29–6–141–1; Flintoff 30–4–99–4; Giles 25–2–91–1; Bell 1–0–12–0; Pietersen 9–1–28–0. *Second Innings*—Hoggard 11–2–43–0; Anderson 9–1–54–0; Flintoff 5–2–11–0; Harmison 12.1–1–54–0; Giles 5–0–22–0; Pietersen 3–0–14–0.

England

A. J. Strauss c Hussey b McGrath	12	– c sub (R. A. Broad) b Clark	11
A. N. Cook c Warne b McGrath	11	– c Hussey b Warne	43
I. R. Bell c Ponting b Clark	50	– lbw b Warne	0
P. D. Collingwood c Gilchrist b Clark	5	– st Gilchrist b Warne	96
K. P. Pietersen lbw b McGrath	16	– c Martyn b Lee	92
*A. Flintoff c Gilchrist b Lee	0	– c Langer b Warne	16
†G. O. Jones lbw b McGrath	19	– b McGrath	33
A. F. Giles c Hayden b McGrath	24	– c Warne b Clark	23
M. J. Hoggard c Gilchrist b Clark	0	– c Warne b Clark	8
S. J. Harmison c Gilchrist b McGrath	0	– c McGrath b Clark	13
J. M. Anderson not out	2	– not out	4
B 2, l-b 8, w 2, n-b 6	18	B 8, l-b 10, w 2, n-b 11	31

1/28 (1) 2/28 (2) 3/42 (4) 4/78 (5)   157   1/29 (1) 2/36 (3) 3/91 (2)   370
5/79 (6) 6/126 (7) 7/149 (3)   4/244 (4) 5/271 (6) 6/293 (5)
8/153 (9) 9/154 (10) 10/157 (8)   7/326 (7) 8/346 (8) 9/361 (9) 10/370 (10)

Lee 15–3–51–1; McGrath 23.1–8–50–6; Clark 14–5–21–3; Warne 9–0–25–0. *Second Innings*—Lee 22–1–98–1; McGrath 19–3–53–1; Clark 24.1–6–72–4; Warne 34–7–124–4; Hussey 1–0–5–0.

Umpires: B. F. Bowden *(New Zealand)* (38) and S. A. Bucknor *(West Indies)* (114).
Third umpire: P. D. Parker *(Australia)*.   Referee: J. J. Crowe *(New Zealand)* (15).

Close of play: First day, Australia 346-3 (Ponting 137, Hussey 63); Second day, England 53-3 (Bell 13, Pietersen 6); Third day, Australia 181-1 (Langer 88, Ponting 51); Fourth day, England 293-5 (Pietersen 92, Jones 12).

AUSTRALIA v ENGLAND 2006-07 (2nd Test)

At Adelaide Oval on 1, 2, 3, 4, 5 December.
Toss: England.   Result: AUSTRALIA won by six wickets.
Debuts: none.
Man of the Match: R. T. Ponting.

Shane Warne conjured up perhaps the most astounding victory of even his glittering career. England began with 551 for 6, Collingwood becoming only the third Englishman to score a Test double-century in Australia, after "Tip" Foster (1903-04) and Wally Hammond, who made three. He and Pietersen, who made 158 for the third time in a Test, put on 310, a fourth-wicket record for England against Australia. Later Australia were struggling at 65 for 3, and would have been worse off had Giles (controversially preferred to Panesar again) not dropped Ponting at deep midwicket when he had 35. Ponting went on to yet another century, as did Clarke. Australia finished only 38 behind – Hoggard took seven wickets in a lion-hearted performance – but with little more than a day left a draw seemed certain. But Warne had other ideas. He was helped by the match's first bad umpiring decision: Steve Bucknor despatched Strauss, caught off his pad. From that moment, demons started to play inside the batsmen's heads – and the biggest demon of all was bowling at them. From 69 for 1, England suddenly found run-making almost impossible, managing only 60 more in 43 overs. Australia's task – 168 in 36 overs – was no certainty. But the force was with them, and they won with 19 balls to spare. Only three higher first-innings totals had led to defeat in a Test, although Flintoff should perhaps have been told that one of them was Australia's 556 against India at Adelaide three years previously.

England

A. J. Strauss c Martyn b Clark	14	– c Hussey b Warne	34
A. N. Cook c Gilchrist b Clark	27	– c Gilchrist b Clark	9
I. R. Bell c and b Lee	60	– run out	26
P. D. Collingwood c Gilchrist b Clark	206	– not out	22
K. P. Pietersen run out	158	– b Warne	2
*A. Flintoff not out	38	– c Gilchrist b Lee	2
†G. O. Jones c Martyn b Warne	1	– c Hayden b Lee	10
A. F. Giles not out	27	– c Hayden b Warne	0
M. J. Hoggard (did not bat)		– b Warne	4
S. J. Harmison (did not bat)		– lbw b McGrath	8
J. M. Anderson (did not bat)		– lbw b McGrath	1
L-b 10, w 2, n-b 8	20	B 3, l-b 5, w 1, n-b 2	11

1/32 (1) 2/45 (2) 3/158 (3)   (6 wkts dec.) 551   1/31 (2) 2/69 (1) 3/70 (3)   129
4/468 (4) 5/489 (5) 6/491 (7)   4/73 (5) 5/77 (6) 6/94 (7)
7/97 (8) 8/105 (9) 9/119 (10) 10/129 (11)

Lee 34–1–139–1; McGrath 30–5–107–0; Clark 34–6–75–3; Warne 53–9–167–1; Clarke 17–2–53–0. *Second Innings*—Lee 18–3–35–2; McGrath 10–6–15–2; Warne 32–12–49–4; Clark 13–4–22–1.

Australia

J. L. Langer c Pietersen b Flintoff	4	– c Bell b Hoggard	7
M. L. Hayden c Jones b Hoggard	12	– c Collingwood b Flintoff	18
*R. T. Ponting c Jones b Hoggard	142	– c Strauss b Giles	49
D. R. Martyn c Bell b Hoggard	11	– (5) c Strauss b Flintoff	5
M. E. K. Hussey b Hoggard	91	– (4) not out	61
M. J. Clarke c Giles b Hoggard	124	– not out	21
†A. C. Gilchrist c Bell b Giles	64		
S. K. Warne lbw b Hoggard	43		
B. Lee not out	7		
S. R. Clark b Hoggard	0		
G. D. McGrath c Jones b Anderson	1		
B 4, l-b 2, w 1, n-b 7	14	B 2, l-b 2, w 1, n-b 2	7

1/8 (1) 2/35 (2) 3/65 (4) 4/257 (3)   513   1/14 (1) 2/33 (2)   (4 wkts) 168
5/286 (5) 6/384 (7) 7/502 (8)   3/116 (3) 4/121 (5)
8/505 (6) 9/507 (10) 10/513 (11)

Hoggard 42–6–109–7; Flintoff 26–5–82–1; Harmison 25–5–96–0; Anderson 21.3–3–85–1; Giles 42–7–103–1; Pietersen 9–0–32–0. *Second Innings*—Hoggard 4–0–29–1; Flintoff 9–0–44–2; Giles 10–0–46–1; Harmison 4–0–15–0; Anderson 3.5–0–23–0; Pietersen 2–0–7–0.

Umpires: S. A. Bucknor *(West Indies)* (115) and R. E. Koertzen *(South Africa)* (78).
Third umpire: S. J. Davis *(Australia)*.   Referee: J. J. Crowe *(New Zealand)* (16).

Close of play: First day, England 266-3 (Collingwood 98, Pietersen 60); Second day, Australia 28-1 (Hayden 12, Ponting 11); Third day, Australia 312-5 (Clarke 30, Gilchrist 13); Fourth day, England 59-1 (Strauss 31, Bell 18).

AUSTRALIA v ENGLAND 2006-07 (3rd Test)

At W. A. C. A. Ground, Perth, on 14, 15, 16, 17, 18 December.
Toss: Australia.   Result: AUSTRALIA won by 206 runs.
Debuts: none.
Man of the Match: M. E. K. Hussey.

After doing without the Ashes for only three Tests and 462 days – the briefest custody in history – Australia regained them at 2.13 p.m. on December 18, when Warne bowled Panesar. England were at their best on the first day, finding a way through Australia's top half without, for once, being inconvenienced by the bottom half. England again could not budge Hussey, but made good progress against some reckless strokes, not least from Symonds, recalled after Damien Martyn's sudden retirement. He top-edged Panesar – who, recalled himself, became only the fourth spinner to take a five-for in a Test at Perth – after hitting him for two straight sixes. Faced with a modest score for once, England did even worse. Pietersen top-scored with 70, but Jones, after 51 Test innings without a duck (an England record), completed the first of a brace with a tame prod to gully. When Langer was gated by the first ball of the second innings, 21 wickets had fallen in 812 deliveries. Ponting and Hayden put a stop to this, then Australia hammered 408 runs on the third day, including Hussey's first Ashes hundred, Clarke's second and Gilchrist's third, which arrived in only 57 balls, one more than the fastest-known Test century, by Viv Richards against England in Antigua in 1985-86. Set an academic 557, England lost Strauss, padding up, fourth ball. Cook and Bell, mixing sound defence with judicious strokes, but after that only Flintoff and Pietersen, undefeated after four hours, delayed the surrender of the Ashes.

Australia

J. L. Langer b Panesar	37	– b Hoggard	0
M. L. Hayden c Jones b Hoggard	24	– c Collingwood b Panesar	92
*R. T. Ponting lbw b Harmison	2	– c Jones b Harmison	75
M. E. K. Hussey not out	74	– c Jones b Panesar	103
M. J. Clarke c and b Harmison	37	– not out	135
A. Symonds c Jones b Panesar	26	– c Collingwood b Panesar	2
†A. C. Gilchrist c Bell b Panesar	0	– not out	102
S. K. Warne c Jones b Panesar	25		
B. Lee lbw b Panesar	10		
S. R. Clark b Harmison	3		
G. D. McGrath c Cook b Harmison	1		
W 1, n-b 4	5	L-b 15, w 2, n-b 1	18

1/47 (2) 2/54 (3) 3/69 (1) 4/121 (5)   **244**   1/0 (1) 2/144 (3)   (5 wkts dec.) **527**
5/172 (6) 6/172 (7) 7/214 (8)   3/206 (2) 4/357 (4)
8/234 (9) 9/242 (10) 10/244 (11)   5/365 (6)

Hoggard 12–2–40–1; Flintoff 9–2–36–0; Harmison 19–4–48–4; Panesar 24–4–92–5; Mahmood 7–2–28–0. *Second Innings*—Hoggard 20–4–85–1; Flintoff 19–2–76–0; Harmison 24–3–116–1; Panesar 34–3–145–3; Mahmood 10–0–59–0; Pietersen 5–1–31–0.

England

A. J. Strauss c Gilchrist b Clark	42	– lbw b Lee	0
A. N. Cook c Langer b McGrath	15	– c Gilchrist b McGrath	116
I. R. Bell c Gilchrist b Lee	0	– c Langer b Warne	87
P. D. Collingwood c Hayden b McGrath	11	– c Gilchrist b Clark	5
K. P. Pietersen c Symonds b Lee	70	– not out	60
*A. Flintoff c Warne b Symonds	13	– (7) b Warne	51
†G. O. Jones c Langer b Symonds	0	– (8) run out	0
S. I. Mahmood c Gilchrist b Clark	10	– (9) lbw b Clark	4
M. J. Hoggard c Hayden b Warne	4	– (6) b McGrath	0
S. J. Harmison c Lee b Clark	23	– lbw b Warne	0
M. S. Panesar not out	16	– b Warne	1
W 1, n-b 10	11	B 11, l-b 4, w 6, n-b 5	26

1/36 (2) 2/37 (3) 3/55 (4) 4/82 (1)   **215**   1/0 (1) 2/170 (3) 3/185 (4)   **350**
5/107 (6) 6/114 (7) 7/128 (8)   4/261 (2) 5/261 (6) 6/336 (7)
8/155 (9) 9/175 (5) 10/215 (10)   7/336 (8) 8/345 (9) 9/346 (10) 10/350 (11)

Lee 18–1–69–2; McGrath 18–5–48–2; Clark 15.1–3–49–3; Warne 9–0–41–1; Symonds 4–1–8–2. *Second Innings*—Lee 22–3–75–1; McGrath 27–9–61–2; Clark 25–7–56–2; Warne 39.2–6–115–4; Symonds 9–1–28–0.

Umpires: Aleem Dar *(Pakistan)* (35) and R. E. Koertzen *(South Africa)* (79).
Third umpire: S. J. Davis *(Australia)*.   Referee: J. J. Crowe *(New Zealand)* (17).

Close of play: First day, England 51-2 (Strauss 24, Collingwood 10); Second day, Australia 119-1 (Hayden 57, Ponting 57); Third day, England 19-1 (Cook 7, Bell 9); Fourth day, England 265-5 (Pietersen 37, Flintoff 2).

AUSTRALIA v ENGLAND 2006-07 (4th Test)

At Melbourne Cricket Ground on 26, 27, 28 December.

Toss: England.   Result: AUSTRALIA won by an innings and 99 runs.

Debuts: none.

Man of the Match: S. K. Warne.

From the moment Shane Warne announced his impending retirement, this Test was always going to be about Melbourne's farewell to its favourite cricketing son. Rain trimmed the crowd figure on Boxing Day to 89,155, an Ashes record, but 1,645 below the 46-year-old high for any properly audited day's Test cricket. It also meant the pitch spent a sweaty Christmas under covers, leaving it underprepared. Warne took five wickets on the opening day, including an unprecedented 700th in Tests (Strauss), which thrilled the crowd but put an end to the match before it had properly begun. It took Australia just two more days to complete victory, forcing the authorities to refund more than £900,000-worth of tickets for the fourth day. Pietersen, again left with the tail, hit out and got out, and England managed only 159. Australia lost Langer and nightwatchman Lee to consecutive balls on the first evening: an hour into the second day, they were 84 for 5. Symonds took 21 balls to break his duck, but he and Hayden composed high-class innings, sharing a pivotal partnership of 279. Hayden made his fifth century in his last six Tests at Melbourne, while Symonds joyously reached his maiden Test hundred by driving Collingwood for six. Australia were quickly out next morning for 419, with six catches for the recalled Read. Mentally crushed, England collapsed so rapidly that it briefly seemed that Warne would not get a bowl on his home farewell, but he nipped in with two late wickets.

England

A. J. Strauss b Warne	50	– c Gilchrist b Lee	31
A. N. Cook c Gilchrist b Lee	11	– b Clark	20
I. R. Bell lbw b Clark	7	– lbw b McGrath	2
P. D. Collingwood c Ponting b Lee	28	– (5) c Langer b Lee	16
K. P. Pietersen c Symonds b Warne	21	– (4) b Clark	1
*A. Flintoff c Warne b Clark	13	– lbw b Clark	25
†C. M. W. Read c Ponting b Warne	3	– not out	26
S. I. Mahmood c Gilchrist b McGrath	0	– lbw b Warne	0
S. J. Harmison c Clarke b Warne	7	– lbw b Warne	4
M. S. Panesar c Symonds b Warne	4	– c Clarke b Lee	14
M. J. Hoggard not out	9	– b Lee	5
B 2, l-b 1, n-b 3	6	L-b 12, w 1, n-b 4	17
	159		**161**

1/23 (2) 2/44 (3) 3/101 (4) 4/101 (1)   159
5/122 (6) 6/135 (7) 7/136 (8)
8/145 (9) 9/146 (5) 10/159 (10)

1/41 (2) 2/48 (3) 3/49 (4)   161
4/75 (5) 5/90 (1) 6/108 (6)
7/109 (8) 8/127 (9) 9/146 (10) 10/161 (11)

Lee 13–4–36–2; McGrath 20–8–37–1; Clark 17–6–27–2; Symonds 7–2–17–0; Warne 17.2–4–39–5. *Second Innings*—Lee 18.5–6–47–4; McGrath 12–2–26–1; Clark 16–6–30–3; Warne 19–3–46–2.

Australia

J. L. Langer c Read b Flintoff	27	S. K. Warne not out	40
M. L. Hayden c Read b Mahmood	153	S. R. Clark c Read b Mahmood	8
B. Lee c Read b Flintoff	0	G. D. McGrath c Bell b Mahmood	0
*R. T. Ponting c Cook b Flintoff	7	L-b 6, w 1, n-b 9	16
M. E. K. Hussey b Hoggard	6		
M. J. Clarke c Read b Harmison	5	1/44 (1) 2/44 (3) 3/62 (4)	**419**
A. Symonds c Read b Harmison	156	4/79 (5) 5/84 (6) 6/363 (2)	
†A. C. Gilchrist c Collingwood b Mahmood	1	7/365 (8) 8/383 (7) 9/417 (10) 10/419 (11)	

Hoggard 21–6–82–1; Flintoff 22–1–77–3; Harmison 28–6–69–2; Mahmood 21.3–1–100–4; Panesar 12–1–52–0; Collingwood 3–0–20–0; Pietersen 1–0–13–0.

Umpires: Aleem Dar *(Pakistan)* (36) and R. E. Koertzen *(South Africa)* (80).
Third umpire: R. L. Parry *(Australia)*.   Referee: R. S. Madugalle *(Sri Lanka)* (93).

Close of play: First day, Australia 48-2 (Hayden 17, Ponting 0); Second day, Australia 372-7 (Symonds 154, Warne 4).

AUSTRALIA v ENGLAND 2006-07 (5th Test)

At Sydney Cricket Ground on 2, 3, 4, 5 January.
Toss: England.   Result: AUSTRALIA won by ten wickets.
Debuts: none.
Man of the Match: S. R. Clark.   Man of the Series: R. T. Ponting.

The final Test fitted into the broad pattern of the entire series. In a match curiously short of compelling indi-vidual achievements – no century and no four-fors, only the fifth such instance in Tests – England were notionally competitive until just after lunch on the third day. Australia were then 325 for 8, only 34 ahead. But yet again their tail wagged, and when the bowlers returned to the day job (for the last time for Warne and McGrath, who had also announced his retirement, as had Langer), the first Ashes whitewash since 1920-21 was soon completed. Flintoff won the toss, but was without Hoggard, whose side strain ended a run of 40 consecutive Tests. Bell batted well before beaten by a classic McGrath nipbacker, and Flintoff played easily his best innings of the series, but Numbers 7-11 made four runs between them as the last six fell for 46. England's bowlers stuck to their task: none of Australia's top six reached 50, but Gilchrist and Warne were in blazing form. England, 102 behind, found trouble right away. Cook went quickly and, two balls later, Lee felled Strauss with a 93mph bouncer. England inched in front, but Warne returned, and just before the third-day close puled Flintoff right forward. He missed, wearily failed to get his foot back, and thus became Warne's 708th and last Test victim. Pietersen was out third ball next day, and Australia wrapped up the whitewash 13 minutes before lunch, before an emotional farewell to their retiring champions.

England

A. J. Strauss c Gilchrist b Lee	29	– lbw b Clark	24
A. N. Cook c Gilchrist b Clark	20	– c Gilchrist b Lee	4
I. R. Bell b McGrath	71	– c Gilchrist b Lee	28
K. P. Pietersen c Hussey b McGrath	41	– c Gilchrist b McGrath	29
P. D. Collingwood c Gilchrist b McGrath	27	– c Hayden b Clark	17
*A. Flintoff c Gilchrist b Clark	89	– st Gilchrist b Warne	7
†C. M. W. Read c Gilchrist b Lee	2	– (8) c Ponting b Lee	4
S. I. Mahmood c Hayden b Lee	0	– (9) b McGrath	4
S. J. Harmison lbw b Clark	2	– (10) not out	16
M. S. Panesar lbw b Warne	0	– (7) run out	0
J. M. Anderson not out	0	– c Hussey b McGrath	5
L-b 5, w 3, n-b 2	10	B 2, l-b 3, w 1, n-b 3	9

1/45 (1) 2/58 (2) 3/166 (4) 4/167 (3)   291   1/5 (2) 2/55 (1) 3/64 (3)   147
5/245 (5) 6/258 (7) 7/258 (8)   4/98 (5) 5/113 (6) 6/114 (4)
8/282 (9) 9/291 (6) 10/291 (10)   7/114 (7) 8/122 (8) 9/123 (9) 10/147 (11)

McGrath 29–8–67–3; Lee 22–5–75–3; Clark 24–6–62–3; Warne 22.4–1–69–1; Symonds 6–2–13–0. *Second Innings*—Lee 14–5–39–3; McGrath 21–11–38–3; Clark 12–4–29–2; Warne 6–1–23–1; Symonds 5–2–13–0.

Australia

J. L. Langer c Read b Anderson	26	– not out	20
M. L. Hayden c Collingwood b Harmison	33	– not out	23
*R. T. Ponting run out	45		
M. E. K. Hussey c Read b Anderson	37		
M. J. Clarke c Read b Harmison	11		
A. Symonds b Panesar	48		
†A. C. Gilchrist c Read b Anderson	62		
S. K. Warne st Read b Panesar	71		
B. Lee c Read b Flintoff	5		
S. R. Clark c Pietersen b Mahmood	35		
G. D. McGrath not out	0		
L-b 10, w 4, n-b 6	20	L-b 3	3

1/34 (1) 2/100 (2) 3/118 (3) 4/155 (5)   393   (no wkt) 46
5/190 (4) 6/260 (6) 7/318 (7)
8/325 (9) 9/393 (10) 10/393 (8)

Flintoff 17–2–56–1; Anderson 26–8–98–3; Harmison 23–5–80–2; Mahmood 11–1–59–1; Panesar 19.3–0–90–2. *Second Innings*—Anderson 4–0–12–0; Harmison 5–1–13–0; Mahmood 1.5–0–18–0.

Umpires: Aleem Dar *(Pakistan)* (37) and B. F. Bowden *(New Zealand)* (39).
Third umpire: P. D. Parker *(Australia)*.   Referee: R. S. Madugalle *(Sri Lanka)* (94).

Close of play: First day, England 234-4 (Collingwood 25, Flintoff 42); Second day, Australia 188-4 (Hussey 37, Symonds 22); Third day, England 114-5 (Pietersen 29, Panesar 0).

NEW ZEALAND v SRI LANKA 2006-07 (1st Test)

At Lancaster Park, Christchurch, on 7, 8, 9 December.
Toss: Sri Lanka.   Result: NEW ZEALAND won by five wickets.
Debuts: Sri Lanka – L. P. C. Silva.
Man of the Match: S. E. Bond.

A low-key Test would have ended with a whimper had New Zealand not ended a gritty second innings with an ungracious act. Sangakkara was playing the game's one great innings, and threatening to set a tricky target of around 150. Then, after Muralitharan completed the easy single that brought up Sangakkara's century – out of just 170 – he strolled back to add his good wishes. But Martin rifled in a long throw, keeper McCullum broke the wicket, and umpire Brian Jerling gave Murali out. The New Zealanders happily accepted the run-out, and a manageable target of 119. Jayawardene admitted Muralitharan was technically out, but said New Zealand had broken the spirit of the game by claiming the dismissal. Some locals argued that Murali's meander was merely the last of Sri Lanka's self-inflicted wounds, and that the first – Jayawardene's decision to bat first on a greenish pitch – was the fatal one: Sri Lanka were shot out before tea for 154. Martin, in his 32nd Test, took his 100th wicket (to go with just 48 runs) when he had Prasanna Jayawardene caught at slip. Murali started a slump, but Fleming and Vettori earned a handy lead. Chamara Silva bagged a debut pair as Sri Lanka lurched to 99 for 8 – only 47 in front – but Sangakkara charged on: only one lower all-out Test total has included a century, New Zealand's 159 (John Reid 100) against England at Christchurch in 1962-63. New Zealand stumbled in their pursuit, losing four wickets for ten, but Astle steadied the ship.

Sri Lanka

W. U. Tharanga	c How b Franklin	33	– c Fleming b Bond		24
S. T. Jayasuriya	c Fleming b Bond	5	– run out		10
K. C. Sangakkara	c Sinclair b Bond	4	– not out		100
*D. P. M. D. Jayawardene	c Franklin b Bond	8	– c Fleming b Franklin		0
C. K. Kapugedera	lbw b Franklin	37	– c Oram b Bond		1
L. P. C. Silva	b Franklin	0	– c Vettori b Bond		0
†H. A. P. W. Jayawardene	c How b Martin	7	– run out		11
W. P. U. J. C. Vaas	c McCullum b Oram	4	– c McCullum b Oram		0
M. F. Maharoof	c Fleming b Oram	15	– c McCullum b Bond		7
S. L. Malinga	not out	7	– c McCullum b Franklin		0
M. Muralitharan	c Astle b Martin	14	– run out		8
	L-b 13, w 1, n-b 6	20	L-b 5, n-b 4		9

1/11 (2) 2/17 (3) 3/37 (4) 4/87 (1)   154   1/18 (2) 2/44 (1) 3/45 (4) 4/46 (5)   170
5/87 (6) 6/106 (5) 7/110 (8)   5/46 (6) 6/74 (7) 7/80 (8) 8/99 (9)
8/121 (7) 9/132 (9) 10/154 (11)   9/143 (10) 10/170 (11)

Bond 13–2–43–3; Martin 16.4–2–37–2; Franklin 12–0–30–3; Oram 10–5–30–2; Astle 1–0–1–0. *Second Innings*—Bond 19.1–5–63–4; Martin 11–2–38–0; Franklin 13–1–34–2; Oram 7–1–19–1; Vettori 2–0–10–0; Astle 1–0–1–0.

New Zealand

C. D. Cumming	b Muralitharan	43	– c H. A. P. W. Jayawardene b Vaas		43
J. M. How	lbw b Malinga	0	– lbw b Muralitharan		11
M. S. Sinclair	c H. A. P. W. Jayawardene b Vaas	36	– c Sangakkara b Muralitharan		4
*S. P. Fleming	c Kapugedera b Maharoof	48	– lbw b Vaas		0
N. J. Astle	lbw b Muralitharan	2	– lbw b Muralitharan		24
J. D. P. Oram	c Silva b Vaas	1	– not out		12
†B. B. McCullum	b Vaas	0	– not out		14
D. L. Vettori	c D. P. M. D. Jayawardene b Malinga	63			
J. E. C. Franklin	lbw b Muralitharan	0			
S. E. Bond	lbw b Muralitharan	1			
C. S. Martin	not out	0			
	L-b 5, n-b 7	12	B 1, l-b 1, w 5, n-b 4		11

1/3 (2) 2/73 (3) 3/106 (1) 4/108 (5)   206   1/58 (2) 2/66 (1) 3/66 (4)   (5 wkts) 119
5/113 (6) 6/113 (7) 7/188 (4)   4/68 (3) 5/103 (5)
8/190 (9) 9/206 (10) 10/206 (8)

Vaas 18–4–49–3; Malinga 19.4–2–43–2; Maharoof 14–3–44–1; Muralitharan 34–7–65–4. *Second Innings*—Vaas 12–3–33–2; Malinga 4–1–35–0; Muralitharan 14–5–34–3; Maharoof 3–0–15–0.

Umpires: B. G. Jerling *(South Africa)* (3) and S. J. A. Taufel *(Australia)* (40).
Third umpire: G. A. V. Baxter *(New Zealand)*.   Referee: J. Srinath *(India)* (3).

Close of play: First day, New Zealand 85-2 (Cumming 37, Fleming 7); Second day, Sri Lanka 125-8 (Sangakkara 63, Malinga 0).

NEW ZEALAND v SRI LANKA 2006-07 (2nd Test)

At Basin Reserve, Wellington, on 15, 16, 17, 18 December.
Toss: Sri Lanka.   Result: SRI LANKA won by 217 runs.
Debuts: none.
Man of the Match: L. P. C. Silva.

Still smarting at the controversial end to the previous Test, Sri Lanka roared back to square the series. Jayawardene might have regretted batting first when Martin grabbed three quick wickets, but again Sangakkara came to the rescue. For the second time in a week he finished unbeaten with a century, his 12th in Tests. Sri Lanka's total looked below par, but New Zealand's innings was soon in ruins. Mixing spearing yorkers with sharp-bouncing lifters, Malinga grabbed three quick wickets before the close, and two more next morning as New Zealand struggled to 130. Malinga extracted some measure of revenge for *that* run-out by hitting McCullum on the hand, heel and shoulder, but he battled on, being last out. Sinclair kept wicket while McCullum's injuries were checked out; Sangakkara also deputised for Prasanna Jayawardene (hit on the elbow while batting) in the second innings, and all four wicketkeepers took at least one catch. Silva energised Sri Lanka's second innings after an early wobble, becoming the first to follow a debut pair with a century in his second Test. When Vettori finished off the innings with four for none in 12 balls, New Zealand needed an unlikely 504, and lost both openers before the close. Vettori and Franklin held Murali up, but he finished with an unprecedented full set of ten in a match against all the Test-playing nations. It gave him 90 wickets in 11 Tests in the calendar year, a tally only ever exceeded by Shane Warne, with 96 in 2005.

Sri Lanka

W. U. Tharanga c McCullum b Martin	7	– lbw b Martin	20
S. T. Jayasuriya c Fleming b Martin	0	– c Fleming b Vettori	31
K. C. Sangakkara not out	156	– c Franklin b Bond	8
*D. P. M. D. Jayawardene b Martin	0	– c Sinclair b Vettori	31
C. K. Kapugedera c Sinclair b Oram	5	– b Vettori	27
L. P. C. Silva c Fleming b Franklin	61	– not out	152
†H. A. P. W. Jayawardene lbw b Vettori	25	– c sub (S. M. Mills) b Martin	37
W. P. U. J. C. Vaas c McCullum b Bond	0	– c McCullum b Vettori	47
M. F. Maharoof c McCullum b Vettori	4	– lbw b Vettori	1
S. L. Malinga c Sinclair b Vettori	0	– lbw b Vettori	0
M. Muralitharan c and b Bond	0	– st McCullum b Vettori	0
B 1, l-b 1, n-b 8	10	L-b 7, n-b 4	11

1/0 (2) 2/27 (1) 3/41 (4) 4/81 (5)　　　　268　　1/44 (1) 2/62 (3) 3/62 (2)　　　　365
5/202 (6) 6/239 (7) 7/240 (8)　　　　　　　　4/100 (5) 5/168 (4) 6/262 (7)
8/251 (9) 9/259 (10) 10/268 (11)　　　　　　7/350 (8) 8/356 (9) 9/365 (10) 10/365 (11)

Bond 16–1–85–2; Martin 13–2–50–3; Franklin 12–2–46–1; Oram 3–0–10–1; Vettori 14–1–53–3; Astle 7–2–22–0.
Second Innings—Bond 19–3–67–1; Martin 23–1–98–2; Vettori 42.3–6–130–7; Franklin 25–8–63–0.

New Zealand

C. D. Cumming b Maharoof	13	– c Sangakkara b Muralitharan	20
J. M. How lbw b Malinga	26	– lbw b Malinga	33
M. S. Sinclair b Malinga	6	– c D. P. M. D. Jayawardene b Muralitharan	37
*S. P. Fleming c H. A. P. W. Jayawardene b Malinga	0	– c Sangakkara b Malinga	27
N. J. Astle b Malinga	17	– lbw b Muralitharan	9
†B. B. McCullum b Muralitharan	43	– b Muralitharan	17
D. L. Vettori b Malinga	0	– (8) lbw b Muralitharan	51
J. D. P. Oram lbw b Muralitharan	1	– (7) lbw b Vaas	4
J. E. C. Franklin lbw b Muralitharan	1	– c Silva b Muralitharan	44
S. E. Bond lbw b Muralitharan	8	– c Sangakkara b Maharoof	6
C. S. Martin not out	0	– not out	4
B 7, l-b 6, n-b 2	15	B 9, l-b 7, w 11, n-b 7	34

1/30 (1) 2/40 (2) 3/40 (4) 4/66 (5)　　　　130　　1/56 (2) 2/60 (1) 3/115 (4)　　　　286
5/75 (3) 6/85 (7) 7/90 (8)　　　　　　　　　4/139 (3) 5/156 (5) 6/161 (7)
8/98 (9) 9/116 (10) 10/130 (6)　　　　　　　7/163 (6) 8/259 (8) 9/278 (10) 10/286 (9)

Vaas 4–0–8–0; Malinga 18–4–68–5; Maharoof 5–2–10–1; Muralitharan 12.1–3–31–4. *Second Innings*—Vaas 18–2–64–1; Malinga 16–1–62–2; Maharoof 11–1–47–1; Muralitharan 34.1–9–87–6; Jayasuriya 6–3–10–0.

Umpires: B. G. Jerling *(South Africa)* (4) and S. J. A. Taufel *(Australia)* (41).
Third umpire: A. L. Hill *(New Zealand)*.   Referee: J. Srinath *(India)* (4).

Close of play: First day, New Zealand 66-4 (Sinclair 6); Second day, Sri Lanka 225-5 (Silva 79, H. A. P. W. Jayawardene 22); Third day, New Zealand 75-2 (Sinclair 10, Fleming 4).

SOUTH AFRICA v INDIA 2006-07 (1st Test)

At The Wanderers, Johannesburg, on 15, 16, 17, 18 December.
Toss: India.   Result: INDIA won by 123 runs.
Debuts: none.
Man of the Match: S. Sreesanth.

India won their first Test in South Africa, with what some observers thought was their best-ever away win. Their hero was Sreesanth, the wild and wacky seamer in only his sixth Test, who started South Africa's first-innings collapse with a maiden five-for. He ended the game with eight wickets, the match award, and a fine for giving Amla an unnecessary sendoff in the second innings. The start was delayed by 90 minutes after the groundstaff overwatered the pitch during a sunny spell. The result was a hard wicket with a wet top. Dravid bravely chose to bat: he and Tendulkar required every iota of their skill – their runs were worth double, at least. Ganguly's emotional return after a year out of favour resulted in a determined innings, during which he was peppered with bouncers. It was soon obvious that 249 was an excellent effort: South Africa's first seven wickets tumbled for 45, as Sreesanth pitched the ball up, and the eventual 84 was their lowest since England twice skittled them for 72 in 1956-57. Twenty wickets fell on the second day, but as the pitch eased slightly India extended their advantage. Pollock's classic late awayswinger had Dravid caught behind, making him the tenth bowler – the first South African – to take 400 Test wickets. Laxman knuckled down, his 73 as valuable as many centuries, and by the time he edged to slip the lead was approaching 400. Sreesanth again flattened the top order, before Prince delayed the inevitable with 97 from 223 balls.

India

Wasim Jaffer lbw b Ntini	9	– c Smith b Nel	4
V. Sehwag c Boucher b Pollock	4	– c Gibbs b Nel	33
*R. Dravid c Smith b Kallis	32	– c Boucher b Pollock	1
S. R. Tendulkar c de Villiers b Kallis	44	– b Pollock	14
V. V. S. Laxman c Boucher b Ntini	28	– c Smith b Ntini	73
S. C. Ganguly not out	51	– c Boucher b Ntini	25
†M. S. Dhoni c Pollock b Ntini	5	– c Boucher b Pollock	18
A. Kumble c Kallis b Nel	6	– c Prince b Nel	1
Zaheer Khan lbw b Pollock	9	– c Boucher b Ntini	37
S. Sreesanth c Amla b Pollock	0	– not out	6
V. R. Singh c and b Pollock	29	– run out	11
L-b 15, w 11, n-b 6	32	B 2, l-b 10, w 1	13

1/14 (1) 2/14 (2) 3/83 (4) 4/110 (3)   249   1/20 (1) 2/37 (3) 3/41 (2)   236
5/156 (5) 6/167 (7) 7/188 (8)   4/61 (4) 5/119 (6) 6/147 (7)
8/205 (9) 9/205 (10) 10/249 (11)   7/148 (8) 8/218 (5) 9/219 (9) 10/236 (11)

Steyn 10.1–3–26–0; Ntini 18–1–57–3; Pollock 17.5–7–39–4; Nel 18.5–5–45–1; Kallis 15–0–67–2. *Second Innings—* Ntini 15.4–2–77–3; Nel 19–4–58–3; Pollock 16–4–33–3; Kallis 11–2–30–0; Smith 3–0–26–0.

South Africa

*G. C. Smith lbw b Sreesanth	5	– (2) c Sehwag b Sreesanth	10
H. H. Gibbs c Sehwag b Zaheer Khan	0	– (1) c Tendulkar b Zaheer Khan	0
H. M. Amla c Laxman b Sreesanth	0	– c Dhoni b Sreesanth	17
J. H. Kallis c Laxman b Sreesanth	12	– c Ganguly b Sreesanth	27
A. G. Prince c Dhoni b Kumble	24	– b Kumble	97
A. B. de Villiers c Sehwag b Zaheer Khan	6	– run out	17
†M. V. Boucher b Sreesanth	5	– lbw b Zaheer Khan	23
S. M. Pollock lbw b Sreesanth	5	– b Kumble	40
A. Nel c Zaheer Khan b Singh	21	– lbw b Kumble	6
M. Ntini b Kumble	0	– (11) c Sehwag b Zaheer Khan	8
D. W. Steyn not out	0	– (10) not out	6
B 2, w 3, n-b 1	6	L-b 8, n-b 19	27

1/5 (1) 2/5 (2) 3/5 (3) 4/21 (4)   84   1/0 (1) 2/22 (2) 3/34 (3) 4/84 (4)   278
5/33 (6) 6/38 (7) 7/45 (8)   5/120 (6) 6/164 (7) 7/231 (8) 8/245 (9)
8/84 (5) 9/84 (10) 10/84 (9)   9/264 (5) 10/278 (11)

Zaheer Khan 10–3–32–2; Sreesanth 10–3–40–5; Singh 3.1–0–8–1; Kumble 2–1–2–2. *Second Innings—Zaheer* Khan 22.5–5–79–3; Sreesanth 25–8–59–3; Singh 18–4–67–0; Ganguly 1–0–11–0; Kumble 20–4–54–3.

Umpires: M. R. Benson *(England)* (14) and D. J. Harper *(Australia)* (62).
Third umpire: K. H. Hurter *(South Africa)*.   Referee: R. S. Mahanama *(Sri Lanka)* (11).

Close of play: First day, India 156-5 (Ganguly 14); Second day, India 146-5 (Laxman 42, Dhoni 17); Third day, South Africa 163-5 (Prince 54, Boucher 23).

SOUTH AFRICA v INDIA 2006-07 (2nd Test)

At Kingsmead, Durban, on 26, 27, 28, 29, 30 December.
Toss: South Africa.   Result: SOUTH AFRICA won by 174 runs.
Debuts: South Africa – M. Morkel.
Man of the Match: M. Ntini.

Although more than 100 overs were lost to the bad light which often characterises Christmas in Durban, South Africa levelled the series with barely ten minutes to spare before cloud and drizzle would have ended the match for good. Prince guided South Africa to 328, then Tendulkar, dropped when 21, and Laxman made subdued half-centuries; but overall India's batsmen struggled, and the eventual deficit would have been even greater but for some late hitting. Fast bowler Morne Morkel caught the eye with an incisive third spell on debut. The third day was shortened by around 40 minutes because a power cut knocked out the floodlights, which had been turned on to illuminate an already grey afternoon. Smith ended a run of low scores with a belligerent 58 as South Africa – without Kallis, nursing a sore back – sought to set an imposing target. Sreesanth took three quick wickets, but Pollock stretched the lead towards 353. India theoretically had 146 overs to face, but several would inevitably be lost to the weather. Ntini dismissed the first five during a shrewd spell before Dhoni counter-attacked, but the final act was all about the swirling clouds and the clock. Sreesanth was struck on the arm late on, and spent an age receiving treatment. Umpires Asad Rauf and Ian Howell (substituting for Mark Benson, taken to hospital with heart palpitations) intervened to keep the match moving. Finally Sreesanth was given out, caught off his own shoulder rather than that of his bat, just as safety loomed.

South Africa

*G. C. Smith c Tendulkar b Zaheer Khan	5	– (2) b Sreesanth	58
A. B. de Villiers c Tendulkar b Sreesanth	9	– (1) c Laxman b Singh	47
H. M. Amla lbw b Zaheer Khan	1	– lbw b Sreesanth	0
H. H. Gibbs c Dhoni b Sreesanth	63	– c sub (K. D. Karthik) b Kumble	9
A. G. Prince c Laxman b Sreesanth	121	– c Ganguly b Sreesanth	0
†M. V. Boucher b Sreesanth	53	– lbw b Zaheer Khan	8
S. M. Pollock c Sehwag b Singh	11	– not out	63
A. J. Hall lbw b Kumble	0	– lbw b Sreesanth	21
A. Nel b Kumble	0		
M. Morkel not out	31	– (9) c Singh b Sehwag	27
M. Ntini lbw b Kumble	16		
L-b 3, w 1, n-b 14	18	B 5, l-b 8, w 7, n-b 12	32

1/8 (1) 2/13 (3) 3/28 (2) 4/122 (4)   328   1/99 (1) 2/108 (3) 3/121 (2)   (8 wkts dec.) 265
5/222 (6) 6/256 (7) 7/257 (8)   4/121 (5) 5/140 (4) 6/143 (6)
8/257 (9) 9/296 (5) 10/328 (11)   7/213 (8) 8/265 (9)

Zaheer Khan 23–7–83–2; Sreesanth 24–4–109–4; Singh 13–1–60–1; Kumble 28.3–1–62–3; Ganguly 3–1–11–0. *Second Innings*—Zaheer Khan 20–5–65–1; Sreesanth 19–3–79–4; Singh 10–2–64–1; Kumble 16–4–37–1; Sehwag 2.4–1–7–1.

India

Wasim Jaffer c de Villiers b Ntini	26	– c Nel b Ntini	28
V. Sehwag c de Villiers b Nel	0	– c Smith b Ntini	8
*R. Dravid lbw b Nel	11	– c Boucher b Ntini	5
S. R. Tendulkar c Boucher b Ntini	63	– lbw b Ntini	0
V. V. S. Laxman not out	50	– b Nel	15
S. C. Ganguly c Gibbs b Ntini	0	– c Gibbs b Ntini	26
†M. S. Dhoni c de Villiers b Morkel	34	– c Boucher b Nel	47
A. Kumble c Boucher b Morkel	0	– c Amla b Hall	11
Zaheer Khan c Amla b Morkel	2	– c Hall b Nel	21
S. Sreesanth c Boucher b Hall	28	– c Boucher b Hall	10
V. R. Singh c Boucher b Pollock	4	– not out	0
B 1, l-b 7, w 2, n-b 12	22	B 2, l-b 1, w 1, n-b 4	8

1/5 (2) 2/35 (3) 3/61 (1) 4/125 (4)   240   1/14 (2) 2/34 (3) 3/38 (4)   179
5/125 (6) 6/179 (7) 7/179 (8)   4/45 (1) 5/83 (6) 6/85 (5)
8/183 (9) 9/235 (10) 10/240 (11)   7/101 (8) 8/160 (7) 9/179 (9) 10/179 (10)

Nel 23–5–60–2; Ntini 15–4–41–3; Morkel 18–1–86–3; Pollock 14.5–10–17–1; Hall 7–0–28–1. *Second Innings*—Nel 16–4–57–3; Ntini 19–6–48–5; Morkel 9–5–20–0; Pollock 9–5–20–0; Hall 5.1–1–26–2.

Umpires: Asad Rauf *(Pakistan)* (8) and M. R. Benson *(England)* (15).
I. L. Howell deputised for Benson from the third day.
Third umpire: I. L. Howell and M. Erasmus *(South Africa)*.   Referee: R. S. Mahanama *(Sri Lanka)* (12).

Close of play: First day, South Africa 257-8 (Prince 98, Morkel 0); Second day, India 103-3 (Tendulkar 46, Laxman 10); Third day, South Africa 64-0 (de Villiers 31, Smith 28); Fourth day, India 38-2 (Wasim Jaffer 22, Tendulkar 0).

SOUTH AFRICA v INDIA 2006-07 (3rd Test)

At Newlands, Cape Town, on 2, 3, 4, 5, 6 January.
Toss: India.   Result: SOUTH AFRICA won by five wickets.
Debuts: South Africa – P. L. Harris.
Man of the Match: G. C. Smith.   Man of the Series: S. M. Pollock.

A compelling series ended with the best contest of the three, as South Africa came from behind to pinch the series. India promoted wicketkeeper Karthik to open – he had replaced the unfit Dhoni (bruised fingers and a chest infection) – and the gamble paid off, as he added 153 with Wasim Jaffer, whose controlled hundred was ended by Kallis's 100th Test catch. India's eventual 414 was therefore slightly disappointing, but the reply was also a mixed bag. Smith made 94, starting with a top-edged six off Zaheer Khan's first ball. Amla lived a charmed but equally swashbuckling life, then Kallis and Boucher inched the total within 41. Sehwag returned to the top of the order but, for the umpteenth time, slashed at a wide half-volley. Jaffer gloved a lifter two balls later, and India were suddenly forced to concentrate on saving face, the Test and the series. Tendulkar was halted on his way in after the second wicket fell. He had spent 18 minutes off the field, but only 13 had been used up, so he was not permitted to bat at that point. Laxman was caught with his pants down – literally – so Ganguly was forced to pad up rapidly: he retained enough composure to make 46, but when he was caught at gully India fell apart. Needing 211, South Africa lost Amla to the fourth day's last ball, but Smith produced a masterstroke next morning by promoting Pollock to No. 4, and he removed any lingering doubts with a whirlwind 37.

India

Wasim Jaffer c Kallis b Steyn	116	– c de Villiers b Ntini	2
†K. D. Karthik c Amla b Harris	63	– (7) not out	38
*R. Dravid c Boucher b Pollock	29	– c and b Harris	47
S. R. Tendulkar c Kallis b Harris	64	– (5) lbw b Pollock	14
V. V. S. Laxman b Steyn	13	– (6) run out	1
S. C. Ganguly c Amla b Pollock	66	– (4) c Gibbs b Kallis	46
V. Sehwag c Ntini b Harris	40	– (2) c Boucher b Steyn	4
A. Kumble lbw b Pollock	0	– c Gibbs b Steyn	6
Zaheer Khan st Boucher b Harris	1	– run out	1
S. Sreesanth c Gibbs b Pollock	3	– c Kallis b Steyn	4
M. M. Patel not out	0	– c Pollock b Steyn	0
B 5, l-b 4, w 2, n-b 8	19	L-b 5, n-b 1	6

1/153 (2) 2/202 (3) 3/240 (1) 4/269 (5)   414 1/6 (2) 2/6 (1) 3/90 (4)   169
5/337 (4) 6/395 (7) 7/395 (8)   4/114 (3) 5/115 (6) 6/121 (5)
8/398 (9) 9/407 (10) 10/414 (6)   7/147 (8) 8/165 (9) 9/169 (10) 10/169 (11)

Steyn 27–12–58–2; Ntini 26–4–107–0; Pollock 29.1–9–75–4; Kallis 12–4–36–0; Harris 37–3–129–4. *Second Innings*—Ntini 8–1–29–1; Steyn 7–0–30–4; Pollock 15–5–24–1; Harris 22–6–50–1; Kallis 12–0–31–1.

South Africa

*G. C. Smith c Sehwag b Kumble	94	– (2) c Karthik b Zaheer Khan	55
A. B. de Villiers c Karthik b Sreesanth	1	– (1) c Karthik b Zaheer Khan	22
H. M. Amla c Karthik b Sreesanth	63	– lbw b Kumble	10
J. H. Kallis c Patel b Tendulkar	54	– (5) c Dravid b Zaheer Khan	32
A. G. Prince b Kumble	26	– (6) not out	38
H. H. Gibbs c Wasim Jaffer b Sehwag	7	– (7) not out	0
†M. V. Boucher c Karthik b Patel	50		
S. M. Pollock c Ganguly b Zaheer Khan	31	– (4) c Laxman b Zaheer Khan	37
P. L. Harris not out	11		
D. W. Steyn b Kumble	1		
M. Ntini lbw b Kumble	0		
B 7, l-b 13, w 1, n-b 14	35	B 11, l-b 1, n-b 5	17

1/14 (2) 2/173 (1) 3/177 (3) 4/260 (4)   373 1/36 (1) 2/55 (3)   (5 wkts) 211
5/260 (5) 6/281 (6) 7/350 (8)   3/127 (2) 4/132 (4)
8/372 (7) 9/373 (10) 10/373 (11)   5/209 (5)

Zaheer Khan 20–3–74–1; Sreesanth 24–9–58–2; Kumble 42.3–6–117–4; Patel 20–5–43–1; Sehwag 12–0–31–1; Tendulkar 10–2–30–1. *Second Innings*—Zaheer Khan 21–2–62–4; Sreesanth 13–2–50–0; Kumble 25–4–74–1; Patel 1–0–2–0; Sehwag 1–0–8–0; Tendulkar 3.1–2–3–0.

Umpires: Asad Rauf *(Pakistan)* (9) and D. J. Harper *(Australia)* (63).
Third umpire: M. Erasmus *(South Africa)*.   Referee: R. S. Mahanama *(Sri Lanka)* (13).

Close of play: First day, India 254-3 (Tendulkar 28, Laxman 4); Second day, South Africa 144-1 (Smith 76, Amla 50); Third day, South Africa 373; Fourth day, South Africa 55-2 (Smith 21).

SOUTH AFRICA v PAKISTAN 2006-07 (1st Test)

At Centurion Park, Pretoria, on 11, 12, 13, 14, 15 January.
Toss: Pakistan.   Result: SOUTH AFRICA won by seven wickets.
Debuts: none.
Man of the Match: H. M. Amla.

South Africa eased to victory before tea on the final day in a high-scoring match. The initiative changed sides frequently: Pakistan made 313 in their first innings, despite regular wickets from Ntini. Yasir Hameed and Younis Khan stood firmest, adding 133, before some lusty lower-order hitting boosted the total. Mohammad Asif knocked over South Africa's top four with just 143 scored, but South Africa regained the advantage through Prince and Gibbs, who stretched their partnership to 213. Prince batted almost six hours for a mature sixth Test hundred, while Gibbs also seemed destined for one before being trapped in front six short, in the middle of a slump during which five wickets fell for 35, three of them to Danish Kaneria. Pakistan's fightback restricted the lead to 104, which they had almost cleared by the end of the third day – but the slide started next morning, and by mid-afternoon Pakistan had slipped to 199 for 7. Pollock and left-arm spinner Paul Harris shared seven wickets, and had it not been for more late-order resistance, South Africa might have been set less than 199. Smith and de Villiers fell on the fourth evening, and night-watchman Harris went early next morning, but that was the extent of the damage. The match was overshadowed by a furore involving Gibbs, who was caught making abusive remarks about some spectators who had become increasingly aggressive in their support of the Pakistan team. He was banned for two Test matches (later reduced on appeal to one).

Pakistan

Mohammad Hafeez c Boucher b Ntini	19	– c Smith b Kallis	15
Imran Farhat c Amla b Ntini	26	– c de Villiers b Harris	68
Yasir Hameed c Ntini b Nel	65	– c Boucher b Kallis	9
Younis Khan c Nel b Pollock	68	– lbw b Pollock	38
*Inzamam-ul-Haq c Amla b Ntini	42	– c de Villiers b Pollock	35
Faisal Iqbal c Boucher b Kallis	1	– c Gibbs b Harris	9
†Kamran Akmal c Pollock b Nel	29	– c Gibbs b Harris	15
Naved-ul-Hasan c and b Nel	30	– c Prince b Pollock	33
Shahid Nazir c Gibbs b Ntini	15	– b Ntini	40
Danish Kaneria c Kallis b Ntini	0	– c Gibbs b Harris	23
Mohammad Asif not out	1	– not out	8
B 6, l-b 6, w 2, n-b 3	17	L-b 5, n-b 4	9

1/48 (2) 2/50 (1) 3/183 (4) 4/193 (3)   313   1/41 (1) 2/58 (3) 3/115 (4)   302
5/204 (6) 6/256 (5) 7/276 (7)   4/154 (2) 5/175 (6) 6/187 (5)
8/300 (9) 9/311 (10) 10/313 (8)   7/199 (7) 8/255 (9) 9/283 (8) 10/302 (10)

Ntini 24–3–83–5; Nel 26.5–3–100–3; Pollock 18–5–38–1; Kallis 15–3–55–1; Harris 13–2–25–0. *Second Innings*—Nel 22–6–69–0; Ntini 16–2–78–1; Pollock 22–7–60–3; Kallis 16–0–44–2; Harris 20.2–6–46–4.

South Africa

A. B. de Villiers c Younis Khan b Mohammad Asif	4	– (2) c Younis Khan b Mohammad Asif	12
*G. C. Smith c Kamran Akmal b Mohammad Asif	0	– (1) lbw b Mohammad Hafeez	32
H. M. Amla c Kamran Akmal b Mohammad Asif	71	– not out	64
J. H. Kallis c Younis Khan b Mohammad Asif	18	– (5) not out	60
A. G. Prince st Kamran Akmal b Danish Kaneria	138		
H. H. Gibbs lbw b Naved-ul-Hasan	94		
†M. V. Boucher c and b Danish Kaneria	2		
S. M. Pollock not out	39		
P. L. Harris b Danish Kaneria	3	– (4) c Faisal Iqbal b Mohammad Asif	7
A. Nel b Naved-ul-Hasan	5		
M. Ntini c Younis Khan b Mohammad Asif	5		
L-b 13, n-b 25	38	B 8, l-b 4, n-b 12	24

1/3 (2) 2/8 (1) 3/53 (4) 4/143 (3)   417   1/20 (2) 2/67 (1)   (3 wkts) 199
5/356 (5) 6/358 (7) 7/383 (6)   3/80 (4)
8/386 (9) 9/391 (10) 10/417 (11)

Mohammad Asif 27.5–4–89–5; Naved-ul-Hasan 17–2–92–2; Shahid Nazir 20–1–96–0; Danish Kaneria 41–8–97–3; Mohammad Hafeez 11–1–24–0; Imran Farhat 1–0–6–0. *Second Innings*—Mohammad Asif 14–2–56–2; Naved-ul-Hasan 7–3–21–0; Shahid Nazir 3–1–13–0; Danish Kaneria 24.5–5–61–0; Mohammad Hafeez 12–2–36–1.

Umpires: S. A. Bucknor *(West Indies)* (116) and B. R. Doctrove *(West Indies)* (10).
Third umpire: K. H. Hurter *(South Africa)*.   Referee: B. C. Broad *(England)* (21).

Close of play: First day, Pakistan 242-5 (Inzamam-ul-Haq 35, Kamran Akmal 18); Second day, South Africa 254-4 (Prince 77, Gibbs 58); Third day, Pakistan 103-2 (Imran Farhat 41, Younis Khan 32); Fourth day, South Africa 69-2 (Amla 17, Harris 1).

SOUTH AFRICA v PAKISTAN 2006-07 (2nd Test)

At St George's Park, Port Elizabeth, on 19, 20, 21, 22 January.
Toss: South Africa.   Result: PAKISTAN won by five wickets.
Debuts: none.
Man of the Match: Inzamam-ul-Haq.

Pakistan's series-levelling victory owed much to Shoaib Akhtar, who made a brief return after a drug ban before going home again with hamstring and knee injuries (and a fine after an altercation about his ailments with coach Bob Woolmer was captured by the TV cameras). But he briefly showed his class: he was ragged in line and length, but his pace was consistently lethal, and South Africa were shot out in 198 minutes for a miserable 124. That looked better when Pakistan reached the close at 135 for 6 on what was throughout a true pitch. Inzamam-ul-Haq proved that next day: he came in at No. 8 after injuring his shoulder, and made a seamless 92 not out, putting on 74 in 92 minutes with last man Mohammad Asif. Still, a lead of 141 was far from commanding. The baton was passed back to the attack, now without Shoaib. But Asif, himself a survivor of the drugs saga, was accurate and penetrative in completing another five-for: he and Danish Kaneria bowled 90 of the 134 overs in the innings. Kallis's 91, and a last-wicket stand of 41, pushed the lead to a respectable 190. Pakistan struggled at first, dipping to 92 for 5 shortly after lunch on the fourth day, before Kamran Akmal, who had dropped numerous catches behind the wicket, joined Younis Khan. Akmal's first few runs came through or over the slips – but luck soon went out of the equation and the target was reached easily enough.

South Africa

A. B. de Villiers c Kamran Akmal b Shoaib Akhtar	. . . .	2	– (2) b Mohammad Asif	15
*G. C. Smith c Younis Khan b Danish Kaneria	. . . .	28	– (1) c Inzamam-ul-Haq b Mohammad Asif	. . . 10
H. M. Amla c Kamran Akmal b Shoaib Akhtar	. . . . . .	5	– b Mohammad Sami	16
J. H. Kallis c Kamran Akmal b Shoaib Akhtar	. . . .	24	– lbw b Mohammad Asif	91
A. G. Prince c Imran Farhat b Mohammad Sami	. . . . .	2	– lbw b Danish Kaneria	22
H. H. Gibbs lbw b Danish Kaneria	. . . .	2	– c Younis Khan b Mohammad Asif	40
†M. V. Boucher c Younis Khan b Danish Kaneria	. . . . .	35	– c Younis Khan b Mohammad Asif	46
S. M. Pollock c Mohammad Sami b Shoaib Akhtar	. . .	4	– c and b Danish Kaneria	36
A. Nel c Danish Kaneria b Mohammad Asif	. . . .	10	– not out	23
M. Ntini not out	. . . .	0	– (11) c Yasir Hameed b Danish Kaneria	 18
P. L. Harris c Yasir Hameed b Mohammad Asif	. . . . . .	4	– (10) c sub (Faisal Iqbal) b Danish Kaneria	 0
L-b 3, n-b 5	. . . .	8	B 3, l-b 5, n-b 6	 14

1/9 (1) 2/27 (3) 3/40 (2) 4/49 (5)   124   1/18 (1) 2/30 (2) 3/61 (3)   331
5/58 (6) 6/83 (4) 7/89 (8)   4/117 (5) 5/195 (6) 6/205 (4)
8/120 (7) 9/120 (9) 10/124 (11)   7/285 (8) 8/289 (7) 9/290 (10) 10/331 (11)

Shoaib Akhtar 11–2–36–4; Mohammad Asif 9–2–34–2; Danish Kaneria 14–3–36–3; Mohammad Sami 6–1–15–1. *Second Innings*—Mohammad Asif 38–16–76–5; Mohammad Sami 29–5–90–1; Danish Kaneria 51.2–14–105–4; Imran Farhat 7–0–20–0; Mohammad Hafeez 8–0–32–0.

Pakistan

Mohammad Hafeez c Amla b Ntini	. . . .	13	– lbw b Pollock	32
Imran Farhat c de Villiers b Ntini	. . . .	0	– c Kallis b Ntini	7
Younis Khan c Gibbs b Ntini	. . . .	45	– (4) not out	67
Yasir Hameed c de Villiers b Ntini	. . . .	2	– (3) run out	6
Mohammad Yousuf lbw b Pollock	. . . .	32	– c Gibbs b Pollock	18
†Kamran Akmal c Prince b Nel	. . . .	33	– (7) not out	57
Mohammad Sami c Boucher b Ntini	. . . .	10		
*Inzamam-ul-Haq not out	. . . .	92	– (6) lbw b Ntini	1
Shoaib Akhtar c Boucher b Kallis	. . . .	4		
Danish Kaneria c Gibbs b Pollock	. . . .	1		
Mohammad Asif b Ntini	. . . .	7		
B 4, l-b 11, w 5, n-b 1, p 5	. . . .	26	L-b 1, w 1, n-b 1	 3

1/0 (2) 2/17 (1) 3/19 (4) 4/79 (5)   265   1/29 (2) 2/35 (3)   (5 wkts) 191
5/135 (3) 6/135 (6) 7/166 (7)   3/48 (1) 4/87 (5)
8/184 (9) 9/191 (10) 10/265 (11)   5/92 (6)

Nel 23–2–68–1; Ntini 21–6–59–6; Kallis 13–0–56–1; Pollock 14–2–42–2; Harris 5–1–20–0. *Second Innings*— Nel 14–2–63–0; Ntini 19–6–50–2; Pollock 13–4–47–2; Kallis 6–0–17–0; Harris 5.3–0–13–0.

Umpires: B. R. Doctrove *(West Indies)* (11) and P. D. Parker *(Australia)* (7).
Third umpire: R. E. Koertzen *(South Africa)*.   Referee: B. C. Broad *(England)* (22).

Close of play: First day, Pakistan 135-6 (Mohammad Sami 0); Second day, South Africa 115-3 (Kallis 50, Prince 21); Third day, Pakistan 8-0 (Mohammad Hafeez 8, Imran Farhat 0).

SOUTH AFRICA v PAKISTAN 2006-07 (3rd Test)

At Newlands, Cape Town, on 26, 27, 28 January.
Toss: South Africa.   Result: SOUTH AFRICA won by five wickets.
Debuts: none.
Man of the Match: J. H. Kallis.   Man of the Series: J. H. Kallis.

When the covers were peeled away to unveil a pitch that was grassy at both ends and barren in the middle, everyone knew that no ordinary match was in prospect. The pitch offered erratic bounce from the start: 32 wickets went down on the first two days, even though the bowling was merely competent rather than excellent. It all meant that Pakistan's chances of becoming the first Asian team to win a Test series in South Africa were dealt a blow some viewed as underhand. Pakistan's first innings ended before tea on the first day for just 157, all ten caught, with Ntini and Kallis sharing eight wickets. Mohammad Yousuf conjured a breathtaking 83 off 90 balls, with ten fours and a six. South Africa squeezed out a lead of 26 before they were dismissed next morning: Smith took Yousuf's lead and bludgeoned an aggressive half-century. Cameos from Yasir Hameed and Inzamam-ul-Haq took Pakistan ahead, but the biggest stand of the innings was 55 for the eighth wicket by Mohammad Sami and Shahid Nazir: no-one was able to survive long enough to make a real difference against an attack gaining in confidence and aggression as each wicket fell. South Africa needed 161 to win, and slipped to 39 for 4 before the sun had cleared the mist off Table Mountain on the third morning. But Kallis, as ever, brought a granite presence to the crease and drew the sting from what remained of the contest in a suitably grim half-century.

Pakistan

Mohammad Hafeez c de Villiers b Ntini	10	– c Prince b Steyn	10
Imran Farhat c Smith b Kallis	20	– lbw b Steyn	13
Yasir Hameed c Kallis b Ntini	7	– c Prince b Hall	35
Younis Khan c de Villiers b Kallis	8	– c Boucher b Ntini	0
Mohammad Yousuf c Prince b Ntini	83	– b Hall	18
*Inzamam-ul-Haq c Boucher b Hall	6	– c Boucher b Steyn	22
†Kamran Akmal c de Villiers b Steyn	0	– st Boucher b Harris	6
Mohammad Sami c Boucher b Kallis	4	– c Amla b Kallis	31
Shahid Nazir c Harris b Ntini	3	– c Boucher b Kallis	27
Danish Kaneria c Boucher b Kallis	0	– not out	1
Mohammad Asif not out	0	– c Prince b Harris	6
L-b 2, w 6, n-b 8	16	B 6, l-b 2, w 5, n-b 4	17

1/13 (1) 2/27 (3) 3/47 (2) 4/54 (4) **157**   1/17 (1) 2/28 (2) 3/44 (4) **186**
5/81 (6) 6/90 (7) 7/150 (8) 4/83 (5) 5/92 (3) 6/111 (7) 7/121 (6)
8/155 (9) 9/157 (10) 10/157 (5) 8/176 (9) 9/179 (8) 10/186 (11)

Steyn 11–3–40–1; Ntini 13.1–2–44–4; Kallis 11–1–42–4; Hall 8–2–29–1. *Second Innings*—Ntini 10–2–41–1; Steyn 13–3–47–3; Kallis 7–0–36–2; Hall 7–1–23–2; Harris 14.2–2–31–2.

South Africa

H. H. Dippenaar lbw b Mohammad Asif	0	– (2) c Kamran Akmal b Danish Kaneria	3
*G. C. Smith c Inzamam-ul-Haq b Shahid Nazir	64	– (1) lbw b Mohammad Asif	33
H. M. Amla c Kamran Akmal b Mohammad Asif	2	– (4) c Kamran Akmal b Mohammad Asif	3
J. H. Kallis c Kamran Akmal b Mohammad Sami	28	– (5) b Shahid Nazir	51
A. G. Prince c Yasir Hameed b Danish Kaneria	19	– (6) not out	59
A. B. de Villiers b Danish Kaneria	11	– (7) not out	4
P. L. Harris c Younis Khan b Mohammad Asif	1	– (3) lbw b Danish Kaneria	0
†M. V. Boucher not out	40		
A. J. Hall c Kamran Akmal b Danish Kaneria	4		
D. W. Steyn run out	3		
M. Ntini lbw b Mohammad Sami	0		
B 4, l-b 4, w 1, n-b 2	11	B 4, l-b 4	8

1/0 (1) 2/12 (3) 3/92 (4) 4/107 (2) **183**   1/30 (2) 2/36 (3) 3/36 (1) **(5 wkts) 161**
5/128 (6) 6/133 (5) 7/133 (7) 4/39 (4) 5/156 (5)
8/140 (9) 9/183 (10) 10/183 (11)

Mohammad Asif 16–2–53–3; Mohammad Sami 9–1–41–2; Shahid Nazir 8–0–37–1; Danish Kaneria 20–6–44–3. *Second Innings*—Mohammad Asif 21–8–43–2; Shahid Nazir 9–1–42–1; Danish Kaneria 28–9–52–2; Mohammad Hafeez 5–1–7–0; Mohammad Sami 1–0–9–0.

Umpires: S. A. Bucknor *(West Indies)* (117) and P. D. Parker *(Australia)* (8).
Third umpire: M. Erasmus *(South Africa)*.   Referee: B. C. Broad *(England)* (23).

Close of play: First day, South Africa 131-5 (Prince 18, Harris 0); Second day, South Africa 36-2 (Smith 33).

ENGLAND v WEST INDIES 2007 (1st Test)

At Lord's, London, on 17, 18, 19, 20, 21 May.
Toss: West Indies.   Result: MATCH DRAWN.
Debuts: England – M. J. Prior.
Man of the Match: A. N. Cook.

Test cricket resumed after the 2007 World Cup – won for the third time running by Australia – with England putting a disappointing tournament behind them to amass 553, including four centuries, a first for any Lord's Test. Cook, still only 22, made his fifth hundred, while the most forthright came from Matt Prior, the first England wicketkeeper to score a century on Test debut, from only 105 balls. Bell made his fourth hundred in five Tests from No. 6. West Indies, captained for the first time by Sarwan after Brian Lara's retirement, looked certain to follow on until Bravo and Ramdin put their heads down alongside the old hand, Chanderpaul. England's pacemen sprayed down 16 wides, a total exceeded only once in Tests, West Indies' 18 at Old Trafford three years earlier. Pietersen, who missed out on a first-innings hundred, made amends in the second: England were only the third team to produce five different centurions in a Test, after Australia at Kingston in 1954-55 and Pakistan against Bangladesh at Multan in 2001-02. The eventual declaration, setting West Indies 401 in just over a day, was on the conservative side: disappointingly, constant weather interruptions allowed only 20 overs on the final day. Strauss was returning as England's captain, as Vaughan had broken a finger and Flintoff, the hapless leader in the winter's Ashes series, was out of favour (and out of the side after another ankle injury). England also had a new coach, Peter Moores, who had replaced Duncan Fletcher.

England

*A. J. Strauss c Smith b Powell	33	– c Morton b Collymore	24
A. N. Cook c Bravo b Taylor	105	– c Ramdin b Collymore	65
O. A. Shah c Smith b Powell	6	– c Ramdin b Collymore	4
K. P. Pietersen c Smith b Collymore	26	– lbw b Gayle	109
P. D. Collingwood b Bravo	111	– c Morton b Bravo	34
I. R. Bell not out	109	– c Ganga b Bravo	3
†M. J. Prior not out	126	– c Bravo b Gayle	21
L. E. Plunkett (did not bat)		– st Ramdin b Gayle	0
S. J. Harmison (did not bat)		– not out	11
M. S. Panesar (did not bat)		– not out	3
B 8, l-b 17, w 8, n-b 4	37	B 1, l-b 3, w 1, n-b 5	10

1/88 (1) 2/103 (3) 3/162 (4)   (5 wkts dec.) 553
4/219 (2) 5/363 (5)

1/35 (1) 2/51 (3)   (8 wkts dec.) 284
3/139 (2) 4/241 (5)
5/248 (6) 6/264 (4) 7/264 (8) 8/271 (7)

M. J. Hoggard did not bat.

Powell 37–9–113–2; Taylor 24–4–114–1; Collymore 32–5–110–1; Bravo 32–8–106–1; Gayle 10–0–48–0; Morton 1–0–4–0; Sarwan 6–0–33–0. *Second Innings*—Powell 9–0–44–0; Collymore 15–1–58–3; Gayle 20.5–4–66–3; Bravo 18–2–91–2; Taylor 4–0–21–0.

West Indies

C. H. Gayle b Plunkett	30	– not out	47
D. Ganga lbw b Panesar	49	– not out	31
D. S. Smith b Panesar	21		
*R. R. Sarwan lbw b Panesar	35		
S. Chanderpaul lbw b Panesar	74		
R. S. Morton lbw b Panesar	14		
D. J. Bravo c Cook b Collingwood	56		
†D. Ramdin c Collingwood b Plunkett	60		
D. B. Powell not out	36		
J. E. Taylor c sub (L. J. Hodgson) b Harmison	21		
C. D. Collymore lbw b Panesar	1		
B 4, l-b 17, w 16, n-b 3	40	B 4, l-b 3, w 3, n-b 1	11

1/38 (1) 2/83 (3) 3/151 (4) 4/165 (2)   437
5/187 (6) 6/279 (7) 7/362 (8)
8/387 (5) 9/424 (10) 10/437 (11)

(no wkt) 89

Hoggard 10.1–3–29–0; Harmison 28–2–117–1; Plunkett 30–7–107–2; Collingwood 11.5–2–34–1; Panesar 36.1–3–129–6. *Second Innings*—Harmison 8–1–21–0; Plunkett 11–1–48–0; Panesar 3–0–13–0.

Umpires: Asad Rauf *(Pakistan)* (10) and R. E. Koertzen *(South Africa)* (81).
Third umpire: N. J. Llong *(England)*.   Referee: A. G. Hurst *(Australia)* (12).

Close of play: First day, England 200-3 (Cook 102, Collingwood 21); Second day, England 553-5 (Bell 109, Prior 126); Third day, West Indies 363-7 (Chanderpaul 63, Powell 0); Fourth day, West Indies 7-0 (Gayle 0, Ganga 4).

ENGLAND v WEST INDIES 2007 (2nd Test)

At Headingley, Leeds, on 25, 26, 27 (*no play*), 28 May.
Toss: England.   Result: ENGLAND won by an innings and 283 runs.
Debuts: none.
Man of the Match: K. P. Pietersen.

Even without firing on all cylinders, England handed West Indies their heaviest Test defeat, in little more than two days' playing time. That the match reached the fourth evening was down to the weather, rather than the visiting batsmen, who were woeful almost throughout. They did have some ill luck: Chanderpaul was missing with tendinitis in his right knee, then Sarwan injured his right shoulder trying to stop a boundary late on the first day, and was forced out of the rest of the tour. England's batting heroes were expected ones: Vaughan, in his first Test for 18 months, made a classical century, his 16th in Tests but the first in front of his home crowd, while Pietersen bull-dozed to 226 – finally passing 158, where he had been out three times – and finished his 25th Test with more runs than anyone at that stage of a career except Don Bradman. But the bowling star was a surprise: Ryan Side-bottom, summoned after Hoggard tweaked his adductor muscle at Lord's. Swinging the ball in, he finished with eight wickets, five of them lbw. On the second day, West Indies lost 12 wickets after England made 204 for two, and, after a third-day washout, when play resumed in Arctic conditions – anecdotal evidence suggested it was the coldest weather in which Test cricket had been played in England since the New Zealand Test at Edgbaston in 1965, when the drinks interval featured hot mugs of coffee – only Bravo showed much stomach for the fight.

England

A. J. Strauss c Ramdin b Powell	15	L. E. Plunkett not out	44
A. N. Cook lbw b Gayle	42		
*M. P. Vaughan c Morton b Taylor	103	B 1, l-b 15, w 9, n-b 6	31
K. P. Pietersen c Taylor b Bravo	226		
P. D. Collingwood c Gayle b Collymore	29	1/38 (1) 2/91 (2) (7 wkts dec.)	570
I. R. Bell c Ramdin b Collymore	5	3/254 (3) 4/316 (5)	
†M. J. Prior b Powell	75	5/329 (6) 6/489 (7) 7/570 (4)	

S. J. Harmison, R. J. Sidebottom and M. S. Panesar did not bat.

Powell 33–5–153–2; Collymore 29–1–110–2; Taylor 22–4–116–1; Bravo 24.3–3–97–1; Gayle 14–1–78–1.

West Indies

C. H. Gayle lbw b Sidebottom	11	– c Prior b Plunkett	13
D. Ganga lbw b Sidebottom	5	– lbw b Sidebottom	9
D. S. Smith c Cook b Plunkett	26	– (4) c Strauss b Sidebottom	16
S. C. Joseph c Strauss b Harmison	13	– (5) lbw b Sidebottom	1
R. S. Morton c Prior b Harmison	5	– (6) c Prior b Harmison	25
D. J. Bravo b Sidebottom	23	– (7) c Plunkett b Panesar	52
†D. Ramdin c Prior b Plunkett	6	– (8) lbw b Harmison	5
D. B. Powell c Collingwood b Plunkett	8	– (3) lbw b Sidebottom	0
J. E. Taylor not out	23	– b Harmison	0
C. D. Collymore c Strauss b Sidebottom	3	– not out	0
*R. R. Sarwan absent hurt		– absent hurt	
L-b 13, w 4, n-b 6	23	B 1, l-b 14, n-b 5	20

1/17 (1) 2/23 (2) 3/68 (4) 4/74 (3)   146   1/20 (2) 2/22 (3) 3/30 (1)   141
5/82 (5) 6/94 (7) 7/114 (8)   4/47 (5) 5/57 (4) 6/120 (6)
8/124 (6) 9/146 (10)   7/141 (8) 8/141 (7) 9/141 (9)

Sidebottom 12–2–42–4; Harmison 12–0–55–2; Plunkett 12–1–35–3; Panesar 1–0–1–0. *Second Innings*—Sidebottom 15–4–44–4; Plunkett 8–2–25–1; Harmison 13.1–3–37–3; Panesar 6–1–20–1.

Umpires: Asad Rauf (*Pakistan*) (11) and R. E. Koertzen (*South Africa*) (82).
Third umpire: I. J. Gould (*England*).   Referee: A. G. Hurst (*Australia*) (13).

Close of play: First day, England 366-5 (Pietersen 130, Prior 13); Second day, West Indies 22-2 (Gayle 9); Third day, No play.

ENGLAND v WEST INDIES 2007 (3rd Test)

At Old Trafford, Manchester, on 7, 8, 9, 10, 11 June.
Toss: England.   Result: ENGLAND won by 60 runs.
Debuts: West Indies – D. J. G. Sammy.
Man of the Match: M. S. Panesar.

England clinched the series, although West Indies competed much better than in the previous match, ending with the second-highest fourth-innings total in an Old Trafford Test. It was Vaughan's 21st victory in 35 Tests as captain, an England record: Peter May won 20 out of 41. England shaded the match in two crucial phases. First the West Indian pacemen got carried away by the bounce they obtained, bowling so short and wide that England reached 112 for 1. Bell and the tail lifted them to 370, before West Indies declined from 216 for 4 to 229 all out. England's bowling was initially wayward: Harmison's first over contained nine deliveries, although the only straight one removed the startled Ganga. Prior conceded 34 byes in the match, and most were not his fault. Harmison gamely sorted out his troubles, and was rewarded with his 200th Test wicket when Taylor received a ferocious lifter. Another Cook century helped England past 300 again, although the dogged medium-pace of Darren Sammy – the first St Lucian to play Test cricket – brought him three wickets in an over, and the second-best figures by a West Indian debutant, after slow left-armer Alf Valentine's 8 for 104 on this same ground in 1950. Set 455, West Indies might have capitulated after Harmison dismissed both openers, but instead fought back gamely, yet again glued together by Chanderpaul. They were only 70 short with three wickets standing when Harmison produced a couple of snorters, then Panesar completed his first ten-wicket haul in Tests.

England

A. J. Strauss lbw b Taylor	6	– lbw b Edwards	0
A. N. Cook c Bravo b Sammy	60	– lbw b Gayle	106
*M. P. Vaughan b Collymore	41	– c and b Sammy	40
K. P. Pietersen c Bravo b Collymore	9	– hit wkt b Bravo	68
P. D. Collingwood lbw b Taylor	10	– c Ganga b Sammy	42
I. R. Bell c Ramdin b Collymore	97	– c Ramdin b Sammy	2
†M. J. Prior c Morton b Bravo	40	– c Ramdin b Sammy	0
L. E. Plunkett b Edwards	13	– c Bravo b Sammy	0
S. J. Harmison c Ramdin b Edwards	18	– c Morton b Sammy	16
R. J. Sidebottom b Edwards	15	– not out	8
M. S. Panesar not out	14	– c Gayle b Sammy	0
B 15, l-b 8, w 6, n-b 18	47	B 2, l-b 6, w 6, n-b 12, p 5	31

1/13 (1) 2/117 (3) 3/132 (4) 4/132 (2)   370   1/1 (1) 2/99 (3) 3/221 (4)   313
5/166 (5) 6/264 (7) 7/285 (8)   4/265 (2) 5/272 (6) 6/272 (7)
8/324 (9) 9/338 (6) 10/370 (10)   7/272 (8) 8/300 (9) 9/313 (5) 10/313 (11)

Taylor 20–1–67–2; Edwards 20.1–2–94–3; Collymore 25–5–60–3; Bravo 23–4–94–1; Sammy 17–7–32–1. *Second Innings*—Edwards 12–0–54–1; Taylor 10–0–42–0; Collymore 7–2–24–0; Sammy 21.3–2–66–7; Chanderpaul 11–1–43–0; Bravo 8–2–14–1; Gayle 16–0–57–1.

West Indies

C. H. Gayle c Cook b Plunkett	23	– c Collingwood b Harmison	16
*D. Ganga lbw b Harmison	5	– lbw b Harmison	0
D. S. Smith c Bell b Panesar	40	– c Cook b Panesar	42
R. S. Morton c Strauss b Harmison	35	– lbw b Panesar	54
S. Chanderpaul c Pietersen b Sidebottom	50	– not out	116
D. J. Bravo c Prior b Sidebottom	24	– c Cook b Panesar	49
†D. Ramdin c Pietersen b Sidebottom	5	– c Collingwood b Panesar	34
D. J. G. Sammy c Collingwood b Panesar	1	– c and b Panesar	25
J. E. Taylor c Strauss b Panesar	0	– c Cook b Harmison	11
C. D. Collymore c Collingwood b Panesar	4	– (11) c Bell b Panesar	0
F. H. Edwards not out	0	– (10) c Bell b Harmison	0
B 20, l-b 10, w 9, n-b 3	42	B 14, l-b 21, w 8, n-b 4	47

1/17 (2) 2/49 (1) 3/116 (4) 4/157 (3)   229   1/4 (2) 2/35 (1) 3/88 (3)   394
5/216 (6) 6/224 (7) 7/225 (8)   4/161 (4) 5/249 (6) 6/311 (7)
8/225 (9) 9/225 (5) 10/229 (10)   7/348 (8) 8/385 (9) 9/385 (10) 10/394 (11)

Sidebottom 12–3–48–3; Harmison 11–2–53–2; Plunkett 12–0–43–1; Panesar 16.4–5–50–4; Collingwood 1–0–5–0. *Second Innings*—Sidebottom 27–8–53–0; Harmison 33–8–95–4; Panesar 51.5–13–137–6; Plunkett 16–2–57–0; Pietersen 5–2–17–0.

Umpires: Aleem Dar *(Pakistan)* (38) and B. F. Bowden *(New Zealand)* (40).
Third umpire: P. J. Hartley *(England)*.   Referee: A. G. Hurst *(Australia)* (14).

Close of play: First day, England 296-7 (Bell 77, Harmison 2); Second day, England 34-1 (Cook 12, Vaughan 10); Third day, West Indies 22-1 (Gayle 11, Smith 10); Fourth day, West Indies 301-5 (Chanderpaul 81, Ramdin 26).

ENGLAND v WEST INDIES 2007 (4th Test)

At Riverside Ground, Chester-le-Street, on 15 *(no play)*, 16, 17, 18, 19 June.
Toss: England.   Result: ENGLAND won by seven wickets.
Debuts: none.
Man of the Match: S. Chanderpaul.   Men of the Series: M. S. Panesar and S. Chanderpaul

Torrential rain prevented any cricket until 2 p.m. on the second day, a Saturday, but not even the redoubtable Chanderpaul could stop England taking the series 3–0. This was West Indies's 20th Test since their last victory, over Pakistan at Bridgetown in May 2005, equalling their previous-longest barren run, between 1969 and 1973, but that included only six defeats: this featured 14. When play did start, Sidebottom removed Ganga with the first ball of the match, but Chanderpaul proved an immovable object once again after being dropped by Bell at third slip when nine. England's batsmen started poorly, slipping to 165 for 6, still 122 behind, before building a commanding lead around Collingwood's century in his first Test on his home ground. West Indies began the final day three down and 30 behind, with Chanderpaul their only realistic hope. During the afternoon a draw looked possible: but the last six wickets tumbled for 60. Chanderpaul finally missed a sweep against Panesar, having batted for 1,074 minutes (six minutes short of 18 hours) since his previous dismissal, in the first innings at Old Trafford. It was the third time he had batted more than 1,000 minutes between dismissals in Test cricket – 1,031 against Bangladesh and England in 2004, and a record 1,513 against India in 2002. It was only the third time in 104 Tests he had been bowled by a spinner. With clouds circling ominously, England's batsmen hit out, and got home with seven wickets and 31 overs to spare.

West Indies

*D. Ganga c Cook b Sidebottom	0	– (3) c Prior b Hoggard		6
C. H. Gayle lbw b Hoggard	28	– (1) c Prior b Hoggard		52
D. S. Smith b Sidebottom	4	– (2) lbw b Hoggard		0
R. S. Morton c Sidebottom b Harmison	6	– b Panesar		7
S. Chanderpaul not out	136	– b Panesar		70
D. J. Bravo b Hoggard	44	– c Sidebottom b Panesar		43
M. N. Samuels b Sidebottom	19	– c Collingwood b Panesar		2
†D. Ramdin c Collingwood b Sidebottom	13	– b Panesar		4
D. B. Powell c Prior b Harmison	1	– c Vaughan b Harmison		4
F. H. Edwards b Sidebottom	5	– b Harmison		0
C. D. Collymore lbw b Panesar	13	– not out		16
B 4, l-b 2, n-b 1	18	B 1, l-b 12, w 2, n-b 3		18

1/0 (1) 2/32 (2) 3/34 (3) 4/55 (4)   287   1/7 (2) 2/15 (3) 3/38 (4)   222
5/141 (6) 6/199 (7) 7/219 (8)   4/94 (1) 5/162 (6) 6/169 (7)
8/220 (9) 9/229 (10) 10/287 (11)   7/175 (8) 8/188 (9) 9/194 (10) 10/222 (5)

Sidebottom 29–10–88–5; Hoggard 26–8–58–2; Harmison 25–4–78–2; Panesar 13.1–2–34–1; Collingwood 4–1–12–0. *Second Innings*—Sidebottom 15–4–40–0; Hoggard 11–4–28–3; Harmison 20–2–92–2; Panesar 16–2–46–5; Pietersen 2–0–3–0.

England

A. J. Strauss c Ramdin b Edwards	77	– b Powell		13
A. N. Cook c Ramdin b Edwards	13	– c Bravo b Powell		7
*M. P. Vaughan c Bravo b Edwards	19	– not out		48
M. J. Hoggard c Gayle b Collymore	0			
K. P. Pietersen c Ramdin b Edwards	0	– (4) c Samuels b Gayle		28
P. D. Collingwood b Collymore	128	– (5) not out		5
I. R. Bell c Morton b Powell	11			
†M. J. Prior c Smith b Edwards	62			
S. J. Harmison c Ganga b Powell	9			
R. J. Sidebottom not out	26			
M. S. Panesar b Powell	4			
B 5, l-b 8, w 15, n-b 23	51	B 4, n-b 6		10

1/37 (2) 2/110 (3) 3/119 (4) 4/121 (5)   400   1/16 (2) 2/29 (1)   (3 wkts) 111
5/133 (1) 6/165 (7) 7/334 (8)   3/105 (4)
8/369 (6) 9/369 (9) 10/400 (11)

Edwards 23–1–112–5; Powell 32–6–89–3; Collymore 29–5–116–2; Gayle 9–3–25–0; Bravo 2–0–10–0; Samuels 5–0–35–0. *Second Innings*—Edwards 7–0–46–0; Powell 7–0–38–2; Samuels 4–0–12–0; Gayle 3.4–0–11–1.

Umpires: Aleem Dar *(Pakistan)* (39) and B. F. Bowden *(New Zealand)* (41).
Third umpire: N. J. Llong *(England)*.   Referee: A. G. Hurst *(Australia)* (15).

Close of play: First day, No play; Second day, West Indies 132-4 (Chanderpaul 44, Bravo 43); Third day, England 121-4 (Strauss 72); Fourth day, West Indies 83-3 (Gayle 52, Chanderpaul 16).

BANGLADESH v INDIA 2007 (1st Test)

At Bir Shrestha Shahid Ruhul Amin Stadium, Chittagong, on 18, 19, 20 *(no play)*, 21, 22 May.
Toss: India.   Result: MATCH DRAWN.
Debuts: Bangladesh – Shakib Al Hasan. India – R. R. Powar.
Man of the Match: Mashrafe bin Mortaza.

Bangladesh achieved their fifth draw in 45 Tests, to go with 39 defeats and their victory over Zimbabwe. Rain is the norm in Chittagong in May, and it dogged this Test throughout: there were only 219 overs in all, including 20 on the second day and none at all on the third. Dravid tried to make a game of it, setting a target of 250 in 43 overs on the last afternoon. Shahriar Nafees fell in the fourth over, but Habibul Bashar and Javed Omar made sure of the draw. The start of the match was far more dramatic. India batted first on what looked a batting-friendly pitch – but Wasim Jaffer never found out. He shouldered arms to the first ball, which came in to hit off stump. In the second innings he lasted three balls, but completed a pair. Dravid responded to Jaffer's first duck by adding 124 with Karthik, the fourth time he had shared a second-wicket century partnership after the first wicket fell at nought. Centuries from Tendulkar – his 36th in Tests, but the first since December 2005 – and Ganguly (who had been waiting three months longer) propelled India to 387. Bangladesh soon ran into trouble: Omar and Habibul fell in the sixth over, and only Rajin Saleh batted as if he knew it was a Test. At 122 for 7, the meagre follow-on target of 188 looked huge, but Mashrafe bin Mortaza batted with refreshing confidence, adding 77, a Bangladesh ninth-wicket record, with his new-ball partner Shahadat Hossain.

India

Wasim Jaffer b Mashrafe bin Mortaza	0	– c Habibul Bashar b Shahadat Hossain	0
K. D. Karthik c Mohammad Ashraful b Mashrafe bin Mortaza	56	– c Shahriar Nafees b Mashrafe bin Mortaza	22
*R. Dravid c Khaled Mashud b Shahadat Hossain	61	– c Rajin Saleh b Shahadat Hossain	2
S. R. Tendulkar c Mohammad Ashraful b Shahadat Hossain	101	– b Mohammad Rafique	31
S. C. Ganguly c Mohammad Rafique b Mashrafe bin Mortaza	100	– c Shahriar Nafees b Mohammad Rafique	13
†M. S. Dhoni c Javed Omar b Mashrafe bin Mortaza	36	– not out	17
R. R. Powar b Mohammad Rafique	7	– st Khaled Mashud b Mohammad Rafique	6
A. Kumble retired ill	1		
Zaheer Khan c Khaled Mashud b Shahadat Hossain	0	– (8) not out	2
V. R. Singh not out	1		
B 2, l-b 8, w 2, n-b 12	24	L-b 1, w 2, n-b 4	7

1/0 (1) 2/124 (2) 3/132 (3)	(8 wkts dec.) 387	1/0 (1) 2/6 (3)	(6 wkts dec.) 100
4/321 (5) 5/366 (4) 6/381 (7)		3/60 (2) 4/64 (4)
7/384 (9) 8/387 (6)		5/78 (5) 6/93 (7)

R. P. Singh did not bat.

In the first innings Kumble retired ill at 384-6.

Mashrafe bin Mortaza 24.5–5–97–4; Shahadat Hossain 18–1–76–3; Mohammad Rafique 24–3–99–1; Enamul Haque 15–0–59–0; Shakib Al Hasan 13–2–29–0; Mohammad Ashraful 1–0–5–0; Rajin Saleh 3–1–12–0. *Second Innings—*Shahadat Hossain 7–3–30–2; Mashrafe bin Mortaza 8–1–36–1; Mohammad Rafique 8–0–27–3; Enamul Haque 1–0–6–0.

Bangladesh

Javed Omar lbw b R. P. Singh	7	– not out	52
Shahriar Nafees c Tendulkar b Zaheer Khan	32	– c Dhoni b R. P. Singh	1
*Habibul Bashar c Tendulkar b R. P. Singh	0	– c R. P. Singh b Powar	37
Rajin Saleh c Ganguly b Powar	41	– not out	7
Mohammad Ashraful c Karthik b R. P. Singh	5		
Shakib Al Hasan b V. R. Singh	27		
†Khaled Mashud lbw b V. R. Singh	2		
Mashrafe bin Mortaza b V. R. Singh	79		
Mohammad Rafique st Dhoni b Powar	9		
Shahadat Hossain b Tendulkar	31		
Enamul Haque, jun. not out	0		
L-b 1, w 3, n-b 1	5	L-b 6, n-b 1	7

1/20 (1) 2/20 (3) 3/47 (2) 4/58 (5)	238	1/12 (2) 2/82 (3)	(2 wkts) 104
5/114 (6) 6/116 (4) 7/122 (7)		
8/149 (9) 9/226 (10) 10/238 (8)		

Zaheer Khan 15–1–63–1; R. P. Singh 17–2–45–3; V. R. Singh 15.2–5–48–3; Powar 17–1–66–2; Tendulkar 4–0–15–1. *Second Innings—*Zaheer Khan 7–0–24–0; R. P. Singh 6–0–29–1; V. R. Singh 5–1–22–0; Powar 7–2–16–1; Tendulkar 3–0–7–0.

Umpires: B. R. Doctrove *(West Indies)* (12) and D. J. Harper *(Australia)* (64).
Third umpire: Nadir Shah *(Bangladesh)*.   Referee: R. S. Mahanama *(Sri Lanka)* (14).

Close of play: First day, India 295-3 (Tendulkar 80, Ganguly 82); Second day, India 384-6 (Dhoni 36, Kumble 1); Third day, No play; Fourth day, India 44-2 (Karthik 15, Tendulkar 24).

BANGLADESH v INDIA 2007 (2nd Test)

At Shere Bangla National Stadium, Mirpur, Dhaka, on 25, 26, 27 May.
Toss: Bangladesh.　　Result: INDIA won by an innings and 239 runs.
Debuts: India – I. Sharma.
Man of the Match: Zaheer Khan.　　Man of the Series: S. R. Tendulkar.

India romped to their biggest Test victory, helped by Habibul Bashar inserting them on a belter at the 95th venue to stage Test cricket: the top four all scored centuries, a Test first. Retirements meant the first wicket did not fall until the score reached 408. The openers put on 175 before Karthik went off with cramp; after adding another 106 with Dravid, Wasim Jaffer also succumbed, and had to be carried off after becoming the 15th player to follow a pair in his previous Test with a hundred; then Dravid and Tendulkar added 127 before Mohammad Rafique finally broke through; Karthik then returned to complete his maiden century. Dravid finally declared at a towering 610 for 3, then Bangladesh were 7 for 4 by the third over. Shakib Al Hasan and Rajin Saleh put up brief resistance, but Bangladesh were soon following on, an overwhelming 492 behind. Javed Omar became the 12th man to bag a king pair in Tests, and the first dismissed by first ball of both innings, although TV replays suggested he did not touch the second one. This time Bangladesh were 10 for 3 by the fourth over, before Mohammad Ashraful raced to the fastest Test fifty by minutes – 27, beating 28 by Jack Brown for England against Australia at Melbourne in 1894-95 – and he had 67 from 41 balls when he flicked Kumble to short midwicket. Bangladesh's highest score of the match again came from Mashrafe bin Mortaza, but it only delayed the bitter end.

India

K. D. Karthik c Habibul Bashar b Mashrafe bin Mortaza	129	S. C. Ganguly c Rajin Saleh b Mohammad Rafique	15
Wasim Jaffer retired ill	138	†M. S. Dhoni not out	51
*R. Dravid c Javed Omar b Mohammad Rafique	129	B 7, l-b 7, w 5, n-b 7	26
S. R. Tendulkar not out	122		
		1/408 (3) 2/493 (1) 3/525 (5) (3 wkts dec.)	610

R. R. Powar, Zaheer Khan, A. Kumble, R. P. Singh and I. Sharma did not bat.

Karthik, when 82, retired ill at 175 and resumed at 408; Wasim Jaffer retired ill at 281.

Mashrafe bin Mortaza 31.4–4–100–1; Syed Rasel 23.4–0–109–0; Mohammad Sharif 25.4–2–109–0; Mohammad Rafique 45–4–181–2; Shakib Al Hasan 19–1–62–0; Mohammad Ashraful 8–0–35–0.

Bangladesh

Javed Omar c Karthik b Zaheer Khan	0	– c Dhoni b Zaheer Khan	0
Shahriar Nafees b Zaheer Khan	2	– c Dhoni b Singh	4
*Habibul Bashar c Dhoni b Singh	4	– c Dravid b Zaheer Khan	5
Rajin Saleh c Wasim Jaffer b Kumble	20	– c Ganguly b Powar	42
Mohammad Ashraful lbw b Zaheer Khan	0	– c Tendulkar b Kumble	67
Shakib Al Hasan lbw b Zaheer Khan	30	– c Dravid b Powar	15
Mohammad Sharif lbw b Kumble	13	– (9) c and b Kumble	17
†Khaled Mashud c Dhoni b Kumble	25	– (7) c Tendulkar b Powar	8
Mashrafe bin Mortaza c Kumble b Sharma	2	– (8) c Dhoni b Tendulkar	70
Mohammad Rafique b Zaheer Khan	12	– lbw b Tendulkar	11
Syed Rasel not out	2	– not out	1
L-b 2, n-b 6	8	L-b 1, w 3, n-b 9	13

1/0 (1) 2/5 (3) 3/7 (2) 4/7 (5)　　　　　　118　　1/0 (1) 2/10 (3) 3/10 (2)　　　　　253
5/40 (4) 6/58 (6) 7/85 (7)　　　　　　　　　　　4/91 (5) 5/135 (4) 6/150 (6)
8/93 (9) 9/110 (10) 10/118 (8)　　　　　　　　7/154 (7) 8/208 (9) 9/223 (10) 10/253 (8)

Zaheer Khan 10–1–34–5; Singh 9–2–28–1; Kumble 9.2–3–32–3; Sharma 7–1–19–1; Powar 2–1–3–0. *Second Innings*—Zaheer Khan 8–1–54–2; Singh 6–1–28–1; Sharma 6–1–30–0; Kumble 15–1–72–2; Powar 16–4–33–3; Tendulkar 6.3–1–35–2.

Umpires: B. R. Doctrove *(West Indies)* (13) and D. J. Harper *(Australia)* (65).
Third umpire: Nadir Shah *(Bangladesh)*.　　Referee: R. S. Mahanama *(Sri Lanka)* (15).

Close of play: First day, India 326-0 (Dravid 88, Tendulkar 9); Second day, Bangladesh 58-5 (Shakib Al Hasan 30, Mohammad Sharif 0).

SRI LANKA v BANGLADESH 2007 (1st Test)

At Sinhalese Sports Club, Colombo, on 25, 26, 27, 28 June.
Toss: Sri Lanka.   Result: SRI LANKA won by an innings and 234 runs.
Debuts: Sri Lanka – B. S. M. Warnapura.
Man of the Match: M. Muralitharan.

Even by Bangladesh's standards, the opening day of their inaugural three-Test series against Sri Lanka was one of their worst. After a quiet first half-hour, they were bowled out 42 minutes after lunch for just 89: by the close, Sri Lanka were already 138 ahead. Malinga and Vaas made the initial inroads before Fernando struck, pinning the former captain Habibul Bashar lbw and hurrying his replacement Mohammad Ashraful, who top-edged a bouncer to deep backward square. Then Muralitharan mesmerised the tail with five wickets in 7.3 overs, four of them falling to the *doosra*. Sri Lanka wobbled to 14 for 2: Malinda Warnapura, the nephew of Sri Lanka's first Test captain, collected a first-ball duck on debut, while Sangakkara was caught behind attempting to pull. Mahela Jayawardene was caught off a no-ball when 17, but once settled he quickly asserted his authority before retiring briefly with leg cramps. Vandort dug in for his third Test century, then Jayawardene returned to complete his 17th. His namesake, Prasanna Jayawardene, reached his first Test hundred during a meandering afternoon, and the declaration finally came when Vaas followed suit for the first time in his 97th Test, beating Jason Gillespie's record of 71 for a maiden Test century (two months later Anil Kumble made one after an even longer wait). Finally, Bangladesh produced a fight. The cause was hopeless – 488 behind with more than three days remaining – but they battled throughout the third day before the last five wickets folded in just 30 minutes on the fourth morning.

Bangladesh

Javed Omar c H. A. P. W. Jayawardene b Vaas	8	– lbw b Malinga	62
Shahriar Nafees c H. A. P. W. Jayawardene b Malinga	15	– c and b Muralitharan	38
Rajin Saleh lbw b Muralitharan	3	– c D. P. M. D. Jayawardene b Dilshan	51
Habibul Bashar lbw b Fernando	2	– c H. A. P. W. Jayawardene b Vaas	17
*Mohammad Ashraful c Warnapura b Fernando	7	– c Vaas b Muralitharan	37
Shakib Al Hasan lbw b Muralitharan	16	– c Warnapura b Malinga	8
†Khaled Mashud not out	12	– b Malinga	1
Shahadat Hossain c Muralitharan b Fernando	1	– (10) st H. A. P. W. Jayawardene b Muralitharan	1
Mashrafe bin Mortaza st H. A. P. W. Jayawardene b Muralitharan	1	– (8) lbw b Muralitharan	9
Mohammad Rafique lbw b Muralitharan	11	– (9) b Malinga	0
Abdul Razzak st H. A. P. W. Jayawardene b Muralitharan	4	– not out	0
L-b 2, n-b 7	9	B 2, l-b 10, w 1, n-b 17	30

1/28 (2) 2/28 (1) 3/32 (4) 4/43 (5)   89   1/86 (2) 2/126 (1) 3/160 (4)   254
5/50 (3) 6/61 (6) 7/64 (8)   4/227 (3) 5/231 (5) 6/238 (7)
8/69 (9) 9/85 (10) 10/89 (11)   7/250 (8) 8/252 (6) 9/253 (9) 10/254 (10)

Vaas 7–3–8–1; Malinga 7–0–31–1; Fernando 11–2–33–3; Muralitharan 7.3–3–15–5. *Second Innings*—Vaas 12–3–36–1; Malinga 17–2–80–4; Muralitharan 36.1–12–87–4; Fernando 15–5–28–0; Dilshan 7–3–11–1.

Sri Lanka

M. G. Vandort c Shahriar Nafees b Mohammad Rafique	117	T. M. Dilshan run out	79
B. S. M. Warnapura lbw b Shahadat Hossain	0	†H. A. P. W. Jayawardene not out	120
K. C. Sangakkara c Khaled Mashud b Shahadat Hossain	6	W. P. U. J. C. Vaas not out	100
		B 6, l-b 7, w 2, n-b 12	27
*D. P. M. D. Jayawardene c Shakib Al Hasan b Mashrafe bin Mortaza	127	1/1 (2) 2/14 (3) (6 wkts dec.)	577
L. P. C. Silva c Mashrafe bin Mortaza b Abdul Razzak	1	3/187 (5) 4/304 (1)	
		5/321 (6) 6/354 (4)	

S. L. Malinga, M. Muralitharan and C. R. D. Fernando did not bat.

D. P. M. D. Jayawardene, when 93, retired hurt at 184 and resumed at 304.

Mashrafe bin Mortaza 19–2–72–1`; Shahadat Hossain 18–0–102–2; Abdul Razzak 30–2–109–1; Mohammad Rafique 28.5–1–138–1; Shakib Al Hasan 16–0–57–0; Mohammad Ashraful 13–0–52–0; Rajin Saleh 3–0–12–0; Habibul Bashar 8–0–22–0.

Umpires: Asad Rauf *(Pakistan)* (12) and S. L. Shastri *(India)* (1).
Third umpire: T. H. Wijewardene *(Sri Lanka)*.   Referee: J. J. Crowe *(New Zealand)* (18).

Close of play: First day, Sri Lanka 227-3 (Vandort 87, Dilshan 27); Second day, Bangladesh 3-0 (Javed Omar 3, Shahriar Nafees 0); Third day, Bangladesh 233-5 (Shakib Al Hasan 4, Khaled Mashud 0).

SRI LANKA v BANGLADESH 2007 (2nd Test)

At P. Saravanamuttu Stadium, Colombo, on 3, 4, 5 July.
Toss: Sri Lanka.   Result: SRI LANKA won by an innings and 90 runs.
Debuts: Bangladesh – Mehrab Hossain, jun.
Man of the Match: K. C. Sangakkara.

This Test followed a near-identical pattern to the First. Bangladesh survived even fewer overs – 111.4 to 119.4 in all – and were bowled out for an even more humiliating 62, their lowest Test total, previously 86 at Colombo's Premadasa Stadium in 2005-06. Rajin Saleh was the only man to reach double figures in that miserable first innings, which lasted two balls beyond lunch on the first day. Malinga cut through the top order and Muralitharan again made easy work of the tail. Warnapura followed his debut duck with a gritty 82, clipping efficiently off his legs and scoring most of his runs square of the wicket. Sangakkara started cautiously, but gradually scored more freely. His double-century, the fifth of his career, was not his most fluent – it took 470 minutes – but it was a masterclass in application and careful shot-selection from a batsman previously struggling for form. It was also the signal for the declaration, with 14 overs left before the close. Bangladesh's openers started in carefree style, racing to 48 in just 41 deliveries. Shahriar Nafees's risk-taking backfired when he nicked a flashy drive, then three more quick blows meant they finished the second day at 69 for 4, still 320 behind. With a seven-session thrashing looming, Mohammad Ashraful and Mushfiqur Rahim dug in for a mature stand of 191, a Bangladesh sixth-wicket record. Ashraful became the first Bangladeshi to make four Test hundreds, but the second new ball brought the match rapidly to a close inside three days.

Bangladesh

Javed Omar c H. A. P. W. Jayawardene b Malinga	8	– lbw b Vaas............................	28
Shahriar Nafees lbw b Malinga...................	0	– c H. A. P. W. Jayawardene b Vaas	20
Rajin Saleh c D. P. M. D. Jayawardene b Muralitharan	21	– c D. P. M. D. Jayawardene b Fernando	0
Habibul Bashar c D. P. M. D. Jayawardene b Malinga ...	5	– (5) b Fernando	12
*Mohammad Ashraful c Warnapura b Malinga	0	– (6) not out............................	129
Mehrab Hossain, jun. b Fernando.................	6	– (4) b Fernando.........................	8
†Mushfiqur Rahim c H. A. P. W. Jayawardene			
b Muralitharan	9	– c and b Muralitharan	80
Mashrafe bin Mortaza c D. P. M. D. Jayawardene			
b Fernando	0	– (9) lbw b Vaas.........................	0
Mohammad Rafique c Vaas b Muralitharan	2	– (10) run out..........................	3
Mohammad Sharif not out......................	4	– (8) lbw b Vaas.........................	2
Shahadat Hossain b Muralitharan	1	– run out...............................	2
L-b 1, w 1, n-b 4.....................	6	B 2, l-b 2, w 2, n-b 9	15
	62		**299**

1/3 (2) 2/14 (1) 3/22 (4) 4/22 (5)
5/33 (6) 6/45 (7) 7/48 (8)
8/51 (9) 9/59 (3) 10/62 (11)

1/48 (2) 2/51 (3) 3/55 (1)
4/59 (4) 5/78 (5) 6/269 (7)
7/276 (8) 8/276 (9) 9/286 (10) 10/299 (11)

Vaas 5–1–6–0; Malinga 9–1–25–4; Fernando 6–1–16–2; Muralitharan 5.2–1–14–4. *Second Innings*—Vaas 20.2–8–55–4; Malinga 15–1–86–0; Fernando 17–2–60–3; Muralitharan 28–6–84–1; Dilshan 6–1–10–0.

Sri Lanka

M. G. Vandort b Mashrafe bin Mortaza.............	14	†H. A. P. W. Jayawardene c Javed Omar
B. S. M. Warnapura c Shahriar Nafees		b Mashrafe bin Mortaza 14
b Shahadat Hossain	82	W. P. U. J. C. Vaas not out 30
K. C. Sangakkara not out	200	
*D. P. M. D. Jayawardene		B 6, l-b 7, w 3, n-b 13......... 29
c Shahriar Nafees b Shahadat Hossain	49	
L. P. C. Silva c Mashrafe bin Mortaza		1/41 (1) 2/169 (2) (6 wkts dec.) 451
b Mehrab Hossain	33	3/267 (4) 4/359 (5)
T. M. Dilshan b Mehrab Hossain	0	5/359 (6) 6/395 (7)

S. L. Malinga, M. Muralitharan and C. R. D. Fernando did not bat.

Mashrafe bin Mortaza 30–7–77–2; Shahadat Hossain 21–3–81–2; Mohammad Sharif 24–4–86–0; Mohammad Rafique 35–3–134–0; Mohammad Ashraful 7–0–31–0; Mehrab Hossain 7.5–0–29–2.

Umpires: Asad Rauf *(Pakistan)* (13) and R. E. Koertzen *(South Africa)* (83).
Third umpire: E. A. R. de Silva *(Sri Lanka)*.   Referee: J. J. Crowe *(New Zealand)* (19).

Close of play: First day, Sri Lanka 154-1 (Warnapura 79, Sangakkara 51); Second day, Bangladesh 69-4 (Habibul Bashar 3, Mohammad Ashraful 7).

SRI LANKA v BANGLADESH 2007 (3rd Test)

At Asgiriya Stadium, Kandy, on 11, 12, 13, 14 July.

Toss: Sri Lanka.   Result: SRI LANKA won by an innings and 193 runs.

Debuts: none.

Man of the Match: M. Muralitharan.   Man of the Series: M. Muralitharan.

Bangladesh could not avert their fourth successive innings defeat after yet more miserable batting. Sri Lanka were only the third team to win all three Tests of a series by an innings, following England against West Indies in 1928 (their first Tests) and India against Sri Lanka in 1993-94. The match lasted four days only because of rain; in terms of overs, it was the shortest of the series. Muralitharan started the match needing 12 wickets for 700 in Tests; with perfect timing, he got there with the last ball, in his home town. It was his 20th ten-wicket haul in Test cricket (Shane Warne is next with ten). Only 29 overs were possible in three short spells on the first day, during which Bangladesh stumbled to 72 for 4. On the second rain-marred day, Murali started with a brilliant one-handed return catch, and ended up with six wickets. The third day started with Bangladesh's best hour of the series with the ball. Shahadat Hossain steamed in, and Syed Rasel maintained an exemplary line and length while swinging the ball both ways. But as the sun dried out the pitch, runs began to flow freely. After a stand of 311 with Mahela Jayawardene, Sangakkara pressed on to his second successive double-century. Sri Lanka scored 470 in 98.2 overs during the day, and declared overnight. Bangladesh started positively, reaching 106 for 2 – but the last eight tumbled for 70, with Murali rounding things off by dismissing Syed Rasel as No. 700.

Bangladesh

Javed Omar lbw b Malinga	8	– c Sangakkara b Malinga	22
Shahriar Nafees c de Silva b Muralitharan	29	– c D. P. M. D. Jayawardene b Muralitharan	64
Habibul Bashar c H. A. P. W. Jayawardene b Maharoof	18	– b Muralitharan	15
Rajin Saleh c D. P. M. D. Jayawardene b Muralitharan	0	– (7) c D. P. M. D. Jayawardene b de Silva	0
*Mohammad Ashraful c H. A. P. W. Jayawardene b de Silva	26	– (4) lbw b Muralitharan	19
Tushar Imran c D. P. M. D. Jayawardene b de Silva	17	– c D. P. M. D. Jayawardene b Malinga	17
†Mushfiqur Rahim not out	11	– (5) c Tharanga b de Silva	1
Mashrafe bin Mortaza c and b Muralitharan	5	– c sub (B. S. M. Warnapura) b Muralitharan	8
Mohammad Rafique c and b Muralitharan	5	– not out	0
Shahadat Hossain c Dilshan b Muralitharan	0	– b Muralitharan	5
Syed Rasel c Silva b Muralitharan	0	– c Maharoof b Muralitharan	4
B 4, l-b 2, w 1, n-b 5	12	B 4, l-b 1, w 3, n-b 13	21
	131		**176**

1/10 (1) 2/50 (3) 3/61 (4) 4/64 (2)
5/98 (6) 6/111 (5) 7/118 (8)
8/130 (9) 9/131 (10) 10/131 (11)

1/47 (1) 2/98 (3) 3/123 (2)
4/138 (4) 5/138 (5) 6/142 (7)
7/166 (8) 8/167 (6) 9/172 (10) 10/176 (11)

Malinga 10–2–41–1; de Silva 12–3–29–2; Maharoof 8–4–21–1; Muralitharan 14.5–6–28–6; Dilshan 4–1–6–0. *Second Innings*—Malinga 10–0–46–2; de Silva 12–4–34–2; Maharoof 16–7–37–0; Muralitharan 21–5–54–6.

Sri Lanka

M. G. Vandort b Syed Rasel	43	T. M. Dilshan not out	17
W. U. Tharanga lbw b Syed Rasel	12		
K. C. Sangakkara not out	222	B 4, l-b 2, w 2, n-b 8	16
*D. P. M. D. Jayawardene c Mohammad Ashraful b Syed Rasel	165	1/47 (2) 2/74 (1) (4 wkts dec.)	500
L. P. C. Silva run out	25	3/385 (4) 4/445 (5)	

†H. A. P. W. Jayawardene, M. F. Maharoof, S. L. Malinga, W. R. S. de Silva and M. Muralitharan did not bat.

Mashrafe bin Mortaza 24–2–125–0; Syed Rasel 31–1–104–3; Shahadat Hossain 16–1–71–0; Mohammad Rafique 14–1–72–0; Mohammad Ashraful 12–0–74–0; Tushar Imran 10–0–48–0.

Umpires: R. E. Koertzen *(South Africa)* (84) and S. L. Shastri *(India)* (2).
Third umpire: R. Martinesz *(Sri Lanka)*.   Referee: J. J. Crowe *(New Zealand)* (20).

Close of play: First day, Bangladesh 72-4 (Mohammad Ashraful 4, Tushar Imran 6); Second day, Sri Lanka 30-0 (Vandort 25, Tharanga 4); Third day, Sri Lanka 500-4 (Sangakkara 222, Dilshan 17).

ENGLAND v INDIA 2007 (1st Test)

At Lord's, London, on 19, 20, 21, 22, 23 July.
Toss: England.   Result: MATCH DRAWN.
Debuts: England – C. T. Tremlett.
Man of the Match: K. P. Pietersen.

The weather toyed with this Test throughout, threatening to submerge Lord's on the second morning, disrupting play on every day bar one, and tantalisingly whisking victory from England on the last afternoon. Not that they could entirely blame the clouds: in dwindling light they should have managed more than 14 overs an hour on the final day. India survived 96 overs, the longest innings of the match, and finished nine down: Panesar was convinced he had Sreesanth lbw just before bad light ended proceedings, but Steve Bucknor disagreed. England had zoomed away on the first day, reaching 218 for 1 during the evening session – Strauss made 96 before Dravid took his 150th Test catch – but with the weather shifting the balance from bat to ball, the next 38 wickets produced just 845 more runs. Anderson and Zaheer Khan moved the ball both ways, and late. In such conditions, Pietersen's second-innings hundred – he said he had never played better – was a masterpiece, even if it could not quite deliver victory. In the first innings, Pietersen had been controversially reinstated after walking for a catch behind: as he trudged towards the pavilion his team-mates were pointing at the replay screen, and the umpires eventually agreed he was not out. Perhaps flustered, Pietersen really was caught behind two balls later, the first of five wickets that clattered for 12 runs. Chris Tremlett became only the sixth grandson to follow his grandfather into Test cricket: Maurice Tremlett played three times against West Indies in 1947-48.

England

A. J. Strauss c Dravid b Kumble	96	– c Tendulkar b Zaheer Khan	18
A. N. Cook lbw b Ganguly	36	– lbw b Zaheer Khan	17
*M. P. Vaughan c Dhoni b Singh	79	– b Singh	30
K. P. Pietersen c Dhoni b Zaheer Khan	37	– b Singh	134
P. D. Collingwood lbw b Kumble	0	– c Laxman b Singh	4
R. J. Sidebottom b Singh	1	– (9) c Dravid b Kumble	9
I. R. Bell b Zaheer Khan	20	– (6) b Singh	9
†M. J. Prior lbw b Sreesanth	1	– (7) c Dhoni b Zaheer Khan	42
C. T. Tremlett lbw b Sreesanth	0	– (8) b Zaheer Khan	0
M. S. Panesar lbw b Sreesanth	0	– lbw b Singh	3
J. M. Anderson not out	0	– not out	4
B 9, l-b 10, w 7, n-b 2	28	B 9, l-b 1, w 2	12

1/76 (2) 2/218 (1) 3/252 (3) 4/255 (5)   298
5/272 (6) 6/286 (4) 7/287 (8)
8/287 (9) 9/297 (10) 10/298 (7)

1/40 (1) 2/43 (2) 3/102 (3)   282
4/114 (5) 5/132 (6) 6/251 (7)
7/251 (8) 8/266 (9) 9/275 (4) 10/282 (10)

Zaheer Khan 18.2–4–62–2; Sreesanth 22–8–67–3; Singh 17–6–58–2; Ganguly 9–3–24–1; Kumble 23–2–60–2; Tendulkar 2–0–8–0. *Second Innings*—Zaheer Khan 28–6–79–4; Sreesanth 16–3–62–0; Singh 16.3–3–59–5; Kumble 17–3–70–1; Tendulkar 1–0–2–0.

India

K. D. Karthik lbw b Sidebottom	5	– (2) c Collingwood b Anderson	60
Wasim Jaffer c and b Tremlett	58	– (1) c Pietersen b Anderson	8
*R. Dravid c Prior b Anderson	2	– lbw b Tremlett	9
S. R. Tendulkar lbw b Anderson	37	– lbw b Panesar	16
S. C. Ganguly b Anderson	34	– lbw b Sidebottom	40
R. P. Singh c Anderson b Sidebottom	17	– (10) b Panesar	2
V. V. S. Laxman c Prior b Sidebottom	15	– (6) b Tremlett	39
†M. S. Dhoni c Bell b Anderson	0	– (7) not out	76
A. Kumble lbw b Sidebottom	11	– (8) lbw b Sidebottom	3
Zaheer Khan c Strauss b Anderson	7	– (9) c Prior b Tremlett	0
S. Sreesanth not out	0	– not out	4
B 4, l-b 7, n-b 4	15	B 13, l-b 5, w 6, n-b 1	25

1/18 (1) 2/27 (3) 3/106 (4) 4/134 (2)   201
5/155 (5) 6/173 (6) 7/175 (8)
8/192 (9) 9/197 (7) 10/201 (10)

1/38 (1) 2/55 (3)   (9 wkts) 282
3/84 (4) 4/143 (5)
5/145 (2) 6/231 (6) 7/247 (8) 8/254 (9) 9/263 (10)

Sidebottom 22–5–65–4; Anderson 24.2–8–42–5; Tremlett 20–8–52–1; Collingwood 3–1–9–0; Panesar 8–3–22–0. *Second Innings*—Sidebottom 19–4–42–2; Anderson 25–4–83–2; Tremlett 21–5–52–3; Panesar 26–7–63–2; Collingwood 1–0–6–0; Vaughan 4–0–18–0.

Umpires: S. A. Bucknor *(West Indies)* (118) and S. J. A. Taufel *(Australia)* (42).
Third umpire: I. J. Gould *(England)*.   Referee: R. S. Madugalle *(Sri Lanka)* (95).

Close of play: First day, England 268-4 (Pietersen 34, Sidebottom 0); Second day, India 145-4 (Ganguly 25, Singh 5); Third day, England 77-2 (Vaughan 16, Pietersen 15); Fourth day, India 137-3 (Karthik 56, Ganguly 36).

ENGLAND v INDIA 2007 (2nd Test)

At Trent Bridge, Nottingham, on 27, 28, 29, 30, 31 July.
Toss: India.   Result: INDIA won by seven wickets.
Debuts: none.
Man of the Match: Zaheer Khan.

India bounced back to secure one of their finest away wins: only their 29th in all (fifth in England) in their 200th Test abroad. The pitch had a smattering of live grass on top, and some moisture beneath. Zaheer Khan soon had Strauss and Vaughan caught at first slip: throughout, Zaheer and his fellow left-armer R. P. Singh showed tremendous control and swung the ball from over and round the wicket. England appeared to have weathered the storm at 94 for 3 by tea on the first day, but they subsided to 198. In a decisive three-hour spell, the openers completed India's first century opening stand in England since 1979, although both fell short of hundreds. Dravid compiled an important 37 when England sensed an opening on the second evening, while Tendulkar made a patchy start but passed 11,000 Test runs. India's eventual lead was 283. England survived a sticky 16 overs on the third evening without loss, but batting for two more days proved well beyond them. The turning-point came when Vaughan shaped to flick Zaheer but the ball bounced down off his thigh-pad and rolled onto his stumps. The remaining wickets fell for 68 as the second new ball caused mayhem, leaving India a simple target. Much was made of a childish prank in which jellybeans were scattered on the pitch when Zaheer came out to bat: the culprit was never unmasked, but his joke backfired as an affronted Zaheer later took five wickets, making nine in the match.

England

A. J. Strauss c Tendulkar b Zaheer Khan	4	– c Dhoni b Zaheer Khan	55
A. N. Cook lbw b Ganguly	43	– lbw b Zaheer Khan	23
*M. P. Vaughan c Tendulkar b Zaheer Khan	9	– b Zaheer Khan	124
K. P. Pietersen lbw b Singh	13	– lbw b Singh	19
P. D. Collingwood b Sreesanth	28	– c Karthik b Zaheer Khan	63
I. R. Bell lbw b Zaheer Khan	31	– lbw b Zaheer Khan	0
†M. J. Prior c Dravid b Kumble	11	– b Singh	7
C. T. Tremlett b Kumble	20	– c Singh b Kumble	5
R. J. Sidebottom not out	18	– not out	25
M. S. Panesar c Laxman b Zaheer Khan	1	– c Karthik b Kumble	4
J. M. Anderson b Kumble	1	– b Kumble	1
B 8, l-b 7, w 1, n-b 3	19	B 7, l-b 6, w 9, n-b 7	29
	198		**355**

1/4 (1) 2/24 (3) 3/47 (4) 4/101 (5)   198
5/109 (2) 6/147 (7) 7/157 (6)
8/186 (8) 9/195 (10) 10/198 (11)

1/49 (2) 2/130 (1) 3/175 (4)   355
4/287 (3) 5/287 (6) 6/304 (7)
7/323 (5) 8/329 (8) 9/333 (10) 10/355 (11)

Zaheer Khan 21–5–59–4; Sreesanth 12–7–16–1; Singh 10–1–56–1; Ganguly 8–4–11–1; Kumble 12.3–2–32–3; Tendulkar 2–0–9–0. *Second Innings*—Zaheer Khan 27–10–75–5; Sreesanth 21–2–60–0; Singh 18–5–52–2; Kumble 25–2–104–3; Ganguly 6–0–22–0; Tendulkar 7–0–29–0.

India

K. D. Karthik c Cook b Panesar	77	– c Prior b Tremlett	22
Wasim Jaffer c Prior b Tremlett	62	– c Pietersen b Tremlett	22
*R. Dravid c Bell b Panesar	37	– not out	11
S. R. Tendulkar lbw b Collingwood	91	– c Cook b Tremlett	1
S. C. Ganguly c Prior b Anderson	79	– not out	2
V. V. S. Laxman c Prior b Tremlett	54		
†M. S. Dhoni c Prior b Sidebottom	5		
A. Kumble c Prior b Tremlett	30		
Zaheer Khan not out	10		
R. P. Singh lbw b Panesar	0		
S. Sreesanth lbw b Panesar	2		
B 16, l-b 16, w 1, n-b 1	34	B 4, l-b 6, w 2, n-b 3	15
	481	(3 wkts)	**73**

1/147 (2) 2/149 (1) 3/246 (3) 4/342 (4)   481
5/409 (5) 6/414 (7) 7/464 (6)
8/473 (8) 9/474 (10) 10/481 (11)

1/47 (2) 2/55 (1) 3/62 (4)   (3 wkts) 73

Sidebottom 36–11–75–1; Anderson 33–4–134–1; Tremlett 40–13–80–3; Collingwood 16–3–59–1; Panesar 33.5–8–101–4. *Second Innings*—Anderson 9–2–23–0; Sidebottom 8–0–28–0; Tremlett 7.1–2–12–3.

Umpires: I. L. Howell *(South Africa)* (7) and S. J. A. Taufel *(Australia)* (43).
Third umpire: N. J. Llong *(England)*.   Referee: R. S. Madugalle *(Sri Lanka)* (96).

Close of play: First day, England 169-7 (Tremlett 16, Sidebottom 0); Second day, India 254-3 (Tendulkar 57, Ganguly 4); Third day, England 43-0 (Strauss 21, Cook 17); Fourth day, India 10-0 (Karthik 6, Wasim Jaffer 3).

ENGLAND v INDIA 2007 (3rd Test)

At Kennington Oval, London, on 9, 10, 11, 12, 13 August.
Toss: India.   Result: MATCH DRAWN.
Debuts: none.
Man of the Match: A. Kumble.   Men of the Series: J. M. Anderson and Zaheer Khan.

Dravid, who stepped down afterwards, became only the third Indian captain to win a series in England, following Ajit Wadekar (1971) and Kapil Dev (1986): it was Vaughan's first home series defeat as captain. India batted solidly throughout, although England still nurtured faint hopes of levelling the series when Tendulkar departed after five hours at 417 for 6: but the last four wickets added 247, as India reached the highest total between these sides. The most exhilarating contribution came from Dhoni, who hit four sixes from 80 balls, and the most surprising from Kumble, the oldest Indian to score a maiden Test century (36 years 297 days) after the longest wait in terms of appearances, his 118 matches beating Chaminda Vaas's recent record of 97. All 11 batsmen reached double figures (the 11th instance in Tests), and there were eight partnerships of 50 or more (no other Test innings had more than six). Prior equalled the record number of byes conceded by a specialist wicketkeeper in a Test. England fought hard, not helped by umpire Ian Howell, who had a poor match. Despite leading by 319 Dravid waived the follow-on, then had to grind out 12 from 96 balls after India nosedived to 11 for 3. England went into the final day needing another 444, and Pietersen ensured the draw with his tenth Test century. This was the first time that both sides were unchanged in a series of three or more Tests. India became the first custodians of the new Pataudi Trophy.

India

K. D. Karthik c Prior b Sidebottom	91	– c Collingwood b Tremlett		8
Wasim Jaffer c Pietersen b Anderson	35	– lbw b Anderson		0
*R. Dravid b Anderson	55	– c Strauss b Collingwood		12
S. R. Tendulkar c Strauss b Anderson	82	– b Anderson		1
S. C. Ganguly lbw b Collingwood	37	– c Strauss b Collingwood		57
V. V. S. Laxman c Prior b Tremlett	51	– not out		46
†M. S. Dhoni c Cook b Pietersen	92	– c Prior b Tremlett		36
A. Kumble not out	110	– not out		8
Zaheer Khan c Anderson b Panesar	11			
R. P. Singh c and b Anderson	11			
S. Sreesanth c Vaughan b Panesar	35			
B 33, l-b 13, w 2, n-b 6	54	B 1, l-b 5, n-b 6		12

1/62 (2) 2/189 (3) 3/199 (1) 4/276 (5)   664   1/10 (2) 2/10 (1)   (6 wkts dec.) 180
5/354 (6) 6/417 (4) 7/508 (7)   3/11 (4) 4/76 (5)
8/570 (9) 9/591 (10) 10/664 (11)   5/89 (3) 6/158 (7)

Sidebottom 32–8–93–1; Anderson 40–5–182–4; Tremlett 40–6–132–1; Panesar 45–5–159–2; Collingwood 7–1–11–1; Pietersen 6–0–41–1. *Second Innings*—Anderson 15–8–34–2; Tremlett 15–2–58–2; Collingwood 10–1–24–2; Panesar 18–1–58–0.

England

A. J. Strauss c Sreesanth b Zaheer Khan	6	– c Laxman b Singh		32
A. N. Cook c Singh b Kumble	61	– c Laxman b Kumble		43
J. M. Anderson lbw b Singh	16			
*M. P. Vaughan c and b Kumble	11	– (3) c Dhoni b Sreesanth		42
K. P. Pietersen c Dravid b Tendulkar	41	– (4) c Karthik b Sreesanth		101
P. D. Collingwood lbw b Sreesanth	62	– (5) lbw b Sreesanth		40
I. R. Bell c Dhoni b Zaheer Khan	63	– (6) lbw b Kumble		67
†M. J. Prior c Tendulkar b Sreesanth	0	– (7) not out		12
R. J. Sidebottom c and b Zaheer Khan	2	– (8) not out		3
C. T. Tremlett not out	25			
M. S. Panesar lbw b Kumble	9			
B 16, l-b 12, w 10, n-b 11	49	B 2, l-b 4, w 9, n-b 14		29

1/12 (1) 2/78 (3) 3/119 (2) 4/124 (4)   345   1/79 (1) 2/86 (2)   (6 wkts) 369
5/202 (5) 6/288 (6) 7/303 (7)   3/152 (3) 4/266 (5)
8/305 (9) 9/305 (8) 10/345 (11)   5/289 (4) 6/363 (6)

Zaheer Khan 22–13–32–3; Sreesanth 21–2–80–2; Kumble 29.1–7–94–3; Singh 18–3–72–1; Ganguly 5–1–8–0; Tendulkar 7–0–26–1; Laxman 1–0–5–0. *Second Innings*—Zaheer Khan 20–3–59–0; Sreesanth 21–7–53–3; Kumble 37–9–123–2; Singh 13–2–50–1; Tendulkar 19–0–78–0.

Umpires: S. A. Bucknor *(West Indies)* (119) and I. L. Howell *(South Africa)* (8).
Third umpire: P. J. Hartley *(England)*.   Referee: R. S. Madugalle *(Sri Lanka)* (97).

Close of play: First day, India 316-4 (Tendulkar 48, Laxman 20); Second day, England 24-1 (Cook 12, Anderson 5); Third day, England 326-9 (Tremlett 18, Panesar 0); Fourth day, England 56-0 (Strauss 23, Cook 27).

PAKISTAN v SOUTH AFRICA 2007-08 (1st Test)

At National Stadium, Karachi, on 1, 2, 3, 4, 5 October.
Toss: South Africa.   Result: SOUTH AFRICA won by 160 runs.
Debuts: Pakistan – Abdur Rahman.
Man of the Match: J. H. Kallis.

South Africa became only the second side to win at Karachi (after England in 2000-01), thanks chiefly to Kallis, who shed his usual introspection in making the fastest of his 25 Test hundreds to date as his side batted solidly to reach 450. Pakistan fielded four spinners, but they found little assistance at first, although Danish Kaneria did finally dismiss Kallis, and then Prince, his 200th Test wicket. South Africa's slow left-armer, Harris, haggled harder with the pitch, getting greater bargains than any Pakistani. Mohammad Yousuf, claiming a lack of practice, had pulled out on the morning of the Test, claiming a lack of practice, and Salman Butt fell ill during it, but this should not detract from Harris's maiden Test five-for. Shoaib Malik's defiance prevented the follow-on, but South Africa had a comfortable lead of 159 and lots of time. Kallis worked his way to his second hundred of the match, only the fourth South African to achieve this in Tests, after Alan Melville and Bruce Mitchell (both in England in 1947), and Gary Kirsten (against India in 1996-97). Debutant slow left-armer Abdur Rahman returned identical figures of 4 for 105 in both innings. Victory was ensured by Steyn – something of a surprise inclusion at the expense of Shaun Pollock – who hurried out both openers within six overs. Younis Khan offered a glimpse of hope with a manic counterattacking hundred in 108 balls, but once he went on the final morning – stumps wrecked by Steyn – the game was up.

South Africa

H. H. Gibbs c Mohammad Hafeez b Umar Gul	54	– (2) c Faisal Iqbal b Danish Kaneria	18
*G. C. Smith lbw b Mohammad Hafeez	42	– (1) c Kamran Akmal b Abdul Rahman	25
H. M. Amla b Mohammad Asif	71	– st Kamran Akmal b Abdul Rahman	0
J. H. Kallis c Kamran Akmal b Danish Kaneria	155	– not out	100
A. G. Prince c and b Danish Kaneria	36	– b Danish Kaneria	45
A. B. de Villiers b Umar Gul	77	– b Abdul Rahman	1
†M. V. Boucher c Kamran Akmal b Abdul Rahman	1	– c Misbah-ul-Haq b Danish Kaneria	29
A. Nel c Misbah-ul-Haq b Abdul Rahman	2	– c Misbah-ul-Haq b Abdul Rahman	33
P. L. Harris c Kamran Akmal b Abdul Rahman	1	– not out	1
D. W. Steyn b Abdul Rahman	0		
M. Ntini not out	0		
B 1, l-b 6, n-b 4	11	B 10, l-b 2	12

1/87 (2) 2/109 (1) 3/279 (3) 4/352 (4) **450** 1/41 (1) 2/43 (3) (7 wkts dec.) **264**
5/373 (5) 6/392 (7) 7/408 (8) 3/43 (2) 4/131 (5)
8/412 (9) 9/448 (10) 10/450 (6) 5/132 (6) 6/188 (7) 7/251 (8)

Mohammad Asif 26–6–83–1; Umar Gul 21.3–6–60–2; Danish Kaneria 36–3–124–2; Abdul Rahman 31–3–105–4; Shoaib Malik 8–2–31–0; Mohammad Hafeez 14–0–40–1. *Second Innings*—Mohammad Asif 6–1–14–0; Umar Gul 12–1–35–0; Abdul Rahman 38–6–105–4; Danish Kaneria 28–3–85–3; Mohammad Hafeez 5–0–13–0.

Pakistan

Mohammad Hafeez c Kallis b Harris	34	– b Steyn	1
†Kamran Akmal lbw b Harris	42	– (8) c Boucher b Harris	9
Younis Khan b Nel	6	– b Steyn	126
Faisal Iqbal b Kallis	7	– c Kallis b Harris	44
Misbah-ul-Haq c Boucher b Steyn	23	– (6) lbw b Nel	23
*Shoaib Malik st Boucher b Harris	73	– (7) c Nel b Ntini	30
Abdul Rahman c Boucher b Nel	9	– (9) lbw b Steyn	0
Salman Butt lbw b Harris	24	– (2) c Amla b Steyn	3
Umar Gul st Boucher b Harris	12	– (10) c Nel b Steyn	8
Danish Kaneria not out	26	– (11) not out	0
Mohammad Asif b Steyn	10	– (5) c Amla b Nel	6
B 15, l-b 7, w 1, n-b 2	25	B 8, l-b 4, n-b 1	13

1/71 (2) 2/82 (1) 3/84 (3) 4/97 (4) **291** 1/1 (1) 2/20 (2) 3/134 (4) **263**
5/120 (5) 6/149 (7) 7/233 (8) 4/161 (5) 5/197 (3) 6/230 (6)
8/238 (6) 9/259 (9) 10/291 (11) 7/239 (8) 8/249 (9) 9/257 (10) 10/263 (7)

Steyn 13.3–2–50–2; Ntini 11–2–48–0; Harris 36–13–73–5; Nel 20–4–59–2; Kallis 11–3–21–1; Smith 6–1–18–0. *Second Innings*—Ntini 12.5–4–34–1; Steyn 15–3–56–5; Nel 19–5–59–2; Harris 30–8–58–2; Smith 3–0–33–0; Kallis 4–3–4–0; Amla 1–0–7–0.

Umpires: M. R. Benson (*England*) (16) and S. J. A. Taufel (*Australia*) (44).
Third umpire: Riazuddin (*Pakistan*).   Referee: A. G. Hurst (*Australia*) (16).

Close of play: First day, South Africa 294-3 (Kallis 118, Prince 3); Second day, Pakistan 127-5 (Shoaib Malik 9, Abdul Rahman 1); Third day, South Africa 76-3 (Kallis 18, Prince 11); Fourth day, Pakistan 146-3 (Younis Khan 93, Mohammad Asif 1).

PAKISTAN v SOUTH AFRICA 2007-08 (2nd Test)

At Gaddafi Stadium, Lahore, on 8, 9, 10, 11, 12 October.
Toss: South Africa.   Result: MATCH DRAWN.
Debuts: none.
Man of the Match: J. H. Kallis.   Man of the Series: J. H. Kallis

As he charged down the track to Harris, Inzamam-ul-Haq was scripting a fairytale in his head. Had he connected, the ball would have sailed over the fence, easing the pressure as Pakistan looked to level the series. But he missed by a distance, was embarrassingly stumped, and trudged off the ground where his international career began late in 1991 for the last time. He ended only two runs behind Javed Miandad's Pakistan-record 8,832 (or three excluding his single for the World XI). Inzamam's dismissal, soon after Younis Khan departed after a disciplined century, briefly gave South Africa hope of another win. Shoaib Malik and Mohammad Yousuf stymied that, but Smith was happy with a first series victory on the subcontinent (excluding Bangladesh) since 2000. Pakistan had done well to restrict South Africa to 259 for 7 by the second morning, but with only two tiring fast bowlers they found the tail hard to dislodge. Harris, with 46 from 132 balls, added 88 with Boucher to swell the total, then took two quick wickets as Pakistan slid from 90 without loss to 206 all out, despite playing seven batsmen. They again trailed by more than 150, which effectively sealed the series. Smith had not scored a Test century since April 2005, and his 12th hundred came 17 Tests after his 11th. He started the fourth day with 75, but it took him 90 more deliveries to reach three figures. Kallis added his third hundred of the series before the eventual declaration, 456 ahead.

South Africa

H. H. Gibbs c Misbah-ul-Haq b Umar Gul	13	– (2) c Kamran Akmal b Umar Gul	16
*G. C. Smith b Danish Kaneria	46	– (1) c sub (Yasir Hameed) b Danish Kaneria	133
H. M. Amla b Mohammad Asif	10	– b Abdul Rahman	17
J. H. Kallis lbw b Danish Kaneria	59	– not out	107
A. G. Prince b Abdul Rahman	63	– b Abdul Rahman	11
A. B. de Villiers run out	45	– not out	8
†M. V. Boucher c Abdul Rahman b Danish Kaneria	54		
A. Nel c Misbah-ul-Haq b Umar Gul	0		
P. L. Harris c Shoaib Malik b Umar Gul	46		
D. W. Steyn b Danish Kaneria	0		
M. Ntini not out	0		
L-b 2, w 7, n-b 7, p 5	21	B 12, n-b 1	13

1/24 (1) 2/47 (3) 3/100 (2) 4/160 (4)   357   1/34 (2) 2/66 (3)   (4 wkts dec.) 305
5/243 (5) 6/259 (6) 7/259 (8)   3/273 (1) 4/290 (5)
8/347 (9) 9/350 (10) 10/357 (7)

Mohammad Asif 34–9–83–1; Umar Gul 29–4–103–3; Danish Kaneria 43.1–5–114–4; Abdul Rahman 14–5–30–1; Shoaib Malik 5–0–20–0. *Second Innings*—Mohammad Asif 4–1–14–0; Umar Gul 16–3–48–1; Danish Kaneria 44.3–11–99–1; Abdul Rahman 42–7–112–2; Younis Khan 4–0–20–0.

Pakistan

Salman Butt c Smith b Harris	40	– c sub (S. M. Pollock) b Ntini	6
†Kamran Akmal c Smith b Harris	52	– b Harris	71
Younis Khan b Nel	3	– c Boucher b Kallis	130
Mohammad Yousuf lbw b Steyn	25	– not out	63
Inzamam-ul-Haq c Boucher b Kallis	14	– st Boucher b Harris	3
Misbah-ul-Haq c Boucher b Ntini	41		
*Shoaib Malik c Amla b Steyn	1	– (6) not out	20
Abdul Rahman not out	25		
Umar Gul lbw b Ntini	0		
Danish Kaneria c Boucher b Ntini	0		
Mohammad Asif c Amla b Harris	4		
L-b 1	1	B 3, l-b 14, w 5, n-b 1	23

1/90 (1) 2/93 (3) 3/99 (2) 4/123 (4)   206   1/15 (1) 2/176 (2)   (4 wkts) 316
5/149 (5) 6/150 (7) 7/189 (6)   3/265 (3) 4/272 (5)
8/189 (9) 9/189 (10) 10/206 (11)

Ntini 8–1–42–3; Steyn 12–3–60–2; Nel 16–3–39–1; Harris 20–5–57–3; Kallis 7–3–7–1. *Second Innings*—Steyn 15–2–56–0; Ntini 17–3–60–1; Kallis 15–0–48–1; Nel 20–1–75–0; Harris 40–14–60–2.

Umpires: M. R. Benson *(England)* (17) and S. J. A. Taufel *(Australia)* (45).
Third umpire: Nadeem Ghauri *(Pakistan)*.   Referee: A. G. Hurst *(Australia)* (17).

Close of play: First day, South Africa 259-6 (Boucher 9, Nel 0); Second day, Pakistan 140-4 (Inzamam-ul-Haq 10, Misbah-ul-Haq 10); Third day, South Africa 154-2 (Smith 75, Kallis 37); Fourth day, Pakistan 108-1 (Kamran Akmal 49, Younis Khan 48).

AUSTRALIA v SRI LANKA 2007-08 (1st Test)

At Woolloongabba, Brisbane, on 8, 9, 10, 11, 12 November.
Toss: Sri Lanka.   Result: AUSTRALIA won by an innings and 40 runs.
Debuts: Australia – M. G. Johnson.
Man of the Match: B. Lee.

Mahela Jayawardene decided to bowl first after winning the toss, but ended up on the wrong end of a thumping defeat. Australia gratefully cantered past 500 for the loss of only four wickets against an attack which, apart from Muralitharan, was as predictable as it was pedestrian after Malinga, their fastest bowler, was surprisingly omitted. After a nervous start – his first run came from his 34th ball – Phil Jaques, in his first Test for 19 months, made the most of the opportunity to replace the retired Justin Langer with a solid maiden century, batting for 17 minutes shy of five hours for his even 100. His departure cleared the way for Hussey to share a thrilling partnership of 245 with Clarke, who lasted seven minutes longer than Sri Lanka managed in their entire first innings. Sensing their demoralisation, Ponting enforced the follow-on for only the second time. In the absence of the injured Sangakkara (torn hamstring), only Atapattu in the first innings and Vandort in the second managed half-centuries. Vandort eventually became MacGill's 200th wicket, in his 41st Test – only Clarrie Grimmett (36 matches), Dennis Lillee and Waqar Younis (both 38) reached the landmark more quickly (Ian Botham also did it in 41, but took only four years to MacGill's ten). Lee spearheaded the Australian attack with considerable aplomb, taking four wickets in each innings. The umpires had pre-match troubles: first Steve Bucknor then Aleem Dar encountered visa problems, and were replaced late on by Tony Hill from New Zealand.

Australia

P. A. Jaques st H. A. P. W. Jayawardene b Muralitharan . . 100	A. Symonds not out	53
M. L. Hayden c Muralitharan b Vaas 43	B 4, l-b 12, w 1, n-b 4	21
*R. T. Ponting st H. A. P. W. Jayawardene b Muralitharan .. 56		
M. E. K. Hussey c Atapattu b Fernando. 133	1/69 (2) 2/183 (3)	(4 wkts dec.) 551
M. J. Clarke not out 145	3/216 (1) 4/461 (4)	

†A. C. Gilchrist, B. Lee, M. G. Johnson, S. R. Clark and S. C. G. MacGill did not bat.

Vaas 28–6–102–1; Maharoof 34–6–107–0; Fernando 34–3–130–1; Muralitharan 50–4–170–2; Jayasuriya 4–0–18–0; Samaraweera 1–0–8–0.

Sri Lanka

M. S. Atapattu c Jaques b Johnson	51	– c Gilchrist b Symonds	16
S. T. Jayasuriya c Gilchrist b Lee	7	– c Ponting b Lee.	39
M. G. Vandort c Gilchrist b Lee	0	– b MacGill	82
*D. P. M. D. Jayawardene c Gilchrist b Clark	14	– c Gilchrist b Johnson	49
T. T. Samaraweera c Gilchrist b Johnson	13	– c Hussey b Johnson	20
L. P. C. Silva c Clarke b Clark	40	– c Hussey b Lee	43
†H. A. P. W. Jayawardene lbw b Lee	37	– lbw b Clark	1
M. F. Maharoof b Symonds.	21	– b Lee	18
W. P. U. J. C. Vaas b MacGill	8	– not out	11
C. R. D. Fernando c Johnson b Lee	7	– b Lee	4
M. Muralitharan not out	6	– b Clark.	4
L-b 1, n-b 6	7	B 4, l-b 3, n-b 6	13

1/7 (2) 2/11 (3) 3/45 (4) 4/65 (5)	211	1/53 (1) 2/65 (2) 3/167 (4)	300
5/119 (6) 6/153 (1) 7/181 (8)		4/213 (3) 5/215 (5) 6/226 (7)
8/198 (9) 9/198 (7) 10/211 (10)		7/259 (8) 8/281 (6) 9/290 (10) 10/300 (11)

Lee 17.5–9–26–4; Johnson 18–2–49–2; MacGill 25–5–79–1; Clark 16–4–46–2; Symonds 5–3–10–1. *Second Innings*—Lee 27–7–86–4; Johnson 19–5–47–2; Clark 22.2–3–75–2; Symonds 6–1–21–1; MacGill 25–3–64–1.

Umpires: A. L. Hill *(New Zealand)* (5) and R. E. Koertzen *(South Africa)* (85).
Third umpire: P. D. Parker *(Australia)*.   Referee: M. J. Procter *(South Africa)* (42).

Close of play: First day, Australia 242-3 (Hussey 28, Clarke 5); Second day, Sri Lanka 31-2 (Atapattu 19, D. P. M. D. Jayawardene 5); Third day, Sri Lanka 80-2 (Vandort 15, D. P. M. D. Jayawardene 8); Fourth day, Sri Lanka 218-5 (Silva 5, H. A. P. W. Jayawardene 0).

AUSTRALIA v SRI LANKA 2007-08 (2nd Test)

At Bellerive Oval, Hobart, on 16, 17, 18, 19, 20 November.
Toss: Australia.   Result: AUSTRALIA won by 96 runs.
Debuts: none.
Man of the Match: B. Lee.   Man of the Series: B. Lee.

Australia completed a clean sweep, dominating the match until Sangakkara, fit again, finally made his presence felt. Australia again ran up more than 500; again Jaques and Hussey scored hundreds. Gilchrist became the first to hit 100 sixes in Tests, the landmark one off Muralitharan flying outside the ground. Malinga, recalled in place of the unfortunate Vaas (who, struggling with a shoulder injury, doubted whether he could get through what would have been his 100th Test), was erratic and expensive – but fast. Jayawardene led from the front with a delightful century, his 19th in Tests but his first in ten matches against Australia, but only Sangakkara followed his example in an innings that lasted only 363 minutes – just 34 longer than Jaques was at the crease for his 150. Ponting did not enforce the follow-on this time, and the eventual target was 507. Sri Lanka were well placed at 247 for 3 at the fourth-day close, and for the first time the restructured Australian attack exhibited some nervousness and uncertainty. Atapattu made an authoritative 80 in his last Test innings, but Jayasuriya's departure next morning provided a reality check. Sangakkara motored on, and was only deprived of a seventh double-century – and the distinction of being the first man to reach 200 in three successive Tests – by poor umpiring. Rudi Koertzen decided he had hit a rising delivery from Clark, which deflected from shoulder and helmet before ballooning into the slips. As Ponting prepared to accept the new Warne-Muralitharan Trophy, Koertzen apologised to Sangakkara.

Australia

P. A. Jaques c Fernando b Jayasuriya	150	– c Vandort b Malinga	68
M. L. Hayden c H. A. P. W. Jayawardene b Fernando	17	– lbw b Muralitharan	33
*R. T. Ponting c D. P. M. D. Jayawardene b Muralitharan	31	– not out	53
M. E. K. Hussey lbw b Fernando	132	– not out	34
M. J. Clarke c H. A. P. W. Jayawardene b Malinga	71		
A. Symonds not out	50		
†A. C. Gilchrist not out	67		
B 5, l-b 1, w 1, n-b 17	24	B 2, l-b 1, n-b 19	22

1/48 (2) 2/133 (3) 3/285 (1)   (5 wkts dec.) 542   1/83 (2) 2/154 (1)   (2 wkts dec.) 210
4/410 (4) 5/447 (5)

B. Lee, M. G. Johnson, S. R. Clark and S. C. G. MacGill did not bat.

Malinga 35–6–156–1; Maharoof 23–4–82–0; Fernando 26–4–134–2; Muralitharan 46–4–140–1; Jayasuriya 9–1–24–1. *Second Innings*—Malinga 12–0–61–1; Fernando 12–1–50–0; Muralitharan 20–1–90–1; Jayasuriya 2–0–6–0.

Sri Lanka

M. S. Atapattu c Clarke b Lee	25	– c Jaques b Lee	80
M. G. Vandort b Lee	14	– c sub (R. J. G. Lockyear) b Johnson	4
K. C. Sangakkara c Hussey b Johnson	57	– c Ponting b Clark	192
*D. P. M. D. Jayawardene c Clarke b Lee	104	– b Lee	0
S. T. Jayasuriya b MacGill	3	– c Gilchrist b Lee	45
L. P. C. Silva c Gilchrist b MacGill	4	– c Ponting b Johnson	0
†H. A. P. W. Jayawardene c Gilchrist b Clark	0	– lbw b Johnson	0
M. F. Maharoof run out	19	– c Lee b MacGill	4
C. R. D. Fernando c Gilchrist b Lee	2	– run out	2
S. L. Malinga b Clark	1	– not out	42
M. Muralitharan not out	1	– b Lee	15
L-b 7, n-b 9	16	B 1, l-b 6, w 6, n-b 13	26

1/41 (2) 2/54 (1) 3/127 (3) 4/134 (5)   246   1/15 (2) 2/158 (1) 3/158 (4)   410
5/152 (6) 6/163 (7) 7/196 (8)   4/265 (5) 5/272 (6) 6/272 (7)
8/207 (9) 9/243 (10) 10/246 (4)   7/284 (8) 8/290 (9) 9/364 (3) 10/410 (11)

Lee 23.2–4–82–4; Johnson 17–3–44–1; Clark 16–6–32–2; MacGill 25–5–81–2. *Second Innings*—Lee 26.3–3–87–4; Johnson 28–4–101–3; Clark 24–5–103–1; MacGill 20–1–102–1; Clarke 6–1–10–0.

Umpires: Aleem Dar *(Pakistan)* (40) and R. E. Koertzen *(South Africa)* (86).
Third umpire: P. D. Parker *(Australia)*.   Referee: M. J. Procter *(South Africa)* (43).

Close of play: First day, Australia 329-3 (Hussey 101, Clarke 8); Second day, Sri Lanka 30-0 (Atapattu 18, Vandort 12); Third day, Australia 111-1 (Jaques 53, Ponting 7); Fourth day, Sri Lanka 247-3 (Sangakkara 109, Jayasuriya 33).

337

SOUTH AFRICA v NEW ZEALAND 2007-08 (1st Test)

At The Wanderers, Johannesburg, on 8, 9, 10, 11 November.
Toss: South Africa.   Result: SOUTH AFRICA won by 358 runs.
Debuts: New Zealand – L. R. P. L. Taylor.
Man of the Match: D. W. Steyn.

When South Africa made only 226 after boldly batting first on a threatening pitch featuring both grass and cracks, there was little to suggest that the match was going to produce their largest Test victory – and New Zealand's heaviest defeat – in terms of runs. South Africa's modest innings included a resolute knock from Gibbs, who stayed more than three hours, but New Zealand responded with a dismal display in which no-one managed to survive even 50 balls. Only Fleming looked remotely comfortable against the pacy Steyn, and no-one else passed 15. However, comfort was something Kallis and Amla oozed later, their partnership of 330 making a mockery of the batsmen's struggles in the first day and a half. Kallis was so dominant after reaching his 28th Test hundred with a six off Vettori that Amla, who had matched him that far, was more than 50 adrift by the time his partner was out, having passed 9,000 runs. Their stand was South Africa's highest for any wicket at the Wanderers and, although both Bond and Oram broke down with injuries, they did bowl more than 30 overs between them. Amla stayed there for 511 minutes, over two hours (and 116 balls) longer than Kallis. New Zealand crumbled again in the face of a theoretical target of 531. Stubborn innings from Oram and Vettori – leading by example in his first Test as captain – prolonged the match beyond lunch on the fourth day, but overall Steyn was simply too good and too fast.

South Africa

*G. C. Smith b Martin	1	– (2) b Martin	9
H. H. Gibbs c Fleming b Martin	63	– (1) c Papps b Bond	8
H. M. Amla c McCullum b Bond	12	– not out	176
J. H. Kallis c McCullum b O'Brien	29	– c McCullum b Oram	186
A. G. Prince c Fleming b Bond	1	– not out	25
A. B. de Villiers c Oram b Bond	33		
†M. V. Boucher c Papps b Vettori	43		
A. Nel c McCullum b Bond	15		
P. L. Harris lbw b Vettori	3		
D. W. Steyn c McCullum b Martin	13		
M. Ntini not out	0		
L-b 6, w 1, n-b 6	13	B 9, l-b 7, w 1, n-b 1	18

1/1 (1) 2/20 (3) 3/73 (4) 4/92 (5) 226   1/8 (1) 2/20 (2)   (3 wkts dec.) 422
5/141 (2) 6/162 (6) 7/182 (8)   3/350 (4)
8/195 (9) 9/219 (7) 10/226 (10)

Bond 17–1–73–4; Martin 17.3–3–67–3; Oram 12–3–31–0; O'Brien 10–4–23–1; Vettori 18–6–26–2. *Second Innings*—Bond 16–1–60–1; Martin 24–6–55–1; Oram 16.4–2–49–1; O'Brien 23–5–91–0; Vettori 37–3–116–0; Styris 6–2–25–0; Taylor 3.2–0–10–0.

New Zealand

C. D. Cumming lbw b Steyn	12	– c Smith b Steyn	7
M. H. W. Papps c de Villiers b Ntini	2	– (7) c de Villiers b Kallis	5
S. P. Fleming c de Villiers b Ntini	40	– (2) c Smith b Nel	17
S. E. Bond b Steyn	1	– absent hurt	
S. B. Styris c Smith b Kallis	11	– (3) c Boucher b Steyn	16
L. R. P. L. Taylor c Gibbs b Kallis	15	– (4) c Kallis b Nel	4
J. D. P. Oram c Kallis b Steyn	1	– (6) c Nel b Harris	40
†B. B. McCullum lbw b Steyn	9	– (5) c Gibbs b Steyn	26
*D. L. Vettori c Harris b Ntini	7	– (8) not out	46
I. E. O'Brien not out	14	– (9) c Amla b Steyn	0
C. S. Martin c Harris b Steyn	0	– (10) b Steyn	0
L-b 5, n-b 1	6	B 7, l-b 1, w 2, n-b 1	11

1/16 (2) 2/40 (1) 3/54 (4) 4/64 (3) 118   1/12 (1) 2/34 (2) 3/39 (4)   172
5/83 (5) 6/84 (7) 7/88 (6)   4/60 (3) 5/90 (5) 6/109 (7)
8/102 (9) 9/118 (8) 10/118 (11)   7/154 (6) 8/170 (9) 9/172 (10)

Steyn 14.3–3–34–5; Ntini 14–3–47–3; Nel 9–1–21–0; Kallis 4–0–11–2. *Second Innings*—Steyn 17–1–59–5; Ntini 13–0–42–0; Nel 12–1–37–2; Kallis 3–0–15–1; Harris 6–2–11–1.

Umpires: M. R. Benson *(England)* (18) and D. J. Harper *(Australia)* (66).
Third umpire: M. Erasmus *(South Africa)*.   Referee: J. Srinath *(India)* (5).

Close of play: First day, New Zealand 41-2 (Fleming 22, Bond 0); Second day, South Africa 179-2 (Amla 85, Kallis 76); Third day, New Zealand 57-3 (Styris 16, McCullum 11).

SOUTH AFRICA v NEW ZEALAND 2007-08 (2nd Test)

At Centurion Park, Pretoria, on 16, 17, 18 November.
Toss: New Zealand.   Result: SOUTH AFRICA won by an innings and 59 runs.
Debuts: New Zealand – M. R. Gillespie.
Man of the Match: D. W. Steyn.   Man of the Series: D. W. Steyn.

After humiliating New Zealand in the First Test South Africa added injury to insult in the Second, when Cumming was hospitalised by a wicked bouncer. At 101 for 2, Vettori's decision to bat first was looking a reasonable one before Steyn unleashed a vicious lifter which Cumming unwisely attempted to hook. He was wretchedly late, and the ball smashed into his helmet visor, shattering his cheekbone and jaw, necessitating reconstructive surgery. Effectively, it ended the contest: New Zealand's collective resolve shattered as surely as Cumming's right cheek, and their misery was completed within three days. Kallis and Amla then became the eighth pair to record consecutive Test partnerships of over 200. Kallis hit his fifth hundred in seven innings; his 29th Test century was the quickest and most dominant of his career, coming from just 143 balls, with 95 between lunch and tea on the second day. He also became the first South African to pass 50 in eight successive Tests. Mark Gillespie led a spirited fightback as the final seven wickets tumbled for 101, 51 from a good old-fashioned slog by Steyn and Nel. Gillespie finished with five wickets (but later became only the fourth man to marry such a debut achievement with a pair). But for Fleming's cussed half-century, New Zealand's second innings – which lasted less than 35 overs – would not have sniffed three figures. Steyn collected six more wickets, with another going to Amla's astonishing reflex back-handed flick from short leg to run out the nonplussed Taylor.

New Zealand

C. D. Cumming retired hurt	48	– absent hurt	
M. H. W. Papps c Gibbs b Ntini	9	– lbw b Steyn	1
L. Vincent c Harris b Steyn	33	– (1) lbw b Steyn	4
S. P. Fleming c Prince b Kallis	43	– (3) lbw b Steyn	54
S. B. Styris lbw b Steyn	3	– (4) c de Villiers b Kallis	29
L. R. P. L. Taylor c Prince b Nel	17	– (5) run out	8
†B. B. McCullum c de Villiers b Nel	13	– (6) c Smith b Steyn	21
*D. L. Vettori not out	17	– (7) c de Villiers b Ntini	8
M. R. Gillespie lbw b Steyn	0	– (8) c Kallis b Steyn	0
I. E. O'Brien c Gibbs b Steyn	0	– (9) b Steyn	0
C. S. Martin c Kallis b Ntini	0	– (10) not out	0
L-b 2, n-b 3	5	B 1, l-b 9, n-b 1	11

1/26 (2) 2/88 (3) 3/105 (5) 4/147 (6)   188   1/4 (1) 2/9 (2) 3/69 (4)   136
5/165 (4) 6/184 (7) 7/187 (9)   4/78 (5) 5/117 (3) 6/128 (6)
8/187 (10) 9/188 (11)   7/128 (8) 8/136 (7) 9/136 (9)

In the first innings Cumming retired hurt at 101.

Steyn 14–5–42–4; Ntini 15.4–4–52–2; Kallis 11–2–35–1; Nel 13–3–42–2; Harris 3–0–15–0. *Second Innings—* Steyn 10.3–1–49–6; Ntini 12–4–39–1; Nel 7–2–20–0; Kallis 5–2–18–1.

South Africa

*G. C. Smith b Martin	2	D. W. Steyn c Papps b O'Brien 25
H. H. Gibbs b Martin	25	M. Ntini not out 0
H. M. Amla c Papps b O'Brien	103	
J. H. Kallis lbw b Gillespie	131	B 6, l-b 4, w 2, n-b 13 25
A. G. Prince c sub (J. M. How) b Gillespie	13	
A. B. de Villiers c McCullum b Gillespie	33	1/2 (1) 2/31 (2) 3/251 (4) 4/282 (5) 383
†M. V. Boucher b Gillespie	1	5/312 (3) 6/325 (7) 7/332 (6)
P. L. Harris c McCullum b Gillespie	0	8/332 (8) 9/383 (9) 10/383 (10)
A. Nel lbw b Vettori	25	

Martin 22–6–81–2; Gillespie 30–7–136–5; O'Brien 21.3–6–78–2; Vettori 20–2–61–1; Styris 4–0–17–0.

Umpires: M. R. Benson *(England)* (19) and D. J. Harper *(Australia)* (67).
Third umpire: K. H. Hurter *(South Africa)*.   Referee: J. Srinath *(India)* (6).

Close of play: First day, New Zealand 187-8 (Vettori 16, Martin 0); Second day, South Africa 272-3 (Amla 89, Prince 8).

INDIA v PAKISTAN 2007-08 (1st Test)

At Feroz Shah Kotla, Delhi, on 22, 23, 24, 25, 26 November.
Toss: Pakistan.   Result: INDIA won by six wickets.
Debuts: Pakistan – Sohail Tanvir.
Man of the Match: A. Kumble.

Anil Kumble returned to the scene of his finest hour – his 10 for 88 against Pakistan in 1998-99 – to enjoy a triumphant beginning to his Test-captaincy career. He took seven wickets in what was a tight, seesawing contest . . . until the fourth morning, when Pakistan lost their last five second-innings wickets for just 34 runs. It was India's seventh successive Test victory at Delhi, but the first time they had successfully chased more than 200 there. Pakistan were 142 for 8 before Misbah-ul-Haq put on 87 with Mohammad Sami. Misbah was in sight of a maiden Test century when he played Ganguly to point and set off for a quick single: as he reached the bowler's end he jumped to avoid Karthik's throw, and both his feet were off the ground when the ball hit the stumps. India stuttered to 93 for 5, before Laxman carried them towards a lead. He batted for 245 minutes, and put on 115 with Dhoni. Shoaib Akhtar, in his first Test for ten months, looked reinvigorated after a series of injuries and controversies, and extracted pace and bounce out of a pitch that was sporting, though never quick. Pakistan started the fourth day with a lead of 167, but once Kamran Akmal fell to the day's fifth ball, the rest soon followed, all to poor shots. India had few scares as they overhauled their target of 203. Bad light prevented a four-day finish, but fewer than seven overs were needed on the fifth morning.

Pakistan

Salman Butt b Zaheer Khan	1	– c Dravid b Kumble		67
Yasir Hameed b Kumble	29	– c Laxman b Kumble		36
Younis Khan c Patel b Zaheer Khan	7	– lbw b Kumble		23
Mohammad Yousuf lbw b Ganguly	27	– c and b Harbhajan Singh		18
Misbah-ul-Haq run out	82	– (7) c Karthik b Ganguly		45
*Shoaib Malik c Dhoni b Patel	0	– (5) b Harbhajan Singh		11
†Kamran Akmal b Kumble	30	– (6) c sub (Yuvraj Singh) b Zaheer Khan		21
Sohail Tanvir lbw b Harbhajan Singh	4	– c Harbhajan Singh b Zaheer Khan		13
Shoaib Akhtar b Kumble	2	– (10) not out		0
Mohammad Sami not out	28	– (9) c Wasim Jaffer b Ganguly		5
Danish Kaneria b Kumble	0	– run out		0
B 6, l-b 12, w 2, n-b 1	21	L-b 6, n-b 2		8

1/13 (1) 2/35 (3) 3/59 (2) 4/76 (4)   231
5/83 (6) 6/122 (7) 7/137 (8)
8/142 (9) 9/229 (5) 10/231 (11)

1/71 (2) 2/114 (3) 3/149 (4)   247
4/155 (1) 5/161 (5) 6/213 (6)
7/229 (8) 8/243 (7) 9/247 (9) 10/247 (11)

Zaheer Khan 20–5–45–2; Patel 24–5–61–1; Kumble 21.2–6–38–4; Ganguly 14–5–28–1; Harbhajan Singh 15–1–37–1; Tendulkar 2–0–4–0. *Second Innings*—Zaheer Khan 18–4–45–2; Patel 10–2–48–0; Kumble 27.1–8–68–3; Ganguly 9–2–20–2; Harbhajan Singh 17–4–56–2; Tendulkar 2–0–4–0.

India

Wasim Jaffer lbw b Shoaib Akhtar	32	– (2) c Salman Butt b Shoaib Akhtar		53
K. D. Karthik c Kamran Akmal b Shoaib Akhtar	9	– (1) c Kamran Akmal b Shoaib Akhtar		1
R. Dravid b Sohail Tanvir	38	– b Shoaib Akhtar		34
S. R. Tendulkar run out	1	– not out		56
S. C. Ganguly b Sohail Tanvir	8	– c Sohail Tanvir b Shoaib Akhtar		48
V. V. S. Laxman not out	72	– not out		6
†M. S. Dhoni c Kamran Akmal b Danish Kaneria	57			
*A. Kumble c Younis Khan b Danish Kaneria	24			
Harbhajan Singh b Sohail Tanvir	1			
Zaheer Khan c Shoaib Akhtar b Danish Kaneria	9			
M. M. Patel lbw b Danish Kaneria	0			
B 11, l-b 8, w 1, n-b 5	25	B 1, l-b 3, n-b 1		5

1/15 (2) 2/71 (1) 3/73 (4) 4/88 (5)   276
5/93 (3) 6/208 (7) 7/262 (8)
8/263 (9) 9/276 (10) 10/276 (11)

1/2 (1) 2/84 (2)   (4 wkts) 203
3/93 (3) 4/181 (5)

Shoaib Akhtar 16–2–44–2; Sohail Tanvir 24–5–83–3; Mohammad Sami 17–1–71–0; Danish Kaneria 21.4–3–59–4. *Second Innings*—Shoaib Akhtar 18.1–4–58–4; Sohail Tanvir 12–4–26–0; Danish Kaneria 16–2–50–0; Mohammad Sami 15–1–65–0.

Umpires: B. R. Doctrove *(West Indies)* (14) and S. J. A. Taufel *(Australia)* (46).
Third umpire: S. L. Shastri *(India)*.   Referee: R. S. Madugalle *(Sri Lanka)* (98).

Close of play: First day, Pakistan 210-8 (Misbah-ul-Haq 71, Mohammad Sami 20); Second day, India 228-6 (Laxman 57, Kumble 7); Third day, Pakistan 212-5 (Kamran Akmal 21, Misbah-ul-Haq 29); Fourth day, India 171-3 (Tendulkar 32, Ganguly 48).

INDIA v PAKISTAN 2007-08 (2nd Test)

At Eden Gardens, Kolkata, on 30 November, 1, 2, 3, 4 December.
Toss: India.   Result: MATCH DRAWN.
Debuts: none.
Man of the Match: Wasim Jaffer.

Sourav Ganguly had passed 50 just once in seven previous Tests at Eden Gardens but now, with his place under pressure, he delivered his first hundred on his home ground. The single to mid-off from Danish Kaneria that took the "Prince of Kolkata" to three figures produced the loudest roar of the match. Wasim Jaffer batted with rare freedom for his second Test double-century, hitting 34 fours, half of them off the left-arm medium-pacer Sohail Tanvir. With Laxman also making a hundred, India declared at 616, their second-highest total against Pakistan, who had personnel problems: Shoaib Malik had twisted his ankle playing football, so Younis Khan captained. Shoaib Akhtar had recently spent a night in hospital with a chest infection, while Mohammad Sami had flu. When they dipped to 150 for 5, 466 behind, defeat seemed certain, but Misbah-ul-Haq (dropped when 22 by Tendulkar at midwicket) and Kamran Akmal (dropped on 87 by Patel at fine leg) put on 207 to kick-start a recovery. Misbah finally reached the maiden Test century he missed at Delhi because of a freak run-out, and proved that, even at 33, he was one for the future. Akmal's hundred was his fifth in Tests and his fourth against India, three of them coming in a crisis. Pakistan needed to survive for most of the final day after India set them 345, but although the dipped to 78 for 4 there were few alarms on a placid pitch once Younis and Mohammad Yousuf settled in.

India

Wasim Jaffer c Kamran Akmal b Sohail Tanvir	202	– b Danish Kaneria 56
K. D. Karthik c Younis Khan b Sohail Tanvir	1	– c Misbah-ul-Haq b Danish Kaneria 28
R. Dravid c Kamran Akmal b Danish Kaneria	50	– (5) not out 8
S. R. Tendulkar b Danish Kaneria	82	
S. C. Ganguly c Sohail Tanvir b Salman Butt	102	– (4) b Shoaib Akhtar 46
V. V. S. Laxman not out	112	
†M. S. Dhoni not out	50	– (3) b Shoaib Akhtar 37
B 8, l-b 5, w 1, n-b 3	17	L-b 3, n-b 6 9

1/2 (2) 2/138 (3) 3/313 (4)   (5 wkts dec.) 616   1/75 (2) 2/95 (1)   (4 wkts dec.) 184
4/375 (1) 5/538 (5)   3/166 (3) 4/184 (4)

*A. Kumble, Harbhajan Singh, Zaheer Khan and M. M. Patel did not bat.

Shoaib Akhtar 24–2–84–0; Sohail Tanvir 39–6–166–2; Mohammad Sami 29–2–99–0; Danish Kaneria 50–7–194–2; Yasir Hameed 4–0–24–0; Salman Butt 6.5–0–36–1. *Second Innings*—Shoaib Akhtar 12.4–0–46–2; Sohail Tanvir 9–0–41–0; Mohammad Sami 5–1–28–0; Danish Kaneria 15–0–61–2; Salman Butt 1–0–5–0.

Pakistan

Salman Butt c Dravid b Harbhajan Singh	42	– (3) lbw b Kumble 11
Yasir Hameed lbw b Kumble	21	– (1) c and b Zaheer Khan 14
*Younis Khan c Dhoni b Patel	43	– (4) not out 107
Mohammad Yousuf b Harbhajan Singh	6	– (6) not out 44
Misbah-ul-Haq not out	161	– b Patel 6
Faisal Iqbal lbw b Kumble	0	
†Kamran Akmal b Harbhajan Singh	119	– (2) b Kumble 14
Mohammad Sami c Wasim Jaffer b Laxman	38	
Sohail Tanvir c Dravid b Kumble	0	
Shoaib Akhtar c Dravid b Harbhajan Singh	0	
Danish Kaneria b Harbhajan Singh	0	
B 8, l-b 7, w 1, n-b 10	26	B 8, l-b 6, n-b 4 18

1/38 (2) 2/77 (1) 3/85 (4) 4/134 (3)   456   1/22 (1) 2/37 (2)   (4 wkts) 214
5/150 (6) 6/357 (7) 7/448 (8)   3/65 (3) 4/78 (5)
8/449 (9) 9/452 (10) 10/456 (11)

Zaheer Khan 25.2–8–69–0; Patel 21–4–85–1; Harbhajan Singh 45.5–9–122–5; Kumble 47–14–122–3; Tendulkar 7–1–32–0; Ganguly 4–1–9–0; Laxman 1–0–2–1. *Second Innings*—Zaheer Khan 8–0–32–1; Kumble 25–4–73–2; Patel 10–3–21–1; Harbhajan Singh 31–5–67–0; Tendulkar 3–0–7–0.

Umpires: B. R. Doctrove *(West Indies)* (15) and R. E. Koertzen *(South Africa)* (87).
A. M. Saheba replaced Doctrove on the fourth day.
Third umpire: A. M. Saheba *(India)*.   Referee: R. S. Madugalle *(Sri Lanka)* (99).

Close of play: First day, India 352-3 (Wasim Jaffer 192, Ganguly 17); Second day, Pakistan 50-1 (Salman Butt 26, Younis Khan 3); Third day, Pakistan 358-6 (Misbah-ul-Haq 108, Mohammad Sami 0); Fourth day, India 141-2 (Dhoni 28, Ganguly 24).

INDIA v PAKISTAN 2007-08 (3rd Test)

At Chinnaswamy Stadium, Bangalore, on 8, 9, 10, 11, 12 December.
Toss: India.   Result: MATCH DRAWN.
Debuts: Pakistan – Yasir Arafat.
Man of the Match: S. C. Ganguly.   Man of the Series: S. C. Ganguly.

India completed their first home Test series win over Pakistan since 1979-80, though the 1–0 scoreline might have been more emphatic but for Kumble's conservative leadership. He prolonged India's second innings midway into the final afternoon before setting Pakistan 374 or, more realistically, allowing only 47 overs to bowl them out. Pakistan seemed to be coasting to safety, but lost four wickets in as many overs and were thankful that bad light ended play 11 overs early. On a cracked pitch where the ball often squatted, Kumble had reverted to medium-pace (which he bowled before converting to leg-spin) and claimed the first five wickets, before Yuvraj Singh added a further two on his birthday, leaving Kumble ruing his delayed closure. Earlier, Yasir Arafat reduced India to 61 for 4, but then Ganguly made his only double-century, in his 99th Test: he put on 300 with Yuvraj, who hit his third Test hundred – all against Pakistan – in his first Test in 18 months (replacing Tendulkar, resting a knee injury ahead of the upcoming Australian tour). Pathan further caned a weakened attack – Shoaib Akhtar limped off with back spasms – to reach his first Test century with his fourth six, as India improved their highest total at home to Pakistan for the second match running. Pakistan batted resolutely to save the follow-on, although they were teetering before Misbah-ul-Haq and Kamran Akmal put on 144. They were helped by 76 extras, beating the 71 conceded by West Indies against Pakistan at Georgetown in 1987-88.

India

Wasim Jaffer lbw b Yasir Arafat	17	– lbw b Yasir Arafat		18
G. Gambhir c Kamran Akmal b Mohammad Sami	5	– b Shoaib Akhtar		3
R. Dravid c Misbah-ul-Haq b Yasir Arafat	19	– lbw b Danish Kaneria		42
S. C. Ganguly b Danish Kaneria	239	– c Faisal Iqbal b Mohammad Sami		91
V. V. S. Laxman b Yasir Arafat	5	– retired hurt		14
Yuvraj Singh c Faisal Iqbal b Mohammad Sami	169	– c Kamran Akmal b Mohammad Sami		2
†K. D. Karthik c Kamran Akmal b Yasir Arafat	24	– c Kamran Akmal b Yasir Arafat		52
I. K. Pathan c Kamran Akmal b Danish Kaneria	102	– not out		21
*A. Kumble lbw b Danish Kaneria	4			
Harbhajan Singh b Yasir Arafat	4			
I. Sharma not out	0			
B 13, l-b 19, n-b 6	38	B 9, l-b 24, w 1, n-b 7		41

1/8 (2) 2/44 (3) 3/51 (1) 4/61 (5)   626   1/17 (2) 2/26 (1)   (6 wkts dec.) 284
5/361 (6) 6/427 (7) 7/605 (4)   3/178 (3) 4/178 (4)
8/615 (9) 9/620 (10) 10/626 (8)   5/184 (6) 6/284 (7)

In the second innings Laxman retired hurt at 225.

Shoaib Akhtar 10–3–23–0; Mohammad Sami 36–5–149–2; Yasir Arafat 39–5–161–5; Danish Kaneria 46.2–8–168–3; Younis Khan 2–0–14–0; Salman Butt 10–1–36–0; Yasir Hameed 7–0–43–0. *Second Innings*—Shoaib Akhtar 17–6–43–1; Mohammad Sami 20–2–63–2; Yasir Arafat 13.3–3–49–2; Danish Kaneria 26–2–96–1.

Pakistan

Salman Butt c Karthik b Ganguly	68	– c Karthik b Kumble		8
Yasir Hameed lbw b Kumble	19	– b Kumble		39
*Younis Khan b Harbhajan Singh	80	– c and b Kumble		0
Mohammad Yousuf c Yuvraj Singh b Pathan	24	– (7) not out		10
Misbah-ul-Haq not out	133	– b Yuvraj Singh		37
Faisal Iqbal c Gambhir b Sharma	22	– (4) c Sharma b Kumble		51
†Kamran Akmal st Karthik b Harbhajan Singh	65	– (6) b Kumble		0
Yasir Arafat b Sharma	44	– b Yuvraj Singh		0
Mohammad Sami b Sharma	1	– not out		4
Shoaib Akhtar c Gambhir b Sharma	1			
Danish Kaneria c and b Sharma	4			
B 35, l-b 26, n-b 15	76	B 12, l-b 1		13

1/59 (2) 2/149 (1) 3/221 (3) 4/227 (4)   537   1/44 (2) 2/44 (3)   (7 wkts) 162
5/288 (6) 6/432 (7) 7/525 (8)   3/73 (1) 4/144 (4)
8/527 (9) 9/529 (10) 10/537 (11)   5/144 (6) 6/148 (5) 7/154 (8)

Pathan 37–14–80–1; Sharma 33.1–10–118–5; Kumble 44–12–116–1; Ganguly 10–2–20–1; Harbhajan Singh 38–7–131–2; Yuvraj Singh 6–2–11–0. *Second Innings*—Pathan 7–4–30–0; Sharma 6–3–22–0; Kumble 14–2–60–5; Harbhajan Singh 6–1–28–0; Yuvraj Singh 3–0–9–2.

Umpires: R. E. Koertzen *(South Africa)* (88) and S. J. A. Taufel *(Australia)* (47).
Third umpire: G. A. Pratapkumar *(India)*.   Referee: R. S. Madugalle *(Sri Lanka)* (100).

Close of play: First day, India 365-5 (Ganguly 125, Karthik 3); Second day, Pakistan 86-1 (Salman Butt 50, Younis Khan 7); Third day, Pakistan 369-5 (Misbah-ul-Haq 54, Kamran Akmal 32); Fourth day, India 131-2 (Dravid 35, Ganguly 63).

SRI LANKA v ENGLAND 2007-08 (1st Test)

At Asgiriya Stadium, Kandy, on 1, 2, 3, 4, 5 December.
Toss: Sri Lanka.   Result: SRI LANKA won by 88 runs.
Debuts: England – R. S. Bopara.
Man of the Match: K. C. Sangakkara.

Muttiah Muralitharan and Kumar Sangakkara, two great cricketing sons of Kandy, were the matchwinners in a classically fluctuating Test, in which England came within 20 minutes of saving a game they had controlled until Vaughan was given out caught off his pad on the second morning. It was Murali's first wicket; he later passed Shane Warne's Test record of 708, when Collingwood was deceived by some extra bounce. The other senior players all made important contributions. Sangakkara extended his amazing run since handing the wicketkeeping gloves to Prasanna Jayawardene to 1,529 in 14 innings; Jayasuriya, in his 110th and final Test – he announced his retirement mid-match – led the second-innings recovery, hitting six fours in an Anderson over; Mahela Jayawardene helped turn recovery into control; and Vaas, in his 100th Test, twice took Cook's wicket in the first over. Hoggard's back injury – after a superb opening spell of four for 21 in ten overs – left England without the necessary penetration to follow up a first-innings lead of 91, which should have been decisive. Jayasuriya signed off with 78, then Sangakkara took command, completing his nap hand of centuries against all nine opponents, and also became the first to reach 150 in four consecutive Tests. England were set 350 in just over a day. Bell looked in control for five hours, and Prior batted calmly through 44 overs, but Murali eventually removed both in the space of three balls. Finally, Malinga's searing yorker removed the incapacitated Hoggard to seal victory with six overs remaining.

Sri Lanka

M. G. Vandort c Vaughan b Hoggard	8	– c Bell b Anderson	49
S. T. Jayasuriya c Pietersen b Sidebottom	10	– lbw b Hoggard	78
K. C. Sangakkara c Collingwood b Anderson	92	– c Vaughan b Collingwood	152
*D. P. M. D. Jayawardene c Prior b Hoggard	1	– c Prior b Hoggard	65
L. P. C. Silva c Prior b Hoggard	2	– lbw b Panesar	37
J. Mubarak c Prior b Hoggard	0	– c sub (G. P. Swann) b Panesar	9
†H. A. P. W. Jayawardene c Cook b Panesar	51	– b Collingwood	20
W. P. U. J. C. Vaas b Panesar	12	– not out	6
C. R. D. Fernando c Vaughan b Panesar	0	– (10) not out	9
S. L. Malinga not out	1	– (9) b Panesar	2
M. Muralitharan run out	1		
L-b 8, n-b 2	10	B 5, l-b 10	15

1/11 (2) 2/29 (1) 3/40 (4) 4/42 (5)   188   1/113 (2) 2/166 (1)   (8 wkts dec.) 442
5/42 (6) 6/148 (7) 7/180 (8)   3/288 (4) 4/359 (5)
8/182 (9) 9/186 (3) 10/188 (11)   5/387 (6) 6/423 (7) 7/426 (3) 8/429 (9)

Sidebottom 15–1–58–1; Hoggard 14–3–29–4; Anderson 15.4–3–39–1; Bopara 1–0–8–0; Panesar 14–4–46–3. *Second Innings*—Hoggard 18–5–55–2; Sidebottom 25–5–65–0; Panesar 45–5–132–3; Anderson 23–4–128–1; Bopara 8–3–16–0; Vaughan 3–0–6–0; Collingwood 8–0–25–2.

England

A. N. Cook lbw b Vaas	0	– c Silva b Vaas	4
*M. P. Vaughan c Silva b Muralitharan	37	– c H. A. P. W. Jayawardene b Vaas	5
I. R. Bell c Silva b Muralitharan	83	– (4) b Muralitharan	74
K. P. Pietersen lbw b Muralitharan	31	– (5) b Fernando	18
P. D. Collingwood b Muralitharan	45	– (6) c Sangakkara b Fernando	16
R. S. Bopara c H. A. P. W. Jayawardene b Muralitharan	8	– (7) lbw b Jayasuriya	34
†M. J. Prior c Mubarak b Fernando	0	– (8) b Muralitharan	63
R. J. Sidebottom c H. A. P. W. Jayawardene b Malinga	31	– (9) lbw b Muralitharan	1
M. J. Hoggard st H. A. P. W. Jayawardene b Muralitharan	15	– (10) b Malinga	8
J. M. Anderson lbw b Vaas	9	– (3) b Vaas	11
M. S. Panesar not out	2	– not out	2
B 6, l-b 1, w 2, n-b 11	20	B 5, l-b 9, n-b 11	25

1/0 (1) 2/107 (2) 3/132 (3) 4/170 (4)   281   1/4 (1) 2/22 (2) 3/27 (3)   261
5/182 (6) 6/185 (7) 7/242 (8)   4/55 (5) 5/90 (6) 6/139 (7)
8/266 (5) 9/272 (9) 10/281 (10)   7/248 (8) 8/249 (4) 9/253 (9) 10/261 (10)

Vaas 18.1–3–76–2; Malinga 20–2–86–1; Muralitharan 35–14–55–6; Jayasuriya 2–0–9–0; Fernando 18–2–48–1. *Second Innings*—Vaas 17–3–56–3; Malinga 15–3–39–1; Muralitharan 36–12–85–3; Jayasuriya 14–6–28–1; Fernando 12–1–39–2.

Umpires: Aleem Dar *(Pakistan)* (41) and Asad Rauf *(Pakistan)* (14).
Third umpire: T. H. Wijewardene *(Sri Lanka)*.   Referee: J. J. Crowe *(New Zealand)* (21).

Close of play: First day, England 49-1 (Vaughan 13, Bell 36); Second day, England 186-6 (Collingwood 14, Sidebottom 1); Third day, Sri Lanka 167-2 (Sangakkara 30, D. P. M. D. Jayawardene 0); Fourth day, England 9-1 (Vaughan 1, Anderson 4).

SRI LANKA v ENGLAND 2007-08 (2nd Test)

At Sinhalese Sports Club, Colombo, on 9, 10, 11, 12, 13 December.
Toss: England.   Result: MATCH DRAWN.
Debuts: England – S. C. J. Broad.
Man of the Match: D. P. M. D. Jayawardene.

A lifeless, grey pitch produced a game to match. Much of the cricket was instantly forgettable, but the Test did not pass without some exceptional performances and a controversial incident. Muralitharan claimed the 62nd five-wicket haul of his remarkable career in England's first-innings 351. He came on with the Test only 11 overs old, and bowled 48 of the next 116, changing ends five times. Vaughan and Cook shared England's first century opening partnership in 15 Tests; they followed up with another to ensure the draw on the final day. Vaughan was fortuitously caught when short leg somehow trapped a flick off the hips between his legs, and later, after a juggling act between Silva at second slip and Sangakkara at first, Pietersen was given out after returning from near the boundary to query the validity of the catch. Vandort played his best Test innings to date, his fourth hundred and second against England. He coped well with a barrage of short-pitched bowling from a rejuvenated Harmison, who returned to England colours alongside the debutant Stuart Broad, the son of the former England batsman (and current match referee) Chris. Mahela Jayawardene's delightful 195 set up a first-innings lead of 197. At 110, he became Sri Lanka's highest Test run-scorer, overtaking the just-retired Sanath Jayasuriya's 6,973. Then, as he went past 150 with a lofted six off the labouring Panesar, he reached 2,019 runs at the Sinhalese Sports Club, a record for a single ground, beating Graham Gooch's 2,015 at Lord's.

England

A. N. Cook lbw b Malinga	81	– c D. P. M. D. Jayawardene b Silva	62
*M. P. Vaughan c Mubarak b Muralitharan	87	– c and b Fernando	61
I. R. Bell c Mubarak b Muralitharan	15	– c Vandort b Muralitharan	54
K. P. Pietersen c Sangakkara b Vaas	1	– not out	45
P. D. Collingwood lbw b Vaas	52	– not out	23
R. S. Bopara b Malinga	0		
†M. J. Prior c and b Muralitharan	79		
S. C. J. Broad lbw b Malinga	2		
R. J. Sidebottom c D. P. M. D. Jayawardene b Muralitharan	17		
S. J. Harmison c Silva b Muralitharan	0		
M. S. Panesar not out	0		
B 8, l-b 2, n-b 7	17	N-b 5	5

1/133 (2) 2/168 (3) 3/171 (4) 4/237 (1)   351   1/107 (2) 2/152 (1)   (3 wkts) 250
5/237 (6) 6/269 (5) 7/272 (8)   3/204 (3)
8/346 (9) 9/350 (10) 10/351 (7)

Vaas 32–8–68–2; Malinga 24–3–78–3; Fernando 23–3–79–0; Muralitharan 47.2–9–116–5. *Second Innings*—Vaas 16–2–56–0; Malinga 8–1–37–0; Fernando 10–0–30–1; Mubarak 1–0–8–0; Muralitharan 27–5–58–1; D. P. M. D. Jayawardene 2–1–4–0; Silva 13–1–57–1.

Sri Lanka

M. G. Vandort lbw b Sidebottom	138	S. L. Malinga lbw b Panesar	9
W. U. Tharanga c Prior b Sidebottom	10	C. R. D. Fernando not out	36
K. C. Sangakkara c Prior b Sidebottom	1	B 7, l-b 9, w 1, n-b 1	18
*D. P. M. D. Jayawardene c Collingwood b Panesar	195		
L. P. C. Silva c Bopara b Harmison	49	1/20 (2) 2/22 (3) (9 wkts dec.) 548	
J. Mubarak c Bell b Harmison	9	3/249 (1) 4/377 (5)	
†H. A. P. W. Jayawardene c Prior b Harmison	79	5/399 (6) 6/420 (4) 7/425 (8)	
W. P. U. J. C. Vaas c Bell b Broad	4	8/450 (9) 9/548 (7)	

M. Muralitharan did not bat.

Sidebottom 36–4–100–3; Broad 36–5–95–1; Harmison 41.5–9–111–3; Panesar 50–7–151–2; Pietersen 15–0–57–0; Collingwood 1–1–0–0; Bopara 7–2–18–0.

Umpires: Aleem Dar *(Pakistan)* (42) and D. J. Harper *(Australia)* (68).
Third umpire: M. G. Silva *(Sri Lanka).*   Referee: J. J. Crowe *(New Zealand)* (22).

Close of play: First day, England 258-5 (Collingwood 49, Prior 10); Second day, Sri Lanka 105-2 (Vandort 50, D. P. M. D. Jayawardene 43); Third day, Sri Lanka 379-4 (D. P. M. D. Jayawardene 167, Mubarak 2); Fourth day, England 48-0 (Cook 19, Vaughan 28).

SRI LANKA v ENGLAND 2007-08 (3rd Test)

At Galle International Stadium on 18, 19, 20, 21, 22 December.
Toss: England.   Result: MATCH DRAWN.
Debuts: Sri Lanka – U. W. M. B. C. A. Welagedara.
Man of the Match: D. P. M. D. Jayawardene.   Man of the Series: D. P. M. D. Jayawardene.

This was the first Test to be played at Galle since the 2004 Boxing Day tsunami which devastated the region. Four days before the start, the game looked in the balance: torrential rain had flooded the outfield, hampering preparations within and beyond the boundary. In the end nothing could prevent an emotional occasion which seemed to inspire Mahela Jayawardene, who hit an exquisite double-century, and his team. However, there were just enough interruptions for England to escape with a draw, despite being bundled out for 81. Oddly, the two matches in the series in which England were outplayed ended in draws, while the one which was much more evenly contested brought them defeat. At the end of an abbreviated first day Sri Lanka, put in, were 147 for 4, but Jayawardene then grabbed control, batting 610 minutes and hitting 25 fours. Prior missed three catches – Jayawardene twice and Dilshan – in a match he would prefer to forget. When the declaration finally came, England were physically shattered and mentally numb. Even so, there was no real excuse for a spineless batting display on a blameless surface: they staggered to lunch at 24 for 4, and were bundled out inside 31 overs. Before the final storm descended, Cook became only the fourth player to make seven Test centuries before turning 23, following a distinguished trio: Don Bradman, Javed Miandad and Sachin Tendulkar. England stuttered when three wickets went down in the 65th over, one of them a schoolboyish run-out as Bopara completed a pair.

Sri Lanka

M. G. Vandort lbw b Sidebottom	18	W. P. U. J. C. Vaas c Vaughan b Hoggard	90
W. U. Tharanga lbw b Harmison	16	S. L. Malinga b Collingwood	5
K. C. Sangakkara c Panesar b Harmison	46	B 1, l-b 14, w 8, n-b 3	26
*D. P. M. D. Jayawardene not out	213		
L. P. C. Silva c Bell b Harmison	1	1/34 (1) 2/44 (2)	(8 wkts dec.) 499
T. M. Dilshan run out	84	3/132 (3) 4/138 (5)	
†H. A. P. W. Jayawardene c Prior b Bopara .	0	5/287 (6) 6/287 (7) 7/470 (8) 8/499 (9)	

U. W. M. B. C. A. Welagedara and M. Muralitharan did not bat.

Sidebottom 34–8–95–1; Hoggard 32–4–121–1; Harmison 34–4–104–3; Panesar 26–3–76–0; Bopara 10–1–39–1; Collingwood 9.5–2–38–1; Pietersen 3–0–11–0.

England

A. N. Cook c H. A. P. W. Jayawardene b Vaas	13	– c H. A. P. W. Jayawardene b Welagedara	118
*M. P. Vaughan lbw b Vaas	1	– c D. P. M. D. Jayawardene b Welagedara	24
I. R. Bell run out	1	– b Muralitharan	34
K. P. Pietersen c H. A. P. W. Jayawardene b Malinga	1	– c D. P. M. D. Jayawardene b Muralitharan	30
P. D. Collingwood b Welagedara	29	– st H. A. P. W. Jayawardene b Muralitharan	0
R. S. Bopara c Welagedara b Vaas	0	– run out	0
†M. J. Prior b Vaas	4	– not out	19
R. J. Sidebottom c Dilshan b Muralitharan	11	– not out	0
S. J. Harmison not out	9		
M. J. Hoggard c D. P. M. D. Jayawardene b Welagedara .	0		
M. S. Panesar run out	0		
B 4, n-b 8	12	B 6, l-b 5, w 1, n-b 14	26
	81		(6 wkts) 251

1/5 (2) 2/9 (3) 3/22 (1) 4/22 (4)   81   1/67 (2) 2/128 (3)   (6 wkts) 251
5/25 (6) 6/33 (7) 7/70 (8)   3/200 (4) 4/200 (5)
8/72 (5) 9/72 (10) 10/81 (11)   5/200 (6) 6/250 (1)

Vaas 9.5–2–28–4; Malinga 9–2–26–1; Welagedara 8–1–17–2; Muralitharan 4–2–6–1. *Second Innings*—Muralitharan 38–8–91–3; Vaas 18–7–37–0; Malinga 20–3–42–0; Welagedara 14–1–59–2; Dilshan 3–1–8–0; Silva 2–1–3–0.

Umpires: Asad Rauf *(Pakistan)* (15) and D. J. Harper *(Australia)* (69).
Third umpire: E. A. R. de Silva *(Sri Lanka)*.   Referee: J. J. Crowe *(New Zealand)* (23).

Close of play: First day, Sri Lanka 147-4 (D. P. M. D. Jayawardene 51, Dilshan 7); Second day, Sri Lanka 384-6 (D. P. M. D. Jayawardene 149, Vaas 46); Third day, England 2-0 (Cook 1, Vaughan 1); Fourth day, England 102-1 (Cook 53, Bell 17).

AUSTRALIA v INDIA 2007-08 (1st Test)

At Melbourne Cricket Ground on 26, 27, 28, 29 December.
Toss: Australia.   Result: AUSTRALIA won by 337 runs.
Debuts: none.
Man of the Match: M. L. Hayden.

After fighting back impressively on the first day, when they took six wickets after tea, India effectively lost the match on the second, when they collapsed against some suffocatingly disciplined bowling. After Ponting declared 498 ahead, India were bowled out for under 200 again as Australia won their ninth successive Test at the MCG, in the 100th match played there. Watched by a Boxing Day crowd of 68,778, Australia surged to 135 before Jaques fell in the 34th over, but some top-class bowling from Kumble pegged them back. Hayden made his sixth hundred in his last seven Tests at Melbourne; it was his 19th on Australian soil (Don Bradman made 18, as had Ponting at the time). India started slowly: Wasim Jaffer faced 27 balls for 4, and Dravid took 41 to get off the mark. Tendulkar counter-attacked thrillingly, targeting Hogg, playing his first Test for more than four years, but when he bottom-edged a cut – the first of three wickets in 12 balls for Clark – a terminal decline set in, during which Lee became the sixth Australian to take 250 Test wickets. Of several useful contributions in Australia's second innings, Clarke's 73 was the best, and Symonds's 44 the most punishing. India, in contrast, crawled along on the fourth day. Gilchrist caught Jaffer, his 396th Test victim to beat Ian Healy's Australian record, and wickets fell regularly against tight bowling and imaginative field placings. Dravid ground out 16 from 114 balls before Symonds beat him with a big off-break.

Australia

P. A. Jaques st Dhoni b Kumble	66	– c and b Kumble	51
M. L. Hayden c Dravid b Zaheer Khan	124	– c Ganguly b Harbhajan Singh	47
*R. T. Ponting b Zaheer Khan	4	– c Dravid b Harbhajan Singh	3
M. E. K. Hussey lbw b Kumble	2	– c Tendulkar b R. P. Singh	36
M. J. Clarke c Laxman b R. P. Singh	20	– st Dhoni b Kumble	73
A. Symonds c sub (K. D. Karthik) b Kumble	35	– lbw b Zaheer Khan	44
†A. C. Gilchrist c Tendulkar b Kumble	23	– c R. P. Singh b Harbhajan Singh	35
G. B. Hogg c Dravid b Zaheer Khan	17	– not out	35
B. Lee lbw b Kumble	0	– not out	11
M. G. Johnson not out	15		
S. R. Clark c Harbhajan Singh b Zaheer Khan	21		
L-b 5, w 2, n-b 9	16	L-b 3, n-b 13	16

1/135 (1) 2/162 (3) 3/165 (4) 4/225 (5)   343   1/83 (2) 2/89 (3)   (7 wkts dec.) 351
5/241 (2) 6/281 (6) 7/288 (7)   3/139 (1) 4/161 (4)
8/294 (9) 9/312 (8) 10/343 (11)   5/243 (6) 6/288 (5) 7/316 (7)

Zaheer Khan 23.4–1–94–4; R. P. Singh 20–3–82–1; Harbhajan Singh 20–3–61–0; Ganguly 3–1–15–0; Kumble 25–4–84–5; Tendulkar 1–0–2–0. *Second Innings*—Zaheer Khan 20–2–93–1; R. P. Singh 16–1–50–1; Kumble 25–2–102–2; Harbhajan Singh 26–0–101–3; Tendulkar 1–0–2–0.

India

Wasim Jaffer c Gilchrist b Lee	4	– (2) c Gilchrist b Lee	15
R. Dravid lbw b Clark	5	– (1) lbw b Symonds	16
V. V. S. Laxman c Ponting b Lee	26	– c Clarke b Clark	42
S. R. Tendulkar b Clark	62	– c Gilchrist b Lee	15
S. C. Ganguly b Hogg	43	– c Ponting b Hogg	40
Yuvraj Singh c Gilchrist b Clark	0	– lbw b Hogg	5
†M. S. Dhoni lbw b Clark	0	– c Gilchrist b Johnson	11
*A. Kumble c Gilchrist b Lee	27	– c Gilchrist b Johnson	8
Harbhajan Singh c Clarke b Hogg	11	– run out	0
Zaheer Khan c Gilchrist b Lee	11	– not out	0
R. P. Singh not out	2	– b Johnson	2
B 4, l-b 3, n-b 7	14	B 1, n-b 6	7

1/4 (1) 2/31 (2) 3/55 (3) 4/120 (4)   196   1/26 (2) 2/54 (1) 3/77 (4)   161
5/122 (6) 6/122 (7) 7/166 (5)   4/118 (3) 5/125 (6) 6/144 (7)
8/173 (9) 9/193 (8) 10/196 (10)   7/157 (8) 8/157 (9) 9/157 (5) 10/161 (11)

Lee 19.5–6–46–4; Johnson 13–5–25–0; Symonds 3–1–8–0; Clark 15–4–28–4; Hogg 21–3–82–2. *Second Innings*—Lee 14–3–43–2; Johnson 15–6–21–3; Clark 15–9–20–1; Hogg 17–3–51–2; Symonds 13–5–25–1.

Umpires: M. R. Benson *(England)* (20) and B. F. Bowden *(New Zealand)* (42).
Third umpire: S. J. Davis *(Australia)*.   Referee: M. J. Procter *(South Africa)* (44).

Close of play: First day, Australia 337-9 (Johnson 10, Clark 21); Second day, Australia 32-0 (Jaques 10, Hayden 22); Third day, India 6-0 (Dravid 3, Wasim Jaffer 2).

AUSTRALIA v INDIA 2007-08 (2nd Test)

At Sydney Cricket Ground on 2, 3, 4, 5, 6 January.
Toss: Australia.   Result: AUSTRALIA won by 122 runs.
Debuts: none.
Man of the Match: A. Symonds.

Australia won with just nine minutes to spare, when Clarke took three wickets in five balls, and equalled the record of 16 consecutive Test victories they themselves set in 2001. However, they would never have won but for several umpiring blunders, most of which went against India, who successfully asked ICC to remove Steve Bucknor from the next Test. India had started well, reducing Australia to 134 for 6 in good batting conditions, before Symonds and Hogg put on 173, a seventh-wicket record for a Sydney Test – but Symonds escaped when Bucknor missed a thick outside edge off Sharma at 30, and at 48 survived a confident stumping appeal. Laxman made his third Test hundred at the SCG, as did Tendulkar, who put on 129 with Harbhajan Singh as the last three wickets added 187. India should have been safe, but more umpiring errors allowed Australia to declare 332 ahead, with a minimum of 72 overs remaining. Until Dravid was fourth out in the 34th over – given out caught when ball only brushed pad – it did not look as if Ponting had given himself enough time. Hogg was ineffective, but the part-timers mopped up: Clarke took three wickets in his second over, two caught at slip, to complete the victory that maintained Australia's hold on the Border-Gavaskar Trophy. The match was overshadowed by allegations that Harbhajan had racially abused Symonds. He was originally suspended for three Tests – incensing the Indians, who threatened to cancel the tour – but this was reduced on appeal.

Australia

P. A. Jaques c Dhoni b R. P. Singh	0	– c Yuvraj Singh b Kumble	42
M. L. Hayden c Tendulkar b R. P. Singh	13	– c Wasim Jaffer b Kumble	123
*R. T. Ponting lbw b Harbhajan Singh	55	– c Laxman b Harbhajan Singh	1
M. E. K. Hussey c Tendulkar b R. P. Singh	41	– not out	145
M. J. Clarke lbw b Harbhajan Singh	1	– c Dravid b Kumble	0
A. Symonds not out	162	– c Dhoni b R. P. Singh	61
†A. C. Gilchrist c Tendulkar b R. P. Singh	7	– c Yuvraj Singh b Kumble	1
G. B. Hogg c Dravid b Kumble	79	– c Dravid b Harbhajan Singh	1
B. Lee lbw b Kumble	59	– not out	4
M. G. Johnson c Ganguly b Kumble	28		
S. R. Clark lbw b Kumble	0		
B 2, l-b 9, w 4, n-b 3	18	B 3, l-b 8, w 3, n-b 9	23

1/0 (1) 2/27 (2) 3/119 (3) 4/119 (4)   463   1/85 (1) 2/90 (3)   (7 wkts dec.) 401
5/121 (5) 6/134 (7) 7/307 (8)   3/250 (2) 4/250 (5)
8/421 (9) 9/461 (10) 10/463 (11)   5/378 (6) 6/393 (7) 7/395 (8)

R. P. Singh 26–3–124–4; Sharma 23–3–87–0; Ganguly 6–1–13–0; Harbhajan Singh 27–3–108–2; Kumble 25.3–0–106–4; Tendulkar 5–0–14–0. *Second Innings*—R. P. Singh 16–2–74–1; Sharma 14–2–59–0; Harbhajan Singh 33–6–92–2; Kumble 40–3–148–4; Tendulkar 2–0–6–0; Yuvraj Singh 2–0–11–0.

India

Wasim Jaffer b Lee	3	– (2) c Clarke b Lee	0
R. Dravid c Hayden b Johnson	53	– (1) c Gilchrist b Symonds	38
V. V. S. Laxman c Hussey b Hogg	109	– lbw b Clark	20
S. R. Tendulkar not out	154	– b Clark	12
S. C. Ganguly c Hussey b Hogg	67	– c Clarke b Lee	51
Yuvraj Singh lbw b Lee	12	– c Gilchrist b Symonds	0
†M. S. Dhoni c Gilchrist b Lee	2	– lbw b Symonds	35
*A. Kumble c Gilchrist b Lee	2	– not out	45
Harbhajan Singh c Hussey b Johnson	63	– c Hussey b Clarke	7
R. P. Singh c Gilchrist b Clark	13	– lbw b Clarke	0
I. Sharma c and b Lee	23	– c Hussey b Clarke	0
B 4, l-b 13, w 6, n-b 8	31	N-b 2	2

1/8 (1) 2/183 (2) 3/185 (3) 4/293 (5)   532   1/3 (2) 2/34 (3) 3/54 (4)   210
5/321 (6) 6/330 (7) 7/345 (8)   4/115 (1) 5/115 (6) 6/137 (5)
8/474 (9) 9/501 (10) 10/532 (11)   7/185 (7) 8/210 (9) 9/210 (10) 10/210 (11)

Lee 32.2–5–119–5; Johnson 37–2–148–2; Clark 25–3–80–1; Symonds 7–1–19–0; Hogg 30–2–121–2; Clarke 7–1–28–0. *Second Innings*—Lee 13–3–34–2; Johnson 11–4–33–0; Clark 12–4–32–2; Hogg 14–2–55–0; Symonds 19–5–51–3; Clarke 1.5–0–5–3.

Umpires: M. R. Benson *(England)* (21) and S. A. Bucknor *(West Indies)* (120).
Third umpire: B. N. J. Oxenford *(Australia)*.   Referee: M. J. Procter *(South Africa)* (45).

Close of play: First day, Australia 376-7 (Symonds 137, Lee 31); Second day, India 216-3 (Tendulkar 9, Ganguly 21); Third day, Australia 13-0 (Jaques 8, Hayden 5); Fourth day, Australia 282-4 (Hussey 87, Symonds 14).

AUSTRALIA v INDIA 2007-08 (3rd Test)

At W. A. C. A. Ground, Perth, on 16, 17, 18, 19 January.
Toss: India.   Result: INDIA won by 72 runs.
Debuts: Australia – C. J. L. Rogers.
Man of the Match: I. K. Pathan.

India inflicted Australia's first Test defeat at Perth since 1996-97, and their first at home since India won at Adelaide in December 2003. It meant Ponting's search for a 17th consecutive victory, to beat Australia's own record of 16, was derailed by India, just as Steve Waugh's side had been in 2000-01. It also helped wipe away some of the bitterness from the previous game. It was the first time in 16 years that Australia had played four fast bowlers without a specialist spinner. Dravid, badly dropped by Clarke at first slip off Lee when 11, played his most fluent innings of the series. He and Tendulkar, whose classy 71 was ended by a poor decision, put on 139. Australia did well to restrict India to 330 after that good start, but started badly when Pathan removed both openers in his second over, before R. P. Singh became the first bowler to dismiss Hussey for a duck in a Test. Symonds, surprised by extra bounce, became Kumble's 600th Test wicket after putting on 102 with Gilchrist. Lee and Clark dragged Australia back into the match: when Pathan was sixth out the lead was only 278, but Laxman made the game safe with a battling 79. Needing 413, more than they had ever managed batting last, Australia again lost both openers in Pathan's new-ball spell. A big innings from Ponting was essential to his side's hopes, but Sharma had him caught at first slip during a magnificent spell on the fourth morning.

India

Wasim Jaffer c Gilchrist b Lee	16	– c Hussey b Clark	11
V. Sehwag c Gilchrist b Johnson	29	– b Clark	43
R. Dravid c Ponting b Symonds	93	– (4) c Gilchrist b Lee	3
S. R. Tendulkar lbw b Lee	71	– (5) lbw b Lee	13
S. C. Ganguly c Hussey b Johnson	9	– (6) c Clarke b Johnson	0
V. V. S. Laxman c Tait b Lee	27	– (7) c Gilchrist b Lee	79
†M. S. Dhoni lbw b Clark	19	– (8) c Gilchrist b Symonds	38
I. K. Pathan lbw b Johnson	28	– (3) c Ponting b Clark	46
*A. Kumble c Rogers b Clark	1	– c Clarke b Symonds	0
R. P. Singh c Hussey b Johnson	0	– c Gilchrist b Clark	30
I. Sharma not out	0	– not out	4
L-b 19, w 9, n-b 9	37	L-b 14, w 5, n-b 8	27

1/57 (2) 2/59 (1) 3/198 (4) 4/214 (5)   330   1/45 (1) 2/79 (2) 3/82 (4)   294
5/278 (3) 6/284 (6) 7/328 (7)   4/116 (5) 5/125 (6) 6/160 (3)
8/330 (8) 9/330 (9) 10/330 (10)   7/235 (8) 8/235 (9) 9/286 (10) 10/294 (7)

Lee 24–5–71–3; Johnson 28.2–7–86–4; Clark 17–4–45–2; Tait 13–1–59–0; Symonds 10–1–36–1; Clarke 6–1–14–0. *Second Innings*—Lee 20.4–4–54–3; Johnson 10–0–58–1; Clark 19–4–61–4; Tait 8–0–33–0; Clarke 13–2–38–0; Symonds 10–2–36–2.

Australia

P. A. Jaques c Laxman b Pathan	8	– (2) c Wasim Jaffer b Pathan	16
C. J. L. Rogers lbw b Pathan	4	– (1) c Dhoni b Pathan	15
*R. T. Ponting c Dravid b Sharma	20	– c Dravid b Sharma	45
M. E. K. Hussey c Dhoni b R. P. Singh	0	– lbw b R. P. Singh	46
M. J. Clarke c Dhoni b Sharma	23	– st Dhoni b Kumble	81
A. Symonds c Dravid b Kumble	66	– lbw b Kumble	12
†A. C. Gilchrist c Dhoni b R. P. Singh	55	– b Sehwag	15
B. Lee c Dhoni b R. P. Singh	11	– c Laxman b Sehwag	0
M. G. Johnson not out	6	– not out	50
S. R. Clark c Dhoni b R. P. Singh	0	– c Dhoni b Pathan	32
S. W. Tait c and b Kumble	8	– b R. P. Singh	4
B 4, l-b 1, w 4, n-b 2	11	L-b 6, w 8, n-b 10	24

1/12 (2) 2/13 (1) 3/14 (4) 4/43 (3)   212   1/21 (1) 2/43 (2) 3/117 (3)   340
5/61 (5) 6/163 (6) 7/192 (7)   4/159 (4) 5/177 (6) 6/227 (7)
8/195 (8) 9/195 (10) 10/212 (11)   7/229 (8) 8/253 (5) 9/326 (10) 10/340 (11)

R. P. Singh 14–2–68–4; Pathan 17–2–63–2; Sharma 7–0–34–2; Kumble 12–1–42–2. *Second Innings*—R. P. Singh 21.5–4–95–2; Pathan 16–2–54–3; Sharma 17–0–63–1; Kumble 24–2–98–2; Sehwag 8–1–24–2.

Umpires: Asad Rauf *(Pakistan)* (16) and B. F. Bowden *(New Zealand)* (43).
Third umpire: B. N. J. Oxenford *(Australia)*.   Referee: M. J. Procter *(South Africa)* (46).

Close of play: First day, India 297-6 (Dhoni 8, Pathan 8); Second day, India 52-1 (Sehwag 29, Pathan 2); Third day, Australia 65-2 (Ponting 24, Hussey 5).

AUSTRALIA v INDIA 2007-08 (4th Test)

At Adelaide Oval on 24, 25, 26, 27, 28 January.
Toss: India.   Result: MATCH DRAWN.
Debuts: none.
Man of the Match: S. R. Tendulkar.   Man of the Series: B. Lee.

Kumble's hopes of squaring the series – high when his side amassed 526 in the first innings – were stymied by some excellent Australian batting. Indeed, India were under pressure themselves on the final day, but Sehwag's century denied Gilchrist victory in his 96th and last Test. After passing Mark Boucher's Test record for wicket-keeping dismissals, Gilchrist stunned his team-mates on the third evening by announcing his imminent retirement. He acted as captain over the next two days as Ponting had a sore back. After winning the toss, India slipped to 156 for 4 on an excellent pitch, but Tendulkar rescued them with another masterly hundred, his 39th in Tests and 80th in all internationals. Kumble made 87 in more than four hours, his first fifty against Australia. Harbhajan Singh played the lead role in a stand of 107: the last three wickets lasted 56 overs and added 167. Australia's batsmen proved equally hard to shift. Hayden and Clarke made centuries, as Ponting – his 34th, but first in a Test since December 2006. He ended up batting with a runner, and resisted for 6½ hours: his fourth-wicket stand of 210 with Clarke guaranteed a draw, at least. India would have been more worried by the fourth-day close had Clarke at second slip not dropped a sitter off Lee when Sehwag was two. It proved a critical miss: Sehwag completed his 13th Test century (the last nine all in excess of 150) out of 128, then dropped anchor for 354 minutes in all.

India

V. Sehwag c Hayden b Lee	63	– c Gilchrist b Symonds		151
I. K. Pathan c Gilchrist b Johnson	9	– lbw b Johnson		0
R. Dravid c Ponting b Johnson	18	– retired hurt		11
S. R. Tendulkar c Hogg b Lee	153	– run out		13
S. C. Ganguly lbw b Hogg	7	– c Hussey b Johnson		18
V. V. S. Laxman c Gilchrist b Lee	51	– c Gilchrist b Lee		12
†M. S. Dhoni c Symonds b Johnson	16	– c Hayden b Lee		20
*A. Kumble c Gilchrist b Johnson	87	– not out		9
Harbhajan Singh c Gilchrist b Symonds	63	– c Ponting b Hogg		7
R. P. Singh c Johnson b Clarke	0			
I. Sharma not out	14	– (10) not out		2
B 8, l-b 21, w 3, n-b 13	45	B 9, l-b 9, w 3, n-b 5		26

1/34 (2) 2/82 (3) 3/122 (1) 4/156 (5)   526   1/2 (2) 2/128 (4)   (7 wkts dec.) 269
5/282 (6) 6/336 (7) 7/359 (4)   3/162 (5) 4/186 (6)
8/466 (9) 9/468 (10) 10/526 (8)   5/237 (7) 6/253 (1) 7/264 (9)

In the second innings Dravid retired hurt at 57.

Lee 36–4–101–3; Johnson 37.5–6–126–4; Clark 31–6–92–0; Hogg 31–2–119–1; Clarke 10–0–39–1; Symonds 7–0–20–1. *Second Innings*—Lee 27–3–74–2; Johnson 16–1–33–2; Symonds 22–4–52–1; Clark 12–3–37–0; Hogg 12–3–53–1; Clarke 1–0–2–0.

Australia

P. A. Jaques b Kumble	60	B. Lee c Dhoni b Pathan		1
M. L. Hayden b Sharma	103	M. G. Johnson c Sharma b Harbhajan Singh		13
*R. T. Ponting b Sehwag	140	S. R. Clark b Sehwag		3
M. E. K. Hussey b Pathan	22	B 10, l-b 12, w 10, n-b 11		43
M. J. Clarke c Laxman b Sharma	118			
A. Symonds b Sharma	30			563
†A. C. Gilchrist c Sehwag b Pathan	14	1/159 (1) 2/186 (2) 3/241 (4)		
G. B. Hogg not out	16	4/451 (3) 5/490 (5) 6/506 (7)		
		7/527 (6) 8/528 (9) 9/557 (10) 10/563 (11)		

R. P. Singh 4–0–14–0; Pathan 36–2–112–3; Sharma 40–6–115–3; Harbhajan Singh 48–5–128–1; Kumble 30–4–109–1; Sehwag 19–2–51–2; Tendulkar 1–0–6–0; Ganguly 3–1–6–0.

Umpires: Asad Rauf *(Pakistan)* (17) and B. F. Bowden *(New Zealand)* (44).
Third umpire: S. J. Davis *(Australia)*.   Referee: M. J. Procter *(South Africa)* (47).

Close of play: First day, India 309-5 (Tendulkar 124, Dhoni 6); Second day, Australia 62-0 (Jaques 21, Hayden 36); Third day, Australia 322-3 (Ponting 79, Clarke 37); Fourth day, India 45-1 (Sehwag 31, Dravid 11).

SOUTH AFRICA v WEST INDIES 2007-08 (1st Test)

At St George's Park, Port Elizabeth, on 26, 27, 28, 29 December.
Toss: South Africa.   Result: WEST INDIES won by 128 runs.
Debuts: none.
Man of the Match: M. N. Samuels.

After bullying the New Zealanders into submission a few weeks previously, South Africa's bowlers adopted a similar bouncer-bouncer-yorker approach on the first morning here – and promptly had the sand kicked back in their faces. West Indies eventually recorded their first Test win in South Africa, their first anywhere for 31 months, and their first overseas outside Zimbabwe and Bangladesh since beating England at Edgbaston in June 2000. It was the best possible start to Gayle's Test-captaincy career. He began by lashing 66 from 49 balls after Smith, in his 50th Test as South Africa's captain (he also led the World XI at Sydney in 2005-06), decided to bowl first. An opening stand of 98 arrived in just 17 overs, helped by Steyn bowling badly. The pace slowed dramatically as Chanderpaul – whose ugly but effective obduracy rubbed off on the normally flashy Samuels – reached 50 for the seventh innings running, equalling the Test record shared by Everton Weekes and Andy Flower. Their stand lasted 40 overs, and was worth 111: Samuels missed a century, but Chanderpaul was not to be denied his 17th, its worth to his team in inverse proportion to the entertainment it provided. Only de Villiers showed much gumption when South Africa batted, but Gayle waived the follow-on and pushed the lead to 388. South Africa wobbled to 45 for 4 on the fourth day, and although Kallis and de Villiers put on 112, the delighted West Indians romped home after Kallis received a dubious decision from umpire Tiffin.

West Indies

*C. H. Gayle	c Kallis b Harris	66	– c Boucher b Ntini	29
D. Ganga	c Boucher b Nel	33	– run out	45
R. S. Morton	c Prince b Ntini	33	– lbw b Kallis	5
M. N. Samuels	c Kallis b Steyn	94	– b Steyn	40
S. Chanderpaul	b Nel	104	– c Kallis b Steyn	8
D. J. Bravo	c and b Ntini	12	– c Gibbs b Harris	10
†D. Ramdin	c Boucher b Ntini	1	– c Gibbs b Steyn	0
D. J. G. Sammy	run out	38	– lbw b Harris	3
J. E. Taylor	b Steyn	9	– c Nel b Harris	22
D. B. Powell	not out	1	– b Harris	6
F. H. Edwards	c Prince b Nel	0	– not out	0
	B 2, l-b 8, w 3, n-b 4	17	B 1, w 1, n-b 5	7

1/98 (2) 2/102 (1) 3/166 (3) 4/277 (4)   408   1/32 (1) 2/57 (3) 3/122 (2)   175
5/296 (6) 6/304 (7) 7/361 (8)   4/123 (4) 5/141 (6) 6/141 (5)
8/385 (9) 9/407 (5) 10/408 (11)   7/144 (8) 8/144 (7) 9/160 (10) 10/175 (9)

Steyn 31–4–121–2; Ntini 30–6–100–3; Nel 25.4–7–85–3; Harris 30–9–69–1; Kallis 17–8–23–0. *Second Innings—* Steyn 17–3–67–3; Ntini 11–3–35–1; Nel 7–1–21–0; Kallis 7–1–16–1; Harris 15.4–5–35–4.

South Africa

*G. C. Smith	lbw b Taylor	28	– (2) c Ganga b Edwards	11
H. H. Gibbs	c Ramdin b Powell	0	– (1) lbw b Powell	0
H. M. Amla	b Powell	29	– c Ramdin b Edwards	8
J. H. Kallis	c Bravo b Taylor	0	– c Ramdin b Edwards	85
A. G. Prince	c Morton b Powell	20	– c Gayle b Taylor	10
A. B. de Villiers	b Bravo	59	– c Samuels b Taylor	60
†M. V. Boucher	c Powell b Taylor	20	– b Taylor	13
P. L. Harris	c Taylor b Bravo	9	– b Bravo	0
A. Nel	c Ganga b Bravo	16	– c Ramdin b Sammy	34
D. W. Steyn	c Powell b Bravo	7	– not out	33
M. Ntini	not out	0	– c Powell b Samuels	1
	B 4, l-b 1, w 1, n-b 1	7	L-b 4, w 1	5

1/1 (2) 2/45 (1) 3/53 (4) 4/63 (3)   195   1/4 (1) 2/17 (3) 3/20 (2)   260
5/96 (5) 6/129 (7) 7/172 (6)   4/45 (5) 5/157 (4) 6/183 (7)
8/181 (8) 9/194 (9) 10/195 (10)   7/190 (8) 8/192 (6) 9/259 (9) 10/260 (11)

Powell 17–4–58–3; Edwards 15–3–56–0; Taylor 13–4–46–3; Bravo 13.1–3–24–4; Sammy 4–2–6–0. *Second Innings—*Powell 14–2–47–1; Edwards 13–3–37–3; Taylor 18–1–66–3; Bravo 16–2–63–1; Sammy 7–0–29–1; Samuels 6.5–1–14–1.

Umpires: Aleem Dar *(Pakistan)* (43) and R. B. Tiffin *(Zimbabwe)* (39).
Third umpire: R. E. Koertzen *(South Africa).*   Referee: R. S. Mahanama *(Sri Lanka)* (16).

Close of play: First day, West Indies 281-4 (Chanderpaul 43, Bravo 0); Second day, South Africa 122-5 (de Villiers 22, Boucher 18); Third day, West Indies 146-8 (Taylor 2, Powell 0).

SOUTH AFRICA v WEST INDIES 2007-08 (2nd Test)

At Newlands, Cape Town, on 2, 3, 4, 5 January.
Toss: West Indies.   Result: SOUTH AFRICA won by seven wickets.
Debuts: none.
Man of the Match: A. G. Prince.

A two-paced pitch was always hard work for batsmen – the run-rate for the first three innings was well below three an over – and South Africa's diligence appeared to have paid off when they reduced West Indies to 167 for 8 in their second innings, just 89 ahead. Smith's side believed they needed just one more wicket, as Gayle had retired earlier, his thumb broken by a Nel lifter after coming in down the order with a hamstring strain. But South Africa's frustration started with Edwards's unlikely career-best 21, and was compounded when Gayle reappeared and slogged three sixes and four fours in a remarkable one-handed 38, as a last-ditch stand of 70 swelled the target to a tricky 185. An angry Smith was still simmering when he came out to bat after tea. The series was at stake and, with runs previously so hard to come by, a back-breaking grind was predicted for the final innings. But Smith smashed his side close to victory, collecting 11 meaty fours in his 85 from 79 balls. He was finally out trying one big hit too many, but had settled the destiny of the match and squared the series. A statistical oddity came at the end of South Africa's first innings, when leg-spinner Rawl Lewis took his second Test wicket, more than nine years after his first. His bowling average of 414 – the worst in Test history – was thus slashed to 207, and he improved it further with two more wickets in the second innings.

West Indies

*C. H. Gayle c McKenzie b Nel	46	– (6) c Harris b Steyn	38
D. Ganga c Boucher b Steyn	3	– (1) b Ntini	22
R. S. Morton c Ntini b Kallis	23	– c Boucher b Steyn	1
M. N. Samuels c Boucher b Ntini	51	– lbw b Nel	18
S. Chanderpaul not out	65	– not out	70
D. J. Bravo c Kallis b Ntini	0	– (7) c Smith b Nel	12
†D. Ramdin lbw b Steyn	21	– (2) c Boucher b Kallis	32
R. N. Lewis b Steyn	0	– c Amla b Harris	1
J. E. Taylor c and b Steyn	8	– c Kallis b Steyn	21
D. B. Powell c Kallis b Nel	0	– c Smith b Steyn	1
F. H. Edwards c de Villiers b Nel	2	– c Harris b Nel	21
B 5, l-b 10, w 1, n-b 8	24	B 4, l-b 20, w 1	25

1/12 (2) 2/71 (3) 3/77 (1) 4/183 (4)   243   1/59 (2) 2/60 (3) 3/81 (1)   262
5/185 (6) 6/220 (7) 7/220 (8)   4/93 (4) 5/126 (7) 6/133 (8)
8/237 (9) 9/241 (10) 10/243 (11)   7/163 (9) 8/167 (10) 9/192 (11) 10/262 (6)

In the second innings Gayle, when 1, retired hurt at 97 and resumed at 192.

Steyn 20–5–60–4; Ntini 22–7–63–2; Nel 22–5–61–3; Kallis 9–1–11–1; Harris 19–5–33–0. *Second Innings*—Nel 27–12–62–3; Ntini 26–8–62–1; Steyn 19.5–7–44–4; Kallis 19–6–34–1; Harris 10–0–36–1.

South Africa

*G. C. Smith c Ramdin b Taylor	28	– c Gayle b Lewis	85
N. D. McKenzie c Gayle b Taylor	23		
H. M. Amla lbw b Bravo	32	– c Gayle b Lewis	37
J. H. Kallis c Ramdin b Bravo	36	– not out	22
A. G. Prince run out	98	– not out	12
A. B. de Villiers c Ramdin b Bravo	2	– (2) c sub (D. J. G. Sammy) b Bravo	23
†M. V. Boucher b Bravo	59		
P. L. Harris c Morton b Powell	4		
A. Nel c Ramdin b Powell	5		
D. W. Steyn c Morton b Lewis	19		
M. Ntini not out	3		
B 4, l-b 5, w 3	12	L-b 5, w 1, n-b 1	7

1/46 (2) 2/61 (1) 3/120 (4) 4/123 (3)   321   1/57 (2) 2/140 (3)   (3 wkts) 186
5/131 (6) 6/260 (7) 7/265 (8)   3/152 (1)
8/284 (9) 9/301 (5) 10/321 (10)

Powell 35–4–123–2; Edwards 4.5–1–12–0; Samuels 8.1–3–18–0; Taylor 21–6–51–2; Bravo 37–9–82–4; Lewis 12.2–3–26–1. *Second Innings*—Powell 11–0–57–0; Taylor 6–0–31–0; Bravo 7–0–34–1; Samuels 3–0–17–0; Lewis 8.2–0–42–2.

Umpires: S. J. A. Taufel *(Australia)* (48) and R. B. Tiffin *(Zimbabwe)* (40).
Third umpire: M. Erasmus *(South Africa)*.   Referee: R. S. Mahanama *(Sri Lanka)* (17).

Close of play: First day, West Indies 240-8 (Chanderpaul 64, Powell 0); Second day, South Africa 218-5 (Prince 55, Boucher 35); Third day, West Indies 96-4 (Chanderpaul 8, Gayle 1).

SOUTH AFRICA v WEST INDIES 2007-08 (3rd Test)

At Kingsmead, Durban, on 10, 11, 12 January.

Toss: South Africa.   Result: SOUTH AFRICA won by an innings and 100 runs.

Debuts: West Indies – B. A. Parchment.

Man of the Match: A. G. Prince.   Man of the Series: D. W. Steyn.

West Indies ended the series with a whimper as pronounced as the bang with which they began it. It was virtually all over in the first session: they were 33 for 5 in the 15th over, and 100 for 7 at lunch. Shaun Pollock, who announced his retirement mid-match, led the way with four wickets in his first Test for almost a year, making good use of a greenish pitch and heavy cloud cover. South Africa were batting before mid-afternoon drinks, and by the close Smith had 122, just 17 short of the West Indians' combined efforts. In all he batted for less than four hours and hit 27 fours. Kallis fell after a stand of 122 with Prince, bowled by a strange-looking ball from Samuels: after the match the umpires reported his bowling action. It mattered little: Prince and de Villiers clubbed fine unbeaten centuries – helped by the tourists' decision to enter the match with just three fit front-line bowlers (Bravo, captaining instead of the injured Gayle, was unable to bowl because of a side strain) – before Smith finally declared with a lead of 417. Samuels and Bravo threatened to take the game into a fourth day, adding 144, before Steyn trapped Bravo with a beauty. He then took the last four wickets for no runs in 15 balls to seal an emphatic victory, and a 2–1 series win. Chanderpaul, suffering from flu, did not bat: in the first innings he had collected his first Test duck since June 2005.

West Indies

D. Ganga c Smith b Steyn	3	– c Kallis b Ntini	11
B. A. Parchment c Gibbs b Pollock	11	– lbw b Steyn	20
R. S. Morton lbw b Pollock	1	– lbw b Pollock	37
M. N. Samuels c Boucher b Ntini	6	– b Steyn	105
S. Chanderpaul c Kallis b Ntini	0	– absent ill	
*D. J. Bravo c Gibbs b Pollock	13	– (5) lbw b Steyn	75
†D. Ramdin c Gibbs b Nel	30	– (6) c Boucher b Nel	25
D. J. G. Sammy c Smith b Nel	28	– (7) c and b Steyn	17
J. E. Taylor c Steyn b Pollock	25	– (8) not out	17
D. B. Powell not out	15	– (9) b Steyn	0
F. H. Edwards c Boucher b Nel	0	– (10) b Steyn	0
B 1, l-b 6	7	L-b 8, w 1, n-b 1	10

1/10 (1) 2/11 (3) 3/22 (2) 4/26 (4)   139   1/33 (2) 2/49 (1) 3/88 (3)   317
5/33 (5) 6/57 (6) 7/74 (7)   4/232 (5) 5/273 (6) 6/292 (4)
8/116 (9) 9/139 (8) 10/139 (11)   7/305 (7) 8/305 (9) 9/317 (10)

Steyn 8–2–18–1; Ntini 7–1–30–2; Pollock 11–2–35–4; Nel 6.3–0–45–3; Kallis 2–1–4–0. *Second Innings*—Steyn 21.5–6–72–6; Ntini 20–4–95–1; Pollock 17–4–50–1; Nel 17–2–67–1; Kallis 8–2–14–0; Amla 3–0–11–0.

South Africa

*G. C. Smith c Ramdin b Taylor	147	A. B. de Villiers not out	103
H. H. Gibbs b Powell	27	B 6, l-b 7	13
H. M. Amla c Bravo b Sammy	69		
J. H. Kallis c Morton b Samuels	74	1/53 (2) 2/252 (3) (4 wkts dec.) 556	
A. G. Prince not out	123	3/252 (1) 4/374 (4)	

†M. V. Boucher, S. M. Pollock, A. Nel, D. W. Steyn and M. Ntini did not bat.

Powell 26–1–128–1; Edwards 23–0–129–0; Taylor 25–3–92–1; Sammy 25–4–104–1; Samuels 21–0–90–1.

Umpires: Aleem Dar *(Pakistan)* (44) and S. J. A. Taufel *(Australia)* (49).
Third umpire: B. G. Jerling *(South Africa)*.   Referee: R. S. Mahanama *(Sri Lanka)* (18).

Close of play: First day, South Africa 213-1 (Smith 122, Amla 55); Second day, West Indies 23-0 (Ganga 6, Parchment 17).

NEW ZEALAND v BANGLADESH 2007-08 (1st Test)

At University Oval, Dunedin, on 4, 5, 6 January.
Toss: New Zealand.   Result: NEW ZEALAND won by nine wickets.
Debuts: Bangladesh – Junaid Siddique, Sajidul Islam, Tamim Iqbal.
Man of the Match: J. D. P. Oram.

Bangladesh's 50th Test match was a disaster for them: it ended with their 44th defeat, to go with five draws and just one victory, over Zimbabwe. Asked to bat in the first Test at the refurbished University Oval, the 96th ground to stage one, they lost all ten wickets before tea on the first day for 137, and lost all their second-innings wickets on the third day for just 93. In between those sad processions New Zealand recovered from losing Cumming to the left-armer Sajidul Islam's eighth ball in Tests to reach 357, with centuries from Oram and Bell, who was playing his first Test for more than six years. However, for a while towards the end of the second day two talented young debutants – Tamim Iqbal and Junaid Siddique – caught the eye with a stylish opening partnership. Both left-handers, they knocked off 148 of the arrears by the close, and extended their stand on the third morning to 161, a record for Bangladesh's first wicket in Tests, beating the 133 of Javed Omar and Nafis Iqbal (Tamim's elder brother) against Zimbabwe at Dhaka in 2004-05. Both collected 12 fours, and Tamim also hit a six. By the time they were separated New Zealand's advantage had been trimmed to 59 – but it was a familiar story after that. Bangladesh eventually capitulated for 254, leaving New Zealand only 35 to win, which they reached in less than nine overs. Fulton ended the match by hitting Mohammad Ashraful's only delivery for six.

Bangladesh

Tamim Iqbal c Fulton b Martin	53	– b Mills		84
Junaid Siddique c Fleming b Martin	1	– c Fleming b Martin		74
Habibul Bashar c McCullum b Martin	23	– c Sinclair b Oram		11
*Mohammad Ashraful lbw b Martin	0	– c Cumming b O'Brien		23
Shahriar Nafees b Vettori	16	– lbw b Vettori		28
Aftab Ahmed b Oram	0	– c Bell b O'Brien		0
†Mushfiqur Rahim c Bell b Mills	7	– lbw b Vettori		6
Mashrafe bin Mortaza b Oram	22	– c McCullum b Vettori		10
Shahadat Hossain c McCullum b Oram	0	– (10) lbw b Vettori		0
Enamul Haque, jun. not out	2	– (9) not out		6
Sajidul Islam c McCullum b Mills	4	– c McCullum b Martin		1
B 1, l-b 2, w 3, n-b 3	9	L-b 4, n-b 7		11

1/5 (2) 2/43 (3) 3/47 (4) 4/82 (5)   **137**   1/161 (1) 2/167 (2) 3/179 (3)   **254**
5/98 (6) 6/100 (1) 7/129 (8)   4/205 (4) 5/205 (6) 6/222 (7)
8/129 (9) 9/133 (7) 10/137 (11)   7/232 (8) 8/252 (5) 9/252 (10) 10/254 (11)

Martin 13–1–64–4; Mills 7.1–1–29–2; Oram 13–4–23–3; O'Brien 7–2–10–0; Vettori 6–2–8–1. *Second Innings—* Martin 20.1–6–56–2; Mills 12–1–54–1; O'Brien 15–2–49–2; Vettori 24–6–70–4; Oram 12–5–21–1.

New Zealand

C. D. Cumming lbw b Sajidul Islam	1	– (2) lbw b Mashrafe bin Mortaza		4
M. D. Bell lbw b Mohammad Ashraful	107	– (1) not out		20
P. G. Fulton b Shahadat Hossain	14	– not out		15
S. P. Fleming c Mushfiqur Rahim b Sajidul Islam	14			
M. S. Sinclair lbw b Mashrafe bin Mortaza	29			
J. D. P. Oram b Mashrafe bin Mortaza	117			
†B. B. McCullum c Junaid Siddique b Mohammad Ashraful	7			
*D. L. Vettori c Enamul Haque b Shahadat Hossain	32			
K. D. Mills c Mushfiqur Rahim b Mashrafe bin Mortaza	0			
I. E. O'Brien c Mushfiqur Rahim b Mashrafe bin Mortaza	5			
C. S. Martin not out	12			
B 4, l-b 10, w 2, n-b 3	19			

1/5 (1) 2/31 (3) 3/58 (4) 4/121 (5)   **357**   1/13 (2)   (1 wkt) **39**
5/260 (2) 6/270 (7) 7/320 (6)
8/320 (9) 9/340 (8) 10/357 (10)

Shahadat Hossain 18–0–95–2; Sajidul Islam 19–2–71–2; Mashrafe bin Mortaza 23–3–74–4; Enamul Haque 22–4–57–0; Mohammad Ashraful 9–0–46–2. *Second Innings—*Mashrafe bin Mortaza 4–0–14–1; Sajidul Islam 3–1–13–0; Shahadat Hossain 1–0–6–0; Mohammad Ashraful 0.1–0–6–0.

Umpires: N. J. Llong *(England)* (1) and P. D. Parker *(Australia)* (9).
Third umpire: A. L. Hill *(New Zealand).*   Referee: B. C. Broad *(England)* (24).

Close of play: First day, New Zealand 156-4 (Bell 74, Oram 17); Second day, Bangladesh 148-0 (Tamim Iqbal 72, Junaid Siddique 69).

NEW ZEALAND v BANGLADESH 2007-08 (2nd Test)

At Basin Reserve, Wellington, on 12, 13, 14 January.
Toss: New Zealand.   Result: NEW ZEALAND won by an innings and 137 runs.
Debuts: none.
Man of the Match: D. L. Vettori.

Vettori decided to bowl first, despite a hard, lightly grassed pitch that looked ideal for batting – and watched his seamers roll Bangladesh over again, setting up another facile victory, completed before lunch on the third day. Martin bustled in with a 60mph wind behind him, and the batsmen were soon flicking and flirting with danger. Mohammad Ashraful hit six fours, while Aftab Ahmed hung on grimly for 108 minutes – after 38 balls he had scored only two – but disaster was always just an edge away. Nine wickets were taken in the cordon from wicket-keeper to widish gully: Mushfiqur Rahim, lbw to Martin, was the only exception. The focus then switched to Fleming, who had never scored a Test century on his adopted home ground: he maintained this record with a careless clout to midwicket for 87 after a grim struggle. Vettori – one of the few batsmen in the match whose bat seemed to have a middle – clouted 17 fours in his 94, five of them off successive legal balls from Sajidul Islam. New Zealand strolled to a lead of 250, then Bangladesh succumbed again to the short-pitched ball. As the second-day close approached they were 45 for 5 and, with Tamim Iqbal absent after breaking his thumb dropping a slip catch, another wicket would probably have persuaded Vettori to claim the extra half-hour. But it was soon over next day: Shakib Al Hasan's last-ditch stand of 30 with Mashrafe bin Mortaza was the highest of another miserable batting display.

Bangladesh

Tamim Iqbal c Sinclair b Mills	15	– absent hurt		
Junaid Siddique c Bell b Martin	13	– c McCullum b Mills		2
Habibul Bashar c McCullum b Martin	1	– lbw b Martin		25
*Mohammad Ashraful c McCullum b O'Brien	35	– c Fleming b Mills		1
Shahriar Nafees c Fulton b O'Brien	6	– (1) c Bell b Martin		12
Aftab Ahmed not out	25	– (5) c Fleming b O'Brien		5
†Mushfiqur Rahim lbw b Martin	8	– (6) c Bell b Oram		0
Shakib Al Hasan c Fulton b Martin	5	– (7) not out		41
Shahadat Hossain c McCullum b O'Brien	1	– (8) c McCullum b O'Brien		5
Sajidul Islam c Fleming b Martin	6	– (9) run out		3
Mashrafe bin Mortaza c Bell b Vettori	15	– (10) c Mills b Oram		6
B 2, l-b 11	13	L-b 2, w 5, n-b 6		13

1/17 (1) 2/18 (3) 3/49 (2) 4/68 (5)   143   1/10 (2) 2/14 (1) 3/30 (4)   113
5/71 (4) 6/86 (7) 7/110 (8)   4/44 (5) 5/45 (6) 6/56 (3)
8/111 (9) 9/122 (10) 10/143 (11)   7/79 (8) 8/83 (9) 9/113 (10)

Martin 16–3–65–5; Mills 9–3–19–1; O'Brien 15–7–34–3; Oram 3–2–2–0; Vettori 2.3–0–10–1. *Second Innings—* Martin 13–1–35–2; Mills 11–4–29–2; Oram 11–3–21–2; O'Brien 11–2–23–2; Vettori 1–0–3–0.

New Zealand

C. D. Cumming lbw b Shakib Al Hasan	42	*D. L. Vettori c and b Aftab Ahmed	94
M. D. Bell c Mushfiqur Rahim b Sajidul Islam	1	K. D. Mills b Mashrafe bin Mortaza	4
P. G. Fulton lbw b Mashrafe bin Mortaza	22	I. E. O'Brien b Aftab Ahmed	4
S. P. Fleming c Aftab Ahmed b Shakib Al Hasan	87	C. S. Martin not out	0
M. S. Sinclair c Mushfiqur Rahim b Shahadat Hossain	47	B 5, l-b 23, w 10, n-b 13	51
J. D. P. Oram c Mushfiqur Rahim b Shahadat Hossain	1		
†B. B. McCullum c Shakib Al Hasan b Shahadat Hossain	40		393

1/2 (2) 2/35 (3)   393
3/118 (1) 4/214 (5) 5/216 (6) 6/242 (4)
7/323 (7) 8/362 (9) 9/390 (8) 10/393 (10)

Mashrafe bin Mortaza 29–5–100–2; Sajidul Islam 14–1–91–1; Shahadat Hossain 27–4–83–3; Aftab Ahmed 12.2–4–31–2; Shakib Al Hasan 19–7–44–2; Mohammad Ashraful 2–0–16–0.

Umpires: N. J. Llong *(England)* (2) and P. D. Parker *(Australia)* (10).
Third umpire: G. A. V. Baxter *(New Zealand)*.   Referee: B. C. Broad *(England)* (25).

Close of play: First day, New Zealand 134-3 (Fleming 39, Sinclair 9); Second day, Bangladesh 51-5 (Habibul Bashar 21, Shakib Al Hasan 4).

BANGLADESH v SOUTH AFRICA 2007-08 (1st Test)

At Shere Bangla National Stadium, Mirpur, Dhaka, on 22, 23, 24, 25 February.
Toss: Bangladesh.   Result: SOUTH AFRICA won by five wickets.
Debuts: none.
Man of the Match: J. H. Kallis.

In the first two days, Bangladesh threatened the unthinkable. They gained only their sixth first-innings lead in a Test, and at 148 for 4 in their second innings, 170 ahead, seemed certain to set a challenging target. But Kallis, who had an unusually quiet game with the bat, produced the key performance with the ball, taking five wickets as Bangladesh crashed to 182 all out. South Africa's second-innings batting was much more assured, and they strode to victory after a no-nonsense innings from Smith. Steyn, who had taken 40 wickets in his previous five Tests, was a handful on the first morning, removing both openers in his first two overs. Morkel unveiled good pace and a lethal yorker, but Bangladesh's middle order eventually worked out an unpredictable pitch, and then their bowlers snatched four wickets in 24 overs on the first evening. Botha and de Villiers dug in next morning before Mohammad Ashraful tried his occasional legspin – and took a return catch after his first ball bounced twice (de Villiers thought it would be called no-ball, but the Law requires *more* than two bounces for that). Shahadat Hossain polished off the tail in a superb spell of reverse-swing, claiming four for three in 27 balls. Steyn soon had Bangladesh back in trouble, but Junaid Siddique survived 4½ hours before Kallis demonstrated that he had also mastered reverse-swing. He provided three of the four catches which lifted Boucher back in front of Adam Gilchrist on the list of most Test wicketkeeping dismissals.

Bangladesh

Tamim Iqbal c and b Steyn	0	– b Steyn	2
Junaid Siddique c Boucher b Steyn	1	– c Boucher b Kallis	74
Shahriar Nafees c Smith b Morkel	25	– lbw b Steyn	16
Habibul Bashar c McKenzie b Morkel	11	– lbw b Steyn	2
*Mohammad Ashraful c and b Botha	34	– c Boucher b Ntini	24
Aftab Ahmed c Ntini b Botha	44	– lbw b Steyn	24
Shakib Al Hasan c de Villiers b Morkel	30	– c Boucher b Kallis	3
†Mushfiqur Rahim b Morkel	7	– c Boucher b Kallis	2
Mohammad Rafique lbw b Morkel	0	– b Kallis	14
Mashrafe bin Mortaza b Steyn	29	– c Smith b Kallis	11
Shahadat Hossain not out	0	– not out	1
B 2, l-b 4, w 2, n-b 3	11	L-b 4, w 1, n-b 4	9

1/0 (1) 2/3 (2) 3/32 (4) 4/60 (3)   192   1/3 (1) 2/25 (3) 3/29 (4)   182
5/82 (5) 6/152 (6) 7/152 (7)   4/85 (5) 5/148 (2) 6/148 (6)
8/152 (9) 9/192 (8) 10/192 (10)   7/151 (8) 8/169 (9) 9/181 (10) 10/182 (7)

Steyn 11.4–2–27–3; Ntini 13–2–47–0; Morkel 13–2–50–5; Kallis 5–2–5–0; Botha 12–0–57–2. *Second Innings*— Steyn 18–2–48–4; Ntini 16–4–35–1; Morkel 17–3–43–0; Kallis 14–4–30–5; Botha 6–0–18–0; McKenzie 2–0–4–0.

South Africa

N. D. McKenzie lbw b Shahadat Hossain	5	– c Habibul Bashar b Shahadat Hossain	26
*G. C. Smith b Shahadat Hossain	10	– lbw b Mohammad Rafique	62
H. M. Amla lbw b Mohammad Rafique	25	– c Junaid Siddique b Mohammad Rafique	46
J. H. Kallis b Mohammad Rafique	17	– c Mashrafe bin Mortaza b Shahadat Hossain	7
A. G. Prince run out	10	– lbw b Shahadat Hossain	38
J. Botha lbw b Shahadat Hossain	25		
A. B. de Villiers c and b Mohammad Ashraful	46	– (6) not out	19
†M. V. Boucher lbw b Shahadat Hossain	11	– (7) not out	2
M. Morkel c Mushfiqur Rahim b Shahadat Hossain	1		
D. W. Steyn b Shahadat Hossain	7		
M. Ntini not out	3		
B 1, l-b 5, w 1, n-b 3	10	B 2, l-b 2, w 1	5

1/12 (2) 2/19 (1) 3/54 (3) 4/69 (4)   170   1/52 (1) 2/125 (2)   (5 wkts) 205
5/77 (5) 6/145 (7) 7/156 (6)   3/144 (3) 4/144 (4)
8/158 (9) 9/163 (8) 10/170 (10)   5/193 (5)

Mashrafe bin Mortaza 9–1–43–0; Shahadat Hossain 15.3–8–27–6; Mohammad Rafique 25–6–55–2; Shakib Al Hasan 10–6–30–0; Mohammad Ashraful 1–0–9–1. *Second Innings*—Mashrafe bin Mortaza 12–0–47–0; Shahadat Hossain 19–0–70–3; Mohammad Rafique 27.5–6–54–2; Shakib Al Hasan 7–0–24–0; Mohammad Ashraful 2–0–6–0.

Umpires: Aleem Dar *(Pakistan)* (45) and S. A. Bucknor *(West Indies)* (121).
Third umpire: A. F. M. Akhtaruddin *(Bangladesh)*.   Referee: R. S. Madugalle *(Sri Lanka)* (101).

Close of play: First day, South Africa 76-4 (Prince 9, Botha 5); Second day, Bangladesh 125-4 (Junaid Siddique 64, Aftab Ahmed 13); Third day, South Africa 178-4 (Prince 24, de Villiers 8).

BANGLADESH v SOUTH AFRICA 2007-08 (2nd Test)

At Bir Shrestha Shahid Ruhul Amin Stadium, Chittagong, on 29 February, 1, 2, 3 March.
Toss: South Africa.   Result: SOUTH AFRICA won by an innings and 205 runs.
Debuts: none.
Man of the Match: G. C. Smith.   Man of the Series: D. W. Steyn.

Neil McKenzie and Graeme Smith put on 415 to beat the 52-year-old Test-record opening stand of 413, by India's Vinoo Mankad and Pankaj Roy against New Zealand, as South Africa took full advantage of batting first on a flat pitch. Smith reached fifty in 65 balls, and needed only 62 more for his hundred; McKenzie reached his third century in 44 Tests – in only his third appearance since March 2004 – with a superb straight six off Mohammad Rafique. They had added 405 by the end of the first day, the most scored by one pair of Test batsmen in a day. The record soon arrived next morning: Smith worked Abdul Razzak to deep square leg for the vital single in the third over, before being bowled, sweeping, in Razzak's next one. McKenzie continued to his maiden first-class double-century, which made him and Smith only the second opening pair to reach 200 in the same Test innings, after Australia's Bill Lawry and Bob Simpson in Barbados in 1964-65. Rafique took the last two wickets to bow out of Test cricket with exactly 100 wickets (to go with 1,059 runs). Steyn soon had Bangladesh in trouble, then after Shahriar Nafees led some stubborn resistance, Ntini uprooted the tail with four wickets for two runs. Following on, Bangladesh were floundering at 54 for 5 by the third-day close, and their fate was sealed when Peterson took two wickets in the first over next morning en route to his first Test five-for.

South Africa

N. D. McKenzie b Shahadat Hossain	226	R. J. Peterson c Junaid Siddique		
*G. C. Smith b Abdul Razzak	232	b Mohammad Rafique		4
H. M. Amla lbw b Shahadat Hossain	38			
J. H. Kallis not out	39	B 10, l-b 7, w 1, n-b 2		20
A. G. Prince b Shahadat Hossain	2			
A. B. de Villiers b Shakib Al Hasan	1	1/415 (2) 2/514 (1)	(7 wkts dec.)	583
†M. V. Boucher c Shakib Al Hasan		3/515 (3) 4/519 (5)		
b Mohammad Rafique	21	5/524 (6) 6/579 (7) 7/583 (8)		

M. Morkel, D. W. Steyn and M. Ntini did not bat.

Mashrafe bin Mortaza 28–6–92–0; Shahadat Hossain 25–1–107–3; Mohammad Rafique 44.1–5–132–2; Abdul Razzak 31–1–129–1; Shakib Al Hasan 25–4–68–1; Mohammad Ashraful 3–0–20–0; Aftab Ahmed 5–0–18–0.

Bangladesh

Tamim Iqbal c de Villiers b Steyn	14	– c Steyn b Peterson		9
Junaid Siddique c Boucher b Steyn	18	– c Boucher b Steyn		0
Shahriar Nafees c Smith b Steyn	69	– c Kallis b Peterson		31
*Mohammad Ashraful c Boucher b Steyn	0	– c Boucher b Steyn		4
Abdul Razzak c Prince b Peterson	33	– (7) not out		32
Aftab Ahmed retired hurt	21	– absent hurt		
Shakib Al Hasan c Boucher b Ntini	40	– (5) c McKenzie b Steyn		2
†Mushfiqur Rahim c Boucher b Ntini	15	– (6) c Kallis b Peterson		4
Mohammad Rafique c Smith b Ntini	10	– (8) c and b Peterson		0
Mashrafe bin Mortaza c Boucher b Ntini	1	– c McKenzie b Morkel		4
Shahadat Hossain not out	13	– (9) c Prince b Peterson		24
L-b 11, w 1, n-b 13	25	B 6, l-b 1, n-b 2		9

1/39 (1) 2/49 (2) 3/49 (4) 4/118 (5)	259	1/0 (2) 2/44 (1) 3/45 (3)	119
5/176 (3) 6/232 (8) 7/241 (7)		4/49 (4) 5/54 (5) 6/58 (6)	
8/246 (9) 9/259 (10)		7/58 (8) 8/114 (9) 9/119 (10)	

In the first innings Aftab Ahmed retired hurt at 176-5.

Steyn 22–7–66–4; Ntini 13.4–3–35–4; Morkel 13–0–71–0; Peterson 16–2–61–1; Kallis 6–1–15–0. *Second Innings*— Ntini 5–3–10–0; Steyn 11–2–35–3; Morkel 4.5–1–21–1; Kallis 6–3–13–0; Peterson 13–2–33–5.

Umpires: Aleem Dar *(Pakistan)* (46) and S. A. Bucknor *(West Indies)* (122).
Third umpire: Nadir Shah *(Bangladesh)*.   Referee: R. S. Madugalle *(Sri Lanka)* (102).

Close of play: First day, South Africa 405-0 (McKenzie 169, Smith 223); Second day, Bangladesh 60-3 (Shahriar Nafees 7, Abdul Razzak 8); Third day, Bangladesh 54-5 (Mushfiqur Rahim 4, Abdul Razzak 0).

NEW ZEALAND v ENGLAND 2007-08 (1st Test)

At Seddon Park, Hamilton, on 5, 6, 7, 8, 9 March.
Toss: New Zealand.   Result: NEW ZEALAND won by 189 runs.
Debuts: England – T. R. Ambrose.
Man of the Match: D. L. Vettori.

This was only New Zealand's eighth Test victory over England, and one of their most convincing. New Zealand, with two front-line spinners, were pleased to win the toss on a dry, sun-kissed pitch likely to turn late on. They stitched together an imposing 470, with Taylor making his maiden Test century and How just missing his. England evidently decided the slow-paced pitch would not produce a result, and spent from 3 p.m. on the second day to 1.36 on the fourth slowly extracting 348 runs from 173 overs. It looked as if Vettori would have to make a ticklish declaration to convert 3½ days of control into victory, but Sidebottom turned the match upside down on the fourth afternoon. In 12 balls, he ripped the heart from New Zealand's second innings, taking four wickets for five runs including England's 11th Test hat-trick – Fleming to the last ball of the 30th over, Sinclair and Oram to the first two balls of the 32nd: in the interim McCullum slogged Panesar to deep midwicket. New Zealand needed a bold 66 from Fleming, and Vettori's second mature innings of the match, to set a final-day target of 300 from 81 overs. England's victory charge began merrily, Cook hitting three fours in the first two overs, but then Mills grabbed four wickets for two runs in 25 balls. Bell looked as if he could bat for ever, but his team-mates were quickly cut down, and New Zealand got home with 26 overs to spare.

New Zealand

J. M. How c Collingwood b Panesar	92	– c Hoggard b Sidebottom	39
M. D. Bell c Cook b Harmison	19	– c Ambrose b Sidebottom	0
S. P. Fleming c Cook b Sidebottom	41	– c Cook b Sidebottom	66
M. S. Sinclair c and b Collingwood	8	– c Cook b Sidebottom	2
L. R. P. L. Taylor c and b Pietersen	120	– (6) c and b Panesar	6
J. D. P. Oram c Cook b Hoggard	10	– (7) lbw b Sidebottom	0
†B. B. McCullum c Ambrose b Sidebottom	51	– (5) c Strauss b Panesar	0
*D. L. Vettori c Strauss b Collingwood	88	– c Cook b Sidebottom	35
K. D. Mills not out	25	– lbw b Panesar	11
J. S. Patel c Strauss b Sidebottom	5	– not out	13
C. S. Martin b Sidebottom	0	– not out	0
B 1, l-b 6, w 1, n-b 3	11	L-b 5	5

1/44 (2) 2/108 (3) 3/129 (4) 4/176 (1)　　470　　1/1 (2) 2/99 (1)　　　　(9 wkts dec.) 177
5/191 (6) 6/277 (7) 7/425 (5)　　　　　　　3/109 (3) 4/110 (5)
8/451 (8) 9/470 (10) 10/470 (11)　　　　　5/115 (4) 6/115 (7) 7/119 (6) 8/141 (9) 9/173 (8)

Sidebottom 34.3–8–90–4; Hoggard 26–2–122–1; Harmison 23–3–97–1; Panesar 37–10–101–1; Collingwood 15–2–42–2; Pietersen 3–1–11–1. *Second Innings*—Sidebottom 17–4–49–6; Hoggard 12–3–29–0; Collingwood 6–1–20–0; Harmison 4–0–24–0; Panesar 16–2–50–3.

England

A. N. Cook c sub (N. K. W. Horsley) b Martin	38	– c McCullum b Mills	13
*M. P. Vaughan c McCullum b Patel	63	– lbw b Mills	9
M. J. Hoggard c Fleming b Martin	2	– (9) c McCullum b Martin	4
A. J. Strauss b Vettori	43	– (3) c McCullum b Mills	2
K. P. Pietersen c and b Vettori	42	– (4) lbw b Mills	6
I. R. Bell b Mills	25	– (5) not out	54
P. D. Collingwood lbw b Oram	66	– (6) b Vettori	2
†T. R. Ambrose c Fleming b Patel	55	– (7) b Martin	0
R. J. Sidebottom not out	3	– (8) c McCullum b Martin	0
S. J. Harmison c Fleming b Patel	0	– c Fleming b Patel	1
M. S. Panesar lbw b Mills	0	– c McCullum b Oram	8
B 4, l-b 1, n-b 6	11	B 4, n-b 7	11

1/84 (1) 2/86 (3) 3/130 (2) 4/159 (4)　　348　　1/19 (1) 2/24 (2) 3/25 (3)　　　110
5/203 (6) 6/245 (5) 7/335 (7)　　　　　　 4/30 (4) 5/59 (6) 6/60 (7)
8/347 (8) 9/347 (10) 10/348 (11)　　　　　7/60 (8) 8/67 (9) 9/77 (10) 10/110 (11)

Martin 32–15–60–2; Mills 21.1–6–61–2; Patel 43–14–107–3; Oram 21–9–27–1; Vettori 56–17–88–2. *Second Innings*—Martin 13–4–33–3; Mills 13–4–16–4; Oram 4–2–2–1; Vettori 14–6–16–1; Patel 11–2–39–1.

Umpires: S. J. Davis *(Australia)* (10) and D. J. Harper *(Australia)* (70).
Third umpire: B. F. Bowden *(New Zealand)*.   Referee: J. Srinath *(India)* (7).

Close of play: First day, New Zealand 282-6 (Taylor 54, Vettori 4); Second day, England 87-2 (Vaughan 44, Strauss 1); Third day, England 286-6 (Collingwood 41, Ambrose 23); Fourth day, New Zealand 147-8 (Vettori 13, Patel 6).

NEW ZEALAND v ENGLAND 2007-08 (2nd Test)

At Basin Reserve, Wellington, on 13, 14, 15, 16, 17 March.
Toss: New Zealand.   Result: ENGLAND won by 126 runs.
Debuts: none.
Man of the Match: T. R. Ambrose.

A firm, well-grassed pitch gave bowlers and batsmen alike the chance to express themselves, which they did in some excellent, cut-and-thrust Test cricket, enjoyed by Wellington's biggest crowd for years: the gates were closed on the third day. England had jettisoned the old (Hoggard and Harmison) and rung in the new (Anderson and Broad) after a slothful display at Hamilton. Anderson's inclusion caused some controversy: he had been allowed to play for Auckland a few days before to get some match-practice. Vettori, with four front-line seamers, felt he had to bowl first, but a wicketless first session had him worried before Oram struck twice soon after lunch. Ambrose and Collingwood combined to spirit England to 300, a stand which underpinned their series-levelling victory. Ambrose, in only his second Test, flayed anything short and wide (of which there was plenty), and drove crisply when the bowlers over-compensated, reaching his maiden century on the second morning after several wild swishes when 97 in Oram's final over of the first day. England's bowlers also enjoyed the conditions, and New Zealand were soon in trouble: Anderson removed the top five in the first innings, and Sidebottom took five wickets in the second. New Zealand were eventually set 438, and Sidebottom cashed in after Broad undermined the upper order with a tormenting off-stump line. McCullum refused to go quietly, finally heaving Panesar to long-on, where Sidebottom pouched the catch to complete England's first overseas victory since winning at Mumbai in March 2006.

England

A. N. Cook c McCullum b Oram	44	– c Fleming b Mills	60
*M. P. Vaughan b Oram	32	– c McCullum b Mills	13
A. J. Strauss c Sinclair b Mills	8	– lbw b Oram	44
K. P. Pietersen b Gillespie	31	– run out	17
I. R. Bell c McCullum b Martin	11	– c Sinclair b Oram	41
P. D. Collingwood lbw b Gillespie	65	– lbw b Gillespie	59
†T. R. Ambrose c Taylor b Mills	102	– b Oram	5
S. C. J. Broad b Oram	1	– c McCullum b Martin	16
R. J. Sidebottom c Bell b Gillespie	14	– c How b Gillespie	0
M. S. Panesar c McCullum b Gillespie	6	– c Taylor b Martin	10
J. M. Anderson not out	0	– not out	12
B 5, l-b 15, n-b 8	28	B 6, l-b 5, n-b 5	16

1/79 (2) 2/82 (1) 3/94 (3) 4/126 (5)   342   1/21 (2) 2/127 (1) 3/129 (3)   293
5/136 (4) 6/300 (7) 7/305 (8)   4/160 (4) 5/219 (5) 6/231 (7)
8/335 (6) 9/342 (9) 10/342 (10)   7/259 (8) 8/260 (9) 9/277 (6) 10/293 (10)

Martin 20–1–80–1; Mills 30–4–86–2; Gillespie 20–2–79–4; Oram 29–11–46–3; Vettori 8–0–31–0. *Second Innings*—Martin 24.4–4–77–2; Mills 23–5–59–2; Oram 20–9–44–3; Gillespie 15–1–63–2; Vettori 15–2–39–0.

New Zealand

J. M. How c Strauss b Anderson	7	– c Bell b Sidebottom	8
M. D. Bell b Anderson	0	– c Ambrose b Broad	29
S. P. Fleming c Pietersen b Anderson	34	– b Broad	31
M. S. Sinclair c Ambrose b Anderson	9	– c Bell b Anderson	39
L. R. P. L. Taylor c Ambrose b Anderson	53	– lbw b Sidebottom	55
J. D. P. Oram lbw b Sidebottom	8	– c Pietersen b Sidebottom	30
†B. B. McCullum c Strauss b Broad	25	– c Sidebottom b Panesar	85
*D. L. Vettori not out	50	– c Cook b Sidebottom	0
K. D. Mills c Bell b Collingwood	1	– lbw b Sidebottom	13
M. R. Gillespie b Collingwood	0	– c Ambrose b Anderson	9
C. S. Martin b Collingwood	1	– not out	0
L-b 8, w 1, n-b 1	10	L-b 11, w 1	12

1/4 (2) 2/9 (1) 3/31 (4) 4/102 (3)   198   1/18 (1) 2/69 (2) 3/70 (3)   311
5/113 (6) 6/113 (5) 7/165 (7)   4/151 (4) 5/173 (5) 6/242 (6)
8/176 (9) 9/180 (10) 10/198 (11)   7/246 (8) 8/270 (9) 9/311 (10) 10/311 (7)

Sidebottom 17–3–36–1; Anderson 20–4–73–5; Broad 12–0–56–1; Collingwood 7.5–1–23–3; Panesar 1–0–2–0. *Second Innings*—Sidebottom 31–10–105–5; Anderson 15–2–57–2; Broad 23–6–62–2; Collingwood 9–2–20–0; Panesar 21.3–1–53–1; Pietersen 1–0–3–0.

Umpires: S. J. Davis *(Australia)* (11) and R. E. Koertzen *(South Africa)* (89).
Third umpire: E. A. Watkin *(New Zealand)*.   Referee: J. Srinath *(India)* (8).

Close of play: First day, England 291-5 (Collingwood 48, Ambrose 97); Second day, England 4-0 (Cook 2, Vaughan 0); Third day, England 277-9 (Panesar 6); Fourth day, New Zealand 242-6 (McCullum 43, Vettori 0).

NEW ZEALAND v ENGLAND 2007-08 (3rd Test)

At McLean Park, Napier, on 22, 23, 24, 25, 26 March.
Toss: England.   Result: ENGLAND won by 121 runs.
Debuts: New Zealand – G. D. Elliott, T. G. Southee.
Man of the Match: R. J. Sidebottom.   Man of the Series: R. J. Sidebottom.

Farewells rarely become fairytales: Stephen Fleming's 111th and final Test ended in defeat, as England came from behind to take the series 2–1, only the third time they had done this in a three-Test series, after beating Australia at home in 1888, and Sri Lanka away in 2000-01. With almost cruel appropriateness, the great "non-converter" Fleming scored two half-centuries, to finish his Test career with 46 fifties but just nine hundreds (only two of them in 54 home Tests). At least his final innings nudged his average above 40. England were struggling at lunch on the second day. They were bowled out for 253 – Pietersen's 11th Test century rescued them from 4 for 3 – then, despite Matthew Bell's third duck of the series, New Zealand scuttled to 93 for 1. But Fleming added just three after lunch before edging to second slip, and the last nine wickets clattered for 65, leaving a crucial deficit of 85. Sidebottom kept steaming in throughout the session, taking 5 for 33 from 13 overs. With the pitch becoming ever more benign, Strauss saved his immediate Test career with a career-best 177, as the lead stretched past 500. New Zealand, with 168 overs to survive, lost wickets regularly enough for England to be reasonably relaxed. Their calm was shaken by Tim Southee, 19, who smote New Zealand's fastest recorded Test fifty (29 balls) and finished with 77 from 40 balls with nine sixes. He had earlier produced New Zealand's best bowling figures on debut for 57 years.

England

A. N. Cook b Martin	2	– c McCullum b Patel	37
*M. P. Vaughan lbw b Southee	2	– c McCullum b Martin	4
A. J. Strauss c How b Southee	0	– c Bell b Patel	177
K. P. Pietersen c How b Southee	129	– c Taylor b Vettori	34
I. R. Bell c and b Elliott	9	– c Sinclair b Vettori	110
P. D. Collingwood c Elliott b Patel	30	– c and b Vettori	22
†T. R. Ambrose c Taylor b Patel	11	– c and b Vettori	31
S. C. J. Broad c McCullum b Southee	42	– not out	31
R. J. Sidebottom c Bell b Southee	14	– not out	12
M. S. Panesar b Martin	1		
J. M. Anderson not out	0		
L-b 9, w 3, n-b 1	13	L-b 3, w 1, n-b 5	9

1/4 (2) 2/4 (3) 3/4 (1) 4/36 (5)   253   1/5 (2) 2/77 (1)   (7 wkts dec.) 467
5/125 (6) 6/147 (7) 7/208 (4)   3/140 (4) 4/327 (5)
8/240 (8) 9/253 (10) 10/253 (9)   5/361 (6) 6/424 (3) 7/425 (7)

Martin 26–6–74–2; Southee 23.1–8–55–5; Elliott 10–2–27–1; Vettori 19–6–51–0; Patel 18–3–37–2. *Second Innings*—Martin 18–2–60–1; Southee 24–5–84–0; Elliott 14–1–58–0; Patel 30.5–4–104–2; Vettori 45–6–158–4.

New Zealand

J. M. How c Strauss b Sidebottom	44	– lbw b Panesar	11
M. D. Bell lbw b Sidebottom	0	– c Broad b Panesar	69
S. P. Fleming c Collingwood b Sidebottom	59	– c Ambrose b Panesar	66
M. S. Sinclair c Broad b Sidebottom	7	– c Ambrose b Broad	6
L. R. P. L. Taylor c Ambrose b Broad	2	– c Collingwood b Panesar	74
G. D. Elliott c Ambrose b Sidebottom	6	– c Bell b Broad	4
†B. B. McCullum b Sidebottom	9	– b Panesar	42
*D. L. Vettori c Cook b Sidebottom	14	– c Ambrose b Anderson	43
T. G. Southee c Pietersen b Broad	5	– (10) not out	77
J. S. Patel c Panesar b Broad	4	– (9) c Broad b Panesar	18
C. S. Martin not out	4	– b Sidebottom	5
L-b 13, w 1	14	B 6, l-b 5, w 4, n-b 1	16

1/1 (2) 2/103 (3) 3/116 (1) 4/119 (5)   168   1/48 (1) 2/147 (2) 3/156 (3)   431
5/119 (4) 6/137 (7) 7/138 (6)   4/160 (4) 5/172 (6) 6/276 (5)
8/152 (9) 9/164 (10) 10/168 (8)   7/281 (7) 8/329 (9) 9/347 (8) 10/431 (11)

Sidebottom 21.4–6–47–7; Anderson 7–1–54–0; Broad 17–3–54–3; Panesar 1–1–0–0; Collingwood 2–2–0–0. *Second Innings*—Sidebottom 19.5–3–83–1; Anderson 17–2–99–1; Broad 32–10–78–2; Panesar 46–17–126–6; Collingwood 2–0–20–0; Pietersen 2–0–14–0.

Umpires: D. J. Harper *(Australia)* (71) and R. E. Koertzen *(South Africa)* (90).
Third umpire: G. A. V. Baxter *(New Zealand)*.   Referee: J. Srinath *(India)* (9).

Close of play: First day, England 240-7 (Broad 42, Sidebottom 3); Second day, England 91-2 (Strauss 42, Pietersen 7); Third day, England 416-5 (Strauss 173, Ambrose 28); Fourth day, New Zealand 222-5 (Taylor 34, McCullum 24).

WEST INDIES v SRI LANKA 2007-08 (1st Test)

At National Stadium, Providence, Guyana, on 22, 23, 24, 25, 26 March.
Toss: Sri Lanka.   Result: SRI LANKA won by 121 runs.
Debuts: West Indies – S. J. Benn.
Man of the Match: W. P. U. J. C. Vaas.

From the time their new opening pair began by putting on 130, Sri Lanka dictated terms on the way to their first Test victory in the Caribbean. It came with just 40 balls remaining, when Powell's expansive drive presented mid-off with a tumbling overhead catch; Gayle, in his first home Test as captain, was left unbeaten and unamused. When West Indies lunched at 170 for 2 on the final day, with Sarwan entrenched, a draw seemed likely – but after Bravo (Gayle had demoted himself to No. 6) and Sarwan put on 134 in 46 overs, the remaining eight wickets occupied less than 56. Gayle battled 215 minutes and 131 balls for his best score against Sri Lanka. Earlier, Warnapura made his maiden Test century (in his third match), and Mahela Jayawardene his 22nd. Taylor evened the balance with two wickets in an over, but the total was an imposing one. Vaas snared Gayle for the seventh time in six Tests, for his fifth duck against Sri Lanka. Sarwan played with stylish assurance for 4½ hours, but it was left to the last four wickets to add 118, just saving the follow-on. Sri Lanka pressed on – there was only one maiden in 57 overs – and West Indies eventually needed to score 437 or resist for 113 overs. The National Stadium at Providence, five miles outside Georgetown, became the world's 97th Test venue. It replaced Bourda which, for all its old-world charm, was located below sea level and notorious for its flooding.

Sri Lanka

M. G. Vandort lbw b Taylor	52	– c Ramdin b Gayle	24
B. S. M. Warnapura c Ramdin b Bravo	120	– c Ramdin b Bravo	62
K. C. Sangakkara c Smith b Taylor	50	– c sub (F. H. Edwards) b Bravo	21
*D. P. M. D. Jayawardene lbw b Gayle	136	– c Chanderpaul b Benn	33
T. T. Samaraweera c sub (T. M. Dowlin) b Taylor	0	– not out	56
T. M. Dilshan lbw b Taylor	20	– lbw b Taylor	4
†H. A. P. W. Jayawardene b Powell	21	– (9) not out	5
W. P. U. J. C. Vaas not out	54	– (7) c Ramdin b Benn	13
M. T. T. Mirando c sub (T. M. Dowlin) b Gayle	0	– (8) c Taylor b Benn	14
H. M. R. K. B. Herath not out	13		
L-b 7, w 1, n-b 2	10	B 2, l-b 1, n-b 5	8

1/130 (1) 2/205 (2) 3/243 (3) (8 wkts dec.) 476
4/243 (5) 5/277 (6) 6/331 (7)
7/457 (4) 8/459 (9)

1/43 (1) 2/94 (3) (7 wkts dec.) 240
3/133 (2) 4/159 (4)
5/171 (6) 6/192 (7) 7/224 (8)

M. Muralitharan did not bat.

Powell 29–3–89–1; Taylor 33–8–110–4; Gayle 27–4–66–2; Bravo 30–3–74–1; Benn 40–6–120–0; Hinds 3–0–10–0. *Second Innings*—Powell 9–0–33–0; Taylor 8–0–37–1; Bravo 14–0–54–2; Benn 13–0–59–3; Gayle 13–1–54–1.

West Indies

*C. H. Gayle lbw b Vaas	0	– (6) not out	51
D. S. Smith c H. A. P. W. Jayawardene b Mirando	14	– (1) c Mirando b Vaas	10
R. R. Sarwan c H. A. P. W. Jayawardene b Vaas	80	– lbw b Mirando	72
M. N. Samuels c H. A. P. W. Jayawardene b Mirando	5	– c Sangakkara b Vaas	10
S. Chanderpaul c Warnapura b Muralitharan	23	– b Vaas	3
D. J. Bravo lbw b Muralitharan	8	– (2) c and b Muralitharan	83
R. O. Hinds c H. A. P. W. Jayawardene b Muralitharan	37	– c Sangakkara b Muralitharan	10
†D. Ramdin c Sangakkara b Vaas	38	– c D. P. M. D. Jayawardene b Mirando	1
S. J. Benn run out	28	– lbw b Muralitharan	7
J. E. Taylor not out	27	– c Dilshan b Vaas	12
D. B. Powell c D. P. M. D. Jayawardene b Mirando	12	– c Muralitharan b Vaas	14
L-b 4, n-b 4	8	B 25, l-b 3, n-b 14	42

1/4 (1) 2/46 (2) 3/58 (4) 4/99 (5) 280
5/109 (6) 6/162 (3) 7/193 (7)
8/236 (8) 9/252 (9) 10/280 (11)

1/22 (1) 2/156 (2) 3/171 (4) 315
4/178 (5) 5/212 (3) 6/229 (7)
7/231 (8) 8/244 (9) 9/291 (10) 10/315 (11)

Vaas 25–7–48–3; Mirando 20.5–3–59–3; Dilshan 1–0–2–0; Muralitharan 40–6–112–3; Herath 25–6–55–0. *Second Innings*—Vaas 22.2–7–61–5; Mirando 17–2–70–2; Herath 22–7–44–0; Muralitharan 45–6–112–3.

Umpires: B. F. Bowden *(New Zealand)* (45) and S. J. A. Taufel *(Australia)* (50).
Third umpire: C. R. Duncan *(West Indies)*.   Referee: B. C. Broad *(England)* (26).

Close of play: First day, Sri Lanka 269-4 (D. P. M. D. Jayawardene 25, Dilshan 15); Second day, West Indies 29-1 (Smith 8, Sarwan 21); Third day, West Indies 269-9 (Taylor 22, Powell 6); Fourth day, West Indies 96-1 (Bravo 46, Sarwan 34).

WEST INDIES v SRI LANKA 2007-08 (2nd Test)

At Queen's Park Oval, Port-of-Spain, Trinidad, on 3, 4, 5, 6 April.
Toss: West Indies.   Result: WEST INDIES won by six wickets.
Debuts: West Indies – S. Chattergoon. Sri Lanka – M. K. D. I. Amerasinghe.
Man of the Match: R. R. Sarwan.   Man of the Series: R. R. Sarwan.

This was the first Test in Trinidad for three years, but the locals were seemingly so disenchanted with five successive West Indian defeats there that only a few thousand turned up over the first three days of an engrossing match.
Just when it appeared that the indifference of a once-passionate public was terminal, the stands suddenly filled
in the hope that West Indies would end the sequence – and level the series – by reaching a challenging goal of
253. There was silent despair as they slipped to 73 for 3 before lunch, but amid rising tension – and with Vaas
seemingly tired and Muralitharan unusually ineffective – Sarwan, with his tenth Test hundred, and Chanderpaul
reversed the team's habit of snatching defeat from the jaws of victory with a stand of 157. With 23 needed, Sarwan
was caught bat-pad at silly point, but Smith settled everyone's nerves by carving Murali for three fours. Both Sri
Lankan innings had been rescued by lower-order partnerships. In the first, 62 without loss turned into 117 for 5
before Dilshan and Silva added 105; in the second, they were 99 for 6 before Samaraweera and Vaas put on 138.
The final over of Sri Lanka's first innings was begun by Taylor, but he was taken off for bowling a beamer; Bravo
needed only three balls to wrap things up. Gayle returned to the top of the order, and opened with Sewnarine
Chattergoon, a diminutive left-hander from Guyana who made his Test debut on his 27th birthday.

Sri Lanka

M. G. Vandort c Ramdin b Edwards	30	– run out		1
B. S. M. Warnapura c Chattergoon b Edwards	35	– c Chattergoon b Taylor		0
†K. C. Sangakkara c Ramdin b Edwards	10	– c Samuels b Powell		14
*D. P. M. D. Jayawardene b Taylor	26	– b Edwards		12
T. T. Samaraweera c Gayle b Taylor	6	– run out		125
T. M. Dilshan c Ramdin b Edwards	62	– b Taylor		25
L. P. C. Silva c Powell b Bravo	76	– c Samuels b Taylor		13
W. P. U. J. C. Vaas c Ramdin b Powell	1	– c Ramdin b Gayle		45
M. T. T. Mirando run out	1	– c Ramdin b Bravo		10
M. Muralitharan c Bravo b Powell	8	– c Powell b Taylor		4
M. K. D. I. Amerasinghe not out	0	– not out		0
L-b 8, w 5, n-b 10	23	B 1, l-b 10, w 6, n-b 2		19

1/62 (2) 2/72 (3) 3/93 (1) 4/112 (5)   278
5/117 (4) 6/222 (6) 7/224 (8)
8/240 (9) 9/255 (10) 10/278 (7)

1/2 (2) 2/4 (1) 3/32 (4)   268
4/32 (3) 5/73 (6) 6/99 (7)
7/237 (8) 8/252 (9) 9/268 (5) 10/268 (10)

Powell 17–7–59–2; Taylor 17.2–7–74–2; Edwards 18–4–84–4; Gayle 2–2–0–0; Bravo 10.3–2–53–1. *Second
Innings*—Powell 13–4–49–1; Taylor 15.1–1–52–4; Edwards 14–1–62–1; Bravo 19–5–64–1; Gayle 14–0–30–1.

West Indies

*C. H. Gayle c Vandort b Mirando	45	– c Dilshan b Mirando		10
S. Chattergoon b Vaas	46	– lbw b Vaas		11
R. R. Sarwan c Warnapura b Muralitharan	57	– c Dilshan b Muralitharan		102
M. N. Samuels lbw b Muralitharan	3	– c Warnapura b Vaas		11
S. Chanderpaul lbw b Mirando	18	– not out		86
D. S. Smith b Muralitharan	47	– not out		14
D. J. Bravo lbw b Amerasinghe	26			
†D. Ramdin c Jayawardene b Muralitharan	13			
J. E. Taylor lbw b Vaas	13			
D. B. Powell lbw b Muralitharan	3			
F. H. Edwards not out	1			
L-b 5, w 2, n-b 15	22	B 11, l-b 2, w 2, n-b 5		20

1/58 (1) 2/137 (2) 3/141 (4) 4/177 (3)   294
5/199 (5) 6/246 (7) 7/266 (6)
8/289 (9) 9/291 (8) 10/294 (10)

1/23 (1) 2/24 (2)   (4 wkts) 254
3/73 (4) 4/230 (3)

Vaas 23–1–76–2; Amerasinghe 12–1–62–1; Mirando 12–0–72–2; Muralitharan 29.2–4–79–5. *Second Innings*—
Vaas 17–2–52–2; Mirando 12–3–49–1; Amerasinghe 13–0–43–0; Muralitharan 24.3–4–92–1; Silva 2–0–5–0.

Umpires: B. F. Bowden *(New Zealand)* (46) and S. J. A. Taufel *(Australia)* (51).
Third umpire: G. E. Greaves *(West Indies)*.   Referee: B. C. Broad *(England)* (27).

Close of play: First day, Sri Lanka 217-5 (Dilshan 58, Silva 37); Second day, West Indies 268-7 (Ramdin 5, Taylor
1); Third day, Sri Lanka 268.

INDIA v SOUTH AFRICA 2007-08 (1st Test)

At M. A. Chidambaram Stadium, Chennai, on 26, 27, 28, 29, 30 March.
Toss: South Africa.   Result: MATCH DRAWN.
Debuts: none.
Man of the Match: V. Sehwag.

Virender Sehwag scored his, and India's, second triple-century to join Sir Don Bradman and Brian Lara on an elite list, and light up a high-scoring draw on a slow, low pitch. McKenzie and Smith, fresh from their record opening stand against Bangladesh, put on 132 this time before Amla grafted to 159. South Africa's 540, at a healthy 3.5 an over, left India a mountain to climb. But Sehwag and Wasim Jaffer rattled off, and on the third day Sehwag made 257 runs himself as the deficit shrank to 72. He reached the third-fastest Test double-hundred by balls (194) and then the fastest triple (278). The first two wickets both put on 200, a Test first: 268 with Dravid was India's best for any wicket against South Africa. Sehwag felt that this innings was even better than his 309 against Pakistan at Multan four years previously. It stood out for the purity of the strokeplay, and the quality of the attack; he also fielded for nearly two days beforehand. Finally, with a healthy crowd hoping to see Sehwag threaten Lara's 400, Ntini found the flashing bat's outside edge, and the assault ended after 530 minutes, 304 balls, 42 fours and five sixes. Tendulkar went for a fifth-ball duck, but Dravid completed 10,000 Test runs. The pace began to flag, but even so India scored at more than four an over. There were four sessions left, during which McKenzie made up for his first-innings near-miss with an unbeaten 155.

South Africa

*G. C. Smith c Laxman b Kumble	73	– (2) lbw b Harbhajan Singh	35
N. D. McKenzie c Dravid b Harbhajan Singh	94	– (1) not out	155
H. M. Amla run out	159	– c Dravid b Kumble	81
J. H. Kallis c Wasim Jaffer b Harbhajan Singh	13	– c R. P. Singh b Harbhajan Singh	19
A. G. Prince c and b Kumble	23	– c Wasim Jaffer b Harbhajan Singh	5
A. B. de Villiers c Dhoni b Sreesanth	44	– c Ganguly b Sehwag	11
†M. V. Boucher c Dravid b Sehwag	70	– not out	11
M. Morkel c and b Harbhajan Singh	35		
P. L. Harris c Dhoni b Harbhajan Singh	5		
D. W. Steyn c R. P. Singh b Harbhajan Singh	15		
M. Ntini not out	1		
B 1, l-b 5, w 1, n-b 1	8	B 8, l-b 5, n-b 1	14

1/132 (1) 2/196 (2) 3/244 (4) 4/291 (5)   540   1/53 (2) 2/210 (3)   (5 wkts dec.) 331
5/357 (6) 6/456 (3) 7/510 (7)   3/264 (4) 4/272 (5)
8/520 (8) 9/529 (9) 10/540 (10)   5/306 (6)

R. P. Singh 23–1–111–0; Sreesanth 26–5–104–1; Kumble 45–11–106–2; Harbhajan Singh 44.5–4–164–5; Sehwag 11–1–37–1; Ganguly 3–0–12–0. *Second Innings*—Sreesanth 12–0–42–0; R. P. Singh 9–1–43–0; Harbhajan Singh 34–1–101–3; Ganguly 2–1–1–0; Kumble 20–2–57–1; Sehwag 22–2–55–1; Laxman 10–2–19–0.

India

Wasim Jaffer c Kallis b Harris	73	R. P. Singh b Steyn	0
V. Sehwag c McKenzie b Ntini	319	S. Sreesanth not out	4
R. Dravid c Kallis b Ntini	111		
S. R. Tendulkar c Kallis b Ntini	0		
S. C. Ganguly c Boucher b Harris	24	B 20, l-b 10, w 4, n-b 4	38
V. V. S. Laxman c and b Harris	39		
†M. S. Dhoni c Boucher b Steyn	16	1/213 (1) 2/481 (2) 3/481 (4)	627
*A. Kumble b Steyn	3	4/526 (5) 5/573 (3) 6/598 (7)	
Harbhajan Singh b Steyn	0	7/610 (8) 8/610 (9)	
		9/612 (10) 10/627 (6)	

Steyn 32–3–103–4; Ntini 28–3–128–3; Morkel 25–4–76–0; Harris 53.1–6–203–3; Kallis 14–0–71–0; Prince 3–0–16–0.

Umpires: Asad Rauf *(Pakistan)* (18) and A. L. Hill *(New Zealand)* (6).
Third umpire: A. M. Saheba *(India)*.   Referee: R. S. Mahanama *(Sri Lanka)* (19).

Close of play: First day, South Africa 304-4 (Amla 85, de Villiers 10); Second day, India 82-0 (Wasim Jaffer 25, Sehwag 52); Third day, India 468-1 (Sehwag 309, Dravid 65); Fourth day, South Africa 131-1 (McKenzie 59, Amla 35).

INDIA v SOUTH AFRICA 2007-08 (2nd Test)

At Sardar Patel Stadium, Motera, Ahmedabad, on 3, 4, 5 April.
Toss: India.   Result: SOUTH AFRICA won by an innings and 90 runs.
Debuts: none.
Man of the Match: A. B. de Villiers.

A hot summer in Ahmedabad meant that grass had to be left on the pitch to bind the surface; the groundsman, the former Test cricketer Dhiraj Parsana, insisted he could not remove it without taking the top off. India won a toss they might have been better off losing, and chose to bat. Steyn and Ntini relished the extra bounce and lateral movement the pitch offered, and tore into the batting, which was lacking Tendulkar, who had aggravated a groin strain. India were demolished for 76, just one run more than their lowest total at home, against West Indies at Delhi in 1987-88. The innings lasted only 20 overs in all, the shortest-ever in a Test on the subcontinent, and South Africa even faced an over before lunch. Suddenly the runs came easily. Kallis helped himself to his 30th Test hundred, putting on 256 – South Africa's highest for any wicket against India – with de Villiers, who tackled pace and spin with aplomb for eight hours in a maiden double-century, South Africa's first against India. Smith eventually declared with a massive lead of 418. India's middle order applied themselves much better in the second innings, but the pressure of being so far behind told. Only a fighting 87 from Ganguly, showing strong technique and sound judgment, and Dhoni's battling 52 pushed India to 328: the three-day defeat was their heaviest at home in nearly 50 years, since Richie Benaud's Australians won by an innings and 127 runs at Delhi in 1959-60.

India

Wasim Jaffer c Smith b Ntini	9	– (2) c de Villiers b Kallis		19
V. Sehwag b Steyn	6	– (1) lbw b Ntini		17
R. Dravid b Steyn	3	– c de Villiers b Morkel		17
V. V. S. Laxman b Ntini	3	– c Boucher b Morkel		35
S. C. Ganguly b Ntini	0	– c Boucher b Steyn		87
†M. S. Dhoni c Boucher b Morkel	14	– c Smith b Ntini		52
I. K. Pathan not out	21	– not out		43
*A. Kumble b Morkel	0	– b Harris		5
Harbhajan Singh lbw b Steyn	1	– lbw b Steyn		4
R. P. Singh c Smith b Steyn	0	– c Kallis b Steyn		8
S. Sreesanth b Steyn	0	– b Ntini		17
B 4, l-b 11, w 2, n-b 2	19	B 5, l-b 7, w 7, n-b 5		24

1/16 (1) 2/24 (2) 3/30 (4) 4/30 (5)   76   1/31 (1) 2/64 (3) 3/70 (2)   328
5/53 (3) 6/55 (6) 7/55 (8)   4/125 (4) 5/235 (5) 6/268 (6)
8/56 (9) 9/76 (10) 10/76 (11)   7/273 (8) 8/292 (9) 9/306 (10) 10/328 (11)

Steyn 8–2–23–5; Ntini 6–1–18–3; Morkel 6–1–20–2. *Second Innings*—Steyn 23–1–91–3; Ntini 16.2–3–44–3; Morkel 20–0–87–2; Kallis 10–3–26–1; Harris 25–4–68–1.

South Africa

*G. C. Smith lbw b Sreesanth	34	M. Morkel lbw b Harbhajan Singh	1
N. D. McKenzie c Dravid b Harbhajan Singh	42	P. L. Harris not out	9
H. M. Amla c Wasim Jaffer b Harbhajan Singh	16	B 2, l-b 14, w 4	20
J. H. Kallis b Sreesanth	132		
A. G. Prince lbw b Harbhajan Singh	2	1/78 (1) 2/100 (2) (7 wkts dec.)	494
A. B. de Villiers not out	217	3/101 (3) 4/117 (5)	
†M. V. Boucher lbw b Kumble	21	5/373 (4) 6/439 (7) 7/452 (8)	

D. W. Steyn and M. Ntini did not bat.

Sreesanth 23–4–87–2; R. P. Singh 21–2–81–0; Pathan 21.2–3–85–0; Harbhajan Singh 40–5–135–4; Kumble 33–2–78–1; Ganguly 3–0–12–0.

Umpires: B. R. Doctrove *(West Indies)* (16) and A. L. Hill *(New Zealand)* (7).
Third umpire: S. L. Shastri *(India)*.   Referee: R. S. Mahanama *(Sri Lanka)* (20).

Close of play: First day, South Africa 223-4 (Kallis 60, de Villiers 59); Second day, South Africa 494-7 (de Villiers 217, Harris 9).

INDIA v SOUTH AFRICA 2007-08 (3rd Test)

At Green Park, Kanpur, on 11, 12, 13 April.
Toss: South Africa.   Result: INDIA won by eight wickets.
Debuts: none.
Man of the Match: S. C. Ganguly.   Man of the Series: Harbhajan Singh.

A pitch to suit India's spinners was part of the plan to level the series, but no-one bargained for the strip that was prepared – or underprepared. Before the first ball was bowled, both sides were privately convinced the pitch would disintegrate and prove dangerous for batting. Kumble had a groin injury, so Dhoni captained India. Smith chose to bat, but by halfway into the first session each delivery was accompanied by a puff of dust. Led by Smith and Amla, South Africa did well to reach 265. When India's turn came, the going was not easy, but Ganguly and Laxman found ways to score where others had failed, and a spirited tenth-wicket stand on the third morning stretched the lead to 60. Harbhajan Singh, who had bowled intelligently and creatively in the first innings, opened the bowling, and South Africa's batsmen attempted to block their way out of trouble rather than trying to put runs on the board, a doomed strategy. While Harbhajan got stuck in, Sehwag tossed up his own offbreaks: his first ball had Kallis caught at short leg, then he produced another peach to bowl Smith round his legs as South Africa were all out for 121. Needing only 62, India sprinted to a three-day victory on a pitch that had come apart. Overjoyed, the Indians presented the groundsman with an impromptu tip of 10,000 rupees. South Africa's coach, Mickey Arthur, was unimpressed: "It was a poor cricket wicket, though I can understand the reason behind it."

South Africa

N. D. McKenzie st Dhoni b Chawla	36	– lbw b Sreesanth		14
*G. C. Smith c Wasim Jaffer b Yuvraj Singh	69	– b Sehwag		35
H. M. Amla b Sharma	51	– c Wasim Jaffer b Harbhajan Singh		0
J. H. Kallis b Harbhajan Singh	1	– c Wasim Jaffer b Sehwag		15
A. G. Prince lbw b Sehwag	16	– not out		22
A. B. de Villiers c Ganguly b Chawla	25	– c Laxman b Harbhajan Singh		7
†M. V. Boucher b Sharma	29	– c Dhoni b Sharma		5
M. Morkel c Dravid b Harbhajan Singh	17	– b Sharma		0
P. L. Harris b Sharma	12	– c Dravid b Harbhajan Singh		0
D. W. Steyn c sub (M. Kaif) b Harbhajan Singh	0	– b Harbhajan Singh		7
M. Ntini not out	0	– c Ganguly b Sehwag		0
L-b 3, w 2, n-b 4	9	B 12, l-b 1, w 1, n-b 2		16

1/61 (1) 2/152 (2) 3/160 (3) 4/161 (4)   265   1/26 (1) 2/27 (3) 3/65 (4)   121
5/199 (6) 6/215 (5) 7/241 (8)   4/72 (2) 5/90 (6) 6/101 (7)
8/264 (7) 9/265 (10) 10/265 (9)   7/101 (8) 8/102 (9) 9/114 (10) 10/121 (11)

Sreesanth 11–0–32–0; Sharma 12.3–1–55–3; Harbhajan Singh 31–9–52–3; Chawla 16–3–66–2; Yuvraj Singh 11–1–39–1; Sehwag 6–2–18–1. *Second Innings*—Harbhajan Singh 23–7–44–4; Sharma 10–2–18–2; Sreesanth 9–4–9–1; Chawla 4–0–18–0; Sehwag 8.5–2–12–3; Yuvraj Singh 1–0–7–0.

India

Wasim Jaffer lbw b Morkel	15	– lbw b Morkel		10
V. Sehwag lbw b Steyn	8	– c Prince b Harris		22
R. Dravid c de Villiers b Morkel	29	– (4) not out		18
V. V. S. Laxman b Morkel	50			
S. C. Ganguly c Amla b Steyn	87	– (3) not out		13
Yuvraj Singh c de Villiers b Harris	32			
*†M. S. Dhoni st Boucher b Harris	32			
Harbhajan Singh lbw b Steyn	6			
P. P. Chawla c Smith b Ntini	4			
S. Sreesanth c Prince b Harris	29			
I. Sharma not out	14			
B 8, l-b 6, w 1, n-b 4	19	N-b 1		1

1/18 (2) 2/35 (1) 3/113 (3) 4/123 (4)   325   1/32 (2) 2/32 (1)   (2 wkts) 64
5/188 (6) 6/248 (7) 7/268 (8)
8/279 (9) 9/279 (5) 10/325 (10)

Steyn 20–1–71–3; Ntini 21–7–47–1; Morkel 15–2–63–3; Harris 32.4–8–101–3; Kallis 9–1–23–0; Amla 2–0–6–0. *Second Innings*—Steyn 2–0–15–0; Ntini 1–0–5–0; Harris 5.1–0–36–1; Morkel 5–1–8–1.

Umpires: Asad Rauf *(Pakistan)* (19) and B. R. Doctrove *(West Indies)* (17).
Third umpire: G. A. Pratapkumar *(India)*.   Referee: R. S. Mahanama *(Sri Lanka)* (21).

Close of play: First day, South Africa 265; Second day, India 288-9 (Sreesanth 9, Sharma 0).

ENGLAND v NEW ZEALAND 2008 (1st Test)

At Lord's, London, on 15, 16, 17, 18, 19 May.
Toss: England.   Result: MATCH DRAWN.
Debuts: New Zealand – D. R. Flynn, A. J. Redmond.
Man of the Match: D. L. Vettori.

Bad weather, which cut the first two days in half and allowed only 8.5 overs on the third, effectively sentenced this match to a draw, although New Zealand – weakened by Stephen Fleming's retirement and the absence of Shane Bond, temporarily banned for joining an unauthorised Indian 20-over league – were grateful to Oram's forthright final-day century to dispel any prospect of defeat. Another attacking innings had lit up the abbreviated first day: after New Zealand slipped to 104 for 5, McCullum smacked 13 fours and two sixes (the second over long-off into the Warner Stand off Broad) in a run-a-ball 97, before falling in the nineties for the second time at Lord's. Sidebottom wrapped things up with four for five in ten overs next morning. England, sporting new ultra-white kit for the first time, started confidently, but after the openers put on 128 only Vaughan – after an elegant 18th (and, as it turned out, last) Test century – batted for long. It was his sixth Test hundred at Lord's, equalling Graham Gooch's record. Vettori finally dismissed him to round off a fine spell with his 250th Test wicket. England still began the final day with victory hopes and, if Strauss had held a straightforward chance at first slip when How had 46, those hopes would have been even higher. Even so, when McCullum retired hurt after being hit on the left elbow by Broad, the lead was only 78, but Oram, who hit 15 fours and two sixes, stopped the rot.

New Zealand

J. M. How c Ambrose b Anderson	7	– c Cook b Broad	68
A. J. Redmond c Cook b Anderson	0	– c Strauss b Anderson	17
J. A. H. Marshall c Strauss b Broad	24	– lbw b Sidebottom	0
L. R. P. L. Taylor c Collingwood b Broad	19	– lbw b Panesar	20
†B. B. McCullum b Panesar	97	– c Ambrose b Anderson	24
D. R. Flynn b Anderson	9	– not out	29
J. D. P. Oram c Strauss b Sidebottom	28	– b Sidebottom	101
*D. L. Vettori b Sidebottom	48	– not out	0
K. D. Mills b Sidebottom	10		
T. G. Southee b Sidebottom	1		
C. S. Martin not out	0		
B 16, l-b 14, w 1, n-b 3	34	B 4, l-b 5, n-b 1	10

1/2 (2) 2/18 (1) 3/41 (4) 4/76 (3)   277   1/47 (2) 2/52 (3)   (6 wkts) 269
5/104 (6) 6/203 (5) 7/222 (7)   3/99 (4) 4/115 (1)
8/258 (9) 9/260 (10) 10/277 (8)   5/252 (7) 6/269 (5)

In the second innings McCullum, when 11, retired hurt at 120 and resumed at 252.

Sidebottom 28.2–12–55–4; Anderson 20–5–66–3; Broad 24–4–85–2; Collingwood 3–1–11–0; Panesar 11–2–30–1. *Second Innings*—Sidebottom 21.2–4–65–2; Anderson 19–5–64–2; Broad 17–4–54–1; Panesar 24–8–56–1; Pietersen 5–0–21–0.

England

A. J. Strauss lbw b Oram	63	R. J. Sidebottom c Taylor b Mills	16
A. N. Cook c McCullum b Martin	61	M. S. Panesar c Flynn b Vettori	0
*M. P. Vaughan c Marshall b Vettori	106	J. M. Anderson not out	0
K. P. Pietersen lbw b Vettori	3	B 3, l-b 7, w 1, n-b 12	23
I. R. Bell c McCullum b Martin	16		
P. D. Collingwood c Taylor b Vettori	6	1/121 (2) 2/148 (1) 3/152 (4)	319
†T. R. Ambrose lbw b Vettori	0	4/180 (5) 5/208 (6) 6/208 (7)	
S. C. J. Broad b Oram	25	7/269 (8) 8/317 (9) 9/318 (10) 10/319 (3)	

Martin 32–8–76–2; Mills 22–3–60–1; Southee 16–2–59–0; Oram 19–5–45–2; Vettori 22.3–4–69–5.

Umpires: S. A. Bucknor *(West Indies)* (123) and S. J. A. Taufel *(Australia)* (52).
Third umpire: N. J. Llong *(England)*.   Referee: R. S. Madugalle *(Sri Lanka)* (103).

Close of play: First day, New Zealand 208-6 (Oram 23, Vettori 5); Second day, England 68-0 (Strauss 24, Cook 43); Third day, England 89-0 (Strauss 31, Cook 53); Fourth day, New Zealand 40-0 (How 26, Redmond 14).

ENGLAND v NEW ZEALAND 2008 (2nd Test)

At Old Trafford, Manchester, on 23, 24, 25, 26 May.
Toss: New Zealand.   Result: ENGLAND won by six wickets.
Debuts: none.
Man of the Match: M. S. Panesar.

England overturned a large first-innings deficit to win inside four days, pulling off their fifth-highest Test run-chase – and Manchester's biggest – to do it. New Zealand had roared away at the start: How and Redmond added 80 in 99 minutes before Sidebottom pegged them back. Taylor batted regally, smiting four of his five sixes after reaching his century. Vettori was run out after failing to ground his bat, while Flynn played no further part in the match after losing two teeth to an Anderson bouncer; later Mills contributed a maiden fifty to a partnership of 89 with Taylor. England surrendered the initiative by batting slowly: Strauss and Vaughan put on 78 in 34 overs, after which only Pietersen and Broad made it past 8 as Vettori took another five wickets. New Zealand were firmly in charge at 85 for 2 – 264 ahead – but suddenly Panesar turned the match: Taylor was his 100th Test wicket, and 6 for 37 his best figures. Sixteen wickets fell on the third day, but England lost only three as they batted more positively next day: Strauss's 12th hundred set up the victory which Collingwood completed on the stroke of tea. It was Old Trafford's last Test for at least three years, which created much local debate, and probably some regret for Panesar, who had taken 25 wickets in three Tests there. Darrell Hair returned from ICC exile to umpire his first Test since The Oval 2006, when he had insisted that Pakistan had forfeited the match.

New Zealand

J. M. How c Ambrose b Anderson	64	– lbw b Panesar	29
A. J. Redmond b Sidebottom	28	– c Collingwood b Anderson	6
J. A. H. Marshall lbw b Sidebottom	0	– lbw b Panesar	28
L. R. P. L. Taylor not out	154	– lbw b Panesar	15
†B. B. McCullum c Collingwood b Panesar	11	– lbw b Panesar	0
D. R. Flynn retired hurt	4	– absent hurt	
J. D. P. Oram run out	38	– (8) c Ambrose b Sidebottom	7
*D. L. Vettori run out	1	– (6) c Broad b Panesar	4
K. D. Mills b Anderson	57	– (7) c Ambrose b Panesar	8
I. E. O'Brien c Bell b Anderson	5	– (9) c Anderson b Sidebottom	6
C. S. Martin b Anderson	0	– (10) not out	0
B 4, l-b 11, w 3, n-b 1	19	L-b 11	11

1/80 (2) 2/86 (3) 3/102 (1) 4/123 (5)   381   1/28 (2) 2/50 (1) 3/85 (3)   114
5/249 (7) 6/250 (8) 7/339 (9)   4/85 (5) 5/91 (6) 6/91 (4)
8/368 (10) 9/381 (11)   7/106 (8) 8/114 (7) 9/114 (9)

In the first innings Flynn retired hurt at 136.

Sidebottom 27–6–86–2; Anderson 20.3–0–118–4; Panesar 22–1–101–1; Broad 20–3–60–0; Collingwood 1–0–1–0.
Second Innings—Sidebottom 12.2–5–26–2; Anderson 8–1–21–1; Panesar 17–5–37–6; Broad 4–0–19–0.

England

A. J. Strauss c McCullum b O'Brien	60	– c Taylor b O'Brien	106
A. N. Cook lbw b O'Brien	19	– c Marshall b Vettori	28
*M. P. Vaughan lbw b Vettori	30	– c McCullum b Martin	48
K. P. Pietersen c Taylor b Vettori	26	– run out	42
R. J. Sidebottom c How b Vettori	4		
I. R. Bell c Taylor b O'Brien	8	– (5) not out	21
P. D. Collingwood lbw b Vettori	2	– (6) not out	24
†T. R. Ambrose c Taylor b Vettori	3		
S. C. J. Broad c sub (J. S. Patel) b Mills	30		
M. S. Panesar c McCullum b Mills	1		
J. M. Anderson not out	3		
B 2, l-b 7, n-b 7	16	B 9, l-b 10, n-b 6	25

1/33 (2) 2/111 (1) 3/141 (3) 4/145 (5)   202   1/60 (2) 2/150 (3)   (4 wkts) 294
5/160 (4) 6/164 (6) 7/164 (7)   3/235 (1) 4/248 (4)
8/179 (8) 9/180 (10) 10/202 (9)

Martin 10–3–31–0; Mills 9.3–1–38–2; O'Brien 23–9–49–3; Vettori 31–5–66–5; Oram 8–3–5–0; Redmond 2–1–4–0. *Second Innings*—Martin 13–1–45–1; Mills 6–0–17–0; Vettori 35–7–111–1; O'Brien 20–2–62–1; How 1–0–4–0; Oram 13–1–36–0.

Umpires: D. B. Hair *(Australia)* (77) and S. J. A. Taufel *(Australia)* (53).
Third umpire: I. J. Gould *(England)*.   Referee: R. S. Madugalle *(Sri Lanka)* (104).

Close of play: First day, New Zealand 202-4 (Taylor 67, Oram 22); Second day, England 152-4 (Pietersen 22, Bell 4); Third day, England 76-1 (Strauss 27, Vaughan 12).

ENGLAND v NEW ZEALAND 2008 (3rd Test)

At Trent Bridge, Nottingham, on 5, 6, 7, 8 June.
Toss: New Zealand.   Result: ENGLAND won by an innings and nine runs.
Debuts: New Zealand – G. J. Hopkins.
Man of the Match: J. M. Anderson.   Men of the Series: A. J. Strauss and D. L. Vettori.

England wrapped up the series 2–0, although victory had looked anything but assured when they lost three wickets in as many overs immediately after lunch on the first day to be 86 for 5. A match-turning stand between Pietersen and Ambrose reclaimed the initiative, then Anderson's superb spell made sure it was not relinquished. At Wellington in March, Ambrose put England on the road to victory by putting on 164 with Collingwood: now his partnership of 161 with Pietersen did likewise. Next morning Broad – reprieved when McCullum, having relinquished the wicketkeeping gloves with a back niggle, turfed a regulation slip catch – went confidently to his first Test fifty. Anderson immediately found his rhythm: Redmond had no answer to a ball angled towards leg stump then swinging away to hit off. In Anderson's third over, McCullum tried a similar shot to a similar ball and lost his off stump too. By the close Anderson had all six wickets for 42 – his best Test figures – but could not quite recapture the magic next day. Sidebottom was the main destroyer in the follow-on, when only McCullum and Flynn, who gritted his remaining teeth for 2½ hours, resisted for long before Oram's defiant 50. The last five wickets tumbled in 41 balls on the fourth morning, Sidebottom taking his tally in six Tests against New Zealand in 2008 to 41. England were unchanged for the fifth Test running, equalling their record from 1884-85, when the same eleven did duty throughout a tour of Australia.

England

A. J. Strauss c Taylor b Mills	37	J. M. Anderson c Hopkins b Oram		28
A. N. Cook b Mills	6	R. J. Sidebottom not out		7
*M. P. Vaughan b O'Brien	16	M. S. Panesar c McCullum b Vettori		0
K. P. Pietersen c Hopkins b O'Brien	115	B 10, l-b 9, w 1, n-b 4		24
I. R. Bell lbw b O'Brien	0			
P. D. Collingwood c Taylor b Mills	0	1/14 (2) 2/44 (3) 3/84 (1) 4/85 (5)		364
†T. R. Ambrose c Hopkins b O'Brien	67	5/86 (6) 6/247 (4) 7/262 (7)		
S. C. J. Broad b Martin	64	8/338 (9) 9/361 (8) 10/364 (11)		

Martin 22–5–83–1; Mills 31–8–76–3; O'Brien 23–4–74–4; Oram 22–7–35–1; Vettori 28.5–4–77–1.

New Zealand

J. M. How c Ambrose b Anderson	40	– c Cook b Sidebottom	19
A. J. Redmond b Anderson	1	– c Ambrose b Broad	2
B. B. McCullum b Anderson	9	– b Anderson	71
L. R. P. L. Taylor c Pietersen b Anderson	21	– lbw b Broad	14
D. R. Flynn lbw b Anderson	0	– c Ambrose b Sidebottom	49
†G. J. Hopkins lbw b Anderson	15	– c Ambrose b Sidebottom	12
J. D. P. Oram c Ambrose b Anderson	7	– not out	50
*D. L. Vettori c Strauss b Sidebottom	7	– c Pietersen b Sidebottom	1
K. D. Mills c Pietersen b Broad	1	– c Strauss b Sidebottom	2
I. E. O'Brien b Broad	0	– c Collingwood b Sidebottom	4
C. S. Martin not out	0	– c Collingwood b Anderson	0
B 8, l-b 8, w 6	22	B 3, l-b 4, w 1	8

1/2 (2) 2/14 (3) 3/62 (4) 4/62 (5)   123
5/77 (1) 6/93 (7) 7/108 (8)
8/123 (9) 9/123 (10) 10/123 (6)

1/21 (2) 2/33 (1) 3/58 (4)   232
4/152 (3) 5/169 (5) 6/197 (6)
7/205 (8) 8/221 (9) 9/225 (10) 10/232 (11)

Sidebottom 17–4–49–1; Anderson 21.3–8–43–7; Collingwood 2–0–5–0; Broad 6–3–10–2. *Second Innings—* Sidebottom 24–7–67–6; Anderson 14.3–3–55–2; Broad 21–4–77–2; Panesar 11–4–21–0; Collingwood 2–1–5–0.

Umpires: S. A. Bucknor *(West Indies)* (124) and D. B. Hair *(Australia)* (78).
Third umpire: P. J. Hartley *(England)*.   Referee: R. S. Madugalle *(Sri Lanka)* (105).

Close of play: First day, England 273-7 (Broad 15, Anderson 1); Second day, New Zealand 96-6 (Hopkins 11, Vettori 3); Third day, New Zealand 177-5 (Hopkins 7, Oram 8).

WEST INDIES v AUSTRALIA 2008 (1st Test)

At Sabina Park, Kingston, Jamaica, on 22, 23, 24, 25, 26 May.
Toss: Australia.   Result: AUSTRALIA won by 95 runs.
Debuts: West Indies – A. S. Jaggernauth. Australia – B. J. Haddin.
Man of the Match: S. R. Clark.

For ten pulsating overs at the end of the third day, the years were rolled back to the heyday of West Indian fast bowling. Edges were clipped, pads rapped and stumps rattled as Edwards and Powell swept aside Australia's first four second-innings wickets for 12. Not even Hall and Griffith, or Marshall and Garner, or Ambrose and Walsh, had reduced Australia to such a shambles. It became 18 for 5 when Powell dismissed Johnson, the nightwatchman, fifth ball next morning: only six times in 694 Tests had Australia lost their first five wickets so cheaply, the most recent for 16 at Brisbane in the 1936-37 Ashes. They led by just 137 but, as in the first innings, Symonds led a recovery, this one bringing 149 for the last five wickets, after which Clark and Lee undermined West Indies' tentative effort at a target of 287. In the respective first innings, Ponting returned to form with a superb 35th Test hundred, one more than Sunil Gavaskar and Brian Lara, behind only Sachin Tendulkar (then 39), while West Indies were 68 for 3 before Chanderpaul rode to their rescue yet again. He had 86 when a Lee bouncer slammed into the back of his helmet: he lay motionless, reporting afterwards that he briefly had no feeling in his hands or legs – but stayed to complete his 18th Test century, batting for 381 minutes in all. With Adam Gilchrist having retired, Brad Haddin became the 400th Australian to wear the baggy green cap.

Australia

P. A. Jaques lbw b Edwards	9	– c Ramdin b Edwards			4
S. M. Katich c Sammy b Edwards	12	– lbw b Edwards			1
*R. T. Ponting c Parchment b Bravo	158	– c Bravo b Powell			5
M. E. K. Hussey c Bravo b Jaggernauth	56	– b Powell			1
B. J. Hodge c Ramdin b Edwards	67	– (6) c Ramdin b Bravo			27
M. G. Johnson c Powell b Sammy	22	– (5) c Ramdin b Powell			4
A. Symonds not out	70	– c Sammy b Bravo			79
†B. J. Haddin c Ramdin b Sammy	11	– c Morton b Bravo			23
B. Lee lbw b Edwards	4	– c Ramdin b Edwards			9
S. R. Clark c Bravo b Powell	3	– not out			1
S. C. G. MacGill b Edwards	2	– c Morton b Bravo			0
B 2, l-b 13, n-b 2	17	B 2, l-b 10, n-b 1			13

1/18 (2) 2/37 (1) 3/174 (4) 4/293 (3)   431   1/5 (1) 2/10 (3) 3/12 (2)   167
5/326 (5) 6/350 (6) 7/368 (8)   4/12 (4) 5/18 (5) 6/70 (6)
8/383 (9) 9/399 (10) 10/431 (11)   7/144 (8) 8/162 (9) 9/166 (7) 10/167 (11)

Powell 29–4–99–1; Edwards 26.5–4–104–5; Sammy 29–7–78–2; Bravo 22–6–61–1; Jaggernauth 20–0–74–1. *Second Innings*—Powell 15–5–36–3; Edwards 16–3–40–3; Bravo 18.5–3–47–4; Jaggernauth 3–0–22–0; Sammy 4–0–10–0.

West Indies

D. S. Smith b Clark	32	– lbw b Clark			28
B. A. Parchment c Haddin b Clark	9	– c Haddin b Clark			15
*R. R. Sarwan c Haddin b Clark	7	– c Symonds b Clark			12
R. S. Morton c Clark b MacGill	67	– lbw b Lee			9
S. Chanderpaul c Hussey b MacGill	118	– c and b Lee			11
D. J. Bravo c Katich b Lee	46	– c Johnson b Clark			0
†D. Ramdin c Haddin b Lee	0	– run out			36
D. J. G. Sammy c Jaques b Johnson	0	– lbw b Clark			35
D. B. Powell b Lee	3	– c Haddin b MacGill			27
F. H. Edwards c Haddin b Johnson	1	– not out			9
A. S. Jaggernauth not out	0	– c Jaques b MacGill			0
B 2, l-b 10, w 3, n-b 14	29	B 4, l-b 2, n-b 3			9

1/47 (1) 2/62 (3) 3/68 (2) 4/196 (4)   312   1/22 (2) 2/55 (3) 3/60 (1)   191
5/260 (6) 6/262 (7) 7/263 (8)   4/74 (4) 5/80 (6) 6/82 (5)
8/268 (9) 9/298 (10) 10/312 (5)   7/149 (7) 8/172 (8) 9/191 (9) 10/191 (11)

Lee 28–7–63–3; Johnson 26–6–63–2; Clark 19–2–59–3; MacGill 22–2–100–2; Symonds 11–4–15–0. *Second Innings*—Lee 22–6–81–2; Clark 20–8–32–5; Johnson 11–3–29–0; MacGill 14–2–43–2.

Umpires: Aleem Dar *(Pakistan)* (47) and R. B. Tiffin *(Zimbabwe)* (41).
Third umpire: N. A. Malcolm *(West Indies)*.   Referee: R. S. Mahanama *(Sri Lanka)* (22).

Close of play: First day, Australia 301-4 (Hodge 53, Johnson 1); Second day, West Indies 115-3 (Morton 23, Chanderpaul 25); Third day, Australia 17-4 (Johnson 4, Hodge 0); Fourth day, West Indies 46-1 (Smith 19, Sarwan 8).

WEST INDIES v AUSTRALIA 2008 (2nd Test)

At Sir Vivian Richards Stadium, North Sound, Antigua, on 30, 31 May, 1, 2, 3 June.
Toss: Australia.　　Result: MATCH DRAWN.
Debuts: none.
Man of the Match: S. Chanderpaul.

With its 18,000 capacity, state-of-the-art stands and surrounding open fields, the 98th ground to stage Test cricket was in direct contrast to its intimate, unpretentious predecessor four miles away in the heart of the island's capital, St John's – except in one important respect. The old ground's pitch, which yielded several batting records (including both Brian Lara's Test-record scores), seemed to have been transported here, completely intact. Flat and feature-less, this one allowed 47.89 runs per wicket: despite declaring twice, Australia could not convert domination into victory. They were not helped by poor drainage, which delayed the third day's play by 5½ hours. Sarwan and Chanderpaul comfortably batted through most of the last day to ensure the first draw between these teams since 1994-95 – almost inevitably at St John's – 25 Tests previously. West Indies' first innings was derailed by Lee, who took five for five in 19 balls as the last six wickets tumbled for 38. That, following centuries from Katich (his first for three years) and Clarke, gave Australia a big lead; Ponting, when 61, became the seventh player (the third Australian after Allan Border and Steve Waugh) to make 10,000 runs in Tests. MacGill announced his imme-diate retirement during the match. He had failed to recover properly from the wrist operation which kept him out of much of the preceding home season, and struggled embarrassingly in the first innings – although ironically his 208th and final Test wicket came from a perfectly pitched ripping legbreak which Sarwan edged to slip.

Australia

P. A. Jaques lbw b Bravo	17	– c Ramdin b Taylor	76
S. M. Katich c Ramdin b Taylor	113		
*R. T. Ponting c Marshall b Taylor	65	– lbw b Taylor	38
M. E. K. Hussey c Chanderpaul b Sammy	10	– (2) c Ramdin b Bravo	40
M. J. Clarke c Marshall b Powell	110	– (4) run out	10
A. Symonds c Ramdin b Edwards	18	– (5) not out	43
†B. J. Haddin c Morton b Taylor	33	– (6) lbw b Edwards	7
B. Lee not out	63	– (7) c Ramdin b Edwards	4
M. G. Johnson not out	29		
L-b 7, w 5, n-b 9	21	B 8, l-b 6, w 3, n-b 9	26

1/36 (1) 2/172 (3) 3/199 (4)　　　　(7 wkts dec.) 479
4/271 (2) 5/296 (6)
6/360 (7) 7/414 (5)

1/74 (2) 2/163 (1)　　　　(6 wkts dec.) 244
3/178 (3) 4/186 (4)
5/222 (6) 6/244 (7)

S. R. Clark and S. C. G. MacGill did not bat.

Powell 29–3–101–1; Edwards 28–6–98–1; Taylor 27–5–95–3; Bravo 24–4–80–1; Sammy 21–2–71–1; Sarwan 7–0–27–0. *Second Innings*—Powell 13–3–47–0; Edwards 7.5–1–28–2; Taylor 12–0–33–2; Sammy 12–1–45–0; Bravo 14–1–59–1; Sarwan 3–0–18–0.

West Indies

D. S. Smith c Symonds b Johnson	16	– c Hussey b Lee	0
X. M. Marshall lbw b Clarke	53	– c Haddin b Clark	5
*R. R. Sarwan c Clarke b MacGill	65	– c Hussey b Johnson	128
R. S. Morton c Katich b Clarke	2	– lbw b Lee	14
S. Chanderpaul not out	107	– not out	77
D. J. Bravo c Haddin b Lee	45	– c sub (B. J. Hodge) b Lee	1
†D. Ramdin lbw b Lee	0	– not out	21
D. J. G. Sammy lbw b Lee	0		
J. E. Taylor b Lee	20		
D. B. Powell lbw b Lee	0		
F. H. Edwards c Haddin b Johnson	0		
B 17, l-b 13, w 2, n-b 12	44	L-b 8, n-b 12	20

1/55 (1) 2/103 (2) 3/105 (4) 4/182 (3)　　　　352
5/314 (6) 6/314 (7) 7/318 (8)
8/341 (9) 9/341 (10) 10/352 (11)

1/4 (1) 2/19 (2)　　　　(5 wkts) 266
3/84 (4) 4/227 (3) 5/236 (6)

Lee 21–7–59–5; Johnson 24–5–72–2; Clark 14–0–39–0; MacGill 21–1–107–1; Clarke 15–7–20–2; Symonds 12–3–25–0. *Second Innings*—Lee 21–5–51–3; Clark 18–8–22–1; Clarke 6–3–16–0; Johnson 20–3–70–1; MacGill 19–2–75–0; Hussey 6–2–14–0; Symonds 3–0–10–0.

Umpires: M. R. Benson *(England)* (22) and R. B. Tiffin *(Zimbabwe)* (42).
Third umpire: N. A. Malcolm *(West Indies)*.　　Referee: R. S. Mahanama *(Sri Lanka)* (23).

Close of play: First day, Australia 259-3 (Katich 113, Clarke 38); Second day, West Indies 125-3 (Sarwan 32, Chan-derpaul 5); Third day, West Indies 255-4 (Chanderpaul 55, Bravo 29); Fourth day, Australia 244-6 (Symonds 43).

WEST INDIES v AUSTRALIA 2008 (3rd Test)

At Kensington Oval, Bridgetown, Barbados, on 12, 13, 14, 15, 16 June.
Toss: West Indies.   Result: AUSTRALIA won by 87 runs.
Debuts: Australia – B. Casson.
Man of the Match: S. M. Katich.   Man of the Series: S. Chanderpaul.

It took two days for the batsmen to come to terms with the pace and bounce of a true pitch. Too eager to indulge themselves, several succumbed to impulsive strokes during two modest first-innings totals. Chanderpaul was the unsurprising exception – and even he clouted one of the first two days' nine sixes. As the surface gradually lost its early life, reality returned. Jaques and Katich built the base for Australia's matchwinning second innings, each scoring hundreds during a careful opening stand of 223. Ponting's declaration, at lunch on the fourth day, set West Indies an unlikely 475 for victory. They did well to get as close as they did, but the quest was over with a session remaining. Sent in, Australia had lost five wickets soon after lunch on the first day, three of them to top-edged hooks, before the consistent Symonds organised another recovery. West Indies regained the initiative through Chanderpaul – who took 18 (440064) off the debutant left-arm wrist-spinner Beau Casson's last over – but the last six wickets tumbled for 48, and from then on Australia dominated. In the second innings Chanderpaul eased past 8,000 runs, joining illustrious West Indian company in Lara, Richards and Sobers. But Clark's third delivery with the new ball pinned him on the back foot, his first dismissal since the First Test, 1,115 minutes and 689 balls earlier. Ponting received the Frank Worrell Trophy on the spot where he had collected the World Cup the previous year. This time the sun was shining.

Australia

P. A. Jaques c Ramdin b Taylor	31	– c Ramdin b Edwards	108
S. M. Katich c Gayle b Edwards	36	– c sub (D. J. G. Sammy) b Benn	157
*R. T. Ponting lbw b Taylor	18	– c sub (R. S. Morton) b Powell	39
M. E. K. Hussey c Powell b Bravo	12	– c Bravo b Benn	18
M. J. Clarke c Ramdin b Bravo	0	– not out	48
A. Symonds c Chattergoon b Bravo	52	– c Chanderpaul b Benn	2
†B. J. Haddin lbw b Benn	32	– not out	45
B. Casson lbw b Edwards	10		
B. Lee not out	23		
M. G. Johnson c Benn b Taylor	0		
S. R. Clark b Edwards	1		
L-b 7, w 21, n-b 8	36	B 5, l-b 2, w 5, n-b 5, p 5	22

1/46 (1) 2/75 (3) 3/96 (4) 4/96 (5)   251   1/223 (1) 2/299 (3)   (5 wkts dec.) 439
5/111 (2) 6/198 (7) 7/213 (6)   3/330 (4) 4/358 (2)
8/244 (8) 9/245 (10) 10/251 (11)   5/360 (6)

Powell 11–5–43–0; Edwards 16.1–3–55–3; Taylor 12–2–46–3; Gayle 7–2–6–0; Bravo 15–5–61–3; Benn 6–0–33–1. *Second Innings*—Powell 16–6–40–1; Edwards 14–3–52–1; Taylor 22–3–64–0; Gayle 16–3–45–0; Benn 47–7–154–3; Bravo 23–4–63–0; Marshall 2–2–0–0; Sarwan 5–0–9–0.

West Indies

*C. H. Gayle c Casson b Lee	14	– c Lee b Clark	26
S. Chattergoon c Haddin b Lee	6	– (8) c Haddin b Lee	13
R. R. Sarwan c Hussey b Clark	20	– lbw b Clarke	43
X. M. Marshall c Casson b Symonds	39	– (2) c Jaques b Casson	85
S. Chanderpaul not out	79	– (4) lbw b Clark	50
D. J. Bravo c Haddin b Johnson	29	– (5) c Jaques b Casson	69
†D. Ramdin c Clarke b Johnson	1	– (6) lbw b Clark	8
J. E. Taylor c Katich b Clarke	0	– (7) c Haddin b Johnson	31
S. J. Benn c Haddin b Johnson	3	– c Hussey b Casson	13
D. B. Powell c Haddin b Lee	9	– c Haddin b Lee	6
F. H. Edwards c Ponting b Johnson	1	– not out	5
L-b 7, n-b 8	15	B 10, l-b 8, w 8, n-b 12	38

1/11 (2) 2/26 (1) 3/64 (3) 4/108 (4)   216   1/64 (1) 2/159 (3) 3/181 (2)   387
5/168 (6) 6/188 (7) 7/189 (8)   4/303 (5) 5/303 (4) 6/345 (6)
8/195 (9) 9/204 (10) 10/216 (11)   7/351 (7) 8/375 (8) 9/375 (9) 10/387 (10)

Lee 15–2–64–3; Clark 15–4–41–1; Johnson 11.5–3–41–4; Symonds 8–4–17–1; Casson 7–1–43–0; Clarke 2–0–3–1. *Second Innings*—Lee 25.4–3–109–2; Clark 24–8–58–3; Johnson 12–0–72–1; Casson 25–3–86–3; Clarke 17–1–38–1; Symonds 2–0–6–0.

Umpires: Aleem Dar *(Pakistan)* (48) and M. R. Benson *(England)* (23).
Third umpire: G. E. Greaves *(West Indies)*.   Referee: R. S. Mahanama *(Sri Lanka)* (24).

Close of play: First day, Australia 226-7 (Casson 6, Lee 7); Second day, Australia 35-0 (Jaques 13, Katich 17); Third day, Australia 330-3 (Katich 148, Clarke 0); Fourth day, West Indies 235-3 (Chanderpaul 27, Bravo 30).

ENGLAND v SOUTH AFRICA 2008 (1st Test)

At Lord's, London, on 10, 11, 12, 13, 14 July.
Toss: South Africa.   Result: MATCH DRAWN.
Debuts: none.
Man of the Match: I. R. Bell.

As the third day ended, England's mastery seemed complete: after scoring 593, they had bowled South Africa out and imposed the follow-on. But between Vaughan and victory lay ten wickets ... and 22 yards of the most curmudgeonly turf ever called a cricket pitch. South Africa drew hope from the Lord's pitch's tendency to get flatter (in 2006, Sri Lanka's follow-on lasted 199 overs). Smith and McKenzie started with 204, the highest opening stand in a Test follow-on. The resistance continued throughout the final day – England's third in a row in the field – and a statistical oddity came when a third different pair (Broad and Collingwood) took the third new ball, thought to be unique in Tests. For the first time, the top three hit hundreds in the second innings (it had happened eight times in the first). It had long become clear that the genuinely remarkable passage of play was South Africa losing all ten wickets on the Saturday. Early that day Smith failed to control the only ball in the whole match that leapt from a length, and scowled back to the pavilion, quickly followed by his team-mates. England had begun the match by gliding to 114 for none, before losing three for three, then Pietersen and Bell (who became the seventh player, but the first Englishman, to be out for 199 in a Test) lifted them past 400. England fielded the same eleven for the sixth match running, a feat unprecedented in 131 years of Test cricket.

England

A. J. Strauss lbw b Morkel	44	R. J. Sidebottom not out	1
A. N. Cook c de Villiers b Morkel	60		
*M. P. Vaughan b Steyn	2	B 14, l-b 12, w 7, n-b 15	48
K. P. Pietersen c Boucher b Morkel	152		
I. R. Bell c and b Harris	199	1/114 (1) 2/117 (3) (8 wkts dec.)	593
P. D. Collingwood c Amla b Harris	7	3/117 (2) 4/403 (4)	
†T. R. Ambrose c Smith b Morkel	4	5/413 (6) 6/422 (7)	
S. C. J. Broad b Harris	76	7/574 (8) 8/593 (5)	

J. M. Anderson and M. S. Panesar did not bat.

Steyn 35–8–117–1; Ntini 29–2–130–0; Morkel 34–3–121–4; Kallis 20–3–70–0; Harris 38.2–8–129–3.

South Africa

*G. C. Smith c Bell b Anderson	8	– c Pietersen b Anderson	107
N. D. McKenzie b Panesar	40	– c Ambrose b Anderson	138
H. M. Amla c Ambrose b Broad	6	– not out	104
J. H. Kallis c Strauss b Sidebottom	7	– b Sidebottom	13
A. G. Prince c Ambrose b Sidebottom	101	– not out	9
A. B. de Villiers c Anderson b Panesar	42		
†M. V. Boucher b Broad	4		
M. Morkel b Panesar	6		
P. L. Harris c Anderson b Panesar	6		
D. W. Steyn c Sidebottom b Pietersen	19		
M. Ntini not out	0		
B 1, l-b 4, w 3	8	B 8, l-b 8, w 5, n-b 1	22

1/13 (1) 2/28 (3) 3/47 (4) 4/83 (2)	247	1/204 (1) 2/329 (2) (3 wkts dec.)	393
5/161 (6) 6/166 (7) 7/191 (8)		3/357 (4)	
8/203 (9) 9/245 (5) 10/247 (10)			

Sidebottom 19–3–41–2; Anderson 21–7–36–1; Broad 23–3–88–2; Panesar 26–4–74–4; Collingwood 4–1–3–0; Pietersen 0.3–0–0–1. *Second Innings*—Panesar 60–15–116–0; Pietersen 7–1–21–0; Sidebottom 30–9–46–1; Anderson 32–7–78–2; Broad 26–7–78–0; Collingwood 11–4–37–0; Cook 1–0–1–0.

Umpires: B. F. Bowden *(New Zealand)* (47) and D. J. Harper *(Australia)* (72).
Third umpire: N. J. Llong *(England)*.   Referee: J. J. Crowe *(New Zealand)* (24).

Close of play: First day, England 309-3 (Pietersen 104, Bell 75); Second day, South Africa 7-0 (Smith 2, McKenzie 5); Third day, South Africa 13-0 (Smith 8, McKenzie 1); Fourth day, South Africa 242-1 (McKenzie 102, Amla 20).

ENGLAND v SOUTH AFRICA 2008 (2nd Test)

At Headingley, Leeds, on 18, 19, 20, 21 July.
Toss: South Africa.   Result: SOUTH AFRICA won by ten wickets.
Debuts: England – D. J. Pattinson.
Man of the Match: A. G. Prince.

In one of Test cricket's most surprising selections England included Darren Pattinson, a swing bowler born in Grimsby but raised in Australia, after only 11 first-class appearances, five of them for Victoria. After the match Vaughan admitted the selection was "confused" and the team lacked "togetherness". Pattinson actually bowled reasonably well after replacing his injured county colleague Sidebottom, but Vaughan's assessment was valid: lack of unity in his 50th Test as captain was the key to England's four-day capitulation. Not even Flintoff's return after 18 months served to inspire. In an abject first-innings display, only two batsmen passed 30 as promising starts were surrendered in an orgy of profligate drives. Boucher took five catches, and finished with nine in the match, equalling the South African record. Spurred on by crowd taunts after claiming a catch off Strauss which the TV cameras showed had hit the ground (later Vaughan also celebrated a tumbling effort off Amla at mid-off, but replays suggested the ball might have touched the floor between his fingers), de Villiers made a resolute 174, putting on 212 with Prince to help South Africa to a lead of 319. Their ability to leave balls outside off stump showed up England, who lost 15 wickets to catches from wicketkeeper to gully. Only the rapidly maturing Broad averted an innings defeat, during a last-wicket stand of 61 with Pattinson, but South Africa needed just seven deliveries to go one up. It was Smith's 28th Test win as captain, passing Hansie Cronje's national record.

England

A. J. Strauss c Boucher b Morkel	27	– c Boucher b Ntini		0
A. N. Cook c Boucher b Morkel	18	– c Amla b Kallis		60
*M. P. Vaughan c Smith b Steyn	0	– c Boucher b Ntini		21
K. P. Pietersen c Smith b Steyn	45	– (5) c Boucher b Kallis		13
I. R. Bell b Kallis	31	– (6) c de Villiers b Morkel		4
†T. R. Ambrose c Boucher b Ntini	12	– (7) c Boucher b Steyn		36
A. Flintoff c Boucher b Steyn	17	– (8) c Kallis b Morkel		38
S. C. J. Broad c de Villiers b Morkel	17	– (9) not out		67
J. M. Anderson not out	11	– (4) lbw b Steyn		34
M. S. Panesar c de Villiers b Morkel	0	– b Steyn		10
D. J. Pattinson c Boucher b Steyn	8	– b Morkel		13
L-b 6, w 6, n-b 5	17	B 4, l-b 11, w 2, n-b 14		31

1/26 (2) 2/27 (3) 3/62 (1) 4/106 (4) 203   1/3 (1) 2/50 (3) 3/109 (4)   327
5/123 (6) 6/150 (5) 7/177 (7)   4/123 (5) 5/140 (6) 6/152 (2)
8/181 (8) 9/186 (10) 10/203 (11)   7/220 (7) 8/238 (8) 9/266 (10) 10/327 (11)

Steyn 18.3–2–76–4; Ntini 11–0–45–1; Morkel 15–4–52–4; Kallis 8–2–24–1. *Second Innings*—Steyn 28–7–97–3; Ntini 25–7–69–2; Morkel 22–4–61–3; Kallis 17–3–50–2; Harris 15–5–35–0.

South Africa

N. D. McKenzie c Flintoff b Anderson	15	– (2) not out		6
*G. C. Smith c Strauss b Flintoff	44	– (1) not out		3
H. M. Amla lbw b Pattinson	38			
J. H. Kallis b Anderson	4			
A. G. Prince c Ambrose b Pattinson	149			
A. B. de Villiers c Flintoff b Broad	174			
†M. V. Boucher b Anderson	34			
M. Morkel b Panesar	0			
P. L. Harris c Anderson b Panesar	24			
D. W. Steyn not out	10			
M. Ntini c Pietersen b Panesar	1			
B 2, l-b 19, w 1, n-b 7	29			

1/51 (1) 2/69 (2) 3/76 (4) 4/143 (3) 522   (no wkt) 9
5/355 (5) 6/422 (7) 7/427 (8)
8/511 (6) 9/511 (9) 10/522 (11)

Anderson 44–9–136–3; Pattinson 30–2–95–2; Flintoff 40–12–77–1; Broad 29–2–114–1; Panesar 29.2–6–65–3; Pietersen 4–0–14–0. *Second Innings*—Broad 1–0–8–0; Pattinson 0.1–0–1–0.

Umpires: B. F. Bowden *(New Zealand)* (48) and D. J. Harper *(Australia)* (73).
Third umpire: R. A. Kettleborough *(England)*.   Referee: J. J. Crowe *(New Zealand)* (25).

Close of play: First day, South Africa 101-3 (Amla 18, Prince 9); Second day, South Africa 322-4 (Prince 134, de Villiers 70); Third day, England 50-2 (Cook 23, Anderson 0).

ENGLAND v SOUTH AFRICA 2008 (3rd Test)

At Edgbaston, Birmingham, on 30, 31 July, 1, 2 August.
Toss: England.   Result: SOUTH AFRICA won by five wickets.
Debuts: none.
Man of the Match: G. C. Smith.

Graeme Smith played one of the great captain's innings to cement South Africa's first series win in England since 1965, single-mindedly and almost single-handedly driving them to the highest fourth-innings Test total at Edgbaston. Five years previously, Smith's 277 here precipitated Nasser Hussain's resignation as captain; this time, his series-winning 154 precipitated Vaughan's departure. In front of a modest crowd for the first Wednesday start to an English Test in modern times, Strauss and Cook were untroubled until Nel (replacing Steyn who broke his left thumb at Headingley), set the dominos falling. Flintoff was just starting to flow when his calling contributed to his last two partners being run out off consecutive balls, but next morning he produced an electrifying spell with the ball. After taking his 200th Test wicket (McKenzie), Flintoff castled Kallis with a superb fast yorker that swung late. However, Boucher – dropped at 12 and 37 – and a Test-record 35 leg-byes swelled the lead. Just as England seemed to be gaining control, Pietersen tried to loft Harris over long-on for his hundred, but fell short. Soon afterwards Collingwood successfully on-drove Harris for six to reach a century which probably saved his Test career. The target of 281 looked distant when South Africa dipped to 93 for 4 ... except to Smith. Panesar over-appealed, and received a warning to calm down – and when Smith seemingly gloved a catch at 85, the appeals were muted. Boucher settled in, and Smith hit the winning four – his 17th – in the extra half-hour.

England

A. J. Strauss hit wkt b Nel	20	– c Kallis b Morkel	25
A. N. Cook c Kallis b Nel	76	– c Boucher b Ntini	9
*M. P. Vaughan c Boucher b Nel	0	– c Amla b Nel	17
K. P. Pietersen c Prince b Kallis	4	– c de Villiers b Harris	94
I. R. Bell c Boucher b Ntini	50	– c Boucher b Ntini	20
P. D. Collingwood c Smith b Kallis	4	– c Boucher b Morkel	135
A. Flintoff not out	36	– c Amla b Harris	2
†T. R. Ambrose b Kallis	22	– b Morkel	19
R. J. Sidebottom c Boucher b Ntini	2	– c Amla b Morkel	22
J. M. Anderson run out	1	– b Kallis	1
M. S. Panesar run out	1	– not out	0
B 1, l-b 7, w 2, n-b 5	15	B 8, l-b 2, w 6, n-b 3	19

1/68 (1) 2/68 (3) 3/74 (4) 4/136 (2)   231   1/15 (2) 2/39 (3) 3/70 (1)   363
5/158 (6) 6/173 (5) 7/212 (8)   4/104 (5) 5/219 (4) 6/221 (7)
8/215 (9) 9/230 (10) 10/231 (11)   7/297 (8) 8/362 (9) 9/363 (10) 10/363 (6)

Morkel 15–2–50–0; Ntini 19–5–70–2; Nel 17–7–47–3; Kallis 15–5–31–3; Harris 11–1–25–0. *Second Innings—* Morkel 19.2–1–97–4; Nel 20–3–79–1; Ntini 18–4–58–2; Kallis 20–5–59–1; Harris 21–3–60–2.

South Africa

N. D. McKenzie lbw b Flintoff	72	– (2) lbw b Flintoff	22
*G. C. Smith c Strauss b Flintoff	7	– (1) not out	154
P. L. Harris c Cook b Sidebottom	19		
H. M. Amla c and b Anderson	9	– (3) lbw b Panesar	6
J. H. Kallis b Flintoff	64	– (4) lbw b Flintoff	5
A. G. Prince c Ambrose b Sidebottom	39	– (5) c Ambrose b Anderson	2
A. B. de Villiers c Sidebottom b Flintoff	5	– (6) c Collingwood b Panesar	27
†M. V. Boucher c Vaughan b Anderson	40	– (7) not out	45
M. Morkel lbw b Anderson	18		
A. Nel b Sidebottom	0		
M. Ntini not out	0		
L-b 35, n-b 6	41	B 10, l-b 8, w 2, n-b 2	22

1/17 (2) 2/94 (3) 3/117 (4) 4/135 (1)   314   1/65 (2) 2/78 (3)   (5 wkts) 283
5/226 (5) 6/238 (7) 7/264 (6)   3/83 (4) 4/93 (5) 5/171 (6)
8/293 (9) 9/298 (10) 10/314 (8)

Sidebottom 25–9–81–3; Anderson 26.2–6–72–3; Flintoff 30–8–89–4; Collingwood 2–0–12–0; Panesar 7–0–25–0. *Second Innings*—Sidebottom 10–1–26–0; Anderson 13–0–60–1; Panesar 33–3–91–2; Flintoff 20–5–72–2; Pietersen 4–0–16–0.

Umpires: Aleem Dar *(Pakistan)* (49) and S. J. Davis *(Australia)* (12).
Third umpire: I. J. Gould *(England)*.   Referee: R. S. Madugalle *(Sri Lanka)* (106).

Close of play: First day, South Africa 38-1 (McKenzie 12, Harris 10); Second day, South Africa 256-6 (Prince 37, Boucher 11); Third day, England 297-6 (Collingwood 101, Ambrose 19).

ENGLAND v SOUTH AFRICA 2008 (4th Test)

At Kennington Oval, London, on 7, 8, 9, 10, 11 August.
Toss: South Africa.   Result: ENGLAND won by six wickets.
Debuts: none.
Man of the Match: K. P. Pietersen.   Men of the Series: K. P. Pietersen and G. C. Smith.

The plot was out of a schoolboy's comic. Kevin Pietersen's first act as England captain was to resurrect Harmison's
Test career, thus completing a five-man bowling attack that dismissed South Africa cheaply. Then he scored a
crucial hundred: all this by tea on the second day. When he dropped Kallis in South Africa's second innings, a
potentially disastrous error, the next ball was edged straight to third slip. Pietersen briefly lost the plot while de
Villiers and Harris added 95 for the eighth wicket in South Africa's second innings, swelling the target to a tricky
197, but England's openers calmed the nerves by putting on 123. Napoleon would have understood the significance of these events: Pietersen, like good generals, had been lucky. It seems churlish to emphasise the fact that
South Africa had already won the series, and batted with uncharacteristic irresolution, especially in the first
innings. One common worry had been the effect captaincy might have on Pietersen's batting, but any fears proved
groundless. He hit 15 fours in becoming only the fourth player (the third born in South Africa, after Allan Lamb
and Andrew Strauss; Archie MacLaren was born in Manchester) to score a century in his first Test as England
captain. Collingwood confirmed his return to form, but England passed 300 only because of Harmison's good
eye and strong shoulders. The only thing missing in Pietersen's fairytale was that he did not hit the winning run
himself: Flintoff did instead, with a four and a six into the pavilion.

South Africa

*G. C. Smith c Anderson b Harmison	46	– lbw b Anderson	0
N. D. McKenzie c Cook b Flintoff	17	– b Broad	29
H. M. Amla b Harmison	36	– c Ambrose b Harmison	76
J. H. Kallis lbw b Anderson	2	– c Collingwood b Harmison	9
A. G. Prince c Bell b Anderson	4	– c Strauss b Flintoff	24
A. B. de Villiers lbw b Panesar	39	– b Panesar	97
†M. V. Boucher c Ambrose b Anderson	3	– c Collingwood b Anderson	12
M. Morkel c Bell b Broad	17	– c Bell b Panesar	10
P. L. Harris not out	13	– c Flintoff b Broad	34
A. Nel c Ambrose b Broad	4	– not out	3
M. Ntini b Panesar	9	– c Collingwood b Broad	2
B 1, l-b 1, n-b 2	4	B 6, l-b 8, w 5, n-b 3	22

1/56 (2) 2/103 (1) 3/103 (3) 4/105 (4)   194   1/0 (1) 2/82 (2) 3/119 (3)   318
5/118 (5) 6/132 (7) 7/158 (6)   4/138 (4) 5/161 (5) 6/201 (7)
8/168 (8) 9/172 (10) 10/194 (11)   7/218 (8) 8/313 (9) 9/313 (6) 10/318 (11)

Harmison 18–6–49–2; Anderson 15–1–42–3; Flintoff 15–2–37–1; Broad 14–3–60–2; Panesar 2.5–0–4–2.
Second Innings—Anderson 22–2–85–2; Harmison 25–6–84–2; Flintoff 18–4–53–1; Panesar 17–5–37–2; Broad
16.2–4–44–3; Pietersen 1–0–1–0.

England

A. J. Strauss c Smith b Ntini	6	– c Smith b Harris	58
A. N. Cook c Boucher b Ntini	39	– c Smith b Ntini	67
I. R. Bell c Smith b Ntini	24	– b Ntini	4
*K. P. Pietersen c Kallis b Ntini	100	– c McKenzie b Harris	13
P. D. Collingwood c and b Kallis	61	– not out	25
A. Flintoff c Boucher b Kallis	9	– not out	11
†T. R. Ambrose c Smith b Kallis	4		
S. C. J. Broad c McKenzie b Ntini	1		
S. J. Harmison not out	49		
J. M. Anderson lbw b Harris	13		
M. S. Panesar run out	0		
L-b 4, w 1, n-b 5	10	B 6, l-b 7, w 1, n-b 6	20

1/7 (1) 2/51 (3) 3/111 (2) 4/219 (4)   316   1/123 (2) 2/147 (3)   (4 wkts) 198
5/233 (6) 6/241 (7) 7/248 (5)   3/147 (1) 4/182 (4)
8/263 (8) 9/316 (10) 10/316 (11)

Morkel 22–3–78–0; Ntini 24–3–94–5; Nel 19.2–5–56–0; Kallis 15–2–51–3; Harris 15–4–33–1. *Second Innings*—
Morkel 13–2–43–0; Ntini 14–4–55–2; Harris 19.5–5–56–2; Nel 5–0–21–0; Kallis 1–0–10–0.

Umpires: Aleem Dar *(Pakistan)* (50) and S. J. Davis *(Australia)* (13).
Third umpire: P. J. Hartley *(England)*.   Referee: R. S. Madugalle *(Sri Lanka)* (107).

Close of play: First day, England 49-1 (Cook 20, Bell 22); Second day, South Africa 37-1 (McKenzie 9, Amla
26); Third day, South Africa 110-2 (Amla 71, Kallis 2); Fourth day, England 0-0 (Strauss 0, Cook 0).

SRI LANKA v INDIA 2008 (1st Test)

At Sinhalese Sports Club, Colombo, on 23, 24, 25, 26 July.
Toss: Sri Lanka.   Result: SRI LANKA won by an innings and 239 runs.
Debuts: Sri Lanka – B. A. W. Mendis.
Man of the Match: M. Muralitharan.

Arguably the world's strongest batting line-up succumbed tamely – twice – as India went down to their heaviest defeat against Sri Lanka in little more than three days' play: only 22 overs survived a rainy first day, and it was all over on the fourth evening. Ajantha Mendis unveiled his mystery mixture of offspinners, legbreaks, and finger-flicked allsorts: he took eight wickets, the best return for Sri Lanka on debut; but Muralitharan managed 11, becoming the first to take 150 Test wickets at a single ground. His dismissals of Gambhir were outstanding: a slower ball provoked an edged drive to short extra, and a flighted ball drew him out to be stumped. Mahela Jayawardene raised eyebrows when he batted first on a pitch that had been under covers in monsoon weather. But he read it correctly: four batsmen scored centuries as the total reached 600. Jayawardene's was his ninth on his home ground, putting him level with Don Bradman's Test-record nine at Melbourne. Dilshan, the fourth centurion, could thank the experimental umpire-review system, trialled for the first time in this series, for saving his Test career. He was the first batsman to have a decision overturned, after being adjudged caught behind off Zaheer Khan for one. Laxman's 56 could not prevent India from following on against Sri Lanka for the first time, then the second-innings 138 was their lowest against them. Jayawardene played the review system to perfection: Sehwag, Tendulkar and Dravid were all given out after the umpires initially spared them.

Sri Lanka

M. G. Vandort c Karthik b Sharma	3	W. P. U. J. C. Vaas not out		22
B. S. M. Warnapura c Dravid b Harbhajan Singh	115	B 4, l-b 5, w 3, n-b 18		30
K. C. Sangakkara c Dravid b Zaheer Khan	12			
*D. P. M. D. Jayawardene c Karthik b Sharma	136	1/7 (1) 2/57 (3)	(6 wkts dec.)	600
T. T. Samaraweera c Laxman b Zaheer Khan	127	3/212 (2) 4/360 (4)		
T. M. Dilshan not out	125	5/454 (5) 6/545 (7)		
†H. A. P. W. Jayawardene c Sharma b Harbhajan Singh	30			

K. M. D. N. Kulasekara, B. A. W. Mendis and M. Muralitharan did not bat.

Zaheer Khan 37–2–156–2; Sharma 33–4–124–2; Ganguly 8–1–24–0; Harbhajan Singh 43–2–149–2; Kumble 37–4–121–0; Sehwag 4–0–17–0.

India

G. Gambhir c Samaraweera b Muralitharan	39	– st H. A. P. W. Jayawardene b Muralitharan		43
V. Sehwag c Warnapura b Kulasekara	25	– lbw b Muralitharan		13
R. Dravid b Mendis	14	– (5) c Warnapura b Mendis		10
S. R. Tendulkar b Muralitharan	27	– c Dilshan b Muralitharan		12
S. C. Ganguly c Kulasekara b Muralitharan	23	– (6) c Dilshan b Muralitharan		4
V. V. S. Laxman b Mendis	56	– (3) lbw b Mendis		21
†K. D. Karthik c and b Muralitharan	9	– c D. P. M. D. Jayawardene b Muralitharan		0
*A. Kumble lbw b Mendis	1	– b Muralitharan		12
Harbhajan Singh c Warnapura b Muralitharan	9	– b Mendis		15
Zaheer Khan lbw b Mendis	5	– b Mendis		3
I. Sharma not out	13	– not out		5
L-b 2	2			
	223			138

1/36 (2) 2/79 (1) 3/79 (3) 4/123 (4)   223
5/138 (5) 6/147 (7) 7/170 (8)
8/181 (9) 9/188 (10) 10/223 (6)

1/25 (2) 2/53 (3) 3/82 (4)   138
4/95 (1) 5/103 (6) 6/103 (5)
7/103 (7) 8/120 (8) 9/133 (10) 10/138 (9)

Vaas 5–0–23–0; Kulasekara 11–2–42–1; Mendis 27.5–5–72–4; Muralitharan 29–4–84–5. *Second Innings*—Vaas 5–0–27–0; Kulasekara 9–3–25–0; Mendis 18–3–60–4; Muralitharan 13–3–26–6.

Umpires: M. R. Benson *(England)* (24) and B. R. Doctrove *(West Indies)* (18).
Third umpire: R. E. Koertzen *(South Africa)*.   Referee: A. G. Hurst *(Australia)* (18).

Close of play: First day, Sri Lanka 85-2 (Warnapura 50, D. P. M. D. Jayawardene 16); Second day, Sri Lanka 422-4 (Samaraweera 111, Dilshan 20); Third day, India 159-6 (Laxman 19, Kumble 1).

SRI LANKA v INDIA 2008 (2nd Test)

At Galle International Stadium on 31 July, 1, 2, 3 August.
Toss: India.   Result: INDIA won by 170 runs.
Debuts: none.
Man of the Match: V. Sehwag.

India completed a stunning turnaround to square the series, mainly thanks to Sehwag. He hurtled to 91 by lunch on the first day then, after the middle session was lost to rain, completed his century despite four wickets tumbling in 20 balls. Next day he passed 5,000 Test runs en route to a magnificent double-hundred, India's first against Sri Lanka, reached with the last man at the crease. Sehwag scored 128 off 158 balls from the spinners, including 70 off 77 from Mendis, and became only the second Indian to carry his bat in a Test, after Sunil Gavaskar at Faisalabad in 1982-83. India's 329 was the lowest Test total to include a double-century, previously England's 344 against West Indies at The Oval in 1950 (Len Hutton 202 not out). Sri Lanka fell 37 short of India's total, despite three of their top four passing 65: Harbhajan Singh matched Mendis's earlier six-wicket haul. India's openers put on 90, but on the fourth morning the last six wickets added only 69, though Ganguly won a brief reprieve after being adjudged lbw to Muralitharan – the only decision of the series overturned in India's favour. Karthik slog-swept to deep midwicket to become Murali's 750th Test wicket, while Mendis completed his first Test ten-for. A target of 307 seemed attainable with two days remaining and the pitch still playing true, but Sri Lanka stumbled to 10 for 3 before lunch. Afterwards only Samaraweera offered resistance as they were bowled out for their lowest total at home to India.

India

G. Gambhir lbw b Mendis	56	– b Mendis		74
V. Sehwag not out	201	– c Dilshan b Vaas		50
R. Dravid c Warnapura b Mendis	2	– lbw b Muralitharan		44
S. R. Tendulkar lbw b Vaas	5	– c D. P. M. D. Jayawardene b Vaas		31
S. C. Ganguly c H. A. P. W. Jayawardene b Vaas	0	– st H. A. P. W. Jayawardene b Muralitharan		16
V. V. S. Laxman c Samaraweera b Mendis	39	– lbw b Mendis		13
†K. D. Karthik lbw b Mendis	7	– c Sangakkara b Muralitharan		20
*A. Kumble st H. A. P. W. Jayawardene b Muralitharan	4	– lbw b Mendis		2
Harbhajan Singh b Mendis	1	– c and b Mendis		11
Zaheer Khan c H. A. P. W. Jayawardene b Muralitharan	2	– (11) not out		1
I. Sharma lbw b Mendis	0	– (10) run out		0
B 1, l-b 4, w 7	12	L-b 7		7

1/167 (1) 2/173 (3) 3/178 (4) 4/178 (5)   329   1/90 (2) 2/144 (1) 3/200 (4)   269
5/278 (6) 6/290 (7) 7/317 (8)   4/200 (3) 5/221 (6) 6/252 (7)
8/318 (9) 9/323 (10) 10/329 (11)   7/255 (5) 8/257 (8) 9/257 (10) 10/269 (9)

Vaas 19–2–74–2; Kulasekara 8–1–40–0; Mendis 28–1–117–6; Muralitharan 27–1–93–2. *Second Innings*—Vaas 13–4–32–2; Kulasekara 5–0–31–0; Muralitharan 31–3–107–3; Mendis 27.2–4–92–4.

Sri Lanka

M. G. Vandort c Dravid b Zaheer Khan	4	– lbw b Harbhajan Singh		10
B. S. M. Warnapura c Gambhir b Harbhajan Singh	66	– c Laxman b Sharma		0
K. C. Sangakkara c and b Harbhajan Singh	68	– c Laxman b Zaheer Khan		1
*D. P. M. D. Jayawardene c Karthik b Kumble	86	– c Dravid b Sharma		5
T. T. Samaraweera lbw b Harbhajan Singh	14	– not out		67
T. M. Dilshan c Gambhir b Harbhajan Singh	0	– c Karthik b Sharma		38
†H. A. P. W. Jayawardene c Laxman b Harbhajan Singh	24	– c Ganguly b Harbhajan Singh		4
W. P. U. J. C. Vaas c Harbhajan Singh b Kumble	1	– lbw b Harbhajan Singh		0
K. M. D. N. Kulasekara not out	5	– c Sharma b Kumble		1
B. A. W. Mendis lbw b Kumble	0	– c Kumble b Harbhajan Singh		2
M. Muralitharan c Ganguly b Harbhajan Singh	0	– c and b Kumble		0
B 10, l-b 12, n-b 2	24	B 4, l-b 2, n-b 2		8

1/4 (1) 2/137 (2) 3/144 (3) 4/192 (5)   292   1/4 (2) 2/5 (3) 3/10 (4) 4/37 (1)   136
5/192 (6) 6/250 (7) 7/255 (8)   5/113 (6) 6/130 (7) 7/131 (8)
8/291 (4) 9/291 (10) 10/292 (11)   8/132 (9) 9/135 (10) 10/136 (11)

Zaheer Khan 9–1–51–1; Sharma 8–1–36–0; Kumble 36–7–81–3; Harbhajan Singh 40.3–8–102–6. *Second Innings*—Zaheer Khan 8–1–18–1; Sharma 15–8–20–3; Kumble 10.3–3–41–2; Harbhajan Singh 14–1–51–4.

Umpires: B. R. Doctrove *(West Indies)* (19) and R. E. Koertzen *(South Africa)* (91).
M. R. Benson replaced Koertzen from the second day
Third umpire: M. R. Benson *(England)* and M. G. Silva *(Sri Lanka)*.   Referee: A. G. Hurst *(Australia)* (19).

Close of play: First day, India 214-4 (Sehwag 128, Laxman 13); Second day, Sri Lanka 215-5 (D. P. M. D. Jayawardene 46, H. A. P. W. Jayawardene 5); Third day, India 200-4 (Ganguly 0, Laxman 0).

SRI LANKA v INDIA 2008 (3rd Test)

At P. Saravanamuttu Stadium, Colombo, on 8, 9, 10, 11 August.
Toss: India.   Result: SRI LANKA won by eight wickets.
Debuts: Sri Lanka – K. T. G. D. Prasad.
Man of the Match: K. C. Sangakkara.   Man of the Series: B. A. W. Mendis.

Sri Lanka showed great character to bounce back to take the series 2–1. Mahela Jayawardene said the difference was that his side enjoyed contributions from different players throughout: here, it was Sangakkara, with 17th Test hundred, and Mendis, with another eight wickets. Ishant Sharma's pace had made Jayawardene realise he needed some extra zip: India's struggling middle order thus had to contend with not only perplexing spin but also the pace of Dammika Prasad, who started his Test career with three impressive scalps: Sehwag, Dravid and Tendulkar. Ironically, Sharma picked up a leg injury and was unable to bowl later on. India got their usual sound start – their lowest opening stand of the series was 25, compared with Sri Lanka's best of 14 – but again the brittle middle order let them down. The second day was dominated by Sangakkara, who concentrated hard for seven hours – at one point he went 55 balls without a boundary – to set up a crucial lead of 147. Sehwag and Gambhir shared their fourth successive half-century opening stand but, once Prasad removed both, the spin twins got to work. Mendis broke Alec Bedser's record of 24 wickets in a maiden series of three Tests, which also came against India, in 1946. The record-breaking victim was Tendulkar, lbw for 14, which gave him an average of 15.83, his lowest for any series in which he played at least two Tests. Sri Lanka were left to score 122, and coasted home comfortably on the fourth evening.

India

G. Gambhir lbw b Mendis	72	– b Prasad	26
V. Sehwag c H. A. P. W. Jayawardene b Prasad	21	– c Samaraweera b Prasad	34
R. Dravid lbw b Prasad	10	– c D. P. M. D. Jayawardene b Mendis	68
S. R. Tendulkar lbw b Prasad	6	– (6) lbw b Mendis	14
S. C. Ganguly c D. P. M. D. Jayawardene b Muralitharan	35	– (4) lbw b Muralitharan	18
V. V. S. Laxman st H. A. P. W. Jayawardene b Mendis	25	– (7) not out	61
†P. A. Patel lbw b Mendis	13	– (5) lbw b Mendis	1
*A. Kumble b Mendis	1	– lbw b Muralitharan	9
Harbhajan Singh c Vandort b Muralitharan	3	– lbw b Vaas	26
I. Sharma not out	17	– (11) c Warnapura b Muralitharan	0
Zaheer Khan st H. A. P. W. Jayawardene b Mendis	32	– (10) run out	0
B 1, l-b 8, n-b 5	14	B 5, l-b 3, w 2, n-b 1	11

1/51 (2) 2/92 (3) 3/102 (4) 4/151 (5)   249   1/62 (2) 2/65 (1) 3/108 (4)   268
5/155 (1) 6/190 (6) 7/195 (7)   4/109 (5) 5/131 (6) 6/216 (3)
8/196 (8) 9/198 (9) 10/249 (11)   7/229 (8) 8/266 (9) 9/268 (10) 10/268 (11)

Vaas 12–1–44–0; Prasad 17–0–82–3; Mendis 28–4–56–5; Muralitharan 23–3–58–2. *Second Innings*—Vaas 5–0–20–1; Prasad 11–0–60–2; Muralitharan 37.5–4–99–3; Mendis 34–7–81–3.

Sri Lanka

M. G. Vandort lbw b Zaheer Khan	14	– b Harbhajan Singh	8
B. S. M. Warnapura b Sharma	8	– not out	54
W. P. U. J. C. Vaas c Sehwag b Harbhajan Singh	47		
K. C. Sangakkara c Patel b Kumble	144	– (3) c Gambhir b Zaheer Khan	4
*D. P. M. D. Jayawardene lbw b Harbhajan Singh	2	– (4) not out	50
T. T. Samaraweera c Patel b Zaheer Khan	35		
T. M. Dilshan lbw b Kumble	23		
†H. A. P. W. Jayawardene c Harbhajan Singh b Zaheer Khan	49		
K. T. G. D. Prasad st Patel b Harbhajan Singh	36		
B. A. W. Mendis lbw b Kumble	17		
M. Muralitharan not out	0		
B 4, l-b 14, w 2, n-b 1	21	B 4, l-b 3	7

1/14 (2) 2/42 (1) 3/137 (3) 4/141 (5)   396   1/11 (1) 2/22 (3)   (2 wkts) 123
5/201 (6) 6/244 (7) 7/324 (4)
8/367 (8) 9/396 (9) 10/396 (10)

Zaheer Khan 32–5–105–3; Sharma 15.3–3–33–1; Harbhajan Singh 40.3–8–104–3; Kumble 41.2–4–123–3; Sehwag 2–0–2–0; Ganguly 3–0–11–0. *Second Innings*—Zaheer Khan 6–1–22–1; Harbhajan Singh 14–2–44–1; Kumble 10–2–34–0; Sehwag 3–0–12–0; Ganguly 0.1–0–4–0.

Umpires: M. R. Benson *(England)* (25) and R. E. Koertzen *(South Africa)* (92).
Third umpire: B. R. Doctrove *(West Indies)*.   Referee: A. G. Hurst *(Australia)* (20).

Close of play: First day, Sri Lanka 14-1 (Vandort 3, Vaas 0); Second day, Sri Lanka 251-6 (Sangakkara 107, H. A. P. W. Jayawardene 1); Third day, India 161-5 (Dravid 46, Laxman 17).

INDIA v AUSTRALIA 2008-09 (1st Test)

At Chinnaswamy Stadium, Bangalore, on 9, 10, 11, 12, 13 October.
Toss: Australia.   Result: MATCH DRAWN.
Debuts: Australia – C. L. White.
Man of the Match: Zaheer Khan.

Doughty partnerships at critical moments delivered a draw on a tediously slow and low pitch, on which runs were crafted rather than freely scored. To general surprise, there was little change to the condition of the terra-cotta mosaic over the five days. Australia's fast bowlers prospered initially to have India 195 for 6, following up the imposing foundation laid by Ponting – who exorcised many of the demons that had beset him on previous tours of India with his sixth century against them, his 36th overall – and Hussey, who lasted for 402 minutes. However, Zaheer Khan and Harbhajan Singh frustrated Australia with half-centuries after Johnson's explosive early burst brought him the prized wickets of Sehwag, Tendulkar and Laxman for 13 runs in the space of 31 balls. India recovered to within 70 of Australia's imposing 430. Harbhajan and Zaheer reverted to their day jobs to give India a sniff of victory, but Watson and Haddin then put on 75 for the sixth wicket. Set 299 from a minimum of 83 overs, India were a shaky 77 for 3 in the 27th before Tendulkar, Laxman and Ganguly pooled their resources to ensure the draw. Towards the end Cameron White brightened an otherwise undistinguished debut by claiming Tendulkar as his first Test wicket. Kumble maintained a brave face despite failing for the first time to take a wicket in a home Test in which he had bowled (in his complete career he would play 63 in India, taking 350 wickets at 24.88).

Australia

M. L. Hayden c Dhoni b Zaheer Khan	0	– lbw b Zaheer Khan	13
S. M. Katich c Dhoni b Sharma	66	– c Laxman b Harbhajan Singh	34
*R. T. Ponting lbw b Harbhajan Singh	123	– c Laxman b Sharma	17
M. E. K. Hussey b Zaheer Khan	146	– b Harbhajan Singh	31
M. J. Clarke lbw b Zaheer Khan	11	– b Sehwag b Sharma	6
S. R. Watson b Sharma	2	– b Sharma	41
†B. J. Haddin c Laxman b Sharma	33	– not out	35
C. L. White c Harbhajan Singh b Sharma	6	– not out	18
B. Lee b Zaheer Khan	27		
M. G. Johnson b Zaheer Khan	1		
S. R. Clark not out	0		
L-b 11, w 1, n-b 3	15	B 13, l-b 10, w 6, n-b 4	33

1/0 (1) 2/166 (2) 3/226 (3) 4/254 (5)   430   1/21 (1) 2/49 (3)   (6 wkts dec.) 228
5/259 (6) 6/350 (7) 7/362 (8)   3/99 (2) 4/115 (5)
8/421 (9) 9/429 (10) 10/430 (4)   5/128 (4) 6/203 (6)

Zaheer Khan 29.5–4–91–5; Sharma 30–7–77–4; Harbhajan Singh 41–8–103–1; Kumble 43–6–129–0; Sehwag 6–0–19–0. *Second Innings*—Zaheer Khan 17–4–46–1; Sharma 14–3–40–3; Harbhajan Singh 27–5–76–2; Sehwag 7–1–12–0; Kumble 8–0–31–0.

India

G. Gambhir lbw b Lee	21	– b Johnson	29
V. Sehwag c Hayden b Johnson	45	– c Hayden b Clark	6
R. Dravid lbw b Watson	51	– c Ponting b Lee	5
S. R. Tendulkar c White b Johnson	13	– c Clarke b White	49
V. V. S. Laxman c Haddin b Johnson	0	– not out	42
S. C. Ganguly lbw b Johnson	47	– not out	26
†M. S. Dhoni b Clarke	9		
Harbhajan Singh c Haddin b Watson	54		
Zaheer Khan not out	57		
*A. Kumble lbw b Watson	5		
I. Sharma b Clarke	6		
B 23, l-b 23, n-b 6	52	B 16, l-b 3, n-b 1	20

1/70 (1) 2/76 (2) 3/94 (4) 4/106 (5)   360   1/16 (2) 2/24 (3)   (4 wkts) 177
5/155 (3) 6/195 (7) 7/232 (6)   3/77 (1) 4/138 (4)
8/312 (8) 9/343 (10) 10/360 (11)

Lee 26–6–64–1; Clark 17–3–58–0; Johnson 27–4–70–4; Watson 19–4–45–3; White 13–2–39–0; Clarke 17–3–38–2. *Second Innings*—Lee 11–3–26–1; Clark 11–6–12–1; Watson 5–2–8–0; Johnson 8–3–23–1; Clarke 20–7–40–0; White 18–4–49–1.

Umpires: Asad Rauf *(Pakistan)* (20) and R. E. Koertzen *(South Africa)* (93).
Third umpire: A. M. Saheba *(India)*.   Referee: B. C. Broad *(England)* (28).

Close of play: First day, Australia 254-4 (Hussey 46); Second day, India 68-0 (Gambhir 20, Sehwag 43); Third day, India 313-8 (Zaheer Khan 35, Kumble 0); Fourth day, Australia 193-5 (Watson 32, Haddin 28).

INDIA v AUSTRALIA 2008-09 (2nd Test)

At Punjab C. A. Stadium, Mohali, Chandigarh, on 17, 18, 19, 20, 21 October.
Toss: India.   Result: INDIA won by 320 runs.
Debuts: India – A. Mishra. Australia – P. M. Siddle.
Man of the Match: M. S. Dhoni.

India outplayed the world's top-ranked team on a glorious batting surface which mysteriously evolved into a mine-field when Australia batted. India's batsmen progressed with such ease that the eventual 469 was a disappointment: still, it was enough to set up their biggest victory over Australia by runs. Fireworks greeted Tendulkar becoming Test cricket's highest runscorer – he passed Brian Lara's 11,953 with a glide for three off the debutant Peter Siddle that took him to 16, and later reached 12,000 with a single off White to go to 61 – although there was widespread disappointment when he became Siddle's first Test wicket 12 short of another century. However Ganguly, who had announced he would retire after this series, took his own aggregate past 7,000 during his 16th Test hundred. Australia were never in the hunt once their first innings went the same way as in the previous game: Hayden again out third ball to Zaheer Khan, and Clarke again falling in the last over. He was defeated by a googly from Amit Mishra, who had replaced Kumble (shoulder soreness) and became only the sixth Indian to take a five-for on debut. Only Watson, who had encountered him in the IPL, picked Mishra's googly. Sehwag and Gambhir piled on 182, then Dhoni spanked a rapid half-century before setting Australia an unlikely 516. Five wickets tumbled for nine runs after a decent start, and although Clarke and Haddin added 84 Zaheer took three wickets in four balls to ensure victory before lunch on the fifth day.

India

G. Gambhir c Haddin b Johnson	67	– c Hussey b White	104
V. Sehwag c Haddin b Johnson	35	– c Haddin b Siddle	90
R. Dravid b Lee	39		
S. R. Tendulkar c Hayden b Siddle	88	– (5) not out	10
V. V. S. Laxman c Haddin b Johnson	12		
S. C. Ganguly c Lee b White	102	– (4) c Clarke b Lee	27
I. Sharma c Katich b Siddle	9		
*†M. S. Dhoni lbw b Siddle	92	– (3) not out	68
Harbhajan Singh b White	1		
Zaheer Khan run out	2		
A. Mishra not out	0		
B 4, l-b 10, w 5, n-b 3	22	B 3, l-b 4, w 5, n-b 3	15

1/70 (2) 2/146 (3) 3/146 (1) 4/163 (5)   469   1/182 (2) 2/224 (1)   (3 wkts dec.) 314
5/305 (4) 6/326 (7) 7/435 (6)   3/290 (4)
8/442 (9) 9/469 (10) 10/469 (8)

Lee 24–5–86–1; Siddle 28–5–114–3; Johnson 27–4–85–3; Watson 24–3–71–0; Clarke 7–0–28–0; White 19–0–71–2. *Second Innings*—Lee 14–0–61–1; Siddle 15–1–62–1; Johnson 14–0–72–0; White 8–0–48–1; Watson 5–0–20–0; Hussey 8–0–38–0; Clarke 1–0–6–0.

Australia

M. L. Hayden b Zaheer Khan	0	– lbw b Harbhajan Singh	29
S. M. Katich b Mishra	33	– c Tendulkar b Harbhajan Singh	20
*R. T. Ponting lbw b Sharma	5	– b Sharma	2
M. E. K. Hussey c Dhoni b Sharma	54	– lbw b Harbhajan Singh	1
M. J. Clarke lbw b Mishra	23	– c Sehwag b Mishra	69
S. R. Watson lbw b Mishra	78	– lbw b Sharma	2
†B. J. Haddin b Harbhajan Singh	9	– b Zaheer Khan	37
C. L. White b Mishra	5	– c Dhoni b Zaheer Khan	1
B. Lee c Dravid b Harbhajan Singh	35	– b Zaheer Khan	0
M. G. Johnson not out	9	– c and b Mishra	26
P. M. Siddle st Dhoni b Mishra	0	– not out	0
L-b 13, n-b 4	17	B 4, n-b 4	8

1/0 (1) 2/17 (3) 3/62 (2) 4/102 (5)   268   1/49 (1) 2/50 (2) 3/52 (4)   195
5/130 (4) 6/146 (7) 7/167 (8)   4/52 (3) 5/58 (6) 6/142 (7)
8/240 (9) 9/262 (6) 10/268 (11)   7/144 (8) 8/144 (9) 9/194 (10) 10/195 (5)

Zaheer Khan 25–7–56–1; Sharma 21–4–68–2; Harbhajan Singh 29–9–60–2; Mishra 26.4–8–71–5. *Second Innings*—Zaheer Khan 15–3–71–3; Sharma 13–4–42–2; Harbhajan Singh 20–3–36–3; Mishra 11.4–2–35–2; Sehwag 5–2–7–0.

Umpires: Asad Rauf *(Pakistan)* (21) and R. E. Koertzen *(South Africa)* (94).
Third umpire: A. M. Saheba *(India)*.   Referee: B. C. Broad *(England)* (29).

Close of play: First day, India 311-5 (Ganguly 54, Sharma 2); Second day, Australia 102-4 (Hussey 37); Third day, India 100-0 (Gambhir 46, Sehwag 53); Fourth day, Australia 141-5 (Clarke 42, Haddin 37).

INDIA v AUSTRALIA 2008-09 (3rd Test)

At Feroz Shah Kotla, Delhi, on 29, 30, 31 October, 1, 2 November.
Toss: India.   Result: MATCH DRAWN.
Debuts: none.
Man of the Match: V. V. S. Laxman.

Few dropped catches have proved as pivotal as Sharma's miss of Clarke from a looping Mishra leg-break early on the fourth morning. Clarke had not added to his overnight 21, and Australia still needed 64 to avoid the follow-on. But the ball burst through Sharma's hands, and India could not land the killer blow. Clarke survived two more chances to reach his hundred: in the end Australia amassed 577, their highest total in India, effectively ensuring the draw. In the absence of Harbhajan Singh (injured toe), Sehwag bowled 40 overs of off-spin and took his first five-for. He was the only bowler who consistently threatened the batsmen's dominance on a pitch that scarcely changed in character over five days in which only 22 wickets fell. The series continued to be played on the edge: Gambhir lightly elbowed Watson after turning for a second run, and was suspended from the final Test. Gambhir's indiscretion overshadowed his second successive century which, to the delight of his home crowd, he converted to his first double. Laxman also reached 200: it was the 14th time a Test innings had included two double-centuries, but the first occasion Australia had been on the receiving end. India's second innings was unexpectedly curtailed when Kumble, who had just announced his retirement, decided he would end his distinguished career with a final bowl. Ignoring the throbbing of a badly lacerated finger which he knew would keep him out of the final Test, Kumble delivered four valedictory overs before the draw was agreed.

India

G. Gambhir b Watson	206	–	lbw b Johnson		36
V. Sehwag lbw b Lee	1	–	b Lee		16
R. Dravid c Hayden b Johnson	11	–	(4) b Lee		11
S. R. Tendulkar c Haddin b Johnson	68	–	(5) c Hayden b White		47
V. V. S. Laxman not out	200	–	(6) not out		59
S. C. Ganguly c Ponting b Katich	5	–	(7) not out		32
†M. S. Dhoni c Haddin b Watson	27				
*A. Kumble lbw b Johnson	45				
Zaheer Khan not out	28				
I. Sharma (did not bat)		–	(3) c Ponting b Clark		1
B 6, l-b 8, w 2, n-b 6	22		L-b 4, w 1, n-b 1		6

1/5 (2) 2/27 (3) 3/157 (4)   (7 wkts dec.) 613   1/29 (2) 2/34 (3)   (5 wkts dec.) 208
4/435 (1) 5/444 (6)   3/53 (4) 4/93 (1)
6/481 (7) 7/579 (8)   5/145 (5)

A. Mishra did not bat.

Lee 30–2–119–1; Clark 33–9–69–0; Johnson 32–4–142–3; Watson 20–4–66–2; White 15–1–73–0; Clarke 14–0–59–0; Katich 15–3–60–1; Ponting 2–0–11–0. *Second Innings*—Lee 17–3–48–2; Clark 12–6–22–1; Clarke 20.3–7–56–0; Katich 1–0–5–0; Johnson 12–0–23–1; White 8–0–23–1; Watson 7–0–27–0.

Australia

M. L. Hayden lbw b Sehwag	83	–	not out		16
S. M. Katich b Mishra	64	–	not out		14
*R. T. Ponting b Sehwag	87				
M. E. K. Hussey b Sehwag	53				
M. J. Clarke c Zaheer Khan b Mishra	112				
S. R. Watson b Sehwag	36				
†B. J. Haddin st Dhoni b Kumble	17				
C. L. White b Sehwag	44				
B. Lee lbw b Kumble	8				
M. G. Johnson c and b Kumble	15				
S. R. Clark not out	1				
B 28, l-b 17, w 2, n-b 10	57		L-b 1		1

1/123 (2) 2/202 (1) 3/284 (3) 4/326 (4)   577   (no wkt) 31
5/399 (6) 6/426 (7) 7/532 (8)
8/555 (9) 9/567 (5) 10/577 (10)

Zaheer Khan 23–5–86–0; Sharma 25–5–84–0; Kumble 43.3–9–112–3; Mishra 47–12–144–2; Sehwag 40–9–104–5; Tendulkar 1–0–2–0. *Second Innings*—Kumble 4–0–14–0; Sehwag 2–0–14–0; Mishra 2–0–2–0.

Umpires: Aleem Dar *(Pakistan)* (51) and B. F. Bowden *(New Zealand)* (49).
Third umpire: S. L. Shastri *(India)*.   Referee: B. C. Broad *(England)* (30).

Close of play: First day, India 296-3 (Gambhir 149, Laxman 54); Second day, Australia 50-0 (Hayden 16, Katich 29); Third day, Australia 338-4 (Clarke 21, Watson 4); Fourth day, India 43-2 (Gambhir 21, Dravid 5).

INDIA v AUSTRALIA 2008-09 (4th Test)

At Vidarbha C. A. Stadium, Jamtha, Nagpur, on 6, 7, 8, 9, 10 November.
Toss: India.   Result: INDIA won by 172 runs.
Debuts: India – M. Vijay. Australia – J. J. Krejza.
Man of the Match: J. J. Krejza.   Man of the Series: I. Sharma.

Australia's 700th Test match ended with their captain fending off accusations that he squandered an unexpected opportunity to level the series by bowling his spinners to boost a sagging over-rate instead of letting his pacemen loose when India were an anxious 166 for 6, only 252 ahead. Dhoni and Harbhajan Singh added 108, the lead swelled to 381, and Australia were brushed aside. Seven wickets fell to Harbhajan and Mishra, who also ran out Ponting. In the first innings Harbhajan had taken his 300th wicket when he dismissed his most frequent victim, Ponting, for the tenth time. India passed 400 for the third Test running. Tendulkar's 40th Test century was his 17th in India (beating Sunil Gavaskar's record) and his tenth against Australia – only Jack Hobbs (12) scored more. Ganguly, in his final Test, mustered a characteristically elegant 85; Laxman, the eighth Indian to win 100 Test caps, made 64 Wheeling away tirelessly, and turning his flighted offbreaks significantly at times, the unheralded Jason Krejza became only the sixth debutant to take eight wickets in a Test innings, and finished with 12 for 358 in the match: only the West Indian legspinner Tommy Scott had ever conceded more runs in a Test, 374 against England in 1929-30. Australia's first innings owed much to Katich, who batted five hours for 102, and Hussey, whose 90 took even longer (315 minutes). The new VCA Stadium became the 99th Test venue (the old ground in the middle of Nagpur staged nine Tests).

India

V. Sehwag b Krejza	66	– c Haddin b Lee		92
M. Vijay c Haddin b Watson	33	– lbw b Watson		41
R. Dravid c Katich b Krejza	0	– c Haddin b Watson		3
S. R. Tendulkar lbw b Johnson	109	– run out		12
V. V. S. Laxman c Haddin b Krejza	64	– b Krejza		4
S. C. Ganguly c Clarke b Krejza	85	– c and b Krejza		0
*†M. S. Dhoni b Krejza	56	– c Hussey b Krejza		55
Harbhajan Singh not out	18	– b Watson		52
Zaheer Khan b Krejza	1	– c Haddin b Krejza		6
A. Mishra b Krejza	0	– b Watson		7
I. Sharma c Katich b Krejza	0	– not out		1
B 4, l-b 2, w 1, n-b 2	9	B 6, l-b 3, w 6, n-b 2, p 5		22

1/98 (2) 2/99 (3) 3/116 (1) 4/262 (5)   441   1/116 (2) 2/132 (3) 3/142 (1)   295
5/303 (4) 6/422 (7) 7/423 (6)   4/163 (5) 5/163 (6) 6/166 (4)
8/437 (9) 9/437 (10) 10/441 (11)   7/274 (7) 8/286 (9) 9/288 (8) 10/295 (10)

Lee 16–2–62–0; Johnson 32–11–84–1; Watson 20–5–42–1; Krejza 43.5–1–215–8; White 10–1–24–0; Katich 3–0–8–0. *Second Innings*—Johnson 14–4–22–0; Lee 10–3–27–1; Krejza 31–3–143–4; Watson 15.4–2–42–4; White 2–0–15–0; Hussey 4–2–3–0; Clarke 6–1–29–0.

Australia

M. L. Hayden run out	16	– lbw b Harbhajan Singh		77
S. M. Katich lbw b Zaheer Khan	102	– c Dhoni b Sharma		16
*R. T. Ponting b Harbhajan Singh	24	– run out		8
M. E. K. Hussey run out	90	– (5) c Dravid b Mishra		19
M. J. Clarke c Dhoni b Sharma	8	– (4) c Dhoni b Sharma		22
S. R. Watson b Harbhajan Singh	2	– c Dhoni b Harbhajan Singh		9
†B. J. Haddin c Dravid b Mishra	28	– c Tendulkar b Mishra		4
C. L. White c Sehwag b Harbhajan Singh	46	– not out		26
J. J. Krejza lbw b Sharma	5	– st Dhoni b Mishra		4
M. G. Johnson c Zaheer Khan b Mishra	5	– (11) lbw b Harbhajan Singh		11
B. Lee not out	1	– (10) c Vijay b Harbhajan Singh		0
B 12, l-b 3, w 2, n-b 6, p 5	28	B 6, l-b 1, w 4, n-b 2		13

1/32 (1) 2/74 (3) 3/229 (2) 4/255 (5)   355   1/29 (2) 2/37 (3) 3/82 (4)   209
5/265 (4) 6/266 (6) 7/318 (7)   4/150 (5) 5/154 (1) 6/161 (7)
8/333 (9) 9/352 (8) 10/355 (10)   7/178 (6) 8/190 (9) 9/191 (10) 10/209 (11)

Zaheer Khan 28–8–68–1; Harbhajan Singh 37–7–94–3; Sharma 26–8–64–2; Mishra 23.4–5–58–2; Sehwag 18–2–38–0; Tendulkar 2–0–13–0. *Second Innings*—Zaheer Khan 8–0–57–0; Sharma 9–0–31–2; Harbhajan Singh 18.2–2–64–4; Sehwag 4–0–23–0; Mishra 11–2–27–3.

Umpires: Aleem Dar *(Pakistan)* (52) and B. F. Bowden *(New Zealand)* (50).
Third umpire: S. L. Shastri *(India)*.   Referee: B. C. Broad *(England)* (31).

Close of play: First day, India 311-5 (Ganguly 27, Dhoni 4); Second day, Australia 189-2 (Katich 92, Hussey 45); Third day, India 0-0 (Sehwag 0, Vijay 0); Fourth day, Australia 13-0 (Hayden 5, Katich 8).

BANGLADESH v NEW ZEALAND 2008-09 (1st Test)

At Bir Shrestha Shahid Ruhul Amin Stadium, Chittagong, on 17, 18, 19, 20, 21 October.
Toss: Bangladesh.   Result: NEW ZEALAND won by three wickets.
Debuts: Bangladesh – Naeem Islam. New Zealand – J. D. Ryder.
Man of the Match: D. L. Vettori.

This Test might not be remembered for the quality of cricket, but it was a gripping contest, another entry on Bangladesh's "almost there" list. They often held the upper hand, but missed out in the end. New Zealand had only once scored more than 300 to win a Test, with 324 against Pakistan at Christchurch in 1993-94; their best on the subcontinent was just 82 at Lahore in 1969-70. It was a superb effort to score the highest total of the match, and no-one showed more character than Vettori, the first player ever to score two fifties and take four wickets in both innings of a Test. In the first innings, he entered at 99 for 6, and his unbeaten 55 limited the deficit to 74. Then, up at No. 4 in the second innings (as nightwatchman, he said), he lasted 260 minutes before misjudging a slog-sweep with just 19 required. Bangladesh had crept along at the start, managing only 34 runs off 32 overs (20 maidens) in the opening session. Three wickets fell for ten runs in 11 overs after lunch, but Mehrab Hossain and Mushfiqur Rahim put on 144 in 55 overs, a national fifth-wicket record, before the last five wickets clattered for 16. New Zealand had their own struggles against a slow left-armer: Shakib Al Hasan (three wickets in six previous Tests) took 7 for 36. He also top-scored in the second innings, and seemed to have done enough to secure Bangladesh's long-awaited second Test win – but Vettori had other ideas.

Bangladesh

Tamim Iqbal c McCullum b Vettori	18	– c and b Vettori	33
Junaid Siddique lbw b O'Brien	0	– c Redmond b Mills	6
Rajin Saleh b O'Brien	20	– lbw b Patel	6
*Mohammad Ashraful lbw b Vettori	2	– c Redmond b Vettori	0
Mehrab Hossain, jun. c Redmond b O'Brien	83	– c Mills b Patel	6
†Mushfiqur Rahim c How b Vettori	79	– b O'Brien	32
Naeem Islam st McCullum b Patel	14	– (8) lbw b Vettori	19
Shakib Al Hasan c Vettori b Patel	5	– (7) c Taylor b Vettori	71
Mashrafe bin Mortaza c Ryder b Vettori	0	– st McCullum b Redmond	44
Abdul Razzak c McCullum b Vettori	11	– c Taylor b O'Brien	18
Shahadat Hossain not out	0	– not out	0
B 12, l-b 1	13	B 4, l-b 1, n-b 2	7

1/0 (2) 2/34 (1) 3/40 (3) 4/44 (4)   245   1/24 (2) 2/36 (3) 3/37 (4)   242
5/188 (5) 6/229 (7) 7/229 (6)   4/49 (5) 5/71 (1) 6/127 (6)
8/229 (9) 9/245 (10) 10/245 (8)   7/175 (7) 8/180 (8) 9/220 (10) 10/242 (9)

Mills 19–7–46–0; O'Brien 23–11–36–3; Oram 20–14–14–0; Ryder 3–1–10–0; Patel 21.1–7–67–2; Vettori 36–15–59–5. *Second Innings*—Mills 18–2–55–1; O'Brien 17–7–28–2; Vettori 42–13–74–4; Patel 20–7–53–2; Oram 8–2–19–0; Redmond 2.3–1–8–1.

New Zealand

A. J. Redmond lbw b Shakib Al Hasan	19	– (2) c Junaid Siddique b Shakib Al Hasan	79
J. M. How c Rajin Saleh b Shakib Al Hasan	16	– (1) b Abdul Razzak	36
J. D. Ryder c Rajin Saleh b Shakib Al Hasan	1	– run out	38
L. R. P. L. Taylor lbw b Abdul Razzak	12	– (5) c sub (Mahbubul Alam)	
		b Mashrafe bin Mortaza	9
†B. B. McCullum c Abdul Razzak b Shakib Al Hasan	25	– (6) lbw b Abdul Razzak	2
D. R. Flynn c Mushfiqur Rahim b Naeem Islam	19	– (7) c Naeem Islam b Shakib Al Hasan	49
J. D. P. Oram c Mashrafe bin Mortaza b Shakib Al Hasan	0	– (8) not out	8
*D. L. Vettori not out	55	– (4) b Abdul Razzak	76
K. D. Mills c Mushfiqur Rahim b Shakib Al Hasan	4	– not out	1
J. S. Patel c Shakib Al Hasan b Mohammad Ashraful	0		
I. E. O'Brien b Shakib Al Hasan	5		
B 8, l-b 6, n-b 1	15	B 13, l-b 3, w 3	19

1/27 (2) 2/29 (3) 3/46 (4) 4/52 (1)   171   1/55 (1) 2/145 (3)   (7 wkts) 317
5/99 (6) 6/99 (5) 7/100 (7)   3/185 (4) 4/209 (5)
8/126 (9) 9/155 (10) 10/171 (11)   5/216 (6) 6/298 (4) 7/316 (7)

Mashrafe bin Mortaza 7–4–13–0; Shahadat Hossain 11–0–35–0; Shakib Al Hasan 25.5–7–36–7; Abdul Razzak 16–1–51–1; Mehrab Hossain 1–0–8–0; Naeem Islam 3–0–11–1; Mohammad Ashraful 1–0–3–1. *Second Innings*—Mashrafe bin Mortaza 14–4–37–1; Shahadat Hossain 11–1–46–0; Abdul Razzak 50–15–93–3; Shakib Al Hasan 44.5–17–79–2; Mehrab Hossain 2–0–6–0; Naeem Islam 12–2–16–0; Mohammad Ashraful 4–0–24–0.

Umpires: E. A. R. de Silva *(Sri Lanka)* (34) and D. J. Harper *(Australia)* (74).
Third umpire: Enamul Haque *(Bangladesh)*.   Referee: J. Srinath *(India)* (10).

Close of play: First day, Bangladesh 183-4 (Mehrab Hossain 79, Mushfiqur Rahim 59); Second day, New Zealand 155-9 (Vettori 48); Third day, Bangladesh 184-8 (Mashrafe bin Mortaza 5, Abdul Razzak 0); Fourth day, New Zealand 145-2 (Redmond 62, Vettori 0).

BANGLADESH v NEW ZEALAND 2008-09 (2nd Test)

At Shere Bangla National Stadium, Mirpur, Dhaka, on 25 *(no play)*, 26 *(no play)*, 27 *(no play)*, 28, 29 October.
Toss: Bangladesh.   Result: MATCH DRAWN.
Debuts: Bangladesh – Mahbubul Alam.
Man of the Match: D. L. Vettori.   Man of the Series: D. L. Vettori.

When the first three days were washed out, only one result seemed possible. But, although it was a draw in the end, there was no shortage of drama. Mohammad Ashraful revealed after the fourth day's play that his side had been unaware that, because it had become a two-day match, the follow-on margin had dropped from 200 runs to 100 under Law 13. By then, they were 13 for 3, needing another 150 to avoid being forced to bat again. All three wickets went in the tenth over, Vettori's first, moments before bad light ended play for the day. A match which had seemed to be of academic interest suddenly turned out to be a serious matter, and questions were asked about the team management's ignorance. The match had started well for Bangladesh: put in on a slightly damp pitch, both New Zealand's openers were gone by the fourth over. Ryder, who just missed a maiden Test century, and McCullum rescued them with a stand of 137 before Vettori declared and sent down his dramatic over. Next morning Bangladesh dipped to 44 for 6: 119 still needed to save the follow-on, against bowlers with their tails up. Shakib Al Hasan and Mashrafe bin Mortaza added 78, but it was Abdul Razzak who inched his side to safety. His joy was short-lived: the umpires reported his bowling action, and he was briefly suspended from international cricket. This match provided only the ninth instance in Tests of the rival captains dismissing each other.

New Zealand

A. J. Redmond lbw b Mashrafe bin Mortaza	2	– (2) not out	30
J. M. How b Mahbubul Alam	8	– (1) c Abdul Razzak b Mashrafe bin Mortaza	8
J. D. Ryder c Mehrab Hossain b Abdul Razzak	91	– not out	39
L. R. P. L. Taylor b Shahadat Hossain	19		
†B. B. McCullum c Mohammad Ashraful b Shakib Al Hasan	66		
D. R. Flynn not out	35		
*D. L. Vettori b Mohammad Ashraful	22		
G. D. Elliott not out	8		
B 6, l-b 3, n-b 2	11	B 1, n-b 1	2

1/10 (1) 2/10 (2) 3/49 (4)   (6 wkts dec.) 262   1/8 (1)   (1 wkt dec.) 79
4/186 (3) 5/201 (5) 6/233 (7)

K. D. Mills, J. S. Patel and I. E. O'Brien did not bat.

Mashrafe bin Mortaza 6–1–21–1; Mahbubul Alam 8–0–37–1; Abdul Razzak 25–2–72–1; Shahadat Hossain 8–0–39–1; Shakib Al Hasan 22–6–57–1; Mehrab Hossain 3–0–20–0; Mohammad Ashraful 3–0–7–1. *Second Innings*—Mashrafe bin Mortaza 5–1–14–1; Mahbubul Alam 3–1–12–0; Shakib Al Hasan 3–0–6–0; Shahadat Hossain 6–0–20–0; Junaid Siddique 2–0–2–0; Mohammad Ashraful 1–0–4–0; Abdul Razzak 6–1–8–0; Mehrab Hossain 4–0–11–0; Tamim Iqbal 1–0–1–0.

Bangladesh

Tamim Iqbal c Taylor b Vettori	24	Shahadat Hossain c Vettori b O'Brien	4
Junaid Siddique st McCullum b Vettori	4	Mahbubul Alam not out	0
*Mohammad Ashraful lbw b Vettori	0		
Rajin Saleh lbw b Vettori	0	L-b 2, w 6, n-b 2	10
Mehrab Hossain, jun. lbw b Patel	7		
†Mushfiqur Rahim c McCullum b O'Brien	7	1/13 (2) 2/13 (3) 3/13 (4) (9 wkts dec.) 169
Shakib Al Hasan lbw b Vettori	49	4/26 (5) 5/44 (1)
Mashrafe bin Mortaza c Flynn b O'Brien	48	6/44 (6) 7/122 (7) 8/155 (8)
Abdul Razzak not out	16	9/169 (10)

Mills 9–4–22–0; O'Brien 13.1–3–31–3; Patel 15–6–45–1; Vettori 19–6–66–5; Redmond 2–0–3–0.

Umpires: E. A. R. de Silva *(Sri Lanka)* (35) and D. J. Harper *(Australia)* (75).
Third umpire: A. F. M. Akhtaruddin *(Bangladesh)*.   Referee: J. Srinath *(India)* (11).

Close of play: First day, No play; Second day, No play; Third day, No play; Fourth day, Bangladesh 13-3 (Tamim Iqbal 8, Mehrab Hossain 0).

SOUTH AFRICA v BANGLADESH 2008-09 (1st Test)

At Springbok Park, Bloemfontein, on 19, 20, 21, 22 November.
Toss: Bangladesh.   Result: SOUTH AFRICA won by an innings and 129 runs.
Debuts: Bangladesh – Imrul Kayes.
Man of the Match: G. C. Smith.

Routine thrashings had been a regular occurrence for Bangladesh ever since they started playing Test cricket, but this one had even fewer sparks of interest than most – even in South Africa, where all minds were on the upcoming tour of Australia. The expected result was duly delivered without a hiccough, let alone a cough: about the only setback came when Harris broke his thumb shortly before the match, after the teams had been announced; he still managed to bowl seven overs and take a catch. A tinge of green in the pitch persuaded Mohammad Ashraful to bowl first, but after some tight new-ball overs, which restricted the score to a modest 61 at lunch, South Africa accelerated to 299 for 1 by the close – and that, effectively, was that. Smith rarely moved out of second gear, but Amla occasionally appeared to be toying with the opposition, flicking and gliding ostensibly tidy deliveries into places they didn't deserve to be hit. When Bangladesh batted, the fast men overwhelmed the top order: by the 25th over it was 88 for 8. Mushfiqur Rahim showed the value of getting into line and, with Shahadat Hossain slogging five fours with completely the opposite technique, the total limped past 150. Extras were a major contributor in the follow-on, which said everything about the gulf in quality between the teams. A violent storm truncated the third day, preventing any play after lunch, but the match was all over shortly before lunch on the fourth.

South Africa

*G. C. Smith b Mahbubul Alam................... 157	D. W. Steyn c Tamim Iqbal
N. D. McKenzie c Mehrab Hossain	b Shakib Al Hasan 1
b Shahadat Hossain 42	M. Ntini c Mushfiqur Rahim
H. M. Amla b Mashrafe bin Mortaza.............. 112	b Mahbubul Alam 5
J. H. Kallis c Mohammad Ashraful	P. L. Harris absent hurt
b Shakib Al Hasan 16	
A. G. Prince not out 59	B 2, l-b 10, n-b 11............. 23
A. B. de Villiers c Mushfiqur Rahim	
b Shakib Al Hasan 3	1/102 (2) 2/327 (3) 441
†M. V. Boucher b Shakib Al Hasan 15	3/327 (1) 4/352 (4)
M. Morkel c Mohammad Ashraful	5/365 (6) 6/404 (7)
b Shakib Al Hasan 8	7/420 (8) 8/427 (9) 9/441 (10)

Mashrafe bin Mortaza 22–4–69–1; Mahbubul Alam 24.5–8–62–2; Shahadat Hossain 25–1–125–1; Shakib Al Hasan 38–4–130–5; Naeem Islam 5–0–19–0; Mehrab Hossain 8–0–24–0.

Bangladesh

Tamim Iqbal b Steyn...........................	7	– c Boucher b Ntini....................	20
Imrul Kayes c Amla b Harris	10	– b Steyn	4
Junaid Siddique c Prince b Morkel................	8	– c Boucher b Kallis..................	27
*Mohammad Ashraful c McKenzie b Steyn........	1	– c McKenzie b Ntini	13
Mehrab Hossain, jun. c Boucher b Ntini	12	– not out............................	43
Shakib Al Hasan c de Villiers b Ntini	14	– c Boucher b Steyn	0
†Mushfiqur Rahim lbw b Kallis	48	– run out............................	0
Naeem Islam c Harris b Ntini....................	8	– c Boucher b Steyn	3
Mashrafe bin Mortaza c and b Morkel..............	5	– b Steyn	6
Shahadat Hossain b Kallis.......................	23	– b Steyn	16
Mahbubul Alam not out.........................	1	– c Prince b Kallis...................	0
B 4, l-b 2, w 4, n-b 6	16	B 7, l-b 17, n-b 3	27

1/8 (1) 2/26 (3) 3/33 (2) 4/33 (4)	153	1/13 (2) 2/45 (1) 3/67 (3) 159
5/50 (6) 6/59 (5) 7/71 (8)		4/80 (4) 5/81 (6) 6/81 (7)
8/88 (9) 9/148 (7) 10/153 (10)		7/92 (8) 8/108 (9) 9/152 (10) 10/159 (11)

Steyn 9–2–36–2; Ntini 8–2–20–3; Morkel 8–0–55–2; Harris 7–1–26–1; Kallis 4.4–1–10–2. *Second Innings*—Steyn 18–4–63–5; Ntini 16–8–19–2; Morkel 13–6–36–0; Kallis 4.5–0–17–2.

Umpires: S. J. Davis *(Australia)* (14) and I. J. Gould *(England)* (1).
Third umpire: M. Erasmus *(South Africa)*.   Referee: A. G. Hurst *(Australia)* (21).

Close of play: First day, South Africa 299-1 (Smith 138, Amla 103); Second day, Bangladesh 20-1 (Tamim Iqbal 5, Junaid Siddique 7); Third day, Bangladesh 67-3 (Mohammad Ashraful 7, Mehrab Hossain 0).

SOUTH AFRICA v BANGLADESH 2008-09 (2nd Test)

At Centurion Park, Pretoria, on 26, 27, 28 November.
Toss: Bangladesh.   Result: SOUTH AFRICA won by an innings and 48 runs.
Debuts: Bangladesh – Raqibul Hasan.
Man of the Match: A. G. Prince.   Man of the Series: A. G. Prince.

Bangladesh subsided meekly once again, a landmark of sorts as it was their 50th defeat in just 57 Tests. After Mohammad Ashraful had bravely decided to bat, Tamim Iqbal and Junaid Siddique resisted stoutly before Mushfiqur Rahim and Shakib Al Hasan thrust and parried towards a semi-decent total on a pitch lacking much pace and bounce. Mushfiqur played Bangladesh's best innings of the series: the smallest man in the squad, he jumped into line to every ball, and backed away from nothing. When South Africa replied, Mahbubul Alam dismissed Smith with a superb delivery – early inswing and sharp off-cut – for the second time running, and later Shakib took three wickets in 17 balls, including de Villiers, stumped by yards for a duck, his first in Tests after a record run of 78 innings without one since his debut. From 134 for 5, Prince and Boucher took complete command: their eventual stand of 271 was a South African sixth-wicket record, beating 200 by Graeme Pollock and Tiger Lance against Australia at Durban in 1969-70. Prince's hundred was his tenth in Tests, while Boucher's fifth was his first for 50 matches. South Africa's innings had a lop-sided look: 429 was the highest to include as many as five ducks. Shakib finished with 6 for 99, the best figures by a Bangladeshi spinner in an away Test. Bangladesh's second innings was over in less than three hours, the highlight McKenzie's one-handed diving catch at backward point to dismiss Tamim, the lowlights three farcical run-outs.

Bangladesh

Tamim Iqbal c Boucher b Morkel	31	– c McKenzie b Morkel	20
Imrul Kayes c Smith b Ntini	6	– c Smith b Ntini	5
Junaid Siddique c McKenzie b Ntini	67	– c Amla b Kallis	16
*Mohammad Ashraful c and b Morkel	1	– run out	21
Mehrab Hossain, jun. c Kallis b Ntini	3	– run out	0
Raqibul Hasan c Smith b Morkel	15	– run out	28
Shakib Al Hasan b Morkel	30	– c Ntini b Morkel	2
†Mushfiqur Rahim c de Villiers b Zondeki	65	– b Ntini	4
Mashrafe bin Mortaza c Kallis b Ntini	12	– not out	23
Shahadat Hossain c Boucher b Steyn	4	– c de Villiers b Zondeki	0
Mahbubul Alam not out	1	– c Boucher b Zondeki	1
L-b 3, n-b 12	15	B 5, l-b 3, w 1, n-b 2	11

1/25 (2) 2/54 (1) 3/57 (4) 4/71 (5)   250
5/122 (6) 6/159 (7) 7/166 (3)
8/186 (9) 9/194 (10) 10/250 (8)

1/8 (2) 2/37 (3) 3/47 (1) 4/57 (5)   131
5/68 (4) 6/77 (7) 7/95 (8)
8/126 (6) 9/127 (10) 10/131 (11)

Steyn 17–4–80–1; Ntini 19.2–8–32–4; Kallis 12–4–30–0; Zondeki 10–2–32–1; Morkel 18–0–73–4. *Second Innings*—Steyn 8–2–23–0; Ntini 11–2–44–2; Kallis 6–1–24–1; Morkel 6–1–21–2; McKenzie 1–0–1–0; Zondeki 4.4–2–10–2.

South Africa

*G. C. Smith lbw b Mahbubul Alam	27	M. Zondeki c Mushfiqur Rahim	
N. D. McKenzie c Raqibul Hasan		b Shakib Al Hasan	0
b Mashrafe bin Mortaza	0	M. Ntini c Mohammad Ashraful	
H. M. Amla c Imrul Kayes		b Shahadat Hossain	0
b Shakib Al Hasan	71	D. W. Steyn b Shahadat Hossain	1
J. H. Kallis b Shakib Al Hasan	24		
A. G. Prince not out	162	L-b 17, w 2, n-b 8	27
A. B. de Villiers st Mushfiqur Rahim			
b Shakib Al Hasan	0	1/3 (2) 2/47 (1) 3/112 (4)	429
†M. V. Boucher c Raqibul Hasan b Shakib Al Hasan	117	4/134 (3) 5/134 (6) 6/405 (7) 7/405 (8)	
M. Morkel b Shakib Al Hasan	0	8/405 (9) 9/412 (10) 10/429 (11)	

Mashrafe bin Mortaza 26–2–74–1; Mahbubul Alam 26–5–85–1; Shakib Al Hasan 28–3–99–6; Shahadat Hossain 22.2–2–89–2; Mehrab Hossain 11–1–50–0; Mohammad Ashraful 2–0–15–0.

Umpires: S. J. Davis *(Australia)* (15) and I. J. Gould *(England)* (2).
Third umpire: B. G. Jerling *(South Africa)*.   Referee: A. G. Hurst *(Australia)* (22).

Close of play: First day, South Africa 20-1 (Smith 15, Amla 5); Second day, South Africa 357-5 (Prince 115, Boucher 102).

AUSTRALIA v NEW ZEALAND 2008-09 (1st Test)

At Woolloongabba, Brisbane, on 20, 21, 22, 23 November.
Toss: New Zealand.   Result: AUSTRALIA won by 149 runs.
Debuts: none.
Man of the Match: M. G. Johnson.

The Australians had barely stepped off the plane from a tough tour of India when they were surprised by a lively, bouncy pitch, spiced up by violent storms. The conditions persuaded Australia to prefer Watson to Krejza, despite his 12-wicket debut a fortnight earlier. Vettori handed his pacemen a welcome gift by winning the toss on a steamy morning, and 19-year-old Southee grabbed three quick wickets. Symonds's return after missing the Indian tour was brief, but action-packed: after three successive fours off Elliott he collected an eight when an all-run four off O'Brien was swelled by four overthrows, but was caught behind two balls later. Replying to Australia's modest total, in which Clarke was last out for a fine 98, New Zealand made only 156: Johnson hastened the end with three wickets in six balls. Australia themselves stumbled to 115 for 6 – 16 wickets fell on the second day – but the determined Katich battled to his fourth century in eight Tests since being recalled, becoming the tenth Australian to carry his bat in a Test, the first since Mark Taylor in 1997-98. The last three wickets added 112, and the eventual target was 327. Taylor ensured the match scraped into the fourth day, but the batting was again underwhelming as Australia stretched their unbeaten run at Brisbane to 20 Tests since West Indies won in 1988-89. Lee became the fourth Australian after Shane Warne, Glenn McGrath and Dennis Lillee to take 300 Test wickets when he bowled How in the first over.

Australia

M. L. Hayden c Taylor b Southee	8	– c McCullum b Martin	0
S. M. Katich c McCullum b Southee	10	– not out	131
*R. T. Ponting c How b Southee	4	– c Redmond b O'Brien	17
M. E. K. Hussey lbw b Martin	35	– c McCullum b O'Brien	0
M. J. Clarke b Ryder	98	– run out	9
A. Symonds c McCullum b O'Brien	26	– c McCullum b Martin	20
S. R. Watson c McCullum b O'Brien	1	– lbw b Martin	5
†B. J. Haddin c How b Ryder	6	– b Vettori	19
B. Lee c McCullum b Southee	4	– b Vettori	7
M. G. Johnson c Taylor b Vettori	5	– c Vettori b Elliott	31
S. R. Clark not out	13	– c Vettori b Southee	18
L-b 2, w 1, n-b 1	4	L-b 10, n-b 1	11

1/13 (1) 2/22 (2) 3/23 (3) 4/96 (4)   214   1/0 (1) 2/40 (3) 3/40 (4)   268
5/132 (6) 6/139 (7) 7/152 (8)   4/53 (5) 5/109 (6) 6/115 (7)
8/160 (9) 9/183 (10) 10/214 (5)   7/156 (8) 8/186 (9) 9/239 (10) 10/268 (11)

Martin 18–4–42–1; Southee 18–3–63–4; O'Brien 19–6–44–2; Elliott 10–4–29–0; Vettori 8–0–27–1; Ryder 4–1–7–2. *Second Innings*—Martin 21–5–69–3; Southee 16.2–5–62–1; O'Brien 17–1–58–2; Elliott 6–1–15–1; Vettori 19–4–46–2; Ryder 2–0–8–0.

New Zealand

A. J. Redmond c Ponting b Clark	3	– c and b Clark	10
J. M. How b Lee	14	– c Ponting b Lee	0
J. D. Ryder c Haddin b Watson	30	– lbw b Johnson	24
L. R. P. L. Taylor lbw b Lee	40	– c Haddin b Johnson	75
†B. B. McCullum c Ponting b Johnson	8	– lbw b Clark	3
D. R. Flynn not out	39	– b Johnson	29
G. D. Elliott b Watson	9	– b Clark	0
*D. L. Vettori c Symonds b Johnson	2	– c Symonds b Johnson	10
T. G. Southee c Symonds b Johnson	0	– not out	12
I. E. O'Brien c Clarke b Johnson	1	– c Clarke b Clark	3
C. S. Martin b Clark	1	– b Johnson	1
L-b 3, n-b 6	9	L-b 5, w 2, n-b 3	10

1/7 (1) 2/44 (2) 3/64 (3) 4/73 (5)   156   1/1 (2) 2/30 (1) 3/40 (3)   177
5/108 (4) 6/127 (7) 7/143 (8)   4/49 (5) 5/133 (6) 6/143 (7)
8/143 (9) 9/149 (10) 10/156 (11)   7/160 (8) 8/161 (4) 9/164 (10) 10/177 (11)

Lee 16–5–38–2; Clark 15–2–46–2; Watson 10–2–35–2; Johnson 8–3–30–4; Symonds 1–0–4–0. *Second Innings*—Lee 9–0–53–1; Clark 17–5–43–4; Johnson 17.3–6–39–5; Watson 5–1–19–0; Symonds 4–0–12–0; Clarke 2–0–6–0.

Umpires: B. R. Doctrove *(West Indies)* (20) and R. E. Koertzen *(South Africa)* (95).
Third umpire: R. J. Tucker *(Australia)*.   Referee: B. C. Broad *(England)* (32).

Close of play: First day, New Zealand 7-0 (Redmond 3, How 2); Second day, Australia 131-6 (Katich 67, Haddin 6); Third day, New Zealand 143-6 (Taylor 67).

AUSTRALIA v NEW ZEALAND 2008-09 (2nd Test)

At Adelaide Oval on 28, 29, 30 November, 1 December.
Toss: New Zealand.   Result: AUSTRALIA won by an innings and 62 runs.
Debuts: none.
Man of the Match: B. J. Haddin.   Man of the Series: M. J. Clarke.

Ponting lost his fifth successive toss, allowing Vettori to hand his team perfect batting conditions a week after his seamers were presented with a bowlers' paradise. Redmond took the long handle to offspinner Nathan Hauritz – called up for his second Test late on, after the unfortunate Jason Krejza missed his chance of a home debut after twisting his ankle – and New Zealand lunched heartily at 101 for 1. But the joy was short-lived: soon after the interval Ryder pulled a long-hop straight to midwicket, then Redmond – in sight of a maiden century – was caught on the midwicket boundary. The sot dismissals continued as New Zealand were bowled out around 200 short of a par score. Hayden, the 11th Australian to win 100 Test caps, ran himself out, but Ponting hit 13 fours before pulling to the 6ft 7ins Fulton at midwicket. "I got it about an inch from the middle," lamented Ponting, "but it just happened to go to the world's tallest man." Hussey and Symonds were out in the same over, but Clarke crafted another fine century, putting on 181 at almost a run a minute with Haddin, who attempted to step out of Adam Gilchrist's giant shadow by playing like him, and reached his first hundred in his ninth Test. His blazing 169 included 24 fours as well as two sixes off Redmond's occasional legspin. Next day New Zealand were destroyed by Lee and incompetence, and only a defiant three-hour innings from McCullum pushed the match beyond tea.

New Zealand

A. J. Redmond c Symonds b Hauritz	83	– c Clarke b Lee	19
J. M. How c Haddin b Johnson	16	– c Ponting b Lee	28
J. D. Ryder c Clarke b Hauritz	13	– c Symonds b Lee	3
L. R. P. L. Taylor lbw b Clark	44	– c and b Lee	1
P. G. Fulton c Katich b Symonds	29	– b Johnson	7
D. R. Flynn b Lee	11	– lbw b Johnson	9
†B. B. McCullum c Haddin b Lee	30	– not out	84
*D. L. Vettori not out	18	– c Hayden b Hauritz	13
T. G. Southee c Katich b Johnson	2	– c Ponting b Hauritz	11
I. E. O'Brien c Haddin b Lee	0	– lbw b Lee	0
C. S. Martin b Lee	0	– b Johnson	0
B 4, l-b 8, w 1, n-b 11	24	B 7, l-b 8, n-b 13	28

1/46 (2) 2/101 (3) 3/130 (1) 4/194 (5)   270   1/39 (1) 2/55 (3) 3/58 (4)   203
5/200 (4) 6/228 (6) 7/266 (7)   4/63 (2) 5/76 (6) 6/84 (5)
8/269 (9) 9/270 (10) 10/270 (11)   7/105 (8) 8/131 (9) 9/181 (10) 10/203 (11)

Lee 25.3–8–66–4; Clark 20–6–56–1; Johnson 25–5–56–2; Hauritz 16–2–63–2; Symonds 12–2–17–1. *Second Innings*—Lee 25–5–105–5; Clark 10–5–22–0; Johnson 15.1–7–29–3; Hauritz 24–11–32–2.

Australia

M. L. Hayden run out	24	N. M. Hauritz b Vettori	1
S. M. Katich c Ryder b Vettori	23	S. R. Clark not out	1
*R. T. Ponting c Fulton b O'Brien	79		
M. E. K. Hussey c Redmond b Martin	70	B 2, l-b 8, w 1, n-b 5	16
M. J. Clarke c Ryder b O'Brien	110		
A. Symonds c McCullum b Martin	0	1/38 (1) 2/49 (2) 3/155 (3)	535
†B. J. Haddin c Fulton b Redmond	169	4/244 (4) 5/247 (6) 6/428 (5)	
B. Lee c Taylor b O'Brien	19	7/470 (8) 8/526 (9)	
M. G. Johnson c McCullum b Redmond	23	9/532 (7) 10/535 (10)	

Martin 27–4–110–2; Southee 27–1–100–0; Vettori 59.4–20–124–2; O'Brien 31–6–111–3; Ryder 7–1–33–0; Redmond 6–0–47–2.

Umpires: B. R. Doctrove *(West Indies)* (21) and R. E. Koertzen *(South Africa)* (96).
Third umpire: B. N. J. Oxenford *(Australia)*.   Referee: B. C. Broad *(England)* (33).

Close of play: First day, New Zealand 262-6 (McCullum 30, Vettori 12); Second day, Australia 241-3 (Hussey 69, Clarke 43); Third day, New Zealand 35-0 (Redmond 15, How 13).

NEW ZEALAND v WEST INDIES 2008-09 (1st Test)

At University Oval, Dunedin, on 11, 12 (*no play*), 13, 14, 15 (*no play*) December.
Toss: New Zealand.   Result: MATCH DRAWN.
Debuts: New Zealand – T. G. McIntosh. West Indies – L. S. Baker, B. P. Nash.
Man of the Match: J. E. Taylor.

The notoriously changeable weather of the nearest Test ground to the South Pole washed out two days' play. The experimental umpire-referral system was trialled for the second time: seven decisions were reconsidered by the TV-watching official – four were reversed, three upheld. The first, an lbw appeal against Flynn, was initially given not out, but he was sent packing by the third umpire. The two innings took contrasting courses. New Zealand, under new coach Andy Moles (his first act was to switch Ryder and Flynn in the batting order: both just missed maiden centuries), looked comfortable on the first day, before losing their last five wickets for 76. West Indies were in some trouble at 173 for 6, but Chanderpaul put on 153 with Taylor, who sailed to a flamboyant hundred in just 97 balls, belying a previous first-class best of just 40: he was the 35th batsman to make his maiden century in a Test, but only the second – after his namesake Bruce Taylor, for New Zealand at Calcutta in 1964-65 – not to have reached 50 before. New Zealand's advantage was just 25, and when Powell bowled How and nightwatchman Mills with successive balls on the fourth evening, an interesting final day was in prospect – but the weather ensured it never materialised. Lionel Baker was the first player from the island of Montserrat to play for West Indies, while Brendan Nash – born in Australia to Jamaican parents – also made his debut: he had returned to Jamaica after losing his place in the Queensland squad.

New Zealand

T. G. McIntosh c Baker b Gayle	34	– not out		24
J. M. How c Chanderpaul b Powell	10	– b Powell		10
D. R. Flynn lbw b Gayle	95	– (4) not out		4
L. R. P. L. Taylor c Marshall b Gayle	15			
J. D. Ryder c Chanderpaul b Powell	89			
†B. B. McCullum c Ramdin b Taylor	25			
J. E. C. Franklin hit wkt b Edwards	7			
*D. L. Vettori c Marshall b Powell	30			
K. D. Mills lbw b Edwards	12	– (3) b Powell		0
M. R. Gillespie not out	16			
I. E. O'Brien c and b Edwards	4			
L-b 16, w 9, n-b 3	28	B 4, l-b 1, n-b 1		6

1/10 (2) 2/97 (1) 3/128 (4) 4/189 (3)   365   1/33 (2) 2/33 (3)   (2 wkts) 44
5/278 (6) 6/289 (7) 7/310 (5)
8/327 (8) 9/347 (9) 10/365 (11)

Taylor 23–7–61–1; Powell 24–7–68–3; Edwards 22–4–91–3; Baker 25–3–85–0; Gayle 21–2–42–3; Nash 1–0–2–0. *Second Innings*—Edwards 5–0–22–0; Powell 5–0–17–2.

West Indies

*C. H. Gayle c Franklin b O'Brien	74	F. H. Edwards c sub (S. W. Eathorne)		
S. Chattergoon c O'Brien b Mills	13	b Vettori		0
R. R. Sarwan c McCullum b Mills	8	L. S. Baker not out		0
X. M. Marshall c Ryder b Vettori	20			
S. Chanderpaul b Vettori	76	B 1, l-b 10, n-b 4		15
B. P. Nash c Ryder b Mills	23			
†D. Ramdin lbw b Vettori	5	1/66 (2) 2/87 (3) 3/114 (1) 4/134 (4)		340
J. E. Taylor c McCullum b Vettori	106	5/162 (6) 6/173 (7) 7/326 (8)		
D. B. Powell lbw b Vettori	0	8/326 (9) 9/334 (10) 10/340 (5)		

Gillespie 21–5–102–0; Mills 24–6–64–3; O'Brien 15–4–46–1; Vettori 25–7–56–6; Franklin 15–2–61–0.

Umpires: M. R. Benson *(England)* (26) and A. M. Saheba *(India)* (1).
Third umpire: R. E. Koertzen *(South Africa)*.   Referee: J. Srinath *(India)* (12).

Close of play: First day, New Zealand 226-4 (Ryder 54, McCullum 4); Second day, No play; Third day, West Indies 39-0 (Gayle 29, Chattergoon 9); Fourth day, New Zealand 44-2 (McIntosh 24, Flynn 4).

NEW ZEALAND v WEST INDIES 2008-09 (2nd Test)

At McLean Park, Napier, on 19, 20, 21, 22, 23 December.
Toss: West Indies.   Result: MATCH DRAWN.
Debuts: none.
Man of the Match: C. H. Gayle.

The players reacted well to the warmth and a hard, reasonably fast pitch, and produced a high-scoring draw. The first to take advantage was Chanderpaul, who reached his 20th Test century late on the first day after putting on 163 with Nash. The lively O'Brien took the last four wickets for 16 in eight overs next morning to complete his first Test five-for: Chanderpaul was left stranded after 340 minutes. New Zealand's latest opener, left-hander Tim McIntosh, had a huge stroke of luck: after toiling to 14 in 21 overs he swished Edwards almost vertically, but Ramdin and the bowler both stopped as they converged for the catch. McIntosh capitalised, moving confidently to his maiden century next morning. Edwards ripped out the tail to finish with his best Test figures, including his 100th wicket (Flynn). Home hopes rose when Marshall and Chanderpaul fell to successive balls from Patel, but Gayle dropped anchor for a century – only his eighth, in 75 matches, and the first since his 317 against South Africa in May 2005 – and next day hurried his side past 300 with four fours in an O'Brien over. Finally, having hit 122 in boundaries, he chopped a ball onto his boot, from where it bounced up gently for McCullum to catch. New Zealand's optimistic quest for 312 in 60 overs was effectively called off after McCullum was given out caught behind: the replays were inconclusive and he had to go. Soon afterwards, the series was left drawn at 0–0.

West Indies

*C. H. Gayle c McCullum b O'Brien	34	– c McCullum b Patel		197
S. Chattergoon c How b Vettori	13	– c Taylor b Patel		25
R. R. Sarwan c McCullum b Patel	11	– lbw b Vettori		1
X. M. Marshall c Ryder b O'Brien	6	– c Taylor b Patel		18
S. Chanderpaul not out	126	– c and b Patel		0
B. P. Nash c Flynn b Franklin	74	– c How b Franklin		65
†D. Ramdin b Vettori	6	– c Flynn b Franklin		6
J. E. Taylor c McCullum b O'Brien	17	– lbw b O'Brien		8
S. J. Benn c McCullum b O'Brien	0	– (11) not out		4
D. B. Powell c McCullum b O'Brien	6	– lbw b Vettori		22
F. H. Edwards lbw b O'Brien	0	– (9) c Taylor b Patel		20
L-b 6, w 1, n-b 7	14	L-b 2, w 1, n-b 6		9

1/43 (1) 2/54 (3) 3/63 (4) 4/74 (2)   307
5/237 (6) 6/257 (7) 7/279 (8)
8/279 (9) 9/299 (10) 10/307 (11)

1/58 (2) 2/61 (3) 3/106 (4)   375
4/106 (5) 5/230 (6) 6/252 (7)
7/272 (8) 8/342 (1) 9/363 (9) 10/375 (10)

Franklin 16–2–57–1; Mills 15–4–48–0; Patel 25–12–41–1; O'Brien 26–6–75–6; Vettori 22–4–71–2; Ryder 3–0–9–0. *Second Innings*—O'Brien 24–3–90–1; Mills 6–1–21–0; Patel 46–16–110–5; Vettori 52–21–91–2; Franklin 17–3–61–2.

New Zealand

T. G. McIntosh b Taylor	136	– lbw b Taylor		3
J. M. How c Chattergoon b Edwards	12	– c Gayle b Edwards		54
D. R. Flynn c and b Edwards	57	– run out		33
L. R. P. L. Taylor c Ramdin b Edwards	4	– lbw b Benn		46
J. D. Ryder c Ramdin b Edwards	57	– not out		59
†B. B. McCullum c Ramdin b Taylor	31	– c Ramdin b Taylor		19
J. E. C. Franklin c Gayle b Powell	0	– not out		2
*D. L. Vettori c Ramdin b Edwards	29			
K. D. Mills lbw b Edwards	18			
J. S. Patel c Marshall b Edwards	2			
I. E. O'Brien not out	0			
L-b 19, n-b 6	25	W 2, n-b 2		4

1/19 (2) 2/137 (3) 3/145 (4) 4/245 (5)   371
5/316 (1) 6/317 (6) 7/319 (7)
8/367 (8) 9/368 (9) 10/371 (10)

1/8 (1) 2/62 (3) 3/96 (2)   (5 wkts) 220
4/170 (4) 5/203 (6)

Taylor 23–6–76–2; Powell 26–7–85–1; Edwards 29.4–6–87–7; Gayle 18–6–33–0; Nash 6–2–22–0; Benn 24–5–49–0. *Second Innings*—Taylor 13–2–67–2; Powell 5–0–30–0; Edwards 11–0–46–1; Benn 17–2–54–1; Gayle 5–0–23–0.

Umpires: R. E. Koertzen *(South Africa)* (97) and A. M. Saheba *(India)* (2).
Third umpire: M. R. Benson *(England)*.   Referee: J. Srinath *(India)* (13).

Close of play: First day, West Indies 258-6 (Chanderpaul 100, Taylor 1); Second day, New Zealand 145-2 (McIntosh 62, Taylor 4); Third day, West Indies 62-2 (Gayle 36, Marshall 0); Fourth day, West Indies 278-7 (Gayle 146, Edwards 1).

INDIA v ENGLAND 2008-09 (1st Test)

At M. A. Chidambaram Stadium, Chennai, on 11, 12, 13, 14, 15 December.
Toss: England.   Result: INDIA won by six wickets.
Debuts: England – G. P. Swann.
Man of the Match: V. Sehwag.

This series faced cancellation after a terrorist attack in Mumbai, but England's players eventually agreed to return to India. This match was switched from volatile Ahmedabad, and a pitch originally meant for a 20-over game produced a classic match, culminating in the highest fourth-innings total to win a Test in Asia. In a century here dedicated to all Indians, Tendulkar masterminded the chase after Sehwag snatched the initiative with 83 from 68 balls. Earlier, Strauss became the first Englishman to score twin Test centuries on the subcontinent (and the eighth player to do so in a losing cause); England reached 164 for 1 before Zaheer Khan began their demise. India then struggled to 102 for 5: Graeme Swann was the second bowler, after Richard Johnson in 2003, to take two wickets in his first Test over, both marginal lbw decisions by Daryl Harper. After Laxman and Tendulkar (Flintoff's 200th Test wicket for England) were out in successive overs, Dhoni made his fifth fifty in six Test innings. Many felt a lead of 75 would be decisive on a disintegrating pitch ... except the pitch did not disintegrate. Strauss and Collingwood put on 214, England's highest fourth-wicket partnership total in Asia, but the longer England batted, the more Zaheer and Sharma slowed it down – only 57 came in 23 overs on the fourth afternoon – and finally Pietersen set India 387. England had been diffident about ramming home the advantage; Sehwag was not, clouting four sixes, and India were always ahead of the rate after that.

England

A. J. Strauss c and b Mishra	123	– c Laxman b Harbhajan Singh		108
A. N. Cook c Zaheer Khan b Harbhajan Singh	52	– c Dhoni b Sharma		9
I. R. Bell lbw b Zaheer Khan	17	– c Gambhir b Mishra		7
*K. P. Pietersen c and b Zaheer Khan	4	– lbw b Yuvraj Singh		1
P. D. Collingwood c Gambhir b Harbhajan Singh	9	– lbw b Zaheer Khan		108
A. Flintoff c Gambhir b Mishra	18	– c Dhoni b Sharma		4
J. M. Anderson c Yuvraj Singh b Mishra	19	– (10) not out		1
†M. J. Prior not out	53	– (7) c Sehwag b Sharma		33
G. P. Swann c Dravid b Harbhajan Singh	1	– (8) b Zaheer Khan		7
S. J. Harmison c Dhoni b Yuvraj Singh	6	– (9) b Zaheer Khan		1
M. S. Panesar lbw b Sharma	6			
L-b 7, n-b 1	8	B 10, l-b 13, w 2, n-b 7		32

1/118 (2) 2/164 (3) 3/180 (4) 4/195 (5)   316   1/28 (2) 2/42 (3)   (9 wkts dec.) 311
5/221 (1) 6/229 (6) 7/271 (7)   3/43 (4) 4/257 (1)
8/277 (9) 9/304 (10) 10/316 (11)   5/262 (6) 6/277 (5) 7/297 (8) 8/301 (9) 9/311 (7)

Zaheer Khan 21–9–41–2; Sharma 19.4–4–32–1; Harbhajan Singh 38–2–96–3; Mishra 34–6–99–3; Yuvraj Singh 15–2–33–1; Sehwag 1–0–8–0. *Second Innings*—Zaheer Khan 27–7–40–3; Sharma 22.5–1–57–3; Mishra 17–1–66–1; Yuvraj Singh 3–1–12–1; Harbhajan Singh 30–3–91–1; Sehwag 6–0–22–0.

India

G. Gambhir lbw b Swann	19	– c Collingwood b Anderson		66
V. Sehwag b Anderson	9	– lbw b Swann		83
R. Dravid lbw b Swann	3	– c Prior b Flintoff		4
S. R. Tendulkar c and b Flintoff	37	– not out		103
V. V. S. Laxman c and b Panesar	24	– c Bell b Swann		26
Yuvraj Singh c Flintoff b Harmison	14	– not out		85
*†M. S. Dhoni c Pietersen b Panesar	53			
Harbhajan Singh c Bell b Panesar	40			
Zaheer Khan lbw b Flintoff	1			
A. Mishra b Flintoff	12			
I. Sharma not out	8			
B 4, l-b 11, n-b 6	21	B 5, l-b 11, n-b 4		20

1/16 (2) 2/34 (1) 3/37 (3) 4/98 (5)   241   1/117 (2) 2/141 (3)   (4 wkts) 387
5/102 (4) 6/137 (6) 7/212 (8)   3/183 (1) 4/224 (5)
8/217 (9) 9/219 (7) 10/241 (10)

Harmison 11–1–42–1; Anderson 11–3–28–1; Flintoff 18.4–2–49–3; Swann 10–0–42–2; Panesar 19–4–65–3. *Second Innings*—Harmison 10–0–48–0; Anderson 11–1–51–1; Panesar 27–4–105–0; Flintoff 22–1–64–1; Swann 28.3–2–103–2.

Umpires: B. F. Bowden *(New Zealand)* (51) and D. J. Harper *(Australia)* (76).
Third umpire: S. L. Shastri *(India)*.   Referee: J. J. Crowe *(New Zealand)* (26).

Close of play: First day, England 229-5 (Flintoff 18, Anderson 2); Second day, India 155-6 (Dhoni 24, Harbhajan Singh 13); Third day, England 172-3 (Strauss 73, Collingwood 60); Fourth day, India 131-1 (Gambhir 41, Dravid 2).

INDIA v ENGLAND 2008-09 (2nd Test)

At Punjab C. A. Stadium, Mohali, Chandigarh, on 19, 20, 21, 22, 23 December.

Toss: India.   Result: MATCH DRAWN.

Debuts: none.

Man of the Match: G. Gambhir.   Man of the Series: Zaheer Khan.

This Test was moved from Mumbai (where it had been due to mark a return to the old Brabourne Stadium) after the terrorist attacks. Had winter morning fog and poor light in the afternoons at chilly not caused more than a day's play to be lost, this could have been another classic. As it was, India held on to their series lead, although England had their moments. Pietersen slammed a glorious 144 despite a cracked rib, and he and Flintoff, who for once batted as robustly as he bowled, worried India on the third afternoon. On a pitch where batting was never easy, Sehwag departed in the second over, but Gambhir and Dravid put on 314, two short of India's all-wicket record against England; India still fell short of the 500 that seemed to be there for the taking. England lost two quick wickets, but Pietersen set about the attack with drives, sweeps and audacious switch-hits, one of which (off Harbhajan Singh) cleared the rope at cover. Dhoni slowed things down with defensive bowling: it wasn't pretty, but it did restrict England to 71 from 25 overs on the third evening, after they made 154 in 36 overs during the afternoon. A lunchtime declaration on the final day, when India were 367 ahead, might have set England a chase of sorts, but Dhoni preferred to let Gambhir and Yuvraj pursue centuries. After England returned home, differences between captain Pietersen and coach Peter Moores became public knowledge, leading to both losing their jobs.

India

G. Gambhir c Cook b Swann	179	– c Bell b Swann	97
V. Sehwag c Prior b Broad	0	– run out	17
R. Dravid c Panesar b Swann	136	– b Broad	0
S. R. Tendulkar lbw b Swann	11	– c Swann b Anderson	5
V. V. S. Laxman lbw b Flintoff	0	– run out	15
Yuvraj Singh c Prior b Panesar	27	– run out	86
*†M. S. Dhoni c sub (O. A. Shah) b Anderson	29	– c and b Panesar	0
Harbhajan Singh c Swann b Panesar	24	– not out	5
Zaheer Khan b Flintoff	7		
A. Mishra b Flintoff	23		
I. Sharma not out	1		
B 5, l-b 5, n-b 6	16	B 10, l-b 8, w 5, n-b 3	26

1/6 (2) 2/320 (1) 3/329 (3) 4/337 (4)   453   1/30 (2) 2/36 (3)   (7 wkts dec.) 251
5/339 (5) 6/379 (6) 7/418 (7)   3/44 (4) 4/80 (5)
8/418 (8) 9/446 (9) 10/453 (10)   5/233 (6) 6/241 (7) 7/251 (1)

Anderson 32–5–84–1; Broad 26–9–84–1; Flintoff 30.2–10–54–3; Panesar 23–2–89–2; Swann 45–11–122–3; Collingwood 2–0–10–0. *Second Innings*—Anderson 19–8–51–1; Broad 14–2–50–1; Flintoff 13–1–39–0; Swann 17–3–49–1; Panesar 10–0–44–1.

England

A. J. Strauss lbw b Zaheer Khan	0	– not out	21
A. N. Cook lbw b Zaheer Khan	50	– c Laxman b Sharma	10
I. R. Bell b Sharma	1	– not out	24
*K. P. Pietersen lbw b Harbhajan Singh	144		
P. D. Collingwood c Dhoni b Mishra	11		
A. Flintoff c Gambhir b Mishra	62		
J. M. Anderson not out	8		
†M. J. Prior c Dhoni b Harbhajan Singh	2		
S. C. J. Broad b Harbhajan Singh	1		
G. P. Swann b Zaheer Khan	3		
M. S. Panesar c Gambhir b Harbhajan Singh	5		
B 1, l-b 7, w 1, n-b 6	15	B 4, w 1, n-b 4	9

1/0 (1) 2/1 (3) 3/104 (2) 4/131 (5)   302   1/18 (2)   (1 wkt) 64
5/280 (4) 6/282 (6) 7/285 (8)
8/290 (9) 9/293 (10) 10/302 (11)

Zaheer Khan 21–3–76–3; Sharma 12–0–55–1; Yuvraj Singh 6–1–20–0; Harbhajan Singh 20.5–2–68–4; Mishra 24–0–75–2. *Second Innings*—Zaheer Khan 3–0–11–0; Sharma 5–1–7–1; Harbhajan Singh 11–3–25–0; Mishra 8–1–16–0; Dhoni 1–0–1–0.

Umpires: Asad Rauf *(Pakistan)* (22) and D. J. Harper *(Australia)* (77).
Third umpire: S. L. Shastri *(India)*.   Referee: J. J. Crowe *(New Zealand)* (27).

Close of play: First day, India 179-1 (Gambhir 106, Dravid 65); Second day, India 453; Third day, England 282-6 (Anderson 1); Fourth day, India 134-4 (Gambhir 44, Yuvraj Singh 39).

AUSTRALIA v SOUTH AFRICA 2008-09 (1st Test)

At W. A. C. A. Ground, Perth, on 17, 18, 19, 20, 21 December.
Toss: Australia.   Result: SOUTH AFRICA won by six wickets.
Debuts: South Africa – J-P. Duminy.
Man of the Match: A. B. de Villiers.

Australia, after recovering from 15 for 3 on the first morning to make 375, controlled the game for the best part of four days – but lost after South Africa marched to the second-highest successful run-chase in Test history. The turnaround owed much to the unwavering belief instilled in the South Africans over a successful year, personified by two 24-year-olds who came together at 303 for 4, within touching distance of the target of 414 yet far enough away to feel the tremors of painful past failures against Australia. Jean-Paul Duminy was a last-minute replacement for Ashwell Prince, whose thumb was broken in the nets the day before the match, while de Villiers was a bundle of energy whose brilliant catching had already helped tame Australia's batsmen. Smith had made his first century in nine Tests against Australia, passing 6,000 runs in the process, and was relieved his dismissal had not precipitated a repeat of the first innings, when Johnson took five for two in 21 balls of express pace and reverse-swing as the last seven wickets tumbled for 47. South Africa's target was swelled by Haddin after the earlier batsmen misfired: Hayden's poor run was compounded by Asad Rauf, who later apologised for giving him out caught off his pad. Johnson, whose first-innings figures were the best by a left-arm fast bowler in any Test, finished with 11 of the 14 wickets to fall, including the only one Australia could manage on the last day on a pitch prone to uneven bounce.

Australia

M. L. Hayden c Smith b Ntini	12	– c and b Steyn		4
S. M. Katich lbw b Morkel	83	– c Boucher b Kallis		37
*R. T. Ponting c de Villiers b Ntini	0	– c Boucher b Harris		32
M. E. K. Hussey c de Villiers b Steyn	0	– b Ntini		8
M. J. Clarke c Smith b Harris	62	– c Kallis b Steyn		25
A. Symonds c McKenzie b Harris	57	– c Smith b Harris		37
†B. J. Haddin c Duminy b Ntini	46	– st Boucher b Harris		94
B. Lee c Duminy b Steyn	29	– c de Villiers b Kallis		5
J. J. Krejza not out	30	– c de Villiers b Kallis		32
M. G. Johnson lbw b Morkel	18	– c Kallis b Morkel		21
P. M. Siddle c Boucher b Ntini	23	– not out		4
L-b 7, w 3, n-b 5	15	B 4, l-b 7, w 2, n-b 7		20

1/14 (1) 2/14 (3) 3/15 (4) 4/164 (2)   375   1/25 (1) 2/59 (2) 3/88 (3)   319
5/166 (5) 6/259 (6) 7/298 (7)   4/88 (4) 5/148 (5) 6/157 (6)
8/303 (8) 9/341 (10) 10/375 (11)   7/162 (8) 8/241 (9) 9/278 (10) 10/319 (7)

Ntini 19.5–1–72–4; Steyn 23–4–81–2; Kallis 15–2–65–0; Morkel 20–1–80–2; Harris 21–2–70–2. *Second Innings—*Steyn 19–3–81–2; Ntini 21–2–76–1; Harris 27–3–85–3; Kallis 14–4–24–3; Morkel 16–4–42–1.

South Africa

N. D. McKenzie c Krejza b Johnson	2	– (2) c Haddin b Johnson		10
*G. C. Smith b Johnson	48	– (1) lbw b Johnson		108
H. M. Amla b Krejza	47	– c Haddin b Lee		53
J. H. Kallis c Haddin b Johnson	63	– c Hussey b Johnson		57
A. B. de Villiers c Haddin b Johnson	63	– not out		106
J-P. Duminy c Haddin b Johnson	1	– not out		50
†M. V. Boucher c Katich b Siddle	26			
M. Morkel c Krejza b Johnson	1			
P. L. Harris c Krejza b Johnson	0			
D. W. Steyn c Haddin b Johnson	8			
M. Ntini not out	5			
L-b 5, w 5, n-b 7	17	B 13, l-b 9, w 2, n-b 6		30

1/16 (1) 2/106 (3) 3/110 (2) 4/234 (5)   281   1/19 (2) 2/172 (1)   (4 wkts) 414
5/237 (4) 6/238 (6) 7/241 (8)   3/179 (3) 4/303 (4)
8/241 (9) 9/256 (10) 10/281 (7)

Lee 21–3–59–0; Johnson 24–4–61–8; Krejza 25–2–102–1; Siddle 16.5–5–44–1; Symonds 3–1–10–0. *Second Innings—*Lee 27–4–73–1; Johnson 34.2–5–98–3; Siddle 26–2–84–0; Krejza 24–2–102–0; Clarke 8–0–35–0.

Umpires: Aleem Dar *(Pakistan)* (53) and E. A. R. de Silva *(Sri Lanka)* (36).
Third umpire: P. R. Reiffel *(Australia)*.   Referee: R. S. Madugalle *(Sri Lanka)* (108).

Close of play: First day, Australia 341-9 (Krejza 19); Second day, South Africa 243-8 (Boucher 2, Steyn 1); Third day, Australia 228-7 (Haddin 39, Krejza 28); Fourth day, South Africa 227-3 (Kallis 33, de Villiers 11).

AUSTRALIA v SOUTH AFRICA 2008-09 (2nd Test)

At Melbourne Cricket Ground on 26, 27, 28, 29, 30 December.
Toss: Australia.   Result: SOUTH AFRICA won by nine wickets.
Debuts: none.
Man of the Match: D. W. Steyn.

The empire had already crumbled by the time Amla sealed South Africa's first-ever series victory in Australia. It was not the scale of the defeat but the manner that was so shocking for the home side, who had seemed completely in control after two days; Ponting ended with nothing to show for two determined innings but becoming Australia's first captain to lose a series at home since Allan Border against West Indies in 1992-93. Few locals could recall a more dispiriting day's cricket in those 16 years than the third here, when Duminy and Steyn humiliated an inexperienced bowling attack. They orchestrated a stunning, series-defining turnaround, putting on 180 in four hours, the third-highest ninth-wicket stand in Tests. Steyn was not done: while Australia laboured for 11 wickets all told, Steyn captured ten on his own with high-class pace and swing. Ponting had started with an imperious century, his 37th in Tests, passing 1,000 runs at the MCG. Clarke's mature 88, and another strong show from the tail, lifted the score to 394, which looked formidable when South Africa stumbled to 184 for 7 – but there was no hint of panic about Duminy during his delightful 166, just self-assurance, precise strokeplay and trust in his partners. South Africa's last three wickets produced 275 runs. Ponting was only the second man, after Geoff Boycott for England at Port-of-Spain in 1973-74, to score a century and 99 in the same Test. South Africa needed 183 and, again led by Smith, coasted home on the final afternoon.

Australia

M. L. Hayden c Duminy b Ntini	8	– c Duminy b Steyn	23
S. M. Katich b Steyn	54	– c Boucher b Steyn	15
*R. T. Ponting c Amla b Harris	101	– c Smith b Morkel	99
M. E. K. Hussey c Boucher b Steyn	0	– c Amla b Morkel	2
M. J. Clarke not out	88	– c McKenzie b Steyn	29
A. Symonds c Kallis b Morkel	27	– c Kallis b Steyn	0
†B. J. Haddin c Smith b Ntini	40	– c Kallis b Ntini	10
B. Lee c Kallis b Steyn	21	– b Kallis	8
M. G. Johnson b Steyn	0	– not out	43
N. M. Hauritz c Smith b Steyn	12	– b Kallis	3
P. M. Siddle c de Villiers b Kallis	19	– c Boucher b Steyn	6
B 5, l-b 12, n-b 7	24	B 1, l-b 3, n-b 5	9

1/21 (1) 2/128 (2) 3/143 (4) 4/184 (3)   **394**   1/37 (1) 2/40 (2) 3/49 (4)   **247**
5/223 (6) 6/277 (7) 7/322 (8)   4/145 (5) 5/145 (6) 6/165 (7)
8/326 (9) 9/352 (10) 10/394 (11)   7/180 (8) 8/212 (3) 9/231 (10) 10/247 (11)

Steyn 29–6–87–5; Ntini 27–7–108–2; Kallis 18.4–4–55–1; Morkel 22–3–89–1; Harris 17–3–38–1. *Second Innings*—Steyn 20.2–3–67–5; Ntini 14–1–26–1; Morkel 15–2–46–2; Harris 21–1–47–0; Kallis 14–1–57–2.

South Africa

*G. C. Smith c Haddin b Siddle	62	– lbw b Hauritz	75
N. D. McKenzie b Siddle	0	– not out	59
H. M. Amla c Symonds b Johnson	19	– not out	30
J. H. Kallis c Haddin b Hauritz	26		
A. B. de Villiers b Siddle	7		
J-P. Duminy c Siddle b Hauritz	166		
†M. V. Boucher c Hussey b Hauritz	3		
M. Morkel b Johnson	21		
P. L. Harris c Johnson b Hussey	39		
D. W. Steyn b Siddle	76		
M. Ntini not out	2		
B 5, l-b 13, n-b 15, p 5	38	L-b 9, w 2, n-b 8	19

1/1 (2) 2/39 (3) 3/102 (4) 4/126 (1)   **459**   1/121 (1)   (1 wkt) **183**
5/132 (5) 6/141 (7) 7/184 (8)
8/251 (9) 9/431 (10) 10/459 (6)

Lee 13–2–68–0; Siddle 34–9–81–4; Johnson 39–6–127–2; Hauritz 43–13–98–3; Clarke 8–0–26–0; Hussey 5–0–22–1; Symonds 11–3–14–0. *Second Innings*—Lee 10–0–49–0; Siddle 14–5–34–0; Johnson 11–1–36–0; Hauritz 10–0–41–1; Clarke 3–0–14–0.

Umpires: Aleem Dar *(Pakistan)* (54) and B. R. Doctrove *(West Indies)* (22).
Third umpire: B. N. J. Oxenford *(Australia)*.   Referee: R. S. Madugalle *(Sri Lanka)* (109).

Close of play: First day, Australia 280-6 (Clarke 36, Lee 0); Second day, South Africa 198-7 (Duminy 34, Harris 8); Third day, Australia 4-0 (Hayden 1, Katich 2); Fourth day, South Africa 30-0 (Smith 25, McKenzie 3).

AUSTRALIA v SOUTH AFRICA 2008-09 (3rd Test)

At Sydney Cricket Ground on 3, 4, 5, 6, 7 January.
Toss: Australia.   Result: AUSTRALIA won by 103 runs.
Debuts: Australia – D. E. Bollinger, A. B. McDonald.
Man of the Match: P. M. Siddle.   Man of the Series: G. C. Smith.

This might have been a dead rubber, but it held great significance for both teams. The No. 1 ranking would have changed hands had South Africa achieved a clean sweep, but it was something more basic that made Smith, by then unable to dress himself, walk out to bat with 8.2 overs remaining. He lasted 26 minutes, wincing with pain when the ball jarred his bat, but finally Johnson found the same crack that had earlier caused a ball to spit up and break Smith's left hand: this time the ball jagged back into the stumps to seal Australia's consolation victory with five minutes and ten balls to spare. "It probably would have got me if I had both arms available," said Smith, after the second successive Sydney cliffhanger: the previous January India's last wicket had fallen with nine minutes left. It was a dramatic finish to a captivating series. Ponting was out first ball after his fine double at Melbourne, but Clarke made an attractive century, putting on 142 with Johnson in Australia's biggest total of the series. Eventually set 375 to win, South Africa slipped to 91 for 3 when McDonald lunged for a return catch from Kallis, who was given out although replays were inconclusive as to whether the ball had scraped the pitch. Some time during Steyn's 65-minute rearguard with Ntini – during which Hayden, shortly to retire, dropped Ntini at slip – the wounded Smith borrowed some whites, and when he emerged at No. 11, the crowd stood and roared.

Australia

M. L. Hayden b Steyn	31	– b Morkel	39
S. M. Katich c de Villiers b Kallis	47	– lbw b Steyn	61
*R. T. Ponting c Boucher b Morkel	0	– b Morkel	53
M. E. K. Hussey c Kallis b Harris	30	– not out	45
M. J. Clarke c and b Duminy	138	– c Amla b Harris	41
A. B. McDonald c Boucher b Ntini	15		
†B. J. Haddin b Steyn	38		
M. G. Johnson c Smith b Steyn	64		
N. M. Hauritz c Duminy b Harris	41		
P. M. Siddle lbw b Harris	23		
D. E. Bollinger not out	0		
L-b 7, w 3, n-b 8	18	B 8, l-b 9, n-b 1	18

1/62 (2) 2/63 (3) 3/109 (1) 4/130 (4)   445   1/62 (1) 2/134 (3)   (4 wkts dec.) 257
5/162 (6) 6/237 (7) 7/379 (5)   3/181 (2) 4/257 (5)
8/381 (8) 9/440 (10) 10/445 (9)

Steyn 27–5–95–3; Ntini 29–5–102–1; Morkel 27–3–89–1; Kallis 20–6–54–1; Harris 29.2–6–84–3; Duminy 4–0–14–1. *Second Innings*—Steyn 13–1–60–1; Ntini 12–1–66–0; Morkel 12–2–38–2; Kallis 10–5–13–0; Harris 20.3–1–63–1.

South Africa

N. D. McKenzie lbw b Siddle	23	– c Hussey b Bollinger	27
*G. C. Smith retired hurt	30	– (11) b Johnson	3
H. M. Amla lbw b McDonald	51	– c Katich b Hauritz	59
J. H. Kallis c Hayden b Johnson	37	– c and b McDonald	4
A. B. de Villiers run out	11	– b Siddle	56
J-P. Duminy lbw b Johnson	13	– lbw b Johnson	16
†M. V. Boucher b Siddle	89	– lbw b Siddle	4
M. Morkel b Siddle	40	– (2) c Johnson b Bollinger	0
P. L. Harris lbw b Siddle	2	– (8) lbw b Siddle	6
D. W. Steyn b Siddle	6	– (9) lbw b McDonald	28
M. Ntini not out	0	– (10) not out	28
L-b 12, w 9, n-b 4	25	B 12, l-b 18, w 4, n-b 2, p 5	41

1/76 (1) 2/131 (4) 3/161 (5)   327   1/2 (2) 2/68 (1) 3/91 (4)   272
4/166 (3) 5/193 (6) 6/308 (8)   4/110 (3) 5/166 (6)
7/310 (9) 8/316 (10) 9/327 (7)   6/172 (7) 7/190 (5) 8/202 (8) 9/257 (9) 10/272 (11)

In the first innings Smith retired hurt at 35.

Siddle 27.5–11–59–5; Bollinger 23–4–78–0; Johnson 28–6–69–2; McDonald 22–8–41–1; Hauritz 20–4–68–0. *Second Innings*—Siddle 27–12–54–3; Bollinger 21–5–53–2; Johnson 23.2–7–49–2; McDonald 13–6–32–2; Hauritz 28–10–47–1; Clarke 2–1–2–0.

Umpires: B. F. Bowden *(New Zealand)* (52) and E. A. R. de Silva *(Sri Lanka)* (37).
Third umpire: R. J. Tucker *(Australia)*.   Referee: R. S. Madugalle *(Sri Lanka)* (110).

Close of play: First day, Australia 267-6 (Clarke 73, Johnson 17); Second day, South Africa 125-1 (Amla 30, Kallis 36); Third day, Australia 33-0 (Hayden 18, Katich 9); Fourth day, South Africa 62-1 (McKenzie 25, Amla 30).

BANGLADESH v SRI LANKA 2008-09 (1st Test)

At Shere Bangla National Stadium, Mirpur, Dhaka, on 26, 27, 28, 30, 31 December.
Toss: Sri Lanka.   Result: SRI LANKA won by 107 runs.
Debuts: none.
Man of the Match: Shakib Al Hasan.

The records will show that Bangladesh lost yet again, their 51st defeat in 58 Tests, but it was not their usual meek surrender. Chasing 521, they briefly threatened the impossible; and at 403 for 6, with Shakib Al Hasan and Mushfiqur Rahim going strong, Mahela Jayawardene (who had earlier scored his 24th Test century) was forced onto the defensive. Shakib also added 112 with Mohammad Ashraful, whose century ended a long drought: in 18 innings since his previous one he had not passed 35. Eventually Shakib dragged a wide one into his stumps: six overs later, the match was over, the last four wickets tumbling for ten. Still, 413 was the 11th-highest fourth-innings total in all Test cricket, the sixth-highest in a losing cause, and the highest on the subcontinent (beating India's 387 against England 16 days earlier); Bangladesh's previous-best was 285 for 5 to draw with Zimbabwe in 2004-05, and in their most recent 13 Tests they had not passed 300 in either innings. Shakib had also been the wrecker-in-chief with his fourth five-for when Sri Lanka batted first, after a two-hour fog delay, and made a modest 293. Muralitharan trumped him with his 66th Test five-wicket haul (and 22nd ten-for). This was the first Test anywhere for seven years to have a scheduled rest day: there was a general election in Bangladesh on December 29. The previous instance was a Poya Day (a Buddhist festival celebrating the full moon) during Sri Lanka's series with Zimbabwe in 2001-02.

Sri Lanka

M. G. Vandort c Shakib Al Hasan b Shahadat Hossain . .	44	– b Mashrafe bin Mortaza	6
B. S. M. Warnapura lbw b Mashrafe bin Mortaza	14	– lbw b Mahbubul Alam	8
K. C. Sangakkara c Mohammad Ashraful			
b Shakib Al Hasan	43	– c Mushfiqur Rahim b Mehrab Hossain	67
*D. P. M. D. Jayawardene b Shakib Al Hasan	3	– c Junaid Siddique b Mehrab Hossain 166
T. T. Samaraweera c Junaid Siddique b Shakib Al Hasan .	90	– b Mashrafe bin Mortaza	62
T. M. Dilshan b Shakib Al Hasan	14	– c Mushfiqur Rahim b Shakib Al Hasan 47
†H. A. P. W. Jayawardene c Tamim Iqbal			
b Shahadat Hossain	6	– not out	3
W. P. U. J. C. Vaas c Mushfiqur Rahim			
b Mashrafe bin Mortaza	37	– not out	15
K. T. G. D. Prasad lbw b Shakib Al Hasan	3		
H. M. R. K. B. Herath run out	1		
M. Muralitharan not out	0		
B 4, l-b 13, w 12, n-b 9	38	B 16, l-b 5, w 2, n-b 8	31

1/24 (2) 2/119 (3) 3/121 (1) 4/135 (4)   293   1/16 (2) 2/18 (1)   (6 wkts dec.) 405
5/155 (6) 6/171 (7) 7/270 (8)   3/153 (3) 4/291 (5)
8/285 (9) 9/291 (10) 10/293 (5)   5/386 (6) 6/388 (4)

Mashrafe bin Mortaza 18–2–67–2; Mahbubul Alam 19–4–56–0; Shahadat Hossain 16–2–55–2; Shakib Al Hasan 28.4–4–70–5; Mehrab Hossain 6–1–22–0; Mohammad Ashraful 2–0–6–0. *Second Innings*—Mashrafe bin Mortaza 21–4–59–2; Mahbubul Alam 17–1–62–1; Shakib Al Hasan 40–10–134–1; Shahadat Hossain 14–1–66–0; Mehrab Hossain 10–0–37–2; Raqibul Hasan 1–0–2–0; Mohammad Ashraful 5–0–24–0.

Bangladesh

Tamim Iqbal c Warnapura b Muralitharan	17	– c H. A. P. W. Jayawardene b Prasad	47
Imrul Kayes c H. A. P. W. Jayawardene b Vaas	33	– run out	13
Junaid Siddique b Muralitharan	29	– c D. P. M. D. Jayawardene b Muralitharan . . . 37
*Mohammad Ashraful c Dilshan b Vaas	12	– (5) lbw b Vaas	101
Raqibul Hasan b Prasad	11	– (4) b Muralitharan	24
Mehrab Hossain, jun. c D. P. M. D. Jayawardene b Herath .	29	– c sub (C. K. Kapugedera) b Muralitharan . .	23
Shakib Al Hasan c D. P. M. D. Jayawardene b Muralitharan.	26	– b Prasad	96
†Mushfiqur Rahim not out	12	– c Dilshan b Muralitharan	61
Mashrafe bin Mortaza lbw b Muralitharan	0	– c H. A. P. W. Jayawardene b Prasad	2
Shahadat Hossain st H. A. P. W. Jayawardene			
b Muralitharan	5	– (11) not out	0
Mahbubul Alam c Warnapura b Muralitharan	0	– (10) run out	2
B 4	4	L-b 3, n-b 4	7

1/44 (1) 2/68 (2) 3/90 (4) 4/95 (3)   178   1/40 (2) 2/72 (1) 3/124 (3)   413
5/117 (5) 6/158 (6) 7/162 (7)   4/144 (4) 5/180 (6) 6/292 (5)
8/162 (9) 9/176 (10) 10/178 (11)   7/403 (7) 8/409 (9) 9/411 (8) 10/413 (10)

Vaas 11–4–33–2; Prasad 13–0–61–1; Dilshan 2–0–2–0; Muralitharan 22–8–49–6; Herath 12–1–29–1. *Second Innings*—Vaas 25–5–74–1; Prasad 25.2–5–105–3; Muralitharan 48–9–141–4; Herath 26–4–86–0; Dilshan 2–0–4–0.

Umpires: S. A. Bucknor *(West Indies)* (125) and N. J. Llong *(England)* (3).
Third umpire: Enamul Haque *(Bangladesh)*.   Referee: J. J. Crowe *(New Zealand)* (28).

Close of play: First day, Sri Lanka 172-6 (Samaraweera 20, Vaas 0); Second day, Bangladesh 177-9 (Mushfiqur Rahim 11, Mahbubul Alam 0); Third day, Sri Lanka 291-4 (D. P. M. D. Jayawardene 129); Fourth day, Bangladesh 254-5 (Mohammad Ashraful 70, Shakib Al Hasan 34).

BANGLADESH v SRI LANKA 2008-09 (2nd Test)

At Bir Shrestha Shahid Ruhul Amin Stadium, Chittagong, on 3, 4, 5, 6 January.
Toss: Sri Lanka.   Result: SRI LANKA won by 465 runs.
Debuts: none.
Man of the Match: T. M. Dilshan.   Man of the Series: T. M. Dilshan.

Sri Lanka prolonged their second innings until lunch on the fourth day, setting a massive target of 624: but after Bangladesh's heroics in the previous Test, it seemed it would go the distance: instead they were bundled out inside 50 overs, as Sri Lanka completed the fifth-largest Test victory by runs. At the start, it had been Sri Lankan wickets tumbling. After Mahela Jayawardene won the toss in his 100th Test, Mashrafe bin Mortaza struck twice in his first two overs, and it was 75 for 4 before Dilshan emerged to make his 50th Test all his own. On a pitch where others found strokemaking difficult, Dilshan batted with amazing freedom and authority. He reached his hundred from only 93 balls, and by the time he was bowled round his legs he had made 162. Sri Lanka lost their last five wickets for 17, but with Mendis back from injury to partner Muralitharan, a total of 384 was enough to give Bangladesh a follow-on scare – the last pair joined forces with 40 still needed, and added 63. Dilshan then scored 143, becoming the fourth Sri Lankan to score two hundreds in a Test. None of the previous batsmen to have scored twin centuries – there were 64 previous instances in all – had taken more then two wickets in the same match (Vijay Hazare took two, including Don Bradman, at Adelaide in 1947-48; despite Hazare's two hundreds, India lost by an innings), but now Dilshan took four to wrap up a 2–0 series victory.

Sri Lanka

B. S. M. Warnapura lbw b Mohammad Ashraful	63	– lbw b Shahadat Hossain	27
†H. A. P. W. Jayawardene lbw b Mashrafe bin Mortaza	0	– c Shakib Al Hasan b Mohammad Ashraful	28
K. C. Sangakkara b Mashrafe bin Mortaza	5	– b Mohammad Ashraful	54
*D. P. M. D. Jayawardene c Mushfiqur Rahim b Shakib Al Hasan	11	– c Imrul Kayes b Enamul Haque	22
T. T. Samaraweera b Shahadat Hossain	19	– lbw b Shakib Al Hasan	77
T. M. Dilshan b Enamul Haque	162	– b Enamul Haque	143
C. K. Kapugedera lbw b Shakib Al Hasan	96	– not out	59
W. P. U. J. C. Vaas lbw b Mashrafe bin Mortaza	3	– not out	20
M. Muralitharan lbw b Shakib Al Hasan	0		
B. A. W. Mendis not out	6		
C. R. D. Fernando lbw b Shakib Al Hasan	0		
B 4, l-b 8, w 1, n-b 6	19	B 3, l-b 4, w 4, n-b 6	17

1/1 (2) 2/7 (3) 3/39 (4) 4/75 (5)   384   1/55 (2) 2/55 (1)   (6 wkts dec.) 447
5/194 (1) 6/367 (6) 7/376 (7)   3/123 (4) 4/165 (3)
8/376 (8) 9/384 (9) 10/384 (11)   5/310 (5) 6/396 (6)

Mashrafe bin Mortaza 22–7–58–3; Shahadat Hossain 14–0–80–1; Shakib Al Hasan 30–6–109–4; Enamul Haque 19–3–70–1; Mehrab Hossain 7–1–36–0; Mohammad Ashraful 2–0–19–1. *Second Innings*—Mashrafe bin Mortaza 15–3–53–0; Shahadat Hossain 28–3–92–1; Shakib Al Hasan 20–2–79–1; Enamul Haque 36–2–109–2; Mohammad Ashraful 17–1–56–2; Mehrab Hossain 8–0–38–0; Raqibul Hasan 1–0–3–0; Imrul Kayes 1–0–7–0; Tamim Iqbal 1–0–3–0.

Bangladesh

Tamim Iqbal c H. A. P. W. Jayawardene b Vaas	0	– c H. A. P. W. Jayawardene b Vaas	17
Imrul Kayes lbw b Vaas	6	– c D. P. M. D. Jayawardene b Mendis	5
Junaid Siddique b Fernando	28	– lbw b Mendis	4
Raqibul Hasan lbw b Mendis	0	– b Fernando	10
*Mohammad Ashraful c H. A. P. W. Jayawardene b Muralitharan	45	– c H. A. P. W. Jayawardene b Mendis	7
Mehrab Hossain, jun. lbw b Mendis	18	– (8) lbw b Dilshan	5
Shakib Al Hasan lbw b Mendis	0	– st H. A. P. W. Jayawardene b Dilshan	46
†Mushfiqur Rahim st H. A. P. W. Jayawardene b Mendis	21	– (6) run out	43
Mashrafe bin Mortaza c Dilshan b Muralitharan	63	– c D. P. M. D. Jayawardene b Dilshan	0
Enamul Haque c H. A. P. W. Jayawardene b Muralitharan	4	– (11) not out	0
Shahadat Hossain not out	5	– (10) b Dilshan	1
B 5, l-b 5, n-b 8	18	B 4, l-b 5, n-b 11	20

1/0 (1) 2/26 (2) 3/33 (4) 4/65 (3)   208   1/18 (2) 2/22 (1) 3/32 (3)   158
5/90 (6) 6/90 (7) 7/122 (5)   4/42 (5) 5/52 (4) 6/144 (7)
8/136 (8) 9/145 (10) 10/208 (9)   7/154 (8) 8/154 (9) 9/156 (10) 10/158 (6)

Vaas 10–5–21–2; Fernando 18–4–44–1; Mendis 28–5–71–4; Muralitharan 20.2–6–62–3. *Second Innings*—Vaas 8–3–16–1; Fernando 12–4–36–1; Mendis 15–4–57–3; Muralitharan 10–0–30–0; Dilshan 4.2–1–10–4.

Umpires: S. A. Bucknor *(West Indies)* (126) and N. J. Llong *(England)* (4).
Third umpire: Nadir Shah *(Bangladesh)*.   Referee: J. J. Crowe *(New Zealand)* (29).

Close of play: First day, Sri Lanka 371-6 (Kapugedera 93, Vaas 1); Second day, Sri Lanka 13-0 (Warnapura 7, H. A. P. W. Jayawardene 6); Third day, Sri Lanka 296-4 (Samaraweera 72, Dilshan 81).

WEST INDIES v ENGLAND 2008-09 (1st Test)

At Sabina Park, Kingston, Jamaica, on 4, 5, 6, 7 February.
Toss: England.   Result: WEST INDIES won by an innings and 23 runs.
Debuts: none.
Man of the Match: J. E. Taylor.

For three days this was a typical Test match ... and then England collapsed on the fourth day for 51. It was their third-lowest total in any Test, after 45 at Sydney in 1886-87 and 46 at Port-of-Spain in 1993-94. In the first one the batsmen were bothered by rain, and in the second they were bothered by Curtly Ambrose, but there were no such excuses this time. Taylor – brisk but no Ambrose – suddenly looked unplayable in a superb second spell, which brought him four for four in six overs, while the tall slow left-armer Benn claimed four wickets, becoming the first West Indian spinner to take eight in a match since Lance Gibbs in 1974-75. Victory ended West Indies' run of 14 defeats and three draws in their previous 17 Tests against England. Strauss, restored as captain after Pietersen's removal, said: "Taylor bowled a fantastic spell, but the wicket wasn't misbehaving terribly so we need to hold our hands up and say it wasn't good enough." The match had started with England overcoming a poor start to move sedately to 318; Pietersen missed out on his 16th Test century when a spiralling top-edge was caught by Ramdin. Gayle then batted for 337 minutes, cutting loose occasionally to hit five sixes to go with five fours, and put on 202 with Sarwan, who lasted even longer (six hours) for 107. Nash applied himself for four hours as West Indies' lead increased to 74 – which no-one dreamed would be enough for victory.

England

*A. J. Strauss c Ramdin b Taylor	7	– c Ramdin b Taylor	9
A. N. Cook c Sarwan b Powell	4	– c Smith b Taylor	0
I. R. Bell c Smith b Gayle	28	– c Ramdin b Benn	4
K. P. Pietersen c Ramdin b Benn	97	– b Taylor	1
P. D. Collingwood lbw b Benn	16	– b Taylor	1
A. Flintoff c Nash b Powell	43	– b Edwards	24
†M. J. Prior c and b Benn	64	– b Taylor	0
S. C. J. Broad c Benn b Taylor	4	– c Marshall b Benn	0
R. J. Sidebottom not out	26	– lbw b Benn	6
S. J. Harmison lbw b Taylor	7	– b Benn	0
M. S. Panesar lbw b Benn	0	– not out	0
B 7, l-b 8, n-b 7	22	B 2, n-b 4	6

1/8 (1) 2/31 (2) 3/71 (3) 4/94 (5)   318   1/1 (2) 2/11 (3)   51
5/180 (4) 6/241 (6) 7/256 (8) 8/288 (7)   3/12 (4) 4/20 (1) 5/23 (5)
9/313 (10) 10/318 (11)   6/23 (7) 7/26 (8) 8/50 (9) 9/51 (6) 10/51 (10)

Taylor 20–4–74–3; Edwards 14–1–58–0; Powell 20–5–54–2; Benn 44.2–13–77–4; Gayle 24–9–40–1. *Second Innings*—Taylor 9–4–11–5; Powell 7–3–5–0; Benn 14.2–2–31–4; Gayle 2–1–1–0; Edwards 1–0–1–1.

West Indies

*C. H. Gayle b Broad	104
D. S. Smith lbw b Flintoff	6
R. R. Sarwan b Flintoff	107
X. M. Marshall lbw b Broad	0
S. Chanderpaul lbw b Broad	20
B. P. Nash c Prior b Broad	55
†D. Ramdin c Collingwood b Panesar	35
J. E. Taylor lbw b Harmison	8
S. J. Benn c Cook b Broad	23
D. B. Powell c Prior b Harmison	9
F. H. Edwards not out	10
B 6, l-b 8, w 1	15

1/18 (2) 2/220 (1) 3/220 (4)   392
4/235 (3) 5/254 (5) 6/320 (7) 7/341 (8)
8/371 (9) 9/376 (6) 10/392 (10)

Sidebottom 24–5–35–0; Flintoff 33–11–72–2; Harmison 20.4–4–49–2; Broad 29–7–85–5; Panesar 47–14–122–1; Pietersen 4–1–15–0.

Umpires: A. L. Hill *(New Zealand)* (8) and R. E. Koertzen *(South Africa)* (98).
Third umpire: N. A. Malcolm *(West Indies)*.   Referee: A. G. Hurst *(Australia)* (23).

Close of play: First day, England 236-5 (Flintoff 43, Prior 27); Second day, West Indies 160-1 (Gayle 71, Sarwan 74); Third day, West Indies 352-7 (Nash 47, Benn 10).

WEST INDIES v ENGLAND 2008-09 (2nd Test)

At Sir Vivian Richards Stadium, North Sound, Antigua, on 13 February.
Toss: West Indies.   Result: MATCH DRAWN.
Debuts: none.
Man of the Match: no award.

This match was abandoned after only ten deliveries because the outfield was unfit for play. It had been dug up the previous October to improve the drainage, which had proved inadequate during the 2007 World Cup, but rain hampered the preparation, and attempts to improve matters with large amounts of sand proved disastrous, as the bowlers found it difficult to make it up to the stumps through the resulting sludge: Edwards aborted his approach three times in his only over, before throwing the ball away in disgust. "The bowlers deemed the run-ups to be a safety hazard," said the referee Alan Hurst. Afterwards, ICC suspended the ground's international status, and warned that a stringent inspection would be needed before it was cleared to stage further matches. "This is not shooting me in the foot," said Viv Richards of the chaos in the stadium which bore his name, "this is shooting me straight through the heart." Mindful of the 8,000 British visitors who had flown to Antigua for the match, the authorities sanctioned a switch to the old Antigua Recreation Ground for an additional Test, to start two days later. This one was the shortest Test in which there was any play, beating the 61 balls of the West Indies-England match at Kingston in 1997-98 – another major embarrassment for the West Indian board – which was called off as the pitch was too dangerous. The shortest Test with a positive result lasted 656 balls, when Australia beat South Africa at Melbourne in 1931-32.

England

*A. J. Strauss not out...........................	6	
A. N. Cook not out	1	
	(no wkt) 7	

O. A. Shah, K. P. Pietersen, P. D. Collingwood, A. Flintoff, †M. J. Prior, S. C. J. Broad, R. J. Sidebottom, J. M. Anderson and M. S. Panesar did not bat.

Taylor 1–0–5–0; Edwards 0.4–0–2–0.

West Indies

*C. H. Gayle, D. S. Smith, R. R. Sarwan, S. Chanderpaul, B. P. Nash, R. O. Hinds, †D. Ramdin, J. E. Taylor, S. J. Benn, D. B. Powell and F. H. Edwards.

Umpires: D. J. Harper *(Australia)* (78) and A. L. Hill *(New Zealand)* (9).
Third umpire: R. E. Koertzen *(South Africa)*. Referee: A. G. Hurst *(Australia)* (24).

WEST INDIES v ENGLAND 2008-09 (3rd Test)

At Antigua Recreation Ground, St John's, on 15, 16, 17, 18, 19 February.
Toss: West Indies.   Result: MATCH DRAWN.
Debuts: none.
Man of the Match: R. R. Sarwan.

There were doubts beforehand about whether a suitable pitch could be prepared for a Test at two days' notice after the previous match was abandoned, but the groundstaff – led by Keith Frederick and overseen by the former Test fast bowler Andy Roberts – performed a minor miracle: their strip lasted well and produced a nailbiting finish. West Indies' unfancied final pair survived the last ten overs (and 36 minutes) in fading light to force a draw which kept their side's series lead intact. Powell took heart from a stubborn first-innings performance as nightwatchman – 22 from 86 balls – while Edwards had been at the crease for a similar last-ditch escape act in the ground's previous Test, against India in June 2006 (*Test No. 1805*). When Strauss led England's march to 566, helped by a five-hour century from Collingwood, it seemed as if the ARG's batsman-friendly reputation – both Brian Lara's Test-record scores were made here – was being maintained. West Indies fared less well as Swann (who had been preferred to Panesar) found some bite, but Strauss decided not to enforce the follow-on, eventually declaring midway through the fourth day. West Indies needed to score 503 or, more realistically, survive what became 128 overs after rain delayed the final day by 75 minutes. Sarwan made another elegant century, while Chanderpaul dug in for almost four hours – but wickets came regularly once they were separated, leading to the exciting finale. Flintoff, who bagged a pair, missed the rest of the series with a hip injury.

England

*A. J. Strauss c and b Edwards	169	– c Smith b Edwards	14
A. N. Cook c Smith b Gayle	52	– c Smith b Hinds	58
O. A. Shah run out	57	– (4) b Powell	14
K. P. Pietersen b Taylor	51	– (5) c Ramdin b Benn	32
J. M. Anderson c Ramdin b Edwards	4	– (3) c Ramdin b Powell	20
P. D. Collingwood c Smith b Hinds	113	– b Hinds	34
A. Flintoff b Taylor	0	– (9) c Hinds b Benn	0
†M. J. Prior c Chanderpaul b Nash	39	– (7) not out	15
S. C. J. Broad c Ramdin b Hinds	44	– (8) run out	1
G. P. Swann not out	20		
S. J. Harmison (did not bat)		– (10) not out	7
B 10, l-b 1, w 1, n-b 5	17	B 12, l-b 3, w 5, n-b 6	26

1/123 (2) 2/276 (3)   (9 wkts dec.) 566   1/23 (1) 2/69 (3)   (8 wkts dec.) 221
3/295 (1) 4/311 (5) 5/405 (4) 6/405 (7)   3/97 (4) 4/145 (2)
7/467 (8) 8/529 (9) 9/566 (6)   5/189 (5) 6/195 (6) 7/201 (8) 8/206 (9)

Taylor 28–7–73–2; Edwards 26–2–75–2; Powell 26–3–103–0; Gayle 13–1–41–1; Benn 39–5–143–0; Hinds 22.2–4–86–2; Nash 11–2–34–1. *Second Innings*—Edwards 9–1–36–1; Taylor 9–2–34–0; Powell 7–0–33–2; Benn 14–1–58–2; Hinds 11–1–45–2.

West Indies

*C. H. Gayle c Anderson b Harmison	30	– lbw b Swann	46
D. S. Smith b Swann	38	– lbw b Harmison	21
D. B. Powell c Collingwood b Swann	22	– (10) not out	22
R. R. Sarwan c Flintoff b Swann	94	– (3) b Broad	106
R. O. Hinds c Prior b Flintoff	27	– (4) c Shah b Broad	6
S. Chanderpaul c Prior b Broad	1	– (5) c Prior b Broad	55
B. P. Nash c Collingwood b Flintoff	18	– (6) lbw b Swann	23
†D. Ramdin c and b Swann	0	– (7) b Anderson	21
J. E. Taylor c and b Flintoff	19	– (8) c sub (I. R. Bell) b Anderson	11
S. J. Benn lbw b Swann	0	– (9) lbw b Swann	21
F. H. Edwards not out	1	– not out	5
B 17, l-b 5, w 2, n-b 11	35	B 21, l-b 7, w 1, n-b 4	33

1/45 (1) 2/109 (2) 3/130 (3)   285   1/59 (2) 2/81 (1)   (9 wkts) 370
4/200 (5) 5/201 (6) 6/251 (4) 7/251 (8)   3/96 (4) 4/244 (3) 5/261 (5)
8/278 (7) 9/279 (10) 10/285 (9)   6/287 (6) 7/313 (8) 8/322 (7) 9/353 (9)

Anderson 19–1–55–0; Flintoff 14.2–3–47–3; Harmison 12–3–44–1; Broad 14–4–24–1; Swann 24–7–57–5; Pietersen 2–0–14–0; Collingwood 4–0–22–0. *Second Innings*—Anderson 25–6–68–2; Broad 21–3–69–3; Swann 39–12–92–3; Harmison 22–3–54–1; Flintoff 15–5–32–0; Pietersen 3–0–15–0; Shah 3–0–12–0.

Umpires: D. J. Harper (*Australia*) (79) and R. E. Koertzen (*South Africa*) (99).
Third umpire: N. A. Malcolm (*West Indies*). Referee: A. G. Hurst (*Australia*) (25).

Close of play: First day, England 301-3 (Pietersen 8, Anderson 3); Second day, West Indies 55-1 (Smith 10, Powell 2); Third day, England 31-1 (Cook 4, Anderson 4); Fourth day, West Indies 143-3 (Sarwan 47, Chanderpaul 1).

WEST INDIES v ENGLAND 2008-09 (4th Test)

At Kensington Oval, Bridgetown, Barbados, on 26, 27, 28 February, 1, 2 March.
Toss: England.   Result: MATCH DRAWN.
Debuts: none.
Man of the Match: R. R. Sarwan.

A pitch that Strauss said "remained incredibly flat" throughout yielded 1,628 runs and only 17 wickets: the average of 95.76 runs per wicket was the fifth-highest for any Test (top of the list is 136.13 by Pakistan and India at Lahore in 2005-06). Strauss led from the front with another century, while Bopara, replacing the injured Flintoff, completed his first after making ducks in his previous three Test innings. Ambrose, in his only Test of the series as Prior had returned home after the birth of his first child, made 76 before the declaration at 600. West Indies were in some danger of following on at 334 for 5, not helped when lbw appeals against Chanderpaul and Nash, which were referred to the third umpire Daryl Harper, were upheld despite both looking doubtful (the regulations provided for a decision to be changed only if there was an obvious error). Sarwan, however, held firm. After reaching his third century of the series he motored past 200 for the second time, beat his previous-highest score (261 not out against Bangladesh in June 2004), and had just equalled Viv Richards's 291 at The Oval in 1976 when, after 698 minutes and 452 balls, he lost his off stump to Sidebottom's late swing. He put on 261 for the sixth wicket with Ramdin, who had little trouble extending his maiden Test century to 166. There was time for Cook to score his first Test century since December 2007, 16 matches previously at Galle.

England

*A. J. Strauss b Powell .... 142 – b Gayle 38
A. N. Cook c Hinds b Taylor .... 94 – not out. 139
O. A. Shah c Smith b Benn........................ 7 – lbw b Benn........................... 21
K. P. Pietersen lbw b Edwards .... 41 – not out. 72
P. D. Collingwood c Nash b Edwards.............. 96
R. S. Bopara c Taylor b Edwards 104
†T. R. Ambrose not out.......................... 76
S. C. J. Broad not out 13
    B 5, l-b 3, w 11, n-b 8 27   B 6, n-b 3......................... 9

1/229 (1) 2/241 (2)   (6 wkts dec.) 600 1/88 (1) 2/129 (3)   (2 wkts dec.) 279
3/259 (3) 4/318 (4) 5/467 (5) 6/580 (6)

G. P. Swann, R. J. Sidebottom and J. M. Anderson did not bat.

Taylor 29.2–7–107–1; Edwards 30–0–151–3; Powell 24–3–107–1; Benn 30–7–106–1; Gayle 15–4–28–0; Hinds 14–2–62–0; Nash 9–1–20–0; Sarwan 2–0–11–0. *Second Innings*—Edwards 10–1–41–0; Powell 12–0–35–0; Benn 21–1–64–1; Taylor 4–0–15–0; Gayle 17–5–46–1; Hinds 14–1–56–0; Sarwan 3–0–16–0.

West Indies

D. S. Smith lbw b Swann 55
*C. H. Gayle lbw b Anderson..................... 6
R. R. Sarwan b Sidebottom...................... 291
R. O. Hinds lbw b Swann 15
S. Chanderpaul lbw b Anderson 70
B. P. Nash lbw b Swann 33
†D. Ramdin b Swann............................ 166
J. E. Taylor b Swann 53
S. J. Benn c Ambrose b Anderson 14
D. B. Powell not out 13
    B 15, l-b 11, w 1, n-b 6 33

1/13 (2) 2/121 (1)   (9 wkts dec.) 749
3/159 (4) 4/281 (5) 5/334 (6)
6/595 (3) 7/672 (8) 8/701 (9) 9/749 (7)

F. H. Edwards did not bat.

Anderson 37–9–125–3; Sidebottom 35–4–146–1; Broad 32–4–113–0; Swann 50.4–8–165–5; Pietersen 9–1–38–0; Bopara 13–0–66–0; Collingwood 16–1–51–0; Shah 2–0–19–0.

Umpires: Aleem Dar *(Pakistan)* (55) and R. B. Tiffin *(Zimbabwe)* (43).
Third umpire: D. J. Harper *(Australia)*. Referee: A. G. Hurst *(Australia)* (26).

Close of play: First day, England 301-3 (Pietersen 32, Collingwood 11); Second day, West Indies 85-1 (Smith 37, Sarwan 40); Third day, West Indies 398-5 (Sarwan 184, Ramdin 25); Fourth day, England 6-0 (Strauss 5, Cook 0).

WEST INDIES v ENGLAND 2008-09 (5th Test)

At Queen's Park Oval, Port-of-Spain, Trinidad, on 6, 7, 8, 9, 10 March.
Toss: England.   Result: MATCH DRAWN.
Debuts: West Indies – L. M. P. Simmons. England – A. Khan.
Man of the Match: M. J. Prior.   Man of the Series: R. R. Sarwan.

West Indies pulled off their second great escape of the series to regain the Wisden Trophy for the first time since 2000. Set 240 in 66 overs after Strauss's cautious lunchtime declaration, defeat looked likely when Chanderpaul departed in the 35th over. But Ramdin survived for two hours, and Gayle, down the order after tearing a hamstring, defended for 51 minutes as the clock ticked down. Powell departed with 20 balls remaining, but Edwards, the other hero of the Antigua rearguard, again clung on to the end. West Indies had gone into a match they needed only to draw with an extra batsman, and several part-timers bowled as England – who had gone the other way and included an extra bowler (Amjad Khan, the first Danish-born Test cricketer) for Bopara, a centurion in the previous match – advanced to 546 against largely defensive fields. Strauss made his third century in successive Tests, then Collingwood put on 218 with Prior, whose hundred was his first since his debut against West Indies at Lord's in 2007. Gayle injured his leg in sprinting the single that completed his tenth Test century, and West Indies were indebted to a stand of 234 between Chanderpaul – himself hobbling after a groin injury – and Nash, who made his maiden Test hundred. Helped by 74 extras (35 of them byes), the second-highest in any Test innings, West Indies almost matched England's score. Pietersen hurried to a century in 88 balls, but there was not quite enough time left to force a result.

England

*A. J. Strauss b Edwards	142	– c and b Gayle			14
A. N. Cook c Ramdin b Powell	12	– c Ramdin b Hinds			24
O. A. Shah run out	33	– c Ramdin b Baker			1
K. P. Pietersen b Hinds	10	– c sub (D. J. Bravo) b Edwards			102
P. D. Collingwood lbw b Baker	161	– c and b Hinds			9
†M. J. Prior not out	131	– b Baker			61
S. C. J. Broad c Simmons b Baker	19	– not out			13
G. P. Swann not out	11				
B 8, l-b 7, w 1, n-b 11	27	B 2, l-b 6, w 1, n-b 4			13

1/26 (2) 2/156 (4)   (6 wkts dec.) 546   1/26 (1)   (6 wkts dec.) 237
3/263 (1) 4/268 (3)   2/27 (3) 3/72 (2) 4/101 (5)
5/486 (5) 6/530 (7)   5/207 (6) 6/237 (4)

A. Khan, J. M. Anderson and M. S. Panesar did not bat.
In the first innings Shah, when 29, retired hurt at 133 and resumed at 263.

Edwards 24–5–63–1; Powell 16–1–79–1; Baker 23–4–77–2; Nash 23–3–77–0; Gayle 26–1–80–0; Hinds 39.5–2–126–1; Smith 1–0–3–0; Simmons 6–0–26–0. *Second Innings*—Edwards 11.4–1–67–1; Baker 8–1–39–2; Gayle 3–0–16–1; Hinds 8–0–57–2; Simmons 5–0–29–0; Nash 3–0–21–0.

West Indies

*C. H. Gayle c Strauss b Swann	102	– (8) lbw b Panesar			4
D. S. Smith b Panesar	28	– (1) lbw b Swann			17
D. B. Powell c Pietersen b Broad	0	– (9) b Anderson			0
R. R. Sarwan lbw b Khan	14	– (3) c Collingwood b Swann			14
L. M. P. Simmons lbw b Panesar	24	– (2) c Collingwood b Anderson			8
S. Chanderpaul not out	147	– (5) lbw b Swann			6
B. P. Nash c Collingwood b Broad	109	– (6) lbw b Anderson			1
R. O. Hinds st Prior b Swann	23	– (4) c Collingwood b Panesar			20
†D. Ramdin lbw b Anderson	15	– (7) not out			17
F. H. Edwards c Prior b Broad	8	– not out			1
L. S. Baker lbw b Swann	0				
B 35, l-b 12, w 11, n-b 16	74	B 17, l-b 6, w 1, n-b 2			26

1/90 (2) 2/96 (3) 3/118 (4)   544   1/25 (2) 2/31 (1)   (8 wkts) 114
4/203 (5) 5/437 (7) 6/482 (8)   3/58 (3) 4/80 (5) 5/85 (6)
7/519 (9) 8/526 (1) 9/543 (10) 10/544 (11)   6/90 (4) 7/107 (8) 8/109 (9)

In the first innings Gayle, when 100, retired hurt at 195 and resumed at 519.

Anderson 32–7–70–1; Broad 30–11–67–3; Khan 25–1–111–1; Swann 45.4–12–130–3; Panesar 43–6–114–2; Pietersen 3–0–5–0. *Second Innings*—Anderson 16–7–24–3; Broad 5–3–9–0; Swann 21–13–13–3; Khan 4–0–11–0; Panesar 19.5–9–34–2.

Umpires: D. J. Harper *(Australia)* (80) and R. B. Tiffin *(Zimbabwe)* (44).
Third umpire: Aleem Dar *(Pakistan)*. Referee: A. G. Hurst *(Australia)* (27).

Close of play: First day, England 258-2 (Strauss 139, Collingwood 54); Second day, West Indies 92-1 (Gayle 49, Powell 0); Third day, West Indies 349-4 (Chanderpaul 52, Nash 70); Fourth day, England 80-3 (Pietersen 34, Collingwood 1).

PAKISTAN v SRI LANKA 2008-09 (1st Test)

At National Stadium, Karachi, on 21, 22, 23, 24, 25 February.
Toss: Sri Lanka.   Result: MATCH DRAWN.
Debuts: Pakistan – Khurram Manzoor, Sohail Khan. Sri Lanka – N. T. Paranavitana.
Man of the Match: Younis Khan.

Other teams' security concerns contributed to Pakistan playing no Test matches at all in 2008, their first blank year since 1970. However, a 14-month layoff did not seem to affect their batsmen, who amassed Pakistan's highest Test total (beating 708 at The Oval in 1987), and the fifth-highest of all. The main contributor was Younis Khan, finally installed as permanent captain, who became Pakistan's third Test triple-centurion, after Hanif Mohammad and Inzamam-ul-Haq. He shared hundred partnerships with Shoaib Malik (his predecessor as captain), Misbah-ul-Haq and Faisal Iqbal, and also passed 5,000 runs. The final-day crowd hoped Younis, 306 overnight, would threaten Brian Lara's 400 – but after seven more runs Fernando jagged one back at him after 760 minutes and 560 balls. Kamran Akmal and Yasir Arafat made sure Pakistan went past Sri Lanka's own sizeable total, which included double-centuries from Mahela Jayawardene and Samaraweera, whose stand of 437 was a Test fourth-wicket record, surpassing the 411 of Peter May and Colin Cowdrey for England against West Indies at Edgbaston in 1957. This was the first Test in which both captains made double-hundreds, and only one other had included three – by Seymour Nurse for West Indies and Australia's Bob Simpson and Bill Lawry at Bridgetown in 1964-65. Ironically, the run-fest had started unpromisingly when the debutant Tharanga Paranavitana was caught at second slip first ball, the fourth of the match, and it finished with a clatter of wickets as Sri Lanka were three down inside seven overs, before Sangakkara made sure of the draw.

Sri Lanka

B. S. M. Warnapura c Misbah-ul-Haq b Yasir Arafat	59	– c Kamran Akmal b Umar Gul..............	2
N. T. Paranavitana c Misbah-ul-Haq b Umar Gul	0	– run out	9
K. C. Sangakkara c Misbah-ul-Haq b Danish Kaneria....	70	– lbw b Danish Kaneria	65
*D. P. M. D. Jayawardene c Kamran Akmal			
b Shoaib Malik....................	240	– (5) c Faisal Iqbal b Danish Kaneria	22
T. T. Samaraweera b Danish Kaneria	231	– (6) not out	24
T. M. Dilshan c Kamran Akmal b Shoaib Malik......	0	– (4) c Faisal Iqbal b Umar Gul............	8
†H. A. P. W. Jayawardene b Danish Kaneria	18	– not out	7
W. P. U. J. C. Vaas not out.......................	12		
L-b 4, w 1, n-b 9..................	14	N-b 7	7

1/3 (2) 2/93 (1) 3/177 (3)   (7 wkts dec.) 644   1/2 (1) 2/32 (2)   (5 wkts) 144
4/614 (4) 5/614 (5)   3/45 (4) 4/103 (5)
6/614 (6) 7/644 (7)   5/120 (3)

M. Muralitharan, B. A. W. Mendis and C. R. D. Fernando did not bat.

Umar Gul 24–2–92–1; Sohail Khan 21–2–131–0; Yasir Arafat 26–2–90–1; Shoaib Malik 36–3–140–2; Danish Kaneria 46.2–5–170–3; Younis Khan 1–0–6–0; Salman Butt 1–0–11–0. *Second Innings*—Umar Gul 9–1–41–2; Sohail Khan 6–0–33–0; Yasir Arafat 6–0–32–0; Danish Kaneria 9–1–35–2; Shoaib Malik 1–0–3–0.

Pakistan

Khurram Manzoor c H. A. P. W. Jayawardene b Mendis	27
Salman Butt c D. P. M. D. Jayawardene	
b Muralitharan	23
*Younis Khan b Fernando........................	313
Shoaib Malik run out............................	56
Misbah-ul-Haq lbw b Fernando	42
Faisal Iqbal lbw b D. P. M. D. Jayawardene..........	57
†Kamran Akmal not out	158
Yasir Arafat not out	50
B 4, l-b 12, w 5, n-b 18	39

1/44 (2) 2/78 (1)   (6 wkts dec.) 765
3/227 (4) 4/357 (5)
5/531 (6) 6/596 (3)

Sohail Khan, Umar Gul and Danish Kaneria did not bat.

Vaas 36–10–66–0; Fernando 39–2–124–2; Mendis 59–14–157–1; Muralitharan 65–14–172–1; Dilshan 19–3–82–0; Paranavitana 5–0–33–0; Sangakkara 10–0–34–0; D. P. M. D. Jayawardene 6.5–0–41–1; Warnapura 9–0–40–0.

Umpires: S. J. Davis *(Australia)* (16) and S. J. A. Taufel *(Australia)* (54).
Third umpire: Zameer Haider *(Pakistan)*.   Referee: B. C. Broad *(England)* (34).

Close of play: First day, Sri Lanka 406-3 (D. P. M. D. Jayawardene 136, Samaraweera 130); Second day, Pakistan 44-1 (Khurram Manzoor 18, Younis Khan 0); Third day, Pakistan 296-3 (Younis Khan 149, Misbah-ul-Haq 20); Fourth day, Pakistan 574-5 (Younis Khan 306, Kamran Akmal 27).

PAKISTAN v SRI LANKA 2008-09 (2nd Test)

At Gaddafi Stadium, Lahore, on 1, 2, 3 *(no play)* March.
Toss: Pakistan.   Result: MATCH DRAWN.
Debuts: Pakistan – Mohammad Talha.
Man of the Match: no award.

The match ended abruptly on what should have been the third morning, when Sri Lanka's team bus was ambushed on the way to the ground. Terrorists sprayed the coach with bullets, while a hand grenade was reportedly rolled underneath but failed to explode. Eight people were killed, including six policemen, and the players were lucky to escape alive. The most seriously injured was Thilan Samaraweera, who needed an operation to remove a bullet from his left thigh, while Ajantha Mendis had shrapnel in his head and back. The fourth umpire Ahsan Raza, who was travelling in the vehicle behind with the other officials, was in intensive care for over a month after being shot in the back: the referee, Chris Broad, was hailed as a hero after throwing himself over Raza to prevent further injury. "I'm angry with the Pakistani security forces," said Broad afterwards. "We were promised high-level security and in our hour of need that security vanished." The preceding two days had been rather better for Samaraweera, who became only the sixth batsman after Wally Hammond, Don Bradman, Vinod Kambli, Graeme Smith and Kumar Sangakkara to score double-centuries in consecutive Tests (Hammond and Bradman both did it twice). He shared successive stands of 204 with Sangakkara and 207 with Dilshan. Pakistan had made a bright start in reply to Sri Lanka's 606, before it all ceased to matter. The match and the tour were immediately abandoned, and Pakistan's hopes of staging more home Tests in the immediate future were seriously damaged.

Sri Lanka

B. S. M. Warnapura	c Misbah-ul-Haq b Umar Gul....	8
N. T. Paranavitana	c Shoaib Malik b Umar Gul.......	21
K. C. Sangakkara	c Kamran Akmal b Yasir Arafat	104
*D. P. M. D. Jayawardene	c Kamran Akmal b Umar Gul ..	30
T. T. Samaraweera	run out.........................	214
T. M. Dilshan	run out	145
†H. A. P. W. Jayawardene	c Kamran Akmal	
	b Umar Gul	15
M. T. T. Mirando	b Umar Gul.....................	10
M. Muralitharan	b Mohammad Talha...............	22
B. A. W. Mendis	b Umar Gul.....................	0
C. R. D. Fernando	not out........................	14
	B 4, l-b 1, w 5, n-b 13	23

1/16 (1) 2/35 (2) 3/96 (4) 4/300 (3)   606
5/507 (5) 6/542 (7) 7/566 (8)
8/572 (6) 9/572 (10) 10/606 (9)

Umar Gul 37–2–135–6; Mohammad Talha 17–0–88–1; Yasir Arafat 20–2–106–1; Danish Kaneria 47–5–183–0; Shoaib Malik 28–3–80–0; Younis Khan 2–0–9–0.

Pakistan

Khurram Manzoor	not out........................	59
Salman Butt	run out..........................	48
	N-b 3..............................	3

1/110 (2)   (1 wkt) 110

*Younis Khan, Shoaib Malik, Misbah-ul-Haq, Faisal Iqbal, †Kamran Akmal, Yasir Arafat, Mohammad Talha, Umar Gul and Danish Kaneria did not bat.

Mirando 8–0–46–0; Fernando 2–0–20–0; Mendis 8–2–21–0; Muralitharan 4.4–0–23–0; Dilshan 1–1–0–0.

Umpires: S. J. Davis *(Australia)* (17) and S. J. A. Taufel *(Australia)* (55).
Third umpire: Nadeem Ghauri *(Pakistan)*. Referee: B. C. Broad *(England)* (35).

Close of play: First day, Sri Lanka 317-4 (Samaraweera 133, Dilshan 3); Second day, Pakistan 110-1 (Khurram Manzoor 59).

SOUTH AFRICA v AUSTRALIA 2008-09 (1st Test)

At The Wanderers, Johannesburg, on 26, 27, 28 February, 1, 2 March.
Toss: Australia.   Result: AUSTRALIA won by 162 runs.
Debuts: Australia – B. W. Hilfenhaus, P. J. Hughes, M. J. North.
Man of the Match: M. G. Johnson.

Australia's fourth consecutive victory at Johannesburg was also the sixth in their last seven Tests in South Africa. The key to their success lay in making 466 on a sporting pitch which encouraged the pacemen throughout. The South Africans had played only Twenty20 cricket since winning in Australia, and it showed. Although they fought back in the second innings, a target of 454 was always unlikely on a surface with some uneven bounce, and they were bowled out with 33 overs unused. A dropped catch on the first morning was undeniably significant: Smith missed Ponting at slip off Steyn when 40. That would have been 67 for 4, and when Ponting – who celebrated by hooking the next ball for six – was eventually out at 151, the ball was 42 overs old. It was a much more comfortable time for Marcus North to come in and, helped by Haddin and Johnson, he became the 18th Australian to score a century on Test debut. South Africa's disappointing reply was dominated by de Villiers, who scored his eighth century in his 50th Test. Ponting went for quick runs instead of enforcing the follow-on. Kallis, not long after becoming the first South African to reach 10,000 Test runs, took three wickets in seven balls to spark a collapse from 99 for 1 to 147 for 8, but the last two wickets stretched the lead to 453. South Africa reached 206 for 2 early on the final day, but the last eight wickets managed only 85 between them.

Australia

P. J. Hughes c Boucher b Steyn	0	– c de Villiers b Harris	75
S. M. Katich c McKenzie b Steyn	3	– c Boucher b Morkel	10
*R. T. Ponting b Ntini	83	– c Amla b Kallis	25
M. E. K. Hussey c Kallis b Morkel	4	– c Ntini b Kallis	0
M. J. Clarke c Boucher b Steyn	68	– c Kallis b Harris	0
M. J. North st Boucher b Harris	117	– b Kallis	5
†B. J. Haddin c Harris b Ntini	63	– c Boucher b Ntini	37
A. B. McDonald c Kallis b Steyn	0	– c Boucher b Ntini	7
M. G. Johnson not out	96	– c Kallis b Ntini	1
P. M. Siddle c Kallis b Morkel	9	– not out	22
B. W. Hilfenhaus c de Villiers b Morkel	0	– b Steyn	16
B 6, l-b 8, w 2, n-b 7	23	L-b 5, w 1, n-b 3	9

1/0 (1) 2/18 (2) 3/38 (4)   466
4/151 (3) 5/182 (5) 6/295 (7)
7/296 (8) 8/413 (6) 9/466 (10) 10/466 (11)

1/38 (2) 2/99 (3) 3/99 (4)   207
4/99 (5) 5/104 (6) 6/138 (1)
7/145 (8) 8/147 (9) 9/174 (7) 10/207 (11)

Steyn 30–4–113–4; Ntini 27–6–71–2; Morkel 28.4–3–117–3; Kallis 8–0–33–0; Harris 18–2–64–1; Duminy 14–2–54–0. *Second Innings*—Steyn 16.4–5–51–1; Ntini 11–3–52–3; Morkel 10–1–41–1; Harris 11–0–36–2; Kallis 5–0–22–3.

South Africa

N. D. McKenzie lbw b Siddle	36	– c Haddin b Johnson	35
*G. C. Smith c Haddin b Johnson	0	– c Johnson b Hilfenhaus	69
H. M. Amla c Ponting b Hilfenhaus	1	– c Hughes b Siddle	57
J. H. Kallis c Hussey b Siddle	27	– b Johnson	45
A. B. de Villiers not out	104	– lbw b McDonald	3
J-P. Duminy c Haddin b Johnson	17	– c Ponting b Siddle	29
†M. V. Boucher c Haddin b Johnson	0	– b Hilfenhaus	24
M. Morkel c and b Siddle	2	– c Hughes b Johnson	2
P. L. Harris lbw b North	1	– c Katich b Siddle	8
D. W. Steyn c North b McDonald	17	– b Johnson	6
M. Ntini b Johnson	1	– not out	0
B 4, l-b 6, n-b 4	14	B 1, l-b 6, w 2, n-b 4	13

1/1 (2) 2/2 (3) 3/49 (4) 4/93 (1)   220
5/138 (6) 6/138 (7) 7/154 (8) 8/156 (9)
9/208 (10) 10/220 (11)

1/76 (1) 2/130 (2) 3/206 (3)   291
4/211 (5) 5/229 (4) 6/268 (6) 7/272 (8)
8/284 (7) 9/289 (9) 10/291 (10)

Johnson 18.1–7–25–4; Hilfenhaus 25–9–58–1; Siddle 21–1–76–3; McDonald 10–4–22–1; North 7–0–29–1. *Second Innings*—Johnson 34.2–2–112–4; Hilfenhaus 31–7–68–2; Siddle 25–8–46–3; McDonald 22–8–31–1; North 7–0–27–0.

Umpires: B. F. Bowden *(New Zealand)* (53) and S. A. Bucknor *(West Indies)* (127).
Third umpire: Asad Rauf *(Pakistan)*. Referee: J. J. Crowe *(New Zealand)* (30).

Close of Play: First day, Australia 254-5 (North 47, Haddin 37); Second day, South Africa 85-3 (McKenzie 35, de Villiers 13); Third day, Australia 51-1 (Hughes 36, Ponting 1); Fourth day, South Africa 178-2 (Amla 43, Kallis 26).

SOUTH AFRICA v AUSTRALIA 2008-09 (2nd Test)

At Kingsmead, Durban, on 6, 7, 8, 9, 10 March.
Toss: Australia.   Result: AUSTRALIA won by 175 runs.
Debuts: none.
Man of the Match: P. J. Hughes.

Australia made up in part for losing at home to Graeme Smith's side shortly before returning the favour, their fourth consecutive series win in South Africa. Phillip Hughes, in only his second Test, became the youngest to make two centuries in the same Test; at 20 years 98 days, he was nearly six months younger than the West Indian George Headley in 1929-30. Hughes's early assault on some poor bowling helped provide the springboard for Australia's triumph. He raced to 75 out of 119 by lunch, and went from 93 to 105 with successive sixes off Harris, becoming the fourth-youngest Australian to make a Test hundred, after Neil Harvey, Archie Jackson and Doug Walters (Don Bradman was elbowed down to fifth). Katich made only 59 of the opening stand of 184. Australia lost their last six wickets for 23, but Johnson quickly wrecked South Africa's innings with some devastating new-ball bowling. He also inflicted Smith's second hand fracture in three Tests – the right hand this time. Kallis also retired hurt briefly for stitches after a Johnson bouncer hit him on the chin. Duminy battled hard, but the innings was beyond repair. Ponting again waived the follow-on, then Hughes resumed, grafting to his second hundred then opening out. Left with 170 overs to survive, South Africa reached 267 for 2 – but the second new ball brought the breakthroughs Australia needed. The part-time spinners mopped up, North taking a brilliant one-handed return catch to dismiss Boucher to atone for dropping Kallis before he had scored.

Australia

P. J. Hughes c McKenzie b Kallis	115	– c Morkel b Ntini		160
S. M. Katich c Smith b Steyn	108	– c Harris b Kallis		30
*R. T. Ponting c McKenzie b Harris	9	– c McKenzie b Morkel		81
M. E. K. Hussey b Morkel	50	– c Kallis b Duminy		19
M. J. Clarke b Harris	3	– not out		23
M. J. North c Steyn b Kallis	38	– c de Villiers b Steyn		0
†B. J. Haddin c Amla b Ntini	5			
A. B. McDonald not out	4			
M. G. Johnson lbw b Ntini	0			
P. M. Siddle c Boucher b Steyn	0			
B. W. Hilfenhaus c Smith b Steyn	0			
B 6, l-b 4, w 2, n-b 8	20	B 12, l-b 2, n-b 4		18

1/184 (1) 2/208 (3) 3/259 (2) 4/266 (5)   352   1/55 (2) 2/219 (3)   (5 wkts dec.) 331
5/329 (4) 6/348 (6) 7/348 (7) 8/348 (9)   3/260 (4) 4/330 (1)
9/352 (10) 10/352 (11)   5/331 (6)

Steyn 25.4–3–83–3; Ntini 19–4–58–2; Morkel 24–4–81–1; Kallis 15–4–49–2; Harris 21–5–66–2; Duminy 3–1–5–0. *Second Innings*—Steyn 15.4–1–75–1; Ntini 15–2–55–1; Morkel 14–1–60–1; Kallis 8–0–21–1; Harris 31–8–68–0; Duminy 11–1–38–1.

South Africa

N. D. McKenzie c Haddin b Johnson	0	– (2) c Haddin b Siddle		31
*G. C. Smith retired hurt	2	– absent hurt		
H. M. Amla lbw b Johnson	0	– (1) c Ponting b Siddle		43
J. H. Kallis c Ponting b McDonald	22	– (3) c Ponting b Johnson		93
A. B. de Villiers lbw b Hilfenhaus	3	– (4) c Haddin b Siddle		84
J-P. Duminy not out	73	– (5) c Haddin b Hilfenhaus		17
†M. V. Boucher b Johnson	1	– (6) c and b North		25
P. L. Harris b McDonald	4	– (7) c Siddle b Katich		5
M. Morkel b McDonald	2	– (8) c Haddin b Katich		24
D. W. Steyn c Haddin b Siddle	8	– (9) st Haddin b Katich		7
M. Ntini lbw b Siddle	0	– (10) not out		4
B 10, l-b 12, n-b 1	23	B 13, l-b 11, w 3, n-b 10		37

1/0 (1) 2/0 (3) 3/6 (5) 4/62 (7)   138   1/63 (2) 2/80 (1) 3/267 (3)   370
5/104 (8) 6/104 (4) 7/106 (9)   4/279 (4) 5/299 (5) 6/307 (7)
8/138 (10) 9/138 (11)   7/345 (6) 8/363 (8) 9/370 (9)

In the first innings, Smith retired hurt at 3; Kallis, when 22, retired hurt at 56 and resumed at 104-5.

Johnson 16–5–37–3; Hilfenhaus 11–2–28–1; McDonald 12–4–25–3; Siddle 13.3–6–20–2; North 4–3–6–0; Clarke 1–1–0–0. *Second Innings*—Johnson 33–9–78–1; Hilfenhaus 24–4–79–1; Siddle 28–12–61–3; McDonald 16–3–47–0; North 20–6–36–1; Katich 11.2–1–45–3.

Umpires: Asad Rauf *(Pakistan)* (23) and B. F. Bowden *(New Zealand)* (54).
Third umpire: S. A. Bucknor *(West Indies)*. Referee: J. J. Crowe *(New Zealand)* (31).

Close of play: First day, Australia 303-4 (Hussey 37, North 17); Second day, South Africa 138-7 (Duminy 73, Steyn 8); Third day, Australia 292-3 (Hughes 136, Clarke 14); Fourth day, South Africa 244-2 (Kallis 84, de Villiers 68).

SOUTH AFRICA v AUSTRALIA 2008-09 (3rd Test)

At Newlands, Cape Town, on 19, 20, 21, 22 March.

Toss: Australia.   Result: SOUTH AFRICA won by an innings and 20 runs.

Debuts: South Africa – I. Khan, J. A. Morkel. Australia – B. E. McGain.

Man of the Match: P. L. Harris.   Man of the Series: M. G. Johnson.

South Africa finally reproduced the form that had won them the preceding series Down Under, inflicting Australia's first innings defeat since Calcutta in 1997-98. Ponting soon fell to Albie Morkel, who had replaced his brother Morne. It was his only wicket of the match, but a vital one: Australia had only five specialist batsmen as they had no replacement for North, who had gastro-enteritis. No Australian batsman convinced on a good pitch, although Katich consumed nearly four hours in making 55. South Africa scored quickly from the outset, taking 20 off Johnson's third over. Prince hammered Bryce McGain's second ball back over his head for six: McGain, making his debut a week before his 37th birthday – Australia's oldest newcomer since another legspinner, Bob Holland, in 1984-85 – conceded eight sixes and 17 fours and failed to take a wicket. After Prince and Kallis put on 160, de Villiers flogged a wilting attack for a brilliant 163, including four successive leg-side sixes off McDonald's medium-pace (a feat previously achieved in Tests only by Kapil Dev and Shahid Afridi). South Africa reached their biggest total against Australia, previously 622 for 9 declared at Durban in 1969-70, including 62 extras, the most ever conceded by Australia. Johnson, whose maiden Test hundred came from 86 balls, and McDonald threatened to take the match into the fifth day during an attacking seventh-wicket stand of 173 in 26 overs, but it was in a lost cause. This was Steve Bucknor's 128th and last Test as an umpire.

Australia

P. J. Hughes lbw b Harris	33	– c Kallis b Harris	32
S. M. Katich c Khan b Harris	55	– c Duminy b Harris	54
*R. T. Ponting c Boucher b Morkel	0	– c Boucher b Steyn	12
M. E. K. Hussey b Steyn	20	– c Duminy b Steyn	39
M. J. Clarke b Steyn	0	– b Steyn	47
†B. J. Haddin lbw b Harris	42	– c Duminy b Harris	18
A. B. McDonald c Kallis b Ntini	13	– c de Villiers b Harris	68
M. G. Johnson c Prince b Steyn	35	– not out	123
P. M. Siddle c de Villiers b Ntini	0	– c de Villiers b Harris	0
B. E. McGain c de Villiers b Steyn	2	– run out	0
B. W. Hilfenhaus not out	0	– c Prince b Harris	12
L-b 6, w 1, n-b 2	9	B 8, l-b 2, w 2, n-b 5	17

1/58 (1) 2/59 (3) 3/81 (4)   209   1/57 (1) 2/76 (3) 3/138 (2)   422
4/81 (5) 5/152 (2) 6/158 (6)   4/146 (4) 5/191 (6) 6/218 (5) 7/381 (7)
7/190 (7) 8/190 (9) 9/209 (8) 10/209 (10)   8/381 (9) 9/388 (10) 10/422 (11)

Steyn 16–5–56–4; Ntini 17–7–38–2; Kallis 10–2–31–0; Morkel 12–3–44–1; Harris 17–5–34–3. *Second Innings—* Steyn 27–5–96–3; Ntini 19–6–66–0; Morkel 20–1–88–0; Harris 42.5–9–127–6; Kallis 10–4–21–0; Duminy 3–1–14–0.

South Africa

I. Khan c and b Siddle	20
A. G. Prince c Haddin b Hilfenhaus	150
H. M. Amla c Haddin b Johnson	46
*J. H. Kallis c and b Hilfenhaus	102
A. B. de Villiers c McDonald b Katich	163
J-P. Duminy b Johnson	7
†M. V. Boucher c Ponting b Johnson	12
J. A. Morkel b McDonald	58
P. L. Harris c Haddin b Johnson	27
D. W. Steyn c Clarke b Katich	0
M. Ntini not out	4
B 19, l-b 24, w 9, n-b 10	62

1/65 (1) 2/162 (3) 3/322 (2)   651
4/415 (4) 5/443 (6) 6/467 (7) 7/591 (8)
8/637 (5) 9/637 (10) 10/651 (9)

Johnson 37.3–5–148–4; Hilfenhaus 34–4–133–2; Siddle 35–15–67–1; McGain 18–2–149–0; McDonald 27–7–102–1; Katich 3–1–9–2.

Umpires: Asad Rauf *(Pakistan)* (24) and S. A. Bucknor *(West Indies)* (128).
Third umpire: B. F. Bowden *(New Zealand)*.   Referee: J. J. Crowe *(New Zealand)* (32).

Close of play: First day, South Africa 57-0 (Khan 15, Prince 37); Second day, South Africa 404-3 (Kallis 102, de Villiers 39); Third day, Australia 102-2 (Katich 44, Hussey 13).

NEW ZEALAND v INDIA 2008-09 (1st Test)

At Seddon Park, Hamilton, on 18, 19, 20, 21 March.
Toss: India.   Result: INDIA won by ten wickets.
Debuts: New Zealand – M. J. Guptill.
Man of the Match: S. R. Tendulkar.

India warmed up for the high-pressure 20-over IPL with a low-key tour of New Zealand, and started by winning their first Test there for 33 years – since Sunil Gavaskar led them to victory at Auckland in January 1976. This one was achieved by sheer weight of runs. New Zealand's first innings had a lop-sided look: from 60 for 6 Ryder and Vettori took them to 246, but the next-best score was just 18. Vettori's hundred was his third in Tests, the second at Hamilton, but Ryder's was his first. He almost didn't get there: he had 77 when Vettori was out, and Mills followed next ball. Ryder nipped to 98 in company with O'Brien, who then blotted his copybook by charging down to Harbhajan Singh and being stumped. Martin, the archetypal No. 11, somehow survived the remaining five balls of Harbhajan's over; a relieved Ryder immediately pulled Sharma for four to reach three figures – and was out himself next ball. Tendulkar led the reply with a sumptuous 160, his 42nd Test century, including 26 fours, and solid contributions down the order swelled the total to an imposing 520. New Zealand lost McIntosh in the first over of their second innings, and although Flynn buckled down for almost five hours, with Harbhajan varying his pace and occasionally getting extra bounce the only other serious resistance came from McCullum, who put on 76 with O'Brien, whose share was 14. India knocked off their tiny target late on the fourth day.

New Zealand

T. G. McIntosh c Sehwag b Sharma	12	– c Tendulkar b Zaheer Khan	0
M. J. Guptill c Dravid b Zaheer Khan	14	– c Sehwag b Harbhajan Singh	48
D. R. Flynn c Dhoni b Zaheer Khan	0	– c Gambhir b Harbhajan Singh	67
L. R. P. L. Taylor b Sharma	18	– (5) c Sehwag b Patel	4
J. D. Ryder c Laxman b Sharma	102	– (6) lbw b Harbhajan Singh	21
J. E. C. Franklin c Dhoni b Sharma	0	– (7) c Patel b Harbhajan Singh	14
†B. B. McCullum c Laxman b Patel	3	– (8) c Laxman b Yuvraj Singh	84
*D. L. Vettori c Dhoni b Patel	118	– (9) c Dhoni b Harbhajan Singh	21
K. D. Mills b Patel	0	– (4) lbw b Patel	2
I. E. O'Brien st Dhoni b Harbhajan Singh	8	– c Laxman b Harbhajan Singh	14
C. S. Martin not out	0	– not out	0
L-b 1, n-b 3	4	B 1, l-b 3	4

1/17 (2) 2/17 (3) 3/40 (1) 4/51 (4)   279
5/51 (6) 6/60 (7) 7/246 (8) 8/246 (9)
9/275 (10) 10/279 (5)

1/0 (1) 2/68 (2) 3/75 (4)   279
4/110 (5) 5/132 (6) 6/154 (7)
7/161 (3) 8/199 (9) 9/275 (10) 10/279 (8)

Zaheer Khan 16–3–70–2; Sharma 19.2–4–73–4; Patel 18–4–60–3; Harbhajan Singh 22–7–57–1; Sehwag 3–0–18–0. *Second Innings*—Zaheer Khan 28–7–79–1; Sharma 22–7–62–0; Patel 17–2–60–2; Harbhajan Singh 28–2–63–6; Yuvraj Singh 7.3–2–11–1.

India

G. Gambhir c McCullum b Martin	72	– not out	30
V. Sehwag run out	24		
R. Dravid b O'Brien	66	– (2) not out	8
S. R. Tendulkar c Taylor b O'Brien	160		
V. V. S. Laxman c Taylor b Martin	30		
Yuvraj Singh b Martin	22		
*†M. S. Dhoni c McCullum b O'Brien	47		
Harbhajan Singh c Vettori b Mills	16		
Zaheer Khan not out	51		
I. Sharma c McCullum b Vettori	6		
M. M. Patel c Martin b Vettori	9		
B 6, l-b 3, n-b 8	17	B 1	1

1/37 (2) 2/142 (1) 3/177 (3)   520
4/238 (5) 5/314 (6) 6/429 (7)
7/443 (4) 8/457 (8) 9/492 (10) 10/520 (11)

(no wkt, 5.2 overs) 39

Martin 30–9–98–3; Mills 22–4–98–1; O'Brien 33–7–103–3; Franklin 23–1–98–0; Vettori 35.4–8–90–2; Ryder 9–5–24–0. *Second Innings*—Martin 3–0–17–0; Mills 2.2–0–21–0.

Umpires: I. J. Gould *(England)* (3) and S. J. A. Taufel *(Australia)* (56).
Third umpire: G. A. V. Baxter *(New Zealand)*.   Referee: A. G. Hurst *(Australia)* (28).

Close of play: First day, India 29-0 (Gambhir 6, Sehwag 22); Second day, India 278-4 (Tendulkar 70, Yuvraj Singh 8); Third day, New Zealand 75-3 (Flynn 24).

NEW ZEALAND v INDIA 2008-09 (2nd Test)

At McLean Park, Napier, on 26, 27, 28, 29, 30 March.
Toss: New Zealand.   Result: MATCH DRAWN.
Debuts: none.
Man of the Match: J. D. Ryder.

New Zealand turned the tables in their 350th Test, although in the end India batted out time for a draw after being forced to follow on. New Zealand made a huge total, despite slipping to 23 for 3 against the new ball. They were rescued by Taylor and Ryder, who put on 271, a New Zealand fourth-wicket record, beating the 243 of Matthew Horne and Nathan Astle against Zimbabwe at Auckland in 1997-98. Fresh from his maiden century in the previous Test, Ryder was a revelation, combining patience with flair and concentrating for 489 minutes to reach 201 (a score already made in Tests by a J. Ryder – Australia's Jack, against England at Adelaide in 1924-25). Another big partnership, between McCullum and Vettori, lifted New Zealand's total past 600 for only the third time in Tests. India barely got halfway there, losing wickets regularly. Dravid dug in for 282 minutes, but Martin and O'Brien mopped up the last five wickets in 14 overs with the new ball. There were more than two days remaining when India went in again, but they batted safely through them. Gambhir settled in for 643 minutes and 436 balls, and later Laxman played a rather freer innings, collecting 25 fours in a delectable unbeaten 124: together they took India to safety as New Zealand maintained their record of never having won a Test at Napier (there had been seven before this). Sehwag captained India as Dhoni dropped out shortly before the start with back trouble.

New Zealand

T. G. McIntosh	c Karthik b Sharma		12
M. J. Guptill	c Sehwag b Zaheer Khan		8
J. M. How	b Zaheer Khan		1
L. R. P. L. Taylor	c Yuvraj Singh b Harbhajan Singh		151
J. D. Ryder	b Zaheer Khan		201
J. E. C. Franklin	run out		52
†B. B. McCullum	c Tendulkar b Sharma		115
*D. L. Vettori	b Sharma		55
J. S. Patel	c Sharma b Harbhajan Singh		1
I. E. O'Brien	not out		1
	B 7, l-b 8, n-b 7		22

1/21 (1) 2/22 (3) 3/23 (2)   (9 wkts dec.) 619
4/294 (4) 5/415 (6) 6/477 (5)
7/605 (8) 8/618 (7) 9/619 (9)

C. S. Martin did not bat.

Zaheer Khan 34–6–129–3; Sharma 27–5–95–3; Patel 28–3–128–0; Harbhajan Singh 41.4–7–120–2; Sehwag 12–0–73–0; Yuvraj Singh 12–0–59–0.

India

G. Gambhir	c Vettori b Patel	16	– lbw b Patel		137
*V. Sehwag	c McCullum b Vettori	34	– lbw b Patel		22
R. Dravid	c McCullum b Ryder	83	– c How b Vettori		62
I. Sharma	lbw b Vettori	0			
S. R. Tendulkar	c Taylor b Patel	49	– (4) c McCullum b Martin		64
V. V. S. Laxman	c McIntosh b Martin	76	– (5) not out		124
Yuvraj Singh	c McIntosh b Martin	0	– (6) not out		54
†K. D. Karthik	c Ryder b Martin	6			
Harbhajan Singh	c Martin b O'Brien	18			
Zaheer Khan	c Ryder b O'Brien	8			
M. M. Patel	not out	0			
	B 1, l-b 7, n-b 7	15	B 9, l-b 1, n-b 3		13

1/48 (2) 2/73 (1) 3/78 (4)   305   1/30 (2) 2/163 (3)   (4 wkts) 476
4/165 (5) 5/246 (3) 6/253 (7)   3/260 (4) 4/356 (1)
7/270 (8) 8/291 (6) 9/305 (9) 10/305 (10)

Martin 24–5–89–3; Franklin 15–4–34–0; Vettori 19–5–45–2; O'Brien 13.5–4–66–2; Patel 19–2–60–2; Ryder 3–1–3–1. *Second Innings*—Martin 30–8–86–1; O'Brien 32–9–94–0; Franklin 21–5–48–0; Patel 45–10–120–2; Ryder 11–5–38–0; Vettori 38–13–76–1; Taylor 2–1–4–0; How 1–1–0–0.

Umpires: B. R. Doctrove *(West Indies)* (23) and I. J. Gould *(England)* (4).
Third umpire: E. A. Watkin *(New Zealand)*.   Referee: A. G. Hurst *(Australia)* (29).

Close of play: First day, New Zealand 351-4 (Ryder 137, Franklin 26); Second day, India 79-3 (Dravid 21, Tendulkar 0); Third day, India 47-1 (Gambhir 14, Dravid 11); Fourth day, India 252-2 (Gambhir 102, Tendulkar 58).

NEW ZEALAND v INDIA 2008-09 (3rd Test)

At Basin Reserve, Wellington, on 3, 4, 5, 6, 7 April.
Toss: New Zealand.   Result: MATCH DRAWN.
Debuts: none.
Man of the Match: G. Gambhir.

New Zealand escaped defeat when the weather closed in 20 minutes after lunch on the final day, although their chances of levelling the series had long since disappeared. India, having set a stratospheric target of 617, had just taken the new ball with eight wickets down – but after one delivery (which O'Brien squeezed through gully for four) the rain started. About an hour later a restart was planned ... but then a final downpour spoiled India's chances of their 100th Test victory. Their massive advantage had been cemented by Gambhir's second-innings 167: he had been one of several to get out when set first time around, when the highest score in a reasonable total of 379 was Tendulkar's attractive 62, which included 11 fours. New Zealand's batsmen, by contrast, were all at sea against Zaheer Khan and Harbhajan Singh: only Taylor survived for more than two hours. It was a similar story in the second innings, when even the rain would not have saved New Zealand had Taylor, who hit his fourth Test century a week after his third, not found an adhesive ally in Franklin, who resisted for more than four hours. Late on, Vettori survived a confident lbw shout from Harbhajan which – with Martin the only batsman to come – might also have led to victory. Dhoni, returning after the back spasm that forced him to miss the previous Test, took six catches in the first innings, equalling Syed Kirmani's Indian record, also set in New Zealand, in 1975-76.

India

G. Gambhir lbw b Franklin	23	– lbw b O'Brien	167
V. Sehwag c McCullum b O'Brien	48	– c Taylor b Martin	12
R. Dravid c Franklin b Martin	35	– c McCullum b Vettori	60
S. R. Tendulkar c McCullum b Martin	62	– c Taylor b Vettori	9
V. V. S. Laxman c McIntosh b Southee	4	– b O'Brien	61
Yuvraj Singh lbw b Ryder	9	– c Taylor b Martin	40
*†M. S. Dhoni c O'Brien b Southee	52	– not out	56
Harbhajan Singh c Vettori b Martin	60	– c Southee b Martin	0
Zaheer Khan c McCullum b O'Brien	33	– not out	18
I. Sharma c McCullum b Martin	18		
M. M. Patel not out	15		
B 2, l-b 8, w 3, n-b 7	20	L-b 5, w 1, n-b 5	11

1/73 (2) 2/75 (1) 3/165 (4) 4/173 (5)   379   1/14 (2) 2/184 (3)   (7 wkts dec.) 434
5/182 (6) 6/204 (3) 7/283 (7)   3/208 (4) 4/314 (1) 5/319 (5)
8/315 (8) 9/347 (9) 10/379 (10)   6/397 (6) 7/397 (8)

Martin 25.1–3–98–4; Southee 18–1–94–2; O'Brien 22–3–89–2; Franklin 14–4–38–1; Vettori 9–1–47–0; Ryder 4–2–3–1. *Second Innings*—Southee 12–2–58–0; Martin 22–7–70–3; O'Brien 25–6–100–2; Franklin 16–3–72–0; Ryder 6–1–21–0; Vettori 35–5–108–2.

New Zealand

T. G. McIntosh c Yuvraj Singh b Zaheer Khan	32	– c Dravid b Zaheer Khan	4
M. J. Guptill b Zaheer Khan	17	– lbw b Harbhajan Singh	49
D. R. Flynn c Dhoni b Zaheer Khan	2	– b Zaheer Khan	10
L. R. P. L. Taylor c Dhoni b Harbhajan Singh	42	– b Harbhajan Singh	107
J. D. Ryder c Dhoni b Zaheer Khan	3	– c Dravid b Harbhajan Singh	0
J. E. C. Franklin c Sehwag b Harbhajan Singh	15	– lbw b Tendulkar	49
†B. B. McCullum c Dhoni b Harbhajan Singh	24	– c Dravid b Tendulkar	6
*D. L. Vettori c Dhoni b Sharma	11	– not out	15
T. G. Southee c and b Zaheer Khan	16	– c Dhoni b Harbhajan Singh	3
I. E. O'Brien c Dhoni b Patel	19	– not out	19
C. S. Martin not out	4		
B 9, l-b 3	12	B 10, l-b 2, w 1, n-b 6	19

1/21 (2) 2/31 (3) 3/80 (1)   197   1/30 (1) 2/54 (3)   (8 wkts) 281
4/98 (5) 5/120 (4) 6/125 (6)   3/84 (2) 4/84 (5) 5/226 (4)
7/138 (8) 8/160 (9) 9/181 (7) 10/197 (10)   6/244 (7) 7/253 (6) 8/258 (9)

Zaheer Khan 18–2–65–5; Sharma 14–3–47–1; Patel 8–2–20–1; Harbhajan Singh 23–4–43–3; Yuvraj Singh 2–0–10–0. *Second Innings*—Zaheer Khan 19.3–6–57–2; Patel 13–4–22–0; Sharma 12–2–57–0; Harbhajan Singh 33–8–59–4; Yuvraj Singh 1–0–4–0; Sehwag 7–0–25–0; Tendulkar 9–0–45–2.

Umpires: D. J. Harper *(Australia)* (81) and S. J. A. Taufel *(Australia)* (57).
Third umpire: A. L. Hill *(New Zealand)*. Referee: A. G. Hurst *(Australia)* (30).

Close of play: First day, India 375-9 (Sharma 15, Patel 14); Second day, India 51-1 (Gambhir 28, Dravid 9); Third day, India 349-5 (Yuvraj Singh 15, Dhoni 16); Fourth day, New Zealand 167-4 (Taylor 69, Franklin 26) .

ENGLAND v WEST INDIES 2009 (1st Test)

At Lord's, London, on 6, 7, 8 May.

Toss: West Indies.   Result: ENGLAND won by ten wickets.

Debuts: England – T. T. Bresnan, G. Onions.

Man of the Match: G. P. Swann.

Less than two months after West Indies hung on for victory in the Caribbean, the two sides met again. West Indies were third-choice opponents for this early-season series (no Test match had ever started earlier in England): after Zimbabwe's tour was cancelled the Sri Lankan board agreed terms before their leading players pointed out they had already been cleared to participate in the 20-over Indian Premier League. Some of the West Indians, notably captain Gayle and strike bowler Edwards, were themselves dragged back from the IPL at the last minute to play. Perhaps because of this, the tourists looked unfocussed and unprepared, and they dropped six catches, two of them sitters, during the first day's final session to let England off the hook. A sizzling spell from Edwards, which included the first-ball dismissal of Pietersen, had set England back – but the dropped catches allowed the last five wickets almost to double the score. Bopara, reprieved twice, made his second century in successive matches, while Swann cashed in with a maiden Test half-century. West Indies also made a decent start, but declined rapidly from 99 for 2 – Chanderpaul was out first ball – against Swann and the debutant fast bowler Graham Onions, whose first three wickets all came in his sixth over (W0W02W). In the follow-on they dipped to 79 for 5 before Nash and Ramdin shared a determined stand, but there was otherwise little resistance as England swept to victory – their first at Lord's since demolishing Bangladesh in 2005 – inside three days.

England

*A. J. Strauss c Ramdin b Taylor	16	– not out		14
A. N. Cook b Edwards	35	– not out		14
R. S. Bopara c Nash b Taylor	143			
K. P. Pietersen c Ramdin b Edwards	0			
P. D. Collingwood c Smith b Edwards	8			
†M. J. Prior c Simmons b Edwards	42			
S. C. J. Broad c Taylor b Benn	38			
T. T. Bresnan lbw b Benn	9			
G. P. Swann not out	63			
J. M. Anderson c Ramdin b Edwards	1			
G. Onions b Edwards	0			
B 1, l-b 5, w 7, n-b 9	22	N-b 4		4

1/28 (1) 2/92 (2) 3/92 (4)   377   (no wkt) 32
4/109 (5) 5/193 (6) 6/262 (7)
7/275 (8) 8/368 (3) 9/377 (10) 10/377 (11)

Taylor 24–2–83–2; Edwards 26.3–4–92–6; Baker 24–5–75–0; Benn 27–4–84–2; Nash 2–1–2–0; Simmons 5–1–24–0; Gayle 3–0–11–0. *Second Innings*—Edwards 3.1–0–12–0; Taylor 3–0–20–0.

West Indies

*C. H. Gayle b Broad	28	– c Swann b Anderson		0
D. S. Smith b Swann	46	– b Onions		41
R. R. Sarwan c Prior b Broad	13	– b Anderson		1
L. M. P. Simmons c Strauss b Onions	16	– c Cook b Onions		21
S. Chanderpaul c Collingwood b Swann	0	– c Bopara b Swann		4
B. P. Nash c Collingwood b Swann	4	– c Cook b Broad		81
†D. Ramdin lbw b Onions	5	– b Broad		61
J. E. Taylor c Prior b Onions	0	– lbw b Swann		15
S. J. Benn c Swann b Onions	2	– b Swann		0
F. H. Edwards not out	10	– c Bresnan b Broad		2
L. S. Baker lbw b Onions	17	– not out		2
L-b 10, w 1	11	B 8, l-b 18, w 2		28

1/46 (1) 2/70 (3) 3/99 (2)   152   1/14 (1) 2/22 (3) 3/70 (4)   256
4/99 (5) 5/117 (6) 6/117 (4)   4/75 (5) 5/79 (2) 6/222 (7)
7/117 (8) 8/119 (9) 9/128 (7) 10/152 (11)   7/243 (8) 8/246 (9) 9/249 (10) 10/256 (6)

Broad 11–0–56–2; Swann 5–2–16–3; Anderson 7–0–32–0; Onions 9.3–1–38–5. *Second Innings*—Anderson 15–6–38–2; Broad 19.2–2–64–3; Bresnan 7–3–17–0; Swann 17–4–39–3; Onions 12–2–64–2; Bopara 2–0–8–0.

Umpires: S. J. Davis *(Australia)* (18) and E. A. R. de Silva *(Sri Lanka)* (38).
Third umpire: I. J. Gould *(England)*. Referee: A. J. Pycroft *(Zimbabwe)* (1).

Close of play: First day, England 289-7 (Bopara 118, Swann 7); Second day, West Indies 39-2 (Smith 26, Simmons 7).

ENGLAND v WEST INDIES 2009 (2nd Test)

At Riverside Ground, Chester-le-Street, on 14, 15 (*no play*), 16, 17, 18 May.
Toss: England.   Result: ENGLAND won by an innings and 83 runs.
Debuts: none.
Man of the Match: J. M. Anderson.   Men of the Series: R. S. Bopara and F. H. Edwards.

Just 69 days after they claimed the Wisden Trophy in Trinidad, West Indies had to hand it back after another anodyne performance. Hardly bothered by the loss of the second day to rain, England sealed a clean sweep in the short series shortly after lunch on the final day. It was their 12th win, to go with two draws, in the last 14 home Tests against once-mighty West Indies. England's foundation was a stand of 213 between the Essex pair of Cook, who batted for more than seven hours, and Bopara, whose third successive century – a run which uniquely followed three successive ducks – nudged Michael Vaughan closer to a retirement he finally confirmed on June 30. Collingwood and Prior swelled the total to the highest in first-class cricket here, then the bowlers set to work. Sarwan made a silky round 100 – his fourth Test century against England in three months – before gloving into the slips, but the only other lengthy resistance came from Chanderpaul and Ramdin, who both lasted for more than two hours. Gayle hammered six fours and two sixes in a defiant 43-ball onslaught in the follow-on, but from 141 for 3 the last seven wickets added only 35. Tim Bresnan took his first Test wickets, but the outstanding bowler was Anderson, who swung the ball a long way, late, and finished with nine wickets in the match. After Prior injured a finger Collingwood kept wicket from after tea on the fourth day, and ended Chanderpaul's 113-minute second innings.

England

*A. J. Strauss c Ramdin b Gayle	....	26
A. N. Cook c Gayle b Benn	....	160
R. S. Bopara b Baker	....	108
J. M. Anderson b Edwards	....	14
K. P. Pietersen c Simmons b Benn	....	49
†P. D. Collingwood not out	....	60
M. J. Prior c Benn b Simmons	....	63
S. C. J. Broad not out	....	28
B 20, l-b 5, w 8, n-b 28	....	61

1/69 (1) 2/282 (3) 3/326 (4)   (6 wkts dec.) 569
4/410 (2) 5/419 (5) 6/513 (7)

T. T. Bresnan, G. P. Swann and G. Onions did not bat.

Taylor 20–2–68–0; Edwards 25–1–113–1; Baker 30–3–119–1; Gayle 14–2–31–1; Benn 43–8–146–2; Simmons 14–0–60–1; Sarwan 1–0–7–0.

West Indies

D. S. Smith b Anderson	....	7	– lbw b Swann	11
*C. H. Gayle lbw b Anderson	....	19	– c Strauss b Onions	54
R. R. Sarwan c Bresnan b Broad	....	100	– lbw b Onions	22
L. M. P. Simmons c Strauss b Anderson	....	8	– c sub (S. G. Borthwick) b Anderson	10
S. Chanderpaul c Prior b Broad	....	23	– c Collingwood b Anderson	47
B. P. Nash b Anderson	....	10	– c sub (S. G. Borthwick) b Bresnan	1
†D. Ramdin c Swann b Anderson	....	55	– c Anderson b Bresnan	0
J. E. Taylor lbw b Onions	....	10	– b Anderson	5
S. J. Benn run out	....	35	– b Anderson	0
F. H. Edwards c Strauss b Broad	....	11	– c sub (K. Turner) b Bresnan	4
L. S. Baker not out	....	0	– not out	4
B 2, l-b 21, w 2, n-b 7	....	32	B 8, l-b 5, w 5	18

1/18 (1) 2/38 (2) 3/68 (4)   310   1/53 (1) 2/88 (3) 3/89 (2)   176
4/167 (5) 5/188 (3) 6/205 (6)   4/141 (4) 5/142 (6) 6/146 (7)
7/216 (8) 8/286 (9) 9/310 (10) 10/310 (7)   7/163 (8) 8/167 (9) 9/168 (5) 10/176 (10)

Anderson 26.3–5–87–5; Broad 16–2–62–3; Onions 18–6–52–1; Bresnan 10–2–35–0; Swann 14–4–51–0.
Second Innings—Anderson 16–5–38–4; Broad 5–1–21–0; Swann 3–0–13–1; Onions 6–0–46–2; Bresnan 14–2–45–3.

Umpires: S. J. Davis (*Australia*) (19) and E. A. R. de Silva (*Sri Lanka*) (39).
Third umpire: P. J. Hartley (*England*). Referee: A. J. Pycroft (*Zimbabwe*) (1).

Close of play: First day, England 302-2 (Cook 126, Anderson 4); Second day, No play; Third day, West Indies 94-3 (Sarwan 41, Chanderpaul 3); Fourth day, West Indies 115-3 (Simmons 3, Chanderpaul 18).

SRI LANKA v PAKISTAN 2008-09 (1st Test)

At Galle International Stadium on 4, 5, 6, 7 July.
Toss: Pakistan.   Result: SRI LANKA won by 50 runs.
Debuts: Sri Lanka – A. D. Mathews. Pakistan – Abdur Rauf, Mohammad Aamer, Saeed Ajmal.
Man of the Match: H. M. R. K. B. Herath.

Sri Lanka pulled off a remarkable victory after Pakistan had looked certain to win – and for once it wasn't Muttiah Muralitharan doing the demolishing. With Murali absent with a knee injury that kept him out of the series, Sri Lanka's hero was slow left-armer Rangana Herath, who had been playing league cricket in England and arrived home the day before the match after Murali pulled out. Herath took four wickets – including the vital one of Mohammad Yousuf – as Pakistan, chasing only 168, were shot down for 117. Pakistan had made most of the running before the dramatic finale. Sri Lanka were restricted to 292, with Paranavitana top-scoring (as he would also do in the second innings). Salman Butt was out first ball, but Pakistan were propelled towards a handy lead by a silky century from Yousuf, back in favour after flirting with the unauthorised Indian Cricket League. Sri Lanka struggled against the debutant offspinner Saeed Ajmal and Younis Khan's seldom-seen legspin, and Pakistan looked impregnable at 71 for 2 by the end of the fourth day. But Herath struck early next day, dismissing Yousuf and Butt in his first over, and when Mirando removed Shoaib Malik for a duck and Misbah-ul-Haq was run out by Dilshan, the wheels fell off: the last eight wickets tumbled for 46 in 25 overs on the fateful final morning. With Prasanna Jayawardene injured and Sangakkara preoccupied with the captaincy – this was his first match in charge after Mahela Jayawardene stepped down – Dilshan kept wicket.

Sri Lanka

B. S. M. Warnapura b Mohammad Aamer	2	– (2) c Younis Khan b Umar Gul	0
N. T. Paranavitana c Misbah-ul-Haq b Abdur Rauf	72	– (3) c Kamran Akmal b Mohammad Aamer	49
*K. C. Sangakkara c Shoaib Malik b Mohammad Aamer	9	– (4) c Kamran Akmal b Mohammad Aamer	14
D. P. M. D. Jayawardene c Kamran Akmal b Abdur Rauf	30	– (5) c Kamran Akmal b Mohammad Aamer	0
T. T. Samaraweera c Kamran Akmal b Younis Khan	31	– (6) c Misbah-ul-Haq b Saeed Ajmal	34
†T. M. Dilshan c Shoaib Malik b Mohammad Aamer	28	– (7) c Khurram Manzoor b Younis Khan	22
A. D. Mathews c Kamran Akmal b Umar Gul	42	– (8) c Salman Butt b Abdur Rauf	27
K. M. D. N. Kulasekara c Kamran Akmal b Younis Khan	38	– (9) lbw b Saeed Ajmal	25
H. M. R. K. B. Herath not out	20	– (1) lbw b Younis Khan	15
M. T. T. Mirando c Khurram Manzoor b Saeed Ajmal	10	– not out	15
B. A. W. Mendis st Kamran Akmal b Saeed Ajmal	5	– b Saeed Ajmal	1
B 1, l-b 3, n-b 1	5	L-b 7, w 1, n-b 7	15

1/3 (1) 2/21 (3) 3/96 (4) 4/139 (2) **292**   1/0 (2) 2/68 (1) 3/86 (3) **217**
5/160 (5) 6/194 (6) 7/241 (7)   4/88 (5) 5/101 (4) 6/138 (7)
8/271 (8) 9/282 (10) 10/292 (11)   7/156 (6) 8/191 (8) 9/211 (9) 10/217 (11)

Umar Gul 14–3–45–1; Mohammad Aamer 19–3–74–3; Abdur Rauf 14–1–59–2; Younis Khan 7–2–23–2; Saeed Ajmal 23.2–4–79–2; Shoaib Malik 3–1–8–0. *Second Innings*—Mohammad Aamer 11–2–38–3; Umar Gul 10–2–62–1; Abdur Rauf 13–1–49–1; Younis Khan 10–1–27–2; Saeed Ajmal 12.2–0–34–3.

Pakistan

Khurram Manzoor lbw b Mirando	2	– c Jayawardene b Mendis	15
Salman Butt b Kulasekara	0	– c Paranavitana b Herath	28
*Younis Khan c Dilshan b Mathews	25	– lbw b Mathews	3
Abdur Rauf c Dilshan b Kulasekara	31	– (8) c Jayawardene b Herath	13
Mohammad Yousuf run out	112	– (4) lbw b Herath	12
Misbah-ul-Haq c Jayawardene b Herath	56	– (5) run out	7
Shoaib Malik b Kulasekara	38	– (6) c Dilshan b Mirando	0
†Kamran Akmal run out	31	– (7) lbw b Mirando	6
Umar Gul b Kulasekara	7	– b Mendis	9
Mohammad Aamer c Paranavitana b Mirando	4	– c Dilshan b Herath	6
Saeed Ajmal not out	1	– not out	1
B 12, l-b 15, w 1, n-b 7	35	B 13, l-b 3, w 1	17

1/1 (2) 2/5 (1) 3/55 (4) 4/80 (3) **342**   1/36 (1) 2/39 (3) 3/71 (4) **117**
5/219 (6) 6/294 (5) 7/303 (7)   4/72 (2) 5/72 (6) 6/80 (7)
8/329 (8) 9/339 (8) 10/342 (10)   7/85 (5) 8/95 (9) 9/110 (10) 10/117 (8)

Kulasekara 24–3–71–4; Mirando 21–3–77–2; Mendis 25–2–89–0; Mathews 8–2–26–1; Herath 16–2–52–1. *Second Innings*—Kulasekara 7–1–25–0; Mirando 12–4–21–2; Mathews 4–0–13–1; Mendis 10–0–27–2; Herath 11.3–5–15–4.

Umpires: I. J. Gould *(England)* (5) and D. J. Harper *(Australia)* (82).
Third umpire: H. D. P. K. Dharmasena *(Sri Lanka)*. Referee: A. G. Hurst *(Australia)* (31).

Close of play: First day, Pakistan 15-2 (Younis Khan 7, Abdur Rauf 0); Second day, Sri Lanka 0-0 (Herath 0, Warnapura 0); Third day, Pakistan 71-2 (Salman Butt 28, Mohammad Yousuf 12).

SRI LANKA v PAKISTAN 2008-09 (2nd Test)

At P. Saravanamuttu Stadium, Colombo, on 12, 13, 14 July.

Toss: Pakistan.   Result: SRI LANKA won by seven wickets.

Debuts: Pakistan – Fawad Alam.

Men of the Match: Fawad Alam and K. M. D. N. Kulasekara.

Sri Lanka clinched their first home series victory over Pakistan in another match with a sudden, dramatic end. Pakistan had been bundled out for 90 – their tenth sub-100 total in Tests but the first against Sri Lanka – by the new-ball pair of Kulasekara and Mirando, but they were sailing along in their second innings at 285 for 1, seemingly on course to set a testing target. Then, in a scene reminiscent of the 1987 World Cup final, when Mike Gatting fatally reverse-swept Allan Border's first ball, Younis Khan tried a similar shot against the first delivery from part-time offspinner Paranavitana and, like Gatting, was caught behind off a top edge. Armed with the new ball, Herath and Kulasekara shared the next eight wickets, and Pakistan were dismissed for 320, their last nine wickets contributing only 35. It was a huge letdown for Fawad Alam, promoted to open for the first time in any first-class match on his Test debut: after criticism of his shuffling-across-the-crease technique in the first innings, he scored a superb 168 in the second. Previously considered a Twenty20 specialist, Fawad, who batted for 384 minutes and put on 200 with Younis, was the tenth Pakistani to score a century on Test debut, but the first to do so away from home. Only Yasir Hameed, with 170 against Bangladesh in 2003, has made a higher score for Pakistan on debut. Sri Lanka needed only 171, and hurtled to a three-day victory at more than five an over.

Pakistan

Khurram Manzoor c Dilshan b Kulasekara	3	– c Dilshan b Herath	38
Fawad Alam lbw b Mathews	16	– c Warnapura b Herath	168
*Younis Khan b Mirando	0	– c Dilshan b Paranavitana	82
Mohammad Yousuf c Herath b Kulasekara	10	– lbw b Herath	6
Misbah-ul-Haq c Dilshan b Kulasekara	0	– lbw b Kulasekara	3
Shoaib Malik not out	39	– b Herath	6
†Kamran Akmal c Dilshan b Mirando	9	– lbw b Kulasekara	3
Abdur Rauf lbw b Kulasekara	0	– lbw b Kulasekara	0
Umar Gul c Samaraweera b Mendis	1	– lbw b Herath	2
Mohammad Aamer lbw b Mendis	2	– not out	1
Saeed Ajmal lbw b Mendis	0	– lbw b Kulasekara	0
B 4, l-b 2, w 2, n-b 2	10	B 8, l-b 1, w 1, n-b 1	11

1/4 (1) 2/6 (3) 3/17 (4) 4/19 (5)   90   1/85 (1) 2/285 (3) 3/294 (4)   320
5/51 (2) 6/67 (7) 7/74 (8) 8/80 (9)   4/303 (5) 5/303 (2) 6/306 (7)
9/90 (10) 10/90 (11)   7/312 (6) 8/316 (8) 9/319 (9) 10/320 (11)

Kulasekara 9–3–21–4; Mirando 8–3–23–2; Mendis 10–3–20–3; Mathews 3–0–15–1; Herath 6–3–5–0. *Second Innings*—Kulasekara 19.4–6–37–4; Mirando 13–0–48–0; Mathews 6–0–20–0; Mendis 17–0–81–0; Herath 35–5–99–5; Paranavitana 6–0–26–1.

Sri Lanka

B. S. M. Warnapura lbw b Umar Gul	11	– c Kamran Akmal b Abdur Rauf	54
N. T. Paranavitana c Kamran Akmal b Saeed Ajmal	26	– b Saeed Ajmal	17
*K. C. Sangakkara b Umar Gul	87	– c Misbah-ul-Haq b Shoaib Malik	46
D. P. M. D. Jayawardene c Khurram Manzoor b Saeed Ajmal	19	– not out	37
T. T. Samaraweera run out	21	– not out	6
†T. M. Dilshan c Kamran Akmal b Saeed Ajmal	20		
A. D. Mathews c Mohammad Yousuf b Saeed Ajmal	27		
K. M. D. N. Kulasekara c Misbah-ul-Haq b Umar Gul	11		
H. M. R. K. B. Herath c and b Umar Gul	0		
M. T. T. Mirando lbw b Abdur Rauf	1		
B. A. W. Mendis not out	0		
B 8, l-b 1, n-b 8	17	L-b 7, n-b 4	11

1/28 (1) 2/82 (2) 3/133 (4)   240   1/60 (2)   (3 wkts) 171
4/177 (5) 5/188 (3) 6/203 (6) 7/220 (8)   2/100 (1)
8/220 (9) 9/227 (10) 10/240 (7)   3/160 (3)

Umar Gul 18–1–43–4; Mohammad Aamer 13–2–36–0; Abdur Rauf 11–1–38–1; Saeed Ajmal 31–5–87–4; Younis Khan 7–1–27–0. *Second Innings*—Umar Gul 6–0–38–0; Mohammad Aamer 6–0–33–0; Saeed Ajmal 12–1–56–1; Abdur Rauf 4–1–13–1; Younis Khan 2–0–11–0; Shoaib Malik 1.5–0–13–1.

Umpires: D. J. Harper *(Australia)* (83) and S. J. A. Taufel *(Australia)* (58).
Third umpire: H. D. P. K. Dharmasena *(Sri Lanka)*. Referee: A. G. Hurst *(Australia)* (32).

Close of play: First day, Sri Lanka 164-3 (Sangakkara 81, Samaraweera 13); Second day, Pakistan 178-1 (Fawad Alam 102, Younis Khan 35).

SRI LANKA v PAKISTAN 2008-09 (3rd Test)

At Sinhalese Sports Club, Colombo, on 20, 21, 22, 23, 24 July.
Toss: Sri Lanka.   Result: MATCH DRAWN.
Debuts: none.
Man of the Match: K. C. Sangakkara.   Man of the Series: K. M. D. N. Kulasekara.

A brave rearguard from Sangakkara, who survived for 471 minutes and hit only seven fours, staved off defeat. He was helped by Paranavitana, Jayawardene and Mathews, who all batted for around three hours as Sri Lanka batted out half the fourth day and all the last after being set 492 on a placid pitch. Pakistan managed only one wicket on the final day, after earlier making most of the running. Khurram Manzoor and Mohammad Yousuf both reached 90 in their first innings without making it to three figures, but Mirando's first Test five-for restricted them to 299. Sri Lanka's batsmen were even more disappointing. Warnapura fell to the first ball of the innings, and only Jayawardene batted for longer than 90 minutes as Pakistan's spinners gave their side a lead of 66. Danish Kaneria, restored to the side, took five wickets but was reprimanded for abusing Mathews after dismissing him. Pakistan dipped to 67 for 4 when they batted again, but Shoaib Malik shared hundred partnerships with Misbah-ul-Haq and Kamran Akmal en route to his second Test century. Sangakkara's match-saving innings – his 19th Test hundred – was all the more meritorious as he was forced to keep wicket for most of Pakistan's second innings after Dilshan broke his finger attempting a catch (he also needed stitches after being hit in the face while batting). Sangakkara passed 7,000 Test runs during his innings, as did Yousuf earlier in the match. Chaminda Vaas, in his 111th and avowedly final Test, took his 355th wicket.

Pakistan

Khurram Manzoor c Jayawardene b Vaas	93	– b Herath	2
Fawad Alam c Dilshan b Mirando	16	– c and b Mirando	16
*Younis Khan b Mirando	2	– lbw b Kulasekara	19
Mohammad Yousuf run out	90	– c Sangakkara b Herath	23
Misbah-ul-Haq c Dilshan b Kulasekara	27	– c Sangakkara b Mathews	65
Shoaib Malik lbw b Mirando	45	– c sub (R. A. S. Lakmal) b Herath	134
†Kamran Akmal b Mirando	1	– c Jayawardene b Kulasekara	74
Umar Gul b Kulasekara	2	– c Vaas b Herath	46
Danish Kaneria lbw b Kulasekara	1	– c Mirando b Herath	5
Mohammad Aamer not out	2	– not out	22
Saeed Ajmal b Mirando	8	– not out	3
B 10, n-b 2	12	B 10, l-b 2, w 2, n-b 2	16

1/34 (2) 2/36 (3) 3/203 (1) 4/210 (4)   299
5/285 (6) 6/285 (5) 7/287 (8)
8/289 (9) 9/289 (7) 10/299 (11)

1/16 (1) 2/22 (2)   (9 wkts dec.) 425
3/54 (3) 4/67 (4) 5/186 (5) 6/319 (7)
7/371 (6) 8/399 (8) 9/405 (9)

Vaas 20–6–43–1; Kulasekara 16–2–47–3; Mirando 20.4–2–83–5; Herath 23–4–76–0; Mathews 8–2–31–0; Jayawardene 2–0–9–0. *Second Innings*—Kulasekara 20–5–55–2; Mirando 28–2–121–1; Herath 46–6–157–5; Vaas 19–6–47–0; Mathews 10–1–33–1.

Sri Lanka

B. S. M. Warnapura b Umar Gul	0	– (2) c Shoaib Malik b Danish Kaneria	31
N. T. Paranavitana b Younis Khan	5	– (1) c Fawad Alam b Shoaib Malik	73
*K. C. Sangakkara lbw b Saeed Ajmal	45	– not out	130
D. P. M. D. Jayawardene b Danish Kaneria	79	– c Kamran Akmal b Danish Kaneria	2
T. T. Samaraweera b Saeed Ajmal	6	– c Kamran Akmal b Saeed Ajmal	73
A. D. Mathews c Misbah-ul-Haq b Danish Kaneria	31	– not out	64
W. P. U. J. C. Vaas lbw b Danish Kaneria	4		
†T. M. Dilshan c Kamran Akmal b Danish Kaneria	44		
K. M. D. N. Kulasekara c Misbah-ul-Haq b Saeed Ajmal	1		
H. M. R. K. B. Herath lbw b Danish Kaneria	7		
M. T. T. Mirando not out	5		
L-b 2, n-b 4	6	B 1, l-b 7, w 1, n-b 9	18

1/0 (1) 2/23 (2) 3/63 (3)   233
4/82 (5) 5/153 (6) 6/171 (7)
7/174 (4) 8/181 (9) 9/204 (10) 10/233 (8)

1/83 (2)   (4 wkts) 391
2/139 (1) 3/155 (4)
4/277 (5)

Umar Gul 10–0–55–1; Mohammad Aamer 10–2–34–0; Younis Khan 3–1–10–1; Saeed Ajmal 25–5–70–3; Danish Kaneria 20.3–3–62–5. *Second Innings*—Umar Gul 12–0–65–0; Mohammad Aamer 21–5–46–0; Younis Khan 8–0–25–0; Saeed Ajmal 43–9–95–1; Shoaib Malik 14–1–38–1; Danish Kaneria 36–3–114–2.

Umpires: I. J. Gould *(England)* (6) and S. J. A. Taufel *(Australia)* (59).
Third umpire: M. G. Silva *(Sri Lanka)*. Referee: A. G. Hurst *(Australia)* (33).

Close of play: First day, Pakistan 289-7 (Kamran Akmal 1, Danish Kaneria 1); Second day, Pakistan 16-1 (Fawad Alam 14, Younis Khan 0); Third day, Pakistan 300-5 (Shoaib Malik 106, Kamran Akmal 60); Fourth day, Sri Lanka 183-3 (Sangakkara 50, Samaraweera 20).

ENGLAND v AUSTRALIA 2009 (1st Test)

At Sophia Gardens, Cardiff, on 8, 9, 10, 11, 12 July.
Toss: England.   Result: MATCH DRAWN.
Debuts: none.
Man of the Match: R. T. Ponting.

England looked dead and buried at 70 for 5 on the final morning, but somehow they hung on for a nerve-shredding, morale-boosting draw. Collingwood was the main stumbling-block, resisting for 344 minutes, but when his first mistake resulted in a gully catch, exposing the No. 11 with 69 balls remaining, all England feared the worst. But Panesar and Anderson, who batted for over an hour after extending his sequence of innings without a duck to 52, survived without much trouble as the clock ticked down. Halfway through the mandatory final hour England crept in front, and with ten minutes left they were finally safe, as there was then no time for Australia to start their innings. All this drama seemed unlikely on the first day of the first Test at Cardiff, the 100th ground to stage one. Against an inexperienced attack lacking Brett Lee (side injury), England eased to 327 for 5 on a bland, flat pitch – but two late wickets set them back, and only Swann's forthright hitting next morning pushed them to 435. Australia's batsmen soon put that into perspective. Four made hundreds, only the second instance in Ashes Tests (England did it at Trent Bridge in 1938). Katich and Ponting put on 239, then both North and Haddin reached three figures on debut against England. Australia's fourth-highest Ashes total – the other three all required significant input from Don Bradman – gave them a lead of 239, which seemed plenty when England collapsed ... but there was a twist in the tail.

England

*A. J. Strauss c Clarke b Johnson	30	– c Haddin b Haurtiz	17
A. N. Cook c Hussey b Hilfenhaus	10	– lbw b Johnson	6
R. S. Bopara c Hughes b Johnson	35	– lbw b Hilfenhaus	1
K. P. Pietersen c Katich b Hauritz	69	– b Hilfenhaus	8
P. D. Collingwood c Haddin b Hilfenhaus	64	– c Hussey b Siddle	74
†M. J. Prior b Siddle	56	– c Clarke b Hauritz	14
A. Flintoff b Siddle	37	– c Ponting b Johnson	26
J. M. Anderson c Hussey b Hauritz	26	– (10) not out	21
S. C. J. Broad b Johnson	19	– (8) lbw b Hauritz	14
G. P. Swann not out	47	– (9) lbw b Hilfenhaus	31
M. S. Panesar c Ponting b Hauritz	4	– not out	7
B 13, l-b 11, w 2, n-b 12	38	B 9, l-b 9, w 4, n-b 11	33

1/21 (2) 2/67 (1) 3/90 (3) 4/228 (5)   435
5/241 (4) 6/327 (7) 7/329 (6)
8/355 (9) 9/423 (8) 10/435 (11)

1/13 (2) 2/17 (3)   (9 wkts) 252
3/31 (4) 4/46 (1) 5/70 (6)
6/127 (7) 7/159 (8) 8/221 (9) 9/233 (5)

Johnson 22–2–87–3; Hilfenhaus 27–5–77–2; Siddle 27–3–121–2; Hauritz 23.5–1–95–3; Clarke 5–0–20–0; Katich 2–0–11–0. *Second Innings*—Johnson 22–4–44–2; Hilfenhaus 15–3–47–3; Siddle 18–2–51–1; Hauritz 37–12–63–3; Clarke 3–0–8–0; North 7–4–14–0; Katich 3–0–7–0.

Australia

P. J. Hughes c Prior b Flintoff	36
S. M. Katich lbw b Anderson	122
*R. T. Ponting b Panesar	150
M. E. K. Hussey c Prior b Anderson	3
M. J. Clarke c Prior b Broad	83
M. J. North not out	125
†B. J. Haddin c Bopara b Collingwood	121
B 9, l-b 14, w 4, n-b 7	34

1/60 (1) 2/299 (2) 3/325 (4)   (6 wkts dec.) 674
4/331 (3) 5/474 (5) 6/674 (7)

M. G. Johnson, N. M. Hauritz, P. M. Siddle and B. W. Hilfenhaus did not bat.

Anderson 32–6–110–2; Broad 32–6–129–1; Swann 38–8–131–0; Flintoff 35–3–128–1; Panesar 35–4–115–1; Collingwood 9–0–38–1.

Umpires: Aleem Dar *(Pakistan)* (56) and B. R. Doctrove *(West Indies)* (24).
Third umpire: R. A. Kettleborough *(England)*. Referee: J. J. Crowe *(New Zealand)* (33).

Close of play: First day, England 336-7 (Anderson 2, Broad 4); Second day, Australia 249-1 (Katich 104, Ponting 100); Third day, Australia 479-5 (North 54, Haddin 4); Fourth day, England 20-2 (Strauss 6, Pietersen 3).

ENGLAND v AUSTRALIA 2009 (2nd Test)

At Lord's, London, on 16, 17, 18, 19, 20 July.
Toss: England.   Result: ENGLAND won by 115 runs.
Debuts: none.
Man of the Match: A. Flintoff.

England bounced back from near-defeat at Cardiff to record their first victory over Australia at Lord's since 1934, and only the second since 1896. On another flat pitch Strauss made hay after winning an important toss, putting on 196 with Cook and batting throughout the first day before being bowled second ball next morning. His 18th Test century ought to have laid the foundations for a huge total, but for the second match running the end result was rather disappointing. Conditions on the overcast second day were the worst of the match for batting, and Australia effectively lost the game in slipping to 156 for 8, latterly under floodlights; five wickets went to attempted pulls as the batsmen mislaid the discipline of Cardiff. In sunshine next morning Australia's tail reduced the deficit to 210, and Strauss decided against the follow-on, instead extending the lead to an imposing 521. Pietersen, who needed an Achilles operation and missed the rest of the series, looked out of sorts in making 44 from 101 balls, but Prior smacked 61 from 42 towards the end. Crushing defeat loomed when Australia dipped to 128 for 5 – not helped by some contentious umpiring decisions from Rudi Koertzen, in his 100th Test – but Clarke and Haddin shared a defiant stand of 185, setting English nerves fluttering. But Haddin fell without addition on an adrenalin-packed final morning as Flintoff, who had announced his imminent Test retirement before the match, completed an emotional five-for in a superb spell of lightning pace.

England

*A. J. Strauss b Hilfenhaus	161	– c Clarke b Hauritz	32
A. N. Cook lbw b Johnson	95	– lbw b Hauritz	32
R. S. Bopara lbw b Hilfenhaus	18	– c Katich b Hauritz	27
K. P. Pietersen c Haddin b Siddle	32	– c Haddin b Siddle	44
P. D. Collingwood c Siddle b Clarke	16	– c Haddin b Siddle	54
†M. J. Prior b Johnson	8	– run out	61
A. Flintoff c Ponting b Hilfenhaus	4	– not out	30
S. C. J. Broad b Hilfenhaus	16	– not out	0
G. P. Swann c Ponting b Siddle	4		
J. M. Anderson c Hussey b Johnson	29		
G. Onions not out	17		
B 15, l-b 2, n-b 8	25	B 16, l-b 9, w 1, n-b 5	31

1/196 (2) 2/222 (3) 3/267 (4)   425   1/61 (2) 2/74 (1)   (6 wkts dec.) 311
4/302 (5) 5/317 (6) 6/333 (7) 7/364 (1)   3/147 (3) 4/174 (4)
8/370 (9) 9/378 (8) 10/425 (10)   5/260 (6) 6/311 (5)

Hilfenhaus 31–12–103–4; Johnson 21.4–2–132–3; Siddle 20–1–76–2; Hauritz 8.3–1–26–0; North 16.3–2–59–0; Clarke 4–1–12–1. *Second Innings*—Hilfenhaus 19–5–59–0; Johnson 17–2–68–0; Siddle 15.2–4–64–2; Hauritz 16–1–80–3; Clarke 4–0–15–0.

Australia

P. J. Hughes c Prior b Anderson	4	– c Strauss b Flintoff	17
S. M. Katich c Broad b Onions	48	– c Pietersen b Flintoff	6
*R. T. Ponting c Strauss b Anderson	2	– b Broad	38
M. E. K. Hussey b Flintoff	51	– c Collingwood b Swann	27
M. J. Clarke c Cook b Anderson	1	– b Swann	136
M. J. North b Anderson	0	– b Swann	6
†B. J. Haddin c Cook b Broad	28	– c Collingwood b Flintoff	80
M. G. Johnson c Cook b Broad	4	– b Swann	63
N. M. Hauritz c Collingwood b Onions	24	– b Flintoff	1
P. M. Siddle c Strauss b Onions	35	– b Flintoff	7
B. W. Hilfenhaus not out	6	– not out	4
B 4, l-b 6, n-b 2	12	B 5, l-b 8, n-b 8	21

1/4 (1) 2/10 (3) 3/103 (2)   215   1/17 (2) 2/34 (1) 3/78 (3)   406
4/111 (4) 5/111 (5) 6/139 (6)   4/120 (4) 5/128 (6) 6/313 (7)
7/148 (8) 8/152 (7) 9/196 (9) 10/215 (10)   7/356 (5) 8/363 (9) 9/388 (10) 10/406 (8)

Anderson 21–5–55–4; Flintoff 12–4–27–1; Broad 18–1–78–2; Onions 11–1–41–3; Swann 1–0–4–0. *Second Innings*—Anderson 21–4–86–0; Flintoff 27–4–92–5; Onions 9–0–50–0; Broad 16–3–49–1; Swann 28–3–87–4; Collingwood 6–1–29–0.

Umpires: B. R. Doctrove *(West Indies)* (25) and R. E. Koertzen *(South Africa)* (100).
Third umpire: N. J. Llong *(England)*. Referee: J. J. Crowe *(New Zealand)* (34).

Close of play: First day, England 364-6 (Strauss 161, Broad 7); Second day, Australia 156-8 (Hauritz 3, Siddle 3); Third day, England 311-6 (Flintoff 30, Broad 0); Fourth day, Australia 313-5 (Clarke 125, Haddin 80).

ENGLAND v AUSTRALIA 2009 (3rd Test)

At Edgbaston, Birmingham, on July 30, 31, August 1 *(no play)*, 2, 3, 2009.
Toss: Australia. Result: MATCH DRAWN.
Debuts: Australia – G. A. Manou.
Man of the Match: M. J. Clarke.

Two superb sessions gave England the upper hand, but they could not conjure up a third when they needed one on the final day. Australia survived comfortably enough, helped by the loss of the entire third day and most of the first to rain, and by the end they were arguably better placed. England's first purple passage was the second day's morning session, when after a lacklustre bowling performance in the two hours possible the day before they claimed seven wickets for 77, Onions starting by striking with the first two balls of the day. The tail stretched the total to 263 before Anderson completed his first five-for against Australia, but England (without Pietersen, who had undergone an operation on his troublesome Achilles and missed the rest of the series) struggled until their second fine session – after lunch on the fourth day, following the third-day washout – when, led by Flintoff, they added 157 in 32.1 overs. Again the momentum could not quite be maintained. Watson (the first right-hander to open in a Test for Australia since Michael Slater in 2001, after Phillip Hughes was dropped), played his second resolute innings in his first Test as an opener, Hussey also passed 50 after narrowly escaping a king pair, then Clarke and North made the match safe. Minutes before the start, Brad Haddin broke a finger in practice. The toss had just taken place, but England agreed that the reserve wicketkeeper, Graham Manou, could play instead. It was believed to be the first time a Test side had been changed after the toss.

Australia

S. R. Watson lbw b Onions	62	– c Prior b Anderson	53
S. M. Katich lbw b Swann	46	– c Prior b Onions	26
*R. T. Ponting c Prior b Onions	38	– b Swann	5
M. E. K. Hussey b Onions	0	– c Prior b Broad	64
M. J. Clarke lbw b Anderson	29	– not out	103
M. J. North c Prior b Anderson	12	– c Anderson b Broad	96
†G. A. Manou b Anderson	8	– not out	13
M. G. Johnson lbw b Anderson	0		
N. M. Hauritz not out	20		
P. M. Siddle c Prior b Anderson	13		
B. W. Hilfenhaus c Swann b Onions	20		
B 5, l-b 7, w 2, n-b 1	15	B 4, l-b 6, w 2, n-b 3	15
	263	**(5 wkts)**	**375**

1/85 (2) 2/126 (1) 3/126 (4)   263
4/163 (3) 5/193 (5) 6/202 (6)
7/202 (8) 8/203 (7) 9/229 (10) 10/263 (11)

1/47 (2) 2/52 (3)   (5 wkts) 375
3/137 (1) 4/161 (4)
5/346 (6)

Anderson 24–7–80–5; Flintoff 15–2–58–0; Onions 16.4–2–58–4; Broad 13–2–51–0; Swann 2–0–4–1. *Second Innings*—Anderson 21–8–47–1; Flintoff 15–0–35–0; Onions 19–3–74–1; Swann 31–4–119–1; Broad 16–2–38–2; Bopara 8.2–1–44–0; Collingwood 2–0–8–0.

England

*A. J. Strauss c Manou b Hilfenhaus	69
A. N. Cook c Manou b Siddle	0
R. S. Bopara b Hilfenhaus	23
I. R. Bell lbw b Johnson	53
P. D. Collingwood c Ponting b Hilfenhaus	13
†M. J. Prior c sub (P. J. Hughes) b Siddle	41
A. Flintoff c Clarke b Hauritz	74
S. C. J. Broad c and b Siddle	55
G. P. Swann c North b Johnson	24
J. M. Anderson c Manou b Hilfenhaus	1
G. Onions not out	2
B 2, l-b 4, w 6, n-b 9	21
	376

1/2 (2) 2/60 (3) 3/141 (1) 4/159 (5)   376
5/168 (4) 6/257 (6) 7/309 (7)
8/348 (9) 9/355 (10) 10/376 (8)

Hilfenhaus 30–7–109–4; Siddle 21.3–3–89–3; Hauritz 18–2–57–1; Johnson 21–1–92–2; Watson 3–0–23–0.

Umpires: Aleem Dar *(Pakistan)* (57) and R. E. Koertzen *(South Africa)* (101).
Third umpire: R. A. Kettleborough *(England)*. Referee: J. J. Crowe *(New Zealand)* (35).

Close of play: First day, Australia 126-1 (Watson 62, Ponting 17); Second day, England 116-2 (Strauss 64, Bell 26); Third day, No play; Fourth day, Australia 88-2 (Watson 34, Hussey 18).

ENGLAND v AUSTRALIA 2009 (4th Test)

At Headingley, Leeds, on August 7, 8, 9, 2009.
Toss: England. Result: AUSTRALIA won by an innings and 80 runs.
Debuts: none.
Man of the Match: M. J. North.

Australia squared the series with an emphatic three-day victory. England won the toss on the first morning, but staggered to lunch on a pitch helpful to the seamers at 72 for 6. They were all out soon afterwards, most of the damage being done by Siddle and Clark, playing his first match of the series in place of Hauritz. The pitch seemed to lose its early demons when Australia batted, although Harmison (recalled in place of Flintoff, whose chronic knee injury was rested) took an early wicket and Broad mopped up well to finish with Test-best figures. In between, though, Clarke and the upright North, who made his third century in his sixth Test, put on 152 as Australia stretched their lead to a massive 343. England's openers made a reasonable start, but Strauss and Bopara were trapped in front by successive balls from Hilfenhaus, who obtained more swing than any of the England bowlers, and there was no comeback from 82 for 5 by the end of the second day. Some happy-go-lucky hitting prolonged the match beyond lunch on the third day – England actually scored 163 runs in 24 overs in the morning session, rather ruining Clark's figures – but it was all over soon afterwards. Johnson, who had been wild and unimpressive earlier in the series, wrapped things up to complete his first five-for against England. Australia were in the ascendant, and now needed only to avoid defeat in the final Test at The Oval to retain the Ashes.

England

*A. J. Strauss c North b Siddle	3	– lbw b Hilfenhaus	32
A. N. Cook c Clarke b Clark	30	– c Haddin b Johnson	30
R. S. Bopara c Hussey b Hilfenhaus	1	– lbw b Hilfenhaus	0
I. R. Bell c Haddin b Johnson	8	– c Ponting b Johnson	3
P. D. Collingwood c Ponting b Clark	0	– lbw b Johnson	4
†M. J. Prior not out	37	– (7) c Haddin b Hilfenhaus	22
S. C. J. Broad c Katich b Clark	3	– (8) c Watson b Siddle	61
G. P. Swann c Clarke b Siddle	0	– (9) c Haddin b Johnson	62
S. J. Harmison c Haddin b Siddle	0	– (10) not out	19
J. M. Anderson c Haddin b Siddle	3	– (6) c Ponting b Hilfenhaus	4
G. Onions c Katich b Siddle	0	– b Johnson	0
B 5, l-b 8, w 1, n-b 3	17	B 5, l-b 5, w 5, n-b 11	26

1/11 (1) 2/16 (3) 3/39 (4) 4/42 (5)   102
5/63 (2) 6/72 (7) 7/92 (8) 8/98 (9)
9/102 (10) 10/102 (11)

1/58 (1) 2/58 (3) 3/67 (4)   263
4/74 (5) 5/78 (2) 6/86 (6)
7/120 (7) 8/228 (8) 9/259 (9) 10/263 (11)

Hilfenhaus 7–0–20–1; Siddle 9.5–0–21–5; Johnson 7–0–30–1; Clark 10–4–18–3. *Second Innings*—Hilfenhaus 19–2–60–4; Siddle 12–2–50–1; Clark 11–1–74–0; Johnson 19.3–3–69–5.

Australia

S. R. Watson lbw b Onions	51
S. M. Katich c Bopara b Harmison	0
*R. T. Ponting lbw b Broad	78
M. E. K. Hussey lbw b Broad	10
M. J. Clarke lbw b Onions	93
M. J. North c Anderson b Broad	110
†B. J. Haddin c Bell b Harmison	14
M. G. Johnson c Bopara b Broad	27
P. M. Siddle b Broad	0
S. R. Clark b Broad	32
B. W. Hilfenhaus not out	0
B 9, l-b 14, w 4, n-b 3	30

1/14 (2) 2/133 (1) 3/140 (3)   445
4/151 (4) 5/303 (5) 6/323 (7)
7/393 (8) 8/394 (9) 9/440 (10) 10/445 (6)

Anderson 18–3–89–0; Harmison 23–4–98–2; Onions 22–5–80–2; Broad 25.1–6–91–6; Swann 16–4–64–0.

Umpires: Asad Rauf *(Pakistan)* (25) and B. F. Bowden *(New Zealand)* (55).
Third umpire: I. J. Gould *(England)*. Referee: R. S. Madugalle *(Sri Lanka)* (111).

Close of play: First day, Australia 196-4 (Clarke 34, North 7); Second day, England 82-5 (Anderson 0, Prior 4).

ENGLAND v AUSTRALIA 2009 (5th Test)

At Kennington Oval, London, on August 20, 21, 22, 23, 2009.
Toss: England. Result: ENGLAND won by 197 runs.
Debuts: England – I. J. L. Trott.
Man of the Match: S. C. J. Broad. Men of the Series: M. J. Clarke and A. J. Strauss.

After their mauling at Headingley England bounced back with a convincing win of their own to reclaim the Ashes with a 2-1 series victory. As at Lord's, one seismic session shifted the initiative England's way. Many felt that England's first-innings 332 – on a dry pitch on which Australia surprisingly decided to omit their specialist spinner – was below par, but that assessment was hastily revised when Australia, after sailing to 61 for 0 by lunch on the overcast second day, lost eight wickets for 75 in 25 overs before tea, five of them in a superb spell from Broad. Strauss dropped anchor as England built on their lead of 172, before a superb innings from the South African-born Jonathan Trott, who became the 18th batsman to make a century on Test debut for England: three of his predecessors were playing in this match (Cook, Prior and Strauss), but few of the others came in such pressurised circumstances. Needing 546 to win, Australia purred with ominous ease to 217 for 2, before Flintoff made the one significant contribution of his farewell Test, hitting the stumps direct from mid-on to run Ponting out. Clarke was narrowly run out in the next over after smart work from Strauss at leg slip, and England motored to victory despite Hussey's century, his tenth in Tests but the first for 16 matches spread over 11 months. Ponting was only the second Australian captain to lose two Test series in England, after Billy Murdoch in the 19th century.

England

*A. J. Strauss c Haddin b Hilfenhaus	55	– c Clarke b North	75
A. N. Cook c Ponting b Siddle	10	– c Clarke b North	9
I. R. Bell b Siddle	72	– c Katich b Johnson	4
P. D. Collingwood c Hussey b Siddle	24	– c Katich b Johnson	1
I. J. L. Trott run out	41	– c North b Clark	119
†M. J. Prior c Watson b Johnson	18	– run out	4
A. Flintoff c Haddin b Johnson	7	– c Siddle b North	22
S. C. J. Broad c Ponting b Hilfenhaus	37	– c Ponting b North	29
G. P. Swann c Haddin b Siddle	18	– c Haddin b Hilfenhaus	63
J. M. Anderson lbw b Hilfenhaus	0	– not out	15
S. J. Harmison not out	12		
B 12, l-b 5, w 3, n-b 18	38	B 1, l-b 15, w 7, n-b 9	32

1/12 (2) 2/114 (1) 3/176 (4)   332   1/27 (2) 2/34 (3)   (9 wkts dec.) 373
4/181 (3) 5/229 (6) 6/247 (7)   3/39 (4) 4/157 (1) 5/168 (6)
7/268 (5) 8/307 (9) 9/308 (10) 10/332 (8)   6/200 (7) 7/243 (8) 8/333 (9) 9/373 (5)

Hilfenhaus 21.5–5–71–3; Siddle 21–6–75–4; Clark 14–5–41–0; Johnson 15–0–69–2; North 14–3–33–0; Watson 5–0–26–0. *Second Innings*—Hilfenhaus 11–1–58–1; Siddle 17–3–69–0; North 30–4–98–4; Johnson 17–1–60–2; Katich 5–2–9–0; Clark 12–2–43–1; Clarke 3–0–20–0.

Australia

S. R. Watson lbw b Broad	34	– lbw b Broad	40
S. M. Katich c Cook b Swann	50	– lbw b Swann	43
*R. T. Ponting b Broad	8	– run out	66
M. E. K. Hussey lbw b Broad	0	– c Cook b Swann	121
M. J. Clarke c Trott b Broad	3	– run out	0
M. J. North lbw b Swann	8	– st Prior b Swann	10
†B. J. Haddin b Broad	1	– c Strauss b Swann	34
M. G. Johnson c Prior b Swann	11	– c Collingwood b Harmison	0
P. M. Siddle not out	26	– c Flintoff b Harmison	10
S. R. Clark c Cook b Swann	6	– c Cook b Harmison	0
B. W. Hilfenhaus b Flintoff	6	– not out	4
B 1, l-b 5, n-b 1	7	B 7, l-b 7, n-b 6	20

1/73 (1) 2/85 (3) 3/89 (4)   160   1/86 (2) 2/90 (1) 3/217 (3)   348
4/93 (5) 5/108 (6) 6/109 (2)   4/220 (5) 5/236 (6) 6/327 (7)
7/111 (7) 8/131 (8) 9/143 (10) 10/160 (11)   7/327 (8) 8/343 (9) 9/343 (10) 10/348 (4)

Anderson 9–3–29–0; Flintoff 13.5–4–35–1; Swann 14–3–38–4; Harmison 4–1–15–0; Broad 12–1–37–5. *Second Innings*—Anderson 12–2–46–0; Flintoff 11–1–42–0; Harmison 16–5–54–3; Swann 40.2–8–120–4; Broad 22–4–71–1; Collingwood 1–0–1–0.

Umpires: Asad Rauf *(Pakistan)* (26) and B. F. Bowden *(New Zealand)* (56).
Third umpire: P. J. Hartley *(England)*. Referee: R. S. Madugalle *(Sri Lanka)* (112).

Close of play: First day, England 307-8 (Broad 26); Second day, England 58-3 (Strauss 32, Trott 8); Third day, Australia 80-0 (Watson 31, Katich 42).

WEST INDIES v BANGLADESH 2009 (1st Test)

At Arnos Vale, Kingstown, St Vincent, on 9, 10, 11, 12, 13 July.
Toss: Bangladesh. Result: BANGLADESH won by 95 runs.
Debuts: West Indies – R. A. Austin, T. M. Dowlin, N. O. Miller, O. J. Phillips, D. M. Richards,
K. A. J. Roach, C. A. K. Walton. Bangladesh – Mahmudullah, Rubel Hossain.
Man of the Match: Tamim Iqbal.

A long-running and bitter contracts dispute between the West Indian board and the players' association finally boiled over when all the first-choice players – and, reportedly, several second-choice ones too – declined invitations to play. At a day's notice the board cobbled together a side containing seven debutants: the other four players had 22 caps between them, 12 of those Best's; the captain, 36-year-old Floyd Reifer, had played the last of his four Tests more than a decade previously. Not surprisingly, this scratch combination struggled – although they did claim a first-innings lead – and Bangladesh eventually completed only their second victory in 60 Tests, their first overseas, after a win over Zimbabwe in 2004-05 (*Test No. 1735*). It was a close-run affair, eventually decided deep into the final session (rain had restricted the first day to 18.5 overs, and shortened the second day too). West Indies' inexperienced batsmen could not cope with off-spinner Mahmudullah, who took eight wickets on his Test debut, and slow left-armer Shakib Al Hasan. Dave Bernard, a veteran of one previous Test, resisted for 198 minutes, but finally Best heaved at a full-toss and missed. There were some bright moments for West Indies: Omar Phillips narrowly missed a debut hundred, while his opening partner Dale Richards, another Barbadian, opened his account in Tests by pulling his fourth ball, from Mashrafe bin Mortaza, for six. Mortaza, captaining Bangladesh for the first time after Mohammad Ashraful was sacked, later went off with a knee injury, leaving Shakib in charge for the exciting climax.

Bangladesh

Tamim Iqbal c Reifer b Best	14	– c Dowlin b Bernard	128
Imrul Kayes lbw b Sammy	33	– c Roach b Austin	24
Junaid Siddique c Dowlin b Bernard	27	– c Richards b Sammy	78
Raqibul Hasan c Sammy b Bernard	14	– b Sammy	18
Mohammad Ashraful c Walton b Best	6	– lbw b Roach	3
Shakib Al Hasan c Richards b Roach	17	– c Austin b Sammy	30
†Mushfiqur Rahim run out	36	– b Roach	37
Mahmudullah c Phillips b Roach	9	– lbw b Roach	8
*Mashrafe bin Mortaza c Walton b Roach	39	– c Roach b Sammy	0
Shahadat Hossain c Walton b Austin	33	– not out	0
Rubel Hossain not out	3	– lbw b Sammy	1
B 2, l-b 2, w 1, n-b 2	7	L-b 9, w 2, n-b 7	18

1/45 (1) 2/49 (2) 3/79 (4) 4/98 (3)   238   1/82 (2) 2/228 (1) 3/258 (3)   345
5/100 (5) 6/121 (6) 7/149 (8)   4/261 (5) 5/267 (4) 6/327 (6)
8/172 (7) 9/207 (9) 10/238 (10)   7/342 (8) 8/344 (9) 9/344 (7) 10/345 (11)

Best 17–4–58–2; Roach 23–11–46–3; Sammy 19–7–38–1; Bernard 11–2–30–2; Austin 13.2–5–35–1; Miller 5–1–27–0. *Second Innings*—Roach 26–4–67–3; Best 13–3–49–0; Austin 30–4–78–1; Sammy 30.1–6–70–5; Miller 17–4–40–0; Bernard 4–0–32–1.

West Indies

D. M. Richards lbw b Shakib Al Hasan	13	– run out	14
O. J. Phillips c Raqibul Hasan b Rubel Hossain	94	– lbw b Shakib Al Hasan	14
R. A. Austin c Imrul Kayes b Rubel Hossain	17	– (9) lbw b Mahmudullah	0
T. M. Dowlin lbw b Shakib Al Hasan	22	– (3) c Imrul Kayes b Mahmudullah	19
*F. L. Reifer c Shakib Al Hasan b Mahmudullah	25	– (4) lbw b Mahmudullah	19
D. E. Bernard c sub (Mehrab Hossain, jun.) b Shahadat Hossain	53	– (5) not out	52
†C. A. K. Walton c Shakib Al Hasan b Mahmudullah	0	– (6) lbw b Mahmudullah	10
D. J. G. Sammy b Mahmudullah	48	– (7) c Shahadat Hossain b Shakib Al Hasan	19
N. O. Miller c Mushfiqur Rahim b Rubel Hossain	0	– (8) c Mushfiqur Rahim b Mohammad Ashraful	5
K. A. J. Roach c sub (Mehrab Hossain, jun.) b Mohammad Ashraful	6	– c Mushfiqur Rahim b Mahmudullah	3
T. L. Best not out	1	– lbw b Shakib Al Hasan	9
B 4, l-b 3, w 2, n-b 19	28	B 5, l-b 5, w 2, n-b 5	17

1/15 (1) 2/94 (3) 3/142 (4)   307   1/20 (1) 2/33 (2) 3/69 (4)   181
4/176 (2) 5/227 (5) 6/227 (7)   4/72 (3) 5/82 (6) 6/119 (7)
7/267 (6) 8/267 (9) 9/306 (10) 10/307 (8)   7/151 (8) 8/164 (6) 9/172 (10) 10/181 (11)

Mashrafe bin Mortaza 6.3–0–26–0; Shahadat Hossain 13–2–48–1; Shakib Al Hasan 35–10–76–2; Rubel Hossain 15–1–76–3; Mahmudullah 19.4–2–59–3; Mohammad Ashraful 6–0–15–1. *Second Innings*—Shahadat Hossain 12–2–32–0; Rubel Hossain 10–1–45–0; Shakib Al Hasan 28.1–11–39–3; Mahmudullah 15–4–51–5; Mohammad Ashraful 5–1–4–1.

Umpires: E. A. R. de Silva *(Sri Lanka)* (40) and A. L. Hill *(New Zealand)* (10).
Third umpire: C. R. Duncan *(West Indies)*. Referee: A. J. Pycroft *(Zimbabwe)* (3).

Close of play: First day, Bangladesh 42-0 (Tamim Iqbal 14, Imrul Kayes 26); Second day, West Indies 17-1 (Phillips 0, Austin 1); Third day, Bangladesh 26-0 (Tamim Iqbal 11, Imrul Kayes 14); Fourth day, Bangladesh 321-5 (Shakib Al Hasan 26, Mushfiqur Rahim 28).

WEST INDIES v BANGLADESH 2009 (2nd Test)

At National Cricket Stadium, Queen's Park, St George's, Grenada, on 17, 18, 19, 20 July.
Toss: Bangladesh. Result: BANGLADESH won by four wickets.
Debuts: none.
Man of the Match: Shakib Al Hasan. Man of the Series: Shakib Al Hasan.

Bangladesh won a Test series for only the second time, their first overseas after beating Zimbabwe at home in 2004-05. "This is the biggest thing that has happened to Bangladesh cricket," said Shakib Al Hasan, their stand-in captain. However, their third Test victory was completed late on the fourth day against a makeshift West Indian side still lacking any established players, although it was boosted (in theory, if not in practice) by the inclusion of 14-Test veteran Ryan Hinds. West Indies again started reasonably, with Travis Dowlin, a 32-year-old from Guyana, unlucky to miss a maiden Test century when well caught at cover. But Bangladesh's trio of spinners kept chipping away, and the eventual total was a disappointment. Bangladesh batted equally unimpressively, struggling against the short ball – of which there were plenty from Best and his fellow Barbadian, Kemar Roach, who took six wickets – and again conceding a first-innings lead. West Indies were propped up by Dowlin and Bernard, but the others made heavy weather of the left-arm spin of Shakib and Enamul Haque, who had replaced the injured Mashrafe bin Mortaza. Facing a tricky target of 215, Bangladesh made a poor start, and home hopes were high at 67 for 4. But Shakib put on 106 in an attacking partnership with Raqibul Hasan then, after Raqibul and Mushfiqur Rahim fell during a superb spell from Sammy, Shakib took his side home with four, four, two and six off successive balls from Roach in what turned out to be the last over.

West Indies

D. M. Richards c and b Mahmudullah	69	– lbw b Shakib Al Hasan	12
O. J. Phillips c Tamim Iqbal b Shakib Al Hasan	23	– c Mohammad Ashraful b Shakib Al Hasan	29
T. M. Dowlin c Tamim Iqbal b Shakib Al Hasan	95	– lbw b Enamul Haque	49
R. O. Hinds c and b Mahmudullah	2	– c Mahmudullah b Shakib Al Hasan	2
*F. L. Reifer lbw b Mahmudullah	1	– lbw b Mahmudullah	3
D. E. Bernard c Mohammad Ashraful b Shakib Al Hasan	17	– st Mushfiqur Rahim b Enamul Haque	69
D. J. G. Sammy lbw b Enamul Haque	1	– c Raqibul Hasan b Enamul Haque	22
†C. A. K. Walton c Mohammad Ashraful b Enamul Haque	2	– c Mahmudullah b Shakib Al Hasan	1
R. A. Austin hit wkt b Shahadat Hossain	19	– c Tamim Iqbal b Shahadat Hossain	3
T. L. Best b Enamul Haque	0	– c Mushfiqur Rahim b Shakib Al Hasan	12
K. A. J. Roach not out	4	– not out	1
L-b 1, n-b 3	4	L-b 2, n-b 4	6

1/60 (2) 2/104 (1) 3/106 (4) 4/114 (5)   237   1/20 (1) 2/72 (2) 3/84 (4)   209
5/157 (6) 6/158 (7) 7/160 (8)   4/95 (5) 5/110 (3) 6/166 (7)
8/219 (9) 9/220 (10) 10/237 (3)   7/167 (8) 8/187 (9) 9/201 (6) 10/209 (10)

Shahadat Hossain 9–2–30–1; Rubel Hossain 6–0–27–0; Enamul Haque 24–2–62–3; Shakib Al Hasan 21.1–7–59–3; Mahmudullah 13–2–44–3; Mohammad Ashraful 3–0–14–0. *Second Innings*—Rubel Hossain 9–1–34–0; Shahadat Hossain 4–0–18–1; Enamul Haque 17–3–48–3; Shakib Al Hasan 24.5–3–70–5; Mahmudullah 15–1–37–1; Mohammad Ashraful 1–1–0–0.

Bangladesh

Tamim Iqbal c Walton b Bernard	37	– c Walton b Sammy	18
Imrul Kayes c Walton b Sammy	14	– c Sammy b Roach	8
Enamul Haque, jun. c Walton b Roach	13		
Junaid Siddique b Austin	7	– (3) c Reifer b Sammy	5
Raqibul Hasan c Walton b Roach	44	– (4) c and b Sammy	65
Mohammad Ashraful c Sammy b Hinds	12	– (5) c Walton b Sammy	3
*Shakib Al Hasan c Austin b Roach	16	– (6) not out	96
†Mushfiqur Rahim c Walton b Roach	48	– (7) c and b Sammy	12
Mahmudullah c Austin b Roach	28	– (8) not out	0
Shahadat Hossain c Richards b Roach	0		
Rubel Hossain not out	1		
L-b 2, w 3, n-b 7	12	B 1, l-b 3, w 2, n-b 4	10

1/26 (2) 2/51 (3) 3/75 (1) 4/77 (4)   232   1/27 (2) 2/29 (1)   (6 wkts) 217
5/106 (6) 6/150 (5) 7/157 (7) 8/219 (8)   3/49 (3) 4/67 (5)
9/223 (10) 10/232 (9)   5/173 (4) 6/201 (7)

Roach 23.5–8–48–6; Best 17–3–47–0; Sammy 15–3–45–1; Bernard 8–0–29–1; Austin 8–0–29–1; Hinds 8–1–32–1. *Second Innings*—Best 9–0–38–0; Bernard 9–1–33–0; Roach 13.4–4–68–1; Sammy 16–1–55–5; Austin 3–0–13–0; Hinds 4–0–6–0.

Umpires: E. A. R. de Silva *(Sri Lanka)* (41) and A. L. Hill *(New Zealand)* (11).
Third umpire: N. A. Malcolm *(West Indies)*. Referee: A. J. Pycroft *(Zimbabwe)* (4).

Close of play: First day, Bangladesh 35-1 (Tamim Iqbal 14, Enamul Haque 5); Second day, West Indies 56-1 (Phillips 17, Dowlin 23); Third day, West Indies 192-8 (Bernard 61, Best 4).

SRI LANKA v NEW ZEALAND 2009 (1st Test)

At Galle International Stadium on August 18, 19, 20, 21, 22, 2009.
Toss: New Zealand. Result: SRI LANKA won by 202 runs.
Debuts: none.
Man of the Match: T. M. Dilshan.

Sri Lanka continued their good home form with a comprehensive victory, set up by a big first-innings total which included a stand of 176 between century-makers Samaraweera and Mahela Jayawardene. Dilshan, relieved of the wicketkeeping gloves he had worn in the preceding series against Pakistan, now moved up to open, and made 92: he followed that with an unbeaten century in the second innings. New Zealand batted consistently, but apart from McIntosh, who survived for nearly five hours, no-one played the big innings required. Muralitharan, back after missing the Pakistan series with a knee injury, took four wickets, including his 100th in Tests at Galle (O'Brien). Murali already occupies first and second place on this particular list, with 117 at Kandy and (by the end of this series) 166 at the Sinhalese Sports Club in Colombo: next comes Heath Streak with 83 at Harare. Dilshan led the way as Sri Lanka built on a lead of 153, and New Zealand were eventually set 413: they were soon 45 for 4. Vettori played his second steadfast innings of the match, batting for 148 minutes to add to 97 in the first innings, but even that only pushed his side just past the halfway point of their chase. Vettori did receive belated support from Ryder and McCullum, who both batted down the order after suffering from stomach trouble: seven players were hit by it in all, and the uncapped substitute Reece Young kept wicket in the second innings, with Sri Lanka's permission.

Sri Lanka

N. T. Paranavitana c McCullum b Martin	0	– c Taylor b O'Brien		5
T. M. Dilshan b O'Brien	92	– not out		123
*K. C. Sangakkara c Flynn b Martin	8	– run out		46
D. P. M. D. Jayawardene c Taylor b O'Brien	114	– c and b Patel		27
T. T. Samaraweera c Patel b Vettori	159	– c Taylor b Vettori		20
A. D. Mathews c McCullum b Vettori	39			
†H. A. P. W. Jayawardene c Flynn b Vettori	7	– (6) not out		30
K. M. D. N. Kulasekara c McCullum b Martin	18			
M. T. T. Mirando c O'Brien b Vettori	0			
M. Muralitharan c McCullum b Martin	8			
B. A. W. Mendis not out	0			
B 1, l-b 2, w 2, n-b 2	7	B 5, l-b 3		8

1/0 (1) 2/16 (3) 3/134 (2)   **452**   1/19 (1) 2/120 (3)   (4 wkts dec.) **259**
4/300 (4) 5/386 (6) 6/408 (7)   3/174 (4)
7/444 (5) 8/444 (8) 9/452 (10) 10/452 (9)   4/205 (5)

Martin 23–5–77–4; O'Brien 21–1–125–2; Oram 7–1–25–0; Vettori 37.4–9–78–4; Patel 24–3–120–0; Ryder 5–1–24–0. *Second Innings*—Martin 5–1–25–0; O'Brien 8–1–45–1; Oram 5–0–31–0; Vettori 19–3–81–1; Patel 12–0–69–1.

New Zealand

T. G. McIntosh lbw b Muralitharan	69	– (4) c Samaraweera b Mirando		0
M. J. Guptill b Mirando	24	– (1) b Mirando		18
D. R. Flynn b Mendis	14	– (2) c D. P. M. D. Jayawardene b Kulasekara		0
J. S. Patel lbw b Muralitharan	26	– (9) st H. A. P. W. Jayawardene b Muralitharan		22
L. R. P. L. Taylor c H. A. P. W. Jayawardene b Mirando	35	– (3) c H. A. P. W. Jayawardene b D. P. M. D. Jayawardene		16
J. D. Ryder b Kulasekara	42	– (7) c H. A. P. W. Jayawardene b Muralitharan		24
†B. B. McCullum b Mirando	1	– (8) run out		29
J. D. P. Oram c sub B. S. M. Warnapura b Muralitharan	12	– (5) lbw b Mendis		21
*D. L. Vettori b Mirando	42	– (6) c H. A. P. W. Jayawardene b Mendis		67
I. E. O'Brien c H. A. P. W. Jayawardene b Muralitharan	9	– c Paranavitana b Muralitharan		5
C. S. Martin not out	2	– not out		0
B 6, l-b 5, w 1, n-b 11	23	B 4, l-b 1, n-b 3		8

1/45 (2) 2/80 (3) 3/129 (4)   **299**   1/1 (2) 2/37 (1) 3/39 (4)   **210**
4/180 (5) 5/188 (1) 6/195 (7)   4/45 (3) 5/86 (5) 6/134 (7)
7/223 (8) 8/259 (6) 9/290 (10) 10/299 (9)   7/167 (6) 8/204 (9) 9/210 (10) 10/210 (8)

Kulasekara 10–2–41–1; Mirando 23–2–81–4; Mendis 39–8–85–1; Muralitharan 42–10–73–4; Paranavitana 2–0–8–0. *Second Innings*—Kulasekara 8–2–20–1; Mirando 14–3–37–2; Mendis 18.5–4–50–2; Muralitharan 27–4–88–3; D. P. M. D. Jayawardene 4–1–10–1.

Umpires: D. J. Harper *(Australia)* (84) and N. J. Llong *(England)* (5).
Third umpire: E. A. R. de Silva *(Sri Lanka)*. Referee: A. J. Pycroft *(Zimbabwe)* (5).

Close of play: First day, Sri Lanka 293-3 (Jayawardene 108, Samaraweera 82); Second day, New Zealand 87-2 (McIntosh 36, Patel 6); Third day, New Zealand 281-8 (Vettori 33, O'Brien 3); Fourth day, New Zealand 30-1 (Guptill 17, Taylor 8).

SRI LANKA v NEW ZEALAND 2009 (2nd Test)

At Sinhalese Sports Club, Colombo, on August 26, 27, 28, 29, 30, 2009.
Toss: Sri Lanka. Result: SRI LANKA won by 96 runs.
Debuts: none.
Man of the Match: D. P. M. D. Jayawardene. Man of the Series: T. T. Samaraweera.

Sri Lanka completed the 12th win in their last 16 home Tests and swept the short series, although New Zealand – set a stiff target of 494 – made a gallant attempt to win a Test in Sri Lanka for the first time since May 1998. The main resistance came, almost inevitably, from their captain, Vettori, who battled more than four hours for his fourth and highest Test century, after becoming the second New Zealander (after Richard Hadlee) to take 300 Test wickets when he dismissed Sangakkara earlier in the match. But Sri Lanka's batting proved too strong: Jayawardene shared another big partnership with Samaraweera, who continued a triumphant year with the bat – punctuated by being shot in the leg in Pakistan – with his fourth century (two of them doubles) in eight Tests, and 1,083 runs at 83 in the year so far. Only Taylor got going in New Zealand's first innings as Muralitharan and slow left-armer Herath (preferred to Ajantha Mendis) twirled away. It was a similar story in the second innings, Herath completing the third five-for in his last three Tests (after none in his first 15). Jayawardene was dismissed in the nineties twice in the match, only the fifth such instance in Tests, following Clem Hill of Australia (who made 98 and 97 against England at Adelaide in 1901-02, after scoring 99 in his previous innings of the series), England's Frank Woolley of England in 1921, and West Indies' Gordon Greenidge (who did it twice, in 1976-77 and 1979-80).

Sri Lanka

N. T. Paranavitana c Taylor b Vettori	19	– (2) c McCullum b Vettori	34
T. M. Dilshan c and b O'Brien	29	– (1) c Guptill b Patel	33
*K. C. Sangakkara c Oram b Vettori	50	– c Taylor b Patel	109
D. P. M. D. Jayawardene c McCullum b O'Brien	92	– c Taylor b O'Brien	96
T. T. Samaraweera c McCullum b Patel	143	– lbw b Vettori	25
C. K. Kapugedera c Vettori b Patel	35	– not out	7
†H. A. P. W. Jayawardene c O'Brien b Martin	17		
K. T. G. D. Prasad c Taylor b Patel	6		
H. M. R. K. B. Herath lbw b Patel	0		
M. Muralitharan not out	17		
M. T. T. Mirando c Patel b Vettori	0		
B 2, l-b 5, n-b 1	8	L-b 1, w 2, n-b 4	7

1/34 (1) 2/75 (2) 3/115 (3)   416   1/56 (1) 2/89 (2)   (5 wkts dec.) 311
4/295 (4) 5/367 (6) 6/389 (7)   3/262 (3) 4/301 (5)
7/396 (8) 8/396 (9) 9/415 (5) 10/416 (11)   5/311 (4)

Martin 24–3–81–1; O'Brien 22–3–73–2; Vettori 40.3–12–104–3; Oram 21–7–56–0; Patel 20–3–78–4; Ryder 3–1–17–0. *Second Innings*—Vettori 24–4–62–2; O'Brien 15.2–1–77–1; Martin 9–0–34–0; Patel 34–2–122–2; Ryder 3–0–15–0.

New Zealand

T. G. McIntosh lbw b Prasad	5	– b Prasad	7
M. J. Guptill c Muralitharan b Mirando	35	– c H. A. P. W. Jayawardene b Herath	28
D. R. Flynn c H. A. P. W. Jayawardene b Mirando	13	– lbw b Herath	50
L. R. P. L. Taylor c H. A. P. W. Jayawardene b Herath	81	– c D. P. M. D. Jayawardene b Herath	27
J. D. Ryder c Paranavitana b Herath	23	– lbw b Herath	38
J. S. Patel c D. P. M. D. Jayawardene b Muralitharan	1	– (9) c Kapugedera b Muralitharan	12
†B. B. McCullum c D. P. M. D. Jayawardene b Muralitharan	18	– (6) b Muralitharan	13
J. D. P. Oram c Kapugedera b Herath	24	– (7) c Sangakkara b Dilshan	56
*D. L. Vettori c Kapugedera b Dilshan	23	– (8) c Herath b Muralitharan	140
I. E. O'Brien lbw b Muralitharan	4	– c H. A. P. W. Jayawardene b Herath	12
C. S. Martin not out	0	– not out	0
L-b 3, w 2, n-b 2	7	L-b 13, n-b 1	14

1/14 (1) 2/49 (3) 3/63 (2)   234   1/36 (1) 2/41 (2) 3/97 (4)   397
4/148 (5) 5/149 (6) 6/183 (7)   4/131 (3) 5/158 (6) 6/176 (5)
7/183 (4) 8/226 (9) 9/234 (8) 10/234 (10)   7/300 (7) 8/318 (9) 9/387 (10) 10/397 (8)

Dilshan 3–0–12–1; Mirando 9–2–37–2; Prasad 6–0–41–1; Herath 34–11–70–3; Muralitharan 25.4–2–71–3. *Second Innings*—Paranavitana 1–0–2–0; Mirando 23.3–1–78–0; Prasad 15–1–56–1; Herath 48–9–139–5; Muralitharan 28.2–2–85–3; Dilshan 6–0–15–1; Kapugedera 2–0–9–0.

Umpires: D. J. Harper *(Australia)* (85) and N. J. Llong *(England)* (6).
Third umpire: H. D. P. K. Dharmasena *(Sri Lanka)*. Referee: A. J. Pycroft *(Zimbabwe)* (6).

Close of play: First day, Sri Lanka 262-3 (Jayawardene 79, Samaraweera 78); Second day, New Zealand 159-5 (Taylor 70, McCullum 5); Third day, Sri Lanka 157-2 (Sangakkara 64, Jayawardene 23); Fourth day, New Zealand 182-6 (Oram 7, Vettori 5).

423

Individual Test Career Records

Compiled by Philip Bailey

These career records for all players appearing in official Test matches are complete to
November 15, 2009.

Symbols: * not out; † in the Innings column denotes a left-hand batsman, in the
Balls column a left-arm bowler;
‡ marks a player who appeared in official Test matches for more than one team (his record
for each team is given under that country, while combined totals are shown at the
end of this section).

INDIVIDUAL CAREER RECORDS – ENGLAND

	First Test	Last Test	Tests		BATTING AND FIELDING									BOWLING					
				Inns	NO	Runs	HS	Avge	100	50	Ct	St	Balls	Runs	Wkts	Avge	BB	5wI	10wM
Abel, R.	1888	1902	13	22	2	744	132*	37.20	2	2	13	–	120	59	1	59.00	1-42	–	–
Absolom, C.A.	1878-79	1878-79	1	2	0	58	52	29.00	–	1	–	–	–	–	–	–	–	–	–
Adams, C.J.	1999-00	1999-00	5	8	0	104	31	13.00	–	–	6	–	54†	49	1	49.00	1-49	–	–
Afzaal, U.	2001	2001	3	6†	1	83	54	16.60	–	1	–	–	552	373	4	93.25	2-51	–	–
Agnew, J.P.	1984	1985	3	4	3	10	5	10.00	–	–	–	–	216	136	5	27.20	3-80	–	–
Ali, K.	2003	2003	1	2	0	10	9	5.00	–	–	–	–	–	–	–	–	–	–	–
Allen, D.A.	1959-60	1966	39	51	15	918	88	25.50	–	5	10	–	11297	3779	122	30.97	5-30	4	–
Allen, G.O.B.	1930	1947-48	25	33	2	750	122	24.19	1	3	20	–	4386	2379	81	29.37	7-80	5	1
Allom, M.J.C.	1929-30	1930-31	5	3	2	14	8*	14.00	–	–	–	–	817	265	14	18.92	5-38	1	–
Allott, P.J.W.	1981	1985	13	18	3	213	52*	14.20	–	1	4	–	2225	1084	26	41.69	6-61	1	–
Ambrose, T.R.	2007-08	2008-09	11	16	1	447	102	29.80	1	1	31	–	–	–	–	–	–	–	–
Ames, L.E.G.	1929	1938-39	47	72	12	2434	149	40.56	8	7	74	23	–	–	–	–	–	–	–
Amiss, D.L.	1966	1977	50	88	10	3612	262*	46.30	11	11	24	–	–	–	–	–	–	–	–
Anderson, J.M.	2003	2009	42	56†	27	412	34	14.20	–	–	17	–	8453	4883	140	34.87	7-43	7	–
Andrew, K.V.	1954-55	1963	2	4	1	29	15	9.66	–	–	1	–	–	–	–	–	–	–	–
Appleyard, R.	1954	1956	9	9	6	51	19*	17.00	–	–	4	–	1596	554	31	17.87	5-51	1	–
Archer, A.G.	1898-99	1898-99	1	2	1	31	24*	31.00	–	–	–	–	–	–	–	–	–	–	–
Armitage, T.	1876-77	1876-77	2	3	0	33	21	11.00	–	–	–	–	12	15	0	–	–	–	–
Arnold, E.G.	1903-04	1907	10	15	3	160	40	13.33	–	–	8	–	1677	788	31	25.41	5-37	1	–
Arnold, G.G.	1967	1975	34	46	11	421	59	12.02	–	1	9	–	7650	3254	115	28.29	6-45	6	–
Arnold, J.	1931	1931	1	2	0	34	34	17.00	–	–	–	–	–	–	–	–	–	–	–
Astill, W.E.	1927-28	1929-30	9	15	0	190	40	12.66	–	–	7	–	2182	856	25	34.24	4-58	–	–
Atherton, M.A.	1989	2001	115	212	7	7728	185*	37.69	16	46	83	–	408	302	2	151.00	1-20	–	–
Athey, C.W.J.	1980	1988	23	41	1	919	123	22.97	1	4	13	–	–	–	–	–	–	–	–
Attewell, W.	1884-85	1891-92	10	15	6	150	43*	16.66	–	–	9	–	2850	626	28	22.35	4-42	–	–
Bailey, R.J.	1988	1989-90	4	8	0	119	43	14.87	–	–	–	–	–	–	–	–	–	–	–
Bailey, T.E.	1949	1958-59	61	91	14	2290	134*	29.74	1	10	32	–	9712	3856	132	29.21	7-34	5	1
Bairstow, D.L.	1979	1980-81	4	7	1	125	59	20.83	–	1	12	1	–	–	–	–	–	–	–
Bakewell, A.H.	1931	1935	6	9	0	409	107	45.44	1	3	3	–	18	8	0	–	–	–	–
Balderstone, J.C.	1976	1976	2	4	0	39	35	9.75	–	–	1	–	96†	80	1	80.00	1-80	–	–
Barber, R.W.	1960	1968	28	45†	3	1495	185	35.59	1	9	21	–	3426	1806	42	43.00	4-132	–	–
Barber, W.	1935	1935	2	5†	0	83	44	20.75	–	–	1	–	2	0	1	0.00	1-0	–	–
Barlow, G.D.	1976-77	1977	3	5†	1	17	7*	4.25	–	–	–	–	–	–	–	–	–	–	–
Barlow, R.G.	1881-82	1886-87	17	30	4	591	62	22.73	–	2	14	–	2456†	767	34	22.55	7-40	3	–
Barnes, S.F.	1901-02	1913-14	27	39	9	242	38*	8.06	–	–	12	–	7873	3106	189	16.43	9-103	24	7
Barnes, W.	1880	1890	21	33	2	725	134	23.38	1	5	19	–	2289	793	51	15.54	6-28	3	–
Barnett, C.J.	1933	1948	20	35	4	1098	129	35.41	2	5	14	–	256	93	0	–	–	–	–
Barnett, K.J.	1988	1989	4	7	1	207	80	29.57	–	2	1	–	36	32	0	–	–	–	–
Barratt, F.	1929	1929-30	5	4	1	28	17	9.33	–	–	2	–	750	235	5	47.00	1-8	–	–
Barrington, K.F.	1955	1968	82	131	15	6806	256	58.67	20	35	58	–	2715	1300	29	44.82	3-4	–	–
Barton, V.A.	1891-92	1891-92	1	1	0	23	23	23.00	–	–	–	–	–	–	–	–	–	–	–

INDIVIDUAL CAREER RECORDS – ENGLAND *continued*

	First Test	Last Test	Tests	BATTING AND FIELDING									BOWLING						
				Inns	NO	Runs	HS	Avge	100	50	Ct	St	Balls	Runs	Wkts	Avge	BB	5wI	10wM
Bates, W.	1881-82	1886-87	15	26	2	656	64	27.33	–	5	9		2364	821	50	16.42	7-28	4	1
Batty, G.J	2003-04	2005	7	8	1	144	38	20.57	–	–	3		1394	733	11	66.63	3-55	–	–
Bean, G.	1891-92	1891-92	3	5	0	92	50	18.40	–	–	4		–	–	–	–	–	–	–
Bedser, A.V.	1946	1955	51	71	15	714	79	12.75	–	1	26		15918	5876	236	24.89	7-44	15	5
Bell, I.R.	2004	2009	49	88	9	3144	199	39.79	8	21	45		108	76	1	76.00	1-33	–	–
Benjamin, J.E.	1994	1994	1	1	0	0	0	0.00	–	–	–		168	80	4	20.00	4-42	–	–
Benson, M.R.	1986	1986	1	2†	0	51	30	25.50	–	–	–		–	–	–	–	–	–	–
Berry, R.	1950	1950	2	4†	2	6	4*	3.00	–	–	2		653†	228	9	25.33	5-63	1	–
Bicknell, M.P.	1993	2003	4	7	0	45	15	6.42	–	–	2		1080	543	14	38.78	4-84	–	–
Binks, J.G.	1963-64	1963-64	2	4	0	91	55	22.75	–	–	8		–	–	–	–	–	–	–
Bird, M.C.	1909-10	1913-14	10	16	1	280	61	18.66	–	1	5		259	120	8	15.00	3-11	–	–
Birkenshaw, J.	1972-73	1973-74	5	7†	0	148	64	21.14	–	1	3		1017	469	13	36.07	5-57	1	–
Blackwell, I.D.	2005-06	2005-06	1	1†	0	4	4	4.00	–	–	–		114†	71	0	–	–	–	–
Blakey, R.J.	1992-93	1992-93	2	4	0	7	6	1.75	–	–	2		–	–	–	–	–	–	–
Bligh, Hon. I.F.W.	1882-83	1882-83	4	7	1	62	19	10.33	–	–	7		–	–	–	–	–	–	–
Blythe, C.	1901-02	1909-10	19	31	12	183	27	9.63	–	–	6		4546†	1863	100	18.63	8-59	9	4
Board, J.H.	1898-99	1905-06	6	12	2	108	29	10.80	–	–	8	3	–	–	–	–	–	–	–
Bolus, J.B.	1963	1963-64	7	12	0	496	88	41.33	–	4	2		18†	16	0	–	–	–	–
Booth, M.W.	1913-14	1913-14	2	2	0	46	32	23.00	–	–	–		312	130	7	18.57	4-49	–	–
Bopara, R.S.	2007-08	2009	10	15	0	502	143	33.46	3	–	5		296	199	1	199.00	1-39	–	–
Bosanquet, B.J.T.	1903-04	1905	7	14	3	147	27	13.36	–	–	9		970	604	25	24.16	8-107	2	–
Botham, I.T.	1977	1992	102	161	6	5200	208	33.54	14	22	120		21815	10878	383	28.40	8-34	27	4
Bowden, M.P.	1888-89	1888-89	2	2	0	25	25	12.50	–	–	1		–	–	–	–	–	–	–
Bowes, W.E.	1932	1946	15	11	5	28	10*	4.66	–	–	2		3655	1519	68	22.33	6-33	6	–
Bowley, E.H.	1929	1929-30	5	7	0	252	109	36.00	1	–	2		252	116	0	–	–	–	–
Boycott, G.	1964	1981-82	108	193	23	8114	246*	47.72	22	42	33		944	382	7	54.57	3-47	–	–
Bradley, W.M.	1899	1899	2	2	1	23	23*	23.00	–	–	–		625	233	6	38.83	5-67	1	–
Braund, L.C.	1901-02	1907-08	23	41	3	987	104	25.97	3	2	39		3805	1810	47	38.51	8-81	3	–
Brearley, J.M.	1976	1981	39	66	3	1442	91	22.88	–	9	52		–	–	–	–	–	–	–
Brearley, W.	1905	1912	4	5	2	21	11*	7.00	–	–	–		705	359	17	21.11	5-110	1	–
Brennan, D.V.	1951	1951	2	2	0	16	16	8.00	–	–	–		–	–	–	–	–	–	–
Bresnan, T.T.	2009	2009	2	2	0	9	9	9.00	–	–	2		186	97	3	32.33	3-45	–	–
Briggs, J.	1884-85	1899	33	50	5	815	121	18.11	–	2	12		5332†	2095	118	17.75	8-11	9	4
Broad, B.C.	1984	1989	25	44†	2	1661	162	39.54	6	6	10		6	4	0	–	–	–	–
Broad, S.C.J.	2007-08	2009	22	31†	6	767	76	30.68	–	5	5		4187	2290	64	35.78	6-91	3	–
Brockwell, W.	1893	1899	7	12	0	202	49	16.83	–	–	6		582	309	5	61.80	3-33	–	–
Bromley-Davenport, H.R.	1895-96	1898-99	4	6	0	128	84	21.33	–	–	1		155†	98	4	24.50	2-46	–	–
Brookes, D.	1947-48	1947-48	1	2	0	17	10	8.50	–	–	1		–	–	–	–	–	–	–
Brown, A.	1961-62	1961-62	2	1	1	3	3*	–	–	–	1		323	150	3	50.00	3-27	–	–
Brown, D.J.	1965	1969	26	34	5	342	44*	11.79	–	–	7		5098	2237	79	28.31	5-42	2	–
Brown, F.R.	1931	1953	22	30	1	734	79	25.31	–	5	22		3260	1398	45	31.06	5-49	1	–
Brown, G.	1921	1922-23	7	12†	2	299	84	29.90	–	2	9	3	35	22	0	–	–	–	–
Brown, J.T.	1894-95	1899	8	16	3	470	140	36.15	1	2	7		–	–	–	–	–	–	–
Brown, S.J.E.	1996	1996	1	2	1	11	10*	11.00	–	–	1		198†	138	2	69.00	1-60	–	–

INDIVIDUAL CAREER RECORDS – ENGLAND continued

				BATTING AND FIELDING									BOWLING						
	First Test	Last Test	Tests	Inns	NO	Runs	HS	Avge	100	50	Ct	St	Balls	Runs	Wkts	Avge	BB	5wI	10wM
Buckenham, C.P.	1909-10	1909-10	4	7	0	43	17	6.14	–	–	2	–	1182	593	21	28.23	5-115	1	1
Butcher, A.R.	1979	1979	1	2†	0	34	20	17.00	–	–	–	–	12†	9	0	–	–	–	–
Butcher, M.A.	1997	2004-05	71	131†	7	4288	173*	34.58	8	23	61	–	901	541	15	36.06	4-42	–	–
Butcher, R.O.	1980-81	1980-81	3	5	0	71	32	14.20	–	–	3	–	–	–	–	–	–	–	–
Butler, H.J.	1947	1947-48	2	2	1	15	15*	15.00	–	–	1	–	552	215	12	17.91	4-34	–	–
Butt, H.R.	1895-96	1895-96	3	4	1	22	13	7.33	–	–	1	1	–	–	–	–	–	–	–
Caddick, A.R.	1993	2002-03	62	95	12	861	49*	10.37	–	–	21	–	13558	6999	234	29.91	7-46	13	1
Calthorpe, Hon. F.S.G.	1929-30	1929-30	4	7	0	129	49	18.42	–	–	3	–	204	91	1	91.00	1-38	–	–
Capel, D.J.	1987	1989-90	15	25	1	374	98	15.58	–	2	6	–	2000	1064	21	50.66	3-88	–	–
Carr, A.W.	1922-23	1929	11	13	1	237	63	19.75	–	1	3	–	–	–	–	–	–	–	–
Carr, D.B.	1951-52	1951-52	2	4	0	135	76	33.75	–	1	–	–	210†	140	2	70.00	2-84	–	–
Carr, D.W.	1909	1909	1	1	0	0	0	0.00	–	–	–	–	414	282	7	40.28	5-146	1	–
Cartwright, T.W.	1964	1965	5	7	2	26	9	5.20	–	–	2	–	1611	544	15	36.26	6-94	1	–
Chapman, A.P.F.	1924	1930-31	26	36†	4	925	121	28.90	1	5	32	–	40†	20	0	–	–	–	–
Charlwood, H.R.J.	1876-77	1876-77	2	4	0	63	36	15.75	–	–	–	–	–	–	–	–	–	–	–
Chatterton, W.	1891-92	1891-92	1	2	0	48	48	48.00	–	–	1	–	–	–	–	–	–	–	–
Childs, J.H.	1988	1988	2	4†	4	2	2*	–	–	–	1	–	516†	183	3	61.00	1-13	–	–
Christopherson, S.	1884	1884	1	1	0	17	17	17.00	–	–	–	–	136	69	1	69.00	1-52	–	–
Clark, E.W.	1929	1934	8	9†	5	36	10	9.00	–	–	1	–	1931†	899	32	28.09	5-98	1	–
Clarke, R.	2003-04	2003-04	2	3	0	96	55	32.00	–	1	1	–	174	60	4	15.00	2-7	–	–
Clay, J.C.	1935	1935	1	–	–	–	–	–	–	–	1	–	192	75	0	–	–	–	–
Close, D.B.	1949	1976	22	37†	2	887	70	25.34	–	4	24	–	1212	532	18	29.55	4-35	–	–
Coldwell, L.J.	1962	1964	7	7	5	9	6*	4.50	–	–	1	–	1668	610	22	27.72	6-85	1	–
Collingwood, P.D.	2003-04	2009	53	93	9	3565	206	42.44	9	16	67	–	1527	846	15	56.40	3-23	–	–
Compton, D.C.S.	1937	1956-57	78	131	15	5807	278	50.06	17	28	49	–	2710†	1410	25	56.40	5-70	1	–
Cook, A.N.	2005-06	2009	48	87†	5	3509	160	42.79	9	20	44	–	6	1	0	–	–	–	–
Cook, C.	1947	1947	1	2	0	4	4	2.00	–	–	–	–	180†	127	0	–	–	–	–
Cook, G.	1981-82	1982-83	7	13	0	203	66	15.61	–	2	9	–	42†	27	0	–	–	–	–
Cook, N.G.B.	1983	1989	15	25	4	179	31	8.52	–	–	5	–	4174†	1689	52	32.48	6-65	4	1
Cope, G.A.	1977-78	1977-78	3	3	0	40	22	13.33	–	–	1	–	864	277	8	34.62	3-102	1	–
Copson, W.H.	1939	1947	3	3	2	6	6	6.00	–	–	–	–	762	297	15	19.80	5-85	1	–
Cork, D.G.	1995	2002	37	56	8	864	59	18.00	–	3	18	–	7678	3906	131	29.81	7-43	5	–
Cornford, W.L.	1929-30	1929-30	4	4	0	36	18	9.00	–	–	5	3	–	–	–	–	–	–	–
Cottam, R.M.H.	1968-69	1972-73	4	5	1	27	13	6.75	–	–	2	–	903	327	14	23.35	4-50	–	–
Coventry, Hon. C.J.	1888-89	1888-89	2	2	1	13	12	13.00	–	–	–	–	–	–	–	–	–	–	–
Cowans, N.G.	1982-83	1985	19	29	7	175	36	7.95	–	–	9	–	3452	2003	51	39.27	6-77	2	–
Cowdrey, C.S.	1984-85	1988	6	8	1	101	38	14.42	–	–	5	–	399	309	4	77.25	2-65	–	–
Cowdrey, M.C.	1954-55	1974-75	114	188	15	7624	182	44.06	22	38	120	–	119	104	0	–	–	–	–
Coxon, A.	1948	1948	1	2†	0	19	19	9.50	–	–	1	–	378	172	3	57.33	2-90	–	–
Cranston, J.	1890	1890	1	2	0	31	16	15.50	–	–	1	–	–	–	–	–	–	–	–
Cranston, K.	1947	1948	8	14	0	209	45	14.92	–	1	3	–	1010	461	18	25.61	4-12	–	–
Crapp, J.F.	1948-49	1948-49	7	13†	2	319	56	29.00	–	3	7	–	–	–	–	–	–	–	–
Crawford, J.N.	1905-06	1907-08	12	23	2	469	74	22.33	–	2	13	–	2203	1150	39	29.48	5-48	3	–

INDIVIDUAL CAREER RECORDS – ENGLAND *continued*

| | | | | | | BATTING AND FIELDING | | | | | | | BOWLING | | | | | | |
	First Test	Last Test	Tests	Inns	NO	Runs	HS	Avge	100	50	Ct	St	Balls	Runs	Wkts	Avge	BB	5wI	10wM
Crawley, J.P.	1994	2002-03	37	61	9	1800	156*	34.61	4	9	29	—	—	—	—	—	—	—	—
Croft, R.D.B.	1996	2001	21	34	8	421	37*	16.19	—	—	10	—	4619	1825	49	37.24	5-95	1	—
Curtis, T.S.	1988	1989	5	9	0	140	41	15.55	—	—	3	—	18	7	0	—	—	—	—
Cuttell, W.R.	1898-99	1898-99	2	4	0	65	21	16.25	—	—	2	—	285	73	6	12.16	3-17	—	—
Dawson, E.W.	1927-28	1929-30	5	9	0	175	55	19.44	—	1	—	—	—	—	—	—	—	—	—
Dawson, R.K.J.	2001-02	2002-03	7	13	3	114	19*	11.40	—	—	3	—	1116	677	11	61.54	4-134	—	—
Dean, H.	1912	1912	3	4†	2	10	8	5.00	—	—	2	—	447†	153	11	13.90	4-19	—	—
DeFreitas, P.A.J.	1986-87	1995	44	68	5	934	88	14.82	—	4	14	—	9838	4700	140	33.57	7-70	4	—
Denness, M.H.	1969	1975	28	45	3	1667	188	39.69	4	7	28	—	—	—	—	—	—	—	—
Denton, D.	1905	1909-10	11	22	1	424	104	20.19	1	1	8	—	—	—	—	—	—	—	—
Dewes, J.G.	1948	1950-51	5	10†	0	121	67	12.10	—	1	—	—	—	—	—	—	—	—	—
Dexter, E.R.	1958	1968	62	102	8	4502	205	47.89	9	27	29	—	5317	2306	66	34.93	4-10	—	—
Dilley, G.R.	1979-80	1989	41	58†	19	521	56	13.35	—	2	10	—	8192	4107	138	29.76	6-38	6	—
Dipper, A.E.	1921	1921	1	2	0	51	40	25.50	—	—	—	—	—	—	—	—	—	—	—
Doggart, G.H.G.	1950	1950	2	4	0	76	29	19.00	—	—	3	—	—	—	—	—	—	—	—
D'Oliveira, B.L.	1966	1972	44	70	8	2484	158	40.06	5	15	29	—	5706	1859	47	39.55	3-46	—	—
Dollery, H.E.	1947	1950	4	7	0	72	37	10.28	—	—	1	—	—	—	—	—	—	—	—
Dolphin, A.	1920-21	1920-21	1	2	0	1	1	0.50	—	—	1	—	—	—	—	—	—	—	—
Douglas, J.W.H.T.	1911-12	1924-25	23	35	2	962	119	29.15	1	6	9	—	2812	1486	45	33.02	5-46	1	—
Downton, P.R.	1980-81	1988	30	48	8	785	74	19.62	—	4	70	5	—	—	—	—	—	—	—
Druce, N.F.	1897-98	1897-98	5	9	0	252	64	28.00	—	1	5	—	—	—	—	—	—	—	—
Ducat, A.	1921	1921	1	2	0	5	3	2.50	—	—	—	—	—	—	—	—	—	—	—
Duckworth, G.	1924	1936	24	28	12	234	39*	14.62	—	—	45	15	—	—	—	—	—	—	—
Duleepsinhji, K.S.	1929	1931	12	19	2	995	173	58.52	3	5	10	—	6	7	0	—	—	—	—
Durston, F.J.	1921	1921	1	2	1	8	6*	8.00	—	—	—	—	202	136	5	27.20	4-102	—	—
Ealham, M.A.	1996	1998	8	13	3	210	53*	21.00	—	2	4	—	1060	488	17	28.70	4-21	—	—
Edmonds, P.H.	1975	1987	51	65	15	875	64	17.50	—	2	42	—	12028†	4273	125	34.18	7-66	2	—
Edrich, J.H.	1963	1976	77	127†	9	5138	310*	43.54	12	24	43	—	30	23	0	—	—	—	—
Edrich, W.J.	1938	1954-55	39	63	2	2440	219	40.00	6	13	39	—	3234	1693	41	41.29	4-68	—	—
Elliott, H.	1927-28	1933-34	4	5	1	61	37*	15.25	—	—	8	3	—	—	—	—	—	—	—
Ellison, R.M.	1984	1986	11	16†	1	202	41	13.46	—	—	2	—	2264	1048	35	29.94	6-77	3	—
Emburey, J.E.	1978	1995	64	96	20	1713	75	22.53	—	10	34	—	15391	5646	147	38.40	7-78	6	—
Emmett, G.M.	1948	1948	1	1	0	10	10	5.00	—	—	—	—	—	—	—	—	—	—	—
Emmett, T.	1876-77	1881-82	7	13†	1	160	48	13.33	—	—	9	—	728†	284	9	31.55	7-68	1	—
Evans, A.J.	1921	1921	1	2	0	18	14	9.00	—	—	—	—	—	—	—	—	—	—	—
Evans, T.G.	1946	1959	91	133	14	2439	104	20.49	2	8	173	46	—	—	—	—	—	—	—
Fagg, A.E.	1936	1939	5	8	0	150	39	18.75	—	—	5	—	—	—	—	—	—	—	—
Fairbrother, N.H.	1987	1992-93	10	15†	1	219	83	15.64	—	1	4	—	12†	9	0	—	—	—	—
Fane, F.L.	1905-06	1909-10	14	27	1	682	143	26.23	1	3	6	—	—	—	—	—	—	—	—
Farnes, K.	1934	1938-39	15	17	5	58	20	4.83	—	—	1	—	3932	1719	60	28.65	6-96	3	—
Farrimond, W.	1930-31	1935	4	7	0	116	35	16.57	—	—	5	2	—	—	—	—	—	—	—

INDIVIDUAL CAREER RECORDS – ENGLAND continued

				Batting and Fielding									Bowling						
	Tests	First Test	Last Test	Inns	NO	Runs	HS	Avge	100	50	Ct	St	Balls	Runs	Wkts	Avge	BB	5wI	10wM
Fender, P.G.H.	13	1920-21	1929	21	1	380	60	19.00	–	2	14	–	2178	1185	29	40.86	5-90	2	–
Ferris, J.J. ‡	1	1891-92	1891-92	1†	0	16	16	16.00	–	–	–	–	272†	91	13	7.00	7-37	2	1
Fielder, A.	6	1903-04	1907-08	12	5	78	20	11.14	–	–	4	–	1491	711	26	27.34	6-82	1	–
Fishlock, L.B.	4	1936	1946-47	5†	1	47	19*	11.75	–	–	1	–	–	–	–	–	–	–	–
Flavell, J.A.	4	1961	1964	6†	2	31	14	7.75	–	–	–	–	792	367	7	52.42	2-65	–	–
Fletcher, K.W.R.	59	1968	1981-82	96	14	3272	216	39.90	7	19	54	–	285	193	2	96.50	1-6	–	–
Flintoff, A. ‡	79	1998	2009	128	9	3795	167	31.89	5	26	52	–	14747	7303	219	33.34	5-58	3	–
Flowers, W.	8	1884-85	1893	14	0	254	56	18.14	–	1	2	–	858	296	14	21.14	5-46	1	–
Ford, F.G.J.	5	1894-95	1894-95	9†	0	168	48	18.66	–	–	5	–	204†	129	1	129.00	1-47	–	–
Foster, F.R.	11	1911-12	1912	15	1	330	71	23.57	–	3	11	–	2447†	926	45	20.57	6-91	4	–
Foster, J.S.	7	2001-02	2002-03	12	3	226	48	25.11	–	1	17	1	–	–	–	–	–	–	–
Foster, N.A.	29	1983	1993	45	7	446	39	11.73	–	1	7	–	6261	2891	88	32.85	8-107	5	1
Foster, R.E.	8	1903-04	1907	14	0	602	287	46.30	1	1	13	–	–	–	–	–	–	–	–
Fothergill, A.J.	2	1888-89	1888-89	2†	0	33	32	16.50	–	–	–	–	321†	90	8	11.25	4-19	–	–
Fowler, G.	21	1982	1984-85	37†	0	1307	201	35.32	3	8	10	–	18	11	0	–	–	–	–
Fraser, A.R.C.	46	1989	1998-99	67	15	388	32	7.46	–	–	9	–	10876	4836	177	27.32	8-53	13	2
Freeman, A.P.	12	1924-25	1929	16	5	154	50*	14.00	–	–	4	–	3732	1707	66	25.86	7-71	5	3
French, B.N.	16	1986	1987-88	21	4	308	59	18.11	–	1	38	1	–	–	–	–	–	–	–
Fry, C.B.	26	1895-96	1912	41	3	1223	144	32.18	2	7	17	–	10	3	0	–	–	–	–
Gallian, J.E.R.	3	1995	1995-96	6	0	74	28	12.33	–	–	1	–	84	62	0	–	–	–	–
Gatting, M.W.	79	1977-78	1994-95	138	14	4409	207	35.55	10	21	59	–	752	317	4	79.25	1-14	–	–
Gay, L.H.	1	1894-95	1894-95	2	0	37	33	18.50	–	–	3	1	–	–	–	–	–	–	–
Geary, G.	14	1924	1934	20	4	249	66	15.56	–	2	13	–	3810	1353	46	29.41	7-70	4	1
Gibb, P.A.	8	1938-39	1946-47	13	0	581	120	44.69	2	3	3	1	–	–	–	–	–	–	–
Giddins, E.S.H.	4	1999	2000	7	3	10	7	2.50	–	–	–	–	444	240	12	20.00	5-15	1	–
Gifford, N.	15	1964	1973	20†	9	179	25*	16.27	–	–	8	–	3084†	1026	33	31.09	5-55	1	–
Giles, A.F.	54	1998	2006-07	81	13	1421	59	20.89	–	4	33	–	12180†	5806	143	40.60	5-57	5	1
Gilligan, A.E.R.	11	1922-23	1924-25	16	3	209	39*	16.07	–	1	3	–	2404	1046	36	29.05	6-7	2	–
Gilligan, A.H.H.	4	1929-30	1929-30	4	0	71	32	17.75	–	–	–	–	–	–	–	–	–	–	–
Gimblett, H.	3	1936	1939	5	1	129	67*	32.25	–	1	1	–	–	–	–	–	–	–	–
Gladwin, C.	8	1947	1949	11	5	170	51*	28.33	–	1	1	–	2129	571	15	38.06	3-21	–	–
Goddard, T.W.J.	8	1930	1939	5	3	13	8	6.50	–	–	3	–	1563	588	22	26.72	6-29	1	–
Gooch, G.A.	118	1975	1994-95	215	6	8900	333	42.58	20	46	103	–	2655	1069	23	46.47	3-39	–	–
Gough, D.	58	1994	2003	86	18	855	65	12.57	–	2	13	–	11821	6503	229	28.39	6-42	9	–
Gover, A.R.	4	1936	1946	2	1	2	2*	2.00	–	–	1	–	816	359	8	44.87	3-85	–	–
Gower, D.I.	117	1978	1992	204†	18	8231	215	44.25	18	39	74	–	36	20	1	20.00	1-1	–	–
Grace, E.M.	1	1880	1880	2	0	36	36	18.00	–	–	1	–	–	–	–	–	–	–	–
Grace, G.F.	1	1880	1880	2	0	0	0	0.00	–	–	–	–	–	–	–	–	–	–	–
Grace, W.G.	22	1880	1899	36	2	1098	170	32.29	2	5	39	–	666	236	9	26.22	2-12	–	–
Graveney, T.W.	79	1951	1969	123	13	4882	258	44.38	11	20	80	–	260	167	1	167.00	1-34	–	–
Greenhough, T.	4	1959	1960	4	1	4	4	1.33	–	–	1	–	1129	357	16	22.31	5-35	1	–
Greenwood, A.	2	1876-77	1876-77	4	0	77	49	19.25	–	–	2	–	–	–	–	–	–	–	–
Greig, A.W.	58	1972	1977	93	4	3599	148	40.43	8	20	87	–	9802	4541	141	32.20	8-86	6	2

INDIVIDUAL CAREER RECORDS – ENGLAND *continued*

	First Test	Last Test	Tests	Inns	NO	Runs	HS	Avge	100	50	Ct	St	Balls	Runs	Wkts	Avge	BB	5wI	10wM
						BATTING AND FIELDING							BOWLING						
Greig, I.A.	1982	1982	2	4	0	26	14	6.50	–	–	–	–	188	114	4	28.50	4-53	–	–
Grieve, B.A.F.	1888-89	1888-89	2	3	2	40	14*	40.00	–	–	–	–	–	–	–	–	–	–	–
Griffith, S.C.	1947-48	1948-49	3	5	0	157	140	31.40	1	–	5	–	–	–	–	–	–	–	–
Gunn, G.	1907-08	1929-30	15	29	1	1120	122*	40.00	2	7	15	–	12	8	0	–	–	–	–
Gunn, J.R.	1901-02	1905	6	10†	2	85	24	10.62	–	–	3	–	999†	387	18	21.50	5-76	1	–
Gunn, W.	1886-87	1899	11	20	2	392	102*	21.77	1	1	5	–	–	–	–	–	–	–	–
Habib, A.	1999	1999	2	3	0	26	19	8.66	–	–	–	–	–	–	–	–	–	–	–
Haig, N.E.	1921	1929-30	5	9	0	126	47	14.00	–	–	4	–	1026	448	13	34.46	3-73	–	–
Haigh, S.	1898-99	1912	11	18	3	113	25	7.53	–	–	8	–	1294	622	24	25.91	6-11	1	–
Hallows, C.	1921	1928	2	2†	0	42	26	42.00	–	–	–	–	–	–	–	–	–	–	–
Hamilton, G.M.	1999-00	1999-00	1	2†	0	0	0	0.00	–	–	–	–	90	63	0	–	–	–	–
Hammond, W.R.	1927-28	1946-47	85	140	16	7249	336*	58.45	22	24	110	–	7969	3138	83	37.80	5-36	2	–
Hampshire, J.H.	1969	1975	8	16	1	403	107	26.86	1	2	9	–	–	–	–	–	–	–	–
Hardinge, H.T.W.	1921	1921	1	2	0	30	25	15.00	–	–	1	–	–	–	–	–	–	–	–
Hardstaff, J., sen.	1907-08	1907-08	5	10	0	311	72	31.10	–	3	–	–	–	–	–	–	–	–	–
Hardstaff, J., jun.	1935	1948	23	38	3	1636	205*	46.74	4	10	9	–	–	–	–	–	–	–	–
Harmison, S.J. ‡	2002	2009	62	84	23	742	49*	12.16	–	–	7	–	13192	7091	222	31.94	7-12	8	1
Harris, Lord	1878-79	1884	4	6	1	145	52	29.00	–	1	2	–	32	29	0	–	–	–	–
Hartley, J.C.	1905-06	1905-06	2	4	0	15	9	3.75	–	–	2	–	192	115	1	115.00	1-62	–	–
Hawke, Lord	1895-96	1898-99	5	8	1	55	30	7.85	–	–	3	–	–	–	–	–	–	–	–
Hayes, E.G.	1905-06	1912	5	9	1	86	35	10.75	–	–	2	–	90	52	1	52.00	1-28	–	–
Hayes, F.C.	1973	1976	9	17	1	244	106*	15.25	1	–	7	–	–	–	–	–	–	–	–
Hayward, T.W.	1895-96	1909	35	60	2	1999	137	34.46	3	12	19	–	893	514	14	36.71	4-22	1	–
Headley, D.W.	1997	1999	15	26	4	186	31	8.45	–	–	7	–	3026	1671	60	27.85	6-60	1	–
Hearne, A.	1891-92	1891-92	1	2	0	9	9	9.00	–	–	1	–	–	–	–	–	–	–	–
Hearne, F. ‡	1888-89	1888-89	2	2	0	47	27	23.50	–	–	1	–	–	–	–	–	–	–	–
Hearne, G.G.	1891-92	1891-92	1	1†	0	0	0	0.00	–	–	1	–	–	–	–	–	–	–	–
Hearne, J.T.	1891-92	1899	12	18	4	126	40	9.00	–	–	4	–	2976	1082	49	22.08	6-41	4	1
Hearne, J.W.	1911-12	1926	24	36	5	806	114	26.00	1	2	13	–	2926	1462	30	48.73	5-49	1	–
Hegg, W.K.	1998-99	1998-99	2	4	0	30	15	7.50	–	–	8	–	–	–	–	–	–	–	–
Hemmings, E.E.	1982	1990-91	16	21	4	383	95	22.52	–	2	5	–	4437	1825	43	42.44	6-58	1	–
Hendren, E.H.	1920-21	1934-35	51	83	9	3525	205*	47.63	7	21	33	–	47	31	1	31.00	1-27	–	–
Hendrick, M.	1974	1981	30	35	15	128	15	6.40	–	–	25	–	6208	2248	87	25.83	4-28	–	–
Heseltine, C.	1895-96	1895-96	2	2	0	18	18	9.00	–	–	3	–	157	84	5	16.80	5-38	1	–
Hick, G.A.	1991	2000-01	65	114	6	3383	178	31.32	6	18	90	–	3057	1306	23	56.78	4-126	–	–
Higgs, K.	1965	1968	15	19†	3	185	63	11.56	–	1	4	–	4112	1473	71	20.74	6-91	2	–
Hill, A.	1876-77	1876-77	2	4	2	101	49	50.50	–	–	1	–	340	130	7	18.57	4-27	–	–
Hill, A.J.L.	1895-96	1895-96	3	4	0	251	124	62.75	1	1	1	–	40	8	4	2.00	4-8	–	–
Hilton, M.J.	1950	1951-52	4	6	1	37	15	7.40	–	–	1	–	1244†	477	14	34.07	5-61	3	–
Hirst, G.H.	1897-98	1909	24	38	3	790	85	22.57	–	5	18	–	4010†	1770	59	30.00	5-48	3	–
Hitch, J.W.	1911-12	1921	7	10	3	103	51*	14.71	–	1	4	–	462	325	7	46.42	2-31	–	–
Hobbs, J.B.	1907-08	1930	61	102	7	5410	211	56.94	15	28	17	–	376	165	1	165.00	1-19	–	–
Hobbs, R.N.S.	1967	1971	7	8	3	34	15*	6.80	–	–	8	–	1291	481	12	40.08	3-25	–	–

INDIVIDUAL CAREER RECORDS – ENGLAND *continued*

	First Test	Last Test	Tests	BATTING AND FIELDING									BOWLING						
				Inns	NO	Runs	HS	Avge	100	50	Ct	St	Balls	Runs	Wkts	Avge	BB	5wI	10wM
Hoggard, M.J.	2000	2007-08	67	92	27	473	38	7.27	–	–	24	–	13909	7564	248	30.50	7-61	7	1
Hollies, W.E.	1934-35	1950	13	15	8	37	18*	5.28	–	–	2	–	3554	1332	44	30.27	7-50	5	–
Hollioake, A.J.	1997	1997-98	4	6	0	65	45	10.83	–	–	4	–	144	67	2	33.50	2-31	–	–
Hollioake, B.C.	1997	1998	2	4	0	44	28	11.00	–	1	2	–	252	199	4	49.75	2-105	–	–
Holmes, E.R.T.	1934-35	1935	5	9	2	114	85*	16.28	–	1	4	–	108	76	2	38.00	1-10	–	–
Holmes, P.	1921	1932	7	14	1	357	88	27.46	–	4	3	–	–	–	–	–	–	–	–
Hone, L.	1878-79	1878-79	1	2	0	13	7	6.50	–	–	2	–	–	–	–	–	–	–	–
Hopwood, J.L.	1934	1934	2	3	1	12	8	6.00	–	–	–	–	462†	155	0	–	–	–	–
Hornby, A.N.	1878-79	1884	3	6	0	21	9	3.50	–	–	2	–	28	0	1	0.00	1-0	–	–
Horton, M.J.	1959	1959	2	2	0	60	58	30.00	–	1	–	–	238	59	2	29.50	2-24	–	–
Howard, N.D.	1951-52	1951-52	4	6	1	86	23	17.20	–	–	4	–	–	–	–	–	–	–	–
Howell, H.	1920-21	1924	5	8	6	15	5	7.50	–	–	–	–	918	559	7	79.85	4-115	1	–
Howorth, R.	1947	1947-48	5	10†	1	145	45*	18.12	–	1	2	–	1536†	635	19	33.42	6-124	1	–
Humphries, J.	1907-08	1907-08	3	6	1	44	16	8.80	–	–	7	3	–	–	–	–	–	–	–
Hunter, J.	1884-85	1884-85	5	7	2	93	39*	18.60	–	–	8	3	–	–	–	–	–	–	–
Hussain, N.	1989-90	2004	96	171	16	5764	207	37.18	14	33	67	–	30	15	0	–	–	–	–
Hutchings, K.L.	1907-08	1909	7	12	0	341	126	28.41	1	1	9	–	90	81	1	81.00	1-5	–	–
Hutton, L.	1937	1954-55	79	138	15	6971	364	56.67	19	33	57	–	260	232	3	77.33	1-2	–	–
Hutton, R.A.	1971	1971	5	8	2	219	81	36.50	–	2	9	–	738	257	9	28.55	3-72	–	–
Iddon, J.	1934-35	1935	5	7	1	170	73	28.33	–	2	–	–	66†	27	0	–	–	–	–
Igglesden, A.P.	1989	1993-94	3	5	3	6	3*	3.00	–	–	–	–	555	329	6	54.83	2-91	–	–
Ikin, J.T.	1946	1955	18	31†	2	606	60	20.89	–	3	31	–	572	354	3	118.00	1-38	–	–
Illingworth, R.	1958	1973	61	90	11	1836	113	23.24	2	5	45	–	11934	3807	122	31.20	6-29	3	–
Illingworth, R.K.	1991	1995-96	9	14	7	128	28	18.28	–	–	5	–	1485†	615	19	32.36	4-96	–	–
Ilott, M.C.	1993	1995-96	5	6	2	28	15	7.00	–	–	5	–	1042†	542	12	45.16	3-48	–	–
Insole, D.J.	1950	1957	9	17	2	408	110*	27.20	1	1	8	–	–	–	–	–	–	–	–
Irani, R.C.	1996	1999	3	5	0	86	41	17.20	–	1	2	–	192	112	3	37.33	1-22	–	–
Jackman, R.D.	1980-81	1982	4	6	0	42	17	7.00	–	–	–	–	1070	445	14	31.78	4-110	–	–
Jackson, F.S.	1893	1905	20	33	4	1415	144*	48.79	5	6	10	–	1587	799	24	33.29	5-52	1	–
Jackson, H.L.	1949	1961	2	2	1	15	8	15.00	–	–	1	–	498	155	7	22.14	2-26	–	–
James, S.P.	1998	1998	2	4	0	71	36	17.75	–	–	–	–	–	–	–	–	–	–	–
Jameson, J.A.	1971	1973-74	4	8	0	214	82	26.75	–	–	26	–	42	17	1	17.00	1-17	–	–
Jardine, D.R.	1928	1933-34	22	33	6	1296	127	48.00	1	10	4	–	6	10	–	–	–	–	–
Jarvis, P.W.	1987-88	1992-93	9	15	5	132	29*	10.15	–	–	2	–	1912	965	21	45.95	4-107	1	–
Jenkins, R.O.	1948-49	1952	9	12	2	198	39	18.00	–	–	4	–	2118	1098	32	34.31	5-116	2	–
Jessop, G.L.	1899	1912	18	26	0	569	104	21.88	1	3	11	–	732	354	10	35.40	4-68	–	–
Johnson, R.L.	2003	2003-04	3	4	0	59	26	14.75	–	–	–	–	547	275	16	17.18	6-33	2	–
Jones, A.O.	1899	1909	12	21	0	291	34	13.85	–	–	15	–	228	133	3	44.33	3-73	–	–
Jones, G.O.	2003-04	2006-07	34	53	4	1172	100	23.91	1	6	128	5	–	–	–	–	–	–	–
Jones, I.J.	1963-64	1967-68	15	17	9	38	16	4.75	–	–	4	–	3546†	1769	44	40.20	6-118	1	–
Jones, S.P.	2002	2005	18	18†	5	205	44	15.76	–	1	4	–	2821	1666	59	28.23	6-53	3	–
Jupp, H.	1876-77	1876-77	2	4	0	68	63	17.00	–	–	2	–	–	–	–	–	–	–	–

INDIVIDUAL CAREER RECORDS – ENGLAND *continued*

Name	First Test	Last Test	Tests	Inns	NO	Runs	HS	Avge	100	50	Ct	St	Balls	Runs	Wkts	Avge	BB	5wI	10wM
				BATTING AND FIELDING									*BOWLING*						
Jupp, V.W.C.	1921	1928	8	13	1	208	38	17.33			5		1301	616	28	22.00	4-37		
Keeton, W.W.	1934	1939	2	4	0	57	25	14.25											
Kennedy, A.S.	1922-23	1922-23	5	8	2	93	41*	15.50			5		1683	599	31	19.32	5-76	2	
Kenyon, D.	1951-52	1955	8	15	0	192	87	12.80		1	5								
Key, R.W.T.	2002	2004-05	15	26	0	775	221	31.00	1	3	11								
Khan, A.	2008-09	2008-09	1	–	–	–	–	–					174	122	1	122.00	1-111		
Killick, E.T.	1929	1929	2	4	0	81	31	20.25			2								
Kilner, R.	1924	1926	9	8†	1	233	74	33.28		2	6		2368†	734	24	30.58	4-51		
King, J.H.	1909	1909	1	2†	0	64	60	32.00		1			162†	99	1	99.00	1-99		
Kinneir, S.P.	1911-12	1911-12	1	2†	0	52	30	26.00											
Kirtley, R.J.	2003	2003-04	4	7	1	32	12	5.33					1079	561	19	29.52	6-34	1	
Knight, A.E.	1903-04	1903-04	3	6	1	81	70*	16.20		1	3								
Knight, B.R.	1961-62	1969	29	38	7	812	127	26.19	2	1	14		5377	2223	70	31.75	4-38		
Knight, D.J.	1921	1921	2	4	0	54	38	13.50			1								
Knight, N.V.	1995	2001	17	30†	0	719	113	23.96	1	4	26								
Knott, A.P.E.	1967	1981	95	149	15	4389	135	32.75	5	30	250	19							
Knox, N.A.	1907	1907	2	4	1	24	8*	8.00					126	105	3	35.00	2-39		
Laker, J.C.	1947-48	1958-59	46	63	15	676	63	14.08		2	12		12027	4101	193	21.24	10-53	9	3
Lamb, A.J.	1982	1992	79	139	10	4656	142	36.09	14	18	75		30	23	1	23.00	1-6		
Langridge, J.	1933	1946	8	9†	0	242	70	26.88		1	6		1074†	413	19	21.73	7-56	2	
Larkins, W.	1979-80	1990-91	13	25	1	493	64	20.54		3	8								
Larter, J.D.F.	1962	1965	10	7	2	16	10	3.20			5		2172	941	37	25.43	5-57	2	
Larwood, H.	1926	1932-33	21	28	3	485	98	19.40		2	15		4969	2212	78	28.35	6-32	4	
Lathwell, M.N.	1993	1993	2	4	0	78	33	19.50											
Lawrence, D.V.	1988	1991-92	5	6	0	60	34	10.00					1089	676	18	37.55	5-106	1	
Leadbeater, E.	1951-52	1951-52	2	2	0	40	38	20.00			3		289	218	2	109.00	1-38		
Lee, H.W.	1930-31	1930-31	1	2	0	19	18	9.50											
Lees, W.S.	1905-06	1905-06	5	9	3	66	25*	11.00			2		1256	467	26	17.96	6-78	2	
Legge, G.B.	1927-28	1929-30	5	7	1	299	196	49.83	1	1	1		30	34	0	–	–		
Leslie, C.F.H.	1882-83	1882-83	4	7	0	106	54	15.14		1	1		96	44	4	11.00	3-31		
Lever, J.K.	1976-77	1986	21	31	5	306	53	11.76			11		4433†	1951	73	26.72	7-46	3	1
Lever, P.	1970-71	1975	17	18	2	350	88*	21.87		1	11		3571	1509	41	36.80	6-38	2	
Leveson Gower, H.D.G.	1909-10	1909-10	3	6	2	95	31	23.75			3								
Levett, W.H.V.	1933-34	1933-34	1	2	1	7	5	7.00											
Lewis, A.R.	1972-73	1973	9	16	2	457	125	32.64	1	3	25								
Lewis, C.C.	1990	1996	32	51	3	1105	117	23.02	1	4	13		6852	3490	93	37.52	6-111	3	
Lewis, J.	2006	2006	2	2	0	27	20	13.50					246	122	3	40.66	3-68		
Leyland, M.	1928	1938	41	65†	5	2764	187	46.06	9	10	13		1103†	585	6	97.50	3-91		
Lilley, A.F.A.	1896	1909	35	52	8	903	84	20.52		4	70	22	25	23	1	23.00	1-23		
Lillywhite, J.	1876-77	1876-77	2	3†	1	16	10	8.00					340†	126	8	15.75	4-70		
Lloyd, D.	1974	1974-75	9	15†	2	552	214*	42.46	1	1	11		24†	17	0	–	–		
Lloyd, T.A.	1984	1984	1	1†	1	10	10*	–											
Loader, P.J.	1954	1958-59	13	19	6	76	17	5.84			2		2662	878	39	22.51	6-36	1	

INDIVIDUAL CAREER RECORDS – ENGLAND continued

	First Test	Last Test	Tests	Inns	NO	Runs	HS	Avge	100	50	Ct	St	Balls	Runs	Wkts	Avge	BB	5wI	10wM
Lock, G.A.R.	1952	1967-68	49	63	9	742	89	13.74	—	3	59	—	13147†	4451	174	25.58	7-35	9	3
Lockwood, W.H.	1893	1902	12	16	3	231	52*	17.76	—	1	4	—	1973	883	43	20.53	7-71	5	1
Lohmann, G.A.	1886	1896	18	26	2	213	62*	8.87	—	1	28	—	3830	1205	112	10.75	9-28	9	5
Lowson, F.A.	1951	1955	7	13	0	245	68	18.84	—	2	5	—						—	—
Lucas, A.P.	1878-79	1884	5	9	1	157	55	19.62	—	1	1	—	120	54	0	—	—	—	—
Luckhurst, B.W.	1970-71	1974-75	21	41	5	1298	131	36.05	4	5	14	—	57†	32	1	32.00	1-9	—	—
Lyttelton, Hon. A.	1880	1884	4	7	1	94	31	15.66	—	—	2	—	48	19	4	4.75	4-19	—	—
Macaulay, G.G.	1922-23	1933	8	10	4	112	76	18.66	—	1	5	—	1701	662	24	27.58	5-64	1	—
MacBryan, J.C.W.	1924	1924	1	—	—				—	—	—	—						—	—
McCague, M.J.	1993	1994-95	3	5	0	21	11	4.20	—	—	1	—	593	390	6	65.00	4-121	—	—
McConnon, J.E.	1954	1954	2	3	1	18	11	9.00	—	—	4	—	216	74	4	18.50	3-19	—	—
McGahey, C.P.	1901-02	1901-02	2	4	0	38	18	9.50	—	—	2	—						—	—
McGrath, A.	2003	2003	4	5	0	201	81	40.20	—	—	3	—	102	56	4	14.00	3-16	—	—
MacGregor, G.	1890	1893	8	11	3	96	31	12.00	—	—	14	3						—	—
McIntyre, A.J.W.	1950	1955	3	6	0	19	7	3.16	—	—	8	—						—	—
MacKinnon, F.A.	1878-79	1878-79	1	2	0	5	5	2.50	—	—	—	—						—	—
MacLaren, A.C.	1894-95	1909	35	61	4	1931	140	33.87	5	8	29	—						—	—
McMaster, J.E.P.	1888-89	1888-89	1	1	0	0	0	0.00	—	—	—	—						—	—
Maddy, D.L.	1999	1999-00	3	4	0	46	24	11.50	—	—	4	—	84	40	0	—	—	—	—
Mahmood, S.I.	2006	2006-07	8	11	1	81	34	8.10	—	—		—	1130	762	20	38.10	4-22	—	—
Makepeace, J.W.H.	1920-21	1920-21	4	8	0	279	117	34.87	1	2	7	—						—	—
Malcolm, D.E.	1989	1997	40	58	19	236	29	6.05	—	—	7	—	8480	4748	128	37.09	9-57	5	2
Mallender, N.A.	1992	1992	2	3	0	8	4	2.66	—	—	3	—	449	215	10	21.50	5-50	1	—
Mann, F.G.	1948-49	1949	7	12	2	376	136*	37.60	1	2	3	—						—	—
Mann, F.T.	1922-23	1922-23	5	9	1	281	84	35.12	—	2	4	—						—	—
Marks, V.J.	1982	1983-84	6	10	1	249	83	27.66	—	3	1	—	1082	484	11	44.00	3-78	—	—
Marriott, C.S.	1933	1933	1	2†	0	0	0	0.00	—	—	1	—	247	96	11	8.72	6-59	2	1
Martin, F.	1890	1891-92	2	2	0	14	13	7.00	—	—	2	—	410†	141	14	10.07	6-50	2	1
Martin, J.W.	1947	1947	1	2	0	26	26	13.00	—	—	—	—	270	129	1	129.00	1-111	—	—
Martin, P.J.	1995	1997	8	13	0	115	29	8.84	—	—	6	—	1452	580	17	34.11	4-60	—	—
Mason, J.R.	1897-98	1897-98	5	10	0	129	32	12.90	—	—	3	—	324	149	2	74.50	1-8	—	—
Matthews, A.D.G.	1937	1937	1	1	1	2	2*	—	—	—	—	—	180	65	2	32.50	1-13	—	—
May, P.B.H.	1951	1961	66	106	9	4537	285*	46.77	13	22	42	—						—	—
Maynard, M.P.	1988	1993-94	4	8	0	87	35	10.87	—	—	3	—						—	—
Mead, C.P.	1911-12	1928-29	17	26†	2	1185	182*	49.37	4	3	4	—						—	—
Mead, W.	1899	1899	1	2	0	7	7	3.50	—	—	1	—	265	91	1	91.00	1-91	—	—
Midwinter, W.E. ‡	1881-82	1881-82	4	7	0	95	36	13.57	—	—	5	—	776	272	10	27.20	4-81	—	—
Milburn, C.	1966	1968-69	9	16	2	654	139	46.71	2	2	7	—						—	—
Miller, A.M.	1895-96	1895-96	1	2	0	24	20*	—	—	—	—	—						—	—
Miller, G.	1976	1984	34	51	4	1213	98*	25.80	—	7	17	—	5149	1859	60	30.98	5-44	1	—
Milligan, F.W.	1898-99	1898-99	2	4	0	58	38	14.50	—	—	1	—	45	29	0	—	—	—	—
Millman, G.	1961-62	1962	6	7	2	60	32*	12.00	—	—	13	2						—	—
Milton, C.A.	1958	1959	6	9	1	204	104*	25.50	1	—	5	—	24	12	0	—	—	—	—

INDIVIDUAL CAREER RECORDS – ENGLAND continued

Name	First Test	Last Test	Tests	Inns	NO	Runs	HS	Avge	100	50	Ct	St	Balls	Runs	Wkts	Avge	BB	5wI	10wM
				BATTING AND FIELDING									**BOWLING**						
Mitchell, A.	1933-34	1936	6	10	0	298	72	29.80	–	2	9	–	6	4	0	–	–	–	–
Mitchell, F. ‡	1898-99	1898-99	2	4	0	88	41	22.00	–	–	2	–	–	–	–	–	–	–	–
Mitchell, T.B.	1932-33	1935	5	6	2	20	9	5.00	–	–	1	–	894	498	8	62.25	2-49	–	–
Mitchell-Innes, N.S.	1935	1935	1	1	0	5	5	5.00	–	–	1	–	–	–	–	–	–	–	–
Mold, A.W.	1893	1893	3	3	1	0	0*	0.00	–	–	1	–	491	234	7	33.42	3-44	–	–
Moon, L.J.	1905-06	1905-06	4	8	0	182	36	22.75	–	–	4	–	–	–	–	–	–	–	–
Morley, F.	1880	1882-83	4	6†	2	6	2*	1.50	–	–	4	–	972†	296	16	18.50	5-56	1	–
Morris, H.	1991	1991	3	6†	2	115	44	19.16	–	–	3	–	–	–	–	–	–	–	–
Morris, J.E.	1990	1990	3	5	0	71	32	23.66	–	1	3	–	–	–	–	–	–	–	–
Mortimore, J.B.	1958-59	1964	9	12	2	243	73*	24.30	–	1	3	–	2162	733	13	56.38	3-36	–	–
Moss, A.E.	1953-54	1960	9	7	1	61	26	10.16	–	–	1	–	1657	626	21	29.80	4-35	–	–
Moxon, M.D.	1986	1989	10	17	1	455	99	28.43	–	3	10	–	48	30	0	–	–	–	–
Mullally, A.D.	1996	2001	19	27	4	127	24	5.52	–	–	6	–	4525†	1812	58	31.24	5-105	1	–
Munton, T.A.	1992	1992	2	2	1	25	25*	25.00	–	–	–	–	405	200	4	50.00	2-22	–	–
Murdoch, W.L. ‡	1891-92	1891-92	1	2	0	12	12	12.00	–	–	1	1	–	–	–	–	–	–	–
Murray, J.T.	1961	1967	21	28	5	506	112	22.00	1	2	52	3	–	–	–	–	–	–	–
Newham, W.	1887-88	1887-88	1	2	0	26	17	13.00	–	–	1	–	–	–	–	–	–	–	–
Newport, P.J.	1988	1990-91	3	5	1	110	40*	27.50	–	–	1	–	669	417	10	41.70	4-87	–	–
Nichols, M.S.	1929-30	1939	14	19†	7	355	78*	29.58	–	2	11	–	2565	1152	41	28.09	6-35	2	–
Oakman, A.S.M.	1956	1956	2	2	0	14	10	7.00	–	–	7	–	48	21	0	–	–	–	–
O'Brien, T.C.	1884	1895-96	5	8	0	59	20	7.37	–	–	4	–	–	–	–	–	–	–	–
O'Connor, J.	1929	1929-30	4	7	0	153	51	21.85	–	1	2	–	162	72	1	72.00	1-31	–	–
Old, C.M.	1972-73	1981	46	66†	9	845	65	14.82	–	2	22	–	8858	4020	143	28.11	7-50	4	–
Oldfield, N.	1939	1939	1	2	0	99	80	49.50	–	1	–	–	–	–	–	–	–	–	–
Onions, G.	2009	2009	5	5	2	19	17*	6.33	–	–	–	–	739	503	20	25.15	5-38	1	–
Ormond, J.	2001	2001-02	2	4	1	38	18	12.66	–	–	–	–	372	185	2	92.50	1-70	–	–
Padgett, D.E.V.	1960	1960	2	4	0	51	31	12.75	–	–	–	–	–	–	–	–	–	–	–
Paine, G.A.E.	1934-35	1934-35	4	7	1	97	49	16.16	–	–	5	–	1044†	467	17	27.47	5-168	1	–
Palairet, L.C.H.	1902	1902	2	4	0	49	20	12.25	–	–	2	–	–	–	–	–	–	–	–
Palmer, C.H.	1953-54	1953-54	1	2	0	22	22	11.00	–	–	–	–	30	15	0	–	–	–	–
Palmer, K.E.	1964-65	1964-65	1	1	0	10	10	10.00	–	–	–	–	378	189	1	189.00	1-113	–	–
Panesar, M.S.	2005-06	2009	39	51†	17	187	26	5.50	–	–	9	–	9042†	4331	126	34.37	6-37	8	1
Parfitt, P.H.	1961-62	1972	37	52†	6	1882	131*	40.91	7	6	42	–	1326	574	12	47.83	2-5	–	–
Parker, C.W.L.	1921	1921	1	1	0	3	3*	–	–	–	–	–	168†	32	2	16.00	2-32	–	–
Parker, P.W.G.	1981	1981	1	2	0	13	13	6.50	–	–	3	–	–	–	–	–	–	–	–
Parkhouse, W.G.A.	1950	1959	7	13	0	373	78	28.69	–	2	3	–	–	–	–	–	–	–	–
Parkin, C.H.	1920-21	1924	10	16	3	160	36	12.30	–	–	3	–	2095	1128	32	35.25	5-38	2	–
Parks, J.H.	1937	1937	1	2	0	29	22	14.50	–	–	–	–	126	36	3	12.00	2-26	–	–
Parks, J.M.	1954	1967-68	46	68	7	1962	108*	32.16	2	9	103	11	54	51	1	51.00	1-43	–	–
Pataudi, Nawab of, sen. ‡	1932-33	1934	3	5	0	144	102	28.80	1	–	–	–	–	–	–	–	–	–	–
Patel, M.M.	1996	1996	2	2	0	45	27	22.50	–	–	2	–	276†	180	1	180.00	1-101	–	–

INDIVIDUAL CAREER RECORDS – ENGLAND continued

	First Test	Last Test	Tests	Inns	NO	Runs	HS	Avge	100	50	Ct	St	Balls	Runs	Wkts	Avge	BB	5wI	10wM
								BATTING AND FIELDING									*BOWLING*		
Pattinson, D.J.	2008	2008	1	2	0	21	13	10.50	–	–	–	–	181	96	2	48.00	2-95	–	–
Paynter, E.	1931	1939	20	31†	5	1540	243	59.23	4	7	7	–	–	–	–	–	–	–	–
Peate, E.	1881-82	1886	9	14†	8	70	13	11.66	–	–	2	–	2096†	683	31	22.03	6-85	2	–
Peebles, I.A.R.	1927-28	1931	13	17	8	98	26	10.88	–	–	5	–	2882	1391	45	30.91	6-63	3	–
Peel, R.	1884-85	1896	20	33†	4	427	83	14.72	–	3	17	–	5216†	1715	101	16.98	7-31	5	1
Penn, F.	1880	1880	1	2	1	50	27*	50.00	–	–	–	–	12	2	0	–	–	–	–
Perks, R.T.D.	1938-39	1939	2	2†	2	3	2*	–	–	–	1	–	829	355	11	32.27	5-100	2	–
Philipson, H.	1891-92	1894-95	5	8	1	63	30	9.00	–	–	8	3	–	–	–	–	–	–	–
Pietersen, K.P.	2005	2009	54	97	4	4647	226	49.96	16	15	32	–	735	518	4	129.50	1-0	–	–
Pigott, A.C.S.	1983-84	1983-84	1	2	1	12	8*	12.00	–	–	–	–	102	75	2	37.50	2-75	–	–
Pilling, R.	1881-82	1888	8	13	1	91	23	7.58	–	–	10	4	–	–	–	–	–	–	–
Place, W.	1947-48	1947-48	3	6	1	144	107	28.80	1	–	3	–	–	–	–	–	–	–	–
Plunkett, L.E.	2005-06	2007	9	13	2	126	44*	11.45	–	–	3	–	1538	916	23	39.82	3-17	–	–
Pocock, P.I.	1967-68	1984-85	25	37	4	206	33	6.24	–	–	15	–	6650	2976	67	44.41	6-79	3	–
Pollard, R.	1946	1948	4	3	2	13	10*	13.00	–	–	3	–	1102	378	15	25.20	5-24	1	–
Poole, C.J.	1951-52	1951-52	3	5†	1	161	69*	40.25	–	2	1	–	30†	9	0	–	–	–	–
Pope, G.H.	1947	1947	1	1	1	8	8*	–	–	–	–	–	218	85	1	85.00	1-49	–	–
Pougher, A.D.	1891-92	1891-92	1	1	0	17	17	17.00	–	–	2	–	105	26	3	8.66	3-26	1	–
Price, J.S.E.	1963-64	1972	15	15†	6	66	32	7.33	–	–	7	–	2724	1401	40	35.02	5-73	1	–
Price, W.F.F.	1938	1938	1	2	0	6	6	3.00	–	–	2	–	–	–	–	–	–	–	–
Prideaux, R.M.	1968	1968-69	3	6	1	102	64	20.40	–	1	3	–	12	0	0	–	–	–	–
Pringle, D.R.	1982	1992	30	50	8	695	63	15.10	–	1	10	–	5287	2518	70	35.97	5-95	3	–
Prior, M.J.	2007	2009	23	37	7	1326	131*	44.20	2	10	51	2	–	–	–	–	–	–	–
Pullar, G.	1959	1962-63	28	49†	4	1974	175	43.86	4	12	2	–	66	37	1	37.00	1-1	–	–
Quaife, W.G.	1899	1901-02	7	13	1	228	68	19.00	–	1	4	–	15	6	0	–	–	–	–
Radford, N.V.	1986	1987-88	3	4	1	21	12*	7.00	–	–	–	–	678	351	4	87.75	2-131	–	–
Radley, C.T.	1977-78	1978	8	10	0	481	158	48.10	2	2	4	–	–	–	–	–	–	–	–
Ramprakash, M.R.	1991	2001-02	52	92	6	2350	154	27.32	2	12	39	–	895	477	4	119.25	1-2	–	–
Randall, D.W.	1976-77	1984	47	79	5	2470	174	33.37	7	12	31	–	16	3	0	–	–	–	–
Ranjitsinhji, K.S.	1896	1902	15	26	4	989	175	44.95	2	6	13	–	97	39	1	39.00	1-23	–	–
Read, C.M.W.	1999	2006-07	15	23	4	360	55	18.94	–	1	48	6	–	–	–	–	–	–	–
Read, H.D.	1935	1935	1	–	–	–	–	–	–	–	–	–	270	200	6	33.33	4-136	–	–
Read, J.M.	1882	1893	17	29	2	461	57	17.07	–	2	8	–	–	–	–	–	–	–	–
Read, W.W.	1882-83	1893	18	27	1	720	117	27.69	1	5	16	–	60	63	0	–	–	–	–
Reeve, D.A.	1991-92	1991-92	3	5	0	124	59	24.80	–	1	–	–	149	60	2	30.00	1-4	–	–
Relf, A.E.	1903-04	1913-14	13	21	3	416	63	23.11	–	1	14	–	1764	624	25	24.96	5-85	1	–
Rhodes, H.J.	1959	1959	2	1	1	0	0*	–	–	–	–	–	449	244	9	27.11	4-50	–	–
Rhodes, S.J.	1994	1994-95	11	17	5	294	65*	24.50	–	2	46	3	–	–	–	–	–	–	–
Rhodes, W.	1899	1929-30	58	98	21	2325	179	30.19	2	11	60	–	8225†	3425	127	26.96	8-68	6	1
Richards, C.J.	1986-87	1988	8	13	0	285	133	21.92	1	2	20	1	–	–	–	–	–	–	–
Richardson, D.W.	1957	1957	1	1†	0	33	33	33.00	–	–	1	–	120	48	3	16.00	2-10	–	–
Richardson, P.E.	1956	1963	34	56†	1	2061	126	37.47	5	9	6	–	–	–	–	–	–	–	–

INDIVIDUAL CAREER RECORDS – ENGLAND continued

	First Test	Last Test	Tests	BATTING AND FIELDING												BOWLING			
				Inns	NO	Runs	HS	Avge	100	50	Ct	St	Balls	Runs	Wkts	Avge	BB	5wI	10wM
Richardson, T.	1893	1897-98	14	24	8	177	25*	11.06	-	-	5	-	4498	2220	88	25.22	8-94	11	4
Richmond, T.L.	1921	1921	1	2	0	6	4	3.00	-	-	-	-	114	86	2	43.00	2-69	-	-
Ridgway, F.	1951-52	1951-52	5	6	2	49	24	8.16	-	-	3	-	793	379	7	54.14	4-83	-	-
Robertson, J.D.B.	1947	1951-52	11	21	2	881	133	46.36	2	6	6	-	138	58	2	29.00	2-17	-	-
Robins, R.W.V.	1929	1937	19	27	4	612	108	26.60	1	4	12	-	3318	1758	64	27.46	6-32	1	-
Robinson, R.T.	1984-85	1989	29	49	5	1601	175	36.38	4	6	8	-	6	0	0	-	-	-	-
Roope, G.R.J.	1972-73	1978	21	32	4	860	77	30.71	-	7	35	-	172	76	0	-	-	-	-
Root, C.F.	1926	1926	3	-	-	-	-	-	-	-	1	-	642	194	8	24.25	4-84	-	-
Rose, B.C.	1977-78	1980-81	9	16†	2	358	70	25.57	-	2	4	-	16	6	0	-	-	-	-
Royle, V.P.F.A.	1878-79	1878-79	1	2	0	21	18	10.50	-	-	2	-	-	-	-	-	-	-	-
Rumsey, F.E.	1964	1965	5	5	3	30	21*	15.00	-	-	-	-	1145†	461	17	27.11	4-25	-	-
Russell, C.A.G.	1920-21	1922-23	10	18	2	910	140	56.87	5	2	8	-	-	-	-	-	-	-	-
Russell, R.C.	1988	1997-98	54	86†	16	1897	128*	27.10	2	6	153	12	-	-	-	-	-	-	-
Russell, W.E.	1961-62	1967	10	18	1	362	70	21.29	-	2	4	-	144	44	0	-	-	-	-
Saggers, M.J.	2003-04	2004	3	3	0	1	1	0.33	-	-	1	-	493	247	7	35.28	2-29	-	-
Salisbury, I.D.K.	1992	2000-01	15	25	3	368	50	16.72	-	1	5	-	2492	1539	20	76.95	4-163	1	-
Sandham, A.	1921	1929-30	14	23	0	879	325	38.21	2	3	4	-	-	-	-	-	-	-	-
Schofield, C.P.	2000	2000	2	3†	0	67	57	22.33	-	1	-	-	108	73	0	-	-	-	-
Schultz, S.S.	1878-79	1878-79	1	1	0	20	20	20.00	-	-	-	-	34	26	1	26.00	1-16	-	-
Scotton, W.H.	1881-82	1886-87	15	25†	2	510	90	22.17	-	3	4	-	20†	20	0	-	-	-	-
Selby, J.	1876-77	1881-82	6	12	1	256	70	23.27	-	2	-	-	-	-	-	-	-	-	-
Selvey, M.W.W.	1976	1976-77	3	5	3	15	5*	7.50	-	-	1	-	492	343	6	57.16	4-41	-	-
Shackleton, D.	1950	1963	7	13	7	113	42	18.83	-	-	1	-	2078	768	18	42.66	4-72	-	-
Shah, O.A.	2005-06	2008-09	6	10	0	269	88	26.90	-	2	2	-	30	31	0	-	-	-	-
Sharp, J.	1909	1909	3	6	2	188	105	47.00	1	1	1	-	183†	111	3	37.00	3-67	-	-
Sharpe, J.W.	1890	1891-92	3	6	4	44	26	22.00	-	-	2	-	975	305	11	27.72	6-84	1	-
Sharpe, P.J.	1963	1969	12	21	4	786	111	46.23	1	4	17	-	-	-	-	-	-	-	-
Shaw, A.	1876-77	1881-82	7	12	1	111	40	10.09	-	-	4	-	1096	285	12	23.75	5-38	1	-
Sheppard, D.S.	1950	1962-63	22	33	2	1172	119	37.80	3	6	12	-	-	-	-	-	-	-	-
Sherwin, M.	1886-87	1893	3	6	4	30	21*	15.00	-	-	5	2	-	-	-	-	-	-	-
Shrewsbury, A.	1881-82	1888	23	40	4	1277	164	35.47	3	4	29	-	12	2	0	-	-	-	-
Shuter, J.	1888	1888	1	1	0	28	28	28.00	-	-	-	-	-	-	-	-	-	-	-
Shuttleworth, K.	1970-71	1971	5	6	0	46	21	7.66	-	-	1	-	1071	427	12	35.58	5-47	1	-
Sidebottom, A.	1985	1985	1	1	0	2	2	2.00	-	-	-	-	112	65	1	65.00	1-65	-	-
Sidebottom, R.J.	2001	2008-09	21	29†	11	298	31	16.55	-	1	5	-	4626†	2133	77	27.70	7-47	5	-
Silverwood, C.E.W.	1996-97	2002-03	6	7	3	29	10	7.25	-	-	5	-	828	444	11	40.36	5-91	1	-
Simpson, R.T.	1948-49	1954-55	27	45	3	1401	156*	33.35	4	6	5	-	45	22	2	11.00	2-4	-	-
Simpson-Hayward, G.H.T.	1909-10	1909-10	5	8	1	105	29*	15.00	-	-	-	-	898	420	23	18.26	6-43	2	-
Sims, J.M.	1935	1936-37	4	4	0	16	12	4.00	-	-	6	-	887	480	11	43.63	5-73	1	-
Sinfield, R.A.	1938	1938	1	1	0	6	6	6.00	-	-	1	-	378	123	2	61.50	1-51	-	-
Slack, W.N.	1985-86	1986	3	6†	0	81	52	13.50	-	1	3	-	-	-	-	-	-	-	-
Smailes, T.F.	1946	1946	1	1†	0	25	25	25.00	-	-	-	-	120	62	3	20.66	3-44	-	-
Small, G.C.	1986	1990-91	17	24	7	263	59	15.47	-	1	9	-	3927	1871	55	34.01	5-48	2	-

INDIVIDUAL CAREER RECORDS – ENGLAND continued

				BATTING AND FIELDING									BOWLING						
	Tests	First Test	Last Test	Inns	NO	Runs	HS	Avge	100	50	Ct	St	Balls	Runs	Wkts	Avge	BB	5wI	10wM
Smith, A.C.	6	1962-63	1962-63	7	3	118	69*	29.50	-	1	20	-							
Smith, A.M.	1	1997	1997	2	1	4	4*	4.00	-	-	-	-	138†	89	0	-	-	-	-
Smith, C.A.	1	1888-89	1888-89	1	0	3	3	3.00	-	-	1	-	154	61	7	8.71	5-19	1	-
Smith, C.I.J.	5	1934-35	1937	10	0	102	27	10.20	-	-	-	-	930	393	15	26.20	5-16	1	-
Smith, C.L.	8	1983	1986	14	1	392	91	30.15	-	2	1	-	102	39	3	13.00	2-31	-	-
Smith, D.	2	1935	1935	4†	0	128	57	32.00	-	1	-	-							
Smith, D.M.	2	1985-86	1985-86	4†	0	80	47	20.00	-	-	-	-	972	359	6	59.83	2-60	-	-
Smith, D.R.	5	1961-62	1961-62	5	1	38	34	9.50	-	-	2	-	270†	97	1	97.00	1-12	-	-
Smith, D.V.	3	1957	1957	4†	1	25	16*	8.33	-	-	-	-							
Smith, E.J.	11	1911-12	1913-14	14	1	113	22	8.69	-	-	17	3							
Smith, E.T.	3	2003	2003	5	0	87	64	17.40	-	1	5	-							
Smith, H.	1	1928	1928	1	0	7	7	7.00	-	-	1	-							
Smith, M.J.K.	50	1958	1972	78	6	2278	121	31.63	3	11	53	-	214	128	1	128.00	1-10	-	-
Smith, R.A.	62	1988	1995-96	112	15	4236	175	43.67	9	28	39	-	24	6	0	-	-	-	-
Smith, T.P.B.	4	1946	1946-47	5	0	33	24	6.60	-	-	1	-	538	319	3	106.33	2-172	-	-
Smithson, G.A.	2	1947-48	1947-48	3†	0	70	35	23.33	-	-	-	-							
Snow, J.A.	49	1965	1976	71	14	772	73	13.54	-	2	16	-	12021	5387	202	26.66	7-40	8	1
Southerton, J.	2	1876-77	1876-77	3	1	7	6	3.50	-	-	2	-	263	107	7	15.28	4-46	-	-
Spooner, R.H.	10	1905	1912	15	0	481	119	32.06	1	4	4	-							
Spooner, R.T.	7	1951-52	1955	14†	1	354	92	27.23	-	3	10	2							
Stanyforth, R.T.	4	1927-28	1927-28	6	1	13	6*	2.60	-	-	7	2							
Staples, S.J.	3	1927-28	1927-28	5	0	65	39	13.00	-	-	-	-	1149	435	15	29.00	3-50	-	-
Statham, J.B.	70	1950-51	1965	87†	28	675	38	11.44	-	-	28	-	16056	6261	252	24.84	7-39	9	1
Steel, A.G.	13	1880	1888	20	3	600	148	35.29	2	5	5	-	1360	605	29	20.86	3-27	1	-
Steele, D.S.	8	1975	1976	16	0	673	106	42.06	1	-	7	-	88†	39	2	19.50	1-1	-	-
Stephenson, J.P.	1	1989	1989	2	0	36	25	18.00	-	-	-	-							
Stevens, G.T.S.	10	1922-23	1929-30	17	0	263	69	15.47	-	1	9	-	1186	648	20	32.40	5-90	2	-
Stevenson, G.B.	2	1979-80	1980-81	2	1	28	27*	28.00	-	-	-	-	312	183	5	36.60	3-111	-	-
Stewart, A.J.	133	1989-90	2003	235	21	8463	190	39.54	15	45	263	14	20	13	0	-	-	-	-
Stewart, M.J.	8	1962	1963-64	12	1	385	87	35.00	-	2	6	-							
Stoddart, A.E.	16	1887-88	1897-98	30	2	996	173	35.57	2	3	6	-	162	94	2	47.00	1-10	-	-
Storer, W.	6	1897-98	1899	11	0	215	51	19.54	-	1	11	-	168	108	2	54.00	1-24	-	-
Strauss, A.J.	67	2004	2009	123†	5	5266	177	44.62	18	17	75	-							
Street, G.B.	1	1922-23	1922-23	2	1	11	7*	11.00	-	-	-	1							
Strudwick, H.	28	1909-10	1926	42	13	230	24	7.93	-	-	61	12							
Studd, C.T.	5	1882	1882-83	9	1	160	48	20.00	-	-	5	-	384	98	3	32.66	2-35	-	-
Studd, G.B.	4	1882-83	1882-83	7	0	31	9	4.42	-	-	8	-							
Subba Row, R.	13	1958	1961	22†	1	984	137	46.85	3	4	5	-	6	2	0	-	-	-	-
Such, P.M.	11	1993	1999	16	5	67	14*	6.09	-	-	4	-	3124	1242	37	33.56	6-67	2	-
Sugg, F.H.	2	1888	1888	2	0	55	31	27.50	-	-	-	-							
Sutcliffe, H.	54	1924	1935	84	9	4555	194	60.73	16	23	23	-							
Swann, G.P.	12	2008-09	2009	14	4	354	63*	35.40	-	3	7	-	2941	1459	48	30.39	5-57	2	-
Swetman, R.	11	1958-59	1959-60	17	2	254	65	16.93	-	1	24	2							

				BATTING AND FIELDING									BOWLING						
	First Test	Last Test	Tests	Inns	NO	Runs	HS	Avge	100	50	Ct	St	Balls	Runs	Wkts	Avge	BB	5wI	10wM
Tate, F.W.	1902	1902	1	2	1	9	5*	9.00	—	—	2	—	96	51	2	25.50	2-7	—	—
Tate, M.W.	1924	1935	39	52	5	1198	100*	25.48	1	5	11	—	12523	4055	155	26.16	6-42	7	1
Tattersall, R.	1950-51	1954	16	17†	7	50	10*	5.00	—	—	8	—	4228	1513	58	26.08	7-52	4	1
Tavaré, C.J.	1980	1989	31	56	2	1755	149	32.50	2	12	20	—	30	11	0	—	—	—	—
Taylor, J.P.	1992-93	1994	2	4†	2	34	17*	17.00	—	—	—	—	288†	156	3	52.00	1-18	—	—
Taylor, K.	1959	1964	3	5	0	57	24	11.40	—	—	1	—	12	6	0	—	—	—	—
Taylor, L.B.	1985	1985	2	1	1	1	1*	—	—	—	—	—	381	178	4	44.50	2-34	—	—
Taylor, R.W.	1970-71	1983-84	57	83	12	1156	97	16.28	—	3	167	7	12	6	0	—	—	—	—
Tennyson, Hon. L.H.	1913-14	1921	9	12	1	345	74*	31.36	—	4	6	—	6	1	0	—	—	—	—
Terry, V.P.	1984	1984	2	3	0	16	8	5.33	—	—	2	—	—	—	—	—	—	—	—
Thomas, J.G.	1985-86	1986	5	10	4	83	31*	13.83	—	—	—	—	774	504	10	50.40	4-70	—	—
Thompson, G.J.	1909	1909-10	6	10	1	273	63	30.33	—	2	5	—	1367	638	23	27.73	4-50	—	—
Thomson, N.I.	1964-65	1964-65	5	4	1	69	39	23.00	—	—	3	—	1488	568	9	63.11	2-55	—	—
Thorpe, G.P.	1993	2005	100	179†	28	6744	200*	44.66	16	39	105	—	138	37	0	—	—	—	—
Titmus, F.J.	1955	1974-75	53	76	11	1449	84*	22.29	—	10	35	—	15118	4931	153	32.22	7-79	7	—
Tolchard, R.W.	1976-77	1976-77	4	7	2	129	67	25.80	—	1	5	—	—	—	—	—	—	—	—
Townsend, C.L.	1899	1899	2	3†	0	51	38	17.00	—	—	—	—	140	75	3	25.00	3-50	—	—
Townsend, D.C.H.	1934-35	1934-35	3	6	0	77	36	12.83	—	—	1	—	6	9	0	—	—	—	—
Townsend, L.F.	1929-30	1933-34	4	6	0	97	40	16.16	—	—	2	—	399	205	6	34.16	2-22	—	—
Tremlett, C.T.	2007	2007	3	5	1	50	25*	12.50	—	—	1	—	859	386	13	29.69	3-12	—	—
Tremlett, M.F.	1947-48	1947-48	3	5	2	20	18*	6.66	—	—	—	—	492	226	4	56.50	2-98	—	—
Trescothick, M.E.	2000	2006	76	143†	10	5825	219	43.79	14	29	95	—	300	155	1	155.00	1-34	—	—
Trott, A.E. ‡	1898-99	1898-99	2	4	0	23	16	5.75	—	—	—	—	474	198	17	11.64	5-49	1	—
Trott, I.J.L.	2009	2009	1	2	0	160	119	80.00	1	—	1	—	—	—	—	—	—	—	—
Trueman, F.S.	1952	1965	67	85	14	981	39*	13.81	—	—	64	—	15178	6625	307	21.57	8-31	17	3
Tudor, A.J.	1998-99	2002-03	10	16	4	229	99*	19.08	—	1	3	—	1512	963	28	34.39	5-44	1	—
Tufnell, N.C.	1909-10	1909-10	1	1	0	14	14	14.00	—	—	—	1	—	—	—	—	—	—	—
Tufnell, P.C.R.	1990-91	2001	42	59	29	153	22*	5.10	—	—	12	—	11288†	4560	121	37.68	7-47	5	2
Turnbull, M.J.L.	1929-30	1936	9	13	2	224	61	20.36	—	1	1	—	—	—	—	—	—	—	—
Tyldesley, G.E.	1921	1928-29	14	20	2	990	122	55.00	3	6	2	—	2	2	0	—	—	—	—
Tyldesley, J.T.	1898-99	1909	31	55	1	1661	138	30.75	4	9	16	—	—	—	—	—	—	—	—
Tyldesley, R.K.	1924	1930	7	7	1	47	29	7.83	—	—	1	—	1615	619	19	32.57	3-50	—	—
Tylecote, E.F.S.	1882-83	1886	6	9	1	152	66	19.00	—	1	5	5	—	—	—	—	—	—	—
Tyler, E.J.	1895-96	1895-96	1	1†	0	0	0	0.00	—	—	—	—	145†	65	4	16.25	3-49	—	—
Tyson, F.H.	1954	1958-59	17	24	3	230	37*	10.95	—	—	4	—	3452	1411	76	18.56	7-27	4	1
Udal, S.D.	2005-06	2005-06	4	7	1	109	33*	18.16	—	—	1	—	596	344	8	43.00	4-14	—	—
Ulyett, G.	1876-77	1890	25	39	0	949	149	24.33	1	7	19	—	2627	1020	50	20.40	7-36	1	—
Underwood, D.L.	1966	1981-82	86	116	35	937	45*	11.56	—	—	44	—	21862†	7674	297	25.83	8-51	17	6
Valentine, B.H.	1933-34	1938-39	7	9	2	454	136	64.85	2	1	2	—	—	—	—	—	—	—	—
Vaughan, M.P.	1999-00	2008	82	147	9	5719	197	41.44	18	18	44	—	978	561	6	93.50	2-71	—	—
Verity, H.	1931	1939	40	44	12	669	66*	20.90	—	3	30	—	11173†	3510	144	24.37	8-43	5	2
Vernon, G.F.	1882-83	1882-83	1	2	1	14	11*	14.00	—	—	—	—	—	—	—	—	—	—	—

INDIVIDUAL CAREER RECORDS – ENGLAND continued

	First Test	Last Test	Tests	Inns	NO	Runs	HS	Avge	100	50	Ct	St	Balls	Runs	Wkts	Avge	BB	5wI	10wM
Vine, J.	1911-12	1911-12	2	3	2	46	36	46.00	—	1	—	—	—	—	—	—	—	—	—
Voce, W.	1929-30	1946-47	27	38	15	308	66	13.39	—	—	15	—	6360†	2733	98	27.88	7-70	3	2
Waddington, A.	1920-21	1920-21	2	4	0	16	7	4.00	—	—	1	—	276†	119	1	119.00	1-35	—	—
Wainwright, E.	1893	1897-98	5	9	0	132	49	14.66	—	—	2	—	127	73	0	—	—	—	—
Walker, P.M.	1960	1960	3	4	0	128	52	32.00	—	1	5	—	78†	34	0	—	—	—	—
Walters, C.F.	1933	1934	11	18	3	784	102	52.26	1	7	6	—	—	—	—	—	—	—	—
Ward, Alan	1969	1976	5	6	1	40	21	8.00	—	—	3	—	761	453	14	32.35	4-61	—	—
Ward, Albert	1893	1894-95	7	13	0	487	117	37.46	1	3	—	—	—	—	—	—	—	—	—
Ward, I.J.	2001	2001	5	9†	1	129	39	16.12	—	—	1	—	—	—	—	—	—	—	—
Wardle, J.H.	1947-48	1957	28	41†	8	653	66	19.78	—	2	12	—	6597†	2080	102	20.39	7-36	5	1
Warner, P.F.	1898-99	1912	15	28	2	622	132*	23.92	1	3	3	—	—	—	—	—	—	—	—
Warr, J.J.	1950-51	1950-51	2	4	0	4	4	1.00	—	—	—	—	584	281	1	281.00	1-76	—	—
Warren, A.	1905	1905	1	1	0	7	7	7.00	—	—	—	—	236	113	6	18.83	5-57	1	—
Washbrook, C.	1937	1956	37	66	6	2569	195	42.81	6	12	12	—	36	33	1	33.00	1-25	—	—
Watkin, S.L.	1991	1993	3	5	6	25	13	5.00	—	—	1	—	534	305	11	27.72	4-65	—	—
Watkins, A.J.	1948	1952	15	24†	4	810	137*	40.50	2	4	17	—	1364†	554	11	50.36	3-20	—	—
Watkinson, M.	1995	1995-96	4	6	1	167	82*	33.40	—	1	—	—	672	348	10	34.80	3-64	—	—
Watson, W.	1951	1958-59	23	37†	3	879	116	25.85	2	3	8	—	—	—	—	—	—	—	—
Webbe, A.J.	1878-79	1878-79	1	2	0	4	4	2.00	—	—	2	—	—	—	—	—	—	—	—
Wellard, A.W.	1937	1938	2	4	0	47	38	11.75	—	—	2	—	456	237	7	33.85	4-81	—	—
Wells, A.P.	1995	1995	1	2	1	3	3*	3.00	—	—	—	—	—	—	—	—	—	—	—
Wharton, A.	1949	1949	1	2†	0	20	13	10.00	—	—	1	—	—	—	—	—	—	—	—
Whitaker, J.J.	1986-87	1986-87	1	1	0	11	11	11.00	—	—	—	—	—	—	—	—	—	—	—
White, C.	1994	2002-03	30	50	7	1052	121	24.46	1	5	14	—	3959	2220	59	37.62	5-32	3	—
White, D.W.	1961-62	1961-62	2	2†	2	0	0	0.00	—	—	—	—	220	119	4	29.75	3-65	—	—
White, J.C.	1921	1930-31	15	22	9	239	29	18.38	—	2	6	—	4801†	1581	49	32.26	8-126	3	1
Whysall, W.W.	1924-25	1930	4	7	0	209	76	29.85	—	2	7	—	16	9	0	—	—	—	—
Wilkinson, L.L.	1938-39	1938-39	3	2	1	3	2	3.00	—	—	—	—	573	271	7	38.71	2-12	—	—
Willey, P.	1976	1986	26	50	6	1184	102*	26.90	2	5	3	—	1091	456	7	65.14	2-73	—	—
Williams, N.F.	1990	1990	1	2	0	38	38	38.00	—	—	—	—	246	148	2	74.00	2-148	—	—
Willis, R.G.D.	1970-71	1984	90	128	55	840	28*	11.50	—	—	39	—	17357	8190	325	25.20	8-43	16	—
Wilson, C.E.M.	1898-99	1898-99	2	4	1	42	18	14.00	—	—	1	—	—	—	—	—	—	—	—
Wilson, D.	1963-64	1970-71	6	7†	1	75	42	12.50	—	—	1	—	1472†	466	11	42.36	2-17	—	—
Wilson, E.R.	1920-21	1920-21	1	2	1	10	5	5.00	—	—	—	—	123	36	3	12.00	2-28	—	—
Wood, A.	1938	1939	4	5	1	80	53	20.00	—	1	10	1	—	—	—	—	—	—	—
Wood, B.	1972	1978	12	21	0	454	90	21.61	—	2	6	—	98	50	0	—	—	—	—
Wood, G.E.C.	1924	1924	3	4	1	7	6	3.50	—	—	5	1	—	—	—	—	—	—	—
Wood, H.	1888	1891-92	4	4	0	204	134*	68.00	1	1	2	1	—	—	—	—	—	—	—
Wood, R.	1886-87	1886-87	1	2†	0	6	6	3.00	—	—	—	—	—	—	—	—	—	—	—
Woods, S.M.J. ‡	1895-96	1895-96	3	4	1	122	53	30.50	—	1	4	—	195	129	5	25.80	3-28	—	—
Woolley, F.E.	1909	1934	64	98†	7	3283	154	36.07	5	23	64	—	6495†	2815	83	33.91	7-76	4	1
Woolmer, R.A.	1975	1981	19	34	2	1059	149	33.09	3	2	10	—	546	299	4	74.75	1-8	—	—
Worthington, T.S.	1929-30	1936-37	9	11	2	321	128	29.18	1	1	8	—	633	316	8	39.50	2-19	—	—
Wright, C.W.	1895-96	1895-96	3	4	0	125	71	31.25	—	1	—	—	—	—	—	—	—	—	—

	First Test	Last Test	Tests	Inns	NO	Runs	HS	Avge	100	50	Ct	St	Balls	Runs	Wkts	Avge	BB	5wI	10wM
								BATTING AND FIELDING								*BOWLING*			
Wright, D.V.P.	1938	1950-51	34	39	13	289	45	11.11	–	–	10	–	8135	4224	108	39.11	7-105	6	1
Wyatt, R.E.S.	1927-28	1936-37	40	64	6	1839	149	31.70	2	12	16	–	1395	642	18	35.66	3-4	–	–
Wynyard, E.G.	1896	1905-06	3	6	0	72	30	12.00	–	–	–	–	24	17	0	–	–	–	–
Yardley, N.W.D.	1938-39	1950	20	34	2	812	99	25.37	–	4	14	–	1662	707	21	33.66	3-67	–	–
Young, H.I.	1899	1899	2	2	0	43	43	21.50	–	–	1	–	556†	262	12	21.83	4-30	–	–
Young, J.A.	1947	1949	8	10	5	28	10*	5.60	–	–	5	–	2368†	757	17	44.52	3-65	–	–
Young, R.A.	1907-08	1907-08	2	4	0	27	13	6.75	–	–	6	–	–	–	–	–	–	–	–

INDIVIDUAL CAREER RECORDS – AUSTRALIA

	First Test	Last Test	Tests	Inns	NO	Runs	HS	Avge	100	50	Ct	St	Balls	Runs	Wkts	Avge	BB	5wI	10wM
								BATTING AND FIELDING								*BOWLING*			
a'Beckett, E.L.	1928-29	1931-32	4	7	0	143	41	20.42	–	–	4	–	1062	317	3	105.66	1-41	–	–
Alderman, T.M.	1981	1990-91	41	53	22	203	26*	6.54	–	–	27	–	10181	4616	170	27.15	6-47	14	1
Alexander, G.	1880	1884-85	2	4	0	52	33	13.00	–	–	2	–	168	93	2	46.50	2-69	–	–
Alexander, H.H.	1932-33	1932-33	1	2	1	17	17*	17.00	–	–	–	–	276	154	1	154.00	1-129	–	–
Allan, F.E.	1878-79	1878-79	1	1	0	5	5	5.00	–	–	–	–	180†	80	4	20.00	2-30	–	–
Allan, P.J.	1965-66	1965-66	1	–	–	–	–	–	–	–	–	–	192	83	2	41.50	2-58	–	–
Allen, R.C.	1886-87	1886-87	1	2	0	44	30	22.00	–	–	2	–	–	–	–	–	–	–	–
Andrews, T.J.E.	1921	1926	16	23	1	592	94	26.90	–	4	12	–	156	116	1	116.00	1-23	–	–
Angel, J.	1992-93	1994-95	4	7†	1	35	11	5.83	–	–	1	–	748	463	10	46.30	3-54	–	–
Archer, K.A.	1950-51	1951-52	5	9	0	234	48	26.00	–	2	–	–	–	–	–	–	–	–	–
Archer, R.G.	1952-53	1956-57	19	30	1	713	128	24.58	1	2	20	–	3576	1318	48	27.45	5-53	1	–
Armstrong, W.W.	1901-02	1921	50	84	10	2863	159*	38.68	6	8	44	–	8022	2923	87	33.59	6-35	3	–
Badcock, C.L.	1936-37	1938	7	12	1	160	118	14.54	1	–	3	–	–	–	–	–	–	–	–
Bannerman, A.C.	1878-79	1893	28	50	2	1108	94	23.08	–	8	21	–	292	163	4	40.75	3-111	–	–
Bannerman, C.	1876-77	1878-79	3	6	2	239	165*	59.75	1	–	–	–	–	–	–	–	–	–	–
Bardsley, W.	1909	1926	41	66†	5	2469	193*	40.47	6	14	12	–	–	–	–	–	–	–	–
Barnes, S.G.	1938	1948	13	19	2	1072	234	63.05	3	5	14	–	594	218	4	54.50	2-25	–	–
Barnett, B.A.	1938	1938	4	8†	1	195	57	27.85	–	1	3	2	–	–	–	–	–	–	–
Barrett, J.E.	1890	1890	2	4†	1	80	67*	26.66	–	1	1	–	–	–	–	–	–	–	–
Beard, G.R.	1979-80	1979-80	3	5	0	114	49	22.80	–	–	–	–	259	109	1	109.00	1-26	–	–
Benaud, J.	1972-73	1972-73	3	5	0	223	142	44.60	1	1	–	–	24	12	2	6.00	2-12	–	–
Benaud, R.	1951-52	1963-64	63	97	7	2201	122	24.45	3	9	65	–	19108	6704	248	27.03	7-72	16	1
Bennett, M.J.	1984-85	1985	3	5	2	71	23	23.66	–	–	5	–	664†	325	6	54.16	3-79	–	–
Bevan, M.G.	1994-95	1997-98	18	30†	3	785	91	29.07	–	6	8	–	1285†	703	29	24.24	6-82	1	1
Bichel, A.J.	1996-97	2003-04	19	22	1	355	71	16.90	–	1	16	–	3337	1870	58	32.24	5-60	1	–
Blackham, J.M.	1876-77	1894-95	35	62	11	800	74	15.68	–	4	37	24	–	–	–	–	–	–	–
Blackie, D.D.	1928-29	1928-29	3	6†	3	24	11*	8.00	–	–	2	–	1260	444	14	31.71	6-94	1	–
Blewett, G.S.	1994-95	1999-00	46	79	4	2552	214	34.02	4	15	45	–	1436	720	14	51.42	2-9	–	–
Bollinger, D.E.	2008-09	2008-09	1	1†	1	0	0*	–	–	–	–	–	264†	131	2	65.50	2-53	–	–
Bonnor, G.J.	1880	1888	17	30	0	512	128	17.06	1	2	16	–	164	84	2	42.00	1-5	–	–

INDIVIDUAL CAREER RECORDS – AUSTRALIA *continued*

	First Test	Last Test	Tests	Inns	NO	Runs	HS	Avge	100	50	Ct	St	Balls	Runs	Wkts	Avge	BB	5wI	10wM
				BATTING AND FIELDING									BOWLING						
Boon, D.C.	1984-85	1995-96	107	190	20	7422	200	43.65	21	32	99	–	36	14	0	–	–	–	–
Booth, B.C.	1961	1965-66	29	48	6	1773	169	42.21	5	10	17	–	436	146	3	48.66	2-33	–	–
Border, A.R.	1978-79	1993-94	156	265†	44	11174	205	50.56	27	63	156	–	4009†	1525	39	39.10	7-46	2	1
Boyle, H.F.	1878-79	1884-85	12	16	4	153	36*	12.75	–	–	10	–	1743	641	32	20.03	6-42	1	–
Bracken, N.W.	2003-04	2005-06	5	6	2	70	37	17.50	–	–	2	–	1110†	505	12	42.08	4-48	–	–
Bradman, D.G.	1928-29	1948	52	80	10	6996	334	99.94	29	13	32	–	160	72	2	36.00	1-8	–	–
Bright, R.J.	1977	1986-87	25	39	8	445	33	14.35	–	–	13	–	5541†	2180	53	41.13	7-87	4	1
Bromley, E.H.	1932-33	1934	2	4†	0	38	26	9.50	–	–	2	–	60†	19	0	–	–	–	–
Brown, W.A.	1934	1948	22	35	1	1592	206*	46.82	4	9	14	–	–	–	–	–	–	–	–
Bruce, W.	1884-85	1894-95	14	26†	2	702	80	29.25	–	5	12	–	988†	440	12	36.66	3-88	–	–
Burge, P.J.P.	1954-55	1965-66	42	68	8	2290	181	38.16	4	12	23	–	–	–	–	–	–	–	–
Burke, J.W.	1950-51	1958-59	24	44	7	1280	189	34.59	3	5	18	–	814	230	8	28.75	4-37	–	–
Burn, E.J.K.	1890	1890	2	4	0	41	19	10.25	–	–	1	–	–	–	–	–	–	–	–
Burton, F.J.	1886-87	1887-88	2	4	2	4	2*	2.00	–	–	1	1	–	–	–	–	–	–	–
Callaway, S.T.	1891-92	1894-95	3	6	1	87	41	17.40	–	–	–	–	471	142	6	23.66	5-37	1	–
Callen, I.W.	1977-78	1977-78	1	2†	2	26	22*	–	–	–	1	–	440	191	6	31.83	3-83	–	–
Campbell, G.D.	1989	1989-90	4	4	0	10	6	2.50	–	–	–	–	951	503	13	38.69	3-79	–	–
Carkeek, W.	1912	1912	6	5†	1	16	6*	5.33	–	–	6	–	–	–	–	–	–	–	–
Carlson, P.H.	1978-79	1978-79	2	4	0	23	21	5.75	–	–	2	–	368	99	2	49.50	2-41	–	–
Carter, H.	1907-08	1921-22	28	47	9	873	72	22.97	–	4	44	21	–	–	–	–	–	–	–
Casson, B.	2008	2008	1	1	0	10	10	10.00	–	–	2	–	192†	129	3	43.00	3-86	–	–
Chappell, G.S.	1970-71	1983-84	87	151	19	7110	247*	53.86	24	31	122	–	5327	1913	47	40.70	5-61	1	–
Chappell, I.M.	1964-65	1979-80	75	136	10	5345	196	42.42	14	26	105	–	2873	1316	20	65.80	2-21	–	–
Chappell, T.M.	1981	1981	3	6	0	79	27	15.80	–	–	2	–	–	–	–	–	–	–	–
Charlton, P.C.	1890	1890	2	4	0	29	11	7.25	–	–	1	–	45	24	3	8.00	3-18	–	–
Chipperfield, A.G.	1934	1938	14	20	3	552	109	32.47	1	2	15	–	924	437	5	87.40	3-91	–	–
Clark, S.R.	2005-06	2009	24	26	7	248	39	13.05	–	–	4	–	5146	2243	94	23.86	5-32	2	–
Clark, W.M.	1977-78	1978-79	10	19	2	98	33	5.76	–	–	6	–	2793	1265	44	28.75	4-46	–	–
Clarke, M.J.	2004-05	2009	52	84	10	3652	151	49.35	12	15	47	–	1540†	755	19	39.73	6-9	1	–
Colley, D.J.	1972	1972	3	4	0	84	54	21.00	–	1	1	–	729	312	6	52.00	3-83	–	–
Collins, H.L.	1920-21	1926	19	31	1	1352	203	45.06	4	6	13	–	654†	252	4	63.00	2-47	–	–
Coningham, A.	1894-95	1894-95	1	2†	0	13	10	6.50	–	–	–	–	186†	76	2	38.00	2-17	–	–
Connolly, A.N.	1963-64	1970-71	29	45	20	260	37	10.40	–	–	17	–	7818	2981	102	29.22	6-47	4	–
Cook, S.H.	1997-98	1997-98	2	2†	2	3	3*	–	–	–	–	–	224	142	7	20.28	5-39	1	–
Cooper, B.B.	1876-77	1876-77	1	2	0	18	15	9.00	–	–	2	–	–	–	–	–	–	–	–
Cooper, W.H.	1881-82	1884-85	2	3	1	13	7	6.50	–	–	1	–	446	226	9	25.11	6-120	1	–
Corling, G.E.	1964	1964	5	4	1	5	3	1.66	–	–	–	–	1159	447	12	37.25	4-60	–	–
Cosier, G.J.	1975-76	1978-79	18	32	1	897	168	28.93	2	3	14	–	899	341	5	68.20	2-26	–	–
Cottam, J.T.	1886-87	1886-87	1	2	0	4	3	2.00	–	–	–	–	–	–	–	–	–	–	–
Cotter, A.	1903-04	1911-12	21	37	2	457	45	13.05	–	–	8	–	4633	2549	89	28.64	7-148	7	–
Coulthard, G.	1881-82	1881-82	1	1	1	6	6*	–	–	–	–	–	–	–	–	–	–	–	–

INDIVIDUAL CAREER RECORDS – AUSTRALIA *continued*

	First Test	Last Test	Tests	Inns	NO	Runs	HS	Avge	100	50	Ct	St	Balls	Runs	Wkts	Avge	BB	5wI	10wM
				BATTING AND FIELDING									*BOWLING*						
Cowper, R.M.	1964	1968	27	46†	2	2061	307	46.84	5	10	21	–	3005	1139	36	31.63	4-48	–	–
Craig, I.D.	1952-53	1957-58	11	18	0	358	53	19.88	–	2	2	–	437	107	7	15.28	3-28	–	–
Crawford, W.P.A.	1956	1956-57	4	5	2	53	34	17.66	–	–	1	–	84	54	1	54.00	1-25	–	–
Cullen, D.J.	2005-06	2005-06	1	–	–	–	–	–	–	–	–	–	–	–	–	–	–	–	–
Dale, A.C.	1997-98	1998-99	2	3†	0	6	5	2.00	–	–	–	–	348	187	6	31.16	3-71	–	–
Darling, J.	1894-95	1905	34	60†	2	1657	178	28.56	3	8	27	–	–	–	–	–	–	–	–
Darling, L.S.	1932-33	1936-37	12	18†	1	474	85	27.88	–	3	8	–	162	65	0	–	–	–	–
Darling, W.M.	1977-78	1979-80	14	27	1	697	91	26.80	–	6	5	–	–	–	–	–	–	–	–
Davidson, A.K.	1953	1962-63	44	61†	7	1328	80	24.59	–	5	42	–	11587†	3819	186	20.53	7-93	14	2
Davis, I.C.	1973-74	1977	15	27	1	692	105	26.61	1	4	9	–	–	–	–	–	–	–	–
Davis, S.P.	1985-86	1985-86	1	1	1	0	0	0.00	–	–	–	–	150	70	0	–	–	–	–
de Courcy, J.H.	1953	1953	3	6	1	81	41	16.20	–	–	3	–	–	–	–	–	–	–	–
Dell, A.R.	1970-71	1973-74	2	2	2	6	3*	–	–	–	–	–	559†	160	6	26.66	3-65	–	–
Dodemaide, A.I.C.	1987-88	1992	10	15	6	202	50	22.44	–	1	6	–	2184	953	34	28.02	6-58	1	–
Donnan, H.	1891-92	1896	5	10	1	75	15	8.33	–	–	2	–	54	22	0	–	–	–	–
Dooland, B.	1946-47	1947-48	3	5	1	76	29	19.00	–	–	3	–	880	419	9	46.55	4-69	–	–
Duff, R.A.	1901-02	1905	22	40	3	1317	146	35.59	2	6	14	–	180	85	4	21.25	2-43	–	–
Duncan, J.R.F.	1970-71	1970-71	1	1	0	3	3	3.00	–	–	–	–	112	30	0	–	–	–	–
Dyer, G.C.	1986-87	1987-88	6	6	0	131	60	21.83	–	–	22	2	–	–	–	–	–	–	–
Dymock, G.	1973-74	1979-80	21	32†	7	236	31*	9.44	–	–	1	–	5545†	2116	78	27.12	7-67	5	1
Dyson, J.	1977-78	1984-85	30	58	7	1359	127*	26.64	2	5	10	–	–	–	–	–	–	–	–
Eady, C.J.	1896	1901-02	2	4	1	20	10*	6.66	–	–	2	–	223	112	7	16.00	3-30	–	–
Eastwood, K.H.	1970-71	1970-71	1	2†	0	5	5	2.50	–	–	–	–	40†	21	1	21.00	1-21	–	–
Ebeling, H.I.	1934	1934	1	2	0	43	41	21.50	–	–	1	–	186	89	3	29.66	3-74	–	–
Edwards, J.D.	1888	1888	3	6	1	48	26	9.60	–	–	1	–	–	–	–	–	–	–	–
Edwards, R.	1972	1975	20	32	3	1171	170*	40.37	2	9	7	–	12	20	0	–	–	–	–
Edwards, W.J.	1974-75	1974-75	3	6†	0	68	30	11.33	–	–	–	–	–	–	–	–	–	–	–
Elliott, M.T.G.	1996-97	2004	21	36†	1	1172	199	33.48	3	4	14	–	12†	4	0	–	–	–	–
Emery, P.A.	1994-95	1994-95	1	1†	1	8	8*	–	–	–	5	1	–	–	–	–	–	–	–
Emery, S.H.	1912	1912	4	2	0	6	5	3.00	–	–	2	–	462	249	5	49.80	2-46	–	–
Evans, E.	1881-82	1886	6	10	2	82	33	10.25	–	–	5	–	1237	332	7	47.42	3-64	–	–
Fairfax, A.G.	1928-29	1930-31	10	12	4	410	65	51.25	–	4	15	–	1520	645	21	30.71	4-31	–	–
Favell, L.E.	1954-55	1960-61	19	31	3	757	101	27.03	1	5	9	–	–	–	–	–	–	–	–
Ferris, J.J. ‡	1886-87	1890	8	16†	4	98	20*	8.16	–	–	4	–	2030†	684	48	14.25	5-26	4	–
Fingleton, J.H.W.	1931-32	1938	18	29	1	1189	136	42.46	5	3	13	–	–	–	–	–	–	–	–
Fleetwood-Smith, L.O'B.	1935-36	1938	10	11	5	54	16*	9.00	–	–	–	–	3093†	1570	42	37.38	6-110	2	1
Fleming, D.W.	1994-95	2000-01	20	19	3	305	71*	19.06	–	2	9	–	4129	1942	75	25.89	5-30	3	–
Francis, B.C.	1972	1972	3	5	0	52	27	10.40	–	–	1	–	–	–	–	–	–	–	–
Freeman, E.W.	1967-68	1969-70	11	18	0	345	76	19.16	–	2	5	–	2183	1128	34	33.17	4-52	–	–
Freer, F.A.W.	1946-47	1946-47	1	1	1	28	28*	–	–	–	–	–	160	74	3	24.66	2-49	–	–
Gannon, J.B.	1977-78	1977-78	3	5	4	3	3*	3.00	–	–	3	–	726†	361	11	32.81	4-77	–	–
Garrett, T.W.	1876-77	1887-88	19	33	6	339	51*	12.55	–	1	7	–	2728	970	36	26.94	6-78	2	2

INDIVIDUAL CAREER RECORDS – AUSTRALIA continued

	First Test	Last Test	Tests	BATTING AND FIELDING									BOWLING						
				Inns	NO	Runs	HS	Avge	100	50	Ct	St	Balls	Runs	Wkts	Avge	BB	5wI	10wM
Gaunt, R.A.	1957-58	1963-64	3	4†	2	6	3	3.00	–	–	–	–	716	310	7	44.28	3-53	–	–
Gehrs, D.R.A.	1903-04	1910-11	6	11	0	221	67	20.09	–	2	6	–	6	4	0	–	–	–	–
Giffen, G.	1881-82	1896	31	53	0	1238	161	23.35	1	6	24	–	6391	2791	103	27.09	7-117	7	1
Giffen, W.F.	1886-87	1891-92	3	6	0	11	3	1.83	–	–	1	–	–	–	–	–	–	–	–
Gilbert, D.R.	1985	1986-87	9	12	4	57	15	7.12	–	–	1	–	1647	843	16	52.68	3-48	–	–
Gilchrist, A.C.	1999-00	2007-08	96	137†	20	5570	204*	47.60	17	26	379	37	–	–	–	–	–	–	–
Gillespie, J.N.	1996-97	2005-06	71	93	28	1218	201*	18.73	1	2	27	–	14234	6770	259	26.13	7-37	8	3
Gilmour, G.J.	1973-74	1976-77	15	22†	1	483	101	23.00	1	3	8	–	2661†	1406	54	26.03	6-85	3	–
Gleeson, J.W.	1967-68	1972	29	46	8	395	45	10.39	–	–	17	–	8857	3367	93	36.20	5-61	3	–
Graham, H.	1893	1896	6	10	0	301	107	30.10	2	–	3	–	–	–	–	–	–	–	–
Gregory, D.W.	1876-77	1878-79	3	5	2	60	43	20.00	–	–	1	–	20	9	0	–	–	–	–
Gregory, E.J.	1876-77	1876-77	1	2	0	11	11	5.50	–	–	–	–	–	–	–	–	–	–	–
Gregory, J.M.	1920-21	1928-29	24	34†	3	1146	119	36.96	2	7	37	–	5582	2648	85	31.15	7-69	4	–
Gregory, R.G.	1936-37	1936-37	2	3	0	153	80	51.00	–	2	1	–	24	14	0	–	–	–	–
Gregory, S.E.	1890	1912	58	100	7	2282	201	24.53	4	8	25	–	30	33	0	–	–	–	–
Grimmett, C.V.	1924-25	1935-36	37	50	10	557	50	13.92	–	1	17	–	14513	5231	216	24.21	7-40	21	7
Groube, T.U.	1880	1880	1	2	0	11	11	5.50	–	–	–	–	–	–	–	–	–	–	–
Grout, A.T.W.	1957-58	1965-66	51	67	8	890	74	15.08	–	3	163	24	–	–	–	–	–	–	–
Guest, C.E.J.	1962-63	1962-63	1	1	0	11	11	11.00	–	–	–	–	144	59	0	–	–	–	–
Haddin, B.J.	2008	2009	19	32	2	1179	169	39.30	2	3	70	1	–	–	–	–	–	–	–
Hamence, R.A.	1946-47	1947-48	3	4	1	81	30*	27.00	–	–	1	–	–	–	–	–	–	–	–
Hammond, J.R.	1972-73	1972-73	5	5	2	28	19	9.33	–	–	2	–	1031	488	15	32.53	4-38	–	–
Harry, J.	1894-95	1894-95	1	2	0	8	6	4.00	–	–	1	–	–	–	–	–	–	–	–
Hartigan, M.J.	1907-08	1907-08	2	4	0	170	116	42.50	1	1	1	–	12	7	0	–	–	–	–
Hartkopf, A.E.V.	1924-25	1924-25	1	2	0	80	80	40.00	–	1	–	–	240	134	1	134.00	1-120	–	–
Harvey, M.R.	1946-47	1946-47	1	2	0	43	31	21.50	–	–	–	–	–	–	–	–	–	–	–
Harvey, R.N.	1947-48	1962-63	79	137†	10	6149	205	48.41	21	24	64	–	414	120	3	40.00	1-8	–	–
Hassett, A.L.	1938	1953	43	69	3	3073	198*	46.56	10	11	30	–	111	78	0	–	–	–	–
Hauritz, N.M.	2004-05	2009	7	9	1	117	41	14.62	–	–	1	–	1628	773	24	32.20	3-16	–	–
Hawke, N.J.N.	1962-63	1968	27	37	15	365	45*	16.59	–	–	9	–	6974	2677	91	29.41	7-105	6	1
Hayden, M.L.	1993-94	2008-09	103	184†	14	8625	380	50.73	30	29	128	–	54	40	0	–	–	–	–
Hazlitt, G.R.	1907-08	1912	9	12	4	89	34*	11.12	–	–	4	–	1563	623	23	27.08	7-25	1	–
Healy, I.A.	1988-89	1999-00	119	182	23	4356	161*	27.39	4	22	366	29	–	–	–	–	–	–	–
Hendry, H.S.T.L.	1921	1928-29	11	18	2	335	112	20.93	1	1	10	–	1706	640	16	40.00	3-36	–	–
Hibbert, P.A.	1977-78	1977-78	1	2†	0	15	13	7.50	–	–	1	–	–	–	–	–	–	–	–
Higgs, J.D.	1977-78	1980-81	22	36	16	111	16	5.55	–	–	1	–	4752	2057	66	31.16	7-143	2	–
Hilditch, A.M.J.	1978-79	1985-86	18	34	0	1073	119	31.55	2	6	13	–	–	–	–	–	–	–	–
Hilfenhaus, B.W.	2008-09	2009	8	11	5	68	20	11.33	–	–	1	–	1835	970	29	33.44	4-60	–	–
Hill, C.	1896	1911-12	49	89†	2	3412	191	39.21	7	19	33	–	–	–	–	–	–	–	–
Hill, J.C.	1953	1954-55	3	6	3	21	8*	7.00	–	–	2	–	606	273	8	34.12	3-35	–	–
Hoare, D.E.	1960-61	1960-61	1	2	0	35	35	17.50	–	–	2	–	232	156	2	78.00	2-68	–	–
Hodge, B.J.	2005-06	2008	6	11	2	503	203*	55.88	1	2	9	–	12	8	0	–	–	–	–
Hodges, J.R.	1876-77	1876-77	2	4†	1	10	8	3.33	–	–	–	–	136†	84	6	14.00	2-7	–	–

INDIVIDUAL CAREER RECORDS – AUSTRALIA *continued*

	First Test	Last Test	Tests	BATTING AND FIELDING									BOWLING						
				Inns	NO	Runs	HS	Avge	100	50	Ct	St	Balls	Runs	Wkts	Avge	BB	5wI	10wM
Hogan, T.G.	1982-83	1983-84	7	12	1	205	42*	18.63	–	–	2	–	1436†	706	15	47.06	5-66	1	–
Hogg, G.B.	1996-97	2007-08	7	10†	3	186	79	26.57	–	1	1	–	1524†	933	17	54.88	2-40	–	–
Hogg, R.M.	1978-79	1984-85	38	58	13	439	52	9.75	–	1	7	–	7633	3503	123	28.47	6-74	6	2
Hohns, T.V.	1988-89	1989	7	7†	1	136	40	22.66	–	–	3	–	1528	580	17	34.11	3-59	–	–
Hole, G.B.	1950-51	1954-55	18	33	2	789	66	25.45	–	6	21	–	398	126	1	42.00	1-9	–	–
Holland, R.G.	1984-85	1985-86	11	15	4	35	10	3.18	–	–	5	–	2889	1352	34	39.76	6-54	3	2
Hookes, D.W.	1976-77	1985-86	23	41†	3	1306	143*	34.36	1	8	12	–	96†	41	1	41.00	1-4	–	–
Hopkins, A.J.Y.	1901-02	1909	20	33	2	509	43	16.41	–	–	11	–	1327	696	26	26.76	4-81	1	–
Horan, T.P.	1876-77	1884-85	15	27	2	471	124	18.84	1	1	6	–	373	143	11	13.00	6-40	1	–
Hordern, H.V.	1910-11	1911-12	7	13	2	254	50	23.09	–	1	6	–	2148	1075	46	23.36	7-90	5	2
Hornibrook, P.M.	1928-29	1930	6	7†	1	60	26	10.00	–	–	7	–	1579†	664	17	39.05	7-92	1	–
Howell, W.P.	1897-98	1903-04	18	27†	6	158	35	7.52	–	–	12	–	3892	1407	49	28.71	5-81	7	1
Hughes, K.J.	1977	1984-85	70	124	6	4415	213	37.41	9	22	50	–	85	28	0	–	–	–	–
Hughes, M.G.	1985-86	1993-94	53	70	8	1032	72*	16.64	–	2	23	–	12285	6017	212	28.38	8-87	7	1
Hughes, P.J.	2008-09	2009	5	9†	0	472	160	52.44	2	1	3	–							
Hunt, W.A.	1931-32	1931-32	1	1†	0	0	0	0.00	–	–	1	–	96†	39	0	–	–	–	–
Hurst, A.G.	1973-74	1979-80	12	20	3	102	26	6.00	–	–	3	–	3054	1200	43	27.90	5-28	2	–
Hurwood, A.	1930-31	1930-31	2	2	0	5	5	2.50	–	–	2	–	517	170	11	15.45	4-22	1	–
Hussey, M.E.K.	2005-06	2009	42	72†	9	3317	182	52.65	10	16	37	–	168	100	1	100.00	1-22	–	–
Inverarity, R.J.	1968	1972	6	11	1	174	56	17.40	–	1	4	–	372†	93	4	23.25	3-26	–	–
Iredale, F.A.	1894-95	1899	14	23	1	807	140	36.68	2	4	16	–	12	3	0	–	–	–	–
Ironmonger, H.	1928-29	1932-33	14	21†	5	42	12	2.62	–	–	3	–	4695†	1330	74	17.97	7-23	4	2
Iverson, J.B.	1950-51	1950-51	5	7	3	3	1*	0.75	–	–	2	–	1108	320	21	15.23	6-27	1	1
Jackson, A.A.	1928-29	1930-31	8	11	1	474	164	47.40	1	2	7	–							
Jaques, P.A.	2005-06	2008	11	19†	0	902	150	47.47	3	6	7	–							
Jarman, B.N.	1959-60	1968-69	19	30	3	400	78	14.81	–	2	50	4							
Jarvis, A.H.	1884-85	1894-95	11	21	3	303	82	16.83	–	1	9	9							
Jenner, T.J.	1970-71	1975-76	9	14	5	208	74	23.11	–	–	5	–	1881	749	24	31.20	5-90	1	–
Jennings, C.B.	1912	1912	6	8	2	107	32	17.83	–	–	5	–							
Johnson, I.W.G.	1945-46	1956-57	45	66	12	1000	77	18.51	–	6	30	–	8780	3182	109	29.19	7-44	3	–
Johnson, L.J.	1947-48	1947-48	1	1	1	25	25*	–	–	–	2	–	282	74	6	12.33	3-8	–	–
Johnson, M.G.	2007-08	2009	26	34†	8	799	123*	30.73	1	4	6	–	6285†	3284	114	28.80	8-61	3	1
Johnston, W.A.	1947-48	1954-55	40	49†	25	273	29	11.37	–	–	16	–	11048†	3826	160	23.91	6-44	7	–
Jones, D.M.	1983-84	1992	52	89	11	3631	216	46.55	11	14	34	–	198	64	1	64.00	1-5	–	–
Jones, E.	1894-95	1902-03	19	26	4	126	20	5.04	–	–	21	–	3754	1857	64	29.01	7-88	3	1
Jones, S.P.	1881-82	1887-88	12	24	4	428	87	21.40	–	1	12	–	262	112	6	18.66	4-47	–	–
Joslin, L.R.	1967-68	1967-68	1	2†	0	9	7	4.50	–	–	–	–							
Julian, B.P.	1993	1995-96	7	9	1	128	56*	16.00	–	1	4	–	1098†	599	15	39.93	4-36	–	–
Kasprowicz, M.S.	1996-97	2005-06	38	54	12	445	25	10.59	–	–	16	–	7140	3716	113	32.88	7-36	4	–
Katich, S.M.	2001	2009	43	74†	5	2990	157	43.33	8	16	32	–	919†	560	18	31.11	6-65	1	–
Kelleway, C.	1910-11	1928-29	26	42	4	1422	147	37.42	3	6	24	–	4363	1683	52	32.36	5-33	1	–
Kelly, J.J.	1896	1905	36	56	17	664	46*	17.02	–	–	43	20							
Kelly, T.J.D.	1876-77	1878-79	2	3	0	64	35	21.33	–	–	–	–							
Kendall, T.K.	1876-77	1876-77	2	4†	1	39	17*	13.00	–	–	2	–	563†	215	14	15.35	7-55	1	–

445

INDIVIDUAL CAREER RECORDS – AUSTRALIA *continued*

	First Test	Last Test	Tests	BATTING AND FIELDING									BOWLING						
				Inns	NO	Runs	HS	Avge	100	50	Ct	St	Balls	Runs	Wkts	Avge	BB	5wI	10wM
Kent, M.F.	1981	1981	3	6	0	171	54	28.50	–	2	6	–	72	19	0	–	–	–	–
Kerr, R.B.	1985-86	1985-86	2	4	0	31	17	7.75	–	–	1	–	–	–	–	–	–	–	–
Kippax, A.F.	1924-25	1934	22	34	1	1192	146	36.12	2	8	13	–	2373†	776	34	22.82	7-75	1	–
Kline, L.F	1957-58	1960-61	13	16†	9	58	15*	8.28	–	–	9	–	743	562	13	43.23	8-215	1	1
Kreiza, J.J.	2008-09	2008-09	2	4	1	71	32	23.66	–	–	4	–	–	–	–	–	–	–	–
Laird, B.M.	1979-80	1982-83	21	40	2	1341	92	35.28	–	11	16	–	18	12	0	–	–	–	–
Langer, J.L.	1992-93	2006-07	105	182†	12	7696	250	45.27	23	30	73	–	6	3	0	–	–	–	–
Langley, G.R.A.	1951-52	1956-57	26	37	12	374	53	14.96	–	1	83	15	–	–	–	–	–	–	–
Laughlin, T.J.	1977-78	1978-79	3	5†	0	87	35	17.40	–	–	3	–	516	262	6	43.66	5-101	1	–
Laver, F.J.	1899	1909	15	23	6	196	45	11.52	–	–	8	–	2361	964	37	26.05	8-31	2	–
Law, S.G.	1995-96	1995-96	1	1	1	54	54*	–	–	1	1	–	18	9	0	–	–	–	–
Lawry, W.M.	1961	1970-71	67	123†	12	5234	210	47.15	13	27	30	–	14†	6	0	–	–	–	–
Lawson, G.F.	1980-81	1989-90	46	68	12	894	74	15.96	–	4	10	–	11118	5501	180	30.56	8-112	11	2
Lee, B	1999-00	2008-09	76	90	18	1451	64	20.15	–	5	23	–	16531	9554	310	30.81	5-30	10	–
Lee, P.K.	1931-32	1932-33	2	3	0	57	42	19.00	–	–	1	–	436	212	5	42.40	4-111	–	–
Lehmann, D.S.	1997-98	2004-05	27	42†	2	1798	177	44.95	5	10	11	–	974†	412	15	27.46	3-42	–	–
Lillee, D.K.	1970-71	1983-84	70	90	24	905	73*	13.71	–	1	23	–	18467	8493	355	23.92	7-83	23	7
Lindwall, R.R.	1945-46	1959-60	61	84	13	1502	118	21.15	2	5	26	–	13650	5251	228	23.03	7-38	12	–
Love, H.S.B.	1932-33	1932-33	1	2	0	8	5	4.00	–	–	3	–	–	–	–	–	–	–	–
Love, M.L.	2002-03	2003	5	8	3	233	100*	46.60	1	1	7	–	–	–	–	–	–	–	–
Loxton, S.J.E.	1947-48	1950-51	12	15	0	554	101	36.93	1	3	7	–	906	349	8	43.62	3-55	1	–
Lyons, J.J.	1886-87	1897-98	14	27	0	731	134	27.07	1	3	3	–	316	149	6	24.83	5-30	1	–
McAlister, P.A.	1903-04	1909	8	16	1	252	41	16.80	–	–	10	–	–	–	–	–	–	–	–
Macartney, C.G.	1907-08	1926	35	55	4	2131	170	41.78	7	9	17	–	3561†	1240	45	27.55	7-58	2	1
McCabe, S.J.	1930	1938	39	62	5	2748	232	48.21	6	13	41	–	3746	1543	36	42.86	4-13	–	–
McCool, C.L.	1945-46	1949-50	14	17	4	459	104*	35.30	1	1	14	–	2504	958	36	26.61	5-41	3	–
McCormick, E.L.	1935-36	1938	12	14†	5	54	17*	6.00	–	–	8	–	2107	1079	36	29.97	4-101	–	–
McCosker, R.B.	1974-75	1979-80	25	46	5	1622	127	39.56	4	9	21	–	–	–	–	–	–	–	–
McDermott, C.J.	1984-85	1995-96	71	90	13	940	42*	12.20	–	–	19	–	16586	8332	291	28.63	8-97	14	2
McDonald, A.B.	2008-09	2008-09	4	6	1	107	68	21.40	–	1	2	–	732	300	9	33.33	3-25	–	–
McDonald, C.C.	1951-52	1961	47	83	4	3107	170	39.32	5	17	14	–	8	3	0	–	–	–	–
McDonald, E.A.	1920-21	1921-22	11	12	5	116	36	16.57	–	–	3	–	2885	1431	43	33.27	5-32	2	–
McDonnell, P.S.	1880	1888	19	34	1	955	147	28.93	3	2	6	–	52	53	0	–	–	–	–
McGain, B.E.	2008-09	2008-09	1	2	0	2	2	1.00	–	–	–	–	108	149	0	–	–	–	–
MacGill, S.C.G.	1997-98	2008	44	47	11	349	43	9.69	–	1	16	–	11237	6038	208	29.02	8-108	12	2
McGrath, G.D.	1993-94	2006-07	124	138	51	641	61	7.36	–	–	38	–	29248	12186	563	21.64	8-24	29	3
McIlwraith, J.	1886	1886	1	2	0	9	7	4.50	–	–	1	–	–	–	–	–	–	–	–
McIntyre, P.E.	1994-95	1996-97	2	4	1	22	16	7.33	–	–	–	–	393	194	5	38.80	3-103	–	–
Mackay, K.D.	1956	1962-63	37	52†	7	1507	89	33.48	–	13	16	–	5792	1721	50	34.42	6-42	2	–
McKenzie, G.D.	1961	1970-71	60	89	12	945	76	12.27	–	2	34	–	17681	7328	246	29.78	8-71	16	3
McKibbin, T.R.	1894-95	1897-98	5	8†	2	88	28*	14.66	–	–	4	–	1032	496	17	29.17	3-35	–	–

INDIVIDUAL CAREER RECORDS – AUSTRALIA *continued*

	First Test	Last Test	Tests	BATTING AND FIELDING									BOWLING						
				Inns	NO	Runs	HS	Avge	100	50	Ct	St	Balls	Runs	Wkts	Avge	BB	5wI	10wM
McLaren, J.W.	1911-12	1911-12	1	2	1	0	0*	0.00	–	–	–	–	144	70	1	70.00	1-23	–	–
Maclean, J.A.	1978-79	1978-79	4	8	1	79	33*	11.28	–	–	18	–	–	–	–	–	–	–	–
McLeod, C.E.	1894-95	1905	17	29	5	573	112	23.87	1	4	9	–	3374	1325	33	40.15	5-65	2	–
McLeod, R.W.	1891-92	1893	6	11†	0	146	31	13.27	–	–	3	–	1089	382	12	31.83	5-53	1	–
McShane, P.G.	1884-85	1887-88	3	6†	1	26	12*	5.20	–	–	2	1	108†	48	1	48.00	1-39	–	–
Maddocks, L.V.	1954-55	1956-57	7	12	2	177	69	17.70	–	1	19	1	–	–	–	–	–	–	–
Maguire, J.N.	1983-84	1983-84	3	5	1	28	15*	7.00	–	–	2	–	616	323	10	32.30	4-57	–	–
Mailey, A.A.	1920-21	1926	21	29	9	222	46*	11.10	–	–	14	–	6119	3358	99	33.91	9-121	6	2
Mallett, A.A.	1968	1980	38	50	13	430	43*	11.62	–	–	30	–	9990	3940	132	29.84	8-59	6	1
Malone, M.F.	1977	1977	1	1	0	46	46	46.00	–	–	–	–	342	77	6	12.83	5-63	1	–
Mann, A.L.	1977-78	1977-78	4	8†	0	189	105	23.62	1	1	2	–	552	316	4	79.00	3-12	–	–
Manou, G.A.	2009	2009	1	2	1	21	13*	21.00	–	–	3	1	–	–	–	–	–	–	–
Marr, A.P.	1884-85	1884-85	1	2	0	5	5	2.50	–	–	–	–	48	14	0	–	–	–	–
Marsh, G.R.	1985-86	1991-92	50	93	7	2854	138	33.18	4	15	38	–	–	–	–	–	–	–	–
Marsh, R.W.	1970-71	1983-84	96	150†	13	3633	132	26.51	3	16	343	12	72	54	0	–	–	–	–
Martin, J.W.	1960-61	1966-67	8	13†	1	214	55	17.83	–	1	5	–	1846†	832	17	48.94	3-56	–	–
Martyn, D.R.	1992-93	2006-07	67	109	14	4406	165	46.37	13	23	36	–	348	168	2	84.00	1-0	–	–
Massie, H.H.	1881-82	1884-85	9	16	0	249	55	15.56	–	1	5	–	–	–	–	–	–	–	–
Massie, R.A.L.	1972	1972-73	6	8†	1	78	42	11.14	–	–	1	–	1739	647	31	20.87	8-53	2	1
Matthews, C.D.	1986-87	1988-89	3	5†	0	54	32	10.80	–	–	–	–	570†	313	6	52.16	3-95	–	–
Matthews, G.R.J.	1983-84	1992-93	33	53†	8	1849	130	41.08	4	12	17	–	6271	2942	61	48.22	5-103	2	1
Matthews, T.J.	1911-12	1912	8	10	1	153	53	17.00	–	1	7	–	1081	419	16	26.18	4-29	–	–
May, T.B.A.	1987-88	1994-95	24	28	12	225	42*	14.06	–	–	6	–	6577	2606	75	34.74	5-9	3	–
Mayne, E.R.	1912	1921-22	4	4	1	64	25*	21.33	–	–	2	–	6	6	0	–	–	–	–
Mayne, L.C.	1964-65	1969-70	6	11†	3	76	13	9.50	–	–	3	–	1251	628	19	33.05	4-43	–	–
Meckiff, I.	1957-58	1963-64	18	20	7	154	45*	11.84	–	–	9	–	3734†	1423	45	31.62	6-38	2	–
Meuleman, K.D.	1945-46	1945-46	1	1	0	0	0	0.00	–	–	1	–	–	–	–	–	–	–	–
Midwinter, W.E. ‡	1876-77	1886-87	8	14	1	174	37	13.38	–	–	5	–	949	333	14	23.78	5-78	1	–
Miller, C.R.	1998-99	2000-01	18	24	3	174	43	8.28	–	–	6	–	4091	1805	69	26.15	5-32	3	1
Miller, K.R.	1945-46	1956-57	55	87	7	2958	147	36.97	7	13	38	–	10461	3906	170	22.97	7-60	7	1
Minnett, R.B.	1911-12	1912	9	15	0	391	90	26.06	–	3	–	–	589	290	11	26.36	4-34	–	–
Misson, F.M.	1960-61	1961	5	5	3	38	25*	19.00	–	–	6	–	1197	616	16	38.50	4-58	–	–
Moody, T.M.	1989-90	1992	8	14	0	456	106	32.57	2	3	9	–	432	147	2	73.50	1-17	–	–
Moroney, J.	1949-50	1951-52	7	12	1	383	118	34.81	2	1	–	–	–	–	–	–	–	–	–
Morris, A.R.	1946-47	1954-55	46	79†	3	3533	206	46.48	12	12	15	–	111†	50	2	25.00	1-5	–	–
Morris, S.	1884-85	1884-85	1	2	1	14	10*	14.00	–	–	1	–	136	73	2	36.50	2-73	–	–
Moses, H.	1886-87	1894-95	6	10†	0	198	33	19.80	–	–	1	–	–	–	–	–	–	–	–
Moss, J.K.	1978-79	1978-79	1	2†	1	60	38*	60.00	–	–	1	–	–	–	–	–	–	–	–
Moule, W.H.	1880	1880	1	2	0	40	34	20.00	–	–	1	–	51	23	3	7.66	3-23	–	–
Muller, S.A.	1999-00	1999-00	2	2	2	6	6*	–	–	–	–	–	348	258	7	36.85	3-68	–	–
Murdoch, W.L. ‡	1876-77	1890	18	33	5	896	211	32.00	2	1	14	1	–	–	–	–	–	–	–
Musgrove, H.A.	1884-85	1884-85	1	2	0	13	9	6.50	–	–	–	–	–	–	–	–	–	–	–
Nagel, L.E.	1932-33	1932-33	1	2	1	21	21*	21.00	–	–	–	–	262	110	2	55.00	2-110	–	–
Nash, L.J.	1931-32	1936-37	2	2	0	30	17	15.00	–	–	6	–	311	126	10	12.60	4-18	–	–

INDIVIDUAL CAREER RECORDS – AUSTRALIA *continued*

	Tests	First Test	Last Test	Inns	NO	Runs	HS	Avge	100	50	Ct	St	Balls	Runs	Wkts	Avge	BB	5wI	10wM
								BATTING AND FIELDING								BOWLING			
Nicholson, M.J.	1	1998-99	1998-99	2	0	14	9	7.00	–	–	–	–	150	115	4	28.75	3-56	–	–
Nitschke, H.C.	2	1931-32	1931-32	2†	0	53	47	26.50	–	–	3	–							
Noble, M.A.	42	1897-98	1909	73	7	1997	133	30.25	1	16	26	–	7159	3025	121	25.00	7-17	9	2
Noblet, G.	3	1949-50	1952-53	4	1	22	13*	7.33	–	–	1	–	774	183	7	26.14	3-21	–	–
North, M.J.	7	2008-09	2009	12†	1	527	125*	47.90	3	1	5	–	633	302	6	50.33	4-98	–	–
Nothling, O.E.	1	1928-29	1928-29	2	0	52	44	26.00	–	–	–	–	276	72	0				
O'Brien, L.P.J.	5	1932-33	1936-37	8†	0	211	61	26.37	–	2	3	–							
O'Connor, J.D.A.	4	1907-08	1909	8†	1	86	20	12.28	–	–	3	–	692	340	13	26.15	5-40	1	–
O'Donnell, S.P.	6	1985	1985-86	10	3	206	48	29.42	–	–	4	–	940	504	6	84.00	3-37	–	–
Ogilvie, A.D.	5	1977-78	1977-78	10	0	178	47	17.80	–	–	5	–							
O'Keeffe, K.J.	24	1970-71	1977	34	9	644	85	25.76	–	1	15	–	5384	2018	53	38.07	5-101	1	–
Oldfield, W.A.S.	54	1920-21	1936-37	80	17	1427	65*	22.65	–	4	78	52							
O'Neill, N.C.	42	1958-59	1964-65	69	8	2779	181	45.55	6	15	21	–	1392	667	17	39.23	4-41	–	–
O'Reilly, W.J.	27	1931-32	1945-46	39†	7	410	56*	12.81	–	1	7	–	10024	3254	144	22.59	7-54	11	3
Oxenham, R.K.	7	1928-29	1931-32	10	0	151	48	15.10	–	–	4	–	1802	522	14	37.28	4-39	–	–
Palmer, G.E.	17	1880	1886	25	4	296	48	14.09	–	–	13	–	4517	1678	78	21.51	7-65	6	2
Park, R.L.	1	1920-21	1920-21	1	0	0	0	0.00	–	–	–	–	6	9	0				
Pascoe, L.S.	14	1977	1981-82	19	9	106	30*	10.60	–	–	2	–	3403	1668	64	26.06	5-59	1	–
Pellew, C.E.	10	1920-21	1921-22	14	1	484	116	37.23	2	1	4	–	78	34	0				
Phillips, W.B.	27	1983-84	1985-86	48†	2	1485	159	32.28	2	7	52	–							
Phillips, W.N.	1	1991-92	1991-92	2	0	22	14	11.00	–	–	–	–							
Philpott, P.I.	8	1964-65	1965-66	10	2	93	22	10.33	–	–	5	–	2262	1000	26	38.46	5-90	1	–
Ponsford, W.H.	29	1924-25	1934	48	4	2122	266	48.22	7	6	21	–							
Ponting, R.T.	136	1995-96	2009	229	26	11345	257	55.88	38	48	159	–	539	242	5	48.40	1-0	–	–
Pope, R.J.	1	1884-85	1884-85	2	0	3	3	1.50	–	–	–	–							
Rackemann, C.G.	12	1982-83	1990-91	14	4	53	15*	5.30	–	–	2	–	2719	1137	39	29.15	6-86	3	1
Ransford, V.S.	20	1907-08	1911-12	38†	6	1211	143*	37.84	1	7	10	–	43†	28	1	28.00	1-9	–	–
Redpath, I.R.	66	1963-64	1975-76	120	11	4737	171	43.45	8	31	83	–	64	41	0				
Reedman, J.C.	1	1894-95	1894-95	2	0	21	17	10.50	–	–	1	–	57	24	1	24.00	1-12	–	–
Reid, B.A.	27	1985-86	1992-93	34†	14	93	13	4.65	–	–	5	–	6244†	2784	113	24.63	7-51	5	2
Reiffel, P.R.	35	1991-92	1997-98	50	14	955	79*	26.52	–	6	15	–	6403	2804	104	26.96	6-71	5	–
Renneberg, D.A.	8	1966-67	1967-68	13	7	22	9	3.66	–	–	2	–	1598	830	23	36.08	5-39	2	–
Richardson, A.J.	9	1924-25	1926	13	0	403	100	31.00	1	2	1	–	1812	521	12	43.41	2-20	–	–
Richardson, V.Y.	19	1924-25	1935-36	30	0	706	138	23.53	1	1	24	–							
Rigg, K.E.	8	1930-31	1936-37	12	0	401	127	33.41	1	1	5	–							
Ring, D.T.	13	1947-48	1953	21	2	426	67	22.42	–	4	5	–	3024	1305	35	37.28	6-72	2	–
Ritchie, G.M.	30	1982-83	1986-87	53	5	1690	146	35.20	3	7	14	–	6	10	0				
Rixon, S.J.	13	1977-78	1984-85	24	3	394	54	18.76	–	2	42	5							
Robertson, G.R.	4	1997-98	1998-99	7	0	140	57	20.00	–	1	1	–	898	515	13	39.61	4-72	–	–
Robertson, W.R.	1	1884-85	1884-85	2	0	2	2	1.00	–	–	–	–	44	24	0				
Robinson, R.D.	3	1977	1977	6	0	100	34	16.66	–	–	4	–							
Robinson, R.H.	1	1936-37	1936-37	2	0	5	3	2.50	–	–	1	–							

INDIVIDUAL CAREER RECORDS – AUSTRALIA continued

Column groups: *BATTING AND FIELDING* spans Inns–St; *BOWLING* spans Balls–10wM.

Player	First Test	Last Test	Tests	Inns	NO	Runs	HS	Avge	100	50	Ct	St	Balls	Runs	Wkts	Avge	BB	5wI	10wM
Rogers, C.J.L.	2007-08	2007-08	1	2†	0	19	15	9.50	–	–	1	–	–	–	–	–	–	–	–
Rorke, G.F.	1958-59	1959-60	4	4†	2	9	7	4.50	–	–	1	–	703	203	10	20.30	3-23	–	–
Rutherford, J.W.	1956-57	1956-57	1	1	0	30	30	30.00	–	–	–	–	36	15	1	15.00	1-11	–	–
Ryder, J.	1920-21	1928-29	20	32	5	1394	201*	51.62	3	9	17	–	1897	743	17	43.70	2-20	–	–
Saggers, R.A.	1948	1949-50	6	5	2	30	14	10.00	–	–	16	8	–	–	–	–	–	–	–
Saunders, J.V.	1901-02	1907-08	14	23†	6	39	11*	2.29	–	–	5	–	3565†	1796	79	22.73	7-34	6	1
Scott, H.J.H.	1884	1886	8	14	1	359	102	27.61	1	1	8	–	28	26	0	–	–	–	–
Sellers, R.H.D.	1964-65	1964-65	1	1	0	0	0	0.00	–	–	1	–	30	17	0	–	–	–	–
Serjeant, C.S.	1977	1977-78	12	23	1	522	124	23.72	1	2	13	–	–	–	–	–	–	–	–
Sheahan, A.P.	1967-68	1973-74	31	53	6	1594	127	33.91	2	7	17	–	–	–	–	–	–	–	–
Shepherd, B.K.	1962-63	1964-65	9	14†	2	502	96	41.83	–	5	2	–	–	–	–	–	–	–	–
Siddle, P.M.	2008-09	2009	12	18	4	197	35	14.07	–	–	7	–	2837	1418	49	28.93	5-21	2	–
Sievers, M.W.	1936-37	1936-37	3	6	1	67	25*	13.40	–	–	4	–	602	161	9	17.88	5-21	1	–
Simpson, R.B.	1957-58	1977-78	62	111	7	4869	311	46.81	10	27	110	–	6881	3001	71	42.26	5-57	2	–
Sincock, D.J.	1964-65	1965-66	3	4	1	80	29	26.66	–	–	2	–	724†	410	8	51.25	3-67	–	–
Slater, K.N.	1958-59	1958-59	1	1	1	1	1*	–	–	–	–	–	256	101	2	50.50	2-40	–	–
Slater, M.J.	1993	2001	74	131	7	5312	219	42.83	14	21	33	–	25	10	1	10.00	1-4	–	–
Sleep, P.R.	1978-79	1989-90	14	21	1	483	90	24.15	–	3	4	–	2982	1397	31	45.06	5-72	1	–
Slight, J.	1880	1880	1	2	0	11	11	5.50	–	–	–	–	–	–	–	–	–	–	–
Smith, D.B.M.	1912	1912	2	3	1	30	24*	15.00	–	–	1	–	–	–	–	–	–	–	–
Smith, S.B.	1983-84	1983-84	3	5	0	41	12	8.20	–	1	–	–	–	–	–	–	–	–	–
Spofforth, F.R.	1876-77	1886-87	18	29	6	217	50	9.43	–	–	11	–	4185	1731	94	18.41	7-44	7	4
Stackpole, K.R.	1965-66	1973-74	43	80	5	2807	207	37.42	7	14	47	–	2321	1001	15	66.73	2-33	–	–
Stevens, G.B.	1959-60	1959-60	4	7	0	112	28	16.00	–	–	2	–	–	–	–	–	–	–	–
Symonds, A.	2003-04	2008-09	26	41	5	1462	162*	40.61	2	10	22	–	2094	896	24	37.33	3-50	–	–
Taber, H.B.	1966-67	1969-70	16	27	5	353	48	16.04	–	–	56	4	–	–	–	–	–	–	–
Tait, S.W.	2005	2007-08	3	5	2	20	8	6.66	–	–	1	–	414	302	5	60.40	3-97	–	–
Tallon, D.	1945-46	1953	21	26	3	394	92	17.13	–	2	50	8	–	–	–	–	–	–	–
Taylor, J.M.	1920-21	1926	20	28	0	997	108	35.60	1	8	11	–	114	45	1	45.00	1-25	–	–
Taylor, M.A.	1988-89	1998-99	104	186†	13	7525	334*	43.49	19	40	157	–	42	26	1	26.00	1-11	–	–
Taylor, P.L.	1986-87	1991-92	13	19†	3	431	87	26.93	–	2	10	–	2227	1068	27	39.55	6-78	1	–
Thomas, G.	1964-65	1965-66	8	12	1	325	61	29.54	–	3	3	–	–	–	–	–	–	–	–
Thoms, G.R.	1951-52	1951-52	1	2	0	44	28	22.00	–	–	–	–	–	–	–	–	–	–	–
Thomson, A.L.	1970-71	1970-71	4	5	4	22	12*	22.00	–	–	–	–	1519	654	12	54.50	3-79	–	–
Thomson, J.R.	1972-73	1985	51	73	20	679	49	12.81	–	–	20	–	10535	5601	200	28.00	6-46	8	–
Thomson, N.F.D.	1876-77	1876-77	2	4	0	67	41	16.75	–	–	3	–	112	31	1	31.00	1-14	–	–
Thurlow, H.M.	1931-32	1931-32	1	1	0	0	0	0.00	–	–	–	–	234	86	0	–	–	–	–
Toohey, P.M.	1977-78	1979-80	15	29	1	893	122	31.89	1	7	9	–	4	4	0	–	–	–	–
Toshack, E.R.H.	1945-46	1948	12	11	6	73	20*	14.60	–	–	4	–	3140†	989	47	21.04	6-29	4	1
Travers, J.P.F.	1901-02	1901-02	1	2†	0	10	9	5.00	–	–	1	–	48†	14	1	14.00	1-14	–	–
Tribe, G.E.	1946-47	1946-47	3	3†	1	35	25*	17.50	–	–	–	–	760†	330	2	165.00	2-48	–	–
Trott, A.E. ‡	1894-95	1894-95	3	5	3	205	85*	102.50	–	2	4	–	474	192	9	21.33	8-43	1	–
Trott, G.H.S.	1888	1897-98	24	42	0	921	143	21.92	1	4	21	–	1891	1019	29	35.13	4-71	–	–

INDIVIDUAL CAREER RECORDS – AUSTRALIA continued

	First Test	Last Test	Tests	Inns	NO	Runs	HS	Avge	100	50	Ct	St	Balls	Runs	Wkts	Avge	BB	5wI	10wM
Trumble, H.	1890	1903-04	32	57	14	851	70	19.79	–	4	45	–	8099	3072	141	21.78	8-65	9	3
Trumble, J.W.	1884-85	1886	7	13	1	243	59	20.25	–	1	3	–	600	222	10	22.20	3-29	–	–
Trumper, V.T.	1899	1911-12	48	89	8	3163	214*	39.04	8	13	31	–	546	317	8	39.62	3-60	–	–
Turner, A.	1975	1976-77	14	27†	1	768	136	29.53	1	3	15	–	–	–	–	–	–	–	–
Turner, C.T.B.	1886-87	1894-95	17	32	4	323	29	11.53	–	–	8	–	5179	1670	101	16.53	7-43	11	2
Veivers, T.R.	1963-64	1966-67	21	30†	4	813	88	31.26	–	7	7	–	4191	1375	33	41.66	4-68	–	–
Veletta, M.R.J.	1987-88	1989-90	8	11	0	207	39	18.81	–	–	12	–	–	–	–	–	–	–	–
Waite, M.G.	1938	1938	2	3	0	11	8	3.66	–	–	1	–	552	190	1	190.00	1-150	–	–
Walker, M.H.N.	1972-73	1977	34	43	13	586	78*	19.53	–	1	12	–	10094	3792	138	27.47	8-143	6	–
Wall, T.W.	1928-29	1934	18	24	5	121	20	6.36	–	–	11	–	4812	2010	56	35.89	5-14	3	–
Walters, F.H.	1884-85	1884-85	1	2	0	12	7	6.00	–	–	2	–	–	–	–	–	–	–	–
Walters, K.D.	1965-66	1980-81	74	125	14	5357	250	48.26	15	33	43	–	3295	1425	49	29.08	5-66	1	–
Ward, F.A.	1936-37	1938	4	8	2	36	18	6.00	–	–	1	–	1268	574	11	52.18	6-102	1	–
Warne, S.K.	1991-92	2006-07	145	199	17	3154	99	17.32	–	12	125	–	40704	17995	708	25.41	8-71	37	10
Watkins, J.R.	1972-73	1972-73	1	2	1	39	36	39.00	–	–	–	–	48	21	0	–	–	–	–
Watson, G.D.	1966-67	1972	5	9	0	97	50	10.77	–	–	1	–	552	254	6	42.33	2-67	–	–
Watson, S.R.	2004-05	2009	11	18	0	497	78	27.61	–	4	2	–	1018	547	14	39.07	4-42	–	–
Watson, W.J.	1954-55	1954-55	4	7	1	106	30	17.66	–	–	2	–	6	5	0	–	–	–	–
Waugh, M.E.	1990-91	2002-03	128	209	17	8029	153*	41.81	20	47	181	–	4853	2429	59	41.16	5-40	1	–
Waugh, S.R.	1985-86	2003-04	168	260	46	10927	200	51.06	32	50	112	–	7805	3445	92	37.44	5-28	3	–
Wellham, D.M.	1981	1986-87	6	11	1	257	103	23.36	1	–	5	–	–	–	–	–	–	–	–
Wessels, K.C. ‡	1982-83	1985-86	24	42†	1	1761	179	42.95	4	9	18	–	90	42	0	–	–	–	–
Whatmore, D.F.	1978-79	1979-80	7	13	0	293	77	22.53	–	2	13	–	30	11	0	–	–	–	–
White, C.L.	2008-09	2008-09	4	7	2	146	46	29.20	–	–	–	–	558	342	5	68.40	2-71	–	–
Whitney, M.R.	1981	1992-93	12	19	8	68	13	6.18	–	–	2	–	2672†	1325	39	33.97	7-27	2	1
Whitty, W.J.	1909	1912	14	19	7	161	39*	13.41	–	–	8	–	3357†	1373	65	21.12	6-17	3	–
Wiener, J.M.	1979-80	1979-80	6	11	0	281	93	25.54	–	2	4	–	78	41	0	–	–	–	–
Williams, B.A.	2003-04	2003-04	4	6	3	23	10*	7.66	–	–	4	–	852	406	9	45.11	4-53	–	–
Wilson, J.W.	1956-57	1956-57	1	2	1	10	10*	10.00	–	–	–	–	216†	64	1	64.00	1-25	–	–
Wilson, P.	1997-98	1997-98	1	2	2	0	0*	–	–	–	–	–	–	–	–	–	–	–	–
Wood, G.M.	1977-78	1988-89	59	112†	6	3374	172	31.83	9	13	41	–	72	50	0	–	–	–	–
Woodcock, A.J.	1973-74	1973-74	1	1	0	27	27	27.00	–	–	–	–	–	–	–	–	–	–	–
Woodfull, W.M.	1926	1934	35	54	4	2300	161	46.00	7	13	7	–	–	–	–	–	–	–	–
Woods, S.M.J. ‡	1888	1888	3	6	0	32	18	5.33	–	–	5	–	217	121	5	24.20	2-35	–	–
Woolley, R.D.	1982-83	1983-84	2	2	0	21	13	10.50	–	–	2	–	–	–	–	–	–	–	–
Worrall, J.	1884-85	1899	11	22	3	478	76	25.15	–	5	13	–	255	127	1	127.00	1-97	–	–
Wright, K.J.	1978-79	1979-80	10	18	5	219	55*	16.84	–	1	31	4	–	–	–	–	–	–	–
Yallop, G.N.	1975-76	1984-85	39	70†	3	2756	268	41.13	8	9	23	–	192†	116	1	116.00	1-21	–	–
Yardley, B.	1977-78	1982-83	33	54	4	978	74	19.56	–	4	31	–	8909	3986	126	31.63	7-98	6	1
Young, S.	1997	1997	1	2†	1	4	4*	4.00	–	–	–	–	48	13	0	–	–	–	–
Zoehrer, T.J.	1985-86	1986-87	10	14	2	246	52*	20.50	–	1	18	1	–	–	–	–	–	–	–

INDIVIDUAL CAREER RECORDS – SOUTH AFRICA

	First Test	Last Test	Tests	BATTING AND FIELDING									BOWLING						
				Inns	NO	Runs	HS	Avge	100	50	Ct	St	Balls	Runs	Wkts	Avge	BB	5wI	10wM
Ackerman, H.D.	1997-98	1997-98	4	8	0	161	57	20.12	-	1	1	-	8850†	4405	134	32.87	7-128	4	1
Adams, P.R.	1995-96	2003-04	45	55	15	360	35	9.00	-	-	29	-	6391	2195	104	21.10	6-43	5	-
Adcock, N.A.T.	1953-54	1961-62	26	39	12	146	24	5.40	-	-	4	-	42	28	0	-	-	-	-
Amla, H.M.	2004-05	2008-09	37	65	4	2460	176*	40.32	6	14	34	-	-	-	-	-	-	-	-
Anderson, J.H.	1902-03	1902-03	1	2	0	43	32	21.50	-	-	1	-	-	-	-	-	-	-	-
Ashley, W.H.	1888-89	1888-89	1	2	0	1	1	0.50	-	-	-	-	173†	95	7	13.57	7-95	1	-
Bacher, A.	1965	1969-70	12	22	1	679	73	32.33	-	6	10	-	-	-	-	-	-	-	-
Bacher, A.M.	1996-97	1999-00	19	33	1	833	96	26.03	1	5	11	-	6	4	0	-	-	-	-
Balaskas, X.C.	1930-31	1938-39	9	13	1	174	122*	14.50	-	-	5	-	1572	806	22	36.63	5-49	1	-
Barlow, E.J.	1961-62	1969-70	30	57	2	2516	201	45.74	6	15	35	-	3021	1362	40	34.05	5-85	1	-
Baumgartner, H.V.	1913-14	1913-14	1	2	0	19	16	9.50	-	-	1	-	166†	99	2	49.50	2-99	-	-
Beaumont, R.	1912	1913-14	5	9	0	70	31	7.77	-	-	2	-	6	0	0	-	-	-	-
Begbie, D.W.	1948-49	1949-50	5	7	0	138	48	19.71	-	-	2	-	160	130	1	130.00	1-38	-	-
Bell, A.J.	1929	1935	16	23	12	69	26*	6.27	-	-	6	-	3342	1567	48	32.64	6-99	4	-
Bisset, M.	1898-99	1909-10	3	6	2	103	35	25.75	-	-	2	1	-	-	-	-	-	-	-
Bisset, G.F.	1927-28	1927-28	4	4	2	38	23	19.00	-	-	-	-	989	469	25	18.76	7-29	2	-
Blanckenberg, J.M.	1913-14	1924	18	30	7	455	59	19.78	-	2	9	-	3888	1817	60	30.28	6-76	4	-
Bland, K.C.	1961-62	1966-67	21	39	5	1669	144*	49.08	3	9	10	-	394	125	2	62.50	2-16	-	-
Bock, E.G.	1935-36	1935-36	1	2	2	11	9*	-	-	-	-	-	138	91	0	-	-	-	-
Boje, N.	1999-00	2006	43	62†	10	1312	85	25.23	-	4	18	-	8620†	4265	100	42.65	5-62	3	-
Bond, G.E.	1938-39	1938-39	1	1	0	0	0	0.00	-	-	-	-	16	16	0	-	-	-	-
Bosch, T.	1991-92	1991-92	1	2	2	5	5*	-	-	-	-	-	237	104	3	34.66	2-61	-	-
Botha, J.	2005-06	2007-08	2	2	1	45	25	45.00	-	-	1	-	225	178	4	44.50	2-57	-	-
Botten, J.T.	1965	1965	3	6	0	65	33	10.83	-	-	-	-	828	337	8	42.12	2-56	-	-
Boucher, M.V. ‡	1997-98	2008-09	125	176	21	4671	125	30.13	5	29	451	22	8	6	1	6.00	1-6	-	-
Brann, W.H.	1922-23	1922-23	3	5	0	71	50	14.20	-	1	2	-	-	-	-	-	-	-	-
Briscoe, A.W.	1935-36	1938-39	2	3	0	33	16	11.00	-	-	1	-	-	-	-	-	-	-	-
Bromfield, H.D.	1961-62	1965	9	12	7	59	21	11.80	-	-	13	-	1810	599	17	35.23	5-88	1	-
Brown, L.S.	1931-32	1931-32	2	3	0	17	8	5.66	-	-	-	-	318	189	3	63.00	1-30	-	-
Burger, C.G.D.	1957-58	1957-58	2	4	1	62	37*	20.66	-	-	1	-	-	-	-	-	-	-	-
Burke, S.F.	1961-62	1964-65	2	4	1	42	20	14.00	-	-	-	-	660	257	11	23.36	6-128	2	1
Buys, I.D.	1922-23	1922-23	1	2	1	4	4*	4.00	-	-	-	-	144†	52	0	-	-	-	-
Cameron, H.B.	1927-28	1935	26	45	4	1239	90	30.21	-	10	39	12	-	-	-	-	-	-	-
Campbell, T.	1909-10	1912	5	9	3	90	48	15.00	-	-	7	1	-	-	-	-	-	-	-
Carlstein, P.R.	1957-58	1963-64	8	14	1	190	42	14.61	-	-	3	-	-	-	-	-	-	-	-
Carter, C.P.	1912	1924	10	15	5	181	45	18.10	-	-	2	-	1475†	694	28	24.78	6-50	2	-
Catterall, R.H.	1922-23	1930-31	24	43	2	1555	120	37.92	3	11	12	-	342	162	7	23.14	3-15	-	-
Chapman, H.W.	1913-14	1921-22	2	4	0	39	17	13.00	-	-	1	-	126	104	1	104.00	1-51	-	-
Cheetham, J.E.	1948-49	1955	24	43	6	883	89	23.86	-	5	13	-	6	2	0	-	-	-	-
Chevalier, G.A.	1969-70	1969-70	1	2	1	0	0*	0.00	-	-	1	-	253†	100	5	20.00	3-68	-	-
Christy, J.A.J.	1929	1931-32	10	18	0	618	103	34.33	1	5	3	-	138	92	2	46.00	1-15	-	-
Chubb, G.W.A.	1951	1951	5	9	3	63	15*	10.50	-	-	-	-	1425	577	21	27.47	6-51	2	-

INDIVIDUAL CAREER RECORDS – SOUTH AFRICA continued

				BATTING AND FIELDING									BOWLING						
	Tests	First Test	Last Test	Inns	NO	Runs	HS	Avge	100	50	Ct	St	Balls	Runs	Wkts	Avge	BB	5wI	10wM
Cochran, J.A.K.	1	1930-31	1930-31	1	0	4	4	4.00	–	–	–	–	138	47	0	–	–	–	–
Coen, S.K.	2	1927-28	1927-28	4	2	101	41*	50.50	–	–	1	–	12	7	0	–	–	–	–
Commaille, J.M.M.	12	1909-10	1927-28	22	1	355	47	16.90	–	–	1	–	–	–	–	–	–	–	–
Commins, J.B.	3	1994-95	1994-95	6	1	125	45	25.00	–	–	2	–	–	–	–	–	–	–	–
Conyngham, D.P.	1	1922-23	1922-23	2	2	6	3*	–	–	–	1	–	366	103	2	51.50	1-40	–	–
Cook, F.J.	1	1895-96	1895-96	2	0	7	7	3.50	–	–	–	–	–	–	–	–	–	–	–
Cook, S.J.	3	1992-93	1993	6	0	107	43	17.83	–	–	1	–	–	–	–	–	–	–	–
Cooper, A.H.C.	1	1913-14	1913-14	2	0	6	6	3.00	–	–	1	–	–	–	–	–	–	–	–
Cox, J.L.	3	1913-14	1913-14	6	1	17	12*	3.40	–	–	–	–	576	245	4	61.25	2-74	–	–
Cripps, G.	1	1891-92	1891-92	2	0	21	18	10.50	–	–	–	–	15	23	0	–	–	–	–
Crisp, R.J.	9	1935	1935-36	13	1	123	35	10.25	–	–	3	–	1429	747	20	37.35	5-99	1	–
Cronje, W.J.	68	1991-92	1999-00	111	9	3714	135	36.41	6	23	33	–	3800	1288	43	29.95	3-14	–	–
Cullinan, D.J.	70	1992-93	2000-01	115	12	4554	275*	44.21	14	20	67	–	120	71	2	35.50	1-10	–	–
Curnow, S.H.	7	1930-31	1931-32	14	0	168	47	12.00	–	–	5	–	–	–	–	–	–	–	–
Dalton, E.L.	15	1929	1938-39	24	2	698	117	31.72	2	3	5	–	864	490	12	40.83	4-59	–	–
Davies, E.Q.	5	1935-36	1938-39	8†	3	9	3	1.80	–	–	–	–	768	481	7	68.71	4-75	–	–
Dawson, A.C.	2	2003	2003	1	0	10	10	10.00	–	–	–	–	252	117	5	23.40	2-20	–	–
Dawson, O.C.	9	1947	1948-49	15	1	293	55	20.92	–	1	10	–	1294	578	10	57.80	2-57	–	–
Deane, H.G.	17	1924	1930-31	27	2	628	93	25.12	–	3	8	–	–	–	–	–	–	–	–
de Bruyn, Z.	3	2004-05	2004-05	5	1	155	83	38.75	–	1	–	–	216	92	3	30.66	2-32	–	–
de Villiers, A.B.	52	2004-05	2008-09	89	8	3559	217*	43.92	9	17	75	1	198	99	2	49.50	2-49	–	–
de Villiers, P.S.	18	1993-94	1997-98	26	7	359	67*	18.89	–	2	11	–	4805	2063	85	24.27	6-23	5	–
Dippenaar, H.H.	38	1999-00	2006-07	62	5	1718	177*	30.14	3	7	27	–	12	1	0	–	–	–	–
Dixon, C.D.	1	1913-14	1913-14	2	0	0	0	0.00	–	–	1	–	240	118	3	39.33	2-62	–	–
Donald, A.A.	72	1991-92	2001-02	94	33	652	37	10.68	–	–	18	–	15519	7344	330	22.25	8-71	20	3
Dower, R.R.	1	1898-99	1898-99	2	0	9	9	4.50	–	–	2	–	–	–	–	–	–	–	–
Draper, R.G.	2	1949-50	1949-50	3	0	25	15	8.33	–	–	3	–	–	–	–	–	–	–	–
Duckworth, C.A.R.	2	1956-57	1956-57	4	0	28	13	7.00	–	–	3	–	–	–	–	–	–	–	–
Dumbrill, R.	5	1965	1966-67	10	0	153	36	15.30	–	–	3	–	816	336	9	37.33	4-30	–	–
Duminy, J.P.	3	1927-28	1929	6†	0	30	12	5.00	–	–	2	–	60†	39	1	39.00	1-17	–	–
Duminy, J-P.	6	2008-09	2008-09	10†	2	389	166	48.62	1	2	9	–	210	125	2	62.50	1-14	–	–
Dunell, O.R.	2	1888-89	1888-89	4	1	42	26*	14.00	–	–	–	–	–	–	–	–	–	–	–
du Preez, J.H.	2	1966-67	1966-67	2	0	0	0	0.00	–	–	1	–	144	51	3	17.00	2-22	–	–
du Toit, J.F.	1	1891-92	1891-92	2	2	2	2*	–	–	–	2	–	85†	47	1	47.00	1-47	–	–
Dyer, D.V.	3	1947	1947	6	0	96	62	16.00	–	1	1	–	–	–	–	–	–	–	–
Eksteen, C.E.	7	1993	1999-00	11	2	91	22	10.11	–	–	5	–	1536†	494	8	61.75	3-12	–	–
Elgie, M.K.	3	1961-62	1961-62	6	0	75	56	12.50	–	1	4	–	66†	46	0	–	–	–	–
Elworthy, S.	4	1998	2002-03	5	1	72	48	18.00	–	–	1	–	867	444	13	34.15	4-66	–	–
Endean, W.R.	28	1951	1957-58	52	4	1630	162*	33.95	3	8	41	–	–	–	–	–	–	–	–
Farrer, W.S.	6	1961-62	1963-64	10	2	221	40	27.62	–	–	2	–	–	–	–	–	–	–	–
Faulkner, G.A.	25	1905-06	1924	47	4	1754	204	40.79	4	8	20	–	4227	2180	82	26.58	7-84	4	–
Fellows-Smith, J.P.	4	1960	1960	8	2	166	35	27.66	–	–	2	–	114	61	0	–	–	–	–

	First Test	Last Test	Tests	BATTING AND FIELDING									BOWLING						
				Inns	NO	Runs	HS	Avge	100	50	Ct	St	Balls	Runs	Wkts	Avge	BB	5wI	10wM
Fichardt, C.G.	1891-92	1895-96	2	4	0	15	10	3.75	–	–	2	–	12	7	0	–	–	–	–
Finlason, C.E.	1888-89	1888-89	1	2	0	6	6	3.00	–	–	–	–	48	24	0	–	–	–	–
Floquet, C.E.	1909-10	1909-10	1	2	1	12	11*	12.00	–	–	–	–	–	–	–	–	–	–	–
Francis, H.H.	1898-99	1898-99	2	4	0	39	29	9.75	–	–	1	–	–	–	–	–	–	–	–
Francois, C.M.	1922-23	1922-23	5	9	1	252	72	31.50	–	1	5	–	684	225	6	37.50	3-23	–	–
Frank, C.N.	1921-22	1921-22	3	6	0	236	152	39.33	1	–	–	–	–	–	–	–	–	–	–
Frank, W.H.B.	1895-96	1895-96	1	2	0	7	5	3.50	–	–	–	–	58	52	1	52.00	1-52	–	–
Fuller, E.R.H.	1952-53	1957-58	7	9	1	64	17	8.00	–	–	3	–	1898	668	22	30.36	5-66	1	–
Fullerton, G.M.	1947	1951	7	13	0	325	88	25.00	–	3	10	2	–	–	–	–	–	–	–
Funston, K.J.	1952-53	1957-58	18	33	1	824	92	25.75	–	5	7	–	–	–	–	–	–	–	–
Gamsy, D.	1969-70	1969-70	2	3	1	39	30*	19.50	–	–	5	–	–	–	–	–	–	–	–
Gibbs, H.H.	1996-97	2007-08	90	154	7	6167	228	41.95	14	26	94	–	6	4	0	–	–	–	–
Gleeson, R.A.	1895-96	1895-96	1	2	1	4	3	4.00	–	–	2	–	–	–	–	–	–	–	–
Glover, G.K.	1895-96	1895-96	1	2	1	21	18*	21.00	–	–	–	–	65	28	1	28.00	1-28	–	–
Goddard, T.L.	1955	1969-70	41	78†	5	2516	112	34.46	1	18	48	–	11736†	3226	123	26.22	6-53	5	–
Gordon, N.	1938-39	1938-39	5	6	5	8	7*	2.00	–	–	1	–	1966	807	20	40.35	5-103	2	–
Graham, R.	1898-99	1898-99	2	4	0	6	4	1.50	–	–	2	–	240	127	3	42.33	2-22	–	–
Grieveson, R.E.	1938-39	1938-39	2	2	0	114	75	57.00	–	1	7	3	–	–	–	–	–	–	–
Griffin, G.M.	1960	1960	2	4	0	25	14	6.25	–	–	–	–	432	192	8	24.00	4-87	–	–
Hall, A.E.	1922-23	1930-31	7	8†	2	11	5	1.83	–	–	4	–	2361†	886	40	22.15	7-63	3	1
Hall, A.J.	2001-02	2006-07	21	33	4	760	163	26.20	1	3	16	–	3001	1617	45	35.93	3-1	1	–
Hall, G.G.	1964-65	1964-65	1	1	0	0	0	0.00	–	–	–	–	186	94	1	94.00	1-94	–	–
Halliwell, E.A.	1891-92	1902-03	8	15	1	188	57	12.53	–	1	10	2	–	–	–	–	–	–	–
Halse, C.G.	1963-64	1963-64	3	3	3	30	19*	–	–	–	1	–	587	260	6	43.33	3-50	–	–
Hands, P.A.M.	1913-14	1924	7	12	0	300	83	25.00	–	2	3	–	37	18	0	–	–	–	–
Hands, R.H.M.	1913-14	1913-14	1	2	0	7	7	3.50	–	–	–	–	–	–	–	–	–	–	–
Hanley, M.A.	1948-49	1948-49	1	1	1	0	0	0.00	–	–	–	–	232	88	1	88.00	1-57	–	–
Harris, P.L.	2006-07	2008-09	24	33	4	304	46	10.48	–	–	12	–	5080†	2315	71	32.60	6-127	2	–
Harris, T.A.	1947	1948-49	3	5	1	100	60	25.00	–	1	1	–	–	–	–	–	–	–	–
Hartigan, G.P.D.	1912	1913-14	5	10	0	114	51	11.40	–	1	1	–	252	141	1	141.00	1-72	–	–
Harvey, R.L.	1935-36	1935-36	2	4	0	51	28	12.75	–	–	5	–	–	–	–	–	–	–	–
Hathorn, C.M.H.	1902-03	1910-11	12	20	1	325	102	17.10	1	–	4	–	–	–	–	–	–	–	–
Hayward, M.	1999-00	2004	16	17	8	66	14	7.33	–	–	2	–	2821	1609	54	29.79	5-56	1	–
Hearne, F. ‡	1891-92	1895-96	4	8	0	121	30	15.12	–	–	3	–	62	40	2	20.00	2-40	–	–
Hearne, G.A.L.	1922-23	1924	3	5	0	59	28	11.80	–	–	8	–	–	–	–	–	–	–	–
Heine, P.S.	1955	1961-62	14	24	3	209	31	9.95	–	–	2	–	3890	1455	58	25.08	6-58	4	–
Henderson, C.W.	2001-02	2002-03	7	7	0	65	30	9.28	–	–	2	–	1962†	928	22	42.18	4-116	–	–
Henry, O.	1992-93	1992-93	3	3†	0	53	34	17.66	–	–	3	–	427†	189	3	63.00	2-56	–	–
Hime, C.F.W.	1895-96	1895-96	1	2	0	8	8	4.00	–	–	–	–	55	31	1	31.00	1-20	–	–
Hudson, A.C.	1991-92	1997-98	35	63	3	2007	163	33.45	4	13	36	–	–	–	–	–	–	–	–
Hutchinson, P.	1888-89	1888-89	2	4	0	14	11	3.50	–	–	3	–	–	–	–	–	–	–	–
Ironside, D.E.J.	1953-54	1953-54	3	4	2	37	13	18.50	–	–	1	–	986	275	15	18.33	5-51	1	–

	First Test	Last Test	Tests	BATTING AND FIELDING Inns	NO	Runs	HS	Avge	100	50	Ct	St	BOWLING Balls	Runs	Wkts	Avge	BB	5wI	10wM
Irvine, B.L.	1969-70	1969-70	4	7†	0	353	102	50.42	1	2	2	—	—	—	—	—	—	—	—
Jack, S.D.	1994-95	1994-95	2	2	0	7	7	3.50	—	—	1	—	462	196	8	24.50	4-69	—	—
Johnson, C.L.	1895-96	1895-96	1	2	0	10	7	5.00	—	—	1	—	140	57	0	—	—	—	—
Kallis, J.H. ‡	1995-96	2008-09	130	219	32	10194	189*	54.51	31	51	143	—	16980	7983	257	31.06	6-54	5	—
Keith, H.J.	1952-53	1956-57	8	16†	1	318	73	21.20	—	2	9	—	108†	63	0	—	—	—	—
Kemp, J.M.	2000-01	2005-06	4	6	1	80	55	13.33	—	1	3	—	479	222	9	24.66	3-33	—	—
Kempis, G.A.	1888-89	1888-89	1	1†	0	0	0*	0.00	—	—	—	—	168†	76	4	19.00	3-53	—	—
Khan, I.	2008-09	2008-09	1	1†	0	20	20	20.00	—	—	1	—	—	—	—	—	—	—	—
Kirsten, G.	1993-94	2003-04	101	176†	15	7289	275	45.27	21	34	83	—	349	142	2	71.00	1-0	—	—
Kirsten, P.N.	1991-92	1994	12	22	2	626	104	31.30	1	4	8	—	54	30	0	—	—	—	—
Klusener, L.	1996-97	2004	49	69†	11	1906	174	32.86	4	8	34	—	6887	3033	80	37.91	8-64	1	—
Kotze, J.J.	1902-03	1907	3	5	1	2	2	0.40	—	—	3	—	413	243	6	40.50	3-64	—	—
Kuiper, A.P.	1991-92	1991-92	1	2	0	34	34	17.00	—	—	1	—	—	—	—	—	—	—	—
Kuys, F.	1898-99	1898-99	1	2	0	26	26	13.00	—	—	—	—	60	31	2	15.50	2-31	—	—
Lance, H.R.	1961-62	1969-70	13	22	1	591	70	28.14	—	5	7	—	948	479	12	39.91	3-30	—	—
Langeveldt, C.K.	2004-05	2005-06	6	4	2	16	10	8.00	—	—	2	—	999	593	16	37.06	5-46	1	—
Langton, A.C.B.	1935	1938-39	15	23	4	298	73*	15.68	—	2	8	—	4199	1827	40	45.67	5-58	1	—
Lawrence, G.B.	1961-62	1961-62	5	8	0	141	43	17.62	—	—	2	—	1334	512	28	18.28	8-53	2	—
le Roux, F.L.	1913-14	1913-14	1	2	0	1	1	0.50	—	—	—	—	54	24	0	—	—	—	—
Lewis, P.T.	1913-14	1913-14	1	2	0	0	0	0.00	—	—	—	—	—	—	—	—	—	—	—
Liebenberg, G.F.J.	1997-98	1998	5	8	0	104	45	13.00	—	—	—	—	—	—	—	—	—	—	—
Lindsay, D.T.	1963-64	1969-70	19	31	1	1130	182	37.66	3	5	57	2	—	—	—	—	—	—	—
Lindsay, J.D.	1947	1947	3	5	2	21	9*	7.00	—	—	4	1	—	—	—	—	—	—	—
Lindsay, N.V.	1921-22	1921-22	1	2	0	35	29	17.50	—	—	1	—	—	—	—	—	—	—	—
Ling, W.V.S.	1921-22	1922-23	6	10	0	168	38	16.80	—	—	1	—	18	20	0	—	—	—	—
Llewellyn, C.B.	1895-96	1912	15	28†	1	544	90	20.14	—	4	7	—	2292†	1421	48	29.60	6-92	4	1
Lundie, E.B.	1913-14	1913-14	1	2	1	1	1	1.00	—	—	1	—	286	107	4	26.75	4-101	—	—
Macaulay, M.J.	1964-65	1964-65	1	2	0	33	21	16.50	—	—	—	—	276†	73	2	36.50	1-10	—	—
McCarthy, C.N.	1948-49	1951	15	24	15	28	5	3.11	—	—	6	—	3499	1510	36	41.94	6-43	2	—
McGlew, D.J.	1951	1961-62	34	64	6	2440	255*	42.06	7	10	18	—	32	23	0	—	—	—	—
McKenzie, N.D.	2000	2008-09	58	94	7	3253	226	37.39	5	16	54	—	90	68	0	—	—	—	—
McKinnon, A.H.	1960	1966-67	8	13	7	107	27	17.83	—	—	1	—	2546†	925	26	35.57	4-128	—	—
McLean, R.A.	1951	1964-65	40	73	3	2120	142	30.28	5	10	23	—	4	1	0	—	—	—	—
McMillan, B.M.	1992-93	1998	38	62	12	1968	113	39.36	3	13	49	—	6048	2537	75	33.82	4-65	—	—
McMillan, Q	1929	1931-32	13	21	4	306	50*	18.00	—	1	8	—	2021	1243	36	34.52	5-66	2	—
Mann, N.B.F.	1947	1951	19	31	1	400	52	13.33	—	1	8	—	5796†	1920	58	33.10	6-59	1	—
Mansell, P.N.F.	1951	1955	13	22	2	355	90	17.75	—	2	15	—	1506	736	11	66.90	3-58	—	—
Markham, L.A.	1948-49	1948-49	1	2	1	20	20	20.00	—	—	—	—	104	72	1	72.00	1-34	—	—
Marx, W.F.E.	1921-22	1921-22	3	6†	0	125	36	20.83	—	—	—	—	228	144	4	36.00	3-85	—	—
Matthews, C.R.	1992-93	1995-96	18	25	6	348	62*	18.31	—	1	4	—	3980	1502	52	28.88	5-42	2	—
Meintjes, D.J.	1922-23	1922-23	2	3	0	43	21	14.33	—	—	3	—	246	115	6	19.16	3-38	—	—

INDIVIDUAL CAREER RECORDS – SOUTH AFRICA *continued*

	First Test	Last Test	Tests	BATTING AND FIELDING									BOWLING						
				Inns	NO	Runs	HS	Avge	100	50	Ct	St	Balls	Runs	Wkts	Avge	BB	5wI	10wM
Melle, M.G.	1949-50	1952-53	7	12	4	68	17	8.50	–	–	4	–	1667	851	26	32.73	6-71	2	1
Melville, A.	1938-39	1948-49	11	19	2	894	189	52.58	4	3	8	–	–	–	–	–	–	–	–
Middleton, J.	1895-96	1902-03	6	12	5	52	22	7.42	–	–	1	–	1064†	442	24	18.41	5-51	2	–
Mills, C.H.	1891-92	1891-92	1	2	0	25	21	12.50	–	–	–	–	140	83	2	41.50	2-83	–	–
Milton, W.H.	1888-89	1891-92	3	6	0	68	21	11.33	–	–	2	–	79	48	2	24.00	1-5	–	–
Mitchell, B.	1929	1948-49	42	80	9	3471	189*	48.88	8	21	56	–	2525	1380	27	51.11	5-87	1	–
Mitchell, F. ‡	1912	1912	3	6	0	28	12	4.66	–	–	–	–	–	–	–	–	–	–	–
Morkel, D.P.B.	1927-28	1931-32	16	28	1	663	88	24.55	–	4	13	–	1704	821	18	45.61	4-93	–	–
Morkel, J.A.	2008-09	2008-09	1	1†	0	58	58	58.00	–	1	–	–	192	132	1	132.00	1-44	–	–
Morkel, M.	2006-07	2008-09	17	22†	1	263	40	12.52	–	–	3	–	3101	1920	55	34.90	5-50	1	–
Murray, A.R.A.	1952-53	1953-54	10	14	1	289	109	22.23	1	1	3	–	2374	710	18	39.44	4-169	–	–
Nel, A.	2001-02	2008	36	42	8	337	34	9.91	–	–	16	–	7630	3919	123	31.86	6-32	3	–
Nel, J.D.	1949-50	1957-58	6	11	0	150	38	13.63	–	–	1	–	–	–	–	–	–	–	–
Newberry, C.	1913-14	1913-14	4	8	0	62	16	7.75	–	–	3	–	558	268	11	24.36	4-72	–	–
Newson, E.S.	1930-31	1938-39	3	5	1	30	16	7.50	–	–	3	–	874	265	4	66.25	2-58	–	–
Ngam, M.	2000-01	2000-01	3	1	1	0	0*	–	–	–	1	–	392	189	11	17.18	3-26	–	–
Nicholson, F.	1935-36	1935-36	4	8	1	76	29	10.85	–	–	3	–	24	17	0	–	–	–	–
Nicolson, J.F.W.	1927-28	1927-28	3	5†	0	179	78	35.80	–	1	–	–	90	47	4	11.75	4-47	–	–
Norton, N.O.	1909-10	1909-10	1	2	0	9	7	4.50	–	–	–	–	20	9	0	–	–	–	–
Nourse, A.D.	1935	1951	34	62	7	2960	231	53.81	9	14	12	–	3234†	1553	41	37.87	4-25	–	–
Nourse, A.W.	1902-03	1924	45	83†	8	2234	111	29.78	1	15	43	–	–	–	–	–	–	–	–
Ntini, M.	1997-98	2008-09	99	113	42	688	32*	9.69	–	–	25	–	20414	11009	388	28.37	7-37	18	4
Nupen, E.P.	1921-22	1935-36	17	31	7	348	69	14.50	–	2	9	–	4159	1788	50	35.76	6-46	5	1
Ochse, A.E.	1888-89	1888-89	2	4	0	16	8	4.00	–	–	1	–	649	362	10	36.20	4-79	–	–
Ochse, A.L.	1927-28	1929	3	4	1	11	4*	3.66	–	–	–	–	–	–	–	–	–	–	–
O'Linn, S.	1960	1961-62	7	12†	1	297	98	27.00	–	2	4	–	–	–	–	–	–	–	–
Ontong, J.L.	2001-02	2004-05	2	4	1	57	32	19.00	–	–	–	–	185	133	1	133.00	1-79	–	–
Owen-Smith, H.G.	1929	1929	5	8	2	252	129	42.00	1	2	4	–	156	113	0	–	–	–	–
Palm, A.W.	1927-28	1927-28	1	2	0	15	13	7.50	–	–	1	–	366	273	8	34.12	6-152	1	–
Parker, G.M.	1924	1924	2	4	2	3	2*	1.50	–	–	–	–	130	82	3	27.33	3-82	–	–
Parkin, D.C.	1891-92	1891-92	1	2	0	6	6	3.00	–	–	1	–	–	–	–	–	–	–	–
Partridge, J.T.	1963-64	1964-65	11	12	5	73	13*	10.42	–	–	6	–	3684	1373	44	31.20	7-91	3	–
Pearse, C.O.C.	1910-11	1910-11	3	6	0	55	31	9.16	–	–	–	–	144	106	3	35.33	3-56	–	–
Pegler, S.J.	1909-10	1924	16	28	5	356	35*	15.47	–	–	5	–	2989	1572	47	33.44	7-65	2	–
Peterson, R.J.	2003	2007-08	6	7†	1	163	61	27.16	–	1	5	–	959†	497	14	35.50	5-33	1	–
Pithey, A.J.	1956-57	1964-65	17	27	1	819	154	31.50	1	4	3	–	12	5	0	–	–	–	–
Pithey, D.B.	1963-64	1966-67	8	12	1	138	55	12.54	–	1	6	–	1424	577	12	48.08	6-58	1	–
Plimsoll, J.B.	1947	1947	1	2	1	16	8*	16.00	–	–	–	–	237†	143	3	47.66	3-128	–	–
Pollock, P.M.	1961-62	1969-70	28	41	13	607	75*	21.67	–	2	9	–	6522	2806	116	24.18	6-38	9	1
Pollock, R.G.	1963-64	1969-70	23	41†	4	2256	274	60.97	7	11	17	–	414	204	4	51.00	2-50	–	–
Pollock, S.M.	1995-96	2007-08	108	156	39	3781	111	32.31	2	16	72	–	24353	9733	421	23.11	7-87	16	1
Poore, R.M.	1895-96	1895-96	3	6	0	76	20	12.66	–	–	3	–	9	4	1	4.00	1-4	–	–
Pothecary, J.E.	1960	1960	3	4	0	26	12	6.50	–	–	2	–	828	354	9	39.33	4-58	–	–

455

	First Test	Last Test	Tests	BATTING AND FIELDING									BOWLING						
				Inns	NO	Runs	HS	Avge	100	50	Ct	St	Balls	Runs	Wkts	Avge	BB	5wI	10wM
Powell, A.W.	1898-99	1898-99	1	2	0	16	11	8.00	—	—	2	—	20	10	1	10.00	1-10	—	—
Pretorius, D.	2001-02	2003	4	4	1	22	9	7.33	—	—	2	—	570	430	6	71.66	4-115	—	—
Prince, A.G.	2001-02	2008-09	48	77†	12	3074	162*	47.29	11	8	29	—	96	47	1	47.00	1-2	—	—
Pringle, M.W.	1991-92	1995-96	4	6	2	67	33	16.75	—	—	—	—	652	270	5	54.00	2-62	—	—
Procter, M.J.	1966-67	1969-70	7	10	1	226	48	25.11	—	—	4	—	1514	616	41	15.02	6-73	1	—
Prommitz, H.L.E.	1927-28	1927-28	2	4	0	14	5	3.50	—	—	2	—	528	161	8	20.12	5-58	1	—
Quinn, N.A.	1929	1931-32	12	18†	3	90	28	6.00	—	—	1	—	2922†	1145	35	32.71	6-92	1	—
Reid, N.	1921-22	1921-22	1	2	0	17	11	8.50	—	—	—	—	126	63	2	31.50	2-63	—	—
Rhodes, J.N.	1992-93	2000	52	80	9	2532	117	35.66	3	17	34	—	12	5	0	—	—	—	—
Richards, A.R.	1895-96	1895-96	1	2	0	6	6	3.00	—	—	—	—							
Richards, B.A.	1969-70	1969-70	4	7	0	508	140	72.57	2	2	3	—	72	26	1	26.00	1-12	—	—
Richards, W.H.M.	1888-89	1888-89	1	2	0	4	4	2.00	—	—	—	—							
Richardson, D.J.	1991-92	1997-98	42	64	8	1359	109	24.26	1	8	150	2							
Robertson, J.B.	1935-36	1935-36	3	6	1	51	17	10.20	—	—	2	—	738	321	6	53.50	3-143	—	—
Rose-Innes, A.	1888-89	1888-89	2	4	0	14	13	3.50	—	—	2	—	128†	89	5	17.80	5-43	1	—
Routledge, T.W.	1891-92	1895-96	4	8	0	72	24	9.00	—	—	2	—							
Rowan, A.M.B.	1947	1951	15	23	6	290	41	17.05	—	—	7	—	5193	2084	54	38.59	5-68	4	—
Rowan, E.A.B.	1935	1951	26	50	5	1965	236	43.66	3	12	14	—	19	7	0	—	—	—	—
Rowe, G.A.	1895-96	1902-03	5	9	3	26	13*	4.33	—	—	4	—	998†	456	15	30.40	5-115	1	—
Rudolph, J.A.	2003	2006	35	63†	7	2028	222*	36.21	5	8	22	—	664	432	4	108.00	1-1	—	—
Rushmere, M.W.	1991-92	1991-92	1	2	0	6	3	3.00	—	—	—	—							
Samuelson, S.V.	1909-10	1909-10	1	2	0	22	15	11.00	—	—	1	—	108	64	0	—	—	—	—
Schultz, B.N.	1992-93	1997-98	9	8†	2	9	6	1.50	—	—	—	—	1733†	749	37	20.24	5-48	2	—
Schwarz, R.O.	1905-06	1912	20	35	8	374	61	13.85	—	1	18	—	2639	1417	55	25.76	6-47	2	—
Seccull, A.W.	1895-96	1895-96	1	2	1	23	17*	23.00	—	—	1	—	60	37	2	18.50	2-37	—	—
Seymour, M.A.	1963-64	1969-70	7	10	3	84	36	12.00	—	—	3	—	1458	588	9	65.33	3-80	—	—
Shalders, W.A.	1898-99	1907	12	23	1	355	42	16.13	—	—	2	—	115	47	1	6.00	1-6	—	—
Shepstone, G.H.	1895-96	1898-99	2	4	0	38	21	9.50	—	—	3	—							
Sherwell, P.W.	1905-06	1910-11	13	22	4	427	115	23.72	1	1	20	16							
Siedle, I.J.	1927-28	1935-36	18	34	0	977	141	28.73	1	5	7	—	19	7	1	7.00	1-7	—	—
Sinclair, J.H.	1895-96	1910-11	25	47	1	1069	106	23.23	3	3	9	—	3598	1996	63	31.68	6-26	1	—
Smith, C.J.E.	1902-03	1902-03	3	6	1	106	45	21.20	—	—	2	—							
Smith, F.W.	1888-89	1895-96	3	6	1	45	12	9.00	—	—	2	—							
Smith, G.C. ‡	2001-02	2008-09	76	133†	9	6330	277	51.04	18	25	101	—	1319	801	8	100.12	2-145	—	—
Smith, V.I.	1947	1957-58	9	16	6	39	11*	3.90	—	—	3	—	1655	769	12	64.08	4-143	—	—
Snell, R.P.	1991-92	1994-95	5	8	1	95	48	13.57	—	—	1	—	1025	538	19	28.31	4-74	—	—
Snooke, S.D.	1907	1907	1	1	0	0	0	0.00	—	—	2	—							
Snooke, S.J.	1905-06	1922-23	26	46	0	1008	103	22.40	1	5	24	—	1620	702	35	20.05	8-70	1	1
Solomon, W.R.T.	1898-99	1898-99	1	2	0	4	2	2.00	—	—	—	—							
Stewart, R.B.	1888-89	1888-89	1	2	0	13	9	6.50	—	—	2	—							
Steyn, D.W.	2004-05	2008-09	33	41	8	393	76	11.90	—	1	9	—	6676	4029	170	23.70	6-49	11	3

INDIVIDUAL CAREER RECORDS – SOUTH AFRICA continued

	First Test	Last Test	Tests	BATTING AND FIELDING									BOWLING						
				Inns	NO	Runs	HS	Avge	100	50	Ct	St	Balls	Runs	Wkts	Avge	BB	5wI	10wM
Steyn, P.J.R.	1994-95	1994-95	3	6	0	127	46	21.16	–	–	–	–	174	105	1	105.00	1-36	–	–
Stricker, L.A.	1909-10	1912	13	24	0	344	48	14.33	–	–	3	–	36†	27	0	–	–	–	–
Strydom, P.C.	1999-00	1999-00	2	3	0	35	30	11.66	–	–	1	–	–						
Susskind, M.J.	1924	1924	5	8	0	268	65	33.50	–	4	1	–	–						
Symcox, P.L.	1993	1998-99	20	27	1	741	108	28.50	1	4	5	–	3561	1603	37	43.32	4-69	–	–
Taberer, H.M.	1902-03	1902-03	1	1	0	2	2	2.00	–	–	–	–	60	48	1	48.00	1-25	–	–
Tancred, A.B.	1888-89	1888-89	2	4	1	87	29	29.00	–	–	2	–	–						
Tancred, L.J.	1902-03	1913-14	14	26	1	530	97	21.20	–	2	3	–	–						
Tancred, V.M.	1898-99	1898-99	1	2	0	25	18	12.50	–	–	1	–	–						
Tapscott, G.L.	1913-14	1913-14	1	2	0	5	4	2.50	–	–	–	–	–						
Tapscott, L.E.	1922-23	1922-23	2	3	1	58	50*	29.00	–	1	1	–	12	2	0	–	–	–	–
Tayfield, H.J.	1949-50	1960	37	60	9	862	75	16.90	–	2	26	–	13568	4405	170	25.91	9-113	14	2
Taylor, A.I.	1956-57	1956-57	1	2	0	18	12	9.00	–	–	–	–	–						
Taylor, D.	1913-14	1913-14	2	4†	0	85	36	21.25	–	–	–	–	–						
Taylor, H.W.	1912	1931-32	42	76	4	2936	176	40.77	7	17	19	–	342	156	5	31.20	3-15	–	–
Terbrugge, D.J.	1998-99	2003-04	7	8	5	16	4*	5.33	–	–	4	–	1012	517	20	25.85	5-46	1	–
Theunissen, N.H.C.D.	1888-89	1888-89	1	2	1	2	2*	2.00	–	–	1	–	80	51	1	20.00	1-20	–	–
Thornton, G.	1902-03	1902-03	1	1†	0	1	1*	–	–	–	–	–	24†	20	0	–	–	–	–
Tomlinson, D.S.	1935	1935	1	1	0	9	9	9.00	–	–	4	–	60	38	0	–	–	–	–
Traicos, A.J. ‡	1969-70	1969-70	3	4	2	8	5*	4.00	–	–	7	–	470	207	4	51.75	2-70	–	–
Trimborn, P.H.J.	1966-67	1969-70	4	4	2	13	11*	6.50	–	–	6	–	747	257	11	23.36	3-12	–	–
Tsolekile, T.L.	2004-05	2004-05	3	5	0	47	22	9.40	–	–	9	–	–						
Tuckett, L.	1947	1948-49	9	14	3	131	40*	11.90	–	–	2	–	2104	980	19	51.57	5-68	2	–
Tuckett, L.R.	1913-14	1913-14	1	2	1	0	0*	0.00	–	–	–	–	120	69	0	–	–	–	–
Twentyman-Jones, P.S.	1902-03	1902-03	1	2	0	0	0	0.00	–	–	–	–	–						
van der Bijl, P.G.V.	1938-39	1938-39	5	9	0	460	125	51.11	1	2	1	–	–						
van der Merwe, E.A.	1929	1935-36	2	4	1	27	19	9.00	–	–	3	–	–						
van der Merwe, P.L.	1963-64	1966-67	15	23	2	533	76	25.38	–	3	11	–	79†	22	1	22.00	1-6	–	–
van Jaarsveld, M.	2002-03	2004-05	9	15	2	397	73	30.53	–	3	11	–	42	28	0	–	–	–	–
van Ryneveld, C.B.	1951	1957-58	19	33	6	724	83	26.81	–	3	14	–	1554	671	17	39.47	4-67	–	–
Varnals, G.D.	1964-65	1964-65	3	6	0	97	23	16.16	–	–	–	–	12	2	0	–	–	–	–
Viljoen, K.G.	1930-31	1948-49	27	50	2	1365	124	28.43	2	9	5	–	48	23	0	–	–	–	–
Vincent, C.L.	1927-28	1935	25	38†	12	526	60	20.23	–	2	27	–	5851†	2631	84	31.32	6-51	3	–
Vintcent, C.H.	1888-89	1891-92	3	6†	0	26	9	4.33	–	–	1	–	369†	193	4	48.25	3-88	–	–
Vogler, A.E.E.	1905-06	1910-11	15	26	6	340	65	17.00	–	2	20	–	2764	1455	64	22.73	7-94	5	1
Wade, H.F.	1935	1935-36	10	18	2	327	40*	20.43	–	3	4	–	–						
Wade, W.W.	1938-39	1949-50	11	19	1	511	125	28.38	1	3	15	2	–						
Waite, J.H.B.	1951	1964-65	50	86	7	2405	134	30.44	4	16	124	17	–						
Walter, K.A.	1961-62	1961-62	2	3	0	11	10	3.66	–	–	3	–	495	197	6	32.83	4-63	–	–
Ward, T.A.	1912	1924	23	42	9	459	64	13.90	–	2	19	13	–						
Watkins, J.C.	1949-50	1956-57	15	27	1	612	92	23.53	–	3	12	–	2805	816	29	28.13	4-22	–	–
Wesley, C.	1960	1960	3	5†	0	49	35	9.80	–	–	1	–	–						
Wessels, K.C. ‡	1991-92	1994	16	29†	2	1027	118	38.03	2	6	12	–	–						

	First Test	Last Test	Tests	Inns	NO	Runs	HS	Avge	100	50	Ct	St	Balls	Runs	Wkts	Avge	BB	5wI	10wM
								BATTING AND FIELDING								BOWLING			
Westcott, R.J.	1953-54	1957-58	5	9	0	166	62	18.44	–	1	1	–	32	22	0	–	–	–	–
White, G.C.	1905-06	1912	17	31	2	872	147	30.06	2	4	10	–	498	301	9	33.44	4-47	1	–
Willoughby, C.M.	2003	2003	2	0†	0	–	–	–	–	–	–	–	300†	125	1	125.00	1-47	–	–
Willoughby, J.T.	1895-96	1895-96	2	4	0	8	5	2.00	–	–	–	–	275	159	6	26.50	2-37	–	–
Wimble, C.S.	1891-92	1891-92	1	2	0	0	0	0.00	–	–	1	–	–	–	–	–	–	–	–
Winslow, P.L.	1949-50	1955	5	9	0	186	108	20.66	1	–	1	–	–	–	–	–	–	–	–
Wynne, O.E.	1948-49	1949-50	6	12	0	219	50	18.25	–	1	3	–	–	–	–	–	–	–	–
Zondeki, M.	2003	2008-09	6	5	0	82	59	16.40	–	1	1	–	780	480	19	25.26	6-39	1	–
Zulch, J.W.	1909-10	1921-22	16	32	2	983	150	32.76	2	4	4	–	24	28	0	–	–	–	–

INDIVIDUAL CAREER RECORDS – WEST INDIES

	First Test	Last Test	Tests	Inns	NO	Runs	HS	Avge	100	50	Ct	St	Balls	Runs	Wkts	Avge	BB	5wI	10wM
								BATTING AND FIELDING								BOWLING			
Achong, E.E.	1929-30	1934-35	6	11†	1	81	22	8.10	–	–	6	–	918†	378	8	47.25	2-64	–	–
Adams, J.C.	1991-92	2000-01	54	90†	17	3012	208*	41.26	6	14	48	5	2853†	1336	27	49.48	5-17	1	–
Alexander, F.C.M.	1957	1960-61	25	38	6	961	108	30.03	1	7	85	5	–	–	–	–	–	–	–
Ali, Imtiaz	1975-76	1975-76	1	1†	0	1	1*	–	–	–	–	–	204	89	2	44.50	2-37	–	–
Ali, Inshan	1970-71	1976-77	12	18†	2	172	25	10.75	–	–	7	–	3718†	1621	34	47.67	5-59	1	–
Allan, D.W.	1961-62	1966	5	7	2	75	40*	12.50	–	–	15	3	–	–	–	–	–	–	–
Allen, I.B.A.	1991	1991	2	2	2	5	4*	–	–	–	1	–	282	180	5	36.00	2-69	–	–
Ambrose, C.E.L.	1987-88	2000	98	145†	29	1439	53	12.40	–	1	18	–	22103	8501	405	20.99	8-45	22	3
Arthurton, K.L.T.	1988	1995	33	50†	5	1382	157*	30.71	2	8	22	–	473†	183	1	183.00	1-17	–	–
Asgarali, N.S.	1957	1957	2	4	0	62	29	15.50	–	–	–	–	–	–	–	–	–	–	–
Atkinson, D.S.	1948-49	1957-58	22	35	6	922	219	31.79	1	5	11	–	5201	1647	47	35.04	7-53	3	–
Atkinson, E.S.	1957-58	1958-59	8	9	1	126	37	15.75	–	–	2	–	1634	589	25	23.56	5-42	1	–
Austin, Richard A.	1977-78	1977-78	2	2	0	22	20	11.00	–	–	2	–	6	5	0	–	–	–	–
Austin, Ryan A.	2009	2009	2	4	0	39	19	9.75	–	–	3	–	326	155	3	51.66	1-29	–	–
Bacchus, S.F.A.F.	1977-78	1981-82	19	30	0	782	250	26.06	1	3	17	–	6	3	0	–	–	–	–
Baichan, L.	1974-75	1975-76	3	6†	2	184	105*	46.00	1	–	2	–	–	–	–	–	–	–	–
Baker, L.S.	2008-09	2009	4	6†	4	23	17	11.50	–	–	1	–	–	–	–	–	–	–	–
Banks, O.A.C.	2002-03	2005	10	16	4	318	50*	26.50	–	1	6	–	660	395	5	79.00	2-39	–	–
Baptiste, E.A.E.	1983-84	1989-90	10	11	1	233	87*	23.30	–	1	2	–	2401	1367	28	48.82	4-87	–	–
Barrett, A.G.	1970-71	1974-75	6	7	1	40	19	6.66	–	–	–	–	1362	563	16	35.18	3-31	–	–
Barrow, I.M.	1929-30	1939	11	19	2	276	105	16.23	1	1	17	5	–	–	–	–	–	–	–
Bartlett, E.L.	1928	1930-31	5	8	1	131	84	18.71	–	1	4	–	–	–	–	–	–	–	–
Baugh, C.S.	2002-03	2004	5	10	0	196	68	19.60	–	1	4	1	–	–	–	–	–	–	–
Benjamin, K.C.G.	1991-92	1997-98	26	36	8	222	43*	7.92	–	–	2	–	5132	2785	92	30.27	6-66	4	1
Benjamin, W.K.M.	1987-88	1994-95	21	26	1	470	85	18.80	–	2	12	–	3694	1648	61	27.01	4-46	–	–
Benn, S.J	2007-08	2009	9	14†	1	150	35	11.53	–	–	4	–	2278†	1178	24	49.08	4-31	–	–
Bernard, D.E.	2002-03	2009	3	6	1	202	69	40.40	–	3	–	–	258	185	4	46.25	2-30	–	–
Best, C.A.	1985-86	1990-91	8	13	1	342	164	28.50	1	1	8	–	30	21	0	–	–	–	–

	First Test	Last Test	Tests	BATTING AND FIELDING Inns	NO	Runs	HS	Avge	100	50	Ct	St	BOWLING Balls	Runs	Wkts	Avge	BB	5wI	10wM
Best, T.L.	2002-03	2009	14	23	3	196	27	9.80	—	—	1	—	2187	1363	28	48.67	4-46	—	—
Betancourt, N.	1929-30	1929-30	1	2	0	52	39	26.00	—	—	—	3							
Binns, A.P.	1952-53	1955-56	5	8	1	64	27	9.14	—	—	14	3							
Birkett, L.S.	1930-31	1930-31	4	8	0	136	64	17.00	—	1	4	—	126	71	1	71.00	1-16	—	—
Bishop, I.R.	1988-89	1997-98	43	63	11	632	48	12.15	—	—	8	—	8407	3909	161	24.27	6-40	6	—
Black, M.I.	2000-01	2001-02	6	11	3	21	6	2.62	—	—	4	—	954	597	12	49.75	4-83	—	—
Boyce, K.D.	1970-71	1975-76	21	30	3	657	95*	24.33	—	4	5	—	3501	1801	60	30.01	6-77	2	1
Bradshaw, I.D.R.	2005-06	2006	5	8†	1	96	33	13.71	—	—	3	—	1021†	540	9	60.00	3-73	—	—
Bravo, D.J.	2004	2008	31	57	1	1833	113	32.73	2	11	30	—	5139	2771	70	39.58	6-55	2	—
Breese, G.R.	2002-03	2002-03	1	2	0	5	5	2.50	—	—	1	—	188	135	2	67.50	2-108	—	—
Browne, C.O.	1994-95	2004-05	20	30	6	387	68	16.12	—	1	79	2							
Browne, C.R.	1928	1929-30	4	8	1	176	70*	25.14	—	1	1	—	840	288	6	48.00	2-72	—	—
Butcher, B.F.	1958-59	1969	44	78	6	3104	209*	43.11	7	16	15	—	256	90	5	18.00	5-34	1	—
Butler, L.S.	1954-55	1954-55	1	1	0	16	16	16.00	—	—	—	—	240	151	2	75.50	2-151	—	—
Butts, C.G.	1984-85	1987-88	7	8	1	108	38	15.42	—	—	2	—	1554	595	10	59.50	4-73	—	—
Bynoe, M.R.	1958-59	1966-67	4	6	0	111	48	18.50	—	—	4	—	30†	5	1	5.00	1-5	—	—
Camacho, G.S.	1967-68	1970-71	11	22	0	640	87	29.09	—	4	4	—	18	12	0	—	—		
Cameron, F.J.	1948-49	1948-49	5	7	1	151	75*	25.16	—	1	—	—	786	278	3	92.66	2-74	—	—
Cameron, J.H.	1939	1939	2	3	0	6	5	2.00	—	—	—	—	232	88	3	29.33	3-66	—	—
Campbell, S.L.	1994-95	2001-02	52	93	4	2882	208	32.38	4	18	47	—							
Carew, G.M.	1934-35	1948-49	4	7	1	170	107	28.33	1	—	1	—	18†	2	0	—	—		
Carew, M.C.	1963	1971-72	19	36†	3	1127	109	34.15	1	5	13	—	1174	437	8	54.62	1-11	—	—
Challenor, G.	1928	1928	3	6	0	101	46	16.83	—	—	—	—							
Chanderpaul, S.	1993-94	2009	121	206†	32	8576	203*	49.28	21	52	50	—	1680	845	8	105.62	1-2	—	—
Chang, H.S.	1978-79	1978-79	1	2†	0	8	6	4.00	—	—	—	—							
Chattergoon, S.	2007-08	2008-09	4	7†	0	127	46	18.14	—	—	4	—							
Christiani, C.M.	1934-35	1934-35	4	7	2	98	32*	19.60	—	—	6	1							
Christiani, R.J.	1947-48	1953-54	22	37	3	896	107	26.35	1	4	19	2							
Clarke, C.B.	1939	1939	3	4	1	3	2	1.00	—	—	—	—	234	108	3	36.00	3-52	—	—
Clarke, S.T.	1977-78	1981-82	11	16	5	172	35*	15.63	—	—	2	—	456	261	6	43.50	3-59	—	—
Collins, P.T.	1998-99	2006	32	47	7	235	24	5.87	—	—	7	—	2477	1170	42	27.85	5-126	1	—
Collymore, C.D.	1998-99	2007	30	52	27	197	16*	7.88	—	—	6	—	6964†	3671	106	34.63	6-53	3	1
Constantine, L.N.	1928	1939	18	33	0	635	90	19.24	—	4	28	—	6337	3004	93	32.30	7-57	4	—
Croft, C.E.H.	1976-77	1981-82	27	37	22	158	33	10.53	—	—	8	—	3583	1746	58	30.10	5-75	2	—
Cuffy, C.E.	1994-95	2002-03	15	23	9	58	15	4.14	—	—	8	—	6165	2913	125	23.30	8-29	3	—
Cummins, A.C.	1992-93	1994-95	5	6	1	98	50	19.60	—	1	5	—	3366	1455	43	33.83	4-82	—	—
Da Costa, O.C.	1929-30	1934-35	5	9	1	153	39	19.12	—	—	5	—	372	175	3	58.33	1-14	—	—
Daniel, W.W.	1975-76	1983-84	10	11	4	46	11	6.57	—	—	3	—	1754	910	36	25.27	5-39	1	—
Davis, B.A.	1964-65	1964-65	4	8	0	245	68	30.62	—	3	1	—							
Davis, C.A.	1968-69	1972-73	15	29	5	1301	183	54.20	4	4	4	—	894	330	2	165.00	1-27	—	—
Davis, W.W.	1982-83	1987-88	15	17	4	202	77	15.53	—	1	10	—	2773	1472	45	32.71	4-19	—	—
de Caires, F.I.	1929-30	1929-30	3	6	0	232	80	38.66	—	2	1	—	12	9	0	—	—		
Deonarine, N.	2004-05	2005	4	6†	1	107	40	21.40	—	—	2	—	341	151	2	75.50	1-5	—	—

INDIVIDUAL CAREER RECORDS – WEST INDIES *continued*

	First Test	Last Test	Tests	Inns	NO	Runs	HS	Avge	100	50	Ct	St	Balls	Runs	Wkts	Avge	BB	5wI	10wM
Depeiza, C.C.	1954-55	1955-56	5	8	2	187	122	31.16	1	–	7	4	30	15	0	–	–	–	–
Dewdney, D.T.	1954-55	1957-58	9	12	5	17	5*	2.42	–	–	7	–	1641	807	21	38.42	5-21	1	–
Dhanraj, R.	1994-95	1995-96	4	4	2	17	9	4.25	–	–	–	–	1087	595	8	74.37	2-49	–	–
Dillon, M.	1996-97	2003-04	38	68	3	549	43	8.44	–	–	16	–	8704	4398	131	33.57	5-71	2	–
Dowe, U.G.	1970-71	1972-73	4	3	2	8	5*	8.00	–	–	3	–	1014	534	12	44.50	4-69	–	–
Dowlin, T.M.	2009	2009	2	4	0	185	95	46.25	–	1	2	–							
Drakes, V.C.	2002-03	2003-04	12	20	2	386	67	21.44	–	1	2	–	2617	1362	33	41.27	5-93	1	–
Dujon, P.J.L.	1981-82	1991	81	115	11	3322	139	31.94	5	16	267	5							
Edwards, F.H.	2003	2009	43	69	21	248	21	5.16	–	–	7	–	7259	4811	122	39.43	7-87	8	–
Edwards, R.M.	1968-69	1968-69	5	8	1	65	22	9.28	–	–	–	–	1311	626	18	34.77	5-84	1	–
Ferguson, W.	1947-48	1953-54	8	10	3	200	75	28.57	–	2	11	–	2568	1165	34	34.26	6-92	3	1
Fernandes, M.P.	1928	1929-30	2	4	0	49	22	12.25	–	–	–	–							
Findlay, T.M.	1969	1972-73	10	16	3	212	44*	16.30	–	–	19	2							
Foster, M.L.C.	1969	1977-78	14	24	5	580	125	30.52	1	1	3	–	1776	600	9	66.66	2-41	–	–
Francis, G.N.	1928	1933	10	18	4	81	19*	5.78	–	–	7	–	1619	763	23	33.17	4-40	–	–
Frederick, M.C.	1953-54	1953-54	1	2	0	30	30	15.00	–	–	–	–							
Fredericks, R.C.	1968-69	1976-77	59	109†	7	4334	169	42.49	8	26	62	–	1187†	548	7	78.28	1-12	–	–
Fuller, R.L.	1934-35	1934-35	1	1	0	1	1	1.00	–	–	–	–	48	12	0	–	–	–	–
Furlonge, H.A.	1954-55	1955-56	3	5	0	99	64	19.80	–	1	–	–							
Ganga, D.	1998-99	2007-08	48	86	2	2160	135	25.71	3	9	30	–	186	106	1	106.00	1-20	–	–
Ganteaume, A.G.	1947-48	1947-48	1	1	0	112	112	112.00	1	–	–	–							
Garner, J.	1976-77	1986-87	58	68	14	672	60	12.44	–	1	42	–	13169	5433	259	20.97	6-56	7	–
Garrick, L.V.	2000-01	2000-01	1	2	0	27	27	13.50	–	–	2	–							
Gaskin, B.B.M.	1947-48	1947-48	2	3	0	17	10	5.66	–	–	2	–	474	158	2	79.00	1-15	–	–
Gayle, C.H.	1999-2000	2009	82	144†	5	5502	317	39.58	10	31	79	–	6707	2929	71	41.25	5-34	2	–
Gibbs, G.L.	1954-55	1954-55	1	2†	0	12	12	6.00	–	–	1	–	24†	7	0	–	–	–	–
Gibbs, L.R.	1957-58	1975-76	79	109	39	488	25	6.97	–	–	52	–	27115	8989	309	29.09	8-38	18	2
Gibson, O.D.	1995	1998-99	2	4	0	93	37	23.25	–	–	1	–	472	275	3	91.66	2-81	–	–
Gilchrist, R.	1957	1958-59	13	14	3	60	12	5.45	–	–	4	–	3227	1521	57	26.68	6-55	1	–
Goddard, J.D.C.	1947-48	1957	27	39†	11	859	83*	30.67	–	4	22	–	2931	1050	33	31.81	5-31	1	–
Gomes, H.A.	1976	1986-87	60	91†	11	3171	143	39.63	9	13	18	–	2401	930	15	62.00	2-20	–	–
Gomez, G.E.	1939	1953-54	29	46	5	1243	101	30.31	1	8	18	–	5236	1590	58	27.41	7-55	1	1
Grant, G.C.	1930-31	1934-35	12	22	6	413	71*	25.81	–	3	10	–	24	18	0	–	–	–	–
Grant, R.S.	1934-35	1939	7	11	1	220	77	22.00	–	1	13	–	986	353	11	32.09	3-68	–	–
Gray, A.H.	1986-87	1986-87	5	8	2	48	12*	8.00	–	–	6	–	888	377	22	17.13	4-39	–	–
Greenidge, A.E.	1977-78	1978-79	6	10	0	222	69	22.20	–	2	5	–	26	4	0	–	–	–	–
Greenidge, C.G.	1974-75	1990-91	108	185	16	7558	226	44.72	19	34	96	–	156	75	0	–	–	–	–
Greenidge, G.A.	1971-72	1972-73	5	9	2	209	50	29.85	–	1	3	–	30	17	0	–	–	–	–
Grell, M.G.	1929-30	1929-30	1	2	0	34	21	17.00	–	–	–	–							
Griffith, A.F.G.	1996-97	2000	14	27†	1	638	114	24.53	1	4	5	–							
Griffith, C.C.	1959-60	1968-69	28	42	10	530	54	16.56	–	1	16	–	5631	2683	94	28.54	6-36	5	–
Griffith, H.C.	1928	1933	13	23	5	91	18	5.05	–	–	4	–	2663	1243	44	28.25	6-103	2	–
Guillen, S.C. ‡	1951-52	1951-52	5	6	2	104	54	26.00	–	1	9	2							

INDIVIDUAL CAREER RECORDS – WEST INDIES continued

	First Test	Last Test	Tests	BATTING AND FIELDING Inns	NO	Runs	HS	Avge	100	50	Ct	St	BOWLING Balls	Runs	Wkts	Avge	BB	5wI	10wM
Hall, W.W.	1958-59	1968-69	48	66	14	818	50*	15.73	–	2	11	–	10421	5066	192	26.38	7-69	9	1
Harper, R.A.	1983-84	1993-94	25	32	3	535	74	18.44	–	3	36	–	3615	1291	46	28.06	6-57	1	1
Haynes, D.L.	1977-78	1993-94	116	202	25	7487	184	42.29	18	39	65	–	18	8	1	8.00	1-2	–	–
Headley, G.A.	1929-30	1953-54	22	40	4	2190	270*	60.83	10	5	14	–	398	230	0	–	–	–	–
Headley, R.G.A.	1973	1973	2	4†	0	62	42	15.50	–	–	2	–	–	–	–	–	–	–	–
Hendriks, J.L.	1961-62	1969	20	32	8	447	64	18.62	–	2	42	5	–	–	–	–	–	–	–
Hinds, R.O.	2001-02	2009	15	25†	1	505	84	21.04	–	2	7	–	1743†	870	13	66.92	2-45	–	–
Hinds, W.W.	1999-00	2005-06	45	80†	1	2608	213	33.01	5	14	32	–	1123	590	16	36.87	3-79	–	–
Hoad, E.L.G.	1928	1933	4	8	0	98	36	12.25	–	–	1	–	–	–	–	–	–	–	–
Holder, R.I.C.	1996-97	1998-99	11	17	2	380	91	25.33	–	2	9	–	–	–	–	–	–	–	–
Holder, V.A.	1969	1978-79	40	59	11	682	42	14.20	–	–	16	–	9095	3627	109	33.27	6-28	3	–
Holding, M.A.	1975-76	1986-87	60	76	10	910	73	13.78	–	6	22	–	12680	5898	249	23.68	8-92	13	2
Holford, D.A.J.	1966	1976-77	24	39	5	768	105*	22.58	1	3	18	–	4816	2009	51	39.39	5-23	2	–
Holt, J.K.C.	1953-54	1958-59	17	31	2	1066	166	36.75	2	5	8	–	30	20	1	20.00	1-20	–	–
Hooper, C.L.	1987-88	2002-03	102	173	15	5762	233	36.46	13	27	115	–	13794	5635	114	49.42	5-26	4	–
Howard, A.B.	1971-72	1971-72	1	0†	–	–	–	–	–	–	–	–	372	140	2	70.00	2-140	–	–
Hunte, C.C.	1957-58	1966-67	44	78	6	3245	260	45.06	8	13	16	–	270	110	2	55.00	1-17	–	–
Hunte, E.A.C.	1929-30	1929-30	3	6	1	166	58	33.20	–	2	5	–	–	–	–	–	–	–	–
Hylton, L.G.	1934-35	1939	6	8	2	70	19	11.66	–	–	1	–	965	418	16	26.12	4-27	–	–
Jacobs, R.D.	1998-99	2004	65	112†	21	2577	118	28.31	3	14	207	12	–	–	–	–	–	–	–
Jaggernauth, A.S.	2008	2008	1	2†	1	0	0*	0.00	–	–	–	–	138	96	1	96.00	1-74	2	–
Johnson, H.H.H.	1947-48	1950	3	4	0	38	22	9.50	–	–	1	–	789	238	13	18.30	5-41	1	–
Johnson, T.F.	1939	1939	1	1†	0	9	9*	–	–	–	1	–	240†	129	3	43.00	2-53	–	–
Jones, C.E.L.	1929-30	1934-35	4	7†	2	63	19	9.00	–	–	3	–	102†	11	0	–	–	–	–
Jones, P.E.W.	1947-48	1951-52	9	11	2	47	10*	5.22	–	–	4	–	1842	751	25	30.04	5-85	1	–
Joseph, D.R.E.	1998-99	1998-99	4	7	0	141	50	20.14	–	1	10	–	–	–	–	–	–	–	–
Joseph, S.C.	2004	2007	5	10	0	147	45	14.70	–	–	3	–	12	8	0	–	–	–	–
Julien, B.D.	1973	1976-77	24	34	6	866	121	30.92	2	3	14	–	4542†	1868	50	37.36	5-57	1	–
Jumadeen, R.R.	1971-72	1978-79	12	14	10	84	56	21.00	–	1	4	–	3140†	1141	29	39.34	4-72	–	–
Kallicharran, A.I.	1971-72	1980-81	66	109†	10	4399	187	44.43	12	21	51	–	406	158	4	39.50	2-16	–	–
Kanhai, R.B.	1957	1973-74	79	137	6	6227	256	47.53	15	28	50	–	183	85	0	–	–	–	–
Kentish, E.S.M.	1947-48	1953-54	2	2	1	1	1*	1.00	–	–	1	–	540	178	8	22.25	5-49	1	–
King, C.L.	1976	1980	9	16	3	418	100*	32.15	1	2	5	–	582	282	3	94.00	1-30	–	–
King, F.M.	1952-53	1955-56	14	17	3	116	21	8.28	–	–	5	–	2869	1159	29	39.96	5-74	1	–
King, L.A.	1961-62	1967-68	2	4	0	41	20	10.25	–	–	2	–	476	154	9	17.11	5-46	1	–
King, R.D.	1998-99	2004-05	19	27	8	66	12*	3.47	–	–	2	–	3442	1733	53	32.69	5-51	–	–
Lambert, C.B.	1991	1998-99	5	9†	0	284	104	31.55	1	1	8	–	10	5	1	5.00	1-4	–	–
Lara, B.C. ‡	1990-91	2006-07	130	230†	6	11912	400*	53.17	34	48	164	–	60	28	0	–	–	–	–
Lashley, P.D.	1960-61	1966	4	7†	0	159	49	22.71	–	–	4	–	18	1	1	1.00	1-1	–	–
Lawson, J.J.C.	2002-03	2005-06	13	21	6	52	14	3.46	–	–	3	–	2364	1512	51	29.64	7-78	2	–

461

INDIVIDUAL CAREER RECORDS – WEST INDIES *continued*

				BATTING AND FIELDING									BOWLING						
	First Test	Last Test	Tests	Inns	NO	Runs	HS	Avge	100	50	Ct	St	Balls	Runs	Wkts	Avge	BB	5wI	10wM
Legall, R.A.	1952-53	1952-53	4	5	0	50	23	10.00	–	–	8	1						–	–
Lewis, D.M.	1970-71	1970-71	3	5	2	259	88	86.33	–	3	8	–						–	–
Lewis, R.N.	1997-98	2007-08	5	10	0	89	40	8.90	–	–	–	–	883	456	4	114.00	2-42	–	–
Lloyd, C.H.	1966-67	1984-85	110	175†	14	7515	242*	46.67	19	39	90	–	1716	622	10	62.20	2-13	–	–
Logie, A.L.	1982-83	1991	52	78	9	2470	130	35.79	2	16	57	–	7	4	0	–	–	–	–
McGarrell, N.C.	2000-01	2001-02	4	6	2	61	33	15.25	–	–	2	–	1212†	453	17	26.64	4-23	–	–
McLean, N.A.M.	1997-98	2000-01	19	32†	2	368	46	12.26	–	3	5	–	3299	1873	44	42.56	3-53	–	–
McMorris, E.D.A.S.	1957-58	1966	13	21	0	564	125	26.85	1	3	5	–	24	16	1	16.00	1-16	–	–
McWatt, C.A.	1953-54	1954-55	6	9†	2	202	54	28.85	–	2	9	1	210	108	0	–	–	–	–
Madray, I.S.	1957-58	1957-58	2	3	0	2	2	1.00	–	–	2	–						–	–
Marshall, M.D.	1978-79	1991	81	107	11	1810	92	18.85	–	10	25	–	17584	7876	376	20.94	7-22	22	4
Marshall, N.E.	1954-55	1954-55	1	2	0	8	8	4.00	–	–	1	–	279	62	2	31.00	1-22	–	–
Marshall, R.E.	1951-52	1951-52	4	7	0	143	30	20.42	–	–	–	–	52	15	0	–	–	–	–
Marshall, X.M.	2005	2008-09	7	12	0	243	85	20.25	–	2	7	–	12	0	0	–	–	–	–
Martin, F.R.	1928	1930-31	9	18†	1	486	123*	28.58	1	–	5	–	1346†	619	8	77.37	3-91	–	–
Martindale, E.A.	1933	1939	10	14	3	58	22	5.27	–	–	5	–	1605	804	37	21.72	5-22	3	–
Mattis, E.H.	1980-81	1980-81	4	5	0	145	71	29.00	–	1	3	–	36	14	0	–	–	–	–
Mendonca, I.L.	1961-62	1961-62	2	2	0	81	78	40.50	–	1	8	2						–	–
Merry, C.A.	1933	1933	2	4	0	34	13	8.50	–	–	1	–						–	–
Miller, N.O.	2009	2009	1	2	0	5	5	2.50	–	–	–	–	132†	67	0	–	–	–	–
Miller, R.	1952-53	1952-53	1	1	0	23	23	23.00	–	–	1	–	96	28	0	–	–	–	–
Mohammed, D.	2003-04	2006-07	5	8†	1	225	52	32.14	–	1	1	–	1065†	668	13	51.38	3-98	–	–
Morais, G.G.	1929-30	1929-30	1	1†	1	12	12*	–	–	–	–	–	300†	189	1	189.00	1-139	–	–
Morton, R.S.	2005	2008	15	27	1	573	70*	22.03	–	4	20	–	66	50	0	–	–	–	–
Moseley, E.A.	1989-90	1989-90	2	4	0	35	26	8.75	–	–	1	–	522	261	6	43.50	2-70	–	–
Mudie, G.H.	1934-35	1934-35	1	1	0	5	5	5.00	–	–	–	–	174†	40	3	13.33	2-23	–	–
Murray, D.A.	1977-78	1981-82	19	31	3	601	84	21.46	–	3	57	5						–	–
Murray, D.L.	1963	1980	62	96	9	1993	91	22.90	–	11	181	8						–	–
Murray, J.R.	1992-93	2001-02	33	45	4	918	101*	22.39	1	3	99	3						–	–
Nagamootoo, M.V.	2000	2002-03	5	8†	1	185	68	26.42	–	1	2	–	1494	637	12	53.08	3-119	–	–
Nanan, R.	1980-81	1980-81	1	2	0	16	8	8.00	–	–	2	–	216	91	4	22.75	2-37	–	–
Nash, B.P.	2008-09	2009	9	13†	1	497	109	38.23	1	4	3	–	330†	178	1	178.00	1-34	–	–
Neblett, J.M.	1934-35	1934-35	1	2	1	16	11*	16.00	–	–	–	–	216	75	1	75.00	1-44	–	–
Noreiga, J.M.	1970-71	1970-71	4	5	2	11	9	3.66	–	–	2	–	1322	493	17	29.00	9-95	2	–
Nunes, R.K.	1928	1929-30	4	8†	1	245	92	30.62	–	2	2	–	42	7	0	–	–	–	–
Nurse, S.M.	1959-60	1968-69	29	54	1	2523	258	47.60	6	10	21	–						–	–
Padmore, A.L.	1975-76	1976	2	2	1	8	8*	8.00	–	–	–	–	474	135	1	135.00	1-36	–	–
Pagon, D.I.	2004-05	2004-05	2	3	0	37	35	12.33	–	–	–	–						–	–
Pairaudeau, B.H.	1952-53	1957	13	21	0	454	115	21.61	1	3	6	–	6	3	0	–	–	–	–
Parchment, B.A.	2007-08	2008	2	4	0	55	20	13.75	–	–	–	–						–	–
Parry, D.R.	1977-78	1979-80	12	20	3	381	65	22.41	–	3	4	–	1909	936	23	40.69	5-15	1	–
Passailaigue, C.C.	1929-30	1929-30	1	2	1	46	44	46.00	–	–	3	–	12	15	0	–	–	–	–

INDIVIDUAL CAREER RECORDS – WEST INDIES *continued*

	First Test	Last Test	Tests	BATTING AND FIELDING									BOWLING						
				Inns	NO	Runs	HS	Avge	100	50	Ct	St	Balls	Runs	Wkts	Avge	BB	5wI	10wM
Patterson, B.P.	1985-86	1992-93	28	38	16	145	21*	6.59	—	—	5	—	4829	2874	93	30.90	5-24	5	—
Payne, T.R.O.	1985-86	1985-86	1	1†	0	5	5	5.00	—	—	5	—	—	—	—	—	—	—	—
Perry, N.O.	1998-99	1999-00	4	7	1	74	26	12.33	—	—	1	—	804	446	10	44.60	5-70	1	—
Phillip, N.	1977-78	1978-79	9	15	5	297	47	29.70	—	—	5	—	1820	1041	28	37.17	4-48	1	—
Phillips, O.J.	2009	2009	2	4†	0	160	94	40.00	—	1	1	—	—	—	—	—	—	—	—
Pierre, L.R.	1947-48	1947-48	1	—	—	—	—	—	—	—	—	—	42	28	0	—	—	—	—
Powell, D.B.	2002	2008-09	37	57	5	407	36*	7.82	—	—	8	—	7077	4068	85	47.85	5-25	1	—
Powell, R.L.	1999-00	2003-04	2	3	0	53	30	17.66	—	—	1	—	78	49	0	—	—	—	—
Rae, A.F.	1948-49	1952-53	15	24†	2	1016	109	46.18	4	4	10	—	—	—	—	—	—	—	—
Ragoonath, S.	1998-99	1998-99	2	4	1	13	9	4.33	—	—	—	—	—	—	—	—	—	—	—
Ramadhin, S.	1950	1960-61	43	58	14	361	44	8.20	—	—	9	—	13939	4579	158	28.98	7-49	10	1
Ramdass, R.R.	2005	2005	1	2	0	26	23	13.00	—	—	2	—	—	—	—	—	—	—	—
Ramdin, D.	2005	2009	36	62	7	1323	166	24.05	1	7	103	2	—	—	—	—	—	—	—
Ramnarine, D.	1997-98	2001-02	12	21†	4	106	35*	6.23	—	—	8	—	3495	1383	45	30.73	5-78	1	—
Reifer, F.L.	1996-97	2009	6	12†	0	111	29	9.25	—	—	6	—	—	—	—	—	—	—	—
Richards, D.M.	2009	2009	2	4	0	108	69	27.00	—	—	3	—	—	—	—	—	—	—	—
Richards, I.V.A.	1974-75	1991	121	182	12	8540	291	50.23	24	45	122	—	5170	1964	32	61.37	2-17	1	—
Richardson, R.B.	1983-84	1995	86	146	12	5949	194	44.39	16	27	90	—	66	18	0	—	—	—	—
Rickards, K.R.	1947-48	1951-52	2	3	0	104	67	34.66	—	1	—	—	—	—	—	—	—	—	—
Roach, C.A.	1928	1934-35	16	32	1	952	209	30.70	2	6	5	—	222	103	2	51.50	1-18	—	—
Roach, K.A.J	2009	2009	2	2	0	14	6	7.00	—	—	2	—	519	229	13	17.61	6-48	1	—
Roberts, A.M.E.	1973-74	1983-84	47	62	11	762	68	14.94	—	3	9	—	11135	5174	202	25.61	7-54	11	2
Roberts, A.T.	1955-56	1955-56	1	2	0	28	28	14.00	—	—	—	—	—	—	—	—	—	—	—
Roberts, L.A.	1998-99	1998-99	1	1	0	0	0	0.00	—	—	—	—	—	—	—	—	—	—	—
Rodriguez, W.V.	1961-62	1967-68	5	7	0	96	50	13.71	—	1	3	—	573	374	7	53.42	3-51	—	—
Rose, F.A.	1996-97	2000	19	28	2	344	69	13.23	—	1	4	—	3124	1637	53	30.88	7-84	2	—
Rowe, L.G.	1971-72	1979-80	30	49	2	2047	302	43.55	7	7	17	—	86†	44	0	—	—	—	—
St Hill, E.L.	1929-30	1929-30	2	4	0	18	12	4.50	—	—	—	—	558	221	3	73.66	2-110	—	—
St Hill, W.H.	1928	1929-30	3	6	0	117	38	19.50	—	—	1	—	12	9	0	—	—	—	—
Sammy, D.J.G.	2007	2009	7	13	0	237	48	18.23	—	—	8	—	1324	649	25	25.96	7-66	3	—
Samuels, M.N.	2000-01	2007-08	29	53	4	1408	105	28.73	2	9	13	—	1596	889	7	127.00	2-49	—	—
Samuels, R.G.	1995-96	1996-97	6	12†	2	372	125	37.20	1	1	8	—	—	—	—	—	—	—	—
Sanford, A.	2001-02	2003-04	11	17	2	72	18*	4.80	—	—	4	—	2217	1316	30	43.86	4-132	—	—
Sarwan, R.R.	1999-00	2009	81	142	8	5671	291	42.32	15	31	47	—	2022	1163	23	50.56	4-37	—	—
Scarlett, R.O.	1959-60	1959-60	3	4	1	54	29*	18.00	—	—	2	—	804	209	2	104.50	1-46	—	—
Scott, A.H.P.	1952-53	1952-53	1	1	0	5	5	5.00	—	—	—	—	264	140	0	—	—	—	—
Scott, O.C.	1928	1930-31	8	13	3	171	35	17.10	—	—	—	—	1405	925	22	42.04	5-266	1	—
Sealey, B.J.	1933	1933	1	2	0	41	29	20.50	—	—	—	—	30	10	1	10.00	1-10	—	—
Sealey, J.E.D.	1929-30	1939	11	19	2	478	92	28.11	—	3	6	1	156	94	3	31.33	2-7	—	—
Shepherd, J.N.	1969	1970-71	5	8†	0	77	32	9.62	—	—	4	—	1445	479	19	25.21	5-104	1	—
Shillingford, G.C.	1969	1971-72	7	7	0	57	25	8.14	—	—	2	—	1181	537	15	35.80	3-63	—	—
Shillingford, I.T.	1976-77	1977-78	4	7	0	218	120	31.14	1	—	1	—	—	—	—	—	—	—	—
Shivnarine, S.	1977-78	1978-79	8	14	1	379	63	29.15	—	4	6	—	336†	167	1	167.00	1-13	—	—

INDIVIDUAL CAREER RECORDS – WEST INDIES continued

	First Test	Last Test	Tests	BATTING AND FIELDING									BOWLING						
				Inns	NO	Runs	HS	Avge	100	50	Ct	St	Balls	Runs	Wkts	Avge	BB	5wI	10wM
Simmons, L.M.P.	2008-09	2009	3	6	0	87	24	14.50	-	-	3	-	180	139	4	139.00	1-60	-	-
Simmons, P.V.	1987-88	1997-98	26	47	2	1002	110	22.26	1	4	26	-	624	257	4	64.25	2-34	-	-
Singh, C.K.	1959-60	1959-60	2	3†	0	11	11	3.66	-	-	2	-	506†	166	5	33.20	2-28	-	-
Small, J.A.	1928	1929-30	3	6	0	79	52	13.16	-	1	3	-	366	184	3	61.33	2-67	-	-
Small, M.A.	1983-84	1984	2	1	1	3	3*	-	-	-	1	-	270	153	4	38.25	3-40	-	-
Smith, C.W.	1960-61	1961-62	5	10	1	222	55	24.66	-	1	4	-	-	-	-	-	-	-	-
Smith, D.R.	2003-04	2005-06	10	14	1	320	105*	24.61	1	-	9	-	651	344	7	49.14	3-71	-	-
Smith, D.S.	2002-03	2009	31	55†	2	1315	108	24.81	1	4	27	-	6	3	0	-	-	-	-
Smith, O.G.	1954-55	1958-59	26	42	0	1331	168	31.69	4	6	9	-	4431	1625	48	33.85	5-90	1	-
Sobers, G.S.	1953-54	1973-74	93	160†	21	8032	365*	57.78	26	30	109	-	21599†	7999	235	34.03	6-73	6	-
Solomon, J.S.	1958-59	1964-65	27	46	7	1326	100*	34.00	1	9	13	-	702	268	4	67.00	1-20	-	-
Stayers, S.C.	1961-62	1961-62	4	4	5	58	35*	19.33	-	-	-	-	636	364	9	40.44	3-65	-	-
Stollmeyer, J.B.	1939	1954-55	32	56	5	2159	160	42.33	4	12	20	-	990	507	13	39.00	3-32	-	-
Stollmeyer, V.H.	1939	1939	1	1	0	96	96	96.00	-	1	-	-	-	-	-	-	-	-	-
Stuart, C.E.L.	2000-01	2001-02	6	9	2	24	12*	3.42	-	-	2	-	1116	628	20	31.40	3-33	-	-
Taylor, J.E.	2003	2009	28	44	6	621	106	16.34	1	1	5	-	4881	2880	81	35.55	5-11	3	-
Taylor, J.O.	1957-58	1958-59	3	5	3	4	4*	2.00	-	-	-	-	672	273	10	27.30	5-109	1	-
Thompson, P.I.C.	1995-96	1996-97	2	3	1	17	10*	8.50	-	-	-	-	228	215	5	43.00	2-58	-	-
Trim, J.	1947-48	1951-52	4	5	1	21	12	5.25	-	-	2	-	794	291	18	16.16	5-34	1	-
Valentine, A.L.	1950	1961-62	36	51	21	141	14	4.70	-	-	13	-	12953†	4215	139	30.32	8-104	8	2
Valentine, V.A.	1933	1933	2	4	1	35	19*	11.66	-	-	-	-	288	104	1	104.00	1-55	-	-
Walcott, C.L.	1947-48	1959-60	44	74	7	3798	220	56.68	15	14	53	11	1194	408	11	37.09	3-50	-	-
Walcott, L.A.	1929-30	1929-30	1	2	1	40	24	40.00	-	-	-	-	48	32	1	32.00	1-17	-	-
Wallace, P.A.	1997-98	1998-99	7	13	0	279	92	21.46	-	2	9	-	-	-	-	-	-	-	-
Walsh, C.A.	1984-85	2000-01	132	185	61	936	30*	7.54	-	-	29	-	30019	12688	519	24.44	7-37	22	3
Walton, C.A.K.	2009	2009	2	4	0	13	10	3.25	-	-	3	-	-	-	-	-	-	-	-
Washington, D.M.	2004-05	2004-05	1	1	1	7	7*	-	-	-	-	-	174	93	0	-	-	-	-
Watson, C.D.	1959-60	1961-62	7	6	1	12	5	2.40	-	-	1	-	1458	724	19	38.10	4-62	1	-
Weekes, E.D.	1947-48	1957-58	48	81	5	4455	207	58.61	15	19	49	-	122	77	1	77.00	1-8	-	-
Weekes, K.H.	1939	1939	2	3†	0	173	137	57.66	1	-	-	-	-	-	-	-	-	-	-
White, A.W.	1964-65	1964-65	2	4	1	71	57*	23.66	-	-	1	-	491	152	3	50.66	2-34	-	-
Wight, C.V.	1928	1929-30	2	4	1	67	23	22.33	-	-	1	-	30	6	0	-	-	-	-
Wight, G.L.	1952-53	1952-53	1	2	0	21	21	21.00	-	-	-	-	-	-	-	-	-	-	-
Wiles, C.A.	1933	1933	1	2	0	2	2	1.00	-	-	-	-	-	-	-	-	-	-	-
Willett, E.T.	1972-73	1974-75	5	8†	3	74	26	14.80	-	-	5	-	1326†	482	11	43.81	3-33	-	-
Williams, A.B.	1977-78	1978-79	7	12	0	469	111	39.08	2	1	-	-	-	-	-	-	-	-	-
Williams, D.	1991-92	1997-98	11	19	1	242	65	13.44	-	1	40	2	-	-	-	-	-	-	-
Williams, E.A.V.	1939	1947-48	4	6	0	113	72	18.83	-	1	-	-	796	241	9	26.77	3-51	-	-
Williams, S.C.	1993-94	2001-02	31	52	3	1183	128	24.14	1	3	27	-	18	19	0	-	-	-	-
Wishart, K.L.	1934-35	1934-35	1	2†	0	52	52	26.00	-	-	-	-	-	-	-	-	-	-	-
Worrell, F.M.M.	1947-48	1963	51	87	9	3860	261	49.48	9	22	43	-	7141†	2672	69	38.72	7-70	2	-

INDIVIDUAL CAREER RECORDS – NEW ZEALAND

	First Test	Last Test	Tests	BATTING AND FIELDING									BOWLING						
				Inns	NO	Runs	HS	Avge	100	50	Ct	St	Balls	Runs	Wkts	Avge	BB	5wI	10wM
Adams, A.R.	2001-02	2001-02	1	2	0	18	11	9.00	–	–	1	–	190	105	6	17.50	3-44	–	–
Alabaster, J.C.	1955-56	1971-72	21	34	6	272	34	9.71	–	–	7	–	3992	1863	49	38.02	4-46	–	–
Allcott, C.F.W.	1929-30	1931-32	6	7†	2	113	33	22.60	–	–	3	–	1206†	541	6	90.16	2-102	–	–
Allott, G.I.	1995-96	1999	10	15	7	27	8*	3.37	–	–	2	–	2023†	1111	19	58.47	4-74	–	–
Anderson, R.W.	1976-77	1978	9	18	0	423	92	23.50	–	3	1	–	–						
Anderson, W.M.	1945-46	1945-46	1	2†	0	5	4	2.50	–	–	1	–	–						
Andrews, B.	1973-74	1973-74	2	3	2	22	17	22.00	–	–	1	–	256	154	2	77.00	2-40	–	–
Astle, N.J.	1995-96	2006-07	81	137	10	4702	222	37.02	11	24	70	–	5688	2143	51	42.01	3-27	–	–
Badcock, F.T.	1929-30	1932-33	7	9	2	137	64	19.57	–	2	1	–	1608	610	16	38.12	4-80	–	–
Barber, R.T.	1955-56	1955-56	1	2	0	17	12	8.50	–	–	1	–	–						
Bartlett, G.A.	1961-62	1967-68	10	18	1	263	40	15.47	–	–	8	–	1768	792	24	33.00	6-38	1	–
Barton, P.T.	1961-62	1962-63	7	14	0	285	109	20.35	1	1	4	–	–						
Beard, D.D.	1951-52	1955-56	4	7	2	101	31	20.20	–	–	2	–	806	302	9	33.55	3-22	–	–
Beck, J.E.F.	1953-54	1955-56	8	15†	0	394	99	26.26	–	3	–	–	–						
Bell, M.D.	1998-99	2007-08	18	32	2	729	107	24.30	2	3	19	–	–						
Bell, W.	1953-54	1953-54	2	3	0	21	21*		–	–	1	–	491	235	2	117.50	1-54	–	–
Bilby, G.P.	1965-66	1965-66	2	4	0	55	28	13.75	–	–	3	–	–						
Blain, T.E.	1986	1993-94	11	20	3	456	78	26.82	–	2	19	2	–						
Blair, R.W.	1952-53	1963-64	19	34	6	189	64*	6.75	–	–	5	–	3525	1515	43	35.23	4-85	–	1
Blunt, R.C.	1929-30	1931-32	9	13	1	330	96	27.50	1	1	5	–	936	472	12	39.33	3-17	–	–
Bolton, B.A.	1958-59	1958-59	2	3	0	59	33	19.66	–	–	1	–	–						
Bond, S.E.	2001-02	2007-08	17	18	7	139	41*	12.63	–	–	6	–	3079	1769	79	22.39	6-51	4	1
Boock, S.L.	1977-78	1988-89	30	41	8	207	37	6.27	–	–	14	–	6598†	2564	74	34.64	7-87	4	–
Bracewell, B.P.	1978	1984-85	6	12	2	24	8	2.40	–	–	1	–	1036	585	14	41.78	3-110	–	–
Bracewell, J.G.	1980-81	1990	41	60	11	1001	110	20.42	1	4	31	–	8403	3653	102	35.81	6-32	4	1
Bradburn, G.E.	1990-91	2000-01	7	10	2	105	30*	13.12	–	–	6	–	867	460	6	76.66	3-134	–	–
Bradburn, W.P.	1963-64	1963-64	2	4	0	62	32	15.50	–	–	2	–	–						
Brown, V.R.	1985-86	1985-86	2	3†	1	51	36*	25.50	–	–	3	–	342	176	1	176.00	1-17	–	–
Burgess, M.G.	1967-68	1980-81	50	92	6	2684	119*	31.20	5	14	34	–	498	212	6	35.33	3-23	–	–
Burke, C.	1945-46	1945-46	1	2	0	4	3	2.00	–	–	–	–	66	30	2	15.00	2-30	–	–
Burtt, T.B.	1946-47	1952-53	10	15	3	252	42	21.00	–	–	2	–	2593†	1170	33	35.45	6-162	3	–
Butler, I.G.	2001-02	2004-05	8	10	2	76	26	9.50	–	–	4	–	1368	884	24	36.83	6-46	1	–
Butterfield, L.A.	1945-46	1945-46	1	2	0	0	0	0.00	–	–	–	–	78	24	0	–	–	–	–
Cairns, B.L.	1973-74	1985-86	43	65	8	928	64	16.28	–	2	30	–	10628	4279	130	32.91	7-74	6	1
Cairns, C.L.	1989-90	2004	62	104	5	3320	158	33.53	5	22	14	–	11698	6410	218	29.40	7-27	13	1
Cameron, F.J.	1961-62	1965	19	30	20	116	27*	11.60	–	–	1	–	4570	1849	62	29.82	5-34	3	–
Cave, H.B.	1949	1958	19	31	5	229	22*	8.80	–	–	8	–	4074	1467	34	43.14	4-21	–	–
Chapple, M.E.	1952-53	1965-66	14	27	1	497	76	19.11	–	3	10	–	248†	84	1	84.00	1-24	–	–
Chatfield, E.J.	1974-75	1988-89	43	54	33	180	21*	8.57	–	–	7	–	10360	3958	123	32.17	6-73	3	1
Cleverley, D.C.	1931-32	1945-46	2	4†	3	19	10*	19.00	–	–	–	–	222	130	0	–	–	–	–
Collinge, R.O.	1964-65	1978	35	50	13	533	68*	14.40	–	2	10	–	7689†	3393	116	29.25	6-63	3	–

INDIVIDUAL CAREER RECORDS – NEW ZEALAND continued

	First Test	Last Test	Tests	Inns	NO	Runs	HS	Avge	100	50	Ct	St	Balls	Runs	Wkts	Avge	BB	5wI	10wM
								BATTING AND FIELDING							BOWLING				
Colquhoun, I.A.	1954-55	1954-55	2	4	2	1	1*	0.50	–	–	4	–	–	–	–	–	–	–	–
Coney, J.V.	1973-74	1986-87	52	85	14	2668	174*	37.57	3	16	64	–	2835	966	27	35.77	3-28	1	–
Congdon, B.E.	1964-65	1978	61	114	7	3448	176	32.22	7	19	44	–	5620	2154	59	36.50	5-65	1	1
Cowie, J.	1937	1949	9	13	4	90	45	10.00	–	–	3	–	2028	969	45	21.53	6-40	4	1
Cresswell, G.F.	1949	1950-51	3	5†	3	14	12*	7.00	–	–	1	–	650	292	13	22.46	6-168	1	–
Cromb, I.B.	1931	1931-32	5	8	2	123	51*	20.50	–	1	1	–	960	442	8	55.25	3-113	–	–
Crowe, J.J.	1982-83	1989-90	39	65	4	1601	128	26.24	3	6	41	–	18	9	0	–	–	–	–
Crowe, M.D.	1981-82	1995-96	77	131	11	5444	299	45.36	17	18	71	–	1377	676	14	48.28	2-25	–	–
Cumming, C.D.	2004-05	2007-08	11	19	2	441	74	25.94	–	1	3	–	–	–	–	–	–	–	–
Cunis, R.S.	1963-64	1971-72	20	31	8	295	51	12.82	–	1	1	–	4250	1887	51	37.00	6-76	1	–
D'Arcy, J.W.	1958	1958	5	10	0	136	33	13.60	–	–	4	–	–	–	–	–	–	–	–
Davis, H.T.	1994	1997-98	5	7	4	20	8*	6.66	–	–	–	–	1010	499	17	29.35	5-63	1	–
de Groen, R.P.	1993-94	1994-95	5	10	4	45	26	7.50	–	–	4	–	1060	505	11	45.90	3-40	–	–
Dempster, C.S.	1929-30	1932-33	10	15	4	723	136	65.72	2	5	2	–	5	10	0	–	–	–	–
Dempster, E.W.	1952-53	1953-54	5	8†	2	106	47	17.66	–	1	2	–	544†	219	2	109.50	1-24	–	–
Dick, A.E.	1961-62	1965	17	30	4	370	50*	14.23	–	1	47	4	–	–	–	–	–	–	–
Dickinson, G.R.	1929-30	1931-32	3	5	0	31	11	6.20	–	–	3	–	451	245	8	30.62	3-66	–	–
Donnelly, M.P.	1937	1949	7	12†	1	582	206	52.90	1	4	7	–	30†	20	0	–	–	–	–
Doull, S.B.	1992-93	1999-00	32	50	11	570	46	14.61	–	–	16	–	6053	2872	98	29.30	7-65	6	–
Dowling, G.T.	1961-62	1971-72	39	77	3	2306	239	31.16	3	11	23	–	36	19	1	19.00	1-19	–	–
Drum, C.J.	2000-01	2001-02	5	5	2	10	4	3.33	–	–	4	–	806	482	16	30.12	3-36	–	–
Dunning, J.A.	1932-33	1937	4	6	1	38	19	7.60	–	–	2	–	830	493	5	98.60	2-35	–	–
Edgar, B.A.	1978	1986	39	68†	4	1958	161	30.59	3	12	14	–	18	3	0	–	–	–	–
Edwards, G.N.	1976-77	1980-81	8	15	0	377	55	25.13	–	3	7	–	–	–	–	–	–	–	–
Elliott, G.D.	2007-08	2008-09	3	5	1	27	9	6.75	–	–	2	–	240	129	2	64.50	1-15	–	–
Emery, R.W.G.	1951-52	1951-52	2	4	0	46	28	11.50	–	–	–	–	46	52	2	26.00	2-52	–	–
Fisher, F.E.	1952-53	1952-53	1	2	0	23	14	11.50	–	–	–	–	204†	78	1	78.00	1-78	–	–
Fleming, S.P.	1993-94	2007-08	111	189†	10	7172	274*	40.06	9	46	171	–	–	–	–	–	–	–	–
Flynn, D.R.	2008	2009	13	24†	5	627	95	33.00	–	4	6	–	–	–	–	–	–	–	–
Foley, H.	1929-30	1929-30	1	2†	0	4	2	2.00	–	–	–	–	–	–	–	–	–	–	–
Franklin, J.E.C.	2000-01	2008-09	26	36†	6	644	122*	21.46	1	2	11	–	4399†	2612	80	32.65	6-119	3	–
Franklin, T.J.	1983	1990-91	21	37	1	828	101	23.00	1	4	8	–	–	–	–	–	–	–	–
Freeman, D.L.	1932-33	1932-33	2	2	0	2	1	1.00	–	–	–	–	240	169	1	169.00	1-91	–	–
Fulton, P.G.	2005-06	2008-09	8	12	1	272	75	24.72	–	1	8	–	–	–	–	–	–	–	–
Gallichan, N.	1937	1937	1	2	0	32	30	16.00	–	–	–	–	264†	113	3	37.66	3-99	–	–
Gedye, S.G.	1963-64	1964-65	4	8	0	193	55	24.12	–	2	–	–	–	–	–	–	–	–	–
Germon, L.K.	1995-96	1996-97	12	21	3	382	55	21.22	–	1	27	2	–	–	–	–	–	–	–
Gillespie, M.R.	2007-08	2008-09	3	5	1	25	16*	6.25	–	–	–	–	516	380	11	34.54	5-136	1	–
Gillespie, S.R.	1985-86	1985-86	1	1	0	28	28	28.00	–	–	–	–	162	79	1	79.00	1-79	–	–
Gray, E.J.	1983	1988-89	10	16	0	248	50	15.50	–	1	6	–	2076†	886	17	52.11	3-73	–	–
Greatbatch, M.J.	1987-88	1996-97	41	71†	5	2021	146*	30.62	3	10	27	–	6	0	0	–	–	–	–

Name	First Test	Last Test	Tests	Inns	NO	Runs	HS	Avge	100	50	Ct	St	Balls	Runs	Wkts	Avge	BB	5wI	10wM
								BATTING AND FIELDING							BOWLING				
Guillen, S.C. ‡	1955-56	1955-56	3	6	0	98	41	16.33	–	–	4	1	–						
Guptill, M.J.	2008-09	2009	5	9	0	241	49	26.77	–	3	1	–	–						
Guy, J.W.	1955-56	1961-62	12	23†	2	440	102	20.95	1	3	2	–	–						
Hadlee, D.R.	1969	1977-78	26	42	5	530	56	14.32	–	1	8	–	4883	2389	71	33.64	4-30	–	–
Hadlee, R.J.	1972-73	1990	86	134†	19	3124	151*	27.16	2	15	39	–	21918	9611	431	22.29	9-52	36	9
Hadlee, W.A.	1937	1950-51	11	19	1	543	116	30.16	1	2	6	–	–						
Harford, N.S.	1955-56	1958	8	15	0	229	93	15.26	–	2	11	–	–						
Harford, R.I.	1967-68	1967-68	3	5†	2	7	6	2.33	–	–	14	–	–						
Harris, C.Z.	1992-93	2002	23	42†	4	777	71	20.44	–	5	6	–	2560	1170	16	73.12	2-16	–	–
Harris, P.G.Z.	1955-56	1964-65	9	18	1	378	101	22.23	1	1	9	–	42	14	0	–	–	–	–
Harris, R.M.	1958-59	1958-59	2	3	0	31	13	10.33	–	–	–	–	–						
Hart, M.N.	1993-94	1995-96	14	24†	4	353	45	17.65	–	1	9	–	3086†	1438	29	49.58	5-77	1	–
Hart, R.G.	2002	2003-04	11	19	3	260	57*	16.25	–	1	29	1	–						
Hartland, B.R.	1991-92	1994	9	18	0	303	52	16.83	–	1	5	–	–						
Haslam, M.J.	1992-93	1995-96	4	2†	1	4	3	4.00	–	–	2	–	493†	245	2	122.50	1-33	–	–
Hastings, B.F.	1968-69	1975-76	31	56	6	1510	117*	30.20	4	7	23	–	22	9	0	–	–	–	–
Hayes, J.A.	1950-51	1958	15	22	7	73	19	4.86	–	–	3	–	2675	1217	30	40.56	4-36	–	–
Henderson, M.	1929-30	1929-30	1	2†	1	8	6	8.00	–	–	1	–	90†	64	2	32.00	2-38	–	–
Hopkins, G.J.	2008	2008	1	2	0	27	15	13.50	–	–	3	–	–						
Horne, M.J.	1996-97	2003	35	65	2	1788	157	28.38	4	5	17	–	66	26	0	–	–	–	–
Horne, P.A.	1986-87	1990-91	4	7†	0	71	27	10.14	–	–	3	–	–						
Hough, K.W.	1958-59	1958-59	2	3	2	62	31*	62.00	–	–	1	–	462	175	6	29.16	3-79	–	–
How, J.M.	2005-06	2008-09	19	35	1	772	92	22.70	–	4	18	–	12	4	0	–	–	–	–
Howarth, G.P.	1974-75	1984-85	47	83	5	2531	147	32.44	6	11	29	–	614	271	3	90.33	1-13	–	–
Howarth, H.J.	1969	1976-77	30	42†	18	291	61	12.12	–	1	33	–	8833†	3178	86	36.95	5-34	2	–
James, K.C.	1929-30	1932-33	11	13	2	52	14	4.72	–	–	11	5	–						
Jarvis, T.W.	1964-65	1972-73	13	22	1	625	182	29.76	1	2	3	–	12	3	0	–	–	–	–
Jones, A.H.	1986-87	1994-95	39	74	8	2922	186	44.27	7	11	25	–	328	194	1	194.00	1-40	–	–
Jones, R.A.	2003-04	2003-04	1	2	0	23	16	11.50	–	–	–	–	–						
Kennedy, R.J.	1995-96	1995-96	4	5	1	28	22	7.00	–	–	2	–	636	380	6	63.33	3-28	–	–
Kerr, J.L.	1931	1937	7	12	1	212	59	19.27	–	1	4	–	–	67	1	67.00	1-50	–	–
Kuggeleijn, C.M.	1988-89	1988-89	2	4	0	7	7	1.75	–	–	1	–	97						
Larsen, G.R.	1994	1995-96	8	13	4	127	26*	14.11	–	–	5	–	1967	689	24	28.70	3-57	–	–
Latham, R.T.	1991-92	1992-93	4	7	0	219	119	31.28	1	1	5	–	18	6	0	–	–	–	–
Lees, W.K.	1976-77	1983	21	37	4	778	152	23.57	1	1	52	7	5	4	0	–	–	–	–
Leggat, I.B.	1953-54	1953-54	1	1	0	0	0	0.00	–	–	2	–	24	6	0	–	–	–	–
Leggat, J.G.	1951-52	1955-56	9	18	2	351	61	21.93	–	2	1	–	–						
Lissette, A.F.	1955-56	1955-56	2	4	2	2	1*	1.00	–	–	1	–	288†	124	3	41.33	2-73	–	–
Loveridge, G.R.	1995-96	1995-96	1	1	1	4	4*	–	–	–	–	–	–						
Lowry, T.C.	1929-30	1931	7	8	0	223	80	27.87	–	2	8	–	12	5	0	–	–	–	–

INDIVIDUAL CAREER RECORDS – NEW ZEALAND continued

Name	First Test	Last Test	Tests	BATTING AND FIELDING Inns	NO	Runs	HS	Avge	100	50	Ct	St	BOWLING Balls	Runs	Wkts	Avge	BB	5wI	10wM
McCullum, B.B.	2003-04	2009	46	76	4	2283	143	31.70	3	13	139	9	36	13	0	–	–	–	–
McEwan, P.E.	1979-80	1984-85	4	7	1	96	40*	16.00	–	–	5								
MacGibbon, A.R.	1950-51	1958	26	46	5	814	66	19.85	–	1	13		5659	2160	70	30.85	5-64	1	–
McGirr, H.M.	1929-30	1929-30	2	4	3	51	51	51.00	–	1	–		180	115	1	115.00	1-65	–	–
McGregor, S.N.	1954-55	1964-65	25	47	2	892	111	19.82	1	3	9								
McIntosh, T.G.	2008-09	2009	7	13†	1	338	136	28.16	1	1	3								
McLeod, E.G.	1929-30	1929-30	1	2†	1	18	16	18.00	–	–	–	1	12	5	0	–	–	–	–
McMahon, T.G.	1955-56	1955-56	5	7	4	7	4*	2.33	–	–	7	1							
McMillan, C.D.	1997-98	2004-05	55	91	10	3116	142	38.46	6	19	22		2502	1257	28	44.89	3-48	–	–
McRae, D.A.N.	1945-46	1945-46	1	2†	0	8	8	4.00	–	–	1		84†	44	0	–	–	–	–
Marshall, H.J.H.	2000-01	2005-06	13	19	2	652	160	38.35	2	2	5		6	4	0	–	–	–	–
Marshall, J.A.H.	2004-05	2008	7	11	0	218	52	19.81	–	1	11								
Martin, C.S.	2000-01	2009	50	72	37	82	12*	2.34	–	–	11		9773	5574	165	33.78	6-54	8	1
Mason, M.J.	2003-04	2003-04	1	2	0	3	3	1.50	–	–	–		132	105	0	–	–	–	–
Matheson, A.M.	1929-30	1931	2	2	1	7	7	7.00	–	–	2		282	136	2	68.00	2-7	–	–
Meale, T.	1958	1958	2	4†	0	21	10	5.25	–	–	–								
Merritt, W.E.	1929-30	1931	6	8	1	73	19	10.42	–	–	2		936	617	12	51.41	4-104	–	–
Meuli, E.M.	1952-53	1952-53	1	2	0	38	23	19.00	–	–	–								
Milburn, B.D.	1968-69	1968-69	3	3	2	8	4*	8.00	–	–	6	2							
Miller, L.S.M.	1952-53	1958	13	25†	0	346	47	13.84	–	–	1		2†	1	0	–	–	–	–
Mills, J.E.	1929-30	1932-33	7	10†	1	241	117	26.77	1	–	4								
Mills, K.D.	2004	2008-09	19	30	5	289	57	11.56	–	1	4		2902	1453	44	33.02	4-16	–	–
Moir, A.M.	1950-51	1958-59	17	30	8	327	41*	14.86	–	1	3		2650	1418	28	50.64	6-155	2	–
Moloney, D.A.R.	1937	1937	3	6	0	156	64	26.00	–	1	3		12	9	0	–	–	–	–
Mooney, F.L.H.	1949	1953-54	14	22	2	343	46	17.15	–	5	22	8	8	0	0	–	–	–	–
Morgan, R.W.	1964-65	1971-72	20	34	1	734	97	22.24	–	5	12		1114	609	5	121.80	1-16	–	–
Morrison, B.D.	1962-63	1962-63	1	2†	0	10	10	5.00	–	–	–		186	129	2	64.50	2-129	–	–
Morrison, D.K.	1987-88	1996-97	48	71	26	379	42	8.42	–	–	14		10064	5549	160	34.68	7-89	10	–
Morrison, J.F.M.	1973-74	1981-82	17	29	0	656	117	22.62	1	3	9		264†	71	2	35.50	2-52	–	–
Motz, R.C.	1961-62	1969	32	56	3	612	60	11.54	–	3	9		7034	3148	100	31.48	6-63	5	–
Murray, B.A.G.	1967-68	1970-71	13	26	1	598	90	23.92	–	5	21		6	0	1	0.00	1-0	–	–
Murray, D.J.	1994-95	1994-95	8	16	1	303	52	20.20	–	1	6								
Nash, D.J.	1992-93	2001-02	32	45	14	729	89*	23.51	–	4	13		6196	2649	93	28.48	6-27	3	1
Newman, J.	1931-32	1932-33	3	4	0	33	19	8.25	–	–	–		425†	254	2	127.00	2-76	–	–
O'Brien, I.E.	2004-05	2009	19	29	4	152	19*	6.08	–	–	6		3533	1981	58	34.15	6-75	1	–
O'Connor, S.B.	1997-98	2001-02	19	27†	9	103	20	5.72	–	–	6		3667†	1724	53	32.52	5-51	1	–
Oram, J.D.P.	2002-03	2009	33	59†	10	1780	133	36.32	5	6	15		4964	1983	60	33.05	4-41	–	–
O'Sullivan, D.R.	1972-73	1976-77	11	21	4	158	23*	9.29	–	–	2		2744†	1221	18	67.83	5-148	1	–
Overton, G.W.F.	1953-54	1953-54	3	6†	1	8	3*	1.60	–	–	1		729	258	9	28.66	3-65	–	–
Owens, M.B.	1992-93	1994	8	12	6	16	8*	2.66	–	–	3		1074	585	17	34.41	4-99	–	–

	First Test	Last Test	Tests	Inns	NO	Runs	HS	Avge	100	50	Ct	St	Balls	Runs	Wkts	Avge	BB	5wI	10wM
								BATTING AND FIELDING								BOWLING			
Page, M.L.	1929-30	1937	14	20	0	492	104	24.60	1	2	6	—	379	231	5	46.20	2-21	—	—
Papps, M.H.W.	2003-04	2007-08	8	16	1	246	86	16.40	—	2	11	—	—	—	—	—	—	—	—
Parker, J.M.	1972-73	1980-81	36	63	2	1498	121	24.55	3	5	30	—	40	24	1	24.00	1-24	—	—
Parker, N.M.	1976-77	1976-77	3	6	0	89	40	14.83	—	—	2	—	—	—	—	—	—	—	—
Parore, A.C.	1990	2001-02	78	128	19	2865	110	26.28	2	14	197	7	—	—	—	—	—	—	—
Patel, D.N.	1986-87	1996-97	37	66	8	1200	99	20.68	—	5	15	—	6594	3154	75	42.05	6-50	3	—
Patel, J.S.	2005-06	2009	9	12	2	131	27*	13.10	—	—	5	—	2556	1289	33	39.06	5-110	1	—
Petherick, P.J.	1976-77	1976-77	6	11	4	34	13	4.85	—	—	4	—	1305	685	16	42.81	3-90	—	—
Petrie, E.C.	1955-56	1965-66	14	25	5	258	55	12.90	—	1	25	—	—	—	—	—	—	—	—
Playle, W.R.	1958	1962-63	8	15	0	151	65	10.06	—	1	4	—	—	—	—	—	—	—	—
Pocock, B.A.	1993-94	1997-98	15	29	0	665	85	22.93	—	6	5	—	24	20	0	—	—	—	—
Pollard, V.	1964-65	1973	32	59	7	1266	116	24.34	2	7	19	—	4421	1853	40	46.32	3-3	—	—
Poore, M.B.	1952-53	1955-56	14	24	1	355	45	15.43	—	—	1	—	788	367	9	40.77	2-28	—	—
Priest, M.W.	1990	1998	3	4†	0	56	26	14.00	—	—	—	—	377†	158	3	52.66	2-42	—	—
Pringle, C.	1990-91	1994-95	14	21	4	175	30	10.29	—	—	3	—	2985	1389	30	46.30	7-52	1	1
Puna, N.	1965-66	1965-66	3	5	3	31	18*	15.50	—	—	1	—	480	240	4	60.00	2-40	—	—
Rabone, G.O.	1949	1954-55	12	20	2	562	107	31.22	1	2	5	—	1385	635	16	39.68	6-68	1	—
Redmond, A.J.	2008	2008-09	7	14	1	299	83	23.00	—	2	5	—	75	62	3	20.66	2-47	—	—
Redmond, R.E.	1972-73	1972-73	1	2†	0	163	107	81.50	1	1	—	—	—	—	—	—	—	—	—
Reid, J.F.	1978-79	1985-86	19	31†	3	1296	180	46.28	6	2	9	—	18	7	0	—	—	—	—
Reid, J.R.	1949	1965	58	108	5	3428	142	33.28	6	22	43	1	7725	2835	85	33.35	6-60	1	—
Richardson, M.H.	2000-01	2004-05	38	65†	3	2776	145	44.77	4	19	26	—	66†	21	0	21.00	1-16	—	—
Roberts, A.D.G.	1975-76	1976-77	7	12	1	254	84*	23.09	—	1	4	—	440	182	4	45.50	1-12	—	—
Roberts, A.W.	1929-30	1937	5	10	1	248	66*	27.55	—	3	4	—	459	209	7	29.85	4-101	—	—
Robertson, G.K.	1985-86	1985-86	1	1	0	12	12	12.00	—	—	—	—	144	91	1	91.00	1-91	—	—
Rowe, C.G.	1945-46	1945-46	1	2	0	0	0	0.00	—	—	1	—	—	—	—	—	—	—	—
Rutherford, K.R.	1984-85	1994-95	56	99	8	2465	107*	27.08	3	18	32	—	256	161	1	161.00	1-38	—	—
Ryder, J.D.	2008-09	2009	11	20†	2	898	201	49.88	2	4	8	—	378	212	4	53.00	2-7	—	—
Scott, R.H.	1946-47	1946-47	1	1	0	18	18	18.00	—	—	—	—	138	74	1	74.00	1-74	—	—
Scott, V.J.	1945-46	1951-52	10	17	1	458	84	28.62	—	3	7	—	18	14	0	—	—	—	—
Sewell, D.G.	1997-98	1997-98	1	1	0	1	1*	—	—	—	—	—	138†	90	0	—	—	—	—
Shrimpton, M.J.F.	1962-63	1973-74	10	19	0	265	46	13.94	—	—	2	—	257	158	5	31.60	3-35	—	—
Sinclair, B.W.	1962-63	1967-68	21	40	1	1148	138	29.43	3	3	8	—	60	32	2	16.00	2-32	—	—
Sinclair, I.M.	1955-56	1955-56	2	4†	1	25	18*	8.33	—	—	1	—	233	120	1	120.00	1-79	—	—
Sinclair, M.S.	1999-00	2007-08	32	54	5	1595	214	32.55	3	4	31	—	24	13	0	—	—	—	—
Smith, F.B.	1946-47	1951-52	4	6	1	237	96	47.40	—	2	1	—	—	—	—	—	—	—	—
Smith, H.D.	1932-33	1932-33	1	1	0	4	4	4.00	—	—	—	—	120	113	1	113.00	1-113	—	—
Smith, I.D.S.	1980-81	1991-92	63	88	17	1815	173	25.56	2	6	168	8	18	5	0	—	—	—	—
Snedden, C.A.	1946-47	1946-47	1	—	—	—	—	—	—	—	—	—	96	46	0	—	—	—	—
Snedden, M.C.	1980-81	1990	25	30†	8	327	33*	14.86	—	—	7	—	4775	2199	58	37.91	5-68	1	—
Southee, T.G.	2007-08	2008-09	5	9	2	127	77*	18.14	—	1	2	—	927	575	12	47.91	5-55	1	—
Sparling, J.T.	1958	1963-64	11	20	2	229	50	12.72	—	1	4	—	708	327	5	65.40	1-9	—	—
Spearman, C.M.	1995-96	2000-01	19	37	2	922	112	26.34	1	3	21	—	6	1	0	—	—	—	—
Stead, G.R.	1998-99	1999-00	5	8	0	278	78	34.75	—	2	2	—	—	—	—	—	—	—	—

INDIVIDUAL CAREER RECORDS – NEW ZEALAND continued

	First Test	Last Test	Tests	Inns	NO	Runs	HS	Avge	100	50	Ct	St	Balls	Runs	Wkts	Avge	BB	5wI	10wM
				BATTING AND FIELDING									*BOWLING*						
Stirling, D.A.	1984-85	1986	6	9	2	108	26	15.42	–	–	1	–	902	601	13	46.23	4-88	–	–
Styris, S.B.	2002	2007-08	29	48	4	1586	170	36.04	5	6	23	–	1960	1015	20	50.75	3-28	–	–
Su'a, M.L.	1991-92	1994-95	13	18†	5	165	44	12.69	–	–	8	–	2843†	1377	36	38.25	5-73	2	–
Sutcliffe, B.	1946-47	1965	42	76†	8	2727	230*	40.10	5	15	20	–	538†	344	4	86.00	2-38	–	–
Taylor, B.R.	1964-65	1973	30	50†	6	898	124	20.40	2	2	10	–	6334	2953	111	26.60	7-74	4	–
Taylor, D.D.	1946-47	1955-56	3	5	0	159	77	31.80	1	1	2	–	–	–	0	–	–	–	–
Taylor, L.R.P.L.	2007-08	2009	19	35	1	1343	154*	39.50	4	5	34	–	32	14	1	9.00	1-9	–	–
Thomson, K.	1967-68	1967-68	2	4	1	94	69	31.33	–	1	–	–	21	9	0	–	–	–	–
Thomson, S.A.	1989-90	1995-96	19	35	4	958	120*	30.90	1	5	7	–	1990	953	19	50.15	3-63	–	–
Tindill, E.W.T.	1937	1946-47	5	9†	1	73	37*	9.12	–	–	6	1	–	–	–	–	–	–	–
Troup, G.B.	1976-77	1985-86	15	18	6	55	13*	4.58	–	–	2	–	3183†	1454	39	37.28	6-95	1	–
Truscott, P.B.	1964-65	1964-65	1	2	0	29	26	14.50	–	–	1	–	–	–	–	–	–	–	–
Tuffey, D.R.	1999-00	2004	22	30	7	263	35	11.43	–	–	12	–	4110	2057	66	31.16	6-54	2	–
Turner, G.M.	1968-69	1982-83	41	73	6	2991	259	44.64	7	14	42	–	12	5	0	–	–	–	–
Twose, R.G.	1995-96	1999	16	27†	2	628	94	25.12	–	6	5	–	211	130	3	43.33	2-36	–	–
Vance, R.H.	1987-88	1989-90	4	7	0	207	68	29.57	–	1	–	–	–	–	–	–	–	–	–
Vaughan, J.T.C.	1992-93	1996-97	6	12†	1	201	44	18.27	–	–	4	–	1040	450	11	40.90	4-27	–	–
Vettori, D.L. ‡	1996-97	2009	93	139†	22	3484	140	29.77	4	20	48	–	22963†	10045	302	33.26	7-87	18	3
Vincent, L.	2001-02	2007-08	23	40	1	1332	224	34.15	3	9	19	–	6	2	0	–	–	–	–
Vivian, G.E.	1964-65	1971-72	5	6†	6	110	43	18.33	–	–	3	–	198	107	1	107.00	1-14	–	–
Vivian, H.G.	1931	1937	7	10†	0	421	100	42.10	1	5	4	–	1311†	633	17	37.23	4-58	–	–
Wadsworth, K.J.	1969	1975-76	33	51	4	1010	80	21.48	–	5	92	4	–	–	–	–	–	–	–
Walker, B.G.K.	2000-01	2002	5	8	2	118	27*	19.66	–	–	5	–	669	399	5	79.80	2-92	–	–
Wallace, W.M.	1937	1952-53	13	21	0	439	66	20.90	–	5	5	–	6	5	0	–	–	–	–
Walmsley, K.P.	1994-95	2000-01	3	5	0	13	5	2.60	–	–	–	–	774	391	9	43.44	3-70	–	–
Ward, J.T.	1963-64	1967-68	8	12	6	75	35*	12.50	–	–	16	1	–	–	–	–	–	–	–
Watson, W.	1986	1993-94	15	18	6	60	11	5.00	–	–	4	–	3486	1387	40	34.67	6-78	1	–
Watt, L.	1954-55	1954-55	1	2	0	2	2	1.00	–	–	–	–	–	–	–	–	–	–	–
Webb, M.G.	1970-71	1973-74	3	2	0	12	12	6.00	–	–	–	–	732	471	4	117.75	2-114	–	–
Webb, P.N.	1979-80	1979-80	2	3	0	11	5	3.66	–	–	2	–	–	–	–	–	–	–	–
Weir, G.L.	1929-30	1937	11	16	2	416	74*	29.71	–	3	3	–	342	209	7	29.85	3-38	–	–
White, D.J.	1990-91	1990-91	2	4	0	31	18	7.75	–	–	–	–	3	5	0	–	–	–	–
Whitelaw, P.E.	1932-33	1932-33	2	4	2	64	30	32.00	–	–	–	–	–	–	–	–	–	–	–
Wiseman, P.J.	1998	2004-05	25	34	8	366	36	14.07	–	–	11	–	5660	2903	61	47.59	5-82	2	–
Wright, J.G.	1977-78	1992-93	82	148†	7	5334	185	37.82	12	23	38	–	30	5	0	–	–	–	–
Young, B.A.	1993-94	1998-99	35	68	4	2034	267*	31.78	2	12	54	–	–	–	–	–	–	–	–
Yuile, B.W.	1962-63	1969-70	17	33	6	481	64	17.81	–	1	12	–	2897†	1213	34	35.67	4-43	–	–

	First Test	Last Test	Tests	Inns	NO	Runs	HS	Avge	100	50	Ct	St	Balls	Runs	Wkts	Avge	BB	5wI	10wM
							BATTING AND FIELDING									*BOWLING*			
Abid Ali, S.	1967-68	1974-75	29	53	3	1018	81	20.36	–	6	32	–	4164	1980	47	42.12	6-55	1	–
Adhikari, H.R.	1947-48	1958-59	21	36	8	872	114*	31.14	1	4	8	–	170	82	3	27.33	3-68	–	–
Agarkar, A.B.	1998-99	2005-06	26	39	5	571	109*	16.79	–	–	6	–	4857	2745	58	47.32	6-41	1	–
Amarnath, L.	1933-34	1952-53	24	40	4	878	118	24.38	1	4	13	–	4241	1481	45	32.91	5-96	2	–
Amarnath, M.	1969-70	1987-88	69	113	10	4378	138	42.50	11	24	47	–	3676	1782	32	55.68	4-63	–	–
Amarnath, S.	1975-76	1978-79	10	18†	0	550	124	30.55	1	3	4	–	11	5	1	5.00	1-5	–	–
Amir Singh, L.	1932	1936	7	14	1	292	51	22.46	–	1	3	–	2182	858	28	30.64	7-86	2	–
Amir Elahi ‡	1947-48	1947-48	1	2	0	17	13	8.50	–	–	–	–	–	–	–	–	–	–	–
Amre, P.K.	1992-93	1993	11	13	3	425	103	42.50	1	3	9	–	–	–	–	–	–	–	–
Ankola, S.A.	1989-90	1989-90	1	1	0	6	6	6.00	–	–	–	–	180	128	2	64.00	1-35	–	–
Apte, A.L.	1959	1959	1	2	0	15	8	7.50	–	–	–	–	–	–	–	–	–	–	–
Apte, M.L.	1952-53	1952-53	7	13	2	542	163*	49.27	1	3	2	–	6	3	0	–	–	–	–
Arshad Ayub	1987-88	1989-90	13	19	4	257	57	17.13	–	1	2	–	3663	1438	41	35.07	5-50	3	–
Arun, B.	1986-87	1986-87	2	2	1	4	2*	4.00	–	–	2	–	252	116	4	29.00	3-76	–	–
Arun Lal	1982-83	1988-89	16	29	1	729	93	26.03	–	6	13	–	16	7	0	–	–	–	–
Azad, K.	1980-81	1983-84	7	12	0	135	24	11.25	–	–	3	–	750	373	3	124.33	2-84	–	–
Azharuddin, M.	1984-85	1999-00	99	147	9	6215	199	45.03	22	21	105	–	13	16	0	–	–	–	–
Badani, H.K.	2001	2001	4	7†	1	94	38	15.66	–	–	6	–	48†	17	0	–	–	–	–
Bahutule, S.V.	2000-01	2001	2	4†	0	39	21*	13.00	–	–	1	–	366	203	3	67.66	1-32	–	–
Baig, A.A.	1959	1966-67	10	18	0	428	112	23.77	1	2	6	–	18	15	0	–	–	–	–
Balaji, L.	2003-04	2004-05	8	9	0	51	31	5.66	–	–	1	–	1756	1004	27	37.18	5-76	1	–
Banerjee, S.A.	1948-49	1948-49	1	2	0	0	0	0.00	–	–	3	–	306	181	5	36.20	4-120	–	–
Banerjee, S.N.	1948-49	1948-49	1	2	0	13	8	6.50	–	–	–	–	273	127	5	25.40	4-54	–	–
Banerjee, S.T.	1991-92	1991-92	1	1	0	3	3	3.00	–	–	–	–	108	47	3	15.66	3-47	–	–
Bangar, S.B.	2001-02	2002-03	12	18	2	470	100*	29.37	1	3	4	–	762	343	7	49.00	2-23	–	–
Baqa Jilani, M.	1936	1936	1	2	0	16	12	16.00	–	–	–	–	90	55	0	–	–	–	–
Bedi, B.S.	1966-67	1979	67	101	28	656	50*	8.98	–	1	26	–	21364†	7637	266	28.71	7-98	14	1
Bhandari, P.	1954-55	1956-57	3	4	0	77	39	19.25	–	–	1	–	78	39	0	–	–	–	–
Bharadwaj, R.V.	1999-00	1999-00	3	3	1	28	22	9.33	–	–	3	–	247	107	1	107.00	1-26	–	–
Bhat, A.R.	1983-84	1983-84	2	3†	1	6	6	3.00	–	–	–	–	438†	151	4	37.75	2-65	–	–
Binny, R.M.H.	1979-80	1986-87	27	41	5	830	83*	23.05	–	5	11	–	2870	1534	47	32.63	6-56	2	–
Borde, C.G.	1958-59	1969-70	55	97	11	3061	177*	35.59	5	18	37	–	5695	2417	52	46.48	5-88	1	–
Chandrasekhar, B.S.	1963-64	1979	58	80	39	167	22	4.07	–	–	25	–	15963	7199	242	29.74	8-79	16	2
Chauhan, C.P.S.	1969-70	1980-81	40	68	2	2084	97	31.57	–	16	38	–	174	106	2	53.00	1-4	–	–
Chauhan, R.K.	1992-93	1997-98	21	17	3	98	23	7.00	–	–	12	–	4749	1857	47	39.51	4-48	–	–
Chawla, P.P.	2005-06	2007-08	2†	2†	0	5	4	2.50	–	–	–	–	205	137	3	45.66	2-66	–	–
Chopra, A.	2003-04	2004-05	10	19	0	437	60	23.00	–	2	15	–	–	–	–	–	–	–	–
Chopra, N.	1999-00	1999-00	1	2	0	7	4	3.50	–	–	–	–	144	78	0	–	–	–	–
Chowdhury, N.R.	1948-49	1951-52	2	2	1	3	3*	3.00	–	–	–	–	516	205	1	205.00	1-130	–	–
Colah, S.H.M.	1932	1933-34	2	4	0	69	31	17.25	–	–	2	–	–	–	–	–	–	–	–
Contractor, N.J.	1955-56	1961-62	31	52†	1	1611	108	31.58	1	11	18	–	186	80	1	80.00	1-9	–	–

	First Test	Last Test	Tests	BATTING AND FIELDING									BOWLING						
				Inns	NO	Runs	HS	Avge	100	50	Ct	St	Balls	Runs	Wkts	Avge	BB	5wI	10wM
Dahiya, V.	2000-01	2000-01	2	1	–	2	2*	–	–	–	6	–	60	19	1	19.00	1-9	–	–
Dani, H.T.	1952-53	1952-53	1	1	–	–	–	–	–	–	1	–	66	35	0	–	–	–	–
Das, S.S.	2000-01	2001-02	23	40	2	1326	110	34.89	2	9	34	–	–	–	–	–	–	–	–
Dasgupta, D.	2001-02	2001-02	8	13	1	344	100	28.66	1	2	13	–	–	–	–	–	–	–	–
Desai, R.B.	1958-59	1967-68	28	44	13	418	85	13.48	–	1	9	–	5597	2761	74	37.31	6-56	2	–
Dhoni, M.S.	2005-06	2008-09	37	59	7	1962	148	37.73	1	16	92	18	12	14	0	–	–	–	–
Dighe, S.S.	2000-01	2001	6	10	1	141	47	15.66	–	–	12	2	–	–	–	–	–	–	–
Dilawar Hussain	1933-34	1936	3	6	0	254	59	42.33	–	3	6	1	–	–	–	–	–	–	–
Divecha, R.V.	1951-52	1952-53	5	5	0	60	26	12.00	–	–	5	–	1044	361	11	32.81	3-102	–	–
Doshi, D.R.	1979-80	1983-84	33	38†	10	129	20	4.60	–	–	10	–	9322†	3502	114	30.71	6-102	6	–
Dravid, R.	1996	2008-09	133	231	27	10800	270	52.94	26	57	183	–	120	39	1	39.00	1-18	–	–
Durani, S.A.	1959-60	1972-73	29	50†	2	1202	104	25.04	1	7	14	–	6446†	2657	75	35.42	6-73	3	1
Engineer, F.M.	1961-62	1974-75	46	87	3	2611	121	31.08	2	16	66	16	–	–	–	–	–	–	–
Gadkari, C.V.	1952-53	1954-55	6	10	4	129	50*	21.50	–	1	6	–	102	45	0	–	–	–	–
Gaekwad, A.D.	1974-75	1984-85	40	70	4	1985	201	30.07	2	10	15	–	334	187	2	93.50	1-4	–	–
Gaekwad, D.K.	1952	1960-61	11	20	1	350	52	18.42	–	1	5	–	12	12	0	–	–	–	–
Gaekwad, H.G.	1952-53	1952-53	1	2†	0	22	14	11.00	–	–	–	–	222†	47	0	–	–	–	–
Gambhir, G.	2004-05	2008-09	25	45†	3	2271	206	54.07	6	10	23	–	–	–	–	–	–	–	–
Gandhi, D.J.	1999-00	1999-00	4	7	1	204	88	34.00	–	2	3	–	–	–	–	–	–	–	–
Gandotra, A.	1969-70	1969-70	2	4†	0	54	18	13.50	–	–	1	–	6†	5	0	–	–	–	–
Ganesh, D.	1996-97	1996-97	4	7	3	25	8	6.25	–	–	–	–	461	287	5	57.40	2-28	–	–
Ganguly, S.C.	1996	2008-09	113	188†	17	7212	239	42.17	16	35	71	–	3117	1681	32	52.53	3-28	–	–
Gavaskar, S.M.	1970-71	1986-87	125	214	16	10122	236*	51.12	34	45	108	–	380	206	1	206.00	1-34	–	–
Ghavri, K.D.	1974-75	1980-81	39	57†	14	913	86	21.23	–	2	16	–	7036†	3656	109	33.54	5-33	4	–
Ghorpade, J.M.	1952-53	1959	8	15	0	229	41	15.26	–	1	4	–	150	131	0	–	–	–	–
Ghulam Ahmed	1948-49	1958-59	22	31	9	192	50	8.72	–	1	11	–	5650	2052	68	30.17	7-49	4	–
Gopalan, M.J.	1933-34	1933-34	1	2	1	18	11*	18.00	–	–	3	–	114	39	1	39.00	1-39	–	–
Gopinath, C.D.	1951-52	1959-60	8	12†	1	242	50*	22.00	–	1	2	–	48	11	1	11.00	1-11	–	–
Guard, G.M.	1958-59	1959-60	2	2†	0	11	7	5.50	–	–	2	–	396†	182	3	60.66	2-69	–	–
Guha, S.	1967	1969-70	4	7	2	17	6	3.40	–	–	2	–	674	311	3	103.66	2-55	–	–
Gul Mahomed ‡	1946	1952-53	8	15†	0	166	34	11.06	–	1	3	–	77†	24	2	12.00	2-21	–	–
Gupte, B.P.	1960-61	1964-65	3	3	2	28	17*	28.00	–	–	–	–	678	349	3	116.33	1-54	–	–
Gupte, S.P.	1951-52	1961-62	36	42	13	183	21	6.31	–	–	14	–	11284	4403	149	29.55	9-102	12	1
Gursharan Singh	1989-90	1989-90	1	1	0	18	18	18.00	–	–	2	–	–	–	–	–	–	–	–
Hafeez, A.: see A.H.Kardar																			
Hanumant Singh	1963-64	1969-70	14	24	2	686	105	31.18	1	5	11	–	66	51	0	–	–	–	–
Harbhajan Singh	1997-98	2008-09	77	108	20	1496	66	17.00	–	7	38	–	21471	10040	330	30.42	8-84	23	5
Hardikar, M.S.	1958-59	1958-59	2	4	1	56	32*	18.66	–	–	3	–	108	55	1	55.00	1-9	–	–
Harvinder Singh	1997-98	2001	3	4	1	6	6	2.00	–	–	–	–	273	185	4	46.25	2-62	–	–

INDIVIDUAL CAREER RECORDS – INDIA continued

	First Test	Last Test	Tests	BATTING AND FIELDING									BOWLING						
				Inns	NO	Runs	HS	Avge	100	50	Ct	St	Balls	Runs	Wkts	Avge	BB	5wI	10wM
Hazare, V.S.	1946	1952-53	30	52	6	2192	164*	47.65	7	9	11	–	2840	1220	20	61.00	4-29	–	1
Hindlekar, D.D.	1936	1946	4	7	2	71	26	14.20	–	–	3	–	–						
Hirwani, N.D.	1987-88	1996-97	17	22	12	54	17	5.40	–	–	5	–	4298	1987	66	30.10	8-61	4	1
Ibrahim, K.C.	1948-49	1948-49	4	8	0	169	85	21.12	–	1	–	–	–						
Indrajitsinhji, K.S.	1964-65	1969-70	4	7	1	51	23	8.50	–	–	6	3	–						
Irani, J.K.	1947-48	1947-48	2	3	2	3	2*	3.00	–	–	2	1	–						
Jadeja, A.	1992-93	1999-00	15	24	2	576	96	26.18	–	4	5	–	606	255	4	63.75	4-60	–	–
Jahangir Khan, M.	1932	1936	4	7	0	39	13	5.57	–	–	4	–	–						
Jai, L.P.	1933-34	1933-34	1	2	0	19	19	9.50	–	–	–	–	–						
Jaisimha, M.L.	1959	1970-71	39	71	4	2056	129	30.68	3	12	17	–	2097	829	9	92.11	2-54	–	–
Jamshedji, R.J.D.	1933-34	1933-34	1	2	2	5	4*	–	–	–	2	–	210†	137	3	45.66	3-137	–	–
Jayantilal, K.	1970-71	1970-71	1	1	0	5	5	5.00	–	–	–	–	–						
Johnson, D.J.	1996-97	1996-97	2	3	1	8	5	4.00	–	–	–	–	240	143	3	47.66	2-52	–	–
Joshi, P.G.	1951-52	1960-61	12	20	1	207	52*	10.89	–	1	18	9	–						
Joshi, S.B.	1996	2000-01	15	19†	2	352	92	20.70	–	1	7	–	3451†	1470	41	35.85	5-142	1	–
Kaif, M.	1999-00	2006	13	22	3	624	148*	32.84	1	3	14	–	18	4	0	–	–	–	–
Kambli, V.G.	1992-93	1995-96	17	21†	1	1084	227	54.20	4	3	7	–	–						
Kanitkar, H.H.	1999-00	1999-00	2	4†	0	74	45	18.50	–	–	–	–	6	2	0	–	–	–	–
Kanitkar, H.S.	1974-75	1974-75	2	4	0	111	65	27.75	–	1	–	–	–						
Kapil Dev	1978-79	1993-94	131	184	15	5248	163	31.05	8	27	64	–	27740	12867	434	29.64	9-83	23	2
Kapoor, A.R.	1994-95	1996-97	4	6	1	97	42	19.40	–	–	1	–	642	255	6	42.50	2-19	–	–
Kardar, A.H. ‡	1946	1946	3	5†	0	80	43	16.00	–	–	1	–	–						
Karim, S.S.	2000-01	2000-01	1	1	0	15	15	15.00	–	–	1	–	–						
Karthik, K.D.	2004-05	2008-09	22	35	1	973	129	28.61	1	7	47	5	–						
Kartik, M.	1999-00	2004-05	8	10†	1	88	43	9.77	–	–	2	–	1932†	820	24	34.16	4-44	–	–
Kenny, R.B.	1958-59	1959-60	5	10	1	245	62	27.22	–	3	1	–	–						
Kirmani, S.M.H.	1975-76	1985-86	88	124	22	2759	102	27.04	2	12	160	38	19	13	1	13.00	1-9	–	–
Kishenchand, G.	1947-48	1952-53	5	10	0	89	44	8.90	–	–	1	–	–						
Kripal Singh, A.G.	1955-56	1964-65	14	20	5	422	100*	28.13	1	2	4	–	1518	584	10	58.40	3-43	–	–
Krishnamurthy, P.	1970-71	1970-71	5	6	0	33	20	5.50	–	–	7	1	–						
Kulkarni, N.M.	1997	2000-01	3	2†	0	5	4	5.00	–	–	1	–	738†	332	2	166.00	1-70	–	–
Kulkarni, R.R.	1986-87	1986-87	3	2	0	2	2	1.00	–	–	1	–	366	227	5	45.40	3-85	–	–
Kulkarni, U.N.	1967-68	1967-68	4	8†	5	13	7	4.33	–	–	1	–	448†	238	5	47.60	2-37	–	–
Kumar, V.V.	1960-61	1961-62	2	2	0	6	6	3.00	–	–	2	–	605	202	7	28.85	5-64	1	–
Kumble, A.	1990	2008-09	132	173	32	2506	110*	17.77	–	5	60	–	40850	18355	619	29.65	10-74	35	8
Kunderan, B.K.	1959-60	1967	18	34	4	981	192	32.70	2	3	23	7	24	13	0	–	–	–	–
Kuruvilla, A.	1996-97	1997-98	10	11	1	66	35*	6.60	–	–	2	–	1765	892	25	35.68	5-68	1	–
Lall Singh	1932	1932	1	2	0	44	29	22.00	–	–	1	–	–						
Lamba, R.	1986-87	1987-88	4	5	0	102	53	20.40	–	1	5	–	–						
Laxman, V.V.S.	1996-97	2008-09	105	174	25	6741	281	45.24	14	39	111	–	324	126	2	63.00	1-2	–	–
Madan Lal	1974	1986	39	62	16	1042	74	22.65	–	5	15	–	5997	2846	71	40.08	5-23	4	–

INDIVIDUAL CAREER RECORDS – INDIA *continued*

	First Test	Last Test	Tests	Inns	NO	Runs	HS	Avge	100	50	Ct	St	Balls	Runs	Wkts	Avge	BB	5wI	10wM
Maka, E.S.	1952-53	1952-53	2	1	1	2	2*	–	–	–	2	1	18	3	0	–	–	–	–
Malhotra, A.O.	1981-82	1984-85	7	10	1	226	72*	25.11	–	1	2	–							
Maninder Singh	1982-83	1992-93	35	38	12	99	15	3.80	–	–	9	–	8218†	3288	88	37.36	7-27	3	2
Manjrekar, S.V.	1987-88	1996-97	37	61	6	2043	218	37.14	4	9	25	–	17	15	0	–	–	–	–
Manjrekar, V.L.	1951-52	1964-65	55	92	10	3208	189*	39.12	7	15	19	1	204	44	1	44.00	1-16	–	–
Mankad, A.V.	1969-70	1977-78	22	42	3	991	97	25.41	–	6	12	–	41	43	0	–	–	–	–
Mankad, M.H.	1946	1958-59	44	72	5	2109	231	31.47	5	6	33	–	14686†	5236	162	32.32	8-52	8	2
Mantri, M.K.	1951-52	1954-55	4	8	1	67	39	9.57	–	–	8	1							
Meherhomji, K.R.	1936	1936	1	1	1	0	0*	–	–	–	1	–							
Mehra, V.L.	1955-56	1963-64	8	14	1	329	62	25.30	–	2	1	–	36	6	0	–	–	–	–
Merchant, V.M.	1933-34	1951-52	10	18	0	859	154	47.72	3	3	7	–	54	40	0	–	–	–	–
Mhambrey, P.L.	1996	1996	2	3	1	58	28	29.00	–	–	1	–	258	148	2	74.00	1-43	–	–
Milkha Singh, A.G.	1959-60	1961-62	4	6†	0	92	35	15.33	–	–	2	–	6	2	0	–	–	–	–
Mishra, A.	2008-09	2008-09	5	5	1	42	23	10.50	–	–	2	–	1230	593	20	29.65	5-71	1	–
Modi, R.S.	1946	1952-53	10	17	1	736	112	46.00	1	6	3	–	30	14	0	–	–	–	–
Mohanty, D.S.	1997	1997-98	2	1	–	0	0*	–	–	–	–	–	430	239	4	59.75	4-78	–	–
Mongia, N.R.	1993-94	2000-01	44	68	8	1442	152	24.03	1	6	99	8	12	12	0	–	–	–	–
More, K.S.	1986	1993	49	64	14	1285	73	25.70	–	7	110	20							
Muddiah, V.M.	1959-60	1960-61	2	3	1	11	11	5.50	–	–	–	–	318	134	3	44.66	2-40	–	–
Mushtaq Ali, S.	1933-34	1951-52	11	20	1	612	112	32.21	2	3	7	–	378†	202	3	67.33	1-45	–	–
Nadkarni, R.G.	1955-56	1967-68	41	67†	12	1414	122*	25.70	1	7	22	–	9165†	2559	88	29.07	6-43	4	1
Naik, S.S.	1974	1974-75	3	6	0	141	77	23.50	–	1	–	–							
Naoomal Jeoomal	1932	1933-34	3	5	1	108	43	27.00	–	1	–	–	108	68	2	34.00	1-4	–	–
Narasimha Rao, M.V.	1978-79	1979-80	4	6	1	46	20*	9.20	–	–	8	–	463	227	3	75.66	2-46	–	–
Navle, J.G.	1932	1933-34	2	4	0	42	13	10.50	–	–	1	–							
Nayak, S.V.	1982	1982	2	3†	1	19	11	9.50	–	–	1	–	231	132	1	132.00	1-16	–	–
Nayudu, C.K.	1932	1936	7	14	0	350	81	25.00	–	2	4	–	858	386	9	42.88	3-40	–	–
Nayudu, C.S.	1933-34	1951-52	11	19	3	147	36	9.18	–	–	3	–	522	359	2	179.50	1-19	–	–
Nazir Ali, S.	1932	1933-34	2	4	0	30	13	7.50	–	–	–	–	138	83	4	20.75	4-83	–	–
Nehra, A.	1998-99	2003-04	17	25	11	77	19	5.50	–	–	5	–	3447†	1866	44	42.40	4-72	–	–
Nissar, M.	1932	1936	6	11	3	55	14	6.87	–	–	2	–	1211	707	25	28.28	5-90	3	–
Nyalchand, S.	1952-53	1952-53	1	2†	1	7	6*	7.00	–	–	–	–	384†	97	3	32.33	3-97	–	–
Pai, A.M.	1969-70	1969-70	1	2†	0	10	9	5.00	–	–	–	–	114	31	2	15.50	2-29	–	–
Palia, P.E.	1932	1936	2	4†	1	29	16	9.66	–	–	–	–	42†	13	0	–	–	–	–
Pandit, C.S.	1986	1991-92	5	8	1	171	39	24.42	–	–	14	2							
Parkar, G.A.	1982	1982	1	2	0	7	6	3.50	–	–	1	–							
Parkar, R.D.	1972-73	1972-73	2	4	0	80	35	20.00	–	–	–	–							
Parsana, D.D.	1978-79	1978-79	2	2†	0	1	1	0.50	–	–	1	–	120†	50	1	50.00	1-32	–	–
Patankar, C.T.	1955-56	1955-56	1	2	1	14	13	14.00	–	–	3	1							
Pataudi, Nawab of, sen. ‡	1946	1946	3	5	0	55	22	11.00	–	–	–	–							
Pataudi, Nawab of, jun.	1961-62	1974-75	46	83	3	2793	203*	34.91	6	16	27	–	132	88	1	88.00	1-10	–	–
Patel, B.P.	1974	1977-78	21	38	5	972	115*	29.45	1	5	17	–							
Patel, J.M.	1954-55	1959-60	7	10	1	25	12	2.77	–	–	2	–	1725	637	29	21.96	9-69	2	1

INDIVIDUAL CAREER RECORDS – INDIA *continued*

	First Test	Last Test	Tests	Inns	NO	Runs	HS	Avge	100	50	Ct	St	Balls	Runs	Wkts	Avge	BB	5wI	10wM
Patel, M.M.	2005-06	2008-09	12	13	5	56	15*	7.00	–	–	6	–	2394	1230	34	36.17	4-25	–	–
Patel, P.A.	2002	2008	20	30†	7	683	69	29.69	–	4	41	8	–	–	–	–	–	–	–
Patel, R.	1988-89	1988-89	1	2†	0	0	0	0.00	–	–	1	–	84†	51	0	–	–	–	–
Pathan, I.K.	2003-04	2007-08	29	40†	5	1105	102	31.57	1	6	8	–	5884†	3226	100	32.26	7-59	7	2
Patiala, Yuvraj of	1933-34	1933-34	1	2	0	84	60	42.00	–	1	2	–	–	–	–	–	–	–	–
Patil, S.M.	1979-80	1984-85	29	47	4	1588	174	36.93	4	7	12	–	645	240	9	26.66	2-28	–	–
Patil, S.R.	1955-56	1955-56	1	1	1	14	14*	–	–	–	–	–	138	51	2	25.50	1-15	–	–
Phadkar, D.G.	1947-48	1958-59	31	45	7	1229	123	32.34	2	8	21	–	5994	2285	62	36.85	7-159	3	–
Powar, R.R.	2007	2007	2	2	0	13	7	6.50	–	–	–	–	252	118	6	19.66	3-33	–	–
Prabhakar, M.	1984-85	1995-96	39	58	9	1600	120	32.65	1	9	20	–	7475	3581	96	37.30	6-132	3	1
Prasad, B.K.V.	1996	2001	33	47	20	203	30*	7.51	–	–	6	–	7041	3360	96	35.00	6-33	7	–
Prasad, M.S.K.	1999-00	2001	6	10	1	106	19	11.77	–	–	15	1	–	–	–	–	–	–	–
Prasanna, E.A.S.	1961-62	1978-79	49	84	20	735	37	11.48	–	–	18	–	14353	5742	189	30.38	8-76	10	2
Punjabi, P.H.	1954-55	1954-55	5	10	0	164	33	16.40	–	–	5	–	–	–	–	–	–	–	–
Rai Singh, K.	1947-48	1947-48	1	2	0	26	24	13.00	–	–	–	–	–	–	–	–	–	–	–
Rajindernath, V.	1952-53	1952-53	1	–	–	–	–	–	–	–	–	4	–	–	–	–	–	–	–
Rajinder Pal	1963-64	1963-64	1	2	1	6	3*	6.00	–	–	–	–	78	22	0	–	–	–	–
Rajput, L.S.	1985	1985	2	4	0	105	61	26.25	–	1	1	–	–	–	–	–	–	–	–
Raju, S.L.V.	1989-90	2000-01	28	34	10	240	31	10.00	–	–	6	–	7602†	2857	93	30.72	6-12	5	1
Raman, W.V.	1987-88	1996-97	11	19†	1	448	96	24.88	–	4	6	–	348†	129	2	64.50	1-7	–	–
Ramaswami, C.	1936	1936	2	4†	1	170	60	56.66	–	1	–	–	–	–	–	–	–	–	–
Ramchand, G.S.	1952	1959-60	33	53	5	1180	109	24.58	2	5	20	–	4976	1899	41	46.31	6-49	1	–
Ramesh, S.	1998-99	2001	19	37†	1	1367	143	37.97	2	8	18	–	54	43	0	–	–	–	–
Ramji, L.	1933-34	1933-34	1	2	1	1	1	0.50	–	–	1	–	138	64	0	–	–	–	–
Rangachari, C.R.	1947-48	1948-49	4	6	3	8	8*	2.66	–	–	1	–	846	493	9	54.77	5-107	1	–
Rangnekar, K.M.	1947-48	1947-48	3	6†	0	33	18	5.50	–	–	1	–	–	–	–	–	–	–	–
Ranjane, V.B.	1958-59	1964-65	7	9	3	40	16	6.66	–	–	1	–	1265	649	19	34.15	4-72	–	–
Rathour, V.	1996	1996-97	6	10	0	131	44	13.10	–	–	12	–	–	–	–	–	–	–	–
Ratra, A.	2001-02	2002	6	10	1	163	115*	18.11	1	–	11	2	6	1	0	–	–	–	–
Razdan, V.	1989-90	1989-90	2	2	1	6	6*	6.00	–	–	–	–	240	141	5	28.20	5-79	1	–
Reddy, B.	1979	1979	4	5	1	38	21	9.50	–	–	9	2	–	–	–	–	–	–	–
Rege, M.R.	1948-49	1948-49	1	2	0	15	15	7.50	–	–	1	–	–	–	–	–	–	–	–
Roy, A.K.	1969-70	1969-70	4	7†	0	91	48	13.00	–	–	–	–	–	–	–	–	–	–	–
Roy, Pankaj	1951-52	1960-61	43	79	4	2442	173	32.56	5	9	16	–	104	66	1	66.00	1-6	–	–
Roy, Pranab	1981-82	1981-82	2	3	1	71	60*	35.50	–	1	1	–	–	–	–	–	–	–	–
Sandhu, B.S.	1982-83	1983-84	8	11	4	214	71	30.57	–	2	1	–	1020	557	10	55.70	3-87	–	–
Sanghvi, R.L.	2000-01	2000-01	1	2†	1	2	2	1.00	–	–	1	–	74†	78	2	39.00	2-67	–	–
Sarandeep Singh	2000-01	2001-02	3	2	1	43	39*	43.00	–	–	1	–	678	340	10	34.00	4-136	–	–
Sardesai, D.N.	1961-62	1972-73	30	55	4	2001	212	39.23	5	9	4	–	59	45	0	–	–	–	–
Sarwate, C.T.	1946	1951-52	9	17	1	208	37	13.00	–	–	3	–	658	374	3	124.66	1-16	–	–
Saxena, R.C.	1967	1967	1	2	0	25	16	12.50	–	–	–	–	12	11	0	–	–	–	–
Sehwag, V. ‡	2001-02	2008-09	68	117	7	5674	319	50.21	15	17	54	–	2455	1265	29	43.62	5-104	1	–
Sekhar, T.A.	1982-83	1982-83	2	1	1	0	0*	–	–	–	1	–	204	129	0	–	–	–	–

INDIVIDUAL CAREER RECORDS – INDIA *continued*

	First Test	Last Test	Tests	*Inns*	*NO*	*Runs*	*HS*	*Avge*	*100*	*50*	*Ct*	*St*	*Balls*	*Runs*	*Wkts*	*Avge*	*BB*	*5wI*	*10wM*
				BATTING AND FIELDING									BOWLING						
Sen, P.K.	1947-48	1952-53	14	18	4	165	25	11.78	–	–	20	11	–	–	–	–	–	–	–
Sengupta, A.K.	1958-59	1958-59	1	2	0	9	8	4.50	–	–	1	–	–	–	–	–	–	–	–
Sharma, A.K.	1987-88	1987-88	1	2	0	53	30	26.50	–	–	–	–	24†	9	0	–	–	–	–
Sharma, C.	1984-85	1988-89	23	27	9	396	54	22.00	–	1	7	–	3470	2163	61	35.45	6-58	4	1
Sharma, G.	1984-85	1990-91	5	4	1	11	10*	3.66	–	–	2	–	1307	418	10	41.80	4-88	–	–
Sharma, I.	2007	2008-09	18	24	12	142	23	11.83	–	1	6	–	3234	1724	52	33.15	5-118	1	–
Sharma, P.H.	1974-75	1976-77	5	10	0	187	54	18.70	–	–	1	–	24	8	0	–	–	–	–
Sharma, S.K.	1988-89	1990	2	3	1	56	38	28.00	–	–	–	–	414	247	6	41.16	3-37	–	–
Shastri, R.J.	1980-81	1992-93	80	121	14	3830	206	35.79	11	12	36	–	15751†	6185	151	40.96	5-75	2	–
Shinde, S.G.	1946	1952	7	11	5	85	14	14.16	–	–	1	–	1515	717	12	59.75	6-91	1	–
Shodhan, R.H.	1952-53	1952-53	3	4†	1	181	110	60.33	1	–	1	–	60†	26	0	–	–	–	–
Shukla, R.C.	1982-83	1982-83	1	–	–	–	–	–	–	–	–	–	294	152	2	76.00	2-82	–	–
Siddiqui, I.R.	2001-02	2001-02	1	2	1	29	24	29.00	–	–	1	–	114	48	1	48.00	1-32	–	–
Sidhu, N.S.	1983-84	1998-99	51	78	2	3202	201	42.13	9	15	9	–	6	9	0	–	–	–	–
Singh, Robin, jun.	1998-99	1998-99	1	1	0	0	0	0.00	–	–	–	–	240	176	3	58.66	2-74	–	–
Singh, R.P.	2005-06	2007-08	13	17	3	91	30	6.50	–	–	6	–	2330†	1564	40	39.10	5-59	1	–
Singh, R.R. ("Robin")	1998-99	1998-99	1	2†	–	27	15	13.50	–	–	5	–	60	32	0	–	–	–	–
Singh, V.R.	2006	2007	1	6	2	47	29	11.75	–	–	–	–	669	427	8	53.37	3-48	–	–
Sivaramakrishnan, L.	1982-83	1985-86	9	9	1	130	25	16.25	–	–	9	–	2367	1145	26	44.03	6-64	3	1
Sohoni, S.W.	1946	1951-52	4	7	2	83	29*	16.60	–	–	2	–	532	202	2	101.00	1-16	–	–
Solkar, E.D.	1969-70	1976-77	27	48†	6	1068	102	25.42	1	6	53	–	2265†	1070	18	59.44	3-28	–	–
Sood, M.M.	1959-60	1959-60	1	2	0	3	3	1.50	–	–	–	–	–	–	–	–	–	–	–
Sreesanth, S.	2005-06	2007-08	14	21	7	217	35	15.50	–	–	7	–	2873	1573	50	31.46	5-40	1	–
Srikkanth, K.	1981-82	1991-92	43	72	3	2062	123	29.88	2	12	40	–	216	114	0	–	–	–	–
Srinath, J.	1991-92	2002-03	67	92	21	1009	76	14.21	–	4	22	–	15104	7196	236	30.49	8-86	10	1
Srinivasan, T.E.	1980-81	1980-81	1	2	0	48	29	24.00	–	–	–	–	–	–	–	–	–	–	–
Subramanya, V.	1964-65	1967-68	9	15	1	263	75	18.78	–	2	9	–	444	201	3	67.00	2-32	–	–
Sunderam, G.R.	1955-56	1955-56	2	1	1	3	3*	–	–	–	–	–	396	166	3	55.33	2-46	–	–
Surendranath	1958-59	1960-61	11	20	7	136	27	10.46	–	–	4	–	2602	1053	26	40.50	5-75	2	–
Surti, R.F.	1960-61	1969-70	26	48†	4	1263	99	28.70	–	9	26	–	3870†	1962	42	46.71	5-74	2	–
Swamy, V.N.	1955-56	1955-56	1	–	–	–	–	–	–	–	–	–	108	45	0	–	–	–	–
Tamhane, N.S.	1954-55	1960-61	21	27	5	225	54*	10.22	–	1	35	16	–	–	–	–	–	–	–
Tarapore, K.K.	1948-49	1948-49	1	1	0	2	2	2.00	–	–	–	–	114†	72	0	–	–	–	–
Tendulkar, S.R.	1989-90	2008-09	159	261	27	12773	248*	54.58	42	53	102	–	3934	2272	44	51.63	3-10	–	–
Umrigar, P.R.	1948-49	1961-62	59	94	8	3631	223	42.22	12	14	33	–	4725	1473	35	42.08	6-74	2	–
Vengsarkar, D.B.	1975-76	1991-92	116	185	22	6868	166	42.13	17	35	78	–	47	36	0	–	–	–	–
Venkataraghavan, S.	1964-65	1983-84	57	76	12	748	64	11.68	–	2	44	–	14877	5634	156	36.11	8-72	3	1
Venkataramana, M.	1988-89	1988-89	1	2	0	0	0*	–	–	–	1	–	70	58	1	58.00	1-10	–	–
Vijay, M.	2008-09	2008-09	1	2	0	74	41	37.00	–	–	–	–	–	–	–	–	–	–	–
Viswanath, G.R.	1969-70	1982-83	91	155	10	6080	222	41.93	14	35	63	–	70	46	1	46.00	1-11	–	–
Viswanath, S.	1985	1985	3	5	0	31	20	6.20	–	–	11	–	–	–	–	–	–	–	–
Vizianagram, Maharajkumar of	1936	1936	3	6	2	33	19*	8.25	–	–	1	–	–	–	–	–	–	–	–

INDIVIDUAL CAREER RECORDS – INDIA continued

	First Test	Last Test	Tests	BATTING AND FIELDING									BOWLING						
				Inns	NO	Runs	HS	Avge	100	50	Ct	St	Balls	Runs	Wkts	Avge	BB	5wI	10wM
Wadekar, A.L.	1966-67	1974	37	71†	3	2113	143	31.07	1	14	46	–	61†	55	0	–	–	–	–
Wasim Jaffer	1999-00	2007-08	31	58	1	1944	212	34.10	5	11	27	–	66	18	2	9.00	2-18	–	–
Wassan, A.S.	1989-90	1990	4	5	1	94	53	23.50	–	1	1	–	712	504	10	50.40	4-108	–	–
Wazir Ali, S.	1932	1936	7	14	0	237	42	16.92	–	–	1	–	30	25	0	–	–	–	–
Yadav, N.S.	1979-80	1986-87	35	40	12	403	43	14.39	–	–	10	–	8360	3580	102	35.09	5-76	3	–
Yadav, V.	1992-93	1992-93	1	1	0	30	30	30.00	–	–	–	2	–	–	–	–	–	–	–
Yajurvindra Singh	1976-77	1979-80	4	7	1	109	43*	18.16	–	–	11	–	120	50	0	–	–	–	–
Yashpal Sharma	1979	1983-84	37	59	11	1606	140	33.45	2	9	16	–	30	17	1	17.00	1-6	–	–
Yograj Singh	1980-81	1980-81	1	2	0	10	6	5.00	–	–	–	–	90	63	1	63.00	1-63	–	–
Yohannan, T.	2001-02	2002-03	3	4	4	13	8*	–	–	–	1	–	486	256	5	51.20	2-56	–	–
Yuvraj Singh	2003-04	2008-09	28	45†	6	1387	169	35.56	3	6	27	–	561†	316	7	45.14	2-9	–	–
Zaheer Khan	2000-01	2008-09	65	86	22	884	75	13.81	–	3	18	–	12962†	7107	210	33.84	5-29	7	–

INDIVIDUAL CAREER RECORDS – PAKISTAN

	First Test	Last Test	Tests	BATTING AND FIELDING									BOWLING						
				Inns	NO	Runs	HS	Avge	100	50	Ct	St	Balls	Runs	Wkts	Avge	BB	5wI	10wM
Aamer Malik	1987-88	1994-95	14	19	3	565	117	35.31	2	3	15	1	156	89	1	89.00	1-0	–	–
Aamir Nazir	1992-93	1995-96	6	11	6	31	11	6.20	–	–	2	–	1057	597	20	29.85	5-46	1	–
Aamir Sohail	1992	1999-00	47	83†	3	2823	205	35.28	5	13	36	–	2383†	1049	25	41.96	4-54	–	–
Abdul Kadir	1964-65	1964-65	4	8	0	272	95	34.00	–	2	15	1	8	6	0	–	–	–	–
Abdul Qadir	1977-78	1990-91	67	77	11	1029	61	15.59	–	3	15	–	17126	7742	236	32.80	9-56	15	5
Abdul Razzaq	1999-00	2006-07	46	77	9	1946	134	28.61	3	7	15	–	7008	3694	100	36.94	5-35	1	–
Abdur Rauf	2009	2009	2	4	0	44	31	11.00	–	–	1	–	252	159	5	31.80	2-59	–	–
Abdur Rehman	2007-08	2007-08	2	3†	1	34	25*	17.00	–	–	1	–	750†	352	11	32.00	4-105	–	–
Afaq Hussain	1961-62	1964-65	2	4	4	66	35*	–	–	–	2	–	240	106	1	106.00	1-40	–	–
Aftab Baloch	1969-70	1974-75	2	3	1	97	60*	48.50	–	1	3	–	44	17	0	–	–	–	–
Aftab Gul	1968-69	1971	6	8	0	182	33	22.75	–	–	3	–	6	4	0	–	–	–	–
Agha Saadat Ali	1955-56	1955-56	1	1	1	8	8*	–	–	–	3	–	–	–	–	–	–	–	–
Agha Zahid	1974-75	1974-75	1	2	0	15	14	7.50	–	–	–	–	–	–	–	–	–	–	–
Akram Raza	1989-90	1994-95	9	12	2	153	32	15.30	–	–	8	–	1526	732	13	56.30	3-46	–	–
Alimuddin	1954	1962	25	45	2	1091	109	25.37	2	7	8	–	84	75	1	75.00	1-17	–	–
Ali Hussain Rizvi	1997-98	1997-98	1	–	–	–	–	–	–	–	–	–	111	72	2	36.00	2-72	–	–
Ali Naqvi	1997-98	1997-98	5	9	1	242	115	30.25	1	1	1	–	12	11	0	–	–	–	–
Amir Elahi ‡	1952-53	1952-53	5	7	1	65	47	10.83	–	–	1	–	400	248	7	35.42	4-134	–	–
Anil Dalpat	1983-84	1984-85	9	12	1	167	52	15.18	–	1	22	3	–	–	–	–	–	–	–
Anwar Hussain	1952-53	1952-53	4	6	0	42	17	7.00	–	–	–	–	36	29	1	29.00	1-25	–	–
Anwar Khan	1978-79	1978-79	1	2	1	15	12	15.00	–	–	–	–	32	12	0	–	–	–	–
Aqib Javed	1988-89	1998-99	22	27	7	101	28*	5.05	–	–	2	–	3918	1874	54	34.70	5-84	1	–
Arif Butt	1964-65	1964-65	3	5	0	59	20	11.80	–	–	–	–	666	288	14	20.57	6-89	1	–
Arshad Khan	1997-98	2004-05	9	8	2	31	9*	5.16	–	–	–	–	2538	960	32	30.00	5-38	1	–

INDIVIDUAL CAREER RECORDS – PAKISTAN continued

	First Test	Last Test	Tests	BATTING AND FIELDING									BOWLING						
				Inns	NO	Runs	HS	Avge	100	50	Ct	St	Balls	Runs	Wkts	Avge	BB	5wI	10wM
Ashfaq Ahmed	1993-94	1993-94	1	2	1	1	1*	1.00	—	—	—	—	138	53	2	26.50	2-31	—	—
Ashraf Ali	1981-82	1987-88	8	8	3	229	65	45.80	—	2	17	5	—	—	—	—	—	—	—
Asif Iqbal	1964-65	1979-80	58	99	7	3575	175	38.85	11	12	36	—	3864	1502	53	28.33	5-48	2	—
Asif Masood	1968-69	1976-77	16	19	10	93	30*	10.33	—	—	5	—	3038	1568	38	41.26	5-111	1	—
Asif Mujtaba	1986-87	1996-97	25	41†	3	928	65*	24.42	—	8	19	—	666†	303	4	75.75	1-0	—	—
Asim Kamal	2003-04	2005-06	12	20†	1	717	99	37.73	—	8	10	—	—	—	—	—	—	—	—
Ata-ur-Rehman	1992	1996	13	15	6	76	19	8.44	—	—	2	—	1973	1071	31	34.54	4-50	—	—
Atif Rauf	1993-94	1993-94	1	2	0	25	16	12.50	—	—	—	—	—	—	—	—	—	—	—
Atiq-uz-Zaman	1999-00	1999-00	1	2	0	26	25	13.00	—	—	5	—	—	—	—	—	—	—	—
Azam Khan	1996-97	1996-97	1	1	0	14	14	14.00	—	—	—	—	—	—	—	—	—	—	—
Azeem Hafeez	1983-84	1984-85	18	21†	5	134	24	8.37	—	—	1	—	4351†	2204	63	34.98	6-46	4	—
Azhar Khan	1979-80	1979-80	1	1	0	14	14	14.00	—	—	1	—	18	2	1	2.00	1-1	—	—
Azhar Mahmood	1997-98	2001	21	34	4	900	136	30.00	3	1	14	—	3015	1402	39	35.94	4-50	—	—
Azmat Rana	1979-80	1979-80	1	1†	0	49	49	49.00	—	—	—	—	—	—	—	—	—	—	—
Basit Ali	1992-93	1995-96	19	33	1	858	103	26.81	1	5	6	—	6	6	0	—	—	—	—
Bazid Khan	2004-05	2004-05	1	2	0	32	23	16.00	—	—	2	—	—	—	—	—	—	—	—
Danish Kaneria	2000-01	2009	54	71	31	266	29	6.65	—	—	16	—	15947	8022	232	34.57	7-77	13	2
D'Souza, A.	1958-59	1962	6	10	8	76	23*	38.00	—	—	3	—	1587	745	17	43.82	5-112	1	—
Ehteshamuddin	1979-80	1982	5	3	1	2	2	1.00	—	—	2	—	940	375	16	23.43	5-47	1	—
Faisal Iqbal	2000-01	2008-09	23	38	2	954	139	26.50	1	7	17	—	6	7	0	—	—	—	—
Farhan Adil	2003-04	2003-04	1	2	0	33	25	16.50	—	—	—	—	—	—	—	—	—	—	—
Farooq Hamid	1964-65	1964-65	1	2	0	3	3	1.50	—	—	—	—	184	107	1	107.00	1-82	—	—
Farrukh Zaman	1976-77	1976-77	1	—	—	—	—	—	—	—	—	—	80†	15	0	—	—	—	—
Fawad Alam	2009	2009	2	4†	0	216	168	54.00	1	1	—	—	—	—	—	—	—	—	—
Fazal Mahmood	1952-53	1962	34	50	6	620	60	14.09	—	1	11	—	9834	3434	139	24.70	7-42	13	4
Fazl-e-Akbar	1997-98	2003-04	5	8	4	52	25	13.00	—	—	2	—	882	511	11	46.45	3-85	—	—
Ghazali, M.E.Z.	1954	1954	2	4	0	32	18	8.00	—	—	—	—	48	18	0	—	—	—	—
Ghulam Abbas	1967	1967	1	2†	0	12	12	6.00	—	—	—	—	—	—	—	—	—	—	—
Gul Mahomed ‡	1956-57	1956-57	1	2†	1	39	27*	39.00	—	—	—	—	—	—	—	—	—	—	—
Hanif Mohammad	1952-53	1969-70	55	97	8	3915	337	43.98	12	15	40	—	206	95	1	95.00	1-1	—	—
Haroon Rashid	1976-77	1982-83	23	36	1	1217	153	34.77	3	4	16	—	8	3	0	—	—	—	—
Hasan Raza	1996-97	2005-06	7	16	1	235	68	26.11	—	2	5	—	6	3	0	—	—	—	—
Haseeb Ahsan	1957-58	1961-62	12	16	7	61	14	6.77	—	—	1	—	2835	1330	27	49.25	6-202	2	—
Humayun Farhat	2000-01	2000-01	1	2	0	54	28	27.00	—	—	—	—	—	—	—	—	—	—	—
Iftikhar Anjum	2005-06	2005-06	1	1	1	9	9*	—	—	—	—	—	84	62	0	—	—	—	—
Ijaz Ahmed, sen.	1986-87	2000-01	60	92	4	3315	211	37.67	12	12	45	—	180†	77	2	38.50	1-9	—	—
Ijaz Ahmed, jun.	1995-96	1995-96	2	3	0	29	16	9.66	—	—	3	—	24	6	0	—	—	—	—
Ijaz Butt	1958-59	1962	8	16	2	279	58	19.92	—	1	5	—	—	—	—	—	—	—	—

INDIVIDUAL CAREER RECORDS – PAKISTAN continued

	First Test	Last Test	Tests	Inns	NO	Runs	HS	Avge	100	50	Ct	St	Balls	Runs	Wkts	Avge	BB	5wI	10wM
								BATTING AND FIELDING								*BOWLING*			
Ijaz Faqih	1980-81	1987-88	5	8	1	183	105	26.14	1	2	–	–	534	299	4	74.75	1-38	–	–
Imran Farhat	2000-01	2006-07	27	51†	1	1655	128	33.10	2	11	30	–	295	218	3	72.66	2-69	–	–
Imran Khan	1971	1991-92	88	126	25	3807	136	37.69	6	18	28	–	19458	8258	362	22.81	8-58	23	6
Imran Nazir	1998-99	2002-03	8	13	0	427	131	32.84	1	1	4	–	6	0	0	–	–	–	–
Imtiaz Ahmed	1952-53	1962	41	72	1	2079	209	29.28	3	11	77	16	6	0	0	–	–	–	–
Intikhab Alam	1959-60	1976-77	47	77	10	1493	138	22.28	1	8	20	–	10474	4494	125	35.95	7-52	5	2
Inzamam-ul-Haq ‡	1992	2007-08	119	198	22	8829	329	50.16	25	46	81	–	9†	8	0	–	–	–	–
Iqbal Qasim	1976-77	1988-89	50	57†	15	549	56	13.07	–	1	42	–	13019†	4807	171	28.11	7-49	8	2
Irfan Fazil	1999-00	1999-00	1	2	1	4	3	4.00	–	–	2	–	48	65	2	32.50	1-30	–	–
Israr Ali	1952-53	1959-60	4	8†	1	33	10	4.71	–	–	1	–	318†	165	6	27.50	2-29	–	–
Jalal-ud-Din	1982-83	1985-86	6	3	2	3	2	3.00	–	–	–	–	1197	537	11	48.81	3-77	–	–
Javed Akhtar	1962	1962	1	2	1	4	2*	4.00	–	–	–	–	96	52	0	–	–	–	–
Javed Burki	1960-61	1969-70	25	48	4	1341	140	30.47	3	4	7	–	42	23	0	–	–	–	–
Javed Miandad	1976-77	1993-94	124	189	21	8832	280*	52.57	23	43	93	1	1470	682	17	40.11	3-74	–	–
Kabir Khan	1994	1994-95	4	5	2	24	10	8.00	–	–	1	–	655†	370	9	41.11	3-26	–	–
Kamran Akmal	2002-03	2009	43	72	5	2226	158*	33.22	6	9	142	20							
Kardar, A.H. ‡	1952-53	1957-58	23	37†	3	847	93	24.91	–	5	15	–	2712†	954	21	45.42	3-35	–	–
Khalid Hassan	1954	1954	1	2	1	17	10	17.00	–	–	–	–	126	116	2	58.00	2-116	–	–
Khalid Ibadulla	1964-65	1967	4	8	0	253	166	31.62	1	–	3	–	336	99	1	99.00	1-42	–	–
Khalid Wazir	1954	1954	2	3	1	14	9*	7.00	–	–	–	–							
Khan Mohammad	1952-53	1957-58	13	17	7	100	26*	10.00	–	–	4	–	3157	1292	54	23.92	6-21	4	–
Khurram Manzoor	2008-09	2009	5	8	1	239	93	34.14	–	2	3	–							
Liaqat Ali	1974-75	1978	5	7	3	28	12	7.00	–	–	1	–	808†	359	6	59.83	3-80	–	–
Mahmood Hussain	1952-53	1962	27	39	6	336	35	10.18	–	–	5	–	5910	2628	68	38.64	6-67	2	–
Majid Khan	1964-65	1982-83	63	106	5	3931	167	38.92	8	19	70	–	3584	1456	27	53.92	4-45	–	–
Mansoor Akhtar	1980-81	1989-90	19	29	3	655	111	25.19	1	3	9	–							
Manzoor Elahi	1984-85	1994-95	6	10	2	123	52	15.37	–	1	7	–	444	194	7	27.71	2-38	–	–
Maqsood Ahmed	1952-53	1955-56	16	27	1	507	99	19.50	–	2	13	–	462	191	3	63.66	2-12	–	–
Masood Anwar	1990-91	1990-91	1	2†	0	39	37	19.50	–	–	–	–	161†	102	3	34.00	2-59	–	–
Mathias, W.	1955-56	1962	21	36	3	783	77	23.72	–	3	22	–	24	20	0	–	–	–	–
Miran Bakhsh	1954-55	1954-55	2	3	2	1	1*	1.00	–	–	–	–	348	115	2	57.50	2-82	–	–
Misbah-ul-Haq	2000-01	2009	15	25	3	871	161*	37.86	2	3	18	–							
Mohammad Aamer	2009	2009	3	6†	3	37	22*	12.33	–	–	4	–	480†	261	6	43.50	3-38	1	–
Mohammad Akram	1995-96	2000-01	9	15	6	24	10*	2.66	–	–	2	–	1477	859	17	50.52	5-138	1	–
Mohammad Asif	2004-05	2007-08	11	16†	6	60	12*	6.00	–	–	–	–	2334	1180	51	23.13	6-44	4	1
Mohammad Aslam	1954	1954	1	2	0	34	18	17.00	–	–	–	–							
Mohammad Farooq	1960-61	1964-65	7	9	4	85	47	17.00	–	–	1	–	1422	682	21	32.47	4-70	–	–
Mohammad Hafeez	2003-04	2007-08	11	21	0	677	104	33.85	2	3	4	–	750	319	4	79.75	1-11	–	–
Mohammad Hussain	1996-97	1998-99	2	3†	0	18	17	6.00	–	–	1	–	180†	87	3	29.00	2-66	–	–
Mohammad Ilyas	1964-65	1968-69	10	19	0	441	126	23.21	1	2	6	–	84	63	0	–	–	–	–
Mohammad Khalil	2004-05	2004-05	2	4†	0	9	5	3.00	–	–	1	–	290†	200	0	–	–	–	–
Mohammad Munaf	1959-60	1961-62	4	7	2	63	19	12.60	–	–	–	–	769	341	11	31.00	4-42	–	–

INDIVIDUAL CAREER RECORDS – PAKISTAN *continued*

				BATTING AND FIELDING									BOWLING						
Player	First Test	Last Test	Tests	Inns	NO	Runs	HS	Avge	100	50	Ct	St	Balls	Runs	Wkts	Avge	BB	5wI	10wM
Mohammad Nazir	1969-70	1983-84	14	18	10	144	29*	18.00	–	–	4	–	3262	1124	34	33.05	7-99	3	–
Mohammad Ramzan	1997-98	1997-98	1	2	0	36	29	18.00	–	–	1	–							
Mohammad Sami	2000-01	2007-08	33	51	13	458	49	12.05	–	–	7	–	6984	4161	81	51.37	5-36	2	–
Mohammad Talha	2008-09	2008-09	1	1	–	–	–	–	–	–	–	–	102	88	1	88.00	1-88	–	–
Mohammad Wasim	1996-97	2000	18	28	2	783	192	30.11	2	2	22	–	6	3	0	–	–	–	–
Mohammad Yousuf	1997-98	2009	82	140	12	7023	223	54.86	24	29	60	–							
Mohammad Zahid	1996-97	2002-03	5	6	1	7	6*	1.40	–	–	–	–	792	502	15	33.46	7-66	1	1
Mohsin Kamal	1983-84	1994-95	9	11	7	37	13*	9.25	–	–	4	–	1348	822	24	34.25	4-116	–	–
Mohsin Khan	1977-78	1986-87	48	79	6	2709	200	37.10	7	9	34	–	86	30	0	–	–	–	–
Moin Khan	1990-91	2004-05	69	104	8	2741	137	28.55	4	15	128	20							
Mudassar Nazar	1976-77	1988-89	76	116	8	4114	231	38.09	10	17	48	–	5967	2532	66	38.36	6-32	1	–
Mufassir-ul-Haq	1964-65	1964-65	1	1	1	8	8*	–	–	–	1	–	222†	84	3	28.00	2-50	–	–
Munir Malik	1959-60	1962	3	4	1	7	4	2.33	–	–	1	–	684	358	3	39.77	5-128	1	–
Mushtaq Ahmed	1989-90	2003-04	52	72	16	656	59	11.71	–	2	23	–	12532	6100	185	32.97	7-56	10	3
Mushtaq Mohammad	1958-59	1978-79	57	100	7	3643	201	39.17	10	19	42	–	5260	2309	79	29.22	5-28	3	–
Nadeem Abbasi	1989-90	1989-90	3	2	0	46	36	23.00	–	–	6	–							
Nadeem Ghauri	1989-90	1989-90	1	1	0	0	0	0.00	–	–	–	–	48†	20	0	–	–	–	–
Nadeem Khan	1992-93	1998-99	2	3	1	34	25	17.00	–	–	–	–	432†	230	2	115.00	2-147	–	–
Nasim-ul-Ghani	1957-58	1972-73	29	50†	5	747	101	16.60	1	2	11	–	4406†	1959	52	37.67	6-67	2	–
Naushad Ali	1964-65	1964-65	6	11	0	156	39	14.18	–	–	9	–							
Naved Anjum	1989-90	1990-91	2	3	0	44	22	14.66	–	–	–	–	342	162	4	40.50	2-57	–	–
Naved Ashraf	1998-99	1999-00	2	3	0	64	32	21.33	–	–	–	–							
Naved Latif	2001-02	2001-02	1	2	0	20	20	10.00	–	–	–	–							
Naved-ul-Hasan	2004-05	2006-07	9	15	3	239	42*	19.91	–	1	3	–	1565	1044	18	58.00	3-30	–	–
Nazar Mohammad	1952-53	1952-53	5	8	1	277	124*	39.57	1	1	7	–	12	4	0	–	–	–	–
Niaz Ahmed	1967	1968-69	2	3	3	17	16*	–	–	–	1	–	294	94	3	31.33	2-72	–	–
Pervez Sajjad	1964-65	1972-73	19	20	11	123	24	13.66	–	–	9	–	4145†	1410	59	23.89	7-74	3	–
Qaiser Abbas	2000-01	2000-01	1	1†	0	2	2	2.00	–	–	–	–	96†	35	0	–	–	–	–
Qasim Omar	1983-84	1986-87	26	43	2	1502	210	36.63	3	5	15	–	6	0	0	–	–	–	–
Ramiz Raja	1983-84	1996-97	57	94	5	2833	122	31.83	2	22	34	–							
Rashid Khan	1981-82	1984-85	4	6	3	155	59	51.66	–	1	2	–	738	360	8	45.00	3-129	–	–
Rashid Latif	1992	2003-04	37	57	9	1381	150	28.77	1	7	119	11	12	10	0	–	–	–	–
Rehman, S.F.	1957-58	1957-58	1	2	0	10	8	5.00	–	–	–	–	204	99	1	99.00	1-43	–	–
Riaz Afridi	2004-05	2004-05	1	1	0	9	9	9.00	–	–	–	–	186	87	2	43.50	2-42	–	–
Rizwan-uz-Zaman	1981-82	1988-89	11	19	1	345	60	19.16	–	3	4	–	132	46	4	11.50	3-26	–	–
Sadiq Mohammad	1969-70	1980-81	41	74†	2	2579	166	35.81	5	10	28	–	200	98	0	–	–	–	–
Saeed Ahmed	1957-58	1972-73	41	78	4	2991	172	40.41	5	16	13	–	1980	802	22	36.45	4-64	–	–
Saeed Ajmal	2009	2009	3	6	3	13	8	4.33	–	–	–	–	880	421	14	30.07	4-87	–	–
Saeed Anwar	1990-91	2001-02	55	91†	2	4052	188*	45.52	11	25	18	–	48†	23	0	–	–	–	–
Salahuddin	1964-65	1969-70	5	8	2	117	34*	19.50	–	–	3	–	546	187	7	26.71	2-36	–	–

INDIVIDUAL CAREER RECORDS – PAKISTAN continued

	First Test	Last Test	Tests	BATTING AND FIELDING									BOWLING						
				Inns	NO	Runs	HS	Avge	100	50	Ct	St	Balls	Runs	Wkts	Avge	BB	5wI	10wM
Saleem Jaffer	1986-87	1991-92	14	14	6	42	10*	5.25	–	–	2	–	2531†	1139	36	31.63	5-40	1	–
Salim Altaf	1967	1978-79	21	31	12	276	53*	14.52	–	1	3	–	4001	1710	46	37.17	4-11	–	–
Salim Elahi	1995-96	2002-03	13	24	1	436	72	18.95	–	1	10	1	–	–	–	–	–	–	–
Salim Malik	1981-82	1998-99	103	154	22	5768	237	43.69	15	29	65	–	734	414	5	82.80	1-3	–	–
Salim Yousuf	1981-82	1990-91	32	44	5	1055	91*	27.05	–	5	91	13	–	–	–	–	–	–	–
Salman Butt	2003-04	2009	22	40†	0	1146	122	28.65	2	6	9	–	137	106	1	106.00	1-36	–	–
Saqlain Mushtaq	1995-96	2003-04	49	78	14	927	101*	14.48	1	2	15	–	14070	6206	208	29.83	8-164	13	3
Sarfraz Nawaz	1968-69	1983-84	55	72	13	1045	90	17.71	–	4	26	–	13951	5798	177	32.75	9-86	4	1
Shabbir Ahmed	2003-04	2005-06	10	15	5	88	24*	8.80	–	–	3	–	2576	1175	51	23.03	5-48	2	–
Shadab Kabir	1996	2001-02	5	7†	0	148	55	21.14	–	1	11	–	6	9	0	–	–	–	–
Shafiq Ahmed	1974	1980-81	6	10	1	99	27*	11.00	–	–	–	–	8	1	0	–	–	–	–
Shafqat Rana	1964-65	1969-70	5	7	0	221	95	31.57	–	2	5	–	36	9	1	9.00	1-2	–	–
Shahid Afridi	1998-99	2006	26	46	1	1683	156	37.40	5	8	10	–	3092	1640	47	34.89	5-52	1	–
Shahid Israr	1976-77	1976-77	1	1	1	7	7*	–	–	–	2	–	–	–	–	–	–	–	–
Shahid Mahboob	1989-90	1989-90	1	2†	0	25	16	12.50	–	–	–	–	294	131	2	65.50	2-131	–	–
Shahid Mahmood	1962	1962	1	2	0	16	16	8.00	–	–	–	–	36†	23	0	–	–	–	–
Shahid Nazir	1996-97	2006-07	15	19	3	194	40	12.12	–	–	5	–	2234	1272	36	35.33	5-53	1	–
Shahid Saeed	1989-90	1989-90	1	1	0	12	12	12.00	–	–	–	–	90	43	0	–	–	–	–
Shakeel Ahmed, sen.	1992-93	1994-95	3	5	0	74	33	14.80	–	–	4	–	–	–	–	–	–	–	–
Shakeel Ahmed, jun.	1998-99	1998-99	1	1†	0	1	1	1.00	–	–	1	–	325†	139	4	34.75	4-91	–	–
Sharpe, D.A.	1959-60	1959-60	3	6	0	134	56	22.33	–	1	2	–	–	–	–	–	–	–	–
Shoaib Akhtar	1997-98	2007-08	46	67	13	544	47	10.07	–	–	12	–	8143	4574	178	25.69	6-11	12	2
Shoaib Malik	2001-02	2009	26	42	6	1394	148*	38.72	2	7	13	–	2010	1153	17	67.82	4-42	–	–
Shoaib Mohammad	1983-84	1995-96	45	68	7	2705	203*	44.34	7	13	22	–	396	170	5	34.00	2-8	–	–
Shujauddin	1954	1961-62	19	32	6	395	47	15.19	–	–	8	–	2313†	801	20	40.05	3-18	–	–
Sikander Bakht	1976-77	1982-83	26	35	12	146	22*	6.34	–	–	7	–	4870	2412	67	36.00	8-69	3	1
Sohail Khan	2008-09	2008-09	1	2	0	3	3	1.50	–	–	–	–	162	164	0	–	–	–	–
Sohail Tanvir	2007-08	2007-08	2	3†	0	17	13	5.66	–	–	2	–	504†	316	5	63.20	3-83	–	–
Tahir Naqqash	1981-82	1984-85	15	19	5	300	57	21.42	–	1	3	–	2800	1398	34	41.11	5-40	2	–
Talat Ali	1972-73	1978-79	10	18	2	370	61	23.12	–	2	4	–	20	7	0	–	–	–	–
Taslim Arif	1979-80	1980-81	6	10	2	501	210*	62.62	1	2	6	3	30	28	1	28.00	1-28	–	–
Taufeeq Umar	2001-02	2006	25	46†	2	1729	135	39.29	4	9	33	–	78	44	0	–	–	–	–
Tauseef Ahmed	1979-80	1993-94	34	38	20	318	35*	17.66	–	–	9	–	7778	2950	93	31.72	6-45	3	–
Umar Gul	2003-04	2009	21	26	2	203	46	8.45	–	–	5	–	4452	2690	83	32.40	6-135	4	–
Wajahatullah Wasti	1998-99	1999-00	6	10	1	329	133	36.55	2	–	7	–	18	8	0	–	–	–	–
Waqar Hassan	1952-53	1959-60	21	35	1	1071	189	31.50	1	6	10	–	6	10	0	–	–	–	–
Waqar Younis	1989-90	2002-03	87	120	21	1010	45	10.20	–	–	18	–	16224	8788	373	23.56	7-76	22	5
Wasim Akram	1984-85	2001-02	104	147†	19	2898	257*	22.64	3	7	44	–	22627†	9779	414	23.62	7-119	25	5
Wasim Bari	1967	1983-84	81	112	26	1366	85	15.88	–	6	201	27	8	2	0	–	–	–	–
Wasim Raja	1972-73	1984-85	57	92†	14	2821	125	36.16	4	18	20	–	4082	1826	51	35.80	4-50	–	–
Wazir Mohammad	1952-53	1959-60	20	33	4	801	189	27.62	2	3	5	–	24	15	0	–	–	–	–

INDIVIDUAL CAREER RECORDS – PAKISTAN continued

	First Test	Last Test	Tests	Inns	NO	Runs	HS	Avge	100	50	Ct	St	Balls	Runs	Wkts	Avge	BB	5wI	10wM
Yasir Ali	2003-04	2003-04	1	2	2	1	1*	–	–	–	–	–	120	55	2	27.50	1-12	–	–
Yasir Arafat	2007-08	2008-09	3	3	1	94	50*	47.00	–	1	–	–	627	438	9	48.66	5-161	1	–
Yasir Hameed	2003-04	2007-08	23	45	3	1450	170	34.52	2	8	16	–	72	72	0	–	–	–	–
Younis Ahmed	1969-70	1986-87	4	7†	1	177	62	29.50	–	1	–	–	6†	6	0	–	–	–	–
Younis Khan	1999-00	2009	63	112	7	5260	313	50.09	16	21	67	–	540	341	7	48.71	2-23	–	–
Yousuf Youhana: see Mohammad Yousuf																			
Zaheer Abbas	1969-70	1985-86	78	124	11	5062	274	44.79	12	20	34	–	370	132	3	44.00	2-21	–	–
Zahid Fazal	1990-91	1995-96	9	16	0	288	78	18.00	–	1	5	–							
Zahoor Elahi	1996-97	1996-97	2	3	0	30	22	10.00	–	–	1	–							
Zakir Khan	1985-86	1989-90	2	2	2	9	9*	–	–	–	1	–	444	259	5	51.80	3-80	–	–
Zulfiqar Ahmed	1952-53	1956-57	9	10	4	200	63*	33.33	–	1	5	–	1285	366	20	18.30	6-42	2	1
Zulqarnain	1985-86	1985-86	3	4	0	24	13	6.00	–	–	8	2							

INDIVIDUAL CAREER RECORDS – SRI LANKA

	First Test	Last Test	Tests	Inns	NO	Runs	HS	Avge	100	50	Ct	St	Balls	Runs	Wkts	Avge	BB	5wI	10wM
Ahangama, F.S.	1985	1985	3	3†	1	11	11	5.50	–	–	1	–	801	348	18	19.33	5-52	1	–
Amalean, K.N.	1985-86	1987-88	2	3	2	9	7*	9.00	–	–	1	–	244	156	7	22.28	4-97	–	–
Amerasinghe, A.M.J.G.	1983-84	1983-84	2	4	1	54	34	18.00	–	–	3	–	300†	150	3	50.00	2-73	–	–
Amerasinghe, M.K.D.I.	2007-08	2007-08	1	2	2	0	0*	–	–	–	–	–	150	105	1	105.00	1-62	–	–
Anurasiri, S.D.	1985-86	1997-98	18	22	5	91	24	5.35	–	–	4	–	3973†	1548	41	37.75	4-71	–	–
Arnold, R.P.	1996-97	2004	44	69†	4	1821	123	28.01	3	10	51	–	1334	598	11	54.36	3-76	–	–
Atapattu, M.S.	1990-91	2007-08	90	156	15	5502	249	39.02	16	17	58	–	48	24	1	24.00	1-9	–	–
Bandara, C.M.	1998	2005-06	8	11	3	124	43	15.50	–	–	4	–	1152	633	16	39.56	3-84	–	–
Bandaratilleke, M.R.C.N.	1998	2001-02	7	9	1	93	25	11.62	–	–	–	–	1722†	698	23	30.34	5-36	1	–
Chandana, U.D.U.	1998-99	2004-05	16	24	1	616	92	26.78	–	2	7	–	2685	1535	37	41.48	6-179	3	1
Dassanayake, P.B.	1993	1994-95	11	17	2	196	36	13.06	–	–	19	5							
de Alwis, R.G.	1982-83	1987-88	11	19	0	152	28	8.00	–	–	21	2							
de Mel, A.L.F.	1981-82	1986-87	17	28	5	326	34	14.17	–	–	9	–	3518	2180	59	36.94	6-109	3	–
de Saram, S.I.	1999-00	1999-00	4	5	0	117	39	23.40	–	–	–	1							
de Silva, A.M.	1992-93	1993	3	3	0	10	9	3.33	–	–	4	1							
de Silva, D.S.	1981-82	1984	12	22	3	406	61	21.36	–	2	5	–	3031	1347	37	36.40	5-59	1	–
de Silva, E.A.R.	1985	1990-91	10	16†	4	185	50	15.41	–	1	4	–	2328	1032	8	129.00	2-67	–	–
de Silva, G.R.A.	1981-82	1982-83	4	7†	2	41	14	8.20	–	–	–	–	962†	385	7	55.00	2-38	–	–
de Silva, K.S.C.	1996-97	1998-99	8	12†	5	65	27	9.28	–	–	5	–	1585†	889	16	55.56	5-85	1	–
de Silva, P.A.	1984	2002	93	159	11	6361	267	42.97	20	22	43	–	2595	1208	29	41.65	3-30	–	–
de Silva, S.K.L.	1997-98	1997-98	3	4	2	36	20*	18.00	–	–	1	–							
de Silva, W.R.S.	2002	2007	3	2	1	10	5*	10.00	–	–	–	–	432†	209	11	19.00	4-35	–	–
Dharmasena, H.D.P.K.	1993	2003-04	31	51	7	868	62*	19.72	–	3	14	–	6939	2920	69	42.31	6-72	3	1

INDIVIDUAL CAREER RECORDS – SRI LANKA *continued*

	First Test	Last Test	Tests	BATTING AND FIELDING									BOWLING						
				Inns	NO	Runs	HS	Avge	100	50	Ct	St	Balls	Runs	Wkts	Avge	BB	5wI	10wM
Dias, R.L.	1981-82	1986-87	20	36	1	1285	109	36.71	3	8	6	-	24	17	0	-	-	-	-
Dilshan, T.M.	1999-00	2009	57	90	10	3443	168	43.03	9	13	66	-	878	433	13	33.30	4-10	-	-
Dunusinghe, C.I.	1994-95	1995-96	5	10	0	160	91	16.00	-	1	13	2	-					-	-
Fernando, C.R.D.	2000	2008-09	33	40	13	198	36*	7.33	-	-	10	-	5126	3072	88	34.90	5-42	3	-
Fernando, E.R.N.S.	1982-83	1983-84	5	10	0	112	46	11.20	-	1	-	-	126	107	1	107.00	1-29	-	-
Fernando, K.A.D.M.	2003-04	2003-04	2	3	1	56	51*	28.00	-	1	1	-	234	108	4	27.00	3-63	-	-
Fernando, K.H.R.K.	2002-03	2002-03	2	4	0	38	24	9.50	-	-	1	-	1270	792	18	44.00	4-27	-	-
Fernando, T.C.B.	2001-02	2002	9	8	3	132	45	26.40	-	-	4	-	-					-	-
Gallage, I.S.	1999-00	1999-00	1	1	0	3	3	3.00	-	-	-	-	150	77	0	-		-	-
Goonatillake, H.M.	1981-82	1982-83	5	10	2	177	56	22.12	-	1	10	3	-					-	-
Gunasekera, Y.	1982-83	1982-83	2	4†	0	48	23	12.00	-	-	6	-	-					-	-
Gunawardene, D.A.	1998-99	2005-06	6	11†	0	181	43	16.45	-	-	2	-	-					-	-
Guneratne, R.P.W.	1982-83	1982-83	1	2	2	0	0*	-	-	-	-	-	102	84	0	-		-	-
Gurusinha, A.P.	1985-86	1996	41	70†	7	2452	143	38.92	7	8	33	-	1408	681	20	34.05	2-7	-	-
Hathurusinghe, U.C.	1990-91	1998-99	26	44	1	1274	83	29.62	-	8	7	-	1962	789	17	46.41	4-66	-	-
Herath, H.M.R.K.B.	1999	2009	18	23†	4	179	33*	9.42	-	-	4	-	4222†	2031	59	34.42	5-99	3	1
Hettiarachchi, D.	2000-01	2000-01	1	2	1	0	0*	0.00	-	-	-	-	162†	41	2	20.50	2-36	-	-
Jayasekera, R.S.A.	1981-82	1981-82	1	2	0	2	2	1.00	-	-	-	-	-					-	-
Jayasuriya, S.T.	1990-91	2007-08	110	188†	14	6973	340	40.07	14	31	78	-	8188†	3366	98	34.34	5-34	2	-
Jayawardene, D.P.M.D.	1997	2009	107	177	13	8747	374	53.33	26	35	151	-	547	292	6	48.66	2-32	-	-
Jayawardene, H.A.P.W.	2000	2009	27	35	5	747	120*	24.90	1	2	59	19	-					-	-
Jeganathan, S.	1982-83	1982-83	2	4	0	19	8	4.75	-	-	2	-	30†	12	0	-		-	-
John, V.B.	1982-83	1984	6	10	5	53	27*	10.60	-	-	2	-	1281	614	28	21.92	5-60	2	-
Jurangpathy, B.R.	1985	1986-87	2	4	0	1	1	0.25	-	-	2	-	150	93	1	93.00	1-69	-	-
Kalavitigoda, S.	2004-05	2004-05	1	2	0	8	7	4.00	-	-	2	-	-					-	-
Kalpage, R.S.	1993	1998-99	11	18†	2	294	63	18.37	-	2	10	-	1576	774	12	64.50	2-27	-	-
Kaluperuma, L.W.S.	1981-82	1981-82	2	4	1	12	11*	4.00	-	-	2	-	162	93	0	-		-	-
Kaluperuma, S.M.S.	1983-84	1987-88	4	8	0	88	23	11.00	-	-	6	-	240	124	2	62.00	2-17	-	-
Kaluwitharana, R.S.	1992	2004-05	49	78	4	1933	132*	26.12	3	9	93	26	-					-	-
Kapugedera, C.K.	2006	2009	8	15	3	418	96	34.83	-	4	6	-	12	9	0	-		-	-
Kulasekara, K.M.D.N.	2004-05	2009	10	14	1	214	64	16.46	-	-	2	-	1492	757	24	31.54	4-21	-	-
Kuruppu, D.S.B.P.	1986-87	1991	4	7	1	320	201*	53.33	1	2	1	-	-					-	-
Kuruppuarachchi, A.K.	1985-86	1986-87	2	2	2	0	0*	-	-	-	1	-	272†	149	8	18.62	5-44	1	-
Labrooy, G.F.	1986-87	1990-91	9	14	3	158	70*	14.36	-	1	3	-	2158	1194	27	44.22	5-133	1	-
Lakshitha, M.K.G.C.P.	2002	2002-03	2	3	0	42	40	14.00	-	-	1	-	288	158	5	31.60	2-33	-	-
Liyanage, D.K.	1992	2001	9	9†	1	69	23	7.66	-	-	1	-	1355	666	17	39.17	4-56	-	-
Lokuarachchi, K.S.	2003	2003-04	4	5	1	94	28*	23.50	-	-	1	-	594	295	5	59.00	2-47	-	-
Madugalle, R.S.	1981-82	1988	21	39	4	1029	103	29.40	1	7	9	-	84	38	0	-	-	-	-
Madurasinghe, M.A.W.R.	1988	1992	3	6†	1	24	11	4.80	-	-	-	-	396	172	3	57.33	3-60	-	-

	First Test	Last Test	Tests	BATTING AND FIELDING									Balls	Runs	Wkts	BOWLING		5wI	10wM
				Inns	NO	Runs	HS	Avge	100	50	Ct	St				Avge	BB		
Mahanama, R.S.	1985-86	1997-98	52	89	1	2576	225	29.27	4	11	56	—	36	30	0	—	—	—	—
Maharoof, M.F.	2004	2007-08	20	31	4	538	72	19.92	—	3	6	—	2628	1458	24	60.75	4-52	1	—
Malinga, S.L.	2004	2007-08	28	34	13	192	42*	9.14	—	—	7	—	4777	3076	91	33.80	5-68	2	—
Mathews, A.D.	2009	2009	4	6	1	230	64*	46.00	—	1	1	—	234	138	4	34.50	1-13	—	—
Mendis, B.A.W.	2008	2009	9	9	3	31	17	5.16	—	—	1	—	2358	1136	42	27.04	6-117	2	1
Mendis, L.R.D.	1981-82	1988	24	43	1	1329	124	31.64	4	8	9	—	—	—	—	—	—	—	—
Mirando, M.T.T.	2003	2009	9	13†	2	90	15*	8.18	—	—	3	—	1542†	961	28	34.32	5-83	1	—
Mubarak, J.	2002	2007-08	10	17†	1	254	48	15.87	—	—	13	—	84	50	0	—	—	—	—
Muralitharan, M. ‡	1992	2009	128	157	54	1201	67	11.66	—	1	68	—	42434	17241	778	22.16	9-51	66	22
Nawaz, M.N.	2002	2002	1	2†	1	99	78*	99.00	—	1	—	—	—	—	—	—	—	—	—
Nissanka, R.A.P.	2003	2003	4	5	2	18	12*	6.00	—	—	—	—	587	366	10	36.60	5-64	1	—
Paranavitana, N.T.	2008-09	2009	7	13†	0	330	73	25.38	—	2	4	—	84	69	1	69.00	1-26	—	—
Perera, A.S.A.	1998	2001	3	4	1	77	43*	25.66	—	—	1	—	408	180	1	180.00	1-104	—	—
Perera, P.D.R.L.	1998-99	2002-03	8	9†	6	33	11*	11.00	—	—	2	—	1130†	661	17	38.88	3-40	—	—
Prasad, K.T.G.D.	2008	2009	3	3	0	45	36	15.00	—	—	—	—	524	405	11	36.81	3-82	—	—
Pushpakumara, K.R.	1994	2001-02	23	31	12	166	44	8.73	—	—	10	—	3792	2242	58	38.65	7-116	4	—
Ramanayake, C.P.H.	1987-88	1993	18	24	9	143	34*	9.53	—	—	6	—	3654	1880	44	42.72	5-82	1	—
Ramyakumara, W.M.G.	2005	2005	2	3†	0	38	14	12.66	—	—	—	—	114†	66	2	33.00	2-49	—	—
Ranasinghe, A.N.	1981-82	1982-83	2	4	0	88	77	22.00	—	1	—	—	114†	69	1	69.00	1-23	—	—
Ranatunga, A.	1981-82	2000	93	155†	12	5105	135*	35.69	4	38	47	—	2373	1040	16	65.00	2-17	—	—
Ranatunga, D.	1989-90	1989-90	2	3	0	87	45	29.00	—	—	—	—	—	—	—	—	—	—	—
Ranatunga, S.	1994	1996-97	9	17†	1	531	118	33.18	2	2	2	—	—	—	—	—	—	—	—
Ratnayake, R.J.	1982-83	1991-92	23	36	6	433	56	14.43	—	2	9	—	4961	2563	73	35.10	6-66	5	—
Ratnayeke, J.R.	1981-82	1989-90	22	38†	6	807	93	25.21	—	5	1	—	3833	1972	56	35.21	8-83	4	—
Samarasekera, M.A.R.	1988	1991-92	4	7	0	118	57	16.85	—	1	3	—	192	104	3	34.66	2-38	—	—
Samaraweera, D.P.	1993-94	1994-95	7	14	0	211	42	15.07	—	—	5	—	—	—	—	—	—	—	—
Samaraweera, T.T.	2001	2009	54	85	12	3787	231	51.87	11	19	35	—	1291	679	14	48.50	4-49	—	—
Sangakkara, K.C.	2000	2009	85	142†	10	7308	287	55.36	20	32	156	20	66	38	0	—	—	—	—
Senanayake, C.P.	1990-91	1990-91	3	5†	0	97	64	19.40	—	1	2	—	—	—	—	—	—	—	—
Silva, K.J.	1995-96	1997-98	7	4	1	6	6*	2.00	—	—	7	—	1533†	647	20	32.35	4-16	—	—
Silva, L.P.C.	2006-07	2007-08	11	17	1	537	152*	33.56	1	2	7	—	102	65	1	65.00	1-57	—	—
Silva, S.A.R.	1982-83	1988	9	16†	2	353	111	25.21	2	—	33	1	—	—	—	—	—	—	—
Tharanga, W.U.	2005-06	2007-08	15	26†	1	713	165	28.52	1	3	11	—	—	—	—	—	—	—	—
Thushara, T.: see M.T.T.Mirando																			
Tillekeratne, H.P.	1989-90	2003-04	83	131†	25	4545	204*	42.87	11	20	122	2	76	25	0	—	—	—	—
Upashantha, K.E.A.	1998-99	2002	2	3	0	10	6	3.33	—	—	—	—	306	200	4	50.00	2-41	—	—
Vaas, W.P.U.J.C.	1994	2009	111	162†	35	3089	100*	24.32	1	13	31	—	23438†	10501	355	29.58	7-71	12	2
Vandort, M.G.	2001-02	2008-09	20	33†	2	1144	140	36.90	4	4	6	—	—	—	—	—	—	—	—

INDIVIDUAL CAREER RECORDS – SRI LANKA continued

				BATTING AND FIELDING									BOWLING						
	First Test	Last Test	Tests	Inns	NO	Runs	HS	Avge	100	50	Ct	St	Balls	Runs	Wkts	Avge	BB	5wI	10wM
Warnapura, B.	1981-82	1982-83	4	8	0	96	38	12.00	-	-	2	-	90	46	0	-	-	-	-
Warnapura, B.S.M.	2007	2009	14	24†	1	821	120	35.69	2	7	14	-	54	40	0	-	-	-	-
Warnaweera, K.P.J.	1985-86	1994	10	12†	3	39	20	4.33	-	-	-	-	2333	1021	32	31.90	4-25	-	-
Weerasinghe, C.D.U.S.	1985	1985	1	1	0	3	3	3.00	-	-	1	-	114	36	0	-	-	-	-
Welagedara, U.W.M.B.C.A.	2007-08	2007-08	1	-	-	-	-	-	-	-	-	-	132†	76	4	19.00	2-17	-	-
Wettimuny, M.D.	1982-83	1982-83	2	4	0	28	17	7.00	-	-	1	-	-	-	-	-	-	-	-
Wettimuny, S.	1981-82	1986-87	23	43	3	1221	190	29.07	2	6	10	-	24	37	0	-	-	-	-
Wickremasinghe, A.G.D.	1989-90	1992-93	3	3	1	17	13*	8.50	-	-	9	1	-	-	-	-	-	-	-
Wickremasinghe, G.P.	1991-92	2000-01	40	64	5	555	51	9.40	-	1	18	-	7260	3559	85	41.87	6-60	3	-
Wijegunawardene, K.I.W.	1991	1991-92	2	4	1	14	6*	4.66	-	-	-	-	364	147	7	21.00	4-51	-	-
Wijekoon, G.: see W.M.G.Ramyakumara																			
Wijesuriya, R.G.C.E.	1981-82	1985-86	4	7	2	22	8	4.40	-	-	1	-	586†	294	1	294.00	1-68	-	-
Wijetunge, P.K.	1993	1993	1	2	0	10	10	5.00	-	-	-	-	312†	118	2	59.00	1-58	-	-
Zoysa, D.N.T.	1996-97	2004	30	40†	6	288	28*	8.47	-	-	4	-	4422†	2157	64	33.70	5-20	1	-

INDIVIDUAL CAREER RECORDS – ZIMBABWE

				BATTING AND FIELDING									BOWLING						
	First Test	Last Test	Tests	Inns	NO	Runs	HS	Avge	100	50	Ct	St	Balls	Runs	Wkts	Avge	BB	5wI	10wM
Arnott, K.J.	1992-93	1992-93	4	8	1	302	101*	43.14	1	1	4	-	-	-	-	-	-	-	-
Blignaut, A.M.	2000-01	2005-06	19	36†	3	886	92	26.84	-	6	13	-	3173	1964	53	37.05	5-73	3	-
Brain, D.H.	1992-93	1994-95	9	13	2	115	28	10.45	-	-	-	-	1810†	915	30	30.50	5-42	1	-
Brandes, E.A.	1992-93	1999-00	10	15	3	121	39	10.08	-	-	4	-	1996	951	26	36.57	3-45	-	-
Brent, G.B.	1999-00	2001-02	4	6	0	35	25	5.83	-	-	1	-	818	314	7	44.85	3-21	-	-
Briant, G.A.	1992-93	1992-93	1	2	0	17	16	8.50	-	-	-	-	-	-	-	-	-	-	-
Bruk-Jackson, G.K.	1993-94	1993-94	2	4	0	39	31	9.75	-	-	1	-	-	-	-	-	-	-	-
Burmester, M.G.	1992-93	1992-93	3	4	2	54	30*	27.00	-	-	1	-	436	227	3	75.66	3-78	-	-
Butchart, I.P.	1994-95	1994-95	1	2	0	23	15	11.50	-	-	-	-	18	11	0	-	-	-	-
Campbell, A.D.R.	1992-93	2002-03	60	109†	4	2858	103	27.21	2	18	60	-	66	28	0	-	-	-	-
Carlisle, S.V.	1994-95	2005-06	37	66	6	1615	118	26.91	2	8	34	-	-	-	-	-	-	-	-
Chigumbura, E.	2004	2004-05	6	12	0	187	71	15.58	-	1	2	-	829	498	9	55.33	5-54	1	-
Coventry, C.K.	2005-06	2005-06	2	4	0	88	37	22.00	-	-	3	-	-	-	-	-	-	-	-
Cremer, A.G.	2005-06	2005-06	6	12	1	29	12	2.63	-	-	3	-	870	595	13	45.76	3-86	-	-
Crocker, G.J.	1992-93	1992-93	3	4†	1	69	33	23.00	-	-	3	-	456†	217	3	72.33	2-65	-	-
Dabengwa, K.M.	2005-06	2005-06	3	6†	0	90	35	15.00	-	-	1	-	438†	249	5	49.80	3-127	-	-
Dekker, M.H.	1993-94	1996-97	14	22†	1	333	68*	15.85	-	2	12	-	60†	15	0	-	-	-	-
Duffin, T.	2005-06	2005-06	2	4†	0	80	56	20.00	-	1	1	-	-	-	-	-	-	-	-
Ebrahim, D.D.	2000-01	2005-06	29	55	1	1226	94	22.70	-	10	16	-	-	-	-	-	-	-	-
Ervine, S.M.	2003	2003-04	5	8†	0	261	86	32.62	-	3	7	-	570	388	9	43.11	4-146	-	-

INDIVIDUAL CAREER RECORDS – ZIMBABWE continued

	First Test	Last Test	Tests	BATTING AND FIELDING									BOWLING						
				Inns	NO	Runs	HS	Avge	100	50	Ct	St	Balls	Runs	Wkts	Avge	BB	5wI	10wM
Evans, C.N.	1996	2003-04	3	6	0	52	22	8.66	–	–	1	–	54	35	0	–	–	–	–
Ewing, G.M.	2003-04	2005-06	3	6	0	108	71	18.00	–	1	1	–	426	260	2	130.00	1-27	–	–
Ferreira, N.R.	2005-06	2005-06	1	2†	0	21	16	10.50	–	–	–	–							
Flower, A.	1992-93	2002-03	63	112†	19	4794	232*	51.54	12	27	151	9	3	4	0	–	–	–	–
Flower, G.W.	1992-93	2003-04	67	123	6	3457	201*	29.54	6	15	43	–	3378†	1537	25	61.48	4-41	–	–
Friend, T.J.	2001	2003-04	13	19	4	447	81	29.80	–	3	2	–	2000	1090	25	43.60	5-31	1	–
Goodwin, M.W.	1997-98	2000	19	37	4	1414	166*	42.84	3	8	10	–	119	69	0	–	–	–	–
Gripper, T.R.	1999-00	2003-04	20	38	1	809	112	21.86	1	5	14	–	793	509	6	84.83	2-91	–	–
Hondo, D.T.	2001-02	2004-05	9	15	6	83	19	9.22	–	–	5	–	1486	774	21	36.85	6-59	1	–
Houghton, D.L.	1992-93	1997-98	22	36	2	1464	266	43.05	4	4	17	–	5	0	0	–	–	–	–
Huckle, A.G.	1997-98	1998-99	8	14	3	74	28*	6.72	–	–	3	–	1568	872	25	34.88	6-109	2	1
James, W.R.	1993-94	1994-95	4	4	0	61	33	15.25	–	–	16	–							
Jarvis, M.P.	1992-93	1994-95	5	3	1	4	2*	2.00	–	–	2	–	1273†	393	11	35.72	3-30	–	–
Johnson, N.C.	1998-99	2000	13	23†	1	532	107	24.18	1	4	12	–	1186	594	15	39.60	4-77	–	–
Lock, A.C.I.	1995-96	1995-96	1	2	1	8	8*	8.00	–	–	–	–	180	105	5	21.00	3-68	–	–
Madondo, T.N.	1997-98	2000-01	3	4	1	90	74*	30.00	–	1	1	–							
Mahwire, N.B.	2002-03	2005-06	10	17	6	147	50*	13.36	–	1	1	–	1287	915	18	50.83	4-92	–	–
Maregwede, A.	2004	2004	2	4	0	74	28	18.50	–	–	1	–							
Marillier, D.A.	2000-01	2001-02	5	7	1	185	73	30.83	–	2	2	–	616	322	11	29.27	4-57	–	–
Masakadza, H.	2001	2005-06	15	30	1	785	119	27.06	1	3	8	–	126	39	2	19.50	1-9	–	–
Matambanadzo, E.Z.	1996-97	1999-00	3	5	1	17	7	4.25	–	–	–	–	384	250	4	62.50	2-62	–	–
Matsikenyeri, S.	2003-04	2004-05	8	16	1	351	57	23.40	–	2	7	–	483	345	2	172.50	1-58	–	–
Mbangwa, M.	1996-97	2000-01	15	25	8	34	8	2.00	–	–	7	–	2596	1006	32	31.43	3-23	–	–
Mpofu, C.B.	2004-05	2005-06	6	12	6	17	7	2.83	–	–	2	–	830	556	8	69.50	4-109	–	–
Mupariwa, T.	2004	2004	1	2	1	15	14	15.00	–	–	–	–	204	136	0	–	–	–	–
Murphy, B.A.	1999-00	2001-02	11	15	3	123	30	10.25	–	–	11	–	2153	1113	18	61.83	3-32	–	–
Mutendera, D.T.	2000-01	2000-01	1	2	0	10	10	5.00	–	–	–	–	84	29	0	–	–	–	–
Mwayenga, W.	2005-06	2005-06	1	2	1	15	14*	15.00	–	–	–	–	126	79	1	79.00	1-79	–	–
Nkala, M.L.	2000	2004-05	10	15	2	187	47	14.38	–	–	4	–	1452	727	11	66.09	3-82	–	–
Olonga, H.K.	1994-95	2002-03	30	45	11	184	24	5.41	–	–	10	–	4502	2620	68	38.52	5-70	2	–
Panyangara, T.	2004	2004-05	3	6	2	128	40*	32.00	–	–	1	–	535	286	8	35.75	3-28	–	–
Peall, S.G.	1993-94	1994-95	4	6†	2	60	30	15.00	–	–	1	–	888	303	4	75.75	2-89	–	–
Price, R.W.	1999-00	2003-04	18	30	7	224	36	9.73	–	–	3	–	5135†	2475	69	35.86	6-73	5	1
Pycroft, A.J.	1992-93	1992-93	3	5	0	152	60	30.40	–	1	2	–							
Ranchod, U.	1992-93	1992-93	1	2	0	8	7	4.00	–	–	–	–	72	45	1	45.00	1-45	–	–

INDIVIDUAL CAREER RECORDS – ZIMBABWE *continued*

	First Test	Last Test	Tests	BATTING AND FIELDING									BOWLING						
				Inns	NO	Runs	HS	Avge	100	50	Ct	St	Balls	Runs	Wkts	Avge	BB	5wI	10wM
Rennie, G.J.	1997-98	2001-02	23	46†	1	1023	93	22.73	–	7	13	–	126†	84	1	84.00	1-40	–	–
Rennie, I.A.	1993-94	1997-98	4	6	1	62	22	12.40	–	–	1	–	724	293	3	97.66	2-22	–	–
Rogers, B.G.	2004-05	2004-05	4	8†	0	90	29	11.25	–	–	1	–	18	17	0	–	–	–	–
Shah, A.H.	1992-93	1996	3	5†	0	122	62	24.40	–	1	–	–	186	125	1	125.00	1-46	–	–
Sibanda, V.	2003-04	2004-05	3	6	0	48	18	8.00	–	–	4	–	–	–	–	–	–	–	–
Strang, B.C.	1994-95	2001	26	45	9	465	53	12.91	–	1	11	–	5433†	2203	56	39.33	5-101	1	–
Strang, P.A.	1994-95	2001-02	24	41	10	839	106*	27.06	1	2	15	–	5720	2522	70	36.02	8-109	4	1
Streak, H.H.	1993-94	2005-06	65	107	18	1990	127*	22.35	1	11	17	–	13559	6079	216	28.14	6-73	7	–
Taibu, T.	2001	2005-06	24	46	3	1273	153	29.60	1	9	48	4	48	27	1	27.00	1-27	–	–
Taylor, B.R.M.	2004	2005-06	10	20	0	422	78	21.10	–	3	7	–	42	38	–	–	–	–	–
Traicos, A.J. ‡	1992-93	1992-93	4	6	2	11	5	2.75	–	–	4	–	1141	562	14	40.14	5-86	1	–
Utseya, P.	2004	2004	1	2	0	45	45	22.50	–	–	2	–	72	55	0	–	–	–	–
Vermeulen, M.A.	2002-03	2004	8	16	0	414	118	25.87	1	2	6	–	6	5	0	–	–	–	–
Viljoen, D.P.	1997-98	2000-01	2	4†	0	57	38	14.25	–	–	1	–	105†	65	1	65.00	1-14	–	–
Waller, A.C.	1996-97	1996-97	2	3	0	69	50	23.00	–	1	1	–	–	–	–	–	–	–	–
Watambwa, B.T.	2000-01	2001-02	6	8	5	11	4*	3.66	–	–	–	–	931	490	14	35.00	4-64	–	–
Whittall, A.R.	1996	1999-00	10	18	3	114	17	7.60	–	–	8	–	1562	736	7	105.14	3-73	–	–
Whittall, G.J.	1993-94	2002-03	46	82	7	2207	203*	29.42	4	10	19	–	4686	2088	51	40.94	4-18	–	–
Wishart, C.B.	1995-96	2005-06	27	50	0	1098	114	22.40	1	5	15	–	–	–	–	–	–	–	–

INDIVIDUAL CAREER RECORDS – BANGLADESH

	First Test	Last Test	Tests	BATTING AND FIELDING									BOWLING						
				Inns	NO	Runs	HS	Avge	100	50	Ct	St	Balls	Runs	Wkts	Avge	BB	5wI	10wM
Abdur Razzak	2005-06	2008-09	5	9	3	129	33	21.50	–	–	2	–	1128†	561	7	80.14	3-93	–	–
Aftab Ahmed	2004-05	2007-08	14	27	3	514	82*	21.41	–	1	6	–	314	225	5	45.00	2-31	–	–
Akram Khan	2000-01	2003	8	16	0	259	44	16.18	–	–	3	–	–	–	–	–	–	–	–
Alamgir Kabir	2002	2003-04	3	5	1	8	4	2.00	–	–	–	–	261	221	0	–	–	–	–
Alok Kapali	2002	2005-06	17	34	0	584	85	17.69	–	2	5	–	1103	709	6	118.16	3-3	–	–
Al Sahariar	2000-01	2003	15	30	0	683	71	22.76	–	4	10	–	–	–	–	–	–	–	–
Aminul Islam	2000-01	2002-03	13	26	1	530	145	21.20	1	2	5	–	198	149	1	149.00	1-66	–	–
Anwar Hossain Monir	2003	2005	3	6	3	22	13	7.33	–	–	–	–	348	307	0	–	–	–	–
Anwar Hossain Piju	2002-03	2002-03	1	2	0	14	12	7.00	–	–	–	–	–	–	–	–	–	–	–
Bikash Ranjan Das	2000-01	2000-01	1	2	0	2	2	1.00	–	–	1	–	132†	72	1	72.00	1-64	–	–
Ehsanul Haque	2002	2002	1	2	0	7	5	3.50	–	–	–	–	18	18	0	–	–	–	–
Enamul Haque, sen.	2000-01	2003	10	19†	4	180	24*	12.00	–	–	1	–	2230†	1027	18	57.05	4-136	–	–
Enamul Haque, jun.	2003-04	2009	14	24	15	53	13	5.88	–	–	3	–	3189†	1609	41	39.24	7-95	3	1
Fahim Muntasir	2001-02	2002	3	6	0	52	33	8.66	–	–	1	–	576	342	5	68.40	3-131	–	–

INDIVIDUAL CAREER RECORDS – BANGLADESH *continued*

	First Test	Last Test	Tests	BATTING AND FIELDING									BOWLING						
				Inns	NO	Runs	HS	Avge	100	50	Ct	St	Balls	Runs	Wkts	Avge	BB	5wI	10wM
Faisal Hossain	2004	2004	1	2†	0	7	5	3.50	–	–	–	–	–	–	–	–	–	–	–
Habibul Bashar	2000-01	2007-08	50	99	1	3026	113	30.87	3	24	22	–	282	217	0	–	–	–	–
Hannan Sarkar	2002	2004-05	17	33	0	662	76	20.06	–	5	7	–	–	–	–	–	–	–	–
Hasibul Hossain	2000-01	2001-02	5	10	1	97	31	10.77	–	–	1	–	780	571	6	95.16	2-125	–	–
Imrul Kayes	2008-09	2009	6	12†	0	161	33	13.41	–	–	4	–	6	7	0	–	–	–	–
Javed Omar	2000-01	2007	40	80	2	1720	119	22.05	1	8	10	–	6	12	0	–	–	–	–
Junaid Siddique	2007-08	2009	12	23†	0	526	78	22.86	–	4	6	–	12	2	0	–	–	–	–
Khaled Mahmud	2001-02	2003-04	12	23	1	266	45	12.09	–	–	2	–	1620	832	13	64.00	4-37	–	–
Khaled Mashud	2000-01	2007	44	84	10	1409	103*	19.04	1	3	78	9	–	–	–	–	–	–	–
Mahbubul Alam	2008-09	2008-09	4	7	3	5	2	1.25	–	–	–	–	587	314	5	62.80	2-62	–	–
Mahmudullah	2009	2009	2	4	1	45	28	15.00	–	–	4	–	376	191	12	15.91	5-51	1	–
Manjural Islam	2000-01	2003-04	17	33†	11	81	21	3.68	–	–	4	–	2970†	1605	28	57.32	6-81	1	–
Manjural Islam Rana	2003-04	2004-05	6	11†	1	257	69	25.70	–	1	3	–	749†	401	5	80.20	3-84	–	–
Mashrafe bin Mortaza	2001-02	2009	36	67	5	797	79	12.85	–	3	9	–	5990	3239	78	41.52	4-60	–	–
Mehrab Hossain, sen.	2000-01	2003	9	18	0	241	71	13.38	–	1	6	–	12	–	0	–	–	–	–
Mehrab Hossain, jun.	2007	2008-09	7	13†	1	243	83	20.25	–	1	2	–	407†	281	4	70.25	2-29	–	–
Mohammad Ashraful	2001-02	2009	50	97	4	2149	158*	23.10	5	7	22	–	1495	1114	19	58.63	2-42	–	–
Mohammad Rafique	2000-01	2007-08	33	63†	6	1059	111	18.57	1	4	7	–	8744†	4076	100	40.76	6-77	7	–
Mohammad Salim	2003	2003	2	4	0	49	26	16.33	–	–	3	1	–	–	–	–	–	–	–
Mohammad Sharif	2000-01	2009	10	20	3	122	24*	7.17	–	–	5	–	1651	1106	14	79.00	4-98	–	–
Mushfiqur Rahim	2005	2009	16	31	2	679	80	23.41	–	4	21	2	–	–	–	–	–	–	–
Mushfiqur Rahman	2000-01	2004-05	10	19	2	232	46*	13.64	–	–	6	–	1365	823	13	63.30	4-65	–	–
Naeem Islam	2008-09	2008-09	2	4	0	44	19	11.00	–	–	1	–	120	46	1	46.00	1-11	–	–
Nafis Iqbal	2004-05	2005-06	11	22	0	518	121	23.54	1	2	2	–	–	–	–	–	–	–	–
Naimur Rahman	2000-01	2002-03	8	15	1	210	48	15.00	–	–	4	–	1321	718	12	59.83	6-132	1	–
Nazmul Hossain	2004-05	2004-05	1	2	1	8	8*	8.00	–	–	–	–	155	114	2	57.00	2-114	–	–
Rafiqul Islam	2002-03	2002-03	1	2	0	7	6	3.50	–	–	–	–	–	–	–	–	–	–	–
Rajin Saleh	2003-04	2008-09	24	46	2	1141	89	25.93	–	7	15	–	438	268	2	134.00	1-9	–	–
Raqibul Hasan	2008-09	2009	5	10	0	229	65	22.90	–	1	4	–	12	5	0	–	–	–	–
Rubel Hossain	2009	2009	2	3	2	5	3*	5.00	–	–	–	–	240	182	3	60.66	3-76	–	–
Sajidul Islam	2007-08	2007-08	2	4	0	14	6	3.50	–	–	–	–	216†	175	3	58.33	2-71	–	–
Sanwar Hossain	2001-02	2003-04	9	18	0	345	49	19.16	–	–	1	–	444	310	5	62.00	2-128	–	–
Shahadat Hossain	2005	2009	23	43	13	231	33	7.70	–	–	4	–	3344	2316	53	43.69	6-27	2	–
Shahriar Hossain	2000-01	2003-04	3	5	0	99	48	19.80	–	–	–	–	–	–	–	–	–	–	–
Shahriar Nafees	2005-06	2007-08	15	30†	0	810	138	27.00	1	4	11	–	–	–	–	–	–	–	–
Shakib Al Hasan	2007	2009	14	26†	2	715	96*	29.79	–	3	8	–	2991†	1357	48	28.27	7-36	5	–
Syed Rasel	2005-06	2007	6	12†	4	37	19	4.62	–	–	–	–	879†	573	12	47.75	4-129	–	–
Talha Jubair	2002	2004-05	7	14	6	52	31	6.50	–	–	1	–	1090	771	14	55.07	3-135	–	–

INDIVIDUAL CAREER RECORDS – BANGLADESH continued

	First Test	Last Test	Tests	Inns	NO	Runs	HS	Avge	100	50	Ct	St	BOWLING Balls	Runs	Wkts	Avge	BB	5wI	10wM
Tamim Iqbal	2007-08	2009	12	22†	0	608	128	27.63	1	2	5	–	12	4	0	–	–	–	–
Tapash Baisya	2002	2005	21	40	6	384	66	11.29	–	2	6	–	3376	2137	36	59.36	4-72	–	–
Tareq Aziz	2004	2004-05	3	6	4	22	10*	11.00	–	–	1	–	360	261	1	261.00	1-76	–	–
Tushar Imran	2002	2007	5	10	0	89	28	8.90	–	–	1	–	60	48	0	–	–	–	–

INDIVIDUAL CAREER RECORDS – ICC WORLD XI

	First Test	Last Test	Tests	Inns	NO	Runs	HS	Avge	100	50	Ct	St	BOWLING Balls	Runs	Wkts	Avge	BB	5wI	10wM
Boucher, M.V.	2005-06	2005-06	1	2	0	17	17	8.50	–	–	2	–							
Dravid, R.S.	2005-06	2005-06	1	2	0	23	23	11.50	–	–	1	–							
Flintoff, A.	2005-06	2005-06	1	2	0	50	35	25.00	–	–	–	–	204	107	7	15.28	4-59	–	–
Harmison, S.J.	2005-06	2005-06	1	2	0	1	1	0.50	–	–	–	–	183	101	4	25.25	3-41	–	–
Inzamam-ul-Haq	2005-06	2005-06	1	2	1	1	1	0.50	–	–	–	–	60	38	1	38.00	1-3	–	–
Kallis, J.H.	2005-06	2005-06	1	2	1	83	44	83.00	–	–	4	–							
Lara, B.C.	2005-06	2005-06	1	2†	0	41	36	20.50	–	–	–	–							
Muralitharan, M.	2005-06	2005-06	1	2	0	2	2	1.00	–	–	2	–	324	157	5	31.40	3-55	–	–
Sehwag, V.	2005-06	2005-06	1	2	0	83	76	41.50	–	1	1	–							
Smith, G.C.	2005-06	2005-06	1	2†	0	12	12	6.00	–	–	3	–							
Vettori, D.L.	2005-06	2005-06	1	2†	1	8	8*	8.00	–	–	–	–	162†	111	1	111.00	1-73	–	–

COMPLETE TEST RECORD FOR PLAYERS REPRESENTING TWO TEAMS

	First Test	Last Test	Tests	Inns	NO	Runs	HS	Avge	100	50	Ct	St	BOWLING Balls	Runs	Wkts	Avge	BB	5wI	10wM
Amir Elahi (I/P)	1947-48	1952-53	6	9	1	82	47	10.25	–	–	–	–	400	248	7	35.42	4-134	–	–
Ferris, J.J. (A/E)	1886-87	1891-92	9	17†	4	114	20*	8.76	–	–	4	–	2302†	775	61	12.70	7-37	6	1
Guillen, S.C. (WI/NZ)	1951-52	1955-56	8	12	2	202	54	20.20	–	1	13	3							
Gul Mahomed (I/P)	1946	1956-57	9	17†	1	205	34	12.81	–	–	3	–	77†	24	2	12.00	2-21	–	–
Hearne, F. (E/SA)	1888-89	1895-96	6	10	0	168	30	16.80	–	–	3	–	62	40	2	20.00	2-40	–	–
Kardar, A.H. (I/P)	1946	1957-58	26	42†	3	927	93	23.76	–	5	16	–	2712†	954	21	45.42	3-35	–	–
Midwinter, W.E. (E/A)	1876-77	1886-87	12	21	1	269	37	13.45	–	–	10	–	1725	605	24	25.20	5-78	1	–
Mitchell, F. (E/SA)	1898-99	1912	5	10	0	116	41	11.60	–	–	2	–							
Murdoch, W.L. (A/E)	1876-77	1891-92	19	34	5	908	211	31.31	2	1	14	1							
Pataudi, Nawab of, sen. (E/I)	1932-33	1946	6	10	0	199	102	19.90	1	1	–	–							
Traicos, A.J. (SA/Z)	1969-70	1992-93	7	10	4	19	5*	3.16	–	–	8	–	1611	769	18	42.72	5-86	1	–
Trott, A.E. (A/E)	1894-95	1898-99	5	9	3	228	85*	38.00	–	2	4	–	948	390	26	15.00	8-43	2	–
Wessels, K.C. (A/SA)	1982-83	1994	40	71†	3	2788	179	41.00	6	15	30	–	90	42	0	–	–	–	–
Woods, S.M.J. (A/E)	1888	1895-96	6	10	0	154	53	15.40	–	1	5	–	412	250	10	25.00	3-28	–	–
Boucher, M.V. (SA/World XI)	1997-98	2008-09	126	178	21	4688	125	29.85	5	29	453	22	8	6	1	6.00	1-6	–	–
Dravid, R.S. (I/World XI)	1996	2008-09	134	233	27	10823	270	52.53	26	57	184	–	120	39	1	39.00	1-18	–	–

COMPLETE TEST RECORD FOR PLAYERS REPRESENTING TWO TEAMS *continued*

	First Test	Last Test	Tests	Inns	NO	Runs	HS	Avge	100	50	Ct	St	Balls	Runs	Wkts	Avge	BB	5wI	10wM
								BATTING AND FIELDING								*BOWLING*			
Flintoff, A. (E/World XI)	1998	2009	79	130	9	3845	167	31.77	5	26	52	–	14951	7410	226	32.78	5-58	3	1
Harmison, S.J. (E/World XI)	2002	2009	63	86	23	743	49*	11.79	–	–	7	–	13375	7192	226	31.82	7-12	8	1
Inzamam-ul-Haq (P'/World XI)	1992	2007-08	120	200	22	8830	329	49.60	25	46	81	–	9†	8	0	–	–	–	–
Kallis, J.H. (SA/World XI)	1995-96	2008-09	131	221	33	10277	189*	54.66	31	51	147	–	17040	8021	258	31.08	6-54	5	–
Lara, B.C. (WI/World XI)	1990-91	2006-07	131	232†	6	11953	400*	52.88	34	48	164	–	60	28	0	–	–	–	–
Muralitharan, M. (SL/World XI)	1992	2009	129	159	54	1203	67	11.45	–	1	70	–	42758	17398	783	22.21	9-51	66	22
Sehwag, V. (I/World XI)	2001-02	2008-09	69	119	4	5757	319	50.06	15	18	55	–	2455	1265	29	43.62	5-104	1	–
Smith, G.C. (SA/World XI)	2001-02	2008-09	77	135†	9	6342	277	50.33	18	25	104	–	1319	801	8	100.12	2-145	–	–
Vettori, D.L. (NZ/World XI)	1996-97	2009	94	141†	23	3492	140	29.59	4	20	48	–	23125†	10156	303	33.51	7-87	18	3

Index

Every cricketer who appeared in official Test matches since September 12, 2000 is listed alphabetically within his country's section of the index. Players who appeared for two countries are listed within both sections. The numbers that follow are the reference numbers of the matches in which the cricketer played; only the prefix of each match is listed; e.g. Test No. 1759/309 (E837/A668) is shown as 1759.

ENGLAND

1692, 1693, 1694, 1700, 1701,
1702, 1707, 1708, 1709, 1710,
1730, 1731, 1732, 1733, 1734,
1751, 1752, 1757, 1758, 1759,
1760, 1761, 1772, 1773, 1774,
1786, 1787, 1788, 1802, 1803,
1804, 1809, 1810, 1811, 1812,
1818, 1819, 1820, 1821, 1831,
1834, 1886
HUSSAIN, Nasser 1513, 1514, 1515,
1530, 1531, 1532, 1546, 1550,
1553, 1554, 1574, 1575, 1576,
1595, 1596, 1597, 1604, 1605,
1606, 1611, 1612, 1613, 1614,
1623, 1624, 1625, 1626, 1627,
1646, 1647, 1652, 1653, 1654,
1655, 1656, 1667, 1671, 1672,
1691, 1692, 1693, 1694, 1700

JOHNSON, Richard Leonard 1647,
1667, 1670
JONES, Geraint Owen 1694, 1700,
1701, 1702, 1707, 1708, 1709,
1710, 1730, 1731, 1732, 1733,
1734, 1751, 1752, 1757, 1758,
1759, 1760, 1761, 1772, 1773,
1774, 1786, 1787, 1788, 1802,
1803, 1804, 1809, 1810, 1818,
1819, 1820
JONES, Simon Philip 1611, 1623, 1691,
1692, 1693, 1694, 1700, 1707,
1730, 1731, 1732, 1734, 1751,
1752, 1757, 1758, 1759, 1760

KEY, Robert William Trevor 1612,
1613, 1624, 1625, 1626, 1627,
1646, 1647, 1707, 1708, 1709,
1710, 1732, 1733, 1734
KHAN, Amjad 1910
KIRTLEY, Robert James 1654, 1655,
1671, 1672
KNIGHT, Nicholas Verity 1547

LEWIS, Jonathan 1804

McGRATH, Anthony 1646, 1647,
1652, 1653
MAHMOOD, Sajid Iqbal 1802, 1803,
1810, 1811, 1812, 1820, 1821,
1822
MULLALLY, Alan David 1553

ONIONS, Graham 1919, 1920, 1925,
1926, 1927
ORMOND, James 1554, 1574

PANESAR, Mudhsuden Singh 1786,
1787, 1788, 1802, 1803, 1804,
1809, 1810, 1811, 1812, 1820,
1821, 1822, 1831, 1832, 1833,
1834, 1840, 1841, 1842, 1852,
1853, 1854, 1866, 1867, 1868,
1874, 1875, 1876, 1880, 1881,
1882, 1883, 1899, 1900, 1906,
1907, 1910, 1924

PATTINSON, Darren John 1881
PIETERSEN, Kevin Peter 1757, 1758,
1759, 1760, 1761, 1772, 1773,
1774, 1786, 1787, 1788, 1802,
1803, 1804, 1809, 1810, 1811,
1812, 1818, 1819, 1820, 1821,
1822, 1831, 1832, 1833, 1834,
1840, 1841, 1842, 1852, 1853,
1854, 1866, 1867, 1868, 1874,
1875, 1876, 1880, 1881, 1882,
1883, 1899, 1900, 1906, 1907,
1908, 1909, 1910, 1919, 1920,
1924, 1925
PLUNKETT, Liam Edward 1774,
1787, 1802, 1803, 1804, 1809,
1831, 1832, 1833
PRIOR, Matthew James 1831, 1832,
1833, 1834, 1840, 1841, 1842,
1852, 1853, 1854, 1899, 1900,
1906, 1907, 1908, 1910, 1919,
1920, 1924, 1925, 1926, 1927,
1928

RAMPRAKASH, Mark Ravin 1551,
1552, 1553, 1554, 1574, 1575,
1576, 1595, 1596, 1597
READ, Christopher Mark Wells 1666,
1667, 1670, 1671, 1672, 1691,
1692, 1693, 1811, 1812, 1821,
1822

SAGGERS, Martin John 1667, 1701,
1702
SALISBURY, Ian David Kenneth 1513,
1514, 1515
SHAH, Owais Alam 1788, 1831, 1907,
1908, 1909, 1910
SIDEBOTTOM, Ryan Jay 1546, 1832,
1833, 1834, 1840, 1841, 1842,
1852, 1853, 1854, 1866, 1867,
1868, 1874, 1875, 1876, 1880,
1882, 1906, 1907, 1909
SILVERWOOD, Christopher Eric
Wilfred 1625
SMITH, Edward Thomas 1654, 1655,
1656
STEWART, Alec James 1513, 1514,
1515, 1530, 1531, 1532, 1546,
1547, 1550, 1551, 1552, 1553,
1554, 1604, 1605, 1606, 1611,
1612, 1613, 1614, 1623, 1624,
1625, 1627, 1646, 1647, 1652,
1653, 1654, 1655, 1656
STRAUSS, Andrew John 1700, 1701,
1702, 1707, 1708, 1709, 1710,
1730, 1731, 1732, 1733, 1734,
1751, 1752, 1757, 1758, 1759,
1760, 1761, 1772, 1773, 1786,
1787, 1788, 1802, 1803, 1804,
1809, 1810, 1811, 1812, 1818,
1819, 1820, 1821, 1822, 1831,
1832, 1833, 1834, 1840, 1841,
1842, 1866, 1867, 1868, 1874,
1875, 1876, 1880, 1881, 1882,
1883, 1899, 1900, 1906, 1907,

1908, 1909, 1910, 1919, 1920,
1924, 1925, 1926, 1927, 1928
SWANN, Graeme Peter 1899, 1900,
1908, 1909, 1910, 1919, 1920,
1924, 1925, 1926, 1927, 1928

THORPE, Graham Paul 1513, 1514,
1515, 1530, 1531, 1532, 1546,
1547, 1551, 1574, 1595, 1596,
1597, 1604, 1605, 1606, 1611,
1656, 1666, 1667, 1670, 1671,
1672, 1691, 1692, 1693, 1694,
1700, 1701, 1702, 1707, 1708,
1709, 1730, 1731, 1732, 1733,
1734, 1751, 1752
TREMLETT, Christopher Timothy
1840, 1841, 1842
TRESCOTHICK, Marcus Edward
1513, 1514, 1515, 1530, 1531,
1532, 1546, 1547, 1550, 1551,
1552, 1553, 1554, 1574, 1575,
1576, 1595, 1596, 1597, 1604,
1605, 1606, 1614, 1623, 1624,
1625, 1626, 1627, 1646, 1647,
1652, 1653, 1654, 1655, 1656,
1666, 1667, 1670, 1671, 1672,
1691, 1692, 1693, 1694, 1700,
1701, 1702, 1707, 1708, 1709,
1710, 1730, 1731, 1732, 1733,
1734, 1751, 1752, 1757, 1758,
1759, 1760, 1761, 1772, 1773,
1774, 1802, 1803, 1804, 1809,
1810, 1811, 1812
TROTT, Ian Jonathan Leonard 1928
TUDOR, Alex Jeremy 1552, 1553,
1605, 1606, 1613, 1614, 1625
TUFNELL, Philip Clive Roderick 1554

UDAL, Shaun David 1772, 1773,
1774, 1788

VAUGHAN, Michael Paul 1532, 1546,
1547, 1575, 1576, 1595, 1596,
1597, 1604, 1605, 1606, 1611,
1612, 1613, 1614, 1623, 1624,
1625, 1626, 1627, 1646, 1647,
1652, 1653, 1654, 1655, 1656,
1666, 1667, 1670, 1671, 1672,
1691, 1692, 1693, 1694, 1701,
1702, 1707, 1708, 1709, 1710,
1730, 1731, 1732, 1733, 1734,
1751, 1752, 1757, 1758, 1759,
1760, 1761, 1773, 1774, 1832,
1833, 1834, 1840, 1841, 1842,
1852, 1853, 1854, 1866, 1867,
1868, 1874, 1875, 1876, 1880,
1881, 1882

WARD, Ian James 1546, 1547, 1550,
1551, 1552
WHITE, Craig 1513, 1514, 1515,
1530, 1531, 1532, 1550, 1551,
1552, 1574, 1575, 1576, 1611,
1612, 1623, 1624, 1625, 1626

AUSTRALIA

BICHEL, Andrew John 1521, 1524,
1578, 1616, 1617, 1623, 1624,
1627, 1638, 1639, 1640, 1641,
1662, 1663, 1673, 1674
BOLLINGER, Douglas Erwin 1903
BRACKEN, Nathan Wade 1673, 1675,
1676, 1769, 1778

CASSON, Beau 1879
CLARK, Stuart Rupert 1792, 1793,
1794, 1797, 1818, 1819, 1820,

1821, 1822, 1845, 1846, 1855,
1856, 1857, 1858, 1877, 1878,
1879, 1887, 1889, 1895, 1896,
1927, 1928
CLARKE, Michael John 1713, 1714,
1715, 1716, 1721, 1722, 1727,
1728, 1729, 1742, 1743, 1744,
1757, 1758, 1759, 1760, 1761,
1768, 1769, 1770, 1797, 1798,
1818, 1819, 1820, 1821, 1822,
1845, 1846, 1855, 1856, 1857,

1858, 1878, 1879, 1887, 1888,
1889, 1890, 1895, 1896, 1901,
1902, 1903, 1913, 1914, 1915,
1924, 1925, 1926, 1927, 1928
CULLEN, Daniel James 1798

ELLIOTT, Matthew Thomas Gray 1705

FLEMING, Damien William 1533

GILCHRIST, Adam Craig 1521, 1522,

1523, 1524, 1525, 1533, 1534,
1535, 1550, 1551, 1552, 1553,
1554, 1566, 1567, 1568, 1577,
1578, 1579, 1591, 1592, 1593,
1615, 1616, 1617, 1623, 1624,
1625, 1626, 1627, 1638, 1639,
1640, 1641, 1650, 1651, 1662,
1663, 1673, 1674, 1675, 1676,
1685, 1686, 1687, 1705, 1706,
1713, 1714, 1715, 1716, 1721,
1722, 1727, 1728, 1729, 1742,
1743, 1744, 1757, 1758, 1759,
1760, 1761, 1768, 1769, 1770,
1771, 1778, 1779, 1780, 1792,
1793, 1794, 1797, 1798, 1818,
1819, 1820, 1821, 1822, 1845,
1846, 1855, 1856, 1857, 1858
GILLESPIE, Jason Neil 1522, 1523,
1524, 1525, 1533, 1534, 1535,
1550, 1551, 1552, 1553, 1554,
1566, 1567, 1568, 1577, 1591,
1592, 1593, 1615, 1623, 1624,
1625, 1626, 1627, 1638, 1639,
1640, 1641, 1650, 1651, 1662,
1673, 1674, 1676, 1685, 1686,
1687, 1705, 1706, 1713, 1714,
1715, 1716, 1721, 1722, 1727,
1728, 1729, 1742, 1743, 1744,
1757, 1758, 1759, 1797, 1798

HADDIN, Bradley James 1877, 1878,
1879, 1887, 1888, 1889, 1890,
1895, 1896, 1901, 1902, 1903,
1913, 1914, 1915, 1924, 1925,
1927, 1928
HAURITZ, Nathan Michael 1716,
1896, 1902, 1903, 1924, 1925,
1926
HAYDEN, Matthew Lawrence 1521,
1522, 1523, 1525, 1533, 1534,
1535, 1550, 1551, 1552, 1553,
1554, 1566, 1567, 1568, 1577,
1578, 1579, 1591, 1592, 1593,
1615, 1616, 1617, 1623, 1624,
1625, 1626, 1627, 1638, 1639,
1640, 1641, 1650, 1651, 1662,
1663, 1673, 1674, 1675, 1676,
1685, 1686, 1687, 1705, 1706,
1713, 1714, 1715, 1716, 1721,
1722, 1727, 1728, 1729, 1742,
1743, 1744, 1757, 1758, 1759,
1760, 1761, 1768, 1769, 1770,
1771, 1778, 1779, 1780, 1792,
1793, 1794, 1797, 1798, 1818,
1819, 1820, 1821, 1822, 1845,
1846, 1855, 1856, 1858, 1887,
1888, 1889, 1890, 1895, 1896,
1901, 1902, 1903
HILFENHAUS, Benjamin William
1913, 1914, 1915, 1924, 1925,
1926, 1927, 1928
HODGE, Bradley John 1770, 1771,
1778, 1779, 1780, 1877
HOGG, George Bradley 1638, 1639,
1663, 1855, 1856, 1858
HUGHES, Philip Joel 1913, 1914,
1915, 1924, 1925
HUSSEY, Michael Edward Killeen
1769, 1770, 1771, 1778, 1779,
1780, 1792, 1793, 1794, 1797,
1798, 1818, 1819, 1820, 1821,
1822, 1845, 1846, 1855, 1856,
1857, 1858, 1877, 1878, 1879,
1887, 1888, 1889, 1890, 1895,
1896, 1901, 1902, 1903, 1913,
1914, 1915, 1924, 1925, 1926,
1927, 1928

JAQUES, Philip Anthony 1779, 1798,
1845, 1846, 1855, 1856, 1857,
1858, 1877, 1878, 1879

JOHNSON, Mitchell Guy 1845, 1846,
1855, 1856, 1857, 1858, 1877,
1878, 1879, 1887, 1888, 1889,
1890, 1895, 1896, 1901, 1902,
1903, 1913, 1914, 1915, 1924,
1925, 1926, 1927, 1928

KASPROWICZ, Michael Scott 1534,
1685, 1686, 1687, 1705, 1706,
1713, 1714, 1715, 1716, 1721,
1722, 1727, 1728, 1742, 1743,
1744, 1758, 1760, 1792, 1793,
1794
KATICH, Simon Mathew 1553, 1663,
1673, 1674, 1675, 1676, 1687,
1705, 1706, 1713, 1714, 1715,
1716, 1742, 1743, 1744, 1757,
1758, 1759, 1760, 1761, 1768,
1769, 1877, 1878, 1879, 1887,
1888, 1889, 1890, 1895, 1896,
1901, 1902, 1903, 1913, 1914,
1915, 1924, 1925, 1926, 1927,
1928
KREJZA, Jason John 1890, 1901

LANGER, Justin Lee 1521, 1522,
1523, 1524, 1525, 1533, 1534,
1535, 1554, 1566, 1567, 1568,
1577, 1578, 1579, 1591, 1592,
1593, 1615, 1616, 1617, 1623,
1624, 1625, 1626, 1627, 1638,
1639, 1640, 1641, 1650, 1651,
1662, 1663, 1673, 1674, 1675,
1676, 1685, 1686, 1687, 1705,
1706, 1713, 1714, 1715, 1716,
1721, 1722, 1727, 1728, 1729,
1742, 1743, 1744, 1757, 1758,
1759, 1760, 1761, 1768, 1771,
1778, 1792, 1793, 1794, 1818,
1819, 1820, 1821, 1822
LEE, Brett 1521, 1522, 1550, 1551,
1552, 1553, 1554, 1566, 1567,
1568, 1577, 1578, 1579, 1591,
1592, 1593, 1615, 1616, 1617,
1625, 1626, 1627, 1638, 1639,
1640, 1641, 1650, 1651, 1662,
1663, 1675, 1676, 1757, 1758,
1759, 1760, 1761, 1768, 1769,
1770, 1771, 1778, 1779, 1780,
1792, 1793, 1794, 1797, 1798,
1818, 1819, 1820, 1821, 1822,
1845, 1846, 1855, 1856, 1857,
1858, 1877, 1878, 1879, 1887,
1888, 1889, 1890, 1895, 1896,
1901, 1902
LEHMANN, Darren Scott 1623, 1624,
1625, 1638, 1639, 1640, 1641,
1650, 1651, 1662, 1685, 1686,
1687, 1705, 1706, 1713, 1714,
1715, 1721, 1722, 1727
LOVE, Martin Lloyd 1626, 1627,
1641, 1650, 1651

McDONALD, Andrew Barry 1903,
1913, 1914, 1915
McGAIN, Bryce Edward 1915
MacGILL, Stuart Charles Glyndwr
1521, 1522, 1523, 1525, 1579,
1626, 1627, 1638, 1639, 1640,
1641, 1650, 1651, 1662, 1673,
1674, 1675, 1676, 1685, 1686,
1729, 1768, 1770, 1771, 1779,
1780, 1797, 1798, 1845, 1846,
1877, 1878
McGRATH, Glenn Donald 1521, 1522,
1523, 1524, 1525, 1533, 1534,
1535, 1550, 1551, 1552, 1553,
1554, 1566, 1567, 1568, 1577,
1578, 1579, 1591, 1592, 1593,
1615, 1616, 1617, 1623, 1624,
1625, 1626, 1640, 1641, 1650,

1651, 1705, 1706, 1713, 1714,
1715, 1716, 1721, 1722, 1727,
1728, 1729, 1742, 1743, 1744,
1757, 1759, 1761, 1768, 1769,
1770, 1771, 1778, 1779, 1780,
1818, 1819, 1820, 1821, 1822
MANOU, Graham Allan 1926
MARTYN, Damien Richard 1523,
1550, 1551, 1552, 1553, 1554,
1566, 1567, 1568, 1577, 1578,
1579, 1591, 1592, 1593, 1615,
1616, 1617, 1623, 1624, 1625,
1627, 1662, 1663, 1673, 1674,
1675, 1676, 1685, 1686, 1687,
1705, 1706, 1713, 1714, 1715,
1716, 1721, 1722, 1727, 1728,
1729, 1742, 1743, 1744, 1757,
1758, 1759, 1760, 1761, 1792,
1793, 1794, 1797, 1818, 1819
MILLER, Colin Reid 1523, 1524,
1525, 1535

NORTH, Marcus James 1913, 1914,
1924, 1925, 1926, 1927, 1928

PONTING, Ricky Thomas 1521, 1522,
1523, 1524, 1525, 1533, 1534,
1535, 1550, 1551, 1552, 1553,
1554, 1566, 1567, 1568, 1577,
1578, 1579, 1591, 1592, 1593,
1615, 1616, 1617, 1623, 1624,
1625, 1626, 1627, 1638, 1639,
1640, 1641, 1651, 1662, 1663,
1673, 1674, 1675, 1676, 1685,
1686, 1687, 1706, 1716, 1721,
1722, 1727, 1728, 1729, 1742,
1743, 1744, 1757, 1758, 1759,
1760, 1761, 1768, 1769, 1770,
1771, 1778, 1779, 1780, 1792,
1793, 1794, 1797, 1798, 1818,
1819, 1820, 1821, 1822, 1845,
1846, 1855, 1856, 1857, 1858,
1877, 1878, 1879, 1887, 1888,
1889, 1890, 1895, 1896, 1901,
1902, 1903, 1913, 1914, 1915,
1924, 1925, 1926, 1927, 1928

ROGERS, Christopher John Llewellyn
1857

SIDDLE, Peter Matthew 1888, 1901,
1902, 1903, 1913, 1914, 1915,
1924, 1925, 1926, 1927, 1928
SLATER, Michael Jonathon 1521, 1522,
1523, 1524, 1525, 1533, 1534,
1535, 1550, 1551, 1552, 1553
SYMONDS, Andrew 1685, 1686,
1770, 1771, 1778, 1779, 1780,
1792, 1793, 1794, 1820, 1821,
1822, 1845, 1846, 1855, 1856,
1857, 1858, 1877, 1878, 1879,
1895, 1896, 1901, 1902

TAIT, Shaun William 1760, 1761, 1857

WARNE, Shane Keith 1533, 1534,
1535, 1550, 1551, 1552, 1553,
1554, 1566, 1567, 1568, 1577,
1578, 1579, 1591, 1592, 1593,
1615, 1616, 1617, 1623, 1624,
1625, 1685, 1686, 1687, 1705,
1706, 1713, 1714, 1715, 1721,
1722, 1727, 1728, 1729, 1742,
1743, 1744, 1757, 1758, 1759,
1760, 1761, 1768, 1769, 1770,
1771, 1778, 1779, 1780, 1792,
1793, 1794, 1797, 1798, 1818,
1819, 1820, 1821, 1822
WATSON, Shane Robert 1729, 1768,
1769, 1887, 1888, 1889, 1890,
1895, 1926, 1927, 1928

WAUGH, Mark Edward 1521, 1522, 1523, 1524, 1525, 1533, 1534, 1535, 1550, 1551, 1552, 1553, 1554, 1566, 1567, 1568, 1577, 1578, 1579, 1591, 1592, 1593, 1615, 1616, 1617

WAUGH, Stephen Rodger 1521, 1522, 1524, 1525, 1533, 1534, 1535, 1550, 1551, 1554, 1566, 1567, 1568, 1577, 1578, 1579, 1591, 1592, 1593, 1615, 1616, 1617, 1623, 1624, 1625, 1626, 1627,

1638, 1639, 1640, 1641, 1650, 1651, 1662, 1663, 1673, 1675, 1676
WHITE, Cameron Leon 1887, 1888, 1889, 1890
WILLIAMS, Brad Andrew 1663, 1674, 1675, 1687

SOUTH AFRICA

ADAMS, Paul Regan 1543, 1592, 1593, 1642, 1643, 1653, 1654, 1656, 1664, 1665, 1679, 1688
AMLA, Hashim Mahomed 1724, 1731, 1732, 1800, 1801, 1813, 1814, 1825, 1826, 1827, 1828, 1829, 1830, 1843, 1844, 1847, 1848, 1859, 1860, 1861, 1864, 1865, 1871, 1872, 1873, 1880, 1881, 1882, 1883, 1893, 1894, 1901, 1902, 1903, 1913, 1914, 1915

BOJE, Nico 1516, 1517, 1518, 1527, 1528, 1529, 1539, 1540, 1541, 1542, 1564, 1565, 1579, 1591, 1636, 1637, 1689, 1690, 1711, 1712, 1731, 1732, 1733, 1734, 1737, 1738, 1745, 1746, 1747, 1748, 1779, 1792, 1793, 1794, 1799, 1800, 1813, 1814
BOTHA, Johan 1780, 1864
BOUCHER, Mark Verdon 1516, 1517, 1518, 1527, 1528, 1529, 1539, 1540, 1541, 1542, 1543, 1562, 1563, 1564, 1565, 1577, 1578, 1579, 1591, 1592, 1593, 1621, 1622, 1628, 1629, 1636, 1637, 1642, 1643, 1652, 1653, 1654, 1655, 1656, 1664, 1665, 1677, 1678, 1679, 1680, 1688, 1689, 1690, 1711, 1712, 1733, 1734, 1737, 1738, 1745, 1746, 1747, 1748, 1778, 1779, 1780, 1792, 1793, 1794, 1799, 1800, 1801, 1813, 1814, 1825, 1826, 1827, 1828, 1829, 1830, 1843, 1844, 1847, 1848, 1859, 1860, 1861, 1864, 1865, 1871, 1872, 1873, 1880, 1881, 1882, 1883, 1893, 1894, 1901, 1902, 1903, 1913, 1914, 1915

CULLINAN, Daryll John 1516, 1517, 1518, 1527, 1528, 1529, 1539, 1540, 1541, 1542, 1543

DAWSON, Alan Charles 1642, 1643
de BRUYN, Zander 1723, 1724, 1730
de VILLIERS, Abraham Benjamin 1730, 1731, 1732, 1733, 1734, 1737, 1738, 1745, 1746, 1747, 1748, 1778, 1779, 1780, 1792, 1793, 1794, 1799, 1800, 1801, 1813, 1814, 1825, 1826, 1827, 1828, 1829, 1830, 1843, 1844, 1847, 1848, 1859, 1860, 1861, 1864, 1865, 1871, 1872, 1873, 1880, 1881, 1882, 1883, 1893, 1894, 1901, 1902, 1903, 1913, 1914, 1915
DIPPENAAR, Hendrik Human 1516, 1517, 1518, 1527, 1529, 1562, 1563, 1564, 1565, 1577, 1578, 1579, 1591, 1636, 1637, 1642, 1643, 1652, 1653, 1654, 1664, 1665, 1711, 1712, 1723, 1724, 1730, 1732, 1733, 1747, 1748, 1794, 1799, 1800, 1801, 1830
DONALD, Allan Anthony 1516, 1517, 1529, 1539, 1540, 1541, 1543, 1578, 1579, 1591

DUMINY, Jean-Paul 1901, 1902, 1903, 1913, 1914, 1915

ELWORTHY, Steven 1629

GIBBS, Herschelle Herman 1528, 1529, 1539, 1540, 1541, 1542, 1543, 1562, 1563, 1564, 1565, 1577, 1578, 1579, 1591, 1592, 1593, 1621, 1622, 1629, 1636, 1637, 1642, 1643, 1652, 1653, 1654, 1655, 1656, 1664, 1665, 1677, 1678, 1679, 1680, 1688, 1689, 1690, 1712, 1731, 1732, 1733, 1734, 1737, 1738, 1745, 1746, 1747, 1748, 1778, 1779, 1780, 1792, 1793, 1794, 1799, 1813, 1814, 1825, 1826, 1827, 1828, 1829, 1843, 1844, 1847, 1848, 1859, 1861

HALL, Andrew James 1592, 1593, 1628, 1629, 1653, 1654, 1655, 1656, 1678, 1680, 1723, 1724, 1730, 1734, 1745, 1792, 1801, 1813, 1814, 1826, 1830
HARRIS, Paul Lee 1827, 1828, 1829, 1830, 1843, 1844, 1847, 1848, 1859, 1860, 1871, 1872, 1873, 1880, 1881, 1882, 1883, 1893, 1901, 1902, 1903, 1913, 1914, 1915
HAYWARD, Mornantau 1564, 1565, 1577, 1578, 1621, 1622, 1636, 1637, 1711, 1712
HENDERSON, Claude William 1562, 1563, 1577, 1578, 1579, 1621, 1622

KALLIS, Jacques Henry 1516, 1517, 1518, 1527, 1528, 1529, 1539, 1540, 1541, 1542, 1543, 1562, 1563, 1564, 1565, 1577, 1578, 1579, 1591, 1592, 1593, 1621, 1622, 1628, 1629, 1636, 1637, 1654, 1655, 1656, 1664, 1665, 1677, 1678, 1679, 1680, 1688, 1689, 1690, 1711, 1712, 1723, 1724, 1730, 1731, 1732, 1733, 1734, 1737, 1738, 1745, 1746, 1747, 1748, 1779, 1792, 1793, 1794, 1799, 1800, 1801, 1825, 1827, 1828, 1829, 1830, 1843, 1844, 1847, 1848, 1859, 1860, 1861, 1864, 1865, 1871, 1872, 1873, 1880, 1881, 1882, 1883, 1893, 1894, 1901, 1902, 1903, 1913, 1914, 1915
KEMP, Justin Miles 1529, 1542, 1543, 1778
KHAN, Imraan 1915
KIRSTEN, Gary 1516, 1517, 1518, 1527, 1528, 1539, 1540, 1541, 1542, 1543, 1562, 1563, 1564, 1565, 1577, 1578, 1579, 1591, 1592, 1593, 1621, 1622, 1628, 1629, 1636, 1637, 1652, 1653, 1655, 1656, 1664, 1665, 1678, 1679, 1680, 1688, 1689, 1690
KLUSENER, Lance 1516, 1517, 1518, 1527, 1528, 1539, 1540,

1541, 1542, 1543, 1562, 1563, 1564, 1565, 1577, 1578, 1711

LANGEVELDT, Charl Kenneth 1732, 1737, 1738, 1745, 1778, 1780

McKENZIE, Neil Douglas 1516, 1517, 1518, 1527, 1528, 1529, 1539, 1540, 1541, 1542, 1543, 1562, 1563, 1564, 1565, 1577, 1578, 1579, 1591, 1592, 1593, 1628, 1629, 1636, 1637, 1642, 1643, 1654, 1655, 1656, 1664, 1665, 1677, 1678, 1679, 1680, 1688, 1689, 1860, 1864, 1865, 1871, 1872, 1873, 1880, 1881, 1882, 1883, 1893, 1894, 1901, 1902, 1903, 1913, 1914
MORKEL, Johannes Albertus 1826, 1864, 1865, 1871, 1872, 1873, 1880, 1881, 1882, 1883, 1893, 1894, 1901, 1902, 1903, 1913, 1914, 1915
MORKEL, Morne

NEL, Andre 1562, 1563, 1591, 1664, 1677, 1678, 1679, 1680, 1688, 1690, 1734, 1738, 1745, 1746, 1747, 1778, 1779, 1780, 1792, 1793, 1794, 1800, 1813, 1825, 1826, 1828, 1829, 1843, 1844, 1847, 1848, 1859, 1860, 1861, 1882, 1883
NGAM, Mfuneko 1518, 1527, 1528
NTINI, Makhaya 1516, 1517, 1518, 1527, 1528, 1529, 1539, 1540, 1541, 1542, 1562, 1563, 1564, 1565, 1577, 1591, 1592, 1593, 1621, 1622, 1628, 1629, 1636, 1637, 1642, 1643, 1652, 1653, 1654, 1655, 1656, 1664, 1665, 1677, 1678, 1679, 1680, 1688, 1689, 1690, 1711, 1712, 1723, 1724, 1730, 1731, 1732, 1733, 1734, 1737, 1745, 1746, 1747, 1748, 1778, 1779, 1792, 1793, 1794, 1799, 1801, 1813, 1814, 1825, 1826, 1827, 1828, 1829, 1830, 1843, 1844, 1847, 1859, 1860, 1861, 1864, 1865, 1871, 1872, 1873, 1880, 1881, 1882, 1883, 1893, 1894, 1901, 1902, 1903, 1913, 1914, 1915

ONTONG, Justin Lee 1579, 1724

PETERSON, Robin John 1643, 1652, 1665, 1677, 1723, 1865
POLLOCK, Shaun Maclean 1516, 1517, 1518, 1527, 1528, 1529, 1539, 1540, 1541, 1542, 1543, 1562, 1563, 1564, 1565, 1577, 1578, 1579, 1622, 1628, 1629, 1636, 1637, 1642, 1643, 1652, 1653, 1654, 1656, 1664, 1665, 1677, 1678, 1679, 1680, 1688, 1689, 1690, 1711, 1712, 1723, 1724, 1730, 1731, 1732, 1733, 1734, 1737, 1748, 1778, 1779, 1780, 1793, 1794, 1799, 1801,

1814, 1825, 1826, 1827, 1828,
1829, 1861
PRETORIUS, Dewald 1592, 1652,
1653, 1655
PRINCE, Ashwell Gavin 1591, 1592,
1593, 1621, 1622, 1628, 1629,
1737, 1738, 1746, 1747, 1748,
1778, 1779, 1780, 1792, 1793,
1794, 1799, 1800, 1801, 1813,
1814, 1825, 1826, 1827, 1828,
1829, 1830, 1843, 1844, 1847,
1848, 1859, 1860, 1861, 1864,
1865, 1871, 1872, 1873, 1880,
1881, 1882, 1883, 1893, 1894,
1915

RUDOLPH, Jacobus Andries 1642,
1643, 1652, 1653, 1654, 1655,
1656, 1677, 1678, 1679, 1680,
1688, 1689, 1690, 1711, 1712,
1723, 1724, 1730, 1731, 1732,
1733, 1734, 1737, 1738, 1745,

1746, 1778, 1779, 1780, 1792,
1793, 1794, 1813, 1814

SMITH, Graeme Craig 1592, 1593,
1621, 1622, 1628, 1629, 1636,
1637, 1642, 1643, 1652, 1653,
1654, 1655, 1656, 1664, 1665,
1677, 1678, 1679, 1680, 1688,
1689, 1690, 1711, 1712, 1723,
1724, 1730, 1731, 1732, 1733,
1734, 1737, 1738, 1745, 1746,
1747, 1748, 1778, 1779, 1780,
1792, 1793, 1799, 1800, 1801,
1825, 1826, 1827, 1828, 1829,
1830, 1843, 1844, 1847, 1848,
1859, 1860, 1861, 1864, 1865,
1871, 1872, 1873, 1880, 1881,
1882, 1883, 1893, 1894, 1901,
1902, 1903, 1913, 1914
STEYN, Dale Willem 1730, 1731,
1733, 1799, 1801, 1813, 1814,
1825, 1827, 1830, 1843, 1844,

1847, 1859, 1860, 1861, 1864,
1865, 1871, 1872, 1873, 1880,
1881, 1893, 1894, 1901, 1902,
1903, 1913, 1914, 1915

TERBRUGGE, David John 1593,
1621, 1689
TSOLEKILE, Thami Lungisa 1723,
1724, 1730

van JAARSVELD, Martin 1621, 1622,
1628, 1677, 1690, 1711, 1712,
1723, 1731

WILLOUGHBY, Charl Myles 1642,
1652

ZONDEKI, Monde 1655, 1738, 1746,
1747, 1748, 1894

WEST INDIES

ADAMS, James Clive 1521, 1522,
1523, 1524, 1525
AUSTIN, Ryan Anthony 1929, 1930

BAKER, Lionel Sionne 1897, 1910,
1919, 1920
BANKS, Omari Ahmed Clemente
1640, 1641, 1648, 1649, 1669,
1704, 1707, 1708, 1755, 1756
BAUGH, Carlton Seymour 1639, 1640,
1678, 1709, 1710
BENN, Sulieman Jamaal 1869, 1879,
1898, 1906, 1907, 1908, 1909,
1919, 1920
BERNARD, David Eddison 1639,
1929, 1930
BEST, Tino la Bertram 1640, 1691,
1692, 1693, 1694, 1703, 1704,
1707, 1748, 1754, 1755, 1756,
1929, 1930
BLACK, Marlon Ian 1521, 1522, 1523,
1556, 1573, 1599
BRADSHAW, Ian David Russell 1789,
1790, 1791, 1805, 1806
BRAVO, Dwayne John 1707, 1708,
1709, 1710, 1746, 1747, 1748,
1770, 1771, 1789, 1790, 1791,
1805, 1806, 1807, 1808, 1815,
1816, 1817, 1831, 1832, 1833,
1834, 1859, 1860, 1861, 1869,
1870, 1877, 1878, 1879
BREESE, Gareth Rohan 1619
BROWNE, Courtney Oswald 1556,
1745, 1746, 1747, 1748, 1753, 1754

CAMPBELL, Sherwin Legay 1521,
1522, 1523, 1524, 1525, 1587
CHANDERPAUL, Shivnarine 1521,
1542, 1543, 1555, 1556, 1587,
1588, 1598, 1599, 1600, 1601,
1602, 1607, 1608, 1618, 1619,
1620, 1632, 1633, 1638, 1640,
1641, 1668, 1669, 1677, 1678,
1680, 1691, 1692, 1693, 1703,
1704, 1707, 1708, 1709, 1710,
1745, 1746, 1747, 1748, 1753,
1754, 1755, 1756, 1769, 1770,
1771, 1789, 1790, 1791, 1805,
1806, 1807, 1808, 1815, 1816,
1817, 1831, 1833, 1834, 1859,
1860, 1861, 1869, 1870, 1877,
1878, 1879, 1897, 1898, 1906,
1907, 1908, 1909, 1910, 1919,
1920

CHATTERGOON, Sewnarine 1870,
1879, 1897, 1898
COLLINS, Pedro Tyrone 1555, 1572,
1573, 1587, 1588, 1600, 1601,
1602, 1607, 1608, 1618, 1619,
1632, 1633, 1638, 1639, 1692,
1693, 1694, 1703, 1704, 1707,
1708, 1709, 1745, 1746, 1806,
1807, 1808
COLLYMORE, Corey Dalanelo 1648,
1649, 1668, 1669, 1677, 1680,
1691, 1692, 1693, 1694, 1708,
1709, 1710, 1753, 1754, 1769,
1770, 1771, 1805, 1806, 1807,
1808, 1815, 1816, 1817, 1831,
1832, 1833, 1834
CUFFY, Cameron Eustace 1541, 1543,
1587, 1588, 1598, 1599, 1600,
1601, 1602, 1608, 1618, 1620

DEONARINE, Narsingh 1745, 1748,
1755, 1756
DILLON, Mervyn 1521, 1522, 1523,
1524, 1539, 1540, 1541, 1542,
1543, 1571, 1572, 1573, 1587,
1588, 1598, 1599, 1600, 1601,
1602, 1607, 1618, 1619, 1620,
1638, 1639, 1641, 1648, 1669,
1677, 1678, 1680
DOWLIN, Travis Montague 1929,
1930
DRAKES, Vasbert Conniel 1632, 1633,
1638, 1639, 1640, 1641, 1649,
1668, 1677, 1678, 1679, 1680

EDWARDS, Fidel Henderson 1649,
1668, 1669, 1677, 1678, 1679,
1680, 1691, 1693, 1694, 1703,
1704, 1707, 1709, 1710, 1747,
1753, 1769, 1770, 1771, 1789,
1790, 1791, 1805, 1815, 1833,
1834, 1859, 1860, 1861, 1870,
1877, 1878, 1879, 1897, 1898,
1906, 1907, 1908, 1909, 1910,
1919, 1920

GANGA, Daren 1521, 1522, 1523,
1524, 1555, 1556, 1571, 1572,
1573, 1587, 1588, 1632, 1633,
1638, 1639, 1640, 1641, 1648,
1668, 1669, 1677, 1678, 1679,
1680, 1693, 1694, 1745, 1789,
1790, 1791, 1805, 1806, 1807,
1808, 1815, 1816, 1817, 1831,

1832, 1833, 1834, 1859, 1860,
1861
GARRICK, Leon Vivian 1543
GAYLE, Christopher Henry 1539, 1540,
1541, 1542, 1543, 1555, 1556,
1571, 1572, 1573, 1587, 1588,
1598, 1599, 1600, 1601, 1602,
1607, 1608, 1618, 1619, 1620,
1632, 1633, 1640, 1641, 1648,
1649, 1668, 1669, 1677, 1679,
1680, 1691, 1692, 1693, 1694,
1703, 1704, 1707, 1708, 1709,
1710, 1746, 1747, 1748, 1753,
1754, 1769, 1770, 1789, 1790,
1791, 1805, 1806, 1807, 1808,
1815, 1816, 1817, 1831, 1832,
1833, 1834, 1859, 1860, 1869,
1870, 1879, 1897, 1898, 1906,
1907, 1908, 1909, 1910, 1919, 1920

HINDS, Ryan O'Neal 1587, 1588,
1618, 1619, 1691, 1693, 1694,
1745, 1747, 1869, 1907, 1908,
1909, 1910, 1930
HINDS, Wavell Wayne 1522, 1523,
1524, 1525, 1539, 1540, 1541,
1542, 1587, 1588, 1601, 1602,
1607, 1608, 1618, 1619, 1620,
1632, 1633, 1638, 1639, 1648,
1649, 1668, 1669, 1677, 1678,
1679, 1745, 1746, 1747, 1748,
1753, 1754, 1771
HOOPER, Carl Llewellyn 1539, 1540,
1541, 1542, 1543, 1555, 1556,
1571, 1572, 1573, 1587, 1588,
1598, 1599, 1600, 1601, 1602,
1607, 1608, 1618, 1619, 1620

JACOBS, Ridley Delamore 1521,
1522, 1523, 1524, 1525, 1539,
1540, 1541, 1542, 1543, 1555,
1571, 1572, 1573, 1587, 1588,
1600, 1601, 1602, 1607, 1608,
1618, 1619, 1620, 1632, 1633,
1638, 1641, 1648, 1649, 1668,
1669, 1677, 1678, 1679, 1680,
1691, 1692, 1693, 1694, 1703,
1704, 1707, 1708
JAGGERNAUTH, Amit Sheldon 1877
JOSEPH, Sylvester Cleofoster 1709,
1710, 1755, 1756, 1832

KING, Reon Dane 1555, 1556, 1745,
1746, 1747, 1753, 1754

495

LARA, Brian Charles 1521, 1522, 1523, 1524, 1525, 1539, 1540, 1541, 1542, 1543, 1571, 1572, 1573, 1598, 1599, 1600, 1601, 1602, 1607, 1608, 1638, 1639, 1640, 1641, 1648, 1649, 1668, 1669, 1677, 1678, 1679, 1680, 1691, 1692, 1693, 1694, 1703, 1704, 1707, 1708, 1709, 1710, 1746, 1747, 1748, 1753, 1754, 1769, 1770, 1771, 1789, 1790, 1791, 1805, 1806, 1807, 1808, 1815, 1816, 1817

LAWSON, Jermaine Jay Charles 1619, 1620, 1632, 1633, 1638, 1640, 1641, 1703, 1708, 1710, 1755, 1756, 1769

LEWIS, Rawl Nicholas 1790, 1860

McGARRELL, Neil Christopher 1542, 1555, 1556, 1571

McLEAN, Nixon Alexei McNamara 1521, 1522, 1523, 1524, 1525, 1539, 1540

MARSHALL, Xavier Melbourne 1755, 1756, 1878, 1879, 1897, 1898, 1906

MILLER, Nikita O'Neil 1929

MOHAMMED, Dave 1679, 1709, 1805, 1815, 1816

MORTON, Runako Shakur 1755, 1756, 1790, 1791, 1816, 1817, 1831, 1832, 1833, 1834, 1859, 1860, 1861, 1877, 1878

MURRAY, Junior Randalph 1598, 1599

NAGAMOOTOO, Mahendra Veeren 1525, 1598, 1608, 1618

NASH, Brendan Paul 1897, 1898, 1906, 1907, 1908, 1909, 1910, 1919, 1920

PAGON, Donovan Jomo 1745, 1746

PARCHMENT, Brenton Anthony 1861, 1877

PHILLIPS, Omar Jamel 1929, 1930

POWELL, Daren Brentlyle 1607, 1620, 1632, 1633, 1694, 1745, 1746, 1747, 1748, 1753, 1754, 1755, 1756, 1769, 1770, 1771, 1790, 1791, 1816, 1817, 1831, 1832, 1834, 1859, 1860, 1861, 1869, 1870, 1877, 1878, 1879, 1897, 1898, 1906, 1907, 1908, 1909, 1910

RAMDASS, Ryan Rakesh 1756

RAMDIN, Denesh 1755, 1756, 1769, 1770, 1771, 1789, 1790, 1791, 1805, 1806, 1807, 1808, 1815, 1816, 1817, 1831, 1832, 1833, 1834, 1859, 1860, 1861, 1869, 1870, 1877, 1878, 1879, 1897, 1898, 1906, 1907, 1908, 1909, 1910, 1919, 1920

RAMNARINE, Dinanath 1539, 1540, 1541, 1542, 1543, 1571, 1572, 1573, 1588

REIFER, Floyd Lamonte 1929, 1930

RICHARDS, Dale Maurice 1929, 1930

ROACH, Kemar Andre Jamal 1929, 1930

SAMMY, Darren Julius Garvey 1833, 1859, 1861, 1877, 1878, 1929, 1930

SAMUELS, Marlon Nathaniel 1523, 1524, 1525, 1539, 1540, 1541, 1543, 1555, 1556, 1571, 1572, 1573, 1620, 1632, 1633, 1638, 1639, 1648, 1649, 1769, 1770, 1807, 1808, 1834, 1859, 1860, 1861, 1869, 1870

SANFORD, Adam 1598, 1599, 1600, 1601, 1602, 1607, 1608, 1678, 1679, 1691, 1692

SARWAN, Ramnaresh Ronnie 1521, 1522, 1525, 1539, 1540, 1541, 1542, 1555, 1556, 1571, 1572, 1573, 1598, 1599, 1600, 1601, 1602, 1607, 1608, 1618, 1619, 1620, 1632, 1633, 1639, 1640, 1641, 1648, 1649, 1668, 1669, 1677, 1678, 1679, 1680, 1691, 1692, 1693, 1694, 1703, 1704, 1707, 1708, 1709, 1710, 1746, 1747, 1748, 1753, 1754, 1769, 1770, 1771, 1789, 1805, 1806, 1807, 1808, 1815, 1817, 1831, 1832, 1869, 1870, 1877, 1878, 1879, 1897, 1898, 1906, 1907, 1908, 1909, 1910, 1919, 1920

SIMMONS, Lendl Mark Platter 1910, 1919, 1920

SMITH, Devon Sheldon 1638, 1639, 1640, 1641, 1691, 1692, 1703, 1704, 1707, 1708, 1745, 1753, 1754, 1769, 1770, 1771, 1831, 1832, 1833, 1834, 1869, 1870, 1877, 1878, 1906, 1907, 1908, 1909, 1910, 1919, 1920

SMITH, Dwayne Romel 1679, 1680, 1692, 1703, 1704, 1710, 1755, 1771, 1789, 1791

STUART, Colin Ellsworth Laurie 1524, 1525, 1555, 1556, 1571, 1572

TAYLOR, Jerome Everton 1648, 1649, 1668, 1789, 1806, 1807, 1808, 1815, 1816, 1817, 1831, 1832, 1833, 1859, 1860, 1861, 1869, 1870, 1878, 1879, 1897, 1898, 1906, 1907, 1908, 1909, 1919, 1920

WALSH, Courtney Andrew 1521, 1522, 1523, 1524, 1525, 1539, 1540, 1541, 1542, 1543

WALTON, Chadwick Antonio Kirkpatrick 1929, 1930

WASHINGTON, Dwight Marlon 1748

WILLIAMS, Stuart Clayton 1598, 1599, 1600

NEW ZEALAND

ADAMS, Andre Richard 1597

ASTLE, Nathan John 1510, 1511, 1516, 1517, 1518, 1526, 1536, 1537, 1538, 1566, 1567, 1568, 1580, 1595, 1596, 1597, 1607, 1608, 1635, 1660, 1661, 1700, 1701, 1702, 1717, 1718, 1721, 1722, 1742, 1743, 1744, 1749, 1750, 1762, 1763, 1789, 1790, 1791, 1799, 1800, 1801, 1823, 1824

BELL, Matthew David 1536, 1537, 1538, 1566, 1567, 1862, 1863, 1866, 1867, 1868

BOND, Shane Edward 1567, 1568, 1580, 1581, 1607, 1608, 1634, 1635, 1644, 1645, 1763, 1789, 1791, 1823, 1824, 1847

BRADBURN, Grant Eric 1537, 1538

BUTLER, Ian Gareth 1595, 1596, 1607, 1608, 1661, 1681, 1682, 1717

CAIRNS, Christopher Lance 1510, 1511, 1566, 1567, 1568, 1580, 1581, 1595, 1681, 1688, 1689, 1690, 1700, 1701, 1702

CUMMING, Craig Derek 1742, 1743, 1744, 1749, 1750, 1823, 1824, 1847, 1848, 1862, 1863

DRUM, Christopher James 1537, 1581, 1595, 1596, 1597

ELLIOTT, Grant David 1868, 1892, 1895

FLEMING, Stephen Paul 1510, 1511, 1516, 1517, 1518, 1526, 1536, 1537, 1538, 1566, 1567, 1568, 1580, 1581, 1595, 1596, 1597, 1603, 1607, 1608, 1634, 1635, 1644, 1645, 1660, 1661, 1681, 1682, 1688, 1689, 1690, 1700, 1701, 1702, 1717, 1718, 1721, 1722, 1742, 1743, 1744, 1749, 1750, 1762, 1763, 1789, 1790, 1791, 1799, 1800, 1801, 1823, 1824, 1847, 1848, 1862, 1863, 1866, 1867, 1868

FLYNN, Daniel Raymond 1874, 1875, 1876, 1891, 1892, 1895, 1896, 1897, 1898, 1916, 1918, 1931, 1932

FRANKLIN, James Edward Charles 1536, 1538, 1702, 1717, 1718, 1722, 1742, 1743, 1744, 1749, 1750, 1762, 1763, 1789, 1790, 1791, 1799, 1800, 1801, 1823, 1824, 1897, 1898, 1916, 1917, 1918

FULTON, Peter Gordon 1789, 1790, 1791, 1799, 1800, 1862, 1863, 1896

GILLESPIE, Mark Raymond 1848, 1867, 1897

GUPTILL, Martin James 1916, 1917, 1918, 1931, 1932

HARRIS, Chris Zinzan 1597, 1603, 1607, 1608

HART, Robert Garry 1603, 1607, 1608, 1634, 1635, 1644, 1645, 1660, 1661, 1681, 1682

HOPKINS, Gareth James 1876

HORNE, Matthew Jeffery 1510, 1526, 1581, 1595, 1596, 1603, 1644, 1645

HOW, Jamie Michael 1789, 1790, 1791, 1801, 1823, 1824, 1866, 1867, 1868, 1874, 1875, 1876, 1891, 1892, 1895, 1896, 1897, 1898, 1917

JONES, Richard Andrew 1682

McCULLUM, Brendon Barrie 1688, 1689, 1690, 1700, 1701, 1702, 1717, 1718, 1721, 1722, 1742, 1743, 1744, 1749, 1750, 1762, 1763, 1789, 1790, 1791, 1799, 1800, 1801, 1823, 1824, 1847,

1848, 1862, 1863, 1866, 1867,
1868, 1874, 1875, 1876, 1891,
1892, 1895, 1896, 1897, 1898,
1916, 1917, 1918, 1931, 1932
McINTOSH, Timothy Gavin 1897,
1898, 1916, 1917, 1918, 1931, 1932
McMILLAN, Craig Douglas 1510,
1511, 1516, 1517, 1518, 1526,
1536, 1537, 1538, 1566, 1567,
1568, 1580, 1581, 1595, 1596,
1597, 1603, 1607, 1608, 1634,
1635, 1660, 1661, 1681, 1682,
1688, 1689, 1700, 1702, 1721,
1742, 1743
MARSHALL, Hamish John Hamilton
1518, 1718, 1742, 1743, 1744,
1749, 1750, 1762, 1763, 1789,
1790, 1791, 1799
MARSHALL, James Andrew Hamilton
1744, 1749, 1750, 1762, 1763,
1874, 1875
MARTIN, Christopher Stewart 1516,
1517, 1536, 1537, 1538, 1568,
1580, 1596, 1603, 1689, 1690,
1700, 1701, 1702, 1721, 1722,
1742, 1743, 1744, 1749, 1763,
1789, 1790, 1791, 1799, 1800,
1801, 1823, 1824, 1847, 1848,
1862, 1863, 1866, 1867, 1868,
1874, 1875, 1876, 1895, 1896,
1916, 1917, 1918, 1931, 1932
MASON, Michael James 1690
MILLS, Kyle David 1702, 1721, 1749,
1750, 1790, 1799, 1801, 1862,
1863, 1866, 1867, 1874, 1875,
1876, 1891, 1892, 1897, 1898,
1916

NASH, Dion Joseph 1511, 1566

O'BRIEN, Iain Edward 1742, 1743,
1847, 1848, 1862, 1863, 1875,
1876, 1891, 1892, 1895, 1896,
1897, 1898, 1916, 1917, 1918,
1931, 1932
O'CONNOR, Shayne Barry 1510,
1511, 1516, 1517, 1566

ORAM, Jacob David Philip 1634,
1635, 1644, 1645, 1660, 1681,
1682, 1688, 1689, 1690, 1700,
1701, 1702, 1717, 1718, 1721,
1722, 1799, 1800, 1801, 1823,
1824, 1847, 1862, 1863, 1866,
1867, 1874, 1875, 1876, 1891,
1931, 1932

PAPPS, Michael Hugh William 1688,
1689, 1690, 1701, 1800, 1801,
1847, 1848
PARORE, Adam Craig 1510, 1511,
1516, 1517, 1518, 1526, 1536,
1537, 1538, 1566, 1568, 1580,
1581, 1595, 1596, 1597
PATEL, Jeetan Shashi 1800, 1866,
1868, 1891, 1892, 1898, 1917,
1931, 1932

REDMOND, Aaron James 1874,
1875, 1876, 1891, 1892, 1895,
1896
RICHARDSON, Mark Hunter 1510,
1511, 1516, 1517, 1518, 1526,
1536, 1537, 1538, 1566, 1567,
1568, 1580, 1581, 1595, 1596,
1597, 1603, 1607, 1608, 1634,
1635, 1644, 1645, 1660, 1661,
1681, 1682, 1688, 1689, 1690,
1700, 1701, 1702, 1717, 1718,
1721, 1722
RYDER, Jesse Daniel 1891, 1892,
1895, 1896, 1897, 1898, 1916,
1917, 1918, 1931, 1932

SINCLAIR, Mathew Stuart 1510,
1511, 1516, 1517, 1518, 1526,
1536, 1537, 1538, 1566, 1567,
1568, 1580, 1581, 1644, 1645,
1690, 1717, 1718, 1721, 1722,
1823, 1824, 1862, 1863, 1866,
1867, 1868
SOUTHEE, Timothy Grant 1868, 1874,
1895, 1896, 1918
SPEARMAN, Craig Murray 1511,
1516, 1517

STYRIS, Scott Bernard 1608, 1634,
1635, 1644, 1645, 1660, 1661,
1681, 1682, 1688, 1689, 1690,
1700, 1701, 1702, 1717, 1718,
1721, 1722, 1762, 1763, 1789,
1790, 1791, 1799, 1800, 1801,
1847, 1848

TAYLOR, Luteru Ross Poutoa Lote
1847, 1848, 1866, 1867, 1868,
1874, 1875, 1876, 1891, 1892,
1895, 1896, 1897, 1898, 1916,
1917, 1918, 1931, 1932
TUFFEY, Daryl Raymond 1516, 1518,
1536, 1537, 1538, 1567, 1597,
1603, 1607, 1634, 1635, 1644,
1645, 1660, 1661, 1681, 1682,
1688, 1689, 1700, 1701

VETTORI, Daniel Luca 1510, 1566,
1568, 1580, 1581, 1595, 1596,
1597, 1603, 1607, 1608, 1634,
1635, 1644, 1645, 1660, 1661,
1681, 1682, 1688, 1689, 1690,
1700, 1701, 1717, 1718, 1721,
1722, 1742, 1743, 1744, 1762,
1763, 1789, 1790, 1791, 1799,
1800, 1801, 1823, 1824, 1847,
1848, 1862, 1863, 1866, 1867,
1868, 1874, 1875, 1876, 1891,
1892, 1895, 1896, 1897, 1898,
1916, 1917, 1918, 1931, 1932
VINCENT, Lou 1568, 1580, 1581,
1595, 1596, 1597, 1603, 1607,
1608, 1634, 1635, 1660, 1661,
1681, 1682, 1742, 1743, 1744,
1749, 1750, 1762, 1763, 1848

WALKER, Brooke Graeme Keith
1516, 1517, 1518, 1526, 1603
WALMSLEY, Kerry Peter 1517
WISEMAN, Paul John 1510, 1511,
1526, 1536, 1644, 1645, 1660,
1661, 1688, 1717, 1718, 1722,
1744, 1749

INDIA

AGARKAR, Ajit Bhalchandra 1512,
1519, 1520, 1533, 1549, 1565,
1611, 1612, 1613, 1614, 1634,
1673, 1674, 1675, 1676, 1696,
1715, 1775, 1776, 1777, 1781

BADANI, Hemang Kamal 1549, 1557,
1558, 1559
BAHUTULE, Sairaj Vasant 1535, 1559
BALAJI, Lakshmipathy 1660, 1661,
1695, 1696, 1697, 1739, 1740, 1741
BANGAR, Sanjay Bapusaheb 1574,
1589, 1590, 1598, 1599, 1613,
1614, 1618, 1619, 1620, 1634, 1635

CHAWLA, Piyush Pramod 1787, 1873
CHOPRA, Aakash 1660, 1661, 1673,
1674, 1675, 1676, 1695, 1696,
1713, 1715

DAHIYA, Vijay 1519, 1520
DAS, Shiv Sunder 1512, 1519, 1520,
1533, 1534, 1535, 1548, 1549,
1557, 1558, 1559, 1564, 1565,
1574, 1575, 1576, 1589, 1590,
1598, 1599, 1600, 1601, 1602
DASGUPTA, Deep 1564, 1565, 1574,
1575, 1576, 1589, 1590, 1598
DHONI, Mahendra Singh 1775, 1776,

1777, 1781, 1782, 1783, 1786,
1787, 1788, 1805, 1806, 1807,
1808, 1825, 1826, 1835, 1836,
1840, 1841, 1842, 1849, 1850,
1855, 1856, 1857, 1858, 1871,
1872, 1873, 1887, 1888, 1889,
1890, 1899, 1900, 1916, 1918
DIGHE, Sameer Sudhakar 1535, 1548,
1549, 1557, 1558, 1559
DRAVID, Rahul 1512, 1519, 1520,
1533, 1534, 1535, 1548, 1549,
1557, 1558, 1559, 1564, 1565,
1574, 1575, 1576, 1589, 1590,
1598, 1599, 1600, 1601, 1602,
1611, 1612, 1613, 1614, 1618,
1619, 1620, 1634, 1635, 1660,
1661, 1673, 1674, 1675, 1676,
1695, 1696, 1697, 1713, 1714,
1715, 1716, 1723, 1724, 1725,
1726, 1739, 1740, 1741, 1766,
1767, 1775, 1776, 1781, 1782,
1783, 1786, 1787, 1788, 1805,
1806, 1807, 1808, 1825, 1826,
1827, 1835, 1836, 1840, 1841,
1842, 1849, 1850, 1851, 1855,
1856, 1857, 1858, 1871, 1872,
1873, 1884, 1885, 1886, 1887,
1888, 1889, 1890, 1899, 1900,
1916, 1917, 1918

GAMBHIR, Gautam 1716, 1723, 1724,
1725, 1726, 1739, 1740, 1741,
1766, 1767, 1775, 1776, 1777,
1851, 1884, 1885, 1886, 1887,
1888, 1889, 1899, 1900, 1916,
1917, 1918
GANGULY, Sourav Chandidas 1512,
1519, 1520, 1533, 1534, 1535,
1548, 1549, 1557, 1558, 1559,
1564, 1565, 1574, 1575, 1576,
1589, 1590, 1598, 1599, 1600,
1601, 1602, 1611, 1612, 1613,
1614, 1618, 1619, 1620, 1634,
1635, 1660, 1673, 1674, 1675,
1676, 1697, 1713, 1714, 1723,
1724, 1725, 1726, 1739, 1740,
1741, 1766, 1767, 1775, 1776,
1781, 1783, 1825, 1826, 1827,
1835, 1836, 1840, 1841, 1842,
1849, 1850, 1851, 1855, 1856,
1857, 1858, 1871, 1872, 1873,
1884, 1885, 1886, 1887, 1888,
1889, 1890

HARBHAJAN SINGH 1533, 1534,
1535, 1548, 1549, 1557, 1558,
1559, 1565, 1574, 1575, 1576,
1589, 1590, 1599, 1600, 1602,
1612, 1613, 1614, 1618, 1619,

1620, 1634, 1635, 1660, 1661,
1673, 1713, 1714, 1716, 1723,
1724, 1725, 1726, 1740, 1741,
1766, 1767, 1775, 1776, 1777,
1781, 1782, 1786, 1787, 1788,
1807, 1808, 1849, 1850, 1851,
1855, 1856, 1858, 1871, 1872,
1873, 1884, 1885, 1886, 1887,
1888, 1890, 1899, 1900, 1916,
1917, 1918
HARVINDER SINGH 1558

JOSHI, Sunil Bandacharya 1512, 1519,
1520

KAIF, Mohammad 1557, 1558, 1559,
1714, 1715, 1716, 1777, 1786,
1805, 1806, 1807, 1808
KARIM, Syed Saba 1512
KARTHIK, Krishnakumar Dinesh
1716, 1723, 1724, 1725, 1726,
1739, 1740, 1741, 1766, 1767,
1827, 1835, 1836, 1840, 1841,
1842, 1849, 1850, 1851, 1884,
1885, 1917
KARTIK, Murali 1512, 1519, 1676,
1715, 1716, 1723
KULKARNI, Nilesh Moreshwar
1535
KUMBLE, Anil 1564, 1565, 1574,
1575, 1576, 1589, 1590, 1598,
1601, 1611, 1613, 1614, 1618,
1619, 1620, 1660, 1661, 1674,
1675, 1676, 1695, 1696, 1697,
1713, 1714, 1715, 1716, 1723,
1724, 1725, 1726, 1739, 1740,
1741, 1766, 1767, 1775, 1776,
1777, 1781, 1782, 1783, 1786,
1787, 1788, 1805, 1806, 1807,
1808, 1825, 1826, 1827, 1835,
1836, 1840, 1841, 1842, 1849,
1850, 1851, 1855, 1856, 1857,
1858, 1871, 1872, 1884, 1885,
1886, 1887, 1889

LAXMAN, Vangipurappu Venkata Sai
1519, 1533, 1534, 1535, 1548,
1549, 1564, 1565, 1574, 1575,
1576, 1589, 1598, 1599, 1600,
1601, 1602, 1611, 1612, 1613,
1614, 1618, 1619, 1620, 1634,
1635, 1660, 1661, 1673, 1674,
1675, 1676, 1695, 1696, 1697,
1713, 1714, 1715, 1716, 1723,
1724, 1725, 1726, 1739, 1740,
1741, 1766, 1767, 1775, 1776,
1777, 1781, 1782, 1783, 1786,
1805, 1806, 1807, 1808, 1825,
1826, 1827, 1840, 1841, 1842,
1849, 1850, 1851, 1855, 1856,
1857, 1858, 1871, 1872, 1873,
1884, 1885, 1886, 1887, 1888,
1889, 1890, 1899, 1900, 1916,
1917, 1918

MISHRA, Amit 1888, 1889, 1890,
1899, 1900
MONGIA, Nayan Ramlal 1533, 1534

NEHRA, Ashish 1548, 1549, 1564,
1599, 1600, 1601, 1602, 1611,
1612, 1620, 1634, 1635, 1673,
1674, 1675, 1697

PATEL, Munaf Musa 1618, 1787,
1788, 1805, 1806, 1807, 1808,
1827, 1849, 1850, 1916, 1917,
1918
PATEL, Parthiv Ajay 1612, 1613,
1619, 1620, 1634, 1635, 1660,
1661, 1673, 1674, 1675, 1676,
1695, 1696, 1697, 1713, 1714,
1715, 1886
PATHAN, Irfan Khan 1674, 1676,
1695, 1696, 1697, 1713, 1714,
1724, 1725, 1726, 1739, 1740,
1741, 1766, 1767, 1775, 1776,
1777, 1781, 1782, 1783, 1786,
1787, 1788, 1806, 1851, 1857,
1858, 1872
POWAR, Ramesh Rajaram 1835,
1836
PRASAD, Bapu Krishnarao Venkatesh
1534, 1557, 1558, 1559

RAJU, Sagi Lakshmi Venkatapathy
1534
RAMESH, Sadogoppan 1512, 1519,
1520, 1533, 1534, 1535, 1548,
1557, 1558, 1559
RATRA, Ajay 1599, 1600, 1601, 1602,
1611, 1614

SANGHVI, Rahul Laxman 1533
SARANDEEP SINGH 1520, 1576,
1598
SEHWAG, Virender 1564, 1565, 1575,
1576, 1590, 1611, 1612, 1613,
1614, 1618, 1619, 1620, 1634,
1635, 1660, 1661, 1673, 1674,
1675, 1676, 1695, 1696, 1697,
1713, 1714, 1715, 1716, 1723,
1724, 1725, 1726, 1739, 1740,
1741, 1766, 1767, 1775, 1777,
1781, 1782, 1783, 1786, 1787,
1788, 1805, 1806, 1807, 1808,
1825, 1826, 1827, 1857, 1858,
1871, 1872, 1873, 1884, 1885,
1886, 1887, 1888, 1889, 1890,
1899, 1900, 1916, 1917, 1918
SHARMA, Ishant 1836, 1851, 1856,
1857, 1858, 1873, 1884, 1885,
1886, 1887, 1888, 1889, 1890,
1899, 1900, 1916, 1917, 1918
SIDDIQUI, Iqbal Rashid 1574
SINGH, Rudra Pratap 1782, 1783,
1835, 1836, 1840, 1841, 1842,
1855, 1856, 1857, 1858, 1871,
1872

SINGH, Vikram Rajvir 1805, 1806,
1825, 1826, 1835
SREESANTH, Shanthakumaran 1786,
1788, 1805, 1807, 1808, 1825,
1826, 1827, 1840, 1841, 1842,
1871, 1872, 1873
SRINATH, Javagal 1512, 1519, 1520,
1533, 1548, 1549, 1557, 1564,
1565, 1575, 1576, 1589, 1590,
1598, 1599, 1600, 1601, 1602,
1618, 1619, 1620

TENDULKAR, Sachin Ramesh 1512,
1519, 1520, 1533, 1534, 1535,
1548, 1549, 1564, 1565, 1574,
1575, 1576, 1589, 1590, 1598,
1599, 1600, 1601, 1602, 1611,
1612, 1613, 1614, 1618, 1619,
1620, 1634, 1635, 1660, 1661,
1673, 1674, 1675, 1676, 1695,
1696, 1697, 1715, 1716, 1723,
1724, 1725, 1726, 1739, 1740,
1741, 1775, 1776, 1777, 1781,
1782, 1783, 1786, 1787, 1788,
1825, 1826, 1827, 1835, 1836,
1840, 1841, 1842, 1849, 1850,
1855, 1856, 1857, 1858, 1871,
1884, 1885, 1886, 1887, 1888,
1889, 1890, 1899, 1900, 1916,
1917, 1918

VIJAY, Murali 1890

WASIM JAFFER 1600, 1601, 1602,
1611, 1612, 1786, 1787, 1788,
1805, 1806, 1807, 1808, 1825,
1826, 1827, 1835, 1836, 1840,
1841, 1842, 1849, 1850, 1851,
1855, 1856, 1857, 1871, 1872,
1873

YOHANNAN, Tinu 1574, 1575, 1635
YUVRAJ SINGH 1661, 1695, 1696,
1697, 1713, 1714, 1766, 1767,
1776, 1777, 1781, 1782, 1783,
1787, 1788, 1805, 1806, 1807,
1808, 1851, 1855, 1856, 1873,
1899, 1900, 1916, 1917, 1918

ZAHEER KHAN 1512, 1520, 1534,
1535, 1548, 1557, 1558, 1559,
1564, 1589, 1590, 1598, 1599,
1600, 1601, 1602, 1611, 1612,
1613, 1614, 1618, 1619, 1634,
1635, 1660, 1661, 1673, 1675,
1695, 1713, 1714, 1715, 1716,
1723, 1724, 1725, 1726, 1739,
1766, 1767, 1782, 1783, 1825,
1826, 1827, 1835, 1836, 1840,
1841, 1842, 1849, 1850, 1855,
1884, 1885, 1886, 1887, 1888,
1889, 1890, 1899, 1900, 1916,
1917, 1918

PAKISTAN

ABDUL RAZZAQ 1513, 1514, 1515,
1546, 1547, 1560, 1585, 1586,
1587, 1588, 1594, 1603, 1615,
1616, 1636, 1665, 1681, 1682,
1695, 1719, 1720, 1727, 1728,
1739, 1740, 1741, 1753, 1754,
1782, 1783, 1795, 1796, 1809,
1810, 1815, 1816, 1817
ABDUR RAUF 1921, 1922
ABDUR REHMAN 1843, 1844
ARSHAD KHAN 1514, 1741
ASIM KAMAL 1664, 1665, 1696,

1697, 1719, 1729, 1739, 1740,
1741, 1753, 1754, 1774
AZHAR MAHMOOD 1546, 1547

BAZID KHAN 1753

DANISH KANERIA 1514, 1515,
1560, 1585, 1586, 1587, 1588,
1603, 1616, 1617, 1657, 1658,
1664, 1665, 1681, 1682, 1696,
1697, 1719, 1720, 1727, 1728,
1729, 1739, 1740, 1741, 1753,

1754, 1772, 1773, 1781, 1782,
1783, 1795, 1796, 1809, 1810,
1811, 1812, 1815, 1816, 1817,
1828, 1829, 1830, 1843, 1844,
1849, 1850, 1851, 1911, 1912,
1923

FAISAL IQBAL 1536, 1537, 1538,
1547, 1560, 1615, 1616, 1617,
1636, 1637, 1783, 1795, 1796,
1809, 1810, 1811, 1812, 1828,
1843, 1850, 1851, 1911, 1912

FARHAN ADIL 1659
FAWAD ALAM 1922, 1923
FAZL-E-AKBAR 1537, 1538, 1697

HASAN RAZA 1617, 1630, 1631,
  1772, 1774
HUMAYUN FARHAT 1538

IFTIKHAR ANJUM 1796
IJAZ AHMED, sen. 1537, 1538
IMRAN FARHAT 1536, 1537, 1538,
  1617, 1664, 1665, 1681, 1682,
  1695, 1696, 1697, 1719, 1720,
  1727, 1728, 1783, 1795, 1796,
  1809, 1810, 1812, 1815, 1816,
  1817, 1828, 1829, 1830
IMRAN NAZIR 1515, 1603, 1615, 1616
INZAMAM-UL-HAQ 1513, 1514,
  1515, 1537, 1538, 1546, 1547,
  1560, 1585, 1586, 1587, 1588,
  1594, 1603, 1630, 1631, 1636,
  1637, 1657, 1658, 1659, 1665,
  1681, 1682, 1695, 1696, 1697,
  1719, 1720, 1727, 1739, 1740,
  1741, 1754, 1772, 1773, 1774,
  1781, 1782, 1795, 1796, 1809,
  1810, 1811, 1812, 1815, 1816,
  1817, 1828, 1829, 1830, 1844

KAMRAN AKMAL 1630, 1631, 1636,
  1637, 1696, 1697, 1720, 1727,
  1728, 1729, 1739, 1740, 1741,
  1753, 1754, 1772, 1773, 1774,
  1781, 1782, 1783, 1795, 1796,
  1809, 1810, 1811, 1812, 1815,
  1816, 1817, 1828, 1829, 1830,
  1843, 1844, 1849, 1850, 1851,
  1911, 1912, 1921, 1922, 1923
KHURRAM MANZOOR 1911, 1912,
  1921, 1922, 1923

MISBAH-UL-HAQ 1536, 1615, 1616,
  1617, 1657, 1843, 1844, 1849,
  1850, 1851, 1911, 1912, 1921,
  1922, 1923
MOHAMMAD AAMER 1921, 1922,
  1923
MOHAMMAD AKRAM 1538
MOHAMMAD ASIF 1729, 1782,
  1783, 1795, 1796, 1812, 1828,
  1829, 1830, 1843, 1844
MOHAMMAD HAFEEZ 1657, 1658,
  1659, 1812, 1815, 1816, 1817,
  1828, 1829, 1830, 1843
MOHAMMAD KHALIL 1727, 1740
MOHAMMAD SAMI 1536, 1537,
  1594, 1615, 1617, 1630, 1631,
  1636, 1637, 1664, 1681, 1682,
  1695, 1696, 1697, 1719, 1727,
  1728, 1739, 1740, 1741, 1772,
  1773, 1774, 1781, 1809, 1810,

1811, 1829, 1830, 1849, 1850,
  1851
MOHAMMAD TALHA 1912
MOHAMMAD YOUSUF (formerly
  Yousuf Youhana) 1513, 1514,
  1515, 1536, 1537, 1538, 1546,
  1547, 1560, 1585, 1586, 1587,
  1588, 1594, 1603, 1630, 1631,
  1636, 1637, 1657, 1658, 1664,
  1681, 1682, 1695, 1696, 1697,
  1719, 1720, 1727, 1728, 1729,
  1739, 1740, 1741, 1772, 1773,
  1774, 1781, 1782, 1783, 1796,
  1809, 1810, 1811, 1812, 1815,
  1816, 1817, 1829, 1830, 1844,
  1849, 1850, 1851, 1921, 1922,
  1923
MOHAMMAD ZAHID 1637
MOIN KHAN 1513, 1514, 1515, 1536,
  1537, 1664, 1665, 1681, 1682,
  1695, 1719
MUSHTAQ AHMED 1513, 1536,
  1664, 1665

NAVED LATIF 1587
NAVED-UL-HASAN 1720, 1729,
  1739, 1753, 1754, 1773, 1774,
  1781, 1828

QAISER ABBAS 1513

RASHID LATIF 1546, 1547, 1560,
  1585, 1586, 1587, 1588, 1594,
  1603, 1615, 1616, 1617, 1657,
  1658, 1659
RIAZ AFRIDI 1720

SAEED AJMAL 1921, 1922, 1923
SAEED ANWAR 1513, 1514, 1515,
  1546, 1547, 1560
SALIM ELAHI 1513, 1514, 1515,
  1536, 1546, 1630, 1631, 1636,
  1637
SALMAN BUTT 1659, 1727, 1728,
  1729, 1739, 1753, 1772, 1773,
  1774, 1781, 1782, 1783, 1809,
  1811, 1843, 1844, 1849, 1850,
  1851, 1911, 1912, 1921
SAQLAIN MUSHTAQ 1513, 1514,
  1515, 1536, 1537, 1538, 1547,
  1585, 1586, 1587, 1588, 1603,
  1615, 1616, 1617, 1630, 1631,
  1636, 1637, 1659, 1695
SHABBIR AHMED 1657, 1658, 1659,
  1665, 1681, 1682, 1695, 1753,
  1754, 1772
SHADAB KABIR 1585, 1586
SHAHID AFRIDI 1513, 1514, 1515,
  1588, 1594, 1603, 1729, 1740,
  1741, 1753, 1754, 1773, 1781,
  1782, 1783, 1795, 1809, 1810

SHAHID NAZIR 1811, 1812, 1815,
  1816, 1817, 1828, 1830
SHOAIB AKHTAR 1546, 1586, 1587,
  1588, 1603, 1615, 1630, 1631,
  1657, 1658, 1664, 1682, 1695,
  1696, 1697, 1719, 1727, 1728,
  1729, 1772, 1773, 1774, 1781,
  1782, 1783, 1829, 1849, 1850,
  1851
SHOAIB MALIK 1560, 1594, 1658,
  1664, 1665, 1719, 1720, 1728,
  1754, 1772, 1774, 1781, 1782,
  1795, 1815, 1816, 1817, 1843,
  1844, 1849, 1911, 1912, 1921,
  1922, 1923
SOHAIL KHAN 1911
SOHAIL TANVIR 1849, 1850

TAUFEEQ UMAR 1560, 1585, 1586,
  1587, 1588, 1594, 1615, 1616,
  1617, 1630, 1631, 1636, 1637,
  1657, 1658, 1664, 1665, 1681,
  1682, 1695, 1696, 1697, 1739,
  1740, 1811

UMAR GUL 1657, 1658, 1659, 1681,
  1696, 1795, 1796, 1809, 1810,
  1811, 1812, 1815, 1816, 1817,
  1843, 1844, 1911, 1912, 1921,
  1922, 1923

WAQAR YOUNIS 1515, 1536, 1537,
  1538, 1546, 1547, 1560, 1585,
  1586, 1587, 1588, 1594, 1603,
  1615, 1616, 1617, 1630, 1631,
  1636, 1637
WASIM AKRAM 1513, 1514, 1546,
  1547, 1560, 1585

YASIR ALI 1659
YASIR ARAFAT 1851, 1911, 1912
YASIR HAMEED 1657, 1658, 1659,
  1664, 1665, 1681, 1682, 1695,
  1696, 1697, 1719, 1720, 1728,
  1729, 1741, 1753, 1754, 1828,
  1829, 1830, 1849, 1850, 1851
YOUNIS KHAN 1536, 1537, 1538,
  1546, 1547, 1585, 1586, 1587,
  1588, 1594, 1603, 1615, 1616,
  1617, 1630, 1631, 1636, 1637,
  1659, 1720, 1727, 1728, 1729,
  1739, 1740, 1741, 1753, 1754,
  1772, 1773, 1781, 1782, 1783,
  1795, 1796, 1810, 1811, 1812,
  1815, 1816, 1817, 1828, 1829,
  1830, 1843, 1844, 1849, 1850,
  1851, 1911, 1912, 1921, 1922,
  1923
YOUSUF YOUHANA see
  MOHAMMAD YOUSUF
  (formerly Yousuf Youhana)

SRI LANKA

AMERASINGHE, Merenna Koralage
  Don Ishara 1870
ARNOLD, Russel Premakumaran
  1527, 1528, 1529, 1530, 1531,
  1532, 1557, 1558, 1559, 1571,
  1572, 1573, 1582, 1583, 1584,
  1594, 1604, 1605, 1606, 1609,
  1628, 1629, 1705
ATAPATTU, Marvan Samson 1527,
  1528, 1529, 1530, 1531, 1532,
  1557, 1558, 1559, 1561, 1571,
  1572, 1573, 1582, 1583, 1584,
  1594, 1604, 1605, 1606, 1609,
  1628, 1629, 1644, 1645, 1648,
  1649, 1670, 1671, 1672, 1685,

1686, 1687, 1698, 1699, 1705,
  1706, 1711, 1712, 1719, 1720,
  1749, 1750, 1755, 1756, 1765,
  1775, 1776, 1777, 1845, 1846

BANDARA, Charitha Malinga 1775,
  1776, 1777, 1784, 1785, 1795,
  1796
BANDARATILLEKE, Mapa Rallage
  Chandima Niroshan 1571, 1572,
  1573
BUDDHIKA, Charitha see
  FERNANDO, Thudellage Charitha
  Buddhika

CHANDANA, Umagiliya Durage Upul
  1584, 1610, 1670, 1672, 1685,
  1705, 1706, 1711, 1712, 1749,
  1750

de SILVA, Pinnaduwage Aravinda
  1529, 1530, 1531, 1532, 1604,
  1605, 1606, 1609
de SILVA, Weddikkara Ruwan Sujeewa
  1609, 1610
DHARMASENA, Handunnettige
  Deepthi Priyantha Kumar 1530,
  1531, 1644, 1645, 1649, 1670,
  1671, 1685
DILSHAN, Tillekeratne Mudiyanselage

499

1527, 1528, 1530, 1531, 1532, 1671, 1672, 1685, 1686, 1687, 1698, 1699, 1705, 1706, 1711, 1712, 1749, 1750, 1755, 1756, 1764, 1765, 1775, 1776, 1777, 1784, 1785, 1795, 1796, 1802, 1803, 1804, 1813, 1814, 1837, 1838, 1839, 1854, 1869, 1870, 1884, 1885, 1886, 1904, 1905, 1911, 1912, 1921, 1922, 1923, 1931, 1932

FERNANDO, Congenige Randhi
Dilhara 1527, 1528, 1529, 1530, 1532, 1557, 1558, 1559, 1606, 1609, 1628, 1629, 1672, 1719, 1720, 1764, 1765, 1775, 1776, 1784, 1785, 1795, 1813, 1837, 1838, 1845, 1846, 1852, 1853, 1905, 1911, 1912
FERNANDO, Kandage Hasantha
Ruwan Kumara 1628, 1629
FERNANDO, Kandana Arachchige
Dinusha Manoj 1670, 1671
FERNANDO, Thudellage Charitha
Buddhika 1571, 1582, 1583, 1584, 1594, 1604, 1605, 1609, 1610

GAMAGE, Chamila see LAKSHITHA,
Materba Kanatha Gamage Chamila
Premanath
GUNAWARDENE, Dihan Avishka
1528, 1686, 1775, 1776

HERATH, Herath Mudiyanselage
Rangana Keerthi Bandara 1687, 1712, 1719, 1720, 1749, 1755, 1756, 1764, 1765, 1869, 1904, 1921, 1922, 1923, 1932
HETTIARACHCHI, Dinuka 1532

JAYASURIYA, Sanath Teran 1527, 1528, 1529, 1530, 1531, 1532, 1557, 1558, 1559, 1561, 1571, 1572, 1573, 1582, 1583, 1584, 1594, 1604, 1605, 1606, 1609, 1610, 1628, 1644, 1645, 1648, 1649, 1670, 1671, 1672, 1685, 1686, 1687, 1698, 1699, 1705, 1706, 1711, 1712, 1719, 1720, 1749, 1750, 1755, 1756, 1764, 1765, 1795, 1796, 1804, 1813, 1814, 1823, 1824, 1845, 1846, 1852
JAYAWARDENE, Denagamage
Proboth Mehela de Silva 1527, 1528, 1529, 1530, 1531, 1532, 1557, 1558, 1559, 1561, 1571, 1572, 1573, 1582, 1583, 1584, 1594, 1604, 1605, 1606, 1609, 1628, 1629, 1644, 1645, 1648, 1649, 1670, 1671, 1672, 1685, 1686, 1687, 1698, 1699, 1705, 1706, 1711, 1712, 1719, 1720, 1749, 1750, 1755, 1756, 1764, 1765, 1775, 1776, 1777, 1784, 1785, 1795, 1796, 1802, 1803, 1804, 1813, 1814, 1823, 1824, 1837, 1838, 1839, 1845, 1846, 1852, 1853, 1854, 1869, 1870, 1884, 1885, 1886, 1904, 1905, 1911, 1912, 1921, 1922, 1923, 1931, 1932
JAYAWARDENE, Hewasandatchige
Asiri Prasanna Wishvanath 1609, 1610, 1698, 1699, 1813, 1814, 1823, 1824, 1837, 1838, 1839, 1845, 1846, 1852, 1853, 1854, 1869, 1884, 1885, 1886, 1905, 1911, 1912, 1931, 1932

KALAVITIGODA, Shantha 1750
KALUWITHARANA, Romesh
Shantha 1527, 1529, 1644, 1645, 1648, 1649, 1706, 1711, 1712, 1719, 1720
KAPUGEDERA, Chamara Kantha
1802, 1804, 1813, 1814, 1823, • 1824, 1905, 1932
KULASEKARA, Kulasekara
Mudiyanselage Dinesh Nuwan
1749, 1796, 1802, 1803, 1884, 1885, 1921, 1922, 1923, 1931

LAKSHITHA, Materba Kanatha
Gamage Chamila Premanath 1610, 1629
LIYANAGE, Dulip Kapila 1559
LOKUARACHCHI, Kaushal
Samaraweera 1644, 1645, 1648, 1686

MAHAROOF, Mohamed Farveez 1699, 1711, 1720, 1750, 1777, 1784, 1785, 1795, 1796, 1802, 1803, 1804, 1813, 1814, 1823, 1824, 1839, 1845, 1846
MALINGA, Separamadu Lasith 1705, 1706, 1712, 1719, 1749, 1750, 1755, 1756, 1764, 1777, 1784, 1785, 1795, 1796, 1803, 1804, 1813, 1814, 1823, 1824, 1837, 1838, 1839, 1846, 1852, 1853, 1854
MATHEWS, Angelo Davis 1921, 1922, 1923, 1931
MENDIS, Balapuwaduge Ajantha
Winslo 1884, 1885, 1886, 1905, 1911, 1912, 1921, 1922, 1931
MIRANDO, Magina Thilan Thushara
1649, 1869, 1870, 1912, 1921, 1922, 1923, 1931, 1932
MUBARAK, Jehan 1610, 1629, 1719, 1720, 1775, 1776, 1777, 1802, 1852, 1853
MURALITHARAN, Muttiah 1527, 1528, 1530, 1531, 1532, 1557, 1558, 1559, 1561, 1571, 1572, 1573, 1582, 1583, 1584, 1594, 1605, 1606, 1609, 1628, 1629, 1644, 1645, 1648, 1649, 1670, 1671, 1672, 1685, 1686, 1687, 1699, 1711, 1755, 1756, 1764, 1765, 1775, 1776, 1777, 1784, 1785, 1795, 1796, 1802, 1803, 1804, 1813, 1814, 1823, 1824, 1837, 1838, 1839, 1845, 1846, 1852, 1853, 1854, 1869, 1870, 1884, 1885, 1886, 1904, 1905, 1911, 1912, 1931, 1932

NAWAZ, Mohamed Naveed 1610
NISSANKA, Ratnayake Arachchige
Prabath 1644, 1645, 1648, 1649

PARANAVITANA, Nishad Tharanga
1911, 1912, 1921, 1922, 1923, 1931, 1932
PERERA, Anhettige Suresh Asanka
1557, 1558
PERERA, Panagodage Ruchira Don
Laksiri 1529, 1557, 1558, 1561, 1604, 1628
PRASAD, Kariyawasam Tirana
Gamage Dammika 1886, 1904, 1932
PUSHPAKUMARA, Karuppiahyage
Ravindra 1561

RAMYAKUMARA, Wijekoon
Mudiyanselage Gayan 1755, 1756

SAMARAWEERA, Thilan Thusara
1559, 1561, 1571, 1572, 1573, 1582, 1583, 1584, 1594, 1610, 1648, 1670, 1671, 1672, 1685, 1687, 1698, 1699, 1705, 1706, 1711, 1712, 1719, 1720, 1749, 1750, 1755, 1756, 1764, 1765, 1775, 1776, 1777, 1784, 1785, 1795, 1796, 1802, 1803, 1845, 1869, 1870, 1884, 1885, 1886, 1904, 1905, 1911, 1912, 1921, 1922, 1923, 1931, 1932
SANGAKKARA, Kumar Chokshanada
1527, 1528, 1529, 1530, 1531, 1532, 1557, 1558, 1559, 1561, . 1571, 1572, 1573, 1582, 1583, 1584, 1594, 1604, 1605, 1606, 1609, 1628, 1629, 1644, 1645, 1648, 1649, 1670, 1671, 1672, 1685, 1686, 1687, 1698, 1699, 1705, 1706, 1711, 1712, 1719, 1720, 1749, 1750, 1755, 1756, 1764, 1765, 1775, 1776, 1777, 1784, 1785, 1795, 1796, 1802, 1803, 1804, 1813, 1814, 1823, 1824, 1837, 1838, 1839, 1846, 1852, 1853, 1854, 1869, 1870, 1884, 1885, 1886, 1904, 1905, 1911, 1912, 1921, 1922, 1923, 1931, 1932
SILVA, Lindamlilage Prageeth
Chamara 1823, 1824, 1837, 1838, 1839, 1845, 1846, 1852, 1853, 1854, 1870

THARANGA, Warushavithana Upul
1777, 1784, 1785, 1795, 1796, 1802, 1803, 1804, 1813, 1814, 1823, 1824, 1839, 1853, 1854
THUSHARA, Thilan see
MIRANDO, Magina Thilan
Thushara
TILLEKERATNE, Hashan Prasantha
1557, 1558, 1559, 1561, 1571, 1572, 1573, 1582, 1583, 1584, 1594, 1604, 1605, 1606, 1610, 1628, 1629, 1644, 1645, 1648, 1649, 1670, 1671, 1672, 1685, 1686, 1687

UPASHANTHA, Kalutarage Eric
Amila 1606

VAAS, Warnakulasuriya Patabendige
Ushantha Joseph Chaminda 1527, 1528, 1530, 1531, 1532, 1557, 1558, 1559, 1561, 1571, 1572, 1573, 1582, 1583, 1584, 1594, 1604, 1605, 1606, 1628, 1629, 1644, 1645, 1648, 1649, 1670, 1671, 1672, 1685, 1686, 1687, 1698, 1699, 1705, 1706, 1711, 1712, 1719, 1720, 1749, 1750, 1755, 1756, 1764, 1765, 1775, 1776, 1802, 1803, 1804, 1814, 1823, 1824, 1837, 1838, 1845, 1852, 1853, 1854, 1869, 1870, 1884, 1885, 1886, 1904, 1905, 1911, 1923
VANDORT, Michael Graydon 1561, 1610, 1784, 1785, 1803, 1804, 1837, 1838, 1839, 1845, 1846, 1852, 1853, 1854, 1869, 1870, 1884, 1885, 1886, 1904

WARNAPURA, Basnayake Shalith
Malinda 1837, 1838, 1869, 1870, 1884, 1885, 1886, 1904, 1905, 1911, 1912, 1921, 1922, 1923
WELAGEDARA, Uda Walawwe

Mahim Bandaralage Chanaka
Asanka 1854
WICKREMASINGHE, Gallage
Pramodya 1529

WIJEKOON, Gayan *see*
RAMYAKUMARA, Wijekoon
Mudiyanselage Gayan

ZOYSA, Demuni Nuwan Tharanga
1527, 1528, 1529, 1531, 1572,
1573, 1582, 1583, 1594, 1604,
1605, 1686, 1687, 1699, 1705, 1706

ZIMBABWE

BLIGNAUT, Arnoldus Mauritius 1544,
1545, 1548, 1549, 1555, 1556,
1630, 1631, 1646, 1647, 1662,
1663, 1668, 1669, 1683, 1737,
1738, 1766, 1767
BRENT, Gary Bazil 1570, 1582

CAMPBELL, Alistair Douglas Ross
1510, 1511, 1519, 1520, 1526,
1544, 1545, 1548, 1549, 1555,
1556, 1562, 1563, 1589, 1590,
1630, 1631
CARLISLE, Stuart Vance 1510, 1511,
1519, 1520, 1526, 1544, 1545,
1548, 1549, 1555, 1563, 1569,
1570, 1582, 1583, 1584, 1589,
1590, 1646, 1647, 1662, 1663,
1668, 1669, 1683, 1684, 1762,
1763
CHIGUMBURA, Elton 1698, 1699,
1735, 1736, 1737, 1738
COVENTRY, Charles Kevin 1766,
1767
CREMER, Alexander Graeme 1735,
1736, 1737, 1738, 1762, 1763

DABENGWA, Keith Mbusi 1763,
1766, 1767
DUFFIN, Terrence 1766, 1767

EBRAHIM, Dion Digby 1544, 1545,
1548, 1549, 1555, 1556, 1562,
1563, 1569, 1570, 1584, 1590,
1630, 1631, 1646, 1647, 1662,
1663, 1683, 1684, 1698, 1699,
1736, 1737, 1738, 1762, 1763,
1766, 1767
ERVINE, Sean Michael 1646, 1647,
1662, 1683, 1684
EVANS, Craig Neil 1662
EWING, Gavin Mackie 1663, 1683,
1766

FERREIRA, Neil Robert 1762
FLOWER, Andrew 1510, 1511, 1519,
1520, 1526, 1544, 1545, 1548,
1549, 1562, 1563, 1569, 1570,
1582, 1583, 1584, 1589, 1590,
1630, 1631
FLOWER, Grant William 1510, 1511,
1519, 1520, 1544, 1545, 1548,
1549, 1555, 1556, 1562, 1563,

1569, 1570, 1582, 1583, 1584,
1589, 1590, 1630, 1631, 1646,
1647, 1683, 1684
FRIEND, Travis John 1549, 1562,
1563, 1569, 1570, 1582, 1583,
1584, 1589, 1590, 1646, 1647,
1684

GRIPPER, Trevor Raymond 1569,
1570, 1582, 1583, 1584, 1589,
1590, 1662, 1663, 1668, 1669,
1683, 1684

HONDO, Douglas Tafadzwa 1562,
1646, 1647, 1683, 1684, 1698,
1699, 1735, 1736

MADONDO, Trevor Nyasha 1526
MAHWIRE, Ngonidzasha Blessing
1630, 1663, 1668, 1669, 1684,
1698, 1762, 1763, 1766, 1767
MAREGWEDE, Alester 1698, 1699
MARILLIER, Douglas Anthony 1526,
1569, 1570, 1583, 1584
MASAKADZA, Hamilton 1556, 1562,
1563, 1582, 1583, 1630, 1631,
1735, 1736, 1737, 1738, 1762,
1763, 1766, 1767
MATSIKENYERI, Stuart 1668, 1669,
1698, 1699, 1735, 1736, 1737,
1738
MBANGWA, Mpumelelo 1511
MPOFU, Christopher Bobby 1735,
1736, 1737, 1738, 1762, 1763
MUPARIWA, Tawanda 1699
MURPHY, Brian Andrew 1519, 1520,
1526, 1544, 1548, 1549, 1569
MUTENDERA, David Travolta 1510
MWAYENGA, Waddington 1767

NKALA, Mluleki Luke 1510, 1511,
1520, 1544, 1545, 1631, 1698,
1699, 1735

OLONGA, Henry Khaaba 1511, 1519,
1520, 1526, 1548, 1569, 1570,
1582, 1583, 1584, 1630, 1631

PANYANGARA, Tinashe 1698, 1699,
1736
PRICE, Raymond William 1545, 1555,
1556, 1562, 1563, 1589, 1590,

1630, 1631, 1646, 1647, 1662,
1663, 1668, 1669, 1683, 1684

RENNIE, Gavin James 1510, 1511,
1519, 1520, 1526, 1582, 1583,
1584, 1589
ROGERS, Barney Guy 1735, 1736,
1737, 1738

SIBANDA, Vusimuzi 1668, 1669,
1735
STRANG, Bryan Colin 1510, 1519,
1526, 1555, 1556
STRANG, Paul Andrew 1510, 1511,
1519, 1563
STREAK, Heath Hilton 1510, 1511,
1519, 1520, 1526, 1544, 1545,
1548, 1549, 1555, 1556, 1562,
1563, 1569, 1570, 1582, 1583,
1584, 1589, 1590, 1646, 1647,
1662, 1663, 1668, 1669, 1683,
1684, 1737, 1738, 1762, 1763,
1766, 1767

TAIBU, Tatenda 1555, 1556, 1589,
1590, 1630, 1631, 1646, 1647,
1662, 1663, 1668, 1669, 1683,
1684, 1698, 1699, 1735, 1736,
1737, 1738, 1762, 1763, 1766,
1767
TAYLOR, Brendan Ross Murray 1698,
1699, 1735, 1736, 1737, 1738,
1762, 1763, 1766, 1767

UTSEYA, Prosper 1698

VERMEULEN, Mark Andrew 1631,
1646, 1647, 1662, 1663, 1668,
1669, 1699
VILJOEN, Dirk Peter 1520

WATAMBWA, Brighton Tonderai
1544, 1545, 1548, 1549, 1589,
1590
WHITTALL, Guy James 1511, 1519,
1520, 1526, 1544, 1545, 1548,
1549, 1555, 1556, 1562, 1563,
1630
WISHART, Craig Brian 1510, 1555,
1556, 1562, 1569, 1570, 1582,
1583, 1584, 1662, 1663, 1668,
1669, 1762, 1763

BANGLADESH

ABDUR RAZZAK 1798, 1837, 1865,
1891, 1892
AFTAB AHMED 1718, 1726, 1735,
1736, 1751, 1752, 1764, 1765,
1797, 1798, 1862, 1863, 1864,
1865
AKRAM KHAN 1512, 1544, 1545,
1560, 1570, 1609, 1642, 1643
ALAMGIR KABIR 1609, 1658, 1684
ALOK KAPALI 1610, 1621, 1622,
1632, 1633, 1642, 1643, 1650,
1651, 1657, 1658, 1659, 1666,
1667, 1717, 1718, 1784
AL SAHARIAR 1512, 1545, 1561,
1569, 1570, 1580, 1581, 1585,

1586, 1609, 1610, 1621, 1622,
1633, 1650
AMINUL ISLAM 1512, 1544, 1545,
1560, 1561, 1569, 1570, 1580,
1581, 1585, 1586, 1609, 1632
ANWAR HOSSAIN MONIR 1651,
1751, 1752
ANWAR HOSSAIN PIJU 1632

BIKASH RANJAN DAS 1512

EHSANUL HAQUE 1609
ENAMUL HAQUE, sen. 1545, 1560,
1569, 1570, 1585, 1586, 1609,
1632, 1633, 1642

ENAMUL HAQUE, jun. 1666, 1667,
1718, 1735, 1736, 1764, 1765,
1784, 1785, 1797, 1835, 1862,
1905, 1930

FAHIM MUNTASIR 1585, 1586,
1610
FAISAL HOSSAIN 1703

HABIBUL BASHAR 1512, 1544,
1545, 1560, 1561, 1569, 1570,
1580, 1581, 1585, 1586, 1609,
1610, 1621, 1622, 1632, 1633,
1642, 1643, 1650, 1651, 1657,
1658, 1659, 1666, 1667, 1683,

1684, 1703, 1704, 1725, 1726,
1735, 1736, 1751, 1752, 1764,
1765, 1784, 1785, 1797, 1798,
1835, 1836, 1837, 1838, 1839,
1862, 1863, 1864
HANNAN SARKAR 1609, 1610,
1622, 1632, 1633, 1650, 1651,
1657, 1658, 1659, 1666, 1667,
1683, 1684, 1703, 1704, 1717
HASIBUL HOSSAIN 1512, 1544,
1560, 1561, 1581

IMRUL KAYES 1893, 1894, 1904,
1905, 1929, 1930

JAVED OMAR 1544, 1545, 1560,
1561, 1569, 1570, 1580, 1581,
1586, 1621, 1642, 1643, 1650,
1651, 1657, 1658, 1659, 1666,
1667, 1703, 1704, 1717, 1718,
1725, 1726, 1735, 1736, 1751,
1752, 1764, 1765, 1784, 1785,
1797, 1798, 1835, 1836, 1837,
1838, 1839
JUNAID SIDDIQUE 1862, 1863,
1864, 1865, 1891, 1892, 1893,
1894, 1904, 1905, 1929, 1930

KHALED MAHMUD 1569, 1580,
1581, 1642, 1643, 1650, 1651,
1657, 1658, 1659, 1666, 1667
KHALED MASHUD 1512, 1544,
1560, 1561, 1569, 1570, 1580,
1581, 1585, 1586, 1609, 1610,
1621, 1622, 1632, 1633, 1650,
1651, 1657, 1658, 1659, 1666,
1667, 1683, 1684, 1703, 1704,
1717, 1718, 1725, 1726, 1735,
1736, 1751, 1752, 1764, 1765,
1784, 1785, 1797, 1798, 1835,
1836, 1837

MAHBUBUL ALAM 1893, 1894,
1904
MAHMUDULLAH 1929, 1930
MANJURAL ISLAM 1544, 1545,
1560, 1561, 1569, 1580, 1581,
1585, 1586, 1609, 1610, 1621,
1622, 1633, 1650, 1659, 1683
MANJURAL ISLAM RANA 1683,

1684, 1704, 1717, 1725, 1726
MASHRAFE BIN MORTAZA 1569,
1570, 1580, 1581, 1642, 1643,
1650, 1651, 1657, 1658, 1666,
1667, 1725, 1726, 1735, 1736,
1751, 1752, 1797, 1798, 1835,
1836, 1837, 1838, 1839, 1862,
1863, 1864, 1865, 1891, 1892,
1893, 1894, 1904, 1905, 1929
MEHRAB HOSSAIN, sen. 1512, 1544,
1545, 1560, 1561, 1585, 1586,
1642, 1643, 1892, 1893, 1894
MEHRAB HOSSAIN, jun. 1838, 1891,
1904, 1905
MOHAMMAD ASHRAFUL 1561,
1569, 1570, 1580, 1581, 1585,
1610, 1632, 1633, 1642, 1643,
1650, 1651, 1658, 1659, 1683,
1684, 1703, 1704, 1717, 1718,
1725, 1726, 1735, 1736, 1751,
1752, 1764, 1765, 1784, 1785,
1797, 1798, 1835, 1836, 1837,
1838, 1839, 1862, 1863, 1864,
1865, 1891, 1892, 1893, 1894,
1904, 1905, 1929, 1930
MOHAMMAD RAFIQUE 1512, 1621,
1643, 1657, 1658, 1659, 1666,
1667, 1683, 1684, 1703, 1704,
1717, 1718, 1725, 1726, 1735,
1736, 1751, 1752, 1764, 1765,
1784, 1785, 1797, 1798, 1835,
1836, 1837, 1838, 1839, 1864,
1865
MOHAMMAD SALIM 1642, 1643
MOHAMMAD SHARIF 1544, 1545,
1560, 1561, 1570, 1580, 1585,
1586, 1836, 1838
MUSHFIQUR RAHIM 1751, 1785,
1838, 1839, 1862, 1863, 1864,
1865, 1891, 1892, 1893, 1894,
1904, 1905, 1929, 1930
MUSHFIQUR RAHMAN 1544, 1545,
1666, 1667, 1683, 1684, 1703,
1704, 1718, 1725

NAEEM ISLAM 1891, 1893
NAFIS IQBAL 1717, 1718, 1725,
1726, 1735, 1736, 1751, 1752,
1765, 1784, 1785
NAIMUR RAHMAN 1512, 1544,

1545, 1560, 1561, 1569, 1570,
1632
NAZMUL HOSSAIN 1726

RAFIQUL ISLAM 1622
RAJIN SALEH 1657, 1658, 1659,
1666, 1667, 1683, 1684, 1703,
1704, 1717, 1718, 1725, 1735,
1736, 1752, 1797, 1798, 1835,
1836, 1837, 1838, 1839, 1891,
1892
RAQIBUL HASAN 1894, 1904, 1905,
1929, 1930
RUBEL HOSSAIN 1929, 1930

SAJIDUL ISLAM 1862, 1863
SANWAR HOSSAIN 1580, 1581,
1585, 1586, 1621, 1622, 1633,
1651, 1657
SHAHADAT HOSSAIN 1751, 1764,
1765, 1784, 1785, 1797, 1798,
1835, 1837, 1838, 1839, 1862,
1863, 1864, 1865, 1893, 1894,
1904, 1905, 1929, 1930
SHAHRIAR HOSSAIN 1512, 1683,
1684
SHAHRIAR NAFEES 1764, 1765,
1784, 1785, 1797, 1798, 1835,
1836, 1837, 1838, 1839, 1862,
1863, 1864, 1865
SHAKIB AL HASAN 1835, 1836,
1837, 1863, 1864, 1865, 1891,
1892, 1893, 1894, 1904, 1905,
1929, 1930
SYED RASEL 1764, 1765, 1784,
1785, 1836, 1839

TALHA JUBAIR 1609, 1610, 1621,
1622, 1632, 1633, 1726
TAMIM IQBAL 1862, 1863, 1864,
1865, 1891, 1892, 1893, 1894,
1904, 1905, 1929, 1930
TAPASH BAISYA 1610, 1621, 1622,
1632, 1633, 1642, 1643, 1650,
1651, 1657, 1659, 1683, 1684,
1703, 1704, 1717, 1718, 1725,
1735, 1736, 1752
TAREQ AZIZ 1703, 1704, 1717
TUSHAR IMRAN 1610, 1621, 1622,
1764, 1839

ICC WORLD XI

BOUCHER, Mark Verdon 1768

DRAVID, Rahul 1768

FLINTOFF, Andrew 1768

HARMISON, Stephen James 1768

INZAMAM-UL-HAQ 1768

KALLIS, Jacques Henry 1768

LARA, Brian Charles 1768

MURALITHARAN, Muttiah 1768

SEHWAG, Virender 1768
SMITH, Graeme Craig 1768

VETTORI, Daniel Luca 1768

Additions and Amendments

The following are additions and amendments to the Fifth Edition of *The Wisden Book of Test Cricket*, as published in 2000 by Headline in three volumes (volume 1: 1877-1970; volume 2: 1970-1996; volume 3: 1996-2000).

Most of these corrections and additions to the scorecards printed in previous volumes have come to light thanks to the tireless researches of the Association of Cricket Historians and Statisticians.

Test No.

38/3   SA v Eng 1891–92 (Only Test): Eng 1st inns G. G. Hearne c Milton, not Mills.

46/43   Aust v Eng 1894–95 (5th Test): Eng 2nd inns G. H. S. Trott 20.1 overs (not 20).

47/4   SA v Eng 1895–96 (1st Test): Eng 1st inns Woods c Halliwell (not bowled), 8–175 (not 145).

48/5   SA v Eng 1895–96 (2nd Test): Miller's colleagues as umpires included H. R. Butt (who was also playing), W. B. Woolley and G. Beves, as well as G. Allsop.

52/46   Eng v Aust 1896 (3rd Test): Eng 1st inns Peel c Donnan (not bowled).

89/10   SA v Eng 1905–06 (2nd Test): SA 2nd inns extras 6 (lb5, nb1), total 33 (not 7 and 34).

108/19   SA v Eng 1909–10 (3rd Test): SA 1st inns Stricker 3, Zulch 1 (not 1 and 3), SA 2nd inns Bird 0.1–0–0–0 (not 1–1–0–0).

110/21   SA v Eng 1909–10 (5th Test): SA 1st inns 4–38 (not 30)

111/4   Aust v SA 1910–11 (1st Test): SA 1st inns extras lb6, nb6 (not lb7, nb5).

115/8   Aust v SA 1910–11 (5th Test): SA 1st inns extras b1, lb8, nb1 (not b1, lb9).

132/27   SA v Eng 1913–14 (3rd Test): 3rd day close SA(2) 132–0 (Taylor 53, Zulch 66) (not Eng 308 all out).

145/12   SA v Aust 1921–22 (1st Test): 3rd day close SA(2) 6–1 (Frank 1, Marx 0) (not Aus 324–7).

155/37   Eng v SA 1924 (3rd Test): SA 2nd inns batting order Susskind 3, Nourse 4 (not 4 and 3).

172/44   SA v Eng 1927–28 (5th Test): SA 2nd inns extras lb2, w1 (not b3).

217/1   NZ v SA 1931–32 (1st Test): 1st day close SA(1) 29–0 (Christy 14, Mitchell 13) (not NZ 293 all out).

222/127   Aust v Eng 1932–33 (3rd Test): Aust 1st inns, Oldfield retired hurt at 218–7 (not 222).

247/20   SA v Aust 1935–36 (1st Test): SA 2nd inns 9–265 (not 263), batting order Nicholson 8, Langton 9 (not vice versa), Aust 1st inns batting order Brown 2, Fingleton 1 (not vice versa).

250/23   SA v Aust 1935–36 (4th Test): Aust 1st inns Mitchell 15 overs (not 14).

251/24   SA v Aust 1935–36 (5th Test): Aust 1st inns 5–338 (not 333); SA 2nd inns 7–216 (not 220).

260/10   Eng v NZ 1937 (1st Test): NZ 1st inns Kerr retired hurt on 6* from 20–1 (probably) to 66–3.

286/66   Eng v SA 1947 (2nd Test): SA 2nd inns Compton 31 overs (not 32).

403/11   WI v Aust 1954–55 (1st Test): WI 2nd inns King c Maddocks (not bowled).

412/84   Eng v SA 1955 (5th Test): Eng 1st inns Ikin retired hurt on 15* from 43–0 to 59–2.

415/3   Pak v NZ 1955–56 (3rd Test): there was no play on the third day (Nov 9), but some on the fifth (Nov 12); report should read ". . . prevented play until the fourth day".

454/22   Eng v NZ 1958 (1st Test): NZ 2nd inns Harford had 23* when he retired at 81–4.

462/14   India v WI 1958–59 (4th Test): India 1st inns batting order Ramchand 6, Kripal Singh 7, Mankad 8, Borde 9; Ramchand retired hurt (probably on 0*) at 121–4, and returned at 147–7); India 2nd inns batting order (2) Ramchand 6, Kripal Singh 7.

501/15   India v Pak 1960–61 (5th Test): India 1st inns Contractor retired hurt on 89* from 217–3 to 324–4.

512/5   Pak v Eng 1961–62 (1st Test): Pak 1st inns 7–337 (not 327).

532/10   Eng v Pak 1962 (3rd Test): Pak 1st inns Javed Burki retired hurt on 1* from 90–4 to 118–6; 2nd inns Javed Burki retired hurt on 21* from 173–6 to 179–8.

544/42   Eng v WI 1963 (2nd Test): Eng 2nd inns Cowdrey retired hurt on 19* from 72–3 to 228–9.

608/49   Eng v WI 1966 (4th Test): Eng 1st inns Milburn retired hurt on 0* from 11–1 to 179–7.

615/47   SA v Aust 1966–67 (3rd Test): Aust 1st inns Lawry retired hurt on 7* at 14–0 and resumed at 45–3.

623/15   Eng v Pak 1967 (3rd Test): Pak 2nd inns batting order Mohammad Ilyas 1, Wasim Bari 2.

684/21   WI v India 1970–71 (5th Test): the close-of-play score given for the fourth day was in fact the score at the end of the fifth day in this six–day Test; at the end of the fourth day India were 94–1 (Gavaskar 57, Wadekar 29).

818/49   NZ v Eng 1977–78 (2nd Test): NZ 2nd inns Burgess had 1* when he retired hurt.

820/42   WI v Aust 1977–78 (1st Test): Aust 1st inns Garner 14 overs, 6 maidens (not 15, 7); Aust 2nd inns Roberts 16.2 overs (not 16.3).

822/44   WI v Aust 1977–78 (3rd Test): WI 1st inns Thomson 56 runs conceded (not 57), Clark 65 (not 64); Aust 1st inns Phillip 75 runs conceded (not 76), Clarke 58 (not 57).

894/38   Aust v India 1980–81 (2nd Test): Aust bowling order 1st innings Pascoe 4, Yardley 3; 2nd inns Hogg 4, Yardley 3, Chappell 6, Border 5.

984/56   WI v Aust 1983–84 (4th Test): WI 1st inns Rackemann 7 maidens (not 8), Hogan 10 maidens (not 9).

985/57   WI v Aust 1983–84 (5th Test): Aust 1st inns Marshall 5 maidens (not 4), Garner 5 maidens (not 4).

999/60   Aust v WI 1984–85 (3rd Test): Aust 2nd inns 5–123 (not 126).

1169/71   WI v Aust 1990–91 (4th Test): Aust 2nd inns Hooper 19 overs (not 18).

1336/7   Pak v Zim 1996–97 (1st Test): Pak 1st inns B. C. Strang 10 overs (not 20); Zim 2nd inns Wishart c Wasim Akram (not bowled).

1347/86   Aust v WI 1996–97 (5th Test): WI 2nd inns Bichel 1.3 overs (not 1.2).

1379/6   Zim v NZ 1997–98 (2nd Test): NZ 1st inns O'Connor 7 (not 9), extras 15, lb9 (not 13, lb7), Huckle 109 runs conceded (not 111).

1380/2   Pak v SA 1997–98 (1st Test): Pak 1st inns Mohammad Wasim c Bacher (not Kirsten).

1414/5   SA v SL 1997–98 (2nd Test): the referee was H. A. B. Gardiner of Zimbabwe (in his only match as referee), not J. R. Reid; the 1998–1999 Australia–England series were thus Reid's 36th, 37th, 38th, 39th and 40th matches as referee, the 1999–2000 Australia–Pakistan series his 41st, 42nd and 43rd, and the 2000–01 Sri Lanka–Pakistan series his 44th, 45th and 46th, not as shown.

1437/6   SA v WI 1998–99 (5th Test): this was R. E. Koertzen's 11th Test as an umpire, not his 10th; Match 1441/37 (NZ v India 1998–99, 3rd Test) was his 10th.

1484/11   India v SA 1999–2000 (1st Test): SA 2nd inns extras b4, lb9 (not lb13).

1492/1   WI v Zim 1999–2000 (1st Test): WI 2nd inns Streak 17 overs, 27 runs (not 16, 23), Murphy 15 overs, 23 runs (not 16, 27).

1508/7   SL v SA 2000–01 (2nd Test): the debutant umpire was M. G. Silva, not as shown.

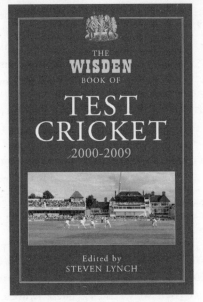